Research-Doctorate Programs in the United States

Continuity and Change

MARVIN L. GOLDBERGER, BRENDAN A. MAHER, AND PAMELA EBERT FLATTAU, *Editors*

Committee for the Study of Research-Doctorate
Programs in the United States

sponsored by

The Conference Board
of
Associated Research Councils

and
conducted by

Studies and Surveys Unit
Office of Scientific and Engineering Personnel
National Research Council

NATIONAL ACADEMY PRESS
Washington, D.C. 1995

NATIONAL ACADEMY PRESS • 2101 CONSTITUTION AVENUE, N.W. • WASHINGTON, DC 20418

NOTICE: The project that is the subject of this report was approved by the Governing Board of the National Research Council, whose members are drawn from the councils of the National Academy of Sciences, the National Academy of Engineering, and the Institute of Medicine. The members of the committee responsible for the report were chosen for their special competencies and with regard to appropriate balance.

This report has been reviewed by persons other than the authors according to procedures approved by a Report Review Committee consisting of members of the National Academy of Sciences, the National Academy of Engineering, and the Institute of Medicine.

This material is based on work supported by the Andrew W. Mellon, Alfred P. Sloan, William and Flora Hewlett and Ford, Foundations, and the National Academy of Sciences.

Library of Congress Cataloging-in-Publication Data

National Research Council (U.S.). Committee for the Study of Research-Doctorate Programs in the United States.

Research-doctorate programs in the United States : continuity and change / Marvin L. Goldberger, Brendan A. Maher, and Pamela Ebert Flattau, editors ; Committee for the Study of Research-Doctorate Programs in the United States ; sponsored by the Congerence Board of Associated Research Councils ; and conducted by Studies and Surveys Unit, Office of Scientific and Engineering Personnel, National Research Council.

p. cm.

Includes bibliographical references and index.

ISBN 0-309-05094-4 (hard)

1. Research—United States—Evaluation. 2. Doctor of philosophy degree—United States—Evaluation. 3. Science—Study and teaching (Higher)—United States—Evaluation. 4. Engineering—Study and teaching (Higher)—United States—Evaluation. 5. Humanities—Study and teaching (Higher)—United States—Evaluation. I. Goldberger, Marvin L. II. Maher, Brendan A. (Brendan Arnold), 1924- . III. Flattau, Pamela Ebert. IV. Conference Board of the Associated Research Councils. V. National Research Council (U.S.). Office of Scientific and Engineering Personnel. Studies and Surveys Unit. VI. Title.

Q180.N334 1995

378.1′553′0973—dc20 95-35154

Printed in the United States of America.

COMMITTEE FOR THE STUDY OF RESEARCH-DOCTORATE PROGRAMS IN THE UNITED STATES

Marvin L. Goldberger, *Co-chair*
Dean, Natural Sciences
University of California, San Diego

Brendan Maher, *Co-chair*
Edward C. Henderson Professor
of the Psychology of Personality
Harvard University

Richard Atkinson
Chancellor
University of California, San Diego

Norman Bradburn
Senior Vice President for Research
National Opinion Research Center

Joseph Cerny
Provost for Research
Dean of the Graduate Division
University of California, Berkeley

Jonathan R. Cole
Provost and Dean of Faculties
Columbia University

John D'Arms
Vice Provost for Academic Affairs
Dean of the Rackham School
of Graduate Studies
University of Michigan

Jane S. de Hart
Professor of History
University of California, Santa Barbara

Elsa Garmire
Director, Center for Laser Studies
University of Southern California

Gardner Lindzey
Director Emeritus
Center for Advanced Study
in the Behavioral Sciences

Pamela L. Mellon
Professor of Reproductive
Medicine and Neuroscience
University of California, San Diego

Lincoln Moses
Professor Emeritus of Statistics
Stanford University

Ernest T. Smerdon
Vice Provost and Dean of Engineering
University of Arizona

Debra W. Stewart
Dean of the Graduate School
North Carolina State University

Stephen M. Stigler
Professor of Statistics
University of Chicago

James H. Wyche
Associate Provost
Brown University

Ex-officio Members

Elaine El-Khawas
Vice President
Policy Analysis and Research
American Council on Education

Douglas Greenberg
President and Director
Chicago Historical Society

David L. Featherman
President
Social Science Research Council
(and Chairman, Conference Board of
Associated Research Councils)

THE CONFERENCE BOARD OF ASSOCIATED RESEARCH COUNCILS REPRESENTATIVES: 1994

American Council on Education

Robert Atwell
President
American Council on Education

Myles Brand
President
Indiana University

Elaine El-Khawas
Vice President
Policy Analysis and Research
American Council on Education

American Council of Learned Societies

Douglas Greenberg
President and Director
Chicago Historical Society

Stanley N. Katz
President
American Council of Learned Societies

National Research Council

Bruce Alberts
Chairman
National Research Council

Barbara Boyle Torrey
Executive Director
Commission on Behavioral and Social Sciences
and Education

Social Science Research Council

David L. Featherman
President
Social Science Research Council
(and Chairman, Conference Board of Associated Research Councils)

Gardner Lindzey
Director Emeritus
Center for Advanced Study in the Behavioral Sciences

PROJECT STAFF FOR THE STUDY OF RESEARCH-DOCTORATE PROGRAMS IN THE UNITED STATES

Pamela Ebert Flattau
Director, Studies and Surveys Unit

James Voytuk
Senior Staff Officer

Elaine Lawson
Research Associate

George Boyce
Director, Data Processing Unit

Eileen Milner
Manager, Data Services Unit

Anthony Quinn De Santis
Patricia Kirchner
Dimitria Satterwhite
Administrative Assistants

OFFICE OF SCIENTIFIC AND ENGINEERING PERSONNEL
ADVISORY COMMITTEE

The National Academy of Sciences is a private, nonprofit, self-perpetuating society of distinguished scholars engaged in scientific and engineering research, dedicated to the furtherance of science and technology and to their use for the general welfare. Upon the authority of the charter granted to it by the Congress in 1863, the Academy has a mandate that requires it to advise the federal government on scientific and technical matters. Dr. Bruce Alberts is president of the National Academy of Sciences.

The National Academy of Engineering was established in 1964, under the charter of the National Academy of Sciences, as a parallel organization of outstanding engineers. It is autonomous in its administration and in the selection of its members, sharing with the National Academy of Sciences the responsibility for advising the federal government. The National Academy of Engineering also sponsors engineering programs aimed at meeting national needs, encourages education and research, and recognizes the superior achievements of engineers. Dr. Harold Liebowitz is president of the National Academy of Engineering.

The Institute of Medicine was established in 1970 by the National Academy of Sciences to secure the services of eminent members of appropriate professions in the examination of policy matters pertaining to the health of the public. The Institute acts under the responsibility given to the National Academy of Sciences by its congressional charter to be an adviser to the federal government and, upon its own initiative, to identify issues of medical care, research, and education. Dr. Kenneth Shine is president of the Institute of Medicine.

The National Research Council was organized by the National Academy of Sciences in 1916 to associate the broad community of science and technology with the Academy's purposes of furthering knowledge and advising the federal government. Functioning in accordance with general policies determined by the Academy, the Council has become the principal operating agency of both the National Academy of Sciences and the National Academy of Engineering in providing services to the government, the public, and the scientific and engineering communities. The Council is administered jointly by both Academies and the Institute of Medicine. Dr. Bruce Alberts and Dr. Harold Liebowitz are chairman and vice chairman, respectively, of the National Research Council.

PREFACE

Opportunities abound for talented individuals to seek advanced education in the United States. In 1993, over 300 universities offered the Ph.D. or related research doctorates in many fields of Science, Engineering, and Arts and Humanities. Of the 39,000 individuals who completed their doctoral studies that same year, about 30,000 earned a degree in one of those areas.

This vast educational enterprise grew significantly during the past century. From time to time, scholars and administrators alike have been prompted to examine the quality of doctoral programs available to students. At first, these analyses were modest studies based on faculty opinions of programs in their field. Over time, however, these reviews of programs of doctoral study became more and more sophisticated. Allan Cartter (1966) and then Kenneth Roose and Charles Andersen (1970) framed the first formal, national assessments of research-doctorate programs; Lyle Jones, Gardner Lindzey, and Porter Coggeshall (1982) expanded the scope of the effort. (See Chapter 1 for a more detailed description of some of these earlier studies.) Our study builds on those earlier efforts and serves to provide the interested reader with a fresh look at doctoral programs as they appeared in academic year 1992-1993.

Specifically, the authors of the 1982 study expressed hope that their work would become one of a recurring series of assessments. Our study was intended to provide some continuity of form and data with the 1982 assessment, but we have also included significant modifications and improvements suggested by the experience gained from preparing and using previous reports.

Both the 1982 and 1993 studies have similar purposes:

- To assist students and advisers in matching students' career goals with the facilities and opportunities available in the relevant research-doctorate programs;
- To inform the practical judgment of university administrators, national and state level policymakers, and managers of public and private funding agencies; and
- To provide a large, recent data base that can be used by scholars who focus their work on characteristics of the national higher learning educational system and its associated research enterprise.

In keeping with these previous studies, we have collected information of two types: descriptive statistics of selected characteristics of research-doctorate programs (such as the number of faculty and students), and the views of faculty "peers" relative to program quality.

Because of the elements of continuity with the 1982 study, it is now also possible for the first time to examine some of the changes that have taken place in various aspects of higher education during the past decade. The richness of the data makes the potential range of such analyses very broad. Within the limits of the present report, we could not conduct more than a few of these analyses. However, the data base will be available to interested scholars, and we look forward to many sophisticated analyses of these data in the next few years. From these, we hope to gain insights into the factors that are associated with increased or reduced quality in the conduct of research-doctorate programs.

AUDIENCES FOR THE REPORT

In addition to scholars, we have kept in mind that there are several audiences for the information contained in this report, and that each of these audiences may choose to focus on subsets of data that are most important to them.

The potential graduate student, for example, may be most interested in comparing a subset of programs on the profile of variables most likely to affect his or her choice: years to degree, student/faculty ratio, financial aid, research publishing activities of the faculty, availability of research funding, and so on.

Administrators may be most interested in how their own programs have evolved since the 1982 assessment compared to those with which they regard themselves as competitive or in the kinds of objective characteristics that appear to be associated with perceived improvement.

For institutional planners, these data may help inform decisions about resource allocation. Department chairs and deans will be able to compare the size, faculty research activities, and other characteristics of their doctoral program with those of other departments in the same field, and bring this information to bear when advancing, or evaluating, requests for additional resources, or for internal resource allocation.

Policymakers may find it useful to focus on national and regional trends over time and across disciplines, such as changes in the median number of years required for students to receive the doctoral degree, changes in faculty size, and other factors that reflect the allocation and effective use of human resources in higher education. The nature of these changes may be analyzed across disciplines, institutional type (public and private), and so on. This report also includes data on the percentages of women, minorities, and United States citizens enrolled in each field and receiving degrees in that field. While no direct comparison of these variables can be made between the 1982 and 1993 assessments, the present findings should provide a useful benchmark for the analysis of future trends.

ANALYTICAL ISSUES

The committee has given serious attention to certain dilemmas and issues that are inherent in the attempt to assess the quality of an enterprise as complex as that of doctoral education. The contents and format of this report are the best testimony as to how we have addressed these dilemmas. However, in the interest of encouraging readers and users of the report to develop a realistic view of the limitations and subtleties of the data, in this section we enumerate some of the issues that we have identified and wrestled with throughout the study process.

First, although the central purpose of the present study was to assess the quality of individual doctoral programs in terms of their effectiveness in preparing graduates for careers in research and scholarship, the committee recognizes that the careers of many graduates develop outside academic settings. A comprehensive study would ideally include assessments from those who are familiar with the work of graduates in other settings, such as industry, business, government services, and the public sector generally. It would also involve direct assessment of the effectiveness of the programs in which they have been educated. Such assessments involve complexities arising from the interactions of many variables that contribute to individual performance; to conduct these assessments adequately requires resources that were unavailable to the committee. They remain as important goals for further effort.

In considering the central purpose of the present study, there is the fundamental question of whether it is possible to achieve this purpose by providing a description of a program by single numbers, or whether it is necessary to provide a range of indices reflecting the many ways in which programs differ from each other. *The committee judged that it is not possible to provide a valid description of the quality of program by any method that relies exclusively on a single number. Rather than merely reporting where a given program ranks in its own field, it is critically important to indicate its relative standing on a number of measures. It is also important to report certain absolute quantitative measures of attributes that we believe are related to the quality of the education and training that the doctoral student receives at an institution.*

Second, many thorny problems surround the assessment of quality of a particular research program or department. Given that a research career may be only one outcome of a doctoral program, what factors should we assess? Is it more valid to look at the research of a faculty member or of the institution as a whole? Should we consider the performance of students after their formal education is complete, in the course of their careers? How should we balance the elements of quality and quantity when examining the faculty of a particular research program? How can we distinguish the reputational effect of the contributions of one or two outstanding scholars in a program composed of otherwise less remarkable colleagues? Is such a program likely to be as effective as one in which the majority of the faculty have active programs of research and scholarship, even though no one of their number may have achieved great international prominence? Should I, as a potential graduate student, be as concerned about the density of quality at a graduate program as with its size and coverage—in short, how can summary numbers adequately capture the actual education environment of academic programs that vary greatly in their characteristics?

Based on the review of these issues and the measures

available to the committee, we selected a combination of factors we believed to be most important in determining the effectiveness of a doctoral program for preparing students for careers in research and scholarship.

Third, to make this report as useful as possible to the widest possible audience, the committee sought to include a very large number of programs. The report covers more than 3,600 programs at over 270 institutions in 41 fields of study.

This approach provides for a review of the many different experiences students may have in a research-doctorate program and should assist students in determining which experience would be appropriate for them. While for most students the key factors in selecting a particular program relate to the career goals of becoming researchers, scholars, and college teachers, issues such as a department's commitment to achieving a diverse student body, and to the mentoring of doctoral students, can also play a large role in the choice of an institution.

Fourth, the committee emphasizes that a major component of this study is reputational measures, and that these are subjective measures that depend on the perception of the raters. When the judgments of numerous individual raters are pooled, there tends to be strong agreement about which programs are the strongest and which are the weakest; there is considerably less agreement about the programs in the middle range.

Because of the nature of reputational ratings, the committee also points out that differences in ranked order between two programs may reflect very small, unreliable, or insignificant differences in the actual quality of a program, and should be regarded by readers with great caution. Appendix Q illustrates this situation. Simple reputational rankings similar to those reported in the popular media may make for easier reading than the tables in this report. But because they mask subtleties that may be important to the reader, they also make for poorer information.

Fifth, the committee wishes to draw attention to the existence of significant differences among the different disciplines. Patterns of research and scholarship in the Arts and Humanities, for example, differ considerably from those in the Physical Sciences and Mathematics. These differences include the manner in which research findings are disseminated (books, articles, monographs, conferences, etc.), the expected period of time to complete a doctoral degree, the significance of the role of post-doctoral appointments in the education of the student, the role of the individual versus research-team contributions, and so on. These differences will be evident in the pages that follow. It is crucial that the reader interpret the meaning of particular indices in terms of the disciplinary field of a particular program rather than against some absolute ideal standard of graduate education in general.

In addition, since 1982, new fields of study—particularly in interdisciplinary combinations—have emerged. The number of programs in some others has declined, and yet others (most notably in the Biological Sciences) have undergone internal reorganization of sub-units leading to the creation of new doctoral programs. These changes betoken a lively evolution of concepts and methods in the fields concerned, but make simple comparisons between 1982 and 1993 problematic.

In sum, after considering all of these issues the committee concluded that it would be of most value to the readers of this volume to report and emphasize the importance of multiple indices of quality, and the lack of importance of minor differences in ranking. We have been particularly careful to incorporate a range of quantitative indices into our assessment variables, thereby placing reputational ratings into a proper and modest perspective. In a word, there is no single agreed index of a unitary attribute called "quality"; there are several "qualities," and the importance of them is largely a function of the needs of the reader.

ACKNOWLEDGMENTS

We are grateful to the many individuals who gave generously of their time to our undertaking. We would especially like to thank the 274 individuals who served as "Institutional Coordinators" and to the presidents of those universities who agreed to participate in this study. Without their assistance this study would not have been possible.

We are also grateful for the thoughtful responses we received from over 8,000 university faculty who participated in the National Survey of Graduate Faculty conducted in 1993. Their review of programs in each of the 41 fields included in the study generated the core statistics from which many other analyses were made possible.

We would also like to thank the members and representatives of the Conference Board of Associated Research Councils who provided useful guidance throughout the study. The committee also benefited from the wise counsel of Drs. Harriet Zuckerman, Michael Teitelbaum, and Sheila Biddle, representing several of the sponsoring agencies.

At key stages of this project, the committee sought and received information and advice from many more individuals than it is possible to list here. The help of some of these experts is acknowledged specifically in the series of endnotes found throughout the text. In addition to these individuals, we would like to thank representatives of a number of organizations who offered their expert views at various times throughout the study process. These include Ms. Elizabeth Aversa, Institute for Scientific Information, and Ms. Sarah Pritchard, Association of Research Libraries, who spent considerable time explaining the intricacies of their data systems to the committee. Dr. John Vaughn, Association of American Universities, and Dr. Jules LaPidus, Council of Graduate Schools, kept the committee informed of important developments in the graduate education sector and facilitated committee and staff contact with their members. The committee also benefited from suggestions by representatives of the U.S. Department of Education, the National Science Foundation, and the National Institutes of Health relative to their plans for gathering and presenting statistics on trends in graduate education. Other federal staff, such as those at the U.S. Department of Defense, provided statistical information directly utilized by the committee.

In looking back on this four-year project, it is remarkable to consider that every one of the committee members assisted with some aspect of the work. In particular, however, we all came to depend on a number of members for their technical guidance in the organization of the statistics found in this report. We are specifically thankful to Drs. Jonathan Cole, Norman Bradburn, and Stephen Stigler for their help in this regard.

The staff of the National Research Council are to be commended for their diligence in designing the data collection plan, and in gathering and analyzing the statistics. We were especially fortunate to have the assistance of Mr. George Boyce and Ms. Eileen Milner, both of whom were closely involved in the data processing activities of the 1982 assessment.

Dr. Paula Ries, former Manager of the Doctorate Records Project, and her staff, most notably Ms. Delores Thurgood, played a crucial role in making data available to the committee in a timely fashion.

Mr. Alan Fechter, Executive Director of the Office of Scientific and Engineering Personnel, wisely guided the committee and staff in completing the project. We are grateful for his help.

We would also like to acknowledge the careful work of Dr. James Voytuk who formulated the electronic files and created the charts and tables found in this report. Together with our administrative assistants Mr. Anthony Quinn De Santis and Ms. Patricia Kirchner, Dr. Voytuk made it possible for all of us to review quickly and efficiently the vast amounts of information collected by the committee over the past four years. His hard work and diligence played a crucial role in this undertaking.

Ms. Elaine Lawson played an important role in keeping the committee informed during critical phases of our work. We are also indebted to Mr. De Santis for his tireless attention to the many details involved in producing this volume. Ms. Ellen Hoffman is to be commended, too, for her expert editorial assistance; her suggestions for organizing the material in this report were gratefully received.

We recommend this report to educators, students and policymakers alike, and look forward to its use in policy and planning activities.

Marvin L. Goldberger,
Brendan A. Maher,
and
Pamela Ebert Flattau,
Editors.

CONTENTS

EXECUTIVE SUMMARY 1

1 HISTORY AND CONTEXT OF THE 1993 STUDY 8

History of the Project /8
The Context of the 1993 Study /12
Project Goals /14
Organization of the Report /14
Notes /14

2 STUDY DESIGN 16

Field Coverage /16
Eligibility Criteria /17
Characteristics of Participating Institutions /19
Data Collection Strategies /19
Notes /28

3 SELECTED FINDINGS 30

The National Survey of Graduate Faculty /30
Program Characteristics Associated with "Quality" /34
The Calculation of "Change" Measures /41
Selected Information About Program Graduates /49
Interpreting the Findings /56
Notes /56

4 SUMMARY AND FUTURE DIRECTIONS 58

Updating the 1982 Assessment /58
Expanding the "Objective" Measures /58
Calculating "Change" Measures /59
Electronic Data Access /59
Presentation of Findings /60
Need for Periodic Updates /60

REFERENCES 62

APPENDIXES
A Conference Board of Associated Research Councils /67
B Summary of 1991 Project Planning Meeting /71
C Field Coverage /79
D Sample Letters to University Presidents and Institutional Coordinators /85
E Characteristics of Institutions Participating in the 1993 Study /103
F The National Survey of Graduate Faculty /115
G Data Sources Utilized in Profiles of Participating Programs /143
H Faculty Quality Ratings of Research-Doctorate Programs /147
I Effectiveness Ratings of Research-Doctorate Programs /197
J Selected Characteristics of Research-Doctorate Programs in the Arts and Humanities /247
K Selected Characteristics of Research-Doctorate Programs in Engineering /279
L Selected Characteristics of Research-Doctorate Programs in the Physical Sciences and Mathematics /311
M Selected Characteristics of Research-Doctorate Programs in the Social and Behavioral Sciences /349
N Selected Characteristics of Research-Doctorate Programs in the Biological Sciences /383
O Correlation Tables for Selected Characteristics of Research-Doctorate Programs /427
P Relative Rankings of Research-Doctorate Programs Along Selected Dimensions /469
Q Mean Scores with Confidence Intervals for the Scholarly Quality of Program Faculty /625
R Change in Magnitude of Selected Measures /699
S Committee for the Study of Research-Doctorate Programs in the United States /731

INDEX 737

LIST OF TABLES AND FIGURES

TABLES

ES-1 Percentage of Programs Whose "Scholarly Quality of Program Faculty" Rated on Average as "Distinguished," "Strong," or "Good" /3

ES-2 Relative Distribution of Research-Doctorate Programs Appearing in Both the 1982 and 1993 Studies by Mean Rating of "Scholarly Quality of Program Faculty" in Quality Grouping /4

ES-3 Percentage of Research-Doctorate Programs Remaining in the "Top Quarter" Between 1982 and 1993 When Mean Rating of "Scholarly Quality of Program Faculty" Is Considered by Broad Field and Quality Grouping /4

ES-4 Relative Distribution of Graduates from Participating HBCU/HSI Institutions by Quality Grouping (for All Fields) /6

1-1 Scores on Graduate Record Examination (GRE) and Subject Matter Tests: 1980-1992 /12

1-2 Number of Ph.D.s Awarded by U.S. Universities (1920-1992) by Reporting Period and Year in Which the Doctorate Records File Recorded the First Ph.D. Awarded by that Institution /13

2-1 Ph.D. Production in Selected Fields in the Biological Sciences by Field, Institution, and Program Within Institution, 1986-1990 /18

2-2 Estimated Range of Institutional Coverage by 1993 Study of Research-Doctorate Programs in the United States by Field /20

2-3 Distribution of Participating Institutions by Carnegie Classification and Broad Field /21

2-4 Selected Characteristics of Research-Doctorate Programs in the 1993 Study /25

3-1 Distribution of Program Ratings on the Variable "Scholarly Quality of Program Faculty" /32

3-2 Distribution of Program Ratings on the Variable "Effectiveness of Program in Educating Research Scholars/Scientists" /33

3-3 Average Number of Program Faculty by Field and Quality Grouping /36

3-4 Average Number of Students Enrolled in Doctoral Studies in Fall 1992 and (in parentheses) the Percentage of Female Students, by Field and Quality Grouping /38

3-5 Average Percentage of Faculty in the Social and Behavioral Sciences Having Had Federal Grants (1986-1992) by Quality Grouping /40

3-6 Publication and Citation Information for Selected Fields by Quality Grouping /40

3-7 Average Number of Awards and Honors Among Faculty in the Arts and Humanities by Field and Quality Grouping /41

3-8 Relative Distribution of Research-Doctorate Programs Appearing in Both the 1982 and 1993 Studies by Mean Rating of "Scholarly Quality of Program Faculty" in Quality Grouping /42

3-9 Percentage of Research-Doctorate Programs Remaining in the "Top Quarter" Between 1982 and 1993 When Mean Rating of "Scholarly Quality of Program Faculty" Is Considered by Broad Field and Quality Grouping /43

3-10 Change in the Average Number of Faculty in the Arts and Humanities by Field and 1982 Quality Grouping, Fall 1980 and Fall 1992 /44
3-11 Average Number Faculty in Selected Fields of Engineering Based on 1982 Quality Grouping /46
3-12 Average Percentage of Doctoral Recipients With Research or Teaching Assistantships as a Primary Source of Support by Field and Quality Grouping /52
3-13: Summary Information on Patterns of Doctoral Degrees Earned by Women from Programs Participating in the 1993 Study by Broad Field and Quality Grouping /53
3-14 Summary Information on Patterns of Doctoral Degrees Earned by Minorities from Programs Participating in the 1993 Study by Broad Field and Quality Grouping /53
3-15 Relative Distribution of Programs from Participating HBCU/HSI Institutions by Quality Grouping (for All Fields) /55
3-16 Relative Distribution of Graduates from Participating HBCU/HSI Institutions by Quality Grouping (for All Fields) /55

FIGURES

ES-1 Relative Distribution of Research-Doctorate Programs Appearing in the 1993 Study for the First Time in Fields Included in Both the 1982 and 1993 Study, by Broad Field and 1993 Quality Grouping /5
ES-2 Relative Distribution of Minority Ph.D. Recipients by Broad Field and by Quality Grouping (1986-1992) /6
1-1 Doctorate Recipients, Total and by Gender, 1963-1993 /9
2-1 Excerpt from the 1993 NRC National Survey of Graduate Faculty /21
3-1 Distribution of Program Ratings Across All Programs by "Scholarly Quality of Program Faculty" /31
3-2 Average Number of Program Faculty by Quality Grouping and Broad Field /35
3-3 Average Number of Students Enrolled by Broad Field and Quality Grouping 37
3-4 Average Percentage of Faculty in Programs Rated in the "Top Quarter" Having Had Federal Grant Support Between 1986 and 1992, by Field /39
3-5 Relative Distribution of Research-Doctorate Programs Appearing in the 1993 Study for the First Time in Fields Included in Both the 1982 and 1993 Study, by Broad Field and 1993 Quality Grouping /43
3-6 Change in the Average Number of Program Graduates in the Arts and Humanities by Field and Quality Grouping: 1975-1980 and 1986-1992 /45
3-7 Average Number of Program Graduates in Engineering by Quality Grouping: 1975-1980 and 1987-1992 /47
3-8 Average Number of Program Graduates in the Physical Sciences and Mathematics by Field and Quality Grouping: 1975-1980 and 1986-1992 /48
3-9 Average Number of Program Graduates in the Social and Behavioral Sciences by Field and 1982 Quality Grouping: 1975-1980 and 1986-1992 /50
3-10 Median Time to Degree by Broad Field and by Quality Grouping: 1986-1992 /51
3-11 Percentage of Female Doctorates Who Come From Programs Rated in the "Top Quarter" on the "Scholarly Quality of Program Faculty" Variable /54
3-12 Relative Distribution of Minority Ph.D. Recipients by Broad Field and by Quality Grouping (1986-1992) /55

Research-Doctorate Programs in the United States

Continuity and Change

EXECUTIVE SUMMARY

Many changes have taken place in size and structure of the research-doctorate enterprise in this country since 1982, when the National Research Council (NRC) issued its first report on the status of research-doctorate programs in the Sciences (including the broad fields of Biological Sciences, Physical Sciences and Mathematics, and Social and Behavioral Sciences), Engineering, and Arts and Humanities in the United States (Jones, Lindzey, and Coggeshall, 1982). From 1980 to 1992, for example, the number of institutions awarding a Ph.D. grew from 325 to 364, an increase of more than ten percent. In 1993, the number of doctoral degree recipients in all fields in the United States reached an all-time high of 39,754. Aware of these changes and of the academic community's interest in the earlier assessment of research-doctorate programs, the Conference Board of Associated Research Councils in 1990 asked the NRC, as a member of the board, to update the 1982 study.

After a planning phase in 1991, the NRC appointed the Committee for the Study of Research-Doctorate Programs in the United States and asked that they undertake a four-year study, taking the 1982 assessment as their starting point. This report represents an effort to build upon and update the information collected for the 1982 study, to collect new information, to analyze key components of the new data base, and to make that data base available to interested researchers and scholars for further analysis. It focuses on "research training programs" although we recognized that doctoral education has a range of purposes, and graduates follow a variety of career paths in academia, industry, and government. The study examines programs in the following 41 fields:

Arts and Humanities: Art History, Classics, Comparative Literature, English Language and Literature, French Language and Literature, German Language and Literature, Linguistics, Music, Philosophy, Religion, Spanish and Portuguese Language and Literature.

Biological Sciences: Biochemistry and Molecular Biology; Cell and Developmental Biology; Ecology, Evolution, and Behavior; Molecular and General Genetics; Neurosciences; Pharmacology; Physiology.

Engineering: Aerospace Engineering, Biomedical Engineering, Chemical Engineering, Civil Engineering, Electrical Engineering, Industrial Engineering, Materials Science, Mechanical Engineering.

Physical Sciences and Mathematics: Astrophysics and Astronomy, Chemistry, Computer Sciences, Geosciences, Mathematics, Oceanography, Physics, Statistics and Biostatistics.

Social and Behavioral Sciences: Anthropology, Economics, Geography, History, Political Science, Psychology, Sociology.

STUDY DESIGN

A critical step in designing a study of research-doctorate programs in the U.S. is to define the target population both to establish the boundaries of the analysis and to assure that a cost-effective procedure can be developed for collecting information about the programs included in the study. The concentration of available resources on a limited number of disciplines seemed to the committee both practical and necessary, although inevitably resulting in the exclusion of some important areas of graduate study.

Field Coverage

The committee selected fields to include in the 1993 study based on a combination of three factors:

- The number of Ph.D.s produced nationally;
- The number of programs training Ph.D.s within a particular field; and
- The average number of Ph.D.s produced per program.

Fields included in the study also have met a criterion of "robustness," that is, they have awarded a minimum of about 500 degrees in about 50 programs for the years 1986 to 1990.

The 41 fields covered in this report consist of:

- All fields in the 1982 report, although the Biological Sciences are represented differently;
- Eight new fields: Comparative Literature, Religion, Aerospace Engineering, Biomedical Engineering, Industrial Engineering, Materials Sciences, Astronomy and Astrophysics, and Oceanography; and
- Some new fields in the broad area of Biological Sciences.

Eligibility Criteria

Based on the analysis of degree production patterns and on reports from "Institutional Coordinators" (ICs) who compiled and submitted information about programs at their institutions, the committee identified 3,634 research-doctorate programs at 274 U.S. universities—105 private and 169 public institutions—which met the criteria and are included in the study. This sample represents about 35 percent more programs than the number included in the 1982 study. Taken together, these programs involved about 78,000 faculty members and trained about 90 percent of the total number of Ph.D.s produced in these fields between 1986 and 1992. Of the 228 institutions in the 1982 study, 214 participated in this one and many added more programs for review.

Data Collection Strategies

The committee used diverse strategies for collecting the two primary types of data contained in this report.

To generate reputational measures—faculty opinion of program quality—the committee conducted the National Survey of Graduate Faculty in Spring 1993. The survey instrument was a questionnaire designed to elicit ratings on the scholarly quality of the program faculty, the effectiveness of each program in educating research scholars and scientists, and the relative change in program quality over the years. The questionnaire replicated key questions appearing on the 1982 survey form thus permitting the calculation of "change" measures for the 1,916 programs appearing in both studies.

To collect data on the characteristics of the 3,634 programs included in this study, the committee decided to update some statistics from the 1982 study (such as number of faculty and number of graduates) and include, exclude, or improve upon other 1982 data depending on whether the data sets were still available and/or relevant. In many cases, a careful matching of faculty lists with various sources of information occurred. In other cases data were drawn from the Doctorate Records File (DRF) on a program by program basis. Among the new data included in this report are statistics related to the participation of women in research-doctorate education. Appendix G describes the chief data sets used in generating the descriptive statistics found in this report.

SELECTED FINDINGS

Educators and policymakers agree that certain distinctive features of the doctoral training environment facilitate the preparation of research scholars and scientists. These include a blend of well-prepared graduate students, talented faculty, and sufficient institutional resources to permit the independent exploration of promising new research directions.

The National Survey of Graduate Faculty

Survey forms were sent to a sample of faculty raters chosen from lists provided by ICs in all 41 fields included in the study. Each rater received a questionnaire with approximately 50 programs in their field selected at random from the roster of participating programs. For each institution they were asked to rate, raters were given a faculty roster provided by the ICs. The committee set as its goal a total of at least 100 ratings per program. Raters were asked to comment on two dimensions of program quality: (1) "scholarly quality of program faculty," and (2) "effectiveness in educating research scholars/scientists." Ratings for "scholarly quality of program faculty" were pooled and an average rating calculated using a five-point scale ranging from 0 to 5, with 0 signifying "not sufficient for doctoral education" and 5 signifying "distinguished." Of the 3,634 program included in the study, about 62 percent were rated as "distinguished," "strong," or "good," although this varied by field:

TABLE ES-1 Percentage of Programs Whose "Scholarly Quality of Program Faculty" Rated on Average as "Distinguished," "Strong," or "Good"

Arts and Humanities	68%
Biological Sciences	65%
Engineering	63%
Physical Sciences and Mathematics	59%
Social and Behavioral Sciences	56%

Each rater was also asked to comment on the effectiveness of a program in "educating research scholars/scientists." Mean ratings were calculated using a five-point scale with 0 representing "not effective" and 5 representing "extremely effective." About two-thirds of the programs were considered to be "extremely effective" or "reasonably effective." Fewer than 10 percent were considered to be "not effective" in this regard.

Program Rankings and Use of Quality Groupings by Quarter

Responding to comments that the presentation of study results by alphabetical listing of programs in the 1982 report created some difficulties for readers, the committee decided that providing a rank ordering of programs within fields is a more convenient way for readers to review and interpret the 1993 information.

The committee chose the mean rating of the "scholarly quality of program faculty" as the dimension along which to array program information. Thus, replies from respondents to the National Survey of Graduate Faculty were pooled, a mean rating was calculated for each program, and a rank ordering was produced within each of the 41 fields in the study.

Rank ordered information requires careful interpretation, of course. A program may be ranked first with respect to "scholarly quality of program faculty," but well down the list with respect to another dimension. As a result the committee created a separate appendix that illustrates the relative standing of programs with respect to a number of variables.

Given the large number of programs within a field, and to facilitate a broad understanding of the data and findings, the committee organized institutions within each field into four groups or "quarters" based on the mean rating of the "scholarly quality of program faculty." Admittedly these are arbitrary groupings. However, these quality groupings represent an efficient way to highlight differences in program characteristics within a field or across fields.

What follows is a brief overview of some of the more interesting observations that can be made from the data collected by the committee and organized in the numerous companion appendix tables.

Program Characteristics Associated with "Quality"

A strong positive correlation between the number of faculty and its reputational standing has been demonstrated in the past but has not been explored thoroughly. From data collected by the committee, the size-"quality grouping" relationship was found to be the strongest in the Biological Sciences and weakest in the Arts and Humanities. By and large, however, top-rated programs in most fields tended to have a larger number of faculty and more graduate students than lower-rated programs.

Another factor thought to be associated with the relative rating of the "scholarly quality of program faculty" is faculty involvement in research and scholarship. Owing to differences in patterns of scholarship across participating fields, the committee developed three measures in these area: (1) patterns of federal grant support for the period 1986-1992; (2) publication and citation patterns for the period 1988-1992; and (3) selected "awards and honors" among faculty in the Arts and Humanities.

As would be expected from the important role academia has come to play in conducting research in the national interest, the vast majority of research-doctorate programs included in the study had faculty who received some type of federal grant support between 1986 and 1992. A large fraction of top-rated programs in most fields had faculty who had received federal support during that period, although the relationship between "quality grouping" and grant support was weaker in the Arts and Humanities and a number of disciplines comprising the Social and Behavioral Sciences.

Analysis of publication/citation patterns in the Sciences and Engineering showed a similar pattern. However, the clearest relationship between ratings of the "scholarly quality of program faculty" and these productivity measures occurred with respect to "citation"—with faculty in top-rated programs cited much more often than faculty in lower-rated programs who published.

To explore the relationship between "quality" scores in the Arts and Humanities and "scholarship," the committee compiled a list of awards and honors using a variety of sources. The list was matched against a list of faculty members provided by the ICs. From this analysis, the committee observed that a larger share of faculty in top-rated programs in the Arts and Humanities were likely to have received a prestigious award than faculty in lower-rated programs. This relationship was most evident in the fields of Classics, Comparative Literature, Philosophy, and English Language and Literature, reflecting in part the sources of information that were used to compile this listing of awards and honors. There is a need to extend the analysis begun by the committee to include other types of awards and honors to explore institutional differences across all fields of the Arts and Humanities.

TABLE ES-2 Relative Distribution of Research-Doctorate Programs Appearing in Both the 1982 and 1993 Studies by Mean Rating of "Scholarly Quality of Program Faculty" in Quality Grouping[a]

Quality Grouping in 1982	Quality Grouping of 1982 Set in 1993: Top	2nd	3rd	4th	Total
Top	***399***	66	3	0	468
2nd	81	***287***	103	12	483
3rd	8	112	***248***	110	478
4th	0	11	113	***363***	487
					1,916

[a]Based on average ratings for "Scholarly Quality of Program Faculty." See Appendix R for details.

"Change" Measures

Because of the care that was taken in designing the 1993 National Survey of Graduate Faculty, it was possible to identify 1,916 doctoral programs in 27 fields appearing in both the 1982 and 1993 studies and to analyze changes in program ratings since 1982. The committee found a remarkable degree of stability in those ratings, with 85 percent of participating programs that appeared in the top quarter in 1982 appearing again in the top quarter in 1993. (See Table ES-2.)

Patterns of stability and change were analyzed across each of the 27 fields, where it was found, overall, that somewhat fewer programs rated in the top quarter in the Arts and Humanities in 1982 remained in the top quarter in 1993 (80 percent) than the fraction observed in some of the other broad fields (e.g. 89 percent in the Social and Behavioral Sciences). (See Table ES-3.)

The committee also considered the relative distribution by "quality grouping" for programs appearing for the first time in the 1993 study in one of these 27 fields. They found that these programs received a mix of high, medium, and low ratings, although the chances were much higher that these newly participating programs would appear at the bottom half of the quality distribution in 1993. (See Figure ES-1.)

Changes in selected characteristics of the 1,916 programs since 1982 were analyzed in three areas: (1) average number of faculty (Fall 1980 versus Fall 1992); (2) average number of graduates (1975-1980 versus 1987-1992); and (3) median time to degree. With the exception of most fields in the Arts and Humanities and in the Social and Behavioral Sciences, the number of faculty and of graduates increased for programs appearing in the 1982 study regardless of quality grouping.

In the Arts and Humanities and in the Social and Behavioral Sciences, faculty rosters were essentially the same size in 1992, but the relative number of program graduates dropped considerably especially from programs rated in the top-quarter in 1982.

It took graduates in the 1980s longer to earn a degree on average than graduates of these programs took 10 years earlier. The longer time to degree was more pronounced for graduates from programs rated in the bottom quarter in 1982 for most fields.

Selected Information About Program Graduates

The committee generated a variety of statistics about graduates of these 3,634 programs. These data revealed that:

- Ph.D. recipients completing their doctoral studies in programs rated in the top quarter in 1993 typically completed their studies more rapidly than graduates of lower-rated programs regardless of field. However, graduates in the Arts and Humanities took longer to complete their studies than graduates in other fields, although the relationship of "quality grouping" and "time to degree" still holds.

The reasons for this observation are complex and linked in part to differences in the readiness of students to under-

TABLE ES-3 Percentage of Research-Doctorate Programs Remaining in the "Top Quarter" Between 1982 and 1993 When Mean Rating of "Scholarly Quality of Program Faculty" Is Considered by Broad Field and Quality Grouping[a]

Broad Fields	Total Number in Both Studies	Total Number in Top Quarter in 1982	Number Remaining in Top Quarter 1993 (%)
Arts and Humanities	431	103	82 (80)
Engineering	301	74	64 (86)
Physical Sciences and Mathematics	535	132	116 (88)
Social and Behavioral Sciences	576	141	125 (89)

NOTE: Biological Sciences are excluded from this table since only one field, Physiology, is common to both studies.

[a]Based on average ratings for "Scholarly Quality of Program Faculty" in 1982 and in 1993. See Appendix R for details.

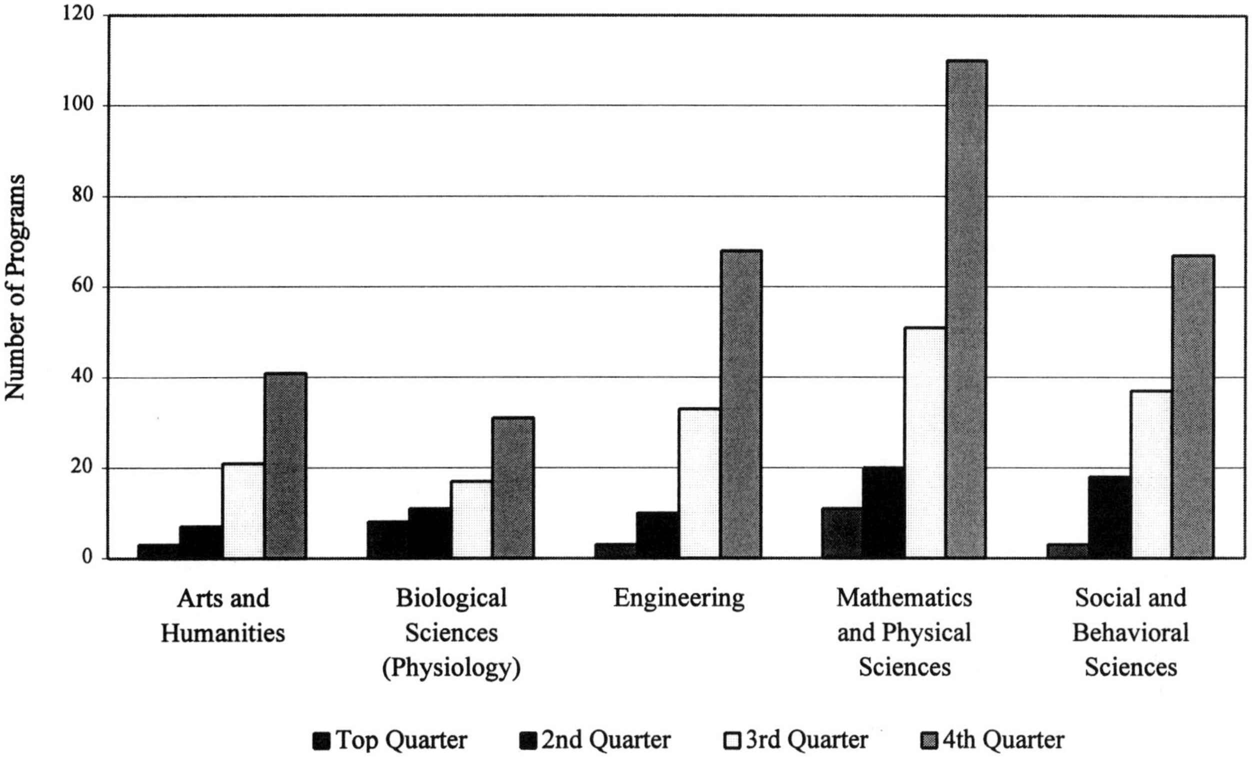

FIGURE ES-1 Relative distribution of research-doctorate programs appearing in the 1993 study for the first time in fields included in both the 1982 and 1993 study, by broad field and 1993 quality grouping. Based on "Scholarly Quality of Program Faculty." See Appendixes J–N.

take doctoral studies and differences in the academic culture. Another factor is thought to be differences in patterns of student support, in which greater dependence on teaching assistantships (TAs) than on research assistantships (RAs) may account for the time it takes a student to earn a degree. From data collected by the committee it was observed that:

- Graduates from lower-rated programs in many fields tended to utilize TAs as a primary source of student support at a greater rate than graduates of higher-rated programs.

The committee also reviewed information about patterns of doctorates awarded to women and to individuals from racial/ethnic minority groups relative to the "scholarly quality of program faculty." Overall, the committee found essentially no relationship between "quality" and patterns of enrollment and degree attainment for women. Although top-rated programs in most fields enroll and graduate many more students on average than lower-rated programs, women tend to be represented in the same percentages across quality groupings within a field. An exception appears to be certain subfields of Engineering in which top-rated programs are slightly more likely than lower-rated programs to enroll and graduate women. However, the total fraction of women remains quite low in those fields in comparison to other fields included in this study.

Approximately 143,000 individuals earned their doctorates between 1986 and 1992 from the 3,634 programs in this study. Of these, about 6,000 graduates were members of a racial/ethnic minority group. As Figure ES-2 reveals, the majority of these graduates earned their degrees in the Social and Behavioral Sciences. When analyzed by "quality grouping," the overall picture that emerges is that minority students tended to come from top-rated programs. Approximately twice as many minority doctorates come from the Social and Behavioral Sciences as from any other broad field.

The analysis of minority participation in doctoral studies by "quality" grouping is complicated by the fact that there was a tendency in 1993 for the 48 participating programs located at Historically Black Colleges and Universities (HBCU) or Hispanic-Serving Institutions (HSI) to be rated in the bottom half of the "quality groupings." Added to that, larger programs associated with top-rated institutions graduated more individuals from racial/ethnic minority groups. However, as seen in Table ES-4, the majority of

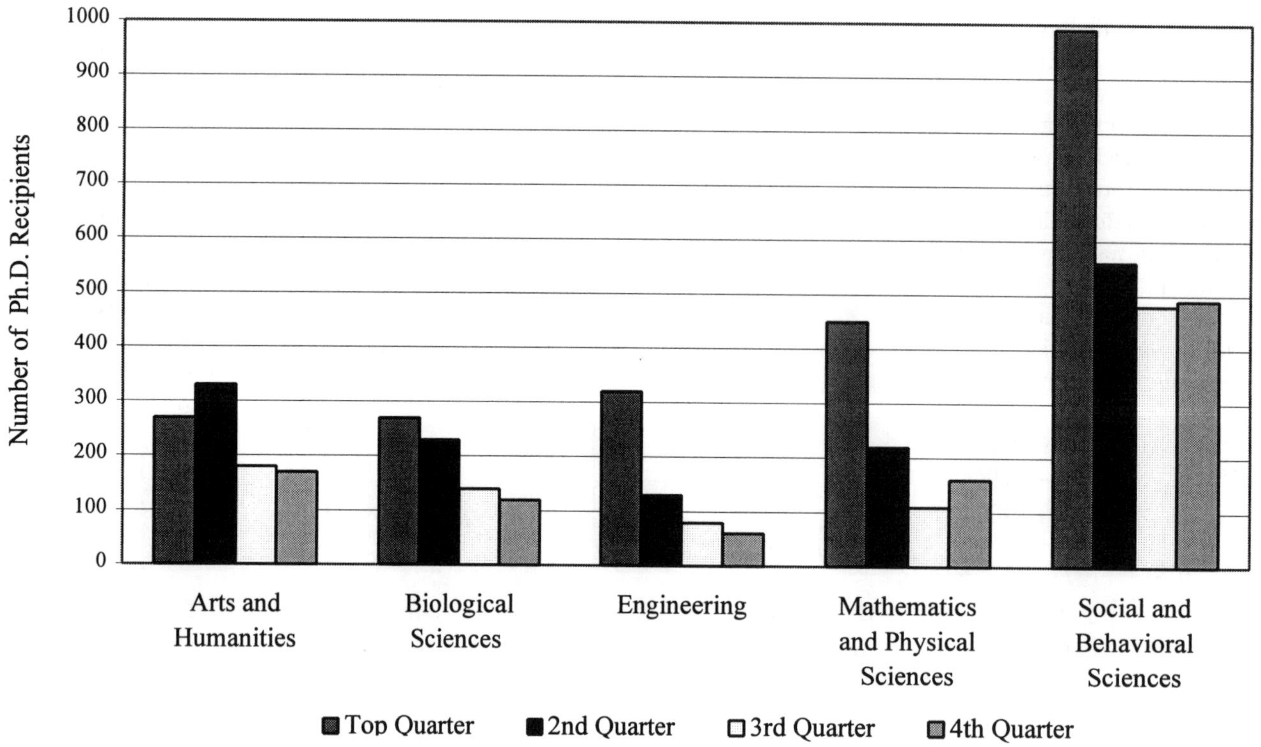

FIGURE ES-2 Relative distribution of minority Ph.D. recipients by broad field and by quality grouping (1986-1992). Based on "Scholarly Quality of Program Faculty." See Appendixes J–N.

graduates from racial/ethnic minority groups completed their doctoral studies at institutions whose programs were rated in the top half of doctoral programs included in the study.

Electronic Data Access

Many types of analysis are possible beyond those reported by the committee. To facilitate further exploration of the data, the committee has prepared an electronic file of the statistics report, which is available through the NRC. (See Note 12 of Chapter 1 for details.)

FUTURE DIRECTIONS

The committee accomplished the five goals established at the outset of the project, namely:

(1) updating the 1982 Assessment,

(2) expanding the "objective" measures developed by the previous committee,

(3) calculating "change" measures and demonstrating their potential for monitoring trends in graduate education,

(4) preparing a selection of findings and making them available in electronic form, and

TABLE ES-4 Relative Distribution of Graduates from Participating HBCU/HSI Institutions by Quality Grouping[a] (for All Fields)

Type of Institutions	Top Quarter	2nd Quarter	3rd Quarter	4th Quarter
All (1986-1992)	66,220	36,800	22,600	17,500
U.S. Citizens	41,200	23,600	14,800	12,100
Minorities	2,300	1,500	1,000	1,000
Minority Graduates from HBCU/HSI Institutions	—	50	50	200

[a]Based on the 1993 average of "Scholarly Quality of Program Faculty."

(5) presenting findings in a format understandable to most readers, namely rank ordered and by quality groupings.

We believe that the information contained here will be useful to general readers, policymakers, current or potential research-doctorate students and advisers, a range of educators and administrators, and researchers although each of these groups may have specialized interests and needs for that information.

The committee encourages researchers to use this data base to conduct additional analyses that could yield important insights into the nature of and changes in research-doctorate education over the last decade. A list of priority issues for analysis appears in the last chapter of this report, as does a list of additional types of studies that the committee believes should be incorporated into future assessments of research-doctorate education.

It is not within the purview of this report to recommend changes in educational policies or practices to address what seem to be negative trends, nor to encourage positive developments. Rather, these data are presented to encourage the debate that is needed to assure all who have an interest in and concern about the quality of advanced study—whether members of the academic or policy community, or of the general citizenry—that the training provided to research scholars and scientists is strong enough to meet the challenges that face our nation and our world in the coming decades.

1

HISTORY AND CONTEXT OF THE 1993 STUDY

The Doctor of Philosophy degree (Ph.D.) or its equivalent represents the highest academic degree offered by universities in the United States. It is a research degree and signals that an individual has mastered the advanced concepts of a field of inquiry and has developed the capacity to make independent intellectual contributions to that field.

As a formal area of study within the university, doctoral preparation typically takes place within the framework of a research-doctorate program, located in turn within a department or similar academic unit. Programs of doctoral study may vary in size or with respect to their general organization, but all share the common goal of preparing a student to become a scholar: "to discover, integrate and apply knowledge as well as to communicate and disseminate it" (Council of Graduate Schools, 1990).

Data from a variety of sources indicate that the enterprise of doctoral education continues to grow. More universities offer doctoral degrees than in the past (Carnegie Foundation for the Advancement of Teaching, 1994), and many institutions have expanded the number of Ph.D. programs they offer (Bowen and Rudenstine, 1992). As might be expected, this expansion of the doctoral education enterprise has led to a significant increase in the number of Ph.D.s awarded each year by U.S. colleges and universities. By 1993, Ph.D. production reached an all-time high of about 39,754 degrees, continuing the upward trend in degree production which, after a stable period from the early 1970s until the mid-1980s, again accelerated. (See Figure 1-1.)

Aware of these developments, and of the interest within the academic community in assessment of doctoral education, the Conference Board of Associated Research Councils asked the National Research Council (NRC or Research Council) in 1990 to undertake a study that would update and expand *An Assessment of Research-Doctorate Programs in the United States* (Jones, Lindzey, and Coggeshall, 1982). That study generated a variety of statistics describing the characteristics of 2,699 research-doctorate programs in 32 fields of study and proved to be a rich source of information for educators and policymakers (Webster, 1983 and 1992).

The Research Council, as a member of the Conference Board, agreed to serve as the institutional base for the ensuing study and spent the following year developing a study plan that would reflect the changes that had occurred in the size and organization of doctoral education since the 1982 report. A study plan was needed that would build upon the 1982 assessment while responding to the new set of policy and planning issues confronting the academic community in the 1990s. This chapter describes the history of the project, identifies key planning issues identified by the Research Council, discusses the goals of the 1993 study, and concludes with an overview of the design of this report.

HISTORY OF THE PROJECT

Each year numerous organizations produce statistical profiles of various aspects of higher education in the United States, such as the human and financial resources involved in the delivery of post-secondary education (U.S. Department of Education, 1993), research and development expenditures at U.S. colleges and universities [National Science Foundation (NSF), 1992], and the total number of doctoral degrees conferred (Ries and Thurgood, 1993). Thus a reader

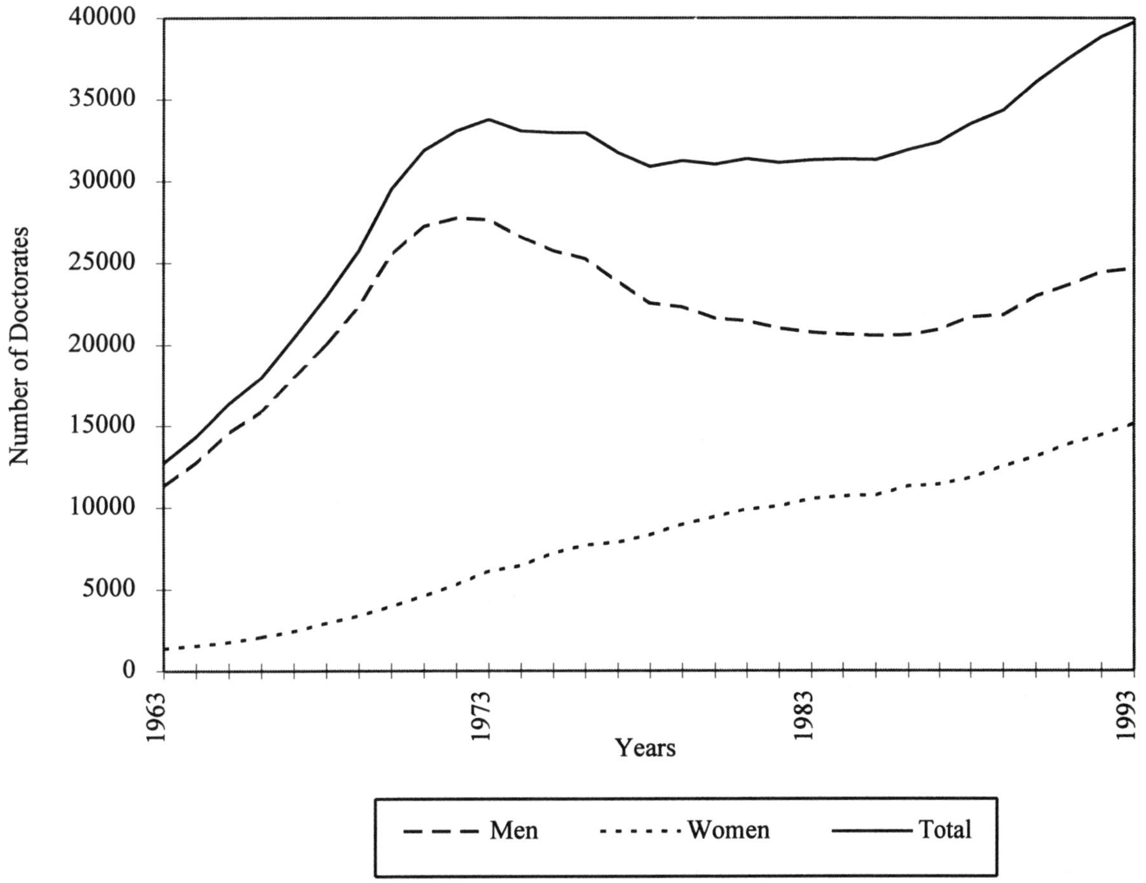

FIGURE 1-1 Doctorate recipients, total and by gender, 1963-1993. SOURCE: National Research Council, Doctorate Records File, Special Tabulations, 1993.

might well ask: Given the number of statistical reports, is there a need for more statistics on doctoral education?

The answer is yes. While many national databases provide a useful overview of trends, they often lack the detail required to address highly specific policy or planning questions. As a result, from time to time educators and administrators have found it useful to conduct more specialized studies that can contribute to the resolution of long-range policy and planning issues. For example, the recent volume by William G. Bowen and Neil L. Rudenstine (1992) demonstrates the value of carefully gathered statistics for developing strategies to increase the rate of degree completion and reduce the time it takes to earn a degree among doctoral students in the Sciences and Humanities.[1]

The study that is the subject of this report is an example of one type of specialized analysis sought by educators and administrators. Specifically, its purpose was to gather statistics about the characteristics of research-doctorate programs in the early 1990s following a decade of continued expansion in course offerings. Data collected for this study are based on two types of quality measures: quantitative data that describe institutional and program characteristics such as size of faculty, library resources and number of years required for a student to complete a degree; and reputational data—judgments of program quality by faculty peers within a given discipline.

To understand the selection and intended use of the two types of statistics found in this volume, it is necessary to consider the design and information goals of preceding studies upon which the current analysis is built. The sections that follow focus on several factors that were considered in creating this study: the emergence of reputational measures (faculty opinion) in the study of doctoral education, how problems of sampling bias have been addressed through national surveys, and contemporary interest in the identification of "objective correlates" of reputational measures.

The Emergence of Reputational Measures

Most studies identify Raymond M. Hughes, then president of Miami University of Ohio, as one of the first analysts to suggest that faculty opinions could be used to document the relative quality of doctoral programs within U.S. colleges and universities.[2] As he said in his report to the Association of American Colleges in 1925:

> At the present time every college president in the country is spending a large portion of his time in seeking men to fill vacancies on the staff of his institution, and every man is confronted with the question of where he can hope to get the best prepared man of the particular type he desires (p. 3).

To guide these personnel decisions, Hughes conducted a study in which 20 to 60 faculty in a field ranked about 38 institutions with respect to their "esteem at the present time for graduate work in your subject." The raters reviewed 20 fields of instruction; the results were published in a monograph. While Hughes' study "stirred up considerable interest, and no little criticism" (Cartter, 1966), the ultimate impact it had on personnel selection decisions is unknown.

Although Hughes conducted another assessment in 1934 for the American Council on Education[3] (Cartter, 1966), a number of years passed before faculty opinion once again achieved national prominence in the form of "reputational ratings" as a tool for policy and planning.

Around 1960, following a period of rapid expansion in higher education, and graduate education in particular, Hayward Keniston, Dean of Graduate Studies of the University of Pennsylvania, conducted a study of doctoral programs designed to reappraise "the goals of graduate study and their relevance to the intellectual needs of our time" (Keniston, 1959). In his study, Keniston invited department chairs from 25 institutions to rate the "strongest departments" in their field on "the basis of the quality of Ph.D. work and the quality of the faculty as scholars." The list of raters was compiled on the basis of: (1) membership in the Association of American Universities, (2) number of Ph.D.s awarded, and (3) geographical distribution. The list did not include "technical schools, like the Massachusetts Institute of Technology and the California Institute of Technology" nor state colleges. Keniston tabulated rankings based on 500 returns in four broad fields: (1) the Biological Sciences (Botany and Zoology), (2) the Humanities (eleven fields including Classics and English), (3) the Physical Sciences (six including Chemistry, Physics, and Mathematics), and (4) the Social Sciences (five, including Economics and Psychology). Keniston compared the results of his rank ordering with that generated by Hughes in 1925 and commented on the changes in relative rankings based on earlier standings.

Problems of Sampling Bias

Each of the studies described above produced ratings of only a fraction of the doctoral programs in existence at the time, programs that the authors included in their studies because they deemed them to be the most prestigious.

The issue of sampling bias in studies of doctoral education—referred to as "geographical bias" by some authors—surfaced as an issue in academic circles in the 1960s. In his presidential address to the American Statistical Association in 1965, for example, Albert Bowker of the City University of New York suggested that future studies should look to sources such as the National Merit Scholarship Program or the Woodrow Wilson Fellowship Program to "identify [other] institutions where a large number of the ablest young people go to college or graduate school" and include them in national assessments of doctoral education (Bowker, 1965).

Around the same time, Allan Cartter, then vice president of the American Council on Education (ACE) and director of the ACE Commission on Plans and Objectives for Higher Education, expressed a similar concern to members of the commission (Cartter, 1966). As a result, Cartter and his colleagues designed a more extensive data-gathering effort involving 5,400 faculty in 30 disciplines at 106 major universities. The Cartter study was designed:

1. To bring earlier qualitative studies of graduate education up to date;
2. To widen the assessment to include all major universities in the United States on the assumption that major expansion would not come from the 10-15 traditionally distinguished universities; and
3. To learn as much as possible about the vagaries and pitfalls of subjective assessments in the interest of improving such measures for the future.

Cartter overcame the problem of what he called institutional "representativeness" by including the 100 charter members of the Council of Graduate Schools plus six institutions that awarded more than 100 doctoral degrees between 1953 and 1962. A sample of faculty members nominated by deans at those institutions was invited to record their opinions of about 33 departments in their fields in response to three questions:

1. Which of the terms below describe your judgment of *the quality of the graduate faculty* in your field at each institution listed?[4]
2. How would you rate the institutions below if you were selecting a graduate school to work for a doctorate in your field? Take into account . . . [the] factors that contribute to the *effectiveness of the doctoral program.*[5]
3. What *change in relative position* of departments in your field do you anticipate in the next 5-10 years?[6]

Thus, Cartter's study may be considered to be the first serious attempt to generate "better information" on graduate and professional education for the public, government agencies, and private foundations through a nationally representative sample of faculty opinion. In 1970, to avoid "freezing" the reputations of various universities by failing to update the results of earlier studies, Kenneth Roose and Charles Andersen—again under the auspices of the American Council on Education—replicated and expanded the Cartter study (Roose and Andersen, 1970). Thus, by the 1970s, surveys of faculty opinion had become established as a formal tool for gathering information about the status of doctoral education study in the United States. Furthermore, the Roose-Andersen report suggested that, given the nature and use of the results of those surveys, such studies might profitably be conducted periodically.

Seeking Objective Correlates of Subjective Ratings

The studies of Hughes, Keniston, Cartter, and Roose and Andersen relied entirely on "reputational" measures and were criticized for this. (See, for example, Dolan, 1976; Hartnett, Clark, and Baird, 1978.) Nonetheless, these studies have been used widely and for a variety of purposes. Participants at a 1976 Conference on the Assessment of Quality Graduate Education Programs organized by the Conference Board of Associated Research Councils[7] identified some of the uses to be:

> [B]y students and their advisors, by the institutions of higher education as aides to planning and the allocation of education functions, as a check of unwarranted claims of excellence, and in social science research.

What was needed, the 1976 conferees concluded, was a study "limited to research-doctorate programs and designed to improve upon the methodologies utilized in earlier studies" (Jones, Lindzey, and Coggeshall, 1982).

The Role of the Conference Board of Associated Research Councils

Established in 1944 to foster occasional broad-scale studies of the nation's scholarly, educational, and scientific infrastructures, the Conference Board consists of the chief executive officers and one representative each from the American Council on Education (ACE), the American Council of Learned Societies (ACLS), the Social Science Research Council (SSRC), and the National Research Council. (See Appendix A.)

> Some years after the release of the Roose-Andersen Report, it was decided that the effort to assess the quality of research-doctorate programs should be renewed, and the Conference Board of Associated Research Councils agreed to sponsor the assessment. The Board of Directors of the American Council on Education concurred with the notion that the next step should be issued under these broader auspices. The NRC agreed to serve as secretariat for a new study. (From the Preface: Jones, Lindzey, and Coggeshall, 1982.).

The board proposed to improve upon previous studies of doctoral program quality by: (1) providing raters with information about key features of each program (such as names of faculty members in those programs) and (2) collecting information about the characteristics of those programs to complement the substantive assessments embodied in reputational ratings with "objective measures" of program quality (D. Featherman, personal communication, 1994).

In June 1980, the National Research Council appointed an 18-member committee to oversee a study of research-doctorate programs.

Committee on an Assessment of Quality-Related Characteristics of Research-Doctorate Programs in the United States

A very different atmosphere surrounded the design of the 1982 study than those of the 1960s. The work of the 1982 study committee was undertaken at a time when the education and social science communities were involved in significant efforts to develop new techniques for increasing knowledge about graduate education. One example of these efforts was a study by Clark, Hartnett, and Baird (1978) who, looking at graduate programs in three fields, identified "as many as 30 possible measures significant for assessing the quality of graduate education" (Jones, Lindzey, and Coggeshall, 1982).

As a result of the greater emphasis on the use of multiple criteria for educational assessment, the study that was published in 1982 differed from previous studies by:

1. Focusing only on programs awarding research-doctorates, acknowledging that other purposes of doctoral training are important but were outside the scope of the 1982 study;
2. Employing multidimensional measures, explicitly recognizing the limitations of studies that rate programs solely on the "perceived quality" ratings of faculty peers; and
3. Improving the survey methodology by providing faculty raters with selected information about each of the programs included in the study.

The results of the study, *An Assessment of Research-Doctorate Programs in the United States*, were issued in five volumes, each containing results in one of five areas: Arts and Humanities, Biological Sciences, Engineering, Physical Sciences and Mathematics, and Social and Behavioral Sciences. The study was considered by many to represent the most comprehensive review of doctoral programs at that time (Webster, 1983).[8]

THE CONTEXT OF THE 1993 STUDY

Several important developments have occurred since the release of the 1982 report that have a bearing on the design of the present study. Two of the most important of these changes, discussed in the following sections of this chapter, are the expansion of the doctoral education enterprise and the emergence of new insights into data presentation.

Expansion of Graduate Education

By several measures, the extent of graduate education in general and the doctoral enterprise in particular, has increased substantially in the U.S. in recent years. The following data document some aspects of this expansion:

- The number of colleges and universities in the U.S. increased from 3,300 to 3,600 between 1987 and 1994.
- Enrollment in graduate education[9] increased from 450,436 in 1967 to 669,641 in 1992, an increase of approximately 50 percent in 25 years.
- The number of institutions awarding a Ph.D. increased from 325 in 1980 to 364 in 1992.
- From 1982 to 1994, the number of institutions in the most research-intensive categories established by the Carnegie Classification grew from 184 to 236—an increase of 52 institutions. Of this group of new institutions, 37 (or 71 percent) are in the Research I, or most research-intensive, category.
- The number of Ph.D.s awarded each year increased from 31,020 in 1980 to 39,754 in 1993, an increase of more than 25 percent.

Along with expansion in student enrollment and higher education institutions, the number of students considering graduate education has also increased in recent years. The number of individuals taking the Graduate Record Examination (GRE), which is required for entrance into most graduate schools, increased from 272,000 in 1980 to 412,000 in 1992. (See Table 1-1.) Average scores also improved during that time following a period of decline. This has been taken to imply an improvement in the quality of doctoral candidates, although no data sources are available to determine the relationship between scores for those who "intend" to pursue an advanced degree and those who actually "enroll" in doctoral programs.[10]

Just as the GRE data provide more useful information about students and potential students, data in the Doctorate Records File (DRF) illuminate changes in the institutional infrastructure of the graduate enterprise. (See Appendix G.) Questionnaires filled out by graduates completing their degrees show that most earn their degrees at institutions that first awarded doctorates before 1930.[11] (See Table 1-2.) However, since the 1970s the number of doctorates conferred by newer institutions has gradually expanded. Between 1990 and 1992, 8.2 percent of the doctorates conferred were awarded by institutions which had recorded the first doctorate after 1970.

TABLE 1-1 Scores on Graduate Record Examination (GRE) and Subject Matter Tests: 1980-1992

Academic Year End	Number of GRE Takers	GRE Takers as % of BA Degree	Verbal	Quantitative	Analytical
1980	272,281	29.3	474	522	—
1981	262,855	28.1	473	523	—
1982	256,381	26.9	469	533	498
1983	263,674	27.2	473	541	504
1984	265,221	27.2	475	541	512
1985	271,972	27.8	474	545	516
1986	279,428	28.3	475	552	520
1987	293,560	29.6	477	550	521
1988	303,703	30.5	483	557	528
1989	326,096	32.0	484	560	530
1990	344,572	32.8	486	562	534
1991	379,882	34.7	485	562	536
1992	411,528	37.2	483	561	537

NOTE: GRE scores for the verbal, quantitative and analytical sections range from 200 to 800.

SOURCES: Graduate Record Examination Board, *Examinee and Score Trends for the GRE General Test*, various years; *A Summary of Data Collected From Graduate Record Examinations Test-Takers During 1986-1987*; and U.S. Department of Education, National Center for Education Statistics, "Degrees and Other Formal Awards Conferred" surveys, and Integrated Postsecondary Education Data System (IPEDS), "Competitions" surveys.

TABLE 1-2 Number of Ph.D.s Awarded by U.S. Universities (1920-1992) by Reporting Period and Year in Which the Doctorate Records File Recorded the First Ph.D. Awarded by that Institution

			Institution Awarded First Ph.D.							
Reporting Period		Total	Before 1930	In the: 1930s	1940s	1950s	1960s	1970s	1980s	1990-1992
1920-1929	N	11,935	11,935							
	Ann Avg		1,194							
	%	*100.0*	*100.0*							
1930-1939	N	25,674	25,256	418						
	Ann Avg		2,526	42						
	%	*100.0*	*98.4*	*1.6*						
1940-1949	N	30,629	28,571	1,850	208					
	Ann Avg		2,875	185	21					
	%	*100.0*	*93.3*	*6.0*	*0.7*					
1950-1959	N	80,266	68,601	7,483	3,165	1,017				
	Ann Avg		6,860	749	317	102				
	%	*100.0*	*85.5*	*9.3*	*3.9*	*1.3*				
1960-1969	N	162,071	123,417	15,608	10,711	8,481	3,854			
	Ann Avg		12,342	1,561	1,071	848	385			
	%	*100.0*	*76.1*	*9.6*	*6.6*	*5.2*	*2.4*			
1970-1979	N	320,936	206,424	30,803	25,537	23,754	26,484	7,934		
	Ann Avg		20,642	3,080	2,554	2,375	2,648	793		
	%	*100.0*	*64.3*	*9.6*	*8.0*	*7.4*	*8.3*	*2.5*		
1980-1989	N	319,493	186,283	28,473	27,545	24,275	32,997	18,183	1,737	
	Ann Avg		18,628	2,847	2,755	2,428	3,300	1,818	174	
	%	*100.0*	*58.3*	*8.9*	*8.6*	*7.6*	*10.3*	*5.7*	*0.5*	
1990-1992	N	112,438	62,874	9,597	10,075	8,622	12,140	7,395	1,416	319
	Ann Avg		20,958	3,166	3,358	2,877	4,047	2,665	472	106
	%	*100.0*	*55.9*	*8.5*	*9.0*	*7.7*	*10.8*	*6.6*	*1.3*	*0.3*
Total	N	1,063,442	713,361	94,232	77,241	66,149	75,475	33,512	3,153	319
1920-1992	%	*100.0*	*67.1*	*8.9*	*7.3*	*6.2*	*7.1*	*3.2*	*0.3*	[a]

NOTE: Percentages for Reporting Period do not total to 100% due to rounding. "Ann Avg" refers to annual average of the total number of Ph.D.s produced in a period of time.

[a]Less than .1%.

SOURCE: National Research Council, Doctorate Records File, Special Tabulations, 1994.

The documented increases in many dimensions of graduate education, the creation of new degree-granting institutions, and the continuing apparent demand for doctoral education all underscored the importance of conducting a study designed to address issues of quality and quantity in the current research-doctorate education enterprise.

Data Presentation

In addition to the growth in doctoral education over the years, another factor that influenced the design of the 1993 NRC study was the possibility of both updating and improving the measures utilized in the 1982 study.

To discuss ways to enhance the next report, the Research Council invited a group of experts to a planning meeting in April 1991. (See Appendix B.) At the meeting conferees addressed a broad range of topics including the lessons learned from the design and impact of the earlier study. In general, conferees noted that the 1982 assessment represented a significant improvement over previous reputational studies in that raters were provided information about each doctoral program to be rated and that the statistics the committee had collected about each program were quite informative. However, many participants observed that the presentation of the data in the 1982 report (alphabetical listings by institution) created a source of frustration for many users. Thus, the conferees recommended strongly that the report prepared by the next study committee take a more "user friendly" form.

To improve understanding of the contributions of graduate programs to the preparation of research scholars and scientists, the conferees also suggested that the 1993 report include more data about each program ("input" measures). They also recommended that the committee try to gather information about the relationship between the 1982 reputational ratings and student "outcome."

A number of conferees suggested that as many features of the 1982 survey of graduate faculty as possible be maintained in order to permit statistical comparisons between the two surveys.

PROJECT GOALS

In 1991, the National Research Council established the Committee for the Study of Research-Doctorate Programs in the United States. With funding from the Andrew W. Mellon, Alfred P. Sloan, Ford, and William and Flora Hewlett Foundations, as well as from the National Academy of Sciences, a four-year study was launched to gather information about the present status of doctoral programs at U.S. universities. Like its predecessor, this study committee decided to restrict its analysis to "research-doctorate" programs at U.S. universities, thus paving the way for the possibility of calculating "change."

The overall objectives of the present study are to:

1. Update the 1982 *An Assessment of Research-Doctorate Programs in the United States*, which includes gathering peer views of program quality through a national survey;
2. Explore the feasibility of replicating and/or improving the "objective" measures of program quality included in the 1982 assessment;
3. Compare data from 1982 and the current study in cases where it is possible to calculate the "change" measures;
4. Create a data base that would permit interested analysts to explore the data beyond the analyses provided by this committee; and
5. Present findings in a way that is accessible to educators, administrators, students, and policymakers alike.

The information gathered by the committee has been collected on a field-by-field basis. A variety of statistics may be found in the appendixes located at the end of this report. Appendix G describes some of the data sets utilized by the committee. In addition, the committee has prepared an electronic file of detailed statistics that should permit meaningful comparisons of the data from the 1982 and 1993 studies.[12]

The committee intends that interested educational and social scientists will make extensive use of this data base to generate analyses that go well beyond the work of this committee.

ORGANIZATION OF THE REPORT

In the pages that follow, the committee presents the results of its data gathering activities and subsequent deliberations. The next chapter (Chapter 2) summarizes the steps that were taken to circumscribe the group of programs included in this study. Detailed information is also provided about the institutions in which these programs are located for those interested in exploring the relationship between relative program standing and institutional resources.

In Chapter 3, the committee presents key findings. These findings represent just a small subset of the tabulations that are possible given the size of the data set. The report concludes with a consideration of new directions future analysts might take in assessing the relative standing of research-doctorate programs.

NOTES

1. See, also, J. D'Arms (1994) for a brief discussion of those findings. A more general analysis of the relationship of student support and time to degree may be found in Tuckman, Coyle, and Bae (1980). Flattau (in preparation) addresses the overall need for better university-based statistics in the area of doctoral degree attainment for policy and planning.

2. Before reputational studies, there were assessments, but they were not systematic and broad in scope. See A. Granbard, "Notes Toward a New History," in J. Cole, E. Barber, and A. Granbard, 1994 (pages 361-390).

3. Cartter notes that the second report by Hughes introduced a bivariate classification scheme: adequate or distinguished. The results were published in the April 1934 issue of the *Educational Record.*

4. Categories included: "Distinguished," "Strong," "Good," "Adequate," "Marginal," "Not sufficient to provide acceptable doctoral training," and "Insufficient information."

5. Categories were: "Extremely attractive," "Attractive," "Acceptable," "Not attractive," and "Insufficient information."

6. Response categories included: "Relative improvement," "Same relative position," "Relative decline," and "Insufficient information."

7. See Appendix A for a description of the Conference Board. The results of the 1976 Conference are summarized in Jones, Lindzey, and Coggeshall, 1982.

8. In recent years, other reputational studies have been undertaken, the most prominent of which may be those conducted by the *U.S. News and World Report* (USNWR). The surveys by USNWR differ in a few important ways from those conducted by the NRC. For example, like the earlier studies by Hughes, USNWR samples the opinion of department chairs and other academic administrators rather than a random sample of the faculty and focuses on departments rather than specific degree programs. USNWR also provides information about selected characteristics of departments, but these measures often vary by field, making comparison across disciplines difficult.

9. This figure excludes enrollment in professional schools.

10. One exception is the joint study under way by the Association of Graduate Schools and the Graduate Record Examination Board, which is collecting information of this sort from member institutions. Information on the difference between "applicants" and "enrollments" on such items as GRE score should be available in the coming years. (Charlotte Kuh, personal communication, 1994.)

11. Based on reports from these graduates. Owing to the history of the Doctorate Records File, this technique records the first time a Ph.D. degree was awarded by an institution and recorded by the DRF. It does not serve as a record of the year in which the degree program was established. (See Appendix G.)

12. For information about the electronic data use file developed by the committee, readers are invited to contact:

National Research Council
Office of Scientific and Engineering Personnel
2101 Constitution Avenue, NW
Washington, DC 20418
E-mail: osepinq@nas.edu

2

STUDY DESIGN

A critical step in designing a study of "research-doctorate programs in the United States" is to define the target population, both to establish the boundaries of the analysis and to assure that a cost-effective procedure can be developed for collecting information about the programs included in the study. The decision to restrict the study to a limited number of doctoral fields is, of course, a difficult one because it results inevitably in the exclusion of some important areas of graduate study. Nonetheless, in the interest of providing useful information about the status of research-doctorate programs in the Sciences (including the broad fields of Biological Sciences, Physical Sciences and Mathematics, and Social and Behavioral Sciences), Engineering, and Arts and Humanities, the concentration of available resources on a more limited number of disciplines seemed both practical and necessary to the committee.

The work of this committee builds on the analytic foundations laid by the 1982 study committee (see Jones, Lindzey, and Coggeshall, 1982). Thus, the current data collection plan began with a review of the 32 disciplines included in the earlier study. The committee agreed that it would include the same set of fields found in the 1982 assessment, but also decided to include nine additional fields based on aggregate counts of doctoral degrees awarded between 1986 and 1990. This chapter reviews the overall study design and concludes with a statement of data collection goals.

FIELD COVERAGE

At the outset of the project, the committee selected fields to include in the present study based on a combination of three factors:

- The number of Ph.D.s produced nationally;
- The number of programs training Ph.D.s within a particular field; and
- The average number of Ph.D.s produced per program.[1]

For purposes of generating comparisons and insights into the trends over the last decade, the committee wanted to include as many fields as possible from the 1982 assessment in the 1993 study. The committee also wanted to produce a study that would be as national in scope as possible by capturing information on the fields that are currently attracting and awarding Ph.D.s to the greatest number of students.

After reviewing and analyzing the data from the 1982 study and Doctorate Records File data on Ph.D.s awarded from 1986 to 1990, the committee adopted a criterion of "robustness"—namely that, to be included in the 1993 study, a field must have awarded a minimum of about 500 degrees in about 50 programs for the years 1986 to 1990. (A detailed description of this analysis may be found in Appendix C.)

As a result of this analysis, field coverage in this report consists of:

- All fields in the 1982 report, although the Biological Sciences are presented differently;
- These new fields:
  - Comparative Literature
  - Religion
  - Aerospace Engineering
  - Biomedical Engineering
  - Industrial Engineering
  - Materials Science
  - Astronomy and Astrophysics
  - Oceanography; and
- Some new fields in the Biological Sciences.[2]

ELIGIBILITY CRITERIA

As part of its study design, the committee reviewed and approved criteria for determining which programs to include in the study. The first step was to identify those universities eligible for inclusion in the study. The next step was to invite those institutions to add and delete programs from that list. The number of doctoral degrees awarded by a given institution played a crucial role in determining eligibility.

Level of Degree Production

Once "field coverage" was determined, the committee then decided to invite to participate in the study any institution within a field that produced at least three Ph.D.s between 1988 and 1990 and one Ph.D. in 1991 or that had a rating of 2.0 or better in that field in the 1982 study (in the event the institution did not produce one Ph.D. in 1991). Under these criteria, institutions were eligible to participate in the study even if they had only one program in only one of the fields included in the study. Three hundred universities were identified as having at least one doctoral program that met those criteria.

Invitation to Participate in the Study

The committee next wrote to presidents of the eligible universities inviting them to participate in the study. (See Appendix D.) Sixteen universities did not respond to the invitation or declined to participate.[3]

The committee also asked each university president to identify an individual at the university to serve as the Institutional Coordinator for the study—someone with whom staff could work at succeeding stages of program selection. The Institutional Coordinator (IC) most often was the Graduate Dean at the university. These individuals made a major contribution to the success of this study through their diligence and care in responding to subsequent requests for information.

Program Selection by Participating Institutions

Institutional Coordinators at 284 universities were sent a list of programs at their institutions eligible for inclusion in the study based on the criterion of Ph.D. production described above. A form also was sent to each IC for each eligible program to collect information as outlined in Appendix D. Ten institutions failed to provide information within the timeframe established by the committee.[4]

The committee also invited ICs to nominate programs in one of the fields included in the study in the event that the committee's criteria had overlooked especially strong programs at their institutions.

The committee acknowledges that this procedure may have resulted in the omission of a number of meritorious programs whose representatives have subsequently expressed interest in having been included in the study.[5] When individuals, early in the process, indicated to the committee that the study did not include a program that they considered eligible, the committee adopted a specific guideline for staff: to correct any errors that may have been introduced in the handling of program information, such as overlooking a program listed by an IC. However, the committee concluded that it was not feasible to correct (or even anticipate) errors of omission or commission that might have occurred at the campus level, and thus directed staff to refrain from modifying lists provided by the ICs.

Perhaps the most frequent question raised by faculty members who corresponded with the committee about eligibility criteria was the issue of including "new" programs whose faculty were clearly strong scholars but which had not yet produced a Ph.D. or fell below the criteria outlined in the earlier section. Again, the committee decided that unless an IC specifically nominated a new program for review, it would not be included in the 1993 study. We would like to point out, however, that future studies of research-doctorate programs will undoubtedly include some of the new programs deemed ineligible for the present study. Omission from the list does not signal that a program is "poor" or "not distinguished." It simply means that the program may not have been included because patterns of degree production as recorded by the Doctorate Records File did not identify it as eligible and/or the Institutional Coordinator did not include it in the list of programs to be rated at that institution.

The Biological Sciences

In his 1966 report, Cartter noted that the taxonomy of Biological Sciences represented a special challenge to analysts because of the wide variation in their administrative organization on campuses throughout the United States. In the 1990s, the variation is even greater than that encountered by Cartter. The committee notes, for example, that important changes in the underlying knowledge base in the last decade have been accompanied once again by changes in the organization of the graduate experience in this area. Interested in reflecting contemporary campus arrangements in the Biological Sciences, the committee began the process of naming the appropriate "target population" in this area by reviewing aggregate Ph.D. information from the Doctorate Records File. A sample set of data from the Biological Sciences as reviewed by the committee may be found in Table 2-1.

TABLE 2-1 Ph.D. Production in Selected Fields in the Biological Sciences by Field, Institution, and Program Within Institution, 1986-1990

Specialty	Number of Ph.D.s	Number of Institutions
Biochemistry†	3,113	211
Microbiology†	2,553	192
Cellular/Molecular Biology†	2,441	181
Botany†	1,947	103
Physiology†	1,261	164
Human and Animal Pharmacology	1,215	137
Ecology	823	131
Neurosciences	809	118
Zoology†	715	91
Total Biological Sciences	14,877	248

NOTE: "Number of Institutions" refers to a count of universities awarding degrees in that area based on reports from individuals earning degrees in a DRF field between 1986 and 1990.

†Designates fields included in the 1982 Study.

SOURCE: National Research Council, Doctorate Records File, Special Tabulations, 1992.

The 1982 study included six fields in the Biological Sciences: Biochemistry, Microbiology, Cellular/Molecular Biology, Botany, Physiology, and Zoology. As a result of changes in Ph.D. production since the release of the 1982 report, we found that now three disciplines (including the "Neurosciences") exceeded "Zoology" in the number of degrees awarded between 1986 and 1990. This suggested to the committee that changes were needed in the "Biological Sciences" field list to permit the inclusion of these other fields.

In the course of expanding the Biological Sciences field coverage, the committee also considered whether it would be necessary to adapt the DRF field list to reflect contemporary doctoral program arrangements. The committee consulted with a number of professional organizations in the course of considering the various options, and, based on its own focus group analysis, decided to abandon the 1982 study taxonomy in favor of one believed to reflect more accurately current campus conditions. The committee defined the target population by assigning the 1982 DRF categories to a new set of categories and creating a disciplinary "crosswalk" that was subsequently presented to the Institutional Coordinators for purposes of providing information to the committee about their programs. This list that was developed is presented below:

- Biochemistry and Molecular Biology
  - Biochemistry
  - Cellular/**Molecular** Biology
- Cell and Developmental Biology
  - Microbiology
  - **Cellular**/Molecular Biology
- Molecular and General Genetics
  - Human and Animal Genetics
- Neurosciences
- Pharmacology
  - Human and Animal Pharmacology
  - Toxicology
- Ecology, Evolution, and Behavior
  - Zoology
  - Botany
  - Ecology
- Physiology[6]

The decision to use this taxonomy caused problems for some institutions. At first, universities were told that the programs included in the study were identified by the DRF classification, which had been used initially to establish institutional eligibility. The committee subsequently replaced the DRF classification system with the categories reported in Appendix C, but took the step of creating a "crosswalk" that allowed participating institutions to understand the relationship of the DRF fields with the new classification system. This was a listing of DRF fields within the list generated by the committee (shown in the preceding paragraph).

A few institutions found that their research-doctorate programs in some biological subfields resembled the original DRF field designation more closely than the new listing. In those cases institutions were allowed to submit information about the program using the DRF rubric. They were informed, however, that the committee would retain their program designation solely for purposes of conducting the National Survey of Graduate Faculty (described later) and would present composite information using the committee's Biological Sciences listing in the published report.[7] Thus, an effort was made on a case-by-case basis to address problems encountered by institutions in responding to the new field designations while retaining the committee's classification system.

Faculty Lists

Institutional Coordinators were asked to provide a limited amount of information about each program included in the study. (See Appendix D.) A key piece of information was a list of faculty members associated with each doctoral program included in the study. These faculty lists were included in the National Survey of Graduate Faculty and were also used to generate statistics about faculty research and publication activities.[8]

Most ICs compiled faculty lists that reflected the mix of

faculty involved in doctoral studies—including staff from other programs in the same department or from other departments on the same campus. Owing to the increasingly multidisciplinary nature of doctoral studies, the way in which ICs approached the task occasionally had the effect of overlooking some faculty members who might otherwise have been included in a program listing. The committee became aware of this problem during the course of conducting a limited number of focus group discussions of sample questionnaires in anticipation of the National Survey of Graduate Faculty, described in the next section. The committee asked staff to check carefully that faculty lists provided by ICs were handled correctly at each stage of data processing and were satisfied that they had done so.[9] The committee concluded, however, that it was infeasible to introduce changes into faculty lists once they had been processed by the NRC staff.

The interdisciplinary nature of doctoral studies is evident especially in the faculty lists submitted in the Biological Sciences. The committee is aware that many programs are "large" because of the multiple listing of the same faculty in related fields. It is important to understand how differences occurred in the formation of faculty lists in order to guide the interpretation and use of data presented in this report.

Overall Results of Eligibility Determination

At the conclusion of this entire process, a total of 3,634 programs in 41 fields at 274 universities were included in the entire study. This represents about 35 percent more programs than the number included in the 1982 study. About 78,000 faculty members provided training through these programs, and trained about 90 percent of the total number of Ph.D.s produced in these fields between 1986 and 1992, although this ranged from a low of 79 percent in Religion to a high of 98 percent in Electrical Engineering. (See Table 2-2.)

CHARACTERISTICS OF PARTICIPATING INSTITUTIONS

Appendix E lists the institutions participating in the study and compares them with those participating in the 1982 study. Of the 228 institutions in the 1982 study, 214 participated once again in the 1993 update. Another 60 institutions participated in the present analysis for the first time.[10] Most institutions involved in the 1982 study increased the number of programs being reviewed, a reflection in part of the expansion of field coverage from 32 disciplines in 1982 to 41 in 1993.

Of the 274 universities in the 1993 study, 105 were private and 169 were public universities.

The Doctorate Records File provides a useful source of information about the year in which an institution awarded its first Ph.D.—or, more precisely, when the first Ph.D. was recorded by the DRF. In keeping with the degree patterns discussed in Chapter 1, about half of the doctoral programs included in the study are located at universities awarding the first Ph.D. before 1930. It is interesting to note, however, that in the Biological Sciences a significant share of research-doctorate programs may be found at institutions awarding the Ph.D. for the first time in 1950 or thereafter. (See Table 2-2.)

The Carnegie Classification system is widely used for categorizing institutions according to the range and number of programs they offer, the number and types of degrees they award, and the amount of federal research funding they receive. The broadest, most research-intensive institutions fall into the following categories: Research Universities I and II, and Doctoral Universities I and II, with Research Universities I including the largest, most research-intensive institutions.

It is possible to array the 274 institutions participating in this study by that system, and for institutions within the five "broad fields" comprising this study. As Table 2-3 reveals, the widest dispersion by Carnegie category occurs in the Biological Sciences, which have programs in 34 out of 60 institutions classified as "other." For each of the broad fields, a large share of the programs are at institutions in the Research University I and II category.

When considered by Carnegie Classification (Research University I, and so on), a considerable range in research resources is evident among participating institutions, as indicated in Appendix E. Total Federal research and development (R&D) expenditures in fiscal 1992 ranged from a low of $4 million to a high of $215 million among Research I institutions. Fiscal 1992 Federal R&D expenditures seldom exceeded $10 million at the remaining institutions, with a few exceptions.

Another important feature of the doctoral education environment involves access to resources for conducting research. The committee had hoped initially to gather information about specialized collections, museums, non-degree-granting research institutes, and other campus resources, but was unable to do so.[11] Instead it has reported basic information about campus libraries. (See Appendix E.) This information, it is hoped, can be used by interested analysts to calculate changes in those measures as reported by the 1982 study committee.[12]

DATA COLLECTION STRATEGIES

In addition to the overall goals outlined in the first chapter, the committee identified several goals and strategies for collecting data. This section states each goal and describes how the committee implemented it.

TABLE 2-2 Estimated Range of Institutional Coverage by 1993 Study of Research-Doctorate Programs in the United States by Field

	Number of Institutions			Number of Study Institutions Awarding 1st Ph.D.		
Field of Study	Awarding Ph.D. Between 1986 and 1992	In the NRC Study	% of Total Ph.D.s 1986 to 1992[a]	Before 1930	1930-1949	1950 and After
Art History	58	38	93	31	4	3
Classics	47	29	88	26	2	1
Comparative Literature[b]	71	44	90	34	4	6
English Language and Literature	146	127	96	62	20	45
French Language and Literature	79	45	84	38	5	2
German Language and Literature	59	32	83	26	3	3
Linguistics	77	41	91	28	7	6
Music	89	65	89	40	10	15
Philosophy	110	71	88	52	10	9
Religion[b]	72	38	79	23	7	8
Spanish and Portuguese Lang and Lit	84	54	84	37	7	10
Total	*192*	*148*		*65*	*71*	*56*
Biochemistry and Molecular Biology[b]	227	187	95	64	29	94
Cell and Developmental Biology[b]	217	165	93	61	27	77
Ecology, Evolution, and Behavior[b]	159	127	96	50	24	53
Molecular and General Genetics[b]	110	102	85	45	20	37
Neurosciences[b]	154	98	83	46	15	37
Pharmacology[b]	164	121	88	48	22	51
Physiology	176	135	87	51	24	60
Total	*256*	*203*		*66*	*33*	*106*
Aerospace Engineering[b]	56	33	90	20	7	6
Biomedical Engineering[b]	86	38	83	24	4	10
Chemical Engineering	121	93	96	48	24	21
Civil Engineering	130	86	93	45	20	21
Electrical Engineering	154	126	98	52	24	50
Industrial Engineering[b]	69	37	81	17	12	8
Materials Science[b]	97	62	92	35	12	15
Mechanical Engineering	143	110	95	52	24	34
Total	*256*	*193*		*57*	*25*	*61*
Astrophysics and Astronomy[b]	76	33	83	24	5	4
Chemistry	203	168	97	68	30	70
Computer Sciences	156	107	93	58	18	31
Geosciences	127	95	95	49	17	29
Mathematics	169	135	83	61	24	50
Oceanography[b]	50	26	97	10	5	11
Physics	182	146	97	67	24	55
Statistics and Biostatistics	122	58	80	32	14	12
Total	*245*	*197*		*71*	*34*	*92*
Anthropology	95	69	93	45	10	14
Economics	135	106	95	61	19	26
Geography	53	36	84	22	10	4
History	158	111	93	62	16	33
Political Science	129	97	96	58	17	22
Psychology	228	185	91	69	33	83
Sociology	125	95	93	53	16	26
Total	*252*	*198*		*72*	*35*	*90*

NOTE: Biological Sciences cannot be estimated accurately owing to recombination of DRF fields to create study taxonomy. See also Appendix D.

[a]See Appendix C.

[b]Fields added to the study since the 1982 assessment (Jones, Lindzey, and Coggeshall, 1982).

SOURCE: National Research Council, Doctorate Records File, Special Tabulations, 1992.

TABLE 2-3 Distribution of Participating Institutions by Carnegie Classification and Broad Field

Broad Field	Research I and II (N=127)	Doctoral I and II (N=87)	Other (N=60)
Arts and Humanities	100	38	11
Biological Sciences	123	49	34
Engineering	104	33	3
Physical Sciences and Mathematics	123	64	11
Social and Behavioral Sciences	123	49	34

NOTE: "N" refers to number of institutions participating in this study. See Appendix E for definitions and detailed statistics. Entries do not total to "N" because institutions may have had programs in more than one broad field.

National Survey of Graduate Faculty

Goal: Mail questionnaire to a probability sample of faculty in participating research-doctorate programs. This questionnaire should replicate key questions that appeared on the 1982 survey form or improve upon items that had proven less useful in the prior study.

The National Survey of Graduate Faculty was conducted in the Spring of 1993. The survey form (see Appendix F) was designed to replicate much of the material included in the 1982 study to permit the calculation of "change" measures as discussed in Appendix B. That is, the questionnaire included approximately 50 randomly selected programs in a field, asked for background information on each rater, provided a clear set of instructions, and listed selected information about each program being rated, such as university, city and state location, number of doctoral recipients between 1987 and 1992, and a list of faculty involved in doctoral training as provided by the Institutional Coordinator. Faculty were asked to record selected background information and a rating along certain dimensions as shown below. (See Figure 2-1).

Survey forms were sent to a sample of faculty raters, chosen from lists provided by the ICs, in all 41 fields included in the study. Approximately 19 percent of the faculty included in the study were sent a questionnaire.

B1. **Familiarity with work of Program Faculty**
Mark (x) One

1. ___Considerable familiarity
2. ___Some familiarity
3. ___Little or no familiarity

B2. **Scholarly Quality of Program Faculty**
Mark (x) One

1. ___Distinguished
2. ___Strong
3. ___Good
4. ___Adequate
5. ___Marginal
6. ___Not sufficient for doctoral education

9. ___Don't know well enough to evaluate

B3. **Familiarity with Graduates of this Program**
Mark (x) One

1. ___Considerable familiarity
2. ___Some familiarity
3. ___Little or no familiarity

B4. **Effectiveness of Program in Educating Research Scholars/Scientists**
Mark (x) One

1. ___Extremely effective
2. ___Reasonably effective
3. ___Minimally effective
4. ___Not effective

9. ___Don't know well enough to evaluate

B5. **Change in Program Quality in Last Five Years**
Mark (x) One

1. ___Better than five years ago
2. ___Little or no change in the last five years
3. ___Poorer than five years ago

9. ___Don't know well enough to evaluate

FIGURE 2-1 Excerpt from the 1993 NRC National Survey of Graduate Faculty.

The committee set as its goal a total of at least 100 ratings per program. To achieve that goal, each program appeared once on at least 200 questionnaires. More details regarding the sampling method may be found in Appendix F.

Based on responses from each faculty member to the National Survey of Graduate Faculty, the committee generated a variety of measures that describe research-doctorate programs. For example, one measure utilized most often in this survey and in previous surveys of this type is the reputational rating of the "scholarly quality of program faculty." This rating is calculated for each program and the findings used to describe how programs vary with respect to that characteristic.

The other reputational measure calculated from this survey is the reputational rating of the "effectiveness of programs in educating research scholars and scientists." Whereas a variety of more quantifiable characteristics are thought to contribute to the emergence of the faculty rating—such as research and publication activities, contributions to the intellectual advancement of a field, and location of employment (Merton, 1968; Coser, 1975; Cole, 1979)—the "effectiveness" rating is less well explored. This measure is believed by many to correlate closely with the career outcomes of program graduates (See Appendix B.) The committee regrets that constraints of time and resources prevented a systematic survey of program graduates to check this hypothesis.

What Reputational Measures Do and Don't Tell Us

The data generated from this study will permit analysts to extend their work on the nature of "reputational ratings" or the opinions of faculty peers about a program. Multivariate analyses can be conducted to explore in detail the factors thought to contribute to the emergence of "reputation" among doctoral programs.

In 1991, NRC staff generated an internal working plan that analyzed the correlation of various measures found in the 1982 report.[13] From that analysis—and based on the expert views of committee members—there are several statements that can be made with reasonable certainty about the interpretation of the reputational measures provided in this report.

- *Reputational measures correlate positively with program size.*

Larger programs tend to have higher reputational scores than smaller programs, although this phenomenon varies by field. The reasons for this correlation are complex but are related to the fact that larger programs are more likely to have faculty engaged in research and scholarship, who publish and who have impact on a field. This in turn attracts more resources for those faculty. Furthermore, a community of scholars also emerges as active faculty attract other faculty who are active in research and scholarship, which in turn attracts good students. Thus, as Robert K. Merton (1968) has said, the reward system without deliberate attempt influences the "class structure" within a field by providing the opportunity for faculty in some programs to enlarge their roles in a field.

- *The reputational rating of a program is related to the level of involvement of faculty in research and scholarly activities.*

A certain visibility accrues when faculty not only achieve success in getting national support for their endeavors, but also when they disseminate the findings of their work through publications. The relationship between research and scholarly reputation has been described most extensively by such authors as Merton (1968), Cole and Cole (1973), and Cole and Lipton (1977). However, the relationship between the relative standing of programs within fields relative to this dimension merits further analysis in light of the findings from this study.

The strong positive correlation between the size of a faculty in a program and its reputational standing has not been explored thoroughly. It is possible that reputations of a department or program are built almost entirely upon the reputations of those members of a faculty who are highly visible and who have been widely recognized for their scientific or scholarly contributions. Those members of the same department who have not achieved strong individual reputations may not detract from the overall reputational evaluation of the program by peers. People judge those that they know, not those who are "invisible" to them. If a program has none or few visible faculty members—that is few with strong scientific or scholarly reputations—the department is apt to be rated poorly, or not rated at all by peers.

But among those raters who are aware of the reputation of faculty members at rated programs, the general reputational assessment may be determined more often by the sheer number of visible scholars and scientists with lofty reputations than by the ratio of visible scientists and scholars to the total size of the department or program. Consider a simple example. A program with 50 members, 10 of whom have *individual* distinguished reputations, may be more likely to be rated as "distinguished" by a rater than a department with 20 members, 6 of whom have distinguished individual reputations. In the first case, there are 10 distinguished faculty, but the ratio—or density of distinction—is 10 of 50 or 20 percent. In the second case, there are fewer distinguished individuals, 6, but the ratio is 6 of 20, or 30 percent. But differences in density of distinction within a program can translate into many differences in the environment for graduate study. We do not know yet how the reputations of individuals relate to the generalized reputation of a program.

Does the presence of one Nobel laureate equate to some larger number of National Academy of Sciences members, or some other number of faculty receiving other forms of honorific recognition from their peers? Understanding the determinants of individual as opposed to collective reputational standings remains for further analysis.

- *Reputational ratings do not tell us how well a program is structured, whether it offers a nurturing environment for students, or if the job placement experiences of its graduates are satisfactory.*

Students using this report should be aware that the reputational ratings of these programs reflect, for the most part, the research activity of faculty associated with a doctoral program. For example, students interested in a strong research-training experience will be able to identify programs whose faculty are esteemed by peers because of their scholarly contributions to the field and because of their strong ratings. However, it should not be overlooked that there are some programs with lower ratings that have faculty engaged in research of interest to students. These lower-rated programs may be located in institutions whose primary missions differ from those of large research universities. Thus, to determine whether a particular program offers the experience they are seeking, students should draw upon the information found in this report along with other types of available information. In the next section we describe a number of measures to be used for this purpose—such as number of graduates or patterns of student support—although these are by no means the only types of information available to students interested in doctoral training at a particular institution.

- *Reputational ratings are influenced by a number of other factors that limit their usefulness in judging quality.*

Survey experts have documented that individuals asked to rate others on the basis of reputation are influenced by a number of subtle factors (Cole, 1979). Although it is impossible to determine the precise amount of influence, it is important to keep these factors in mind in analyzing the results of reputational ratings. These factors include:

- There are "stars" in fields who have been anointed as such by virtue of their actual achievements, by their appointment to various high-ranking departments, or by their honorific recognition. Many members within the scholarly community accept these individuals as "stars" on the basis of "authority," not on the basis of their own reading and evaluation of work.
- Just as an institution with a lofty reputation may create a "halo effect" for the reputation of its individual members, universities with distinguished reputations can create "halo effects" for the evaluation of the reputations of individual departments. An institution with many very highly rated programs may cast a "halo" over some that do not merit as lofty a reputation. Thus, there may be some upward, or downward, bias in reputational measures resulting from the overall evaluation of the larger university.
- Reputational scores may be influenced by the visibility of a department or university. Without adequate information, an evaluator may assume if she or he does not know of the department, that its doctoral programs must be less than distinguished. It would be valuable to examine the relationship between levels of information about programs and their actual evaluations.
- Reputational ratings may be influenced by the detailed analysis that should be carried out on the attributes of the raters. For example, are alumni of programs more or less apt to rate their alma mater as distinguished? Does the current location of her or his academic rank or standing influence the judgments made?

Detailed correlation studies of the ratings and raters in the 1993 study could provide significantly more insight into these phenomena.

- *Reputational standing does not take into account other elements in the "quality of faculty performance," such as contributions to teaching of graduate and undergraduate students or contributions to the welfare of departments, the institution, or the larger academic community.*

Most faculty members in research-doctorate programs teach graduate or undergraduate students as well as conduct research. They also are expected to contribute to the welfare of the department or program and the university through service on a committee or by taking on administrative or other duties. In many cases they are expected to contribute to the local community, as well as the broader academic community. Since these activities rarely result in products known to the national community of scholars (like publications, grants, or honors and awards), they cannot be measured through a national reputational survey. The relationship of these elements to the quality of the education of graduate students is unknown.

In summary, reputational measures provide only one tool, albeit a valuable one, for reviewing the relative standing of doctoral programs in a field. There are many features of doctoral programs not captured by these ratings and readers should have a clear understanding of this limitation.

Program Characteristics

Goal: Identify and collect data describing key features of each of the 3,634 participating programs. Focus on variables thought to be related to perceived quality of program faculty or program effectiveness.

In 1982, the NRC contributed to the development of national studies of research-doctorate programs by expanding such analyses beyond the use of a simple measure, such as "reputation," to the use of multiple measures of program quality. In selecting variables, the 1982 study committee drew on work by the Educational Testing Service (Clark, Hartnett, and Baird, 1976) and "was aided by the many suggestions received from university administrators and others within the academic community" (Jones, Lindzey, and Coggeshall, 1982).

In its 1991 planning meeting (see Appendix B), the NRC initiated a review of the measures used by the 1982 study committee and considered other types of data that might be collected in the 1993 study. Subsequent discussion by the project committee led to the development of these general guidelines:

- Identify measures that were presented in the 1982 report that can be updated in 1992-1993, but consider recasting the presentation of some of those measures;
- Include other measures to the extent they are available; and
- Generate new measures.

Updating and Refining the 1982 "Objective Measures"

Participants in the 1991 project planning meeting offered a number of interesting comments about the usefulness of the objective measures presented in the 1982 report. Those data were useful—especially to Graduate Deans to assess the standing of their programs relative to other programs with respect to the number of graduates or levels of student support. (See Appendix B.) Conferees asked that attention be given to the further refinement of some of the earlier measures. The variables listed in Table 2-4 reflect some of the changes that were suggested. Appendix G describes several of the data sources that were used by the committee in updating the 1982 measures and adding new ones.

Like the earlier study group, this committee's selection of data for "updating" was influenced by the availability of some measures and lack of availability of others. For example, the Association of Research Libraries (ARL) continues to serve as an important source of information about characteristics of university libraries; however, data are restricted to member libraries. To expand the data set, the present committee abandoned the use of the ARL composite index (Jones, Lindzey, and Coggeshall, 1982) and presents instead basic statistics about volumes, serials, and expenditures, which permits the addition of library data from other sources, such as the Association of College and Research Libraries and the U.S. Department of Education. (See Appendixes E and G.)

Since the last study on this topic was published, changes have taken place in some data systems, which had a bearing on the selection and use of statistics in this report. For example, the Institute for Scientific Information (ISI) has continued to expand and improve its data regarding publications and citations since the 1982 study.

Early in its deliberations the committee commissioned an analysis of the potential use of the expanded ISI files within the context of the present study. Through this work and subsequent committee discussion, the committee is able to present more detailed information about publication/citation patterns among program faculty than that found in the earlier report.[14] Like the 1982 study committee, this committee found data in the area of the Arts and Humanities to be lacking and has not reported information in that area.[15]

The Survey of Earned Doctorates (SED), which generates the statistics found in the Doctorate Records File, has dropped an item from the questionnaire that was used by the earlier committee—the name of the thesis adviser. This item was particularly useful to generate counts of "program" graduates by linking names of faculty on lists provided by ICs with adviser names found in the DRF. In the absence of such information, the committee had to adopt a different strategy for presenting statistics about the "characteristics" of graduates. (See Table 2-4.) The tables in this report present statistics on the number of Ph.D.s from a program based on information provided by the IC.

Because the committee wanted to present information about patterns of student support [such as Research Assistantships (RA) or Teaching Assistantships (TA)] but no longer could link advisers with graduates, another method for generating those statistics was adopted. The committee generated its own counts of Ph.D.s by field and by institution from the Doctorate Records File and then generated statistics on "Doctoral Recipients" (Table 2-4). For example, the statistic on Research Assistantships (%RA) is the percentage of graduates who reported research assistantships as their primary source of financial support in the DRF. An internal review of the Ph.D. counts generated by the ICs and by NRC staff suggest that small but systematic differences occur in the number of graduates per program.

The differences are sufficiently small to suggest that the data reported under the "Doctoral Recipients" category are reliable. Nonetheless, in the absence of information about thesis adviser from the SED, these statistics should be interpreted as an indicator of relative standing of programs along these dimensions. The calculation of change measures is possible only to the extent the 1982 data are retabulated to conform to the 1993 estimation method. Thus, readers are once again cautioned to refrain from making comparisons between proportion of students with support, for example, using the two studies.[16]

TABLE 2-4 Selected Characteristics of Research-Doctorate Programs in the 1993 Study

	Institution
Institution:	U.S. Universities participating in the 1993 NRC Study, ranked in descending order based on the scholarly rating of the program faculty (93Q).
	1993 Ratings
93Q:	1993 trimmed mean for scholarly quality of program faculty. The trimmed mean is obtained by dropping the two highest and two lowest scores on the survey before computing the average. For purposes of analysis, scores were converted to a scale of 0 to 5, with 0 denoting "Not sufficient for doctoral education" and 5 denoting "Distinguished." Source: NRC National Survey of Graduate Faculty.
93E:	1993 trimmed mean for program effectiveness in educating research scholars and scientists. The trimmed mean is obtained by dropping the two highest and two lowest scores on the survey before computing the average. For purposes of analysis, scores were converted to a scale of 0 to 5 with 0 denoting "Not Effective" and 5 denoting "Extremely Effective." Source: NRC National Survey of Graduate Faculty.
93C:	1993 trimmed mean for change in program quality in the last five years. The trimmed mean is obtained by dropping the two highest and two lowest scores on the survey before computing the average. For purposes of analysis, scores were converted to a scale of –1 to 1 with –1 denoting "Poorer than 5 years ago" and 1 denoting "Better than 5 years ago." Source: NRC National Survey of Graduate Faculty.
	Faculty
Tot Fac:	Total number of faculty participating in the program. Source: Institutional Coordinators.
%Full:	Percentage of full professors participating in the program. Source: Institutional Coordinators.
%Supp	Percentage of program faculty (Tot Fac) with research support (1986-1992). Source: Federal Agencies.
For Arts and Humanities:	
No. Awd:	Total number of awards and honors attributed to program faculty for the period 1986-1992. Source: See Appendix G for award organizations.
Awd Fac:	Percentage of program faculty that have received at least one honor or award for the period 1986-1992. Source: See Appendix G for award organizations.
For the fields in Engineering and the Sciences:	
%Pub:	Percentage of program faculty (Tot Fac) publishing in the period 1988 to 1992. Source: Institute of Scientific Information.
Pub/Fac:	The ratio of the total number of program publications in the period 1988-1992 to the number of program faculty (Tot Fac). Source: Institute of Scientific Information.
Gini Pub:	Gini coefficient for program publications, 1988-1992. The Gini coefficient is an indicator of the concentration of publications on a small number of the program faculty during the period 1988-92. The largest possible value, or maximum concentration, is 100 (only one individual in the program registered a positive count); the smallest value, or minimum concentration, is 100/Fac [All the faculty (Tot Fac) in the program contribute equally]. Source: Institute of Scientific Information.
Cite/Fac:	The ratio of the total number of program citations in the period 1988-1992 to the number of program faculty (Tot Fac). Source: Institute of Scientific Information.
Gini Cite:	Gini coefficient for program citations, 1988-1992. The Gini coefficient is an indicator of the concentration of citations on a small number of the program faculty during the period 1988-1992. The largest possible value, or maximum concentration, is 100 (only one individual in the program registered a positive count); the smallest value, or minimum concentration, is 100/Fac [All the faculty (Tot Fac) in the program contribute equally]. Source: Institute of Scientific Information.

continued

TABLE 2-4 *Continued*

	Students
Tot Stu:	The number of full and part time graduate students enrolled in the Fall of 1992. Source: Institutional Coordinators.
%Fem:	The percentage of full and part time female graduate students enrolled in the Fall of 1992. Source: Institutional Coordinators.
Rpt Ph.D.s:	The number of Ph.D.s produced by that program for the period academic year 1987-1988 to 1991-1992. Source: Institutional Coordinators.
	Doctoral Recipients
%Fem:	The percentage of Ph.D.s awarded to women during the period July 1986-June 1992. Source: Doctorate Records File.
%Min:	The percentage of Ph.D.s known to be awarded to underrepresented minorities (only U.S. Citizens or Permanent Residents) during the period July 1986-June 1992. Source: Doctorate Records File.
%US:	The percentage of Ph.D.s known to be awarded to U.S. Citizens and Permanent Residents during the period July 1986-June 1992. Source: Doctorate Records File.
%RA:	The percentage of Ph.D.s having research assistantships who reported their primary form of support. Source: Doctorate Records File.
%TA:	The percentage of Ph.D.s having teaching assistantships who reported their primary form of support. Source: Doctorate Records File.
MYD:	Median time lapse from entering graduate school to receipt of Ph.D. in years. This is a distributed median with multiple degrees awarded in the median year proportioned over the year. Source: Doctorate Records File.

Exploratory Studies

Goal: Add new measures to the data base by conducting studies that would generate those statistics.

The 1982 study committee identified several areas in which new or "other" statistics would advance our knowledge about research-doctorate programs. One area that they identified involves information about graduates of these research-doctorate programs, a measure subsequently mentioned again by participants attending the 1991 planning meeting. (See Appendix B.) Other innovations explored by the committee, and described below, include industrial views of Ph.D. programs relative to employer needs, and enhanced survey techniques.

Career Outcomes of Program Graduates

An important but missing element in both the 1982 and 1993 assessments of research-doctorate programs is the analysis of the career outcomes of program graduates. Such an analysis would help to determine the effectiveness of those programs in preparing research scholars/scientists: Is there a relationship between program factors and the subsequent involvement by graduates in research and scholarship?

The present committee discussed two possible strategies for the design of an "alumni" study to generate such data. The first was a survey of a sample of graduates from programs rated in the 1982 study. The second approach involved exploring publication patterns of program graduates. Unfortunately, the committee was unable to raise the funds needed to conduct this work within the time frame allotted for this study. However, the committee is aware of a number of studies being planned or conducted that explore the relationship between doctoral training and career outcomes.[17]

Furthermore, committee members were not in complete agreement that patterns of research and development activity or of publishing among program graduates could be attributed to program factors. Sociologists who have studied "stratification" in science as an area of knowledge and as an occupation point out that over the career of a doctoral scientist, many factors influence the level of research and development involvement and output (Cole and Cole, 1973; Long, Allison, and McGinnis, 1980; Stephan and Levin, 1992). This is not to deny that research-intensive programs are more likely to produce graduates who gravitate toward research careers; they do. However, we might ask whether research-intensive programs attract students with strong research ability or does the program confer research skills on program graduates that predispose them to careers in scholarship? This question is of interest to analysts who assess the effectiveness of research-doctorate programs in producing research scholars/scientists. In short, the question of the relationship of program factors and the career outcomes of program graduates remains unanswered by this report.

National Survey of Industrial Employers

Another area of considerable interest to both the 1982 and the 1993 study committees was how the industrial sector views the quality of program graduates. Aware that there has been an increase in the number of doctoral workers employed in industry, the committee undertook an exploratory study to determine the feasibility of conducting a national Survey of Industrial Employers.[18] In 1992 and 1993, the committee gathered information through site visits and structured interviews[19] at a sample of four large firms specializing in electronics and/or aerospace research and development. Based on these interviews the committee received a report that suggested that a national survey of industrial employers in the "electronics" area would be feasible but that more work was needed before an appropriate questionnaire and sampling plan could be designed. Thus, the recommendation was made to solicit funds for a pilot effort that would request technical/research and development/laboratory directors to respond to a questionnaire on which research-doctorate programs in Engineering and the Physical Sciences are effective in producing research scientists for employment in industry. Constraints of time and resources did not permit the committee to explore this issue further.

Innovations in the National Survey of Graduate Faculty

The 1993 National Survey of Graduate Faculty provided an opportunity for the committee to explore the potential contribution of new data to the interpretation of survey results. Prior to conducting the survey, the committee invited three specialists to conduct structured interviews of a sample of faculty in Economics, History, Engineering, and Chemistry to determine the feasibility of soliciting new information from faculty raters.[20] Following this work, and as a result of committee discussions, a survey questionnaire was developed and tested through a series of focus group discussions.[21] The following information, which represents new sources of information for analysis, was collected on the survey forms:

(1) Information About the Rater
- "In what program or field was [your] degree awarded?"
- For the Biological Sciences only: "What is the location of your primary academic employment?"
- For the Biological Sciences only: "What is the name of the doctoral degree program with which you are most closely affiliated?"

(2) Instructions to the Raters
- A sample (10 percent) of the 8,000 questionnaires contained verbatim those instructions used in the 1982 survey for purposes of research.
- The remainder of the questionnaires contained an expanded form of one of the instructions:

  Effectiveness of Program in Educating Research Scholars/Scientists. Please consider the accessibility of the faculty, the curricula, the instructional and research facilities, the quality of graduate students, the performance of graduates, the clarity of stated program objectives and expectations, the appropriateness of program requirements and timetables, the adequacy of graduate advising and mentorship, the commitment of the program in assuring access and promoting success of students historically underrepresented in graduate education, the quality of associated personnel (postdoctorates, research scientists, et al.), and other factors that contribute to the effectiveness of the research-doctorate program.

(3) Familiarity with Graduates of the Program
- This was a new item added to each of the 50 program ratings.

(4) Visibility of Faculty
- A sample (10 percent) of the questionnaires asked raters to write in a number in response to this instruction at the bottom of each program faculty list:

  "Indicate the number of faculty whose work is familiar to you."

  These findings, it is hoped, will be used by analysts to explore the relationship of faculty "visibility" to perceived quality of those faculty regardless of program size.

(5) Expanding the Peer Ratings
- In an effort to determine the feasibility of conducting a companion survey of the opinions of international colleagues, survey respondents were asked to provide the following information at the end of every questionnaire:

  "Please nominate at least two faculty peers in your field who might serve in an international assessment of research-doctorate programs in the United States. (Exclude U.S. citizens working abroad.) Please print and provide address if known."

Appendix F reproduces a portion of the questionnaire, which includes many of these elements. The results of many of these tabulations are intended for use by future investigators, and are not included by the committee in this report.

Nonetheless, a preliminary review of certain of these survey elements enables the following conclusions to be drawn:

- No differences were evident in response patterns when "instructions" for rating program effectiveness was considered.
- Raters tended to be more familiar with program faculty than they were with graduates.
- While respondents were able to generate information about peers for an international assessment, the majority listed researchers only in northern European countries. Further, while the questionnaire was intended to generate names of colleagues working abroad, many respondents also gave names of non-U.S. citizens working in the United States. Further work is needed in the design of an international assessment, although its feasibility is suggested by these responses.

In conclusion, the committee initiated several explorations of new data collection in the area of doctoral program studies. Important statistics have been collected and await use by other investigators. Other studies suggested by this work remain to be done.

Like the 1982 study of research-doctorate programs, the present report aims to:

- Assist students and advisers in matching students' career goals with the facilities and opportunities available in the relevant research-doctorate programs;
- Inform the practical judgment of university administrators, national and state-level policymakers, and managers of public and private funding agencies; and
- Provide a large, recent data base that can be used by scholars who focus their work on characteristics of the national higher learning educational system and its associated research enterprise.

The next chapter presents the overall results of this study in the context of these goals.

NOTES

1. Joint JD/Ph.D. and MD/Ph.D. programs were included in these numbers.

2. This area presented special problems and is discussed in detail later in this chapter in *The Biological Sciences* section.

3. California Institute of Integral Studies, Graduate Theological Union, The Juilliard School, Indiana State University—Terre Haute, Long Island University—Brooklyn, Manhattan College, Marquette University, Middlebury College, Midwestern Baptist Theological Seminary, New School for Social Research, Nova University, Peabody Institute—Johns Hopkins, Southwestern Baptist Theological Seminary, U.S. International University, Villanova University, Wright Institute.

4. Caribbean Center for Advanced Studies, Cornell University Medical School, Cleveland State University, University of Dallas, Depaul University, Louisiana Technical, Memphis State University, Oregon Health Sciences, South Dakota State University, Wright State University.

5. The committee and their staff received expressions of concern from representatives in a few fields. For example, faculty members in Astronomy and Astrophysics at one institution were particularly concerned that their program had not been included in the list of programs reviewed. The committee acknowledges that the smaller size of the doctoral programs in this area could have resulted in the omission of otherwise vigorous research-training sites. However, upon discussion, the committee concluded that it was not feasible in the context of the present study to modify the eligibility criteria for one discipline. The committee urges professional societies—or other organizations—to extend the work of this committee to include a review of programs not included in this list.

6. "Physiology" appeared in both the 1982 and 1993 studies and was the only field so identified.

7. The area of "Ecology, Evolution, and Behavior" was especially problematic in this regard. The results of specialized cases, we should add, were collapsed into a single composite rating as reported in Appendix Tables H-2, I-2, and N-3.

8. Details about the use of these lists are provided later in this chapter.

9. An erroneous questionnaire printing involving two programs at the same institution was corrected by the staff during the course of the survey.

10. This includes Peabody College and the Mayo Graduate School, which previously had been reported as part of their parent institutes in 1982.

11. Owing to the lack of readily available information about institutional resources in this area, a campus inventory would be needed to generate this type of information. The committee considered conducting such an inventory but restrictions of time and resources prevented such an undertaking.

12. The committee recognizes that the 1982 committee utilized a "composite" measure. However, it is possible to access the component statistics and compare them to those reported in Appendix E of this report.

13. Dr. James Voytuk generated the analysis in March 1991 advised by Conference Board member Dr. David Featherman.

14. The committee is grateful for the work of Dr. James Simmons, who prepared a background paper for the committee on the potential use of ISI data in this study and to Dr. Elizabeth Aversa, a representative of ISI, who met with the committee on a number of occasions to discuss technical matters arising in the use of the data. Mr. George Boyce and Dr. James Voytuk, it should be noted, undertook and successfully completed the matching of 4.5 million ISI records with the 78,000 names of faculty in the current study.

15. ACLS, with support from the Andrew W. Mellon Foundation, is overseeing a project to organize and make more widely available data sets bearing on the humanities. The project will identify some statistics not now being collected, but by itself will not add to the data sets currently being compiled.

16. For purposes of this study, staff were able to generate comparable calculations of Median Year to Degree, which are reported in the next chapter.

17. In the area of sciences, the National Research Council has related work under way by the Commission on Life Sciences and the Commission on Physical Sciences, Mathematics, and Applications. The Committee on Science, Engineering, and Public Policy recently published a report which addressed doctoral education in general: *Reshaping the Graduate Education of Scientists and Engineers.*

18. The committee is indebted to Dr. William G. Howard who served as a consultant to the project and to committee members Drs. Elsa Garmire, Ernest Smerdon, and Marvin Goldberger, who participated in the exploratory work in 1992. Six undergraduate students from Worcester Polytechnic Institute also served as interns on this project and generated useful background documents. These were: Kathleen Lamkin, Peter Sargent, and Khanh Nguyen (Fall 1991) and David Fitts, Chris Franz, and Prabhjot Anand (Fall 1992).

19. The committee is grateful for the expert assistance provided by Ms. Susan Mitchell in conducting these interviews and to Ms. Dimitria Satterwhite for arranging the visits.

20. These interviews were conducted by Dr. Georgine Pion (Vanderbilt University), Professor Helen Astin (UCLA), and Dr. Pamela Atkinson (UC-Berkeley) in the Fall and Winter of 1992. The committee is grateful for the work they performed under extremely tight time constraints.

21. This work was performed by Dr. John Boyle through Klemm Associates, Washington, D.C. Focus group sites included: Washington, D.C.; Philadelphia; New York City; and Boston.

3

SELECTED FINDINGS

Educators and policymakers agree that certain distinctive features of the doctoral training environment facilitate the preparation of research scholars and scientists. These include a blend of well-prepared graduate students, talented faculty, and sufficient institutional resources to permit the independent exploration of promising new research directions. Doctoral programs ought to be "effective" too, in the sense that students who enter the programs complete their doctoral studies and do so in a timely manner.

In this chapter we present just a small sample of observations based on the wide variety of data found in the appendixes to this report. We begin with an overview of the results of the National Survey of Graduate Faculty. This is followed by a brief description of "changes" in selected aspects of research-doctorate programs between 1982 and 1993 on a field-by-field basis. The chapter closes with highlights of selected program graduates, including the time it takes them to earn a degree, patterns of support, and their gender and racial/ethnic diversity.

Throughout this chapter, data regarding characteristics of participating programs are presented by "quality" groupings. That is, the committee has adopted a framework which groups programs within a field on the basis of the average ratings assigned to the "scholarly quality of program faculty" for purposes of pattern analysis. Data have been summarized using "quarter" groupings. There are, of course, many other ways to partition the data, but we have concluded that grouping data within a field into four "quarters" represents an efficient, easily understood approach for presenting this large body of data. The interested reader is encouraged to explore the information found in this report using this chapter as a guide to some of the analyses that are possible. We also hope, however, that independent assessments will be generated using other analytic techniques.

The cornerstone of our analyses is the National Survey of Graduate Faculty, whose results are summarized in the following section.

THE NATIONAL SURVEY OF GRADUATE FACULTY

The NRC Committee for the Study of Research-Doctorate Programs in the United States launched the National Survey of Graduate Faculty in May 1993. The first set of questionnaires was mailed to about 11,400 raters in 34 fields, or approximately 18 percent of the total number of program faculty listed by participating institutions in all non-biological science fields. Later, a second set of questionnaires was mailed to about 5,300 raters in the Biological Sciences, or approximately 25 percent of all faculty associated with those programs included in the study.[1] In some fields, it was necessary to mail a second wave of questionnaires to faculty. The final disposition of the response outcome is described in detail in Appendix F.

Scholarly Quality of Program Faculty

Raters were asked to comment on two dimensions of quality for about 50 randomly selected programs in their fields: (1) "scholarly quality of program faculty," and (2) "effectiveness in educating research scholars/scientists." Ratings for "scholarly quality of program faculty" ranged from 0 to 5 with 0 signifying "not sufficient for doctoral education" and 5 signifying "distinguished." Raters were asked to designate no more than five programs as "distinguished." From these responses, the committee calculated a mean rating for each program appearing in the study.[2] Appendix H summarizes the results alphabetically by institution and broad field.

Figure 3-1 presents the overall ratings for the 3,634 programs included in the study. As can be seen from this figure, more than 60 percent of the programs rated as "distinguished," "strong," or "good."

However, raters identified some programs with faculty whose scholarly quality they considered "marginal" or "not sufficient for doctoral education." Of the five broad fields included in the study, the Social and Behavioral Sciences had the largest share of programs whose faculty were rated as "marginal" or "not sufficient"—23 percent or 165 out of 701. (See Table 3-1.) Within that broad field, economists tended to be the hardest graders[3]: about 44 percent of their programs had faculty rated in one of those two categories. Comparable figures in Sociology and in Political Science were 27 percent and 23 percent, respectively. Geography had the smallest fraction of programs with an average rating of "marginal" or "not sufficient for doctoral education"—about 8 percent of the total number participating in the study.

The following summary shows the percentage of programs in the other four broad fields with faculty whose scholarly quality was considered "marginal" or "not sufficient for doctoral education."

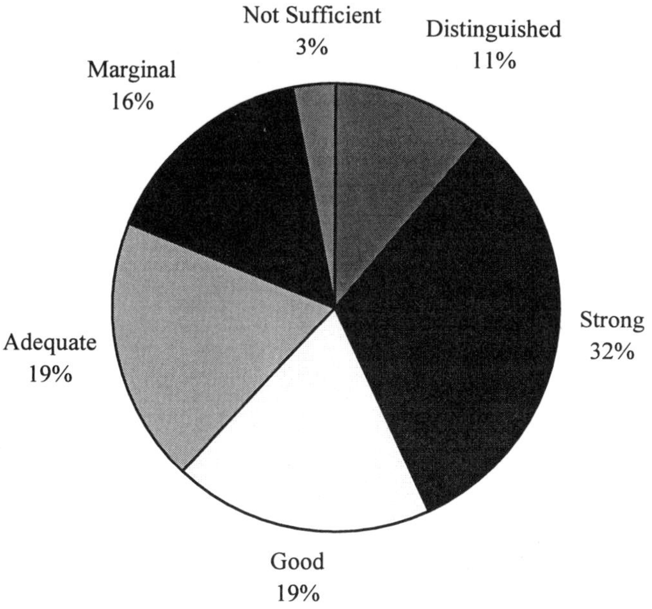

FIGURE 3-1 Distribution of program ratings across all programs by "Scholarly Quality of Program Faculty."

Physical Sciences and Mathematics: 21 percent, ranging from 9 percent in Astrophysics and Astronomy to 34 percent in the Computer Sciences.

Biological Sciences: 19 percent, ranging from about 5 percent in Pharmacology to 27 percent in Biochemistry and Molecular Biology.

Engineering: 17 percent, ranging from 3 percent in Aerospace Engineering to 25 percent in Chemical Engineering.

Arts and Humanities: 13 percent, ranging from 4 percent in Spanish and Portuguese Language and Literature to 25 percent in English Language and Literature.

Effectiveness in Educating Research Scholars/Scientists

Each rater was also asked to comment on the "effectiveness of a program in educating research scholars/scientists." Mean ratings were calculated, and the results presented alphabetically by institution in Appendix I for each broad field. Table 3-2 provides an overview of the mean ratings of program effectiveness for each of the 41 fields. The majority (about two-thirds) of the programs were considered in 1993 to be "extremely effective" or "reasonably effective" in preparing research scholars and scientists. Fewer than 10 percent were considered to be "not effective" in this regard.

A Technical Note

Readers will note that survey results found in Tables 3-1 and 3-2 have been re-scaled from the scoring system presented to the raters. (See Figure 2-1.) Ratings for both the "scholarly quality of program faculty" and the "effectiveness of programs in educating research scholars/scientists" are presented using a five-point scale, with the highest score associated with the highest rating. This modification permits comparison with the 1982 findings, which used a similar scoring procedure.[4]

Program Rankings

The committee spent considerable time discussing the format for generating an effective presentation of data from this study. They were aware that the 1982 study committee restricted the presentation of survey returns to an alphabetical listing by university within each of 32 disciplines (Jones, Lindzey, and Coggeshall, 1982) and that this format created considerable difficulty for readers interested in comparative analysis. (See Appendix B.) The present study committee concluded that a rank ordering of programs within fields provides a more convenient way for readers to review and interpret the information collected during the past three years. The committee selected the mean rating of the "schol-

TABLE 3-1 Distribution of Program Ratings on the Variable "Scholarly Quality of Program Faculty"

Field of Study	Total Number of Programs Surveyed	Number of Programs with Average Ratings of: Distinguished (4.01 +)	Strong (3.01-4.00)	Good (2.51 3.00)	Adequate (2.00-2.50)	Marginal (1.00-1.99)	Not Sufficient (less than 1)
Art History	38	6	14	8	8	1	1
Classics	29	6	11	6	4	1	1
Comparative Literature	44	9	10	9	13	3	0
English Language and Literature	127	13	37	24	21	27	5
French Language and Literature	45	8	14	13	7	3	0
German Language and Literature	32	4	17	4	3	4	0
Linguistics	41	5	13	12	3	7	1
Music	65	12	22	14	13	4	0
Philosophy	72	10	22	9	16	15	0
Religion	38	5	16	9	3	5	0
Spanish and Portuguese Lang and Lit	54	1	27	10	14	2	0
Total Arts and Humanities	*585*	*79*	*203*	*118*	*105*	*72*	*8*
Percent	100%	14%	35%	20%	18%	12%	1%
Biochemistry and Molecular Biology	194	19	48	35	40	38	14
Cell and Developmental Biology	179	16	46	39	33	32	13
Ecology, Evolution, and Behavior	129	12	43	36	21	15	2
Molecular and General Genetics	103	15	37	18	13	13	7
Neurosciences	102	14	39	13	14	12	10
Pharmacology	127	10	72	21	18	5	1
Physiology	140	10	60	29	15	20	6
Total Biological Sciences	*974*	*96*	*345*	*191*	*154*	*135*	*53*
Percent	100%	10%	35%	20%	16%	14%	5%
Aerospace Engineering	33	5	15	6	6	1	0
Biomedical Engineering	38	8	20	5	3	2	0
Chemical Engineering	93	10	21	19	20	21	2
Civil Engineering	86	7	27	20	19	13	0
Electrical Engineering	126	9	34	25	28	28	2
Industrial Engineering	37	4	11	8	9	5	0
Materials Science	65	8	25	17	8	7	0
Mechanical Engineering	110	11	32	22	25	18	2
Total Engineering	*588*	*62*	*185*	*122*	*119*	*94*	*6*
Percent	100%	11%	31%	21%	20%	16%	1%
Astrophysics and Astronomy	33	7	13	6	4	3	0
Chemistry	168	15	41	27	34	44	7
Computer Sciences	108	9	26	20	16	35	2
Geosciences	100	14	28	23	25	10	0
Mathematics	139	17	35	29	27	27	4
Oceanography	26	4	13	5	1	3	0
Physics	147	18	44	26	36	21	2
Statistics and Biostatistics	65	9	25	11	10	8	2
Total Physical Sciences and Mathematics	*786*	*93*	*225*	*147*	*153*	*151*	*17*
Percent	100%	12%	29%	19%	19%	19%	2%
Anthropology	69	5	32	12	14	6	0
Economics	107	14	14	16	16	34	13
Geography	36	5	16	7	5	3	0
History	111	13	29	27	21	16	5
Political Science	98	11	21	17	26	20	3
Psychology	185	17	53	34	42	31	8
Sociology	95	11	24	14	20	25	1
Total Social and Behavioral Sciences	*701*	*76*	*189*	*127*	*144*	*135*	*30*
Percent	100%	11%	27%	18%	21%	19%	4%
Totals	*3634*	*406*	*1147*	*705*	*675*	*587*	*114*
Percent	100%	11%	32%	19%	19%	16%	3%

TABLE 3-2 Distribution of Program Ratings on the Variable "Effectiveness of Program in Educating Research Scholars/Scientists"

Field of Study	Total Number of Programs Surveyed	Number of Programs with Average Ratings of: Extremely Effective (3.5-5.0)	Reasonably Effective (2.5-3.49)	Minimally Effective (1.5-2.49)	Not Effective[a] (0.0-1.49)
Art History	38	9	18	10	1
Classics	29	6	14	6	3
Comparative Literature	44	11	26	7	0
English Language and Literature	127	23	58	35	11
French Language and Literature	45	12	23	9	1
German Language and Literature	32	9	15	8	0
Linguistics	41	10	19	8	4
Music	65	15	32	16	2
Philosophy	72	14	33	21	4
Religion	38	8	22	7	1
Spanish and Portuguese Lang and Lit	54	9	32	13	0
Total Arts and Humanities	*585*	*126*	*292*	*140*	*27*
Percent	100%	22%	50%	24%	5%
Biochemistry and Molecular Biology	194	42	85	49	18
Cell and Developmental Biology	179	39	80	39	21
Ecology, Evolution, and Behavior	129	28	68	25	8
Molecular and General Genetics	103	30	49	13	11
Neurosciences	102	27	47	14	14
Pharmacology	127	32	81	11	3
Physiology	140	35	82	17	6
Total Biological Sciences	*974*	*233*	*492*	*168*	*81*
Percent	100%	24%	51%	17%	8%
Aerospace Engineering	33	7	20	5	1
Biomedical Engineering	38	15	20	3	0
Chemical Engineering	93	16	38	31	8
Civil Engineering	86	16	44	21	5
Electrical Engineering	126	20	52	36	18
Industrial Engineering	37	8	14	14	1
Materials Science	65	14	39	7	5
Mechanical Engineering	110	18	55	29	8
Total Engineering	*588*	*114*	*282*	*146*	*46*
Percent	100%	19%	48%	25%	8%
Astrophysics and Astronomy	33	9	19	5	0
Chemistry	168	34	67	51	16
Computer Sciences	108	15	37	36	20
Geosciences	100	21	53	22	4
Mathematics	139	26	58	39	16
Oceanography	26	5	16	5	0
Physics	147	29	74	28	16
Statistics and Biostatistics	65	18	26	18	3
Total Physical Sciences and Mathematics	*786*	*157*	*350*	*204*	*75*
Percent	100%	20%	44%	26%	10%
Anthropology	69	8	42	18	1
Economics	107	16	28	30	33
Geography	36	12	17	6	1
History	111	23	49	30	9
Political Science	98	16	34	33	15
Psychology	185	38	81	51	15
Sociology	95	14	36	27	18
Total Social and Behavioral Sciences	*701*	*127*	*287*	*195*	*92*
Percent	100%	18%	41%	28%	13%
Totals	*3634*	*757*	*1703*	*853*	*321*
Percent	100%	21%	47%	23%	9%

[a]Includes programs that received no scores.

arly quality of program faculty" as the dimension along which to array most program information. Thus, replies from the respondents to the National Survey of Graduate Faculty were pooled, a mean rating for each program was calculated,[5] and a rank ordering produced within each of the 41 fields in the study.[6] The results of that rank ordering may be found in Appendixes J (Arts and Humanities) through Appendix N (Biological Sciences).

"Rank ordered" information requires careful interpretation, however. A program may be ranked first with respect to "scholarly quality of program faculty" but well down the list with respect to another dimension, such as the number of publications per faculty in that field. Admittedly, many of the measures utilized in this study are believed to correlate with "scholarly quality of program faculty." This point is illustrated in Appendix O, which provides an analysis of the correlation within a field of all the variables selected by the committee. Thus, large differences in rank ordering across most variables rarely occur. Nonetheless, the committee created Appendix P to remind the reader that the relative standing of a program may change significantly depending on which variable is being considered.

The committee is also aware that "rank ordering" magnifies small differences in raw scores, a point illustrated in Appendix Q. In that appendix, one notes that the average ratings for some programs are indistinguishable from each other. That is, overlapping "confidence intervals" found in that appendix indicate that there is statistically no difference (or little difference) in the results of ratings for adjacent institutions in a list. The "confidence intervals" found in that appendix will give the reader a rough indication of the uncertainty to be attached to the absolute level of the measures used, although these tend to overstate the uncertainty of relative rankings (because the same raters were asked to rate 50 programs in a field).[7]

Use of Quality Groupings by "Quarter"

Given the large number of programs within a field, it is impractical to review statistics about all research-doctorate programs by rank. Thus, to facilitate a broad understanding of the data and findings, we have organized institutions into four groups or "quarters" within a field based on the mean rating of the scholarly quality of program faculty.[8] Each table in Appendixes J through N provides summary statistics for programs ranked within a field in the "top quarter," "second," "third," or "fourth" quarters.

Admittedly, these are arbitrary groupings. However, these groupings offer an efficient way to highlight differences in program characteristics within a field and across the numerous fields included in this study. The rest of the findings presented in this chapter are organized on the basis of these four quality groupings.

PROGRAM CHARACTERISTICS ASSOCIATED WITH "QUALITY"

In Chapter 2, we noted that several variables correlate strongly with "scholarly quality of program faculty." These are:

1. "size" as defined by number of faculty, number of enrolled students, and number of graduates; and
2. "level of faculty research and scholarship," as measured by publications, citations, and grants.

Using data gathered from the 1993 National Survey of Graduate Faculty, the committee explored the relationship between differences in ratings of the "scholarly quality" and program size and between "scholarly quality" and level of faculty research activity.

Program Size

Research-doctorate programs at U.S. universities vary significantly in size. Among the 3,634 programs included in this study, some had fewer than 10 faculty and as many students in Fall 1992, while others comprise more than 50 faculty and occasionally twice as many students.

The Biological Sciences tend to have larger numbers of doctoral program faculty than other fields (Figure 3-2), especially in areas like Biochemistry and Molecular Biology. (See Table 3-3.) This is due, in part, to the way in which the committee collected information in this area. Faculty rosters at the same institution often included faculty names from a wide variety of programs within the same department or from several departments on the same campus. The overall effect was to generate faculty lists much longer, as a rule, than those found in other fields.

Among the remaining broad fields, programs in English Language and Literature tended to involve a large number of faculty, as did doctoral programs in Physics, Electrical Engineering, and History. It is interesting to note that within the Arts and Humanities, doctoral programs that prepare scholars in modern European languages (German, French, Spanish) had fewer faculty on average than many of the other fields included in the study.

Doctoral enrollments in the Fall 1992 presented quite another pattern (Figure 3-3). While certain fields with large faculties like Electrical Engineering, English Language and Literature, Physics, and Psychology also revealed a sizeable number of doctoral students, many of the component fields in the Biological Sciences fields—while having large numbers of faculty—had proportionately fewer students. (See Table 3-4.) The reason for this difference in the Biological Sciences doctoral enrollments was not explored by the committee, but is thought to be related to enrollment restrictions imposed by laboratory requirements not found in many other

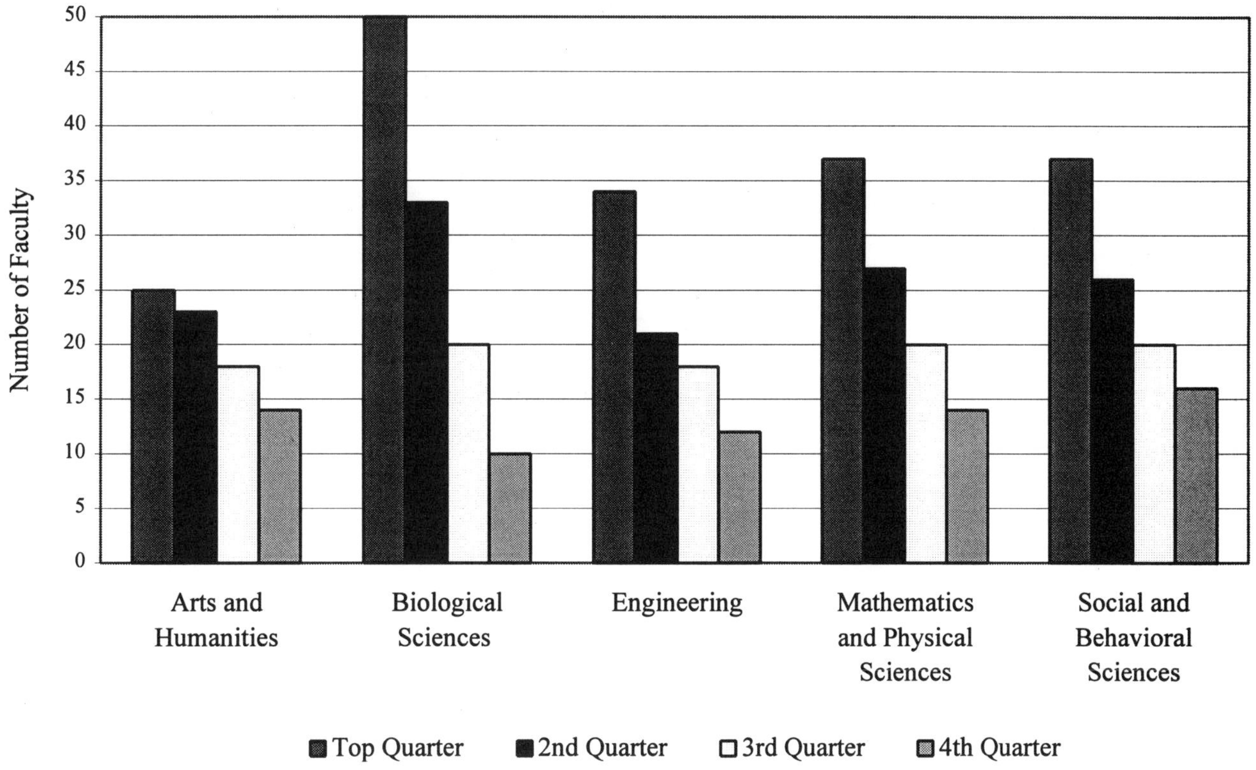

FIGURE 3-2 Average number of program faculty by quality grouping and broad field. Based on the "Scholarly Quality of Program Faculty." See Appendixes J-N.

participating disciplines and multiple appearance of faculty across programs within an institution.

Table 3-4 also provides information about patterns of enrollment by women across field and quality grouping. This is the only demographic variable for which information was requested by the committee from the Institutional Coordinator.

Differences are evident across fields with respect to the relative share of women among doctoral students in the Fall 1992—with the fields of Aerospace and Mechanical Engineering, Computer Sciences, and Physics having a relatively small percentage of female doctoral students. Art History and French Language and Literature have a significant larger share of women graduates among the Arts and Humanities, and Oceanography, Anthropology, Biomedical Engineering, and the Biological Sciences, in general, have a higher share of women. What is perhaps most interesting about these data is the fairly symmetrical distribution of female enrollments across quality groupings. Although the average number of doctoral students is positively correlated with "scholarly quality of program faculty," there appears to be no relationship between faculty "quality" and the share of women typically enrolled in these doctoral programs.

One thing is clear from a review of these data by quality grouping:

- *Top-rated programs in most fields tend to have a larger number of faculty and more graduate students than lower-rated programs. While certain fields have a tendency to enroll more women in graduate studies, there is no apparent relationship between quality grouping and patterns of enrollment in doctoral study by women within any of the 41 fields analyzed by the committee.*

The size-"quality grouping" relationship, it must be noted, is markedly weakest in the Arts and Humanities and strongest in the Biological Sciences. This is evident in the information provided by Tables 3-3 and 3-4 and companion appendix tables (J-N). Nonetheless, these results generally support the notion that perceived "scholarly quality of program faculty" is positively correlated with the size of the program whether measured in terms of faculty numbers or total number of doctoral students.

Faculty Involvement in Research and Scholarship

Another factor thought to be associated with relative rating of the "scholarly quality of program faculty" is faculty involvement in research and scholarship. The committee assembled a variety of measures related to faculty in-

TABLE 3-3 Average Number of Program Faculty by Field and Quality Grouping[a]

Field	Top Quarter	2nd Quarter	3rd Quarter	4th Quarter
Art History	18	15	15	9
Classics	17	17	11	7
Comparative Literature	25	23	17	17
English Language and Literature	44	36	29	20
French Language and Literature	14	13	14	11
German Language and Literature	12	12	12	8
Linguistics	22	12	13	13
Music	22	27	22	16
Philosophy	19	21	16	13
Religion	32	26	19	20
Spanish and Portuguese Lang and Lit	14	16	12	10
Average Program Size	*25*	*23*	*18*	*14*
Biochemistry and Molecular Biology	60	31	23	11
Cell and Developmental Biology	61	38	19	9
Ecology, Evolution, and Behavior	53	41	20	13
Molecular and General Genetics	43	42	20	7
Neurosciences	46	34	25	11
Pharmacology	36	24	14	10
Physiology	37	22	18	8
Average Program Size	*50*	*33*	*20*	*10*
Aerospace Engineering	22	24	15	15
Biomedical Engineering	40	27	26	10
Chemical Engineering	19	15	12	9
Civil Engineering	36	21	17	13
Electrical Engineering	46	26	23	15
Industrial Engineering	25	18	10	9
Materials Science	29	19	13	13
Mechanical Engineering	39	23	19	13
Average Program Size	*34*	*21*	*18*	*12*
Astrophysics and Astronomy	21	19	15	9
Chemistry	33	27	19	14
Computer Sciences	32	22	19	12
Geosciences	31	21	16	14
Mathematics	46	34	29	20
Oceanography	45	37	15	15
Physics	49	32	22	14
Statistics and Biostatistics	21	18	12	10
Average Program Size	*37*	*27*	*20*	*14*
Anthropology	28	21	17	14
Economics	36	27	20	17
Geography	20	18	13	11
History	46	31	25	17
Political Science	34	27	20	16
Psychology	43	27	21	19
Sociology	29	24	21	13
Average Program Size	*37*	*26*	*20*	*16*

[a]Based on average ratings for "Scholarly Quality of Program Faculty." See Appendixes J through N for details.

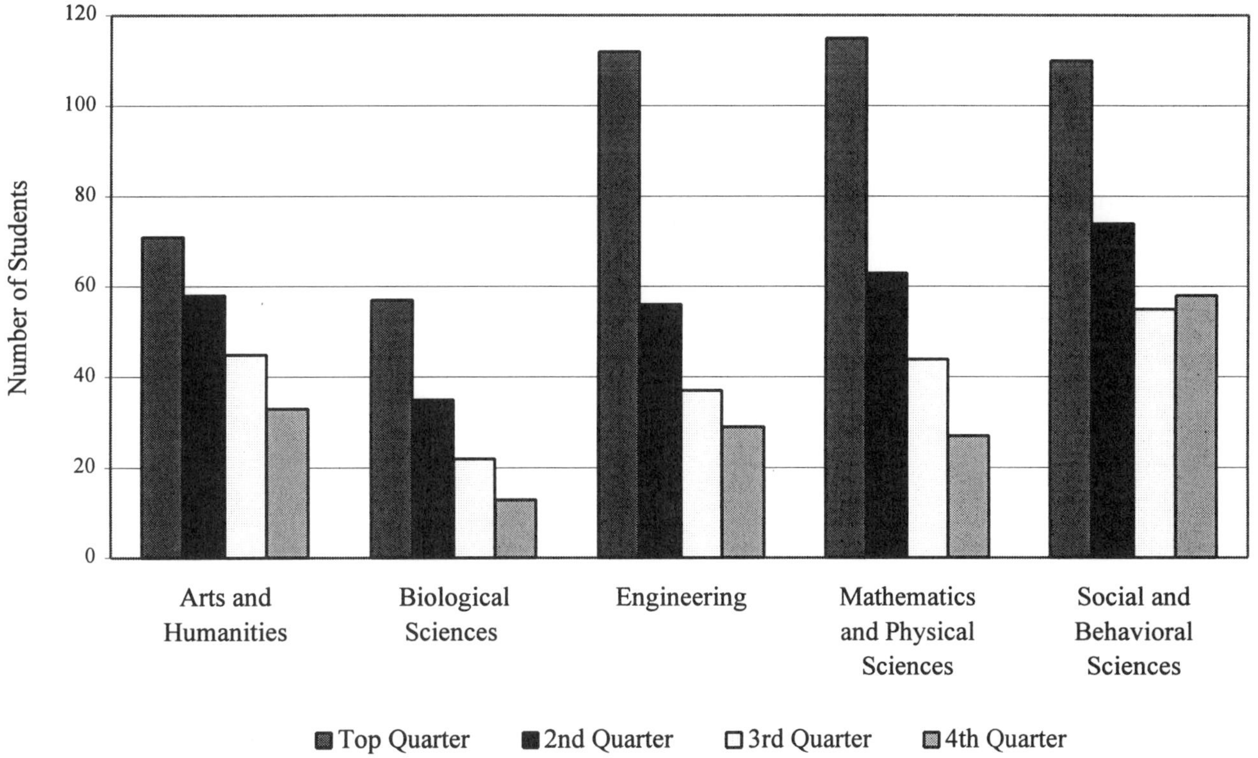

FIGURE 3-3 Average number of students enrolled by broad field and quality grouping. Based on the "Scholarly Quality of Program Faculty." See Appendixes J-N.

volvement in research and scholarship. (See Appendix G.) The first measure involves federal support for research. For these analyses, it was possible to generate lists of grant support from data provided by federal agencies and to match those lists with faculty lists provided by Institutional Coordinators. In addition, large files from the Institute for Scientific Information (ISI) were used to generate publication/citation patterns for all 78,000 faculty members who were involved in doctoral training in Fall 1992 in the 41 fields included in this study. Selected highlights from those tabulations are presented below.

Federal Grant Support

The federal government has been the primary source of support for academic research and development for over a half a century. In recent years, three agencies accounted for nearly three-fourths of total federal support in this area, namely, the National Institutes of Health, the National Science Foundation, and the Department of Defense (National Science Board, 1993). To analyze patterns of federal support, the committee matched the names of principal investigators supported between 1986 and 1992 by these three—and four other—key agencies (see Appendix G) against faculty lists provided by 274 Institutional Coordinators. From this effort, it was possible to identify doctoral program faculty having had some form of federal support. The results of this analysis are presented by institution on a field-by-field basis in Appendixes J through N.

- *The vast majority of research-doctorate programs included in the study had faculty who received some type of federal support for research between 1986 and 1992.*

Doctoral programs in the Arts and Humanities revealed significantly less evidence of federal support, with an exception being the field of English Language and Literature (Appendix J-4). This finding reflects in part the limitations of the present analysis and suggests that a separate, more focused study of faculty research support patterns in the Arts and Humanities is needed before conclusions can be drawn about faculty activity along this dimension.

The committee also analyzed patterns of federal support by quality groupings in the Sciences and Engineering. As was to be expected, research activities in the Sciences and Engineering were concentrated in top-rated programs. (See Figure 3-4.) This relationship is weaker in the Social and Behavioral Sciences as seen in Table 3-5.

TABLE 3-4 Average Number of Students Enrolled in Doctoral Studies in Fall 1992 and (in parentheses) the Percentage of Female Students, by Field and Quality Grouping[a]

Fields	Top Quarter	2nd Quarter	3rd Quarter	4th Quarter
Art History	74 (67%)	60 (77%)	35 (74%)	26 (74%)
Classics	27 (39)	25 (52)	20 (46)	16 (50)
Comparative Literature	47 (57)	46 (63)	34 (60)	31 (66)
English Language and Literature	140 (59)	94 (61)	56 (65)	50 (61)
French Language and Literature	37 (66)	24 (76)	35 (66)	17 (76)
German Language and Literature	28 (52)	32 (54)	26 (65)	15 (59)
Linguistics	46 (50)	52 (57)	32 (64)	27 (51)
Music	75 (43)	60 (46)	51 (45)	23 (90)
Philosophy	44 (28)	53 (26)	42 (25)	37 (25)
Religion	96 (38)	48 (29)	105 (36)	75 (17)
Spanish and Portuguese Lang and Lit	35 (63)	41 (59)	38 (66)	21 (66)
Average Program Size	*71*	*57*	*46*	*33*
Biochemistry and Molecular Biology	84 (42)	45 (44)	28 (41)	18 (42)
Cell and Developmental Biology	77 (44)	42 (48)	26 (48)	17 (40)
Ecology, Evolution, and Behavior	82 (42)	41 (36)	27 (40)	21 (40)
Molecular and General Genetics	43 (45)	48 (48)	23 (41)	11 (43)
Neurosciences	44 (41)	22 (38)	20 (38)	8 (42)
Pharmacology	35 (47)	23 (42)	15 (44)	12 (50)
Physiology	23 (40)	18 (43)	15 (42)	8 (36)
Average Program Size	*59*	*35*	*23*	*14*
Aerospace Engineering	84 (7)	82 (6)	47 (10)	21 (8)
Biomedical Engineering	60 (21)	38 (23)	34 (24)	17 (26)
Chemical Engineering	83 (22)	46 (19)	27 (16)	23 (17)
Civil Engineering	81 (15)	54 (12)	31 (10)	29 (11)
Electrical Engineering	220 (11)	77 (12)	53 (10)	42 (10)
Industrial Engineering	73 (22)	47 (21)	23 (17)	28 (15)
Materials Science	85 (24)	52 (12)	38 (17)	27 (12)
Mechanical Engineering	121 (8)	57 (7)	46 (10)	26 (10)
Average Program Size	*118*	*58*	*39*	*29*
Astrophysics and Astronomy	38 (22)	27 (22)	21 (25)	17 (19)
Chemistry	180 (31)	88 (34)	53 (30)	31 (33)
Computer Sciences	123 (16)	73 (16)	81 (17)	43 (19)
Geosciences	67 (29)	39 (24)	24 (21)	17 (17)
Mathematics	93 (21)	51 (28)	37 (28)	22 (33)
Oceanography	98 (35)	45 (32)	26 (37)	17 (34)
Physics	150 (13)	74 (12)	51 (16)	27 (16)
Statistics and Biostatistics	34 (29)	33 (39)	22 (38)	27 (34)
Average Program Size	*116*	*62*	*45*	*27*
Anthropology	93 (59)	75 (59)	55 (53)	34 (63)
Economics	114 (26)	76 (27)	42 (28)	45 (27)
Geography	53 (38)	39 (36)	21 (36)	21 (28)
History	152 (44)	67 (39)	56 (37)	31 (35)
Political Science	112 (33)	68 (32)	48 (35)	48 (33)
Psychology	113 (57)	90 (65)	81 (63)	116 (63)
Sociology	80 (51)	64 (58)	43 (58)	31 (60)
Average Program Size	*110*	*73*	*56*	*58*

[a]Based on average ratings for "Scholarly Quality of Program Faculty." See Appendixes J through N for details.

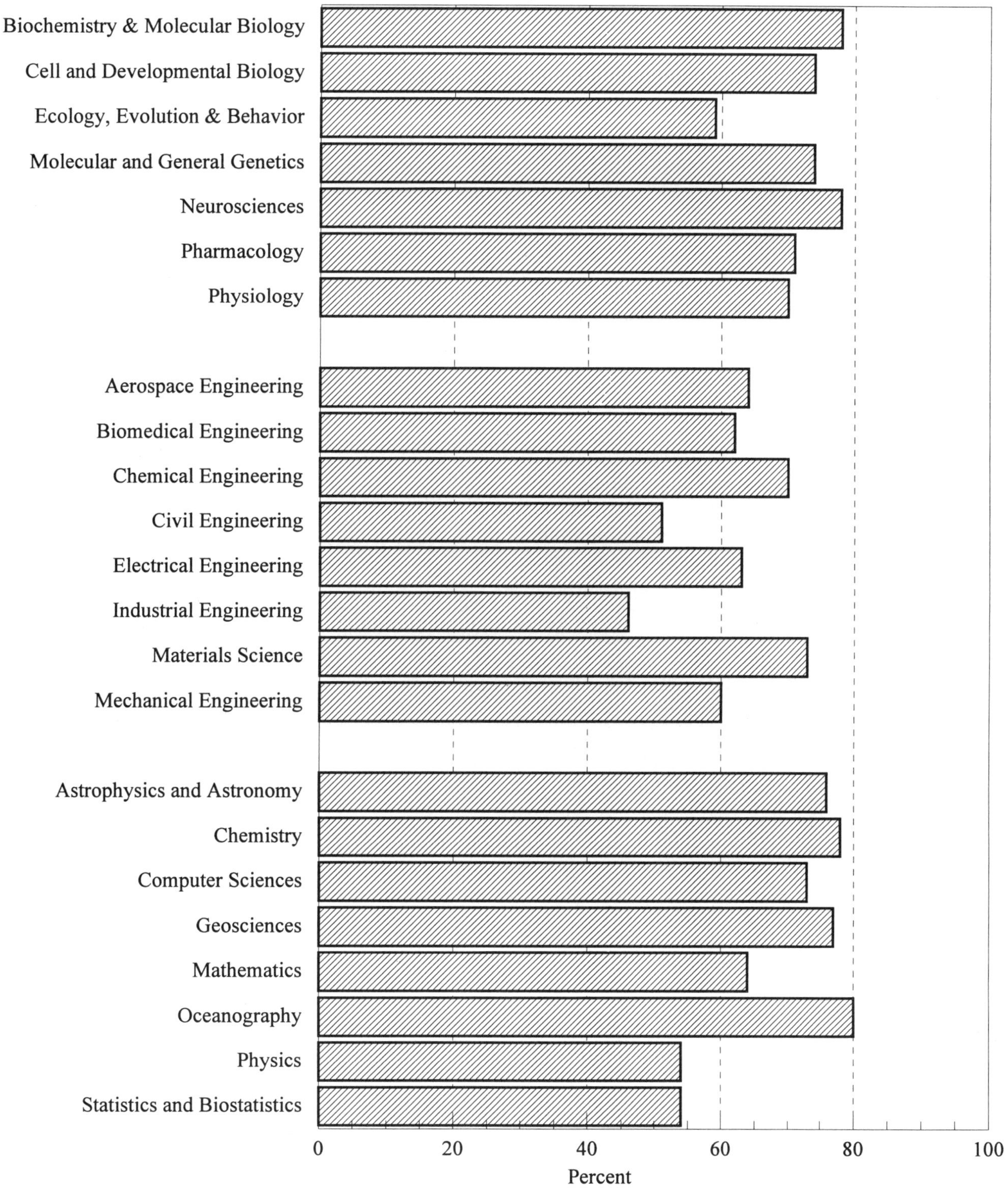

FIGURE 3-4 Average percentage of faculty in programs rated in the "Top Quarter" having had federal grant support between 1986 and 1992, by field. Based on the "Scholarly Quality of Program Faculty." See Appendix Tables K, L, and N for details.

TABLE 3-5 Average Percentage of Faculty in the Social and Behavioral Sciences Having Had Federal Grants (1986-1992) by Quality Grouping[a]

Fields	Top Quarter	2nd Quarter	3rd Quarter	4th Quarter
Anthropology	31%	29%	22%	16%
Economics	27	14	5	3
Geography	35	33	34	22
History	4	3	2	1
Political Science	14	7	6	1
Psychology	43	27	18	7
Sociology	28	19	11	10

[a]Based on average ratings for "Scholarly Quality of Program Faculty." See Appendix M for details.

Publication and Citation Patterns

University research and scholarship produces knowledge that is disseminated in a variety of ways. In the Sciences and Engineering, faculty—often in collaboration with their graduate students—present the results of their analytic work through papers given at professional meetings, through the publication of those papers in scholarly journals, and/or through patenting activities. In the Arts and Humanities the publication of books and monographs tends to be emphasized.

Like the previous study committee, this committee sought to analyze patterns of publishing among faculty at institutions participating in this study. Faculty lists provided by Institutional Coordinators were matched against files containing publication and citation information compiled by the Institute for Scientific Information. (See Appendix G.)

Although the contents of the ISI files have been expanded since the 1982 study to include more information about publication activities in the Social and Behavioral Sciences, the committee concluded that the more limited listing of books and monographs compared to journal articles yielded little useful information about faculty scholarship in the Arts and Humanities. Thus, the publication and citation information presented in this section is restricted to the activities of faculty in the Sciences and Engineering. A separate measure was generated, however, for faculty scholarship in the Arts and Humanities and is presented subsequently.

Based on an analysis of the ISI files, the committee offers the following observation:

- *Most doctoral programs in the Sciences and Engineering have faculty actively engaged in the publication of scholarly work. However, there is evidence for a strong positive correlation between the "scholarly quality of program faculty" and the citation of their work.*

As data in Appendixes K through N reveal, nearly every doctoral program included in this study had faculty who had published between 1986 and 1992. When analyzed by "quality grouping," patterns of publication varied to some extent. Lower rated programs tend to have fewer faculty who are responsible for the publication rates observed by an institution. (This is evident in higher *Gini coefficients*—or "concentration measures"— which are described in the keys to Appendixes K through N).[9]

- *Faculty in top-rated programs are cited more often than faculty who publish and are located in lower-rated programs.*

While space does not permit a detailed analysis, differences in citation patterns by quality groups are illustrated in Table 3-6. In that table, the positive correlation between the "scholarly quality of program faculty" and rates of citation are shown for four large fields: Economics, Electrical Engineering, Neurosciences, and Physics.

Numerous other analyses of these data are possible and await work by interested scholars. For example, tabulations are needed of the extent to which program size, publication

TABLE 3-6 Publication and Citation Information for Selected Fields by Quality Grouping[a]

Field (Quarter)	Percent Publishing[b]	Pubs per Faculty[c]	Cites per Faculty[d]
Economics			
Top Quarter	76.56	3.63	12.83
2nd Quarter	70.68	2.82	4.75
3rd Quarter	70.20	2.74	2.58
4th Quarter	56.41	1.68	1.36
Electrical Engineering			
Top Quarter	83.66	8.89	32.87
2nd Quarter	78.10	5.71	16.23
3rd Quarter	65.85	3.11	4.56
4th Quarter	58.63	2.54	3.17
Neurosciences			
Top Quarter	88.16	11.97	136.51
2nd Quarter	89.62	9.31	69.40
3rd Quarter	85.76	6.23	36.84
4th Quarter	81.00	5.21	20.26
Physics			
Top Quarter	86.36	9.75	71.49
2nd Quarter	83.41	8.65	47.58
3rd Quarter	81.57	7.14	31.11
4th Quarter	80.14	5.82	23.91

[a]Based on average ratings for "Scholarly Quality of Program Faculty." See Appendix Tables K-5, L-7, M-2, and N-5 for details.
[b]Fraction of all faculty in that quarter having published one article between 1988 and 1992.
[c]Average number of publications per faculty member for program faculty between 1988 and 1992.
[d]Average number of articles cited per faculty member for program faculty between 1988 and 1992.

TABLE 3-7 Average Number of Awards and Honors Among Faculty in the Arts and Humanities by Field and Quality Grouping[a]

	Top Quarter		2nd Quarter		3rd Quarter		4th Quarter	
Fields	**Avg Nm of Awds**	*% of Faculty*	**Avg Nm of Awds**	*% of Faculty*	**Avg Nm of Awds**	*% of Faculty*	**Avg Nm of Awds**	*% of Faculty*
Art History	**7.40**	*39%*	**3.67**	*21%*	**2.40**	*14%*	**2.33**	*22%*
Classics	**7.13**	*35*	**5.71**	*27*	**2.00**	*18*	**0.71**	*12*
Comparative Literature	**10.00**	*33*	**4.18**	*18*	**2.91**	*15*	**2.45**	*11*
English Language and Literature	**10.00**	*21*	**5.41**	*14*	**2.03**	*8*	**1.32**	*6*
French Language and Literature	**3.42**	*19*	**1.36**	*15*	**1.27**	*11*	**0.82**	*6*
German Language and Literature	**2.75**	*18*	**1.63**	*15*	**1.00**	*7*	**0.13**	*2*
Linguistics	**3.64**	*17*	**1.50**	*10*	**0.80**	*5*	**1.40**	*9*
Music	**4.12**	*23*	**1.06**	*5*	**0.75**	*5*	**0.25**	*2*
Philosophy	**6.28**	*27*	**3.28**	*15*	**1.44**	*9*	**0.67**	*4*
Religion	**7.45**	*20*	**3.25**	*8*	**1.30**	*8*	**0.33**	*4*
Spanish and Portuguese Language and Literature	**1.71**	*14*	**0.93**	*6*	**0.85**	*5*	**0.46**	*5*

[a]Based on average ratings for "Scholarly Quality of Program Faculty." See Appendix J for details.

rates, and the concentration of "publishing faculty" (as suggested by the Gini coefficient) interact with the rating of program faculty. Are there instances in which relatively small doctoral programs are rated higher than very large programs in the same field due in part to greater rates of publication and citation by faculty in those smaller programs? A type of "density" measure is needed to probe more deeply into the relationship between publications/citation activities and perceived faculty quality. The data gathered by the committee and presented in this volume should offer an interesting starting point for such an analysis.

Awards and Honors in the Arts and Humanities

Unlike the situation in the Sciences and Engineering, few federal sources of support are available to faculty in the Arts and Humanities to support their scholarly activities. Furthermore, conventional approaches to estimating the impact of knowledge dissemination (i.e., "publishing") fail to capture the contributions of scholars in these fields—whose product might be a musical composition, a film, or a book summarizing many years of thought on a subject. Thus, the committee sought another measure that would reflect faculty involvement in research and scholarship, and settled on a measure of "awards and honors."

The committee collected and reviewed information from a variety of sources about the distribution of a selected number of prestigious awards and honors among faculty in the Arts and Humanities.[10] Names of faculty were matched against lists of awardees, and the number of faculty with such awards or honors was tabulated on a program-by-program basis.

- *A larger share of faculty in top-rated programs in the Arts and Humanities are likely to have received a prestigious award or honor than faculty in lower-rated programs, although this pattern varies by field.*

This pattern was especially evident in Classics, Comparative Literature, Philosophy, English Language and Literature, and Music. (See Table 3-7.) The relationship was weaker in Art History and Linguistics.

As can be seen in Table 3-7, more faculty in top-rated programs received an honor or award than faculty in lower-rated programs, varying from an average high of 10 awards in the top quarter of programs in Comparative Literature to an average low of 2.45 awards in the last quarter of that field. Overall, in percentage terms, fields in Arts and Humanities ranged from 33 percent of Comparative Literature faculty in the top quarter receiving an award or honor to a low 2 percent in the last quarter for German Language and Literature, and Music. It is notable that the committee's analysis failed to identify awardees among faculty appearing in the last quarter of German Language and Literature, possibly reflecting the limitations of the data base developed by the committee.

Although this analysis must be viewed as "preliminary" pending the expansion and refinement of such data bases, it illustrates the potential role for the analysis of awards and honors in understanding institutional differences in the scholarly environment where doctoral preparation occurs.

THE CALCULATION OF "CHANGE" MEASURES

Because of the care that was taken in designing the 1993 survey form and sampling plan, it is possible to calculate "change measures" for programs appearing in 27 of the 41 fields included in the study. (See Appendix C.) From the list of 3,634 research-doctorate programs in the study, 1,916 were included in both studies:

430 programs in Arts and Humanities
301 programs in Engineering
535 programs in Physical Sciences and Mathematics
577 programs in Social and Behavioral Sciences
73 programs in Physiology[11]

From these data, it is possible to calculate mean ratings of the "scholarly quality of program faculty" for programs appearing in both the 1982 and 1993 surveys. The results may be found in Appendix P.

Owing to the availability of faculty ratings for these 1,916 programs it is possible to tabulate changes in the relative standing of those programs between 1982 and 1993.

The calculation is relatively simple: We first consider the order of the average program ratings based on "scholarly quality of program faculty" in 1982 and assign the ratings to one of four quality groupings (or quarters) and then consider the relative order of ratings for the *same* set of programs in 1993. We then determine the number of programs that remain in the top quarter (or second quarter, etc.) in 1993 based on their standing in 1982. The results of this analysis are summarized in Table 3-8.

- *Analysis of 1993 program ratings for programs appearing in both studies indicates a remarkable stability among programs rated in the top and bottom quarter in 1982 based on the "scholarly quality of program faculty."*

Of the 1,916 appearing in both studies, 399 (or 85 percent) remained in the top quarter, 287 (or 59 percent) in the second quarter, 248 (or 52 percent) in the third quarter, and 363 (or 75 percent) in the last quarter. Most programs increased their relative standing between 1982 and 1993, evident in the number of programs shifting from the bottom half of the quality groupings in 1982 to the second or third quarters as estimated in 1993. For example, 81 programs rated in the second quarter in 1982 appeared among "top-rated" programs in 1993; 112 programs rated in the third quarter were among those in the second quarter in 1993.

TABLE 3-8 Relative Distribution of Research-Doctorate Programs Appearing in Both the 1982 and 1993 Studies by Mean Rating of "Scholarly Quality of Program Faculty" in Quality Grouping[a]

Quality Grouping in 1982	Quality Grouping in 1993				
	Top	2nd	3rd	4th	Total
Top	***399***	66	3	0	468
2nd	81	***287***	103	12	483
3rd	8	112	***248***	110	478
4th	0	11	113	***363***	487
					1,916

[a]Based on average ratings for "Scholarly Quality of Program Faculty." See Appendix R for details.

Patterns of stability and change are evident across each of the 27 fields listed in Appendix R.[12] There was a tendency, however, for programs appearing in the "top quarter" in 1982 in the Social and Behavioral Sciences to remain in the "top quarter" in 1993, as shown in Table 3-9. Slightly fewer "top-rated" programs remained in the "top quarter" on average in the Arts and Humanities than in the other fields.

Of course, as new programs were added to the study in 1993, the quarter groupings reported elsewhere in the chapter are based on the total number of programs included in the study. It is interesting to consider, then, the distribution of the 317 programs appearing for the first time in the 1993 NRC study in these 27 fields by the 1993 quality groupings. Figure 3-5 summarizes the distribution of those programs appearing in one of the 27 fields analyzed in 1982. From this analysis we conclude:

- *Programs appearing in the 1993 study for the first time in one of the 27 fields studied in 1982 received a mix of high, medium, and low ratings, although the chances were much higher that these newly participating programs would appear in the bottom half of the 1993 quality groupings.*

It is also possible to analyze the relative standing of programs appearing in the 1982 study within the new quality groupings of the entire 1993 data set in these 27 fields into quarters. In general, the evidence for "grade inflation" for programs rated in 1982 (see Appendix R) has resulted in a general shift upwards in the relative rankings for the majority of programs appearing in both studies. Evidence for this tendency may be found in the detailed appendixes on a discipline-by-discipline basis. (See Appendixes J through N and Appendix P.) This phenomenon merits closer analysis by interested researchers in the years to come.

The "change" measures included in this section are only illustrative of the data exploration that is possible using the information collected by the committee. Nonetheless, the committee is persuaded that careful attention to study design has created the potential for conducting longitudinal analysis of changes in program standings using data gathered by the committee.

The fields utilized in the 1993 study that are "new" to the series become the basis for future analyses in the same way that the 1982 fields served as the benchmark for change analysis in 27 fields.

We now turn to a consideration of changes in the characteristics of those doctoral programs included in both the 1982 and 1993 studies.

TABLE 3-9 Percentage of Research-Doctorate Programs Remaining in the "Top Quarter" Between 1982 and 1993 When Mean Rating of "Scholarly Quality of Program Faculty" Is Considered by Broad Field and Quality Grouping[a]

Broad Fields	Total Number in Both Studies	Total Number in Top Quarter in 1982	Number Remaining in Top Quarter 1993 (%)
Arts and Humanities	431	103	82 (80)
Engineering	301	74	64 (86)
Physical Sciences and Mathematics	535	132	116 (88)
Social and Behavioral Sciences	576	141	125 (89)

NOTE: Biological Sciences are excluded from this table since only one field, Physiology, is common to both studies.

[a]Based on average ratings for "Scholarly Quality of Program Faculty" in 1982 and in 1993. See Appendix R for details.

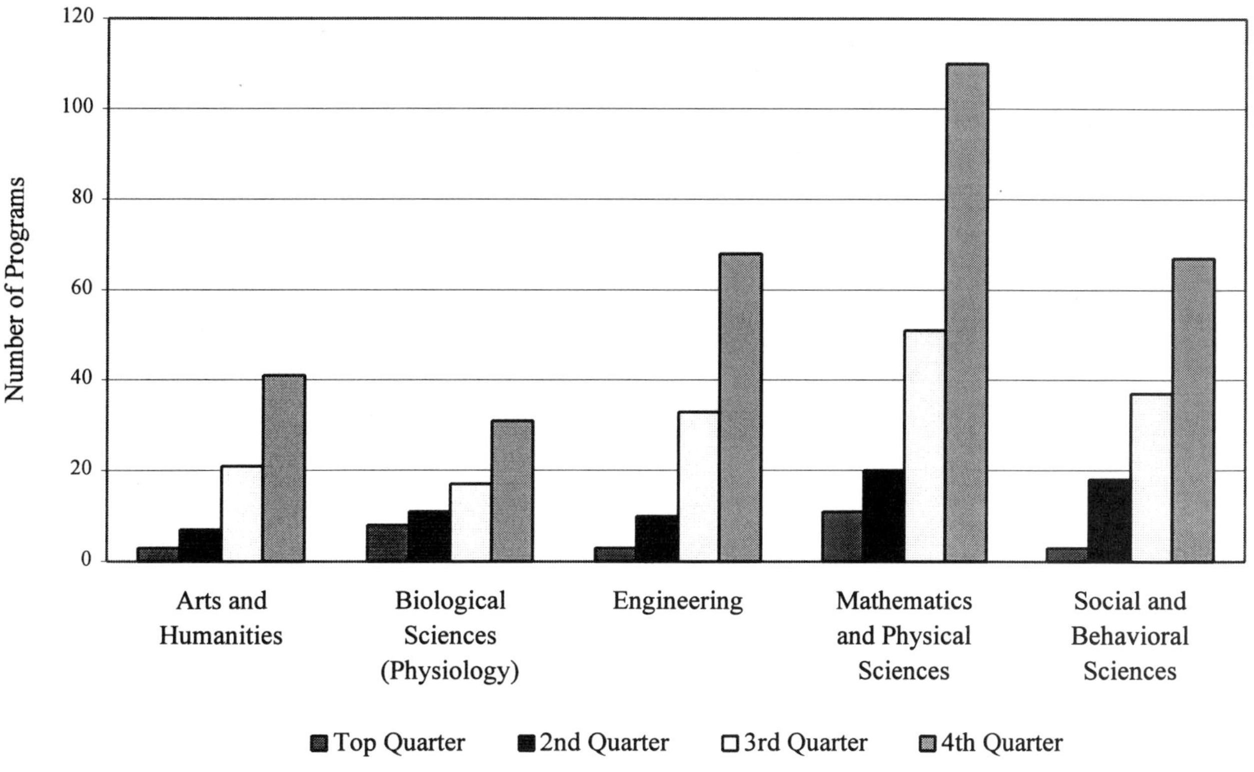

FIGURE 3-5 Relative distribution of research-doctorate programs appearing in the 1993 study for the first time in fields included in both the 1982 and 1993 study, by broad field and 1993 quality grouping. Based on the "Scholarly Quality of Program Faculty." See Appendixes J-N.

"Changes" in Selected Program Characteristics for Programs Appearing in the 1982 Study

The availability of 1982 program ratings coupled with more recent information about the characteristics of those programs provides a unique opportunity to review changes in program characteristics across quality groupings. Differences in data collection procedures between 1982 and 1993 restricted the number of program variables that could be analyzed over time. However, the committee identified three variables thought to be relatively stable and available for analysis: (1) the number of program faculty, (2) the number of program graduates, and (3) the median years to degree (from entering graduate school). Details related to these measures are presented in Appendix R, where limitations surrounding the "change" analysis are also described.

Throughout this section, "change" measures are reported only for those programs appearing in both the 1982 and the 1993 study. All "quality grouping" measures refer to program standings in 1982. Thus, "changes" in degree production for programs in the "top quarter" refer to differences in degree output for those programs rated in the "top quarter" in 1982 *regardless of their standing in 1993.*

Arts and Humanities

It is possible to analyze changes for programs in those fields in the Arts and Humanities included in both studies, which are:

- Art History
- Classics
- English Language and Literature
- French Language and Literature
- German Language and Literature
- Linguistics
- Music
- Philosophy
- Spanish and Portuguese Language and Literature

Number of Faculty. Information in Appendix R suggests a small but positive correlation in the Arts and Humanities between the average number of faculty providing doctoral training and the "scholarly quality" of those faculty as measured in 1982. Top rated programs in English Language and Literature, for example, had an average of 43 faculty in 1982 while programs rated in the last quarter averaged 22 faculty. (See Appendix Table R-10.) Similar patterns are evident in such fields as Classics and the modern European languages. The relationship between quality grouping and number of faculty was substantially weaker in a number of fields, including Music (Appendix Table R-19) which had an average of 22 faculty in the top quarter in 1982 and 21 in the fourth quarter.

A modest increase in the average number of faculty in the Arts and Humanities was evident for programs participating in both the 1982 and the 1993 studies. (See Table 3-10.) For the most part, the average number of faculty in English Language and Literature, Music, Philosophy, and Spanish and Portuguese Language and Literature revealed the most significant growth.

Number of Graduates. Restricting our analysis to the number of Ph.D.s produced on average between 1975-1980 and 1987-1992, it is possible to calculate an estimate of "change" by 1982 "quality groupings."

As Figure 3-6 reveals, programs rated in the top quality grouping in 1982 awarded many fewer doctorates between 1987 and 1992 than in the earlier comparable six year period, although degree production in Linguistics actually increased in that time. These data suggest that programs rated in the top quarter in 1982 in the Arts and Humanities actively restricted graduate activity in the 1980s, possibly in response to changing employment conditions. (See, for example, Bowen and Sosa, 1989.)

Median Years to Degree. Information from the Doctorate Records File (see Appendix G) reveals that individuals graduating between 1986 and 1992 in the Arts and Humanities typically took longer to complete their doctoral studies than graduates between 1975 and 1979. For those programs participating in both studies, there appears to be a relationship between 1982 quality grouping and changes in time to degree, such that "time to degree" increased more in programs rated in the last quarter in many fields. In the field of

TABLE 3-10 Change in the Average Number of Faculty in the Arts and Humanities by Field and 1982 Quality Grouping,[a] Fall 1980 and Fall 1992

Fields	Top Quarter	2nd Quarter	3rd Quarter	4th Quarter
Art History	0.13	0.67	3.23	-1.00
Classics	0.43	4.72	3.00	-0.43
English Language and Literature	2.92	5.80	1.29	2.48
French Language and Literature	0.20	2.18	2.60	1.18
German Language and Literature	0.14	-0.63	2.38	0.25
Linguistics	3.50	-2.86	1.71	1.12
Music	2.09	6.36	5.42	-3.46
Philosophy	1.82	6.06	0.50	2.18
Spanish and Portuguese Language and Literature	2.25	3.00	2.54	2.38

[a]Based on average ratings for "Scholarly Quality of Program Faculty" in 1982. See Appendix R for details.

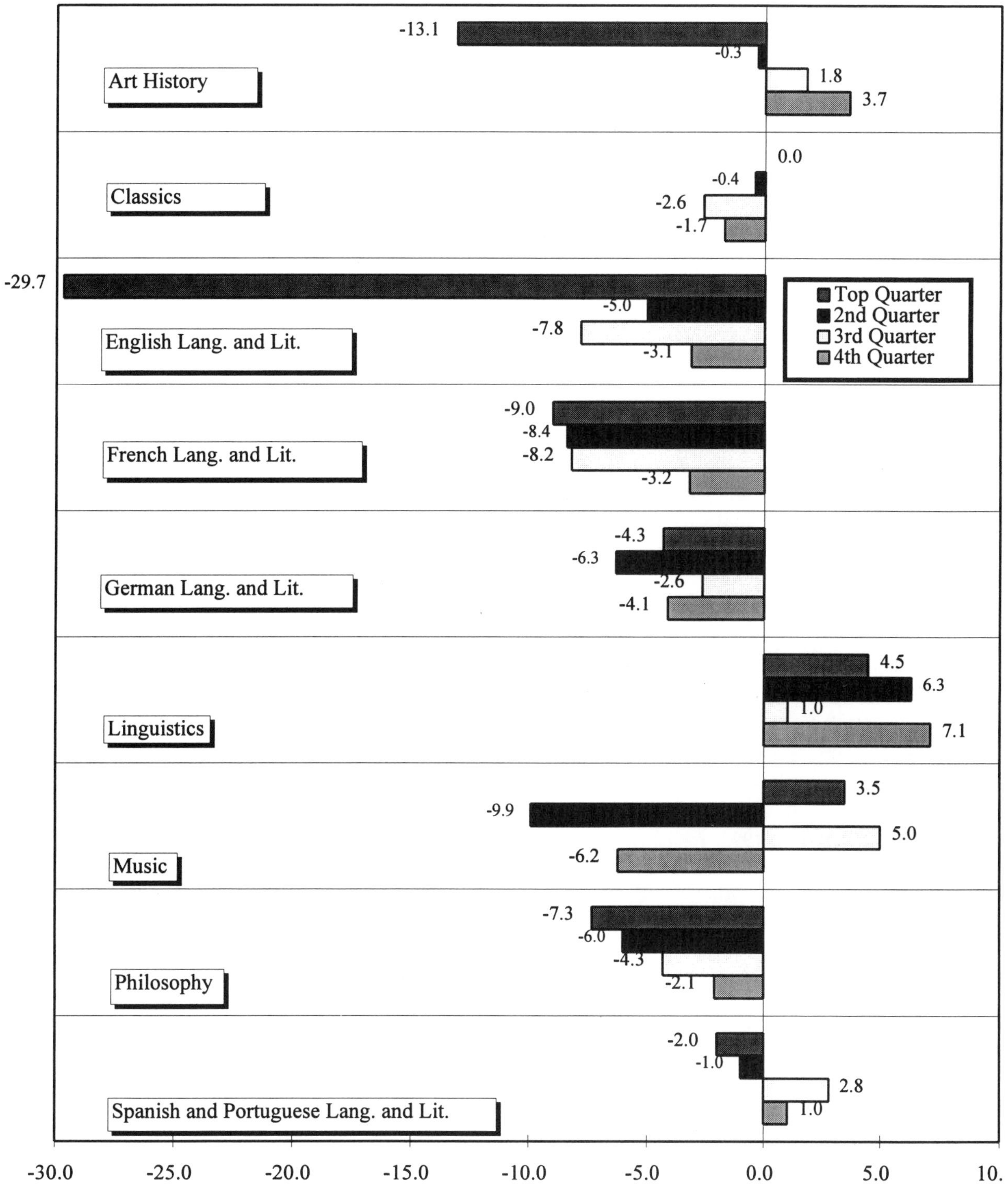

FIGURE 3-6 Change in the average number of program graduates in the Arts and Humanities by field and quality grouping: 1975-1980 and 1987-1992. Based on the average rating of "Scholarly Quality of Program Faculty" in 1982. See Appendix R for details.

Philosophy (Appendix Table R-20), for example, the median years to degree for graduates in the top quarter increased by an average of about 1.8 years, while graduates in programs rated in the bottom quarter in 1982 took about 2.5 years longer.

- *Research-doctorate programs in the Arts and Humanities appearing in both the 1982 and 1993 studies produced fewer Ph.D.s between 1986 and 1992 than during an earlier, comparable period regardless of quality groupings. The most significant decline occurred in programs rated in the top quarter in 1982. While it took most individuals longer to earn a doctorate in the Arts and Humanities in recent years, time to degree tended to lengthen more for graduates of programs rated in the bottom quarter in 1982.*

Engineering

Among the eight fields included in the 1993 study, four appeared both in the 1982 and 1993 studies, namely:

- Chemical Engineering
- Civil Engineering
- Electrical Engineering
- Mechanical Engineering

Change measures for a number of variables have been tabulated and presented in Appendix R. Among the 27 fields included in that appendix, doctoral programs in these four engineering fields are notable for their growth between 1982 and 1993, as described below.

Number of Faculty. Doctoral faculty rosters are larger in 1993 in these four Engineering fields than they were in the earlier study. Between 1982 and 1993, for example, the average number of doctoral program faculty in participating Chemical Engineering programs grew from about 13 to 14. (See Appendix Table R-3.) This pattern was also evident in the fields of Civil Engineering (Appendix Table R-5), Electrical Engineering (Appendix Table R-9), and Mechanical Engineering (Appendix Table R-18).

Patterns of faculty growth are related to 1982 ratings of the "scholarly quality of program faculty," with more growth occurring in top rated programs. Coupled with the fact that top rated programs in 1982 also had a larger number of faculty at that time, the growth that occurred between 1982 and 1993 accentuated differences in faculty size by quality grouping. (See Table 3-11).

Number of Program Graduates. As doctoral faculty grew, the number of graduates in these four fields of Engineering also grew. (See Appendix R.) However, as Figure 3-7 reveals the actual number of graduates increased more in programs in the top quarter in 1982 than in other quarters.

TABLE 3-11 Average Number Faculty in Selected Fields of Engineering Based on 1982 Quality Grouping[a]

	Top Quarter	2nd Quarter	3rd Quarter	4th Quarter
Chemical Engineering				
Fall 1980	16.05	12.32	12.47	9.17
Fall 1992	18.95	15.11	13.89	10.47
Civil Engineering				
Fall 1980	36.60	21.25	15.75	10.94
Fall 1992	37.27	26.63	18.94	13.94
Electrical Engineering				
Fall 1980	41.52	22.86	16.71	15.26
Fall 1992	47.29	33.10	24.67	22.91
Mechanical Engineering				
Fall 1980	31.32	19.79	17.68	12.85
Fall 1992	35.47	30.11	20.89	15.50

[a]Based on average ratings for "Scholarly Quality of Program Faculty" in 1982. See Appendix R for details.

This means that just over 50 percent of degree recipients in Chemical, Civil, Electrical, and Mechanical Engineering who were awarded their degrees at participating programs between 1987 and 1992 earned them at institutions rated in the top quarter in 1982.

Median Years to Degree. In the late 1970s, graduates in these four fields of Engineering took about 7 years to complete their doctorates from the time of entering graduate school. (See Appendix R.) Graduates from programs rated in the top quarter tended to complete their doctoral studies faster than graduates from lower-rated programs. Looking at the same set of programs 10 years later, 1986 to 1992 program graduates took longer to earn their degrees in these four fields, now averaging about 8 years. This lengthening of time to degree was more evident for graduates in participating programs rated in the fourth quarter regardless of field.

- *Degree production essentially doubled across all quality groupings in the four Engineering fields included in both the 1982 and 1993 studies. Furthermore, programs rated in the top quarter in 1982 contributed more doctorates on average to the Ph.D. labor force than all other quality groupings combined.*

Physical Sciences and Mathematics

It is possible to analyze changes in the size of doctoral programs in the Physical Sciences and Mathematics for those fields which appeared in both the 1982 and the 1993 studies, which are:

- Chemistry
- Computer Sciences

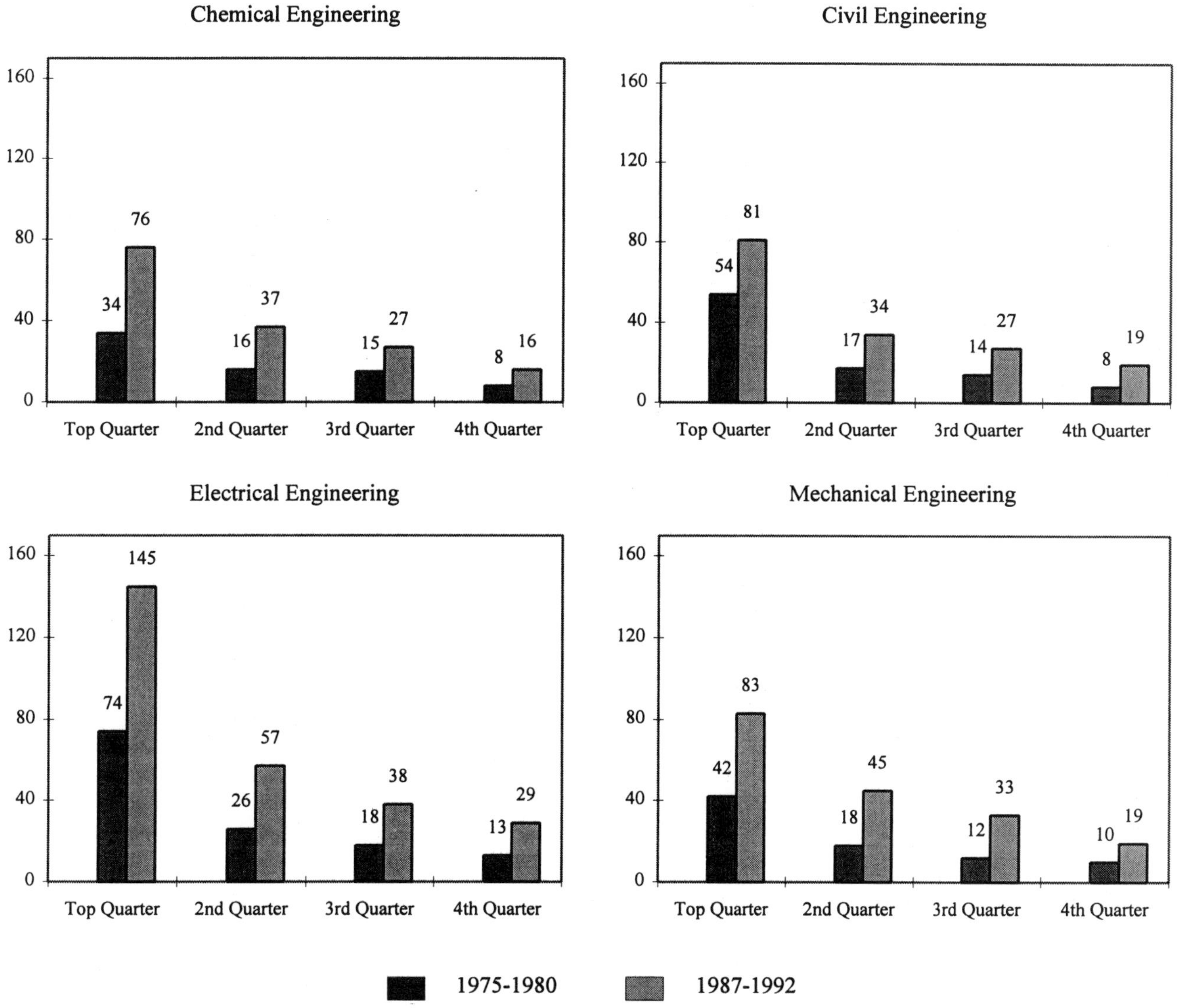

FIGURE 3-7 Average number of program graduates in Engineering by quality grouping: 1975-1980 and 1987-1992. Based on the average rating of "Scholarly Quality of Program Faculty" in 1982. See Appendix R for details.

- Geosciences
- Mathematics
- Physics
- Statistics and Biostatistics

For the most part, information included in Appendix R points to a significant expansion during the past decade with respect to the number of faculty involved in doctoral training and the number of program graduates. Programs rated in the top quarter in 1982 grew slightly more than other programs, as illustrated in data found in Appendix R.

Number of Faculty. Like Engineering, the number of faculty providing doctoral training in these selected fields of Physical Sciences and Mathematics increased between 1982 and 1993. (See Appendix R.) Growth occurred regardless of the 1982 quality grouping. However, owing to the fact that participating programs rated in the top quarter in 1982 had a larger number of faculty than lower rated programs, patterns of growth retained this difference.

Number of Program Graduates. As Figure 3-8 indicates, doctoral programs in the Computer Sciences, especially programs rated in the top quarter in 1982, experienced the most significant expansion between 1982 and 1993. Chemistry and Geosciences also increased the number of program graduates from 1982 top-rated programs. In Mathematics and in Statistics and Biostatistics, more modest expansion occurred in the number of degrees produced. In Physics,

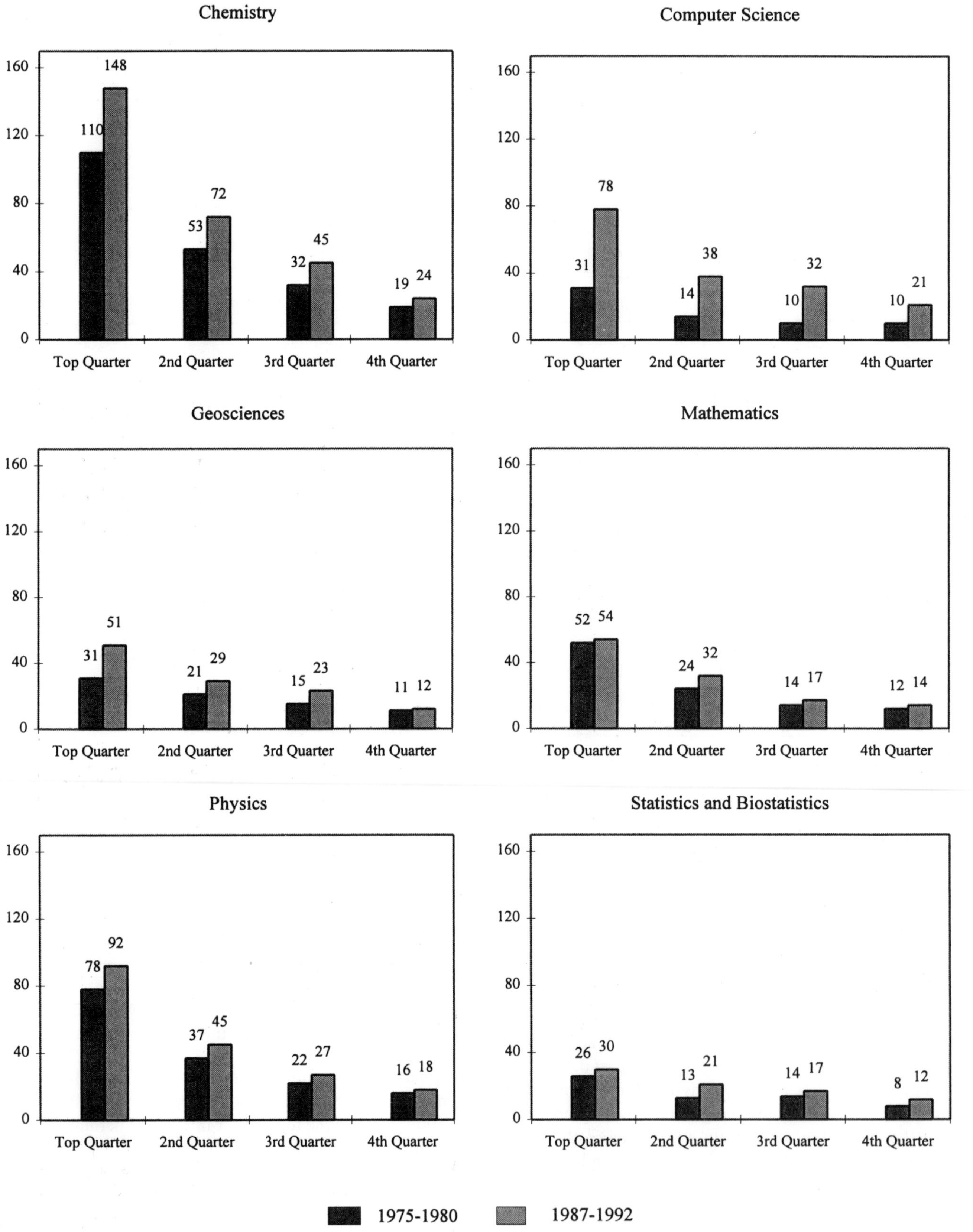

FIGURE 3-8 Average number of program graduates in the Physical Sciences and Mathematics by field and quality grouping: 1975-1980 and 1987-1992. Based on the average rating for "Scholarly Quality of Program Faculty" in 1982. See Appendix R for details.

more significant expansion occurred among programs rated in the top quarter in 1982.

Median Years to Degree. The lengthening of time to the doctorate observed in participating programs in Engineering (discussed earlier) also occurred in these fields of the Physical Sciences and Mathematics. For programs participating in both the 1982 and the 1993 studies, there appears to be a relationship between 1982 quality grouping and changes in time to degree: "time to degree" lengthened more in programs in the last quarter in 1982 in most component fields.

- *Degree production increased in the Physical Sciences and Mathematics between 1982 and 1993 regardless of 1982 quality groupings. However, the number of degrees produced by programs in the top quarter in 1982 in Chemistry, Computer Sciences, and Physics increased more between 1982 and 1993 than degree production by lower rated programs. Students graduating from programs rated in the bottom quarter in 1993 typically took longer to earn their doctorates than those graduating from the same programs a decade earlier.*

Social and Behavioral Sciences

It is possible to analyze changes in the size of doctoral programs between 1982 and 1993 for all eight fields comprising the Social and Behavioral Sciences in 1993.

Number of Faculty. Data from Appendix R indicate that the average number of program faculty involved in doctoral training in the Social and Behavioral Sciences grew only slightly between 1982 and 1992. The one exception occurs in Psychology, where the average number of faculty active in programs rated in the bottom quarter in 1982 grew more than for 1982 top-rated programs (Appendix Table R-24).

Number of Program Graduates. For most fields in the Social and Behavioral Sciences, degree production declined in the last decade—with a slightly greater decline occurring at programs rated in the top quarter in 1982, except in Geography. (See Figure 3-9). Programs in Psychology receiving lower ratings in 1982 displayed an especially notable expansion of degree production in the 1980s.[13]

Median Years to Degree. Information presented in Appendix R points to a substantial lengthening of "time to degree" for graduates in participating programs. In Anthropology (Appendix Table R-1), for example, graduates completing their degrees between 1975 and 1979 at these institutions took about 8.3 years to do so; for 1986-1992 graduates, the figure was 11.6 years on average. The greatest increase occurred for graduates from programs rated in the bottom quarter. This pattern was evident in most of the other fields in this area.

- *While most doctoral programs in the Social and Behavioral Sciences produced fewer graduates between 1987 and 1992 compared to an earlier, comparable period, degree production markedly increased in Psychology from programs appearing in the last quarter in 1982. It took program graduates more time to complete their degrees in the 1980s, with "time to degree" lengthening more in programs rated in the bottom quarter in 1982.*

SELECTED INFORMATION ABOUT PROGRAM GRADUATES

In this chapter we have reviewed thus far the overall results of the National Survey of Graduate Faculty, discussed differences in both the size of doctoral programs and the level of research and scholarship among faculty based on differences perceived in the quality of those programs, and pointed to changes that have taken place in faculty size, degree production, and time to degree for doctoral programs by their 1982 quality grouping. We conclude this brief analysis of our data by focusing on information about program graduates. This analysis includes the entire set of 3,634 programs participating in the 1993 study.

We begin with a consideration of the length of time it took program graduates to earn their degrees, then a examination of patterns of student support, and participation of women and of racial/ethnic minority groups in doctoral training in recent years.

Time to Degree

Fields vary, of course, with respect to the length of time required by students to earn a doctorate. This is due in part to differences in expectation about the rate of progress of doctoral students through degree programs and the intended purpose of the dissertation.[14] In the Biological Sciences, Engineering, and most Physical Sciences, where students generally engage collaboratively with faculty in research projects from the early phases of doctoral study, time to degree is shortest. In general, doctoral students earning degrees in the Arts and Humanities and in the Social and Behavioral Sciences, where the research activity is less collaborative and more individual, take considerably longer to complete the Ph.D.[15] However, when degree progress is analyzed by quality grouping (Figure 3-10), a common pattern emerges:

- *Students completing their doctoral studies in top-rated programs, regardless of field, typically complete their studies more rapidly than students emerging from lower-rated programs.*

The factors behind this phenomenon are not well under-

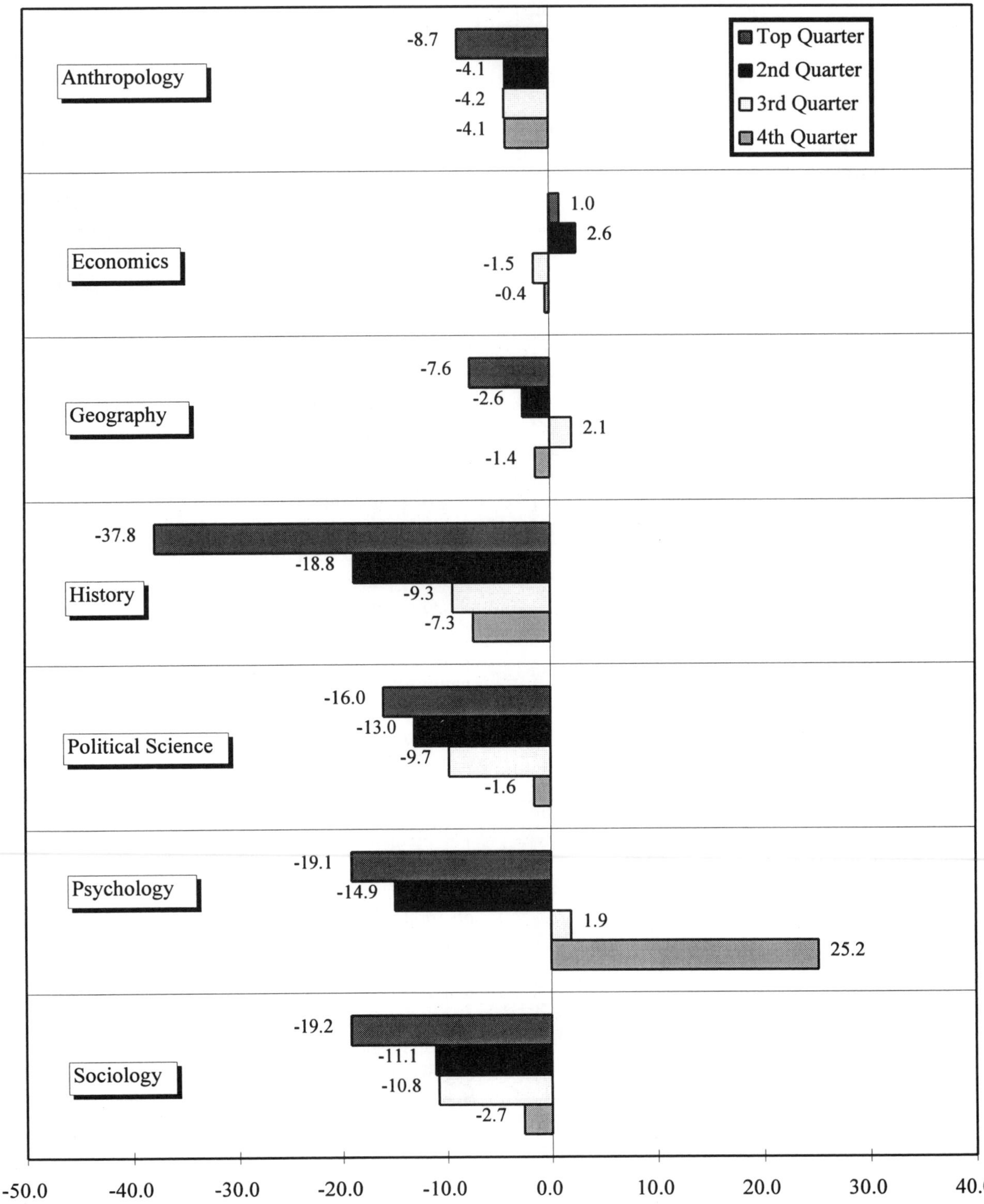

FIGURE 3-9 Average number of program graduates in the Social and Behavioral Sciences by field and 1982 quality grouping: 1975-1980 and 1987-1992. Based on average rating for "Scholarly Quality of Program Faculty" in 1982. See Appendix R for details.

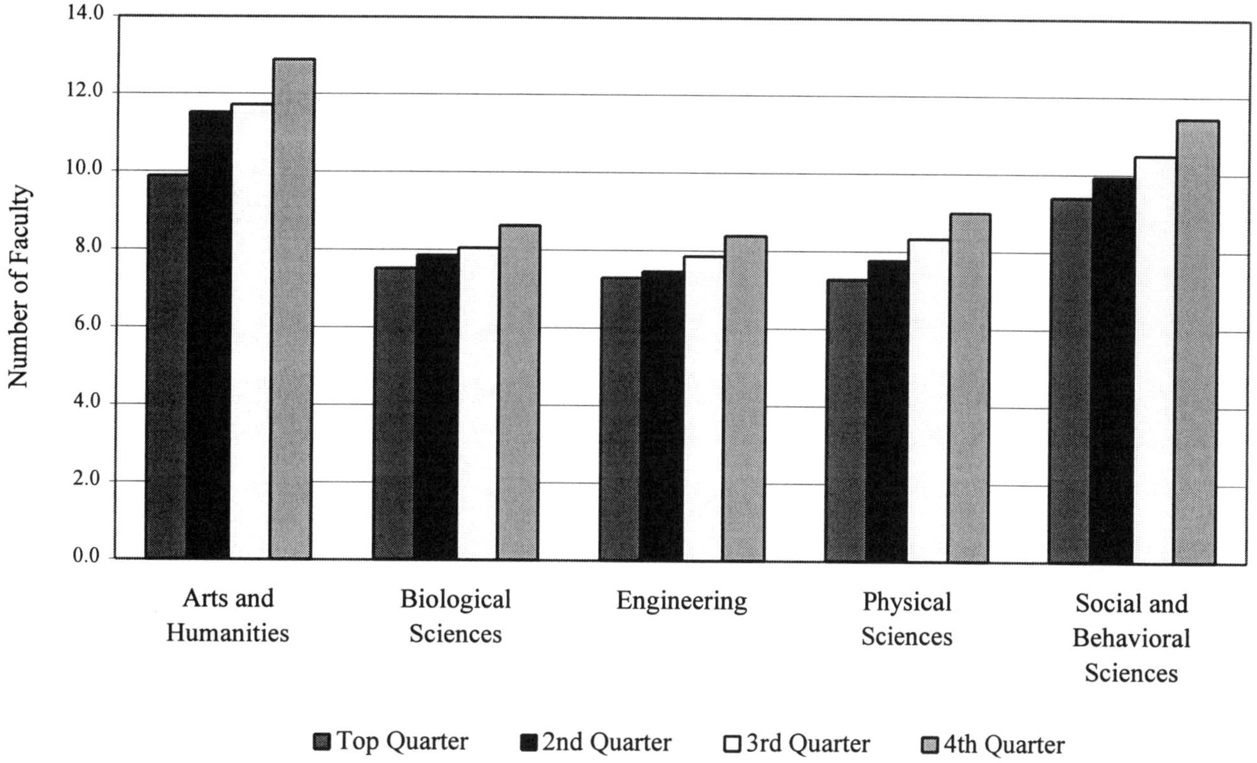

FIGURE 3-10 Median time to degree by broad field and by quality grouping: 1987-1992. Based on the "Scholarly Quality of Program Faculty" in 1982. See Appendixes J-N for details.

stood. One factor may be differences in the availability of student support. (See Table 3-12.)

Patterns of Student Support

- *Degree recipients in the Sciences and Engineering are more likely to have received research assistantship (RA) support to complete their training than students in the Arts and Humanities; those earning degrees in top-rated institutions were more likely to have had some form of RA support.*

Because students often focus their dissertation work on the subjects in which they engaged during their research assistantships, greater access to grant support in top-rated doctoral programs facilitates the completion of doctoral studies in most of the Sciences and Engineering fields. Graduates in the Arts and Humanities and in the Social and Behavioral Sciences do not have access to external support at the same rate as students in the other fields. Coupled with differences in degree requirements and in the character of the overall structure of doctoral programs, graduate students in the Arts and Humanities and in the Social and Behavioral Sciences, even in top-rated programs, may be expected to take longer to complete degree requirements.

Both the Association of American Universities (1990) and the Council of Graduate Schools (1990) have observed that student progress toward the doctorate is slowed by excessive involvement in teaching. Thus, it is interesting to note that (Table 3-12):

- *Graduates from lower-rated programs across many fields included in the study tended to have utilized teaching assistantships at a higher rate than graduates of higher-rated programs, a factor likely to contribute to longer times to degree.*

Diversity

In the past few decades, U.S. universities have made a special effort to recruit women and individuals from racial/ethnic minority groups into postsecondary education. The fruits of these efforts are reflected in part in the number of students who complete their baccalaureate education and continue to pursue advanced degrees, especially the doctorate. In this section, we focus on the diversification of doctoral degree production among the 41 fields included in the

TABLE 3-12 Average Percentage of Doctoral Recipients With Research or Teaching Assistantships as a Primary Source of Support by Field and Quality Grouping[a]

	Top Quarter		2nd Quarter		3rd Quarter		4th Quarter	
Fields	**RA**	*TA*	**RA**	*TA*	**RA**	*TA*	**RA**	*TA*
Art History	2	12	3	14	1	22	2	24
Classics	0	38	4	24	0	50	0	30
Comparative Literature	0	46	0	53	3	48	1	37
English Language and Literature	0	47	1	46	1	40	0	33
French Language and Literature	0	53	1	43	0	70	3	52
German Language and Literature	2	63	4	65	4	68	0	44
Linguistics	12	42	10	35	9	27	4	20
Music	0	29	1	23	0	26	0	22
Philosophy	1	55	0	51	7	40	1	33
Religion	1	7	0	10	2	11	1	8
Spanish and Portuguese Lang and Lit	1	69	1	56	1	58	0	52
Biochemistry and Molecular Biology	42	5	46	18	38	24	36	28
Cell and Developmental Biology	31	6	35	18	23	24	25	29
Ecology, Evolution, and Behavior	28	29	30	35	20	35	25	31
Molecular and General Genetics	29	2	33	15	43	22	26	27
Neurosciences	23	5	28	15	41	24	23	42
Pharmacology	24	3	31	8	27	12	22	14
Physiology	30	7	26	21	26	18	29	24
Aerospace Engineering	63	7	59	7	53	14	34	10
Biomedical Engineering	45	1	48	2	47	7	48	7
Chemical Engineering	68	6	58	14	59	15	46	26
Civil Engineering	53	9	41	16	43	18	26	17
Electrical Engineering	58	9	46	20	30	22	26	35
Industrial Engineering	36	17	43	28	17	35	12	33
Materials Science	79	2	68	5	68	3	55	7
Mechanical Engineering	57	12	48	19	41	21	28	22
Astrophysics and Astronomy	65	11	68	13	56	23	52	31
Chemistry	61	17	44	34	32	45	26	43
Computer Sciences	52	13	46	21	20	32	12	28
Geosciences	54	14	41	22	32	30	25	30
Mathematics	14	57	10	67	5	68	6	59
Oceanography	77	1	53	3	70	4	49	11
Physics	69	12	60	23	46	34	39	30
Statistics and Biostatistics	22	41	16	44	12	49	14	40
Anthropology	6	16	6	17	7	26	4	15
Economics	2	33	11	47	18	36	11	32
Geography	12	36	26	31	18	29	6	26
History	2	26	2	35	2	30	2	24
Political Science	7	30	7	31	4	29	5	22
Psychology	15	21	14	18	10	14	7	9
Sociology	17	21	16	29	11	30	7	24

[a]Based on average ratings for "Scholarly Quality of Program Faculty" in 1993. See Appendix J-N for details.

study. We ask the question: Can any conclusions be drawn about relative patterns of degree attainment for women and for minorities when 1993 quality grouping is considered? The results that emerge are preliminary but suggest that further analysis of the data would yield high payoff for educational planners and policymakers.

Female Graduates

Earlier in the chapter, we pointed out that in the Fall 1992 women tended to be enrolled in graduate study in comparable proportions across quality groupings within a field of study. In English Language and Literature, for example,

TABLE 3-13 Summary Information on Patterns of Doctoral Degrees Earned by Women from Programs Participating in the 1993 Study by Broad Field and Quality Grouping[a]

Broad Field (Quarter)	Average Number Degrees Awarded[b]	Average Percentage to Women[c]
Arts and Humanities		
Top	31.7	47.1%
2nd	24.0	49.2
3rd	16.4	46.5
4th	14.3	48.0
Biological Sciences		
Top	36.1	36.3
2nd	20.7	35.3
3rd	13.0	35.3
4th	8.4	31.7
Engineering		
Top	77.5	9.2
2nd	32.8	8.0
3rd	23.6	7.6
4th	10.9	7.8
Physical Sciences and Mathematics		
Top	72.9	17.4
2nd	35.7	18.7
3rd	20.0	17.9
4th	12.4	19.6
Social and Behavioral Sciences		
Top	55.0	43.4
2nd	31.5	44.7
3rd	26.8	46.1
4th	29.2	46.8

[a]Based on average ratings for "Scholarly Quality of Program Faculty" in 1993.
[b]From information provided by Institutional Coordinators.
[c]From information drawn from the Doctorate Records File.

TABLE 3-14 Summary Information on Patterns of Doctoral Degrees Earned by Minorities from Programs Participating in the 1993 Study by Broad Field and Quality Grouping[a]

Broad Field (Quarter)	Average Number Degrees Awarded[b]	Average Percentage to Minorities[c]
Arts and Humanities		
Top	31.7	4.3%
2nd	24.0	7.0
3rd	16.4	5.5
4th	14.3	6.9
Biological Sciences		
Top	36.1	2.4
2nd	20.7	3.3
3rd	13.0	3.7
4th	8.4	6.0
Engineering		
Top	77.5	2.2
2nd	32.8	2.0
3rd	23.6	2.0
4th	10.9	2.7
Physical Sciences and Mathematics		
Top	72.9	2.3
2nd	35.7	2.3
3rd	20.0	2.2
4th	12.4	4.9
Social and Behavioral Sciences		
Top	55.0	6.3
2nd	31.5	5.9
3rd	26.8	6.8
4th	29.2	6.5

[a]Based on average ratings for "Scholarly Quality of Program Faculty" in 1993.
[b]From information provided by Institutional Coordinators.
[c]From information drawn from the Doctorate Records File.

women accounted for about 60 percent of the enrollments in each of the four quarters. (See Table 3-4.) However, due to the fact that top-rated programs in many fields have a larger number of doctoral students on average than lower-rated programs, more women will be enrolled for graduate study in top-rated programs in most fields.

An analysis of degree production reveals a similar pattern across quality groupings. Table 3-13 shows that the percentage of women doctorates does not vary appreciably across quality groupings in any of the broad fields. However, since the top-rated programs produce a higher total number of graduates, they also produce a disproportionately higher number of women. (See Figure 3-11.) As a result, women enrolled in top-rated programs are as likely to earn a degree as those in lower-rated programs. An exception appears to occur in Engineering, where on average, a slightly larger fraction of graduates in top-rated programs were women than the fraction emerging from programs in the bottom quarter. Subfield differences are illustrated in Figure 3-11.

- *In 27 of the 41 fields included in the study, over 40 percent of the women earning their Ph.D.s between 1986 and 1992 earned them at top-rated institutions in their field of study. This percentage was especially high in Electrical Engineering (65 percent), Oceanography (62 percent), and Geosciences (60 percent). However, taking into account the fact that top-rated programs tend to be larger, there appears to be little relationship between quality and patterns of degree attainment for women.*

Graduates from Racial/Ethnic Minority Groups

Information regarding the participation of individuals

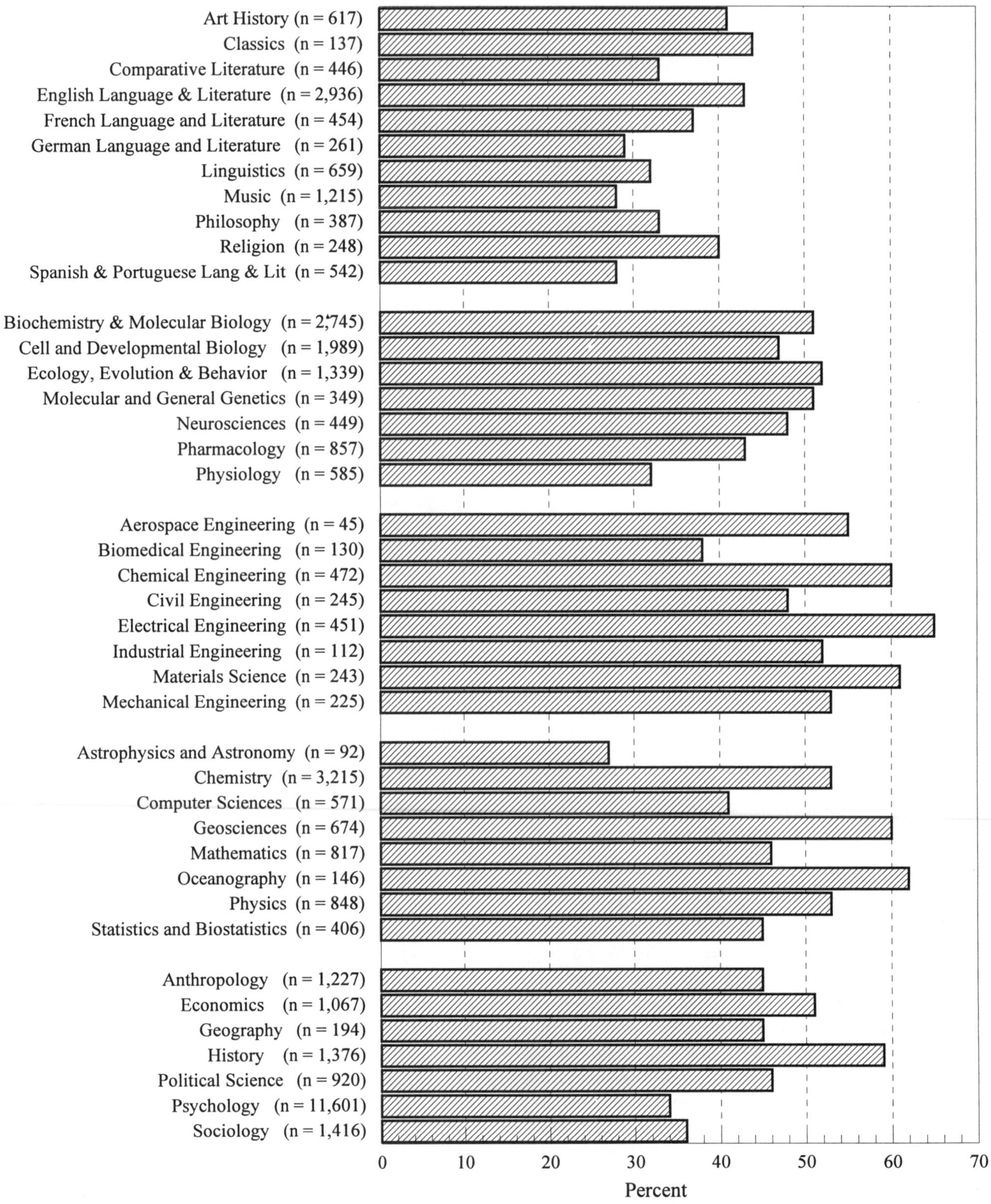

FIGURE 3-11 Percentage of female doctorates who come from programs rated in the "Top Quarter" on the "Scholarly Quality of Program Faculty" variable. Note: The numbers in parentheses are the total number of Ph.D.s awarded to women between 1986 and 1992. SOURCE: National Research Council, Doctorate Records File, Special Tabulations Files, 1994.

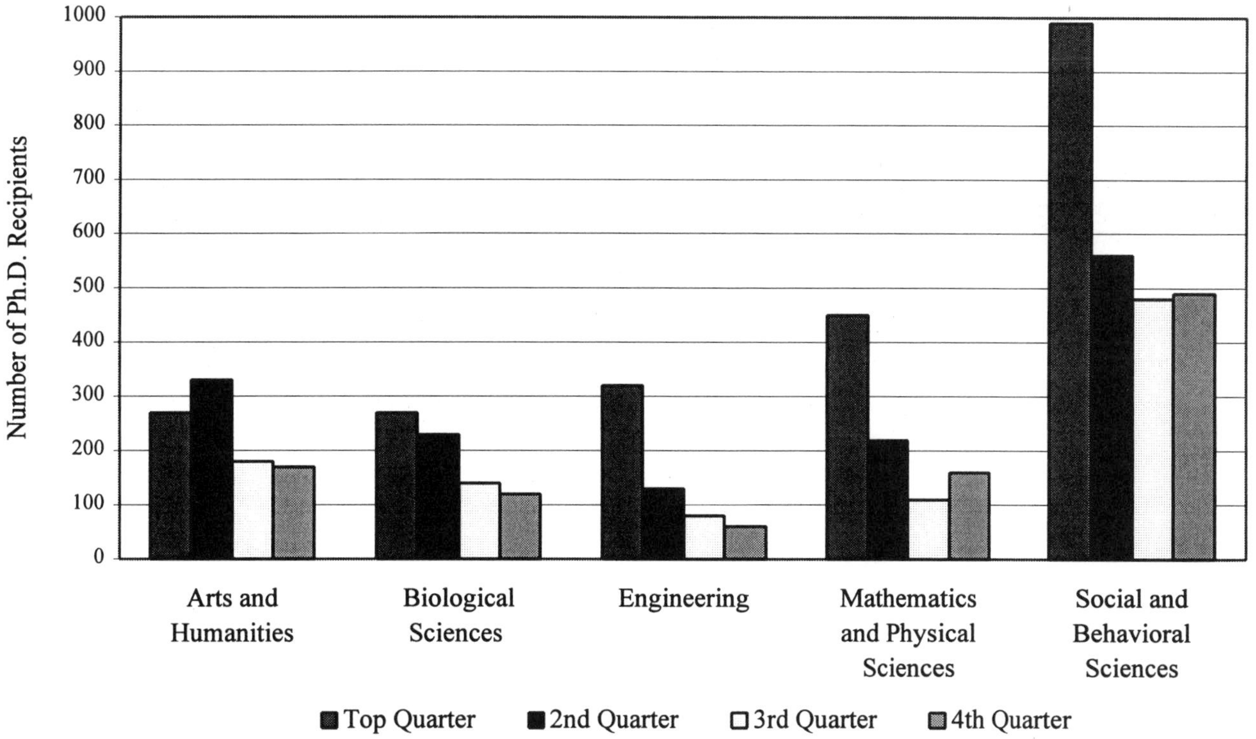

FIGURE 3-12 Relative distribution of minority Ph.D. recipients by broad field and by quality grouping (1986-1992). Based on the "Scholarly Quality of Program Faculty." See Appendixes J-N.

from historically underrepresented racial/ethnic minority groups was more difficult to obtain. Owing to differences in recordkeeping practices across campuses, the committee did not approach Institutional Coordinators in this area for information. Rather, the committee relied on the Doctorate Records File for the purpose of developing some understanding of the distribution of program graduates by quality group within fields. These data have been summarized and presented in Appendixes J through N.

Between 1986 and 1992, approximately 143,000 individuals earned their doctorates from the 3,634 programs included in this study. Of these graduates, about 6,000 (4 percent) were members of racial/ethnic minority groups. The majority completed their doctorates in the Social and Behavioral Sciences. (See Figure 3-12.)

When analyzed by "quality grouping," the overall picture that emerges (Figure 3-12) is that minority graduates tended to emerge from top-rated programs. Approximately twice as many minority doctorates come from the Social and Behavioral Sciences as from any other broad field.

The evidence found in Table 3-14, for example, reveals a larger proportion of the graduates of programs rated in the bottom quarter are from racial/ethnic minority groups. This

TABLE 3-15 Relative Distribution of Programs from Participating HBCU/HSI Institutions by Quality Grouping[a] (for All Fields)

Type of Institutions	Top Quarter	2nd Quarter	3rd Quarter	4th Quarter
All	897	918	897	923
HBCU/HSI	0	3	6	39

[a]Based on the 1993 average of "Scholarly Quality of Program Faculty."

TABLE 3-16 Relative Distribution of Graduates from Participating HBCU/HSI Institutions by Quality Grouping[a] (for All Fields)

Type of Institutions	Top Quarter	2nd Quarter	3rd Quarter	4th Quarter
All (1986-1992)	66,220	36,800	22,600	17,500
US Citizens	41,200	23,600	14,800	12,100
Minorities	2,300	1,500	1,000	1,000
Minority Graduates from HBCU/HSI Institutions	—	50	50	200

[a]Based on the 1993 average of "Scholarly Quality of Program Faculty."

finding is thought to be related to the rating of programs located at Historically Black Colleges/Universities (HBCU) or Hispanic-Serving Institutions (HSI).[16]

To investigate this hypothesis, the committee analyzed the relative distribution of the 48 programs located at institutions primarily serving minority students.

As Table 3-15 indicates, there was a tendency for the faculty in those programs to be rated in the lower half of quality groupings.

It must be kept in mind, of course, that top-rated programs—regardless of the type of institution—produce more doctorates on average than lower-rated programs. Thus, while a smaller *share* of graduates from top-rated programs may be members of racial/ethnic minority groups, they may actually *outnumber* the number of minority graduates from programs rated in the bottom quarter. For example, more than half the minority graduates in Electrical Engineering between 1986 and 1992 completed their doctoral work at top-rated programs (see Appendix Table K-5).[17] Thus, a degree of complexity is introduced into the interpretation of the relationship between "program quality" and degree patterns among minority graduates. This point is underscored in Table 3-16. In summary:

- *The relationship between "quality" and patterns of minority degree production is complex and merits further analysis. There is a tendency for faculty in doctoral programs located at HBCU/HSI universities to be rated lower. However, the effects of this phenomenon on patterns of degree production can be eclipsed by the significantly larger volume of doctorates awarded by top-rated programs in a field.*

INTERPRETING THE FINDINGS

The findings presented in the preceding pages are initial explorations of the data that have been gathered by the committee in the course of this three-year study. At one level, the findings reveal that quality groupings based on the perceived quality of program faculty offer a useful tool for examining differences in research-doctorate programs along a variety of dimensions: faculty, research and scholarship, awards and honors, time to degree, and diversity. Likewise, the "change" measures summarized here can be extended and interpreted further. In the next chapter we conclude our study with some observations as to the types of analysis that might be conducted using the data gathered and summarized in this report. The committee hopes that educators and planners will actively explore the data set that has been compiled by the committee and undertake additional analyses.

NOTES

1. The design of the survey is discussed in the previous chapter, "Study Design," and more fully in Appendix F.

2. A total of 3,736 programs was reviewed. However, owing to the problems encountered by some institutions in reporting their programs in the Biological Sciences (as discussed in Chapter 2), separate scores were gathered for multiple programs in the same field at some institutions. Composite scores were then calculated as described in Appendix F. Separate scores for two or more programs in the same field at the same institution were retained only if these involved programs offered in separate academic units—such as "Neurosciences" in a medical school and in a liberal arts college at the same university. In the end, scores for a total of 3,634 programs are reported in this volume.

3. Cartter (1966) also found that half the programs in Economics included in his study appeared in the two lowest groupings.

4. Selected results from the 1982 study are presented in Appendix P. The 1993 study committee recalculated the 1982 ratings of "program effectiveness" to conform to the five-point scaling system. See, also, Jones, Lindzey, and Coggeshall, 1982.

5. A "trimmed mean" was calculated for each program, in effect, ignoring the two highest and the two lowest scores assigned to a program. See Table 2-4 or the definition "key" located at the front of each of the Appendixes J through N for further details.

6. Programs have been ranked on the basis of a program's average rating on the measure "Scholarly Quality of Program Faculty." For programs with identical scores, programs were then ordered on the basis of the score "Percent Distinguished" and "Percent Distinguished or Strong" as reported in Appendix P.

7. See the key to Appendix Q for a further discussion of the general matter of calculating confidence intervals.

8. In calculating the "breaking points" between quarters, consideration was given to the assignment of programs with tied scores. Average ratings of the "scholarly quality of program faculty" were made to three decimal places. If a program fell below a break point but shared the same score as the last program in the preceding quarter, that program was moved into the preceding quarter. However, it is possible to observe in some tables that programs appear above and below a breaking point having what seem to be the same average rating. In fact, rounding procedures mask differences in scores, which would account for the arrangement of programs that is observed.

9. The Gini coefficient $= \dfrac{\sum_{i-1}^{n} (P_i)^2}{\left(\sum_{i=1}^{n} P_i\right)^2} \times 100$

where P_i equals the number of publications or citations for faculty member i.

The higher the Gini coefficient, the less the dispersion. For example, consider three programs each having 20 faculty members who together publish 40 articles during a certain period of time. In program A, each of the 20 faculty members published 2 articles for a Gini coefficient of 5. In program B, 2 faculty members each produced 11 articles (for a total of 22 articles) and the remaining 18 faculty members each published one article; the Gini coefficient would be 16.3. In program C, one faculty member published 40 articles and the remainder published none; the Gini coefficient would be 100.

10. See Appendix G for a list of those awards and honors identified by the committee for purposes of this analysis.

11. Only 1 field in the Biological Sciences appeared by that designation in both the 1982 and 1993 studies, namely Physiology. A total of 73 Physiology programs appeared in both studies. The results of the change calculations for Physiology appear in Appendix Table R-22. An interpretation of the "change" measures is addressed in a technical note prepared by committee member and co-chair Brendan Maher which appears in Appendix R.

12. A technical note in Appendix R also addresses the issue of rater response patterns in 1982 and 1993.

13. It is likely that lower-rated programs in Psychology include a large percentage of those which emphasize doctoral preparation in clinical psychology. Data from the Doctorate Records File indicates degree production in that area increased significantly in recent years. Further analysis of the factors behind this finding is needed before conclusions may be drawn about its meaning.

14. Factors related to the time it takes to earn a doctorate have been discussed by a variety of authors, most notably, Berelson (1960), Nerad and Cerny (1992), Tuckman, Coyle, and Bae (1980), and the Association of American Universities (1990).

15. Bowen and Rudenstine (1992) address this phenomenon. Differences occur by discipline within these broad groupings.

16. The list of "Historically Black Colleges and Universities" can be obtained from the U.S. Department of Education, National Center for Education Statistics (NCES). The list of "Hispanic-Serving Institutions" can be obtained from the Hispanic Association of Colleges and Universities (HACU), Washington, D.C. Information is current as of January 1995.

17. Based on special tabulations from the Doctorate Records Files, similar patterns may be observed in History, Anthropology, Geosciences, and Neurosciences, although the numbers of minority graduates are smaller in those fields.

4

SUMMARY AND FUTURE DIRECTIONS

Chapter 1 of this report enumerates five goals that the committee formulated for the 1993 Study of Research-Doctorate Programs in the United States. In this chapter we summarize the committee's study design and presentation of findings to achieve these goals. Within the discussion of each of the goals, the committee also identifies additional data collection and analyses that might be conducted in the future. The chapter concludes with a broad proposal for the future that the committee believes would greatly enhance the knowledge and understanding of the quality of research-doctorate education: periodic updating and refining of the types of data contained in this report.

UPDATING THE 1982 ASSESSMENT

The committee conducted the National Survey of Graduate Faculty in Spring 1993 to secure faculty opinions of research-doctorate programs in their field in the same way faculty opinions were tapped by the 1982 study committee. The survey instrument was a questionnaire designed to elicit ratings of the "scholarly quality of program faculty," the "effectiveness of the program in educating research scholars and scientists," and the "relative change in program quality over the years." Like the 1982 study, all of these ratings were provided by faculty peers. In addition to providing raters with the same set of questions presented in the earlier questionnaire, the 1993 survey solicited more information about raters and, for the first time, asked about their familiarity with graduates of those doctoral programs. (See Appendix F for a description of the 1993 survey methodology.)

The 1993 study differs from the earlier study in its size. In 1993, approximately 8,000 faculty participants rated 3,634 programs in all of the five broad fields, compared with the 1982 survey, in which approximately 5,000 faculty members rated about 2,200 programs. Ratings were gathered, furthermore, in 41 disciplines, compared to 32 fields in 1982. In addition significant changes were made to the collection of program statistics in the Biological Sciences (see Chapter 2).

The committee also hoped to expand reputational ratings in this study to include program ratings by peers in industry. An exploratory study undertaken by the committee in 1992 suggests that it is feasible to survey peer views in industry in much the same way as faculty views are tapped. Unfortunately, the committee was prevented by limits of time and resources from conducting the study. Clearly, this is a promising area for future exploration.

The committee was also encouraged by the preliminary findings from the National Survey of Graduate Faculty, which indicated that it is not only feasible to collect views from faculty peers in other countries but that such a study would have value in expanding the base from which we can assess the relative standing of doctoral programs in the United States. The growing momentum toward "globalization" in academia—and in industry—makes it especially important to conduct this type of analysis.

EXPANDING THE "OBJECTIVE" MEASURES

The 1982 assessment included the following measures of individual research-doctorate programs: number of faculty members, students enrolled and graduates; several characteristics of graduates, including the number of years it took to earn a degree at a particular institution; and university library size. The 1993 study also measured most of these characteristics, but made some adjustments in the measures collected due to changes in or the availability of other data bases. Among the new data included in this study are statistics related to the participation of women in graduate studies and patterns of degree production by race/ethnicity.

The committee also identified at least two other important types of information that it would be useful to collect in future analyses of the quality of research-doctorate programs: student career outcomes and analyses of interdisciplinary programs.

At the 1991 planning meeting for this study, participants expressed interest in adding information about students' career outcomes to the data base. The committee conducted a preliminary exploration of how to calculate "career outcomes" as a means to validate the 1982 ratings and determined that such a study would require tracking individuals from a sample of institutions in the various quality groupings. The primary questions to be answered, the committee determined, are: Do differences in "scholarly quality of program faculty" (or other ratings) result in measurable differences in careers of research and scholarship among program graduates? Are these differences attributable to program factors? Are other factors at work?

It was not possible to conduct an "outcomes" study in the context of the 1993 assessment. But the committee believes that it would be prudent to use the 1993 rankings in a sample of fields as the basis for another study. For example, a sample of fields could be identified, a sample of programs selected based on the quality ratings of program faculty, and a prospective study conducted that would track individuals graduating from those programs over the next few years. Such information would play a useful role in guiding the design and interpretation of future studies which aim to assess the relative contributions of doctoral programs on career attainment.

During the design phase of the present study, committee members repeatedly emphasized that research-doctorate programs have become increasingly interdisciplinary since the appearance of the last report. This became evident in the emergence of new campus arrangements in the Biological Sciences. This tendency was also reflected in those fields included for the first time in the study: Comparative Literature, Neurosciences, and Materials Science, all of which require participation of faculty from more than one discipline.

In addition, the committee saw considerable value in undertaking an inventory of the campuses in the study to identify non-degree granting programs—such as Women's Studies, International Area Studies, Biophysics Programs, African and Afro-American Studies, and Humanities Institutes so as to gauge the impact of such programs on more traditional courses and degree granting programs. Such a study seems to be of great importance, and the committee hopes that an inventory like this will be available in advance of any future studies of research-doctorate programs in the United States.

CALCULATING "CHANGE" MEASURES

The committee's decision to follow the 1982 study format as closely as possible has resulted in the production of change measures in the following categories:

- ratings of the "scholarly quality of program faculty";
- number of faculty on a program-by-program basis;
- number of program graduates; and
- time to degree.

This study traces its origins, of course, to early attempts to sorting programs within a field on the basis of the reputational ratings of those programs. Tables found in Appendix P continue and extend the tradition. They continue the tradition in the sense that programs are rank ordered along those measures gathered by Cartter, Roose, and Andersen and Jones, Lindzey, and Coggeshall; that is, by perceived "scholarly quality of program faculty" and program effectiveness.

With this report, however, the committee expands the tradition by suggesting that there is an opportunity to learn much more about these reputational ratings than has been learned to date owing to the availability of "change" measures. In Chapter 3, the committee presents an early analysis of the findings using these data but concludes that much more work is needed to exploit fully the potential analyses inherent in these data. We encourage interested readers to engage in this undertaking.

ELECTRONIC DATA ACCESS

In preceding sections the committee has reported a selection of findings that emerge from the statistics collected for this report. Many of the analyses in the text of this report are based on a division of the programs in a field into four quarters—the top one-fourth being those deemed to have the highest "scholarly quality of program faculty" by the faculty raters. Obviously, many other types of analyses are possible and encouraged. The committee has prepared an electronic file to make it possible for educators and administrators to undertake additional analyses. This file is available through the National Research Council. (See Note 12 in Chapter 1.)

On the basis of our review of available data, the committee recommends the following activities as priority studies and analyses for the coming years using this electronic data base:

- *Reputational ratings—what accounts for the changes observed between 1982 and 1993?*

- *Arts and Humanities—What factors contribute to the changes observed in relative rankings of programs and degree output? Are there changes in the organization of degree programs in this area that account for the changes observed in the more traditional disciplines? What impact have non-degree granting programs had—Women's Studies, International Area Studies, Humanities Institutes—on the character and quality of Ph.D. programs?*

- *Biological Sciences—What accounts for the pattern of program ratings in this area?*

- *Validity—What is the predictive validity of these reputational ratings? That is, what differences occur in the careers of program graduates which might be related to difference in scholarly environment among these programs?*

- *Missing Information—In advance of future, periodic updates of studies such as this and the 1982 study, further work is needed to expand the national data set. Information is needed on the characteristics of entering students on a program-by-program basis in order to determine "program effects" on student outcomes. Peer views in industry and from abroad would round out our understanding of the status of our research-doctorate programs.*

PRESENTATION OF FINDINGS

When a report must convey large quantities of complex information to diverse audiences—some of which were identified in the Preface of the report—the clear accessible presentation of findings can be a difficult task. This committee's response to the challenge has been to organize and present some basic information on trends or significant changes in the text of the report; and to provide data on and rankings of programs by institution in a set of appendixes.

Perhaps the most significant contribution this committee has made to the interpretation and use of the data found in this report is to present much of it in ranked order. This is a significant departure from the presentation of the data collected by the 1982 study committee, and—in recognition of the utility of this approach—the committee has reproduced in ranked order selected information from the earlier report.

Appendixes H and I present two key reputational ratings:

- Appendix H shows the "scholarly quality of program faculty" ratings by program within each of the five broad fields. The ratings range from 0, signifying that a program is "not sufficient for doctoral education" to 5, for "distinguished."
- Appendix I lists "effectiveness ratings" by program within each of the 5 broad fields. The ratings range from 0, signifying that a program is "not effective," to 5, for "extremely effective."

In succeeding tables, the reader will be able to review both the "quality" and "effectiveness" ratings as well as numerous other data—program size, research support available, etc.—for each program in the study.

The committee hopes that the following summary of the contents of the report and appendixes will facilitate readers' search for the information they seek:

- For the general reader or policymaker seeking background information or information about trends, the text of the report outlines the history, methodology, and an overview of findings in each of the five academic program areas without reference to any specific programs or institutions;
- For current or potential research-doctorate students and advisers, the appendixes provide a variety of information about specific programs at specific institutions. The best sources for this information are Appendixes J through N, which provide the reader with each program's "quality" and "effectiveness" ratings, as well as characteristics such as size of faculty and student body, amount of research assistance available, etc.;
- For deans, department chairs, and other educators and administrators, the same tables referred to above will provide a basis for comparing the characteristics of specific departments ranked at different levels in the quality ratings; and
- For researchers, the technical and methodological notes in Appendixes F and G, as well as the program tables in the report should be useful. An electronic data base summarizing these statistics will be available to analysts.

NEED FOR PERIODIC UPDATES

This report contains a variety of statistics that describe the status of a large sample of research-doctorate programs in the United States. Based on the experience of preparing this assessment, the committee strongly recommends that a means be found to conduct, regular, periodic assessments of research-doctorate education in the U.S.

The analyses presented in this report demonstrate that periodic updates of faculty ratings provide a benchmark against which changes in quality of doctoral education can be monitored by the public sector, the private sector, and professional groups.

Periodic updates also allow faculty and administrators with new or emerging programs to assess the relative standing of their own programs from time to time. The committee heard from many faculty who were eager to have their newly established programs rated in the 1993 study but could not for reasons which were related to the eligibility criteria established by the committee. This experience suggests that more frequent updates—or supplemental studies—are needed to provide the feedback faculty, administrators, and students are seeking.

In making this recommendation, we do not underestimate the magnitude of the task. On the one hand, the committee was pleased that improvements have been made in a number of data sets beyond those utilized by the 1982 study committee, and that it was possible to create "change" measures. On the other hand, the continuing inability to find statistics in a number of areas is a serious problem. More work is needed prior to any future "updates" to assure that data problems encountered by this committee are resolved.

The committee presents the data in the many appendixes that follow in the spirit of encouraging debate and analysis by all who have an interest in and concern about advanced study at U.S universities—whether members of the academic or policy community, or of the general citizenry.

REFERENCES

Association of American Universities
1990 *Institutional Policies to Improve Doctoral Education.* Washington, D.C.: AAU.

Berelson, B.
1960 *Graduate Education in the United States.* New York: McGraw-Hill.

Bowen, W., and N. Rudenstine
1992 *In Pursuit of the Ph.D.* Princeton, NJ: Princeton University Press.

Bowen, W.G., and J.A. Sosa
1989 *Prospectus for Faculty in the Arts and Sciences.* Princeton: Princeton University Press.

Bowker, A.
1965 "Quality and Quantity in Higher Education," *Journal of American Statistical Association* 60.

Bradburn, N.
1987 "The Ranking of Universities in the United States and Its Effect on Their Achievement," *Freiheit der Wissenschaft.*

Carnegie Foundation for the Advancement of Teaching
1994 *The Academic Profession: An International Perspective.* Princeton, N.J.: Foundation for the Advancement of Teaching.

Cartter, A.
1966 *An Assessment of Quality In Graduate Education.* Washington, D.C.: American Council on Education.

Clark, M.J., R.T. Hartnett, and L.L. Baird
1976 *Assessing the Dimensions of Quality in Doctoral Education: A Technical Report on a National Study in Three Fields.* Princeton, N.J.: Educational Testing Service.

Cole, J.
1979 *Fair Science.* New York: Free Press.

Cole, J., E. Barber, and A. Granbard
1994 *The Research University in a time of Discontent.* Baltimore, Md.: Johns Hopkins University Press.

Cole, J., and S. Cole
1973 *Social Stratification in Science.* Chicago: The University of Chicago Press.

Cole, J., and J. Lipton
1977 "The Reputations of American Medical Schools," *Social Forces* 55:3.

Committee on Science, Engineering and Public Policy
1995 *Reshaping Graduate Education of Scientists and Engineers.* Washington, D.C.: National Academy Press.

Coser, L.A. (Ed.)
1975 *The Idea of Social Structure: Papers in Honor of Robert K. Merton.* New York: Harcourt, Brace and Jovanovich.

Council of Graduate Schools (CGS)
1990 *The Doctor of Philosophy Degree.* Washington, D.C.: CGS.
1991 *The Role and Nature of the Doctoral Dissertation.* Washington, D.C.: CGS.

D'Arms, J.
1994 "Letters to the Editor," *Change Magazine* 26:52.

Dolan, W. P.
1976 *The Ranking Game: The Power of the Academic Elite.* Lincoln, Nebr.: University of Nebraska Press.

Hartnett, R.T., M.J. Clark, and L.L. Baird
1978 "Reputational Ratings of Doctoral Programs." *Science* 199:1310-1314.

Hughes, R.M.
1925 *A Study of the Graduate Schools of America.* Oxford, Ohio: Miami University.

Jones, L.V., G. Lindzey, and P.E. Coggeshall
1982 *An Assessment of Research-Doctorate Programs in the United States*. Five Volumes. Washington, D.C.: National Academy Press.

Keniston, H.
1959 *Graduate Study and Research in the Arts and Sciences at the University of Pennsylvania*. Philadelphia: University of Pennsylvania Press.

Long, J.S., P.D. Allison, and R. McGinnis
1980 "Entrance into the Academic Career." *American Sociological Review* 43: 816-830.

Merton, R.
1968a "The Matthew Effect in Science." *Science* 159:156-163.
1968b "The Self-Fulfilling Prophecy." *Social Theory and Social Structure*. New York: Free Press.

National Science Board (NSB)
1993 *Science and Engineering Indicators — 1993*. Washtington D.C.: U.S. Goverment Printing Office.

National Science Foundation (NSF)
1992 *Federal Support to Universities, College and Nonprofits. FY 1990*. NSF 92-234. Washington, D.C.: National Science Foundation.

Nerad, M., and J. Cerny
1989 "From Facts to Action: Expanding the Educational Role of the Graduate Division." Paper presented at the XIV Annual Meeting of the Association of for the Study of Higher Education. Atlanta, Ga. November.

Ries, P., and D.H. Thurgood
1993 *Summary Report 1992*. Washington, D.C.: National Academy Press.

Roose, K.D., and C.J. Andersen
1970 *A Rating of Graduate Programs*. Washington, D.C.: American Council on Education.

Stephan, P., and S. Levin
1992 *Striking the Motherlode in Science: The Importance of Age, Place and Time*. New York: Oxford University Press.

Tuckman, H., S. Coyle, and Y. Bae
1980 *On Time to the Doctorate*. Washington, D.C.: National Academy Press.

U.S. Department of Education
1993 *Digest of Education Statistics*. NCES 93-292. Washington, D.C.: National Center for Education Statistics.

Webster, D.S.
1983 "America's Highest Ranked Graduate Schools, 1925-1982," *Change* 15.
1986 *Academic Quality Rankings of American Colleges and Universities*. Springfield, Ill.: Charles C. Thomas.
1992 "Reputational Ratings of Colleges, Universities, and Individual Disciplines and Fields of Study from Their Beginnings to the Present." In *Education: Handbook of Theory and Research*, J.C. Smart (ed.). New York: Agathon Press.

APPENDIXES

APPENDIX A

Conference Board of Associated Research Councils

REPRESENTATIVES: 1994

American Council on Education
- Robert Atwell, President, American Council on Education (ACE)
- Myles Brand, President, Indiana University
- Elaine El-Khawas, Vice President, Policy Analysis and Research, American Council on Education

American Council of Learned Societies
- Stanley N. Katz, President, American Council of Learned Societies (ACLS)
- Douglas Greenberg, President and Director, Chicago Historical Society

National Research Council
- Bruce Alberts, President, National Academy of Sciences (NAS) and Chairman, National Research Council (NRC)
- Barbara Boyle Torrey, Executive Director, NRC Commission on Behavioral and Social Sciences and Education (CBASSE)

Social Science Research Council
- David L. Featherman, President, Social Science Research Council (SSRC) and Chairman, Conference Board of Associated Research Councils
- Gardner Lindzey, Director Emeritus, Center for Advanced Study in the Behavioral Sciences

AMERICAN COUNCIL ON EDUCATION

President: Robert Atwell
One Dupont Circle, N.W., Suite 800
Washington, D.C. 20036
(202) 939-9300

The American Council on Education is the major representative organization in higher education in the United States. An independent, nonprofit association founded in 1918, the Council represents all accredited, degree-granting institutions of higher education as well as national and regional higher education associations. Through its programs, activities, and policy-setting functions, it strives to ensure quality education on the nation's campuses and equal educational opportunity for all American citizens.

The Council serves as the focus for discussion and decision-making on higher education issues of national importance. By bringing together major constituent groups under a single umbrella, it works to coordinate the interests of all segments of the higher education community into a single voice.

The Council regularly convenes such groups as the Washington Higher Education Secretariat, as a forum for higher education associations to discuss issues of national importance; the Association Council for Policy Analysis and Research, a forum for the discussion, planning, and implementation of both short and long-range research projects affecting higher education; and the Action Committee for Higher Education, which serves as the public affairs arm of higher education's national efforts on student aid funding and related issues.

Among the many activities of the American Council on Education are those of the Division of Policy Analysis and Research (DPAR) in developing an information base for educational policymaking by the higher educational community. DPAR issues special reports that monitor trends in higher education on enrollment, finances, and academic programs. In addition, the Division coordinates information sharing among 27 educational associations belonging to the Association Council for Policy Analysis and Research, and maintains an Information Service, including a clearinghouse, the Higher Education and the Handicapped Resource Center, to improve access to post-secondary institutions for persons with disabilities.

Other activities of the American Council on Education include: administering the international General Educational Development high school equivalency testing program in cooperation with the states, trust territories, and Canadian provinces; holding the Business-Higher Education Forum, which provides an opportunity for interchange among leading corporate and academic chief executives on issues of mutual concern; and the publication of a magazine and a newsletter for higher education.

ACE's membership stands at approximately 1,440 institutions. This broad mix of two- and four-year, public and private institutions represents 72 percent of all full-time enrollments in the United States. Including non-institutional members, ACE counts more than 1,802 organizations on its roster.

AMERICAN COUNCIL OF LEARNED SOCIETIES

President: Stanley N. Katz
228 E. 45th Street
New York, New York 10017
(212) 697-1505

The American Council of Learned Societies (ACLS) is the preeminent private humanities organization in the United States. Founded in 1919, ACLS supports humanistic research through awards to individual scholars, serves as a national representative for 54 constituent societies, and helps to identify and meet the present and future needs of humanistic scholarship. By bringing together learned societies concerned with the humanities and with humanistic aspects of the social sciences, ACLS enables these organizations to speak with a single voice on matters of common interest.

Although ACLS is best known for its program of fellowships and grants, its activities take many other forms. Through programs such as the Council for International Exchange of Scholars and the Committee on Scholarly Communication with the People's Republic of China, and the Vietnam Fulbright Program, ACLS serves as a channel for the funding of postdoctoral academic exchanges—including the Fulbright Scholar (Faculty) Program. Its publishing projects have resulted in the *Dictionary of the Middle Ages* and the *Dictionary of American Biography*, soon to be completely redone as the *American National Biography*. The ACLS has also conducted a major international scholarly project on comparative constitutionalism, and it is sponsoring a national project to improve the humanities content of the elementary and secondary schools.

As an advocate for the humanities, ACLS has broadened support for the humanistic study in the United States. In 1962, R.M. Lumiansky, then chairman of the ACLS Board of Directors proposed the creation of the National Endowment for the Humanities (NEH) and led the movement toward its establishment in 1965. As a nexus for the exchange of ideas, the ACLS provides a forum for discussion of current and future trends in scholarship. It does so through the publication of a quarterly newsletter, a series of Occasional Papers, and through sessions at its Annual Meetings.

The ACLS maintains liaisons with a number of other organizations. With the Social Science Research Council, it jointly sponsors 11 committees related to international and foreign area studies. It serves as the United States representative to the Union Academique Internationale (International Union of Academies) and is a member of the Conference Board of Associated Research Councils. The ACLS is also an observer at the meetings of the Humanities Subcommittee of the European Science Foundation.

The ACLS is a private non-profit federation of 54 national scholarly organizations. Its governing body consists of a 15-member Board of Directors and one delegate from each constituent society. The Board of Directors sets policies, administers funds, oversees the investment of endowed funds, and reports on all decisions to the constituent societies. The ACLS is supported by income from endowment, dues from constituent societies, subscriptions from organizations that are Affiliates, subscriptions from universities, colleges, and research libraries that are Associates, private and public grants, government grants and contracts, and private gifts.

NATIONAL RESEARCH COUNCIL

Chairman: Bruce M. Alberts
2101 Constitution Avenue, N.W.
Washington, D.C. 20418
(202) 334-2100

The National Research Council (NRC) is the working arm of the National Academy of Sciences (NAS) and the National Academy of Engineering (NAE), carrying out most of the studies done in their names. The Research Council is not a membership organization. It was organized in 1916 in response to the increased need for scientific and technical services caused by World War I. The Research Council is administered jointly by the National Academy of Sciences, the National Academy of Engineering, and the Institute of Medicine, and its work is overseen by a Governing Board and an Executive Committee.

The basic mission of the National Research Council is to provide most of the services to government agencies and Congress that are undertaken by the National Academy of Sciences and the National Academy of Engineering in their role as advisers to the federal government. The Research Council does this primarily through its committee structure, calling upon a wide cross-section of the nation's leading scientists, engineers, and other professionals who serve on its committees. These committees are administered through a series of commissions, offices, and boards which constitute the operational units of National Research Council.

Through its various study committees, the National Research Council performs many advisory roles as an arbiter, assessor, reviewer, evaluator or prognosticator, depending on the issue before it. The NRC clarifies, informing the debate on a scientific, technological, or public policy matter. Research Council committees are often the definitive authority on the state of knowledge on a particular topic. Their critical analysis and carefully drawn recommendations are guides for action. The Research Council maintains no laboratory facilities of its own. In most instances, committees collect and critically evaluate the available scientific evidence. If information is lacking, committees sometimes conduct surveys or assemble new data bases.

Most of the requests for studies come from governmental agencies or from Congress; some are initiated internally; a few are proposed by other external sources. About 85 percent of the funding comes from the federal government through contracts and grants from agencies, and 15 percent from state governments, private foundations, industrial organizations, and funds provided by the National Academy of Sciences, the National Academy of Engineering, and the Institute of Medicine for internally generated projects of a critical nature. The process by which studies are conducted is crucial to the validity of the results. Therefore, care is taken in selection of the study committee and in review procedures for the reports that are issued.

In a typical year there are more than 1,000 functioning committees with approximately 10,000 volunteers serving on them. The activities of these committees are supported by a National Research Council staff of about 1,200 employees.

SOCIAL SCIENCE RESEARCH COUNCIL

President: David L. Featherman
605 Third Avenue
New York, New York 10158
(212) 661-0280

Founded in 1923, the Social Science Research Council (SSRC) is an independent, nongovernmental, not-for-profit international association of over 300 social scientists. Its purpose is to provide opportunities for scholars in separate disciplines—i.e., anthropologists, economists, historians, political scientists, psychologists, sociologists—to work together to advance interdisciplinary social science research. The SSRC accomplishes this through a wide variety of workshops and conferences, research consortia, fellowships and grants, summer training institutes, scholarly exchanges, and publications.

Throughout its history, the SSRC has worked on the frontiers of social science and in most of the substantive areas that have been of scientific interest, many of which have also been of pressing public and national concern. Both basic academic and applied policy-oriented approaches have prevailed. Exploring the new theoretical and methodological opportunities for social science, and its use in the public interest, constitutes the SSRC's mandate. Its eclectic program reflects a tendency toward "mission-oriented" basic research. The emphasis is on collaboration among scholars—those with area and disciplinary expertise, and among scholars from different regions of the world. In selecting topics for investigation, the SSRC gives priority to those scholarly and public policy questions that address the fundamentals of human behavior and of society's institutions; involve potential contributions of several disciplines; show promise of responding to collaborative effort and discussion; and that might profit from transnational and/or comparative research.

Historically, the SSRC has been best known to social science communities in the United States and abroad through its fellowship and grant programs. These cover graduate training, dissertation work, postdoctoral training and research, professional foreign travel, and institutional support. In addition, the SSRC often serves as a forum for international conferences and collaborative, international research projects; it works as a partner with other national and institutional interdisciplinary bodies.

The Council is governed by a board of directors, drawn from the academe, which regularly reviews and approves the SSRC's scientific and intellectual program and elects the president. Practically speaking, however, the operational arm of the SSRC is a continually changing group of some 309 social scientists, who, together with a salaried professional staff of about 15 program officers, create and direct the Council's program. This program is vested in approximately 30 different committees, working groups, and research consortia that are devoted to research planning and grants sponsorship, doctoral and postdoctoral fellowship administration, and advanced training for the evolving frontiers of interdisciplinary research.

An average of 2,000-3,000 researchers and graduate students per year participate in SSRC-sponsored activities around the globe, and more than 300 receive significant financial support in any given year. Seventy to 80 conferences, workshops, and training institutes take place annually.

APPENDIX B

Summary of 1991 Project Planning Meeting

WORKSHOP ON THE ASSESSMENT OF
RESEARCH-DOCTORATE PROGRAMS IN THE UNITED STATES

Convened by the National Research Council
Office of Scientific and Engineering Personnel
Studies and Surveys Unit

April 5 and 6, 1991
NAS/NAE Beckman Center
Irvine, California

AGENDA

Friday, April 5

8:30 a.m. Call to order and opening remarks
Chair, Philip Converse

Welcome
Jack Peltason, *Chancellor, University of California, Irvine*

Alan Fechter
Executive Director, OSEP

RETROSPECTIVE ANALYSIS

9:00 a.m. Lessons from Design of Earlier Assessments of Research-Doctorate Programs in the United States

In this session panelists will be asked to summarize their views on the strengths and weaknesses of the 1982 assessment, how it represented an improvement over earlier studies, and possible directions for improvement in the 1991 study.

Michael Pelczar, Lincoln Moses, Jack Peltason
Discussion Leader: Porter Coggeshall

10:30 a.m. BREAK

10:45 a.m. Lessons from the Presentation and Use of Data from the 1982 Assessment

The 1982 assessment presented data in five volumes, choosing to avoid "rankings" in favor of alphabetical arrangement of institutional measures. Data have been used subsequently for institutional planning and in higher education research. Panelists will be asked to comment on the effectiveness of data presentation in the 1982 reports and possible new approaches in 1991.

R. Duncan Luce, David Webster
Discussion Leader: Stephen Fienberg

Noon LUNCHEON
Guest Speaker, Roger Heyns
President, William Hewlett Foundation

BACKGROUND TO THE 1991 ASSESSMENT

1:30 p.m. Issues Related to the Quality of Research-Doctorate Programs in the 1990s

Institutions of higher education have changed over the years and research-doctorate programs have responded to a variety of internal and external pressures. Panelists will be asked to comment on the changes in higher education that are most likely to affect the

perception of program quality by peers—and the implications for design of the 1991 study and subsequent analysis.

David Breneman, Brendan Maher, Harrison Shull, George Wetherill
Discussion Leader: Robert Rosenzweig

3:00 p.m. BREAK

3:30 p.m. The European Experience in Assessing Research-Doctorate Programs

European institutions have taken an active interest in studying and enhancing programs of doctoral training. Various factors motivate these assessments including the need to respond to budget austerity measures while maintaining and/or building strong research institutions. Panelists will be asked to review studies under way in Europe with special reference to those measures that might be incorporated into the 1991 U.S. assessment.

T.G. Whiston (U.K.), John Irvine (U.K.),
Discussion Leader: Carlos Kruytbosch

4:30 p.m. General Discussion
Chair, Philip Converse

5:00 p.m.- 7:30 p.m Cocktails/Dinner at the Beckman Center

Guest Speaker, Richard Atkinson
Chancellor, University of California, San Diego

Saturday, April 6

8:30 a.m. Call to Order and Opening Remarks
Chair, Philip Converse

PLANNING THE 1991 ASSESSMENT

9:00 a.m. 1991-1992 Survey Design: Considerations in Selecting Fields, Institutions, and Programs

Assessments of research-doctorate programs include a very large array of fields and institutions, not to mention programs within institutions. Panelists drawn from representative disciplines to discuss changes in cross-departmental treatment of certain degrees and the implications for catching new/non-traditional fields in study design.

David A. Patterson (Computer Science), Douglas Greenberg (Humanities), Karl Pister (Engineering), Norman Hackerman (Physical Science)
Discussion Leader: Pamela Ebert Flattau

10:30 a.m. BREAK

10:45 a.m. 1991-1992 Survey Design: Instrument Design/Analysis, Change Measures

In order for the findings from the 1991 study to be compared to the 1982 assessment, it will be necessary to use the same survey instrument. Must all the features of the earlier instrument be retained to permit change analysis? If not, which features should be maintained and which abandoned? What change measures should be developed?

David Featherman, John F. Kihlstrom
Discussion Leader: Thomas D. Cook

Noon LUNCHEON

1:30 p.m. Correlates of Quality: Selecting, Analyzing, and Presenting Objective Measures of Subjective Phenomena

Research in higher education suggests that it is possible to select certain measures of institutional/student/program characteristics that may be analyzed relative to perceived program quality. What guidelines should be established for selecting and analyzing measures in 1991?

Harriet Zuckerman, Joseph Cerny
Discussion Leader: Charlotte Kuh

2:45 p.m. BREAK

LOOKING TO THE FUTURE

3:00 p.m. Measures that Should be Developed for the Assessment of 2001

Given the widespread interest in—and use of—measures of program quality, a goal of

the 1991 assessment will be to pave the way for another study in the year 2001. Panelists will be asked to comment on those features of research-doctorate programs that merit further scrutiny—if not in 1991, then in 2001.

Lincoln Moses, Lyle Jones
Discussion Leader: Jules LaPidus

4:30 p.m. Summary and Charge to the 1991 Committee Chair, Philip Converse

5:30 p.m. Adjournment

MEETING SUMMARY

The meeting opened with welcoming remarks by Philip Converse, workshop Chair; Jack Peltason, Chancellor, University of California, Irvine; and Alan Fechter, Executive Director, OSEP. A summary of the discussions of eight panels—addressing four major themes—follows.

Retrospective Analysis

Lessons from the Design of Earlier Assessments of Research-Doctorate Programs in the United States:
P. Coggeshall (Chair), M. Pelczar, L. Moses, and J. Peltason

Studies of research-doctorate programs become important because educators sense a need for "accountability." The scholarly community is asking: "How well are our programs doing in preparing people to do research or to engage in scholarly activity?" Peltason reported that, in the 1970s when ACE asked the NAS to conduct an assessment, he was surprised that not everyone in the community was enthusiastic about such a study. This was due partly to concerns that the findings might be used to cut back programs or divert resources from some departments to others. Or, as some other meeting participants put it, assessment findings may motivate lesser-rated programs to emulate highly-rated ones, regardless of whether this fits with the institutional mission.

Panelists noted that the 1982 assessment had several notable "strengths": (1) there was an excellent chain of communication set up between the study committee and the institutions, which involved institutional coordinators, deans, department chairs, and faculty; (2) program raters were given "data" on which to base their assessment of the programs in their field; (3) the statistics on the data were quite good; and (4) the fields that were selected tended to "hang together."

On the negative or "weak" side of the 1982 assessment, panelists observed that: (1) the study did not really assess the contribution of the "learning environment" to the success of graduate programs; (2) land grant institutions were somewhat less well involved in the study than other institutions; (3) bigger programs may fare better than smaller programs in this kind of study; (4) while the 1982 committee attempted to study other dimensions of graduate programs, there were severe limitations to the measures selected (for example, the "library holdings" measure is largely meaningless as applied in this study); and (5) the study did not tap student views—which may be as valuable if not more so than peer views of a research-doctorate program.

Lessons from the Presentation and Use of Data from the 1982 Assessment:
S. Fienberg (Chair), R.D. Luce, and D. Webster

The 1982 assessment presented data in five disciplinary based volumes, choosing to avoid "rankings" in favor of alphabetical presentation of institutional measures. Panelists provided feedback from the user community with the following comments: (1) Measure 8 (faculty reputation) tends to be the most frequently used measure from all the data provided by the 1982 report; (2) the failure of the 1982 information to be circulated widely (at least as reflected in Webster's review of the popular press) suggests that the next committee should consider producing a summary of findings for the "general public"; (3) the next committee might consider arraying institutions alphabetically within certain groupings (e.g., by quartile)—but there was no consensus on that suggestion; and (4) upon use, many of the attendant measures were found to be meaningless (e.g., number of publications per program) or absent (e.g., number of fellowships among humanities programs as an equivalent measure to "grant getting"). These other measures, it might be added, did not capture the attention of scholars or the press, according to Webster.

Background to the 1991 Assessment

Issues Related to the Quality of Research-Doctorate Programs in the 1990s:
R. Rosenzweig (Chair), D. Breneman, B. Maher, H. Shull, and G. Wetherill

Several important changes have taken place in higher education that merit consideration before launching the next NRC study: (1) programs in certain fields are more likely to operate through a consortium arrangement than was the case 10 years ago, and this should be reflected in program descriptors that are collected and analyzed; (2) technological advances—such as the introduction of self-contained work stations—have changed the way students and faculty do their work; (3) computers also allow faculty to exchange research information between institutions and countries—again suggesting some need to collect other kinds of program descriptors; (4) faculties have "aged" since the last study, suggesting that this feature of the educational environment might be analyzed in 1991; and (5) likewise, program participants have diversified (more women, minorities, and foreign students) and that diversification might be captured in this study as a relevant aspect of research-doctorate programs in the 1990s.

The European Experience in Assessing Research-Doctorate Programs:
C. Kruytbosch (Chair), T.G. Whiston, and J. Irvine

In recent years, the British Government has developed a keen interest in measuring and analyzing the performance of university-based research and graduate programs. Speakers from the University of Sussex, Science Policy Research Unit, described several of their projects in this area and the conceptual advances arising from their work. Of particular interest to workshop participants was the view that many of the measures arrayed in the 1982 assessment would be considered "program descriptors," not measures of "quality." In lieu of measures of quality, the British Government (through its unique grant system of "research councils") has turned to the development of "indicators of effectiveness" and "indicators of efficiency." Studies begin with a review of the purpose or function of a research/research-doctorate program, which in turn defines the output measures that need to be gathered to assess output relative to the stated mission. Once program descriptors have been created, information is assembled in much the same way it is assembled at the NRC so that an expert committee can make judgments about program effectiveness or efficiency. [While workshop participants were somewhat intrigued by the concept of indicators of "effectiveness," there was generally negative reaction toward the concept of indicators of "efficiency"—which were more "economically" oriented.]

The speakers also described how output measures like publication profiles can be used to assess the effectiveness of university-based programs. British researchers reported the need for very focused survey work (of Ph.D. program drop-outs, for example) which suggested certain limitations in the application of their work to the next NRC study of research-doctorate programs.

Planning the 1991 Assessment

1991-1992 Survey Design: Considerations in Selecting Fields, Institutions, and Programs:
P. Flattau (Chair), D.A. Patterson, D. Greenberg, K. Pister, and N. Hackerman.

In the 1982 assessment, the committee concentrated its efforts on 32 disciplines in 5 broad fields and decided that the selection of programs within each area should be based primarily on the number of doctorates awarded nationally in recent years. The dynamics of these fields have changed substantially, and the challenge to the 1991 study committee will be to address the special character and present state of research-doctorate programs in the various fields, and to design the study accordingly.

The computer sciences, for example, have undergone very rapid changes over the past decade, with a heritage that can be traced both to engineering and to mathematics—making them a "mismatch" with the rest of academia. Likewise, the humanities have been through a severe "job crisis" over the past decade. Coupled with low rates of funding and high diversification of the student body and faculty, this may make it difficult to find stable measures that relate to peer views of research-doctorate programs in the humanities. At the same time, engineering, a professional discipline with diverse—at times competing—program goals, has been occupied with training issues unrelated to the preparation of researchers. This again suggests the need to tailor the study to recognize the special needs of each field.

As Hackerman suggested, the 1982 study—and studies prior to that time—did not really represent "assessments of research-doctorate programs" because none of the reports has defined a route to improvement. Thus, Hackerman suggested: "Change the title or change the procedure." Along those lines, the suggestion for improvement most frequently voiced by these panelists was: increase the amount of program information given to each rater—even if it means reducing the number of programs rated. In addition, Hackerman and others suggested that the study should look at research-doctorate programs in terms of the "value" they "add" to students passing through them.

1991-1992 Survey Design: Instrument Design/Analysis, Change Measures:
T.D. Cook (Chair), D.F. Featherman, and J.F. Kihlstrom

Featherman led workshop participants through a discussion of the 1982 assessment with regard to the variables included in the questionnaire and in the instructions to raters. In Featherman's view, Measure 8 (scholarly quality of program faculty) should be retained and an effort made to refine attendant objective measures. Measure 9 (effectiveness of program in educating research scholars/scientists) should be dropped—partly because the instructions for that item were flawed (so one isn't certain what was measured in 1982) and also because, as the British researchers suggested, program effectiveness can be measured through means other than peer review.

Panelists also commented on the intercorrelations of the

various measures on the survey and between the survey and the selected measures. The suggestion was made that correlational analysis should assist the next study committee to select and reject measures in a more informed manner.

In addition, the suggestion was made that Measure 8 should be retained to begin building a time series—but opinion was divided on the extent to which the 1991 study should "replicate" the peer measures. As Cook summarized, the 1991 effort should do everything possible to preserve the best parts of the 1982 assessment.

Correlates of Quality: Selecting, Analyzing, and Presenting Objective Measures of Subjective Phenomena:
C. Kuh (Chair), H. Zuckerman, and J. Cerny

Panelists spent considerable time discussing the objective measures (that is, non-peer review measures) that they would like to include in the study. Zuckerman challenged the next committee to think about gathering data about program alumni—measures that might indicate how well alumni perform as scholars or researchers (indicators of effectiveness). This kind of analysis could be restricted to recent graduates—possibly no more than 5 years out of these programs. The committee was also challenged to think about developing measures of the "quality of students" attracted to and completing their doctoral preparation in these programs—looking for program effects.

From his perspective as a graduate dean, Cerny suggested specific measures that would allow him to ascertain where certain of his programs stand relative to other programs in the U.S. institutions. Some of these new measures focused on the presence of specific kinds of student support, for example. Clearly, implementation of these and other suggestions would be constrained by time and funding.

Looking to the Future

Measures That Should be Developed for the Assessment of 2001:
J. LaPidus (Chair), L. Moses, and L. Jones

The meeting concluded with a discussion about conducting a continuous activity relative to research-doctorate programs in U.S. institutions. Moses suggested that the 1991 committee ought to consider introducing new respondents for new information. While peer studies are helpful, certain dimensions of the research-doctorate process would benefit from a survey of other individuals—such as students or nonacademic peers (industrialists, for example). In addition, it would be helpful, in Moses' view, to maintain a small staff that in the interim years would work on the development of new measures, paving the way for regular updates and tracing their origins to the 1982 assessment.

Agreeing with earlier speakers, Jones endorsed the idea of dropping Measure 9 but at the same time looking for better measures of the "effectiveness" of research-doctorate programs in producing scholars/researchers. Both panelists offered suggestions for approaching the selection of variables in future studies (including the 1991 study) and also in presenting the findings in a more interesting, possibly more usable, way. Jones warned against the "tyranny of the decile"—meaning that the next study committee will need to grapple with the issue of alphabetical versus rank-order presentation of the results of the peer review portion of the upcoming studies.

OVERALL CONCLUSIONS

In the course of the two-day workshop, several important suggestions emerged for enhancing the next assessment of research-doctorate programs. These suggestions will be submitted for consideration to the NRC study committee which will oversee the next assessment when it is convened in 1991:

Retain Measure 08: Measure 8 (as it appeared in the summary tables in each of the five disciplinary volumes) addresses the "scholarly quality of program faculty." Specifically, survey respondents were asked to:

> "Check the box next to the term that most closely corresponds to your judgment of the quality of faculty in the research-doctorate program described. Consider only the scholarly competence and achievements of the faculty. It is suggested that no more than five programs be designated 'distinguished.'"
>
> This measure has proven to be positively correlated with numerous other statistics summarizing the characteristics of doctoral programs (such as length of time to degree, number of publications per faculty, etc.).

Information on the scholarly quality of program faculty should be collected in a manner as consistent as possible with its measurement in 1982. The committee should consider, however, adding as many additional measures of scholarly quality of faculty as are feasible given time and costs of the project, to augment analysis through peer ratings.

Drop Measure 09: Measure 09 (as it appeared in the 1982 summary tables) addresses the "effectiveness of the program in educating research scholars/scientists." Respondents were asked to:

> Check the box next to the term that most closely corresponds to your judgment of the doctoral program's effectiveness in educating research scholars/scientists. Consider the accessibility of the faculty, the curricula, the instructional and research facilities, the quality of the graduate students, the performance of the graduates, and other factors that contribute to the effectiveness of the research-doctorate program.

Workshop participants considered the item to be poorly conceived and the instructions too vague to ascertain the objective correlates that led the rater to provide a subjective rating. Furthermore, according to a number of participants, there are sufficient sources of information available to generate "effectiveness measures" through objective analytic techniques, rather than through this type of questionnaire.

Generate More Data on Graduate Student Characteristics: Participants suggested that more data are needed on the attributes of students in the graduate programs and on post-Ph.D. performance. This type of information would add some dimensions to our understanding of the contributions of the graduate program to the preparation of students.

Arrange for Ongoing Data Collection: A number of workshop participants commented that, in the 10 years since the last assessment, very little has been done to stimulate the collection of data that might serve to ascertain changes in the nature/quality of graduate education in the fields that are the subject of this study. Participants suggested that this type of assessment ought to be updated every 10 years (or some regular period) and that, in the meantime, biennial review of data on certain aspects of research-doctorate programs ought to be analyzed and disseminated. The work of the study committee should be institutionalized in some way to permit continuity in analysis and to avoid the expense of starting up an effort every 10 years.

Disseminating Survey Results to the Public: Some participants suggested that the study committee should consider new modes of packaging and disseminating its findings. A few participants recommended that the committee consider preparing a clearly written one-volume overview containing detailed findings. A press conference when the report is released and presentations at appropriate disciplinary meetings might be part of a Report Dissemination Plan (although this feature of committee work would be determined by the study committee and its staff when the project is launched).

Change the Survey Timetable: Based on the kinds of changes that might be made to the peer-survey and correlational analyses, workshop participants suggested that the formal survey of peers be delayed one year (1992-1993 academic year) to permit the development of a modified procedure. The peer study would be replicated to as large an extent as possible, however.

Prepared by
Pamela Ebert Flattau,
June 3, 1991

PARTICIPANTS

Richard Atkinson
Chancellor
University of California, San Diego
La Jolla, California

Richard E. Attiyeh, Dean
Office of Graduate Studies & Research
University of California, San Diego
La Jolla, California

George A. Boyce
Office of Scientific and Engineering Personnel
Director, Data Processing Section
National Research Council
Washington, DC

David Breneman
Harvard University
Graduate School of Education
Cambridge, Massachusetts

Joseph Cerny
Provost for Research
Dean, Graduate Division
University of California, Berkeley
Berkeley, California

David Chananie
Policy Planning and Research Branch
National Institutes of Health
Bethesda, Maryland

Porter Coggeshall
Assistant Director
Report Review Committee
National Research Council
Washington, DC

Philip E. Converse
Center for Advanced Study in
the Behavioral Sciences
Stanford, California

Thomas D. Cook
Northwestern University
Center for Urban Affairs
Evanston, Illinois

Elaine El-Khawas
Vice President
Policy Analysis and Research
American Council on Education
Washington, DC

David L. Featherman
President
Social Science Research Council
New York, New York

Alan Fechter
Executive Director
Office of Scientific and Engineering Personnel
National Research Council
Washington, DC

Stephen Fienberg
Dean, College of Humanities and
Social Sciences
Carnegie Mellon University
Pittsburgh, Pennsylvania

Pamela Ebert Flattau
Director, Studies and Surveys Unit
Office of Scientific and Engineering Personnel
National Research Council
Washington, DC

Douglas Greenberg
Vice President
American Council of Learned Societies
New York, New York

Norman Hackerman
Chairman
Scientific Advisory Board
Robert A. Welch Foundation
Houston, Texas

Roger W. Heyns
President
William Hewlett Foundation
Menlo Park, California

John H. Irvine
Director
Science Policy Research Consultants
East Sussex, United Kingdom

Lyle V. Jones
Director
L.L. Thurstone Psychometric Laboratory
University of North Carolina, Chapel Hill
Chapel Hill, North Carolina

John F. Kihlstrom
Department of Psychology
University of Arizona
Tucson, Arizona

Carlos Kruytbosch
Study Director
Science Indicators Studies Group
National Science Foundation
Washington, DC

Charlotte Kuh
Executive Director
Graduate Records Examination Program
Educational Testing Service
Princeton, New Jersey

Jules B. LaPidus
President
Council of Graduate Schools
Washington, DC

Gardner Lindzey
Director Emeritus
Center for Advanced Study in
the Behavioral Sciences
Stanford, California

R. Duncan Luce
Director, Irvine Research Unit
Mathematical Behavioral Science
Social Science Tower
Irvine, California

Brendan A. Maher
Dean, Graduate School of Arts and Sciences
Harvard University
Cambridge, Massachusetts

Lincoln Moses
Professor of Statistics
Stanford University
Stanford, California

David A. Patterson
Chairman, Computer Science Division
Department of Electrical Engineering
and Computer Science
University of California, Berkeley
Berkeley, California

Michael J. Pelczar, Jr.
Professor Emeritus and Emeritus
Vice President for Graduate Studies
University of Maryland
Chester, Maryland

Jack W. Peltason
Chancellor
University of California, Irvine
Irvine, California

Karl S. Pister
Dean, College of Engineering
Department of Civil Engineering
University of California, Berkeley
Berkeley, California

Robert M. Rosenzweig
President
Association of American Universities
Washington, DC

Dimitria Satterwhite
Administrative Secretary
Office of Scientific and Engineering Personnel
National Research Council
Washington, DC

Harrison Shull
Provost and Academic Dean
Naval Postgraduate School
Monterey, California

David Webster
Department of Educational
Administration and Higher Education
College of Education
Oklahoma State University
Stillwater, Oklahoma

Joanne M. Weinman
Manager Doctorate Records File
Office of Scientific and Engineering Personnel
National Research Council
Washington, DC

George Wetherill
Department of Terrestrial Magnetism
Carnegie Institution of Washington
Washington, DC

Thomas G. Whiston
Science Policy Research Unit
University of Sussex
East Sussex, United Kingdom

Harriet Zuckerman
Columbia University
Department of Sociology
New York, New York

APPENDIX C

Field Coverage

The following disciplinary specialties have been included in the current Study of Research-Doctorate Programs in the United States. Those marked with a dagger (†) appear this year for the first time; all others were part of the 1982 study. (See Jones, Lindzey, and Coggeshall, 1982.) The number of doctoral programs included in this study is shown in **bold type** next to each field. The fraction of total Ph.D.s awarded between 1986 and 1992 by programs participating in this study is presented.

	Programs in This Study:	
Field	Number	Percent of All 1986-1992 Ph.D.s
Art History	**38**	93
Classics	**29**	88
Comparative Literature †	**44**	90
English Language and Literature	**127**	96
French Language and Literature	**45**	84
German Language and Literature	**32**	83
Linguistics	**41**	91
Music	**65**	89
Philosophy	**72**	88
Religion †	**38**	79
Spanish and Portuguese Language and Literature	**54**	84
Total Arts and Humanities	**585**	
Biochemistry and Molecular Biology †	**193**	95
Cell and Developmental Biology †	**180**	93
Ecology, Evolution, and Behavior †	**129**	96
Molecular and General Genetics †	**103**	85
Neurosciences †	**102**	83
Pharmacology †	**127**	88
Physiology	**140**	87
Total Biological Sciences	**974**	

continued

Field	Programs in This Study: Number	Percent of All 1986-1992 Ph.D.s
Aerospace Engineering †	**33**	90
Biomedical Engineering †	**38**	83
Chemical Engineering	**93**	96
Civil Engineering	**86**	93
Electrical Engineering	**126**	98
Industrial Engineering †	**37**	81
Materials Science †	**65**	92
Mechanical Engineering	**110**	95
Total Engineering	**588**	
Astrophysics and Astronomy †	**33**	83
Chemistry	**168**	97
Computer Sciences	**108**	93
Geosciences	**100**	95
Mathematics	**139**	97
Oceanography †	**26**	83
Physics	**147**	97
Statistics and Biostatistics	**65**	80
Total Physical Sciences and Mathematics	**786**	
Anthropology	**69**	93
Economics	**107**	95
Geography	**36**	84
History	**111**	93
Political Science	**98**	96
Psychology	**185**	91
Sociology	**95**	93
Total Social and Behavioral Sciences	**701**	
TOTAL	**3634**	

The committee's selection of fields for inclusion in the present study involved a review and consideration of three factors, the first of which was patterns of Ph.D. production in the five broad fields comprising the 1982 study: Arts and Humanities, the Biological Sciences, Engineering, the Physical Sciences and Mathematics, and the Social and Behavioral Sciences.

The committee considered as possible "new" fields those fields whose degree counts during a certain period of time exceeded Ph.D. production in fields that had been included in the 1982 study. In 1991, when the present study was initiated, aggregate counts of Ph.D. production were available for the period 1986 through 1990 from the Doctorate Records File (DRF).[1] It was possible to generate a count of Ph.D.s awarded in component disciplines and then to rank order fields on the basis of those statistics. From this listing emergent "new" fields could be identified. The results are described below by broad field.

ARTS AND HUMANITIES

Information in the Arts and Humanities is given in Table C-1. Nine fields [marked with an asterisk (*)] were included in the 1982 study, based on the volume of degrees produced in the 1970s. (See Jones, Lindzey, and Coggeshall, 1982.) Our committee considered the number of degrees awarded between 1986 and 1990 on a field-by-field basis. A table was prepared showing Ph.D. production in rank order through the field of Classics (the smallest field included in the 1982 study).

Four fields not included in the earlier study were found in this new listing: Religion, Comparative Literature, The-

TABLE C-1 Ph.D. Production in Selected Fields in the Arts and Humanities by Field, 1986-1990

Specialty	Number of Ph.D.s	Number of Institutions
English Language and Literature*	3,620	143
Music*	2,573	87
Philosophy*	1,215	105
Religion	1,014	63
Linguistics*	909	72
Spanish and Portuguese Lang and Lit*	699	83
Art History*	683	53
Comparative Literature	561	61
French Language and Literature*	535	76
Theatre	447	51
German Language and Literature*	383	54
American Studies	361	34
Classics*	272	42
Total Arts and Humanities	13,272	187

NOTE: "Number of Institutions" refers to a count of universities awarding degrees in that area based on reports from individuals earning degrees in a DRF field between 1986 and 1990.

SOURCE: National Research Council, Doctorate Records File, Special Tabulations, 1991.

atre, and American Studies. This finding led the committee to enunciate a second principle for purposes of guiding field selection, namely, the participation of a significant number of programs across U.S. universities.

As in earlier studies of doctoral education, the present study focused on a review of the "reputational ratings" of programs within a field suggesting that participating programs should have achieved some level of visibility within the scholarly community. Furthermore, and perhaps more important, the committee considered the success of their National Survey of Graduate Faculty to depend on the availability of a pool of faculty from which "raters" could be drawn. The committee found that it was possible to review institutional patterns of degree production by studying data from the Doctorate Records File. Thus, the committee considered differences in degree production this way: How many institutions were involved in awarding 100 percent of the degrees in the Arts and Humanities between 1986 and 1990? How many were involved in awarding 90 percent of the degrees? How many at 80 percent? The results are presented in Table C-2.

As can be seen from Table C-2, 120 universities awarded 90 percent (3,288) of the degrees in English Language and Literature, and another 23 institutions awarded the remaining 10 percent or about 340 degrees. In Religion, 34 institutions awarded 90 percent (915) of the Ph.D.s between 1986 and 1990, and another 29 institutions awarded the remaining 10 percent of the degrees or about 100.

The picture that emerged from this review, and from a review of degree production in other fields, suggested to the committee that there was a need to establish a criterion that assured the inclusion of relatively "robust" fields; this is,

TABLE C-2 Ph.D. Production in Selected Fields in the Arts and Humanities by Field, and by Proportion of Degrees Produced, 1986-1990

	Fraction of Ph.D.s (1986-1990)					
	80 Percent		90 Percent		100 Percent	
Specialty	Number of Ph.D.s	Number of Institutions	Number of Ph.D.s	Number of Institutions	Number of Ph.D.s	Number of Institutions
English Language and Literature*	2,922	95	3,288	120	3,620	143
Music*	2,083	39	2,337	52	2,57	387
Philosophy*	976	53	1,101	68	1,215	105
Religion	807	23	915	34	1,014	63
Linguistics*	725	25	826	36	909	72
Spanish and Portuguese Lang and Lit*	561	44	636	58	699	83
Art History*	551	25	615	32	683	53
Comparative Literature	450	28	507	38	561	61
French Language and Literature*	432	38	486	51	535	76
Theatre	361	24	402	31	447	51
German Language and Literature*	307	27	348	35	383	54
American Studies	291	15	327	19	361	34
Classics*	220	22	244	27	272	42
Total Arts and Humanities	10,686	133	12,032	151	13,272	187

NOTE: "Number of Institutions" refers to a count of the universities awarding degrees in that area based on reports from individuals earning degrees in a DRF field between 1986 and 1990.

SOURCE: National Research Council, Doctorate Records File, Special Tabulations, 1991.

that a field should be selected for inclusion in the study not only on the basis of the volume of degrees produced but also on the number of institutions awarding those degrees. Thus, the committee considered as "robust" those fields having awarded about 500 degrees in about 50 programs for the period 1986-1990. In the Arts and Humanities, the fields of Religion and Comparative Literature were added to the 1982 field listing using those criteria. American Studies and Theater were excluded.

PHYSICAL SCIENCES AND MATHEMATICS

The committee reviewed doctoral degree production in the Physical Sciences and Mathematics for the period 1986 through 1990. The top fields in the 1982 study continued to represent the largest fields within this broad area. (See Table C-3.) However, it was apparent that a number of smaller fields that had not been included in the 1982 study had reached a sufficient level of degree production to be considered in this round of analysis. Within the Physical Sciences and Mathematics, Astronomy and Astrophysics, and Oceanography were included in the 1993 study owing to the fact that they met or were sufficiently near to meeting the criteria of about 500 degrees awarded between 1986 and 1990 from 50 programs.

TABLE C-3 Ph.D. Production in Selected Fields in the Physical Sciences and Mathematics by Field, 1986-1990

Specialty	Number of Ph.D.s	Number of Institutions
Chemistry*	9,965	201
Physics*	5,812	177
Mathematics*	3,149	164
Computer Sciences*	2,740	144
Geosciences*	1,983	118
Statistics and Biostatistics*	967	112
Astronomy and Astrophysics	580	73
Oceanography	561	43
Atmospheric Sciences	438	61
Environmental Sciences	335	74
Total Physical Sciences and Mathematics	26,530	239

NOTE: "Number of Institutions" refers to a count of universities awarding degrees in that area based on reports from individuals earning degrees in a DRF field between 1986 and 1990.

SOURCE: National Research Council, Doctorate Records File, Special Tabulations, 1991.

ENGINEERING

The fields comprising the 1982 list in Engineering revealed a similar pattern to that found in the Physical Sciences and Mathematics. That is, the four large fields of Engineering (Electrical, Mechanical, Chemical and Civil) continued to dominate doctoral degree production in that area. (See Table C-4.) Relatively large fields were also identified for inclusion in the present study. Applying the criteria described earlier, fields added to the 1982 list in Engineering included: Materials Science, Aerospace Engineering, Industrial Engineering, and Biomedical Engineering.

TABLE C-4 Ph.D. Production in Selected Fields in Engineering by Field, 1986-1990

Specialty	Number of Ph.D.s	Number of Institutions
Electrical Engineering*	5,008	149
Mechanical Engineering*	3,550	137
Chemical Engineering*	2,813	118
Civil Engineering*	2,530	125
Materials Science	1,240	99
Aerospace, Astronautical	780	54
Industrial	661	62
Bioengineering and Biomedical Engineering	500	76
Nuclear	487	35
Metallurgical	476	51
Agricultural	599	32
Operations Research	263	46
Total Engineering	28,714	171

NOTE: "Number of Institutions" refers to a count of universities awarding degrees in that area based on reports from individuals earning degrees in a DRF field between 1986 and 1990.

SOURCE: National Research Council, Doctorate Records File, Special Tabulations, 1991.

SOCIAL AND BEHAVIORAL SCIENCES

Ph.D. production patterns in the Social and Behavioral Sciences also revealed that the fields included in the 1982 study field continued to represent the largest Ph.D. fields in this broad area (see Table C-5). However, unlike the other broad fields discussed thus far, degree production and institutional involvement remained sufficiently small in the remaining fields that the committee decided to retain only those fields found in the 1982 study.

Although the committee recognized that there was a sufficient number of programs in "Public Policy Studies" to warrant inclusion in this study, they concluded that the heterogeneity of those programs could not assure the validity of the peer review that took place through the National Survey of Graduate Faculty. A separate study of the quality of doctoral preparation through those programs is needed, in their view.

It should also be noted that the committee is aware of

TABLE C-5 Ph.D. Production in Selected Fields in the Social and Behavioral Sciences by Field, 1986-1990

Specialty	Number of Ph.D.s	Number of Institutions
Psychology*	15,827	218
Economics*	4,296	132
History*	2,901	152
Political Science*	2,527	126
Sociology*	2,226	121
Anthropology*	1,837	89
Geography*	596	53
Public Policy Studies	404	67
Urban Studies	337	40
Statistics	299	69
Criminology	170	29
Demographics	102	22
Area Studies	100	32
Total Social and Behavioral Sciences	32,516	249

NOTE: "Number of Institutions" refers to a count of universities awarding degrees in that area based on reports from individuals earning degrees in a DRF field between 1986 and 1990.

SOURCE: National Research Council, Doctorate Records File, Special Tabulations, 1991.

the fact that 299 students indicated that they had earned their doctorates in "statistics" between 1986 and 1990. The committee assumes that some fraction of programs indicated here (perhaps, all) have been included in the program/faculty lists provided by the Institutional Coordinators and reported by the committee under the heading "Physical Sciences and Mathematics."

BIOLOGICAL SCIENCES

Information regarding the designation of fields in the Biological Sciences is described in detail in Chapter 2.

NOTE

1. The Doctorate Records File is a compilation of responses to the Survey of Earned Doctorates that has been conducted each year since 1958 by the NRC's Office of Scientific and Engineering Personnel and its predecessor organizations. Questionnaires, distributed with the cooperation of the graduate deans of U.S. universities, are filled in by graduates as they complete requirements for their doctoral degrees. The doctorates are reported by academic year and include research and applied-research doctorates in all fields. See Ries and Thurgood, 1993.

APPENDIX D

Sample Letters to University Presidents and Institutional Coordinators

The following pages contain reproductions of different correspondence with universities in the process of organizing the study. They include:

Exhibit I: A letter to university presidents asking for their participation in the study and the name of a person to serve as an Institutional Coordinator (IC).

Exhibit II: A letter to the IC with instructions and forms for programs in the study.

Exhibit III: A second letter to the IC asking for amended information in the Biological Sciences.

Exhibit IV: A letter to the IC asking for information about programs in the four new fields added to the study.

EXHIBIT I

NATIONAL RESEARCH COUNCIL
OFFICE OF SCIENTIFIC AND ENGINEERING PERSONNEL
2101 Constitution Avenue Washington, D.C. 20418

Committee for the Study of
Research-Doctorate Programs
in the United States

PHONE: (202) 334-2293
FAX: (202) 334-2753

September 4, 1992

Dr. Frederick E. Hutchinson
President
University of Maine
Orono, ME 04469

Dear President Hutchinson:

The National Research Council (NRC) has undertaken a three-year study of research-doctorate programs in the United States under the aegis of the Conference Board of Associated Research Councils. The primary goal of the study is to develop and disseminate a compendium of measures which characterize the essential features of the nation's Ph.D. programs in the sciences, engineering, and the humanities, in their present state. Members of the Board include: the American Council on Education (ACE), American Council of Learned Societies (ACLS), Social Science Research Council (SSRC), and the NRC. The anticipated summary will be of use to educational planners, policy makers, faculty and students alike. We have the privilege of co-chairing an 18-person committee of experts who oversee the project—which is outlined in more detail in the enclosed "Project Summary."

We have identified approximately 300 universities which play a major role in preparing skilled research scholars and scientists. The University of Maine at Orono is among those key institutions.

To a large extent, the present study updates the earlier work of the National Research Council, which resulted in the report *An Assessment of Research-Doctorate Programs in the United States,* (L. Jones, G. Lindzey, and P. Coggeshall, eds., 1982). Based on that earlier study, we know that an important step in the process of soliciting the information we request is for one person at each university to be designated the Institutional Coordinator.

Dr. Frederick E. Hutchinson
September 4, 1992
Page Two

The Institutional Coordinator, who at many institutions is the Graduate Dean or Provost, will work closely with NRC staff in generating the information needed. We require the assistance of an Institutional Coordinator in a number of ways:

(1) to identify Ph.D. programs at your institution which should be included in the planned compendium;

(2) to furnish us with names of the graduate faculty comprising the doctoral programs that are identified; and

(3) to nominate graduate faculty to participate in the national survey.

We recognize that your institution may not have a program in every field included in this study. However, our goal is to develop a comprehensive profile of research-doctorate programs at U.S. universities, and we hope to include the appropriate set of graduate programs from your institution. Please identify an Institutional Coordinator at your institution as soon as possible in order for us to proceed with this important project.

The University of Maine at Orono is an important component of the U.S. graduate education enterprise. Your participation in this study is crucial to its success. Therefore, we hope you will respond favorably to this invitation to join us in this important undertaking.

Sincerely,

Marvin Goldberger

Brendan Maher
Co-chairs

EXHIBIT II

NATIONAL RESEARCH COUNCIL
OFFICE OF SCIENTIFIC AND ENGINEERING PERSONNEL
2101 Constitution Avenue Washington, D.C. 20418

Committee for the Study of
Research-Doctorate Programs
in the United States

PHONE: (202) 334-2293
FAX: (202) 334-2753

November 17, 1992

Dr. P. Bruce Pipes
Associate Provost for Academic Affairs
Provost's Office
204 Parkhurst
Dartmouth College
Hanover, NH 03755

Dear Dr. Pipes:

We are pleased to learn that you have been designated to coordinate the efforts of your institution in assisting our committee with our study of research-doctorate programs in U.S. universities. A project summary describing the goals and procedures for this study is enclosed. The cooperation of universities and their faculties is essential for the study to be carried out in an objective and accurate fashion.

The study is being conducted under the aegis of the Conference Board of Associated Research Councils and is housed administratively within the National Research Council. Financial support has been provided by the Alfred P. Sloan Foundation, the Andrew W. Mellon Foundation, and the Ford Foundation. The study will examine more than 3,200 programs in 41 fields in the physical sciences, engineering, life sciences, social sciences, and humanities. Approximately 10,000 faculty members will be asked to evaluate programs in their own fields. In addition to the reputational evaluations by faculty, information will be compiled from national data banks on the achievements of both the faculty involved in each program and the program graduates.

The product of this study will report descriptive data on institutional programs in each of 41 fields to be covered. The report will present several different measures of the characteristics of each program being evaluated. Some of the measures will be adjusted for program size. With the cooperation of your institution and that of other universities, we plan to produce a report to be published in 1994. This report should prove to be quite valuable for an assessment of the particular strengths and weaknesses of individual programs at your institution.

For the past few months the committee has deliberated over what fields are to be covered in the study and which programs within each field are to be evaluated. The financial resources available limit us to an assessment of approximately 3,200 programs in 41 fields. The fields to be included have been determined on the basis of the total number of doctorates awarded by U.S. universities during the FY 1988-91 period and the feasibility of identifying and evaluating comparable programs in a particular field. Within each of the 41 fields, programs which awarded more than a specified number of doctorates during the period have been designated for inclusion in the study.

Dr. Pipes
November 17, 1992
Page Two

For each of the programs at your institution, we ask that you furnish the names and ranks of all faculty members who participate significantly in education toward the research doctorate. We also ask that you provide basic information about the program itself. A set of instructions and a response form for each program are enclosed.

In addition, we would like to give you the opportunity to nominate other programs at the institution that are not on the roster but belong to one of the 41 fields included in the study.

The information supplied by your institution will be used for two purposes. First, a sample of the faculty members identified with each program will be selected to evaluate research-doctorate programs in their fields at other universities. The selection will be made in such a way as to ensure that all institutional programs and faculty ranks are adequately represented in each field category. Secondly, a list of names of faculty and some of the program information you supply will be provided to evaluators selected from other institutions. Thus, it is important that you provide accurate and up-to-date information.

You may wish to ask department chairs or other appropriate persons at your institution to assist in providing the information requested. If you do so, we ask that your office coordinate the effort by collecting the information on each program and sending a single package to us in the envelope provided.

We need you to return all the requested material by Thursday, December 24, at the latest. Should you have any questions regarding our request, please call Dr. Pamela Ebert Flattau at (202) 334-3186.

We look forward to having your contributions to this important effort.

Sincerely,

Brendan Maher

Marvin Goldberger
Co-chairs

GENERAL INSTRUCTIONS TO THE INSTITUTIONAL COORDINATOR

Purpose and Scope

The NRC Committee for the Study of Research-Doctorate Programs in the United States has identified 41 fields whose Ph.D. programs will be included in this study. These are listed on the enclosed yellow Field Coverage List.

Not every institution offers Ph.D. preparation in all 41 fields. Therefore, we have identified with an asterisk (*) those fields for which we request information from your institution.

Program Response Form (Tan)

For every field designated, we have also enclosed a separate Program Response Form. This form has been designed to collect descriptive information about a program as well as to generate a roster of faculty members who participate significantly in doctoral education in that field.

Multiple Programs

It is possible that your institution offers more than one research-doctorate program in a designated field. If your institution offers more than one program, please use the extra tan Program Response Form, specify the field in the space allocated, and provide information separately for that program.

For example, if your university offers one doctoral program in statistics and another in biostatistics, include both. Do not, however, consider different specialty areas within the same department to be separate programs.

No Program

If your institution currently does not offer a research-doctorate program in a field we have designated, please check the appropriate box on the front of the Program Response Form and return the form with the others.

(over)

Program Fit

The list of 41 fields included in the study has been generated from the Doctorate Records File maintained by the National Research Council on behalf of the Federal Government. We believe that most Ph.D. programs will fit the Field Coverage List as provided.

However, not all doctoral programs may fit this list. We are aware that many campuses have established new arrangements in the biological sciences. For this reason, the Field Coverage List (yellow sheet) presents on the reverse side what we believe to be possible new arrangements. Please compare the field designation on the front of the Program Response Form and the Optional Biological Sciences List as you complete the tan form.

Program Nomination Form (Peach)

We recognize the possibility that we may have failed to designate one or more research-doctorate specialties at your institution which you believe belongs on the list of fields found on the Field Coverage List. Therefore, we have enclosed a Program Nomination Form to permit you to nominate an additional program(s). You are asked to provide all the information about the program as indicated on the form. Should you decide to nominate more than one program, it will be necessary to make additional copies of the Program Nomination Form.

Please restrict your nominations to programs in your institution that you consider to be of uncommon distinction and that have awarded no fewer than three doctorates during the past three years. Only programs which fall under one of the 41 field categories will be considered for inclusion in the study.

Your Role

Please follow the instructions found on the front of each form:

- Please type or print clearly the information as requested; and
- Please return all forms in the return envelope provided no later than December 24, 1992.

Thank you.

National Research Council
Office of Scientific and Engineering Personnel
Committee for the Study of Research-Doctorate Programs in the United States
2101 Constitution Avenue N.W. - GR 415
Washington, DC 20418

Field Coverage List

Dartmouth College/NH

Arts and Humanities
- Art History
- Classics
- Comparative Literature
- English Language and Literature
- French Language and Literature
- German Language and Literature
- Linguistics
- Music
- Philosophy
- Religion
- Spanish and Portuguese Language and Literature

Biological Sciences
- * Biochemistry
- Botany (including Plant Physiology, Plant Pathology)
- Cellular Biology / Molecular Biology
- * Ecology
- Genetics (Animal, Human)
- Microbiology (including Immunology, Bacteriology, Parasitology)
- Neurosciences
- Pharmacology (Animal, Human)
- * Physiology (Animal, Human)
- Toxicology
- Zoology

Engineering
- Chemical Engineering
- Civil Engineering
- Electrical Engineering
- Materials Science
- Mechanical Engineering

Physical Sciences
- Astrophysics / Astronomy
- * Chemistry
- Computer Sciences
- * Geosciences (including Geology, Geochemistry, Geophysics, Gen Earth)
- * Mathematics
- * Physics
- Statistics / Biostatistics

Social and Behavioral Sciences
- Anthropology
- Economics
- Geography
- History
- Political Science
- * Psychology
- Sociology

* Designates fields for which you are requested to provide information on **Research-Doctorate Programs** in your institution. (See instruction sheet regarding nomination of additional programs to be included in the study.)

(over)

INSTRUCTIONS FOR THE OPTIONAL BIOLOGICAL SCIENCES LIST

In the course of designating fields for inclusion in this study, the Committee became aware of the fact that some institutions have organized traditional biological science disciplines into new campus arrangements. Not all universities have introduced new research-doctorate programs in the biological sciences. However, in the event that you provide research training in the biological sciences under a nontraditional heading, we have formulated the "Optional Biological Sciences List" (found below) for your use.

The list presents what we believe to be new programmatic designations. Within each designation is the discipline title—from the Doctorate Records File (DRF)—which we consider to be included in that new designation.

Please use this list when responding to the Program Response Form. In the space provided, please indicate the "Optional Biological Sciences List" from this sheet which captures the alternate designation for the field of training listed by us at the top of the Program Response Form.

For example, microbiology may be offered as part of a new program entitled "cell and developmental biology." Indicate this on the form, and provide doctorate information and faculty names for all graduate faculty in the new designation.

OPTIONAL BIOLOGICAL SCIENCES LIST (DRF Field)

Biochemistry and Molecular Biology
- (Biochemistry)
- (Celluar/Molecular Biology)

Cell and Developmental Biology
- (Microbiology)
- (Cellular/Molecular Biology)

Molecular and General Genetics
- (Human and Animal Genetics)

Neurosciences
- (Neurosciences)

Pharmacology
- (Human and Animal Pharmacology)
- (Toxicology)

Ecology, Evolution and Behavior
- (Zoology)
- (Botany)
- (Ecology)

Physiology
- (Physiology)

Dartmouth College 006
Chemistry 23

NATIONAL RESEARCH COUNCIL
Office of Scientific and Engineering Personnel
COMMITTEE FOR THE STUDY OF RESEARCH-DOCTORATE PROGRAMS IN THE UNITED STATES

PROGRAM RESPONSE FORM

Check One.

☐ We no longer offer doctoral training in this field. (Stop here. Return form "as is.")

☐ We offer doctoral training in this field as specified above.

☐ INSTRUCTION FOR BIOLOGICAL SCIENCES: We offer doctoral training in this field under another designation.
Specify: ______________________________

(1) What is the name of the department (or equivalent academic unit) in which this research-doctorate program is offered?

Department: ______________________________

Address: ______________________________

____

____

(2) How many Ph.D.'s (or equivalent research-doctorates) have been awarded in the program in each of the last five academic years?

1987-88 _______ 1990-91 _______

1988-89 _______ 1991-92 _______

1989-90 _______

(3) Approximately how many full-time and part-time graduate students enrolled in the program at the present time (Fall 1992) intend to earn doctorates?

	TOTAL	FEMALES
Full-Time Students	______	________
Part-Time Students	______	________
TOTAL	______	________

(4) In approximately what year was this research-doctorate program initiated? _____

Instructions for the faculty roster: The section which follows has been designed to gather information about the faculty members who participate significantly in doctoral education.

COLUMNS 1 and 2: Include those individuals who (a) are members of the regular academic faculty (typically holding the rank of assistant, associate, or full professor), and (b) regularly teach doctoral students and/or serve on doctoral committees. Include members of the faculty who are currently on leave of absence but meet the above criteria.

Exclude visiting faculty members or emeritus or adjunct faculty (or faculty with other comparable ranks) unless they currently participate significantly in doctoral education.

Members of the faculty who participate significantly in doctoral education in more than one program should be listed on every form that lists a program in which they participate.

Faculty names should be provided in the form in which they are most likely to be recognized by colleagues in their field. We prefer that, within each academic rank, you list the faculty alphabetically by last name.

COLUMN 3: Please check the names of at least two faculty members within each academic rank who would be available and, in your opinion, well-qualified to evaluate research-doctorate programs in their field.

A sample of evaluators will be selected from the list of faculty you provide for each program. In selecting evaluators, preference will be given to those whose names you have checked. If no names are checked, a random sample will be selected from the faculty list.

COLUMN 4: In order to help us match faculty names you provide with records in the Doctorate Records File (maintained by the National Research Council), we ask that you identify those faculty who do not hold a Ph.D. or equivalent research-doctorate from a university in the United States. This information will be used only for the purposes of collating records and will not be released to those who are selected to evaluate your institution's programs. Nor will this information in any way affect the selection of program evaluators from your institution's faculty.

1	2	3	4
List below *all faculty who participate significantly in doctoral education* in this program. Please **PRINT** or **TYPE** names in the following format: Examples: Mary A. Jones A.B. Smith, Jr.	Indicate the academic rank of each faculty member. Professor Associate Professor	Check at least 2 faculty in each rank qualified to evaluate other programs.	Check any faculty who do not hold a Ph.D. or other research doctorate from a U.S. university
01			
02			
03			
04			
05			
06			
07			
08			
09			
10			
11			
12			
13			
14			
15			
16			
17			
18			
19			
20			
21			
22			
23			
24			
25			

1	2	3	4
List below *all faculty who participate significantly in doctoral education* in this program. Please PRINT or TYPE names in the following format: **Examples: Mary A. Jones A.B. Smith, Jr.**	**Indicate the academic rank of each faculty member.** **Professor Associate Professor**	**Check at least 2 faculty in each rank qualified to evaluate other programs.**	**Check any faculty who do not hold a Ph.D. or other research doctorate from a U.S. university**
26			
27			
28			
29			
30			
31			
32			
33			
34			
35			
36			
37			
38			
39			
40			
41			
42			
43			
44			
45			
46			
47			
48			
49			
50			

EXHIBIT III

NATIONAL RESEARCH COUNCIL
OFFICE OF SCIENTIFIC AND ENGINEERING PERSONNEL
2101 Constitution Avenue Washington, D.C. 20418

Committee for the Study of
Research-Doctorate Programs
in the United States

PHONE: (202) 334-2293
FAX: (202) 334-2753

December 15, 1992

URGENT NOTICE

Harry J. Richards
Associate Dean, Graduate School
108 Thompson Hall
University of New Hampshire
Durham, NH 03824

NATIONAL RESEARCH COUNCIL
OFFICE OF SCIENTIFIC AND
ENGINEERING PERSONNEL
2101 CONSTITUTION AVENUE, NW
WASHINGTON, DC 20418

Dear Mr. Richards:

By this time you've received a set of materials from us asking for information about research-doctorate programs at your institution. We are writing to amend the instructions with regard to the Biological Sciences. These amendments supersede all previous correspondence from us about the Biological Sciences.

After further consultation with the biological sciences community and in recognition of the various ways in which the biological sciences are organized at participating universities, the Committee has decided that information about the Biological Sciences will be presented exclusively using the SEVEN BIOLOGICAL SCIENCE FIELDS designated in our November 17 mailing and listed below:

- Biochemistry and Molecular Biology
- Cell and Developmental Biology
- Molecular and General Genetics
- Neurosciences
- Pharmacology
- Ecology, Evolution and Behavior
- Physiology

We have enclosed with this letter one Biological Sciences Response Form for each of the seven fields. We ask that you use these forms in responding to our request for information in this area. The information presented below has been designed to assist you in completing this task.

Harry J. Richards
Page 2
December 15, 1992

In our November 17 mailing, we provided most institutions with at least one "Program Response Form" which carried a biological science designation derived from a count of Ph.D.s from the Doctorate Records File (DRF). We also indicated that the DRF fields could be used to interpret the composition of the seven Biological Science Fields of interest to the Committee as shown below:

- Biochemistry and Molecular Biology
  (Biochemistry)
  (Cellular/Molecular Biology)*

- Cell and Developmental Biology
  (Microbiology)
  (Cellular/Molecular Biology)*

- Molecular and General Genetics
  (Human and Animal Genetics)

- Neurosciences
  (Neurosciences)

- Pharmacology
  (Human and Animal Pharmacology)
  (Toxicology)

- Ecology, Evolution and Behavior
  (Zoology)
  (Botany)

- Physiology
  (Physiology)

We now request that for each of the seven forms that have been enclosed, you list ALL FACULTY at your institution who participate significantly in doctoral education in that area. Restrict your responses to those seven component subfields we've designate even

*The categorization of "Cellular/Molecular Biology" is that of the DRF. For our purposes, faculty members conducting graduate education in Cellular/Molecular Biology who specialize primarily in Molecular Biology would be listed under Biochemistry and Molecular Biology. Those specializing in Cellular Biology would be listed under Cell and Developmental Biology. Those who specialization spans both fields would be listed in both fields.

Harry J. Richards
Page 3
December 15, 1992

if the program boundaries at your institution are drawn differently. These faculty lists will be used first to select and then to advise raters in each of the seven Biological Sciences Fields for the National Survey of Graduate Faculty.

It is possible that your institution provides graduate training in one or all of these seven Biological Sciences Fields at two locations on your campus, such as the Medical School and the College of Arts and Sciences. In that case, you may provide information separately for each location though we do not encourage you to do so.

If your institution currently does not offer doctoral training in one of the seven Biological Science Fields, please check the appropriate box on the front of the form and return the form with the others.

Understanding that we are attempting to recast work that you already have undertaken in response to our mailing of November 17, we have established a new deadline for responding in the Biological Sciences. We ask that you return the enclosed forms in the return envelope no later than January 25.

The revised approach to the Biological Science Fields makes it possible for us to add four new fields to this study—providing a more accurate reflection of the composition of doctoral training at U.S. universities. In the next week, we will send you material asking for information (as appropriate to your institution, about oceanography/marine sciences and three additional fields in engineering: aerospace/aeronautical; industrial; and bioengineering/biomedical) The deadline for providing information about those programs will also be extended to January 25.

We certainly thank you for your cooperation in providing the Biological Sciences Field information using the forms enclosed. We understand that we are increasing the burden we have already placed on you by virtue of our earlier mailing. We trust, however, that you share our view that the proposed presentation of information about the Biological Sciences more accurately reflects the shifting character of graduate studies in this area.

Thank you for your assistance.

Brendan Maher

Marvin Goldberger

EXHIBIT IV

NATIONAL RESEARCH COUNCIL
OFFICE OF SCIENTIFIC AND ENGINEERING PERSONNEL
2101 Constitution Avenue Washington, D.C. 20418

Committee for the Study of
Research-Doctorate Programs
in the United States

PHONE: (202) 334-2293
FAX: (202) 334-2753

December 22, 1992

Dr. Joyce E. Sirianni
Dean of the Graduate School
SUNY at Buffalo
552 Capen Hall
Buffalo, NY 14260

Dear Dr. Sirianni:

As we mentioned in our correspondence of December 15, the Committee for the Study of Research-Doctorate Programs in the United States has added four fields to our National Survey of Graduate Faculty:

- oceanography/marine sciences
- aerospace/aeronautical engineering
- bioengineering/biomedical engineering
- industrial engineering

Based on recent patterns of doctoral degree production, we have determined that your institution has at least one research-doctorate program in these areas eligible for inclusion in the survey. We have enclosed a form for each of the programs for which you are eligible and one Program Nomination Form.

We have included another set of instructions which remain the same as those sent to you in an earlier mailing. We ask that you provide the information we request and return the forms to us in the envelope that has been enclosed no later than January 25.

Thank you for your cooperation in this matter. If you have any questions about this phase of our work, please don't hesitate to telephone me at 202-334-3186.

Sincerely

Pamela Ebert Flattau
Director, Studies and Surveys Unit

The National Research Council is the principal operating agency of the National Academy of Sciences and the National Academy of Engineering to serve government and other organizations.

APPENDIX E

Characteristics of Institutions Participating in the 1993 Study

The following pages contain information describing each of the 274 universities participating in the 1993 *Study of Research-Doctorate Programs in the United States*. This includes:

Institutions

Institution: U.S. universities participating in the 1993 Study, alphabetical order within Carnegie Class.

Number of Programs

1982 Study: Number of programs at that institution reviewed by the 1982 study committee. Source: *An Assessment of Research-Doctorate Programs in the United States*, 1982.

1993 Study Number of programs at that institution reviewed by the 1993 study committee. Source: NRC National Survey of Graduate Faculty.

Institutional Profile

Year of First Ph.D.: The year in which the Doctorate Records File (DRF) first recorded a Ph.D. Since the DRF information dates back only to 1920, institutions awarding a Ph.D. prior to 1920 were identified by other sources, such as university catalogs or direct inquiries to the institutions. Because of the historic limitations of this file, "Year of First Ph.D." should be considered a general indicator not an institutional record. Source: Doctorate Records File.

Carn Class: 1994 Carnegie Classification of the Institution. Classes included:

RI	Research Universities I
RII	Research Universities II
DI	Doctoral Universities I
DII	Doctoral Universities II
MAI	Master's Universities and Colleges I
BAI	Baccalaureate Colleges I
ENG	Schools of Engineering and technology
MED	Medical schools and medical centers
HLT	Other separate health-professional schools
REL	Theological seminaries, Bible colleges, and other institutions offering degrees in religion.
OTH	Other specialized institutions

Source: Carnegie Foundation for the Advancement of Teaching.

Institutional Profile (Cont'd)

Control:	Type of "Institutional Control": PR= private institution; PU= public institution. Source: U.S. Department of Education.

Research and Development Expenditures

Total R&D:	Average annual expenditure for research and development at the institution for the period 1986-1992 in thousands of 1988 dollars. Source: National Science Foundation.
Federal R&D:	Average annual federal expenditure for research and development at the institution for the period 1986-1992 in thousands of 1988 dollars. Source: National Science Foundation.

Library

Volumes:	Total number of printed, typewritten, mimeographed or processed works contained in one binding or portfolio that has been cataloged, classified and made ready for use in 1992-1993 academic year. Sources: Association of Research Libraries, Association of College and Research Libraries, and Department of Education.
Serials:	Total number of serial subscriptions for the 1992-1993 academic year. Serials includes periodicals, newspapers, annuals, memoirs, and proceedings and transactions of societies. Sources: Association of Research Libraries, Association of College and Research Libraries, and Department of Education.
Expend:	Total library expenditure of funds from regular institutional budgets and other sources such as research grants, special projects, gifts, endowments, and fees for services for the 1992-1993 academic year. Sources: Association of Research Libraries, Association of College and Research Libraries, and Department of Education.
Enrollment Total:	Total full- and part-time students enrolled in Fall 1992 in courses creditable toward a diploma, certificate, degree, or other formal award. Source: Department of Education.
Grad:	Full- and part-time students in Fall 1992 in non-professional programs seeking a graduate degree. Source: Department of Education.

> Notice to Reader: Blank spaces in Table E reflect a situation where data were not available from the source or the data was aggregated with other institutions, for example, all data from a state system were added together.

Appendix Table E Characteristics of Institutions Participating in the 1993 Study

Institution	Number of Programs in: 1982 Study	1993 Study	Institutional Profile: Year of First PhD	Carn Class	Control	Average Research Expenditure 1986-92 [1]: Total R&D (x $1,000)	Federal R&D (x $1,000)	Library 1992 [2]: Volumes	Serials	Expend (x $1,000)	Enrollment Fall 1992 [3]: Total	Graduate Students
University of Alabama-Birmingham	3	13	1971	R1	Pu	$86,037	$60,642	923,096	5,447	$6,288	15,735	3,125
Albert Einstein College of Med	6	6	1971	R1	Pr							
Arizona State University	10	26	1954	R1	Pu	45,382	20,062	2,922,157	32,241	16,106	43,628	11,205
University of Arizona	26	29	1922	R1	Pu	159,949	75,978	4,018,071	28,662	16,152	35,118	7,726
Boston University	23	29	1877	R1	Pr	61,848	51,305	1,895,723	28,512	10,802	28,375	8,178
Brown University	24	30	1889	R1	Pr	40,215	31,238	2,606,259	13,533	11,215	7,593	1,388
California Institute Technology	11	19	1920	R1	Pr	90,574	77,112	498,812	4,600	4,347	2,009	1,097
Univ of California-Berkeley	38	37	1885	R1	Pu	196,547	114,702	7,981,724	89,730	32,382	30,616	7,857
University of California-Davis	26	27	1949	R1	Pu	158,430	64,036	2,659,270	50,298	15,232	22,880	4,021
University of California-Irvine	19	24	1967	R1	Pu	62,454	42,816	1,598,488	17,550	12,248	17,181	3,045
Univ of California-Los Angeles	32	36	1937	R1	Pu	204,757	140,714	6,390,409	94,612	29,346	35,403	9,852
Univ of California-San Diego	23	29	1961	R1	Pu	201,715	157,742	2,241,696	24,414	15,623	18,239	2,992
Univ of California-San Francisco	4	9	1961	R1	Pu	199,826	142,044	700,389	4,778	4,375	3,746	2,238
Univ of California-Santa Barbara	20	32	1964	R1	Pu	47,223	36,936	2,126,774	24,325	11,448	18,651	2,374
Carnegie Mellon University	12	15	1920	R1	Pr	87,390	55,581	828,109	4,061	4,533	7,139	2,664
Case Western Reserve Univ	21	21	1895	R1	Pr	79,286	59,982	1,802,042	14,344	8,625	9,059	4,076
University of Chicago	31	30	1893	R1	Pr	96,971	79,962	5,578,937	45,613	17,492	11,286	6,921
University of Cincinnati	22	28	1909	R1	Pu	60,963	37,192	1,947,773	19,574	11,831	34,660	6,165
Colorado State University	14	16	1955	R1	Pu	61,164	43,601	1,505,169	20,868	7,769	27,306	6,263
University of Colorado	25	31	1885	R1	Pu	128,266	95,317	2,504,405	27,727	13,501		
Columbia University	28	34	1882	R1	Pr	158,444	137,116	6,386,712	65,000	27,158	19,290	11,237
University of Connecticut	27	28	1949	R1	Pu	94,218	38,680	2,442,215	16,924	13,258		
Cornell University	30	37	1872	R1	Pr	256,272	146,896	5,579,629	61,015	25,860	20,359	4,877
Duke University	23	33	1928	R1	Pr	117,781	86,373	4,234,985	32,732	17,347	11,426	3,722
Emory University	13	16	1948	R1	Pr	66,673	44,594	2,212,507	22,842	14,265	9,958	2,727
Florida State University	18	24	1952	R1	Pu	47,941	23,902	2,028,509	18,420	8,755	28,424	5,900
University of Florida	23	32	1934	R1	Pu	111,866	53,893	3,022,768	24,191	14,577	36,447	6,972
Georgetown University	11	14	1897	R1	Pr	44,262	30,321	1,965,113	24,763	14,134	12,075	2,977
Georgia Institute of Technology	8	16	1950	R1	Pu	139,871	77,909	1,771,934	11,381	5,327		
University of Georgia	19	22	1940	R1	Pu	131,938	37,788	3,131,402	47,993	13,593	28,493	5,285

Appendix Table E (Continued)

Institution	Number of Programs in 1982 Study	Number of Programs in 1993 Study	Institutional Profile: Year of First PhD	Institutional Profile: Carn Class	Control	Average Research Expenditure 1986-92 [1]: Total R&D (x $1,000)	Average Research Expenditure 1986-92 [1]: Federal R&D (x $1,000)	Library 1992 [2]: Volumes	Library 1992 [2]: Serials	Library 1992 [2]: Expend (x $1,000)	Enrollment Fall 1992 [3]: Total	Enrollment Fall 1992 [3]: Graduate Students
Harvard University	25	30	1873	R1	Pr	187,012	130,208	12,605,537	96,357	57,978	25,012	11,626
University of Hawaii at Manoa	17	21	1933	R1	Pu	63,644	37,362	2,718,618	36,592	12,107	19,799	6,075
Howard University	7	16	1958	R1	Pr	15,578	10,768	1,905,110	25,564	9,600	10,667	1,717
U of Illinois at Urbana-Champaign	31	37	1903	R1	Pu	193,703	102,227	8,281,456	91,026	19,668	38,396	10,118
University of Illinois at Chicago	12	22	1971	R1	Pu	72,828	37,260	1,782,637	21,119	12,311	25,335	6,790
Indiana University	27	28	1912	R1	Pu	76,798	50,264	5,438,860	39,929	20,832		
Iowa State University	21	23	1916	R1	Pu	94,448	27,316	1,994,376	21,547	12,007	25,695	4,777
University of Iowa	28	33	1903	R1	Pu	95,103	65,009	3,317,265	40,047	14,060	28,145	7,057
Johns Hopkins University	26	34	1878	R1	Pr	198,606	157,052	3,012,364	21,172	17,624	14,506	8,745
University of Kansas	33	33	1895	R1	Pu	53,684	23,841	3,193,850	33,047	13,131		
University of Kentucky	25	30	1930	R1	Pu	64,867	26,699	2,515,874	26,889	11,018	11,858	
Louisiana State U & A&M College	17	27	1935	R1	Pu	113,383	37,685	2,709,757	16,169	8,967		
University of Maryland College Park	26	28	1920	R1	Pu	143,766	57,490	2,231,552	19,433	14,212	32,916	9,241
Massachusetts Inst of Technology	17	23	1907	R1	Pr	268,033	203,560	2,320,524	21,136	11,703	9,798	5,198
U of Massachusetts at Amherst	25	31	1902	R1	Pu	7,493	3,974	2,575,292	15,546	9,260	24,185	5,815
University of Miami	10	18	1961	R1	Pr	76,000	52,172	1,875,556	18,890	12,266	14,156	3,202
Michigan State University	28	31	1925	R1	Pu	112,209	49,969	2,939,376	27,876	12,957	39,138	7,094
University of Michigan	32	41	1876	R1	Pu	261,942	156,975	6,699,359	70,691	27,843		
University of Minnesota	37	39	1888	R1	Pu	243,425	122,525	5,008,637	52,018	24,534		
University of Missouri-Columbia	27	24	1899	R1	Pu	70,733	21,363	2,630,419	22,688	9,800	23,418	4,928
University of Nebraska-Lincoln	19	21	1896	R1	Pu	64,939	22,739	2,164,254	21,671	9,194	24,573	4,381
New Mexico State University	5	10	1960	R1	Pu	61,122	43,798	924,614	8,389	4,396	22,916	2,543
University of New Mexico	13	6	1947	R1	Pu			1,904,107	21,795	13,392		
New York University	21	25	1866	R1	Pr	97,509	73,087	3,273,708	28,689	21,043	33,695	15,508
North Carolina State University	18	23	1947	R1	Pu	110,882	36,353	1,485,041	18,086	10,414	27,766	4,459
U of North Carolina-Chapel Hill	29	34	1883	R1	Pu	109,119	81,503	4,059,441	38,288	18,082	23,977	7,029
Northwestern University	28	30	1896	R1	Pr	105,856	52,782	3,642,790	37,424	15,857	17,285	6,245
Ohio State University	38	39	1890	R1	Pu	149,064	68,643	4,693,081	33,010	18,021		
Oregon State University	14	20	1935	R1	Pu	83,712	45,746	1,246,307	18,800	6,975	14,355	2,808
Pennsylvania State University	33	39	1926	R1	Pu	198,662	108,466	3,421,370	31,707	20,340		

Institution	Number of Programs in 1982 Study	Number of Programs in 1993 Study	Institutional Profile Year of First PhD	Institutional Profile Carn Class	Control	Average Research Expenditure 1986-92 [1] Total R&D (x $1,000)	Average Research Expenditure 1986-92 [1] Federal R&D (x $1,000)	Library 1992 [2] Volumes	Library 1992 [2] Serials	Library 1992 [2] Expend (x $1,000)	Enrollment Fall 1992 [3] Total	Enrollment Fall 1992 [3] Graduate Students
University of Pennsylvania	30	36	1880	R1	Pr	164,694	117,285	4,099,548	33,024	19,827	22,418	8,726
University of Pittsburgh	34	40	1886	R1	Pu	100,776	75,913	3,122,798	24,991	15,672		
Princeton University	27	29	1879	R1	Pr	72,497	43,849	5,081,114	30,656	20,714	6,564	1,913
Purdue University	20	25	1928	R1	Pu	113,010	58,227	2,076,302	14,139	10,628		
University of Rochester	21	28	1925	R1	Pr	109,834	88,345	2,812,892	12,885	9,278	9,686	3,864
Rockefeller University	5	4	1959	R1	Pr	65,592	34,946	190,430	529	1,194	132	132
Rutgers State Univ-New Brunswick	29	33	1884	R1	Pu	111,490	34,090	3,441,294	32,564	23,604		
University of Southern California	26	26	1923	R1	Pr	144,562	108,157	3,168,969	24,832	15,479	28,586	10,639
Stanford University	33	43	1894	R1	Pr	263,527	214,815	6,250,671	46,397	35,801	15,674	7,870
State Univ of New York-Buffalo	31	35	1935	R1	Pu	87,861	57,216	2,797,145	22,593	12,092		
State U of New York-Stony Brook	17	30	1966	R1	Pu	70,543	46,824	1,848,618	16,952	10,375	17,125	5,685
Temple University	14	21	1925	R1	Pu	40,992	21,506	2,189,431	15,699	10,883	30,229	7,859
University of Tennessee-Knoxville	22	21	1937	R1	Pu			2,021,903	18,881	10,396	26,579	6,544
Texas A&M University	19	27	1940	R1	Pu	233,023	83,911	2,154,600	16,187	12,398		
University of Texas at Austin	30	37	1916	R1	Pu	179,946	91,103	6,835,983	51,689	22,429	49,253	11,689
Tufts University	6	11	1941	R1	Pr	44,600	35,932	565,082	2,424	3,569	7,896	1,942
Utah State University	7	9	1950	R1	Pu	62,700	38,472	1,177,282	13,994	4,524	16,513	2,682
University of Utah	19	20	1947	R1	Pu	75,855	57,138	2,345,111	19,572	11,459	26,795	3,982
Vanderbilt University	26	26	1879	R1	Pr	59,646	48,674	2,085,652	16,357	12,400	9,640	3,031
Peabody Col at Vanderbilt Univ		1	1916	R1	Pr	59,646	48,674				9,640	3,031
Virginia Commonwealth University	5	2	1974	R1	Pu	48,765	33,620	1,030,463	9,932	8,133	21,939	5,257
Virginia Polytech Inst & State U	16	19	1942	R1	Pu	95,071	36,573	1,849,994	18,288	9,350	26,003	6,832
University of Virginia	26	32	1885	R1	Pu	75,793	47,903	3,948,504	44,349	16,392		
Washington University	26	27	1895	R1	Pr	120,311	88,102	2,979,934	18,601	13,525	11,572	4,399
University of Washington	32	39	1914	R1	Pu	211,698	171,308	5,248,347	54,517	24,754	35,552	7,880
Wayne State University	19	19	1948	R1	Pu	51,512	23,175	2,752,167	24,468	12,532	34,945	12,284
West Virginia University	13	16	1932	R1	Pu	34,269	16,093	1,706,768	11,099	6,437	22,712	5,802
University of Wisconsin-Madison	34	39	1892	R1	Pu	266,703	155,466	5,424,299	46,651	24,065	41,824	10,479
Yale University	31	30	1860	R1	Pr	157,598	124,577	9,327,219	52,971	33,176	10,945	4,380
Yeshiva University	1	1	1929	R1	Pr	72,729	57,362	957,873	9,241	4,682	4,899	1,304

Appendix Table E (Continued)

Institution	Number of Programs in 1982 Study	Number of Programs in 1993 Study	Institutional Profile Year of First PhD	Institutional Profile Carn Class	Control	Average Research Expenditure 1986-92 [1] Total R&D (x $1,000)	Average Research Expenditure 1986-92 [1] Federal R&D (x $1,000)	Library 1992 [2] Volumes	Library 1992 [2] Serials	Library 1992 [2] Expend (x $1,000)	Enrollment Fall 1992 [3] Total	Enrollment Fall 1992 [3] Graduate Students
Univ of Arkansas-Fayetteville	5	10	1953	R2	Pu	31,338	9,042	1,392,403	16,540	6,414	14,582	2,368
Auburn University	14	17	1955	R2	Pu	53,253	13,747	2,140,856	21,611	7,817		
Brandeis University	12	14	1957	R2	Pr	26,446	17,297	938,072	7,142	4,314	3,848	935
Brigham Young University	6	10	1961	R2	Pr	10,884	5,246	2,262,029	17,698	11,540		
Univ of California-Riverside	18	19	1963	R2	Pu	49,488	14,658	1,682,006	13,621	7,494	8,799	1,533
Univ of California-Santa Cruz	3	17	1968	R2	Pu	23,513	12,644	1,065,529	9,663	7,269	10,251	945
Clemson University	8	15	1960	R2	Pu	52,938	11,925	797,997	6,831	5,912	17,666	4,361
University of Delaware	13	13	1948	R2	Pu	34,466	15,203	2,119,899	20,941	9,716	21,136	2,845
George Washington University	8	18	1888	R2	Pr	26,221	21,185	1,291,356	8,020	9,665	18,600	9,415
University of Houston	12	22	1947	R2	Pu	30,277	14,406	1,754,375	14,437	8,872	33,022	6,196
University of Idaho	5	11	1962	R2	Pu	29,688	11,271	805,139	10,296	3,188	11,435	2,715
Kansas State University	13	17	1933	R2	Pu	43,713	13,999	1,276,462	9,609	5,989	20,451	3,277
Kent State University	10	18	1964	R2	Pu	5,955	3,430	2,139,129	11,146	8,811	33,060	5,253
Lehigh University	5	16	1938	R2	Pr	24,364	10,105	1,059,491	10,994	4,872	6,549	2,077
Mississippi State University	5	7	1953	R2	Pu	48,615	17,259	859,306	7,189	3,749	14,619	2,528
University of Mississippi	3	8	1950	R2	Pu	16,765	10,924	896,517	9,131	4,036		
Northeastern University	5	13	1965	R2	Pr	11,863	8,886	738,193	8,698	7,805	27,586	4,750
University of Notre Dame	17	22	1920	R2	Pr	16,835	11,655	2,252,029	21,727	9,038	10,126	1,949
Ohio University	8	15	1959	R2	Pu	10,395	3,467	1,642,952	22,485	8,073	27,249	3,221
Oklahoma State University	21	16	1942	R2	Pu	53,479	12,261	1,705,986	17,553	7,893	26,313	4,626
University of Oklahoma	25	24	1929	R2	Pu	54,147	17,491	2,430,404	17,400	8,430		
University of Oregon	24	20	1926	R2	Pu	20,449	15,433	2,024,323	17,914	10,233	17,285	3,684
Rensselaer Polytechnic Inst	10	14	1917	R2	Pr	34,988	17,637	407,421	3,720	2,426	6,988	2,520
University of Rhode Island	11	10	1960	R2	Pu	31,891	20,316	1,019,029	9,759	4,706	15,449	3,664
Rice University	20	22	1918	R2	Pr	20,804	15,644	1,794,602	13,725	8,284	4,251	1,446
Saint Louis University	8	10	1880	R2	Pr	12,702	10,841	1,338,931	13,183	6,777		
University of South Carolina	8	22	1891	R2	Pu	37,359	16,893	2,576,311	19,232	10,588		
University of South Florida	5	12	1971	R2	Pu	47,642	15,825	880,261	4,542	5,133	34,145	8,469
Southern Illinois University	15	11	1959	R2	Pu	21,405	6,265	2,248,064	17,047	8,956	24,761	3,759
State Univ of New York-Albany	12	16	1963	R2	Pu	20,587	13,875	1,748,697	16,039	7,642	19,001	5,190

Institution	Number of Programs in 1982 Study	Number of Programs in 1993 Study	Institutional Profile: Year of First PhD	Institutional Profile: Carn Class	Control	Average Research Expenditure 1986-92 [1]: Total R&D (x $1,000)	Average Research Expenditure 1986-92 [1]: Federal R&D (x $1,000)	Library 1992 [2]: Volumes	Library 1992 [2]: Serials	Library 1992 [2]: Expend (x $1,000)	Enrollment Fall 1992 [3]: Total	Enrollment Fall 1992 [3]: Graduate Students
Syracuse University	23	24	1875	R2	Pr	29,535	16,554	2,572,485	16,477	9,876		
Texas Tech University	9	17	1952	R2	Pu	29,303	9,824	1,833,658	17,413	8,241	25,417	4,086
Tulane University	21	24	1887	R2	Pr	46,976	24,326	1,943,858	16,934	8,806	10,869	2,453
University of Vermont	4	10	1944	R2	Pu	36,906	24,937	1,105,649	17,229	5,984	10,885	1,230
Washington State University	15	21	1929	R2	Pu	55,965	23,839	1,717,764	24,038	9,208	17,871	2,682
University of Wisconsin-Milwaukee	11	16	1966	R2	Pu	12,850	5,053	1,785,170	8,239	6,472	24,991	4,857
University of Wyoming	7	14	1947	R2	Pu	20,412	10,665	1,096,703	16,090	4,793	12,044	2,535
Adelphi University	2	2	1952	D1	Pr	393	155	473,098	3,514	3,591	8,256	4,105
University of Akron	5	11	1959	D1	Pu	8,753	2,428	897,779	4,826	4,451	28,501	3,725
University of Alabama	4	15	1952	D1	Pu	16,180	5,347	1,949,073	16,164	7,937	19,233	3,298
American University	8	10	1916	D1	Pr	3,564	3,198	598,386	4,877	4,055	11,128	4,488
Andrews University		1	1976	D1	Pr	209	48	554,440	2,957	1,924	2,979	624
Ball State University	2	4	1964	D1	Pu	806	225	1,041,232	5,703	5,972	21,235	2,614
Boston College	7	10	1927	D1	Pr	6,569	5,888	1,318,437	14,619	10,127	14,450	3,430
Bowling Green State University	5	10	1963	D1	Pu	2,816	1,395	1,798,711	7,602	6,680	19,579	2,997
Catholic University of America	17	19	1897	D1	Pr	5,708	5,103	1,321,879	8,961	3,011	6,464	2,916
CUNY - Grad Sch & Univ Center	20	26	1965	D1	Pu	2,599	2,023	224,072	1,697	1,364	4,131	4,131
Claremont Graduate School	8	10	1937	D1	Pr	888	177	1,843,798	4,215	4,633	456	456
Clark Atlanta University	3	3	1969	D1	Pr	6,765	5,461				4,480	1,229
University of Denver	8	6	1944	D1	Pr	9,425	6,835	1,078,325	4,796	2,694	8,201	3,760
Drexel University	5	10	1967	D1	Pr	16,653	6,807	493,537	4,126	2,329	11,055	3,227
East Texas State University		1	1964	D1	Pu	299	39	533,621	2,166	1,691	8,235	2,867
Florida Institute of Technology		5	1979	D1	Pr	3,727	980	187,294	1,707	993	5,769	3,334
Fordham University	8	11	1918	D1	Pr	2,033	1,549	1,574,042	12,677	5,363	14,534	6,767
Georgia State University	3	7	1965	D1	Pu	6,368	2,493	1,185,801	11,157	5,786	24,050	6,323
Hofstra University	1	1	1970	D1	Pr	300	239	1,063,772	2,786	5,405	11,999	3,006
Illinois Institute of Technology	9	9	1939	D1	Pr	6,479	4,267	383,803	1,623	1,446	6,692	2,957
Illinois State University		8	1966	D1	Pu	2,400	962	1,237,815	9,600	5,673	21,761	3,153
Indiana Univ of Pennsylvania		2	1972	D1	Pu						14,357	1,532

Appendix Table E (Continued)

Institution	Number of Programs in 1982 Study	Number of Programs in 1993 Study	Institutional Profile: Year of First PhD	Institutional Profile: Carn Class	Control	Average Research Expenditure 1986-92 [1]: Total R&D (x $1,000)	Average Research Expenditure 1986-92 [1]: Federal R&D (x $1,000)	Library 1992 [2]: Volumes	Library 1992 [2]: Serials	Library 1992 [2]: Expend (x $1,000)	Enrollment Fall 1992 [3]: Total	Enrollment Fall 1992 [3]: Graduate Students
University of Louisville	6	9	1945	D1	Pu	16,679	5,441	1,196,410	12,131	9,240	21,987	3,776
Loyola University of Chicago	9	10	1928	D1	Pr	12,507	7,176	1,309,832	11,843	10,479	15,298	4,491
Miami University	6	10	1970	D1	Pu	2,306	1,426	1,438,750	7,294	5,230	20,603	1,915
Univ of Missouri-Kansas City	2	5	1957	D1	Pu	6,592	1,993	925,453	8,583	3,437	10,483	3,424
University of Missouri-Rolla	11	10	1964	D1	Pu	14,531	3,742	447,229	1,394	1,313	5,651	1,221
U of North Carolina-Greensboro	1	2	1963	D1	Pu	942	728	*830,530	5,525	4,248	13,230	3,002
University of North Texas	7	14	1953	D1	Pu	7,499	2,279	1,557,017	10,525	5,256	26,433	6,820
Northern Arizona University		8	1973	D1	Pu	4,759	2,391	1,023,658	5,398	4,207	18,485	4,435
University of Northern Colorado	1	3	1934	D1	Pu	121	47	609,155	4,289	3,199	12,667	2,698
Northern Illinois University	7	8	1965	D1	Pu	6,858	2,878	1,354,657	13,215	6,555	24,052	6,325
Old Dominion University	1	9	1975	D1	Pu	7,862	5,262	634,435	6,601	3,669	16,507	5,176
Polytechnic University	8	6	1935	D1	Pr	8,900	5,858	192,738	1,762	2,271	3,514	1,948
St. John's University		4	1938	D1	Pr	708	391	1,148,601	15,034	8,939	18,813	4,133
Southern Methodist University	6	10	1963	D1	Pr	7,232	5,354	2,197,215	4,784	7,953	8,978	2,547
Univ of Southern Mississippi	3	8	1963	D1	Pu	4,110	3,172	868,477	4,770	3.273	13,062	2,222
State Univ of New York-Binghamton	10	17	1969	D1	Pu	8,988	3,050	1,471,424	9,443	7,065	11,966	2,834
University of Texas at Arlington	3	9	1972	D1	Pu	7,497	1,830	897,292	8,035	5,283	24,729	4,323
University of Texas at Dallas	3	12	1974	D1	Pu	10,059	6,137	498,661	2,918	4,233	8,993	3,760
Texas Woman's University	3	4	1953	D1	Pu	953	319	782,573	3,072	2,399	9,636	4,026
University of Toledo	2	5	1964	D1	Pu	4,256	1,960	805,149	7,211	5,627	24,539	2,735
Western Michigan University	4	3	1969	D1	Pu	3,107	544	1,104,251	10,016	5,798	27,281	6,606
College of William & Mary	1	2	1967	D1	Pu	11,734	5,251	1,203,718	10,133	6,187	1,264	
University of Alabama-Huntsville		7	1973	D2	Pu	19,782	14,038	406,620	3,182	1,879	8,026	1,860
University of Alaska	1	6	1955	D2	Pu	52,392	24,768	703,051	5,926	4,712	8,116	730
Baylor University	2	5	1954	D2	Pr	1,083	342	1,510,111	9,171	5,839	12,179	1,342
Biola University	1	1	1976	D2	Pr	2		257,517	1,796	696	2,883	584
University of Central Florida		2	1981	D2	Pu	20,467	6,168	628,982	4,981	4,284	21,873	3,906
Clark University	4	9	1891	D2	Pr	1,191	884	505,307	1,891	1,760	3,230	860

Institution	Number of Programs in 1982 Study	Number of Programs in 1993 Study	Institutional Profile: Year of First PhD	Carn Class	Control	Average Research Expenditure 1986-92 [1]: Total R&D (x $1,000)	Federal R&D (x $1,000)	Library 1992 [2]: Volumes	Serials	Expend (x $1,000)	Enrollment Fall 1992 [3]: Total	Graduate Students
Clarkson University	5	7	1964	D2	Pr	7,471	4,230	213,130	2,850	1,176	2,978	373
Colorado School of Mines		7	1922	D2	Pu	9,313	4,925	277,218	2,500	1,305	3,450	946
Dartmouth College	3	11	1885	D2	Pr	36,245	25,665	1,992,074	20,143	10,155	5,017	874
University of Detroit Mercy	1	3	1966	D2	Pr	1,088	149	784,696	5,355	2,943	7,387	1,906
Duquesne University		3	1935	D2	Pr	384	118	491,509	2,112	1,637	8,688	2,812
Florida Atlantic University		1	1972	D2	Pu	3,832	1,620	592,131	4,670	3,690	14,673	3,137
George Mason University		3	1983	D2	Pu	5,306	2,515	580,200	7,780	4,778	20,829	7,067
Hahnemann University	7	1	1946	D2	Pr	10,916	7,406	93,017	1,321	1,297	2,379	711
Idaho State University	1	4	1973	D2	Pu	1,253	392	498,786	3,383	2,401	10,748	1,733
Loma Linda University	2	6	1958	D2	Pr	6,201	3,300	293,409	2,775	2,018	4,451	851
University of Maine	2	5	1960	D2	Pu	19,357	7,886	826,648	14,590	4,334	12,315	2,106
U of Maryland Baltimore County		5	1976	D2	Pu	4,428	3,392	567,159	4,114	3,158	10,650	1,570
University of Mass-Lowell		6	1963	D2	Pu	10,144	5,394	391,058	3,757	2,669	13,233	2,734
Middle Tennessee State University		1	1973	D2	Pu			576,751	3,528	2,836	16,787	1,776
U of Mississippi-Medical Center		2	1971	D2	Pu							
Univ of Missouri-Saint Louis		4	1977	D2	Pu	2,280	984	583,134	8,995	2,588	14,918	2,523
Montana State University	4	10	1956	D2	Pu	24,592	8,858	515,214	5,078	3,145	10,537	867
University of Montana	4	5	1958	D2	Pu	6,612	2,969	649,993	4,656	3,066	10,612	1,480
University of Nevada, Reno	1	6	1964	D2	Pu	19,724	9,278	861,089	12,914	6,165	11,894	2,951
University of New Hampshire	8	14	1957	D2	Pu	22,608	13,892	1,024,911	7,000	4,137	13,872	2,237
New Jersey Inst of Technology	4	3	1964	D2	Pu	11,860	2,084	154,257	1,735	1,557	7,697	2,634
University of New Orleans	1	3	1967	D2	Pu			591,545	5,909	2,604	16,308	3,993
North Dakota State University	3	4	1963	D2	Pu	17,522	4,693	455,338	5,345	2,350	9,640	1,018
University of North Dakota	9	5	1914	D2	Pu	15,409	12,384	847,181	8,673	2,353	14,241	1,393
Portland State University		1	1973	D2	Pu	3,085	2,048	930,693	11,132	5,150	17,357	5,446
Univ of Puerto Rico-Rio Piedras	2	12	1966	D2	Pu	4,192	2,812	1,173,710	6,154	7,572	19,282	3,096
Rutgers State Univ-Newark	3	5	1975	D2	Pu							
Seton Hall University		1	1965	D2	Pr	214	207	631,401	7,833	4,156	10,422	3,016
University of South Dakota	2	4	1959	D2	Pu	1,343	708	445,215	2,687	1,818	8,693	1,715
Univ of Southwestern Louisiana		6	1971	D2	Pu	6,602	732	667,473	6,318	2,559	16,648	1,738

Appendix Table E (Continued)

Institution	Number of Programs in 1982 Study	Number of Programs in 1993 Study	Institutional Profile: Year of First PhD	Institutional Profile: Carn Class	Control	Average Research Expenditure 1986-92 [1]: Total R&D (x $1,000)	Average Research Expenditure 1986-92 [1]: Federal R&D (x $1,000)	Library 1992 [2]: Volumes	Library 1992 [2]: Serials	Library 1992 [2]: Expend (x $1,000)	Enrollment Fall 1992 [3]: Total	Enrollment Fall 1992 [3]: Graduate Students
SUNY Col Environ Sci & Forestry	5	2	1936	D2	Pu	14,272	1,653	109,196	3,234	1,028	1,656	582
Stevens Inst of Technology	5	9	1955	D2	Pr	7,472	3,279	100,397	122	648	3,371	2,062
Texas Christian University	2	5	1964	D2	Pr	1,467	1,069	748,887	3,637	3,397	6,728	807
University of Tulsa	3	8	1954	D2	Pr	3,563	923	762,925	7,756	3,651	4,900	829
Wake Forest University	2	8	1964	D2	Pr	31,910	24,419	1,188,534	19,252	6,539	5,650	974
Wichita State University		3	1963	D2	Pu	3,586	1,631	926,431	6,393	3,785	14,695	2,727
Worcester Polytechnic Inst	1	7	1904	D2	Pr	4,511	2,266	240,416	1,542	1,467	3,913	1,045
Air Force Inst of Technology	1	2	1972	OTH	Pu	1,557	1,557	511,146	4,962	2,928	881	881
Albany Medical College	2	6	1971	MED	Pr	10,288	6,895	117,463	1,183	1,107	654	127
U of Arkansas for Medical Sci	1	2	1971	MED	Pu	10,088	5,652	164,239	1,757	1,614	1,734	323
Baylor College of Medicine	4	6	1971	MED	Pu	114,892	60,973	251,977	4,511	5,252	1,076	378
Bryn Mawr College	11	5	1888	BA1	Pr	1,176	702	760,988	1,980	2,545	1,835	534
Cal Sch Prof Psych-Alameda	1	1	1977	OTH	Pr			1,231,096	10,295	5,997	628	628
Cal Sch Prof Psych-Fresno		1	1978	OTH	Pr	870	620	12,550	210	206	383	383
Cal Sch Prof Psych-Los Angeles		1	1977	OTH	Pr	706	458	20,500	350	216	615	615
Cal Sch Prof Psych-San Diego	1	1	1978	OTH	Pr	41		22,129	275	217	630	630
Creighton University		2	1971	MA1	Pr	6,667	1,997	684,467	6,285	3,185	6,225	551
University of Dayton		4	1972	MA1	Pr	30,998	25,863	698,003	2,840	2,335	10,778	3,507
Drew University		2	1912	BA1	Pr			421,330	2,060	1,698	2,138	643
East Carolina U Sch Medicine		5	1983	MA1	Pu	4,687	2,634	1,058,529	6,788	6,538	19,264	2,893
Fairleigh Dickinson University		1	1973	MA1	Pr	2,338	1,672	564,112	3,288	2,096		
Fielding Institute		1	1982	OTH	Pr							
Fuller Theological Seminary	1	2	1971	REL	Pr	49	6	176,568	18,891	612	4,019	2,888
University of Hartford		1	1977	MA1	Pr			348,711	2,152	1,638	7,837	2,159
Univ of Health Sc/Chicago Med Sch	2	5	1970	MED	Pr	4,192	2,840	110,000	1,079	730	1,070	297
Hebrew Union College		1	1936	REL	Pr			130,200	799	143		
Jewish Theological Seminary		2	1936	REL	Pr			294,558	728	1,086		
Louisiana State U Medical Center	2	5	1971	MED	Pu			274,896	3,551	3,286		

Institution	Number of Programs in 1982 Study	Number of Programs in 1993 Study	Institutional Profile: Year of First PhD	Institutional Profile: Carn Class	Control	Average Research Expenditure 1986-92 [1]: Total R&D (x $1,000)	Average Research Expenditure 1986-92 [1]: Federal R&D (x $1,000)	Library 1992 [2]: Volumes	Library 1992 [2]: Serials	Library 1992 [2]: Expend (x $1,000)	Enrollment Fall 1992 [3]: Total	Enrollment Fall 1992 [3]: Graduate Students
Louisiana St U-Sch Med Shreveport		4	1974	MED	Pu							
Univ of Maryland at Baltimore	3	5	1973	MED	Pu	68,895	32,247	252,967	3,758	1,488	5,064	2,205
U of Massachusetts Med Center		5	1985	MED	Pu	6,345	4,212	162,084	2,546	1,697	644	221
Mayo Graduate School		4	1985	HLTH	Pr	14	5	330,318	4,281	3,861	1,713	128
Medical College of Georgia		3	1966	MED	Pu	11,231	7,136	155,612	1,442	1,455	4,117	519
Medical College of Ohio		4	1982	MED	Pu	7,168	5,349	121,110	1,810	998	962	388
Medical College of Pensylvania		5	1961	MED	Pr	16,290	10,198	90,891	1,814	1,421	615	121
Medical College of Wisconsin	2	5	1973	MED	Pr	31,175	18,876	189,181	2,156	1,677	1,197	394
Medical University South Carolina	3	4	1952	MED	Pu	21,463	11,276	200,351	2,526	2,034	2,290	527
Univ of Med & Dent of NJ	3	4	1965	MED	Pu	51,081	25,063	213,535	4,337	3,868	3,581	1,131
Michigan Technological University		3	1968	ENG	Pu	14,211	5,397	162,857	3,534	1,734	6,961	601
Naval Postgraduate School		4	1959	OTH	Pu	14,974	14,852	301,209	1,297	2,220	1,830	1,830
New Mexico Inst of Mining & Tech	1	4	1956	ENG	Pu	20,453	6,467	230,667	919	805	1,592	328
New Orleans Baptist Theo Seminary		1	1965	REL	Pr			204,791	1,148	365		
New York Medical College		5	1968	MED	Pr	12,140	9,527	148,709	2,290	1,376	1,324	550
Northeast Louisiana University		1	1970	MA1	Pu	742	435	366,805	6,130	2,928	11,732	1,115
Oakland University		1	1978	MA1	Pu	4,216	2,490	572,445	2,456	2,561	13,068	2,517
Oregon Graduate Inst Sci & Tech		6	1974	ENG	Pr	8,227	5,669	655,677	6,792	3,955	413	413
Pacific Grad Sch of Psychology		1	1987	OTH	Pr			432,661	2,504	1,617	372	372
Phila Col of Pharmacy & Science		2	1933	HLT	Pr	642	190	64,856	789	791	1,784	72
Princeton Theological Seminary		1	1967	REL	Pr			368,094	2,220	1,445		
Rush University		1	1980	MED	Pr	19,153	6,795	120,002	10,295	1,713	1,301	625
Saybrook Institute		1	1984	OTH	Pr							
University of South Alabama		1	1983	MA1	Pu	9,228	5,832	413,751	4,500	2,893	12,311	1,506
South Dakota Sch of Mines & Tech		2	1970	ENG	Pu	2,409	1,744	101,544	798	631	2,459	282
Southern Baptist Theological Sem		2	1930	REL	Pr			338,896	1,606	950		
SUNY-Health Science Ctr-Brooklyn	4	6	1960	MED	Pu	21,285	12,209	238,131	4,962	1,704	1,711	215
SUNY Health Science Ctr-Syracuse	3	4	1959	MED	Pu	18,438	7,727	164,269	1,598	1,435	1,095	104
Tennessee Technological Univ		2	1974	MA1	Pu	7,346	851	383,616	3,799	2,027	8,242	884
University of Tennessee - Memphis	3	5	1971	MED	Pu			165,280	1,878	1,134	2,001	348

Appendix Table E (Continued)

Institution	Number of Programs in 1982 Study	Number of Programs in 1993 Study	Institutional Profile: Year of First PhD	Institutional Profile: Carn Class	Control	Average Research Expenditure 1986-92 [1]: Total R&D (x $1,000)	Average Research Expenditure 1986-92 [1]: Federal R&D (x $1,000)	Library 1992 [2]: Volumes	Library 1992 [2]: Serials	Library 1992 [2]: Expend (x $1,000)	Enrollment Fall 1992 [3]: Total	Enrollment Fall 1992 [3]: Graduate Students
University of Texas-El Paso		1	1979	MA1	Pu	4,807	3,542	786,494	11,952	2,916	17,223	2,614
U of Texas, Medical Br-Galveston	2	5	1971	MED	Pu	34,099	18,622	237,364	2,823	2,949	2,112	388
U of Tex-Health Sci Ctr-Houston	6	6	1971	MED	Pu	41,083	26,593				3,203	1,477
U of Tex-Hlth Sci Ct-San Antonio	2	4	1971	MED	Pu	40,759	26,850	203,515	2,945	2,460	2,573	532
U of Texas-Southwestern Med Ctr		7	1971	MED	Pu	71,601	46,929	216,514	2,609	2,559	1,634	459
Thomas Jefferson University	3	4	1972	MED	Pr	24,842	17,315	161,178	2,356	2,927	2,685	453
Uniformed Services U of Hlth Sci		6	1985	MED	Pu	26,782	11,960				806	140
Union Theological Seminary in VA		1	1973	REL	Pr			275,444	1,561	952		
Wesleyan University	2	5	1965	BA1	Pr	3,374	1,958	1,231,096	10,295	5,997	3,332	606

Sources: 1. National Science Foundation Survey of Scientific and Engineering Expenditures at Universities and Colleges, FY 1992
2. Association of Research Libraries 1992 Survey, Association of College and Research Libraries 1992 Survey, and the Department of Education IPEDS Academic Libraries Survey 1992
3. Department of Education IPEDS Fall Enrollment 1992 Survey

APPENDIX F

The National Survey of Graduate Faculty

The National Survey of Graduate Faculty was conducted in 1993 by the National Research Council. The survey was designed to gather the views of a sample of faculty at U.S. universities on the scholarly quality of the program faculty in their field and the effectiveness of those programs in educating research scholars/scientists.

The National Survey of Graduate Faculty traces its origins to the work of Hughes (1925), Keniston (1959), Cartter (1966), and Roose and Andersen (1970). The format and content of the present survey are generally similar to that developed by the 1982 study on the same topic (Jones, Lindzey, and Coggeshall, 1982), with individual faculty acting as "raters" for approximately 50 programs in their field.

THE SAMPLE

The sample of "raters" for the National Survey of Graduate Faculty was drawn from a list of 65,470 faculty members reported by Institutional Coordinators at 274 institutions as participants in research-doctorate training programs. The size of the sample depended on the number of programs in the field. (See Appendix C.) In fields other than the Biological Sciences the number of raters was four times the number of programs for the field. No fewer than 200 raters were selected even in fields with fewer than 50 programs participating in the study. Thus each program was included on 200 questionnaires.

For the Biological Sciences the number of raters was expanded to five times the number of programs, which resulted in each program appearing on 300 questionnaires. This step was taken in recognition of the interdisciplinary nature of the faculty in those programs and in light of our goal of seeking at least 100 ratings for every program included in the study.

THE QUESTIONNAIRE

The survey instrument (see the pages that follow) was a questionnaire that retained many of the features of the one used in the 1982 study, including questions on the "scholarly quality of the program faculty," the "effectiveness of the program in educating research scholars and scientists," and "the relative change in program quality over the years." Each questionnaire contained a random sample of 50 research-doctorate programs except in the Biological Sciences which included 60 programs.

DATA COLLECTION

In May 1993, the first set of questionnaires was mailed to 11,407 raters in 34 fields. The raters in this group represented approximately 18 percent of total faculty in fields other than the Biological Sciences. Later, a second set of questionnaires was mailed to 5,331 raters in the Biological Sciences. This group of evaluators represented approximately 25 percent of the program faculty in that area.

FINAL SAMPLE DISPOSITION

Owing to the fact that the sample was drawn from faculty lists provided by Institutional Coordinators crossing departmental boundaries, respondents occasionally indicated that they did not consider themselves qualified to rate programs in a certain disciplinary area. This effectively reduced the sample and necessitated the use of a second wave mailing in fields in which the sampling problem was particularly evident, for example, in the biological sciences and in biomedical engineering. Appendix Tables F-1 and F-2 summarize the final disposition of the sample and the response outcome.

RESPONSE OUTCOMES

Questionnaires were returned to the staff of the National Research Council during the Summer and Fall of 1993. The committee achieved their goal of soliciting approximately 100 responses for each of the programs included in the study. The overall response rate was about 50 percent in most fields, except in the Biological Sciences which registered a 40 percent return.

The responses to each of the five questions asked of each program were tabulated and entered into a working file. From the working file, the "mean" and a "trimmed mean" for responses to each of the five questions for each program was computed and entered into a data base.

The "trimmed mean" was obtained by dropping the two highest and two lowest scores for each program and computing the resulting mean. In the computation of the means for B2 (Scholarly Quality of Program Faculty) and B4 (Effectiveness of Program in Educating Research Scholars/Scientists) for the response "Don't know well enough to evaluate" was not counted. However, these responses were recorded and used in the computation of the Visibility Index. (See Appendix P for a definition.)

About midway through the survey, the committee asked a subgroup of its membership[1] to review the survey returns and to advise staff on strategies that might be needed to achieve the objective of 100 responses per program. The ad hoc advisory panel in fact suggested an additional mailing of questionnaires in a few fields owing to patterns of non-response thought to be associated with this problem of interdisciplinary faculty lists.

Four fields subsequently selected for follow-up and a second wave mailing were: Biomedical Engineering, Comparative Literature, Religion, and Music. In addition, a second wave follow-up mailing was conducted in nine fields: Electrical Engineering, English Language and Literature, Materials Science, Mechanical Engineering, Computer Sciences, Mathematics, Oceanography, History, and Psychology.

Questionnaires were returned to the staff during the Summer and Fall of 1993. Responses were tabulated and a large file was formed for purposes of analysis. Appendix Table F-1 summarizes the response rate in February 1994, the point at which no further returns were accepted for analysis. Data from that table reveal that just over 7,900 raters returned forms that were usable,[2] or about 51 percent of the raters known to be eligible.[3] The committee achieved its goal of having a minimum of 100 raters per program, with the exception of the same fields noted earlier whose response rates varied from 82 respondents in Comparative Literature (or 43 percent of the total number surveyed) to 98 percent in Linguistics (or 51 percent of the total number surveyed). A further analysis of patterns of response by the ad hoc panel persuaded the committee, however, that patterns of non-response in this field did not reveal a bias, suggesting that the results could be utilized in the study.

The committee also sought to achieve a balance in survey replies on the basis of faculty position. That is, responses were sought from full professors, associate and assistant professors, and other faculty in proportion to their numbers in the sample of respondents. Appendix Table F-2 provides an overview of survey responses by faculty position and reveals a balance with respect to the level of seniority of faculty included in the study.

Analyses were also conducted with respect to geographic region of the rater and whether the rater had been suggested by the Institutional Coordinator or had been selected randomly by the committee in the course of composing the sample.[4] The results of those analyses maybe found in Appendix Table F-3.

The accuracy of the data entry and working file preparation was monitored by cross-checking sample tabulations.

THE DATA BASE

In addition to the overall survey information, the committee created a data base containing information about the characteristics of each rater, such as area of research specialization and the institution where the rater received his or her highest degree. These data have been aggregated to a level which will not identify the rater, but provide researchers with useful information about this dimension of the survey. Plans have been made to prepare these files for release to the public at the conclusion of the project. (See Note 12 of Chapter 1 for more details.)

NOTES

1. Committee members Drs. Norman Bradburn, Jonathan Cole, and Steve Stigler, together with the committee co-chairs, closely monitored the survey and guided staff in the interpretation of response rates. Dr. Rebecca Klemm, of Klemm Associates, provided technical support in the sampling plan and fielding of the questionnaire.

2. See Appendix F for a definition of this term and other terms.

3. Owing to the fact that it is not possible to determine the fraction of non-respondents who might also be considered ineligible.

4. The issue of potential bias associated with the use of faculty as raters who have been recommended by the Institutional Coordinators was discussed in the 1982 NRC study. See Jones, Lindzey, and Coggeshall, 1982

TABLE OF CONTENTS TO SAMPLE NATIONAL SURVEY OF GRADUATE FACULTY AND SUMMARY TABLES:

Cover Letter to the Rater /118
Excerpt from the National Survey Instrument /119
Project Summary /129
Table F-1 Adjusted Response Rate /133
Table F-2 Survey Outcome Summary /136
Table F-3 Selected Characteristics of Rater Responses /137

NATIONAL RESEARCH COUNCIL

COMMITTEE FOR THE STUDY OF RESEARCH-DOCTORATE PROGRAMS
IN THE UNITED STATES

2101 Constitution Avenue Washington, D.C. 20418

May 4, 1993

Physics
Worcester Polytechnic Institute
Worcester, MA 01609

In 1991, the National Research Council established the Committee for the Study of Research-Doctorate Programs in the United States to undertake a study of doctoral programs in the social and behavioral sciences, the physical sciences and mathematics, the biological sciences, engineering, and the humanities. As the enclosed Project Summary indicates, our study is conducted on behalf of the Conference Board of Associated Research Councils and involves over 4,000 research-doctorate programs in 41 fields at 284 universities.

In our capacity as co-chairs of the Committee, we invite you to serve as a reviewer of up to 50 programs in Physics. You have been selected to participate in this study from a list of faculty furnished by your institution. Review by you and your colleagues will constitute an important component of this study.

The purpose of our survey of graduate faculty is to gather the views of peers with regard to several features of Ph.D. programs. These include the scholarly quality of faculty at a sample of institutions, and the effectiveness of these programs in producing research scholars and scientists. The results of this survey will be summarized and presented, along with a number of other measures of these doctoral programs for use by students, administrators, and educators.

We ask that you complete the attached questionnaire as soon as possible **and return it in the enclosed postage paid envelope no later than May 18, 1993.** Your participation is vital to the successful completion of this task, and will be very much appreciated by our Committee.

Sincerely,

Brendan A. Maher

Brendan Maher

Marvin L. Goldberger

Marvin Goldberger

The National Research Council is the principal operating agency of the National Academy of Sciences and the National Academy of Engineering to serve government and other organizations

National Research Council
National Academy of Sciences
National Academy of Engineering
Institute of Medicine

National Survey of Graduate Faculty

Conducted by the
National Research Council
Committee for the Study of Research-Doctorate Programs
in the United States
Washington, D.C.

We solicit this information on behalf of the Conference Board of Associated Research Council whose members include: The American Council on Education, the American Council of Learned Societies, the National Research Council, and the Social Science Research Council. Your response is entirely voluntary, and failure to provide some or all of the information will not in any way adversely affect you. We will use the information you provide to produce statistical summaries from which no one may identify any particular respondent. Your reply is confidential.

Participating Research-Doctorate Programs in the Field of Physics

(* Designates the programs which you are asked to evaluate on the following pages.)

Institution - Program / Department / Academic Unit

* University of Akron, Akron, OH - Polymer Science
University of Alabama, Tuscaloosa, AL - Physics and Astronomy
* University of Alabama-Birmingham, Birmingham, AL - Physics
* University of Alabama-Huntsville, Huntsville, AL - Physics
University of Alaska, Fairbanks, AK - Physics
* American University, Washington, DC - Physics
Arizona State University, Tempe, AZ - Physics and Astronomy
University of Arizona, Tucson, AZ - Physics
* Univ of Arkansas-Fayetteville, Fayetteville, AR - Physics
* Auburn University, Auburn, AL - Physics
* Baylor University, Waco, TX - Physics
Boston College, Chestnut Hill, MA - Physics
* Boston University, Boston, MA - Physics
Brandeis University, Waltham, MA - Physics
Brigham Young University, Provo, UT - Physics and Astronomy
* Brown University, Providence, RI - Physics
Bryn Mawr College, Bryn Mawr, PA - Physics
California Institute Technology, Pasadena, CA - Physics, Mathematics and Astronomy
University of California-Berkeley, Berkeley, CA - Physics
University of California-Davis, Davis, CA - Physics
University of California-Irvine, Irvine, CA - Physics
Univ of California-Los Angeles, Los Angeles, CA - Physics
Univ of California-Riverside, Riverside, CA - Physics
* Univ of California-San Diego, La Jolla, CA - Physics
Univ of California-Santa Barbara, Santa Barbara, CA - Physics
Univ of California-Santa Cruz, Santa Cruz, CA - Physics
Carnegie Mellon University, Pittsburgh, PA - Physics
* Case Western Reserve Univ, Cleveland, OH - Physics
* Catholic University of America, Washington, DC - Physics
University of Chicago, Chicago, IL - Physics
University of Cincinnati, Cincinnati, OH - Physics
CUNY - Grad Sch & Univ Center, New York, NY - Physics
* Clark University, Worcester, MA - Physics
Clarkson University, Potsdam, NY - Physics
Colorado School of Mines, Golden, CO - Physics
Colorado State University, Fort Collins, CO - Physics
University of Colorado, Denver, CO - Physics
* Columbia University, New York, NY - Physics
University of Connecticut, Storrs, CT - Physics
Cornell University, Ithaca, NY - Physics
Dartmouth College, Hanover, NH - Physics & Astronomy
University of Delaware, Newark, DE - Physics & Astronomy
University of Denver, Denver, CO - Physics
* Drexel University, Philadelphia, PA - Physics & Atmospheric Sciences
* Duke University, Durham, NC - Physics
Florida Institute of Technology, Melbourne, FL - Physics
George Washington University, Washington, DC - Physics
Georgia Institute of Technology, Atlanta, GA - Physics
University of Georgia, Athens, GA - Physics and Astronomy
Harvard University, Cambridge, MA - Physics
University of Hawaii at Manoa, Honolulu, HI - Physics
University of Houston, Houston, TX - Physics
Howard University, Washington, DC - Physics and Astronomy
Illinois Institute of Technology, Chicago, IL - Physics
U of Illinois at Urbana-Champaign, Urbana, IL - Physics
University of Illinois at Chicago, Chicago, IL - Physics
Indiana University, Bloomington, IN - Physics
Iowa State University, Ames, IA - Physics and Astronomy
University of Iowa, Iowa City, IA - Physics and Astronomy
* Johns Hopkins University, Baltimore, MD - Physics
* Kansas State University, Manhattan, KS - Physics
University of Kansas, Lawrence, KS - Physics and Astonomy
* Kent State University, Kent, OH - Physics
University of Kentucky, Lexington, KY - Physics and Astronomy
Lehigh University, Bethlehem, PA - Physics
* Louisiana State U & A&M College, Baton Rouge, LA - Physics and Astronomy
University of Maine, Orono, ME - Physics and Astronomy
* University of Maryland, College Park, MD - Physics
Massachusetts Inst of Technology, Cambridge, MA - Physics
* U of Massachusetts at Amherst, Amherst, MA - Physics and Astronomy

(CONTINUED ON REVERSE SIDE)

* University of Mass-Lowell, Lowell, MA - Physics and Applied Physics
University of Miami, Miami, FL - Physics
Michigan State University, East Lansing, MI - Physics and Astronomy
* Michigan Technological University, Houghton, MI - Physics
University of Michigan, Ann Arbor, MI - Physics
University of Minnesota, Minneapolis, MN - School of Physics and Astronomy
University of Mississippi, University, MS - Physics and Astronomy
* University of Missouri-Columbia, Columbia, MO - Physics and Astronomy
University of Missouri-Rolla, Rolla, MO - Physics
* Montana State University, Bozeman, MT - Physics
* University of Nebraska-Lincoln, Lincoln, NE - Physics & Astronomy
University of Nevada, Reno, Reno, NV - Physics
University of New Hampshire, Durham, NH - Physics
* New Mexico Inst of Mining & Tech, Socorro, NM - Physics
New Mexico State University, Las Cruces, NM - Physics
New York University, New York, NY - Physics
U of North Carolina-Chapel Hill, Chapel Hill, NC - Physics and Astronomy
* North Carolina State University, Raleigh, NC - Physics
University of North Texas, Denton, TX - Physics
* Northeastern University, Boston, MA - Physics
Northwestern University, Evanston, IL - Physics & Astronomy
University of Notre Dame, Notre Dame, IN - Physics
Oakland University, Rochester, MI - Medical Physics
* Ohio State University, Columbus, OH - Physics
* Ohio University, Athens, OH - Physics and Astronomy
* Oklahoma State University, Stillwater, OK - Physics
* University of Oklahoma, Norman, OK - Physics and Astronomy
Old Dominion University, Norfolk, VA - Physics
* Oregon Graduate Inst Sci & Tech, Beaverton, OR - Applied Physics
University of Oregon, Eugene, OR - Physics
Oregon State University, Corvallis, OR - Physics
Pennsylvania State University, University Park, PA - Physics
University of Pennsylvania, Philadelphia, PA - Physics
University of Pittsburgh, Pittsburgh, PA - Physics & Astronomy
Polytechnic University, Brooklyn, NY - Physics
* Princeton University, Princeton, NJ - Physics
* Univ of Puerto Rico-Rio Piedras, San Juan, PR - Chemical Physics (Interdisciplinary)
Purdue University, West Lafayette, IN - Physics
Rensselaer Polytechnic Inst, Troy, NY - Physics
* University of Rhode Island, Kingston, RI - Physics
Rice University, Houston, TX - Physics
University of Rochester, Rochester, NY - Optics/Physics
University of Rochester, Rochester, NY - Physics and Astronomy
Rockefeller University, New York, NY - Physics
* Rutgers State Univ-New Brunswick, New Brunswick, NJ - Physics & Astronomy
* University of South Carolina, Columbia, SC - Physics and Astronomy
University of Southern California, Los Angeles, CA - Physics and Astronomy
Stanford University, Stanford, CA - Physics
University of Florida, Gainesville, FL - Physics
* Florida State University, Tallahassee, FL - Physics
Univ at Albany, State Univ of NY, Albany, NY - Physics
State Univ of New York-Buffalo, Buffalo, NY - Physics and Astronomy
State U of New York-Stony Brook, Stony Brook, NY - Physics
* Stevens Inst of Technology, Hoboken, NJ - Physics/Engineering Physics
Syracuse University, Syracuse, NY - Physics
* Temple University, Philadelphia, PA - Physics
University of Tennessee-Knoxville, Knoxville, TN - Physics
* Texas A&M University, College Station, TX - Physics
Texas Christian University, Fort Worth, TX - Physics
Texas Tech University, Lubbock, TX - Physics
* University of Texas at Austin, Austin, TX - Physics
University of Texas at Arlington, Arlington, TX - Physics
University of Texas at Dallas, Richardson, TX - Physics
* Tufts University, Boston, MA - Physics and Astronomy
Tulane University, New Orleans, LA - Physics
University of Utah, Salt Lake City, UT - Physics
Vanderbilt University, Nashville, TN - Physics and Astronomy
Virginia Polytech Inst & State U, Blacksburg, VA - Physics
University of Virginia, Charlottesville, VA - Physics
Washington State University, Pullman, WA - Physics
* Washington University, St. Louis, MO - Physics
* University of Washington, Seattle, WA - Physics
College of William & Mary, Williamsburg, VA - Physics
* University of Wisconsin-Madison, Madison, WI - Physics
* University of Wisconsin-Milwaukee, Milwaukee, WI - Physics
Worcester Polytechnic Inst, Worcester, MA - Physics
Yale University, New Haven, CT - Physics

Part A: EDUCATIONAL INFORMATION

A1. What is the highest degree that you hold?

Mark (x) One

1. ☐ M.A.
2. ☐ M.S.
3. ☐ PhD.
4. ☐ Other, specify:

____

A2. In what program or field was this degree awarded?

____

A3. When was this degree awarded?

__________ 19 __________
MONTH YEAR

A4. From which college or university did you receive this degree?

Please do not abbreviate school name.

____
(SCHOOL NAME)

____
(CITY/TOWN)

____
(STATE OR FOREIGN COUNTRY)

Form No. 03572-00

A5. Using the Employment Specialties List below, indicate your field of specialization as of January 1993.

Mark (x) One

1. ☐ Acoustics
2. ☐ Astronomy/Astrophysics
3. ☐ Atomic/Molecular Physics
4. ☐ Electromagnetism
5. ☐ Elementary Particles
6. ☐ Fluids
7. ☐ Mechanics
8. ☐ Nuclear Structure
9. ☐ Optics
10. ☐ Plasma Physics
11. ☐ Polymer Physics
12. ☐ Solid State Physics
13. ☐ Thermal Physics
14. ☐ Theoretical Physics
15. ☐ Physics, General
16. ☐ Other (Please Specify):

____

Part B: Instructions

On the pages that follow, you are asked to judge up to 50 programs (presented in random sequence) that offer the research-doctorate. A list of the faculty members significantly involved in each program, the name of the program and academic unit in which the program is offered (if different from the field name), and the number of doctorates awarded have been printed on the survey form. Although this information has been furnished to us by the institution and is believed to be accurate, it has not been verified by our study committee and may have a few omissions, misspellings, or other errors.

Before marking your responses on the survey form, you may find it helpful to look over the full set of programs you are being asked to evaluate. Each program is to be evaluated in terms of:

(1) Scholarly Quality of Program Faculty. Please consider only the scholarly competence and achievements of the faculty. It is suggested that no more than five programs be designated "distinguished."

(2) Effectiveness of Program in Educating Research Scholars/Scientists. Please consider the accessibility of the faculty, the curricula, the instructional and research facilities, the quality of graduate students, the performance of graduates, the clarity of stated program objectives and expectations, the appropriateness of program requirements and timetables, the adequacy of graduate advising and mentorship, the commitment of the program in assuring access and promoting success of students historically underrepresented in graduate education, the quality of associated personnel (post-doctorates, research scientists, et. al.), and other factors that contribute to the effectiveness of the research-doctorate program.

(3) Change in Program Quality in the Last Five Years. Please consider both the scholarly quality of the program faculty and the effectiveness of the program in educating research scholars/scientists. Compare the quality of the program today with its quality five years ago -- not the change in the program's relative standing among other programs in the field.

In assessing each of these questions, please check the box next to the phrase that most closely corresponds to your assessment. If you are unfamiliar with that aspect of the program, mark the category "Don't know well enough to evaluate".

Although the assessment is limited to these factors, our committee recognizes that other factors are relevant to the quality of doctoral graduate programs, and that programs serve important purposes in addition to that of educating doctoral candidates. Our committee appreciates your willingness to participate in this survey and welcomes any comments you may wish to provide on the last page of the survey form.

Part B: ASSESSMENT OF RESEARCH-DOCTORATE PROGRAMS

Northeastern University

Boston, MA

Physics

Total Doctorates Awarded in 1987-1992: 33

Professors

Ronald Aaron
Petros Argyres
Arun Bansil
Paul Champion
Alan Cromer
William Faissler
Marvin Friedman
David Garelick
Michael Glaubman
Haim Goldberg
Jorge Jose
Robert P. Lowndes
Marie Machacek
Bertram Malenka
Robert Markiewicz
Pran Nath
Clive Perry
Stephen Reucroft
Carl Shiffman
Jeffrey Sokoloff
Yogendra Srivastava
Michael Vaughn
Eberhard VonGoeler
Allan Widom
Fa-Yueh Wu

Associate Professors

George Alverson
Jacqueline Krim
Sridhar Srinivas

Assistant Professors

Alain Karma
Ian Leedom
Tomasz Taylor

Form No. 03572-01

B1. Familiarity with Work of Program Faculty

Mark (x) One

1. ☐ **Considerable familiarity**
2. ☐ **Some familiarity**
3. ☐ **Little or no familiarity**

B2. Scholarly Quality of Program Faculty

Mark (x) One

1. ☐ **Distinguished**
2. ☐ **Strong**
3. ☐ **Good**
4. ☐ **Adequate**
5. ☐ **Marginal**
6. ☐ **Not sufficient for doctoral education**

9. ☐ **Don't know well enough to evaluate**

B3. Familiarity with Graduates of this Program

Mark (x) One

1. ☐ **Considerable familiarity**
2. ☐ **Some familiarity**
3. ☐ **Little or no familiarity**

B4. Effectiveness of Program in Educating Research Scholars/Scientists

Mark (x) One

1. ☐ **Extremely effective**
2. ☐ **Reasonably effective**
3. ☐ **Minimally effective**
4. ☐ **Not effective**

9. ☐ **Don't know well enough to evaluate**

B5. Change in Program Quality in Last Five Years

Mark (x) One

1. ☐ **Better than five years ago**
2. ☐ **Little or no change in the last five years**
3. ☐ **Poorer than five years ago**

9. ☐ **Don't know well enough to evaluate**

Part B: ASSESSMENT OF RESEARCH-DOCTORATE PROGRAMS

American University

Washington, DC

Physics

Total Doctorates Awarded in 1987-1992: 11

Professors

Raymond Arnold
Peter Bosted
Richard Kay
Howard Reiss
Stephen Rock
Romeo Segnan
Zenon Szalata
John White

Assistant Professors

Bruce Flanders
Robert Kille
Fred Volkening

Form No. 03572-02

B1. Familiarity with Work of Program Faculty

Mark (x) One

1. ☐ Considerable familiarity
2. ☐ Some familiarity
3. ☐ Little or no familiarity

B2. Scholarly Quality of Program Faculty

Mark (x) One

1. ☐ Distinguished
2. ☐ Strong
3. ☐ Good
4. ☐ Adequate
5. ☐ Marginal
6. ☐ Not sufficient for doctoral education

9. ☐ Don't know well enough to evaluate

B3. Familiarity with Graduates of this Program

Mark (x) One

1. ☐ Considerable familiarity
2. ☐ Some familiarity
3. ☐ Little or no familiarity

B4. Effectiveness of Program in Educating Research Scholars/Scientists

Mark (x) One

1. ☐ Extremely effective
2. ☐ Reasonably effective
3. ☐ Minimally effective
4. ☐ Not effective

9. ☐ Don't know well enough to evaluate

B5. Change in Program Quality in Last Five Years

Mark (x) One

1. ☐ Better than five years ago
2. ☐ Little or no change in the last five years
3. ☐ Poorer than five years ago

9. ☐ Don't know well enough to evaluate

Part C: CLOSING INFORMATION

Form No. 03572-99

C1. Please nominate at least two faculty peers in your field who might serve in an international assessment of research doctorate programs in the United States. (Exclude U.S. citizens working abroad.) Please print and provide address if known.

COUNTRY 1: ________________

Name: ________________

University: ________________

Department: ________________

COUNTRY 2: ________________

Name: ________________

University: ________________

Department: ________________

COUNTRY 3: ________________

Name: ________________

University: ________________

Department: ________________

COUNTRY 4: ________________

Name: ________________

University: ________________

Department: ________________

C2. Do you have any comments about this evaluation or is there anything else you would like to add?

____

THANK YOU FOR COMPLETING THE QUESTIONNAIRE.

NATIONAL RESEARCH COUNCIL
OFFICE OF SCIENTIFIC AND ENGINEERING PERSONNEL

COMMITTEE FOR THE STUDY OF RESEARCH-DOCTORATE PROGRAMS IN THE UNITED STATES

PROJECT SUMMARY

The preeminence of this Nation's graduate education enterprise is unquestioned. Each year, more than 30,000 candidates are awarded doctorates in the sciences, engineering and the humanities from over 350 U.S. universities, about one-third to citizens from countries other than the United States.

It has been said that the genius of American higher education is the close association of training and research through formal "research-doctorate programs." Yet, numerous reports point to the fact that increasing pressures on academic institutions run the risk of jeopardizing that relationship--threatening to weaken the effectiveness of the doctoral program in preparing future generations of skilled research scholars and scientists.[1] In particular, available information suggests that fierce competition is underway at U.S. universities relative to the allocation of institutional resources that are needed to sustain the excellence of the graduate education enterprise.[2]

In 1991, the National Research Council (NRC) established the ***Committee for the Study of Research-Doctorate Programs in the United States*** *to undertake a three-year study of doctoral programs which have as a goal the preparation of research scholars/scientists. The Committee predicates its work on the findings of an earlier NRC Committee published in 1982 as the five-volume series:* ***An Assessment of Research-Doctorate Programs in the United States*** *(National Academy Press, Washington, D.C.). Through a combination of survey work and review of available descriptive statistics, the Committee will assemble information which characterizes selected features of research-doctorate programs in the biological sciences, the physical sciences and mathematics, the social and behavioral sciences, engineering, and the humanities.*

---

[1] See, for example, the series of reports by the Association of American Universities (1990) which address methods to enhance doctoral education at U.S. universities; the recent analyses of W. Bowen and N. Rudenstine, In Pursuit of the PhD, Princeton University Press 1992; and the discussion paper Fateful Choices prepared by the National Research Council's Government-University-Research Roundtable, 1992.

[2] See, for example, Science and Engineering Indicators: 1991, National Science Board.

INFORMATION GOALS

There are many aspects of graduate education which merit examination in any study of the research-training enterprise. The present study seeks to provide descriptive statistics and other quantitative indicators of research-doctorate programs in four areas:

(1) the students participating in graduate preparation -- their demographic characteristics and career outcomes;

(2) the faculty who provide the educational and research leadership in research-doctorate programs;

(3) institutional resources brought to bear in creating an enriched environment for preparing research scholars and scientists; and

(4) the views of disciplinary peers regarding the effectiveness of those programs in preparing students for careers as research scholars/scientists.

STRUCTURE

Chaired by Marvin L. Goldberger (University of California, San Diego) and Brendan Maher (Harvard University), the sixteen-member Committee represents a range of scholars and administrators drawn from the five broad fields comprising the study. In addition, Committee membership reflects the addition of specialists familiar with survey research and statistical methods.

OPERATIONS

The study has been undertaken on behalf of the Conference Board of Associated Research Councils whose members include: the American Council on Education, the American Council of Learned Societies, the Social Science Research Council, and the National Research Council. The National Research Council's Office of Scientific and Engineering Personnel (OSEP) provides oversight of the activities of the Committee. Project staff are located in OSEP's Studies and Surveys Unit.

The Committee meets three times a year and will do so through August 1994. The Committee works through ad hoc panels which address technical issues related to data gathering and/or analysis.

PROJECT MILESTONES

The Committee will finalize its data collection plans in 1993. New measures will be identified to attain the information goals outlined above and data gathering will proceed.

The Committee will utilize a variety of data bases to generate descriptive statistics about research-doctorate programs at U.S. universities, including such sources as the Doctorate Records File maintained by the National Research Council on behalf of the National Science Foundation and a number of other federal agencies. Other potential sources of information will be utilized as available.

In addition to examining data from readily available sources, the Committee plans to conduct a number of surveys. The first of these is the National Survey of Graduate Faculty, updating the ratings provided by over 8,100 faculty members in 1982. In addition, the Committee is considering a survey of industrial employers to develop a parallel set of ratings of research-doctorate programs in selected fields by individuals employed in industry who hire and/or direct the research of Ph.D.s.

Emphasis will also be given to the identification and/or development of data sources to track the career outcomes of program graduates.

The Committee will summarize its findings and prepare a report or a series of reports for broad distribution in 1994.

FIELD COVERAGE LIST

Arts and Humanities: Art History, Classics, Comparative Literature, English Language and Literature, French Language and Literature, German Language and Literature, Linguistics, Music, Philosophy, Religion, Spanish and Portuguese Language and Literature.

Biological Sciences: Biochemistry and Molecular Biology; Cell and Developmental Biology; Ecology, Evolution, and Behavior; Molecular and General Genetics; Neurosciences; Pharmacology; Physiology.

Engineering: Aerospace Engineering, Biomedical Engineering, Chemical Engineering, Civil Engineering, Electrical Engineering, Industrial Engineering, Materials Science, Mechanical Engineering.

Physical Sciences: Astrophysics/Astronomy, Chemistry, Computer Sciences, Geosciences, Mathematics, Oceanography, Physics, Statistics/Biostatistics.

Social and Behavioral Sciences: Anthropology, Economics, Geography, History, Political Science, Psychology, Sociology.

NATIONAL RESEARCH COUNCIL
OFFICE OF SCIENTIFIC AND ENGINEERING PERSONNEL

COMMITTEE FOR THE STUDY OF RESEARCH-DOCTORATE PROGRAMS IN THE UNITED STATES

Marvin L. Goldberger, Co-chair
Dean, Natural Sciences
University of California, San Diego

Brendan Maher, Co-chair
Edward C. Henderson Professor of the Psychology of Personality
Harvard University

Richard Atkinson
Chancellor
University of California, San Diego

Gardner Lindzey
Director Emeritus
Center for Advanced Study in the Behavioral Sciences

Norman Bradburn
Director
National Opinion Research Center

Pamela L. Mellon
Professor of Reproductive Medicine and Neuroscience
University of California, San Diego

Joseph Cerny
Provost for Research
Dean Graduate Division
University of California, Berkeley

Lincoln Moses
Professor of Statistics
Stanford University

Jonathan R. Cole
Provost and Dean of Faculties
Columbia University

Ernest T. Smerdon
Vice Provost and Dean of Engineering
University of Arizona

John D'Arms
Vice Provost for Academic Affairs
University of Michigan

Debra W. Stewart
Dean of the Graduate School
North Carolina State University

Jane S. de Hart
Professor of History
University of California, Santa Barbara

Stephen M. Stigler
Professor of Statistics
University of Chicago

Elsa Garmire
Director, Center for Laser Studies
University of Southern California

James H. Wyche
Associate Provost
Brown University

APPENDIX TABLE F-1: KEY

No. Inst.:	Number of institutions included in the study with programs reviewed, by field. [Note: Number of institutions does not add to Grand Total because many institutions had more than one program included in the study.]
No. Prog.:	Number of programs reviewed in the field.
No. Raters:	Number of individuals in the field who were selected as raters.
Adj. No. Raters:	Number of individuals considered qualified raters. This number is the difference between the number of individuals who were originally sent questionnaires and the number of individuals identified as being improperly selected for the rater pool, either as a result of: an incorrect address, they were retired, they did not feel qualified to rate programs, or they were asked to rate programs in an area they felt was not appropriate given their field of expertise.
No. Ind. Rater Resp.:	Number of completed questionnaires returned by individuals originally identified as raters.
Usable Rater Resp.:	Number of questionnaires used to calculate "program rating." This includes questionnaires completed by an individual other than the person sent the questionnaire.
Percent. Rater Resp.	Percentage of usable rater responses after the rater pool was adjusted.
No. Non-Resp.:	Number of questionnaires for which no response was received and no reason is known for the non-response.
No. Other Resp.:	Number of responses received from faculty members who did not complete the questionnaire, because: Lost - The questionnaire was lost and a replacement questionnaire was not returned. Not Avail. - Faculty member was not available, i.e. on leave or out of the country Rfs. - Faculty member refused to complete the questionnaire Time - Faculty member did not have the time to complete the questionnaire. No Info - Questionnaire was returned with no explanation. Misc.- Reason for not completing the questionnaire was different from any of the above.

Appendix Table F - 1 Adjusted Response Rate

Program Field	No. Inst.	No. Prog.	No. Raters	Adj No. Sample	No. Ind. Rater Resp.	Usable Rater Resp.	Percent. Rater Resp.	No. Non-Resp	No. Other Resp.	Outcomes Lost (L)	Not Avl (N)	Rfs (R)	Time (T)	No Info (Z)	Misc (M)
Art History	38	38	204	195	111	112	57%	81	2	0	0	2	0	0	0
Classics	29	29	203	197	109	109	55%	84	4	0	0	1	3	0	0
Comparative Literature	44	44	204	189	82	82	43%	82	25	12	4	2	4	2	1
English Language & Literature	127	127	508	476	264	267	56%	185	24	1	0	14	7	2	0
French Language and Literature	45	45	204	193	99	101	52%	87	5	1	0	0	2	1	1
German Language and Literature	32	32	204	198	118	118	60%	77	3	1	2	0	0	0	0
Linguistics	41	41	204	194	97	98	51%	86	10	1	2	5	2	0	0
Music	65	65	260	255	106	107	42%	129	19	7	7	4	1	0	0
Philosophy	71	72	288	279	144	145	52%	126	8	0	2	1	5	0	0
Religion	38	38	204	190	95	95	50%	86	9	6	0	1	0	2	0
Spanish & Portuguese Lang & Lit	54	54	216	215	108	109	51%	103	3	0	1	0	2	0	0
Total Arts and Humanities	148	585	2699	2581	1333	1343	52%	1126	112	29	18	30	26	7	2
Biochemistry & Molecular Biology	187	220	1092	983	424	424	43%	426	133	20	12	31	64	2	4
Cell and Developmental Biology	165	208	1037	881	355	356	40%	408	117	26	11	25	46	6	3
Ecology, Evolution & Behavioral	127	166	826	709	309	318	45%	298	93	12	11	23	43	3	1
Molecular and General Genetics	102	107	528	458	176	176	38%	219	63	11	5	21	26	0	0
Neurosciences	98	104	511	443	210	211	48%	178	54	6	4	10	31	2	1
Pharmacology	121	130	637	500	220	223	45%	218	59	13	8	14	23	0	1
Physiology	135	141	700	573	259	259	45%	256	58	7	7	22	20	1	1
Total Biological Sciences	205	1076	5331	4547	1953	1967	43%	2001	579	97	58	145	254	14	11
Aerospace Engineering	33	33	202	193	100	100	52%	90	3	0	1	1	0	1	0
Biomedical Engineering	38	38	204	163	80	83	51%	57	23	11	3	4	4	0	1
Chemical Engineering	93	93	372	361	206	206	57%	148	7	1	0	4	1	0	1
Civil Engineering	86	86	344	328	169	170	52%	149	9	2	1	3	2	1	0
Electrical Engineering	126	126	504	477	264	269	56%	191	17	3	1	4	6	2	1
Industrial Engineering	37	37	204	196	103	104	53%	88	4	0	1	2	1	0	0
Materials Science	62	65	260	245	157	156	64%	82	7	0	2	5	0	0	0
Mechanical Engineering	110	110	440	409	230	229	56%	163	17	4	1	8	3	1	0
Total Engineering	143	588	2530	2374	1302	1317	55%	970	87	22	10	30	17	5	3
Astrophysics / Astronomy	33	33	202	193	114	114	59%	72	7	0	1	6	0	0	0
Chemistry	168	168	672	648	329	332	51%	274	42	4	7	14	15	2	0
Computer Sciences	107	108	432	414	220	221	53%	166	27	1	12	6	5	3	0
Geosciences	95	100	400	382	201	203	53%	163	16	1	1	8	4	2	0
Mathematics	135	139	556	526	306	308	59%	197	21	2	0	10	6	2	1
Oceanography	26	26	202	184	116	116	63%	62	6	1	0	2	2	1	0
Physics	146	147	588	561	296	297	53%	241	23	5	1	7	8	2	0
Statistics / Biostatistics	58	65	260	249	149	151	61%	94	4	0	1	1	1	1	0
Total Physical Sciences	197	786	3312	3157	1731	1742	55%	1268	147	15	23	54	41	13	1
Anthropology	69	69	276	268	134	134	50%	119	15	0	6	8	1	0	0
Economics	106	107	428	420	233	234	56%	182	4	1	2	1	0	0	0
Geography	37	37	204	197	127	127	64%	66	4	0	1	2	1	0	0
History	111	111	446	427	251	252	59%	153	22	1	1	13	7	0	0
Political Science	97	98	392	378	207	208	55%	164	6	1	1	1	2	1	0
Psychology	185	185	740	701	402	405	58%	279	17	1	4	5	4	3	0
Sociology	95	95	380	371	196	197	53%	164	10	1	2	3	2	2	0
Total Social & Behavioral Sci	198	702	2866	2762	1550	1557	56%	1128	77	5	17	33	16	6	0
Grand Total	274	3737	16738	15421	7869	7926	51%	6492	1003	168	126	293	354	45	17

APPENDIX TABLE F-2: KEY

Total Raters: Number of faculty members in the field who were sent questionnaires.

The following description of the table headings apply to each of the four categories: Full Professors, Associate Professors, Assistant Professors, and Other Staff.

No. Rtrs.: Number of faculty members at this faculty rank who were sent questionnaires in their field.

% of Rtrs.: Percentage of all raters in this field who were in this faculty rank.

% Good Rec.: Percentage of raters who had been recommended by the Institutional Coordinators and who returned usable questionnaires.

% Good N-Rec: Percentage of raters drawn at random from faculty lists submitted by Institutional Coordinators and who returned usable questionnaires.

Appendix Table F-2 Survey Response by Faculty Rank

Fields	Total Raters	Full Professors No. Rtrs	% of Rtrs	% Good Rec	% Good N-Rc	Associate Professors No. Rtrs	% of Rtrs	% Good Rec	% Good N-Rc	Assistant Professors No. Rtrs	% of Rtrs	% Good Rec	% Good N-Rc	Other Staff No. Rtrs	% of Rtrs	% Good Rec	% Good N-Rc
Art History	204	131	64	71	45	45	22	61	32	27	13	61	78	1			
Classics	203	133	66	59	42	45	22	70	50	23	11	64	67	2	1		
Comparative Literature	204	125	61	54	38	58	28	50	24	20	10	43	31	1			
English Language & Literature	508	320	63	59	52	131	26	54	43	54	11	63	63	3	1		
French Language and Literature	204	130	64	65	45	43	21	56	33	29	14	30	37	2	1		50
German Language and Literature	204	128	63	68	52	48	24	68	43	27	13	46	64	1			
Linguistics	204	130	64	63	38	49	24	59	18	24	12	50	33	1			
Music	260	163	63	58	34	64	25	52	26	28	11	54	60	5	2		20
Philosophy	288	189	66	53	46	60	21	68	46	36	13	47	53	3	1		
Religion	204	140	69	63	41	38	19	77	56	19	9	11	40	7	3		14
Spanish & Portuguese Lang & Lit	216	136	63	56	49	55	25	57	32	25	12	40	53				
Total Arts and Humanities	2699	1725	64	60	44	636	24	61	38	312	12	49	53	26	1		14
Biochemistry & Molecular Biology	1092	654	60	39	37	273	25	37	32	160	15	58	46	5			50
Cell and Developmental Biology	1037	590	57	39	30	285	27	44	24	155	15	40	36	7	1		50
Ecology, Evolution & Behavioral	826	514	62	40	35	208	25	40	30	74	9	43	48	30	4		33
Molecular and General Genetics	528	286	54	36	31	146	28	39	27	87	16	32	39	9	2		22
Neurosciences	511	293	57	45	35	137	27	49	34	80	16	57	44	1			
Pharmacology	637	377	59	37	29	165	26	39	30	83	13	46	33	12	2		50
Physiology	700	432	62	44	34	193	28	38	31	75	11	36	32				
Total Biological Sciences	5331	3146	59	40	33	1407	26	41	29	714	13	46	40	64	1		37
Aerospace Engineering	202	125	62	66	49	54	27	53	29	22	11	30	67	1			
Biomedical Engineering	204	131	64	51	31	47	23	61	24	18	9	43	91	8	4	100	
Chemical Engineering	372	272	73	62	52	57	15	54	35	42	11	64	60	1			
Civil Engineering	344	218	63	53	49	76	22	50	43	45	13	53	50	5	1		
Electrical Engineering	504	312	62	58	49	117	23	53	45	73	14	65	62	2			
Industrial Engineering	204	113	55	53	43	54	26	74	39	34	17	54	48	3	1		33
Materials Science	260	192	74	66	57	39	15	65	59	27	10	45	56	2	1	100	100
Mechanical Engineering	440	289	66	57	53	95	22	54	40	54	12	67	36	2			
Total Engineering	2530	1652	65	59	49	539	21	57	40	315	12	57	55	24	1	67	10
Astrophysics / Astronomy	202	146	72	54	54	37	18	57	57	17	8	75	89	2	1		
Chemistry	672	499	74	61	44	92	14	50	47	79	12	53	47	2			50
Computer Sciences	432	235	54	57	42	103	24	60	50	88	20	62	46	6	1		50
Geosciences	400	287	72	62	43	73	18	48	48	26	7	62	46	14	4		43
Mathematics	556	418	75	63	50	84	15	59	58	47	8	91	47	7	1	67	25
Oceanography	202	138	68	54	58	41	20	56	57	12	6	50	63	11	5	100	70
Physics	588	463	79	51	50	65	11	57	34	51	9	74	59	9	2		
Statistics / Biostatistics	260	185	71	66	57	43	17	52	27	31	12	77	56	1			
Total Physical Sciences	3312	2371	72	59	49	538	16	55	48	351	11	65	52	52	2	60	38
Anthropology	276	183	66	51	41	53	19	63	52	34	12	41	76	6	2		33
Economics	428	294	69	58	50	75	18	64	54	59	14	58	58				
Geography	204	119	58	69	55	55	27	66	42	26	13	88	80	4	2		50
History	446	313	70	62	52	86	19	69	47	46	10	56	75	1			
Political Science	392	252	64	67	45	95	24	71	48	44	11	44	57	1			
Psychology	740	502	68	58	54	159	21	49	52	67	9	64	49	12	2	100	55
Sociology	380	253	67	61	47	90	24	52	46	33	9	65	54	4	1		
Total Social & Behavioral Sci	2866	1916	67	60	50	613	21	60	49	309	11	59	61	28	1	100	37
Grand Total	16738	10810	65	53	44	3733	22	51	38	2001	12	54	49	194	1	35	31

APPENDIX TABLE F-3: KEY

Rtrs.:	Distribution of questionnaires sent to raters, by rater's rank, by source of rater name, and by rater's geographic region.
Non Resp.:	Distribution of nonrespondents by rater's rank, by source of rater name, and by rater's geographic region.
Resp.:	Distribution of individuals responding to the survey by rater's rank, by source of rater name, and by rater's geographic region.
Usable:	Distribution of usable questionnaires, by rater's rank, by source of rater name, and by rater's geographic region.
93Q Resp.:	Distribution of actual number of program ratings submitted by faculty respondents with respect to the "scholarly quality of program faculty," by rater's rank, by source of rater name, and by rater's geographic region.

The rater's geographic region includes the following states and territory:

New England:	Connecticut, Maine, Massachusetts, New Hampshire, Rhode Island, Vermont
Middle Atlantic:	New Jersey, New York, Pennsylvania
East North Central:	Illinois, Indiana, Michigan, Ohio, Wisconsin
West North Central:	Iowa, Kansas, Minnesota, Missouri, Nebraska, North Dakota, South Dakota
South Atlantic:	Delaware, District of Columbia, Florida, Georgia, Maryland, North Carolina, South Carolina, Virginia, West Virginia
East South Central:	Alabama, Kentucky, Mississippi, Tennessee
West South Central:	Arkansas, Louisiana, Oklahoma, Texas
Mountain:	Arizona, Colorado, Idaho, Montana, Nevada, New Mexico, Utah, Wyoming
Pacific & Insular:	Alaska, California, Hawaii, Oregon, Washington, Puerto Rico

APPENDIX TABLE F-3: Distribution of Rater Responses by Selected Charateristics

ARTS AND HUMANITIES

Academic Rank	Rtrs.	Non Resp.	Resp.	Usable	93Q Resp.
Full	1,725	685	1,040	872	28,605
Associate	636	289	347	298	8,743
Assistant	312	134	178	160	4,304
Other	26	18	8	3	88

Source of Rater Name	Rtrs.	Non Resp.	Resp.	Usable	93Q Resp.
IC Recommended	1,062	373	689	623	20,688
IC Not Recommended	1,637	753	884	710	21,052

Region	Rtrs.	Non Resp.	Resp.	Usable	93Q Resp.
New England	266	113	153	132	4,074
Mid-Atlantic	630	289	341	283	8,707
East North Central	516	190	326	285	8,952
West North Central	157	60	97	83	2,773
South Atlantic	373	156	217	179	5,827
East South Central	67	29	38	34	956
West South Central	213	82	131	110	3,496
Mountain	63	34	29	24	706
Pacific & Insular	414	173	241	203	6,249

Total Number	2,699	1,126	1,573	1,333	41,740

APPENDIX TABLE F-3 Continued

BIOLOGICAL SCIENCES

Academic Rank	Rtrs.	Non Resp.	Resp.	Usable	93Q Resp.
Full	3,146	1,134	2,012	1,146	31,648
Associate	1,407	593	814	485	11,018
Assistant	714	251	463	300	6,299
Other	64	24	40	22	469

Source of Rater Name	Rtrs.	Non Resp.	Resp.	Usable	93Q Resp.
IC Recommended	2,435	895	1,590	988	25,807
IC Not Recommended	2,896	1,157	1,739	965	23,627

Region	Rtrs.	Non Resp.	Resp.	Usable	93Q Resp.
New England	394	153	241	111	2,810
Mid-Atlantic	1,010	388	622	334	8,416
East North Central	813	314	499	309	7,926
West North Central	410	152	258	164	4,338
South Atlantic	813	317	496	284	7,030
East South Central	110	172	282	105	2,385
West South Central	182	369	551	241	6,109
Mountain	119	208	327	122	3,346
Pacific & Insular	267	464	731	283	7,074
Total Number	5,331	2,002	3,329	1,953	49,434

APPENDIX TABLE F-3 Continued

ENGINEERING

Academic Rank	Rtrs.	Non Resp.	Resp.	Usable	93Q Resp.
Full	1,652	600	1,052	873	25,206
Associate	539	233	306	256	6,530
Assistant	315	113	202	176	3,884
Other	24	14	10	4	81

Source of Rater Name	Rtrs.	Non Resp.	Resp.	Usable	93Q Resp.
IC Recommended	1,017	349	668	592	17,146
IC Not Recommended	1,513	611	902	717	18,555

Region	Rtrs.	Non Resp.	Resp.	Usable	93Q Resp.
New England	193	85	108	90	2,390
Mid-Atlantic	428	149	279	231	6,788
East North Central	482	171	311	261	7,510
West North Central	187	77	110	95	2,622
South Atlantic	380	145	235	197	5,320
East South Central	120	43	77	61	1,672
West South Central	245	99	146	121	3,326
Mountain	158	63	95	79	2,017
Pacific & Insular	337	128	209	174	4,056
Total Number	2,530	960	1,570	1,309	35,701

APPENDIX TABLE F-3 Continued

SOCIAL AND BEHAVIORAL SCIENCES

Academic Rank	Rtrs.	Non Resp.	Resp.	Usable	93Q Resp.
Full	1,916	742	1,174	1,025	33,981
Associate	613	259	354	328	10,006
Assistant	309	110	199	186	4,964
Other	28	16	12	11	252

Source of Rater Name	Rtrs.	Non Resp.	Resp.	Usable	93Q Resp.
IC Recommended	1,059	364	695	637	20,701
IC Not Recommended	1,807	763	1,044	913	28,502

Region	Rtrs.	Non Resp.	Resp.	Usable	93Q Resp.
New England	259	114	145	127	3,699
Mid-Atlantic	515	211	304	267	8,385
East North Central	536	194	342	304	10,205
West North Central	183	62	121	104	3,340
South Atlantic	412	151	261	234	7,449
East South Central	104	44	60	51	1,552
West South Central	222	83	139	129	4,176
Mountain	175	71	104	96	3,078
Pacific & Insular	460	197	263	238	7,319
Total Number	2,866	1,127	1,739	1,550	49,203

APPENDIX TABLE F-3 Continued

PHYSICAL SCIENCES

Academic Rank	Rtrs.	Non Resp.	Resp.	Usable	93Q Resp.
Full	2,371	891	1,480	1,236	38,150
Associate	538	226	312	274	7,224
Assistant	351	122	229	200	4,985
Other	52	26	26	21	345

Source of Rater Name	Rtrs.	Non Resp.	Resp.	Usable	93Q Resp.
IC Recommended	1,195	413	782	702	21,701
IC Not Recommended	2,117	852	1,265	1,029	29,003

Region	Rtrs.	Non Resp.	Resp.	Usable	93Q Resp.
New England	330	151	197	141	3,804
Mid-Atlantic	553	230	325	274	8,023
East North Central	539	172	367	317	9,768
West North Central	203	70	133	112	3,612
South Atlantic	486	171	315	265	7,698
East South Central	112	38	74	69	2,064
West South Central	313	129	184	155	4,860
Mountain	210	73	137	114	3,160
Pacific & Insular	566	231	335	284	7,715
Total Number	3,312	1,265	2,047	1,731	50,704

APPENDIX G

Data Sources Utilized in Profiles of Participating Programs

The data sets developed for the Study of Research-Doctorate Programs in the United States provide a helpful source of information about the faculty and students who participate in research-doctorate programs and about the institutions sponsoring the programs. The data describing institutional characteristics were obtained from several national data bases, as well as from independently generated data sets which supply descriptive information about the programs, such as lists of faculty members that participate in the programs. However, as mentioned in Appendix E, gaps may occur in the information owing to response patterns to each of the data sources described below. The following sections describe the origins and composition of the data sets.

INSTITUTE FOR SCIENTIFIC INFORMATION

A generally accepted measure for judging the productivity and quality of a research program is the publication record of the faculty. The measure includes both a count of papers published in reviewed journals and monographs printed by recognized publishers, and the impact of those publications on the research in the area as measured by a citation analysis. The Institute for Scientific Information (ISI) maintains a computer file consisting of bibliographic records of papers indexed in the ISI citation indexes: the Science Citation Index, Social Science Citation Index, and Arts and Humanities Citation Index. With this file ISI maintains a citation index which identifies for each publication the other publications on its file that have been cited in the article. By matching the names on ISI's file with the program faculty it is possible to calculate a publication measure and a citation measure. This measure is considered of little value in the Arts and Humanities fields, due to the ISI concentration of papers in journals and monographs, and is only used for the 30 fields outside the Arts and Humanities.

For the Study of Research-Doctorate Programs in the United States, ISI extracted a raw data file which contains over 4.5 million publication records for the period 1981 to 1992. Each record contains bibliographic information about the publication, the author's (s') last name and initials, the author's (s') addresses, and identifying codes that link the publication to a citation file. For the Research-Doctorate Study a computer match was made between the ISI records and the publication of faculty participating in the 3,634 programs. The matching process was done at several stages and under successively stronger criteria. First the last name of each author on the ISI file was matched to the last name of the faculty list, independent of the faculty member's program and institution. Next the Zip Codes of the addresses on the ISI file and the institution of the faculty member were matched using a criterion for area Zip Codes that allowed authors to use an address near their home institution. Finally each journal was assigned an area identifier to be matched against the field of the program faculty. The result of this matching was the identification of approximately 1 million publications that could be credited to the program faculty in the study. The number of publications for each faculty member was then tabulated and the number of citations counted from the citation file. The data for the purpose of this study were aggregated to the program level, but are still available at the individual level for detailed analysis.

FEDERAL RESEARCH SUPPORT

One measure of the research activity for a program is the amount of federal research support that can be attributed to its program faculty. By matching the names of principal investigators on federal grants with the faculty for each program, it is possible to calculate measures such as the amount of grant support and the proportion of the faculty receiving support. While this analysis of research support does not take into consideration funds from private foundations and industry, it does provide information that can be used to compare one program with another.

The primary federal agencies that provide research support for faculty at U.S. universities are the National Science Foundation, the National Institutes of Health, the Department of Defense, the National Endowment for the Humanities, the Department of Energy, the Department of Agriculture, and the National Aeronautics and Space Administration. Analyzing funding for the agencies in the population was complicated by the inclusion of support for instrumentation and facilities as part of a research award. This type of funding, if not specified by a particular category, could not be identified without an examination of each award. Thus the study used the overall funding figure, assuming that development funds of this type have an overall positive benefit to the research program and provide some indication of the research level of the program.

Data files—mainly in computer form—were obtained from each of the above agencies. The amount of grant support for a program was obtained by matching the names of the principal investigator and co-principal investigator, when available, against the program faculty file. The match was made on a last name-first initial basis by computer, using institutional names and a research field to identify faculty for the large NSF and NIH files. For the other files a preliminary match was made using last name and first initial only and a hand match was then done using the institution and area of research. The data available from these matches include the amount of each award, the duration of the award, and the agency supporting the research.

SURVEY OF EARNED DOCTORATES (SED)

The Survey of Earned Doctorates (SED) has collected basic statistics from the universe of doctorate recipients in the United States since the 1920s. Beginning in 1958, SED has been conducted by the National Academy of Sciences/National Research Council and is currently supported by five federal agencies: the National Science Foundation, the U.S. Department of Education, the National Center for Education Statistics, the National Endowment for the Humanities, the Department of Agriculture, and the National Institutes of Health.

Administered annually, SED produces national-level data. The survey form contains 25 questions that obtain information on sex, race/ethnicity, marital status, citizenship, disabilities, dependents, specialty field of doctorate, educational institutions attended, time spent in completion of doctorate, financial support, educational debt, post-graduation plans, and educational attainment of parents of each person who receives a doctorate. These data were compiled and placed in a file called the Doctorate Records File (DRF).

The survey universe is a complete census of all regionally accredited universities in the United States and its territories that confer research doctorates. In 1992, there were 366 such institutions. Approximately 95 percent or more of the annual cohorts of doctoral recipients respond to the survey. Response rates are further delineated by science and/or engineering (S&E) field. In 1991, these varied from 91 percent to 98 percent across science and engineering fields.

To use the SED data for the Research-Doctorate Study, a crosswalk was developed among the 41 fields in the study and the SED Specialties List, the doctorate fields into which graduates classify themselves. Using this crosswalk the number of graduates and the characteristics of the graduates for each of the 3,634 programs in the study were determined. One problem with this procedure is the possibility of incorrect identification of degree field by the graduate. However, this survey is considered to be the most accurate of its type, and the level of this error is small and needs to be taken into consideration only when the number of responses in a particular cell is small. While some characteristics of the graduates, such as the number of portable fellowships held by program graduates were considered to be particularly interesting for the study, the data were considered to be unreliable and were not used. In general the data file is the DRF is extensive and only a fraction of these data were used in the research-doctorate analysis.

HONORS AND AWARDS

The accomplishments of an individual faculty member are often recognized by independent groups, such as foundations and governmental agencies which award competitive fellowships or peer-reviewed research grants, and the national academies and other honorific organizations which confer membership on the basis of academic distinction. One measure of the quality of a program's faculty can be derived by identifying the number of faculty members who have received such awards. In future studies of this kind, it should be possible to assemble lists of the major fellowships, residencies, and academic honors pertinent to each of the five broad subject areas, and to derive one indicator of faculty quality from such lists. Owing to constraints of both time and resources, the authors of the present study have not

Awards, Fellowships and Honors
Organization List

Nobel Prize	MacArthur Awards
John Simon Guggenheim Fellowship	Alexander von Humbolt Fellowship
Fulbright Awards	National Endowment for the Humanities Fellowships
American Council of Learned Societies Fellowships	American Antiquarian Society Fellowships
Huntington Library Research Fellowships	Newberry Library Fellowships
American School of Classical Studies in Athens Fellowships	Folger Library Post Doctoral Fellowships
Residency at the Center for Advance Study in the Behavioral Sciences	Residency at the Institute for Advance Study
Residency at the National Humanities Center	Residency at the Center for the Advance Study in the Visual Arts
Residency at the Getty Center for Humanities and Arts	Residency at the Woodrow Wilson Center for Scholars
American Academy of Arts and Sciences	American Philosophical Society
American Academy at Rome	

been able to make comprehensive use of such data. However, since the Arts and Humanities Citation Index has been judged inadequate to provide a fair measure of scholarly productivity in these fields, in this study data on Honors and Awards have been preferred instead, and so have been substituted from scholarly publication as one measure of quality in the Humanities.

INSTITUTIONAL DATA SOURCES

Three data sources were used to generate institutional statistics on research activity: library data from the professional library associations, R&D expenditures from the National Science Foundation, and fall undergraduate and graduate enrollment data from the U.S. Department of Education.

Association of Research Libraries
Association of Colleges and Research Libraries

The Association of Research Libraries (ARL) collects data on an annual basis from its 113 member libraries. Ninety-five of these are institutions in the U.S. with graduate programs. Data are collected on volumes held (excluding microfilm, uncatalogued government material, and audio-visual materials), current serials held, volumes added and withdrawn, and microfilm and government documents. They also collect data on the size of the library staff, the expenditure for staff and materials, the number of interlibrary loans, and the size of the faculty and the student body. These data are made available through an annual report, *ARL Statistics*. In addition to the data collected by ARL on its member institutions, a survey is conducted by the Association of Colleges and Research Libraries (ACRL) on an additional 110 U.S. libraries. The Research-Doctorate Study used the data from ARL and ACRL, supplemented by Department of Education data for institutions not surveyed by the library organizations, to measure the size of institutional libraries through the number of volumes and serials in each library, and its level of activity and support services through the amount of annual expenditures.

National Science Foundation

NSF conducts an annual survey on research and development expenditures from a sample of 459 institutions of higher education in the United States. In 1992 the sample was generated from the universe of 595 schools that grant a graduate science or engineering degree and/or received at least $50,000 funded from separately budgeted R&D expenditures. This is a very carefully conducted survey with attention given to the recordkeeping process at the institution to ensure consistency from one year to the next. Several items on R&D expenditures are contained in the survey, including allocation of amounts to major subdisciplines and purchases of research equipment. The two main data elements used for the Research-Doctorate Study are the total R&D expenditure and the Federal R&D expenditure. Other data elements are included in the institutional file and can be used by researchers to compare institutional and program characteristics.

U. S. Department of Education

The Integrated Postsecondary Education Data System (IPEDS) consists of several integrated components that obtain information on types of postsecondary institutions, student participants, programs offered and completed, and the human and financial resources involved in the delivery of postsecondary education. The IPEDS Fall Enrollment Survey replaces and extends the previous Higher Education General Information Survey, "Fall Enrollment and Compliance Report of Institutions of Higher Education." The IPEDS Fall Enrollment Survey has two versions designated EF1 and EF2, which are administered to a census of accredited institutions offering degrees at the bachelor's level and above (EF1 survey) and all two-year institutions (EF2 survey). These surveys are conducted annually and are completed by institutional administrators who provide total enrollments and broad field enrollments. For the Research-Doctorate Study the institutional enrollment data were used to compare undergraduate and graduate enrollment as a measure of graduate activity.

APPENDIX H

Faculty Quality Ratings of Research-Doctorate Programs

Respondents to the National Survey of Graduate Faculty rated the "Scholarly Quality of Program Faculty" for each program included in the survey. For purposes of analysis, scores were converted to a scale of 0 to 5, with 0 denoting "Not sufficient for doctoral education" and 5 denoting "Distinguished." Ratings for each program were summed and an average rating computed, as described in Appendix F. In the pages that follow, mean ratings of program faculty in the 41 fields included in the study are reported by broad field and by institution. The first line for each program is the raw score. In the next line, a standardized score is given (in italic) and the program's ranking (in parenthesis) within a field. Standardized scores have been computed from the raw value of mean ratings for all programs in a field. A mean score of 50 represents the middle of the range of scores for that field. One standard deviation around the middle scores represents plus/minus 10 points. Program rankings are drawn from information in Appendixes J through N.

Appendix Table H - 1 Faculty Quality Ratings of Research-Doctorate Programs in Arts and Humanities

Institution	Art History	Classics	Comp Literature	English L & L	French L & L	German L & L	Linguistics	Music	Philosophy	Religion	Spanish L & L
University of Alabama				2.38				2.02			
				47 (79)				*36* (61)			
Andrews University										1.86	
										35 (35)	
Arizona State University				2.38							2.58
				47 (79)							*44* (38)
University of Arizona			2.32	2.81			3.58	2.87	3.99		
			42 (36)	*51* (58)			*56* (12.5)	*47* (39)	*62* (11)		
Univ of Arkansas-Fayetteville				1.47							
				37 (116)							
Auburn University				2.08							
				44 (92.5)							
Ball State University				1.49				2.06			
				38 (115)				*37* (60)			
Baylor University				1.19						2.50	
				35 (119)						*42* (31)	
Boston College				2.72					2.05	3.42	
				50 (65)					*42* (57)	*53* (17)	
Boston University	2.85	2.31		3.20			2.60	2.48	3.12	2.93	2.12
	47 (24.5)	*40* (26)		*55* (38)			*46* (28.5)	*42* (50)	*53* (29)	*47* (22)	*37* (49)
Bowling Green State University				1.82							
				41 (100)							
Brandeis University				3.09				3.85			
				54 (44)				*59* (13)			
Brown University	3.20	4.10	2.98	3.99	3.07		2.94	2.73	3.82	3.55	3.83
	51 (18)	*59* (6)	*49* (20)	*63* (14)	*50* (21)		*50* (20)	*45* (44)	*60* (13.5)	*55* (15)	*64* (3)
Bryn Mawr College	3.28	3.48									
	52 (17)	*52* (14)									
University of California-Berkeley	4.67	4.77	4.00	4.77	4.19	4.32	3.97	4.51	4.66		3.70
	67 (3)	*66* (2)	*61* (10)	*71* (2)	*64* (7)	*65* (1)	*60* (6.5)	*68* (3)	*69* (4)		*62* (9)

Institution	Art History	Classics	Comp Literature	English L & L	French L & L	German L & L	Linguistics	Music	Philosophy	Religion	Spanish L & L
University of California-Davis			2.23	3.04	2.82	2.90					3.43
			40 (38)	*53* (47.5)	*47* (28)	*46* (23)					*58* (14)
University of California-Irvine			4.06	3.95	3.78	3.28			3.30		3.41
			62 (8)	*63* (15)	*58* (10)	*52* (14.5)			*55* (21)		*57* (15)
Univ of California-Los Angeles	3.52	3.89	3.22	4.10	3.13	2.94	4.56	3.56	4.42		3.37
	54 (13)	*57* (9)	*52* (16)	*64* (12)	*50* (18.5)	*47* (22)	*67* (3)	*56* (18)	*67* (6)		*57* (16)
Univ of California-Riverside			2.66	3.27					2.57		
			46 (26)	*56* (34.5)					*47* (39)		
Univ of California-San Diego			3.17	3.21			3.43	3.32	3.79		3.27
			52 (18)	*55* (37)			*55* (14)	*53* (25)	*60* (15)		*55* (18.5)
Univ of California-Santa Barbara	2.98	2.59		3.27		2.77		3.41	2.46	3.82	3.23
	48 (21)	*43* (22)		*56* (34.5)		*45* (24)		*54* (23.5)	*46* (42)	*58* (9)	*54* (20.5)
Univ of California-Santa Cruz				3.10			3.66				
				54 (43)			*57* (10)				
Carnegie Mellon University				2.97					2.31		
				53 (51.5)					*44* (47.5)		
Case Western Reserve Univ	1.79			2.11				2.52			
	35 (37)			*44* (90.5)				*42* (48)			
Catholic University of America		0.93	1.60	1.14	1.13			2.78	2.16	2.90	2.06
		25 (29)	*33* (43)	*34* (121)	*26* (45)			*46* (43)	*43* (53)	*47* (24)	*36* (52)
University of Chicago	3.74	4.00	3.56	4.41	3.30		3.97	4.53	3.88	4.76	2.32
	57 (10)	*58* (7)	*56* (12)	*68* (10)	*52* (16)		*60* (6.5)	*68* (2)	*61* (12)	*69* (1)	*40* (42)
University of Cincinnati		2.10		1.66	1.66	1.99		3.02	1.56		
		37 (27)		*39* (109)	*32* (44)	*34* (29)		*49* (34)	*37* (67)		
CUNY - Grad Sch & Univ Center	3.60		2.18	3.78	3.48		3.41	4.41	3.45		3.27
	55 (12)		*40* (40)	*61* (18.5)	*55* (14)		*55* (15)	*66* (4)	*56* (19)		*55* (18.5)
Claremont Graduate School				2.31				2.23	1.10	3.02	
				46 (81.5)				*39* (56)	*32* (72)	*48* (20.5)	
University of Colorado				2.97			2.15	2.36			2.59
				53 (51.5)			*41* (33)	*40* (53)			*44* (36.5)
Columbia University	4.79	3.86	4.44	4.47	4.40			4.05	3.15	3.57	4.31
	69 (1.5)	*56* (10)	*67* (3)	*68* (8.5)	*66* (4)			*62* (11.5)	*53* (27)	*55* (14)	*72* (1)

Appendix Table H - 1 Arts and Humanities (Continued)

Institution	Art History	Classics	Comp Literature	English L & L	French L & L	German L & L	Linguistics	Music	Philosophy	Religion	Spanish L & L
University of Connecticut			1.93	2.31			3.36				2.13
			37 (42)	*46* (81.5)			*54* (16)				*37* (48)
Cornell University	2.87	3.73	4.31	4.49	4.08	4.19	3.78	4.05	4.11		3.73
	47 (23)	*55* (12)	*65* (6)	*68* (7)	*62* (8)	*64* (3)	*58* (9)	*62* (11.5)	*63* (9)		*62* (8)
University of Delaware	3.40						2.60				
	53 (15)						*46* (28.5)				
University of Denver				1.67						2.65	
				39 (108)						*44* (29)	
Drew University				0.84						3.02	
				31 (124)						*48* (20.5)	
Duke University		3.37	4.51	4.55	4.43			3.42	2.37	4.25	3.87
		51 (15)	*67* (2)	*69* (5.5)	*66* (3)			*54* (22)	*45* (44)	*63* (4)	*65* (2)
Duquesne University									1.29	1.83	
									34 (71)	*34* (36)	
Emory University			2.72	3.33	3.38				2.54	4.05	
			46 (24)	*56* (30.5)	*53* (15)				*47* (40)	*61* (5)	
Florida State University	2.10			2.23				3.26	1.95		2.08
	38 (36)			*45* (85)				*52* (27)	*41* (58)		*36* (50.5)
University of Florida				3.19	2.41		1.78				2.15
				55 (39)	*42* (36.5)		*38* (37)				*37* (47)
Fordham University		1.83		1.64					1.81	2.73	
		34 (28)		*39* (111)					*39* (64)	*45* (28)	
Fuller Theological Seminary										1.74	
										33 (37)	
George Washington University				2.38							
				47 (79)							
Georgetown University						2.15	3.00		2.51		2.92
						36 (28)	*50* (19)		*47* (41)		*50* (30)
University of Georgia	0.90			2.91				2.45	1.86		2.08
	24 (38)			*52* (54)				*41* (51)	*40* (61.5)		*36* (50.5)
University of Hartford								2.44			
								41 (52)			

Institution	Art History	Classics	Comp Literature	English L & L	French L & L	German L & L	Linguistics	Music	Philosophy	Religion	Spanish L & L
Harvard University	4.49	4.79	4.37	4.77	3.19	4.01	2.92	4.59	4.69	4.73	3.63
	65 (4)	*66* (1)	*66* (4)	*71* (2)	*51* (17)	*61* (4)	*49* (21)	*69* (1)	*69* (3)	*69* (2)	*61* (10)
University of Hawaii at Manoa							2.79		1.78		
							48 (25)		*39* (65)		
Hebrew Union College										3.71	
										57 (13)	
University of Houston				2.15							
				44 (88)							
Howard University				1.60							
				39 (112)							
Idaho State University				0.72							
				30 (126)							
Illinois State University				1.72							
				40 (104)							
U of Illinois at Urbana-Champaign	2.67	3.02	2.39	3.38	2.70	3.11	3.10	4.11	2.77		3.22
	45 (26)	*47* (17)	*42* (33)	*57* (28)	*45* (30.5)	*49* (20)	*51* (18)	*63* (10)	*49* (36)		*54* (22)
University of Illinois at Chicago				2.75					3.51		
				51 (64)					*57* (18)		
Indiana University	2.85		3.08	3.78	2.89	3.28	2.66	3.47	3.11		3.23
	47 (24.5)		*50* (19)	*61* (18.5)	*47* (25)	*52* (14.5)	*47* (27)	*54* (20)	*53* (30)		*54* (20.5)
Indiana Univ of Pennsylvania				0.89			0.55				
				31 (123)			*25* (41)				
University of Iowa			2.48	3.07	2.88			3.31	2.23	2.83	
			43 (30)	*54* (45)	*47* (26.5)			*52* (26)	*44* (51)	*46* (26.5)	
Jewish Theological Seminary										3.74	
										57 (10.5)	
Johns Hopkins University	3.93	2.52	4.18	4.33	3.13	3.75			3.03		
	59 (7)	*42* (23)	*63* (7)	*67* (11)	*50* (18.5)	*58* (9)			*52* (31)		
University of Kansas	2.56			2.65	2.12		1.91	2.65	2.10		3.60
	43 (27)			*49* (69)	*38* (42)		*39* (34.5)	*44* (46)	*42* (54)		*60* (11)
Kent State University				2.08				2.20			
				44 (92.5)				*38* (58)			

Appendix Table H - 1 Arts and Humanities (Continued)

Institution	Art History	Classics	Comp Literature	English L & L	French L & L	German L & L	Linguistics	Music	Philosophy	Religion	Spanish L & L
University of Kentucky				3.04				2.33	1.59		2.94
				54 (47.5)				*40* (54)	*37* (66)		*50* (29)
Lehigh University				1.56							
				38 (114)							
Louisiana State U & A&M College				2.80	3.08			2.81			
				51 (60)	*50* (20)			*46* (41)			
Loyola University of Chicago				2.11					2.28		
				44 (90.5)					*44* (49)		
University of Maryland College Park	2.53		2.21	3.18	2.18			2.95	2.86		2.84
	43 (28)		*40* (39)	*55* (40.5)	*39* (41)			*48* (35)	*50* (35)		*48* (32)
Massachusetts Inst of Technology							4.79		4.01		
							69 (1)		*62* (10)		
U of Massachusetts at Amherst			2.35	3.18	2.39	3.18	4.44		3.44		2.63
			42 (35)	*55* (40.5)	*41* (38)	*50* (19)	*65* (4)		*56* (20)		*45* (34)
Miami University				2.49							
				48 (75)							
University of Miami				2.57				2.79	2.22		
				49 (71)				*46* (42)	*43* (52)		
Michigan State University				2.80	2.33		1.76	2.69	1.91		2.59
				51 (60)	*41* (39)		*37* (38)	*45* (45)	*40* (59.5)		*44* (36.5)
University of Michigan	3.71	4.54	3.23	3.93	3.97	3.04	2.37	4.16	4.15		3.46
	56 (11)	*64* (3)	*52* (15)	*63* (16)	*61* (9)	*48* (21)	*44* (31)	*63* (9)	*64* (8)		*58* (13)
Middle Tennessee State University				0.61							
				29 (127)							
University of Minnesota	2.47	2.43	2.53	3.24	2.88	3.68		3.16	3.01		3.06
	42 (30)	*41* (24)	*44* (28)	*56* (36)	*47* (26.5)	*57* (11)		*51* (30.5)	*52* (32)		*52* (27.5)
University of Mississippi				1.95							
				42 (96)							
University of Missouri-Columbia				2.80							2.17
				51 (60)							*38* (46)
Univ of Missouri-Kansas City								1.40			
								28 (65)			

Institution	Art History	Classics	Comp Literature	English L & L	French L & L	German L & L	Linguistics	Music	Philosophy	Religion	Spanish L & L
University of Nebraska-Lincoln				2.53					2.07		
				48 (74)					*42* (56)		
University of New Hampshire				2.55							
				48 (73)							
New Orleans Baptist Theo Seminary										1.24	
										27 (38)	
New York University	4.79	2.33	3.49	3.77	3.66	2.37	1.84	3.53			3.19
	69 (1.5)	*40* (25)	*55* (13)	*61* (20)	*57* (12)	*39* (26)	*38* (36)	*55* (19)			*54* (23)
U of North Carolina-Chapel Hill	2.33	3.81	2.44	3.43	2.63	3.21		3.72	3.67		2.91
	41 (32)	*56* (11)	*43* (32)	*58* (24)	*44* (34)	*51* (18)		*58* (16)	*59* (17)		*49* (31)
U of North Carolina-Greensboro				1.94							
				42 (97)							
University of North Dakota				1.24							
				35 (118)							
University of North Texas				2.05				3.43			
				43 (94)				*54* (21)			
University of Northern Colorado								1.86			
								34 (63)			
Northern Illinois University				1.87							
				41 (98)							
Northwestern University	3.83		3.20	3.37	2.71			3.41	3.18	2.91	
	58 (8)		*52* (17)	*57* (29)	*45* (29)			*54* (23.5)	*54* (25)	*47* (23)	
University of Notre Dame				2.78					3.69	3.73	
				51 (63)					*59* (16)	*57* (12)	
Ohio State University	2.48	2.60		3.28	2.70	3.25	3.80	3.23	3.21		2.83
	42 (29)	*43* (21)		*56* (33)	*45* (30.5)	*51* (17)	*59* (8)	*52* (28)	*54* (24)		*48* (33)
Ohio University				1.69							
				40 (106)							
Oklahoma State University				1.13							
				34 (122)							
University of Oklahoma				2.25				1.84			
				45 (84)				*34* (64)			

Appendix Table H - 1 Arts and Humanities (Continued)

Institution	Art History	Classics	Comp Literature	English L & L	French L & L	German L & L	Linguistics	Music	Philosophy	Religion	Spanish L & L
University of Oregon			2.10	2.71	1.92		2.68	2.55	1.52		
			39 (41)	*50* (66)	*36* (43)		*47* (26)	*43* (47)	*36* (68)		
Pennsylvania State University	2.28		2.65	3.14	2.66	2.31			2.09		3.12
	40 (34)		*45* (27)	*54* (42)	*45* (33)	*39* (27)			*42* (55)		*53* (24.5)
University of Pennsylvania	3.80	3.62	3.99	4.47	4.37	3.26	4.16	4.35	3.15	3.74	3.75
	57 (9)	*54* (13)	*61* (11)	*68* (8.5)	*66* (5)	*51* (16)	*62* (5)	*66* (7)	*53* (27)	*57* (10.5)	*63* (6)
University of Pittsburgh	2.90			3.40	2.21	1.89	2.83	2.83	4.73	2.15	3.11
	47 (22)			*57* (26.5)	*39* (40)	*33* (30)	*49* (23)	*46* (40)	*70* (2)	*38* (33)	*53* (26)
									4.47 [a]		
									67 (5)		
Princeton Theological Seminary										3.84	
										58 (8)	
Princeton University	4.04	4.16	4.32	4.05	4.55	4.22		4.39	4.93	4.33	3.80
	60 (6)	*60* (4)	*65* (5)	*64* (13)	*68* (2)	*64* (2)		*66* (6)	*72* (1)	*64* (3)	*63* (4)
Univ of Puerto Rico-Rio Piedras											3.12
											53 (24.5)
Purdue University				2.83							
				51 (57)							
University of Rhode Island				1.80							
				41 (102)							
Rice University				2.95	2.68		1.72		2.72	2.56	
				53 (53)	*45* (32)		*37* (39)		*49* (37)	*43* (30)	
University of Rochester			2.47	3.05				4.24	2.95		
			43 (31)	*54* (46)				*64* (8)	*51* (33)		
Rutgers State Univ-New Brunswick	3.04		2.92	3.92	3.03	1.69		3.16	3.82		2.61
	49 (20)		*49* (22)	*63* (17)	*49* (22)	*30* (32)		*51* (30.5)	*60* (13.5)		*45* (35)
St. John's University				1.14							
				34 (121)							
Saint Louis University				2.56					1.84		
				49 (72)					*39* (63)		
University of South Carolina			1.55	2.90			1.91	2.13			
			32 (44)	*52* (55)			*39* (34.5)	*38* (59)			

Institution	Art History	Classics	Comp Literature	English L & L	French L & L	German L & L	Linguistics	Music	Philosophy	Religion	Spanish L & L
University of South Florida				1.38							
				37 (117)							
Southern Baptist Theological Sem								1.95		1.96	
								35 (62)		*36* (34)	
University of Southern California			2.86	3.41			3.58	2.91	2.89	2.49	
			48 (23)	*57* (25)			*56* (12.5)	*47* (36.5)	*51* (34)	*42* (32)	
Southern Illinois University				1.64					1.41		
				39 (111)					*35* (69)		
Southern Methodist University										3.53	
										55 (16)	
Univ of Southern Mississippi				2.19							
				45 (86.5)							
Univ of Southwestern Louisiana				1.69							
				40 (106)							
Stanford University	3.49	3.32	4.05	4.55	4.20	3.83	4.59	3.79	4.20	3.05	3.30
	54 (14)	*50* (16)	*62* (9)	*69* (5.5)	*64* (6)	*59* (6)	*67* (2)	*59* (15)	*64* (7)	*49* (19)	*56* (17)
State Univ of New York-Albany						2.59					2.29
						42 (25)					*40* (43)
State Univ of New York-Binghamton			2.36	2.67							
			42 (34)	*50* (67)							
State Univ of New York-Buffalo				3.40		1.80	2.87	2.91	2.24		2.43
				57 (26.5)		*32* (31)	*49* (22)	*47* (36.5)	*44* (50)		*42* (39)
State U of New York-Stony Brook			2.49	3.03			2.82	3.80	2.33		2.33
			44 (29)	*53* (49)			*49* (24)	*59* (14)	*45* (46)		*40* (41)
Syracuse University				2.47					3.28	2.83	2.18
				48 (76)					*55* (22.5)	*46* (26.5)	*38* (45)
Temple University				2.79				2.90	2.31	2.84	1.83
				51 (62)				*47* (38)	*44* (47.5)	*46* (25)	*32* (53)
University of Tennessee-Knoxville				2.66					1.32		
				50 (68)					*34* (70)		
Texas A&M University				2.89							
				52 (56)							

Appendix Table H - 1 Arts and Humanities (Continued)

Institution	Art History	Classics	Comp Literature	English L & L	French L & L	German L & L	Linguistics	Music	Philosophy	Religion	Spanish L & L
Texas Christian University				2.13							
				44 (89)							
Texas Tech University				1.67				2.22			1.80
				39 (108)				*39* (57)			*32* (54)
University of Texas at Arlington				1.83			1.26				
				41 (99)			*32* (40)				
University of Texas at Austin	3.17	3.92	2.96	3.54	2.97	3.40	3.61	3.69	3.15		3.54
	50 (19)	*57* (8)	*49* (21)	*59* (21)	*49* (23)	*53* (13)	*57* (11)	*57* (17)	*53* (27)		*59* (12)
University of Texas at Dallas				1.81							
				41 (101)							
Texas Woman's University				0.80							
				31 (125)							
University of Toledo				1.74							
				40 (103)							
Tufts University				2.64							
				49 (70)							
Tulane University				2.26	2.41				1.86		2.34
				45 (83)	*42* (36.5)				*40* (61.5)		*40* (40)
University of Tulsa				2.02							
				43 (95)							
Union Theological Seminary in VA										3.08	
										49 (18)	
Vanderbilt University				3.33					2.61	3.85	
				56 (30.5)					*48* (38)	*58* (7)	
University of Virginia	3.31	2.98		4.58	3.60	3.77			2.38	3.96	3.76
	52 (16)	*47* (18)		*69* (4)	*56* (13)	*58* (8)			*45* (43)	*60* (6)	*63* (5)
Washington State University				2.19							
				45 (86.5)							
Washington University	2.31		2.70	3.02	2.93	3.81		3.08	2.35		3.06
	40 (33)		*46* (25)	*53* (50)	*48* (24)	*59* (7)		*50* (33)	*45* (45)		*52* (27.5)
University of Washington	2.39	2.89	3.37	3.48	2.60	3.60	3.16	3.22			2.25
	41 (31)	*46* (20)	*54* (14)	*58* (23)	*44* (35)	*56* (12)	*52* (17)	*51* (29)			*39* (44)

Institution	Art History	Classics	Comp Literature	English L & L	French L & L	German L & L	Linguistics	Music	Philosophy	Religion	Spanish L & L
Wayne State University				2.39							
				47 (77)							
Wesleyan University								2.50			
								42 (49)			
West Virginia University				1.58				2.27			
				39 (113)				*39* (55)			
University of Wisconsin-Madison	2.14	2.92	2.25	3.53	3.74	3.74	2.20	3.13	3.28		3.74
	39 (35)	*46* (19)	*41* (37)	*59* (22)	*58* (11)	*58* (10)	*42* (32)	*50* (32)	*55* (22.5)		*63* (7)
University of Wisconsin-Milwaukee				3.31							
				56 (32)							
Yale University	4.44	4.12	4.70	4.77	4.68	3.95	2.57	4.40	1.91		
	65 (5)	*59* (5)	*70* (1)	*71* (2)	*69* (1)	*60* (5)	*46* (30)	*66* (5)	*40* (59.5)		

Source: National Survey of Graduate Faculty

Note: *a* Program in the History and Philosophy of Science

Appendix Table H - 2 Faculty Quality Ratings of Research-Doctorate Programs in Biological Sciences

Institution	Biochem & Molec Bio	Cell & Develop Bio	Eco, Evl & Behavior	Molec & Gen Genetics	Neuro-sciencs	Pharma-cology	Physiology
University of Alabama	1.48		2.57				
	39 (170)		46 (84.5)				
University of Alabama-Birmingham	3.34	3.31	1.68	3.15		3.04	3.81
	57 (49.5)	57 (48.5)	36 (119)	53 (45)		49 (77)	60 (20.5)
University of Alaska	0.15		2.83				2.43
	26 (194)		49 (68.5)				45 (102)
Albany Medical College	2.28	2.59		2.13	2.08	3.04	3.34
	47 (122)	50 (94)		43 (78)	43 (77.5)	49 (77)	55 (44)
Albert Einstein College of Med	3.79	3.76		3.53	3.57	3.59	3.88
	61 (28)	61 (26)		56 (25)	56 (26.5)	57 (30)	61 (17)
Arizona State University	2.47	2.52	3.41	2.50			3.13
	49 (106)	49 (101)	56 (34)	47 (71)			53 (65)
University of Arizona	3.23	3.00	3.80	3.32	3.20	3.71	3.69
	56 (57.5)	54 (63)	61 (21)	54 (34)	53 (47)	59 (22)	59 (23.5)
Univ of Arkansas-Fayetteville	2.30	0.60	2.12				
	47 (121)	30 (175)	41 (108)				
U of Arkansas for Medical Sci	2.38	1.68					
	48 (114)	41 (146)					
Auburn University		1.38 [a]					2.38
		38 (161)					44 (105)
		1.50 [d]					
		39 (157)					
Ball State University	1.33						
	38 (176)						
Baylor College of Medicine	4.04	3.80		4.07	3.75	3.36	4.21
	64 (19)	61 (24)		61 (14)	58 (19.5)	54 (44.5)	65 (5.5)
Boston University	0.53 [a]	1.69	2.54	1.05	0.67		2.96
	30 (187)	41 (145)	46 (88)	33 (96)	31 (98)		51 (76.5)
	2.78 [b]						
	52 (82)						
Bowling Green State University	1.83	1.00	2.40	0.69			1.50
	43 (150)	34 (166)	44 (94)	30 (99)			35 (128)
Brandeis University	4.06	3.73		3.48	3.75		
	64 (17)	61 (28)		56 (27)	58 (19.5)		
Brigham Young University	1.79	2.20	2.14				
	42 (152)	46 (125)	41 (106)				
Brown University	3.09	3.08	3.30		2.98	3.17	3.02
	55 (62)	54 (59)	55 (44)		51 (54)	51 (60.5)	52 (69.5)
California Institute Technology	4.57	4.73	2.35	4.51	4.30		3.98
	69 (7)	70 (4)	44 (99)	65 (4)	63 (10.5)		62 (13)

Appendix Table H - 2 Biological Sciences (Continued)

Institution	Biochem & Molec Bio	Cell & Develop Bio	Eco, Evl & Behavior	Molec & Gen Genetics	Neuro-sciencs	Pharma-cology	Physiology
University of California-Berkeley	4.81	4.16	4.29	4.21	4.32		
	71 (4)	*65* (13)	*67* (8)	*63* (10)	*63* (9)		
University of California-Davis	3.52	3.55	4.42	3.21		3.51	3.64
	59 (35)	*59* (33)	*68* (5)	*53* (42.5)		*56* (35)	*59* (28)
University of California-Irvine	3.31	3.44	3.77	3.09	3.38 [b]	3.04	3.05
	57 (53)	*58* (39)	*61* (22)	*52* (47.5)	*55* (39)	*49* (77)	*52* (68)
					3.72 [a]		
					58 (21)		
Univ of California-Los Angeles	4.20	3.99	3.82		3.91	3.40	4.23
	65 (14)	*63* (17)	*61* (18.5)		*59* (15)	*54* (41)	*65* (4)
Univ of California-Riverside	2.96	2.87	3.60	3.17			1.50
	53 (69)	*52* (75)	*59* (26)	*53* (44)			*35* (128)
Univ of California-San Diego	4.53	4.50	3.82	4.44	4.82	4.36	4.47
	69 (9)	*68* (7)	*61* (18.5)	*65* (6)	*68* (1)	*69* (3)	*68* (2)
Univ of California-San Francisco	4.84	4.76		4.87	4.66		4.21
	72 (1)	*71* (3)		*69* (2)	*66* (4)		*65* (5.5)
Univ of California-Santa Barbara	3.23	2.67	3.81	3.09	0.84	2.13	0.80
	56 (57.5)	*50* (87)	*61* (20)	*52* (47.5)	*32* (95)	*35* (119)	*27* (137)
Univ of California-Santa Cruz	3.33	2.60	2.93	2.97	0.89	0.25	1.69
	57 (51.5)	*50* (92)	*51* (63)	*51* (55.5)	*33* (94)	*6* (127)	*37* (121)
Carnegie Mellon University	3.45						
	58 (41)						
Case Western Reserve Univ	3.35	3.38		3.22	3.83	2.94	3.55
	57 (48)	*57* (42)		*53* (40.5)	*59* (16.5)	*47* (87)	58 (32.5)
Catholic University of America	0.93	1.50					
	34 (181)	*39* (157)					
University of Chicago	3.89	4.10	4.51	4.17	3.63	3.64	4.00
	62 (23.5)	*64* (15)	*69* (1.5)	*62* (11)	*57* (22)	*58* (26)	*63* (11)
University of Cincinnati	2.81	2.68	2.11	2.97		3.34	3.17
	52 (80)	*50* (85)	*41* (109)	*51* (55.5)		*53* (47)	*53* (62.5)
CUNY - Grad Sch & Univ Center	2.51	2.30	2.87		2.43		
	49 (102)	*47* (118)	*50* (65.5)		*46* (70)		
Claremont Graduate School			2.54				
			46 (88)				
Clark Atlanta University	1.08	0.72					
	35 (180)	*31* (173)					
Clark University	*0.56*	1.43	1.20	0.30	0.72		
	30 (186)	*38* (160)	*30* (125)	*26* (101)	*31* (96.5)		
Clemson University	1.41	2.14	2.61	1.45		2.40	2.15
	39 (175)	*45* (126)	*47* (80)	*37* (91)		*39* (110)	*42* (112)
Colorado State University	2.67	2.72	2.99		3.25		3.38
	51 (91.5)	*51* (82.5)	*51* (58)		*54* (45)		*56* (40)

Appendix Table H - 2 Biological Sciences (Continued)

Institution	Biochem & Molec Bio	Cell & Develop Bio	Eco, Evl & Behavior	Molec & Gen Genetics	Neuro-sciencs	Pharma-cology	Physiology
University of Colorado	4.26	2.93 [a]	3.46	3.07	3.40	3.81	2.73
	66 (12)	*53* (69.5)	*57* (31.5)	*52* (50)	*55* (38)	*61* (17.5)	*48* (90.5)
		3.85 [b]					
		62 (22)					
Columbia University	4.38	3.94		4.14	4.58	3.65	4.19
	67 (10.5)	*63* (19)		*62* (12)	*65* (6)	*58* (24.5)	*65* (9.5)
University of Connecticut	2.90	2.48	3.35	2.88	2.89 [b]	2.82 [e]	3.22
	53 (73)	*48* (103)	*56* (40)	*50* (59)	*50* (58)	*45* (94)	*54* (56.5)
					3.14 [a]	3.06 [b]	
					53 (48)	*49* (73)	
Cornell University	3.91	3.53	4.44	3.68	3.59	3.12 [d]	3.59
	63 (22)	*59* (35.5)	*68* (4)	*58* (23)	*57* (24)	*50* (65)	*58* (31)
						3.33 [f]	
						53 (48.5)	
Creighton University	1.74	2.00					
	42 (157)	*44* (132)					
Dartmouth College	3.02		2.65			3.24	3.61
	54 (67)		*47* (77)			*52* (56)	*58* (30)
University of Dayton		0.93	1.16				
		33 (169)	*30* (127)				
University of Delaware	2.78						
	52 (82)						
Drexel University	1.46	0.81	1.83	0.93			
	39 (173)	*32* (171)	*38* (116)	*32* (97)			
Duke University	4.18	4.11	4.49	4.01	3.83	4.18	3.67
	65 (15)	*64* (14)	*69* (3)	*61* (15)	*59* (16.5)	*66* (5)	*59* (26.5)
East Carolina U Sch Medicine	2.00	1.67			1.21	2.58	1.82
	44 (140)	*40* (148)			*35* (90)	*42* (101)	*38* (118)
Emory University	2.86	3.20		3.34	3.45	3.83	3.71
	53 (76)	*56* (52.5)		*55* (32.5)	*55* (33)	*61* (15)	*59* (22)
Florida State University	2.35	2.27	3.41	2.00	2.70		2.75
	48 (116)	*46* (120)	*56* (34)	*42* (81.5)	*49* (63)		*49* (88.5)
University of Florida	2.88	2.77	3.57	3.07	2.84	3.32	3.21
	53 (74)	*51* (78)	*58* (28)	*52* (50)	*50* (60)	*53* (50.5)	*54* (58)
Fordham University		1.16	1.45				
		35 (164)	*33* (123)				
George Mason University			2.41				
			44 (93)				
George Washington University	2.31	1.50			2.00	3.03	
	47 (120)	*39* (157)			*42* (80)	*49* (80)	
Georgetown University	2.70	2.54			3.08	3.52	3.19
	51 (86)	*49* (98.5)			*52* (49.5)	*56* (34)	*53* (60.5)

Appendix Table H - 2 Biological Sciences (Continued)

Institution	Biochem & Molec Bio	Cell & Develop Bio	Eco, Evl & Behavior	Molec & Gen Genetics	Neuro-sciencs	Pharma-cology	Physiology
Georgia Institute of Technology	2.39	0.16		1.55			
	48 (112)	26 (178)		38 (90)			
Georgia State University	1.32	2.00			1.45		
	38 (178)	44 (132)			37 (88)		
University of Georgia	3.03	2.00 [d]	3.87	3.22		2.92	2.80
	54 (66)	44 (132)	62 (16)	53 (40.5)		47 (88)	49 (85.5)
		2.72 [a]					
		51 (82.5)					
Hahnemann University	1.76	2.21		2.00	2.64	1.80	2.58
	42 (156)	46 (124)		42 (81.5)	48 (64.5)	30 (123)	47 (97)
Harvard University	4.80	4.70		4.77	4.73	4.14	3.45
	71 (5)	70 (5)		68 (3)	67 (3)	66 (7)	56 (37.5)
University of Hawaii at Manoa	1.57	1.63	2.94	2.52		2.35	2.75
	40 (167)	40 (152)	51 (61.5)	47 (70)		38 (112)	49 (88.5)
Univ of Health Sc/Chicago Med Sch	2.33	2.30				2.23	2.56
	47 (118)	47 (118)				37 (116)	46 (98)
University of Houston	2.61	2.57	2.24	1.62		2.38	1.59
	50 (95)	49 (96.5)	42 (102)	39 (88)		39 (111)	36 (124)
Howard University	1.67		1.80	1.56		2.08	2.00
	41 (162)		37 (117)	38 (89)		34 (120)	40 (114)
Idaho State University			2.60				
			47 (82)				
University of Idaho	1.87	1.44	2.14	0.24	0.59	1.53	0.42
	43 (146)	38 (159)	41 (106)	26 (102)	30 (99)	26 (126)	23 (139)
Illinois State University	2.10	1.82	1.91	1.25			1.78
	45 (133)	42 (138)	39 (113)	35 (94)			38 (120)
U of Illinois at Urbana-Champaign	3.55	3.74	3.52	3.30	3.33		3.81
	59 (34)	61 (27)	58 (29)	54 (35)	54 (41)		60 (20.5)
University of Illinois at Chicago	2.72	2.97 [a]		2.81		3.18	3.15
	51 (85)	53 (65)		50 (64)		51 (58.5)	53 (64)
		3.11 [b]					
		55 (55)					
Indiana University	3.42	3.59	3.49	3.64		1.89	1.47
	58 (42.5)	59 (32)	57 (30)	57 (24)		31 (122)	34 (130)
Iowa State University	3.00	3.05	3.00	2.82		3.00	2.72
	54 (68)	54 (62)	51 (56.5)	50 (63)		48 (84)	48 (92.5)
University of Iowa	3.36	3.28	2.94	3.21	3.46	3.79	3.99
	57 (47)	56 (50)	51 (61.5)	53 (42.5)	55 (31)	60 (19.5)	62 (12)
Johns Hopkins University	4.38	3.91	2.83	4.26	4.47	4.21	3.86
	67 (10.5)	62 (20)	49 (68.5)	63 (9)	64 (7)	67 (4)	61 (19)
Kansas State University	2.41	2.00	2.57	2.90	0.91		2.50
	48 (111)	44 (132)	46 (84.5)	50 (58)	33 (93)		46 (101)

Appendix Table H - 2 Biological Sciences (Continued)

Institution	Biochem & Molec Bio	Cell & Develop Bio	Eco, Evl & Behavior	Molec & Gen Genetics	Neuro-sciencs	Pharma-cology	Physiology
University of Kansas	2..45 [b]	2.43 [a]	3.46	2.67		3.03 [a]	2.50 [a]
	48 (107)	48 (107)				49 (80)	46 (101)
	2.56 [a]	2.95 [b]				3.70 [b]	3.22 [b]
	50 (98)	53 (68)				59 (23)	54 (56.5)
Kent State University	1.69	1.64	1.88		2.03	2.22	2.62
	41 (160)	40 (150)	38 (115)		43 (79)	36 (117)	47 (96)
University of Kentucky	2.64	2.31 [a]	2.79 [c]			2.87 [b]	3.00
	50 (93.5)	47 (115)	49 (72)			46 (91.5)	51 (72.5)
		2.82 [b]	3.04 [a]			3.56 [a]	
		52 (76)	52 (54.5)			57 (31)	
Lehigh University	1.85	1.33					
	43 (149)	37 (163)					
Loma Linda University	1.47	1.50	1.17		1.17	2.31	2.42
	39 (172)	39 (157)	30 (126)		35 (91)	38 (114)	45 (103)
Louisiana State U & A&M College	2.17	2.53	2.91	2.67	1.47	2.75	2.70
	46 (125)	49 (100)	50 (64)	48 (66.5)	38 (87)	44 (98.5)	48 (95)
Louisiana State U Medical Center	2.12	2.00		2.54		2.76	2.87
	45 (132)	44 (132)		47 (69)		45 (96.5)	50 (83)
Louisiana St U-Sch Med Shreveport	1.48	1.75				2.47	3.00
	39 (170)	41 (141)				40 (107)	51 (72.5)
University of Louisville	2.86	1.33		1.27	1.69	3.10	2.94
	53 (76)	37 (163)		35 (93)	40 (86)	50 (67)	51 (78)
Loyola University of Chicago	1.77	2.11				2.85	2.73
	42 (155)	45 (127)				46 (93)	48 (90.5)
University of Maine			2.52				
			46 (90)				
University of Maryland College Park	2.74	2.67	3.28				
	51 (84)	50 (87)	55 (45)				
Univ of Maryland at Baltimore	2.43	2.96		1.86		3.12	3.33
	48 (108)	53 (67)		41 (85)		50 (65)	55 (45)
U of Maryland Baltimore County	2.31	2.92					
	47 (120)	53 (71)					
Massachusetts Inst of Technology	4.83	4.86		4.88	4.21	3.90	
	71 (2.5)	72 (1)		69 (1)	62 (14)	62 (11)	
U of Massachusetts at Amherst	2.78	3.21	3.39		2.80		
	52 (82)	56 (51)	56 (36.5)		50 (61)		
U of Massachusetts Med Center	3.30	3.33		3.07		3.00	3.63
	57 (54)	57 (46)		52 (50)		48 (84)	58 (29)
University of Mass-Lowell	0.44						
	29 (191)						
Mayo Graduate School	3.34				3.42	3.53	3.87
	57 (49.5)				55 (35)	56 (32.5)	61 (18)

Appendix Table H - 2 Biological Sciences (Continued)

Institution	Biochem & Molec Bio	Cell & Develop Bio	Eco, Evl & Behavior	Molec & Gen Genetics	Neuro-sciencs	Pharma-cology	Physiology
Medical College of Georgia	1.56					3.09	2.71
	40 (168)					*50* (68)	*48* (94)
Medical College of Ohio	1.78				1.86	2.48	1.56
	42 (154)				*41* (84)	*40* (105)	*35* (126)
Medical College of Pensylvania	2.57	1.79			3.04	2.97	2.36
	50 (97)	*42* (139)			*52* (52)	*48* (86)	*44* (107)
Medical College of Wisconsin	2.07	2.88		1.92		3.26	3.27
	45 (134)	*52* (73)		*41* (84)		*52* (53.5)	*54* (52)
Medical University South Carolina	1.32	2.09				3.41	
	38 (178)	*45* (128)				*55* (40)	
Univ of Med & Dent of NJ	2.12	2.39				2.79	2.20
	45 (132)	*48* (110)				*45* (95)	*43* (111)
Miami University	1.65	1.63	2.67	1.33	0.39		1.18
	41 (164)	*40* (152)	*47* (76)	*36* (92)	*28* (102)		*31* (134)
University of Miami	2.49	3.33			2.14	3.42	3.26
	49 (105)	*57* (46)			*44* (76)	*55* (39)	54 (53)
Michigan State University	3.33	3.41	3.41	3.26	2.64	3.50	3.31
	57 (51.5)	*58* (40)	*56* (34)	*54* (36.5)	*48* (64.5)	*56* (36)	*55* (47)
University of Michigan	3.87 [a]	3.66	4.10	3.75	3.79	3.60 [a]	3.89
	62 (26)	*60* (30)	*64* (12)	*58* (21)	*58* (18)	*57* (29)	*61* (15.5)
	3.89 [b]					3.85 [b]	
	62 (23.5)					*61* (13)	
University of Minnesota	3.46	3.49 [a]	3.88	3.23	3.43	3.76	3.00
	58 (39)	*58* (37)	*62* (15)	*54* (39)	*55* (34)	*60* (21)	*51* (72.5)
		3.54 [b]					
		59 (34)					
Mississippi State University			2.00				
			40 (112)				
University of Mississippi						2.47	
						40 (107)	
U of Mississippi-Medical Center	1.73					2.68	
	42 (158)					*43* (100)	
University of Missouri-Columbia	2.92	2.88	2.79	2.44	1.92	2.57	3.02
	53 (71)	*52* (73)	*49* (72)	*46* (72)	*42* (83)	*42* (102)	*52* (69.5)
Univ of Missouri-Kansas City	2.50	2.45					
	49 (104)	*48* (105)					
Univ of Missouri-Saint Louis	0.46		2.33				
	29 (190)		*43* (100)				
Montana State University	1.80	1.67 [a]	1.63	2.30	1.04		0.91
	42 (151)	*40* (148)	*35* (120)	*45* (76)	*34* (92)		*28* (135)
		1.75 [c]					
		41 (141)					

Appendix Table H - 2 Biological Sciences (Continued)

Institution	Biochem & Molec Bio	Cell & Develop Bio	Eco, Evl & Behavior	Molec & Gen Genetics	Neuro-sciencs	Pharma-cology	Physiology
University of Montana	1.15	1.07	2.51				
	36 (179)	*35 (165)*	*46 (91)*				
University of Nebraska-Lincoln	2.84	2.42	2.96	2.00			1.38
	52 (78.5)	*48 (108)*	*51 (59)*	*42 (81.5)*			*33 (132)*
University of Nevada, Reno	2.50		2.74				
	49 (104)		*48 (74)*				
University of New Hampshire	2.60	2.00	1.88	2.08			0.67
	50 (96)	*44 (132)*	*38 (115)*	*43 (79)*			*25 (138)*
New Mexico State University	1.67		2.00				
	41 (162)		*40 (112)*				
University of New Mexico	2.53	2.67	3.24	1.73	2.08		2.27
	49 (100)	*50 (87)*	*54 (47)*	*40 (86.5)*	*43 (77.5)*		*43 (110)*
New York Medical College	1.47	2.25	0.50			2.91	2.72
	39 (172)	*46 (122)*	*22 (128)*			*47 (89)*	48 (92.5)
New York University	3.47	3.86		3.04	2.96	3.84	3.91
	58 (36.5)	*62 (21)*		*52 (52)*	*51 (56)*	*61 (14)*	*61 (14)*
North Carolina State University	3.09	2.88	3.20	3.36		3.53	3.00
	55 (62)	*52 (73)*	*54 (48)*	*55 (30)*		*56 (32.5)*	*51 (72.5)*
U of North Carolina-Chapel Hill	3.83	3.79	3.33	3.78	3.57	3.82 [j]	3.55
	62 (27)	*61 (25)*	*55 (42)*	*59 (20)*	*56 (26.5)*	*61 (16)*	*57 (32.5)*
						4.03 [a]	
						64 (8)	
North Dakota State University	1.69		1.61				0.88
	41 (160)		*35 (121)*				*28 (136)*
University of North Dakota	2.04						
	45 (136)						
University of North Texas	*1.78*	1.75	1.72				2.55
	42 (154)	*41 (141)*	*36 (118)*				*46 (99)*
Northeast Louisiana University						2.55	
						41 (103)	
Northeastern University	2.00						
	44 (140)						
Northern Arizona University	0.21	0.86	3.35	0.17	0.48		1.67
	27 (193)	*33 (170)*	*56 (40)*	*25 (103)*	*29 (101)*		*37 (122)*
Northwestern University	3.59	3.64			3.60		3.67
	60 (31)	*60 (31)*			*57 (23)*		*59 (26.5)*
University of Notre Dame	0.84	1.95	2.37	2.43			1.93
	33 (183)	*43 (135)*	*44 (98)*	*46 (73)*			*40 (115)*
Ohio State University	3.16	3.06	3.27	2.98	2.97	3.26	3.37
	55 (59.5)	*54 (61)*	*55 (46)*	*51 (54)*	*51 (55)*	*52 (53.5)*	*55 (41.5)*
Ohio University	0.63	1.71	2.13	0.47	1.77	1.63	1.80
	31 (185)	*41 (144)*	*41 (107)*	*28 (100)*	*40 (85)*	*27 (125)*	*38 (119)*

Appendix Table H - 2 Biological Sciences (Continued)

Institution	Biochem & Molec Bio	Cell & Develop Bio	Eco, Evl & Behavior	Molec & Gen Genetics	Neuro-sciencs	Pharma-cology	Physiology
Oklahoma State University	2.00	0.94	2.39				2.10
	44 (140)	*33* (168)	*44* (96)				*41* (113)
University of Oklahoma	2.04	2.59	3.11	1.73	1.93	2.76	2.83
	45 (136)	*50* (94)	*53* (50)	*40* (86.5)	*42* (82)	*45* (96.5)	*50* (84)
Old Dominion University	1.91		2.16				
	43 (144)		*41* (104)				
Oregon Graduate Inst Sci & Tech	1.57						
	40 (167)						
Oregon State University	3.46	3.20	3.74	3.00	1.96	3.36	2.90
	58 (39)	*55* (52.5)	*60* (23)	*51* (53)	*42* (81)	*54* (44.5)	*50* (81)
University of Oregon	3.88				3.46		
	62 (25)				*55* (31)		
Pennsylvania State University	3.39	3.10	3.31	3.34	2.50	3.05	3.20 [h]
	58 (45)	*55* (56)	*55* (43)	*55* (32.5)	*47* (67)	*49* (75)	*54* (59)
			3.60 [c]				3.24 [c]
			58 (26)				*54* (55)
							3.45 [i]
							56 (37.5)
University of Pennsylvania	4.11	3.81	3.90	3.81	4.30	4.02	4.27
	65 (16)	*61* (23)	*62* (14)	*59* (19)	*63* (10.5)	*64* (9.5)	*66* (3)
Phila Col of Pharmacy & Science						2.33	
						38 (113)	
University of Pittsburgh	2.64 [b]	2.47 [b]	2.42	2.85 [g]	3.28 [b]	3.36	3.31
	50 (93.5)	*48* (104)	*45* (92)	*50* (60)	*54* (44)	*54* (44.5)	*55* (47)
	2.68 [a]	2.93 [a]		3.11 [a]	3.36 [a]		
	51 (89.5)	*53* (69.5)		*52* (46)	*55* (40)		
Princeton University		4.36	4.34				
		67 (11.5)	*67* (6)				
Univ of Puerto Rico-Rio Piedras	1.67	0.94 [a]	1.31		0.58	1.79	1.85
	41 (162)	*33* (168)	*31* (124)		*30* (100)	*30* (124)	*39* (117)
		1.62 [b]					
		40 (154)					
Purdue University	3.24 [c]	3.33	3.10		2.31	2.89	
	56 (56)	*57* (46)	*53* (51.5)		*45* (72)	*47* (90)	
	3.39 [a]						
	58 (45)						
Rice University	3.39	2.65					
	58 (45)	*50* (89)					
University of Rochester	3.29	3.35	2.95	3.44	3.30	3.79	3.28
	57 (55)	*57* (44)	*51* (60)	*55* (29)	*54* (43)	*60* (19.5)	*54* (50)
Rockefeller University	3.92	4.77			4.23		
	63 (21)	*71* (2)			*62* (13)		

Appendix Table H - 2 Biological Sciences (Continued)

Institution	Biochem & Molec Bio	Cell & Develop Bio	Eco, Evl & Behavior	Molec & Gen Genetics	Neuro-sciencs	Pharma-cology	Physiology
Rush University	1.86						
	43 (147)						
Rutgers State Univ-New Brunswick	3.47	3.07	3.60	3.35	3.22	3.49	3.47
	58 (36.5)	*54* (60)	*59* (26)	*55* (31)	*53* (46)	*56* (37)	*57* (36)
Rutgers State Univ-Newark	1.88		2.61		2.93		
	43 (145)		*47* (80)		*51* (57)		
St. John's University		1.63				2.46	
		40 (152)				*40* (109)	
Saint Louis University	2.91	2.35	2.06			3.33	3.19
	53 (72)	*47* (112)	*40* (110)			*53* (48.5)	53 (60.5)
University of South Alabama		1.74					
		41 (143)					
University of South Carolina	2.84	2.31	2.87			2.75	2.35
	52 (78.5)	*47* (115)	*50* (65.5)			*44* (98.5)	*44* (108)
University of South Dakota	0.50	0.69				2.00	1.45
	30 (189)	*31* (174)				*33* (121)	*34* (131)
University of South Florida	1.85	2.22	2.54			2.50	
	43 (149)	*46* (123)	*46* (88)			*41* (104)	
University of Southern California	3.46	3.31			3.41	2.46	3.25
	58 (39)	*57* (48.5)			*55* (36.5)	*40* (109)	*54* (54)
Southern Illinois University		1.83	2.39			2.16	
		42 (137)	*44* (96)			*36* (118)	
Southern Methodist University	*1.43*						
	39 (174)						
Univ of Southern Mississippi	0.52	0.13	1.50				0.38
	30 (188)	*25* (179)	*34* (122)				*22* (140)
Univ of Southwestern Louisiana			2.64				
			47 (78)				
Stanford University	4.83	4.36 [a]	4.51	4.48	4.64	3.81	4.20
	72 (2.5)	*67* (11.5)	*69* (1.5)	*65* (5)	*66* (5)	*61* (17.5)	*65* (7.5)
		4.55 [b]					
		69 (6)					
State Univ of New York-Albany		2.25	3.10	2.59	2.21	2.87	
		46 (122)	*53* (51.5)	*48* (68)	*44* (75)	*46* (91.5)	
State Univ of New York-Binghamton	0.41	0.33	2.86				1.50
	29 (192)	*27* (177)	*50* (67)				*35* (128)
State Univ of New York-Buffalo	2.52 [b]	2.75 [a]	2.17	2.94	2.24 [a]	3.03	3.40
	49 (101)	*51* (80)	*42* (103)	*51* (57)	*45* (73)	*49* (80)	*56* (39)
	2.67 [a]	2.64 [b]			2.51 [b]		
	51 (91.5)	*50* (90.5)			*47* (66)		
State U of New York-Stony Brook	3.58	3.53	4.12	3.73	3.54	3.62	3.28
	59 (32)	*59* (35.5)	*65* (10.5)	*58* (22)	*56* (28)	*58* (27)	*55* (50)

Appendix Table H - 2 Biological Sciences (Continued)

Institution	Biochem & Molec Bio	Cell & Develop Bio	Eco, Evl & Behavior	Molec & Gen Genetics	Neuro-sciencs	Pharma-cology	Physiology
SUNY Col Environ Sci & Forestry			2.27				
			43 (101)				
SUNY-Health Science Ctr-Brooklyn	2.00	1.67		2.40	2.47	3.36	3.17
	44 (140)	*40* (148)		*46* (74.5)	*47* (68.5)	*54* (44.5)	*53* (62.5)
SUNY Health Science Ctr-Syracuse	2.41	2.57				3.00	2.90
	48 (111)	*49* (96.5)				*48* (84)	*50* (81)
Syracuse University	2.42		3.09	2.40	2.38		
	48 (109)		*52* (53)	*46* (74.5)	*46* (71)		
Temple University	2.27	2.54		2.84		3.08	2.90
	47 (123)	*49* (98.5)		*50* (61)		*49* (69.5)	*50* (81)
University of Tennessee-Knoxville	1.64	2.77	3.35	1.11			
	41 (165)	*51* (78)	*56* (40)	*34* (95)			
University of Tennessee - Memphis	2.86	2.73			3.03	3.25	3.31
	53 (76)	*51* (81)			*52* (53)	*52* (55)	*55* (47)
Texas A&M University	2.69 [a]	2.97	2.61	3.24		3.16	2.32
	51 (87.5)	*53* (65)	*47* (80)	*54* (38)		*51* (62.5)	*44* (109)
	2.95 [c]						
	53 (70)						
Texas Tech University	2.16	2.64	2.79			2.23	2.40
	46 (126)	*50* (90.5)	*49* (72)			*37* (116)	*45* (104)
University of Texas at Austin	3.57	3.37	4.12	3.47	3.08	3.61	3.52
	59 (33)	*57* (43)	*65* (10.5)	*56* (28)	*52* (49.5)	*58* (28)	*57* (34.5)
University of Texas at Dallas	2.13						
	45 (130)						
U of Texas, Medical Br-Galveston	2.55	2.38			3.31	3.12	3.52
	50 (99)	*47* (111)			*54* (42)	*50* (65)	*57* (34.5)
U of Tex-Health Sci Ctr-Houston	3.42	3.46		3.49	3.05	3.47	3.69
	58 (42.5)	*58* (38)		*56* (26)	*52* (51)	*55* (38)	*59* (23.5)
U of Tex-Hlth Sci Ct-San Antonio	3.08	3.09				3.07	3.37
	55 (64)	*54* (57.5)				*49* (71)	55 (41.5)
U of Texas-Southwestern Med Ctr	4.00	3.98		3.91	3.41	4.39	
	63 (20)	*63* (18)		*60* (18)	*55* (36.5)	*69* (2)	
Texas Woman's University	0.86				0.72		
	33 (182)				*31* (96.5)		
Thomas Jefferson University	2.69	3.09				3.30	3.28
	51 (87.5)	*54* (57.5)				*53* (52)	*54* (50)
Tufts University	3.09	2.97 [a]			2.88	3.06	3.10
	55 (62)	*53* (65)			*50* (59)	*49* (73)	*52* (66.5)
		3.16 [b]					
		55 (54)					
Tulane University	2.00	2.32 [a]	2.58			3.02	2.97
	44 (140)	*47* (113)	*46* (83)			*49* (82)	*51* (75)

Appendix Table H - 2 Biological Sciences (Continued)

Institution	Biochem & Molec Bio	Cell & Develop Bio	Eco, Evl & Behavior	Molec & Gen Genetics	Neuro-sciencs	Pharma-cology	Physiology
Tulane University		2.28 [b]					
		46 (119)					
University of Tulsa	0.69	0.80	0.47	0.75			
	32 (184)	*32* (172)	*22* (129)	*31* (98)			
Uniformed Services U of Hlth Sci	2.21	2.77			2.23	3.08	2.96
	46 (124)	*51* (78)			*44* (74)	*50* (69.5)	*51* (76.5)
Utah State University	1.94	0.50	3.39			3.18	1.33
	44 (143)	*29* (176)	*56* (36.5)			*51* (58.5)	*33* (133)
University of Utah	3.72		3.65	4.08		3.37	
	61 (29)		*59* (24)	*61* (13)		*54* (42)	
Vanderbilt University	3.68	3.69	2.73	3.26	3.49	4.17	3.89
	60 (30)	*60* (29)	*48* (75)	*54* (36.5)	*56* (29)	*66* (6)	*61* (15.5)
University of Vermont	2.38	2.70	3.04			3.17	3.35
	48 (114)	*51* (84)	*52* (54.5)			*51* (60.5)	*55* (43)
Virginia Polytech Inst & State U	2.13		2.80				1.56 [d]
	45 (130)		*49* (70)				*35* (126)
							1.85 [c]
							39 (117)
							1.63 [a]
							36 (123)
University of Virginia	3.16	3.39	3.14	2.83	3.46	3.65	4.19
	55 (59.5)	*57* (41)	*53* (49)	*50* (62)	*55* (31)	*58* (24.5)	*65* (9.5)
Wake Forest University	2.33	2.59	2.56	2.29	2.79	3.20	3.10
	47 (118)	*50* (94)	*46* (86)	*45* (77)	*50* (62)	*51* (57)	*53* (66.5)
Washington State University	3.05	2.50	3.37			3.16	2.92
	54 (65)	*49* (102)	*56* (38)			*51* (62.5)	*50* (79)
Washington University	4.22	4.39	3.94	3.98	4.43		
	66 (13)	*67* (9)	*63* (13)	*61* (16)	*64* (8)		
University of Washington	4.05	4.48	4.30	3.93	4.28	4.02	4.20
	64 (18)	*68* (8)	*67* (7)	*60* (17)	*63* (12)	*64* (9.5)	*65* (7.5)
Wayne State University	2.68	2.43	2.39	2.77	2.47	3.06	2.76
	51 (89.5)	*48* (107)	*44* (96)	*49* (65)	*47* (68.5)	*49* (73)	*49* (87)
Wesleyan University	2.15	2.41					
	46 (128)	*48* (109)					
West Virginia University	2.15	2.31		2.00		3.32	2.80
	46 (128)	*47* (115)		*42* (81.5)		*53* (50.5)	*49* (85.5)
University of Wisconsin-Madison	4.55	4.05	4.18	4.33	3.58	3.89	3.68
	69 (8)	*64* (16)	*65* (9)	*64* (7)	*56* (25)	*62* (12)	*59* (25)
University of Wisconsin-Milwaukee	2.37						
	48 (115)						
University of Wyoming	2.00	1.90	3.00		1.42		2.36
	44 (140)	*43* (136)	*51* (56.5)		*37* (89)		*44* (107)

Appendix Table H - 2 Biological Sciences (Continued)

Institution	Biochem & Molec Bio	Cell & Develop Bio	Eco, Evl & Behavior	Molec & Gen Genetics	Neuro-sciencs	Pharma-cology	Physiology
Yale University	4.59	4.37	3.83	4.32	4.76	4.45	4.48
	69 (6)	*67* (10)	*61* (17)	*64* (8)	*67* (2)	*70* (1)	*68* (1)

Source: National Survey of Graduate Faculty

Notes: *a* School of Arts and Sciences
b School of Medicine
c School of Agriculture
d School of Veterinary Medicine
e School of Pharmacology
f School of Engineering
g School of Public Health
h Interdisciplinary with the Schools of Agriculture and Arts and Sciences
i Interdisciplinary with the Schools of Agriculture, Arts and Sciences, and Medicine
j Interdisciplinary with the Schools of Medicine, Pharmacology, and Public Health

Appendix Table H - 3 Faculty Quality Ratings of Research-Doctorate Programs in Engineering

Institution	Aerospace Engineering	Biomedical Engineering	Chemical Engineering	Civil Engineering	Electrical Engineering	Industrial Engineering	Materials Science	Mechanical Engineering
Air Force Inst of Technology	2.45				2.21			
	40 (28)				*45* (86)			
University of Akron		1.92	1.62	1.77	1.40		*3.14*	2.08
		29 (37)	*38* (85)	*36* (78)	*37* (114)		*51* (31)	*42* (86)
University of Alabama				1.41	1.59			1.88
				32 (84.5)	*39* (105)			*40* (96)
University of Alabama-Birmingham		3.27					2.18	
		48 (25)					*38* (55)	
University of Alabama-Huntsville					2.03	1.71	1.85	1.90
					43 (95)	*36* (35)	*34* (61)	*40* (94)
Arizona State University			2.12	2.41	3.17	2.97	3.27 [a]	3.08
			44 (64)	*45* (58)	*56* (37)	*51* (17)	*53* (27)	*54* (37)
							2.97 [b]	
							49 (35)	
University of Arizona			1.86	3.03	3.12		3.25	3.11
			41 (79)	*52* (34)	*55* (40)		*52* (28)	*54* (34)
Univ of Arkansas-Fayetteville					1.56	2.33		
					38 (109)	*44* (27)		
Auburn University	2.15		1.98	2.55	2.61	2.73	1.65	2.29
	36 (32)		*42* (71.5)	*46* (54)	*50* (59)	*48* (20)	*32* (64)	*45* (75)
Boston University					2.29			
					46 (82.5)			
Brigham Young University			2.53	2.42	2.10			
			48 (50)	*45* (57)	*44* (92)			
Brown University					3.22		3.18	3.79
					56 (35)		*51* (30)	*62* (13)
California Institute Technology	4.61		4.41	4.27	4.46		3.75	4.35
	68 (1)		*69* (6)	*68* (7)	*70* (5)		*59* (11.5)	*69* (4)
University of California-Berkeley		4.08	4.63	4.56	4.69	4.44	4.33	4.54
		59 (8)	*71* (3)	*71* (2)	*72* (4)	*68* (2)	*66* (4)	*71* (3)
University of California-Davis		3.37	3.11	3.54	3.24			3.28
		49 (23)	*54* (28)	*59* (16)	*57* (33)			*56* (26)
University of California-Irvine				3.04	2.96			3.11
				52 (33)	*54* (46.5)			*54* (34)
Univ of California-Los Angeles	3.62		2.88	3.37	4.00		3.34	3.76
	56 (10.5)		*52* (39)	*57* (21)	*65* (10.5)		*54* (26)	*62* (14)
Univ of California-San Diego	3.62	4.45			3.57			4.04
	56 (10.5)	*64* (2)			*60* (20)			*65* (10.5)
Univ of California-San Francisco		4.19						
		61 (7)						
Univ of California-Santa Barbara			3.82		3.71		4.18	3.07
			62 (14)		*62* (19)		*64* (8)	*54* (40)
Carnegie Mellon University			3.87	3.85	3.94		3.75	3.59
			63 (12)	*63* (12)	*64* (12)		*59* (11.5)	*60* (19)
Case Western Reserve Univ		3.84	2.59		3.05		3.56	3.48
		56 (13)	*49* (46)		*55* (42)		*56* (18)	*59* (20.5)

Appendix Table H - 3 Engineering (Continued)

Institution	Aerospace Engineering	Biomedical Engineering	Chemical Engineering	Civil Engineering	Electrical Engineering	Industrial Engineering	Materials Science	Mechanical Engineering
Catholic University of America				1.65				2.00
				35 (81)				*41* (91)
University of Central Florida					2.39			
					47 (77)			
University of Cincinnati	2.94		1.97	2.44	2.16		2.22	2.71
	47 (23)		*42* (73.5)	*45* (55)	*45* (87)		*39* (54)	*50* (59)
CUNY - Grad Sch & Univ Center			3.46		2.79			2.76
			58 (19)		*52* (51)			*50* (56)
Clarkson University			2.54	2.84	2.41			2.39
			48 (49)	*50* (42.5)	*48* (74.5)			*46* (68)
Clemson University		2.74	1.74	2.39	2.44	2.08		2.54
		40 (33)	*40* (81)	*44* (62)	*48* (73)	*41* (31.5)		*48* (63)
Colorado School of Mines			2.11				2.64	
			44 (65)				*45* (49)	
Colorado State University				3.23	2.60			2.51
				55 (25)	*50* (60.5)			*47* (65)
University of Colorado	3.35		3.18	3.27	3.17			2.86
	52 (13)		*55* (26)	*55* (24)	*56* (37)			*51* (51)
Columbia University			2.29	3.21	3.79		3.20	3.18
			46 (56)	*55* (27.5)	*63* (15)		*52* (29)	*55* (29.5)
University of Connecticut			2.49	2.22	2.37			2.32
			48 (51)	*42* (68)	*47* (78.5)			*45* (72)
Cornell University	3.93		3.86	4.30	4.35		4.35	4.15
	60 (6)		*63* (13)	*68* (6)	*69* (7)		*67* (3)	*67* (7)
Dartmouth College		2.83						
		42 (32)						
University of Dayton	1.07				1.52			
	22 (33)				*38* (111)			
University of Delaware			4.34	2.80	2.37		2.77	2.94
			68 (8)	*49* (45.5)	*47* (78.5)		*46* (47)	*52* (47.5)
University of Detroit Mercy								0.76
								26 (110)
Drexel University		3.42			2.90		2.91	
		50 (22)			*53* (48)		*48* (39.5)	
Duke University		4.33	1.63	3.21	2.71		2.23	3.06
		63 (4)	*38* (84)	*55* (27.5)	*51* (54.5)		*39* (53)	*54* (42)
Florida Atlantic University					1.25			
					35 (118)			
Florida Institute of Technology					1.56			1.35
					38 (109)			*33* (107)
University of Florida	2.50		2.97	2.93	3.26	2.82	3.65	2.83
	41 (27)		*53* (34)	*51* (36.5)	*57* (30.5)	*49* (19)	*57* (16)	*51* (52)
George Washington University				1.95	2.46			2.52
				39 (75)	*48* (70.5)			*47* (64)

Appendix Table H - 3 Engineering (Continued)

Institution	Aerospace Engineering	Biomedical Engineering	Chemical Engineering	Civil Engineering	Electrical Engineering	Industrial Engineering	Materials Science	Mechanical Engineering
Georgia Institute of Technology	3.66		3.01	3.40	3.93	4.71	2.87	3.62
	56 (9)		*53* (30.5)	*57* (17.5)	*64* (13)	*71* (1)	*47* (44)	*60* (18)
University of Houston			3.66	2.62	2.14	1.61	1.90	3.08
			60 (17)	*47* (51)	*45* (89.5)	*35* (36)	*35* (59)	*54* (37)
Howard University					1.43			1.41
					37 (112)			*34* (105)
University of Idaho			1.33		1.00			
			35 (90.5)		*32* (124)			
Illinois Institute of Technology			2.57	2.21	2.23		*2.06*	2.98
			49 (47.5)	*42* (70)	*46* (84)		*37* (57)	*53* (44)
U of Illinois at Urbana-Champaign	3.34		4.42	4.41	4.70	3.13	4.29	4.07
	52 (14)		*69* (5)	*70* (5)	*72* (3)	*53* (13)	*66* (5)	*66* (9)
University of Illinois at Chicago		2.41	2.15	2.35	2.58			2.97
		36 (35)	*44* (61)	*44* (63.5)	*49* (65)			*53* (45)
Iowa State University	2.96	2.92	2.98	2.80	2.78	2.69		2.96
	47 (21.5)	*43* (30)	*53* (32.5)	*49* (45.5)	*52* (52)	*48* (21)		*53* (46)
University of Iowa		3.35	2.09	3.19	2.73	2.49		2.82
		49 (24)	*43* (66.5)	*54* (29)	*51* (53)	*45* (24)		*51* (53.5)
Johns Hopkins University		4.25	2.95	3.22	3.23		3.02	2.94
		61 (6)	*53* (35.5)	*55* (26)	*56* (34)		*49* (33)	*52* (47.5)
Kansas State University			2.18	1.95	1.58	2.27		2.29
			44 (59.5)	*39* (75)	*39* (107)	*43* (29)		*44* (75)
University of Kansas	2.63		1.94	2.82	2.45			2.16
	43 (26)		*42* (75.5)	*50* (44)	*48* (72)			*43* (80)
University of Kentucky			1.98	2.58	1.85		1.71	2.33
			42 (71.5)	*47* (53)	*42* (97)		*32* (62)	*45* (71)
Lehigh University			3.13	3.39	2.54	3.03	3.44	3.38
			55 (27)	*57* (19.5)	*49* (67)	*52* (15)	*55* (23)	*58* (23)
Louisiana State U & A&M College			2.40	2.23	1.75			1.78
			47 (55)	*42* (67)	*40* (100)			*38* (98)
University of Louisville			1.33					
			35 (90.5)					
University of Maine			1.49					
			37 (87)					
University of Maryland College Park	3.05		2.48	2.92	3.75		2.43	3.11
	48 (20)		*48* (52)	*51* (38)	*62* (17)		*42* (51)	*54* (34)
Massachusetts Inst of Technology	4.54	4.62	4.73	4.61	4.79		4.61	4.65
	68 (2)	*67* (1)	*72* (2)	*72* (1)	*73* (2)		*70* (1)	*73* (2)
U of Massachusetts at Amherst			3.35	2.77	3.28	2.42	4.20	2.70
			57 (21.5)	*49* (47)	*57* (28.5)	*45* (25)	*65* (7)	*49* (60.5)
University of Mass-Lowell					1.15		2.88	
					34 (122)		*47* (42.5)	
University of Miami		2.11		1.68	1.77			1.72
		31 (36)		*35* (79)	*41* (99)			*38* (100)

Appendix Table H - 3 Engineering (Continued)

Institution	Aerospace Engineering	Biomedical Engineering	Chemical Engineering	Civil Engineering	Electrical Engineering	Industrial Engineering	Materials Science	Mechanical Engineering
Michigan State University			2.60	2.85	3.00		2.58	3.02
			49 (45)	*50* (41)	*54* (44)		*44* (50)	*53* (43)
Michigan Technological University								2.40
								46 (67)
University of Michigan	4.05	3.91	3.52	3.90	4.38	4.36	3.66	4.22
	61 (5)	*57* (11)	*59* (18)	*63* (10)	*69* (6)	*67* (4)	*58* (14.5)	*68* (5)
University of Minnesota	3.40	3.49	4.86	3.76	3.73		3.64	4.09
	53 (12)	*51* (17.5)	*73* (1)	*61* (13)	*62* (18)		*57* (17)	*66* (8)
Mississippi State University					1.67			
					40 (102)			
University of Mississippi			0.76	1.22				
			29 (93)	*30* (86)				
University of Missouri-Columbia			1.70	1.95	2.29	1.78		2.12
			39 (83)	*39* (75)	*46* (82.5)	*37* (33)		*42* (83.5)
University of Missouri-Rolla			2.22	2.40	2.32		*2.80*	2.88
			45 (58)	*44* (60)	*47* (80.5)		*47* (45.5)	*52* (50)
Montana State University								1.24
								32 (108)
Naval Postgraduate School	2.42				2.53			
	40 (30)				*49* (68)			
University of Nebraska-Lincoln				2.15		2.28		1.68
				41 (72)		*43* (28)		*37* (102)
University of New Hampshire				2.14	1.31			
				41 (73)	*36* (117)			
New Jersey Inst of Technology			1.75		1.66			1.77
			40 (80)		*39* (103)			*38* (99)
New Mexico State University				1.94	2.41			
				39 (77)	*48* (74.5)			
North Carolina State University	3.19	2.86	3.20	3.17	3.54	3.46	3.44	3.33
	50 (16)	*42* (31)	*55* (25)	*54* (30)	*60* (21)	*57* (11)	*55* (23)	*57* (24)
U of North Carolina-Chapel Hill		3.49		3.58				
		51 (17.5)		*59* (15)				
Northeastern University			1.38	1.67	2.70	2.17		2.03
			36 (89)	*35* (80)	*51* (56)	*42* (30)		*41* (89)
Northwestern University		3.82	3.75	3.96	3.16	3.73	4.47	3.98
		55 (14)	*61* (15)	*64* (9)	*56* (39)	*60* (6)	*68* (2)	*65* (12)
University of Notre Dame	2.76		3.30	2.93	2.98		1.88	3.08
	44 (25)		*57* (24)	*51* (36.5)	*54* (45)		*35* (60)	*54* (37)
Ohio State University	2.84	3.26	2.73	2.88	3.53	3.24	3.48	3.32
	45 (24)	*48* (26)	*50* (41)	*50* (40)	*60* (22)	*54* (12)	*55* (21)	*57* (25)
Ohio University			0.93		2.22			
			31 (92)		*45* (85)			
Oklahoma State University			2.04	2.21	1.63	2.99		2.21
			43 (70)	*42* (70)	*39* (104)	*51* (16)		*44* (78)

Appendix Table H - 3 Engineering (Continued)

Institution	Aerospace Engineering	Biomedical Engineering	Chemical Engineering	Civil Engineering	Electrical Engineering	Industrial Engineering	Materials Science	Mechanical Engineering
University of Oklahoma			2.41	2.43	2.06	2.37		2.43
			47 (54)	*45* (56)	*44* (94)	*44* (26)		*46* (66)
Old Dominion University					1.41			2.35
					37 (113)			*45* (70)
Oregon Graduate Inst Sci & Tech					1.39		2.00	
					37 (115)		*36* (58)	
Oregon State University			1.93	2.61	2.59	1.28		2.14
			42 (77)	*47* (52)	*49* (63)	*31* (37)		*43* (81.5)
Pennsylvania State University	3.12	3.48	3.34	3.12	3.28	3.50	3.97	3.68
	49 (17.5)	*51* (19.5)	*57* (23)	*53* (32)	*57* (28.5)	*57* (9)	*62* (9)	*61* (17)
University of Pennsylvania		4.28	3.97		3.11		3.79	3.40
		62 (5)	*64* (11)		*55* (41)		*59* (10)	*58* (22)
University of Pittsburgh			2.64	2.65	2.59	2.61	2.80	2.36
			49 (44)	*48* (50)	*50* (63)	*47* (23)	*47* (45.5)	*45* (69)
Polytechnic University			2.14		3.42			1.36
			44 (62.5)		*59* (24.5)			*33* (106)
Portland State University					1.19			
					34 (120)			
Princeton University	4.30		4.14	3.99	4.01			4.19
	64 (4)		*66* (9)	*64* (8)	*65* (9)			*67* (6)
Purdue University	3.71		3.67	3.89	4.02	4.43	3.05	4.04
	57 (7)		*60* (16)	*63* (11)	*65* (8)	*68* (3)	*50* (32)	*66* (10.5)
Rensselaer Polytechnic Inst	2.96	2.97	2.95	2.97	3.44	3.12	3.68	3.69
	47 (21.5)	*43* (29)	*53* (35.5)	*52* (35)	*59* (23)	*53* (14)	*58* (13)	*61* (16)
University of Rhode Island			1.42	1.60	2.66			2.59
			36 (88)	*34* (82)	*50* (57)			*48* (62)
Rice University		3.94	3.35	3.28	3.36			3.22
		57 (10)	*57* (21.5)	*55* (23)	*58* (26)			*56* (27.5)
University of Rochester		3.67	2.81		2.96		2.94	2.72
		53 (15)	*51* (40)		*54* (46.5)		*48* (36.5)	*50* (58)
Rutgers State Univ-New Brunswick		3.16	2.66		2.83		3.36 [c]	3.16
		46 (27)	*50* (43)		*52* (50)		*54* (25)	*55* (31)
							2.91 [d]	
							48 (39.5)	
University of South Carolina					1.58			1.94
					39 (107)			*40* (93)
South Dakota Sch of Mines & Tech							2.08	
							37 (56)	
University of South Florida					1.72			
					40 (101)			
University of Southern California			2.25		4.00	2.64	2.73	2.73
			45 (57)		*65* (10.5)	*47* (22)	*46* (48)	*50* (57)
Southern Methodist University					2.40			1.98
					47 (76)			*41* (92)

Appendix Table H - 3 Engineering (Continued)

Institution	Aerospace Engineering	Biomedical Engineering	Chemical Engineering	Civil Engineering	Electrical Engineering	Industrial Engineering	Materials Science	Mechanical Engineering
Univ of Southwestern Louisiana					1.81			
					41 (98)			
Stanford University	4.50	3.86	4.35	4.44	4.83	3.68	4.24	4.77
	67 (3)	*56* (12)	*68* (7)	*70* (3)	*74* (1)	*59* (7)	*65* (6)	*74* (1)
State Univ of New York-Binghamton					1.16			
					34 (121)			
State Univ of New York-Buffalo	2.43		3.08	3.14	2.60	2.86		3.07
	40 (29)		*54* (29)	*54* (31)	*50* (60.5)	*50* (18)		*54* (40)
State U of New York-Stony Brook					2.63		2.90	2.82
					50 (58)		*48* (41)	*51* (53.5)
Stevens Inst of Technology			1.73		2.09		2.40	1.79
			39 (82)		*44* (93)		*41* (52)	*39* (97)
Syracuse University			2.57	2.40	2.86			2.03
			49 (47.5)	*44* (60)	*52* (49)			*41* (89)
Tennessee Technological Univ					0.94			1.89
					32 (125)			*40* (95)
University of Tennessee-Knoxville	2.17		2.18	2.33	2.57			2.23
	37 (31)		*44* (59.5)	*44* (65)	*49* (66)			*44* (77)
Texas A&M University	3.12	2.50	2.91	3.40	3.25	3.81		3.22
	49 (17.5)	*37* (34)	*52* (37)	*57* (17.5)	*57* (32)	*61* (5)		*56* (27.5)
Texas Tech University				2.40	2.47			
				44 (60)	*48* (69)			
University of Texas at Arlington					2.59			2.12
					50 (63)			*42* (83.5)
University of Texas at Austin	3.67	3.48	4.08	4.42	3.88		3.50	3.73
	56 (8)	*51* (19.5)	*65* (10)	*70* (4)	*63* (14)		*56* (20)	*62* (15)
U of Texas-Southwestern Med Ctr		3.13						
		46 (28)						
University of Toledo					1.55			2.17
					38 (110)			*43* (79)
Tulane University			1.91	1.43	0.84			2.03
			41 (78)	*32* (83)	*31* (126)			*41* (89)
University of Tulsa			1.97					0.83
			42 (73.5)					*27* (109)
Utah State University				2.70				
				48 (48)				
University of Utah		3.97	2.47		3.02		2.94	2.70
		57 (9)	*47* (53)		*54* (43)		*48* (36.5)	*49* (60.5)
Vanderbilt University		3.65	1.94	2.84	2.46		2.98	2.31
		53 (16)	*42* (75.5)	*50* (42.5)	*48* (70.5)		*49* (34)	*45* (73)
University of Vermont					1.05		1.43	1.70
					33 (123)		*29* (65)	*37* (101)
Virginia Polytech Inst & State U	3.24		2.67	3.39	3.30	3.66	2.92	3.18
	51 (15)		*50* (42)	*57* (19.5)	*57* (27)	*59* (8)	*48* (38)	*55* (29.5)

Appendix Table H - 3 Engineering (Continued)

Institution	Aerospace Engineering	Biomedical Engineering	Chemical Engineering	Civil Engineering	Electrical Engineering	Industrial Engineering	Materials Science	Mechanical Engineering
University of Virginia		3.44	3.01	2.91	2.71		3.44	3.07
		50 (21)	*53* (30.5)	*51* (39)	*51* (54.5)		*55* (23)	*54* (40)
Washington State University			2.14	2.35	2.32			2.92
			44 (62.5)	*44* (63.5)	*47* (80.5)			*52* (49)
Washington University			2.89	2.66	3.17			2.78
			52 (38)	*48* (49)	*56* (37)			*50* (55)
University of Washington	3.08	4.35	3.44	3.67	3.42		2.88	3.13
	49 (19)	*63* (3)	*58* (20)	*60* (14)	*59* (24.5)		*48* (42.5)	*55* (32)
Wayne State University			2.09	1.41	2.14	2.08		2.29
			43 (66.5)	*32* (84.5)	*45* (89.5)	*41* (31.5)		*45* (75)
West Virginia University			2.08	2.26	2.15			2.10
			43 (68)	*43* (66)	*45* (88)			*42* (85)
Wichita State University					1.24			1.48
					35 (119)			*35* (104)
University of Wisconsin-Madison			4.62	3.34	3.77	3.48	3.52 [d]	3.48
			71 (4)	*56* (22)	*62* (16)	*57* (10)	*56* (19)	*59* (20.5)
							3.66	
							58 (14.5)	
University of Wisconsin-Milwaukee				2.21	2.00	1.77	1.68	2.06
				42 (70)	*43* (96)	*37* (34)	*32* (63)	*42* (87)
Worcester Polytechnic Inst		1.72	2.07		2.12			2.14
		26 (38)	*43* (69)		*44* (91)			*43* (81.5)
University of Wyoming			1.55		1.38			1.57
			37 (86)		*36* (116)			*36* (103)
Yale University			2.98		3.26			
			53 (32.5)		*57* (30.5)			

Source: National Survey of Graduate Faculty

Notes: *a* Program in Science and Engineering of Materials
b Program in Materials Science and Engineering
c Program in Ceramic Scienceand Engineering
d Program in Metallurgical Engineering

Appendix Table H - 4 Faculty Quality Ratings of Research-Doctorate Programs in Physical Sciences and Mathematics

Institution	Astrophysics/ Astronomy	Chemistry	Computer Science	Geosciences	Mathematics	Ocean- ography	Physics	Statistics/ Biostatistics
Adelphi University					1.24			
					35 (133)			
University of Akron		2.02					*2.40*	
		44 (116)					*45* (97)	
University of Alabama		2.26		1.92	1.47		2.08	1.70
		47 (96)		*37* (92)	*37* (126)		*42* (120)	*36* (60)
University of Alabama-Birmingham		1.82	1.29				1.90	1.63
		42 (126)	*38* (97.5)				*40* (127)	*35* (62)
University of Alabama-Huntsville			1.61		1.28		2.13	
			41 (87)		*35* (130)		*42* (114)	
University of Alaska				2.58		2.71	2.50	
				45 (64.5)		*44* (21)	*46* (89)	
American University		1.14					2.00	1.69
		36 (156)					*41* (124)	*36* (61)
Arizona State University		2.88	2.33	3.48	2.43		2.87	
		53 (69)	*48* (61)	*57* (26)	*47* (85)		*50* (70)	
University of Arizona	4.10		3.05	3.87	2.96		3.23	
	59 (7)		*55* (33)	*61* (19)	*52* (54)		*54* (45.5)	
Univ of Arkansas-Fayetteville		2.16					2.12	
		46 (103)					*42* (116)	
Auburn University		1.88			2.31		1.88	
		43 (123)			*45* (93)		*40* (128)	
Baylor University		1.64					1.13	
		41 (141)					*32* (145)	
Boston College		2.37					1.80	
		48 (87)					*39* (131)	
Boston University	2.40	2.36	2.42		3.03		3.28	2.46
	40 (27)	*48* (88.5)	*49* (58)		*53* (51)		*55* (39)	*44* (47)
Bowling Green State University					1.85			
					41 (114)			
Brandeis University		3.26			3.64		3.25	
		56 (45)			*59* (32)		*55* (42.5)	
Brigham Young University		2.64					2.21	
		50 (80.5)					*43* (110)	
Brown University		3.02	3.86	4.11	3.73		3.60	
		54 (56)	*63* (13)	*64* (12)	*60* (27)		*58* (26.5)	
					4.04 [a]			
					63 (16)			
Bryn Mawr College		1.33					1.48	
		38 (150)					*35* (138)	
California Institute Technology	4.91	4.94	3.93	4.87	4.19		4.81	
	69 (1)	*73* (2)	*64* (12)	*74* (1)	*64* (11)		*72* (5)	

Appendix Table H - 4 Physical Sciences and Mathematics (Continued)

Institution	Astrophysics/ Astronomy	Chemistry	Computer Science	Geosciences	Mathematics	Ocean-ography	Physics	Statistics/ Biostatistics
University of California-Berkeley	4.65	4.96	4.88	4.45	4.94		4.87	4.43 [m]
	66 (3)	*73* (1)	*73* (3)	*69* (3)	*72* (1.5)		*72* (3.5)	*65* (3)
								4.76 [l]
								69 (1.5)
University of California-Davis		3.24	2.42	3.25	2.48		2.89	
		56 (47.5)	*49* (58)	*54* (33)	*47* (83.5)		*51* (67)	
University of California-Irvine		3.52	3.03		2.84		3.37	
		59 (36)	*55* (34)		*51* (63.5)		*56* (33.5)	
Univ of California-Los Angeles	3.27	4.46	3.73	4.11	4.14		4.18	3.93
	50 (16)	*68* (10)	*62* (14.5)	*64* (12)	*64* (12)		*65* (15)	*60* (12)
Univ of California-Riverside		2.86		2.69	2.55		2.88	2.75
		53 (70)		*47* (59)	*48* (79)		*51* (68.5)	*47* (39.5)
Univ of California-San Diego		3.95	3.45	4.23	4.02	4.69	4.10	
		63 (18.5)	*59* (22.5)	*66* (6)	*63* (17)	*68* (1)	*64* (16)	
Univ of California-San Francisco		3.86						
		62 (23)						
Univ of California-Santa Barbara		3.57	2.65	3.70	3.04		4.43	2.54
		59 (33)	*51* (48)	*59* (20)	*53* (49.5)		*68* (10)	*45* (44)
Univ of California-Santa Cruz	4.31	2.52	2.59	3.54	2.92		3.22	
	62 (6)	*49* (83)	*50* (50)	*57* (24)	*52* (56)		*54* (47.5)	
Carnegie Mellon University		2.79	4.76		3.41		3.56	3.77
		52 (74)	*72* (4)		*57* (40)		*58* (28)	*58* (16)
Case Western Reserve Univ		2.83	2.04	2.33	2.38		2.96	
		52 (71)	*45* (67.5)	*42* (80.5)	*46* (89)		*52* (65)	
Catholic University of America		1.08					2.33	
		35 (161)					*45* (102)	
University of Central Florida			1.71					
			42 (83)					
University of Chicago	4.36	4.46	3.31	4.22	4.69		4.69	4.34
	62 (5)	*68* (10)	*58* (24.5)	*66* (7)	*69* (5)		*70* (7)	*64* (5)
University of Cincinnati		2.82		2.45	2.06		2.33	
		52 (72)		*44* (69.5)	*43* (106)		*45* (102)	
CUNY - Grad Sch & Univ Center		2.36	2.52	2.33	3.65		3.36	
		48 (88.5)	*50* (54.5)	*42* (80.5)	*59* (30.5)		*56* (35)	
Claremont Graduate School					2.61			
					48 (74)			
Clark University							1.82	
							39 (130)	
Clarkson University		2.10			1.68		2.13	
		45 (110)			*39* (120)		*42* (114)	
Clemson University		2.28			2.34			
		47 (94)			*46* (92)			
Colorado School of Mines		1.12		3.13	1.26		2.25	
		36 (159)		*52* (38)	*35* (132)		*44* (107)	
Colorado State University		3.50		2.60	2.28		2.30	3.13
		59 (37)		*46* (63)	*45* (96)		*44* (105)	*51* (31)

Appendix Table H - 4 Physical Sciences and Mathematics (Continued)

Institution	Astrophysics/ Astronomy	Chemistry	Computer Science	Geosciences	Mathematics	Ocean- ography	Physics	Statistics/ Biostatistics
University of Colorado	3.54	3.30	2.90	3.20	2.83		3.30	2.15
	53 (12)	57 (42)	54 (40.5)	53 (36.5)	51 (65)		55 (38)	41 (55)
Columbia University	3.20	4.54	3.45	4.38	4.23	4.30	4.25	3.44
	49 (18)	69 (7)	59 (22.5)	68 (4)	65 (9.5)	64 (4)	66 (12)	55 (24.5)
University of Connecticut		2.47	1.47		2.16		2.33	2.62
		49 (85)	39 (92)		44 (101)		45 (102)	46 (43)
Cornell University	3.98	4.55	4.64	4.15	4.05		4.75	4.37
	58 (9)	69 (6)	70 (5)	65 (9.5)	63 (15)		71 (6)	65 (4)
Dartmouth College		3.07	2.45	3.08	2.97		2.60	
		54 (54)	49 (56)	52 (40.5)	52 (53)		48 (83.5)	
University of Delaware		2.80			2.54		2.76	
		52 (73)			48 (80)		49 (74)	
University of Denver							1.61	
							37 (133)	
University of Detroit Mercy		0.44						
		29 (167)						
Drexel University		1.99			1.97		2.62	
		44 (118)			42 (110)		48 (81)	
Duke University		3.28	3.17	2.99	3.53	3.22	3.25	
		57 (44)	56 (28)	50 (43)	58 (34.5)	50 (13.5)	55 (42.5)	
Emory University		3.37						2.20
		57 (38)						41 (51)
Florida Institute of Technology					1.09	1.65	0.46	
					33 (135)	31 (25)	24 (147)	
Florida State University		3.11	1.35	2.07 [h]	2.49	3.48	3.25	3.47
		55 (51)	38 (94.5)	39 (88)	47 (82)	54 (9)	55 (42.5)	55 (23)
				2.50 [i]				
				44 (66)				
University of Florida	1.98	3.67	2.70	2.45	2.95		3.35	3.31
	35 (31)	60 (30)	52 (46)	44 (69.5)	52 (55)		56 (36)	53 (27)
George Washington University		0.93	2.04	1.16	1.26		1.45	2.91
		34 (163)	45 (67.5)	28 (100)	35 (132)		35 (140)	49 (36)
Georgetown University		2.17						
		46 (102)						
Georgia Institute of Technology		2.92	3.10	2.36	3.19		3.02	
		53 (64)	55 (32)	43 (76.5)	54 (44)		52 (61.5)	
Georgia State University	1.81							
	34 (33)							
University of Georgia		3.17		2.36	2.90		2.73	
		55 (49)		43 (76.5)	51 (58.5)		49 (75)	
Harvard University	4.49	4.87	3.94	4.20	4.90		4.91	4.17
	64 (4)	72 (3.5)	64 (11)	66 (8)	72 (4)		73 (1)	63 (7)
University of Hawaii at Manoa	3.60	2.26		3.40	2.20	3.50	2.61	
	54 (11)	47 (96)		56 (29.5)	44 (98)	54 (7)	48 (82)	
University of Houston		3.16	1.85	2.58	2.78		3.02	
		55 (50)	43 (75)	45 (64.5)	50 (68)		52 (61.5)	

Appendix Table H - 4 Physical Sciences and Mathematics (Continued)

Institution	Astrophysics/ Astronomy	Chemistry	Computer Science	Geosciences	Mathematics	Ocean-ography	Physics	Statistics/ Biostatistics
Howard University		1.46			1.82		1.60	
		39 (146)			*40* (117)		*37* (135)	
Idaho State University					0.69			
					29 (138)			
University of Idaho		1.80		1.71				
		42 (130)		*35* (96)				
Illinois Institute of Technology			1.52		1.45		2.56	
			40 (91)		*37* (127)		*47* (87.5)	
Illinois State University					0.40			
					26 (139)			
U of Illinois at Urbana-Champaign	3.53	4.48	4.09	3.22	3.93		4.66	3.35
	53 (13)	*68* (8)	*65* (8)	*53* (34)	*62* (21)		*70* (8)	*54* (26)
University of Illinois at Chicago		2.93	2.56		3.58		2.56	2.16
		53 (63)	*50* (51)		*58* (33)		*47* (87.5)	*41* (53.5)
Indiana University	2.16	3.99	3.00	2.97	3.53		3.37	
	37 (28)	*63* (16)	*54* (36)	*50* (45)	*58* (34.5)		*56* (33.5)	
Iowa State University	2.03	3.76	1.81	2.05	2.59		3.17	3.89
	36 (30)	*61* (26)	*43* (77.5)	*39* (89)	*48* (77)		*54* (49.5)	*60* (14)
University of Iowa		2.72	2.31	2.46	2.85		2.79	2.39 [m]
		51 (76)	*48* (62)	*44* (68)	*51* (62)		*50* (73)	*43* (48)
								3.00 [l]
								50 (35)
Johns Hopkins University		3.74	2.96	3.95	3.04 [c]		3.51	3.55
		61 (27)	*54* (37)	*62* (17)	*53* (49.5)		*58* (29)	*56* (21)
					3.65			
					59 (30.5)			
Kansas State University		2.66	1.75		2.35		2.33	2.24
		51 (77)	*42* (82)		*46* (91)		*45* (102)	*42* (50)
University of Kansas		2.89	1.62	2.82			2.46	
		53 (68)	*41* (86)	*48* (51)			*46* (93)	
Kent State University		1.81	1.25	1.78	2.41		2.65	
		42 (128)	*37* (100)	*36* (95)	*46* (86)		*48* (78)	
University of Kentucky		2.20	2.12	2.25	2.72		2.48	2.27
		46 (99)	*46* (65)	*41* (83)	*50* (71)		*46* (91.5)	*42* (49)
Lehigh University		2.48	1.32	2.69	2.22		2.39	
		49 (84)	*38* (96)	*47* (59)	*44* (97)		*45* (98)	
Louisiana State U & A&M College	2.06	2.91	1.81	2.83	2.74	2.42	2.64	
	36 (29)	*53* (65.5)	*43* (77.5)	*49* (50)	*50* (69.5)	*41* (23)	*48* (79.5)	
University of Louisville		1.59						
		40 (144)						
Loyola University of Chicago		1.56						
		40 (145)						
University of Maine		1.60					2.18	
		40 (143)					*43* (112)	
University of Maryland College Park	3.07	3.08	3.69		3.97	3.42	4.02	
	48 (19)	*55* (52.5)	*61* (16)		*62* (18)	*53* (10)	*63* (18)	

Appendix Table H - 4 Physical Sciences and Mathematics (Continued)

Institution	Astrophysics/ Astronomy	Chemistry	Computer Science	Geosciences	Mathematics	Ocean- ography	Physics	Statistics/ Biostatistics
U of Maryland Baltimore County			1.54		1.69			
			40 (89.5)		*39* (119)			
Massachusetts Inst of Technology	4.00	4.86	4.91	4.67	4.92	4.62	4.87	
	58 (8)	*72* (5)	*73* (2)	*71* (2)	*72* (3)	*68* (2)	*72* (3.5)	
U of Massachusetts at Amherst	3.04	2.98	3.59	2.95	2.90	1.77	2.97	2.68
	47 (20)	*54* (58)	*60* (18)	*50* (47)	*51* (58.5)	*33* (24)	*52* (64)	*46* (42)
University of Mass-Lowell		1.80	1.29				1.92	
		42 (130)	*38* (97.5)				*40* (125)	
Medical University South Carolina								1.92
								38 (58)
Miami University		2.06						
		45 (113)						
University of Miami		1.67		2.92	2.12	3.29	2.03	
		41 (138)		*50* (48)	*43* (103)	*51* (11)	*41* (122)	
Michigan State University		3.35	2.53	2.31	3.05		3.43	3.14
		57 (39)	*50* (53)	*42* (82)	*53* (48)		*57* (32)	*51* (30)
Michigan Technological University				2.14			1.47	
				40 (86)			*35* (139)	
University of Michigan	2.65	3.53	3.49	3.94	4.23		*3.96*	3.02 [m]
	43 (25)	*59* (35)	*59* (21)	*62* (18)	*65* (9.5)		*62* (19)	*50* (34)
								3.44 [l]
								55 (24.5)
University of Minnesota	2.89	3.89	2.67	3.35	4.08		3.76	2.52 [m]
	46 (24)	*62* (21)	*51* (47)	*55* (31)	*63* (14)		*60* (22.5)	*45* (45)
								3.91 [l]
								60 (13)
Mississippi State University		1.12	1.26					
		36 (159)	*37* (99)					
University of Mississippi		1.13			0.97		1.42	
		36 (157)			*32* (136)		*35* (141)	
University of Missouri-Columbia		2.13			2.30		2.38	
		45 (107)			*45* (94.5)		*45* (99)	
Univ of Missouri-Kansas City		1.08						
		35 (161)						
University of Missouri-Rolla		2.09	1.10	1.22	1.33		2.00	
		45 (111)	*36* (106)	*28* (99)	*35* (129)		*41* (124)	
Univ of Missouri-Saint Louis		2.02						
		44 (116)						
Montana State University		2.13					2.27	
		45 (107)					*44* (106)	
University of Montana		0.98						
		34 (162)						
Naval Postgraduate School			1.67			2.54		
			41 (84)			*42* (22)		
University of Nebraska-Lincoln		2.91	1.89	1.82	2.40		2.64	
		53 (65.5)	*44* (74)	*36* (93)	*46* (87)		*48* (79.5)	

Appendix Table H - 4 Physical Sciences and Mathematics (Continued)

Institution	Astrophysics/ Astronomy	Chemistry	Computer Science	Geosciences	Mathematics	Ocean- ography	Physics	Statistics/ Biostatistics
University of Nevada, Reno		2.23		2.64			1.31	
		46 (98)		*46* (62)			*33* (142)	
University of New Hampshire		2.29					2.41	
		47 (93)					*45* (96)	
New Mexico Inst of Mining & Tech		0.37	0.52	2.74			1.57	
		28 (168)	*30* (107)	*47* (55)			*36* (136)	
New Mexico State University	1.85	1.91	1.80		1.95		2.19	
	34 (32)	*43* (120)	*43* (79.5)		*42* (111)		*43* (111)	
University of New Orleans		2.17						
		46 (102)						
New York University		2.65	3.60		4.49		3.14	
		50 (78.5)	*60* (17)		*67* (8)		*54* (53.5)	
North Carolina State University		2.64	2.36		2.90	2.86	3.16	3.54
		50 (80.5)	*48* (60)		*51* (58.5)	*46* (19)	*54* (51)	*56* (22)
U of North Carolina-Chapel Hill		3.97	3.16	2.75	3.24	3.22	3.14	3.70 [m]
		63 (17)	*56* (29)	*48* (53)	*55* (42)	*50* (13.5)	*54* (53.5)	*57* (18)
								3.98 [l]
								61 (11)
North Dakota State University		1.62						
		40 (142)						
University of North Dakota		1.31						
		37 (152)						
University of North Texas		1.84	1.35		2.06		*2.30*	
		43 (124)	*38* (94.5)		*43* (106)		*44* (105)	
Northeastern University		2.15			2.52	1.50	2.91	
		46 (105)			*48* (81)	*29* (26)	*51* (66)	
University of Northern Colorado								0.75
								26 (65)
Northern Illinois University		1.78		2.02	1.72			
		42 (133)		*39* (90)	*39* (118)			
Northwestern University		4.23	2.93	3.63	3.71		3.31	3.05
		66 (14)	*54* (38)	*58* (21)	*59* (28)		*55* (37)	*50* (33)
University of Notre Dame		2.94			3.11		3.06	
		53 (62)			*53* (46)		*53* (56)	
Oakland University							1.60	
							37 (135)	
Ohio State University	2.91	3.87	2.92	2.35 [k]	3.66		3.75	3.21
	46 (23)	*62* (22)	*54* (39)	*43* (78)	*59* (29)		*60* (24)	*52* (29)
				2.97				
				50 (45)				
Ohio University		1.42			1.57		2.60	
		39 (147)			*38* (124)		*48* (83.5)	
Oklahoma State University		2.19	0.21				2.07	
		46 (100)	*27* (108)				*42* (121)	
University of Oklahoma		2.26	1.17	2.77	2.18		2.42	
		47 (96)	*37* (101)	*48* (52)	*44* (99.5)		*46* (95)	

Appendix Table H - 4 Physical Sciences and Mathematics (Continued)

Institution	Astrophysics/ Astronomy	Chemistry	Computer Science	Geosciences	Mathematics	Ocean-ography	Physics	Statistics/ Biostatistics
Old Dominion University			1.55		1.39	3.01	1.70	
			40 (88)		*36* (128)	*48* (17)	*38* (132)	
Oregon Graduate Inst Sci & Tech		1.77	2.83				1.27	
		42 (134)	*53* (42)				*33* (143)	
Oregon State University		2.96	2.00	2.69	2.37	3.88	2.69	2.85
		53 (61)	*45* (70.5)	*47* (59)	*46* (90)	*59* (5)	*49* (76)	*48* (37.5)
University of Oregon		3.31	2.20	3.21	3.06		3.03	
		57 (41)	*47* (64)	*53* (35)	*53* (47)		*52* (60)	
Pennsylvania State University	3.00	3.95	2.52	4.11	3.50		3.08	3.65
	47 (21)	*63* (18.5)	*50* (54.5)	*64* (12)	*57* (37)		*53* (55)	*57* (19)
University of Pennsylvania		3.78	2.72 [d]	2.34	3.87		4.09	3.22
		61 (25)	*52* (45)	*42* (79)	*61* (22)		*64* (17)	*52* (28)
			3.31 [e]					
			58 (24.5)					
Phila Col of Pharmacy & Science		0.50						
		30 (166)						
University of Pittsburgh		3.56	2.81	2.41	2.88		3.27	2.19 [m]
		59 (34)	*53* (43)	*43* (75)	*51* (61)		*55* (40)	*41* (52)
								2.85 [l]
								48 (37.5)
Polytechnic University		2.11			2.18		1.91	
		45 (109)			*44* (99.5)		*40* (126)	
Princeton University	4.79	3.92	4.31	4.01	4.94		4.89	
	67 (2)	*63* (20)	*67* (6)	*63* (14)	*72* (1.5)		*73* (2)	
Univ of Puerto Rico-Rio Piedras		1.82					1.22	
		42 (126)					*33* (144)	
Purdue University		3.83	3.28	3.08	3.82		3.44	4.00
		62 (24)	*57* (26)	*52* (40.5)	*61* (24.5)		*57* (31)	*61* (10)
Rensselaer Polytechnic Inst		2.55	2.63	3.03	3.02		2.88	
		49 (82)	*51* (49)	*51* (42)	*53* (52)		*51* (68.5)	
University of Rhode Island		1.65			1.57	3.68	1.85	
		41 (140)			*38* (124)	*56* (6)	*39* (129)	
Rice University		3.70	3.55	3.53	3.49		3.25	
		61 (28.5)	*60* (19)	*57* (25)	*57* (38)		*55* (42.5)	
					3.82 [b]			
					61 (24.5)			
University of Rochester		3.63	3.13	2.42	2.90		3.60	3.09
		60 (31.5)	*56* (30)	*43* (73.5)	*51* (58.5)		*59* (26.5)	*51* (32)
							3.65 [j]	
							59 (25)	
Rockefeller University							3.46	
							57 (30)	
Rutgers State Univ-New Brunswick		2.97	3.25		3.96		3.82	3.76
		54 (59.5)	*57* (27)		*62* (19)		*61* (20)	*58* (17)
Rutgers State Univ-Newark		1.78						
		42 (133)						

Appendix Table H - 4 Physical Sciences and Mathematics (Continued)

Institution	Astrophysics/ Astronomy	Chemistry	Computer Science	Geosciences	Mathematics	Ocean-ography	Physics	Statistics/ Biostatistics
Saint Louis University				2.73	1.63			
				47 (57)	*39* (121)			
Seton Hall University		1.41						
		39 (148)						
University of South Carolina		3.24	1.36	2.74	2.60	2.85	2.58	2.16
		56 (47.5)	*38* (93)	*47* (55)	*48* (75)	*46* (20)	*47* (85.5)	*41* (53.5)
South Dakota Sch of Mines & Tech				1.80				
				36 (94)				
University of South Florida		1.90	2.03		1.90	3.07		
		43 (122)	*45* (69)		*41* (112)	*49* (15)		
University of Southern California		3.34	3.52	3.46	3.23		3.17	
		57 (40)	*60* (20)	*56* (28)	*55* (43)		*54* (49.5)	
Southern Illinois University		1.82			1.98			
		42 (126)			*42* (109)			
Southern Methodist University			1.54	2.74	1.83			2.75
			40 (89.5)	*47* (55)	*41* (116)			*47* (39.5)
Univ of Southern Mississippi		1.22						
		37 (154)						
Univ of Southwestern Louisiana			1.92		1.13			0.92
			44 (72)		*34* (134)			*27* (64)
Stanford University	2.96	4.87	4.97	3.96 [g]	4.68	2.98	4.53	4.76
	47 (22)	*72* (3.5)	*74* (1)	*63* (15.5)	*69* (6)	*47* (18)	*69* (9)	*69* (1.5)
				4.15				
				65 (9.5)				
				4.33 [f]				
				67 (5)				
State Univ of New York-Albany		2.13		2.42	2.48		2.58	
		45 (107)		*43* (73.5)	*47* (83.5)		*47* (85.5)	
State Univ of New York-Binghamton		2.15	1.10	2.44	2.74			
		46 (105)	*36* (106)	*44* (71)	*50* (69.5)			
State Univ of New York-Buffalo		2.99	2.42	2.24	2.79		2.24	1.97
		54 (57)	*49* (58)	*41* (84)	*50* (66.5)		*44* (108)	*39* (56)
State U of New York-Stony Brook	2.58	3.25	3.12	3.40	3.94	3.49	3.76	1.33
	42 (26)	*56* (46)	*56* (31)	*56* (29.5)	*62* (20)	*54* (8)	*60* (22.5)	*32* (63)
SUNY Col Environ Sci & Forestry		1.35						
		38 (149)						
Stevens Inst of Technology		1.21	1.13		1.62		2.23	
		36 (155)	*36* (104)		*38* (122)		*44* (109)	
Syracuse University		2.97	2.80	2.43	2.62		3.04	
		54 (59.5)	*53* (44)	*44* (72)	*49* (73)		*52* (58)	
Temple University		1.73	2.00		2.67		2.43	2.50
		42 (135)	*45* (70.5)		*49* (72)		*46* (94)	*44* (46)
University of Tennessee-Knoxville		2.65		2.65	2.59		2.83	
		50 (78.5)		*46* (61)	*48* (77)		*50* (72)	
Texas A&M University		4.11	2.30	2.86 [h]	2.84	3.26	3.22	3.78
		65 (15)	*48* (63)	*49* (49)	*51* (63.5)	*51* (12)	*54* (47.5)	*58* (15)

Appendix Table H - 4 Physical Sciences and Mathematics (Continued)

Institution	Astrophysics/ Astronomy	Chemistry	Computer Science	Geosciences	Mathematics	Ocean-ography	Physics	Statistics/ Biostatistics
Texas A&M University				3.20[f]				
				53 (36.5)				
Texas Christian University		2.07					0.67	
		45 (112)					*26* (146)	
Texas Tech University		2.35		1.97	2.03		2.10	
		48 (90)		*38* (91)	*43* (107)		*42* (119)	
University of Texas at Arlington		2.05	1.65		2.02		2.11	
		45 (114)	*41* (85)		*42* (108)		*42* (117)	
University of Texas at Austin	3.65	4.28	4.18	3.96	3.85		4.33	
	54 (10)	*66* (13)	*66* (7)	*63* (15.5)	*61* (23)		*67* (11)	
University of Texas at Dallas		1.32	1.84	2.47	0.76		2.48	1.94
		38 (151)	*43* (76)	*44* (67)	*30* (137)		*46* (91.5)	*38* (57)
University of Texas-El Paso				2.16				
				40 (85)				
University of Toledo		1.65						
		41 (140)						
Tufts University		1.69					2.66	
		41 (137)					*48* (77)	
Tulane University		1.90	1.14		2.59		2.12	
		43 (122)	*36* (102)		*48* (77)		*42* (116)	
University of Utah		3.63	2.90	2.97	3.52		3.04	
		60 (31.5)	*54* (40.5)	*50* (45)	*58* (36)		*52* (58)	
Vanderbilt University		2.43	1.90		2.39		*3.04*	
		48 (86)	*44* (73)		*46* (88)		*52* (58)	
University of Vermont		2.34						
		47 (91.5)						
Virginia Commonwealth University		1.69						
		41 (137)						
Virginia Polytech Inst & State U		2.90	2.10	3.47	2.79		2.86	2.74
		53 (67)	*46* (66)	*56* (27)	*50* (66.5)		*50* (71)	*47* (41)
University of Virginia	3.23	3.29	3.02		3.18		3.23	
	50 (17)	*57* (43)	*55* (35)		*54* (45)		*54* (45.5)	
Wake Forest University		1.23						
		37 (153)						
Washington State University		2.73	1.78	2.08	2.10		2.10	
		51 (75)	*43* (81)	*39* (87)	*43* (104)		*42* (119)	
Washington University		3.04	2.54	3.26	3.42		3.15	
		54 (55)	*50* (52)	*54* (32)	*57* (39)		*54* (52)	
University of Washington		3.70	4.04	3.55	3.39[a]	4.31	4.20	4.01[l]
		61 (28.5)	*65* (9)	*58* (23)	*56* (41)	*64* (3)	*65* (14)	*61* (9)
					3.76			4.21[m]
					60 (26)			*63* (6)
Wayne State University		3.08	1.80		2.30			
		55 (52.5)	*43* (79.5)		*45* (94.5)			
Wesleyan University		2.34			2.12			
		47 (91.5)			*43* (103)			

Appendix Table H - 4 Physical Sciences and Mathematics (Continued)

Institution	Astrophysics/ Astronomy	Chemistry	Computer Science	Geosciences	Mathematics	Ocean-ography	Physics	Statistics/ Biostatistics
West Virginia University		1.80		1.57				
		42 (130)		*33* (98)				
Western Michigan University					1.86			
					41 (113)			
Wichita State University		0.81						
		33 (165)						
College of William & Mary							3.00	
							52 (63)	
University of Wisconsin-Madison	3.46	4.46	4.00	3.56	4.10	3.04	3.79	4.06
	52 (14)	*68* (10)	*64* (10)	*58* (22)	*63* (13)	*48* (16)	*61* (21)	*61* (8)
University of Wisconsin-Milwaukee		1.94		1.64	1.84		*2.49*	
		44 (119)		*34* (97)	*41* (115)		*46* (90)	
Worcester Polytechnic Inst		0.81	1.13				1.48	
		33 (165)	*36* (104)				*35* (138)	
University of Wyoming		2.02		3.12	1.53			1.82
		44 (116)		*52* (39)	*38* (125)			*37* (59)
Yale University	3.31	4.38	3.73		4.55		4.21	3.62
	50 (15)	*67* (12)	*62* (14.5)		*68* (7)		*65* (13)	*57* (20)

Source: National Survey of Graduate Faculty

Notes: *a* Program in Applied Mathematics
b Program in Computational and Applied Mathematics
c Program in Mathematical Sciences
d Program in Decision Sciences, Wharton School
e Program in Computer and Information Science
f Program in Geophysics
g Program in Applied Earth Sciences
h Program in Geology
i Program in Meteorology
j Program in Optics
k Program in Geodetic Science and Surveying
l Program in Statistics
m Program in Biostatistics

Appendix Table H - 5 Faculty Quality Ratings of Research-Doctorate Programs in Social and Behavioral Sciences

Institution	Anthro-pology	Economics	Geography	History	Political Science	Psychology	Sociology
Adelphi University						2.04	
						43 (144)	
University of Akron				1.76		2.07	1.30
				40 (95)		*43* (141)	*37* (84)
University of Alabama		0.99		1.88		2.39	
		38 (95)		*41* (92)		*47* (112)	
University of Alabama-Birmingham						2.91	
						52 (74.5)	
American University	1.86	1.72		2.14	2.37	2.28	1.52
	34 (68)	*44* (71)		*44* (88)	*47* (59.5)	*45* (125)	*39* (80)
					1.94 [a]		
					43 (76.5)		
Arizona State University	3.31	1.85	3.35	2.37	2.67	3.35	1.87
	54 (26)	*46* (67)	*53* (15)	*46* (76.5)	*50* (43)	*57* (49)	*42* (73)
University of Arizona	4.11	2.78	3.17	2.88	2.89	3.47	3.78
	65 (5)	*53* (36.5)	*50* (19)	*51* (48.5)	*52* (35)	*58* (43)	*62* (14)
Univ of Arkansas-Fayetteville				1.70		1.89	
				39 (96)		*41* (152)	
Auburn University		1.68		1.22		1.85	
		44 (74)		*34* (105)		*41* (154)	
Ball State University						1.92	
						42 (149)	
Baylor University						1.58	
						38 (165)	
Biola University						0.86	
						31 (180)	
Boston College		2.53		2.57	2.00	2.00	2.32
		51 (43)		*48* (66)	*43* (75)	*43* (146)	*47* (55)
Boston University	2.44	3.39	2.67	2.67	1.69	2.65	2.67
	42 (51)	*59* (21)	*44* (27)	*49* (62)	*40* (82)	*49* (95.5)	*51* (44)
Bowling Green State University				1.66		2.76	1.59
				39 (97)		*51* (86)	*40* (76)
Brandeis University	2.28			3.41	2.41	2.93	2.19
	40 (59)			*56* (28)	*48* (55)	*52* (72)	*46* (60)
Brigham Young University				1.56		2.31	
				38 (99)		*46* (123)	
Brown University	2.73	3.34		3.96		3.62	2.84
	46 (43.5)	*58* (23)		*62* (14)		*60* (37)	*52* (38)
Bryn Mawr College						2.34	
						46 (121)	

Appendix Table H - 5 Social and Behavioral Sciences (Continued)

Institution	Anthro-pology	Economics	Geography	History	Political Science	Psychology	Sociology
California Institute Technology		3.54					
		60 (19)					
Cal Sch Prof Psych-Alameda						1.30	
						35 (171)	
Cal Sch Prof Psych-Fresno						0.91	
						31 (178)	
Cal Sch Prof Psych-Los Angeles						1.04	
						32 (176)	
Cal Sch Prof Psych-San Diego						1.04	
						32 (176)	
University of California-Berkeley	4.51	4.55	3.99	4.79	4.66	4.33	4.56
	71 (3)	*69* (7)	*61* (6.5)	*70* (2)	*70* (2)	*67* (9)	*70* (3)
University of California-Davis	3.51	2.75		3.19	2.61	3.42	
	57 (15)	*53* (38)		*54* (35)	*50* (46)	*57* (47)	
University of California-Irvine				2.99	3.14	3.85	
				52 (43)	*55* (32)	*62* (26)	
Univ of California-Los Angeles	3.67	4.12	3.95	4.59	4.25	4.61	4.36
	59 (9)	*65* (11)	*60* (8)	*68* (6)	*66* (8)	*70* (4)	*68* (5)
Univ of California-Riverside	2.39	1.72		2.62	2.36	3.02	3.27
	42 (55.5)	*44* (71)		*48* (63.5)	*47* (61)	*53* (70)	*57* (27.5)
Univ of California-San Diego	3.67	3.80		3.46	4.13	4.32	3.31
	59 (9)	*62* (16)		*57* (26)	*65* (9)	*67* (10)	*57* (22)
Univ of California-San Francisco						1.60	2.47
						38 (164)	49 (50.5)
Univ of California-Santa Barbara	3.40	2.38	4.16	3.34	2.74	3.28	3.30
	56 (20)	*50* (49)	*63* (4)	*55* (32)	*51* (41)	*56* (52)	*57* (23)
Univ of California-Santa Cruz						3.16	2.41
						55 (59.5)	*48* (53)
Carnegie Mellon University				3.09		4.29	
				53 (40.5)		*67* (11)	
Case Western Reserve Univ				2.05		2.77	
				43 (90)		*51* (85)	
Catholic University of America	1.21			2.36	0.95	2.27	1.12
	25 (69)			*46* (78)	*33* (96)	*45* (127)	*35* (92)
University of Chicago	4.77	4.95		4.49	4.41	3.98	4.77
	74 (1.5)	*72* (1.5)		*67* (8)	*68* (6)	*63* (18)	*72* (1)
University of Cincinnati		0.90	1.39	2.18	1.65	2.46	1.25
		37 (97)	*27* (36)	*44* (86)	*40* (83)	*47* (107)	*36* (87)
CUNY - Grad Sch & Univ Center	3.39	2.26		3.73	2.57	3.48	2.86
	55 (21.5)	*49* (53)		*59* (18)	*49* (47.5)	*58* (42)	*53* (37)
Claremont Graduate School		2.02		2.25	1.80	2.22	
		47 (60)		*45* (82)	*41* (78)	*45* (132)	

Appendix Table H - 5 Social and Behavioral Sciences (Continued)

Institution	Anthro-pology	Economics	Geography	History	Political Science	Psychology	Sociology
Clark Atlanta University					0.60		
					29 (97)		
Clark University		0.59	3.82			3.30	
		35 (106)	*59* (9)			*56* (50)	
Clemson University		1.67					
		44 (75)					
Colorado School of Mines		0.65					
		35 (104)					
Colorado State University		0.81				2.79	1.40
		37 (100)				*51* (82)	*38* (81)
University of Colorado	2.39	2.25	3.57	2.77	2.78	3.94	2.29
	42 (55.5)	*49* (54.5)	*55* (12)	*50* (55)	*51* (39)	*63* (22.5)	*47* (56.5)
Columbia University	3.49	4.07		4.63	3.84	4.04	3.76
	57 (16)	*65* (12)		*69* (5)	*62* (16)	*64* (16.5)	*62* (15)
University of Connecticut	2.80	1.40		2.89	2.31	3.28	2.54
	47 (40)	*42* (84)		*51* (46.5)	*47* (67)	*56* (52)	*49* (49)
Cornell University	3.21	3.56		4.22	3.85	4.15	3.02
	53 (31)	*60* (18)		*64* (13)	*62* (15)	*65* (14)	*54* (35)
Dartmouth College						2.80	
						51 (81)	
University of Delaware						3.18	2.00
						55 (57.5)	44 (69)
University of Denver					2.23	3.14	1.14
					46 (70)	*54* (62)	*35* (90)
University of Detroit Mercy						0.86	
						31 (180)	
Duke University	3.41	3.36		3.93	3.94	3.69	3.42
	56 (18.5)	*58* (22)		*61* (15)	*63* (14)	*60* (33)	*58* (20)
Duquesne University						1.55	
						38 (167)	
East Texas State University						1.04	
						32 (176)	
Emory University				3.39	2.88	3.46	
				56 (31)	*52* (36)	*58* (44)	
Fairleigh Dickinson University						1.40	
						36 (170)	
Fielding Institute						0.84	
						30 (181)	
Florida State University		1.97		2.20	2.82	2.78	2.96
		46 (62)		*44* (83)	*52* (38)	*51* (83.5)	*53* (36)
University of Florida	3.65	2.65	2.86	3.09	2.48	3.60	2.68
	59 (11)	*52* (41)	*46* (24)	*53* (40.5)	*48* (51.5)	*59* (38)	*51* (43)

Appendix Table H - 5 Social and Behavioral Sciences (Continued)

Institution	Anthro-pology	Economics	Geography	History	Political Science	Psychology	Sociology
Fordham University		0.93		1.13	1.12	1.92	1.36
		38 (96)		33 (106)	34 (95)	42 (149)	37 (82)
Fuller Theological Seminary						1.73	
						40 (160)	
George Mason University		2.46				2.49	
		51 (47)				48 (106)	
George Washington University		1.83		2.75	2.57	2.52	
		45 (68)		50 (57)	49 (47.5)	48 (104)	
Georgetown University		2.25		2.84	2.85	2.27	
		49 (54.5)		51 (50)	52 (37)	45 (127)	
Georgia Institute of Technology						2.87	
						52 (77.5)	
Georgia State University		1.77				2.53	1.11
		45 (69)				48 (103)	35 (94)
University of Georgia		1.95	3.02	2.75	2.66	3.10	2.60
		46 (63)	48 (21)	50 (57)	50 (44.5)	54 (65)	50 (47.5)
Hahnemann University						2.13	
						44 (138)	
Harvard University	4.43	4.95		4.71	4.88	4.48	4.18
	70 (4)	72 (1.5)		69 (4)	73 (1)	69 (6)	66 (7)
University of Hawaii at Manoa	2.78	1.38	2.36	2.51	2.49	2.87	1.59
	47 (41)	42 (85)	40 (30)	47 (69)	48 (50)	52 (77.5)	40 (76)
Univ of Health Sc/Chicago Med Sch						2.17	
						44 (135)	
Hofstra University						1.82	
						41 (155)	
University of Houston		2.14		2.62	2.96	3.04	
		48 (57)		48 (63.5)	53 (33)	53 (69)	
Howard University		0.83		1.81	1.62	2.35	1.59
		37 (99)		40 (93)	39 (85)	46 (119)	40 (76)
Idaho State University					0.33		
					26 (98)		
Illinois Institute of Technology						1.79	
						40 (157)	
Illinois State University				0.67			
				29 (108)			
U of Illinois at Urbana-Champaign	3.59	3.07	3.30	3.50	3.20	4.58	3.26
	58 (14)	56 (28)	52 (16)	57 (25)	56 (30)	70 (5)	57 (29)
University of Illinois at Chicago		1.72		2.79		3.05	2.66
		44 (71)		50 (53)		54 (68)	50 (45)
Indiana University	3.24	2.51	2.77	3.57	3.45	3.97	3.94
	53 (29)	51 (44)	45 (25)	58 (24)	58 (20)	63 (19.5)	63 (12)

Appendix Table H - 5 Social and Behavioral Sciences (Continued)

Institution	Anthro-pology	Economics	Geography	History	Political Science	Psychology	Sociology
Iowa State University		2.78				2.82	2.15
		53 (36.5)				*51* (79)	*45* (61.5)
University of Iowa	2.73	2.97	3.23	3.40	3.25	3.64	2.80
	46 (43.5)	*55* (30)	*51* (17)	*56* (29.5)	*56* (25)	*60* (36)	*52* (40.5)
Jewish Theological Seminary				2.07			
				43 (89)			
Johns Hopkins University	3.39	2.87	2.87	4.42	3.37	3.68	3.56
	55 (21.5)	*54* (32)	*46* (23)	*66* (9)	*57* (21)	*60* (34.5)	*60* (17)
Kansas State University						2.15	
						44 (136)	
University of Kansas	2.35	1.71	2.69	3.13	2.33	3.22	2.10
	41 (57.5)	*44* (73)	*44* (26)	*53* (39)	*47* (63)	*55* (55.5)	*45* (66)
Kent State University			1.95	2.19	1.14	2.61	1.18
			35 (35)	*44* (84.5)	*35* (94)	*49* (98)	*36* (88)
University of Kentucky	2.51	1.90	3.10	2.48	2.42	2.69	2.40
	43 (49)	*46* (64)	*49* (20)	*47* (71)	*48* (54)	*50* (89.5)	*48* (54)
Lehigh University		1.16				1.95	
		40 (89)				*42* (147)	
Louisiana State U & A&M College		1.53	3.19	2.46	2.02	2.28	2.12
		43 (81.5)	*51* (18)	*47* (73.5)	*43* (74)	*45* (125)	*45* (65)
University of Louisville						2.41	
						47 (109)	
Loyola University of Chicago				2.34		2.50	2.02
				46 (79.5)		*48* (105)	*44* (68)
University of Maine						2.35	
						46 (119)	
University of Maryland College Park		3.46	2.40	3.40	3.23	3.28	3.06
		59 (20)	*40* (29)	*56* (29.5)	*56* (29)	*56* (52)	*55* (33)
U of Maryland Baltimore County						2.38	
						47 (114)	
Massachusetts Inst of Technology		4.93			3.96		
		72 (3)			*63* (12)		
U of Massachusetts at Amherst	3.04	2.37		2.68	2.37	3.78	2.83
	51 (35)	*50* (50.5)		*49* (61)	*47* (59.5)	*61* (27)	*52* (39)
Miami University				2.34		2.40	
				45 (79.5)		*47* (111)	
University of Miami						3.18	
						55 (57.5)	
Michigan State University	2.58	3.09		2.88	3.24	3.43	2.72
	44 (46)	*56* (27)		*51* (48.5)	*56* (27)	*58* (46)	*51* (42)
University of Michigan	4.77	4.03		4.30	4.60	4.63	4.39
	74 (1.5)	*64* (13)		*65* (11)	*70* (3.5)	*70* (2)	*68* (4)

Appendix Table H - 5 Social and Behavioral Sciences (Continued)

Institution	Anthropology	Economics	Geography	History	Political Science	Psychology	Sociology
University of Minnesota	2.49	4.22	4.22	3.66	3.95	4.46	3.29
	43 (50)	*66* (10)	*64* (3)	*59* (21.5)	*63* (13)	*68* (7)	*57* (24)
Mississippi State University				0.88		0.80	1.27
				31 (107)		*30* (182)	*36* (86)
University of Mississippi						2.18	
						44 (134)	
University of Missouri-Columbia	2.40	1.04		2.81	1.79	3.07	2.14
	42 (53.5)	*39* (93)		*50* (51)	*41* (79)	*54* (67)	*45* (63)
		0.70[b]					
		36 (103)					
Univ of Missouri-Kansas City						1.90	
						41 (151)	
Univ of Missouri-Saint Louis						2.07	
						43 (141)	
University of Montana						1.73	
						40 (160)	
University of Nebraska-Lincoln		1.19	2.32	2.19	2.33	2.65	2.04
		40 (87)	*39* (32)	*44* (84.5)	*47* (63)	*49* (95.5)	*44* (67)
University of Nevada, Reno						2.21	
						45 (133)	
University of New Hampshire		0.74		2.48		2.56	1.99
		36 (101)		*47* (71)		*48* (101)	*44* (70)
New Mexico State University						2.23	
						45 (130)	
University of New Orleans					1.45	1.64	
					38 (88)	*39* (163)	
New York University	3.60	3.62		3.63	2.40	3.68	3.34
	58 (13)	*61* (17)		*58* (23)	*47* (56)	*60* (34.5)	*57* (21)
North Carolina State University		2.61				2.33	2.13
		52 (42)				*46* (122)	*45* (64)
U of North Carolina-Chapel Hill	3.24	3.16	2.89	3.84	3.54	3.90	4.31
	53 (29)	*57* (25)	*47* (22)	*61* (17)	*59* (18)	*63* (25)	*67* (6)
U of North Carolina-Greensboro						2.67	
						50 (92)	
University of North Dakota				0.62		1.50	
				28 (110)		*37* (168)	
University of North Texas				1.48	1.64	1.76	1.12
				37 (100)	*40* (84)	*40* (158)	*35* (92)
Northeastern University		0.47				2.92	1.98
		34 (107)				*52* (73)	*44* (71)
Northern Arizona University				1.29	1.17		
				35 (103)	*35* (93)		

Appendix Table H - 5 Social and Behavioral Sciences (Continued)

Institution	Anthropology	Economics	Geography	History	Political Science	Psychology	Sociology
University of Northern Colorado						1.22	
						34 (172)	
Northern Illinois University		1.02		2.79	1.77	2.06	
		38 (94)		50 (53)	41 (80)	43 (142)	
Northwestern University	3.09	4.39		3.85	3.35	3.91	4.07
	51 (34)	67 (9)		61 (16)	57 (22)	63 (24)	65 (9)
University of Notre Dame		1.53		2.74	2.66	2.70	2.63
		43 (81.5)		49 (59)	50 (44.5)	50 (87.5)	50 (46)
Ohio State University	1.89	2.83	4.07	3.15	3.69	3.95	3.28
	35 (66)	54 (34)	62 (5)	54 (37.5)	61 (17)	63 (21)	57 (25.5)
Ohio University				2.79		2.35	
				50 (53)		46 (119)	
Oklahoma State University		1.23				1.55	0.60
		40 (86)				38 (167)	30 (95)
University of Oklahoma	1.89			2.39	1.94	2.37	1.15
	35 (66)			46 (75)	43 (76.5)	46 (116)	35 (89)
Old Dominion University						1.81	
						41 (156)	
Oregon State University			2.03				
			35 (33)				
University of Oregon	2.66	1.98	2.61	2.58	2.21	3.94	2.29
	45 (45)	47 (61)	43 (28)	48 (65)	45 (71)	63 (22.5)	47 (56.5)
Pacific Grad Sch of Psychology						1.06	
						33 (174)	
Pennsylvania State University	3.18	2.49	4.59	2.46	2.25	3.72	3.51
	53 (32)	51 (45)	69 (1)	47 (73.5)	46 (69)	61 (32)	59 (18)
University of Pennsylvania	3.94	4.43		4.24	2.68	4.35	4.02
	63 (6)	68 (8)		65 (12)	50 (42)	67 (8)	64 (11)
University of Pittsburgh	3.34	2.83		3.15	3.15	3.38	2.21
	55 (25)	54 (34)		54 (37.5)	55 (31)	57 (48)	46 (59)
Princeton University	3.30	4.84		4.75	4.39	4.22	3.79
	54 (27)	71 (5)		70 (3)	68 (7)	66 (13)	62 (13)
Univ of Puerto Rico-Rio Piedras				0.50		1.40	
				27 (111)		36 (170)	
Purdue University		2.37		2.52	2.38	3.74	2.44
		50 (50.5)		47 (68)	47 (58)	61 (29.5)	48 (52)
Rensselaer Polytechnic Inst		0.70					
		36 (103)					
University of Rhode Island						2.57	
						49 (100)	
Rice University		2.47		3.21	2.43	3.08	
		51 (46)		54 (34)	48 (53)	54 (66)	

Appendix Table H - 5 Social and Behavioral Sciences (Continued)

Institution	Anthro-pology	Economics	Geography	History	Political Science	Psychology	Sociology
University of Rochester	1.89	4.01		3.45	4.01	3.73	
	35 (66)	*64* (14)		*57* (27)	*64* (11)	*61* (31)	
Rutgers State Univ-New Brunswick	3.38	2.36	3.39	3.67	3.24	3.76	3.09
	55 (23.5)	*50* (52)	*53* (13)	*59* (20)	*56* (27)	*61* (28)	*55* (31)
Rutgers State Univ-Newark						0.74	
						29 (183)	
St. John's University						2.05	
						43 (143)	
Saint Louis University						2.13	
						44 (138)	
Saybrook Institute						1.08	
						33 (173)	
University of South Carolina		1.89		2.33	2.39	2.67	
		46 (65)		*45* (81)	*47* (57)	*50* (92)	
University of South Florida	2.17					3.22	
	39 (60)					*55* (55.5)	
University of Southern California		2.66		2.48	2.33	3.74	2.80
		52 (40)		*47* (71)	*47* (63)	*61* (29.5)	*52* (40.5)
Southern Illinois University	2.76	1.65				2.58	1.56
	47 (42)	*44* (77)				*49* (99)	*39* (78)
Southern Methodist University	3.10	2.04					
	51 (33)	*47* (59)					
Univ of Southern Mississippi				0.66		1.72	
				29 (109)		*40* (161)	
Stanford University	*3.71*	4.92		4.56	4.50	4.82	4.08
	60 (7)	*72* (4)		*68* (7)	*69* (5)	*72* (1)	*65* (8)
State Univ of New York-Albany	2.82	1.65			2.32	3.16	3.22
	48 (39)	*44* (77)			*47* (65.5)	*55* (59.5)	*56* (30)
State Univ of New York-Binghamton	3.02	1.88		3.04	2.27	2.91	3.03
	50 (36)	*46* (66)		*53* (42)	*46* (68)	*52* (74.5)	*54* (34)
State Univ of New York-Buffalo	3.01	2.09	3.63	2.71	2.06	3.15	1.78
	50 (37)	*48* (58)	*56* (11)	*49* (60)	*44* (72)	*55* (61)	*42* (74)
State U of New York-Stony Brook	2.97	2.73		2.90	2.92	3.59	3.28
	50 (38)	*53* (39)		*51* (45)	*53* (34)	*59* (39)	*57* (25.5)
Stevens Inst of Technology						0.20	
						24 (185)	
Syracuse University	2.09	2.21	3.99	2.75	2.77	2.88	2.22
	38 (61)	*49* (56)	*61* (6.5)	*50* (57)	*51* (40)	*52* (76)	*46* (58)
Temple University	2.40	1.11		2.37	1.54	3.12	2.15
	42 (53.5)	*39* (91)		*46* (76.5)	*39* (86)	*54* (63.5)	*45* (61.5)
University of Tennessee-Knoxville	2.42	1.62		1.89	1.36	2.66	1.55
	42 (52)	*44* (79)		*41* (91)	*37* (90)	*49* (94)	*39* (79)

Appendix Table H - 5 Social and Behavioral Sciences (Continued)

Institution	Anthro-pology	Economics	Geography	History	Political Science	Psychology	Sociology
Texas A&M University		2.83		2.15		2.94	2.47
		54 (34)		*44* (87)		*52* (71)	*49* (50.5)
Texas Christian University				1.40		2.23	
				36 (101)		*45* (130)	
Texas Tech University				1.61	1.20	2.35	
				38 (98)	*35* (91)	*46* (119)	
University of Texas at Arlington						2.55	
						48 (102)	
University of Texas at Austin	3.62	2.91	3.38	3.66	3.49	4.04	3.64
	59 (12)	*55* (31)	*53* (14)	*59* (21.5)	*59* (19)	*64* (16.5)	60 (16)
University of Texas at Dallas		0.89		1.28	1.18	2.23	
		37 (98)		*35* (104)	*35* (92)	*45* (130)	
U of Texas-Southwestern Med Ctr						2.69	
						50 (89.5)	
Texas Woman's University						0.73	
						29 (184)	
University of Toledo						2.00	
						43 (146)	
Tufts University					2.51	2.45	
					49 (49)	*47* (108)	
Tulane University	2.56	1.54		2.53	1.49	2.23	1.91
	44 (47.5)	*43* (80)		*47* (67)	*38* (87)	*45* (130)	*43* (72)
University of Tulsa						2.38	
						46 (114)	
Uniformed Services U of Hlth Sci						3.54	
						59 (41)	
Utah State University		0.64				1.64	1.12
		35 (105)				*39* (163)	*35* (92)
University of Utah	2.56	1.15	1.96		1.74	3.23	1.34
	44 (47.5)	*40* (90)	*35* (34)		*41* (81)	*55* (54)	*37* (83)
Vanderbilt University	2.35	2.40		3.17	2.32	3.55	3.27
	41 (57.5)	*50* (48)		*54* (36)	*47* (65.5)	*59* (40)	*57* (27.5)
Peabody Col at Vanderbilt Univ						3.44	
						58 (45)	
University of Vermont						2.78	
						51 (83.5)	
Virginia Commonwealth University						2.63	
						49 (97)	
Virginia Polytech Inst & State U						2.67	
						50 (92)	
University of Virginia	3.38	3.20		3.68	3.24	3.97	2.60
	55 (23.5)	*57* (24)		*59* (19)	*56* (27)	*63* (19.5)	*50* (47.5)

Appendix Table H - 5 Social and Behavioral Sciences (Continued)

Institution	Anthro-pology	Economics	Geography	History	Political Science	Psychology	Sociology
Washington State University	2.00	1.42		1.78	1.39	2.37	3.08
	36 (63)	*42* (83)		*40* (94)	*37* (89)	*46* (116)	*55* (32)
Washington University	3.42	3.00		2.96	3.29	3.12	
	56 (17)	*55* (29)		*52* (44)	*57* (24)	*54* (63.5)	
University of Washington	3.24	3.15	3.66	3.31	3.34	4.24	4.03
	53 (29)	*57* (26)	*57* (10)	*55* (33)	*57* (23)	*66* (12)	*64* (10)
Wayne State University	1.98				2.04	2.81	
	36 (64)				*44* (73)	*51* (80)	
West Virginia University		1.06		1.37		2.70	
		39 (92)		*36* (102)		*50* (87.5)	
Western Michigan University						1.87	1.29
						41 (153)	*37* (85)
College of William & Mary				2.89			
				51 (46.5)			
University of Wisconsin-Madison	3.41	3.93	4.40	4.37	4.09	4.09	4.74
	56 (18.5)	*63* (15)	*66* (2)	*66* (10)	*65* (10)	*65* (15)	*71* (2)
University of Wisconsin-Milwaukee	2.08	1.17	2.35		2.48	2.12	
	37 (62)	*40* (88)	*40* (31)		*48* (51.5)	*44* (139)	
University of Wyoming		1.65				1.90	
		44 (77)				*41* (151)	
Yale University	*3.67*	4.70		4.89	4.60	4.62	3.49
	59 (9)	*70* (6)		*71* (1)	*70* (3.5)	*70* (3)	*59* (19)
Yeshiva University						2.40	
						47 (111)	

Source: National Survey of Graduate Faculty

Notes: *a* Program in International Relations

b Program in Agricultural Economics

APPENDIX I

Effectiveness Ratings of Research-Doctorate Programs

Respondents to the National Survey of Graduate Faculty rated the "Effectiveness of Program in Educating Research Scholars/Scientists" for each program included in the survey. For purposes of analysis, scores were converted to a scale of 0 to 5, with 0 denoting "Not Effective" and 5 denoting "Extremely Effective." Ratings for each program were summed and an average rating computed, as described in Appendix F. In the pages that follow, mean ratings of program effectiveness in the 41 fields included in the study are reported by broad field and by institution. The first line for each program is the raw score. In the next line, a standardized score is given (in italic) and the program's ranking (in parenthesis) within a field. Standardized scores have been computed from the raw value of mean ratings for all programs in a field. A mean score of 50 represents the middle of the range of scores for that field. One standard deviation around the middle scores represents plus/minus 10 points. Program rankings are drawn from information in Appendixes J through N.

Appendix Table I - 1 Effectiveness Ratings of Research-Doctorate Programs in Arts and Humanities

Institution	Art History	Classics	Comp Literature	English L & L	French L & L	German L & L	Linguistics	Music	Philosophy	Religion	Spanish L & L
University of Alabama				2.61				1.91			
				48 (74.5)				37 (59)			
Andrews University										1.39	
										27 (38)	
Arizona State University				2.76							2.73
				50 (72)							47 (35)
University of Arizona			2.26	2.99			3.51	2.53	3.74		
			38 (40.5)	53 (54.5)			58 (9.5)	46 (44.5)	62 (10)		
Univ of Arkansas-Fayetteville				1.85							
				39 (111)							
Auburn University				2.11							
				42 (103)							
Ball State University				1.85				1.67			
				39 (111)				34 (62.5)			
Baylor University				1.31						2.65	
				33 (119)						46 (25.5)	
Boston College				2.94					2.35	3.12	
				52 (61)					44 (53.5)	53 (17)	
Boston University	2.73	1.78		3.33			2.60	2.50	2.91	2.90	2.57
	47 (26)	39 (26)		57 (32.5)			48 (23)	45 (46.5)	51 (33)	50 (20)	44 (40)
Bowling Green State University				2.38							
				45 (84)							
Brandeis University				3.05				3.73			
				53 (46.5)				62 (11)			
Brown University	3.05	3.46	2.99	3.76	3.11		2.69	2.54	3.62	3.26	3.76
	51 (18)	57 (8)	50 (20)	62 (15)	53 (14.5)		49 (22)	46 (42.5)	60 (12)	55 (12.5)	65 (1.5)
Bryn Mawr College	3.46	3.48									
	56 (12)	57 (7)									
University of California-Berkeley	4.18	4.41	3.83	4.53	3.90	3.88	3.40	4.11	3.66		3.61
	65 (4)	67 (1)	64 (4)	71 (1)	64 (5.5)	63 (2)	56 (13)	67 (4.5)	61 (11)		62 (6)

Institution	Art History	Classics	Comp Literature	English L & L	French L & L	German L & L	Linguistics	Music	Philosophy	Religion	Spanish L & L
University of California-Davis			2.46	2.79	2.83	2.65					3.20
			41 (38)	*50* (70)	*49* (22)	*46* (23)					*55* (20)
University of California-Irvine			3.63	3.60	2.71	3.10			2.96		3.33
			60 (10)	*60* (22)	*47* (27.5)	*52* (14)			*52* (31)		*57* (13.5)
Univ of California-Los Angeles	3.46	3.23	3.29	3.97	2.87	2.88	4.17	3.12	4.01		3.31
	56 (12)	*54* (11)	*55* (12.5)	*64* (11)	*50* (21)	*49* (21.5)	*65* (3)	*53* (25)	*65* (6)		*57* (15)
Univ of California-Riverside			2.56	3.08					2.61		
			43 (34)	*54* (45)					*48* (43)		
Univ of California-San Diego			3.01	3.26			3.08	2.61	3.47		3.07
			50 (18.5)	*56* (35.5)			*53* (16)	*47* (40)	*58* (15)		*53* (27.5)
Univ of California-Santa Barbara	2.78	1.91		3.37		2.60		2.89	2.04	3.33	3.23
	47 (25)	*40* (24)		*57* (28.5)		*45* (24)		*50* (29.5)	*41* (60)	*56* (11)	*56* (18)
Univ of California-Santa Cruz				2.97			3.80				
				52 (58)			*61* (6)				
Carnegie Mellon University				3.25					1.67		
				56 (37)					*36* (66)		
Case Western Reserve Univ	2.08			2.33				2.33			
	38 (35)			*45* (87)				*43* (49)			
Catholic University of America		0.56	1.95	1.47	1.09			2.54	2.57	2.74	1.70
		25 (29)	*33* (43)	*34* (117)	*25* (45)			*46* (42.5)	*47* (45)	*47* (23)	*28* (53)
University of Chicago	3.49	3.09	3.29	4.20	3.11		3.64	4.32	3.41	4.01	2.61
	56 (10)	*53* (14)	*55* (12.5)	*67* (7)	*53* (14.5)		*59* (8)	*69* (1)	*58* (17.5)	*66* (2)	*44* (38.5)
University of Cincinnati		1.96		2.17	1.83	2.09		2.81	1.95		
		41 (23)		*43* (99)	*35* (44)	*38* (26)		*49* (31)	*39* (61)		
CUNY - Grad Sch & Univ Center	3.38		2.66	3.62	3.28		2.99	3.79	2.84		3.16
	55 (15)		*45* (30)	*60* (20.5)	*55* (13)		*52* (17.5)	*62* (9.5)	*51* (35)		*54* (22.5)
Claremont Graduate School				2.35				1.82	1.58	2.78	
				45 (86)				*36* (61)	*35* (68)	*48* (21)	
University of Colorado				2.97			2.36	2.35			2.61
				52 (58)			*45* (30)	*43* (48)			*44* (38.5)
Columbia University	4.29	3.15	3.82	3.91	3.90			3.56	2.87	3.40	3.46
	66 (3)	*53* (13)	*63* (5)	*64* (13)	*63* (5.5)			*59* (13)	*51* (34)	*57* (10)	*60* (10)

Appendix Table I - 1 Arts and Humanities Continued)

Institution	Art History	Classics	Comp Literature	English L & L	French L & L	German L & L	Linguistics	Music	Philosophy	Religion	Spanish L & L
University of Connecticut			2.33	2.92			3.51				2.01
			39 (39)	*52* (63)			*58* (9.5)				*34* (51)
Cornell University	2.80	3.38	3.78	4.43	4.03	3.73	3.89	3.90	4.14		3.69
	47 (23)	*56* (10)	*63* (8)	*70* (2.5)	*65* (3)	*61* (4)	*62* (5)	*64* (8)	*67* (4)		*64* (3)
University of Delaware	3.33						2.55				
	54 (16)						*47* (27)				
University of Denver				2.32						2.61	
				45 (88)						*45* (27.5)	
Drew University				0.83						2.76	
				27 (126)						*48* (22)	
Duke University		3.01	3.80	3.98	3.78			3.33	2.58	3.90	3.10
		52 (15)	*63* (7)	*64* (10)	*62* (8)			*56* (19)	*47* (44)	*65* (3)	*53* (24.5)
Duquesne University									1.67	1.91	
									36 (66)	*35* (36)	
Emory University			2.72	3.15	2.71				3.00	3.59	
			46 (27.5)	*54* (41)	*47* (27.5)				*53* (26)	*60* (6)	
Florida State University	1.67			2.25				3.29	1.86		2.13
	33 (37)			*44* (97)				*56* (21)	*38* (63)		*36* (49)
University of Florida				3.26	2.13		1.91				2.10
				56 (35.5)	*39* (36.5)		*41* (35)				*35* (50)
Fordham University		1.38		1.76					2.20	2.61	
		34 (27)		*38* (114)					*43* (56)	*45* (27.5)	
Fuller Theological Seminary										2.04	
										37 (34)	
George Washington University				2.10							
				42 (105)							
Georgetown University						2.14	2.55		2.83		2.95
						39 (25)	*47* (27)		*50* (36)		*51* (31)
University of Georgia	0.79			2.92				2.16	1.81		2.38
	22 (38)			*52* (63)				*41* (53)	*38* (64)		*40* (45.5)
University of Hartford								2.21			
								41 (51)			

Institution	Art History	Classics	Comp Literature	English L & L	French L & L	German L & L	Linguistics	Music	Philosophy	Religion	Spanish L & L
Harvard University	4.11	3.86	3.81	4.14	2.92	3.78	2.99	4.26	3.77	4.10	3.40
	64 (5)	*61* (4)	*63* (6)	*66* (8)	*50* (19)	*62* (3)	*52* (17.5)	*69* (2)	*62* (9)	*68* (1)	*59* (12)
University of Hawaii at Manoa							2.81		1.11		
							50 (20)		*29* (71.5)		
Hebrew Union College										3.53	
										59 (7)	
University of Houston				2.50							
				47 (80)							
Howard University				2.29							
				44 (91.5)							
Idaho State University				0.83							
				27 (126)							
Illinois State University				1.76							
				38 (114)							
U of Illinois at Urbana-Champaign	2.79	2.60	2.50	3.41	2.94	3.05	3.22	3.60	2.78		3.33
	47 (24)	*47* (19)	*42* (36.5)	*58* (26)	*51* (18)	*52* (15)	*55* (15)	*60* (12)	*50* (38)		*57* (13.5)
University of Illinois at Chicago				2.58					3.33		
				48 (76)					*57* (20)		
Indiana University	2.87		2.97	3.62	3.07	3.02	2.50	3.04	3.06		3.24
	48 (22)		*50* (21)	*60* (20.5)	*52* (16)	*51* (16)	*47* (29)	*52* (27)	*53* (23)		*56* (17)
Indiana Univ of Pennsylvania				1.21			0.00				
				31 (122)			*20* (41)				
University of Iowa			2.79	3.13	2.69			3.13	2.68	2.58	
			47 (24)	*54* (42.5)	*47* (31)			*53* (24)	*49* (41)	*45* (29)	
Jewish Theological Seminary										3.26	
										55 (12.5)	
Johns Hopkins University	3.46	1.33	4.12	3.99	2.72	3.33			2.97		
	56 (12)	*34* (28)	*68* (2)	*65* (9)	*47* (26)	*56* (11)			*52* (30)		
University of Kansas	2.57			3.01	2.10		2.02	2.50	2.69		3.76
	44 (27)			*53* (51.5)	*39* (39)		*42* (34)	*45* (46.5)	*49* (40)		*65* (1.5)
Kent State University				2.27				2.10			
				44 (94.5)				*40* (56)			

Appendix Table I - 1 Arts and Humanities Continued)

Institution	Art History	Classics	Comp Literature	English L & L	French L & L	German L & L	Linguistics	Music	Philosophy	Religion	Spanish L & L
University of Kentucky				3.03				2.18	1.67		3.09
				53 (49)				*41* (52)	*36* (66)		*53* (26)
Lehigh University				2.29							
				44 (91.5)							
Louisiana State U & A&M College				2.99	2.73			2.74			
				53 (54.5)	*48* (25)			*48* (34)			
Loyola University of Chicago				2.54					2.50		
				47 (78)					*46* (47)		
University of Maryland	2.25		2.26	3.33	1.87			2.79	2.67		2.75
	40 (32)		*38* (40.5)	*57* (32.5)	*36* (43)			*49* (32)	*48* (42)		*47* (34)
Massachusetts Inst of Technology							4.39		3.91		
							67 (2)		*64* (7)		
U of Massachusetts at Amherst			2.50	3.09	1.88	2.88	4.44		3.37		2.67
			42 (36.5)	*54* (44)	*36* (42)	*49* (21.5)	*68* (1)		*57* (19)		*45* (37)
Miami University				2.82							
				51 (67)							
University of Miami				2.61				2.53	2.56		
				48 (74.5)				*45* (44.5)	*47* (46)		
Michigan State University				2.72	2.69		1.57	2.64	2.15		2.77
				49 (73)	*47* (31)		*37* (37)	*47* (38.5)	*42* (58)		*47* (33)
University of Michigan	3.58	4.26	3.17	3.87	3.73	2.98	2.10	4.03	3.88		3.53
	57 (7)	*65* (2)	*53* (16)	*63* (14)	*61* (9)	*51* (18)	*43* (33)	*66* (6.5)	*64* (8)		*61* (8)
Middle Tennessee State University				1.00							
				29 (123)							
University of Minnesota	2.43	2.33	2.75	3.68	2.91	3.48		2.74	2.98		3.00
	43 (29)	*45* (22)	*46* (26)	*61* (18)	*50* (20)	*58* (10)		*48* (34)	*52* (29)		*51* (30)
University of Mississippi				2.02							
				41 (108)							
University of Missouri-Columbia				2.80							2.19
				50 (69)							*37* (47.5)
Univ of Missouri-Kansas City								1.37			
								30 (65)			

Institution	Art History	Classics	Comp Literature	English L & L	French L & L	German L & L	Linguistics	Music	Philosophy	Religion	Spanish L & L
University of Nebraska-Lincoln				2.78					2.35		
				50 (71)					*45* (53.5)		
University of New Hampshire				2.37							
				45 (85)							
New Orleans Baptist Theo Seminary										1.56	
										30 (37)	
New York University	4.32	1.84	3.19	3.63	3.53	1.89	1.73	3.41			3.07
	67 (2)	*39* (25)	*53* (15)	*60* (19)	*58* (11)	*35* (29)	*39* (36)	*57* (17)			*53* (27.5)
U of North Carolina-Chapel Hill	2.46	3.57	2.76	3.47	2.69	2.91		3.52	3.41		3.01
	43 (28)	*58* (5)	*46* (25)	*58* (25)	*47* (31)	*50* (20)		*59* (14.5)	*58* (17.5)		*52* (29)
U of North Carolina-Greensboro				2.19							
				43 (98)							
University of North Dakota				1.95							
				40 (109)							
University of North Texas				2.05				3.20			
				41 (107)				*54* (22)			
University of Northern Colorado								1.93			
								37 (58)			
Northern Illinois University				2.11							
				42 (103)							
Northwestern University	3.57		3.01	3.37	2.75			3.30	2.99	2.73	
	57 (8)		*50* (18.5)	*57* (28.5)	*48* (24)			*56* (20)	*53* (27.5)	*47* (24)	
University of Notre Dame				2.92					3.61	3.24	
				52 (63)					*60* (13)	*55* (14)	
Ohio State University	1.98	2.38		3.33	2.77	2.97	3.46	2.74	3.07		2.80
	37 (36)	*45* (21)		*57* (32.5)	*48* (23)	*51* (19)	*57* (12)	*48* (34)	*54* (22)		*48* (32)
Ohio University				2.11							
				42 (103)							
Oklahoma State University				1.58							
				36 (115)							
University of Oklahoma				2.15				2.00			
				43 (100)				*38* (57)			

Appendix Table I - 1 Arts and Humanities Continued)

Institution	Art History	Classics	Comp Literature	English L & L	French L & L	German L & L	Linguistics	Music	Philosophy	Religion	Spanish L & L
University of Oregon			2.65	2.95	2.13		2.55	2.26	1.31		
			45 (31.5)	52 (60)	40 (36.5)		47 (27)	42 (50)	31 (69)		
Pennsylvania State University	2.31		2.55	3.16	2.70	2.03			2.17		3.20
	41 (31)		43 (35)	55 (40)	47 (29)	37 (27)			42 (57)		55 (20)
University of Pennsylvania	3.51	2.65	3.57	4.24	3.98	2.99	3.68	3.79	3.04	3.22	3.41
	56 (9)	48 (18)	59 (11)	67 (6)	65 (4)	51 (17)	60 (7)	62 (9.5)	53 (24.5)	55 (15)	59 (11)
University of Pittsburgh	3.04			3.33	2.01	1.57	2.26	2.64	4.43	1.95	3.10
	50 (19.5)			57 (32.5)	38 (41)	31 (32)	44 (31.5)	47 (38.5)	70 (2)	35 (35)	53 (24.5)
									4.26 [a]		
									68 (3)		
Princeton Theological Seminary										3.61	
										60 (5)	
Princeton University	3.78	4.15	3.96	3.94	4.35	3.91		4.18	4.56	3.89	3.65
	60 (6)	64 (3)	66 (3)	64 (12)	70 (2)	64 (1)		68 (3)	72 (1)	65 (4)	63 (5)
Univ of Puerto Rico-Rio Piedras											3.30
											57 (16)
Purdue University				3.05							
				53 (46.5)							
University of Rhode Island				2.50							
				47 (80)							
Rice University				2.98	2.59		1.47		2.80	2.41	
				52 (56)	46 (34)		36 (38)		50 (37)	42 (31)	
University of Rochester			2.14	2.97				4.03	3.04		
			36 (42)	52 (58)				66 (6.5)	53 (24.5)		
Rutgers State Univ-New Brunswick	3.04		2.92	3.71	2.62	1.76		3.03	3.44		2.72
	50 (19.5)		49 (22.5)	61 (16)	46 (33)	33 (30)		52 (28)	58 (16)		46 (36)
St. John's University				0.93							
				28 (124)							
Saint Louis University				2.55					2.46		
				47 (77)					46 (49)		
University of South Carolina			1.50	3.02			1.21	2.11			
			26 (44)	53 (50)			33 (40)	40 (55)			

Institution	Art History	Classics	Comp Literature	English L & L	French L & L	German L & L	Linguistics	Music	Philosophy	Religion	Spanish L & L
University of South Florida				1.28							
				32 (121)							
Southern Baptist Theological Sem								1.85		2.14	
								36 (60)		*38* (33)	
University of Southern California			2.72	3.40			3.39	2.66	2.73	2.22	
			46 (27.5)	*57* (27)			*56* (14)	*47* (37)	*49* (39)	*40* (32)	
Southern Illinois University				2.08					1.17		
				42 (106)					*30* (70)		
Southern Methodist University										3.13	
										53 (16)	
Univ of Southern Mississippi				2.26							
				44 (96)							
Univ of Southwestern Louisiana				1.78							
				38 (112)							
Stanford University	3.45	3.17	3.75	4.30	3.52	3.61	4.01	3.52	4.02	3.00	3.20
	56 (14)	*54* (12)	*62* (9)	*68* (4)	*58* (12)	*60* (7)	*63* (4)	*59* (14.5)	*65* (5)	*51* (19)	*55* (20)
State Univ of New York-Albany						1.96					2.38
						36 (28)					*40* (45.5)
State Univ of New York-Binghamton			2.92	3.04							
			49 (22.5)	*53* (48)							
State Univ of New York-Buffalo				3.51		1.63	2.56	2.67	2.22		2.48
				59 (23)		*32* (31)	*48* (25)	*47* (36)	*43* (55)		*42* (42)
State U of New York-Stony Brook			2.57	3.01			2.78	3.45	2.43		2.50
			43 (33)	*53* (51.5)			*50* (21)	*58* (16)	*45* (50)		*42* (41)
Syracuse University				2.29					3.52	2.65	2.19
				44 (91.5)					*59* (14)	*46* (25.5)	*37* (47.5)
Temple University				2.81				2.58	2.36	2.55	1.82
				50 (68)				*46* (41)	*45* (52)	*44* (30)	*30* (52)
University of Tennessee-Knoxville				2.84					1.11		
				51 (65)					*29* (71.5)		
Texas A&M University				2.83							
				51 (66)							

Appendix Table I - 1 Arts and Humanities Continued)

Institution	Art History	Classics	Comp Literature	English L & L	French L & L	German L & L	Linguistics	Music	Philosophy	Religion	Spanish L & L
Texas Christian University				2.27							
				44 (94.5)							
Texas Tech University				2.12				1.67			1.59
				42 (101)				*34* (62.5)			*26* (54)
University of Texas at Arlington				2.29			1.25				
				44 (91.5)			*34* (39)				
University of Texas at Austin	3.03	3.40	3.14	3.36	2.96	3.26	3.48	3.37	2.99		3.51
	50 (21)	*56* (9)	*53* (17)	*57* (30)	*51* (17)	*55* (12)	*57* (11)	*57* (18)	*53* (27.5)		*61* (9)
University of Texas at Dallas				1.36							
				33 (118)							
Texas Woman's University				0.83							
				27 (126)							
University of Toledo				1.28							
				32 (121)							
Tufts University				3.00							
				53 (53)							
Tulane University				2.31	2.12				2.14		2.47
				44 (89)	*39* (38)				*42* (59)		*42* (43)
University of Tulsa				2.46							
				46 (83)							
Union Theological Seminary in VA										3.10	
										53 (18)	
Vanderbilt University				3.13					2.95	3.50	
				54 (42.5)					*52* (32)	*59* (8)	
University of Virginia	3.07	2.57		4.27	3.61	3.54			2.42	3.46	3.55
	51 (17)	*47* (20)		*68* (5)	*60* (10)	*59* (9)			*45* (51)	*58* (9)	*61* (7)
Washington State University				2.50							
				47 (80)							
Washington University	2.24		2.65	3.18	2.55	3.55		3.14	2.47		3.16
	40 (33)		*45* (31.5)	*55* (39)	*45* (35)	*59* (8)		*54* (23)	*46* (48)		*54* (22.5)
University of Washington	2.15	2.87	3.21	3.48	2.08	3.17	2.92	2.89			2.46
	39 (34)	*50* (16)	*54* (14)	*58* (24)	*39* (40)	*53* (13)	*51* (19)	*50* (29.5)			*42* (44)

Institution	Art History	Classics	Comp Literature	English L & L	French L & L	German L & L	Linguistics	Music	Philosophy	Religion	Spanish L & L
Wayne State University				2.47							
				46 (82)							
Wesleyan University								2.14			
								40 (54)			
West Virginia University				1.57				1.45			
				36 (116)				*31* (64)			
University of Wisconsin-Madison	2.35	2.76	2.68	3.69	3.79	3.65	2.26	3.07	3.11		3.66
	42 (30)	*49* (17)	*45* (29)	*61* (17)	*62* (7)	*60* (6)	*44* (31.5)	*53* (26)	*54* (21)		*63* (4)
University of Wisconsin-Milwaukee				3.23							
				55 (38)							
Yale University	4.36	3.52	4.30	4.43	4.49	3.68	2.59	4.11	1.92		
	67 (1)	*57* (6)	*71* (1)	*70* (2.5)	*72* (1)	*61* (5)	*48* (24)	*67* (4.5)	*39* (62)		

Source: National Survey of Graduate Faculty

Note: *a* Program in the History and Philosophy of Science

Appendix Table I - 2 Effectiveness Ratings of Research-Doctorate Programs in Biological Sciences

Institution	Biochem & Molec Bio	Cell & Develop Bio	Eco, Evl & Behavior	Molec & Gen Genetics	Neuro-sciencs	Pharma-cology	Physiology
University of Alabama	1.50		2.62				
	37 (176)		46 (93)				
University of Alabama-Birmingham	3.54	3.39	2.22	3.33		3.05	3.70
	58 (37.5)	57 (47)	41 (106)	53 (46.5)		48 (84)	59 (17.5)
University of Alaska	0.00		3.16				3.33
	22 (194)		53 (52)				54 (56.5)
Albany Medical College	2.43	3.33		3.33	2.17	3.33	3.33
	47 (132)	56 (51.5)		53 (46.5)	44 (79)	53 (48)	54 (56.5)
Albert Einstein College of Med	3.88	3.64		3.60	3.61	3.44	3.57
	62 (23.5)	59 (26)		56 (27)	57 (23)	55 (38)	57 (29.5)
Arizona State University	2.78	2.67	3.33	2.33			3.33
	50 (98)	49 (111)	55 (42)	43 (81)			54 (56.5)
University of Arizona	3.49	3.25	3.77	3.26	3.21	3.60	3.60
	58 (43)	55 (56)	61 (13)	52 (55)	53 (50)	57 (28)	57 (27.5)
Univ of Arkansas-Fayetteville	2.50	0.83	2.03				
	48 (125)	30 (172)	39 (113)				
U of Arkansas for Medical Sci	2.17	1.67					
	44 (146)	39 (149)					
Auburn University		1.00 [a]					3.33
		32 (165)					54 (56.5)
		1.67 [d]					
		39 (149)					
Ball State University	2.22						
	45 (142)						
Baylor College of Medicine	3.88	3.58		4.05	3.48	3.29	3.84
	62 (23.5)	59 (31)		60 (11)	55 (28)	52 (55)	61 (10)
Boston University	0.00 [a]	2.08	2.75	1.43	0.56		3.10
	22 (194)	43 (133)	48 (84)	34 (93)	29 (97)		50 (86.5)
	2.74 [b]						
	50 (103)						
Bowling Green State University	1.67	1.67	2.50	n/s			2.50
	39 (169)	39 (149)	45 (96)				42 (116)
Brandeis University	3.92	3.57		3.49	3.88		
	62 (21)	58 (32)		54 (31)	59 (15)		
Brigham Young University	*1.67*	1.67	2.22				
	39 (169)	39 (149)	41 (106)				
Brown University	3.39	3.26	3.25		3.38	3.33	3.33
	57 (50)	55 (55)	54 (46.5)		55 (38.5)	53 (48)	54 (56.5)
California Institute Technology	4.41	4.68	2.00	4.47	4.22		3.70
	67 (6)	70 (1)	38 (115)	64 (4)	62 (10)		59 (17.5)

Appendix Table I - 2 Biological Sciences (Continued)

Institution	Biochem & Molec Bio	Cell & Develop Bio	Eco, Evl & Behavior	Molec & Gen Genetics	Neuro-sciencs	Pharma-cology	Physiology
University of California-Berkeley	4.66	4.19	4.15	4.18	4.12		
	70 (3)	*65* (11)	*66* (6)	*62* (9)	*61* (12)		
University of California-Davis	3.65	3.63	4.12	3.56		3.75	3.64
	59 (30.5)	*59* (27.5)	*65* (8)	*55* (29.5)		*60* (20)	*58* (23)
University of California-Irvine	3.30	3.33	3.63	3.33	3.41 [b]	2.99	2.97
	56 (59)	*56* (51.5)	*59* (21.5)	*53* (46.5)	*55* (35.5)	*47* (92)	*48* (95)
					3.72 [a]		
					58 (19)		
Univ of California-Los Angeles	3.93	3.86	3.67		3.69	3.07	4.02
	62 (19.5)	*61* (18)	*60* (17.5)		*57* (20.5)	*48* (81.5)	*63* (5)
Univ of California-Riverside	3.29	2.99	3.51	3.33			1.67
	56 (60)	*52* (80)	*57* (27)	*53* (46.5)			*30* (131)
Univ of California-San Diego	4.37	4.15	3.50	4.17	4.48	3.87	4.25
	67 (7)	*64* (12)	*57* (28)	*61* (10)	*64* (2)	*62* (13)	*67* (2)
Univ of California-San Francisco	4.73	4.57		4.80	4.45		4.00
	71 (1)	*69* (3)		*68* (1)	*64* (3)		*63* (6)
Univ of California-Santa Barbara	3.42	2.74	3.63	2.99	1.19	3.00	1.67
	57 (48)	*50* (105)	*59* (21.5)	*49* (70)	*35* (90)	*47* (88.5)	*30* (131)
Univ of California-Santa Cruz	3.38	2.65	2.93	3.06	1.00	0.33	2.50
	57 (51)	*49* (112)	*50* (69)	*50* (64)	*33* (94.5)	*4* (127)	*42* (116)
Carnegie Mellon University	3.61						
	59 (33)						
Case Western Reserve Univ	3.24	3.40		3.33	3.69	3.00	3.56
	55 (63.5)	*57* (45)		*53* (46.5)	*57* (20.5)	*47* (88.5)	57 (31.5)
Catholic University of America	1.67	1.67					
	39 (169)	*39* (149)					
University of Chicago	3.93	4.03	4.31	4.25	3.60	3.53	3.86
	62 (19.5)	*63* (15)	*68* (2)	*62* (8)	*57* (24)	*56* (31)	*61* (9)
University of Cincinnati	3.00	2.86	2.33	3.33		3.03	3.18
	53 (82)	*51* (93.5)	*43* (101)	*53* (46.5)		*48* (86)	*51* (76)
CUNY - Grad Sch & Univ Center	2.87	2.41	2.99		2.58		
	51 (92)	*47* (123)	*51* (64)		*47* (70.5)		
Claremont Graduate School			3.24				
			54 (49)				
Clark Atlanta University	2.08	n/s					
	43 (149)						
Clark University	*0.93*	2.08	0.95	n/s	1.17		
	31 (185)	*43* (133)	*25* (125)		*35* (92)		
Clemson University	1.85	2.50	2.81	1.19		2.67	2.62
	41 (160)	*47* (118)	*49* (80.5)	*31* (94)		*42* (105)	*43* (109)
Colorado State University	2.72	2.82	2.91		3.47		3.62
	50 (106)	*51* (96)	*50* (71)		*55* (29)		*58* (25)

Appendix Table I - 2 Biological Sciences (Continued)

Institution	Biochem & Molec Bio	Cell & Develop Bio	Eco, Evl & Behavior	Molec & Gen Genetics	Neuro-sciencs	Pharma-cology	Physiology
University of Colorado	4.01	3.22[a]	3.37	3.39	3.33	3.86	3.13
	63 (15)	*55* (59)	*56* (40.5)	*54* (37.5)	*54* (44.5)	*61* (14)	*51* (82.5)
		3.40[b]					
		57 (45)					
Columbia University	4.25	3.89		3.93	4.29	3.33	3.83
	66 (11)	*62* (17)		*59* (14.5)	*63* (8)	*53* (48)	*61* (11.5)
University of Connecticut	2.92	2.90	3.46	3.24	3.10[b]	2.84[e]	3.41
	52 (88)	*52* (89.5)	*57* (31)	*52* (56)	*52* (53.5)	*45* (102)	*55* (42.5)
					3.26[a]	3.12[b]	
					54 (48)	*49* (76)	
Cornell University	3.94	3.75	4.24	3.92	3.74	3.07[d]	3.76
	62 (17.5)	*60* (23)	*67* (3)	*59* (16)	*58* (18)	*49* (81.5)	*60* (16)
						3.46[f]	
						55 (37)	
Creighton University	2.04	2.22					
	43 (152)	*45* (130)					
Dartmouth College	3.23		2.73			3.33	3.56
	55 (65)		*48* (85.5)			*53* (48)	*57* (31.5)
University of Dayton		0.83	1.25				
		30 (172)	*29* (124)				
University of Delaware	3.00						
	53 (82)						
Drexel University	1.67	0.95	0.83	1.67			
	39 (169)	*32* (168)	*24* (126)	*36* (89)			
Duke University	4.16	3.91	4.33	3.83	3.86	4.03	3.49
	65 (12)	*62* (16)	*68* (1)	*58* (18)	*59* (16)	*64* (6)	*56* (37)
East Carolina U Sch Medicine	2.67	1.67			1.19	2.67	2.36
	49 (114)	*39* (149)			*35* (90)	*42* (105)	*40* (118)
Emory University	3.03	3.19		3.28	3.46	3.81	3.49
	53 (77.5)	*55* (61.5)		*52* (54)	*55* (30)	*61* (17)	*56* (37)
Florida State University	2.50	3.33	3.29	3.13	2.90		3.33
	48 (125)	*56* (51.5)	*55* (44)	*51* (62)	*50* (62.5)		*54* (56.5)
University of Florida	3.21	2.94	3.43	3.45	3.04	3.25	3.49
	55 (67)	*52* (84.5)	*57* (36)	*54* (33)	*52* (57)	*51* (59.5)	*56* (37)
Fordham University		0.91	0.63				
		31 (169)	*21* (127)				
George Mason University			2.67				
			47 (89)				
George Washington University	2.59	1.67			2.92	2.99	
	48 (117)	*39* (149)			*50* (61)	*47* (92)	
Georgetown University	2.95	2.86			3.15	3.64	3.33
	52 (86)	*51* (93.5)			*53* (51)	*58* (24.5)	*54* (56.5)

Appendix Table I - 2 Biological Sciences (Continued)

Institution	Biochem & Molec Bio	Cell & Develop Bio	Eco, Evl & Behavior	Molec & Gen Genetics	Neuro-sciencs	Pharma-cology	Physiology
Georgia Institute of Technology	2.69	0.00		1.67			
	50 (112)	*22* (176)		*36* (89)			
Georgia State University	1.33	1.43			2.22		
	35 (179)	*37* (160)			*44* (78)		
University of Georgia	2.96	2.67 [d]	3.72	3.40		3.13	3.01
	52 (85)	*49* (111)	*60* (15)	*54* (36)		*49* (74)	*49* (92)
		3.08 [a]					
		53 (70)					
Hahnemann University	1.83	2.38		2.71	2.90	1.84	2.50
	41 (162)	*46* (124)		*47* (75)	*50* (62.5)	*28* (123)	*42* (116)
Harvard University	4.44	4.33		4.55	4.33	4.00	3.52
	68 (5)	*66* (7)		*65* (3)	*63* (6.5)	*64* (9)	*56* (33)
University of Hawaii at Manoa	2.00	1.67	3.05	2.41		2.92	3.13
	42 (155)	*39* (149)	*52* (60)	*44* (80)		*46* (98.5)	*51* (82.5)
Univ of Health Sc/Chicago Med Sch	2.59	2.50				2.08	2.57
	48 (117)	*47* (118)				*32* (122)	*43* (113)
University of Houston	2.89	2.82	2.12	1.11		2.54	1.67
	52 (90)	*51* (96)	*40* (108)	*30* (95.5)		*40* (111)	*30* (131)
Howard University	2.41		1.33	2.29		2.22	2.17
	47 (134)		*30* (122)	*42* (82)		*35* (120)	37 (123)
Idaho State University			2.71				
			47 (87)				
University of Idaho	1.98	1.67	1.67	0.00	0.00	1.16	0.00
	42 (157)	*39* (149)	*34* (120)	*19* (101)	*24* (101)	*17* (126)	*6* (137)
Illinois State University	2.71	2.29	2.02	1.00			3.33
	50 (109)	*45* (127)	*39* (114)	*29* (97)			*54* (56.5)
U of Illinois at Urbana-Champaign	3.59	3.62	3.62	3.33	3.37		3.92
	59 (35.5)	*59* (29.5)	*59* (23.5)	*53* (46.5)	*55* (40.5)		*62* (8)
University of Illinois at Chicago	3.11	2.92 [a]		3.06		3.33	3.18
	54 (70.5)	*52* (87)		*50* (64)		*53* (48)	*52* (76)
		3.14 [b]					
		54 (64.5)					
Indiana University	*3.40*	3.63	3.49	3.78		1.82	2.00
	57 (49)	*59* (27.5)	*57* (29)	*57* (20.5)		*28* (124)	*35* (124)
Iowa State University	3.33	3.33	3.00	2.87		2.92	3.06
	56 (55)	*56* (51.5)	*51* (62.5)	*48* (71)		*46* (98.5)	*50* (89)
University of Iowa	3.53	3.50	3.14	3.46	3.45	3.97	3.81
	58 (39)	*58* (39)	*53* (54.5)	*54* (32)	*55* (31.5)	*63* (11)	*60* (13)
Johns Hopkins University	4.26	3.79	3.15	4.01	4.33	4.22	3.77
	66 (10)	*61* (19)	*53* (53)	*60* (13)	*63* (6.5)	*67* (2)	*60* (14.5)
Kansas State University	2.78	2.08	3.00	2.78	1.19		2.95
	50 (98)	*43* (133)	*51* (62.5)	*47* (73)	*35* (90)		*48* (97)

Appendix Table I - 2 Biological Sciences (Continued)

Institution	Biochem & Molec Bio	Cell & Develop Bio	Eco, Evl & Behavior	Molec & Gen Genetics	Neuro-sciencs	Pharma-cology	Physiology
University of Kansas	2.71 [b]	2.08 [a]	3.62	2.50		3.20 [a]	3.33 [a]
	50 (109)	43 (133)	59 (23.5)	45 (78)		51 (68)	54 (56.5)
	2.50 [a]	2.69 [b]				3.56 [b]	3.33 [b]
	48 (125)	49 (109)				57 (29)	54 (56.5)
Kent State University	2.29	1.33	2.31		2.00	2.17	2.78
	45 (140)	36 (162)	42 (103)		42 (82.5)	34 (121)	46 (105)
University of Kentucky	2.76	2.08 [a]	2.92 [c]			3.00 [b]	3.23
	50 (101)	43 (133)	50 (70)			47 (88.5)	52 (71)
		2.94 [b]	2.95 [a]			3.64 [a]	
		52 (84.5)	50 (68)			58 (24.5)	
Lehigh University	1.67	1.33					
	39 (169)	36 (162)					
Loma Linda University	1.25	1.67	2.08		1.00	2.38	2.80
	35 (181)	39 (149)	40 (110)		33 (94.5)	37 (117)	46 (103)
Louisiana State U & A&M College	2.53	3.18	3.03	2.22	1.67	3.21	3.11
	48 (122)	55 (63)	52 (61)	42 (83.5)	39 (87)	51 (65)	50 (84)
Louisiana State U Medical Center	2.22	2.50		3.06		3.04	2.78
	45 (142)	47 (118)		50 (64)		48 (85)	46 (105)
Louisiana St U-Sch Med Shreveport	2.33	1.92				2.50	2.92
	46 (136)	42 (139)				39 (113)	48 (99.5)
University of Louisville	2.82	0.72		3.33	1.11	3.00	3.10
	51 (94)	29 (174)		53 (46.5)	34 (93)	47 (88.5)	50 (86.5)
Loyola University of Chicago	2.08	2.45				2.94	3.26
	43 (149)	47 (121)				46 (97)	53 (68)
University of Maine			2.63				
			46 (92)				
University of Maryland College Park	3.06	2.88	3.37				
	53 (74.5)	51 (92)	56 (40.5)				
Univ of Maryland at Baltimore	2.72	3.11		1.67		3.10	3.38
	50 (106)	54 (66)		36 (89)		49 (78.5)	54 (48)
U of Maryland Baltimore County	2.33	3.33					
	46 (136)	56 (51.5)					
Massachusetts Inst of Technology	4.68	4.66		4.75	4.07	3.69	
	70 (2)	70 (2)		67 (2)	61 (14)	59 (22.5)	
U of Massachusetts at Amherst	2.72	3.43	3.43		2.93		
	50 (106)	57 (42)	57 (36)		51 (60)		
U of Massachusetts Med Center	3.33	3.40		3.21		3.33	3.44
	56 (55)	57 (45)		52 (57.5)		53 (48)	55 (41)
University of Mass-Lowell	0.56						
	27 (189)						
Mayo Graduate School	3.08				3.27	3.50	3.68
	54 (73)				54 (47)	56 (32)	59 (19.5)

Appendix Table I - 2 Biological Sciences (Continued)

Institution	Biochem & Molec Bio	Cell & Develop Bio	Eco, Evl & Behavior	Molec & Gen Genetics	Neuro-sciencs	Pharma-cology	Physiology
Medical College of Georgia	1.50					3.26	2.58
	37 (176)					*52* (58)	*43* (112)
Medical College of Ohio	1.82				1.95	2.36	1.91
	40 (163)				*42* (84)	*37* (118)	*33* (126)
Medical College of Pensylvania	2.71	1.67			2.89	3.25	2.83
	50 (109)	*39* (149)			*50* (64.5)	*51* (59.5)	*47* (102)
Medical College of Wisconsin	1.98	2.92		1.67		3.18	3.50
	42 (157)	*52* (87)		*36* (89)		*50* (69.5)	*56* (34.5)
Medical University South Carolina	1.67	1.95				3.39	
	39 (169)	*42* (138)				*54* (41.5)	
Univ of Med & Dent of NJ	2.33	2.73				3.18	2.17
	46 (136)	*50* (107)				*50* (69.5)	*37* (123)
Miami University	2.03	2.78	2.98	2.14	0.00		1.91
	43 (153)	*50* (101)	*51* (65)	*41* (85)	*24* (101)		*33* (126)
University of Miami	3.03	3.33			2.31	3.11	3.23
	53 (77.5)	*56* (51.5)			*45* (76)	*49* (77)	52 (71)
Michigan State University	3.43	3.55	3.45	3.58	2.70	3.81	3.41
	57 (47)	*58* (34)	*57* (32.5)	*55* (28)	*49* (68)	*61* (17)	*55* (42.5)
University of Michigan	3.86 [a]	3.55	3.98	3.93	3.75	3.49 [a]	3.65
	62 (25)	*58* (34)	*63* (9)	*59* (14.5)	*58* (17)	*55* (34)	*58* (21)
	3.96 [b]					3.82 [b]	
	63 (16)					*61* (15)	
University of Minnesota	3.52	3.41 [a]	3.77	3.39	3.37	3.61	3.14
	58 (40)	*57* (43)	*61* (13)	*53* (37.5)	*55* (40.5)	*57* (26.5)	*51* (80.5)
		3.45 [b]					
		57 (40)					
Mississippi State University			1.96				
			38 (116)				
University of Mississippi						2.67	
						42 (105)	
U of Mississippi-Medical Center	1.39					2.98	
	36 (178)					*47* (94.5)	
University of Missouri-Columbia	3.13	3.08	2.78	2.50	1.67	2.88	3.22
	54 (68)	*53* (70)	*48* (83)	*45* (78)	*39* (87)	*45* (100)	*52* (73)
Univ of Missouri-Kansas City	2.59	2.78					
	48 (117)	*50* (101)					
Univ of Missouri-Saint Louis	0.77		2.35				
	30 (186)		*43* (99)				
Montana State University	2.73	1.43 [a]	2.08	3.00	0.83		1.67
	50 (104)	*37* (160)	*40* (110)	*50* (68.5)	*32* (96)		*30* (131)
		1.67 [c]					
		39 (149)					

Appendix Table I - 2 Biological Sciences (Continued)

Institution	Biochem & Molec Bio	Cell & Develop Bio	Eco, Evl & Behavior	Molec & Gen Genetics	Neuro-sciencs	Pharma-cology	Physiology
University of Montana	1.67	1.67	2.82				
	39 (169)	*39* (149)	*49* (79)				
University of Nebraska-Lincoln	3.05	2.82	2.69	3.00			1.67
	53 (76)	*51* (96)	*47* (88)	*50* (68.5)			*30* (131)
University of Nevada, Reno	2.57		2.83				
	48 (120)		*49* (78)				
University of New Hampshire	2.78	2.22	1.95	2.50			n/s
	50 (98)	*45* (130)	*38* (117)	*45* (78)			
New Mexico State University	2.00		2.05				
	42 (155)		*39* (112)				
University of New Mexico	3.00	2.95	3.40	1.67	1.67		2.71
	53 (82)	*52* (83)	*56* (39)	*36* (89)	*39* (87)		*45* (107)
New York Medical College	1.67	2.26	n/s			2.95	2.92
	39 (169)	*45* (128)				*47* (96)	48 (99.5)
New York University	3.50	3.77		3.33	3.33	3.75	3.64
	58 (42)	*60* (21.5)		*53* (46.5)	*54* (44.5)	*60* (20)	*58* (23)
North Carolina State University	3.10	3.22	3.30	3.64		3.30	3.33
	54 (72)	*55* (59)	*55* (43)	*56* (25)		*52* (54)	*54* (56.5)
U of North Carolina-Chapel Hill	3.80	3.78	3.43	3.66	3.57	4.14[j]	3.45
	61 (26)	*61* (20)	*57* (36)	*56* (24)	*56* (26)	*66* (4)	*55* (40)
						3.99[a]	
						64 (10)	
North Dakota State University	1.83		1.67				1.11
	41 (162)		*34* (120)				*22* (135)
University of North Dakota	2.41						
	47 (134)						
University of North Texas	*2.05*	n/s	2.22				3.00
	43 (151)		*41* (106)				*49* (93)
Northeast Louisiana University						2.50	
						39 (113)	
Northeastern University	2.08						
	43 (149)						
Northern Arizona University	0.17	1.11	3.45	0.83	0.00		2.29
	23 (192)	*33* (164)	*57* (32.5)	*28* (98)	*24* (101)		*39* (120)
Northwestern University	3.70	3.62			3.59		3.61
	60 (28)	*59* (29.5)			*56* (25)		*58* (26)
University of Notre Dame	0.74	2.45	2.87	3.33			2.67
	29 (187)	*47* (121)	*49* (75)	*53* (46.5)			*44* (108)
Ohio State University	3.22	3.38	3.11	3.14	3.10	3.33	3.33
	55 (66)	*57* (48)	*52* (57.5)	*51* (61)	*52* (53.5)	*53* (48)	*54* (56.5)
Ohio University	0.67	1.50	2.33	0.33	2.14	2.38	n/s
	28 (188)	*37* (158)	*43* (101)	*23* (100)	*44* (80)	*37* (117)	

Appendix Table I - 2 Biological Sciences (Continued)

Institution	Biochem & Molec Bio	Cell & Develop Bio	Eco, Evl & Behavior	Molec & Gen Genetics	Neuro-sciencs	Pharma-cology	Physiology
Oklahoma State University	2.69	0.97	2.87				2.33
	50 (112)	*32* (166)	*49* (75)				*39* (119)
University of Oklahoma	2.57	2.89	3.11	1.67	1.81	3.22	2.56
	48 (120)	*51* (91)	*53* (57.5)	*36* (89)	*41* (85)	*51* (62)	*43* (114)
Old Dominion University	1.67		2.31				
	39 (169)		*42* (103)				
Oregon Graduate Inst Sci & Tech	1.25						
	35 (181)						
Oregon State University	3.33	3.19	3.64	3.03	2.36	3.39	3.15
	56 (55)	*55* (61.5)	*59* (20)	*50* (66.5)	*45* (75)	*54* (41.5)	*51* (79)
University of Oregon	3.68				3.65		
	60 (29)				*57* (22)		
Pennsylvania State University	3.44	3.22	3.47	3.71	2.88	2.81	3.18[h]
	57 (46)	*55* (59)	*57* (30)	*57* (23)	*50* (66)	*44* (103)	*52* (76)
			3.55[c]	3.71			3.16[c]
			58 (26)				*51* (78)
							3.39[i]
							54 (46)
University of Pennsylvania	3.94	3.74	3.67	3.72	4.17	4.02	3.95
	62 (17.5)	*60* (24)	*60* (17.5)	*57* (22)	*62* (11)	*64* (7)	*62* (7)
Phila Col of Pharmacy & Science						2.26	
						35 (119)	
University of Pittsburgh	2.99[b]	2.64[b]	2.38	3.03[g]	3.33[b]	3.21	3.60
	53 (84)	*49* (114)	*43* (98)	*50* (66.5)	*54* (44.5)	*51* (65)	*57* (27.5)
	3.11[a]	3.08[a]		3.33[a]	3.33[a]		
	54 (70.5)	*53* (70)		*53* (46.5)	*54* (44.5)		
Princeton University		4.45	3.96				
		67 (5)	*63* (10)				
Univ of Puerto Rico-Rio Piedras	1.67	0.95[a]	1.67		0.24	1.39	1.67
	39 (169)	*32* (168)	*34* (120)		*27* (98)	*21* (125)	*30* (131)
		1.25[b]					
		35 (163)					
Purdue University	3.33[c]	3.44	3.25		2.50	3.10	
	56 (55)	*57* (41)	*54* (46.5)		*47* (73.5)	*49* (78.5)	
	3.33[a]						
	56 (55)						
Rice University	3.65	2.92					
	59 (30.5)	*52* (87)					
University of Rochester	3.54	3.14	2.87	3.43	3.40	3.81	3.33
	58 (37.5)	*54* (64.5)	*49* (75)	*54* (35)	*55* (37)	*61* (17)	*54* (56.5)
Rockefeller University	3.91	4.54			4.26		
	62 (22)	*68* (4)			*62* (9)		

Appendix Table I - 2 Biological Sciences (Continued)

Institution	Biochem & Molec Bio	Cell & Develop Bio	Eco, Evl & Behavior	Molec & Gen Genetics	Neuro-sciencs	Pharma-cology	Physiology
Rush University	1.67						
	39 (169)						
Rutgers State Univ-New Brunswick	3.48	3.07	3.24	3.38	3.38	3.69	3.33
	58 (44)	*53* (74)	*54* (49)	*53* (39)	*55* (38.5)	*59* (22.5)	*54* (56.5)
Rutgers State Univ-Newark	1.91		3.10		3.06		
	41 (159)		*52* (59)		*52* (55)		
St. John's University		1.67				2.59	
		39 (149)				*41* (108)	
Saint Louis University	2.93	2.45	1.25			3.40	3.27
	52 (87)	*47* (121)	*29* (124)			*54* (39.5)	53 (67)
University of South Alabama		1.67					
		39 (149)					
University of South Carolina	2.78	2.72	3.14			2.98	2.58
	50 (98)	*50* (108)	*53* (54.5)			*47* (94.5)	*43* (112)
University of South Dakota	0.95	0.83				2.62	1.67
	31 (184)	*30* (172)				*41* (107)	*30* (131)
University of South Florida	2.18	2.03	2.65			2.57	
	44 (144)	*43* (136)	*47* (90.5)			*40* (109)	
University of Southern California	3.51	3.00			3.35	2.56	3.28
	58 (41)	*53* (78.5)			*54* (42)	*40* (110)	*53* (66)
Southern Illinois University		1.89	2.65			2.44	
		41 (140)	*47* (90.5)			*38* (114)	
Southern Methodist University	*1.25*						
	35 (181)						
Univ of Southern Mississippi	0.42	0.00	1.88				0.83
	26 (190)	*22* (176)	*37* (118)				*18* (136)
Univ of Southwestern Louisiana			2.44				
			44 (97)				
Stanford University	4.59	4.08 [a]	4.23	4.44	4.56	3.75	4.17
	69 (4)	*64* (13)	*67* (4)	*64* (5)	*65* (1)	*60* (20)	*66* (3)
		4.39 [b]					
		67 (6)					
State Univ of New York-Albany		2.36	3.12	2.74	2.08	3.21	
		46 (125)	*53* (56)	*47* (74)	*43* (81)	*51* (65)	
State Univ of New York-Binghamton	1.00	1.67	2.81				3.33
	32 (183)	*39* (149)	*49* (80.5)				*54* (56.5)
State Univ of New York-Buffalo	2.50 [b]	2.50 [a]	2.08	3.33	2.78 [a]	3.13	3.40
	48 (125)	*47* (118)	*40* (110)	*53* (46.5)	*49* (67)	*49* (74)	*55* (44)
	2.45 [a]	3.08 [b]			2.89 [b]		
	47 (130)	*53* (70)			*50* (64.5)		
State U of New York-Stony Brook	3.60	3.55	3.86	3.62	3.41	3.33	3.50
	59 (34)	*58* (34)	*62* (11)	*56* (26)	*55* (35.5)	*53* (48)	*56* (34.5)

Appendix Table I - 2 Biological Sciences (Continued)

Institution	Biochem & Molec Bio	Cell & Develop Bio	Eco, Evl & Behavior	Molec & Gen Genetics	Neuro-sciencs	Pharma-cology	Physiology
SUNY Col Environ Sci & Forestry			2.87				
			49 (75)				
SUNY-Health Science Ctr-Brooklyn	2.08	1.67		1.67	2.57	3.15	3.04
	43 (149)	*39* (149)		*36* (89)	*47* (72)	*50* (72)	*49* (90.5)
SUNY Health Science Ctr-Syracuse	3.02	2.29				3.33	3.04
	53 (79.5)	*45* (127)				*53* (48)	*49* (90.5)
Syracuse University	2.67		2.96	2.82	2.50		
	49 (114)		*51* (66.5)	*48* (72)	*47* (73.5)		
Temple University	2.83	2.78		3.33		2.87	3.21
	51 (93)	*50* (101)		*53* (46.5)		*45* (101)	*52* (74)
University of Tennessee-Knoxville	2.17	3.08	3.26	1.11			
	44 (146)	*53* (70)	*54* (45)	*30* (95.5)			
University of Tennessee - Memphis	3.02	2.74			3.01	3.23	3.47
	53 (79.5)	*50* (105)			*51* (58)	*51* (61)	*56* (39)
Texas A&M University	3.06 [a]	2.96	2.80	3.15		3.27	2.78
	53 (74.5)	*52* (81.5)	*49* (82)	*51* (60)		*52* (56.5)	*46* (105)
	3.24 [c]						
	55 (63.5)						
Texas Tech University	2.31	2.74	2.96			2.40	2.59
	46 (138)	*50* (105)	*51* (66.5)			*37* (115)	*43* (110)
University of Texas at Austin	3.59	3.56	3.77	3.56	3.25	3.49	3.39
	59 (35.5)	*58* (34)	*61* (13)	*55* (29.5)	*53* (49)	*55* (34)	*54* (46)
University of Texas at Dallas	2.29						
	45 (140)						
U of Texas, Medical Br-Galveston	2.80	2.80			3.43	3.21	3.68
	51 (95)	*51* (98.5)			*55* (34)	*51* (65)	*59* (19.5)
U of Tex-Health Sci Ctr-Houston	3.28	3.54		3.44	3.14	3.47	3.57
	56 (61.5)	*58* (37)		*54* (34)	*52* (52)	*55* (36)	*57* (29.5)
U of Tex-Hlth Sci Ct-San Antonio	3.12	3.24				2.99	3.39
	54 (69)	*55* (57)				*47* (92)	54 (46)
U of Texas-Southwestern Med Ctr	3.79	3.77		3.78	3.05	4.04	
	61 (27)	*61* (21.5)		*58* (20.5)	*52* (56)	*64* (5)	
Texas Woman's University	1.48				0.00		
	37 (177)				*24* (101)		
Thomas Jefferson University	2.67	2.96				3.21	2.96
	49 (114)	*52* (81.5)				*51* (65)	*48* (96)
Tufts University	3.33	3.07 [a]			2.94	3.27	3.23
	56 (55)	*53* (74)			*51* (59)	*52* (56.5)	*52* (71)
		3.07 [b]					
		53 (74)					
Tulane University	2.45	2.56 [a]	2.57			3.09	2.98
	47 (130)	*48* (115)	*46* (94.5)			*49* (80)	*49* (94)

Appendix Table I - 2 Biological Sciences (Continued)

Institution	Biochem & Molec Bio	Cell & Develop Bio	Eco, Evl & Behavior	Molec & Gen Genetics	Neuro-sciencs	Pharma-cology	Physiology
Tulane University		2.74 [b]					
		50 (105)					
University of Tulsa	0.37	0.83	0.00	0.56			
	25 (191)	*30* (172)	*13* (128)	*25* (99)			
Uniformed Services U of Hlth Sci	2.45	2.80			2.29	3.13	3.10
	47 (130)	*51* (98.5)			*45* (77)	*49* (74)	*50* (86.5)
Utah State University	2.19	0.00	3.41			3.33	n/s
	44 (143)	*22* (176)	*56* (38)			*53* (48)	
University of Utah	3.45		3.56	3.80		3.49	
	57 (45)		*58* (25)	*58* (19)		*55* (34)	
Vanderbilt University	3.63	3.53	2.57	3.21	3.44	4.15	3.77
	59 (32)	*58* (38)	*46* (94.5)	*52* (57.5)	*55* (33)	*66* (3)	*60* (14.5)
University of Vermont	2.50	3.02	2.89			3.40	3.30
	48 (125)	*53* (76.5)	*50* (72)			*54* (39.5)	*53* (65)
Virginia Polytech Inst & State U	2.46		2.87				1.67 [d]
	47 (128)		*49* (75)				*30* (131)
							2.22 [c]
							38 (121)
							3.33 [a]
							54 (56.5)
University of Virginia	3.33	3.69	3.24	2.64	3.45	3.61	3.83
	56 (55)	*60* (25)	*54* (49)	*46* (76)	*55* (31.5)	*57* (26.5)	*61* (11.5)
Wake Forest University	2.89	2.64	2.73	3.33	2.68	3.33	3.25
	52 (90)	*49* (114)	*48* (85.5)	*53* (46.5)	*48* (69)	*53* (48)	*52* (69)
Washington State University	3.28	3.00	3.44			3.16	3.14
	56 (61.5)	*53* (78.5)	*57* (34)			*50* (71)	*51* (80.5)
Washington University	4.15	4.24	3.69	3.86	4.42		
	65 (13)	*65* (8)	*60* (16)	*58* (17)	*64* (5)		
University of Washington	4.05	4.23	4.20	4.02	4.11	4.01	4.10
	64 (14)	*65* (9)	*66* (5)	*60* (12)	*61* (13)	*64* (8)	*65* (4)
Wayne State University	2.89	3.02	2.26	3.20	2.58	3.06	2.94
	52 (90)	*53* (76.5)	*42* (104)	*52* (59)	*47* (70.5)	*48* (83)	*48* (98)
Wesleyan University	2.55	2.90					
	48 (121)	*52* (89.5)					
West Virginia University	1.98	3.10		2.22		3.54	3.10
	42 (157)	*54* (67)		*42* (83.5)		*56* (30)	*50* (86.5)
University of Wisconsin-Madison	4.30	4.06	4.13	4.40	3.53	3.93	3.64
	66 (9)	*64* (14)	*65* (7)	*64* (6)	*56* (27)	*63* (12)	*58* (23)
University of Wisconsin-Milwaukee	2.75						
	50 (102)						
University of Wyoming	2.78	1.97	3.18		2.00		2.88
	50 (98)	*42* (137)	*53* (51)		*42* (82.5)		*47* (101)

Appendix Table I - 2 Biological Sciences (Continued)

Institution	Biochem & Molec Bio	Cell & Develop Bio	Eco, Evl & Behavior	Molec & Gen Genetics	Neuro-sciencs	Pharma-cology	Physiology
Yale University	4.32	4.22	3.66	4.29	4.44	4.32	4.38
	66 (8)	*65* (10)	*59* (19)	*63* (7)	*64* (4)	*69* (1)	*69* (1)

Source: National Survey of Graduate Faculty

Notes: *a* School of Arts and Sciences
b School of Medicine
c School of Agriculture
d School of Veterinary Medicine
e School of Pharmacology
f School of Engineering
g School of Public Health
h Interdisciplinary with the Schools of Agriculture and Arts and Sciences
i Interdisciplinary with the Schools of Agriculture, Arts and Sciences, and Medicine
j Interdisciplinary with the Schools of Medicine, Pharmacology, and Public Health

n/s After trimming no cases remained

Appendix Table I - 3 Effectiveness Ratings of Research-Doctorate Programs in Engineering

Institution	Aerospace Engineering	Biomedical Engineering	Chemical Engineering	Civil Engineering	Electrical Engineering	Industrial Engineering	Materials Science	Mechanical Engineering
Air Force Inst of Technology	2.45				1.93			
	39 (29)				*43* (94)			
University of Akron		2.04	1.58	1.60	1.17		2.92	1.95
		31 (36)	*38* (85)	*34* (80)	*34* (118)		*49* (40)	*40* (90.5)
University of Alabama				1.59	1.77			2.00
				34 (81)	*41* (101)			*41* (89)
University of Alabama-Birmingham		3.33					2.22	
		51 (19)					*40* (55)	
University of Alabama-Huntsville					2.07	1.52	1.67	2.08
					44 (93)	*33* (36)	*32* (60)	*42* (84)
Arizona State University			2.26	2.69	3.09	3.01	2.64 [a]	2.98
			45 (58.5)	*48* (53)	*55* (41)	*52* (17)	*46* (49)	*53* (48)
							2.78 [b]	
							48 (46)	
University of Arizona			2.02	3.09	3.20		3.08	3.11
			43 (69.5)	*53* (32.5)	*57* (35)		*52* (29)	*55* (37.5)
Univ of Arkansas-Fayetteville					1.49	2.15		
					38 (109)	*41* (29)		
Auburn University	2.36		2.07	2.67	2.60	2.71	1.80	2.48
	38 (31)		*43* (66)	*48* (54)	*50* (65)	*48* (21)	*34* (59)	*47* (74)
Boston University					1.88			
					42 (96)			
Brigham Young University			2.85	2.65	2.55			
			52 (39.5)	*47* (55.5)	*49* (68)			
Brown University					3.24		3.05	3.80
					57 (32)		*51* (30)	*63* (12)
California Institute Technology	4.43		4.24	4.42	4.34		3.44	4.30
	69 (1)		*67* (7)	*71* (2)	*69* (5)		*57* (17)	*69* (4)
University of California-Berkeley		3.84	4.43	4.22	4.46	4.31	4.08	4.50
		59 (7)	*70* (2.5)	*68* (6)	*70* (4)	*68* (1)	*65* (4.5)	*72* (1.5)
University of California-Davis		3.15	3.12	3.51	3.02			3.36
		48 (24)	*55* (28)	*59* (15)	*55* (43)			*58* (21)
University of California-Irvine				2.88	3.10			3.01
				50 (44.5)	*55* (40)			*53* (47)
Univ of California-Los Angeles	3.44		2.68	3.28	3.79		3.23	3.51
	54 (10)		*50* (49.5)	*56* (21.5)	*63* (11)		*54* (24)	*60* (17.5)
Univ of California-San Diego	3.27	4.43			3.37			3.59
	52 (15)	*69* (1)			*58* (25)			*60* (13.5)
Univ of California-San Francisco		3.89						
		60 (5)						
Univ of California-Santa Barbara			3.45		3.58		3.65	3.16
			59 (18)		*61* (20)		*59* (10.5)	*55* (34.5)
Carnegie Mellon University			3.80	3.79	4.05		3.72	3.46
			63 (12)	*62* (10)	*66* (8)		*60* (9)	*59* (19)
Case Western Reserve Univ		3.60	2.77		2.86		3.56	3.41
		55 (13)	*51* (42)		*53* (48)		*58* (13)	*58* (20)

Appendix Table I - 3 Engineering (Continued)

Institution	Aerospace Engineering	Biomedical Engineering	Chemical Engineering	Civil Engineering	Electrical Engineering	Industrial Engineering	Materials Science	Mechanical Engineering
Catholic University of America				1.11				2.14
				27 (85)				*43* (82.5)
University of Central Florida					2.47			
					49 (74)			
University of Cincinnati	2.80		2.03	2.65	2.31		2.67	2.91
	45 (25)		*43* (68)	*47* (55.5)	*47* (83)		*46* (48)	*52* (50)
CUNY - Grad Sch & Univ Center			3.15		2.92			2.73
			55 (27)		*53* (46)			*50* (58.5)
Clarkson University			2.69	2.85	2.47			2.50
			50 (48)	*50* (46)	*49* (74)			*47* (72.5)
Clemson University		2.78	1.71	2.82	2.40	2.20		2.57
		42 (30)	*39* (84)	*50* (48)	*48* (77.5)	*42* (28)		*48* (67)
Colorado School of Mines			2.37				2.59	
			46 (57)				*45* (52.5)	
Colorado State University				3.28	2.35			2.73
				56 (21.5)	*47* (82)			*50* (58.5)
University of Colorado	3.17		3.19	3.33	3.14			2.72
	50 (17)		*56* (26)	*56* (20)	*56* (38)			*50* (60)
Columbia University			2.24	3.16	3.75		3.19	3.07
			45 (60)	*54* (28)	*63* (12)		*53* (26.5)	*54* (42)
University of Connecticut			2.53	1.79	2.27			2.07
			48 (54)	*36* (77)	*46* (84)			*42* (85.5)
Cornell University	3.75		3.81	4.08	4.08		4.10	3.99
	59 (6)		*63* (10.5)	*66* (7)	*66* (7)		*65* (3)	*65* (9)
Dartmouth College		3.06						
		47 (26)						
University of Dayton	0.95				1.23			
	17 (33)				*35* (117)			
University of Delaware			4.21	3.01	2.43		2.73	3.24
			67 (8)	*52* (37)	*48* (76)		*47* (47)	*56* (27.5)
University of Detroit Mercy								0.51
								22 (110)
Drexel University		3.04			2.90		2.81	
		47 (27)			*53* (47)		*48* (43)	
Duke University		3.63	1.18	3.12	2.71		2.63	3.17
		56 (12)	*33* (90)	*54* (30)	*51* (58)		*46* (50)	*55* (33)
Florida Atlantic University					1.11			
					34 (119)			
Florida Institute of Technology					2.16			1.14
					45 (90.5)			*30* (107)
University of Florida	2.47		3.03	2.95	3.22	2.87	3.36	3.11
	40 (28)		*54* (32)	*51* (39.5)	*57* (33)	*50* (18)	*55* (19)	*55* (37.5)
George Washington University				1.67	2.50			2.78
				35 (79)	*49* (71)			*50* (55)

Appendix Table I - 3 Engineering (Continued)

Institution	Aerospace Engineering	Biomedical Engineering	Chemical Engineering	Civil Engineering	Electrical Engineering	Industrial Engineering	Materials Science	Mechanical Engineering
Georgia Institute of Technology	3.49		3.07	3.26	3.72	4.30	2.96	3.54
	55 (8)		*54* (30.5)	*55* (25)	*62* (14)	*68* (2)	*50* (36)	*60* (16)
University of Houston			3.37	2.39	2.10	1.83	1.11	3.10
			58 (21)	*44* (65)	*45* (92)	*37* (33)	*25* (65)	*54* (39.5)
Howard University					1.48			1.44
					38 (110)			*34* (105)
University of Idaho			1.39		1.39			
			36 (87.5)		*37* (113)			
Illinois Institute of Technology			2.54	2.45	2.38		*1.48*	3.04
			48 (52.5)	*45* (62)	*48* (80)		*30* (61)	*54* (44.5)
U of Illinois at Urbana-Champaign	3.31		4.28	4.23	4.57	3.25	3.93	4.02
	52 (13)		*68* (6)	*68* (5)	*71* (3)	*55* (13)	*63* (7)	*66* (6)
University of Illinois at Chicago		2.67	2.26	2.30	2.61			3.03
		41 (31.5)	*45* (58.5)	*43* (67)	*50* (64)			*54* (46)
Iowa State University	3.08	2.50	2.85	2.92	2.68	2.83		3.08
	49 (22)	*38* (34.5)	*52* (39.5)	*51* (41)	*51* (60)	*50* (19)		*54* (41)
University of Iowa		3.33	1.84	3.23	3.00	2.49		2.85
		51 (19)	*41* (77)	*55* (27)	*54* (44)	*46* (23)		*51* (52)
Johns Hopkins University		4.09	2.95	3.44	3.26		2.96	2.79
		63 (3)	*53* (38)	*58* (17)	*57* (31)		*50* (36)	*51* (54)
Kansas State University			2.21	1.99	1.67	2.07		2.06
			45 (61)	*39* (74)	*40* (103)	*40* (31)		*42* (87.5)
University of Kansas	2.68		1.95	2.70	2.20			2.54
	43 (27)		*42* (74)	*48* (51.5)	*46* (88)			*47* (68)
University of Kentucky			1.82	2.76	1.83		1.42	2.38
			40 (78)	*49* (49)	*42* (99)		*29* (63)	*46* (78.5)
Lehigh University			3.26	3.37	2.74	3.18	3.45	3.30
			57 (24)	*57* (18)	*51* (56)	*54* (14)	*57* (16)	*57* (23)
Louisiana State U & A&M College			2.47	2.36	1.84			1.67
			48 (55.5)	*44* (66)	*42* (98)			*37* (101)
University of Louisville			1.39					
			36 (87.5)					
University of Maine			1.04					
			32 (91)					
University of Maryland College Park	3.11		2.75	3.09	3.59		2.03	3.10
	49 (19.5)		*51* (45)	*53* (32.5)	*61* (18.5)		*37* (56)	*54* (39.5)
Massachusetts Inst of Technology	4.31	4.17	4.43	4.47	4.61		4.22	4.45
	67 (2)	*65* (2)	*70* (2.5)	*71* (1)	*72* (2)		*67* (1)	*71* (3)
U of Massachusetts at Amherst			3.28	2.64	3.21	2.46	4.21	2.61
			57 (23)	*47* (57)	*57* (34)	*45* (25)	*67* (2)	*48* (65)
University of Mass-Lowell					1.02		3.24	
					33 (121)		*54* (23)	
University of Miami		2.03		1.74	1.60			2.14
		31 (37)		*36* (78)	*39* (105)			*43* (82.5)

Appendix Table I - 3 Engineering (Continued)

Institution	Aerospace Engineering	Biomedical Engineering	Chemical Engineering	Civil Engineering	Electrical Engineering	Industrial Engineering	Materials Science	Mechanical Engineering
Michigan State University			2.74	2.99	3.16		2.80	3.12
			51 (47)	*52* (38)	*56* (36)		*48* (44.5)	*55* (36)
Michigan Technological University								2.61
								48 (65)
University of Michigan	3.80	3.68	3.43	3.82	4.17	4.19	3.47	4.00
	59 (5)	*57* (11)	*58* (19)	*63* (9)	*67* (6)	*67* (3)	*57* (15)	*66* (8)
University of Minnesota	3.33	3.38	4.57	3.62	3.59		3.53	3.85
	53 (12)	*52* (17)	*71* (1)	*60* (14)	*61* (18.5)		*58* (14)	*64* (11)
Mississippi State University					1.57			
					39 (107)			
University of Mississippi			0.61	1.08				
			27 (93)	*27* (86)				
University of Missouri-Columbia			1.78	2.11	2.54	1.72		2.07
			40 (80)	*40* (72.5)	*49* (69)	*36* (34)		*42* (85.5)
University of Missouri-Rolla			2.14	2.40	2.26		2.97	2.76
			44 (62)	*44* (64)	*46* (85)		*50* (34)	*50* (56.5)
Montana State University								0.97
								28 (108)
Naval Postgraduate School	2.43				2.22			
	39 (30)				*46* (86.5)			
University of Nebraska-Lincoln				2.18		2.14		1.60
				41 (70)		*41* (30)		*36* (102)
University of New Hampshire				2.13	0.83			
				41 (71)	*31* (125)			
New Jersey Inst of Technology			1.77		1.60			1.92
			40 (81)		*39* (105)			*40* (93.5)
New Mexico State University				2.22	2.50			
				42 (69)	*49* (71)			
North Carolina State University	3.10	2.50	3.21	3.13	3.43	3.36	3.27	3.24
	49 (21)	*38* (34.5)	*56* (25)	*54* (29)	*59* (23)	*56* (11)	*54* (22)	*56* (27.5)
U of North Carolina-Chapel Hill		3.24		3.50				
		50 (23)		*59* (16)				
Northeastern University			1.40	1.48	2.76	2.28		1.90
			36 (86)	*32* (82)	*52* (55)	*43* (27)		*40* (96)
Northwestern University		3.54	3.67	3.73	3.27	3.62	4.08	3.87
		55 (14)	*61* (14)	*61* (11.5)	*57* (30)	*60* (6)	*65* (4.5)	*64* (10)
University of Notre Dame	2.99		3.38	3.03	2.83		1.84	3.06
	48 (24)		*58* (20)	*52* (35.5)	*52* (51)		*35* (58)	*54* (43)
Ohio State University	3.03	3.25	3.07	3.03	3.63	3.33	3.36	3.28
	48 (23)	*50* (22)	*54* (30.5)	*52* (35.5)	*61* (16)	*56* (12)	*55* (19)	*57* (24)
Ohio University			0.80		2.22			
			29 (92)		*46* (86.5)			
Oklahoma State University			2.08	2.11	1.54	2.78		2.37
			43 (65)	*40* (72.5)	*38* (108)	*49* (20)		*45* (80)

Appendix Table I - 3 Engineering (Continued)

Institution	Aerospace Engineering	Biomedical Engineering	Chemical Engineering	Civil Engineering	Electrical Engineering	Industrial Engineering	Materials Science	Mechanical Engineering
University of Oklahoma			2.57	2.56	2.38	2.47		2.76
			49 (51)	*46* (59)	*48* (80)	*45* (24)		*50* (56.5)
Old Dominion University					1.58			2.53
					39 (106)			*47* (69.5)
Oregon Graduate Inst Sci & Tech					1.39		2.00	
					37 (113)		*37* (57)	
Oregon State University			1.73	2.88	2.62	1.56		2.47
			39 (83)	*50* (44.5)	*50* (62.5)	*34* (35)		*47* (75.5)
Pennsylvania State University	3.37	3.13	3.29	2.95	3.31	3.52	3.83	3.55
	53 (11)	*48* (25)	*57* (22)	*51* (39.5)	*58* (29)	*58* (8)	*62* (8)	*60* (15)
University of Pennsylvania		3.82	3.81		2.95		3.62	3.27
		59 (9)	*63* (10.5)		*54* (45)		*59* (12)	*56* (25)
University of Pittsburgh			2.75	2.75	2.69	2.67	2.61	2.63
			51 (45)	*49* (50)	*51* (59)	*48* (22)	*45* (51)	*49* (62.5)
Polytechnic University			2.04		3.33			1.49
			43 (67)		*58* (27)			*35* (103)
Portland State University					1.23			
					35 (117)			
Princeton University	4.03		4.02	3.89	4.00			4.09
	63 (4)		*65* (9)	*64* (8)	*65* (9)			*67* (5)
Purdue University	3.46		3.63	3.73	3.94	4.07	*2.91*	4.01
	54 (9)		*61* (15)	*61* (11.5)	*65* (10)	*65* (4)	*49* (41)	*66* (7)
Rensselaer Polytechnic Inst	3.20	2.89	2.99	3.04	3.46	3.02	3.65	3.51
	51 (16)	*44* (29)	*54* (34.5)	*53* (34)	*59* (21)	*52* (16)	*59* (10.5)	*59* (17.5)
University of Rhode Island			1.19	1.43	2.57			2.50
			33 (89)	*32* (83)	*50* (67)			*47* (72.5)
Rice University		3.95	3.54	3.24	3.45			3.16
		61 (4)	*60* (16)	*55* (26)	*59* (22)			*55* (34.5)
University of Rochester		3.53	2.98		3.06		3.02	2.47
		54 (15)	*53* (36.5)		*55* (42)		*51* (32)	*47* (75.5)
Rutgers State Univ-New Brunswick		2.99	2.99		2.84		3.15 [c]	3.21
		46 (28)	*54* (34.5)		*53* (50)		*53* (28)	*56* (30)
							2.85 [d]	
							49 (42)	
University of South Carolina					1.74			1.91
					41 (102)			*40* (95)
South Dakota Sch of Mines & Tech							2.59	
							45 (52.5)	
University of South Florida					1.91			
					42 (95)			
University of Southern California			2.47		3.71	2.42	2.94	2.63
			48 (55.5)		*62* (15)	*45* (26)	*50* (38)	*49* (62.5)
Southern Methodist University					2.40			2.06
					48 (77.5)			*42* (87.5)

Appendix Table I - 3 Engineering (Continued)

Institution	Aerospace Engineering	Biomedical Engineering	Chemical Engineering	Civil Engineering	Electrical Engineering	Industrial Engineering	Materials Science	Mechanical Engineering
Univ of Southwestern Louisiana					1.41			
					37 (111)			
Stanford University	4.26	3.83	4.31	4.29	4.68	3.60	4.00	4.50
	66 (3)	*59* (8)	*68* (5)	*69* (3)	*73* (1)	*60* (7)	*64* (6)	*72* (1.5)
State Univ of New York-Binghamton					1.03			
					33 (120)			
State Univ of New York-Buffalo	2.76		3.09	3.11	2.81	3.15		3.19
	44 (26)		*55* (29)	*53* (31)	*52* (52)	*54* (15)		*56* (31)
State U of New York-Stony Brook					2.85		2.96	2.89
					53 (49)		*50* (36)	*52* (51)
Stevens Inst of Technology			1.89		1.87		2.80	1.44
			41 (75)		*42* (97)		*48* (44.5)	*34* (105)
Syracuse University			2.75	2.50	2.73			1.86
			51 (45)	*46* (60)	*51* (57)			*39* (97)
Tennessee Technological Univ					0.91			1.81
					32 (123)			*38* (99)
University of Tennessee-Knoxville	2.26		2.12	2.62	2.64			2.38
	37 (32)		*44* (64)	*47* (58)	*50* (61)			*45* (78.5)
Texas A&M University	3.11	2.58	2.81	3.27	3.33	3.44		3.25
	49 (19.5)	*39* (33)	*51* (41)	*55* (23.5)	*58* (27)	*57* (10)		*56* (26)
Texas Tech University				2.47	2.59			
				45 (61)	*50* (66)			
University of Texas at Arlington					2.47			2.19
					49 (74)			*43* (81)
University of Texas at Austin	3.64	3.33	3.73	4.27	3.74		3.19	3.59
	57 (7)	*51* (19)	*62* (13)	*69* (4)	*62* (13)		*53* (26.5)	*60* (13.5)
U of Texas-Southwestern Med Ctr		2.67						
		41 (31.5)						
University of Toledo					1.25			1.92
					35 (115)			*40* (93.5)
Tulane University			1.81	1.37	0.50			1.85
			40 (79)	*31* (84)	*27* (126)			*39* (98)
University of Tulsa			2.00					0.59
			42 (71.5)					*23* (109)
Utah State University				2.84				
				50 (47)				
University of Utah		3.69	2.54		2.80		3.03	2.70
		57 (10)	*48* (52.5)		*52* (53)		*51* (31)	*49* (61)
Vanderbilt University		3.30	1.74	2.90	2.50		2.47	2.53
		51 (21)	*39* (82)	*51* (42.5)	*49* (71)		*43* (54)	*47* (69.5)
University of Vermont					1.31		1.46	1.67
					36 (114)		*30* (62)	*37* (101)
Virginia Polytech Inst & State U	3.30		2.68	3.36	3.41	3.68	2.93	3.18
	52 (14)		*50* (49.5)	*57* (19)	*59* (24)	*61* (5)	*50* (39)	*55* (32)

Appendix Table I - 3 Engineering (Continued)

Institution	Aerospace Engineering	Biomedical Engineering	Chemical Engineering	Civil Engineering	Electrical Engineering	Industrial Engineering	Materials Science	Mechanical Engineering
University of Virginia		3.40	3.00	2.90	2.78		3.36	3.04
		52 (16)	*54* (33)	*51* (42.5)	*52* (54)		*55* (19)	*54* (44.5)
Washington State University			2.13	2.43	2.62			2.96
			44 (63)	*45* (63)	*50* (62.5)			*53* (49)
Washington University			2.98	2.70	3.11			2.80
			53 (36.5)	*48* (51.5)	*55* (39)			*51* (53)
University of Washington	3.13	3.85	3.48	3.66	3.33		2.99	3.22
	50 (18)	*59* (6)	*59* (17)	*61* (13)	*58* (27)		*50* (33)	*56* (29)
Wayne State University			1.96	1.93	2.18	2.00		2.52
			42 (73)	*38* (75)	*45* (89)	*39* (32)		*47* (71)
West Virginia University			2.02	2.29	1.81			1.93
			43 (69.5)	*43* (68)	*41* (100)			*40* (92)
Wichita State University					0.83			1.39
					31 (125)			*33* (106)
University of Wisconsin-Madison			4.37	3.27	3.62	3.48	3.22 [d]	3.33
			69 (4)	*56* (23.5)	*61* (17)	*58* (9)	*54* (25)	*57* (22)
							3.33	
							55 (21)	
University of Wisconsin-Milwaukee				1.91	2.16	1.44	1.37	2.61
				38 (76)	*45* (90.5)	*32* (37)	*28* (64)	*48* (65)
Worcester Polytechnic Inst		1.56	2.00		2.38			2.43
		23 (38)	*42* (71.5)		*48* (80)			*46* (77)
University of Wyoming			1.88		0.95			1.95
			41 (76)		*32* (122)			*40* (90.5)
Yale University			2.76		3.15			
			51 (43)		*56* (37)			

Source: National Survey of Graduate Faculty

Notes: *a* Program in Science and Engineering of Materials
b Program in Materials Science and Engineering
c Program in Ceramic Scienceand Engineering
d Program in Metallurgical Engineering

Appendix Table I - 4 Effectiveness Ratings of Research-Doctorate Programs in Physical Sciences and Mathematics

Institution	Astrophysics/ Astronomy	Chemistry	Computer Science	Geosciences	Mathematics	Ocean- ography	Physics	Statistics/ Biostatistics
Adelphi University					0.67			
					29 (134)			
University of Akron		2.32					3.13	
		46 (111)					*53* (59.5)	
University of Alabama		2.72		2.04	1.28		1.82	1.96
		50 (84)		*38* (89.5)	*36* (125)		*39* (123)	*38* (56)
University of Alabama-Birmingham		1.80	0.91				1.11	1.30
		40 (137)	*35* (101)				*31* (139)	*30* (64)
University of Alabama-Huntsville			1.39		1.25		1.92	
			40 (94)		*35* (127)		*40* (119)	
University of Alaska				2.50		3.02	2.22	
				44 (73)		*50* (17)	*43* (113)	
American University		1.81					1.45	1.59
		41 (136)					*35* (135)	*34* (61)
Arizona State University		3.07	2.26	3.30	2.32		3.27	
		54 (69)	*48* (59)	*55* (31.5)	*47* (95)		*55* (46.5)	
University of Arizona	3.69		2.99	3.62	2.72		3.39	
	57 (8)		*55* (35)	*59* (20)	*51* (64.5)		*56* (34)	
Univ of Arkansas-Fayetteville		2.50					2.57	
		48 (100)					*47* (98)	
Auburn University		1.82			2.25		1.48	
		41 (134)			*46* (100)		*35* (132)	
Baylor University		1.54					1.46	
		38 (151)					*35* (134)	
Boston College		2.60					1.83	
		49 (95)					*39* (122)	
Boston University	2.56	2.66	2.44		2.93		3.29	2.43
	42 (27)	*49* (88.5)	*50* (55)		*53* (55)		*55* (43)	*44* (48.5)
Bowling Green State University					1.78			
					41 (115)			
Brandeis University		3.33			3.50		3.21	
		57 (47)			*59* (26)		*54* (55)	
Brigham Young University		2.66					2.92	
		49 (88.5)					*51* (78.5)	
Brown University		3.20	3.75	3.96	3.56		3.64	
		55 (57)	*63* (12)	*64* (8.5)	*60* (23)		*59* (25)	
					4.06 [a]			
					65 (9)			
Bryn Mawr College		1.77					1.77	
		40 (141)					*38* (126)	
California Institute Technology	4.75	4.75	3.97	4.63	3.90		4.61	
	71 (1)	*71* (1)	*65* (7)	*73* (1)	*63* (13)		*70* (4)	

Appendix Table I - 4 Physical Sciences and Mathematics (Continued)

Institution	Astrophysics/ Astronomy	Chemistry	Computer Science	Geosciences	Mathematics	Ocean- ography	Physics	Statistics/ Biostatistics
University of California-Berkeley	4.53	4.72	4.58	4.09	4.37		4.49	4.01 [m]
	68 (2)	*71* (2)	*71* (3)	*66* (4)	*68* (6)		*68* (7)	*63* (7)
								4.33 [l]
								67 (2)
University of California-Davis		3.43	2.58	3.07	2.17		3.01	
		58 (37.5)	*51* (51)	*52* (42.5)	*45* (102)		*52* (71)	
University of California-Irvine		3.39	2.98		2.78		*3.54*	
		57 (43.5)	*55* (36)		*51* (61)		*58* (27.5)	
Univ of California-Los Angeles	3.05	4.00	3.48	3.67	3.91		3.77	3.80
	49 (18)	*64* (13)	*60* (16)	*60* (17)	*63* (12)		*60* (18.5)	*61* (11.5)
Univ of California-Riverside		2.95		2.56	2.50		3.13	2.65
		53 (74)		*45* (68)	*49* (83.5)		*53* (59.5)	*46* (43)
Univ of California-San Diego		3.82	3.11	4.06	3.58	4.21	3.82	
		62 (18)	*57* (28)	*65* (5.5)	*60* (22)	*67* (2)	*61* (15)	
Univ of California-San Francisco		3.91						
		63 (15)						
Univ of California-Santa Barbara		3.39	2.18	3.47	2.85		3.91	2.35
		57 (43.5)	*48* (63)	*57* (22)	*52* (57)		*62* (11.5)	*43* (50)
Univ of California-Santa Cruz	4.14	2.81	2.24	3.33	2.07		3.33	
	63 (4)	*51* (79.5)	*48* (61.5)	*56* (29)	*44* (107)		*56* (39)	
Carnegie Mellon University		3.00	4.38		3.48		3.35	3.84
		53 (72.5)	*69* (5)		*59* (28)		*56* (36.5)	*61* (10)
Case Western Reserve Univ		3.18	2.10	2.42	1.95		3.04	
		55 (60.5)	*47* (64)	*43* (78)	*43* (112)		*52* (67)	
Catholic University of America		0.80					2.33	
		30 (165)					*45* (109)	
University of Central Florida			1.52					
			41 (88)					
University of Chicago	3.85	4.20	2.88	4.03	4.64		4.55	4.09
	59 (7)	*66* (11.5)	*54* (43.5)	*65* (7)	*71* (2)		*69* (5)	*64* (3)
University of Cincinnati		2.94		2.53	1.96		2.50	
		52 (75)		*45* (70)	*43* (111)		*46* (103)	
CUNY - Grad Sch & Univ Center		2.57	2.33	2.04	3.08		3.27	
		48 (96)	*49* (57)	*38* (89.5)	*55* (44.5)		*55* (46.5)	
Claremont Graduate School					2.54			
					49 (80.5)			
Clark University							1.67	
							37 (128)	
Clarkson University		2.39			1.79		1.85	
		47 (108)			*41* (114)		*39* (120)	
Clemson University		2.46			2.59			
		47 (103)			*50* (73)			
Colorado School of Mines		0.87		3.12	0.63		2.45	
		31 (163)		*53* (40)	*29* (135)		*46* (105)	
Colorado State University		3.50		2.73	2.46		2.35	3.06
		58 (33.5)		*47* (63)	*48* (86.5)		*45* (108)	*51* (31)

Appendix Table I - 4 Physical Sciences and Mathematics (Continued)

Institution	Astrophysics/ Astronomy	Chemistry	Computer Science	Geosciences	Mathematics	Ocean-ography	Physics	Statistics/ Biostatistics
University of Colorado	3.38	3.22	2.93	3.20	3.06		3.41	2.45
	53 (12)	*55* (55)	*55* (39)	*54* (35)	*54* (49)		*56* (33)	*44* (47)
Columbia University	2.90	4.37	3.36	4.14	3.94	4.00	3.87	3.36
	47 (23)	*67* (8)	*59* (23.5)	*66* (3)	*64* (11)	*64* (4)	*61* (13)	*55* (23)
University of Connecticut		2.68	1.56		2.19		2.18	2.43
		50 (85.5)	*42* (85)		*45* (101)		*43* (114)	*44* (48.5)
Cornell University	3.97	4.40	4.47	3.71	3.96		4.54	4.06
	61 (5)	*68* (6)	*70* (4)	*61* (16)	*64* (10)		*69* (6)	*64* (6)
Dartmouth College		3.28	2.40	3.28	3.09		3.26	
		56 (52)	*50* (56)	*55* (33)	*55* (43)		*55* (49)	
University of Delaware		3.19			2.29		*2.86*	
		55 (58)			*46* (96.5)		*50* (83.5)	
University of Denver							1.67	
							37 (128)	
University of Detroit Mercy		0.89						
		31 (162)						
Drexel University		1.98			1.55		2.94	
		42 (127)			*39* (121)		*51* (76)	
Duke University		3.43	3.08	2.86	3.37	3.11	3.45	
		58 (37.5)	*56* (30)	*49* (55)	*58* (32.5)	*51* (11.5)	*57* (31)	
Emory University		3.47						2.46
		58 (36)						*44* (45.5)
Florida Institute of Technology					0.72	1.83	0.28	
					30 (133)	*32* (26)	*22* (146)	
Florida State University		3.00	0.83	2.36 [h]	2.41	3.28	3.23	3.44
		53 (72.5)	*35* (104)	*42* (80)	*48* (90)	*54* (7.5)	*54* (53.5)	*56* (19.5)
				3.23 [i]				
				54 (34)				
University of Florida	1.92	3.42	2.48	2.50	2.63		3.25	3.11
	34 (32)	*57* (39.5)	*50* (53.5)	*44* (73)	*50* (71)		*55* (50.5)	*52* (29)
George Washington University		1.02	2.25	0.63	0.79		1.21	2.83
		32 (160)	*48* (60)	*19* (100)	*31* (132)		*32* (137)	*49* (38)
Georgetown University		2.43						
		47 (106)						
Georgia Institute of Technology		3.21	3.00	2.75	3.07		3.09	
		55 (56)	*56* (34)	*48* (62)	*55* (47)		*53* (64)	
Georgia State University	2.10							
	36 (29)							
University of Georgia		3.13		2.22	2.38		2.90	
		54 (65)		*41* (84)	*47* (93)		*51* (81)	
Harvard University	3.92	4.57	3.47	3.80	4.58		4.71	3.80
	60 (6)	*70* (4.5)	*60* (17.5)	*62* (14)	*70* (3)		*71* (1)	*61* (11.5)
University of Hawaii at Manoa	3.09	2.45		3.38	2.43	3.11	2.29	
	49 (17)	*47* (104)		*56* (25)	*48* (89)	*51* (11.5)	*44* (111)	
University of Houston		3.18	1.54	2.68	3.01		2.78	
		55 (60.5)	*41* (86)	*47* (66)	*54* (50.5)		*49* (87.5)	

Appendix Table I - 4 Physical Sciences and Mathematics (Continued)

Institution	Astrophysics/ Astronomy	Chemistry	Computer Science	Geosciences	Mathematics	Ocean-ography	Physics	Statistics/ Biostatistics
Howard University		1.60			1.25		1.67	
		38 (148)			*35* (127)		*37* (128)	
Idaho State University					0.42			
					27 (138)			
University of Idaho		1.79		1.61				
		40 (138)		*32* (96)				
Illinois Institute of Technology			1.58		1.67		2.47	
			42 (82.5)		*40* (117)		*46* (104)	
Illinois State University					0.40			
					27 (139)			
U of Illinois at Urbana-Champaign	3.24	4.38	3.93	3.01	3.63		4.39	3.16
	51 (14)	*68* (7)	*65* (8)	*51* (46)	*60* (19)		*67* (8)	*53* (27.5)
University of Illinois at Chicago		3.18	2.86		3.29		2.53	2.03
		55 (60.5)	*54* (46)		*57* (36)		*47* (101)	*39* (55)
Indiana University	2.53	3.74	3.17	2.97	3.33		3.33	
	42 (28)	*61* (22)	*57* (27)	*51* (48)	*57* (34.5)		*56* (39)	
Iowa State University	2.07	3.66	1.80	2.07	2.82		3.42	3.99
	35 (30)	*60* (25)	*44* (72)	*39* (87)	*52* (58)		*56* (32)	*63* (8)
University of Iowa		3.09	2.24	2.87	2.71		3.07	2.32 [m]
		54 (67)	*48* (61.5)	*49* (54)	*51* (66)		*53* (66)	*42* (52)
								3.09 [l]
								52 (30)
Johns Hopkins University		3.57	2.96	3.94	2.98 [c]		3.65	3.58
		59 (29)	*55* (37)	*64* (10)	*54* (52)		*59* (24)	*58* (16.5)
					3.24			
					56 (37.5)			
Kansas State University		3.04	1.58		2.29		2.86	2.46
		53 (70.5)	*42* (82.5)		*46* (96.5)		*50* (83.5)	*44* (45.5)
University of Kansas		3.10	1.83	2.76			2.68	
		54 (66)	*44* (71)	*48* (60.5)			*48* (94)	
Kent State University		2.28	0.52	1.45	2.40		3.03	
		46 (115)	*32* (106)	*30* (98)	*47* (91.5)		*52* (68)	
University of Kentucky		2.78	1.67	2.05	2.47		2.92	2.34
		51 (82)	*43* (78.5)	*38* (88)	*48* (85)		*51* (78.5)	*43* (51)
Lehigh University		2.74	1.67	2.90	2.06		2.75	
		50 (83)	*43* (78.5)	*50* (52.5)	*44* (108)		*49* (89)	
Louisiana State U & A&M College	2.02	3.08	1.87	2.76	2.69	2.65	2.92	
	35 (31)	*54* (68)	*45* (70)	*48* (60.5)	*51* (67)	*44* (21)	*51* (78.5)	
University of Louisville		1.97						
		42 (129)						
Loyola University of Chicago		1.78						
		40 (139)						
University of Maine		1.72					2.38	
		40 (143)					*45* (107)	
University of Maryland College Park	3.02	3.16	3.45		3.64	3.17	3.66	
	48 (19)	*55* (63.5)	*60* (19)		*60* (18)	*52* (9)	*59* (23)	

Appendix Table I - 4 Physical Sciences and Mathematics (Continued)

Institution	Astrophysics/ Astronomy	Chemistry	Computer Science	Geosciences	Mathematics	Ocean- ography	Physics	Statistics/ Biostatistics
U of Maryland Baltimore County			1.53		1.92			
			41 (87)		*42* (113)			
Massachusetts Inst of Technology	3.68	4.70	4.62	4.52	4.57	4.31	4.64	
	57 (9)	*71* (3)	*71* (1)	*72* (2)	*70* (4)	*69* (1)	*70* (3)	
U of Massachusetts at Amherst	3.23	3.33	3.36	3.02	3.08	1.95	3.12	2.78
	51 (15)	*57* (47)	*59* (23.5)	*51* (44.5)	*55* (44.5)	*34* (24)	*53* (61)	*48* (40)
University of Mass-Lowell		2.44	1.16				2.41	
		47 (105)	*38* (97)				*45* (106)	
Medical University South Carolina								1.95
								38 (57.5)
Miami University		2.62						
		49 (94)						
University of Miami		1.67		3.02	2.33	3.05	1.83	
		39 (145)		*51* (44.5)	*47* (94)	*50* (15.5)	*39* (122)	
Michigan State University		3.50	2.74	2.53	2.95		3.37	2.94
		58 (33.5)	*53* (48)	*45* (70)	*53* (53.5)		*56* (35)	*50* (34)
Michigan Technological University				2.44			1.43	
				44 (76.5)			*35* (136)	
University of Michigan	3.00	3.63	3.51	3.89	3.84		3.74	3.02 [m]
	48 (20)	*60* (26.5)	*60* (14)	*63* (11)	*63* (14.5)		*60* (20)	*51* (32)
								3.36 [l]
								55 (23)
University of Minnesota	2.94	3.75	2.87	3.42	3.65		3.54	2.72 [m]
	47 (21)	*61* (21)	*54* (45)	*57* (24)	*61* (17)		*58* (27.5)	*47* (41)
								3.65 [l]
								59 (14)
Mississippi State University		1.28	1.28					
		35 (156)	*39* (95)					
University of Mississippi		1.09			0.56		1.62	
		33 (158)			*28* (136)		*37* (130)	
University of Missouri-Columbia		2.50			2.40		2.80	
		48 (100)			*47* (91.5)		*50* (86)	
Univ of Missouri-Kansas City		1.02						
		32 (160)						
University of Missouri-Rolla		1.97	1.03	1.21	0.94		2.17	
		42 (129)	*36* (100)	*27* (99)	*32* (130)		*43* (115)	
Univ of Missouri-Saint Louis		2.22						
		45 (119)						
Montana State University		2.65					2.62	
		49 (91.5)					*48* (95.5)	
University of Montana		0.80						
		30 (165)						
Naval Postgraduate School			1.40			2.11		
			40 (93)			*36* (23)		
University of Nebraska-Lincoln		3.04	1.89	1.98	2.72		2.96	
		53 (70.5)	*45* (69)	*37* (92)	*51* (64.5)		*52* (75)	

Appendix Table I - 4 Physical Sciences and Mathematics (Continued)

Institution	Astrophysics/ Astronomy	Chemistry	Computer Science	Geosciences	Mathematics	Ocean- ography	Physics	Statistics/ Biostatistics
University of Nevada, Reno		2.32		2.47			0.83	
		46 (111)		*44* (75)			*28* (143)	
University of New Hampshire		2.32					2.56	
		46 (111)					*47* (99)	
New Mexico Inst of Mining & Tech		0.42	0.00	2.72			1.19	
		26 (167)	*26* (108)	*47* (64.5)			*32* (138)	
New Mexico State University	1.82	2.12	1.77		2.55		2.22	
	32 (33)	*44* (122)	*44* (73)		*49* (78.5)		*43* (113)	
University of New Orleans		2.47						
		47 (102)						
New York University		2.68	3.47		4.26		3.15	
		50 (85.5)	*60* (17.5)		*67* (7)		*54* (57)	
North Carolina State University		2.79	1.96		2.86	2.80	3.20	3.36
		51 (81)	*45* (67)		*52* (56)	*46* (20)	*54* (56)	*55* (23)
U of North Carolina-Chapel Hill		3.93	3.40	2.92	3.01	3.13	3.27	3.58 [m]
		63 (14)	*59* (22)	*50* (51)	*54* (50.5)	*51* (10)	*55* (46.5)	*58* (16.5)
								3.69 [l]
								59 (13)
North Dakota State University		1.48						
		37 (153)						
University of North Dakota		1.88						
		41 (131)						
University of North Texas		1.77	1.04		1.99		2.83	
		40 (141)	*37* (98.5)		*43* (109)		*50* (85)	
Northeastern University		2.66			2.80	1.91	3.01	
		49 (88.5)			*52* (59.5)	*33* (25)	*52* (71)	
University of Northern Colorado								0.69
								23 (65)
Northern Illinois University		2.03		2.17	1.31			
		43 (126)		*40* (85)	*36* (124)			
Northwestern University		4.20	2.92	3.60	3.42		3.47	2.92
		66 (11.5)	*55* (40)	*59* (21)	*58* (31)		*57* (30)	*50* (35.5)
University of Notre Dame		3.30			3.17		3.27	
		56 (49.5)			*56* (41)		*55* (46.5)	
Oakland University							n/s	
Ohio State University	2.76	3.79	2.94	2.57 [k]	3.13		3.70	3.23
	45 (24)	*61* (20)	*55* (38)	*45* (67)	*55* (42)		*60* (22)	*54* (25)
				2.83				
				49 (57.5)				
Ohio University		1.62			1.55		2.88	
		39 (147)			*39* (121)		*51* (82)	
Oklahoma State University		2.50	0.11				1.78	
		48 (100)	*28* (107)				*39* (125)	
University of Oklahoma		2.65	1.04	2.83	2.12		2.53	
		49 (91.5)	*37* (98.5)	*49* (57.5)	*45* (103)		*47* (101)	

Appendix Table I - 4 Physical Sciences and Mathematics (Continued)

Institution	Astrophysics/ Astronomy	Chemistry	Computer Science	Geosciences	Mathematics	Ocean- ography	Physics	Statistics/ Biostatistics
Old Dominion University			1.48		1.54	3.05	0.94	
			41 (90)		*38* (123)	*50* (15.5)	*29* (142)	
Oregon Graduate Inst Sci & Tech		1.58	2.80				1.00	
		38 (150)	*54* (47)				*30* (141)	
Oregon State University		3.25	1.57	2.90	2.26	3.46	2.71	2.86
		56 (53.5)	*42* (84)	*50* (52.5)	*46* (98.5)	*56* (6)	*49* (92)	*49* (37)
University of Oregon		3.42	2.01	3.07	2.95		3.24	
		57 (39.5)	*46* (66)	*52* (42.5)	*53* (53.5)		*55* (52)	
Pennsylvania State University	2.75	3.70	2.59	3.85	3.37		3.08	3.53
	45 (25)	*60* (24)	*52* (50)	*63* (13)	*58* (32.5)		*53* (65)	*57* (18)
University of Pennsylvania		3.71	2.88 [d]	2.44	3.52		3.77	3.00
		61 (23)	*54* (43.5)	*44* (76.5)	*59* (25)		*60* (18.5)	*51* (33)
			3.42 [e]					
			60 (21)					
Phila Col of Pharmacy & Science		0.30						
		25 (168)						
University of Pittsburgh		3.52	2.72	2.80	2.58		3.29	2.63 [m]
		58 (32)	*53* (49)	*48* (59)	*49* (75)		*55* (43)	*46* (44)
								2.79 [l]
								48 (39)
Polytechnic University		2.32			2.50		1.97	
		46 (111)			*49* (83.5)		*41* (116)	
Princeton University	4.38	3.83	3.84	3.78	4.69		4.69	
	66 (3)	*62* (16.5)	*64* (10)	*62* (15)	*71* (1)		*70* (2)	
Univ of Puerto Rico-Rio Piedras		2.19					0.67	
		45 (121)					*26* (145)	
Purdue University		3.83	3.31	3.15	3.54		3.50	3.61
		62 (16.5)	*58* (25)	*53* (39)	*59* (24)		*57* (29)	*58* (15)
Rensselaer Polytechnic Inst		2.86	2.90	3.19	3.07		3.11	
		52 (77)	*55* (42)	*54* (36)	*54* (47)		*53* (62.5)	
University of Rhode Island		2.29			1.25	3.53	1.06	
		46 (114)			*35* (127)	*57* (5)	*31* (140)	
Rice University		3.56	3.51	3.46	3.33		3.35	
		59 (30)	*60* (14)	*57* (23)	*57* (34.5)		*56* (36.5)	
					3.84 [b]			
					63 (14.5)			
University of Rochester		3.54	3.51	2.50	2.76		3.63	3.18
		59 (31)	*60* (14)	*44* (73)	*51* (62.5)		*59* (26)	*53* (26)
							3.91 [j]	
							62 (11.5)	
Rockefeller University							2.50	
							46 (103)	
Rutgers State Univ-New Brunswick		2.89	3.05		3.62		3.33	3.16
		52 (76)	*56* (31.5)		*60* (20)		*56* (39)	*53* (27.5)
Rutgers State Univ-Newark		2.08						
		43 (123)						

Appendix Table I - 4 Physical Sciences and Mathematics (Continued)

Institution	Astrophysics/ Astronomy	Chemistry	Computer Science	Geosciences	Mathematics	Ocean-ography	Physics	Statistics/ Biostatistics
Saint Louis University				3.00	1.21			
				51 (47)	*35* (129)			
Seton Hall University		1.53						
		38 (152)						
University of South Carolina		3.33	1.49	2.53	2.61	2.87	2.69	2.24
		57 (47)	*41* (89)	*45* (70)	*50* (72)	*47* (18)	*49* (93)	*42* (54)
South Dakota Sch of Mines & Tech				1.99				
				37 (91)				
University of South Florida		1.77	1.75		2.08	2.83		
		40 (141)	*43* (74)		*44* (105)	*47* (19)		
University of Southern California		3.38	3.19	3.33	3.07		3.00	
		57 (45)	*57* (26)	*56* (29)	*55* (47)		*52* (73.5)	
Southern Illinois University		2.29			1.58			
		46 (114)			*39* (119)			
Southern Methodist University			1.67	3.08	2.11			2.68
			43 (78.5)	*52* (41)	*44* (104)			*47* (42)
Univ of Southern Mississippi		1.11						
		33 (157)						
Univ of Southwestern Louisiana			2.08		0.91			1.37
			47 (65)		*32* (131)			*31* (63)
Stanford University	2.91	4.57	4.60	3.86 [g]	4.41	2.20	4.35	4.44
	47 (22)	*70* (4.5)	*71* (2)	*63* (12)	*69* (5)	*37* (22)	*67* (9)	*68* (1)
				4.06				
				65 (5.5)				
				3.96 [f]				
				64 (8.5)				
State Univ of New York-Albany		2.26		2.72	2.45		2.73	
		45 (117)		*47* (64.5)	*48* (88)		*49* (91)	
State Univ of New York-Binghamton		2.40	0.88	2.38	2.56			
		47 (107)	*35* (102)	*43* (79)	*49* (77)			
State Univ of New York-Buffalo		3.16	2.48	2.08	2.55		2.30	1.94
		55 (63.5)	*50* (53.5)	*39* (86)	*49* (78.5)		*44* (110)	*38* (59)
State U of New York-Stony Brook	2.59	3.40	3.10	3.30	3.61	3.28	3.71	1.52
	42 (26)	*57* (42)	*56* (29)	*55* (31.5)	*60* (21)	*54* (7.5)	*60* (21)	*33* (62)
SUNY Col Environ Sci & Forestry		2.04						
		43 (124)						
Stevens Inst of Technology		1.44	1.23		1.67		1.95	
		37 (154)	*38* (96)		*40* (117)		*40* (117)	
Syracuse University		3.18	2.91	2.30	2.76		3.25	
		55 (60.5)	*55* (41)	*42* (81)	*51* (62.5)		*55* (50.5)	
Temple University		1.86	1.45		2.58		2.59	2.25
		41 (132)	*40* (92)		*49* (75)		*47* (97)	*42* (53)
University of Tennessee-Knoxville		2.85		2.84	2.53		2.78	
		51 (78)		*49* (56)	*49* (82)		*49* (87.5)	
Texas A&M University		3.63	2.30	2.94 [h]	2.58	3.09	3.29	3.44
		60 (26.5)	*49* (58)	*50* (50)	*49* (75)	*51* (13)	*55* (43)	*56* (19.5)

Appendix Table I - 4 Physical Sciences and Mathematics (Continued)

Institution	Astrophysics/ Astronomy	Chemistry	Computer Science	Geosciences	Mathematics	Ocean- ography	Physics	Statistics/ Biostatistics
Texas A&M University				3.18[f]				
				54 (37)				
Texas Christian University		1.81					0.72	
		41 (136)					*27* (144)	
Texas Tech University		2.53		1.85	2.26		2.62	
		48 (97.5)		*36* (94)	*46* (98.5)		*48* (95.5)	
University of Texas at Arlington		2.20	1.67		1.97		1.92	
		45 (120)	*43* (78.5)		*43* (110)		*40* (119)	
University of Texas at Austin	3.39	3.81	3.81	3.64	3.46		3.84	
	53 (11)	*62* (19)	*63* (11)	*60* (19)	*59* (30)		*61* (14)	
University of Texas at Dallas		1.67	1.92	2.29	0.48		3.00	1.95
		39 (145)	*45* (68)	*42* (82)	*27* (137)		*52* (73.5)	*38* (57.5)
University of Texas-El Paso				1.90				
				36 (93)				
University of Toledo		1.40						
		36 (155)						
Tufts University		1.58					2.92	
		38 (150)					*51* (78.5)	
Tulane University		2.27	0.63		2.65		1.53	
		45 (116)	*33* (105)		*50* (69.5)		*36* (131)	
University of Utah		3.58	3.04	2.95	3.19		3.02	
		59 (28)	*56* (33)	*50* (49)	*56* (39)		*52* (69)	
Vanderbilt University		2.81	1.74		2.46		*3.14*	
		51 (79.5)	*43* (75)		*48* (86.5)		*53* (58)	
University of Vermont		2.53						
		48 (97.5)						
Virginia Commonwealth University		1.85						
		41 (133)						
Virginia Polytech Inst & State U		3.25	1.67	3.33	2.80		3.01	2.92
		56 (53.5)	*43* (78.5)	*56* (29)	*52* (59.5)		*52* (71)	*50* (35.5)
University of Virginia	3.16	3.41	3.05		3.18		3.23	
	50 (16)	*57* (41)	*56* (31.5)		*56* (40)		*54* (53.5)	
Wake Forest University		1.67						
		39 (145)						
Washington State University		2.66	1.46	2.27	2.54		1.80	
		49 (88.5)	*41* (91)	*41* (83)	*49* (80.5)		*39* (124)	
Washington University		3.29	2.53	3.37	3.49		3.31	
		56 (51)	*51* (52)	*56* (26)	*59* (27)		*55* (41)	
University of Washington		3.49	4.05	3.36	3.24[a]	4.07	3.81	3.85[l]
		58 (35)	*66* (6)	*56* (27)	*56* (37.5)	*65* (3)	*61* (16.5)	*61* (9)
					3.47			4.08[m]
					59 (29)			*64* (4)
Wayne State University		3.30	1.67		2.07			
		56 (49.5)	*43* (78.5)		*44* (107)			
Wesleyan University		2.64			2.67			
		49 (93)			*50* (68)			

Appendix Table I - 4 Physical Sciences and Mathematics (Continued)

Institution	Astrophysics/ Astronomy	Chemistry	Computer Science	Geosciences	Mathematics	Ocean-ography	Physics	Statistics/ Biostatistics
West Virginia University		1.95		1.49				
		42 (130)		*31* (97)				
Western Michigan University					2.65			
					50 (69.5)			
Wichita State University		0.93						
		31 (161)						
College of William & Mary							3.11	
							53 (62.5)	
University of Wisconsin-Madison	3.47	4.26	3.87	3.65	3.82	3.06	3.81	4.07
	54 (10)	*66* (10)	*64* (9)	*60* (18)	*62* (16)	*50* (14)	*61* (16.5)	*64* (5)
University of Wisconsin-Milwaukee		2.24		1.67	1.54		*2.74*	
		45 (118)		*33* (95)	*38* (123)		*49* (90)	
Worcester Polytechnic Inst		0.65	0.83				1.46	
		28 (166)	*35* (104)				*35* (134)	
University of Wyoming		2.03		3.17	1.59			1.74
		43 (126)		*53* (38)	*39* (118)			*35* (60)
Yale University	3.31	4.31	3.44		4.11		4.03	3.39
	52 (13)	*67* (9)	*60* (20)		*65* (8)		*63* (10)	*56* (21)

Source: National Survey of Graduate Faculty

Notes: *a* Program in Applied Mathematics
b Program in Computational and Applied Mathematics
c Program in Mathematical Sciences
d Program in Decision Sciences, Wharton School
e Program in Computer and Information Science
f Program in Geophysics
g Program in Applied Earth Sciences
h Program in Geology
i Program in Meteorology
j Program in Optics
k Program in Geodetic Science and Surveying
l Program in Statistics
m Program in Biostatistics

n/s After trimming no cases remained

Appendix Table I - 5 Effectiveness Ratings of Research-Doctorate Programs in Social and Behavioral Sciences

Institution	Anthro-pology	Economics	Geography	History	Political Science	Psychology	Sociology
Adelphi University						1.72	
						39 (161)	
University of Akron				1.36		2.22	1.57
				34 (106)		*44* (138)	*39* (77)
University of Alabama		0.69		2.00		2.50	
		36 (98.5)		*41* (93.5)		*47* (118)	
University of Alabama-Birmingham						2.89	
						51 (88)	
American University	2.37	1.53		2.05	2.17	2.03	1.39
	42 (52)	*44* (73)		*42* (92)	*46* (67)	*42* (152)	*37* (82)
					1.85 [a]		
					43 (78)		
Arizona State University	3.22	1.81	3.22	2.66	2.33	3.49	1.74
	56 (21.5)	*46* (64.5)	*52* (15)	*49* (61.5)	*48* (58.5)	*58* (40)	*41* (73)
University of Arizona	3.60	2.44	2.97	2.78	2.50	3.29	3.41
	62 (7)	*52* (48)	*49* (21)	*50* (55)	*50* (48)	*56* (59)	*60* (17)
Univ of Arkansas-Fayetteville				2.14		1.67	
				43 (88.5)		*38* (165)	
Auburn University		1.27		1.80		2.04	
		41 (87)		*39* (96)		*42* (150)	
Ball State University						1.50	
						36 (170)	
Baylor University						1.67	
						38 (165)	
Biola University						0.19	
						22 (183)	
Boston College		2.47		2.46	1.29	2.33	2.45
		52 (46)		*46* (74)	*36* (88.5)	*45* (131)	*49* (53)
Boston University	2.27	2.76	2.74	2.65	1.14	2.78	2.63
	41 (57)	*55* (32)	*45* (27)	*48* (63.5)	*34* (91)	*50* (99.5)	*51* (45)
Bowling Green State University				1.45		3.03	1.62
				35 (103)		*53* (74.5)	*40* (76)
Brandeis University	2.08			3.28	2.08	3.45	2.31
	38 (60)			*55* (30.5)	*45* (72)	*58* (44.5)	*48* (59)
Brigham Young University				2.00		2.44	
				41 (93.5)		*47* (121)	
Brown University	2.59	3.38		3.86		3.57	3.22
	46 (48)	*60* (18)		*62* (14)		*59* (36)	*58* (22)
Bryn Mawr College						2.17	
						44 (142)	

Appendix Table I - 5 Social and Behavioral Sciences (Continued)

Institution	Anthro-pology	Economics	Geography	History	Political Science	Psychology	Sociology
California Institute Technology		3.81					
		64 (13)					
Cal Sch Prof Psych-Alameda						0.69	
						28 (176)	
Cal Sch Prof Psych-Fresno						0.46	
						25 (182)	
Cal Sch Prof Psych-Los Angeles						0.88	
						30 (173)	
Cal Sch Prof Psych-San Diego						0.65	
						27 (179)	
University of California-Berkeley	3.93	4.05	3.73	4.50	4.13	4.03	3.60
	67 (3)	*66* (7)	*60* (7)	*69* (2)	*68* (4)	*64* (14)	*62* (11)
University of California-Davis	3.26	2.34		3.11	2.60	3.42	
	56 (18.5)	*51* (50)		*54* (41.5)	*51* (40)	*57* (48)	
University of California-Irvine				2.94	2.83	3.68	
				52 (49)	*54* (34)	*60* (29)	
Univ of California-Los Angeles	3.50	3.55	3.50	4.07	3.62	4.05	3.79
	60 (8)	*62* (16)	*56* (12)	*64* (10)	*62* (14)	*64* (12)	*64* (6)
Univ of California-Riverside	2.33	1.32		2.53	2.13	2.92	2.87
	42 (54)	*42* (80)		*47* (72)	*46* (69.5)	*52* (82)	*54* (35.5)
Univ of California-San Diego	3.44	3.83		3.41	3.70	4.12	3.01
	59 (10.5)	*64* (12)		*57* (25)	*63* (12)	*65* (8)	*56* (30)
Univ of California-San Francisco						2.22	2.57
						44 (138)	51 (48)
Univ of California-Santa Barbara	3.26	2.46	3.95	3.08	2.55	3.37	3.06
	56 (18.5)	*52* (47)	*63* (4)	*53* (44)	*50* (43.5)	*57* (52)	*56* (27)
Univ of California-Santa Cruz						3.04	2.40
						53 (73)	*49* (55)
Carnegie Mellon University				3.26		4.13	
				55 (32)		*65* (7)	
Case Western Reserve Univ				1.96		2.96	
				41 (95)		*52* (78)	
Catholic University of America	1.50			2.64	0.95	2.69	0.99
	29 (68)			*48* (65.5)	*32* (95)	*49* (107)	*33* (92.5)
University of Chicago	4.19	4.63		4.20	3.83	3.75	4.26
	71 (2)	*71* (3)		*66* (8)	*65* (10)	*61* (22)	*70* (2)
University of Cincinnati		0.75	1.43	2.24	1.02	2.78	0.86
		37 (97)	*25* (36)	*44* (84.5)	*33* (94)	*50* (99.5)	*31* (94)
CUNY - Grad Sch & Univ Center	3.27	2.28		3.24	2.13	3.23	2.62
	56 (17)	*50* (52)		*55* (34)	*46* (69.5)	*55* (63)	*51* (46.5)
Claremont Graduate School		1.90		2.32	1.74	2.33	
		47 (60)		*45* (81.5)	*41* (79)	*45* (131)	

Appendix Table I - 5 Social and Behavioral Sciences (Continued)

Institution	Anthro-pology	Economics	Geography	History	Political Science	Psychology	Sociology
Clark Atlanta University					0.79		
					31 (97)		
Clark University		0.42	3.63			3.44	
		34 (106)	*58* (8)			*57* (47)	
Clemson University		1.95					
		47 (57)					
Colorado School of Mines		0.67					
		36 (100)					
Colorado State University		0.45				2.83	1.45
		34 (105)				*51* (96)	*38* (80.5)
University of Colorado	2.43	2.59	3.61	2.42	2.71	3.67	2.30
	43 (51)	*53* (40.5)	*58* (9)	*46* (75)	*52* (36.5)	*60* (30)	*48* (60)
Columbia University	3.21	3.43		4.29	3.22	3.60	3.25
	55 (23.5)	*61* (17)		*67* (7)	*58* (22.5)	*59* (33)	*58* (20)
University of Connecticut	2.93	1.30		2.67	2.43	3.45	2.24
	51 (38)	*42* (84.5)		*49* (60)	*49* (52)	*57* (44.5)	*47* (61)
Cornell University	3.39	3.36		3.87	3.61	4.04	3.10
	58 (14)	*60* (19)		*62* (13)	*62* (15)	*64* (13)	*57* (25)
Dartmouth College						2.99	
						53 (77)	
University of Delaware						3.21	1.86
						55 (64)	43 (71)
University of Denver					2.33	3.18	1.04
					48 (58.5)	*55* (66.5)	*33* (91)
University of Detroit Mercy						0.56	
						26 (181)	
Duke University	3.12	3.29		3.84	3.68	3.49	3.43
	54 (31)	*59* (20)		*62* (15)	*63* (13)	*58* (40)	*60* (16)
Duquesne University						1.82	
						40 (157)	
East Texas State University						0.83	
						29 (174)	
Emory University				3.33	2.69	3.38	
				56 (26.5)	*52* (38.5)	*57* (51)	
Fairleigh Dickinson University						1.78	
						39 (160)	
Fielding Institute						0.98	
						31 (172)	
Florida State University		1.92		2.47	2.97	2.95	2.95
		47 (59)		*46* (73)	*55* (30)	*52* (79.5)	*55* (32)
University of Florida	3.40	2.57	2.76	3.12	2.33	3.59	2.68
	58 (13)	*53* (42.5)	*45* (26)	*54* (38.5)	*48* (58.5)	*59* (34.5)	*52* (43)

Appendix Table I - 5 Social and Behavioral Sciences (Continued)

Institution	Anthro-pology	Economics	Geography	History	Political Science	Psychology	Sociology
Fordham University		0.94		0.83	1.07	2.19	1.17
		39 (92)		*28* (107)	*34* (92)	*44* (141)	*35* (87.5)
Fuller Theological Seminary						1.50	
						36 (170)	
George Mason University		2.14				2.22	
		49 (54)				*44* (138)	
George Washington University		1.78		2.90	2.50	2.43	
		46 (66)		*51* (50)	*50* (48)	*46* (123)	
Georgetown University		1.93		3.12	2.49	2.67	
		47 (58)		*54* (38.5)	*50* (51)	*49* (109)	
Georgia Institute of Technology						3.06	
						53 (72)	
Georgia State University		1.67				2.41	0.99
		45 (70)				*46* (126)	*33* (92.5)
University of Georgia		1.77	3.08	2.89	2.71	3.30	2.62
		46 (67)	*50* (19)	*51* (51)	*52* (36.5)	*56* (57)	*51* (46.5)
Hahnemann University						2.04	
						42 (150)	
Harvard University	3.67	4.33		4.02	4.17	4.09	3.58
	63 (5)	*69* (5)		*64* (12)	*69* (3)	*64* (10)	62 (12)
University of Hawaii at Manoa	2.63	0.99	2.63	3.15	2.07	2.84	1.18
	46 (45)	*39* (91)	*43* (28)	*54* (36)	*45* (73)	*51* (94)	*35* (86)
Univ of Health Sc/Chicago Med Sch						2.38	
						46 (128)	
Hofstra University						1.67	
						38 (165)	
University of Houston		2.02		2.38	2.69	3.16	
		48 (56)		*46* (77.5)	*52* (38.5)	*54* (68.5)	
Howard University		0.56		2.26	2.05	2.33	1.80
		35 (103)		*44* (83)	*45* (74)	*45* (131)	*42* (72)
Idaho State University					0.28		
					25 (98)		
Illinois Institute of Technology						2.08	
						43 (148)	
Illinois State University				0.77			
				28 (108)			
U of Illinois at Urbana-Champaign	3.47	2.94	3.24	3.67	3.04	4.36	3.07
	59 (9)	*56* (28)	*52* (14)	*60* (20.5)	*56* (28)	*67* (3)	*56* (26)
University of Illinois at Chicago		1.38		2.70		2.93	2.35
		42 (78)		*49* (57.5)		*52* (81)	*48* (58)
Indiana University	3.16	2.68	2.85	3.46	3.45	4.08	3.85
	55 (27)	*54* (36.5)	*47* (25)	*57* (24)	*60* (17)	*64* (11)	*65* (5)

Appendix Table I - 5 Social and Behavioral Sciences (Continued)

Institution	Anthro-pology	Economics	Geography	History	Political Science	Psychology	Sociology
Iowa State University		2.90				3.41	2.81
		56 (30)				*57* (49.5)	*53* (38)
University of Iowa	2.62	2.92	3.33	3.28	3.31	3.63	2.88
	46 (46)	*56* (29)	*54* (13)	*56* (30.5)	*59* (20.5)	*59* (32)	*54* (34)
Jewish Theological Seminary				3.33			
				56 (26.5)			
Johns Hopkins University	3.44	3.00	3.11	4.37	3.14	3.79	3.51
	59 (10.5)	*57* (26)	*51* (18)	*68* (5)	*57* (25)	*61* (20)	*61* (14)
Kansas State University						2.11	
						43 (146)	
University of Kansas	2.56	1.72	2.93	3.11	2.50	3.46	2.07
	45 (50)	*45* (69)	*48* (22)	*54* (41.5)	*50* (48)	*58* (42)	*45* (65.5)
Kent State University			2.13	2.18	1.17	2.83	1.09
			36 (34)	*43* (86.5)	*35* (90)	*51* (96)	*34* (90)
University of Kentucky	2.57	1.87	3.05	2.60	2.58	2.76	2.36
	45 (49)	*47* (61)	*50* (20)	*48* (69)	*51* (41)	*50* (103)	*48* (57)
Lehigh University		1.11				2.00	
		40 (88)				*42* (154)	
Louisiana State U & A&M College		1.74	3.14	2.61	1.99	2.55	2.16
		46 (68)	*51* (17)	*48* (67.5)	*44* (76)	*48* (115)	*46* (63)
University of Louisville						2.43	
						46 (123)	
Loyola University of Chicago				2.69		2.69	1.97
				49 (59)		*49* (107)	*44* (70)
University of Maine						2.43	
						46 (123)	
University of Maryland College Park		2.99	2.37	3.29	3.13	3.41	2.97
		57 (27)	*39* (30)	*56* (29)	*57* (27)	*57* (49.5)	*55* (31)
U of Maryland Baltimore County						2.19	
						44 (141)	
Massachusetts Inst of Technology		4.71			3.74		
		72 (1)			*64* (11)		
U of Massachusetts at Amherst	3.17	2.55		2.70	2.27	3.59	2.85
	55 (26)	*53* (44)		*49* (57.5)	*47* (63)	*59* (34.5)	*54* (37)
Miami University				2.18		2.47	
				43 (86.5)		*47* (120)	
University of Miami						3.11	
						54 (71)	
Michigan State University	2.75	3.09		2.81	3.31	3.45	2.70
	48 (41)	*58* (25)		*50* (54)	*59* (20.5)	*58* (44.5)	*52* (41)
University of Michigan	4.40	3.65		4.09	4.31	4.40	4.08
	74 (1)	*63* (15)		*64* (9)	*70* (1)	*68* (2)	*68* (3)

Appendix Table I - 5 Social and Behavioral Sciences (Continued)

Institution	Anthro-pology	Economics	Geography	History	Political Science	Psychology	Sociology
University of Minnesota	2.35	4.08	3.95	3.83	3.92	4.33	3.20
	42 (53)	*66* (6)	*63* (4)	*62* (16.5)	*66* (7)	*67* (4)	*58* (23)
Mississippi State University				0.56		1.11	1.45
				25 (110)		*32* (171)	*38* (80.5)
University of Mississippi						2.11	
						43 (146)	
University of Missouri-Columbia	2.07	0.91		2.66	1.43	3.29	2.07
	38 (61)	*38* (93)		*49* (61.5)	*38* (85)	*56* (59)	*45* (65.5)
		1.31 [b]					
		42 (81.5)					
Univ of Missouri-Kansas City						2.12	
						43 (144)	
Univ of Missouri-Saint Louis						2.67	
						49 (109)	
University of Montana						2.41	
						46 (126)	
University of Nebraska-Lincoln		0.45	2.34	2.07	2.22	2.90	2.56
		34 (105)	*39* (31)	*42* (91)	*47* (65)	*52* (85.5)	*51* (49)
University of Nevada, Reno						2.38	
						46 (128)	
University of New Hampshire		0.61		2.35		2.95	1.98
		36 (101)		*45* (79.5)		*52* (79.5)	*44* (69)
New Mexico State University						2.73	
						50 (105)	
University of New Orleans					1.67	2.50	
					40 (81.5)	*47* (118)	
New York University	3.36	3.22		3.60	2.56	3.45	2.93
	58 (16)	*59* (22)		*59* (23)	*50* (42)	*58* (44.5)	*55* (33)
North Carolina State University		2.43				2.63	2.38
		52 (49)				*49* (110)	*49* (56)
U of North Carolina-Chapel Hill	2.94	3.16	2.92	3.83	3.54	3.90	4.00
	51 (36.5)	*58* (24)	*48* (23)	*62* (16.5)	*61* (16)	*62* (17)	*67* (4)
U of North Carolina-Greensboro						2.90	
						52 (85.5)	
University of North Dakota				0.64		2.08	
				26 (109)		*43* (148)	
University of North Texas				1.67	1.73	1.67	1.21
				38 (99.5)	*41* (80)	*38* (165)	*35* (85)
Northeastern University		0.14				2.85	2.03
		31 (107)				*51* (92)	*45* (67)
Northern Arizona University				1.67	1.37		
				38 (99.5)	*37* (86)		

Appendix Table I - 5 Social and Behavioral Sciences (Continued)

Institution	Anthro-pology	Economics	Geography	History	Political Science	Psychology	Sociology
University of Northern Colorado						1.67	
						38 (165)	
Northern Illinois University		0.69		2.57	1.98	2.26	
		36 (98.5)		*48* (70)	*44* (77)	*45* (135)	
Northwestern University	3.11	4.04		3.69	3.14	3.64	3.61
	54 (32)	*66* (8)		*60* (19)	*57* (25)	*60* (31)	*62* (10)
University of Notre Dame		1.47		2.84	2.36	2.54	2.55
		43 (76)		*51* (53)	*48* (55.5)	*48* (116)	*50* (50)
Ohio State University	1.81	2.69	3.95	3.11	3.40	3.70	3.24
	34 (65)	*54* (34.5)	*63* (4)	*54* (41.5)	*60* (18)	*60* (26)	*58* (21)
Ohio University				3.00		2.78	
				52 (47.5)		*50* (99.5)	
Oklahoma State University		1.04				1.85	0.73
		39 (89)				*40* (156)	30 (95)
University of Oklahoma	1.67			2.24	2.03	2.58	1.13
	31 (66.5)			*44* (84.5)	*45* (75)	*48* (113)	*35* (89)
Old Dominion University						2.33	
						45 (131)	
Oregon State University			2.29				
			38 (32)				
University of Oregon	2.68	1.59	2.60	2.65	2.11	3.83	2.15
	47 (43)	*44* (71)	*43* (29)	*48* (63.5)	*45* (71)	*62* (19)	*46* (64)
Pacific Grad Sch of Psychology						0.72	
						28 (175)	
Pennsylvania State University	3.21	2.60	4.18	2.32	2.38	3.53	3.47
	55 (23.5)	*53* (39)	*67* (1)	*45* (81.5)	*48* (54)	*58* (37)	*61* (15)
University of Pennsylvania	*3.68*	3.91		4.05	2.41	4.18	3.66
	63 (4)	*65* (11)		*64* (11)	*49* (53)	*65* (6)	*63* (9)
University of Pittsburgh	2.99	2.71		3.25	2.90	3.33	2.17
	52 (35)	*54* (33)		*55* (33)	*54* (31)	*56* (54.5)	*46* (62)
Princeton University	3.15	4.69		4.48	3.91	4.10	3.29
	54 (28)	*72* (2)		*69* (3)	*66* (8)	*65* (9)	*59* (18.5)
Univ of Puerto Rico-Rio Piedras				1.67		n/s	
				38 (99.5)			
Purdue University		2.68		2.61	2.24	3.70	2.42
		54 (36.5)		*48* (67.5)	*47* (64)	*60* (26)	*49* (54)
Rensselaer Polytechnic Inst		0.83					
		38 (95)					
University of Rhode Island						2.87	
						51 (90)	
Rice University		2.21		3.00	2.55	3.16	
		50 (53)		*52* (47.5)	*50* (43.5)	*54* (68.5)	

Appendix Table I - 5 Social and Behavioral Sciences (Continued)

Institution	Anthro-pology	Economics	Geography	History	Political Science	Psychology	Sociology
University of Rochester	2.20	3.96		3.13	4.00	3.73	
	40 (58)	*65* (10)		*54* (37)	*67* (6)	*61* (23)	
Rutgers State Univ-New Brunswick	3.08	2.29	3.17	3.74	3.14	3.70	2.78
	53 (33)	*51* (51)	*51* (16)	*61* (18)	*57* (25)	*60* (26)	*53* (40)
Rutgers State Univ-Newark						0.67	
						27 (178)	
St. John's University						2.12	
						43 (144)	
Saint Louis University						1.80	
						40 (158)	
Saybrook Institute						0.67	
						27 (178)	
University of South Carolina		1.50		2.39	2.52	3.18	
		43 (74)		*46* (76)	*50* (45)	*55* (66.5)	
University of South Florida	1.99					2.91	
	36 (62)					*52* (83)	
University of Southern California		2.57		2.35	2.15	3.71	2.67
		53 (42.5)		*45* (79.5)	*46* (68)	*60* (24)	*52* (44)
Southern Illinois University	2.81	1.30				2.90	1.37
	49 (40)	*42* (84.5)				*52* (85.5)	*37* (83)
Southern Methodist University	3.04	1.81					
	53 (34)	*46* (64.5)					
Univ of Southern Mississippi				0.51		2.33	
				25 (111)		*45* (131)	
Stanford University	*3.63*	4.58		4.44	4.02	4.64	3.77
	62 (6)	*71* (4)		*68* (4)	*67* (5)	*70* (1)	*64* (7)
State Univ of New York-Albany	2.68	1.44			2.31	3.26	3.18
	47 (43)	*43* (77)			*48* (61)	*55* (62)	*58* (24)
State Univ of New York-Binghamton	2.94	1.86		3.11	2.36	3.01	2.80
	51 (36.5)	*47* (62.5)		*54* (41.5)	*48* (55.5)	*53* (76)	*53* (39)
State Univ of New York-Buffalo	2.68	1.86	3.51	2.64	2.50	3.49	1.73
	47 (43)	*47* (62.5)	*57* (11)	*48* (65.5)	*50* (48)	*58* (40)	*41* (74)
State U of New York-Stony Brook	3.14	2.59		3.22	2.88	3.69	3.29
	54 (29.5)	*53* (40.5)		*55* (35)	*54* (32)	*60* (28)	*59* (18.5)
Stevens Inst of Technology						0.00	
						20 (184)	
Syracuse University	1.89	2.13	3.78	2.54	2.84	2.83	2.47
	35 (64)	*49* (55)	*61* (6)	*47* (71)	*54* (33)	*51* (96)	*50* (51)
Temple University	2.30	0.90		2.38	1.30	3.28	2.02
	41 (56)	*38* (94)		*46* (77.5)	*36* (87)	*56* (61)	*45* (68)
University of Tennessee-Knoxville	2.86	1.30		2.14	1.49	2.76	1.17
	50 (39)	*42* (84.5)		*43* (88.5)	*38* (84)	*50* (103)	*35* (87.5)

Appendix Table I - 5 Social and Behavioral Sciences (Continued)

Institution	Anthro-pology	Economics	Geography	History	Political Science	Psychology	Sociology
Texas A&M University		2.69		2.08		2.88	2.69
		54 (34.5)		*42* (90)		*51* (89)	*52* (42)
Texas Christian University				1.67		2.50	
				38 (99.5)		*47* (118)	
Texas Tech University				1.37	0.88	2.02	
				34 (105)	*32* (96)	*42* (153)	
University of Texas at Arlington						2.26	
						45 (135)	
University of Texas at Austin	3.38	2.66	2.88	3.63	3.22	3.96	3.56
	58 (15)	*54* (38)	*47* (24)	*59* (22)	*58* (22.5)	*63* (16)	62 (13)
University of Texas at Dallas		0.57		1.37	1.29	1.88	
		35 (102)		*34* (105)	*36* (88.5)	*41* (155)	
U of Texas-Southwestern Med Ctr						3.13	
						54 (70)	
Texas Woman's University						0.56	
						26 (181)	
University of Toledo						2.22	
						44 (138)	
Tufts University					2.33	2.85	
					48 (58.5)	*51* (92)	
Tulane University	2.61	1.30		3.03	1.60	2.62	1.72
	46 (47)	*42* (84.5)		*53* (46)	*40* (83)	*49* (111)	*41* (75)
University of Tulsa						2.61	
						48 (112)	
Uniformed Services U of Hlth Sci						3.33	
						56 (54.5)	
Utah State University		0.79				1.67	1.25
		37 (96)				*38* (165)	*36* (84)
University of Utah	2.14	1.00	1.76		1.67	3.29	1.47
	39 (59)	*39* (90)	*30* (35)		*40* (81.5)	*56* (59)	*38* (78)
Vanderbilt University	2.32	2.48		3.05	2.30	3.51	2.87
	42 (55)	*52* (45)		*53* (45)	*48* (62)	*58* (38)	*54* (35.5)
Peabody Col at Vanderbilt Univ						3.33	
						56 (54.5)	
University of Vermont						2.78	
						50 (99.5)	
Virginia Commonwealth University						2.73	
						50 (105)	
Virginia Polytech Inst & State U						2.85	
						51 (92)	
University of Virginia	3.14	3.26		3.67	2.72	3.78	2.46
	54 (29.5)	*59* (21)		*60* (20.5)	*52* (35)	*61* (21)	*50* (52)

Appendix Table I - 5 Social and Behavioral Sciences (Continued)

Institution	Anthro-pology	Economics	Geography	History	Political Science	Psychology	Sociology
Washington State University	1.97	1.54		1.77	1.04	2.56	3.04
	36 (63)	*44* (72)		*39* (97)	*33* (93)	*48* (114)	*56* (28.5)
Washington University	3.18	2.82		2.72	3.38	3.19	
	55 (25)	*55* (31)		*49* (56)	*60* (19)	*55* (65)	
University of Washington	3.25	3.17	3.55	3.30	3.02	3.89	3.73
	56 (20)	*58* (23)	*57* (10)	*56* (28)	*56* (29)	*62* (18)	*64* (8)
Wayne State University	1.67				2.19	3.03	
	31 (66.5)				*46* (66)	*53* (74.5)	
West Virginia University		1.35		1.56		2.90	
		42 (79)		*36* (102)		*52* (85.5)	
Western Michigan University						1.79	1.46
						40 (159)	*38* (79)
College of William & Mary				2.87			
				51 (52)			
University of Wisconsin-Madison	3.22	3.79	4.14	4.33	3.86	3.99	4.61
	56 (21.5)	*64* (14)	*66* (2)	*67* (6)	*65* (9)	*63* (15)	*74* (1)
University of Wisconsin-Milwaukee	1.31	1.31	2.21		2.50	3.33	
	26 (69)	*42* (81.5)	*37* (33)		*50* (48)	*56* (54.5)	
University of Wyoming		1.48				1.67	
		43 (75)				*38* (165)	
Yale University	*3.43*	4.01		4.55	4.24	4.31	3.04
	59 (12)	*66* (9)		*70* (1)	*69* (2)	*67* (5)	*56* (28.5)
Yeshiva University						2.03	
						42 (152)	

Source: National Survey of Graduate Faculty

Notes: *a* Program in International Relations
b Program in Agricultural Economics

n/s After trimming no cases remained

APPENDIX J

Selected Characteristics of Research-Doctorate Programs in the Arts and Humanities

In the tables that follow, information from the National Survey of Graduate Faculty is linked to a variety of statistics depicting participating doctoral programs. The tables have been designed to present information about each program in a field in rank order by the average rating of the scholarly quality of program faculty (93Q), with the top-rated institutions appearing at the beginning of the list. A key to the variables in the table is presented below.

Institution

Institution: U.S. universities participating in the 1993 NRC Study, ranked in descending order based on the scholarly rating of the program faculty (93Q).

1993 Ratings

93Q: 1993 trimmed mean for scholarly quality of program faculty. The trimmed mean is obtained by dropping the two highest and two lowest scores on the survey before computing the average. For purposes of analysis, scores were converted to a scale of 0 to 5, with 0 denoting "Not sufficient for doctoral education" and 5 denoting "Distinguished." Source: NRC National Survey of Graduate Faculty.

93E: 1993 trimmed mean for program effectiveness in educating research scholars and scientists. The trimmed mean is obtained by dropping the two highest and two lowest scores on the survey before computing the average. For purposes of analysis, scores were converted to a scale of 0 to 5 with 0 denoting "Not Effective" and 5 denoting "Extremely Effective." Source: NRC National Survey of Graduate Faculty.

93C: 1993 trimmed mean for change in program quality in the last five years. The trimmed mean is obtained by dropping the two highest and two lowest scores on the survey before computing the average. For purposes of analysis, scores were converted to a scale of –1 to 1 with –1 denoting "Poorer than 5 years ago" and 1 denoting "Better than 5 years ago." Source: NRC National Survey of Graduate Faculty.

Faculty

Tot Fac: Total number of faculty participating in the program. Source: Institutional Coordinators.

%Full: Percentage of full professors participating in the program. Source: Institutional Coordinators.

%Supp Percentage of program faculty (Tot Fac) with research support (1986-92). Source: Federal Agencies.

No. Awd: Total number of awards and honors attributed to program faculty for the period 1986-1992. Source: See Appendix G for award organizations.

Awd Fac: Percentage of program faculty that have received at least one honor or award for the period 1986-1992. Source: See Appendix G for award organizations.

Students

Tot Stu: The number of full and part time graduate students enrolled in the Fall of 1992. Source: Institutional Coordinators.

%Fem: The percentage of full and part time female graduate students enrolled in the Fall of 1992. Source: Institutional Coordinators.

Rpt PhDs: The number of PhDs produced by that program for the period academic year 1987-1988 to 1991-1992. Source: Institutional Coordinators.

Doctoral Recipients

%Fem: The percentage of PhDs awarded to women during the period July 1986-June 1992. Source: Doctorate Records File.

%Min: The percentage of PhDs known to be awarded to underrepresented minorities (only US Citizens or Permanent Residents) during the period July 1986-June 1992. Source: Doctorate Records File.

%US:	The percentage of PhDs known to be awarded to U.S. Citizens and Permanent Residents during the period July 1986-June 1992. Source: Doctorate Records File.
%RA:	The percentage of PhDs having research assistantships who reported their primary form of support. Source: Doctorate Records File.
%TA:	The percentage of PhDs having teaching assistantships who reported their primary form of support. Source: Doctorate Records File.
MYD:	Median time lapse from entering graduate school to receipt of Ph.D. in years. This is a distributed median with multiple degrees awarded in the median year proportioned over the year. Source: Doctorate Records File.

NOTICE: **n/a** denotes a case where information was not provided by the Institutional Coordinators or was not available from the Doctorate Records File.

Appendix Table J - 1 Selected Characteristics of Research-Doctorate Programs in Art History

Institution	1993 Ratings[1]			Faculty					Students[2]			Doctorate Recipients[3]					
	93Q	93E	93C	Tot Fac[2]	% Full[2]	% Supp[2]	Nmbr. Awd[5]	Awd Fac[5]	Tot Stu	% Fem	Rpt PhDs	% Fem	% Min	% US	% RA	% TA	MYD
Columbia University	4.79	4.29	0.27	35	57	0	16	43	228	75	57	71	1	96	2	0	12.9
New York University	4.79	4.32	0.05	25	84	0	11	40	23	70	64	74	3	96	0	0	12.9
University of California-Berkeley	4.67	4.18	0.36	12	83	0	7	33	42	74	26	67	3	91	0	15	12.6
Harvard University	4.49	4.11	0.07	15	80	0	7	40	101	56	37	59	6	78	4	19	10.7
Yale University	4.44	4.36	-0.32	23	48	0	2	9	68	49	40	67	4	89	0	7	9.9
Princeton University	4.04	3.78	-0.11	17	71	0	3	18	55	62	37	59	0	87	0	6	12.5
Johns Hopkins University	3.93	3.46	-0.30	5	80	0	6	80	16	63	12	40	0	75	0	0	8.6
Northwestern University	3.83	3.57	0.58	12	58	8	13	83	33	73	16	47	6	94	9	45	11.1
University of Pennsylvania	3.80	3.51	0.22	20	40	0	4	15	66	73	25	58	0	94	4	26	10.7
University of Chicago	3.74	3.49	0.07	14	43	0	5	29	105	77	25	57	7	100	0	0	13.6
Mean Values for the Top Quarter	**4.25**	**3.91**	**0.09**	**17.80**	**64.40**	**0.80**	**7.40**	**39.00**	**73.70**	**67.20**	**33.90**	**59.90**	**3.00**	**90.00**	**1.90**	**11.80**	**11.55**
University of Michigan	3.71	3.58	0.31	25	52	0	5	16	41	78	25	81	7	97	5	18	15.2
CUNY - Grad Sch & Univ Center	3.60	3.38	-0.12	17	82	0	5	18	207	77	24	68	7	93	0	0	15.4
Univ of California-Los Angeles	3.52	3.46	-0.06	16	56	0	5	25	72	85	36	79	5	95	0	19	13.6
Stanford University	3.49	3.45	0.04	17	59	0	5	29	36	78	13	65	0	94	7	0	10.8
University of Delaware	3.40	3.33	0.37	14	57	0	5	29	49	78	13	65	0	95	6	6	14.4
University of Virginia	3.31	3.07	0.19	20	30	0	2	10	32	66	6	75	0	100	0	25	10.7
Bryn Mawr College	3.28	3.46	-0.26	6	83	0	1	17	37	84	6	91	0	100	13	0	10.8
Brown University	3.20	3.05	-0.08	9	44	0	2	22	41	80	13	74	0	79	0	44	10.4
University of Texas at Austin	3.17	3.03	0.47	15	60	0	3	20	22	64	23	96	0	89	0	13	12.3
Mean Values for the 2nd Quarter	**3.41**	**3.31**	**0.10**	**15.44**	**58.11**	**0.00**	**3.67**	**20.67**	**59.67**	**76.67**	**17.67**	**77.11**	**2.11**	**93.56**	**3.44**	**13.89**	**12.62**
Rutgers State Univ-New Brunswick	3.04	3.04	0.38	18	39	0	5	22	53	70	9	71	0	100	0	0	14.4
Univ of California-Santa Barbara	2.98	2.78	0.10	15	53	0	4	20	43	58	13	50	13	89	0	42	10.4
University of Pittsburgh	2.90	3.04	0.11	12	67	0	2	17	32	72	14	100	0	100	0	11	11.0
Cornell University	2.87	2.80	0.07	14	43	7	4	21	23	74	13	47	0	88	8	38	12.9
Indiana University	2.85	2.87	0.00	14	36	0	2	14	38	82	18	57	14	96	0	12	12.8

Institution	1993 Ratings[1] 93Q	93E	93C	Faculty Tot Fac[2]	% Full[2]	% Supp[2]	Nmbr. Awd[5]	Awd Fac[5]	Students[2] Tot Stu	% Fem	Rpt PhDs	Doctorate Recipients[3] % Fem	% Min	% US	% RA	% TA	MYD
Boston University	2.85	2.73	0.00	13	54	0	4	31	34	79	14	86	5	95	0	21	12.7
U of Illinois at Urbana-Champaign	2.67	2.79	-0.02	10	40	0	0	0	42	81	9	60	0	89	0	43	14.8
University of Kansas	2.56	2.57	-0.08	13	31	0	0	0	26	73	21	70	6	78	6	6	13.7
University of Maryland College Park	2.53	2.25	0.18	17	41	0	0	0	37	86	13	81	13	100	0	13	15.4
Ohio State University	2.48	1.98	0.28	20	50	0	3	15	19	68	8	75	0	100	0	38	16.4
Mean Values for the 3rd Quarter	**2.77**	**2.69**	**0.10**	**14.60**	**45.40**	**0.70**	**2.40**	**14.00**	**34.70**	**74.30**	**13.20**	**69.70**	**5.10**	**93.50**	**1.40**	**22.40**	**13.45**
University of Minnesota	2.47	2.43	-0.25	13	38	0	2	8	14	57	9	81	0	100	0	40	17.7
University of Washington	2.39	2.15	-0.04	11	55	9	1	9	19	79	11	75	8	100	0	33	12.4
U of North Carolina-Chapel Hill	2.33	2.46	-0.53	6	50	0	4	33	20	80	9	100	0	100	0	9	11.9
Washington University	2.31	2.24	0.06	9	33	11	2	22	22	68	3	67	0	100	0	33	10.7
Pennsylvania State University	2.28	2.31	-0.12	11	45	0	1	9	46	72	3	60	0	100	0	75	10.5
University of Wisconsin-Madison	2.14	2.35	-0.03	10	50	0	4	40	69	70	5	63	0	100	0	29	12.7
Florida State University	2.10	1.67	0.20	11	18	0	3	18	11	82	9	64	20	91	0	0	17.4
Case Western Reserve Univ	1.79	2.08	-0.11	7	43	0	2	29	23	57	5	50	0	83	17	0	11.6
University of Georgia	0.90	0.79	-0.31	6	17	0	2	33	8	100	9	60	0	93	0	0	14.4
Mean Values for the 4th Quarter	**2.08**	**2.05**	**-0.13**	**9.33**	**38.78**	**2.22**	**2.33**	**22.33**	**25.78**	**73.89**	**7.00**	**68.89**	**3.11**	**96.33**	**1.89**	**24.33**	**13.26**
Mean Values for All Programs	**3.15**	**3.01**	**0.04**	**14.39**	**51.84**	**0.92**	**4.00**	**24.13**	**48.76**	**72.89**	**18.24**	**68.68**	**3.37**	**93.26**	**2.13**	**18.05**	**12.71**

Sources: 1. National Survey of Graduate Faculty
2. Institutional Coordinator Response Data
3. Doctorate Records File
4. Federal Agencies
5. Associations and Organizations Administrating Prestigious Awards and Honors

Appendix Table J - 2 Selected Characteristics of Research-Doctorate Programs in Classics

Institution	1993 Ratings[1]			Faculty					Students[2]			Doctorate Recipients[3]					
	93Q	93E	93C	Tot Fac[2]	% Full[2]	% Supp[2]	Nmbr. Awd[5]	Awd Fac[5]	Tot Stu	% Fem	Rpt PhDs	% Fem	% Min	% US	% RA	% TA	MYD
Harvard University	4.79	3.86	0.01	19	74	0	17	58	41	46	19	47	6	100	0	54	8.7
University of California-Berkeley	4.77	4.41	0.06	18	78	6	7	28	25	40	23	40	4	93	0	52	9.4
University of Michigan	4.54	4.26	0.28	22	64	0	8	23	34	38	16	31	0	100	0	57	8.6
Princeton University	4.16	4.15	-0.22	8	75	0	2	25	24	46	17	38	0	100	0	0	8.8
Yale University	4.12	3.52	-0.30	17	53	0	1	6	35	34	18	52	0	100	0	21	9.0
Brown University	4.10	3.46	0.20	10	80	0	11	80	23	43	14	35	0	94	0	54	7.6
University of Chicago	4.00	3.09	0.27	12	42	0	4	33	23	26	6	64	0	100	0	0	11.8
University of Texas at Austin	3.92	3.40	0.30	31	58	0	7	23	13	38	14	41	0	94	0	65	8.8
Mean Values for the Top Quarter	**4.30**	**3.77**	**0.08**	**17.13**	**65.50**	**0.75**	**7.13**	**34.50**	**27.25**	**38.88**	**15.88**	**43.50**	**1.25**	**97.63**	**0.00**	**37.88**	**9.09**
Univ of California-Los Angeles	3.89	3.23	0.61	19	58	0	6	21	22	59	10	20	0	100	0	33	11.0
Columbia University	3.86	3.15	0.15	13	62	0	6	38	21	76	11	44	0	100	8	31	10.0
U of North Carolina-Chapel Hill	3.81	3.57	-0.03	15	80	0	5	27	25	36	13	33	0	96	0	59	7.8
Cornell University	3.73	3.38	0.29	24	58	4	8	29	16	56	7	58	0	83	0	13	8.2
University of Pennsylvania	3.62	2.65	0.45	24	67	0	9	25	22	32	1	67	0	100	0	33	6.8
Bryn Mawr College	3.48	3.48	-0.14	10	80	0	5	40	55	58	15	60	0	100	0	0	7.8
Duke University	3.37	3.01	0.30	11	55	0	1	9	16	50	10	25	0	100	20	0	10.8
Mean Values for the 2nd Quarter	**3.68**	**3.21**	**0.23**	**16.57**	**65.71**	**0.57**	**5.71**	**27.00**	**25.29**	**52.43**	**9.57**	**43.86**	**0.00**	**97.00**	**4.00**	**24.14**	**8.91**
Stanford University	3.32	3.17	-0.69	11	55	9	2	18	36	78	5	56	0	88	0	14	8.0
U of Illinois at Urbana-Champaign	3.02	2.60	-0.09	15	73	0	5	33	20	35	6	14	0	57	0	100	9.7
University of Virginia	2.98	2.57	0.27	6	83	0	2	33	15	40	4	40	0	100	0	0	15.7
University of Wisconsin-Madison	2.92	2.76	0.32	11	64	0	1	9	13	38	6	14	0	100	0	67	8.0
University of Washington	2.89	2.87	0.69	11	27	0	1	9	20	55	7	18	0	91	0	80	15.7
Ohio State University	2.60	2.38	0.12	16	31	0	2	13	26	35	13	27	0	71	0	92	9.7
Univ of California-Santa Barbara	2.59	1.91	-0.05	8	63	0	1	13	12	42	1	0	100	100	0	0	9.0
Mean Values for the 3rd Quarter	**2.90**	**2.61**	**0.08**	**11.14**	**56.57**	**1.29**	**2.00**	**18.29**	**20.29**	**46.14**	**6.00**	**24.14**	**14.29**	**86.71**	**0.00**	**50.43**	**10.83**

Institution	1993 Ratings[1]			Faculty					Students[2]			Doctorate Recipients[3]					
	93Q	93E	93C	Tot Fac[2]	% Full[2]	% Supp[2]	Nmbr. Awd[5]	Awd Fac[5]	Tot Stu	% Fem	Rpt PhDs	% Fem	% Min	% US	% RA	% TA	MYD
Johns Hopkins University	2.52	1.33	-0.58	9	44	0	0	0	8	88	6	38	0	100	0	67	11.4
University of Minnesota	2.43	2.33	-0.06	13	46	0	1	8	29	41	8	56	0	100	0	50	13.0
New York University	2.33	1.84	0.10	8	50	0	1	13	8	50	2	25	0	100	0	0	14.0
Boston University	2.31	1.78	-0.05	5	60	0	0	0	27	33	7	83	0	83	0	50	13.7
University of Cincinnati	2.10	1.96	-0.67	5	80	0	0	0	16	69	6	57	0	67	0	17	7.4
Fordham University	1.83	1.38	-0.03	5	20	0	1	20	17	47	3	60	0	100	0	25	15.7
Catholic University of America	0.93	0.56	-0.08	5	20	0	2	40	9	22	3	100	0	100	0	0	17.5
Mean Values for the 4th Quarter	**2.06**	**1.60**	**-0.20**	**7.14**	**45.71**	**0.00**	**0.71**	**11.57**	**16.29**	**50.00**	**5.00**	**59.86**	**0.00**	**92.86**	**0.00**	**29.86**	**13.24**
Mean Values for All Programs	**3.27**	**2.83**	**0.05**	**13.14**	**58.62**	**0.66**	**4.00**	**23.24**	**22.45**	**46.59**	**9.34**	**42.86**	**3.79**	**93.69**	**1.00**	**35.66**	**10.47**

Sources: 1. National Survey of Graduate Faculty
2. Institutional Coordinator Response Data
3. Doctorate Records File
4. Federal Agencies
5. Associations and Organizations Administrating Prestigious Awards and Honors

Appendix Table J - 3 Selected Characteristics of Research-Doctorate Programs in Comparative Literature

Institution	1993 Ratings[1] 93Q	93E	93C	Faculty Tot Fac[2]	% Full[2]	% Supp[2]	Nmbr. Awd[5]	Awd Fac[5]	Students[2] Tot Stu	% Fem	Rpt PhDs	Doctorate Recipients[3] % Fem	% Min	% US	% RA	% TA	MYD
Yale University	4.70	4.30	-0.24	18	67	0	9	33	32	n/a	27	38	5	97	0	14	8.6
Duke University	4.51	3.80	0.79	25	68	0	12	28	60	48	10	33	50	67	0	67	7.7
Columbia University	4.44	3.82	0.39	75	51	5	21	27	55	64	18	53	0	89	0	19	9.6
Harvard University	4.37	3.81	0.13	21	86	0	11	48	63	57	34	64	4	86	0	59	8.9
Princeton University	4.32	3.96	0.21	17	76	0	7	29	33	70	18	45	4	83	0	10	8.3
Cornell University	4.31	3.78	0.17	27	63	0	7	22	25	36	17	48	6	95	0	63	9.9
Johns Hopkins University	4.18	4.12	0.09	13	69	0	5	38	25	68	17	67	0	100	0	83	8.6
University of California-Irvine	4.06	3.63	0.68	13	54	0	4	31	40	50	9	75	0	82	0	67	10.1
Stanford University	4.05	3.75	0.10	11	73	9	10	55	32	56	19	57	0	89	0	6	8.7
University of California-Berkeley	4.00	3.83	-0.02	20	60	0	3	10	95	65	43	68	4	89	2	65	11.2
University of Pennsylvania	3.99	3.57	0.48	35	74	0	21	46	52	62	8	63	0	75	0	50	9.2
Mean Values for the Top Quarter	**4.27**	**3.85**	**0.25**	**25.00**	**67.36**	**1.27**	**10.00**	**33.36**	**46.55**	**57.60**	**20.00**	**55.55**	**6.64**	**86.55**	**0.18**	**45.73**	**9.16**
University of Chicago	3.56	3.29	0.08	22	64	0	4	18	38	50	5	38	9	100	0	0	9.6
New York University	3.49	3.19	0.48	18	72	0	4	17	13	77	39	61	10	85	3	3	11.4
University of Washington	3.37	3.21	0.40	25	56	0	2	8	81	59	20	50	7	67	0	36	10.4
University of Michigan	3.23	3.17	0.13	9	44	0	2	22	57	68	13	42	8	80	0	80	11.6
Univ of California-Los Angeles	3.22	3.29	0.31	28	64	0	6	21	49	57	15	50	5	95	0	63	11.3
Northwestern University	3.20	3.01	0.17	29	38	7	11	38	24	67	16	0	0	100	0	100	8.5
Univ of California-San Diego	3.17	3.01	0.00	18	50	0	6	22	33	64	7	22	33	67	0	83	10.0
Indiana University	3.08	2.97	-0.18	24	63	0	4	17	120	58	20	68	5	75	0	64	11.8
Brown University	2.98	2.99	-0.11	8	63	0	2	25	18	67	10	80	0	93	0	67	7.9
University of Texas at Austin	2.96	3.14	0.26	44	50	0	4	7	40	58	15	42	6	71	0	61	11.4
Rutgers State Univ-New Brunswick	2.92	2.92	0.04	21	38	0	1	5	38	63	10	45	0	91	0	25	13.6
Mean Values for the 2nd Quarter	**3.20**	**3.11**	**0.14**	**22.36**	**54.73**	**0.64**	**4.18**	**18.18**	**46.45**	**62.55**	**15.45**	**45.27**	**7.55**	**84.00**	**0.27**	**52.91**	**10.68**
University of Southern California	2.86	2.72	0.06	13	85	0	1	8	20	55	10	89	0	78	0	67	12.7
Emory University	2.72	2.72	-0.06	19	37	0	3	16	31	61	3	64	25	73	0	0	8.6

Institution	1993 Ratings[1]			Faculty					Students[2]			Doctorate Recipients[3]					
	93Q	93E	93C	Tot Fac[2]	% Full[2]	% Supp[2]	Nmbr. Awd[5]	Awd Fac[5]	Tot Stu	% Fem	Rpt PhDs	% Fem	% Min	% US	% RA	% TA	MYD
Washington University	2.70	2.65	0.00	21	62	0	5	19	48	60	9	50	0	80	0	50	12.7
Univ of California-Riverside	2.66	2.56	0.40	35	54	0	2	6	17	47	13	71	15	93	0	17	12.1
Pennsylvania State University	2.65	2.55	0.05	25	52	4	3	12	43	72	17	62	0	38	7	79	9.8
University of Minnesota	2.53	2.75	-0.57	7	57	0	0	0	46	43	10	40	0	73	13	50	12.0
State U of New York-Stony Brook	2.49	2.57	-0.17	16	38	0	6	31	45	51	8	61	7	83	8	50	10.6
University of Iowa	2.48	2.79	-0.08	11	64	0	1	9	30	73	14	45	0	60	0	71	10.4
University of Rochester	2.47	2.14	0.11	19	16	0	4	16	21	71	4	75	0	25	0	0	8.5
U of North Carolina-Chapel Hill	2.44	2.76	-0.14	7	71	0	4	29	41	66	18	58	0	86	0	64	11.2
U of Illinois at Urbana-Champaign	2.39	2.50	-0.37	9	78	0	3	22	34	59	18	57	8	44	0	79	9.0
Mean Values for the 3rd Quarter	**2.58**	**2.61**	**-0.07**	**16.55**	**55.82**	**0.36**	**2.91**	**15.27**	**34.18**	**59.82**	**11.27**	**61.09**	**5.00**	**66.64**	**2.55**	**47.91**	**10.69**
State Univ of New York-Binghamton	2.36	2.92	-0.32	8	75	0	0	0	64	58	24	56	9	92	0	81	11.9
U of Massachusetts at Amherst	2.35	2.50	-0.25	10	70	0	0	0	29	62	9	82	20	45	11	44	11.0
University of Arizona	2.32	2.26	0.47	35	49	6	5	11	21	48	1	100	0	100	0	0	6.0
University of Wisconsin-Madison	2.25	2.68	-0.53	8	38	0	2	13	38	74	18	50	29	78	0	30	10.0
University of California-Davis	2.23	2.46	-0.05	8	63	0	2	25	17	59	4	57	0	57	0	50	9.7
University of Maryland College Park	2.21	2.26	-0.23	58	34	0	10	14	31	74	9	60	14	70	0	33	9.7
CUNY - Grad Sch & Univ Center	2.18	2.66	-0.28	6	33	0	0	0	72	64	29	66	4	97	0	6	13.6
University of Oregon	2.10	2.65	-0.50	14	36	0	4	29	28	75	11	53	10	67	0	64	13.1
University of Connecticut	1.93	2.33	-0.20	16	69	13	3	19	21	62	8	38	0	63	0	43	15.7
Catholic University of America	1.60	1.95	0.00	8	38	0	0	0	3	67	7	88	0	100	0	25	13.7
University of South Carolina	1.55	1.50	0.00	15	47	0	1	7	14	86	5	80	50	80	0	33	9.6
Mean Values for the 4th Quarter	**2.10**	**2.38**	**-0.17**	**16.91**	**50.18**	**1.73**	**2.45**	**10.73**	**30.73**	**66.24**	**11.36**	**66.36**	**12.36**	**77.18**	**1.00**	**37.18**	**11.27**
Mean Values for All Programs	**3.04**	**2.99**	**0.04**	**20.20**	**57.02**	**1.00**	**4.89**	**19.39**	**39.48**	**61.64**	**14.52**	**57.07**	**7.89**	**78.59**	**1.00**	**45.93**	**10.45**

Sources: 1. National Survey of Graduate Faculty
2. Institutional Coordinator Response Data
3. Doctorate Records File
4. Federal Agencies
5. Associations and Organizations Administrating Prestigious Awards and Honors

Appendix Table J - 4 Selected Characteristics of Research-Doctorate Programs in English Language and Literature

Institution	1993 Ratings[1] 93Q	93E	93C	Faculty Tot Fac[2]	% Full[2]	% Supp[2]	Nmbr. Awd[5]	Awd Fac[5]	Students[2] Tot Stu	% Fem	Rpt PhDs	Doctorate Recipients[3] % Fem	% Min	% US	% RA	% TA	MYD
Yale University	4.77	4.43	-0.11	50	52	6	17	26	90	56	47	51	2	88	0	25	7.6
University of California-Berkeley	4.77	4.53	0.28	62	56	3	18	24	220	60	93	62	3	97	0	54	10.1
Harvard University	4.77	4.14	0.43	34	65	3	21	41	134	52	50	46	11	87	0	72	8.0
University of Virginia	4.58	4.27	0.31	71	45	0	9	11	204	50	92	43	3	98	0	34	9.8
Duke University	4.55	3.98	0.52	35	63	0	15	31	141	52	49	41	0	98	0	55	9.7
Stanford University	4.55	4.30	0.30	41	78	7	12	29	99	46	46	54	13	96	2	17	9.0
Cornell University	4.49	4.43	0.14	48	67	4	9	17	83	61	56	63	6	85	1	67	8.4
University of Pennsylvania	4.47	4.24	0.46	49	61	4	21	33	123	56	63	58	0	92	1	45	9.0
Columbia University	4.47	3.91	0.33	48	58	6	16	27	290	62	108	48	1	90	1	30	10.3
University of Chicago	4.41	4.20	0.19	34	47	0	2	6	193	61	49	62	3	98	2	2	12.1
Johns Hopkins University	4.33	3.99	-0.15	11	100	0	12	64	49	41	21	57	0	91	0	28	8.7
Univ of California-Los Angeles	4.10	3.97	0.56	66	59	5	16	21	139	61	69	53	0	94	0	64	10.6
Princeton University	4.05	3.94	-0.31	22	59	9	13	50	53	57	43	60	0	88	0	10	6.8
Brown University	3.99	3.76	0.32	30	60	0	8	27	79	67	56	63	5	87	0	63	9.7
University of California-Irvine	3.95	3.60	0.33	24	79	4	4	13	90	58	31	69	7	100	3	62	9.8
University of Michigan	3.93	3.87	0.61	50	64	10	15	24	156	65	66	55	7	94	0	50	8.6
Rutgers State Univ-New Brunswick	3.92	3.71	0.50	51	53	2	14	25	233	63	38	58	0	92	0	46	10.5
CUNY - Grad Sch & Univ Center	3.78	3.62	0.56	41	78	7	14	24	280	63	40	55	2	96	0	22	11.4
Indiana University	3.78	3.62	0.32	71	49	0	6	8	273	57	84	61	4	90	0	65	11.2
New York University	3.77	3.63	0.39	31	61	0	11	23	109	60	59	59	3	93	0	14	15.4
University of Texas at Austin	3.54	3.36	-0.12	76	53	4	16	18	103	57	58	49	9	88	2	55	11.4
University of Wisconsin-Madison	3.53	3.69	0.13	46	61	13	6	13	127	69	62	53	5	93	0	71	9.8
University of Washington	3.48	3.48	0.25	57	42	5	2	4	183	57	90	58	3	100	0	62	8.8
U of North Carolina-Chapel Hill	3.43	3.47	0.02	55	60	2	11	16	245	64	71	52	4	98	0	49	10.7
University of Southern California	3.41	3.40	0.20	23	48	4	3	13	143	59	49	61	7	95	0	42	12.7
University of Pittsburgh	3.40	3.33	0.57	32	44	0	1	3	64	70	22	75	0	92	0	48	12.8
State Univ of New York-Buffalo	3.40	3.51	-0.15	40	67	0	6	13	200	55	92	45	3	87	0	56	10.2
U of Illinois at Urbana-Champaign	3.38	3.41	0.16	72	51	4	6	8	147	54	39	54	4	92	0	94	8.8
Northwestern University	3.37	3.37	-0.35	25	36	8	6	24	43	60	24	50	3	92	0	66	9.7
Vanderbilt University	3.33	3.13	0.48	29	55	3	5	17	11	73	35	54	10	100	0	55	8.7

Appendix Table J - 4 English Language and Literature (Continued)

Institution	1993 Ratings[1]			Faculty					Students[2]			Doctorate Recipients[3]					
	93Q	93E	93C	Tot Fac[2]	% Full[2]	% Supp[2]	Nmbr. Awd[5]	Awd Fac[5]	Tot Stu	% Fem	Rpt PhDs	% Fem	% Min	% US	% RA	% TA	MYD
Emory University	3.33	3.15	0.23	26	46	8	2	8	91	67	44	66	13	98	0	30	10.9
University of Wisconsin-Milwaukee	3.31	3.23	0.54	47	49	4	3	6	95	53	34	58	3	95	0	42	12.7
Mean Values for the Top Quarter	**3.95**	**3.77**	**0.25**	**43.66**	**58.31**	**3.91**	**10.00**	**20.84**	**140.31**	**58.94**	**55.63**	**56.03**	**4.19**	**93.25**	**0.38**	**46.72**	**10.12**
Ohio State University	3.28	3.33	0.51	65	31	0	2	3	201	61	79	74	8	99	0	71	9.8
Univ of California-Santa Barbara	3.27	3.37	0.46	33	48	6	4	12	81	59	18	60	3	100	0	55	8.7
Univ of California-Riverside	3.27	3.08	0.36	31	45	3	7	19	105	69	31	49	8	97	0	41	9.7
University of Minnesota	3.24	3.68	0.13	38	63	3	5	11	104	52	58	51	0	90	0	57	11.8
Univ of California-San Diego	3.21	3.26	0.22	22	64	5	3	9	43	77	20	48	14	81	0	50	10.3
Boston University	3.20	3.33	0.17	38	45	13	17	34	76	58	23	56	7	97	0	38	10.4
University of Florida	3.19	3.26	0.44	30	77	0	4	10	104	51	32	54	9	89	3	67	8.7
University of Maryland College Park	3.18	3.33	0.56	73	45	3	12	12	142	74	36	64	12	91	0	32	15.6
U of Massachusetts at Amherst	3.18	3.09	0.05	57	75	0	12	18	161	70	42	67	0	88	0	44	11.8
Pennsylvania State University	3.14	3.16	0.31	44	43	7	6	11	100	64	29	50	0	75	0	81	9.3
Univ of California-Santa Cruz	3.10	2.97	0.19	14	71	7	1	7	4	0	4	38	15	95	0	54	11.7
Brandeis University	3.09	3.05	0.11	12	33	0	4	33	76	58	27	68	3	97	0	39	9.7
University of Iowa	3.07	3.13	-0.04	44	66	2	5	11	132	58	173	45	4	90	2	58	13.2
University of Rochester	3.05	2.97	-0.09	18	50	6	5	22	85	62	32	73	0	94	0	7	9.4
University of Kentucky	3.04	3.03	0.11	29	45	7	4	14	73	56	19	65	6	95	0	47	11.6
University of California-Davis	3.04	2.79	0.20	25	56	0	7	28	80	71	32	52	3	92	0	69	12.3
State U of New York-Stony Brook	3.03	3.01	0.14	32	38	0	3	9	164	55	65	66	9	92	0	53	11.4
Washington University	3.02	3.18	0.15	22	64	0	4	14	97	60	9	54	0	92	0	55	11.5
Carnegie Mellon University	2.97	3.25	0.30	16	44	13	2	13	45	82	21	60	0	100	25	13	14.6
University of Colorado	2.97	2.97	0.30	35	43	0	5	14	75	57	23	68	0	100	0	42	11.3
Rice University	2.95	2.98	0.08	21	76	5	7	24	57	77	20	84	8	100	0	0	12.2
University of Georgia	2.91	2.92	0.31	32	31	3	5	16	81	64	19	52	9	96	0	33	12.1
University of South Carolina	2.90	3.02	0.30	43	58	9	8	16	99	57	46	53	4	95	2	39	11.9
Texas A&M University	2.89	2.83	0.57	55	33	2	7	13	80	63	30	58	6	92	0	38	13.3
Purdue University	2.83	3.05	0.27	49	33	2	3	6	157	89	59	41	3	93	0	64	10.3

Institution	1993 Ratings[1] 93Q	93E	93C	Faculty Tot Fac[2]	% Full[2]	% Supp[2]	Nmbr. Awd[5]	Awd Fac[5]	Students[2] Tot Stu	% Fem	Rpt PhDs	Doctorate Recipients[3] % Fem	% Min	% US	% RA	% TA	MYD
University of Arizona	2.81	2.99	0.08	32	59	6	3	6	63	68	24	66	4	83	0	50	11.9
Michigan State University	2.80	2.72	-0.05	46	59	2	4	9	133	59	58	49	5	82	0	46	9.9
Louisiana State U & A&M College	2.80	2.99	0.52	47	40	4	5	11	111	57	32	61	11	90	4	42	10.4
University of Missouri-Columbia	2.80	2.80	0.26	34	56	0	4	12	84	55	39	45	0	84	0	37	11.8
Temple University	2.79	2.81	0.17	42	62	2	5	12	71	61	31	70	4	93	4	30	14.4
University of Notre Dame	2.78	2.92	0.35	38	45	11	4	8	54	48	28	55	3	97	4	70	9.4
University of Illinois at Chicago	2.75	2.58	0.43	29	59	7	6	17	81	52	31	58	26	100	0	37	12.6
Mean Values for the 2nd Quarter	**3.02**	**3.06**	**0.25**	**35.81**	**51.78**	**4.00**	**5.41**	**14.19**	**94.30**	**60.80**	**37.19**	**57.94**	**5.75**	**92.47**	**1.38**	**45.59**	**11.34**
Boston College	2.72	2.94	0.13	34	38	3	1	3	27	70	13	60	0	95	0	0	10.7
University of Oregon	2.71	2.95	0.26	37	38	0	3	8	90	54	28	51	0	88	0	34	12.6
State Univ of New York-Binghamton	2.67	3.04	-0.09	31	45	3	1	3	50	60	42	58	0	90	0	77	9.4
University of Tennessee-Knoxville	2.66	2.84	0.27	35	60	6	5	11	73	55	49	56	4	97	0	57	10.4
University of Kansas	2.65	3.01	0.23	41	63	2	1	2	104	54	18	45	0	95	0	35	10.8
Tufts University	2.64	3.00	0.17	16	44	0	1	6	48	75	16	74	0	87	6	29	13.3
University of Miami	2.57	2.61	0.43	17	59	6	2	12	16	75	19	67	10	91	0	60	14.6
Saint Louis University	2.56	2.55	-0.25	15	47	0	2	13	22	64	19	71	0	100	0	18	16.0
University of New Hampshire	2.55	2.37	0.39	40	47	13	2	5	24	50	10	67	0	100	0	31	15.4
University of Nebraska-Lincoln	2.53	2.78	0.15	55	44	2	1	2	94	64	49	46	4	88	0	36	12.6
Miami University	2.49	2.82	0.36	34	50	3	3	9	30	60	20	60	13	94	0	46	14.0
Syracuse University	2.47	2.29	-0.12	27	37	0	1	4	16	44	13	63	0	72	0	33	12.5
Wayne State University	2.39	2.47	0.04	39	36	3	2	5	39	72	19	67	7	94	0	50	15.7
Arizona State University	2.38	2.76	0.39	28	71	0	2	7	58	62	29	61	5	95	8	33	17.7
George Washington University	2.38	2.10	0.18	23	39	0	4	13	44	84	18	75	10	83	0	11	16.4
University of Alabama	2.38	2.61	0.27	38	47	0	2	5	89	84	16	67	4	96	5	50	15.0
Claremont Graduate School	2.31	2.35	-0.19	3	67	0	2	33	53	79	5	30	0	100	0	0	11.0
University of Connecticut	2.31	2.92	-0.19	33	76	9	5	15	137	53	20	43	0	90	0	50	10.0
Tulane University	2.26	2.31	0.00	23	30	13	4	17	80	71	17	64	10	88	5	30	13.7
University of Oklahoma	2.25	2.15	-0.03	26	31	4	4	15	27	70	8	82	0	100	0	14	19.1

Appendix Table J - 4 English Language and Literature (Continued)

Institution	1993 Ratings[1] 93Q	93E	93C	Faculty Tot Fac[2]	% Full[2]	% Supp[2]	Nmbr. Awd[5]	Awd Fac[5]	Students[2] Tot Stu	% Fem	Rpt PhDs	Doctorate Recipients[3] % Fem	% Min	% US	% RA	% TA	MYD
Florida State University	2.23	2.25	-0.05	33	42	0	6	15	90	62	56	43	5	87	0	35	11.0
Univ of Southern Mississippi	2.19	2.26	0.70	24	42	4	0	0	35	51	18	75	0	100	0	40	15.5
Washington State University	2.19	2.50	-0.14	26	54	12	0	0	61	66	12	17	0	89	0	73	12.6
University of Houston	2.15	2.50	0.00	35	20	3	2	6	93	58	15	56	14	100	0	78	13.0
Texas Christian University	2.13	2.27	0.19	14	86	7	0	0	39	67	24	85	4	100	0	35	7.6
Loyola University of Chicago	2.11	2.54	0.33	28	21	0	2	7	44	55	18	59	0	95	0	38	14.9
Case Western Reserve Univ	2.11	2.33	-0.21	14	50	0	0	0	58	71	12	84	11	100	0	40	12.1
Auburn University	2.08	2.11	0.44	32	25	6	2	6	30	67	6	60	10	100	0	50	13.4
Kent State University	2.08	2.27	0.06	30	57	10	3	10	75	76	27	57	0	81	0	53	11.6
University of North Texas	2.05	2.05	0.44	43	35	5	1	2	77	47	14	81	0	69	0	27	15.6
University of Tulsa	2.02	2.46	-0.07	13	46	15	1	8	28	79	13	71	8	93	0	54	10.9
University of Mississippi	1.95	2.02	-0.05	25	32	8	0	0	51	65	10	50	0	100	0	50	15.0
Mean Values for the 3rd Quarter	**2.35**	**2.51**	**0.13**	**28.50**	**46.22**	**4.28**	**2.03**	**7.56**	**56.31**	**64.50**	**20.41**	**60.78**	**3.72**	**92.41**	**0.75**	**39.59**	**13.25**
U of North Carolina-Greensboro	1.94	2.19	0.42	28	29	7	1	4	56	54	14	72	0	100	0	15	13.1
Northern Illinois University	1.87	2.11	0.00	40	47	3	3	8	64	47	22	69	8	96	0	45	12.7
University of Texas at Arlington	1.83	2.29	-0.14	18	28	11	1	6	87	60	28	50	0	100	0	0	23.5
Bowling Green State University	1.82	2.38	0.00	29	38	0	1	3	37	76	41	56	13	92	0	46	11.4
University of Texas at Dallas	1.81	1.36	-0.17	15	47	0	4	27	45	58	11	n/a	n/a	n/a	n/a	n/a	n/a
University of Rhode Island	1.80	2.50	0.00	20	60	0	1	5	120	67	36	58	0	95	0	29	13.4
University of Toledo	1.74	1.28	0.33	22	64	0	2	9	31	61	9	69	8	92	0	50	14.4
Illinois State University	1.72	1.76	0.11	36	44	0	0	0	59	54	29	63	9	81	5	42	14.3
Ohio University	1.69	2.11	0.08	15	67	0	1	7	23	39	27	44	0	94	0	70	10.4
Univ of Southwestern Louisiana	1.69	1.78	-0.08	28	39	0	3	11	52	52	23	58	10	88	0	50	10.7
Texas Tech University	1.67	2.12	0.25	30	27	7	4	13	46	74	10	57	14	100	0	18	15.0
University of Denver	1.67	2.32	0.09	21	48	0	1	5	27	52	30	63	3	100	0	49	12.6
University of Cincinnati	1.66	2.17	-0.19	17	65	6	0	0	32	69	12	56	0	100	0	55	13.6
Fordham University	1.64	1.76	-0.31	17	29	12	1	6	109	51	25	55	3	97	0	13	13.4
Southern Illinois University	1.64	2.08	-0.41	13	54	0	2	15	50	60	27	44	6	68	0	63	13.1

Institution	1993 Ratings[1] 93Q	93E	93C	Faculty Tot Fac[2]	% Full[2]	% Supp[2]	Nmbr. Awd[5]	Awd Fac[5]	Students[2] Tot Stu	% Fem	Rpt PhDs	Doctorate Recipients[3] % Fem	% Min	% US	% RA	% TA	MYD
Howard University	1.60	2.29	-0.10	12	33	0	1	8	27	74	8	50	80	83	0	0	22.4
West Virginia University	1.58	1.57	0.14	30	40	0	3	10	29	52	9	50	0	100	0	17	15.0
Lehigh University	1.56	2.29	0.00	16	69	6	2	13	54	61	16	45	0	95	0	72	11.6
Ball State University	1.49	1.85	0.00	21	43	0	1	5	18	67	41	72	8	93	0	30	13.9
Univ of Arkansas-Fayetteville	1.47	1.85	0.13	19	53	0	2	11	23	70	14	82	0	100	0	46	12.7
University of South Florida	1.38	1.28	0.00	24	75	0	1	4	82	74	32	63	10	94	0	16	13.1
University of North Dakota	1.24	1.95	0.00	23	39	4	1	4	49	53	11	38	0	75	0	55	13.9
Baylor University	1.19	1.31	-0.33	13	69	0	0	0	13	38	6	67	0	100	0	43	15.7
Catholic University of America	1.14	1.47	-0.27	10	30	0	0	0	39	62	8	65	12	89	0	27	15.6
St. John's University	1.14	0.93	0.00	11	55	0	0	0	35	57	15	60	13	100	0	0	19.8
Oklahoma State University	1.13	1.58	-0.17	15	33	13	2	13	153	54	25	47	0	70	0	50	11.4
Indiana Univ of Pennsylvania	0.89	1.21	0.14	16	44	6	0	0	84	45	25	46	12	75	4	15	14.6
Drew University	0.84	0.83	0.00	12	75	0	0	0	45	76	15	84	0	88	4	0	11.6
Texas Woman's University	0.80	0.83	0.00	11	45	0	0	0	28	89	13	100	31	94	0	27	11.0
Idaho State University	0.72	0.83	-0.20	23	43	0	2	9	12	75	9	58	0	90	0	17	16.4
Middle Tennessee State University	0.61	1.00	0.25	22	45	5	1	5	12	83	11	69	8	100	0	18	16.3
Mean Values for the 4th Quarter	**1.45**	**1.72**	**-0.01**	**20.23**	**47.65**	**2.58**	**1.32**	**6.48**	**49.71**	**61.42**	**19.42**	**60.33**	**8.27**	**91.63**	**0.43**	**32.60**	**14.22**
Mean Values for All Programs	**2.70**	**2.77**	**0.15**	**32.14**	**51.02**	**3.70**	**4.72**	**12.31**	**85.45**	**61.40**	**33.27**	**58.75**	**5.44**	**92.45**	**0.74**	**41.26**	**12.20**

Sources: 1. National Survey of Graduate Faculty
2. Institutional Coordinator Response Data
3. Doctorate Records File
4. Federal Agencies
5. Associations and Organizations Administrating Prestigious Awards and Honors

Appendix Table J - 5 Selected Characteristics of Research-Doctorate Programs in French Language and Literature

Institution	1993 Ratings[1] 93Q	93E	93C	Faculty Tot Fac[2]	% Full[2]	% Supp[2]	Nmbr. Awd[5]	Awd Fac[5]	Students[2] Tot Stu	% Fem	Rpt PhDs	Doctorate Recipients[3] % Fem	% Min	% US	% RA	% TA	MYD
Yale University	4.68	4.49	0.03	18	50	0	6	22	20	n/a	37	67	0	100	0	11	8.6
Princeton University	4.55	4.35	0.00	13	62	0	3	15	26	58	24	64	0	83	0	32	7.8
Duke University	4.43	3.78	0.72	16	56	0	5	19	31	74	9	100	0	100	0	40	10.7
Columbia University	4.40	3.90	0.07	13	54	0	4	31	90	67	16	75	5	88	0	75	10.8
University of Pennsylvania	4.37	3.98	0.33	11	91	0	5	36	36	81	11	73	14	93	0	67	10.5
Stanford University	4.20	3.52	0.10	12	75	0	2	17	35	60	17	52	5	87	0	13	6.7
University of California-Berkeley	4.19	3.90	0.02	13	62	0	3	23	27	52	18	65	7	70	0	64	12.4
Cornell University	4.08	4.03	0.14	17	71	6	3	12	20	75	22	69	7	88	0	81	9.9
University of Michigan	3.97	3.73	0.14	14	57	0	2	7	29	83	10	76	0	73	0	75	9.4
University of California-Irvine	3.78	2.71	0.21	9	78	0	1	11	16	63	3	50	0	100	0	50	9.8
University of Wisconsin-Madison	3.74	3.79	0.35	22	73	5	4	14	94	70	25	79	7	94	0	78	9.9
New York University	3.66	3.53	0.02	12	58	17	3	17	17	47	20	64	0	95	0	50	10.0
Mean Values for the Top Quarter	**4.17**	**3.81**	**0.18**	**14.17**	**65.58**	**2.33**	**3.42**	**18.67**	**36.75**	**66.36**	**17.67**	**69.50**	**3.75**	**89.25**	**0.00**	**53.00**	**9.71**
University of Virginia	3.60	3.61	0.29	17	41	6	3	18	46	85	21	54	0	92	0	79	9.1
CUNY - Grad Sch & Univ Center	3.48	3.28	0.24	13	77	0	2	15	43	72	14	75	6	84	0	0	11.8
Emory University	3.38	2.71	0.25	10	40	0	0	0	25	56	7	91	40	91	0	50	14.0
University of Chicago	3.30	3.11	-0.07	6	67	0	2	33	59*	73*	8*	89	0	100	0	11	11.7
Harvard University	3.19	2.92	-0.57	7	43	0	2	29	34	79	16	67	9	73	0	64	9.8
Johns Hopkins University	3.13	2.72	-0.72	5	60	0	2	40	7	57	7	89	0	71	0	50	10.0
Univ of California-Los Angeles	3.13	2.87	-0.08	12	42	0	1	8	38	89	13	100	0	94	0	36	13.6
Louisiana State U & A&M College	3.08	2.73	0.42	15	47	0	1	7	21	71	11	64	10	91	11	56	11.4
Brown University	3.07	3.11	-0.35	12	58	0	1	8	24	96	17	68	18	89	0	64	8.3
Rutgers State Univ-New Brunswick	3.03	2.62	0.23	18	56	0	0	0	46	80	11	40	10	100	0	0	15.5
University of Texas at Austin	2.97	2.96	0.04	25	40	0	1	4	18	78	11	83	13	67	0	56	12.8
Mean Values for the 2nd Quarter	**3.21**	**2.97**	**-0.03**	**12.73**	**51.91**	**0.55**	**1.36**	**14.73**	**32.82**	**76.00**	**12.36**	**74.55**	**9.64**	**86.55**	**1.00**	**42.36**	**11.64**
Washington University	2.93	2.55	0.21	10	30	0	0	0	32	66	1	50	0	100	0	100	9.4
Indiana University	2.89	3.07	-0.09	23	43	0	1	4	75	87	10	67	10	100	0	67	12.3

Institution	1993 Ratings[1] 93Q	93E	93C	Faculty Tot Fac[2]	% Full[2]	% Supp[2]	Nmbr. Awd[5]	Awd Fac[5]	Students[2] Tot Stu	% Fem	Rpt PhDs	Doctorate Recipients[3] % Fem	% Min	% US	% RA	% TA	MYD
University of Minnesota	2.88	2.91	0.08	12	42	0	1	8	34	65	12	81	11	83	0	57	12.7
University of Iowa	2.88	2.69	0.16	12	58	0	0	0	17	59	6	50	0	92	0	50	16.0
University of California-Davis	2.82	2.83	0.28	8	50	0	2	25	2	50	9	67	0	78	0	0	8.6
Northwestern University	2.71	2.75	0.03	12	58	0	5	42	11	73	10	77	11	85	0	89	11.7
Ohio State University	2.70	2.77	-0.07	20	40	0	0	0	60	63	5	78	17	75	0	100	11.6
U of Illinois at Urbana-Champaign	2.70	2.94	-0.15	17	47	0	0	0	60	62	17	63	0	76	0	92	8.6
Rice University	2.68	2.59	0.24	9	44	0	3	33	11	91	6	86	0	71	0	50	13.0
Pennsylvania State University	2.66	2.70	0.26	18	28	6	2	11	42	60	5	78	0	67	0	100	10.6
U of North Carolina-Chapel Hill	2.63	2.69	-0.36	10	60	0	0	0	44	50	12	63	6	95	0	62	10.8
Mean Values for the 3rd Quarter	**2.77**	**2.77**	**0.05**	**13.73**	**45.45**	**0.55**	**1.27**	**11.18**	**35.27**	**66.00**	**8.45**	**69.09**	**5.00**	**83.82**	**0.00**	**69.73**	**11.39**
University of Washington	2.60	2.08	0.15	8	38	0	1	13	20	80	4	100	0	100	0	0	13.7
Tulane University	2.41	2.12	0.00	12	17	0	5	42	38	76	7	75	0	100	0	86	14.7
University of Florida	2.41	2.13	0.11	8	88	0	0	0	9	78	6	67	0	100	0	83	11.0
U of Massachusetts at Amherst	2.39	1.88	-0.13	15	60	0	0	0	14	86	3	100	33	100	0	100	11.7
Michigan State University	2.33	2.69	-0.03	12	67	0	0	0	31	90	7	80	17	67	0	83	10.0
University of Pittsburgh	2.21	2.01	-0.17	10	40	0	2	10	12	67	2	100	0	100	33	0	25.0
University of Maryland College Park	2.18	1.87	0.11	18	28	0	1	6	14	86	5	92	11	75	0	64	10.4
University of Kansas	2.12	2.10	-0.14	9	44	0	0	0	12	67	6	57	0	100	0	50	14.7
University of Oregon	1.92	2.13	-0.38	10	30	0	0	0	4	75	5	78	0	78	0	75	11.7
University of Cincinnati	1.66	1.83	-0.20	10	50	0	0	0	19	58	13	80	50	80	0	33	12.7
Catholic University of America	1.13	1.09	-0.24	5	0	0	0	0	15**	73**	n/a	83	17	100	0	0	21.0
Mean Values for the 4th Quarter	**2.12**	**1.99**	**-0.08**	**10.64**	**42.00**	**0.00**	**0.82**	**6.45**	**17.09**	**76.00**	**5.80**	**82.91**	**11.64**	**90.91**	**3.00**	**52.18**	**14.24**
Mean Values for All Programs	**3.09**	**2.91**	**0.03**	**12.84**	**51.56**	**0.89**	**1.76**	**12.89**	**30.62**	**71.09**	**11.34**	**73.91**	**7.42**	**87.67**	**0.98**	**54.29**	**11.70**

Sources: 1. National Survey of Graduate Faculty
2. Institutional Coordinator Response Data
3. Doctorate Records File
4. Federal Agencies
5. Associations and Organizations Administrating Prestigious Awards and Honors

* Enrollment and degree data is for the Romance Language Department which includes French, Spanish, and Portuguese Language and Literature programs

** Enrollment data is for the Modern Language Department which includes French, Spanish, and Portuguese Language and Literature programs

Appendix Table J - 6 Selected Characteristics of Research-Doctorate Programs in German Language and Literature

Institution	1993 Ratings[1] 93Q	93E	93C	Faculty Tot Fac[2]	% Full[2]	% Supp[2]	Nmbr. Awd[5]	Awd Fac[5]	Students[2] Tot Stu	% Fem	Rpt PhDs	Doctorate Recipients[3] % Fem	% Min	% US	% RA	% TA	MYD
University of California-Berkeley	4.32	3.88	-0.05	16	81	0	3	13	33	55	28	39	0	87	0	68	10.8
Princeton University	4.22	3.91	-0.04	11	45	0	2	9	22	45	15	35	0	94	8	38	7.9
Cornell University	4.19	3.73	0.30	20	75	0	8	30	27	48	6	56	0	67	0	75	8.8
Harvard University	4.01	3.78	-0.03	10	60	0	1	10	22	50	12	50	0	71	0	80	8.7
Yale University	3.95	3.68	-0.41	9	56	0	1	11	17	53	6	67	0	100	0	11	8.6
Stanford University	3.83	3.61	-0.44	7	100	0	3	29	30	40	14	50	0	79	6	76	8.8
Washington University	3.81	3.55	0.02	10	40	0	2	20	49	59	15	80	0	65	0	67	8.6
University of Virginia	3.77	3.54	-0.03	11	45	0	2	18	23	65	4	60	0	90	0	89	8.7
Mean Values for the Top Quarter	**4.01**	**3.71**	**-0.09**	**11.75**	**62.75**	**0.00**	**2.75**	**17.50**	**27.88**	**51.88**	**12.50**	**54.63**	**0.00**	**81.63**	**1.75**	**63.00**	**8.86**
Johns Hopkins University	3.75	3.33	0.11	5	60	0	1	20	17	29	8	50	0	67	0	83	10.1
University of Wisconsin-Madison	3.74	3.65	-0.52	13	54	0	2	15	66	50	24	38	0	92	0	83	8.7
University of Minnesota	3.68	3.48	0.38	12	58	0	1	8	27	85	10	47	0	100	0	50	13.7
University of Washington	3.60	3.17	0.04	13	54	0	5	31	37	38	15	47	0	88	0	57	9.7
University of Texas at Austin	3.40	3.26	-0.07	25	56	0	0	0	22	45	23	76	0	92	0	47	12.6
Indiana University	3.28	3.02	-0.23	15	60	0	1	7	48	65	7	64	0	100	14	86	10.5
University of California-Irvine	3.28	3.10	-0.02	8	63	0	2	25	12	67	6	50	0	67	0	80	10.4
University of Pennsylvania	3.26	2.99	-0.02	8	75	13	1	13	27	56	11	67	0	87	18	36	11.8
Mean Values for the 2nd Quarter	**3.50**	**3.25**	**-0.04**	**12.38**	**60.00**	**1.63**	**1.63**	**14.88**	**32.00**	**54.38**	**13.00**	**54.88**	**0.00**	**86.63**	**4.00**	**65.25**	**10.94**
Ohio State University	3.25	2.97	-0.23	15	40	0	2	13	34	74	14	63	0	89	0	67	11.1
U of North Carolina-Chapel Hill	3.21	2.91	0.19	11	55	0	0	0	20	60	5	56	0	88	0	100	8.7
U of Massachusetts at Amherst	3.18	2.88	-0.09	10	70	0	0	0	24	83	7	88	0	25	0	83	10.0
U of Illinois at Urbana-Champaign	3.11	3.05	-0.11	13	62	0	4	23	40	55	14	33	0	100	8	75	9.3
University of Michigan	3.04	2.98	-0.15	13	46	0	1	8	26	69	6	43	0	86	0	25	12.8
Univ of California-Los Angeles	2.94	2.88	-0.20	18	89	0	0	0	35	66	17	74	0	86	5	53	9.8
University of California-Davis	2.90	2.65	0.17	7	100	0	1	14	15	60	7	33	0	78	17	67	11.4

Institution	1993 Ratings[1] 93Q	93E	93C	Faculty Tot Fac[2]	% Full[2]	% Supp[2]	Nmbr. Awd[5]	Awd Fac[5]	Students[2] Tot Stu	% Fem	Rpt PhDs	Doctorate Recipients[3] % Fem	% Min	% US	% RA	% TA	MYD
Univ of California-Santa Barbara	2.77	2.60	-0.01	10	60	0	0	0	12	50	9	45	0	60	0	71	12.0
Mean Values for the 3rd Quarter	**3.05**	**2.87**	**-0.05**	**12.13**	**65.25**	**0.00**	**1.00**	**7.25**	**25.75**	**64.63**	**9.88**	**54.38**	**0.00**	**76.50**	**3.75**	**67.63**	**10.64**
State Univ of New York-Albany	2.59	1.96	-0.14	7	86	0	0	0	9	56	7	50	0	60	0	29	13.0
New York University	2.37	1.89	-0.14	11	55	0	0	0	15	40	11	81	0	67	0	0	7.0
Pennsylvania State University	2.31	2.03	0.06	13	23	0	0	0	22	68	4	75	0	100	0	100	15.7
Georgetown University	2.15	2.14	0.38	8	25	0	1	13	17	82	10	88	0	88	0	0	10.7
University of Cincinnati	1.99	2.09	-0.20	6	50	0	0	0	5	20	8	100	0	86	0	33	11.7
University of Pittsburgh	1.89	1.57	-0.11	7	14	0	0	0	12	67	2	50	0	100	0	50	17.5
State Univ of New York-Buffalo	1.80	1.63	-0.38	7	57	0	0	0	6	50	2	100	0	75	0	100	13.7
Rutgers State Univ-New Brunswick	1.69	1.76	-0.22	8	50	0	0	0	30	87	16	76	0	94	0	38	16.0
Mean Values for the 4th Quarter	**2.10**	**1.88**	**-0.09**	**8.38**	**45.00**	**0.00**	**0.13**	**1.63**	**14.50**	**58.75**	**7.50**	**77.50**	**0.00**	**83.75**	**0.00**	**43.75**	**13.16**
Mean Values for All Programs	**3.17**	**2.93**	**-0.07**	**11.16**	**58.25**	**0.41**	**1.38**	**10.31**	**25.03**	**57.41**	**10.72**	**60.34**	**0.00**	**82.13**	**2.38**	**59.91**	**10.90**

Sources: 1. National Survey of Graduate Faculty
2. Institutional Coordinator Response Data
3. Doctorate Records File
4. Federal Agencies
5. Associations and Organizations Administrating Prestigious Awards and Honors

Appendix Table J - 7 Selected Characteristics of Research-Doctorate Programs in Linguistics

Institution	1993 Ratings[1] 93Q	93E	93C	Faculty Tot Fac[2]	% Full[2]	% Supp[2]	Nmbr. Awd[5]	Awd Fac[5]	Students[2] Tot Stu	% Fem	Rpt PhDs	Doctorate Recipients[3] % Fem	% Min	% US	% RA	% TA	MYD
Massachusetts Inst of Technology	4.79	4.39	-0.21	13	77	31	3	23	29	28	37	44	0	39	67	33	6.7
Stanford University	4.59	4.01	0.20	13	85	38	3	23	44	55	32	56	5	62	24	4	9.4
Univ of California-Los Angeles	4.56	4.17	0.24	42	69	33	1	2	85	36	80	52	8	76	4	44	10.7
U of Massachusetts at Amherst	4.44	4.44	0.24	12	67	58	2	17	45	56	25	43	0	54	0	61	8.8
University of Pennsylvania	4.16	3.68	0.47	28	75	36	7	14	61	56	30	56	9	68	8	11	9.4
University of Chicago	3.97	3.64	0.00	25	72	20	9	24	48	60	19	48	0	89	5	0	10.7
University of California-Berkeley	3.97	3.40	0.16	15	60	27	3	20	53	49	27	58	6	76	10	30	12.0
Ohio State University	3.80	3.46	0.32	15	47	27	4	27	20	n/a	12	44	10	67	10	80	9.4
Cornell University	3.78	3.89	0.59	26	58	23	1	4	51	55	27	61	8	56	3	63	9.8
Univ of California-Santa Cruz	3.66	3.80	0.58	5	40	60	1	20	26	50	3	0	0	100	0	100	9.0
University of Texas at Austin	3.61	3.48	-0.08	50	62	18	6	12	46	61	36	56	8	63	4	39	9.4
Mean Values for the Top Quarter	**4.12**	**3.85**	**0.23**	**22.18**	**64.73**	**33.73**	**3.64**	**16.91**	**46.18**	**50.60**	**29.82**	**47.09**	**4.91**	**68.18**	**12.27**	**42.27**	**9.57**
University of Southern California	3.58	3.39	0.28	18	56	11	1	6	56	50	27	49	5	51	0	79	8.0
University of Arizona	3.58	3.51	0.70	17	41	29	0	0	34	62	25	46	21	56	7	60	8.0
Univ of California-San Diego	3.43	3.08	-0.08	16	63	25	2	13	40	58	18	58	6	79	5	52	9.2
CUNY - Grad Sch & Univ Center	3.41	2.99	0.37	15	93	33	3	20	71	73	18	58	10	83	0	5	15.0
University of Connecticut	3.36	3.51	-0.04	7	71	0	0	0	41	51	23	43	0	40	21	26	8.4
University of Washington	3.16	2.92	-0.05	8	50	25	2	25	26	31	28	34	5	50	0	41	9.4
U of Illinois at Urbana-Champaign	3.10	3.22	-0.33	13	85	0	2	15	93	54	49	41	7	44	18	34	9.3
Georgetown University	3.00	2.55	0.16	17	35	6	2	6	132	66	83	64	16	62	1	3	11.3
Brown University	2.94	2.69	0.12	7	57	57	0	0	12	42	11	63	7	79	50	21	7.5
Harvard University	2.92	2.99	-0.35	6	33	0	3	17	19	84	13	46	0	88	0	27	8.6
Mean Values for the 2nd Quarter	**3.25**	**3.09**	**0.08**	**12.40**	**58.40**	**18.60**	**1.50**	**10.20**	**52.40**	**57.10**	**29.50**	**50.20**	**7.70**	**63.20**	**10.20**	**34.80**	**9.47**
State Univ of New York-Buffalo	2.87	2.56	0.55	9	33	33	1	11	33	45	18	42	0	48	10	25	11.0
University of Pittsburgh	2.83	2.26	0.24	10	50	20	0	0	7	71	3	44	0	33	0	38	11.8
State U of New York-Stony Brook	2.82	2.78	0.52	8	13	25	0	0	3	100	0	56	50	44	0	33	9.7

Institution	1993 Ratings[1] 93Q	93E	93C	Faculty Tot Fac[2]	% Full[2]	% Supp[2]	Nmbr. Awd[5]	Awd Fac[5]	Students[2] Tot Stu	% Fem	Rpt PhDs	Doctorate Recipients[3] % Fem	% Min	% US	% RA	% TA	MYD
University of Hawaii at Manoa	2.79	2.81	0.06	23	57	9	1	4	63	51	26	44	0	47	13	4	10.6
University of Oregon	2.68	2.55	0.30	17	35	24	2	6	14	57	8	44	14	78	0	20	8.1
Indiana University	2.66	2.50	0.04	14	29	14	2	14	69	48	51	31	9	49	0	26	9.4
Boston University	2.60	2.60	-0.08	9	33	22	0	0	47	81	9	70	0	80	0	25	9.2
University of Delaware	2.60	2.55	0.72	12	42	17	1	8	31	58	27	56	6	72	5	58	10.8
Yale University	2.57	2.59	-0.62	7	57	0	0	0	19	47	7	67	20	83	60	0	9.8
University of Michigan	2.37	2.10	-0.05	16	25	13	1	6	34	79	20	65	5	56	0	45	10.8
Mean Values for the 3rd Quarter	**2.68**	**2.53**	**0.17**	**12.50**	**37.40**	**17.70**	**0.80**	**4.90**	**32.00**	**63.70**	**16.90**	**51.90**	**10.40**	**59.00**	**8.80**	**27.40**	**10.12**
University of Wisconsin-Madison	2.20	2.26	0.00	10	70	20	0	0	44	59	15	68	11	45	6	33	8.6
University of Colorado	2.15	2.36	0.38	7	29	57	1	14	36	47	4	50	20	100	25	0	16.7
University of South Carolina	1.91	1.21	0.39	28	39	7	4	14	31	52	8	40	0	40	13	38	13.5
University of Kansas	1.91	2.02	0.19	11	55	9	2	18	15	60	11	50	14	44	0	36	9.4
New York University	1.84	1.73	-0.12	7	43	29	1	14	14	50	4	82	27	100	0	20	17.0
University of Florida	1.78	1.91	0.18	18	50	0	5	22	22	50	11	71	17	71	0	46	10.4
Michigan State University	1.76	1.57	-0.13	23	52	0	0	0	15	47	10	41	30	77	0	25	15.1
Rice University	1.72	1.47	0.12	6	67	0	0	0	15	60	9	60	0	70	0	0	7.9
University of Texas at Arlington	1.26	1.25	0.10	5	40	0	0	0	n/a	n/a	n/a	29	0	57	0	0	17.7
Indiana Univ of Pennsylvania	0.55	0.00	n/s	13	69	8	1	8	50	38	53	50	0	82	0	0	18.6
Mean Values for the 4th Quarter	**1.71**	**1.58**	**0.12**	**12.80**	**51.40**	**13.00**	**1.40**	**9.00**	**26.89**	**51.44**	**13.89**	**54.10**	**11.90**	**68.60**	**4.40**	**19.80**	**13.49**
Mean Values for All Programs	**2.97**	**2.79**	**0.15**	**15.15**	**53.27**	**21.07**	**1.88**	**10.41**	**39.85**	**55.82**	**22.93**	**50.73**	**8.63**	**64.83**	**9.00**	**31.34**	**10.64**

Sources: 1. National Survey of Graduate Faculty
2. Institutional Coordinator Response Data
3. Doctorate Records File
4. Federal Agencies
5. Associations and Organizations Administrating Prestigious Awards and Honors

n/s After trimming no cases remained

Appendix Table J - 8 Selected Characteristics of Research-Doctorate Programs in Music

Institution	1993 Ratings[1] 93Q	93E	93C	Faculty Tot Fac[2]	% Full[2]	% Supp[2]	Nmbr. Awd[5]	Awd Fac[5]	Students[2] Tot Stu	% Fem	Rpt PhDs	Doctorate Recipients[3] % Fem	% Min	% US	% RA	% TA	MYD
Harvard University	4.59	4.26	0.14	11	73	0	7	64	44	34	29	20	0	94	0	61	10.3
University of Chicago	4.53	4.32	-0.17	12	50	0	9	58	56	32	28	43	10	94	0	7	10.3
University of California-Berkeley	4.51	4.11	0.02	18	72	0	5	28	35	34	19	25	0	91	0	53	10.4
CUNY - Grad Sch & Univ Center	4.41	3.79	0.18	38	79	0	6	16	145	37	26	26	4	76	0	8	12.0
Yale University	4.40	4.11	-0.08	12	42	0	0	0	55	49	31	34	2	86	0	9	10.3
Princeton University	4.39	4.18	-0.25	11	64	0	5	45	32	41	23	32	0	80	0	18	10.4
University of Pennsylvania	4.35	3.79	0.26	15	73	0	7	40	34	44	22	43	0	81	0	41	9.7
University of Rochester	4.24	4.03	0.28	50	70	0	7	12	119	55	137	33	3	90	0	12	8.9
University of Michigan	4.16	4.03	-0.10	22	59	0	3	14	21	71	25	35	6	87	2	16	8.8
U of Illinois at Urbana-Champaign	4.11	3.60	-0.04	74	61	1	4	4	288	49	99	35	2	92	3	32	11.3
Columbia University	4.05	3.56	0.22	18	33	0	4	22	107	33	14	27	4	96	0	34	12.2
Cornell University	4.05	3.90	0.17	17	47	0	4	24	17	47	27	28	3	89	0	71	9.9
Brandeis University	3.85	3.73	0.36	8	50	0	2	25	13	54	18	30	0	89	0	9	10.4
State U of New York-Stony Brook	3.80	3.45	0.18	32	25	0	1	3	153	51	71	50	0	82	0	57	8.5
Stanford University	3.79	3.52	-0.03	14	36	7	5	29	26	12	11	35	8	81	3	26	9.3
U of North Carolina-Chapel Hill	3.72	3.52	0.14	9	33	11	1	11	35	57	13	39	0	100	0	19	9.9
University of Texas at Austin	3.69	3.37	0.14	21	48	0	0	0	103	37	25	43	6	95	0	15	11.7
Mean Values for the Top Quarter	**4.16**	**3.84**	**0.08**	**22.47**	**53.82**	**1.12**	**4.12**	**23.24**	**75.47**	**43.35**	**36.35**	**34.00**	**2.82**	**88.41**	**0.47**	**28.71**	**10.25**
Univ of California-Los Angeles	3.56	3.12	-0.23	26	69	0	2	8	93	41	47	27	12	90	0	23	11.4
New York University	3.53	3.41	0.04	10	70	0	1	10	2	50	13	46	14	88	5	8	13.6
Indiana University	3.47	3.04	0.18	6	50	0	0	0	6	n/a	8	35	2	91	0	31	12.9
University of North Texas	3.43	3.20	0.21	83	49	0	2	2	118	37	107	30	2	90	0	11	12.2
Duke University	3.42	3.33	0.42	12	33	0	1	8	40	58	8	25	14	88	0	0	8.0
Northwestern University	3.41	3.30	0.07	35	46	0	0	0	25	52	24	35	5	93	1	21	11.9
Univ of California-Santa Barbara	3.41	2.89	0.38	10	40	0	1	10	28	39	15	33	0	94	0	33	9.0
Univ of California-San Diego	3.32	2.61	0.36	24	54	0	1	4	35	23	34	28	13	83	9	53	9.0
University of Iowa	3.31	3.13	0.07	43	53	0	1	2	121	47	107	37	3	93	2	19	12.1
Florida State University	3.26	3.29	0.26	47	72	4	1	2	136	44	94	47	5	93	0	28	10.9

Institution	1993 Ratings[1] 93Q	93E	93C	Faculty Tot Fac[2]	% Full[2]	% Supp[2]	Nmbr. Awd[5]	Awd Fac[5]	Students[2] Tot Stu	% Fem	Rpt PhDs	Doctorate Recipients[3] % Fem	% Min	% US	% RA	% TA	MYD
Ohio State University	3.23	2.74	0.04	50	38	2	3	6	202	58	79	43	10	90	4	41	10.6
University of Washington	3.22	2.89	-0.09	28	50	0	1	4	31	55	10	38	15	95	2	6	12.3
Rutgers State Univ-New Brunswick	3.16	3.03	-0.43	13	54	0	1	8	45	42	9	33	0	94	0	20	13.6
University of Minnesota	3.16	2.74	0.30	15	60	0	0	0	19	63	44	38	4	98	0	12	11.6
University of Wisconsin-Madison	3.13	3.07	0.17	15	33	7	1	7	28	36	12	27	2	100	0	33	10.8
Washington University	3.08	3.14	0.35	9	33	0	1	11	27	52	9	44	38	100	0	21	10.9
Mean Values for the 2nd Quarter	**3.32**	**3.06**	**0.13**	**26.63**	**50.25**	**0.81**	**1.06**	**5.13**	**59.75**	**46.47**	**38.75**	**35.38**	**8.69**	**92.50**	**1.44**	**22.50**	**11.30**
University of Cincinnati	3.02	2.81	0.12	22	77	0	1	5	210	42	89	32	1	92	0	49	11.2
University of Maryland College Park	2.95	2.79	-0.08	45	44	0	1	2	103	57	29	43	2	93	0	12	11.9
University of Southern California	2.91	2.66	0.16	7	14	0	2	29	9	56	0	39	4	93	0	38	10.6
State Univ of New York-Buffalo	2.91	2.67	0.13	20	40	0	2	10	61	36	17	16	0	54	0	29	9.9
Temple University	2.90	2.58	0.04	38	63	0	1	3	47	36	22	47	0	92	0	20	10.4
University of Arizona	2.87	2.53	0.22	47	51	2	2	4	87	39	58	39	5	97	0	14	8.6
University of Pittsburgh	2.83	2.64	0.22	11	36	0	3	27	38	42	17	26	18	74	0	39	11.4
Louisiana State U & A&M College	2.81	2.74	0.48	41	44	0	0	0	21	29	14	25	5	92	3	21	11.1
University of Miami	2.79	2.53	0.16	41	59	0	0	0	60	33	17	37	9	88	0	44	10.9
Catholic University of America	2.78	2.54	0.00	6	67	0	0	0	29	41	11	26	2	85	3	0	14.6
Brown University	2.73	2.54	0.06	5	40	0	0	0	10	60	6	100	0	67	0	100	11.4
Michigan State University	2.69	2.64	-0.27	12	58	0	0	0	16	63	9	31	5	86	0	13	10.9
University of Kansas	2.65	2.50	0.06	11	64	0	0	0	34	44	29	35	0	98	0	14	10.6
University of Oregon	2.55	2.26	0.27	36	36	0	0	0	49	43	24	39	0	100	0	6	15.6
Case Western Reserve Univ	2.52	2.33	-0.05	7	14	0	0	0	14	64	20	38	6	86	0	6	10.7
Wesleyan University	2.50	2.14	-0.50	10	50	0	0	0	24	38	12	9	0	82	0	11	12.7
Mean Values for the 3rd Quarter	**2.78**	**2.56**	**0.06**	**22.44**	**47.31**	**0.13**	**0.75**	**5.00**	**50.75**	**45.19**	**23.38**	**36.38**	**3.56**	**86.19**	**0.38**	**26.00**	**11.41**
Boston University	2.48	2.50	0.00	14	14	0	0	0	7	86	3	37	4	90	0	13	11.6
University of Georgia	2.45	2.16	0.00	11	55	9	0	0	38	47	22	67	14	93	0	73	9.8

Appendix Table J - 8 Music (Continued)

Institution	1993 Ratings[1] 93Q	93E	93C	Faculty Tot Fac[2]	% Full[2]	% Supp[2]	Nmbr. Awd[5]	Awd Fac[5]	Students[2] Tot Stu	% Fem	Rpt PhDs	Doctorate Recipients[3] % Fem	% Min	% US	% RA	% TA	MYD
University of Hartford	2.44	2.21	0.12	28	25	0	0	0	14	57	14	25	10	100	0	25	14.9
University of Colorado	2.36	2.35	0.09	12	33	0	2	8	14	57	10	45	5	94	0	16	12.5
University of Kentucky	2.33	2.18	0.04	14	21	0	0	0	22	68	12	33	5	100	0	29	11.8
West Virginia University	2.27	1.45	-0.11	10	50	0	2	20	5	80	1	50	0	100	0	25	15.7
Claremont Graduate School	2.23	1.82	-0.22	3	67	0	0	0	52	42	11	57	0	100	0	0	14.3
Texas Tech University	2.22	1.67	0.00	33	45	0	0	0	43	47	22	41	6	94	0	23	12.1
Kent State University	2.20	2.10	-0.38	11	45	0	0	0	36	42	21	8	0	92	0	20	10.5
University of South Carolina	2.13	2.11	0.00	20	80	0	0	0	9	133	6	55	7	97	0	27	12.2
Ball State University	2.06	1.67	0.00	36	39	0	0	0	34	41	22	39	3	94	0	7	12.8
University of Alabama	2.02	1.91	0.19	15	67	0	0	0	28	50	19	44	11	100	0	33	11.4
Southern Baptist Theological Sem	1.95	1.85	-0.20	15	53	0	0	0	20	35	25	24	0	97	0	11	13.6
University of Northern Colorado	1.86	1.93	-0.22	21	67	0	0	0	35	23	25	18	0	97	0	14	15.7
University of Oklahoma	1.84	2.00	0.00	6	67	0	0	0	3	533	55	43	3	100	2	22	13.5
Univ of Missouri-Kansas City	1.40	1.37	-0.20	4	0	0	0	0	1	100	0	32	0	96	0	12	13.2
Mean Values for the 4th Quarter	**2.14**	**1.96**	**-0.06**	**15.81**	**45.50**	**0.56**	**0.25**	**1.75**	**22.56**	**90.06**	**16.75**	**38.63**	**4.25**	**96.50**	**0.13**	**21.88**	**12.85**
Mean Values for All Programs	**3.11**	**2.87**	**0.06**	**21.85**	**49.29**	**0.66**	**1.58**	**9.00**	**52.49**	**56.22**	**28.92**	**36.06**	**4.80**	**90.86**	**0.60**	**24.83**	**11.43**

Sources: 1. National Survey of Graduate Faculty
2. Institutional Coordinator Response Data
3. Doctorate Records File
4. Federal Agencies
5. Associations and Organizations Administrating Prestigious Awards and Honors

Appendix Table J - 9 Selected Characteristics of Research-Doctorate Programs in Philosophy

Institution	1993 Ratings[1] 93Q	93E	93C	Faculty Tot Fac[2]	% Full[2]	% Supp[2]	Nmbr. Awd[5]	Awd Fac[5]	Students[2] Tot Stu	% Fem	Rpt PhDs	Doctorate Recipients[3] % Fem	% Min	% US	% RA	% TA	MYD
Princeton University	4.93	4.56	0.03	16	81	13	7	31	34	41	26	25	4	80	4	4	8.0
University of Pittsburgh	4.73	4.43	0.09	30	63	10	9	23	60	25	28	26*	0*	70*	0*	69*	7.6*
Harvard University	4.69	3.77	-0.06	14	64	7	11	57	44	34	10	38	6	85	0	56	8.6
University of California-Berkeley	4.66	3.66	-0.19	16	63	6	7	31	34	18	19	13	0	84	0	73	10.0
University of Pittsburgh [a]	4.47	4.26	-0.07	17	76	18	6	29	38	39	6	26*	0*	70*	0*	69*	7.6*
Univ of California-Los Angeles	4.42	4.01	-0.31	25	64	12	5	16	46	20	18	20	11	88	0	64	10.7
Stanford University	4.20	4.02	0.05	18	50	17	3	17	52	33	22	33	4	73	10	20	7.4
University of Michigan	4.15	3.88	0.13	19	63	5	7	32	48	21	25	19	5	100	0	74	8.8
Cornell University	4.11	4.14	-0.11	15	73	0	9	47	31	32	22	29	0	61	7	41	8.6
Massachusetts Inst of Technology	4.01	3.91	0.00	11	82	36	5	36	29	21	17	37	0	50	0	50	7.1
University of Arizona	3.99	3.74	0.48	19	74	5	3	11	36	25	15	14	6	85	0	53	8.8
University of Chicago	3.88	3.41	-0.05	20	70	30	9	30	59	27	16	21	0	94	0	0	10.3
Rutgers State Univ-New Brunswick	3.82	3.44	0.91	28	75	0	3	11	59	25	10	40	0	90	0	86	10.0
Brown University	3.82	3.62	0.19	13	62	0	6	38	26	31	18	18	16	81	0	38	8.0
Univ of California-San Diego	3.79	3.47	0.43	18	78	6	4	17	40	33	15	20	7	79	0	75	7.9
University of Notre Dame	3.69	3.61	0.70	33	48	9	9	24	67	22	30	17	0	98	3	68	8.6
U of North Carolina-Chapel Hill	3.67	3.41	0.55	20	60	0	3	15	48	29	14	30	0	96	0	61	8.9
University of Illinois at Chicago	3.51	3.33	-0.06	17	41	6	7	29	38	29	15	26	0	95	0	92	8.8
Mean Values for the Top Quarter	**4.14**	**3.82**	**0.15**	**19.39**	**65.94**	**10.00**	**6.28**	**27.44**	**43.83**	**28.06**	**18.11**	**25.11**	**3.28**	**82.17**	**1.33**	**55.17**	**8.65**
CUNY - Grad Sch & Univ Center	3.45	2.84	0.62	32	63	6	4	9	108	32	14	19	10	95	0	14	12.9
U of Massachusetts at Amherst	3.44	3.37	-0.07	15	80	7	5	27	62	27	28	42	0	94	0	56	9.8
University of California-Irvine	3.30	2.96	0.15	12	67	17	2	17	32	13	12	13	7	100	0	60	8.8
University of Wisconsin-Madison	3.28	3.11	-0.13	26	65	12	3	12	126	32	29	24	0	97	0	60	9.8
Syracuse University	3.28	3.52	0.26	20	45	5	5	25	46	24	18	16	6	84	0	65	8.6
Ohio State University	3.21	3.07	0.65	36	50	14	3	8	55	22	13	44	0	86	0	91	10.4
Northwestern University	3.18	2.99	0.36	21	62	14	8	33	35	17	15	20	0	95	0	79	7.6
University of Pennsylvania	3.15	3.04	-0.12	15	67	7	4	20	36	39	20	26	4	89	0	59	9.1
University of Texas at Austin	3.15	2.99	0.07	37	62	11	6	14	61	18	29	26	6	97	0	67	8.7

Appendix Table J - 9 Philosophy (Continued)

Institution	1993 Ratings[1] 93Q	93E	93C	Faculty Tot Fac[2]	% Full[2]	% Supp[2]	Nmbr. Awd[5]	Awd Fac[5]	Students[2] Tot Stu	% Fem	Rpt PhDs	Doctorate Recipients[3] % Fem	% Min	% US	% RA	% TA	MYD
Columbia University	3.15	2.87	-0.48	17	53	0	5	24	75	29	25	21	15	83	3	14	11.4
Boston University	3.12	2.91	0.47	22	55	9	4	14	57	32	19	27	0	88	0	38	12.9
Indiana University	3.11	3.06	0.26	17	59	0	5	29	51	16	18	17	13	55	4	64	10.8
Johns Hopkins University	3.03	2.97	-0.14	9	56	0	1	11	38	34	11	17	7	94	0	25	9.4
University of Minnesota	3.01	2.98	0.22	22	68	14	1	5	41	39	20	30	5	88	0	39	11.0
University of Rochester	2.95	3.04	-0.12	13	31	8	0	0	31	26	16	32	0	75	0	0	8.0
University of Southern California	2.89	2.73	-0.32	13	38	0	1	8	30	23	9	30	0	67	0	67	10.6
University of Maryland College Park	2.86	2.67	0.05	22	55	14	1	5	26	19	6	21	0	64	0	45	11.6
U of Illinois at Urbana-Champaign	2.77	2.78	-0.06	22	41	5	1	5	46	24	11	0	8	93	0	70	9.6
Mean Values for the 2nd Quarter	**3.13**	**2.99**	**0.09**	**20.61**	**56.50**	**7.94**	**3.28**	**14.78**	**53.11**	**25.89**	**17.39**	**23.61**	**4.50**	**85.78**	**0.39**	**50.72**	**10.06**
Rice University	2.72	2.80	0.33	11	36	0	3	18	18	22	11	38	0	92	8	0	11.7
Vanderbilt University	2.61	2.95	-0.06	15	67	0	1	7	58	24	32	31	6	95	0	39	8.9
Univ of California-Riverside	2.57	2.61	0.64	19	68	11	1	5	40	15	6	33	0	100	0	25	8.5
Emory University	2.54	3.00	0.30	14	50	0	4	21	46	24	20	25	0	92	0	25	10.6
Georgetown University	2.51	2.83	0.35	26	35	8	2	8	49	47	31	51	6	87	0	17	11.6
Univ of California-Santa Barbara	2.46	2.04	0.08	11	64	0	1	9	44	18	10	17	0	67	0	78	9.0
University of Virginia	2.38	2.42	-0.15	11	36	27	0	0	34	29	9	21	0	86	0	50	10.3
Duke University	2.37	2.58	0.00	11	36	9	3	27	21	29	8	11	0	89	0	11	10.4
Washington University	2.35	2.47	0.03	14	71	0	3	14	37	49	12	24	0	76	0	56	8.7
State U of New York-Stony Brook	2.33	2.43	-0.25	24	38	4	2	8	54	33	36	21	3	90	0	64	9.8
Temple University	2.31	2.36	0.09	14	50	0	2	14	46	26	16	33	0	91	0	44	11.4
Carnegie Mellon University	2.31	1.67	0.05	13	23	62	0	0	13	15	3	0	0	0	100	0	6.0
Loyola University of Chicago	2.28	2.50	0.26	29	38	0	0	0	75	29	14	28	6	89	8	38	11.0
State Univ of New York-Buffalo	2.24	2.22	-0.06	19	53	0	0	0	54	26	15	29	0	65	0	43	11.2
University of Iowa	2.23	2.68	0.16	11	45	0	2	18	44	16	12	17	0	92	8	75	7.9
University of Miami	2.22	2.56	0.36	8	88	0	0	0	18	11	10	35	25	100	0	67	9.1
Catholic University of America	2.16	2.57	0.00	15	40	7	1	7	66	12	0	8	6	79	0	11	10.7
University of Kansas	2.10	2.69	0.00	16	63	0	1	6	36	17	7	13	0	100	0	77	12.3
Mean Values for the 3rd Quarter	**2.37**	**2.52**	**0.12**	**15.61**	**50.06**	**7.11**	**1.44**	**9.00**	**41.83**	**24.56**	**14.00**	**24.17**	**8.89**	**82.78**	**6.89**	**40.00**	**9.95**

Institution	1993 Ratings[1] 93Q	93E	93C	Faculty Tot Fac[2]	% Full[2]	% Supp[2]	Nmbr. Awd[5]	Awd Fac[5]	Students[2] Tot Stu	% Fem	Rpt PhDs	Doctorate Recipients[3] % Fem	% Min	% US	% RA	% TA	MYD
Pennsylvania State University	2.09	2.17	-0.15	14	50	0	3	14	38	24	22	27	0	80	4	78	10.5
University of Nebraska-Lincoln	2.07	2.35	0.04	10	40	0	0	0	33	18	6	38	0	75	0	43	11.0
Boston College	2.05	2.35	0.19	22	50	0	0	0	73	26	18	27	8	87	0	38	10.4
Florida State University	1.95	1.86	-0.37	10	60	0	0	0	28	21	8	25	9	92	0	20	10.6
Michigan State University	1.91	2.15	0.00	25	64	0	1	4	25	20	9	15	11	82	0	44	10.6
Yale University	1.91	1.92	-0.94	14	21	0	1	7	33	33	26	24	3	89	0	19	9.7
Tulane University	1.86	2.14	-0.10	11	36	0	1	9	41	27	9	33	0	89	0	0	10.0
University of Georgia	1.86	1.81	-0.05	14	43	7	0	0	26	15	6	9	20	91	0	56	9.8
Saint Louis University	1.84	2.46	0.10	17	41	0	1	6	9	11	9	9	0	90	0	50	14.7
Fordham University	1.81	2.20	-0.05	13	31	0	1	8	124	22	18	7	5	81	6	6	12.6
University of Hawaii at Manoa	1.78	1.11	0.23	13	69	0	2	15	34	24	13	14	0	68	8	17	11.9
University of Kentucky	1.59	1.67	0.14	16	38	0	0	0	27	30	4	20	0	100	0	80	9.8
University of Cincinnati	1.56	1.95	-0.23	10	80	10	0	0	17	41	4	0	20	83	0	60	12.6
University of Oregon	1.52	1.31	-0.05	9	56	0	0	0	28	32	7	0	0	100	0	17	7.8
Southern Illinois University	1.41	1.17	-0.06	13	46	0	2	15	14	21	12	6	14	53	0	22	11.7
University of Tennessee-Knoxville	1.32	1.11	0.00	11	64	0	0	0	26	38	13	26	0	94	0	23	11.6
Duquesne University	1.29	1.67	-0.21	9	67	0	0	0	54	17	21	21	9	92	0	13	11.9
Claremont Graduate School	1.10	1.58	-0.25	3	100	0	0	0	40	28	11	31	0	92	0	0	12.6
Mean Values for the 4th Quarter	**1.72**	**1.83**	**-0.10**	**13.00**	**53.11**	**0.94**	**0.67**	**4.33**	**37.22**	**24.89**	**12.00**	**18.44**	**5.50**	**85.44**	**1.00**	**32.56**	**11.10**
Mean Values for All Programs	**2.84**	**2.79**	**0.07**	**17.15**	**56.40**	**6.50**	**2.92**	**13.89**	**44.00**	**25.85**	**15.38**	**22.83**	**4.04**	**84.04**	**2.40**	**44.61**	**9.94**

Sources: 1. National Survey of Graduate Faculty
2. Institutional Coordinator Response Data
3. Doctorate Records File
4. Federal Agencies
5. Associations and Organizations Administrating Prestigious Awards and Honors

Note: *a.* Program in History and Philosophy of Science

* The Doctorate Recipient information cannot be separated for the two programs at the same institution and therefore the total for the combined programs is given.

Appendix Table J - 10 Selected Characteristics of Research-Doctorate Programs in Religion

Institution	1993 Ratings[1] 93Q	93E	93C	Faculty Tot Fac[2]	% Full[2]	% Supp[2]	Nmbr. Awd[5]	Awd Fac[5]	Students[2] Tot Stu	% Fem	Rpt PhDs	Doctorate Recipients[3] % Fem	% Min	% US	% RA	% TA	MYD
University of Chicago	4.76	4.01	-0.07	26	65	0	8	31	224	41	121	22	3	97	1	0	11.6
Harvard University	4.73	4.10	0.05	39	87	3	14	33	59	56	25	24	10	87	0	6	10.9
Princeton University	4.33	3.89	0.21	12	58	0	9	50	28	39	14	8	14	92	0	5	8.7
Duke University	4.25	3.90	0.47	33	61	0	7	18	102	25	73	20	4	99	4	4	11.5
Emory University	4.05	3.59	0.64	43	63	0	10	16	118	33	62	17	6	93	2	2	13.5
University of Virginia	3.96	3.46	0.32	29	48	0	4	14	81	30	39	20	4	100	3	5	12.0
Vanderbilt University	3.85	3.50	0.13	27	63	0	2	7	133	41	57	25	3	95	0	2	12.7
Princeton Theological Seminary	3.84	3.61	0.24	37	54	0	0	0	126	29	68	23	6	76	0	29	12.8
Univ of California-Santa Barbara	3.82	3.33	0.47	18	56	0	0	0	60	42	20	24	17	92	0	22	11.7
Jewish Theological Seminary	3.74	3.26	-0.07	37	35	0	9	16	99	43	32	45	0	80	0	0	12.7
University of Pennsylvania	3.74	3.22	0.07	47	79	2	19	32	28	43	9	31	0	92	0	0	12.8
Mean Values for the Top Quarter	**4.10**	**3.62**	**0.22**	**31.64**	**60.82**	**0.45**	**7.45**	**19.73**	**96.18**	**38.36**	**47.27**	**23.55**	**6.09**	**91.18**	**0.91**	**6.82**	**11.90**
University of Notre Dame	3.73	3.24	-0.03	30	53	0	1	3	83	31	30	0	0	100	0	0	22.0
Hebrew Union College	3.71	3.53	0.14	28	89	0	0	0	47	21	18	10	0	70	0	0	13.8
Columbia University	3.57	3.40	0.10	23	39	0	3	13	55	35	33	41	0	97	0	4	13.6
Brown University	3.55	3.26	0.07	42	74	0	19	33	19	26	4	33	0	83	0	75	11.1
Southern Methodist University	3.53	3.13	0.21	24	71	0	0	0	25	32	13	9	0	90	0	0	14.6
Boston College	3.42	3.12	0.41	31	48	0	1	3	73	34	21	29	0	100	0	0	14.8
Union Theological Seminary in VA	3.08	3.10	0.00	20	70	0	0	0	49	18	26	0	0	86	0	0	13.7
Stanford University	3.05	3.00	-0.18	10	20	0	2	10	30	37	6	30	11	90	0	0	12.6
Mean Values for the 2nd Quarter	**3.46**	**3.22**	**0.09**	**26.00**	**58.00**	**0.00**	**3.25**	**7.75**	**47.63**	**29.25**	**18.88**	**19.00**	**1.38**	**89.50**	**0.00**	**9.88**	**14.53**
Claremont Graduate School	3.02	2.78	-0.47	5	60	0	1	20	106	31	38	21	4	93	2	0	12.3
Drew University	3.02	2.76	0.40	35	43	0	3	9	191	32	111	21	14	90	0	0	14.3
Boston University	2.93	2.90	0.18	11	73	0	2	18	137	36	0	34	15	96	0	5	15.4
Northwestern University	2.91	2.73	0.05	13	77	0	3	15	15	47	13	25	11	100	5	24	12.4
Catholic University of America	2.90	2.74	-0.44	35	46	3	1	3	130	33	0	41	3	100	3	21	14.8

Institution	1993 Ratings[1]			Faculty					Students[2]			Doctorate Recipients[3]					
	93Q	93E	93C	Tot Fac[2]	% Full[2]	% Supp[2]	Nmbr. Awd[5]	Awd Fac[5]	Tot Stu	% Fem	Rpt PhDs	% Fem	% Min	% US	% RA	% TA	MYD
Temple University	2.84	2.55	-0.11	17	41	0	1	6	92	37	52	32	2	71	0	14	13.8
University of Iowa	2.83	2.58	-0.18	13	62	0	0	0	35	26	20	9	0	100	0	27	13.4
Syracuse University	2.83	2.65	-0.24	12	58	0	1	8	58	45	9	27	0	93	0	20	13.7
Fordham University	2.73	2.61	0.28	20	50	0	0	0	207	26	48	25	0	100	0	0	13.0
University of Denver	2.65	2.61	0.47	30	53	0	1	3	78	42	26	38	0	90	13	0	15.6
Mean Values for the 3rd Quarter	**2.87**	**2.69**	**-0.01**	**19.10**	**56.30**	**0.30**	**1.30**	**8.20**	**104.90**	**35.50**	**31.70**	**27.30**	**4.90**	**93.30**	**2.30**	**11.10**	**13.87**
Rice University	2.56	2.41	0.22	7	71	0	1	14	25	44	12	9	0	100	0	0	15.6
Baylor University	2.50	2.65	0.65	36	75	0	0	0	73	5	40	5	3	93	7	7	11.6
University of Southern California	2.49	2.22	-0.44	7	43	0	1	14	58	33	14	31	20	94	0	36	12.3
University of Pittsburgh	2.15	1.95	0.00	16	19	0	1	6	18	22	15	36	8	86	0	10	12.6
Southern Baptist Theological Sem	1.96	2.14	-0.71	33	79	0	0	0	171	12	144	11	0	95	0	0	9.1
Andrews University	1.86	1.39	0.00	41	61	0	0	0	125	2	67	0	17	40	0	0	14.4
Duquesne University	1.83	1.91	0.00	10	50	0	0	0	85	20	15	33	0	33	0	0	12.7
Fuller Theological Seminary	1.74	2.04	0.00	4	100	0	0	0	63	14	19	10	0	63	0	17	19.5
New Orleans Baptist Theo Seminary	1.24	1.56	-0.25	24	46	0	0	0	61	5	30	0	2	100	0	0	9.4
Mean Values for the 4th Quarter	**2.04**	**2.03**	**-0.06**	**19.78**	**60.44**	**0.00**	**0.33**	**3.78**	**75.44**	**17.44**	**39.56**	**15.00**	**5.56**	**78.22**	**0.78**	**7.78**	**13.02**
Mean Values for All Programs	**3.15**	**2.92**	**0.07**	**24.34**	**58.95**	**0.21**	**3.26**	**10.39**	**83.34**	**30.73**	**35.37**	**21.55**	**4.66**	**88.32**	**1.05**	**8.82**	**13.24**

Sources: 1. National Survey of Graduate Faculty
2. Institutional Coordinator Response Data
3. Doctorate Records File
4. Federal Agencies
5. Associations and Organizations Administrating Prestigious Awards and Honors

Appendix Table J - 11 Selected Characteristics of Research-Doctorate Programs in Spanish and Portuguese Language and Literature

Institution	1993 Ratings[1]			Faculty					Students[2]			Doctorate Recipients[3]					
	93Q	93E	93C	Tot Fac[2]	% Full[2]	% Supp[2]	Nmbr. Awd[5]	Awd Fac[5]	Tot Stu	% Fem	Rpt PhDs	% Fem	% Min	% US	% RA	% TA	MYD
Columbia University	4.31	3.46	0.39	11	55	0	2	18	47	68	10	50	45	92	0	56	12.0
Duke University	3.87	3.10	0.29	9	67	0	1	11	22	64	2	0	50	100	0	50	11.5
Brown University	3.83	3.76	0.32	14	57	0	2	14	32	56	11	43	67	86	0	100	9.7
Princeton University	3.80	3.65	0.17	7	71	0	2	29	21	52	13	63	50	88	0	33	9.3
University of Virginia	3.76	3.55	0.31	17	47	0	4	24	31	65	17	68	31	89	6	56	7.8
University of Pennsylvania	3.75	3.41	-0.11	9	67	0	0	0	44	45	26	79	42	83	0	79	10.9
University of Wisconsin-Madison	3.74	3.66	0.06	23	39	0	3	13	49	61	20	67	23	92	0	74	10.4
Cornell University	3.73	3.69	0.00	9	56	0	1	11	15	73	12	82	70	91	0	100	8.4
University of California-Berkeley	3.70	3.61	-0.13	13	62	0	4	23	33	73	19	40	31	80	8	85	9.8
Harvard University	3.63	3.40	-0.18	8	63	0	1	13	41	56	19	67	36	88	0	50	8.6
University of Kansas	3.60	3.76	0.33	15	53	0	2	13	38	74	15	67	20	87	0	71	7.4
University of Texas at Austin	3.54	3.51	-0.27	44	64	0	0	0	49	59	44	43	55	64	3	62	9.5
University of Michigan	3.46	3.53	-0.30	11	45	0	1	9	44	73	14	60	46	68	0	73	12.3
University of California-Davis	3.43	3.20	0.16	8	63	0	1	13	24	67	20	52	64	70	0	81	9.6
Mean Values for the Top Quarter	**3.73**	**3.52**	**0.07**	**14.14**	**57.79**	**0.00**	**1.71**	**13.64**	**35.00**	**63.29**	**17.29**	**55.79**	**45.00**	**84.14**	**1.21**	**69.29**	**9.80**
University of California-Irvine	3.41	3.33	0.30	12	67	0	0	0	36	47	14	69	68	92	0	60	12.7
Univ of California-Los Angeles	3.37	3.31	0.11	21	57	0	3	14	65	69	36	48	45	80	0	76	12.9
Stanford University	3.30	3.20	-0.08	10	50	0	4	30	35	63	8	69	70	85	0	40	10.6
Univ of California-San Diego	3.27	3.07	-0.14	7	43	0	1	14	14	57	7	73	77	93	0	63	9.7
CUNY - Grad Sch & Univ Center	3.27	3.16	0.16	22	64	0	0	0	58	62	21	48	79	97	0	0	13.7
Indiana University	3.23	3.24	0.25	21	43	0	1	5	90	53	17	65	31	81	0	92	11.0
Univ of California-Santa Barbara	3.23	3.23	0.15	17	65	0	0	0	36	53	22	59	40	68	0	76	10.0
U of Illinois at Urbana-Champaign	3.22	3.33	-0.09	22	32	0	2	9	62	69	28	54	29	63	0	94	9.8
New York University	3.19	3.07	0.38	14	57	0	0	0	8	38	21	72	68	93	6	11	13.7
Pennsylvania State University	3.12	3.20	0.44	22	45	0	0	0	46	65	14	75	64	69	0	62	11.0
Univ of Puerto Rico-Rio Piedras	3.12	3.30	0.18	19	84	0	0	0	18	72	29	61	100	95	0	0	20.3
University of Pittsburgh	3.11	3.10	-0.02	10	50	0	0	0	46	57	16	67	33	50	5	67	8.4

Institution	1993 Ratings[1]			Faculty					Students[2]			Doctorate Recipients[3]					
	93Q	93E	93C	Tot Fac[2]	% Full[2]	% Supp[2]	Nmbr. Awd[5]	Awd Fac[5]	Tot Stu	% Fem	Rpt PhDs	% Fem	% Min	% US	% RA	% TA	MYD
Washington University	3.06	3.16	0.36	11	36	0	2	18	26	62	8	40	60	50	0	67	6.7
University of Minnesota	3.06	3.00	-0.18	9	67	0	0	0	32	63	16	53	40	56	0	71	10.1
Mean Values for the 2nd Quarter	**3.21**	**3.19**	**0.13**	**15.50**	**54.29**	**0.00**	**0.93**	**6.43**	**40.86**	**59.29**	**18.36**	**60.93**	**57.43**	**76.57**	**0.79**	**55.64**	**11.47**
University of Kentucky	2.94	3.09	-0.02	11	55	0	1	9	55	82	11	38	20	83	0	64	11.4
Georgetown University	2.92	2.95	0.11	11	36	9	2	9	23	57	11	62	50	77	0	13	9.8
U of North Carolina-Chapel Hill	2.91	3.01	-0.02	14	50	0	0	0	49	31	17	79	36	100	0	60	11.4
University of Maryland College Park	2.84	2.75	-0.11	12	33	0	0	0	32	56	8	77	70	77	0	50	11.6
Ohio State University	2.83	2.80	0.28	18	28	0	2	11	56	79	11	73	38	73	0	80	11.0
U of Massachusetts at Amherst	2.63	2.67	-0.10	15	93	0	3	13	39	85	16	65	57	82	0	67	8.6
Rutgers State Univ-New Brunswick	2.61	2.72	0.09	12	33	0	0	0	28	82	16	84	67	95	0	80	11.6
University of Colorado	2.59	2.61	0.45	13	38	0	0	0	33	55	15	71	90	71	0	25	16.0
Michigan State University	2.59	2.77	0.45	10	60	0	0	0	43	72	8	58	20	50	0	75	10.7
Arizona State University	2.58	2.73	-0.09	13	38	0	2	15	28	57	14	77	63	73	0	60	12.7
State Univ of New York-Buffalo	2.43	2.48	-0.13	8	88	0	0	0	40	63	7	83	33	50	0	75	13.5
Tulane University	2.34	2.47	-0.10	12	17	0	0	0	22	68	11	45	50	73	0	44	11.6
State U of New York-Stony Brook	2.33	2.50	-0.73	9	22	0	1	11	41	71	14	50	75	50	7	57	7.8
Mean Values for the 3rd Quarter	**2.66**	**2.73**	**0.01**	**12.15**	**45.46**	**0.69**	**0.85**	**5.23**	**37.62**	**66.00**	**12.23**	**66.31**	**51.46**	**73.38**	**0.54**	**57.69**	**11.36**
University of Chicago	2.32	2.61	-0.48	5	60	0	2	40	59*	73*	8*	67	50	89	0	0	10.7
State Univ of New York-Albany	2.29	2.38	-0.03	10	50	0	0	0	27	56	14	57	56	76	0	60	9.4
University of Washington	2.25	2.46	-0.24	11	9	0	0	0	16	75	6	57	50	86	0	100	9.8
Syracuse University	2.18	2.19	-0.25	7	71	0	0	0	5	80	6	44	40	56	0	67	7.7
University of Missouri-Columbia	2.17	2.19	0.14	12	42	0	0	0	25	48	4	50	67	75	0	50	10.1
University of Florida	2.15	2.10	-0.20	9	56	0	3	22	21	57	4	67	50	67	0	33	12.7
University of Connecticut	2.13	2.01	-0.20	6	83	0	0	0	26	81	7	56	33	100	0	80	10.4
Boston University	2.12	2.57	-0.18	5	40	0	0	0	9	78	9	73	78	82	0	67	10.1

Appendix Table J - 11 Spanish and Portuguese Language and Literature (Continued)

Institution	1993 Ratings[1]			Faculty					Students[2]			Doctorate Recipients[3]					
	93Q	93E	93C	Tot Fac[2]	% Full[2]	% Supp[2]	Nmbr. Awd[5]	Awd Fac[5]	Tot Stu	% Fem	Rpt PhDs	% Fem	% Min	% US	% RA	% TA	MYD
University of Georgia	2.08	2.38	-0.44	23	35	0	1	4	20	70	11	56	75	44	0	75	8.7
Florida State University	2.08	2.13	-0.14	9	33	0	0	0	19	58	23	71	60	88	0	33	14.3
Catholic University of America	2.06	1.70	-0.20	7	29	0	0	0	15**	73**	n/a	58	56	75	0	50	13.7
Temple University	1.83	1.82	-0.07	12	42	0	0	0	20	65	10	62	60	77	0	30	13.7
Texas Tech University	1.80	1.59	-0.18	11	36	0	0	0	14	43	8	67	22	100	0	25	15.7
Mean Values for the 4th Quarter	**2.11**	**2.16**	**-0.19**	**9.77**	**45.08**	**0.00**	**0.46**	**5.08**	**21.23**	**65.92**	**9.17**	**60.38**	**53.62**	**78.08**	**0.00**	**51.54**	**11.31**
Mean Values for All Programs	**2.95**	**2.92**	**0.01**	**12.96**	**50.85**	**0.17**	**1.00**	**7.69**	**33.83**	**63.54**	**14.49**	**60.76**	**51.85**	**78.13**	**0.65**	**58.69**	**10.97**

Sources: 1. National Survey of Graduate Faculty
2. Institutional Coordinator Response Data
3. Doctorate Records File
4. Federal Agencies
5. Associations and Organizations Administrating Prestigious Awards and Honors

* Enrollment and degree data is for the Romance Language Department which includes French, Spanish, and Portuguese Language and Literature programs
** Enrollment data is for the Modern Language Department which includes French, Spanish, and Portuguese Language and Literature programs

APPENDIX K

Selected Characteristics of Research-Doctorate Programs in Engineering

In the tables that follow, information from the National Survey of Graduate Faculty is linked to a variety of statistics depicting participating doctoral programs. The tables have been designed to present information about each program in a field in rank order by the average rating of the scholarly quality of program faculty (93Q), with the top-rated institutions appearing at the beginning of the list. A key to the variables in the table is presented below.

Institution

Institution: U.S. universities participating in the 1993 NRC Study, ranked in descending order based on the scholarly rating of the program faculty (93Q).

1993 Ratings

93Q: 1993 trimmed mean for scholarly quality of program faculty. The trimmed mean is obtained by dropping the two highest and two lowest scores on the survey before computing the average. For purposes of analysis, scores were converted to a scale of 0 to 5, with 0 denoting "Not sufficient for doctoral education" and 5 denoting "Distinguished." Source: NRC National Survey of Graduate Faculty.

93E: 1993 trimmed mean for program effectiveness in educating research scholars and scientists. The trimmed mean is obtained by dropping the two highest and two lowest scores on the survey before computing the average. For purposes of analysis, scores were converted to a scale of 0 to 5 with 0 denoting "Not Effective" and 5 denoting "Extremely Effective." Source: NRC National Survey of Graduate Faculty.

93C: 1993 trimmed mean for change in program quality in the last five years. The trimmed mean is obtained by dropping the two highest and two lowest scores on the survey before computing the average. For purposes of analysis, scores were converted to a scale of –1 to 1 with –1 denoting "Poorer than 5 years ago" and 1 denoting "Better than 5 years ago." Source: NRC National Survey of Graduate Faculty.

Faculty

Tot Fac: Total number of faculty participating in the program. Source: Institutional Coordinators.

%Full: Percentage of full professors participating in the program. Source: Institutional Coordinators.

%Supp Percentage of program faculty (Tot Fac) with research support (1986-1992). Source: Federal Agencies.

%Pub: Percentage of program faculty (Tot Fac) publishing in the period 1988 to 1992. Source: Institute of Scientific Information.

Pub/Fac: The ratio of the total number of program publications in the period 1988-1992 to the number of program faculty (Tot Fac). Source: Institute of Scientific Information.

Gini Pub: Gini coefficient for program publications, 1988-1992. The Gini coefficient is an indicator of the concentration of publications on a small number of the program faculty during the period 1988-1992. The largest possible value, or maximum concentration, is 100 (only one individual in the program registered a positive count); the smallest value, or minimum concentration, is 100/Fac (All the faculty (Tot Fac) in the program contribute equally). Source: Institute of Scientific Information.

Cite/Fac: The ratio of the total number of program citations in the period 1988-1992 to the number of program faculty (Tot Fac). Source: Institute of Scientific Information.

Gini Cite: Gini coefficient for program citations, 1988-1992. The Gini coefficient is an indicator of the concentration of citations on a small number of the program faculty during the period 1988-1992. The largest possible value, or maximum concentration, is 100 (only one individual in the program registered a positive count); the smallest value, or minimum concentration, is 100/Fac (All the faculty (Tot Fac) in the program contribute equally). Source: Institute of Scientific Information.

Students

Tot Stu:	The number of full and part time graduate students enrolled in the Fall of 1992. Source: Institutional Coordinators.
%Fem:	The percentage of full and part time female graduate students enrolled in the Fall of 1992. Source: Institutional Coordinators.
Rpt PhDs:	The number of Ph.D.s produced by that program for the period academic year 1987-1988 to 1991-1992. Source: Institutional Coordinators.

Doctoral Recipients

%Fem:	The percentage of Ph.D.s awarded to women during the period July 1986-June 1992. Source: Doctorate Records File.
%Min:	The percentage of Ph.D.s known to be awarded to underrepresented minorities (only U.S. Citizens or Permanent Residents) during the period July 1986-June 1992. Source: Doctorate Records File.
%US:	The percentage of Ph.D.s known to be awarded to U.S. Citizens and Permanent Residents during the period July 1986-June 1992. Source: Doctorate Records File.
%RA:	The percentage of Ph.D.s having research assistantships who reported their primary form of support. Source: Doctorate Records File.
%TA:	The percentage of Ph.D.s having teaching assistantships who reported their primary form of support. Source: Doctorate Records File.
MYD:	Median time lapse from entering graduate school to receipt of Ph.D. in years. This is a distributed median with multiple degrees awarded in the median year proportioned over the year. Source: Doctorate Records File.

NOTICE: **n/a** denotes a case where information was not provided by the Institutional Coordinators or was not available from the Doctorate Records File.

Appendix Table K - 1 Selected Characteristics of Research-Doctorate Programs in Aerospace Engineering

Institution	1993 Ratings[1] 93Q	93E	93C	Faculty Tot Fac[2]	% Full[2]	% Supp[2]	% Pub[5]	Pub/ Fac[5]	Gini Pub[5]	Cite/ Fac[5]	Gini Cite[5]	Students[2] Tot Stu	% Fem	Rpt PhDs	Doctorate Recipients[3] % Fem	% Min	% US	% RA	% TA	MYD
California Institute Technology	4.61	4.43	-0.11	15	87	60	80	4.2	19.4	12.6	23.3	54	6	33	7	0	60	73	6	6.9
Massachusetts Inst of Technology	4.54	4.31	-0.03	28	54	54	75	3.5	10.8	4.5	16.3	127	11	85	8	2	67	76	0	6.8
Stanford University	4.50	4.26	-0.03	15	73	80	93	8.3	16.6	18.9	27.1	163	5	83	6	5	54	56	1	7.3
Princeton University	4.30	4.03	0.05	22	73	73	95	6.6	7.6	19.2	14.3	93	12	44	3	11	61	75	0	6.7
University of Michigan	4.05	3.80	0.30	24	50	58	83	5.1	8.7	10.0	14.8	94	4	67	4	5	31	43	18	8.3
Cornell University	3.93	3.75	-0.02	9	89	78	89	5.8	21.2	35.6	36.0	23	9	6	8	0	23	78	11	6.6
Purdue University	3.71	3.46	0.23	23	39	61	74	6.2	15.1	8.8	31.5	61	5	70	0	8	51	53	8	8.3
University of Texas at Austin	3.67	3.64	0.31	38	66	47	68	4.8	9.0	9.2	13.3	57	7	56	3	2	59	46	13	8.3
Mean Values for the Top Quarter	**4.16**	**3.96**	**0.09**	**21.75**	**66.38**	**63.88**	**82.13**	**5.56**	**13.55**	**14.85**	**22.08**	**84.00**	**7.38**	**55.50**	**4.88**	**4.13**	**50.75**	**62.50**	**7.13**	**7.40**
Georgia Institute of Technology	3.66	3.49	0.39	29	59	52	76	5.3	8.4	4.9	21.8	157	5	78	2	3	38	67	1	6.9
Univ of California-San Diego	3.62	3.27	-0.05	20	80	60	75	5.1	9.6	9.9	12.8	16	6	9	0	0	100	100	0	9.0
Univ of California-Los Angeles	3.62	3.44	0.39	20	75	35	80	6.3	7.9	14.4	16.0	46	2	24	0	0	80	43	9	8.6
University of Minnesota	3.40	3.33	0.40	27	56	78	81	4.2	11.1	10.9	19.8	50	4	17	0	0	13	50	25	6.8
University of Colorado	3.35	3.17	0.58	30	50	57	67	3.6	7.6	8.2	12.5	204	12	40	5	0	67	33	2	7.7
U of Illinois at Urbana-Champaign	3.34	3.31	0.18	23	43	48	70	3.1	12.1	12.4	56.2	69	6	22	4	0	54	55	15	8.6
Virginia Polytech Inst & State U	3.24	3.30	0.23	20	40	55	65	5.9	15.5	5.5	18.1	47	6	57	3	5	44	60	2	6.8
North Carolina State University	3.19	3.10	0.14	23	61	48	57	2.5	11.9	4.0	22.3	64	5	20	8	0	77	61	0	7.0
Mean Values for the 2nd Quarter	**3.43**	**3.30**	**0.28**	**24.00**	**58.00**	**54.13**	**71.38**	**4.50**	**10.51**	**8.78**	**22.44**	**81.63**	**5.75**	**33.38**	**2.75**	**1.00**	**59.13**	**58.63**	**6.75**	**7.68**
Texas A&M University	3.12	3.11	0.21	16	38	44	75	3.0	13.8	4.4	31.8	27	19	28	7	0	65	42	16	6.9
Pennsylvania State University	3.12	3.37	0.17	17	29	88	76	3.2	15.1	2.5	17.3	85	9	22	0	0	40	64	18	8.4
University of Washington	3.08	3.13	0.17	20	75	50	75	2.2	9.2	3.8	16.2	27	7	16	0	0	30	76	10	8.6
University of Maryland College Park	3.05	3.11	0.13	13	46	46	69	5.8	15.8	7.6	27.8	124	15	23	0	0	61	36	0	8.6
Iowa State University	2.96	3.08	0.06	15	47	47	53	1.8	19.8	4.7	46.2	16	6	6	0	0	44	78	11	7.8
Rensselaer Polytechnic Inst	2.96	3.20	-0.23	12	33	58	67	3.3	22.1	1.5	35.1	18	0	8	0	17	67	63	0	6.6
University of Cincinnati	2.94	2.80	-0.12	13	85	69	77	5.8	12.8	8.2	25.2	54	9	29	7	0	39	48	24	7.8
Ohio State University	2.84	3.03	0.05	14	57	57	71	2.8	12.4	4.1	22.3	27	11	6	0	0	44	14	29	10.0
Mean Values for the 3rd Quarter	**3.01**	**3.10**	**0.06**	**15.00**	**51.25**	**57.38**	**70.38**	**3.49**	**15.13**	**4.60**	**27.74**	**47.25**	**9.50**	**17.25**	**1.75**	**2.13**	**48.75**	**52.63**	**13.50**	**8.09**

Institution	1993 Ratings[1]			Faculty								Students[2]			Doctorate Recipients[3]					
	93Q	93E	93C	Tot Fac[2]	% Full[2]	% Supp[2]	% Pub[5]	Pub/ Fac[5]	Gini Pub[5]	Cite/ Fac[5]	Gini Cite[5]	Tot Stu	% Fem	Rpt PhDs	% Fem	% Min	% US	% RA	% TA	MYD
University of Notre Dame	2.76	2.99	0.09	7	57	71	100	4.0	18.8	3.4	25.0	18	11	10	0	0	90	56	0	5.6
University of Kansas	2.63	2.68	-0.07	9	56	33	78	2.6	18.3	1.2	42.1	14	14	15	5	0	25	43	14	7.7
University of Florida	2.50	2.47	0.00	24	58	46	58	3.3	13.0	4.8	25.8	52	8	8	33	0	50	44	0	10.3
Air Force Inst of Technology	2.45	2.45	0.10	17	35	0	47	3.5	32.8	3.6	50.9	18	6	10	0	0	100	0	0	9.7
State Univ of New York-Buffalo	2.43	2.76	0.28	22	55	55	86	6.6	9.1	6.4	12.6	11	0	4	0	33	50	33	0	7.4
Naval Postgraduate School	2.42	2.43	-0.03	16	69	0	38	1.1	22.4	0.4	42.8	7	0	6	0	25	80	20	0	10.7
University of Tennessee-Knoxville	2.17	2.26	-0.07	22	73	18	55	1.2	11.6	1.5	20.4	57	11	15	5	17	35	87	0	9.1
Auburn University	2.15	2.36	-0.05	10	30	20	90	2.8	26.2	2.1	69.1	4	0	6	0	33	38	25	75	6.4
University of Dayton	1.07	0.95	-0.18	5	20	40	40	0.6	55.5	0.8	62.5	11	18	3	0	0	100	0	0	13.5
Mean Values for the 4th Quarter	**2.29**	**2.37**	**0.01**	**14.67**	**50.33**	**31.44**	**65.78**	**2.86**	**23.08**	**2.69**	**39.02**	**21.33**	**7.56**	**8.56**	**4.78**	**12.00**	**63.11**	**34.22**	**9.89**	**8.93**
Mean Values for All Programs	**3.19**	**3.16**	**0.11**	**18.73**	**56.30**	**51.09**	**72.21**	**4.06**	**15.79**	**7.58**	**28.16**	**57.42**	**7.55**	**28.06**	**3.58**	**5.03**	**55.67**	**51.45**	**9.33**	**8.05**

Sources: 1. National Survey of Graduate Faculty
2. Institutional Coordinator Response Data
3. Doctorate Records File
4. Federal Agencies
5. Institute for Scientific Information

Appendix Table K - 2 Selected Characteristics of Research-Doctorate Programs in Biomedical Engineering

Institution	1993 Ratings[1] 93Q	93E	93C	Faculty Tot Fac[2]	% Full[2]	% Supp[2]	% Pub[5]	Pub/ Fac[5]	Gini Pub[5]	Cite/ Fac[5]	Gini Cite[5]	Students[2] Tot Stu	% Fem	Rpt PhDs	Doctorate Recipients[3] % Fem	% Min	% US	% RA	% TA	MYD
Massachusetts Inst of Technology	4.62	4.17	0.06	68	79	66	85	13.0	3.4	71.9	5.1	134	0	122	12	0	80	65	0	7.8
Univ of California-San Diego	4.45	4.43	0.60	18	67	67	83	9.4	11.5	34.4	13.4	38	29	25	19	10	68	45	5	7.4
University of Washington	4.35	3.85	0.63	34	47	50	91	9.9	6.6	41.4	20.8	62	32	22	15	0	65	56	0	7.2
Duke University	4.33	3.63	0.18	28	36	46	93	8.5	5.4	31.3	7.3	54	19	26	25	6	80	35	3	6.6
University of Pennsylvania	4.28	3.82	0.48	54	59	70	94	9.8	2.8	41.9	4.2	90	21	51	27	2	89	54	4	7.4
Johns Hopkins University	4.25	4.09	0.38	20	45	100	90	9.5	7.3	43.3	10.0	47	21	17	23	5	84	10	0	7.7
Univ of California-San Francisco	4.19	3.89	0.39	42	67	69	93	19.5	5.6	100.1	5.9	51*	43*	17*	11	20	78	25	0	6.6
University of California-Berkeley	4.08	3.84	0.25	27	93	56	93	12.1	5.5	49.0	6.0	51*	43*	17*	14	0	83	40	0	6.0
University of Utah	3.97	3.69	0.21	67	22	31	73	6.8	4.0	22.5	5.7	n/a	n/a	n/a	20	0	88	71	0	6.8
Mean Values for the Top Quarter	**4.28**	**3.93**	**0.35**	**39.78**	**57.22**	**61.67**	**88.33**	**10.94**	**5.79**	**48.42**	**8.71**	**59.50**	**20.63**	**35.00**	**18.44**	**4.78**	**79.44**	**44.56**	**1.33**	**7.06**
Rice University	3.94	3.95	0.50	11	64	100	82	9.9	16.3	58.2	23.7	54	20	27	67	0	67	50	0	6.8
University of Michigan	3.91	3.68	0.56	59	53	58	93	12.1	3.0	47.6	4.6	70	33	30	15	0	79	69	0	8.0
Stanford University	3.86	3.83	-0.05	6	100	83	83	17.7	26.0	60.5	29.7	n/a	n/a	n/a	0	0	83	67	0	8.5
Case Western Reserve Univ	3.84	3.60	0.04	14	43	43	79	8.9	11.9	20.6	18.7	39	18	37	11	0	63	37	0	8.4
Northwestern University	3.82	3.54	0.42	27	48	48	85	5.2	7.6	16.4	10.2	12	25	30	32	6	68	39	22	7.7
University of Rochester	3.67	3.53	0.45	43	60	81	95	10.4	3.4	37.7	4.7	20	15	24	0	0	33	50	0	6.7
Vanderbilt University	3.65	3.30	0.60	15	33	47	87	7.1	14.8	29.3	25.5	23	26	13	20	0	53	64	0	6.7
University of Minnesota	3.49	3.38	0.61	33	79	48	88	13.7	6.3	77.3	13.1	28	32	7	22	0	100	0	0	7.8
U of North Carolina-Chapel Hill	3.49	3.24	0.43	31	35	19	61	4.2	13.5	20.1	19.9	54	17	14	33	0	93	55	0	6.4
Mean Values for the 2nd Quarter	**3.74**	**3.56**	**0.40**	**26.56**	**57.22**	**58.56**	**83.67**	**9.91**	**11.42**	**40.86**	**16.68**	**37.50**	**23.25**	**22.75**	**22.22**	**0.67**	**71.00**	**47.89**	**2.44**	**7.44**
University of Texas at Austin	3.48	3.33	0.46	33	58	45	85	5.3	8.2	13.3	11.6	21	10	15	6	10	59	46	31	9.4
Pennsylvania State University	3.48	3.13	0.57	28	57	54	100	9.2	8.5	28.6	15.0	30	20	3	14	0	71	86	14	7.6
University of Virginia	3.44	3.40	0.38	19	37	26	74	5.1	9.8	15.9	14.1	47	40	21	38	4	88	50	0	7.1
Drexel University	3.42	3.04	0.04	41	54	51	88	4.8	4.3	8.9	4.8	25	12	13	15	0	75	29	0	8.7
University of California-Davis	3.37	3.15	0.67	27	70	30	89	8.0	7.0	22.1	12.0	21	24	6	0	0	78	43	14	7.8
University of Iowa	3.35	3.33	0.33	10	70	40	80	9.3	17.1	13.7	19.3	32	22	29	5	0	30	50	0	6.8

Institution	1993 Ratings[1]			Faculty								Students[2]			Doctorate Recipients[3]					
	93Q	93E	93C	Tot Fac[2]	% Full[2]	% Supp[2]	% Pub[5]	Pub/ Fac[5]	Gini Pub[5]	Cite/ Fac[5]	Gini Cite[5]	Tot Stu	% Fem	Rpt PhDs	% Fem	% Min	% US	% RA	% TA	MYD
University of Alabama-Birmingham	3.27	3.33	0.64	28	29	46	82	3.4	6.8	13.4	22.8	34	32	9	27	0	73	11	0	7.8
Ohio State University	3.26	3.25	0.19	22	59	55	86	5.9	10.6	11.8	18.5	38	26	12	24	0	73	38	0	8.6
Rutgers State Univ-New Brunswick	3.16	2.99	0.39	30	57	13	83	8.6	8.6	24.8	11.0	67	27	33	24	15	66	33	13	7.6
U of Texas-Southwestern Med Ctr	3.13	2.67	0.25	20	25	45	85	9.0	9.3	36.8	13.4	28	25	5	29	0	43	80	0	7.7
Mean Values for the 3rd Quarter	**3.34**	**3.16**	**0.39**	**25.80**	**51.60**	**40.50**	**85.20**	**6.86**	**9.02**	**18.93**	**14.25**	**34.30**	**23.80**	**14.60**	**18.20**	**2.90**	**65.60**	**46.60**	**7.20**	**7.91**
Rensselaer Polytechnic Inst	2.97	2.89	-0.17	8	38	75	63	4.4	23.2	14.1	33.4	37	78	11	36	0	64	58	17	6.8
Iowa State University	2.92	2.50	0.00	18	56	11	67	1.7	11.1	3.2	35.6	10	40	7	13	0	63	83	0	5.8
North Carolina State University	2.86	2.50	0.00	20	70	0	70	4.1	11.9	4.2	12.3	26	12	29	25	33	75	33	0	8.6
Dartmouth College	2.83	3.06	-0.28	14	7	50	93	6.9	12.0	31.0	22.1	9	22	9	25	0	100	57	0	7.6
Clemson University	2.74	2.78	0.00	8	38	63	88	4.3	19.8	2.3	48.7	18	17	6	0	0	71	67	17	6.8
Texas A&M University	2.50	2.58	0.00	8	38	88	88	2.6	18.8	4.0	32.6	17	18	11	8	29	58	50	10	6.8
University of Illinois at Chicago	2.41	2.67	-0.40	11	55	64	82	5.5	17.4	14.4	27.0	4	25	21	19	15	62	33	13	9.4
University of Miami	2.11	2.03	-0.57	7	43	14	71	1.7	26.3	3.3	35.3	8	25	7	0	14	78	25	0	9.6
University of Akron	1.92	2.04	-0.14	7	29	29	86	2.6	22.8	0.6	37.5	39	26	3	33	0	33	50	0	9.7
Worcester Polytechnic Inst	1.72	1.56	-0.27	3	33	67	100	4.3	38.4	11.7	42.8	1	0	6	9	17	60	25	13	9.7
Mean Values for the 4th Quarter	**2.50**	**2.46**	**-0.18**	**10.40**	**40.70**	**46.10**	**80.80**	**3.81**	**20.17**	**8.88**	**32.73**	**16.90**	**26.30**	**11.00**	**16.80**	**10.80**	**66.40**	**48.10**	**7.00**	**8.08**
Mean Values for All Programs	**3.44**	**3.26**	**0.23**	**25.24**	**51.39**	**51.26**	**84.42**	**7.75**	**11.76**	**28.46**	**18.38**	**35.78**	**23.67**	**19.94**	**18.84**	**4.89**	**70.37**	**46.82**	**4.63**	**7.64**

Sources: 1. National Survey of Graduate Faculty
2. Institutional Coordinator Response Data
3. Doctorate Records File
4. Federal Agencies
5. Institute for Scientific Information

* University of California-San Francisco and University of California-Berkeley reported combined enrollments and degree data

Appendix Table K - 3 Selected Characteristics of Research-Doctorate Programs in Chemical Engineering

Institution	1993 Ratings[1] 93Q	93E	93C	Faculty Tot Fac[2]	% Full[2]	% Supp[2]	% Pub[5]	Pub/ Fac[5]	Gini Pub[5]	Cite/ Fac[5]	Gini Cite[5]	Students[2] Tot Stu	% Fem	Rpt PhDs	Doctorate Recipients[3] % Fem	% Min	% US	% RA	% TA	MYD
University of Minnesota	4.86	4.57	0.18	32	66	84	94	23.0	6.4	117.2	12.5	142	15	98	10	1	58	73	4	6.3
Massachusetts Inst of Technology	4.73	4.43	0.23	31	71	77	90	18.8	5.8	78.6	7.0	190	21	165	13	2	72	72	4	6.3
University of California-Berkeley	4.63	4.43	0.17	19	63	58	95	19.5	9.6	89.3	13.8	95	21	108	16	4	96	72	2	6.2
University of Wisconsin-Madison	4.62	4.37	-0.21	19	63	79	84	13.2	12.7	32.1	14.5	95	20	72	12	10	76	65	5	6.2
U of Illinois at Urbana-Champaign	4.42	4.28	0.31	15	60	60	87	12.6	12.7	45.7	14.0	74	35	67	15	3	80	52	9	5.9
California Institute Technology	4.41	4.24	-0.45	10	60	70	70	17.7	22.8	67.1	23.9	63	24	61	17	3	67	81	1	6.7
Stanford University	4.35	4.31	-0.01	10	60	100	90	20.3	14.6	103.9	16.2	56	32	49	18	0	75	78	0	6.2
University of Delaware	4.34	4.21	0.18	20	65	75	95	12.6	9.3	43.7	16.9	121	20	75	10	7	77	82	2	5.9
Princeton University	4.14	4.02	0.05	15	67	93	87	10.3	10.9	43.7	14.5	62	21	62	20	3	77	63	3	6.3
University of Texas at Austin	4.08	3.73	0.44	30	73	67	83	18.8	9.4	95.8	13.7	91	14	96	16	6	72	68	2	6.3
University of Pennsylvania	3.97	3.81	0.02	16	63	88	100	12.0	10.6	45.2	11.3	53	25	49	30	9	84	70	0	5.7
Carnegie Mellon University	3.87	3.80	0.20	17	65	71	71	8.2	12.6	21.1	16.7	80	29	60	24	2	71	25	8	5.5
Cornell University	3.86	3.81	0.38	19	42	89	89	11.7	8.4	37.6	15.0	197	34	153	8	2	76	87	0	6.4
Univ of California-Santa Barbara	3.82	3.45	0.82	18	83	56	94	11.3	8.2	51.8	16.4	45	13	23	12	6	71	41	24	6.8
Northwestern University	3.75	3.67	0.47	17	71	76	88	10.7	10.1	30.3	17.9	62	16	61	13	6	68	57	10	6.5
Purdue University	3.67	3.63	0.31	25	72	76	76	10.0	10.2	32.1	10.4	69	12	85	7	4	57	80	1	6.6
University of Houston	3.66	3.37	-0.09	18	61	39	83	5.0	10.4	11.0	17.3	67	21	43	12	7	51	62	13	6.2
University of Michigan	3.52	3.43	0.15	18	56	61	94	11.6	11.4	39.3	11.4	71	21	61	12	8	60	65	7	6.1
CUNY - Grad Sch & Univ Center	3.46	3.15	0.67	13	54	62	85	4.2	13.5	11.7	14.2	22	14	20	24	10	48	64	21	7.3
University of Washington	3.44	3.48	0.20	18	61	56	83	11.3	14.2	34.4	23.0	62	23	46	17	6	81	90	0	6.5
U of Massachusetts at Amherst	3.35	3.28	-0.14	13	62	54	77	10.8	17.2	35.0	21.8	52	27	59	18	7	64	90	3	5.9
Rice University	3.35	3.54	0.16	15	73	60	60	5.4	19.7	30.3	33.0	57	18	40	11	5	68	46	2	6.2
Pennsylvania State University	3.34	3.29	0.23	27	44	52	70	7.0	9.8	18.1	12.8	87	21	55	10	3	49	92	6	7.3
Mean Values for the Top Quarter	**3.98**	**3.84**	**0.19**	**18.91**	**63.26**	**69.70**	**84.57**	**12.43**	**11.76**	**48.48**	**16.01**	**83.17**	**21.61**	**69.91**	**15.00**	**4.96**	**69.48**	**68.48**	**5.52**	**6.32**
University of Notre Dame	3.30	3.38	0.31	11	64	64	100	9.7	15.5	28.9	29.4	46	20	34	28	3	68	82	3	5.6
North Carolina State University	3.20	3.21	0.48	17	59	65	88	9.8	10.1	37.2	18.1	53	19	39	14	3	80	34	24	6.8
University of Colorado	3.18	3.19	0.22	15	67	60	80	8.1	17.3	23.4	27.3	57	25	31	19	3	83	66	16	7.8
Lehigh University	3.13	3.26	0.34	19	89	74	95	11.7	10.5	40.0	14.6	69	16	73	8	0	55	43	19	7.4

Institution	1993 Ratings[1] 93Q	93E	93C	Faculty Tot Fac[2]	% Full[2]	% Supp[2]	% Pub[5]	Pub/ Fac[5]	Gini Pub[5]	Cite/ Fac[5]	Gini Cite[5]	Students[2] Tot Stu	% Fem	Rpt PhDs	Doctorate Recipients[3] % Fem	% Min	% US	% RA	% TA	MYD
University of California-Davis	3.11	3.12	0.43	16	69	63	88	10.8	10.2	37.1	15.5	23	17	20	11	0	33	38	38	7.2
State Univ of New York-Buffalo	3.08	3.09	0.22	14	43	71	71	12.5	36.7	39.6	38.7	64	14	51	3	7	24	44	36	7.3
University of Virginia	3.01	3.00	0.40	12	58	75	75	8.8	13.7	31.3	22.7	30	13	32	22	13	86	68	15	6.0
Georgia Institute of Technology	3.01	3.07	0.43	25	56	44	88	8.3	7.5	15.4	13.0	45	33	48	11	11	72	44	38	5.8
Yale University	2.98	2.76	-0.37	8	38	88	100	11.8	19.0	56.3	24.8	29	24	18	4	0	31	79	0	6.9
Iowa State University	2.98	2.85	-0.06	16	88	44	88	5.8	13.2	28.6	23.4	43	37	29	11	0	68	83	4	6.8
University of Florida	2.97	3.03	0.01	14	57	50	71	6.9	17.1	15.6	40.3	28	4	38	9	6	72	78	8	6.3
Rensselaer Polytechnic Inst	2.95	2.99	0.07	14	57	71	93	9.1	11.7	26.4	18.2	69	6	41	12	9	41	49	15	6.4
Johns Hopkins University	2.95	2.95	0.17	8	50	100	88	13.9	27.4	51.9	40.3	30	33	20	8	0	50	82	0	6.0
Texas A&M University	2.91	2.81	0.35	20	80	55	75	8.4	15.8	11.9	17.4	51	8	60	9	0	59	60	10	7.3
Washington University	2.89	2.98	-0.08	12	75	67	75	6.8	17.9	6.3	18.3	45	22	41	3	6	41	57	3	6.8
Univ of California-Los Angeles	2.88	2.68	0.10	23	74	78	87	13.9	12.0	64.6	17.5	50	12	17	18	0	71	94	0	6.0
University of Rochester	2.81	2.98	-0.08	13	54	62	92	8.6	13.7	31.6	26.9	42	10	30	3	8	36	17	7	6.6
Ohio State University	2.73	3.07	0.11	14	43	71	79	9.7	16.4	24.7	18.5	60	18	34	2	4	53	45	21	6.3
Virginia Polytech Inst & State U	2.67	2.68	-0.11	12	58	58	75	7.1	29.3	25.0	36.2	37	19	34	13	5	65	77	5	6.1
Rutgers State Univ-New Brunswick	2.66	2.99	0.40	14	57	57	86	5.6	13.1	13.3	22.8	75	27	47	13	4	64	34	23	7.3
University of Pittsburgh	2.64	2.75	0.12	22	41	50	86	5.5	7.5	9.9	14.7	35	23	40	9	4	43	67	4	5.7
Michigan State University	2.60	2.74	0.15	14	57	93	93	6.4	11.1	12.6	12.2	40	20	24	3	5	88	60	10	6.9
Case Western Reserve Univ	2.59	2.77	-0.15	10	80	80	80	8.8	15.5	59.1	42.7	33	21	24	16	5	70	24	31	7.2
Mean Values for the 2nd Quarter	**2.92**	**2.97**	**0.15**	**14.91**	**61.48**	**66.96**	**84.91**	**9.04**	**15.75**	**30.03**	**24.07**	**45.83**	**19.17**	**35.87**	**10.83**	**4.17**	**58.83**	**57.61**	**14.35**	**6.63**
Syracuse University	2.57	2.75	-0.05	10	80	60	100	14.1	20.8	42.9	22.4	15	33	28	0	17	24	80	13	7.6
Illinois Institute of Technology	2.57	2.54	-0.12	11	64	9	82	8.4	22.2	15.4	25.2	32	38	35	4	8	46	63	13	7.2
Clarkson University	2.54	2.69	-0.16	15	67	67	93	6.3	9.5	14.4	13.8	48	19	30	9	0	37	61	9	6.8
Brigham Young University	2.53	2.85	0.05	12	58	25	83	7.7	15.4	17.2	18.2	13	0	56	0	0	89	77	9	6.5
University of Connecticut	2.49	2.53	0.00	12	67	58	83	8.0	16.2	25.0	19.6	45	18	19	10	0	52	53	13	7.4
University of Maryland College Park	2.48	2.75	0.03	13	46	62	100	7.0	14.6	12.5	16.9	47	26	17	9	0	38	64	18	6.7
University of Utah	2.47	2.54	0.14	24	75	42	79	6.9	7.5	17.3	14.1	66	11	31	4	8	57	69	0	7.0
University of Oklahoma	2.41	2.57	0.05	11	55	36	100	7.9	15.4	26.8	24.9	66	21	24	0	0	57	57	4	6.8

Appendix Table K - 3 Chemical Engineering (Continued)

Institution	1993 Ratings[1] 93Q	93E	93C	Faculty Tot Fac[2]	% Full[2]	% Supp[2]	% Pub[5]	Pub/ Fac[5]	Gini Pub[5]	Cite/ Fac[5]	Gini Cite[5]	Students[2] Tot Stu	% Fem	Rpt PhDs	Doctorate Recipients[3] % Fem	% Min	% US	% RA	% TA	MYD
Louisiana State U & A&M College	2.40	2.47	0.07	27	48	37	78	6.8	6.9	15.5	9.1	39	8	25	7	7	53	59	11	8.3
Columbia University	2.29	2.24	-0.58	6	67	83	100	7.3	29.5	11.5	38.5	19	26	18	23	7	71	12	48	7.7
University of Southern California	2.25	2.47	-0.45	7	57	57	86	11.9	20.5	34.1	27.6	27	11	23	10	0	53	73	0	7.7
University of Missouri-Rolla	2.22	2.14	0.02	13	69	15	46	2.4	29.8	6.4	56.7	11	9	14	8	0	38	53	26	6.5
Kansas State University	2.18	2.21	-0.09	10	70	40	80	6.2	25.4	3.9	25.3	6	0	10	0	0	20	86	7	6.6
University of Tennessee-Knoxville	2.18	2.12	-0.08	15	73	7	40	1.8	20.1	1.3	31.3	28	14	20	12	13	67	41	23	6.8
University of Illinois at Chicago	2.15	2.26	0.06	11	64	45	64	6.8	18.9	17.6	22.6	10	10	21	12	0	42	53	20	7.5
Washington State University	2.14	2.13	0.03	9	56	67	78	6.6	16.4	13.8	20.4	22	9	9	0	0	69	82	9	5.7
Polytechnic University	2.14	2.04	-0.16	9	33	56	67	9.0	25.4	20.9	36.3	19	11	13	6	0	25	64	7	7.6
Arizona State University	2.12	2.26	0.06	13	46	38	77	3.4	23.2	18.2	54.8	20	0	12	18	0	77	36	27	6.6
Colorado School of Mines	2.11	2.37	0.32	14	79	36	57	5.0	15.1	9.1	16.7	9	11	14	16	0	59	64	0	6.6
University of Iowa	2.09	1.84	0.03	8	38	63	88	6.6	24.1	11.3	41.6	32	16	16	14	0	48	47	20	7.6
Wayne State University	2.09	1.96	0.14	12	33	25	83	3.1	17.1	6.9	68.0	15	20	21	10	0	37	36	27	8.6
West Virginia University	2.08	2.02	0.04	15	47	33	87	3.4	12.1	4.9	11.8	11	9	13	19	0	55	72	17	6.5
Worcester Polytechnic Inst	2.07	2.00	-0.10	9	56	89	100	7.3	13.9	16.8	17.4	15	40	16	12	0	82	44	33	6.8
Mean Values for the 3rd Quarter	**2.29**	**2.34**	**-0.03**	**12.43**	**58.61**	**45.65**	**80.48**	**6.69**	**18.26**	**15.81**	**27.53**	**26.74**	**15.65**	**21.09**	**8.83**	**2.61**	**52.00**	**58.52**	**15.39**	**7.09**
Oklahoma State University	2.04	2.08	-0.25	6	83	33	83	4.8	25.0	9.0	26.5	55	4	30	3	0	31	42	19	7.3
University of Kentucky	1.98	1.82	0.02	12	75	50	92	4.0	14.0	9.8	37.4	30	30	9	0	0	50	78	0	6.8
Auburn University	1.98	2.07	0.07	14	57	43	64	5.1	25.0	13.2	43.8	53	6	23	0	0	38	89	4	8.2
University of Cincinnati	1.97	2.03	-0.09	8	88	38	88	9.1	26.8	16.4	25.0	29	14	24	23	0	34	50	33	7.5
University of Tulsa	1.97	2.00	-0.04	9	56	100	56	4.0	36.1	8.2	75.7	18	22	11	27	0	40	46	31	6.0
Vanderbilt University	1.94	1.74	0.07	11	55	27	55	2.7	28.0	2.4	25.4	13	8	8	25	0	63	57	43	5.7
University of Kansas	1.94	1.95	-0.07	12	42	33	75	2.3	12.5	2.0	22.5	5	20	12	10	0	90	38	13	8.4
Oregon State University	1.93	1.73	-0.58	5	40	60	100	4.0	34.0	14.4	47.3	18	0	8	20	0	20	30	20	7.1
Tulane University	1.91	1.81	0.17	9	56	44	89	3.8	18.6	5.6	42.8	38	29	13	25	25	80	40	0	8.0
University of Arizona	1.86	2.02	-0.25	7	57	14	57	4.7	32.0	11.6	37.0	23	4	12	0	0	53	71	14	7.4
New Jersey Inst of Technology	1.75	1.77	-0.04	10	100	10	40	2.6	32.5	3.2	44.3	30	10	16	10	0	35	53	27	7.6
Clemson University	1.74	1.71	0.08	11	64	36	82	2.6	13.4	5.5	37.8	41	5	9	10	0	56	86	0	4.8

Institution	1993 Ratings[1]			Faculty								Students[2]			Doctorate Recipients[3]					
	93Q	93E	93C	Tot Fac[2]	% Full[2]	% Supp[2]	% Pub[5]	Pub/ Fac[5]	Gini Pub[5]	Cite/ Fac[5]	Gini Cite[5]	Tot Stu	% Fem	Rpt PhDs	% Fem	% Min	% US	% RA	% TA	MYD
Stevens Inst of Technology	1.73	1.89	-0.19	7	100	14	86	6.7	31.0	21.0	53.7	6	33	20	4	0	26	30	60	7.8
University of Missouri-Columbia	1.70	1.78	-0.02	18	56	44	89	5.6	11.1	5.8	26.0	18	6	15	15	20	32	0	42	9.2
Duke University	1.63	1.18	0.08	10	40	80	100	8.5	14.4	42.3	24.7	14	43	1	n/a	n/a	n/a	n/a	n/a	n/a
University of Akron	1.62	1.58	0.13	9	33	22	89	5.3	16.1	4.4	22.6	49	12	11	8	0	38	44	56	6.8
University of Wyoming	1.55	1.88	-0.04	7	57	14	57	2.9	32.5	3.7	66.5	9	0	4	0	0	71	60	0	7.7
University of Maine	1.49	1.04	0.00	11	73	9	82	2.5	20.7	4.1	27.1	30	23	5	13	0	83	0	100	12.4
University of Rhode Island	1.42	1.19	-0.21	7	57	29	71	4.7	31.8	4.4	34.6	29	10	12	21	29	50	75	25	7.9
Northeastern University	1.38	1.40	-0.17	7	43	57	71	2.9	26.5	4.0	27.2	2	50	7	0	0	50	0	50	9.7
University of Louisville	1.33	1.39	-0.09	9	89	44	67	3.1	24.2	1.0	35.8	8	25	9	8	43	54	0	33	6.6
University of Idaho	1.33	1.39	-0.06	7	57	29	71	4.6	28.9	5.7	47.8	12	17	12	0	0	50	67	0	7.7
Ohio University	0.93	0.80	-0.24	8	38	50	38	1.4	57.0	2.8	76.4	9	11	4	20	0	60	50	0	7.7
University of Mississippi	0.76	0.61	-0.22	6	33	0	50	2.2	62.1	2.3	64.2	7	29	4	0	0	60	60	20	7.9
Mean Values for the 4th Quarter	**1.66**	**1.62**	**-0.08**	**9.17**	**60.38**	**36.67**	**73.00**	**4.17**	**27.26**	**8.45**	**40.50**	**22.75**	**17.13**	**11.63**	**10.52**	**5.09**	**50.61**	**46.35**	**25.65**	**7.66**
Mean Values for All Programs	**2.70**	**2.68**	**0.05**	**13.81**	**60.92**	**54.55**	**80.66**	**8.04**	**18.35**	**25.51**	**27.17**	**44.39**	**18.38**	**34.38**	**11.29**	**4.21**	**57.73**	**57.74**	**15.23**	**6.93**

Sources: 1. National Survey of Graduate Faculty
2. Institutional Coordinator Response Data
3. Doctorate Records File
4. Federal Agencies
5. Institute for Scientific Information

Appendix Table K - 4 Selected Characteristics of Research-Doctorate Programs in Civil Engineering

Institution	1993 Ratings[1] 93Q	93E	93C	Faculty Tot Fac[2]	% Full[2]	% Supp[2]	% Pub[5]	Pub/ Fac[5]	Gini Pub[5]	Cite/ Fac[5]	Gini Cite[5]	Students[2] Tot Stu	% Fem	Rpt PhDs	Doctorate Recipients[3] % Fem	% Min	% US	% RA	% TA	MYD
Massachusetts Inst of Technology	4.61	4.47	-0.07	40	65	63	78	6.2	6.0	25.9	12.4	78	21	126	10	9	38	76	4	7.0
University of California-Berkeley	4.56	4.22	-0.31	43	60	60	93	6.3	4.0	14.7	10.9	138	19	179	9	3	45	47	3	7.3
Stanford University	4.44	4.29	0.15	23	52	78	91	6.7	8.3	23.0	14.8	106	25	74	11	4	59	57	3	7.9
University of Texas at Austin	4.42	4.27	0.48	93	69	44	80	5.1	4.5	15.1	12.0	79	13	138	3	4	42	55	8	7.7
U of Illinois at Urbana-Champaign	4.41	4.23	-0.04	71	72	44	66	2.6	4.8	5.5	11.0	250	10	112	6	6	38	66	2	7.9
Cornell University	4.30	4.08	0.28	33	73	58	88	6.5	5.5	13.7	11.7	62	13	55	3	0	43	67	3	7.9
California Institute Technology	4.27	4.42	-0.15	12	83	83	75	7.6	20.3	34.1	34.6	35	31	39	23	5	52	77	15	7.2
Princeton University	3.99	3.89	0.15	21	57	71	86	6.2	7.9	14.2	11.7	62	21	42	8	6	42	65	8	7.3
Northwestern University	3.96	3.73	0.24	25	68	56	84	13.8	10.9	23.8	16.1	73	12	57	8	3	34	58	8	7.9
University of Michigan	3.90	3.82	0.16	23	48	70	87	5.9	7.7	10.6	25.5	80	16	72	0	5	24	41	5	6.9
Purdue University	3.89	3.73	0.15	56	46	21	55	3.0	12.7	2.2	22.7	110	17	95	8	5	36	41	17	6.8
Carnegie Mellon University	3.85	3.79	0.24	17	65	100	94	5.1	10.5	8.7	25.7	42	14	33	8	0	61	39	19	7.4
University of Minnesota	3.76	3.62	0.47	32	56	56	72	4.4	7.9	10.6	14.7	72	11	65	10	0	40	63	10	8.0
University of Washington	3.67	3.66	0.39	34	68	50	82	4.3	6.7	11.4	17.6	42	19	49	6	7	47	47	12	9.3
U of North Carolina-Chapel Hill	3.58	3.50	0.36	20	70	15	85	3.1	8.8	9.9	16.7	44	20	29	8	0	85	50	8	9.1
University of California-Davis	3.54	3.51	0.31	27	70	30	78	3.7	9.2	4.1	9.6	50	12	44	4	3	56	26	17	8.2
Texas A&M University	3.40	3.27	0.41	63	43	22	59	2.0	4.3	4.2	15.9	100	8	64	7	19	62	48	10	8.8
Georgia Institute of Technology	3.40	3.26	0.33	41	37	29	56	2.0	7.4	2.7	11.9	99	6	34	3	8	45	44	4	8.6
Virginia Polytech Inst & State U	3.39	3.36	0.33	34	50	35	71	3.1	7.9	4.0	13.1	54	0	14	3	12	43	57	9	7.8
Lehigh University	3.39	3.37	0.00	22	59	45	55	1.4	14.8	1.0	31.9	31	3	23	0	0	19	53	6	8.7
Univ of California-Los Angeles	3.37	3.28	0.11	26	81	46	85	4.0	8.5	9.6	12.1	93	29	48	9	5	72	45	9	8.0
Mean Values for the Top Quarter	**3.91**	**3.80**	**0.19**	**36.00**	**61.52**	**51.24**	**77.14**	**4.90**	**8.50**	**11.86**	**16.79**	**80.95**	**15.24**	**66.29**	**7.00**	**4.95**	**46.81**	**53.43**	**8.57**	**7.89**
University of Wisconsin-Madison	3.34	3.27	-0.04	33	73	42	82	4.4	7.4	13.1	17.9	59	12	51	12	0	43	27	24	8.7
Rice University	3.28	3.24	-0.08	8	63	50	50	3.3	38.7	3.8	59.3	20	0	15	4	0	40	52	0	7.6
University of Colorado	3.27	3.33	0.43	36	47	47	69	3.0	8.2	3.4	7.5	93	18	59	10	16	45	36	0	7.3
Colorado State University	3.23	3.28	-0.18	30	53	47	87	3.9	5.6	2.5	7.8	120	10	110	5	7	45	21	3	9.7
Johns Hopkins University	3.22	3.44	0.21	7	43	100	86	6.7	22.5	6.0	30.0	25	4	14	9	0	62	35	35	6.8
Duke University	3.21	3.12	0.19	16	38	56	88	4.6	9.7	3.6	10.9	63	25	25	9	0	41	41	35	6.3

Institution	1993 Ratings[1] 93Q	93E	93C	Faculty Tot Fac[2]	% Full[2]	% Supp[2]	% Pub[5]	Pub/ Fac[5]	Gini Pub[5]	Cite/ Fac[5]	Gini Cite[5]	Students[2] Tot Stu	% Fem	Rpt PhDs	Doctorate Recipients[3] % Fem	% Min	% US	% RA	% TA	MYD
Columbia University	3.21	3.16	-0.30	12	75	33	83	2.6	11.7	3.8	20.3	17	24	21	14	0	29	50	17	6.4
University of Iowa	3.19	3.23	0.05	18	67	39	78	5.1	11.3	11.7	16.5	45	7	47	6	11	31	51	6	7.9
North Carolina State University	3.17	3.13	0.38	35	49	43	57	2.6	9.6	2.0	11.8	70	7	37	2	6	31	21	10	8.2
State Univ of New York-Buffalo	3.14	3.11	0.58	30	47	37	70	6.6	10.9	16.8	16.0	72	4	42	9	7	31	72	15	7.2
Pennsylvania State University	3.12	2.95	0.31	27	67	15	70	2.5	8.9	2.4	12.8	102	15	27	3	0	48	30	11	8.3
University of California-Irvine	3.04	2.88	0.53	17	47	47	71	2.1	10.1	1.1	14.6	47	19	13	7	13	53	33	0	8.6
University of Arizona	3.03	3.09	0.12	20	35	50	80	5.6	10.4	9.0	12.9	93	8	34	2	0	31	40	40	7.6
Rensselaer Polytechnic Inst	2.97	3.04	-0.11	11	45	73	91	8.6	16.3	24.1	30.4	33	6	13	6	9	32	61	0	8.2
University of Florida	2.93	2.95	0.06	25	48	16	56	1.4	10.1	0.6	38.7	49	6	41	10	22	43	42	4	8.4
University of Notre Dame	2.93	3.03	0.25	13	23	46	85	4.0	13.6	9.9	24.8	17	29	11	0	0	50	57	29	8.0
University of Maryland College Park	2.92	3.09	0.22	29	48	34	52	3.2	11.2	2.6	20.0	82	10	39	18	3	61	36	2	8.3
University of Virginia	2.91	2.90	0.15	15	60	53	53	3.3	22.0	4.6	30.2	16	0	11	17	29	58	60	10	8.4
Ohio State University	2.88	3.03	-0.05	18	44	22	78	4.5	9.8	4.4	13.9	47	4	26	0	0	33	58	10	8.0
Michigan State University	2.85	2.99	0.13	19	47	16	68	2.8	14.7	1.6	29.1	43	12	35	2	8	34	19	0	7.7
Vanderbilt University	2.84	2.90	0.15	18	61	33	67	6.2	16.9	11.5	22.5	37	19	16	13	33	44	18	55	7.6
Clarkson University	2.84	2.85	0.12	17	53	65	82	4.1	9.4	6.2	17.3	35	14	19	18	0	45	50	40	8.2
Mean Values for the 2nd Quarter	**3.07**	**3.09**	**0.14**	**20.64**	**51.50**	**43.82**	**72.86**	**4.14**	**13.14**	**6.58**	**21.15**	**53.86**	**11.51**	**32.09**	**8.00**	**7.45**	**42.27**	**41.36**	**15.73**	**7.88**
University of Kansas	2.82	2.70	0.00	23	74	17	48	2.4	15.5	2.8	19.5	36	6	17	0	0	60	44	6	9.6
Iowa State University	2.80	2.92	-0.10	28	46	25	64	2.1	9.6	1.5	14.3	26	8	17	0	6	67	58	0	7.4
University of Delaware	2.80	3.01	0.23	17	47	47	76	5.5	12.1	10.2	14.8	34	12	14	9	22	43	47	20	7.9
U of Massachusetts at Amherst	2.77	2.64	-0.35	15	60	33	60	4.8	17.0	8.0	18.2	19	16	29	15	0	38	43	11	7.2
Utah State University	2.70	2.84	0.21	31	48	6	68	2.1	9.9	5.7	23.2	64	8	33	5	5	52	60	0	10.8
Washington University	2.66	2.70	-0.21	8	75	38	75	3.3	28.4	2.1	35.6	16	13	12	0	0	47	43	0	8.7
University of Pittsburgh	2.65	2.75	0.37	17	47	47	65	2.4	11.0	3.1	16.0	22	0	24	14	0	28	22	22	8.4
University of Houston	2.62	2.39	0.11	14	36	43	71	4.4	16.7	4.1	21.4	57	14	17	4	25	31	44	17	7.8
Oregon State University	2.61	2.88	0.16	11	55	18	73	3.7	18.8	7.4	31.6	30	27	19	13	0	33	47	5	9.7
University of Kentucky	2.58	2.76	0.14	17	53	29	59	3.1	16.9	3.4	17.4	31	0	13	7	25	29	0	67	7.8
Auburn University	2.55	2.67	0.22	23	39	13	65	2.6	10.2	4.4	16.8	20	10	18	0	0	61	69	8	7.7

Appendix Table K - 4 Civil Engineering (Continued)

Institution	1993 Ratings[1] 93Q	93E	93C	Faculty Tot Fac[2]	% Full[2]	% Supp[2]	% Pub[5]	Pub/ Fac[5]	Gini Pub[5]	Cite/ Fac[5]	Gini Cite[5]	Students[2] Tot Stu	% Fem	Rpt PhDs	Doctorate Recipients[3] % Fem	% Min	% US	% RA	% TA	MYD
University of Cincinnati	2.44	2.65	0.27	13	46	15	77	4.0	18.7	4.5	28.2	56	18	32	17	13	30	31	46	7.6
University of Oklahoma	2.43	2.56	0.08	20	35	35	65	2.6	14.1	1.5	15.5	28	11	81	9	11	41	47	5	9.2
Brigham Young University	2.42	2.65	0.27	13	46	31	54	1.2	22.6	1.7	32.2	10	20	129	0	0	87	64	0	6.9
Arizona State University	2.41	2.69	0.31	13	46	38	62	2.1	15.5	2.7	31.2	39	10	19	0	0	22	50	20	8.0
Texas Tech University	2.40	2.47	0.17	19	58	47	58	2.1	13.2	0.8	27.1	24	4	14	6	14	39	46	23	6.7
University of Missouri-Rolla	2.40	2.40	-0.15	15	53	60	47	1.2	20.3	0.8	31.9	24	0	23	6	8	42	24	16	7.3
Syracuse University	2.40	2.50	-0.03	17	59	65	82	6.9	20.2	31.9	39.2	13	8	10	0	0	70	100	0	8.6
Clemson University	2.39	2.82	0.15	13	62	31	77	2.8	16.6	2.1	26.2	18	22	18	13	6	60	25	39	8.3
Washington State University	2.35	2.43	0.03	17	41	29	65	2.2	14.9	1.7	41.2	49	6	24	17	0	48	38	29	7.6
University of Illinois at Chicago	2.35	2.30	-0.11	11	36	27	55	5.0	27.6	10.3	59.1	28	7	23	9	0	70	0	38	9.5
Mean Values for the 3rd Quarter	**2.55**	**2.65**	**0.08**	**16.90**	**50.57**	**33.05**	**65.05**	**3.17**	**16.66**	**5.27**	**26.70**	**30.67**	**10.48**	**27.90**	**6.86**	**6.43**	**47.52**	**42.95**	**17.71**	**8.22**
University of Tennessee-Knoxville	2.33	2.62	-0.11	18	67	11	61	1.8	13.8	0.9	34.9	38	8	16	0	0	81	17	17	13.6
West Virginia University	2.26	2.29	0.04	19	42	32	32	1.0	21.8	0.3	38.8	25	0	12	0	13	42	36	14	8.4
Louisiana State U & A&M College	2.23	2.36	0.06	23	39	22	65	4.2	15.5	4.0	24.6	46	7	28	8	0	44	42	8	6.9
University of Connecticut	2.22	1.79	0.18	17	41	47	82	2.2	9.8	2.6	16.8	13	8	8	0	0	71	55	9	10.7
Oklahoma State University	2.21	2.11	-0.04	14	79	7	29	0.8	45.4	0.8	53.7	140	9	22	3	13	48	13	25	8.3
Illinois Institute of Technology	2.21	2.45	-0.57	7	43	14	71	2.0	24.4	2.1	66.2	17	6	13	14	9	30	18	43	8.4
University of Wisconsin-Milwaukee	2.21	1.91	0.06	14	64	21	50	1.0	21.4	1.1	59.3	n/a	n/a	n/a	14	0	29	40	20	9.3
University of Nebraska-Lincoln	2.15	2.18	0.14	20	30	30	60	2.5	18.3	2.0	28.5	13	31	7	0	0	44	71	0	7.0
University of New Hampshire	2.14	2.13	0.26	14	14	36	57	1.8	17.4	1.9	19.2	6	17	7	14	0	57	17	17	6.9
University of Missouri-Columbia	1.95	2.11	-0.28	10	40	40	90	2.6	18.0	2.2	26.8	15	7	8	0	0	40	11	0	8.0
Kansas State University	1.95	1.99	0.00	12	58	42	33	0.7	31.2	1.3	28.0	15	0	9	0	33	38	50	0	6.6
George Washington University	1.95	1.67	-0.19	9	56	44	67	3.2	24.1	3.8	38.5	18	6	16	13	0	44	8	8	10.2
New Mexico State University	1.94	2.22	0.27	18	50	22	28	0.5	23.4	1.1	41.8	14	21	10	23	14	64	14	14	9.4
University of Akron	1.77	1.60	0.00	10	50	40	90	5.5	16.2	6.7	24.2	47	9	17	5	11	45	47	24	8.2
University of Miami	1.68	1.74	-0.12	11	36	64	91	2.2	13.1	1.3	22.4	12	8	9	0	0	38	33	11	7.7
Northeastern University	1.67	1.48	0.19	15	40	27	53	1.2	19.1	2.1	58.7	10	10	4	0	0	60	0	40	11.8
Catholic University of America	1.65	1.11	-0.17	7	71	57	57	2.4	41.1	0.7	52.0	n/a	n/a	7	0	0	20	0	0	7.8

Institution	1993 Ratings[1]			Faculty								Students[2]			Doctorate Recipients[3]					
	93Q	93E	93C	Tot Fac[2]	% Full[2]	% Supp[2]	% Pub[5]	Pub/ Fac[5]	Gini Pub[5]	Cite/ Fac[5]	Gini Cite[5]	Tot Stu	% Fem	Rpt PhDs	% Fem	% Min	% US	% RA	% TA	MYD
University of Rhode Island	1.60	1.43	-0.22	6	83	50	67	3.2	40.7	5.7	35.8	64	20	10	8	25	33	45	0	8.7
Tulane University	1.43	1.37	-0.28	10	40	30	30	0.9	35.8	1.4	54.0	41	12	5	0	0	60	0	25	9.7
University of Alabama	1.41	1.59	-0.23	9	44	11	44	1.1	30.0	0.6	100.0	18	33	13	31	0	62	0	45	9.7
Wayne State University	1.41	1.93	-0.21	10	40	50	90	2.2	14.0	2.2	37.1	32	3	7	0	0	25	40	20	8.4
University of Mississippi	1.22	1.08	-0.23	7	57	14	57	1.0	30.6	0.0		4	0	5	0	0	60	25	25	9.7
Mean Values for the 4th Quarter	**1.89**	**1.87**	**-0.07**	**12.73**	**49.27**	**32.32**	**59.27**	**2.00**	**23.87**	**2.04**	**41.01**	**29.40**	**10.75**	**11.10**	**6.05**	**5.36**	**47.05**	**26.45**	**16.59**	**8.88**
Mean Values for All Programs	**2.85**	**2.85**	**0.09**	**21.45**	**53.15**	**40.06**	**68.52**	**3.54**	**15.61**	**6.39**	**26.35**	**49.01**	**12.00**	**34.32**	**6.98**	**6.06**	**45.88**	**40.88**	**14.69**	**8.22**

Sources: 1. National Survey of Graduate Faculty
2. Institutional Coordinator Response Data
3. Doctorate Records File
4. Federal Agencies
5. Institute for Scientific Information

Appendix Table K - 5 Selected Characteristics of Research-Doctorate Programs in Electrical Engineering

Institution	1993 Ratings[1]			Faculty								Students[2]			Doctorate Recipients[3]					
	93Q	93E	93C	Tot Fac[2]	% Full[2]	% Supp[2]	% Pub[5]	Pub/ Fac[5]	Gini Pub[5]	Cite/ Fac[5]	Gini Cite[5]	Tot Stu	% Fem	Rpt PhDs	% Fem	% Min	% US	% RA	% TA	MYD
Stanford University	4.83	4.68	0.10	45	67	80	93	17.3	5.0	80.1	6.5	357	11	323	4	4	72	66	0	7.4
Massachusetts Inst of Technology	4.79	4.61	0.08	72	75	58	86	10.8	3.7	57.6	6.5	400	19	212	10	3	78	72	0	7.2
U of Illinois at Urbana-Champaign	4.70	4.57	0.29	93	61	73	88	13.8	3.4	44.4	4.2	472	11	266	6	3	71	76	4	6.7
University of California-Berkeley	4.69	4.46	0.12	54	76	69	94	12.6	3.6	48.9	5.6	345	13	204	5	3	52	76	0	6.8
California Institute Technology	4.46	4.34	0.02	15	60	67	87	16.8	23.4	93.5	21.4	74	16	53	8	0	41	65	11	6.1
University of Michigan	4.38	4.17	0.41	64	48	69	95	11.7	4.6	29.5	6.3	388	11	174	3	2	49	55	12	7.5
Cornell University	4.35	4.08	0.24	47	57	79	94	9.1	4.9	33.4	12.4	133	10	132	11	11	64	56	10	6.6
Purdue University	4.02	3.94	0.20	59	44	76	85	9.2	5.2	28.0	10.9	250	7	221	5	9	53	52	17	6.4
Princeton University	4.01	4.00	0.28	21	57	95	95	15.6	10.4	91.1	17.4	114	11	46	13	0	60	67	2	5.8
University of Southern California	4.00	3.71	0.26	39	56	79	87	5.8	4.4	12.1	7.1	1282	14	311	5	2	51	41	6	8.2
Univ of California-Los Angeles	4.00	3.79	0.31	50	66	46	80	8.7	8.1	24.7	18.1	302	13	122	9	3	66	41	9	8.0
Carnegie Mellon University	3.94	4.05	0.36	38	68	68	82	8.2	7.3	15.9	10.1	140	11	156	8	2	63	73	0	6.7
Georgia Institute of Technology	3.93	3.72	0.42	79	42	44	72	4.2	3.5	6.0	6.9	383	9	130	6	7	61	57	7	7.2
University of Texas at Austin	3.88	3.74	0.48	73	70	60	86	9.9	4.0	23.3	5.0	114	9	161	4	12	43	53	8	7.3
Columbia University	3.79	3.75	0.12	21	71	43	95	13.4	13.3	56.0	16.5	95	20	67	9	7	48	73	1	7.4
University of Wisconsin-Madison	3.77	3.62	0.33	49	59	65	96	8.3	3.7	18.8	8.2	161	5	80	2	5	46	59	19	7.5
University of Maryland College Park	3.75	3.59	0.46	60	63	53	88	7.6	4.2	23.3	9.6	236	11	98	8	0	47	51	5	7.5
University of Minnesota	3.73	3.59	0.36	47	49	55	85	5.6	4.3	19.3	10.1	96	9	75	2	2	50	44	24	7.1
Univ of California-Santa Barbara	3.71	3.58	0.65	34	59	56	85	16.0	8.0	70.4	16.9	221	11	77	12	5	54	61	7	7.0
Univ of California-San Diego	3.57	3.37	0.49	39	62	67	87	9.8	5.2	36.5	7.8	141	11	75	7	3	52	69	6	8.2
North Carolina State University	3.54	3.43	0.65	71	58	59	83	8.6	4.0	28.6	8.5	146	10	103	4	5	52	51	8	7.9
Ohio State University	3.53	3.63	0.12	41	51	61	78	4.2	4.8	7.8	6.6	94	6	87	6	0	47	56	12	6.9
Rensselaer Polytechnic Inst	3.44	3.46	0.07	42	57	52	79	5.1	5.0	12.2	12.0	124	8	116	4	2	42	47	14	6.8
Polytechnic University	3.42	3.33	-0.10	36	61	42	42	1.3	10.5	2.3	19.7	79	5	64	5	0	43	33	17	8.6
University of Washington	3.42	3.33	0.38	46	67	63	83	6.1	4.6	16.5	8.2	188	10	71	9	0	52	48	15	8.2
Rice University	3.36	3.45	-0.09	18	39	72	67	5.7	14.6	22.2	25.9	80	20	35	11	4	51	49	2	6.8
Virginia Polytech Inst & State U	3.30	3.41	0.16	38	47	66	79	4.6	5.6	6.4	10.5	93	9	74	5	3	44	53	13	7.0
Pennsylvania State University	3.28	3.31	0.31	48	48	52	71	7.7	11.8	19.4	12.0	258	14	71	5	0	43	49	21	7.7
U of Massachusetts at Amherst	3.28	3.21	0.11	30	40	73	80	6.4	6.2	10.7	9.8	124	6	62	6	3	40	75	3	7.5
Yale University	3.26	3.15	-0.33	15	47	67	93	7.3	22.8	20.4	42.2	54	13	30	14	0	42	69	0	7.3

Appendix Table K - 5 Electrical Engineering (Continued)

Institution	1993 Ratings[1] 93Q	93E	93C	Faculty Tot Fac[2]	% Full[2]	% Supp[2]	% Pub[5]	Pub/ Fac[5]	Gini Pub[5]	Cite/ Fac[5]	Gini Cite[5]	Students[2] Tot Stu	% Fem	Rpt PhDs	Doctorate Recipients[3] % Fem	% Min	% US	% RA	% TA	MYD
University of Florida	3.26	3.22	0.21	38	61	50	84	7.2	5.3	17.6	7.2	99	7	108	5	11	28	59	6	7.7
Texas A&M University	3.25	3.33	0.54	46	35	54	78	5.8	4.9	10.8	9.4	8	0	87	2	0	36	53	21	7.8
Mean Values for the Top Quarter	**3.83**	**3.74**	**0.25**	**45.88**	**56.91**	**62.91**	**83.66**	**8.89**	**7.20**	**30.87**	**11.86**	**220.34**	**10.62**	**121.59**	**6.66**	**3.47**	**51.28**	**57.78**	**8.75**	**7.28**
University of California-Davis	3.24	3.02	0.50	36	58	39	78	4.7	6.0	11.2	15.1	69	9	29	6	0	62	32	28	8.8
Johns Hopkins University	3.23	3.26	0.00	16	50	69	88	5.8	12.1	18.5	18.0	53	17	30	16	0	62	43	26	6.5
Brown University	3.22	3.24	-0.24	13	62	54	77	9.1	33.1	26.2	54.5	54	15	17	6	10	61	50	7	7.4
Arizona State University	3.17	3.09	0.40	36	44	53	81	6.4	9.3	11.5	18.2	109	8	59	4	0	37	54	12	7.8
Washington University	3.17	3.11	0.36	35	60	60	63	3.7	9.1	8.5	28.1	206	8	46	7	0	83	56	11	7.0
University of Colorado	3.17	3.14	0.22	37	46	78	76	6.0	6.9	18.7	10.5	158	23	73	5	2	54	52	6	7.5
Northwestern University	3.16	3.27	0.16	29	55	66	83	7.5	9.2	34.2	20.4	101	15	49	6	0	46	32	19	7.6
University of Arizona	3.12	3.20	0.45	40	32	50	75	4.5	4.7	7.4	6.2	101	5	54	0	5	38	63	4	7.7
University of Pennsylvania	3.11	2.95	0.00	17	53	59	88	8.9	10.7	36.1	16.9	67	9	31	2	0	48	66	6	6.6
Case Western Reserve Univ	3.05	2.86	-0.33	13	38	62	85	6.0	14.2	11.1	20.3	33	9	26	2	12	35	55	21	7.6
University of Utah	3.02	2.80	0.04	25	48	48	68	5.4	8.4	10.2	18.2	38	13	35	6	0	56	63	11	8.4
Michigan State University	3.00	3.16	0.04	24	50	50	79	3.7	10.3	13.2	47.2	52	8	49	3	0	38	49	15	6.7
University of Notre Dame	2.98	2.83	0.17	19	42	68	95	7.4	10.2	16.2	16.9	63	10	28	12	5	50	30	36	6.3
University of Rochester	2.96	3.06	-0.11	22	41	59	77	7.7	8.7	25.0	10.9	61	10	29	21	0	36	61	13	6.3
University of California-Irvine	2.96	3.10	0.30	21	38	67	76	4.8	12.5	8.8	28.3	72	7	63	3	3	48	33	2	8.7
Drexel University	2.90	2.90	0.28	39	41	54	74	4.1	5.0	12.4	32.0	40	20	53	5	6	57	47	16	7.9
Syracuse University	2.86	2.73	-0.38	18	56	6	78	6.4	13.7	12.1	18.3	76	14	62	6	3	29	42	26	7.3
Rutgers State Univ-New Brunswick	2.83	2.84	0.37	36	44	42	75	4.6	6.6	11.8	13.4	91	4	33	5	4	60	33	19	8.4
CUNY - Grad Sch & Univ Center	2.79	2.92	-0.12	29	41	45	76	9.3	16.6	34.4	27.1	83	12	45	2	16	70	17	33	7.8
Iowa State University	2.78	2.68	0.19	40	42	35	58	2.6	9.2	2.6	14.8	54	6	19	6	0	43	53	21	5.9
University of Iowa	2.73	3.00	0.39	20	40	65	85	6.1	8.1	14.0	18.5	41	17	25	3	0	26	48	26	6.1
Duke University	2.71	2.71	0.00	22	41	45	73	5.0	10.5	16.5	17.3	52	15	31	17	0	66	47	9	6.9
University of Virginia	2.71	2.78	0.13	20	40	65	85	5.1	10.7	10.6	19.4	145	16	36	11	3	79	63	7	6.9
Northeastern University	2.70	2.76	0.34	41	39	39	68	4.3	14.8	9.3	15.9	73	14	38	14	0	24	45	25	7.7
University of Rhode Island	2.66	2.57	-0.05	13	54	69	100	3.7	11.3	4.0	17.7	109	13	28	6	9	37	35	25	8.8

Institution	1993 Ratings[1] 93Q	93E	93C	Faculty Tot Fac[2]	% Full[2]	% Supp[2]	% Pub[5]	Pub/ Fac[5]	Gini Pub[5]	Cite/ Fac[5]	Gini Cite[5]	Students[2] Tot Stu	% Fem	Rpt PhDs	Doctorate Recipients[3] % Fem	% Min	% US	% RA	% TA	MYD
State U of New York-Stony Brook	2.63	2.85	-0.18	20	35	30	65	2.0	12.1	3.6	16.7	128	9	25	3	0	21	10	80	6.5
Auburn University	2.61	2.60	0.22	24	33	46	88	5.9	7.4	9.4	27.7	34	6	20	0	13	62	29	46	8.0
State Univ of New York-Buffalo	2.60	2.81	0.00	26	35	50	88	8.7	11.1	50.6	34.9	58	17	57	5	3	47	65	24	7.3
Colorado State University	2.60	2.35	0.13	19	53	53	63	6.3	15.0	22.7	18.8	17	12	31	4	4	58	49	9	9.6
Mean Values for the 2nd Quarter	**2.92**	**2.92**	**0.11**	**25.86**	**45.21**	**52.62**	**78.10**	**5.71**	**10.95**	**16.23**	**21.46**	**77.17**	**11.76**	**38.66**	**6.41**	**3.38**	**49.41**	**45.59**	**20.10**	**7.45**
Oregon State University	2.59	2.62	0.25	13	54	77	77	6.2	14.6	10.6	23.7	29	3	36	5	14	21	35	35	7.7
University of Texas at Arlington	2.59	2.47	0.45	30	53	40	67	3.4	6.9	5.4	14.7	98	3	44	5	6	31	40	19	7.8
University of Pittsburgh	2.59	2.69	0.00	19	37	26	79	3.3	9.8	5.2	28.1	165	8	36	6	0	18	20	54	7.5
University of Illinois at Chicago	2.58	2.61	0.19	27	41	41	70	4.5	8.2	11.4	17.3	173	17	39	12	0	60	39	17	8.6
University of Tennessee-Knoxville	2.57	2.64	0.10	27	78	26	67	2.6	7.4	2.5	10.1	35	3	32	3	10	57	31	14	9.0
Lehigh University	2.54	2.74	0.18	18	50	44	67	2.8	21.1	5.3	36.6	31	42	26	3	0	50	46	19	7.8
Naval Postgraduate School	2.53	2.22	0.05	29	31	3	66	1.7	7.7	0.7	19.5	5	20	7	0	0	89	0	0	6.6
Texas Tech University	2.47	2.59	0.04	24	50	17	58	2.9	14.6	3.3	17.5	22	9	23	7	6	55	56	22	5.8
George Washington University	2.46	2.50	-0.09	20	70	25	70	2.5	11.2	1.6	19.3	96	10	39	4	8	50	2	10	10.7
Vanderbilt University	2.46	2.50	0.05	24	67	63	71	3.3	9.0	4.6	18.4	83	10	27	0	7	48	37	22	7.4
University of Kansas	2.45	2.20	0.00	17	47	35	65	3.3	16.2	4.1	17.7	14	21	18	0	0	48	56	6	7.8
Clemson University	2.44	2.40	0.39	31	55	35	48	3.3	16.7	2.1	18.8	36	6	26	13	12	53	46	21	7.5
Clarkson University	2.41	2.47	0.30	16	44	50	88	4.8	13.9	6.4	19.3	49	16	30	0	33	11	8	38	7.9
New Mexico State University	2.41	2.50	0.25	22	50	32	50	1.4	15.2	1.2	38.8	42	7	22	3	4	87	11	7	8.3
Southern Methodist University	2.40	2.40	-0.16	17	53	35	82	2.2	9.2	2.9	24.4	76	13	71	2	0	45	17	9	9.3
University of Central Florida	2.39	2.47	0.79	37	22	24	70	4.3	10.8	6.9	17.1	100	6	10	0	25	80	43	0	7.6
University of Delaware	2.37	2.43	0.00	15	53	27	53	1.5	17.5	2.1	37.1	27	11	25	6	14	71	24	28	7.1
University of Connecticut	2.37	2.27	0.09	19	63	58	79	5.8	10.6	12.4	32.7	63	13	17	7	0	44	45	32	7.8
Washington State University	2.32	2.62	0.47	41	39	32	49	2.3	9.5	2.9	25.5	81	5	18	5	0	32	20	33	8.8
University of Missouri-Rolla	2.32	2.26	0.00	19	68	16	47	1.3	18.0	1.2	62.5	19	5	20	0	0	63	11	33	9.0
Boston University	2.29	1.88	0.04	36	28	39	81	3.6	5.6	10.4	14.3	n/a	n/a	7	0	0	58	75	0	6.9
University of Missouri-Columbia	2.29	2.54	0.00	26	42	27	50	2.3	10.7	2.2	17.8	78	6	33	10	7	36	33	20	8.2
Illinois Institute of Technology	2.23	2.38	-0.35	14	29	0	79	5.7	20.4	5.9	27.8	64	5	38	2	22	37	33	36	7.3

Appendix Table K - 5 Electrical Engineering (Continued)

Institution	1993 Ratings[1] 93Q	93E	93C	Faculty Tot Fac[2]	% Full[2]	% Supp[2]	% Pub[5]	Pub/ Fac[5]	Gini Pub[5]	Cite/ Fac[5]	Gini Cite[5]	Students[2] Tot Stu	% Fem	Rpt PhDs	Doctorate Recipients[3] % Fem	% Min	% US	% RA	% TA	MYD
Ohio University	2.22	2.22	0.15	22	50	14	45	0.9	12.4	0.3	50.0	24	4	17	5	0	37	20	33	8.7
Air Force Inst of Technology	2.21	1.93	0.15	34	24	0	38	1.4	12.9	1.7	24.0	20	5	15	0	0	100	0	0	7.0
University of Cincinnati	2.16	2.31	0.22	13	85	46	77	6.2	17.0	13.1	29.6	73	8	36	10	11	46	57	14	6.8
West Virginia University	2.15	1.81	-0.12	16	44	50	88	3.4	11.3	6.6	46.6	23	13	20	4	0	26	50	33	6.6
Wayne State University	2.14	2.18	0.17	26	35	42	65	2.9	9.7	4.3	16.1	40	8	12	9	0	39	28	28	9.3
University of Houston	2.14	2.10	0.05	28	46	32	82	3.9	8.0	5.2	10.1	58	16	19	14	8	57	42	8	9.1
Worcester Polytechnic Inst	2.12	2.38	-0.05	22	41	36	82	3.8	10.9	4.2	19.7	5	0	23	20	0	47	27	40	7.8
Brigham Young University	2.10	2.55	0.20	21	33	24	33	0.5	18.0	0.2	62.5	1	0	119	0	0	90	29	14	5.8
Stevens Inst of Technology	2.09	1.87	-0.09	14	43	21	71	1.5	16.5	1.4	22.4	28	11	15	0	0	40	0	59	7.7
University of Oklahoma	2.06	2.38	-0.14	17	47	29	59	3.1	14.6	2.2	34.4	25	12	21	4	0	44	25	10	10.6
Mean Values for the 3rd Quarter	**2.35**	**2.37**	**0.11**	**22.85**	**47.64**	**32.30**	**65.85**	**3.11**	**12.61**	**4.56**	**26.50**	**52.59**	**9.88**	**28.52**	**4.82**	**5.67**	**50.61**	**30.48**	**21.64**	**7.93**
University of Alabama-Huntsville	2.03	2.07	0.22	17	53	53	76	3.4	12.3	4.2	40.1	53	9	18	10	0	40	20	27	9.7
University of Wisconsin-Milwaukee	2.00	2.16	0.20	21	14	29	71	2.7	9.6	3.2	12.1	61	11	25	11	0	11	0	80	7.8
University of Kentucky	1.85	1.83	0.00	21	29	24	67	2.7	10.1	1.7	12.9	24	21	18	0	0	37	60	30	8.6
Univ of Southwestern Louisiana	1.81	1.41	0.15	23	35	39	70	2.4	7.9	1.1	19.0	30	3	9	0	0	20	29	43	6.3
University of Miami	1.77	1.60	-0.07	14	57	14	57	2.2	21.1	2.9	31.8	27	11	12	0	29	50	20	20	6.7
Louisiana State U & A&M College	1.75	1.84	0.00	23	26	43	96	4.3	7.0	3.4	10.2	57	9	15	5	14	40	26	42	7.7
University of South Florida	1.72	1.91	0.31	13	85	38	46	0.9	25.0	0.8	42.0	52	4	15	15	0	65	36	21	6.4
Mississippi State University	1.67	1.57	0.00	21	43	29	29	0.6	24.2	0.1	50.0	28	11	19	0	6	59	19	24	7.9
New Jersey Inst of Technology	1.66	1.60	-0.06	14	100	21	43	1.1	26.5	1.5	36.9	48	25	11	0	0	18	25	63	6.9
Oklahoma State University	1.63	1.54	0.00	10	70	20	50	1.6	25.0	1.2	38.8	245	7	18	0	5	70	30	20	6.6
University of Alabama	1.59	1.77	0.00	15	47	20	40	0.9	23.4	0.3	68.0	62	8	7	0	0	50	38	38	7.6
University of South Carolina	1.58	1.74	0.00	20	40	30	60	2.3	15.3	2.4	73.8	35	11	17	4	0	35	32	47	6.4
Kansas State University	1.58	1.67	-0.11	20	50	5	60	2.2	11.8	3.1	25.2	22	0	5	0	0	63	33	17	6.6
Florida Institute of Technology	1.56	2.16	0.11	16	38	13	38	0.6	20.0	0.3	37.5	36	14	19	9	0	59	0	32	10.0
Univ of Arkansas-Fayetteville	1.56	1.49	0.10	16	44	25	50	3.3	23.0	3.3	26.4	14	7	12	17	0	50	33	17	8.3
University of Toledo	1.55	1.25	-0.20	19	32	37	63	2.3	10.9	2.3	25.3	32	9	21	10	0	10	0	83	7.0
University of Dayton	1.52	1.23	-0.19	9	33	0	44	5.4	77.5	14.0	98.4	28	4	16	4	12	74	15	10	13.4

Institution	1993 Ratings[1]			Faculty								Students[2]			Doctorate Recipients[3]					
	93Q	93E	93C	Tot Fac[2]	% Full[2]	% Supp[2]	% Pub[5]	Pub/ Fac[5]	Gini Pub[5]	Cite/ Fac[5]	Gini Cite[5]	Tot Stu	% Fem	Rpt PhDs	% Fem	% Min	% US	% RA	% TA	MYD
Howard University	1.43	1.48	0.13	9	56	67	67	2.9	27.5	2.7	43.7	53	17	10	7	80	77	38	0	10.1
Old Dominion University	1.41	1.58	0.00	18	17	33	50	2.8	17.0	6.8	20.5	70	11	8	0	0	44	57	14	9.3
University of Akron	1.40	1.17	0.06	17	24	18	65	4.1	18.5	14.1	46.7	96	17	11	0	14	58	10	40	9.6
Oregon Graduate Inst Sci & Tech	1.39	1.39	0.00	10	40	40	90	5.9	16.5	14.7	25.8	21	19	11	0	0	27	100	0	6.4
University of Wyoming	1.38	0.95	-0.10	10	60	20	60	2.6	20.4	2.1	26.9	7	14	9	0	0	50	10	60	6.9
University of New Hampshire	1.31	0.83	0.00	16	56	19	56	1.3	13.5	5.1	32.1	4	0	4	0	0	100	50	50	6.0
Florida Atlantic University	1.25	1.11	0.36	7	29	29	86	3.3	29.3	0.6	50.0	26	12	11	6	33	75	29	14	9.0
Wichita State University	1.24	0.83	0.00	14	57	0	50	1.3	18.5	0.5	26.5	23	4	7	8	0	50	0	60	6.7
Portland State University	1.19	1.23	0.22	12	33	42	42	3.0	34.1	5.0	70.4	31	6	5	0	0	75	33	67	13.0
State Univ of New York-Binghamton	1.16	1.03	0.00	13	38	8	38	1.0	30.1	1.4	63.5	43	9	8	0	0	43	0	33	10.4
University of Mass-Lowell	1.15	1.02	0.22	17	53	12	65	3.1	14.5	2.3	19.7	46	11	4	25	0	0	0	67	8.7
University of Vermont	1.05	1.31	-0.27	7	29	43	100	6.3	18.9	13.7	31.2	16	6	9	0	0	89	0	29	11.7
University of Idaho	1.00	1.39	0.14	14	36	0	36	0.7	40.0	1.1	41.3	14	14	13	8	0	75	10	10	10.7
Tennessee Technological Univ	0.94	0.91	-0.27	7	71	71	86	3.7	21.3	2.6	31.4	19	21	13	6	0	63	54	31	7.7
Tulane University	0.84	0.50	-0.23	8	25	0	25	0.5	50.0	0.1	100.0	27	7	4	14	33	43	17	17	5.6
Mean Values for the 4th Quarter	**1.47**	**1.42**	**0.02**	**14.72**	**44.38**	**26.31**	**58.63**	**2.54**	**22.52**	**3.71**	**39.94**	**42.19**	**10.38**	**12.00**	**4.97**	**7.06**	**50.63**	**25.75**	**34.56**	**8.30**
Mean Values for All Programs	**2.63**	**2.60**	**0.12**	**27.33**	**48.60**	**43.23**	**71.36**	**5.03**	**13.37**	**13.71**	**25.03**	**98.58**	**10.63**	**50.29**	**5.69**	**4.94**	**50.51**	**39.69**	**21.29**	**7.75**

Sources: 1. National Survey of Graduate Faculty
2. Institutional Coordinator Response Data
3. Doctorate Records File
4. Federal Agencies
5. Institute for Scientific Information

Appendix Table K - 6 Selected Characteristics of Research-Doctorate Programs in Industrial Engineering

Institution	1993 Ratings[1] 93Q	93E	93C	Faculty Tot Fac[2]	% Full[2]	% Supp[2]	% Pub[5]	Pub/ Fac[5]	Gini Pub[5]	Cite/ Fac[5]	Gini Cite[5]	Students[2] Tot Stu	% Fem	Rpt PhDs	Doctorate Recipients[3] % Fem	% Min	% US	% RA	% TA	MYD
Georgia Institute of Technology	4.71	4.30	0.66	46	35	70	70	3.6	4.6	3.7	9.5	121	28	49	13	4	48	55	15	8.5
University of California-Berkeley	4.44	4.31	0.08	15	87	67	80	6.4	16.1	18.2	23.7	47	19	46	6	0	13	31	0	6.8
Purdue University	4.43	4.07	0.18	31	55	52	74	4.4	7.0	3.5	12.8	66	18	54	13	6	55	53	18	7.5
University of Michigan	4.36	4.19	0.19	22	59	36	95	6.9	9.3	9.2	21.7	84	20	56	17	9	49	32	5	7.9
Texas A&M University	3.81	3.44	0.73	31	52	23	71	3.2	8.0	2.5	10.5	91	14	46	20	9	54	32	12	8.9
Northwestern University	3.73	3.62	0.17	27	63	52	78	4.9	8.5	24.7	28.3	18	39	45	12	11	36	22	22	10.8
Stanford University	3.68	3.60	-0.08	9	78	22	78	6.2	25.0	22.3	39.8	29	28	21	16	0	58	18	35	8.6
Virginia Polytech Inst & State U	3.66	3.68	0.21	24	63	29	71	2.8	12.3	1.6	16.7	70	14	67	21	3	58	46	19	6.4
Pennsylvania State University	3.50	3.52	0.42	22	27	64	82	3.8	7.4	3.1	16.6	135	15	34	4	0	29	31	31	7.6
Mean Values for the Top Quarter	**4.04**	**3.86**	**0.28**	**25.22**	**57.67**	**46.11**	**77.67**	**4.69**	**10.91**	**9.87**	**19.96**	**73.44**	**21.67**	**46.44**	**13.56**	**4.67**	**44.44**	**35.56**	**17.44**	**8.11**
University of Wisconsin-Madison	3.48	3.48	0.37	17	47	47	82	2.6	12.6	6.6	44.5	58	21	25	31	0	45	44	16	6.9
North Carolina State University	3.46	3.36	0.39	21	52	19	81	3.3	9.0	2.6	16.2	36	28	21	17	17	50	50	9	9.3
Ohio State University	3.24	3.33	0.11	21	29	29	86	4.7	10.9	4.4	16.4	51	22	33	8	8	33	52	24	8.2
U of Illinois at Urbana-Champaign	3.13	3.25	0.25	17	53	71	71	6.8	26.9	26.8	59.2	26	12	2	0	0	100	0	100	7.0
Rensselaer Polytechnic Inst	3.12	3.02	0.30	36	42	33	75	3.1	5.9	2.9	11.0	39	10	12	0	0	0	100	0	5.0
Lehigh University	3.03	3.18	0.33	14	43	36	50	1.0	18.3	0.3	100.0	23	30	18	0	40	23	38	19	8.7
Oklahoma State University	2.99	2.78	-0.03	10	70	0	60	1.2	25.0	0.5	52.0	112	15	17	10	10	50	39	28	7.8
Arizona State University	2.97	3.01	0.32	10	50	40	70	2.6	17.1	1.5	28.0	52	21	27	7	10	36	20	15	8.8
State Univ of New York-Buffalo	2.86	3.15	0.22	15	20	33	67	4.8	21.1	4.6	23.8	26	31	12	32	0	42	44	39	7.4
Mean Values for the 2nd Quarter	**3.14**	**3.17**	**0.25**	**17.89**	**45.11**	**34.22**	**71.33**	**3.34**	**16.31**	**5.58**	**39.01**	**47.00**	**21.11**	**18.56**	**11.67**	**9.44**	**42.11**	**43.00**	**27.78**	**7.68**
University of Florida	2.82	2.87	-0.35	7	43	57	86	7.6	22.5	7.3	21.4	22	14	7	9	0	9	33	56	6.8
Auburn University	2.73	2.71	0.15	14	50	7	64	1.7	14.9	0.5	22.4	19	11	22	7	0	29	22	22	7.8
Iowa State University	2.69	2.83	0.19	15	47	27	60	3.1	19.5	4.3	26.3	19	21	24	7	0	14	40	15	7.3
University of Southern California	2.64	2.42	-0.32	8	50	38	50	1.5	37.5	1.3	100.0	24	13	8	19	10	63	23	31	8.3
University of Pittsburgh	2.61	2.67	0.20	14	50	57	57	1.9	21.2	1.2	35.6	36	28	18	20	14	40	12	59	7.6
University of Iowa	2.49	2.49	-0.04	8	50	25	63	4.3	30.7	5.4	49.0	34	15	18	13	0	31	8	46	6.6

Institution	1993 Ratings[1]			Faculty								Students[2]			Doctorate Recipients[3]					
	93Q	93E	93C	Tot Fac[2]	% Full[2]	% Supp[2]	% Pub[5]	Pub/ Fac[5]	Gini Pub[5]	Cite/ Fac[5]	Gini Cite[5]	Tot Stu	% Fem	Rpt PhDs	% Fem	% Min	% US	% RA	% TA	MYD
U of Massachusetts at Amherst	2.42	2.46	-0.31	7	57	57	57	4.0	33.6	3.4	30.9	24	17	15	8	14	58	9	27	8.6
University of Oklahoma	2.37	2.47	-0.13	8	38	75	88	8.5	22.8	4.3	29.2	15	13	18	5	20	25	7	20	9.0
Univ of Arkansas-Fayetteville	2.33	2.15	0.07	9	56	44	89	2.1	18.0	0.4	37.5	14	21	5	0	33	50	0	40	7.1
Mean Values for the 3rd Quarter	**2.57**	**2.56**	**-0.06**	**10.00**	**49.00**	**43.00**	**68.22**	**3.86**	**24.52**	**3.12**	**39.14**	**23.00**	**17.00**	**15.00**	**9.78**	**10.11**	**35.44**	**17.11**	**35.11**	**7.68**
University of Nebraska-Lincoln	2.28	2.14	0.11	10	70	20	80	2.7	21.5	2.2	58.2	11	9	13	20	0	80	0	30	9.1
Kansas State University	2.27	2.07	-0.06	9	44	22	44	3.4	53.7	0.6	100.0	13	8	10	31	0	54	50	8	8.4
Northeastern University	2.17	2.28	-0.07	16	38	19	56	1.6	22.1	4.6	92.1	26	31	1	0	0	50	0	50	8.5
Wayne State University	2.08	2.00	-0.11	9	56	33	78	2.1	27.9	1.4	36.0	36	11	6	0	0	50	50	25	7.5
Clemson University	2.08	2.20	0.11	9	44	33	44	2.3	36.0	0.3	55.5	9	22	12	15	0	54	8	33	8.4
University of Missouri-Columbia	1.78	1.72	-0.28	7	29	29	57	2.7	31.8	0.6	50.0	17	0	9	18	0	45	0	43	10.4
University of Wisconsin-Milwaukee	1.77	1.44	0.00	8	38	0	38	2.1	45.3	2.5	51.5	n/a	n/a	n/a	0	0	25	0	25	12.0
University of Alabama-Huntsville	1.71	1.52	0.04	12	17	17	33	0.9	45.4	0.1	100.0	38	21	16	0	0	50	0	75	9.6
University of Houston	1.61	1.83	-0.14	9	22	11	44	1.0	33.3	0.0		69	9	11	0	0	70	13	0	10.0
Oregon State University	1.28	1.56	-0.39	3	0	67	100	10.3	38.3	0.0		31	26	9	10	0	56	0	40	10.8
Mean Values for the 4th Quarter	**1.90**	**1.88**	**-0.08**	**9.20**	**35.80**	**25.10**	**57.40**	**2.91**	**35.53**	**1.23**	**67.91**	**27.78**	**15.22**	**9.67**	**9.40**	**0.00**	**53.40**	**12.10**	**32.90**	**9.47**
Mean Values for All Programs	**2.88**	**2.84**	**0.09**	**15.41**	**46.59**	**36.78**	**68.35**	**3.68**	**22.19**	**4.85**	**40.75**	**42.81**	**18.75**	**22.42**	**11.05**	**5.89**	**44.11**	**26.54**	**28.43**	**8.27**

Sources: 1. National Survey of Graduate Faculty
2. Institutional Coordinator Response Data
3. Doctorate Records File
4. Federal Agencies
5. Institute for Scientific Information

Appendix Table K - 7 Selected Characteristics of Research-Doctorate Programs in Materials Science

Institution	1993 Ratings[1]			Faculty								Students[2]			Doctorate Recipients[3]					
	93Q	93E	93C	Tot Fac[2]	% Full[2]	% Supp[2]	% Pub[5]	Pub/ Fac[5]	Gini Pub[5]	Cite/ Fac[5]	Gini Cite[5]	Tot Stu	% Fem	Rpt PhDs	% Fem	% Min	% US	% RA	% TA	MYD
Massachusetts Inst of Technology	4.61	4.22	-0.19	36	64	69	92	12.1	5.3	48.5	7.1	125	28	181	19	4	60	82	0	6.8
Northwestern University	4.47	4.08	0.35	35	80	89	94	26.7	4.6	100.3	7.8	124	21	87	17	2	63	77	1	6.9
Cornell University	4.35	4.10	0.04	26	77	85	96	18.1	5.5	83.5	7.4	82	26	73	18	6	74	75	0	6.9
University of California-Berkeley	4.33	4.08	-0.16	25	80	56	96	19.9	7.2	116.2	11.1	95	25	97	16	4	56	68	5	7.5
U of Illinois at Urbana-Champaign	4.29	3.93	0.15	44	64	61	89	12.8	4.9	48.5	8.4	117	16	95	7	0	60	72	0	7.1
Stanford University	4.24	4.00	-0.18	8	75	75	100	17.0	16.8	67.4	19.4	114	22	80	20	1	68	73	1	8.2
U of Massachusetts at Amherst	4.20	4.21	0.00	15	87	80	100	40.5	9.8	154.4	10.9	82	32	74	0	0	50	100	0	6.0
Univ of California-Santa Barbara	4.18	3.65	0.88	27	78	81	100	29.7	6.7	188.3	10.5	71	17	19	9	6	78	86	9	6.4
Pennsylvania State University	3.97	3.83	0.27	85	67	60	82	15.6	2.9	62.4	4.0	168	18	124	12	6	58	72	2	7.7
University of Pennsylvania	3.79	3.62	0.16	20	60	85	95	16.1	8.6	78.7	17.7	62	27	35	22	6	63	75	0	6.8
Carnegie Mellon University	3.75	3.72	-0.10	18	50	78	78	9.5	12.0	21.9	14.6	24	21	44	0	0	53	67	0	7.8
California Institute Technology	3.75	3.44	-0.09	8	50	88	100	34.6	16.6	167.4	20.2	17	24	3	0	25	80	100	0	6.4
Rensselaer Polytechnic Inst	3.68	3.65	0.00	21	76	62	90	10.1	7.9	19.3	8.7	47	30	42	18	6	61	71	2	6.8
University of Wisconsin-Madison	3.66	3.33	0.35	50	52	80	96	13.3	3.6	62.9	7.1	76	22	35	13*	3*	72*	85*	5*	7.3*
University of Michigan	3.66	3.47	0.46	21	67	71	86	9.3	9.7	36.0	15.2	67	43	37	10	0	54	76	0	8.4
University of Florida	3.65	3.36	0.48	27	63	44	96	9.0	6.4	23.9	9.1	95	11	36	17	0	35	85	0	8.8
Mean Values for the Top Quarter	**4.04**	**3.79**	**0.15**	**29.13**	**68.13**	**72.75**	**93.13**	**18.39**	**8.03**	**79.98**	**11.20**	**85.38**	**23.94**	**66.38**	**12.38**	**4.31**	**61.56**	**79.00**	**1.56**	**7.24**
University of Minnesota	3.64	3.53	0.52	26	65	85	96	24.5	7.6	144.3	13.3	79	13	30	13	0	43	90	3	6.8
Case Western Reserve Univ	3.56	3.56	-0.13	10	40	40	80	11.4	23.8	22.6	52.5	46	15	54	15	0	34	51	2	7.7
University of Wisconsin-Madison [a]	3.52	3.22	0.31	14	50	86	100	17.9	12.6	116.1	20.8	31	6	23	13*	3*	72*	85*	5*	7.3*
University of Texas at Austin	3.50	3.19	0.62	38	76	68	97	19.0	5.9	81.0	8.3	36	8	35	9	13	26	70	20	7.2
Ohio State University	3.48	3.36	-0.21	26	58	54	69	5.5	9.6	10.2	13.0	83	10	48	0	0	0	100	0	7.0
University of Virginia	3.44	3.36	0.30	20	80	65	95	11.1	11.1	43.7	23.6	72	17	22	9	0	89	81	0	7.1
Lehigh University	3.44	3.45	0.15	19	84	79	89	12.1	7.3	32.0	10.0	53	21	32	4	0	44	70	0	7.0
North Carolina State University	3.44	3.27	0.31	17	88	82	100	27.9	8.4	134.5	12.6	93	23	55	10	4	40	77	2	8.0
Rutgers State Univ-New Brunswick [b]	3.36	3.15	0.39	20	65	35	90	6.1	10.8	22.4	27.5	57	11	37	14*	0*	45*	43*	7*	8.3*
Univ of California-Los Angeles	3.34	3.23	0.00	22	77	73	95	21.5	8.6	102.9	11.8	93	16	33	6	0	41	76	0	8.8
Arizona State University [c]	3.27	2.64	0.34	36	64	67	86	14.7	6.3	54.2	8.8	24	0	2	0*	0*	17*	70*	0*	6.2*

Institution	1993 Ratings[1] 93Q	93E	93C	Faculty Tot Fac[2]	% Full[2]	% Supp[2]	% Pub[5]	Pub/ Fac[5]	Gini Pub[5]	Cite/ Fac[5]	Gini Cite[5]	Students[2] Tot Stu	% Fem	Rpt PhDs	Doctorate Recipients[3] % Fem	% Min	% US	% RA	% TA	MYD
University of Arizona	3.25	3.08	0.70	16	69	63	88	7.4	12.5	14.3	16.0	77	21	12	20	0	71	33	42	5.8
Columbia University	3.20	3.19	-0.49	13	85	54	85	6.7	26.3	23.1	22.1	12	0	15	8	0	50	83	0	7.6
Brown University	3.18	3.05	-0.15	6	33	67	83	10.7	42.1	69.8	57.1	23	30	14	15	17	46	78	0	7.2
University of Akron	3.14	2.92	0.00	9	78	56	100	24.3	16.1	60.3	20.0	48	8	31	0	0	0	0	0	
Purdue University	3.05	2.91	0.00	8	63	63	88	11.5	56.1	65.3	86.4	10	0	24	17	0	42	83	6	8.3
Mean Values for the 2nd Quarter	**3.36**	**3.19**	**0.17**	**18.75**	**67.19**	**64.81**	**90.06**	**14.52**	**16.57**	**62.29**	**25.24**	**52.31**	**12.42**	**29.19**	**9.56**	**2.31**	**41.25**	**68.13**	**5.44**	**7.35**
Johns Hopkins University	3.02	2.96	-0.11	12	58	67	92	7.8	15.4	18.6	22.0	66	30	33	16	0	90	35	0	7.9
Vanderbilt University	2.98	2.47	0.06	21	48	52	86	6.2	8.5	9.8	9.8	25	24	13	6	11	56	73	0	8.3
Arizona State University [d]	2.97	2.78	0.40	14	57	64	86	11.1	16.0	25.3	28.9	16	13	16	0*	0*	17*	70*	0*	6.2*
University of Utah	2.94	3.03	0.05	10	60	70	80	20.0	21.9	111.1	37.7	81	5	36	0	0	35	81	0	7.9
University of Rochester	2.94	3.02	0.00	9	56	78	89	11.3	18.1	30.7	24.3	19	11	13	12	0	53	57	0	7.4
Virginia Polytech Inst & State U	2.92	2.93	0.26	13	54	31	77	6.2	15.5	13.8	21.1	53	15	48	10	0	50	83	0	8.7
Drexel University	2.91	2.81	0.07	11	64	36	73	8.8	15.4	26.1	24.4	55	24	22	9	13	44	69	0	6.0
Rutgers State Univ-New Brunswick [d]	2.91	2.85	0.34	11	55	82	100	8.6	11.5	16.5	21.1	47	17	19	14*	0*	45*	43*	7*	8.3*
State U of New York-Stony Brook	2.90	2.96	-0.29	11	64	64	82	9.6	17.1	26.4	28.1	47	23	25	12	0	38	67	13	7.6
University of Washington	2.88	2.99	0.00	13	54	54	77	5.5	21.2	89.1	71.0	35	20	33	8	0	57	54	0	8.4
University of Mass-Lowell	2.88	3.24	0.23	12	92	0	67	1.8	29.3	1.7	73.5	35	14	94	n/a	n/a	n/a	n/a	n/a	n/a
Georgia Institute of Technology	2.87	2.96	-0.03	15	40	47	73	3.9	15.0	6.5	19.8	34	15	23	0	0	50	100	0	6.9
University of Pittsburgh	2.80	2.61	0.03	13	62	69	100	6.8	12.0	20.5	24.2	20	20	2	25	33	38	100	0	9.1
University of Missouri-Rolla	2.80	2.97	0.06	15	73	33	73	6.1	17.5	9.9	22.1	22	9	25	n/a	n/a	n/a	n/a	n/a	n/a
University of Delaware	2.77	2.73	0.00	11	64	45	100	10.6	17.7	23.6	26.0	16	19	16	17	0	56	54	8	6.6
University of Southern California	2.73	2.94	-0.31	12	75	67	100	15.5	14.9	54.4	18.3	41	10	20	4	13	33	71	10	8.3
Mean Values for the 3rd Quarter	**2.89**	**2.89**	**0.05**	**12.69**	**61.00**	**53.69**	**84.69**	**8.74**	**16.69**	**30.25**	**29.52**	**38.25**	**16.81**	**27.38**	**9.50**	**5.00**	**47.29**	**68.36**	**2.71**	**7.69**
Colorado School of Mines	2.64	2.59	0.06	18	67	44	56	6.0	19.9	28.0	32.8	22	14	5	20	0	50	67	0	7.1
Michigan State University	2.58	2.80	0.36	23	30	35	74	4.1	9.0	5.5	12.3	18	0	15	6	0	31	33	33	7.6
University of Maryland College Park	2.43	2.03	-0.14	8	50	63	100	7.5	18.3	15.1	29.6	42	17	0	8	0	83	45	0	9.6

Appendix Table K - 7 Materials Science (Continued)

Institution	1993 Ratings[1] 93Q	93E	93C	Faculty Tot Fac[2]	% Full[2]	% Supp[2]	% Pub[5]	Pub/ Fac[5]	Gini Pub[5]	Cite/ Fac[5]	Gini Cite[5]	Students[2] Tot Stu	% Fem	Rpt PhDs	Doctorate Recipients[3] % Fem	% Min	% US	% RA	% TA	MYD
Stevens Inst of Technology	2.40	2.80	0.39	9	78	67	78	4.0	23.7	5.9	34.6	24	0	24	7	13	31	47	6	8.0
Duke University	2.23	2.63	0.07	6	67	33	83	14.0	29.5	89.3	30.0	10	10	15	10	0	70	43	14	4.7
University of Cincinnati	2.22	2.67	0.00	7	71	71	57	7.6	40.1	23.0	44.1	32	19	17	0	0	38	78	11	6.9
University of Alabama-Birmingham	2.18	2.22	0.50	29	41	55	93	7.4	7.9	27.7	16.6	40	25	5	25	0	50	33	0	8.0
South Dakota Sch of Mines & Tech	2.08	2.59	0.00	13	69	38	23	0.6	40.6	0.8	60.3	12	8	18	0	0	11	23	8	7.3
Illinois Institute of Technology	2.06	1.48	-0.54	7	57	0	86	3.3	26.2	2.3	49.2	26	4	9	20	0	60	67	0	9.8
Oregon Graduate Inst Sci & Tech	2.00	2.00	-0.43	10	30	30	50	2.5	27.3	3.7	27.1	29	21	17	0	0	33	82	0	9.0
University of Houston	1.90	1.11	-0.18	12	58	58	92	5.3	14.6	5.6	22.3	25	16	3	0	0	50	50	0	7.0
University of Notre Dame	1.88	1.84	-0.88	5	40	20	80	8.8	32.7	50.8	61.8	14	0	7	0	0	29	80	20	8.0
University of Alabama-Huntsville	1.85	1.67	0.25	28	57	54	71	5.2	9.4	17.4	12.8	23	26	2	50	0	100	50	0	6.0
University of Kentucky	1.71	1.42	-0.33	7	86	29	86	5.4	19.9	13.0	56.3	12	8	10	0	0	29	75	0	7.7
University of Wisconsin-Milwaukee	1.68	1.37	-0.09	7	71	14	71	8.1	26.8	18.6	39.4	n/a	n/a	n/a	10	0	40	50	13	10.6
Auburn University	1.65	1.80	0.17	9	44	67	56	6.6	28.8	6.4	33.8	92	12	16	8	0	17	70	10	6.7
University of Vermont	1.43	1.46	0.00	21	38	43	81	6.8	13.5	12.5	35.5	11	18	7	43	0	57	40	0	14.7
Mean Values for the 4th Quarter	**2.05**	**2.03**	**-0.05**	**12.88**	**56.12**	**42.41**	**72.76**	**6.07**	**22.84**	**19.15**	**35.21**	**27.00**	**12.38**	**10.63**	**12.18**	**0.76**	**45.82**	**54.88**	**6.76**	**8.16**
Mean Values for All Programs	**3.07**	**2.96**	**0.08**	**18.28**	**63.00**	**58.17**	**84.97**	**11.84**	**16.14**	**47.48**	**25.44**	**50.73**	**16.39**	**33.39**	**10.97**	**3.00**	**48.98**	**67.37**	**4.21**	**7.62**

Sources: 1. National Survey of Graduate Faculty
2. Institutional Coordinator Response Data
3. Doctorate Records File
4. Federal Agencies
5. Institute for Scientific Information

Notes: *a.* Program in Metallurgial Engineering
b. Program in Ceramic Science and Engineering
c. Program in Science and Engineering of Materials
d. Program in Materials Science and Engineering

* The Doctorate Recipient information cannot be separated for the two programs at the same institution and therefore the total for the combined programs is given.

Appendix Table K - 8 Selected Characteristics of Research-Doctorate Programs in Mechanical Engineering

Institution	1993 Ratings[1] 93Q	93E	93C	Faculty Tot Fac[2]	% Full[2]	% Supp[2]	% Pub[5]	Pub/ Fac[5]	Gini Pub[5]	Cite/ Fac[5]	Gini Cite[5]	Students[2] Tot Stu	% Fem	Rpt PhDs	Doctorate Recipients[3] % Fem	% Min	% US	% RA	% TA	MYD
Stanford University	4.77	4.50	0.06	31	61	77	90	10.7	6.5	38.4	8.8	219	11	172	7	2	65	61	3	7.9
Massachusetts Inst of Technology	4.65	4.45	0.03	59	58	69	86	6.8	3.5	15.6	4.8	412	11	213	5	4	59	75	1	7.6
University of California-Berkeley	4.54	4.50	0.15	41	59	73	88	8.5	4.6	14.8	5.5	235	9	189	6	5	50	63	6	6.9
California Institute Technology	4.35	4.30	0.02	18	56	72	83	8.0	11.6	22.7	20.1	41	12	22	8	6	62	45	20	6.6
University of Michigan	4.22	4.00	0.15	48	48	56	83	6.3	4.1	8.8	5.7	175	3	141	2	2	30	37	14	7.8
Princeton University	4.19	4.09	-0.02	22	73	77	100	6.9	7.2	20.0	13.4	93	12	43	6	0	58	73	0	6.9
Cornell University	4.15	3.99	0.10	31	74	58	77	4.9	6.5	19.7	14.7	49	10	61	7	7	44	61	18	6.8
University of Minnesota	4.09	3.85	-0.01	38	63	61	84	7.8	5.4	12.7	6.8	109	8	96	4	4	42	68	11	7.6
U of Illinois at Urbana-Champaign	4.07	4.02	0.37	53	53	51	79	5.2	4.5	7.3	8.1	230	6	86	9	2	61	61	19	7.3
Univ of California-San Diego	4.04	3.59	0.40	39	77	69	74	6.6	5.1	12.6	6.2	34	12	18	0	0	73	50	0	6.6
Purdue University	4.04	4.01	0.27	54	57	48	74	5.9	5.3	7.5	11.2	109	4	101	1	5	76	54	13	7.5
Northwestern University	3.98	3.87	0.25	26	77	62	88	12.0	9.3	26.9	12.6	85	7	60	6	0	34	70	10	6.7
Brown University	3.79	3.80	-0.12	18	78	72	89	9.6	11.6	44.7	15.7	54	19	30	8	0	33	86	0	6.7
Univ of California-Los Angeles	3.76	3.51	0.33	33	79	52	88	9.0	6.5	25.2	10.7	94	6	58	1	5	52	51	7	8.7
University of Texas at Austin	3.73	3.59	0.49	85	69	58	82	7.8	4.5	28.0	11.6	92	3	74	7	8	50	58	12	7.8
Rensselaer Polytechnic Inst	3.69	3.51	0.24	34	41	59	74	4.0	6.6	5.4	10.9	99	4	82	4	5	56	59	5	7.5
Pennsylvania State University	3.68	3.55	0.44	78	49	51	79	6.2	3.8	17.3	12.4	259	4	87	2	2	35	66	9	7.6
Georgia Institute of Technology	3.62	3.54	0.26	57	40	49	72	3.4	4.1	4.1	8.0	172	16	77	3	0	45	55	10	7.8
Carnegie Mellon University	3.59	3.46	0.02	24	54	67	75	5.0	8.3	4.8	17.9	45	11	37	5	3	58	60	9	7.4
Case Western Reserve Univ	3.48	3.41	-0.03	16	69	75	75	2.7	13.5	2.4	17.5	34	12	39	2	0	34	61	5	8.4
University of Wisconsin-Madison	3.48	3.33	0.07	32	50	50	72	3.0	8.4	1.7	10.6	76	5	76	1	0	35	46	13	7.8
University of Pennsylvania	3.40	3.27	-0.02	12	67	75	83	6.6	13.6	12.8	18.5	50	12	33	3	17	49	55	14	8.0
Lehigh University	3.38	3.30	-0.05	35	83	37	66	3.8	7.1	5.9	13.1	109	9	34	10	0	25	43	29	8.9
North Carolina State University	3.33	3.24	0.33	56	55	41	61	4.1	6.8	6.3	9.1	106	4	76	4	0	44	28	33	8.0
Ohio State University	3.32	3.28	0.21	30	60	80	83	6.6	5.9	9.2	8.6	86	2	54	0	4	25	63	19	7.5
University of California-Davis	3.28	3.36	0.53	37	68	35	76	6.1	8.4	6.7	15.8	81	5	65	7	0	60	25	31	8.0
Mean Values for the Top Quarter	**3.87**	**3.74**	**0.17**	**38.73**	**62.23**	**60.54**	**80.04**	**6.44**	**7.03**	**14.67**	**11.47**	**121.08**	**8.35**	**77.85**	**4.54**	**3.12**	**48.27**	**56.69**	**11.96**	**7.55**

Appendix Table K - 8 Mechanical Engineering (Continued)

Institution	1993 Ratings[1] 93Q	93E	93C	Faculty Tot Fac[2]	% Full[2]	% Supp[2]	% Pub[5]	Pub/ Fac[5]	Gini Pub[5]	Cite/ Fac[5]	Gini Cite[5]	Students[2] Tot Stu	% Fem	Rpt PhDs	Doctorate Recipients[3] % Fem	% Min	% US	% RA	% TA	MYD
Rice University	3.22	3.16	0.14	15	67	53	80	6.3	15.6	7.5	22.1	75	12	30	7	0	46	48	0	8.9
Texas A&M University	3.22	3.25	0.57	54	39	41	72	4.3	4.2	3.8	8.5	111	4	70	4	0	55	54	15	7.3
Columbia University	3.18	3.07	-0.25	10	60	70	80	5.7	23.1	17.3	45.5	34	3	18	0	14	54	48	14	7.2
Virginia Polytech Inst & State U	3.18	3.18	0.13	24	63	67	79	4.7	11.1	5.7	17.6	51	6	41	4	4	55	66	8	6.9
Rutgers State Univ-New Brunswick	3.16	3.21	0.38	24	50	42	75	5.5	8.9	8.4	13.2	41	15	52	8	0	36	28	32	7.7
University of Washington	3.13	3.22	-0.03	22	68	64	82	5.4	11.1	9.0	16.3	71	4	27	0	3	72	60	9	8.4
University of Maryland College Park	3.11	3.10	0.31	58	41	48	79	4.1	3.2	19.0	64.8	86	8	46	3	0	47	45	18	7.8
University of Arizona	3.11	3.11	0.06	26	58	58	85	3.6	6.9	6.5	16.1	42	7	53	4	17	37	59	12	7.3
University of California-Irvine	3.11	3.01	0.55	22	32	68	86	7.7	10.5	14.2	15.0	59	14	21	10	0	60	44	6	8.4
University of Notre Dame	3.08	3.06	0.10	24	46	58	67	3.0	9.5	3.1	16.8	24	8	8	20	0	30	56	44	6.4
University of Houston	3.08	3.10	-0.03	24	63	38	75	2.2	9.6	2.4	20.2	67	15	28	3	9	30	41	31	8.6
Arizona State University	3.08	2.98	0.25	20	70	90	85	5.2	8.7	7.8	15.0	52	8	33	3	0	39	69	10	8.3
Univ of California-Santa Barbara	3.07	3.16	0.46	22	59	64	86	10.9	16.4	63.9	49.0	86	12	31	0	0	58	42	19	7.9
State Univ of New York-Buffalo	3.07	3.19	0.09	25	60	48	80	6.2	8.5	5.7	12.2	77	6	49	2	4	49	42	18	6.3
University of Virginia	3.07	3.04	0.13	22	45	36	77	3.4	9.0	2.1	26.9	132	0	25	8	0	96	52	4	10.2
Duke University	3.06	3.17	0.29	13	46	62	85	7.8	18.2	12.3	20.6	40	13	13	17	0	57	47	6	5.7
Michigan State University	3.02	3.12	0.22	23	52	52	87	5.7	17.1	9.2	27.6	29	7	38	10	0	34	43	19	8.0
Illinois Institute of Technology	2.98	3.04	-0.20	18	67	22	78	2.1	9.4	4.4	28.2	23	4	27	12	0	32	16	42	9.3
University of Illinois at Chicago	2.97	3.03	0.22	29	28	34	59	5.4	7.2	5.8	11.9	74	8	68	7	0	35	41	21	7.4
Iowa State University	2.96	3.08	0.12	16	50	44	94	3.9	13.5	2.2	14.7	54	6	39	1	0	40	49	28	7.4
Johns Hopkins University	2.94	2.79	0.00	6	33	83	83	15.5	34.0	61.3	52.3	34	9	14	7	0	60	83	0	6.6
University of Delaware	2.94	3.24	0.15	17	41	47	82	5.1	18.0	10.1	23.4	78	9	43	4	5	45	41	15	6.0
Washington State University	2.92	2.96	0.43	34	56	47	74	6.6	7.0	10.2	10.0	57	7	23	6	8	44	24	52	7.4
University of Missouri-Rolla	2.88	2.76	0.17	30	67	53	77	4.5	8.0	6.3	17.2	57	4	17	0	0	20	26	48	7.9
University of Colorado	2.86	2.72	0.27	17	53	59	82	5.5	21.0	12.3	44.8	38	3	23	5	0	19	33	0	8.8
University of Florida	2.83	3.11	0.23	12	50	58	92	3.6	16.7	2.1	37.2	33	3	43	2	6	41	59	13	7.4
State U of New York-Stony Brook	2.82	2.89	-0.20	19	58	53	79	7.2	10.8	29.2	28.5	51	8	31	3	0	23	53	42	7.8
University of Iowa	2.82	2.85	0.00	15	60	53	87	6.8	11.3	6.4	15.1	46	11	67	2	5	20	73	12	8.2

Institution	1993 Ratings[1] 93Q	93E	93C	Faculty Tot Fac[2]	% Full[2]	% Supp[2]	% Pub[5]	Pub/ Fac[5]	Gini Pub[5]	Cite/ Fac[5]	Gini Cite[5]	Students[2] Tot Stu	% Fem	Rpt PhDs	Doctorate Recipients[3] % Fem	% Min	% US	% RA	% TA	MYD
Washington University	2.78	2.80	-0.10	14	71	64	79	5.1	11.7	9.4	16.4	33	3	17	0	0	63	47	0	9.0
Mean Values for the 2nd Quarter	**3.02**	**3.05**	**0.15**	**22.59**	**53.55**	**54.34**	**80.21**	**5.62**	**12.42**	**12.33**	**24.38**	**57.07**	**7.48**	**34.31**	**5.24**	**2.59**	**44.72**	**47.90**	**18.55**	**7.74**
CUNY - Grad Sch & Univ Center	2.76	2.73	0.19	16	63	75	69	4.8	15.5	10.1	27.8	27	19	10	0	0	36	55	18	7.4
University of Southern California	2.73	2.63	-0.36	11	36	64	82	6.7	13.3	14.8	22.6	21	14	13	7	0	45	40	20	8.5
University of Rochester	2.72	2.47	0.16	20	55	65	85	7.7	9.6	25.6	11.7	34	12	17	6	0	29	65	0	9.2
University of Cincinnati	2.71	2.91	0.22	19	89	42	58	3.2	13.8	2.5	23.2	82	9	66	4	0	45	42	27	7.6
U of Massachusetts at Amherst	2.70	2.61	0.04	20	50	60	75	5.0	14.8	5.9	23.1	44	0	26	9	0	38	75	4	7.4
University of Utah	2.70	2.70	0.33	23	39	39	74	3.8	10.8	6.7	13.2	68	9	27	11	0	55	48	9	9.0
University of Rhode Island	2.59	2.50	0.00	16	69	25	63	2.8	19.2	2.5	34.5	55	11	21	4	7	56	47	5	7.8
Clemson University	2.54	2.57	0.25	24	50	50	71	3.2	12.0	2.7	12.3	33	9	15	0	0	37	29	57	6.5
George Washington University	2.52	2.78	-0.05	16	75	50	38	1.5	20.4	1.3	47.3	45	4	23	0	7	70	0	0	11.6
Colorado State University	2.51	2.73	0.10	24	67	33	50	2.6	17.2	4.8	23.8	33	9	23	9	4	72	38	4	7.7
University of Oklahoma	2.43	2.76	0.06	15	47	27	53	3.1	22.0	4.6	31.4	30	13	21	9	33	13	17	28	7.4
Michigan Technological University	2.40	2.61	0.40	40	38	33	65	1.9	17.9	3.6	56.1	29	7	21	7	0	48	35	29	7.4
Clarkson University	2.39	2.50	0.19	19	26	58	63	5.9	22.0	12.4	26.2	66	12	27	0	0	25	21	58	7.9
University of Pittsburgh	2.36	2.63	0.04	14	36	36	57	4.7	25.5	6.0	22.5	42	17	21	4	0	32	30	35	7.2
Old Dominion University	2.35	2.53	0.31	22	41	55	82	3.0	9.4	1.7	23.5	117	11	39	2	6	44	67	7	8.7
University of Kentucky	2.33	2.38	-0.07	19	42	37	74	4.7	11.4	6.4	19.0	32	0	16	0	0	29	76	14	7.3
University of Connecticut	2.32	2.07	0.00	18	33	22	67	2.0	13.8	2.1	30.8	46	9	20	0	0	70	24	33	8.9
Vanderbilt University	2.31	2.53	0.26	12	42	42	83	2.9	18.2	2.3	50.2	46	13	12	8	13	62	70	30	6.9
Auburn University	2.29	2.48	0.24	18	22	50	78	2.3	10.3	1.1	21.8	32	0	13	7	33	21	50	13	7.8
Wayne State University	2.29	2.52	0.10	24	46	50	75	2.6	8.1	3.1	29.7	64	13	19	0	11	41	12	6	9.9
Kansas State University	2.29	2.06	-0.28	16	63	25	50	1.2	23.5	1.3	33.0	13	23	16	6	0	20	53	7	8.6
University of Tennessee-Knoxville	2.23	2.38	0.04	22	73	18	55	1.2	11.6	1.5	20.4	34	6	18	0	14	50	31	31	9.2
Oklahoma State University	2.21	2.37	-0.28	13	100	38	77	2.5	18.3	2.8	24.5	181	2	33	6	0	38	42	16	9.4
University of Toledo	2.17	1.92	-0.10	16	50	44	69	3.1	29.1	2.6	42.6	26	12	17	0	0	50	43	43	10.2
University of Kansas	2.16	2.54	0.00	14	50	7	43	2.4	28.2	2.0	54.0	14	0	9	0	0	58	20	10	6.6

Appendix Table K - 8 Mechanical Engineering (Continued)

Institution	1993 Ratings[1] 93Q	93E	93C	Faculty Tot Fac[2]	% Full[2]	% Supp[2]	% Pub[5]	Pub/ Fac[5]	Gini Pub[5]	Cite/ Fac[5]	Gini Cite[5]	Students[2] Tot Stu	% Fem	Rpt PhDs	Doctorate Recipients[3] % Fem	% Min	% US	% RA	% TA	MYD
Worcester Polytechnic Inst	2.14	2.43	0.28	28	36	18	43	1.5	10.9	1.9	64.4	12	25	16	14	0	36	63	13	8.3
Oregon State University	2.14	2.47	0.00	8	50	38	88	2.6	21.0	1.4	35.5	27	15	39	2	0	38	26	45	8.5
Mean Values for the 3rd Quarter	**2.42**	**2.51**	**0.08**	**18.78**	**51.41**	**40.78**	**66.19**	**3.29**	**16.59**	**4.95**	**30.56**	**46.41**	**10.15**	**22.15**	**4.26**	**4.74**	**42.89**	**41.44**	**20.81**	**8.26**
University of Texas at Arlington	2.12	2.19	0.20	19	47	16	58	2.3	13.9	2.5	15.2	50	12	21	0	0	35	19	38	8.8
University of Missouri-Columbia	2.12	2.07	0.13	22	41	36	55	2.1	30.6	4.0	40.0	40	8	16	0	0	38	26	47	8.8
West Virginia University	2.10	1.93	0.19	34	47	26	82	2.4	6.9	2.4	20.3	35	6	18	5	0	60	67	17	7.4
University of Akron	2.08	1.95	-0.05	19	42	32	74	6.8	14.4	2.9	28.2	125	10	9	6	0	69	31	31	9.4
University of Wisconsin-Milwaukee	2.06	2.61	0.20	13	54	38	62	1.4	17.2	2.4	24.2	n/a	n/a	n/a	0	0	60	11	0	8.0
Tulane University	2.03	1.85	0.00	8	50	38	88	2.3	16.0	2.5	35.0	30	10	6	0	0	80	0	0	8.7
Northeastern University	2.03	1.90	0.17	19	47	5	74	2.2	15.3	3.9	31.3	16	19	7	0	0	50	43	29	8.7
Syracuse University	2.03	1.86	-0.58	16	31	31	75	1.8	9.4	1.0	42.1	21	10	3	0	0	60	33	67	7.5
Catholic University of America	2.00	2.14	-0.08	9	78	33	44	2.8	37.6	2.6	59.5	32	0	18	5	7	67	17	0	12.4
Southern Methodist University	1.98	2.06	-0.25	11	27	27	55	1.0	19.0	1.1	62.5	35	11	20	13	10	63	14	14	10.6
University of South Carolina	1.94	1.91	0.07	17	41	47	47	2.4	17.9	2.4	22.0	18	17	13	6	0	69	18	27	6.3
University of Alabama-Huntsville	1.90	2.08	0.14	24	42	54	58	3.7	14.5	8.4	24.7	56	18	13	6	0	47	58	0	8.2
Tennessee Technological Univ	1.89	1.81	-0.16	9	89	22	67	2.3	28.7	0.7	38.8	27	15	10	0	0	23	56	44	6.6
University of Alabama	1.88	2.00	0.20	12	25	8	42	0.8	22.0	0.3	33.3	8	13	14	3	11	31	21	37	7.7
Stevens Inst of Technology	1.79	1.44	-0.18	14	50	0	43	1.1	30.4	1.1	44.8	24	8	9	9	0	36	45	18	8.7
Louisiana State U & A&M College	1.78	1.67	-0.23	13	46	38	92	8.7	13.2	16.8	19.7	38	8	19	5	0	62	35	20	6.5
New Jersey Inst of Technology	1.77	1.92	0.00	12	100	8	42	0.5	22.2	0.0		34	0	14	0	0	25	43	21	6.9
University of Miami	1.72	2.14	-0.19	9	56	33	78	2.0	23.4	0.9	53.1	14	7	15	11	40	28	11	33	8.6
University of Vermont	1.70	1.67	-0.10	9	44	56	67	1.2	23.9	0.2	50.0	4	25	5	14	0	71	14	0	11.4
University of Nebraska-Lincoln	1.68	1.60	0.18	14	29	14	57	3.7	26.7	11.2	44.0	10	0	6	8	0	42	42	33	9.0
University of Wyoming	1.57	1.95	0.00	11	55	36	45	2.3	41.7	1.4	76.0	5	20	6	13	0	75	0	83	5.4
Wichita State University	1.48	1.39	0.10	11	27	9	45	0.5	20.0	0.0		21	14	5	0	0	44	17	0	7.2
Howard University	1.41	1.44	0.00	8	75	25	50	2.5	36.5	1.5	34.7	27	11	6	0	0	33	67	0	9.8
Polytechnic University	1.36	1.49	-0.36	6	33	50	67	1.0	27.7	0.3	50.0	18	0	6	9	0	55	9	18	9.7

Institution	1993 Ratings[1]			Faculty								Students[2]			Doctorate Recipients[3]					
	93Q	93E	93C	Tot Fac[2]	% Full[2]	% Supp[2]	% Pub[5]	Pub/ Fac[5]	Gini Pub[5]	Cite/ Fac[5]	Gini Cite[5]	Tot Stu	% Fem	Rpt PhDs	% Fem	% Min	% US	% RA	% TA	MYD
Florida Institute of Technology	1.35	1.14	0.22	10	40	30	40	2.2	56.6	7.5	100.0	5	20	6	0	0	43	20	0	9.8
Montana State University	1.24	0.97	0.00	9	44	44	33	0.9	40.6	0.6	100.0	2	0	4	0	0	67	60	40	7.8
University of Tulsa	0.83	0.59	-0.28	9	22	11	67	1.6	23.4	0.0		7	0	2	0	0	100	0	0	5.0
University of Detroit Mercy	0.76	0.51	0.00	7	57	0	0	0.0		0.0		8	0	9	0	0	67	0	0	10.8
Mean Values for the 4th Quarter	**1.74**	**1.72**	**-0.02**	**13.36**	**47.82**	**27.39**	**57.39**	**2.23**	**24.06**	**2.81**	**43.73**	**26.30**	**9.70**	**10.37**	**4.04**	**2.43**	**53.57**	**27.75**	**22.04**	**8.42**
Mean Values for All Programs	**2.75**	**2.74**	**0.09**	**23.12**	**53.62**	**45.62**	**70.92**	**4.38**	**15.05**	**8.65**	**27.17**	**62.07**	**8.90**	**35.75**	**4.53**	**3.20**	**47.36**	**43.26**	**18.44**	**7.99**

Sources: 1. National Survey of Graduate Faculty
2. Institutional Coordinator Response Data
3. Doctorate Records File
4. Federal Agencies
5. Institute for Scientific Information

APPENDIX L

Selected Characteristics of Research-Doctorate Programs in the Physical Sciences and Mathematics

In the tables that follow, information from the National Survey of Graduate Faculty is linked to a variety of statistics depicting participating doctoral programs. The tables have been designed to present information about each program in a field in rank order by the average rating of the scholarly quality of program faculty (93Q), with the top-rated institutions appearing at the beginning of the list. A key to the variables in the table is presented below.

Institution

Institution: U.S. universities participating in the 1993 NRC Study, ranked in descending order based on the scholarly rating of the program faculty (93Q).

1993 Ratings

93Q: 1993 trimmed mean for scholarly quality of program faculty. The trimmed mean is obtained by dropping the two highest and two lowest scores on the survey before computing the average. For purposes of analysis, scores were converted to a scale of 0 to 5, with 0 denoting "Not sufficient for doctoral education" and 5 denoting "Distinguished." Source: NRC National Survey of Graduate Faculty.

93E: 1993 trimmed mean for program effectiveness in educating research scholars and scientists. The trimmed mean is obtained by dropping the two highest and two lowest scores on the survey before computing the average. For purposes of analysis, scores were converted to a scale of 0 to 5 with 0 denoting "Not Effective" and 5 denoting "Extremely Effective." Source: NRC National Survey of Graduate Faculty.

93C: 1993 trimmed mean for change in program quality in the last five years. The trimmed mean is obtained by dropping the two highest and two lowest scores on the survey before computing the average. For purposes of analysis, scores were converted to a scale of –1 to 1 with –1 denoting "Poorer than 5 years ago" and 1 denoting "Better than 5 years ago." Source: NRC National Survey of Graduate Faculty.

Faculty

Tot Fac: Total number of faculty participating in the program. Source: Institutional Coordinators.

%Full: Percentage of full professors participating in the program. Source: Institutional Coordinators.

%Supp Percentage of program faculty (Tot Fac) with research support (1986-1992). Source: Federal Agencies.

%Pub: Percentage of program faculty (Tot Fac) publishing in the period 1988 to 1992. Source: Institute of Scientific Information.

Pub/Fac: The ratio of the total number of program publications in the period 1988-1992 to the number of program faculty (Tot Fac). Source: Institute of Scientific Information.

Gini Pub: Gini coefficient for program publications, 1988-1992. The Gini coefficient is an indicator of the concentration of publications on a small number of the program faculty during the period 1988-1992. The largest possible value, or maximum concentration, is 100 (only one individual in the program registered a positive count); the smallest value, or minimum concentration, is 100/Fac (All the faculty (Tot Fac) in the program contribute equally). Source: Institute of Scientific Information.

Cite/Fac: The ratio of the total number of program citations in the period 1988-1992 to the number of program faculty (Tot Fac). Source: Institute of Scientific Information.

Gini Cite: Gini coefficient for program citations, 1988-1992. The Gini coefficient is an indicator of the concentration of citations on a small number of the program faculty during the period 1988-1992. The largest possible value, or maximum concentration, is 100 (only one individual in the program registered a positive count); the smallest value, or minimum concentration, is 100/Fac (All the faculty (Tot Fac) in the program contribute equally). Source: Institute of Scientific Information.

Students

Tot Stu:	The number of full and part time graduate students enrolled in the Fall of 1992. Source: Institutional Coordinators.
%Fem:	The percentage of full and part time female graduate students enrolled in the Fall of 1992. Source: Institutional Coordinators.
Rpt PhDs:	The number of Ph.D.s produced by that program for the period academic year 1987-1988 to 1991-1992. Source: Institutional Coordinators.

Doctoral Recipients

%Fem:	The percentage of Ph.D.s awarded to women during the period July 1986-June 1992. Source: Doctorate Records File.
%Min:	The percentage of Ph.D.s known to be awarded to underrepresented minorities (only U.S. Citizens or Permanent Residents) during the period July 1986-June 1992. Source: Doctorate Records File.
%US:	The percentage of Ph.D.s known to be awarded to U.S. Citizens and Permanent Residents during the period July 1986-June 1992. Source: Doctorate Records File.
%RA:	The percentage of Ph.D.s having research assistantships who reported their primary form of support. Source: Doctorate Records File.
%TA:	The percentage of Ph.D.s having teaching assistantships who reported their primary form of support. Source: Doctorate Records File.
MYD:	Median time lapse from entering graduate school to receipt of Ph.D. in years. This is a distributed median with multiple degrees awarded in the median year proportioned over the year. Source: Doctorate Records File.

NOTICE: **n/a** denotes a case where information was not provided by the Institutional Coordinators or was not available from the Doctorate Records File.

Appendix Table L - 1 Selected Characteristics of Research-Doctorate Programs in Astrophysics and Astronomy

Institution	1993 Ratings[1]			Faculty								Students[2]			Doctorate Recipients[3]					
	93Q	93E	93C	Tot Fac[2]	% Full[2]	% Supp[2]	% Pub[5]	Pub/ Fac[5]	Gini Pub[5]	Cite/ Fac[5]	Gini Cite[5]	Tot Stu	% Fem	Rpt PhDs	% Fem	% Min	% US	% RA	% TA	MYD
California Institute Technology	4.91	4.75	0.10	22	73	95	95	19.3	6.3	203.8	9.2	31	23	16	9	0	71	83	10	6.8
Princeton University	4.79	4.38	0.00	16	88	63	88	13.3	10.6	99.8	10.9	56	11	47	5	0	62	75	0	5.7
University of California-Berkeley	4.65	4.53	-0.03	17	82	88	94	16.5	9.0	137.0	9.6	40	18	15	9	0	80	61	8	7.2
Harvard University	4.49	3.92	0.20	20	80	50	90	14.2	9.3	100.1	9.8	32	19	17	6	8	86	50	4	6.4
University of Chicago	4.36	3.85	0.25	27	81	70	85	10.5	7.1	74.4	8.7	33	27	14	8	0	91	50	5	7.3
Univ of California-Santa Cruz	4.31	4.14	0.10	17	82	88	100	11.9	7.5	115.5	16.5	32	31	20	20	5	84	70	13	7.8
University of Arizona	4.10	3.69	-0.09	29	52	72	79	9.7	7.1	64.9	9.6	32	34	24	8	3	85	53	27	6.7
Massachusetts Inst of Technology	4.00	3.68	0.38	18	72	83	100	9.3	8.4	88.3	9.9	46	15	21	29	10	71	75	17	6.5
Mean Values for the Top Quarter	**4.45**	**4.12**	**0.11**	**20.75**	**76.25**	**76.13**	**91.38**	**13.09**	**8.16**	**110.48**	**10.53**	**37.75**	**22.25**	**21.75**	**11.75**	**3.25**	**78.75**	**64.63**	**10.50**	**6.80**
Cornell University	3.98	3.97	0.05	25	80	96	100	15.9	4.8	74.4	5.5	34	18	15	6	4	77	61	21	7.3
University of Texas at Austin	3.65	3.39	0.09	23	65	70	83	11.9	7.5	64.5	9.8	29	7	30	22	0	71	61	27	7.8
University of Hawaii at Manoa	3.60	3.09	0.49	32	50	81	97	7.7	4.8	49.3	7.3	30	27	15	11	8	76	87	0	6.8
University of Colorado	3.54	3.38	0.23	16	75	81	94	12.5	9.2	83.9	11.0	33	30	22	19	0	86	74	3	6.7
U of Illinois at Urbana-Champaign	3.53	3.24	0.08	21	71	100	100	10.3	7.2	54.1	9.9	20	30	15	11	5	81	70	26	7.4
University of Wisconsin-Madison	3.46	3.47	0.25	12	75	58	92	9.3	11.6	55.3	16.7	26	27	14	14	0	86	76	8	6.7
Yale University	3.31	3.31	-0.01	10	60	70	100	10.0	15.4	83.9	20.9	20	25	7	25	0	75	33	0	7.4
Univ of California-Los Angeles	3.27	3.05	0.20	15	87	87	100	14.1	8.8	73.2	11.2	23	13	14	27	6	76	78	17	8.8
Mean Values for the 2rd Quarter	**3.54**	**3.36**	**0.17**	**19.25**	**70.38**	**80.38**	**95.75**	**11.46**	**8.66**	**67.33**	**11.54**	**26.88**	**22.13**	**16.50**	**16.88**	**2.88**	**78.50**	**67.50**	**12.75**	**7.36**
University of Virginia	3.23	3.16	0.28	15	47	60	87	8.8	11.9	45.6	11.9	13	8	10	17	0	92	20	30	7.6
Columbia University	3.20	2.90	0.12	14	50	64	93	8.8	10.0	61.4	18.3	19	37	5	6	11	60	77	15	7.4
University of Maryland College Park	3.07	3.02	0.03	19	63	47	89	9.8	10.7	67.2	14.6	31	29	10	13	0	94	54	15	8.0
U of Massachusetts at Amherst	3.04	3.23	0.17	14	64	57	93	14.3	11.3	133.8	13.9	25	36	19	17	6	83	65	25	8.4
Pennsylvania State University	3.00	2.75	0.73	16	63	50	75	6.4	13.3	23.2	23.9	22	27	10	13	0	81	40	47	6.9
Stanford University	2.96	2.91	0.02	7	71	86	100	12.0	16.2	61.7	18.3	16	6	16	0	0	91	75	0	6.5

Institution	1993 Ratings[1]			Faculty								Students[2]			Doctorate Recipients[3]					
	93Q	93E	93C	Tot Fac[2]	% Full[2]	% Supp[2]	% Pub[5]	Pub/ Fac[5]	Gini Pub[5]	Cite/ Fac[5]	Gini Cite[5]	Tot Stu	% Fem	Rpt PhDs	% Fem	% Min	% US	% RA	% TA	MYD
Ohio State University	2.91	2.76	0.23	18	50	67	83	7.3	9.1	50.6	14.8	18	22	8	10	0	80	50	33	6.7
University of Minnesota	2.89	2.94	-0.05	14	93	93	100	12.9	13.3	81.2	25.0	21	33	10	17	0	82	70	20	7.2
Mean Values for the 3rd Quarter	**3.04**	**2.96**	**0.19**	**14.63**	**62.63**	**65.50**	**90.00**	**10.04**	**11.98**	**65.59**	**17.59**	**20.63**	**24.75**	**11.00**	**11.63**	**2.13**	**82.88**	**56.38**	**23.13**	**7.34**
University of Michigan	2.65	3.00	-0.25	8	63	75	88	7.5	17.8	46.8	31.8	13	54	14	17	7	88	31	46	7.8
State U of New York-Stony Brook	2.58	2.59	-0.28	7	57	86	100	10.1	18.4	85.6	24.9	17	24	0	0	0	55	88	0	6.7
Boston University	2.40	2.56	0.32	19	53	53	84	6.6	9.6	23.8	13.0	26	15	8	40	0	25	100	0	7.7
Indiana University	2.16	2.53	-0.09	7	57	71	100	8.6	21.2	50.6	23.7	20	10	7	8	17	92	13	50	8.1
Louisiana State U & A&M College	2.06	2.02	0.00	9	78	89	89	5.8	15.9	33.3	36.8	12	17	6	17	0	33	50	50	6.7
Iowa State University	2.03	2.07	0.38	7	57	86	100	5.9	19.2	46.7	24.1	5	0	4	25	0	75	50	50	8.5
University of Florida	1.98	1.92	0.00	14	57	79	100	6.9	11.6	26.7	16.3	26	15	11	26	0	79	29	50	8.3
New Mexico State University	1.85	1.82	0.53	8	75	63	100	5.0	21.3	7.4	28.0	23	22	6	11	0	89	67	0	7.7
Georgia State University	1.81	2.10	0.32	6	33	67	67	5.5	28.9	14.0	28.8	14	14	8	14	0	86	43	29	11.3
Mean Values for the 4th Quarter	**2.17**	**2.29**	**0.10**	**9.44**	**58.89**	**74.33**	**92.00**	**6.88**	**18.21**	**37.21**	**25.27**	**17.33**	**19.00**	**7.11**	**17.56**	**2.67**	**69.11**	**52.33**	**30.56**	**8.09**
Mean Values for All Programs	**3.27**	**3.16**	**0.14**	**15.82**	**66.79**	**74.09**	**92.27**	**10.26**	**11.95**	**69.15**	**16.50**	**25.39**	**21.94**	**13.88**	**14.55**	**2.73**	**77.06**	**59.97**	**19.58**	**7.42**

Sources: 1. National Survey of Graduate Faculty
2. Institutional Coordinator Response Data
3. Doctorate Records File
4. Federal Agencies
5. Institute for Scientific Information

Appendix Table L - 2 Selected Characteristics of Research-Doctorate Programs in Chemistry

Institution	1993 Ratings[1] 93Q	93E	93C	Faculty Tot Fac[2]	% Full[2]	% Supp[2]	% Pub[5]	Pub/ Fac[5]	Gini Pub[5]	Cite/ Fac[5]	Gini Cite[5]	Students[2] Tot Stu	% Fem	Rpt PhDs	Doctorate Recipients[3] % Fem	% Min	% US	% RA	% TA	MYD
University of California-Berkeley	4.96	4.72	0.23	45	69	73	91	22.3	3.8	187.0	4.4	298	28	352	21	3	90	80	4	5.7
California Institute Technology	4.94	4.75	0.33	25	80	92	92	18.5	6.7	200.1	9.8	177	24	93	20	1	85	62	8	6.6
Harvard University	4.87	4.57	-0.03	20	70	95	95	32.1	7.9	362.6	10.3	196	16	103	14	1	82	79	6	6.6
Stanford University	4.87	4.57	0.13	21	71	81	81	25.2	9.5	172.8	11.5	233	30	152	20	3	81	77	3	6.6
Massachusetts Inst of Technology	4.86	4.70	0.33	36	78	86	92	18.8	4.2	168.4	5.9	245	28	205	24	1	85	79	1	5.7
Cornell University	4.55	4.40	0.10	33	76	79	88	19.8	6.9	124.2	7.5	197	34	126	18	4	81	65	10	6.3
Columbia University	4.54	4.37	-0.07	17	71	76	88	20.0	12.9	147.3	13.9	98	31	96	23	4	66	77	2	5.8
U of Illinois at Urbana-Champaign	4.48	4.38	0.06	44	66	80	91	15.7	3.5	89.3	4.3	277	26	226	19	1	76	58	21	6.3
University of Wisconsin-Madison	4.46	4.26	0.16	42	69	79	88	10.4	4.1	54.5	5.2	275	26	192	21	3	95	67	19	6.2
University of Chicago	4.46	4.20	0.00	30	73	90	93	17.6	5.6	143.0	7.5	135	27	324	20	8	71	78	3	6.2
Univ of California-Los Angeles	4.46	4.00	0.17	52	67	87	96	16.2	3.2	163.8	4.9	186	34	132	27	4	78	70	15	6.2
Yale University	4.38	4.31	-0.04	22	73	77	91	17.5	8.5	165.5	12.0	149	36	114	25	3	83	72	9	6.1
University of Texas at Austin	4.28	3.81	0.38	50	82	74	94	19.2	5.4	117.7	6.7	197	30	171	19	7	76	57	9	6.4
Northwestern University	4.23	4.20	0.11	32	75	88	91	20.2	5.7	144.9	7.0	146	39	128	24	1	83	52	16	5.6
Texas A&M University	4.11	3.63	0.33	53	74	66	87	19.3	5.6	82.3	5.9	298	26	182	22	10	76	42	24	6.1
Indiana University	3.99	3.74	0.22	35	74	77	97	17.4	6.4	100.9	7.2	192	34	131	17	2	87	64	14	5.8
U of North Carolina-Chapel Hill	3.97	3.93	0.28	37	73	78	84	14.2	5.0	98.0	7.6	236	35	168	33	5	85	64	16	5.7
Univ of California-San Diego	3.95	3.82	0.43	52	77	73	90	12.4	3.2	95.0	4.2	95	43	84	24	3	69	67	11	6.4
Pennsylvania State University	3.95	3.70	0.32	39	59	67	74	10.5	7.6	68.8	11.0	227	37	148	23	3	83	76	11	6.6
Princeton University	3.92	3.83	0.06	21	57	95	100	19.0	9.2	118.0	11.2	115	41	99	27	4	64	69	14	6.3
University of Minnesota	3.89	3.75	0.30	45	71	73	82	14.5	5.4	92.3	7.4	256	32	141	23	2	82	54	23	6.5
Ohio State University	3.87	3.79	0.25	41	61	78	93	16.9	7.7	77.9	8.0	291	27	180	19	4	69	46	32	6.4
Univ of California-San Francisco	3.86	3.91	0.36	38	63	87	95	20.6	4.3	161.8	5.5	83	39	55	47	9	84	52	6	6.8
Purdue University	3.83	3.83	0.09	48	75	60	92	15.2	4.8	93.5	8.0	332	31	226	26	3	77	38	48	6.3
University of Pennsylvania	3.78	3.71	0.13	34	74	74	82	14.2	8.4	113.1	11.2	185	38	106	28	5	83	71	9	6.3
Iowa State University	3.76	3.66	0.30	32	75	72	94	20.5	4.7	106.7	5.8	196	26	167	22	4	58	71	17	6.5
Johns Hopkins University	3.74	3.57	0.07	22	91	73	91	11.0	6.9	60.4	10.9	84	37	51	33	2	79	45	32	7.1
University of Washington	3.70	3.49	0.43	46	61	74	85	12.1	4.0	83.9	5.4	169	30	119	26	3	75	44	32	6.4
Rice University	3.70	3.56	0.37	20	65	95	95	12.6	8.7	110.2	24.2	76	39	65	30	10	79	48	4	6.1
University of Florida	3.67	3.42	0.32	37	65	62	86	22.2	12.0	98.5	15.3	189	26	148	23	8	76	48	30	5.9

Institution	1993 Ratings[1] 93Q	93E	93C	Faculty Tot Fac[2]	% Full[2]	% Supp[2]	% Pub[5]	Pub/ Fac[5]	Gini Pub[5]	Cite/ Fac[5]	Gini Cite[5]	Students[2] Tot Stu	% Fem	Rpt PhDs	Doctorate Recipients[3] % Fem	% Min	% US	% RA	% TA	MYD
University of Utah	3.63	3.58	0.31	25	60	92	80	19.9	7.9	138.8	11.4	169	24	105	20	7	80	66	11	6.3
University of Rochester	3.63	3.54	0.22	23	74	83	87	12.5	8.8	80.7	12.7	116	30	93	31	5	80	69	8	6.5
Univ of California-Santa Barbara	3.57	3.39	0.33	31	74	65	84	15.1	7.1	109.4	10.7	107	33	95	25	4	81	28	48	6.6
University of Pittsburgh	3.56	3.52	0.25	27	48	74	89	15.8	10.4	102.7	16.2	205	35	104	14	3	57	58	30	6.6
University of Michigan	3.53	3.63	0.21	42	71	55	86	11.5	4.8	60.5	7.4	194	26	93	25	6	63	33	35	6.3
University of California-Irvine	3.52	3.39	0.50	25	68	80	92	12.9	6.4	86.5	7.8	119	28	71	13	8	92	63	13	5.8
Colorado State University	3.50	3.50	0.46	28	68	71	79	13.9	7.1	82.4	8.2	141	29	84	23	6	93	62	17	5.9
Emory University	3.37	3.47	0.38	19	84	79	89	15.7	11.2	103.6	10.9	119	40	73	29	11	82	64	0	6.0
Michigan State University	3.35	3.50	0.06	38	71	61	87	13.0	4.1	57.7	8.7	185	26	129	23	9	64	40	49	7.1
University of Southern California	3.34	3.38	-0.03	23	70	87	96	17.7	8.2	92.5	9.8	110	31	89	25	6	64	43	43	7.3
University of Oregon	3.31	3.42	-0.09	26	73	92	100	12.0	5.6	80.8	8.0	101	34	50	20	0	63	72	14	6.0
University of Colorado	3.30	3.22	0.63	12	33	75	83	12.4	17.3	165.2	23.4	n/a	n/a	n/a	28	2	97	75	9	6.1
Mean Values for the Top Quarter	**3.99**	**3.86**	**0.22**	**33.05**	**69.74**	**77.98**	**89.29**	**16.63**	**6.92**	**118.17**	**9.40**	**180.46**	**31.37**	**133.41**	**23.67**	**4.48**	**77.95**	**60.60**	**17.29**	**6.29**
University of Virginia	3.29	3.41	0.13	24	67	67	83	10.8	8.0	73.1	11.7	85	41	68	29	1	96	58	19	6.5
Duke University	3.28	3.43	0.43	20	60	70	95	14.3	11.5	55.5	13.6	96	36	71	28	3	95	43	45	5.4
Brandeis University	3.26	3.33	-0.02	18	83	72	89	12.1	10.6	63.2	15.8	45	47	45	41	2	66	43	33	6.6
State U of New York-Stony Brook	3.25	3.40	0.23	30	70	77	97	14.4	8.4	70.2	7.5	158	32	91	25	11	51	72	21	6.9
University of South Carolina	3.24	3.33	0.26	26	73	73	92	17.8	13.6	78.5	9.5	126	30	116	24	5	83	70	16	5.9
University of California-Davis	3.24	3.43	0.20	34	74	53	91	14.1	7.8	61.0	10.0	139	34	101	31	5	76	30	42	6.6
University of Georgia	3.17	3.13	0.35	26	65	58	88	17.2	13.5	79.3	22.2	95	34	49	13	4	62	25	48	6.3
University of Houston	3.16	3.18	0.30	26	65	42	73	18.6	11.0	94.1	14.2	96	28	63	25	4	39	73	20	6.8
Florida State University	3.11	3.00	0.00	35	66	46	83	8.6	7.5	31.7	7.3	110	25	42	19	3	63	47	36	5.9
Wayne State University	3.08	3.30	0.09	32	66	59	81	9.2	7.3	45.3	9.4	143	30	87	21	10	70	40	26	7.3
University of Maryland College Park	3.08	3.16	0.12	35	66	54	86	8.7	5.7	43.8	8.8	104	37	72	30	2	67	47	29	6.2
Dartmouth College	3.07	3.28	0.02	17	71	59	82	6.6	11.8	30.1	17.9	33	33	24	28	10	100	39	13	6.3
Washington University	3.04	3.29	-0.11	23	65	74	83	9.8	10.6	56.0	12.7	76	37	49	34	7	71	41	34	5.9
Brown University	3.02	3.20	-0.14	18	72	56	94	8.2	9.2	43.2	14.0	70	33	69	41	5	74	59	34	6.1
State Univ of New York-Buffalo	2.99	3.16	-0.08	24	63	71	92	16.0	7.3	81.5	9.3	118	31	83	21	2	70	51	40	6.7

Appendix Table L - 2 Chemistry (Continued)

Institution	1993 Ratings[1] 93Q	93E	93C	Faculty Tot Fac[2]	% Full[2]	% Supp[2]	% Pub[5]	Pub/ Fac[5]	Gini Pub[5]	Cite/ Fac[5]	Gini Cite[5]	Students[2] Tot Stu	% Fem	Rpt PhDs	Doctorate Recipients[3] % Fem	% Min	% US	% RA	% TA	MYD
U of Massachusetts at Amherst	2.98	3.33	0.05	35	77	60	91	17.5	6.4	80.7	7.7	98	39	83	26	3	71	56	24	6.7
Rutgers State Univ-New Brunswick	2.97	2.89	0.28	44	64	61	84	9.5	6.3	45.0	6.4	137	47	85	31	3	58	16	49	8.0
Syracuse University	2.97	3.18	0.19	21	71	67	95	10.2	7.8	48.3	9.8	70	40	51	16	4	80	38	38	7.0
Oregon State University	2.96	3.25	0.02	25	76	60	92	9.2	6.2	29.8	8.2	79	24	53	21	0	55	49	39	8.2
University of Notre Dame	2.94	3.30	0.06	27	63	56	81	11.5	7.9	47.6	10.2	97	41	58	27	4	48	50	30	6.5
University of Illinois at Chicago	2.93	3.18	0.18	27	56	63	74	10.6	6.9	40.6	7.7	81	33	82	42	7	65	20	53	7.7
Georgia Institute of Technology	2.92	3.21	0.18	28	64	61	75	6.7	8.3	29.0	12.7	95	35	57	25	5	79	38	41	6.1
Louisiana State U & A&M College	2.91	3.08	0.10	35	51	60	74	9.3	6.3	29.1	8.1	100	36	80	28	8	51	16	66	6.9
University of Nebraska-Lincoln	2.91	3.04	0.00	26	58	62	88	8.5	12.8	37.4	24.5	114	23	65	18	4	71	54	25	7.0
Virginia Polytech Inst & State U	2.90	3.25	0.22	30	53	37	87	10.4	7.4	34.9	10.5	141	35	84	22	2	75	51	36	5.9
University of Kansas	2.89	3.10	0.13	25	64	56	76	7.2	7.7	29.4	9.6	76	37	29	21	5	67	44	16	6.9
Arizona State University	2.88	3.07	0.09	30	67	73	90	15.4	11.7	85.8	15.2	97	49	62	17	6	78	26	43	6.0
Univ of California-Riverside	2.86	2.95	0.23	27	63	52	89	10.0	9.8	58.6	20.3	61	31	49	25	4	88	69	16	6.5
Case Western Reserve Univ	2.83	3.18	-0.16	16	69	75	94	16.4	11.3	82.4	13.3	77	26	71	16	3	53	57	13	7.2
University of Cincinnati	2.82	2.94	0.02	26	88	54	92	16.0	7.6	72.0	11.1	76	38	119	22	2	72	29	49	6.8
University of Delaware	2.80	3.19	0.15	32	59	56	84	15.3	18.4	69.2	24.1	49	37	72	18	2	82	34	47	6.4
Carnegie Mellon University	2.79	3.00	-0.39	20	45	55	85	7.6	10.8	35.5	14.7	45	31	33	35	3	74	67	19	6.6
Washington State University	2.73	2.66	0.05	34	68	68	82	9.4	7.2	37.9	11.4	48	31	21	23	3	90	44	50	5.8
University of Iowa	2.72	3.09	0.06	25	64	64	84	9.8	8.4	42.2	9.4	104	29	62	28	2	71	48	28	5.8
Kansas State University	2.66	3.04	-0.07	17	76	53	82	10.3	18.3	39.4	14.6	48	29	42	8	0	52	48	43	7.3
New York University	2.65	2.68	0.16	33	39	48	76	7.2	7.4	40.5	15.8	69	28	57	33	8	85	13	47	7.4
University of Tennessee-Knoxville	2.65	2.85	0.14	30	67	60	77	14.8	10.6	66.1	27.0	95	35	59	14	4	88	31	47	6.6
North Carolina State University	2.64	2.79	0.51	27	41	19	89	9.3	11.6	47.0	18.4	56	34	37	24	3	82	33	53	6.8
Brigham Young University	2.64	2.66	0.00	26	77	23	65	14.5	14.8	80.6	13.3	34	24	48	12	0	70	60	17	5.6
Rensselaer Polytechnic Inst	2.55	2.86	-0.07	26	69	73	92	8.2	6.4	23.3	10.6	121	29	57	20	3	76	43	32	6.3
Univ of California-Santa Cruz	2.52	2.81	-0.15	17	65	65	88	9.5	10.3	56.9	15.1	78	28	40	29	7	83	27	42	7.5
Lehigh University	2.48	2.74	0.15	22	64	59	82	7.3	8.8	24.0	10.4	68	44	48	30	6	82	54	2	7.2
Mean Values for the 2nd Quarter	**2.92**	**3.10**	**0.09**	**26.64**	**65.33**	**58.83**	**85.17**	**11.38**	**9.55**	**52.85**	**12.95**	**88.29**	**33.83**	**62.71**	**24.79**	**4.17**	**72.12**	**44.12**	**33.83**	**6.62**

Institution	1993 Ratings[1] 93Q	93E	93C	Faculty Tot Fac[2]	% Full[2]	% Supp[2]	% Pub[5]	Pub/ Fac[5]	Gini Pub[5]	Cite/ Fac[5]	Gini Cite[5]	Students[2] Tot Stu	% Fem	Rpt PhDs	Doctorate Recipients[3] % Fem	% Min	% US	% RA	% TA	MYD
University of Connecticut	2.47	2.68	0.11	22	64	36	100	10.6	7.5	49.1	12.2	95	44	49	22	0	69	34	33	6.5
Vanderbilt University	2.43	2.81	0.00	14	50	57	71	19.0	14.4	73.6	14.3	54	41	31	18	3	67	43	43	6.5
Boston College	2.37	2.60	0.36	16	63	63	94	10.4	10.3	54.8	20.3	62	39	23	32	0	72	53	32	7.4
CUNY - Grad Sch & Univ Center	2.36	2.57	-0.38	51	78	49	65	3.1	5.7	11.8	8.6	128	36	79	29	14	56	14	68	7.8
Boston University	2.36	2.66	0.07	21	57	52	81	5.9	9.8	31.1	11.9	67	28	31	30	0	58	41	50	7.8
Texas Tech University	2.35	2.53	0.21	28	36	36	68	8.6	12.4	31.3	16.4	75	28	36	13	0	52	39	29	6.9
Wesleyan University	2.34	2.64	0.07	16	63	63	63	5.7	14.4	25.4	20.7	35	40	26	36	0	82	19	48	7.8
University of Vermont	2.34	2.53	-0.07	15	53	40	93	8.9	15.7	34.8	20.3	37	30	33	28	7	91	25	67	6.8
University of New Hampshire	2.29	2.32	-0.18	15	53	27	87	5.8	9.7	20.5	12.9	36	33	19	52	5	76	33	44	6.5
Clemson University	2.28	2.46	0.24	18	44	39	83	8.6	10.7	33.2	13.7	48	29	39	8	3	65	32	62	5.8
University of Oklahoma	2.26	2.65	0.18	23	61	74	91	12.1	7.5	37.1	9.7	118	30	47	31	6	62	29	33	6.8
University of Alabama	2.26	2.72	-0.22	16	38	44	75	11.0	17.0	40.7	22.0	45	20	32	15	4	61	35	47	5.5
University of Hawaii at Manoa	2.26	2.45	0.08	20	70	55	80	9.4	9.5	33.4	13.2	38	29	29	11	7	56	37	47	6.9
University of Nevada, Reno	2.23	2.32	0.49	14	57	50	79	8.0	18.5	28.0	24.8	31	29	15	10	0	75	56	22	7.7
University of Kentucky	2.20	2.78	0.07	24	58	33	83	8.6	9.7	29.3	9.2	73	27	32	32	3	62	37	42	6.8
Oklahoma State University	2.19	2.50	-0.13	13	85	62	85	15.6	13.0	61.3	20.7	49	0	38	15	6	65	33	48	6.3
Georgetown University	2.17	2.43	-0.05	15	67	60	93	9.6	11.6	42.7	17.1	61	25	38	20	0	49	33	36	8.0
University of New Orleans	2.17	2.47	0.11	20	70	25	70	8.8	16.9	25.8	19.6	42	43	21	28	6	62	25	46	7.7
Univ of Arkansas-Fayetteville	2.16	2.50	0.03	23	61	57	83	8.6	8.7	36.6	9.5	58	34	31	19	6	80	24	59	5.8
Northeastern University	2.15	2.66	-0.19	17	65	53	82	10.0	13.8	71.1	21.7	46	39	50	24	3	50	19	52	8.2
State Univ of New York-Binghamton	2.15	2.40	-0.30	14	43	50	93	6.1	9.5	15.4	18.4	33	15	33	20	6	72	20	63	8.6
State Univ of New York-Albany	2.13	2.26	-0.36	17	76	53	88	8.5	14.6	41.9	13.6	29	28	26	17	10	51	43	53	8.3
University of Missouri-Columbia	2.13	2.50	0.06	26	46	38	81	5.3	7.6	13.5	9.6	74	24	33	32	6	50	40	43	6.8
Montana State University	2.13	2.65	0.11	14	71	50	86	5.5	13.7	25.3	18.0	44	14	37	13	0	86	35	50	6.6
Polytechnic University	2.11	2.32	-0.37	14	57	71	64	8.5	21.5	30.6	25.0	62	19	46	15	6	60	61	11	7.9
Clarkson University	2.10	2.39	-0.08	16	44	38	94	10.0	13.6	16.8	13.0	52	50	36	20	10	67	42	50	7.7
University of Missouri-Rolla	2.09	1.97	-0.12	25	44	36	56	6.5	19.2	25.7	39.7	56	34	32	21	0	55	40	37	7.0
Texas Christian University	2.07	1.81	-0.08	12	75	67	92	9.1	26.4	19.7	35.5	20	30	14	15	21	70	25	0	5.5

Appendix Table L - 2 Chemistry (Continued)

Institution	1993 Ratings[1] 93Q	93E	93C	Faculty Tot Fac[2]	% Full[2]	% Supp[2]	% Pub[5]	Pub/ Fac[5]	Gini Pub[5]	Cite/ Fac[5]	Gini Cite[5]	Students[2] Tot Stu	% Fem	Rpt PhDs	Doctorate Recipients[3] % Fem	% Min	% US	% RA	% TA	MYD
Miami University	2.06	2.62	0.25	25	40	44	80	5.8	7.9	17.0	12.7	38	32	33	18	0	82	17	40	5.2
University of Texas at Arlington	2.05	2.20	0.04	18	67	28	61	7.5	18.3	38.2	25.4	25	20	27	7	14	50	44	39	6.9
Univ of Missouri-Saint Louis	2.02	2.22	0.05	17	35	47	94	5.9	9.3	17.6	13.5	32	31	25	28	0	63	22	44	6.0
University of Akron	2.02	2.32	0.36	17	71	65	100	6.3	9.0	18.4	12.3	86	35	49	13	1	58	23	48	8.6
University of Wyoming	2.02	2.03	0.26	15	47	40	80	5.7	18.3	29.7	26.3	44	23	24	15	4	78	48	35	7.4
Drexel University	1.99	1.98	-0.04	16	63	56	88	7.1	10.8	29.6	14.8	33	33	19	23	0	67	22	56	6.7
University of Wisconsin-Milwaukee	1.94	2.24	0.00	16	69	38	81	10.3	15.1	33.4	26.7	59	32	32	12	0	63	25	63	8.4
New Mexico State University	1.91	2.12	0.11	17	59	59	76	11.0	24.9	48.9	44.1	49	33	33	21	20	76	23	37	6.8
Tulane University	1.90	2.27	-0.20	16	56	38	75	5.6	11.1	17.1	12.0	44	25	21	21	6	62	13	71	6.7
University of South Florida	1.90	1.77	0.45	15	60	47	93	6.9	11.1	15.5	14.7	52	31	16	14	8	89	8	63	6.0
Auburn University	1.88	1.82	0.08	23	35	39	65	6.3	15.9	20.4	24.2	61	43	20	12	0	47	22	70	9.6
University of North Texas	1.84	1.77	0.22	22	55	14	77	8.8	14.1	26.2	16.8	33	36	22	2	22	45	61	18	6.5
Mean Values for the 3rd Quarter	**2.15**	**2.37**	**0.03**	**18.90**	**57.65**	**47.33**	**81.25**	**8.38**	**13.22**	**31.81**	**18.38**	**53.10**	**30.30**	**31.93**	**20.30**	**5.18**	**65.03**	**32.38**	**44.98**	**7.07**
Southern Illinois University	1.82	2.29	-0.13	16	44	25	81	7.1	20.2	23.4	35.8	25	24	24	24	0	30	56	28	8.8
Univ of Puerto Rico-Rio Piedras	1.82	2.19	0.19	23	39	30	61	4.9	13.5	13.4	21.4	39	33	30	36	93	93	35	12	6.8
University of Alabama-Birmingham	1.82	1.80	0.08	25	36	36	76	8.4	9.9	34.4	16.4	22	18	13	20	22	60	8	8	6.9
Kent State University	1.81	2.28	0.07	19	58	21	95	9.1	12.0	20.2	15.4	27	41	21	29	0	53	7	71	9.4
University of Mass-Lowell	1.80	2.44	0.05	26	58	23	58	5.0	12.9	15.9	17.1	114	35	48	13	6	65	15	56	7.4
University of Idaho	1.80	1.79	-0.03	14	50	64	86	12.1	10.6	27.5	11.6	40	18	19	8	7	54	47	47	8.4
West Virginia University	1.80	1.95	0.00	17	35	59	76	6.9	21.6	31.1	24.0	34	26	18	20	7	63	24	62	7.9
Rutgers State Univ-Newark	1.78	2.08	0.04	19	68	11	84	6.0	11.5	21.0	21.0	50	34	24	30	13	86	0	52	9.7
Northern Illinois University	1.78	2.03	-0.20	24	54	46	83	11.7	20.2	44.0	16.0	27	41	34	22	9	73	13	67	6.8
Oregon Graduate Inst Sci & Tech	1.77	1.58	0.00	8	50	63	100	9.0	22.1	69.5	32.4	13	38	5	11	0	89	86	0	7.8
Temple University	1.73	1.86	-0.37	17	47	29	71	4.5	12.3	19.8	29.5	55	31	23	14	0	69	15	52	8.7
Virginia Commonwealth University	1.69	1.85	0.25	15	40	13	87	4.4	13.6	15.3	26.7	45	33	32	24	7	90	23	30	7.3
Tufts University	1.69	1.58	-0.33	12	33	33	75	3.8	18.7	13.5	28.4	40	48	30	36	4	75	18	59	6.4

Institution	1993 Ratings[1] 93Q	93E	93C	Faculty Tot Fac[2]	% Full[2]	% Supp[2]	% Pub[5]	Pub/ Fac[5]	Gini Pub[5]	Cite/ Fac[5]	Gini Cite[5]	Students[2] Tot Stu	% Fem	Rpt PhDs	Doctorate Recipients[3] % Fem	% Min	% US	% RA	% TA	MYD
University of Miami	1.67	1.67	-0.31	11	55	64	100	12.5	16.5	54.1	17.8	34	35	20	47	45	73	50	23	7.3
University of Rhode Island	1.65	2.29	0.00	16	75	31	94	8.0	12.2	26.2	12.3	40	40	24	34	7	66	16	58	6.9
University of Toledo	1.65	1.40	0.21	17	53	24	71	6.0	14.3	14.8	15.6	38	24	15	10	11	43	18	71	7.8
Baylor University	1.64	1.54	0.00	16	69	6	63	6.3	16.7	17.9	32.3	33	24	14	16	0	47	38	38	7.4
North Dakota State University	1.62	1.48	-0.15	13	46	46	77	4.4	15.9	15.5	27.9	36	14	14	17	4	64	56	25	6.7
University of Maine	1.60	1.72	0.04	12	50	42	75	5.3	15.3	15.7	19.1	13	54	17	17	20	22	13	81	6.8
University of Louisville	1.59	1.97	0.00	18	61	44	89	8.6	13.9	38.9	19.0	76	33	24	22	13	47	5	57	9.3
Loyola University of Chicago	1.56	1.78	-0.06	16	44	31	75	3.8	11.7	7.9	18.2	46	50	26	31	11	69	15	60	8.3
Howard University	1.46	1.60	-0.33	20	60	30	70	4.2	14.1	9.5	16.9	45	38	17	16	85	67	8	54	7.9
Ohio University	1.42	1.62	0.07	17	35	12	71	4.1	24.8	13.3	51.3	33	24	18	19	8	44	11	84	6.7
Seton Hall University	1.41	1.53	-0.20	15	47	13	73	2.7	11.7	5.0	19.6	58	17	27	28	10	83	19	29	8.4
SUNY Col Environ Sci & Forestry	1.35	2.04	-0.87	6	67	50	100	8.8	25.9	34.5	29.5	15	33	12	15	0	62	58	17	8.2
Bryn Mawr College	1.33	1.77	-0.13	5	40	60	60	2.6	36.0	10.8	43.4	15	60	8	50	0	83	0	60	5.8
University of Texas at Dallas	1.32	1.67	-0.10	10	40	40	70	7.5	24.1	28.5	27.6	31	29	11	8	0	75	43	29	6.4
University of North Dakota	1.31	1.88	-0.13	15	47	13	53	1.3	19.1	2.0	24.0	25	24	19	15	0	89	26	48	5.7
Wake Forest University	1.23	1.67	-0.15	13	54	77	77	4.4	19.6	21.8	34.9	25	28	6	0	0	80	20	40	8.7
Univ of Southern Mississippi	1.22	1.11	0.00	18	67	56	89	7.1	16.4	20.6	19.2	39	36	15	15	7	76	40	22	6.4
Stevens Inst of Technology	1.21	1.44	-0.54	8	88	63	75	7.5	23.2	31.4	26.4	1	0	15	22	23	76	7	64	10.9
American University	1.14	1.81	0.00	10	60	20	40	0.9	38.2	3.9	38.4	35	46	22	46	9	85	11	5	11.3
University of Mississippi	1.13	1.09	-0.29	12	50	67	83	5.8	14.8	25.5	18.5	22	32	14	14	17	55	35	29	7.8
Mississippi State University	1.12	1.28	0.60	14	29	21	71	4.8	17.5	12.6	16.4	52	31	16	18	23	59	38	38	8.3
Colorado School of Mines	1.12	0.87	-0.07	16	75	19	69	2.8	18.3	6.2	32.6	18	44	7	20	0	100	38	38	6.6
Univ of Missouri-Kansas City	1.08	1.02	-0.31	12	83	17	83	6.2	22.1	22.0	39.5	8	25	8	30	11	47	7	57	8.7
Catholic University of America	1.08	0.80	-0.42	7	43	43	100	9.3	21.7	31.9	47.9	23	57	11	16	0	50	33	22	9.7
University of Montana	0.98	0.80	-0.35	8	63	63	63	6.6	43.8	31.9	52.5	8	38	9	29	0	43	33	67	7.0
George Washington University	0.93	1.02	0.06	10	60	30	70	4.4	29.4	24.7	28.8	21	52	6	29	17	43	13	13	10.3
Worcester Polytechnic Inst	0.81	0.65	-0.10	12	50	83	75	2.0	16.3	5.2	30.6	14	64	5	50	0	17	0	100	12.0
Wichita State University	0.81	0.93	-0.09	10	60	40	80	4.0	16.1	5.2	21.4	18	33	7	17	0	100	0	33	13.7

Appendix Table L - 2 Chemistry (Continued)

Institution	1993 Ratings[1]			Faculty									Students[2]			Doctorate Recipients[3]					
	93Q	93E	93C	Tot Fac[2]	% Full[2]	% Supp[2]	% Pub[5]	Pub/ Fac[5]	Gini Pub[5]	Cite/ Fac[5]	Gini Cite[5]		Tot Stu	% Fem	Rpt PhDs	% Fem	% Min	% US	% RA	% TA	MYD
Phila Col of Pharmacy & Science	0.50	0.30	0.00	12	33	17	83	3.3	19.2	5.0	27.1		8	25	2	0	0	100	0	33	8.6
University of Detroit Mercy	0.44	0.89	-0.20	9	67	11	33	0.9	40.6	0.8	59.1		4	25	8	7	0	44	50	50	7.8
New Mexico Inst of Mining & Tech	0.37	0.42	-0.25	5	60	20	60	3.0	39.5	7.6	65.7		9	11	5	25	0	100	100	0	8.6
Mean Values for the 4th Quarter	**1.38**	**1.54**	**-0.10**	**14.05**	**53.25**	**36.50**	**75.57**	**5.73**	**19.73**	**20.45**	**27.94**		**31.23**	**33.32**	**16.89**	**22.05**	**11.11**	**66.11**	**26.09**	**42.93**	**8.14**
Mean Values for All Programs	**2.61**	**2.71**	**0.06**	**23.14**	**61.54**	**55.21**	**82.76**	**10.52**	**12.39**	**55.88**	**17.17**		**87.83**	**32.29**	**60.84**	**22.71**	**6.34**	**70.56**	**40.63**	**34.77**	**7.03**

Sources: 1. National Survey of Graduate Faculty
2. Institutional Coordinator Response Data
3. Doctorate Records File
4. Federal Agencies
5. Institute for Scientific Information

Appendix Table L - 3 Selected Characteristics of Research-Doctorate Programs in Computer Sciences

Institution	1993 Ratings[1]			Faculty								Students[2]			Doctorate Recipients[3]					
	93Q	93E	93C	Tot Fac[2]	% Full[2]	% Supp[2]	% Pub[5]	Pub/ Fac[5]	Gini Pub[5]	Cite/ Fac[5]	Gini Cite[5]	Tot Stu	% Fem	Rpt PhDs	% Fem	% Min	% US	% RA	% TA	MYD
Stanford University	4.97	4.60	0.12	31	55	84	90	6.0	6.6	16.4	12.2	133	16	85	15	3	71	53	3	7.5
Massachusetts Inst of Technology	4.91	4.62	0.07	39	67	72	77	3.8	5.1	15.7	10.7	170	18	102	9	0	82	70	4	8.4
University of California-Berkeley	4.88	4.58	0.31	40	75	73	95	5.4	4.3	14.5	11.8	169	14	113	9	6	70	63	6	7.2
Carnegie Mellon University	4.76	4.38	-0.04	42	48	71	83	4.2	5.9	8.4	10.3	163	14	89	10	2	74	68	2	7.9
Cornell University	4.64	4.47	0.23	36	33	92	83	5.2	4.7	12.8	11.1	91	15	68	12	2	66	38	21	6.8
Princeton University	4.31	3.84	0.27	18	44	89	83	7.3	10.2	21.7	20.0	45	29	38	11	0	60	53	13	6.0
University of Texas at Austin	4.18	3.81	0.17	56	46	57	73	3.6	4.5	6.4	8.5	92	5	81	7	0	59	30	19	8.9
U of Illinois at Urbana-Champaign	4.09	3.93	0.12	59	39	61	76	4.6	4.9	11.6	11.8	398	13	151	9	3	67	71	7	7.9
University of Washington	4.04	4.05	0.58	29	45	90	86	4.3	7.1	11.5	12.5	100	20	50	11	2	68	61	8	8.2
University of Wisconsin-Madison	4.00	3.87	0.42	35	43	83	97	5.5	4.0	9.8	10.9	142	13	65	6	4	61	49	27	6.8
Harvard University	3.94	3.47	0.29	17	71	59	76	2.7	16.8	14.2	18.5	46	17	33	16	7	50	77	5	6.8
California Institute Technology	3.93	3.97	0.12	10	50	50	60	1.9	29.0	11.0	62.9	25	20	18	16	0	71	67	0	7.6
Brown University	3.86	3.75	0.39	17	47	88	82	4.3	11.5	3.9	12.3	49	18	26	15	0	82	67	7	7.6
Univ of California-Los Angeles	3.73	3.48	-0.07	47	70	36	79	4.3	5.4	6.7	9.0	145	10	99	8	4	59	30	13	8.2
Yale University	3.73	3.44	-0.26	16	38	94	94	4.6	10.3	15.6	22.0	68	15	44	6	0	70	86	0	7.6
University of Maryland College Park	3.69	3.45	0.22	47	34	70	79	5.3	3.4	9.1	4.9	207	17	54	10	2	46	58	9	8.1
New York University	3.60	3.47	0.15	32	56	81	91	6.6	7.8	25.5	12.4	99	9	68	11	2	52	35	10	7.7
U of Massachusetts at Amherst	3.59	3.36	0.41	30	50	83	90	5.1	6.1	11.3	7.8	139	14	57	16	2	77	64	7	9.0
Rice University	3.55	3.51	0.41	15	33	73	87	4.1	16.7	4.6	14.9	48	21	15	17	0	78	53	0	6.9
University of Southern California	3.52	3.19	0.17	45	44	58	62	3.5	5.7	6.8	9.2	133	13	51	19	0	52	37	23	7.3
University of Michigan	3.49	3.51	0.27	30	47	70	77	4.7	9.2	6.5	11.7	242	16	58	16	3	72	41	24	8.2
Columbia University	3.45	3.36	-0.18	22	27	77	77	4.1	16.6	6.3	17.8	67	9	36	17	4	69	64	0	8.0
Univ of California-San Diego	3.45	3.11	0.60	34	44	59	65	3.3	8.4	7.2	18.4	72	13	20	18	0	81	32	21	8.8
University of Chicago	3.31	2.88	0.33	13	38	77	77	2.7	13.7	6.5	25.0	39	21	4	0	0	25	25	50	4.7
University of Pennsylvania [a]	3.31	3.42	0.20	24	50	75	71	4.4	10.9	22.3	25.1	199	21	57	17*	0*	56*	53*	22*	7.8*
Purdue University	3.28	3.31	-0.13	30	47	83	90	6.3	5.7	7.4	11.8	120	22	45	17	0	46	44	32	7.9
Rutgers State Univ-New Brunswick	3.25	3.05	0.29	46	50	63	76	3.8	4.6	7.2	8.8	125	18	35	25	0	63	20	29	10.0
Mean Values for the Top Quarter	**3.91**	**3.70**	**0.20**	**31.85**	**47.81**	**72.89**	**80.59**	**4.50**	**8.86**	**11.14**	**15.27**	**123.19**	**15.96**	**57.85**	**12.70**	**1.70**	**63.96**	**52.19**	**13.41**	**7.70**

Appendix Table L - 3 Computer Sciences (Continued)

Institution	1993 Ratings[1] 93Q	93E	93C	Faculty Tot Fac[2]	% Full[2]	% Supp[2]	% Pub[5]	Pub/ Fac[5]	Gini Pub[5]	Cite/ Fac[5]	Gini Cite[5]	Students[2] Tot Stu	% Fem	Rpt PhDs	Doctorate Recipients[3] % Fem	% Min	% US	% RA	% TA	MYD
Duke University	3.17	3.08	0.33	19	37	84	89	5.2	11.9	19.5	23.0	48	29	31	10	3	77	62	11	7.3
U of North Carolina-Chapel Hill	3.16	3.40	0.19	18	50	56	44	2.1	18.1	6.9	50.5	118	11	40	10	4	72	59	0	8.0
University of Rochester	3.13	3.51	0.24	13	38	69	92	6.2	13.6	13.2	32.1	41	12	32	15	3	63	69	3	7.6
State U of New York-Stony Brook	3.12	3.10	0.02	23	52	91	78	4.7	7.5	12.0	22.3	120	26	33	3	0	19	74	19	6.6
Georgia Institute of Technology	3.10	3.00	0.50	36	17	47	61	2.1	9.3	2.9	12.0	127	15	41	14	3	76	48	24	7.3
University of Arizona	3.05	2.99	0.40	13	31	77	92	4.8	11.7	34.5	52.5	35	20	17	12	3	78	48	19	7.5
University of California-Irvine	3.03	2.98	0.21	26	50	73	88	3.5	6.3	6.1	13.1	132	22	46	14	7	86	37	11	8.3
University of Virginia	3.02	3.05	0.58	18	33	78	67	2.8	12.8	5.1	16.3	60	13	12	18	0	88	80	0	9.8
Indiana University	3.00	3.17	0.16	24	42	63	54	1.7	10.1	2.3	14.3	66	8	15	24	0	64	24	52	8.8
Johns Hopkins University	2.96	2.96	0.07	10	20	100	90	3.5	20.0	6.6	26.1	38	18	15	17	20	50	75	0	8.0
Northwestern University	2.93	2.92	0.20	22	41	59	59	2.9	13.3	7.9	18.4	99	15	101	9	0	44	15	35	7.4
Ohio State University	2.92	2.94	0.09	35	17	49	74	3.6	6.8	9.1	14.0	106	20	82	9	0	53	44	43	8.0
University of Colorado	2.90	2.93	0.55	25	44	76	80	3.0	8.7	10.8	23.4	164	20	34	21	3	71	30	7	7.9
University of Utah	2.90	3.04	-0.13	16	56	81	75	2.0	12.1	2.0	35.9	57	4	19	5	0	59	48	21	7.6
Oregon Graduate Inst Sci & Tech	2.83	2.80	0.72	17	18	47	47	0.7	18.0	1.6	25.2	47	26	9	0	0	70	75	0	6.6
University of Pittsburgh	2.81	2.72	0.42	21	29	71	71	3.6	11.8	5.6	13.0	54	19	17	24	4	82	30	37	9.6
Syracuse University	2.80	2.91	0.25	40	55	28	78	3.4	5.9	5.7	27.6	71	0	28	24	0	57	18	27	10.3
University of Pennsylvania[b]	2.72	2.88	0.00	24	58	67	83	5.4	7.6	12.5	10.0	39	23	36	17*	0*	56*	53*	22*	7.8*
University of Florida	2.70	2.48	0.63	24	29	54	83	3.0	7.7	4.3	25.1	53	13	25	21	9	46	37	26	8.9
University of Minnesota	2.67	2.87	-0.51	16	50	50	88	4.5	11.2	5.0	16.3	77	14	70	11	2	47	11	50	7.8
Univ of California-Santa Barbara	2.65	2.18	0.32	14	43	100	86	6.5	10.2	14.9	30.3	42	26	4	0	0	13	67	33	9.9
Rensselaer Polytechnic Inst	2.63	2.90	0.31	17	41	76	65	2.8	14.0	2.6	28.8	71	11	23	19	6	56	40	16	7.9
Univ of California-Santa Cruz	2.59	2.24	0.39	14	29	71	86	3.8	12.8	11.7	33.9	44	18	6	9	0	64	20	20	7.7
University of Illinois at Chicago	2.56	2.86	0.57	37	38	57	84	3.8	5.1	4.4	9.4	n/a	n/a	n/a	10	9	37	55	25	7.9
Washington University	2.54	2.53	0.18	17	47	76	65	1.4	12.5	5.1	25.1	31	10	14	13	0	60	40	0	9.0
Michigan State University	2.53	2.74	0.26	22	36	68	68	2.6	11.8	2.8	22.9	79	8	29	4	0	38	25	38	8.9
Mean Values for the 2nd Quarter	**2.86**	**2.89**	**0.27**	**21.58**	**38.50**	**68.00**	**74.88**	**3.45**	**11.18**	**8.27**	**23.90**	**72.76**	**16.04**	**31.16**	**12.81**	**2.92**	**58.69**	**45.54**	**20.73**	**8.17**

Institution	1993 Ratings[1]			Faculty								Students[2]			Doctorate Recipients[3]					
	93Q	93E	93C	Tot Fac[2]	% Full[2]	% Supp[2]	% Pub[5]	Pub/ Fac[5]	Gini Pub[5]	Cite/ Fac[5]	Gini Cite[5]	Tot Stu	% Fem	Rpt PhDs	% Fem	% Min	% US	% RA	% TA	MYD
Pennsylvania State University	2.52	2.59	-0.36	19	21	58	63	3.4	14.9	24.5	69.9	77	18	39	6	0	40	34	44	8.7
CUNY - Grad Sch & Univ Center	2.52	2.33	0.00	56	43	36	32	0.6	8.3	1.1	28.5	149	23	29	21	13	67	19	6	10.8
Dartmouth College	2.45	2.40	0.38	14	29	57	57	1.0	17.3	0.9	37.2	26	23	3	0	0	75	0	0	7.0
Boston University	2.42	2.44	0.25	10	30	80	60	2.5	24.4	2.3	27.0	42	17	14	16	0	68	13	19	9.7
University of California-Davis	2.42	2.58	0.25	27	59	48	59	2.5	10.8	4.0	16.0	41	0	23	24	6	75	35	10	8.3
State Univ of New York-Buffalo	2.42	2.48	0.11	20	25	60	75	2.5	9.7	1.6	23.4	123	15	16	21	0	54	48	24	7.8
North Carolina State University	2.36	1.96	0.31	24	38	58	54	2.2	10.9	1.7	18.5	47	13	2	0	0	60	25	75	6.7
Arizona State University	2.33	2.26	0.30	27	37	30	48	1.2	12.6	0.5	18.3	48	10	31	22	0	61	18	26	8.8
University of Iowa	2.31	2.24	0.11	24	42	42	71	3.3	8.0	4.5	13.1	32	22	16	13	0	48	11	68	8.7
Texas A&M University	2.30	2.30	0.37	24	46	54	88	3.0	7.5	2.1	12.8	110	14	25	31	3	77	22	15	8.8
University of Oregon	2.20	2.01	0.16	13	23	92	85	3.1	14.0	5.3	21.4	22	9	5	0	0	71	33	33	9.9
University of Kentucky	2.12	1.67	0.44	15	47	47	60	2.1	17.1	2.3	29.3	35	14	3	75	0	75	25	25	9.6
Virginia Polytech Inst & State U	2.10	1.67	0.05	16	31	63	100	5.4	13.4	3.5	13.0	31	6	14	0	0	57	30	50	8.2
Case Western Reserve Univ	2.04	2.10	-0.17	11	36	45	91	3.7	13.1	2.4	24.8	31	19	33	22	9	30	16	16	9.2
George Washington University	2.04	2.25	0.13	13	46	46	54	1.1	17.3	0.4	100.0	116	13	30	17	3	69	7	2	10.9
University of South Florida	2.03	1.75	0.47	14	36	50	64	2.6	14.0	1.9	34.3	8	13	8	0	0	63	17	0	8.0
Temple University	2.00	1.45	0.00	18	39	22	39	0.7	23.6	0.2	100.0	36	28	12	33	0	91	0	17	12.8
Oregon State University	2.00	1.57	0.14	6	33	83	67	1.7	42.0	4.3	38.4	47	9	8	8	0	35	25	20	9.7
Univ of Southwestern Louisiana	1.92	2.08	-0.07	23	35	43	74	2.5	7.4	1.1	17.7	60	23	48	14	4	51	18	24	7.0
Vanderbilt University	1.90	1.74	-0.04	10	30	60	80	5.8	43.9	18.0	77.4	42	21	17	22	0	72	12	41	8.3
University of Nebraska-Lincoln	1.89	1.89	0.13	17	47	65	76	4.3	11.7	3.4	27.1	13	23	16	18	0	55	17	56	9.3
University of Houston	1.85	1.54	0.00	18	28	22	50	1.4	17.4	0.5	28.3	70	33	9	6	0	58	10	20	10.8
University of Texas at Dallas	1.84	1.92	0.06	14	29	43	64	3.6	14.3	2.7	22.9	534	23	26	24	0	41	4	61	6.8
Louisiana State U & A&M College	1.81	1.87	0.11	29	66	31	86	5.7	8.3	7.6	16.7	66	21	34	6	0	38	27	57	8.9
Iowa State University	1.81	1.80	0.14	15	13	40	80	4.7	21.7	9.9	58.2	28	7	18	19	0	58	10	55	9.0
New Mexico State University	1.80	1.77	0.25	12	25	58	50	1.0	18.0	0.4	36.0	25	20	18	22	10	59	64	14	8.7
Wayne State University	1.80	1.67	-0.12	14	57	14	86	3.4	15.6	3.6	25.1	369	14	13	9	10	45	14	43	9.9

Appendix Table L - 3 Computer Sciences (Continued)

Institution	1993 Ratings[1] 93Q	93E	93C	Faculty Tot Fac[2]	% Full[2]	% Supp[2]	% Pub[5]	Pub/ Fac[5]	Gini Pub[5]	Cite/ Fac[5]	Gini Cite[5]	Students[2] Tot Stu	% Fem	Rpt PhDs	Doctorate Recipients[3] % Fem	% Min	% US	% RA	% TA	MYD
Washington State University	1.78	1.46	0.13	41	37	32	49	2.3	9.5	2.9	25.5	26	15	14	13	0	60	15	62	9.3
Mean Values for the 3rd Quarter	**2.11**	**1.99**	**0.13**	**19.43**	**36.71**	**49.25**	**66.50**	**2.76**	**15.95**	**4.06**	**34.31**	**80.50**	**16.64**	**18.71**	**16.50**	**2.07**	**59.04**	**20.32**	**31.54**	**8.99**
Kansas State University	1.75	1.58	0.35	11	27	45	73	1.5	20.4	1.4	58.2	54	15	6	24	10	63	0	79	9.6
University of Central Florida	1.71	1.52	0.07	16	38	44	81	4.0	11.0	2.5	29.0	28	21	16	21	10	56	25	17	8.3
Naval Postgraduate School	1.67	1.40	-0.27	7	43	43	57	1.9	28.9	2.1	48.4	13	0	4	0	0	86	0	0	9.7
University of Texas at Arlington	1.65	1.67	0.00	19	21	26	53	1.2	13.6	0.2	55.5	36	11	13	37	0	63	4	38	9.6
University of Kansas	1.62	1.83	-0.26	11	45	27	55	1.2	24.2	4.7	85.5	14	29	10	7	0	64	30	20	11.1
University of Alabama-Huntsville	1.61	1.39	0.25	16	31	13	38	1.2	49.0	5.0	100.0	22	41	21	25	5	79	17	4	11.5
Old Dominion University	1.55	1.48	0.32	15	27	53	67	4.7	29.9	3.7	37.9	28	36	9	20	0	33	20	0	9.4
U of Maryland Baltimore County	1.54	1.53	0.67	15	13	13	60	1.3	15.2	1.0	56.4	126	25	12	14	0	64	9	27	11.6
Southern Methodist University	1.54	1.67	-0.15	8	13	38	50	1.5	31.9	1.4	53.7	57	14	26	11	0	41	44	28	10.5
Illinois Institute of Technology	1.52	1.58	-0.27	11	18	9	73	2.0	33.0	0.7	53.1	182	16	82	17	7	52	6	25	8.8
University of Connecticut	1.47	1.56	0.00	15	27	40	53	2.0	31.7	1.1	40.6	42	33	20	21	7	67	33	24	10.6
University of South Carolina	1.36	1.49	-0.08	12	42	25	75	3.6	19.3	3.3	20.2	29	7	7	10	0	40	0	43	7.9
University of North Texas	1.35	1.04	0.53	17	18	18	65	2.4	17.4	2.1	24.7	39	28	12	27	20	58	14	5	10.6
Florida State University	1.35	0.83	0.00	12	42	17	92	2.3	11.1	0.6	18.3	36	28	26	16	15	63	20	16	7.9
Lehigh University	1.32	1.67	0.00	11	45	36	73	0.8	13.5	0.0		26	19	15	5	0	63	27	20	9.9
University of Mass-Lowell	1.29	1.16	0.00	15	33	20	47	0.6	16.0	0.1	100.0	52	19	6	20	0	60	0	25	10.0
University of Alabama-Birmingham	1.29	0.91	0.06	15	27	27	53	1.1	15.6	1.2	54.3	22	18	6	13	0	75	13	0	10.0
Mississippi State University	1.26	1.28	0.00	16	25	38	31	0.6	40.0	0.1	50.0	18	17	2	29	17	86	0	20	10.0
Kent State University	1.25	0.52	0.00	11	27	18	55	1.2	20.7	0.3	55.5	28	7	4	13	0	38	29	43	9.6
University of Oklahoma	1.17	1.04	-0.11	9	33	44	56	1.2	22.3	0.6	68.0	24	17	10	15	0	31	8	42	8.9
Tulane University	1.14	0.63	0.08	8	25	63	50	0.9	26.5	2.5	53.5	46	20	11	31	0	69	10	40	7.0
Stevens Inst of Technology	1.13	1.23	-0.08	11	45	27	45	1.8	26.5	1.0	70.2	50	16	20	7	8	46	4	46	7.6
Worcester Polytechnic Inst	1.13	0.83	-0.10	12	25	42	58	1.1	18.3	0.3	55.5	14	21	3	0	0	67	0	0	6.8
University of Missouri-Rolla	1.10	1.03	-0.12	10	60	20	40	0.6	33.3	0.5	68.0	18	22	15	11	0	76	13	13	9.4

Institution	1993 Ratings[1] 93Q	93E	93C	Faculty Tot Fac[2]	% Full[2]	% Supp[2]	% Pub[5]	Pub/ Fac[5]	Gini Pub[5]	Cite/ Fac[5]	Gini Cite[5]	Students[2] Tot Stu	% Fem	Rpt PhDs	Doctorate Recipients[3] % Fem	% Min	% US	% RA	% TA	MYD
State Univ of New York-Binghamton	1.10	0.88	-0.44	8	38	25	25	0.3	50.0	0.0		33	21	6	24	0	81	0	32	11.4
New Mexico Inst of Mining & Tech	0.52	0.00	-0.60	5	0	20	20	0.4	100.0	0.0		11	18	2	50	0	50	0	100	18.0
Oklahoma State University	0.21	0.11	-0.27	3	67	67	67	1.0	55.5	0.0		116	0	9	22	0	56	0	50	9.5
Mean Values for the 4th Quarter	**1.32**	**1.18**	**-0.02**	**11.81**	**31.67**	**31.78**	**56.00**	**1.57**	**28.70**	**1.35**	**54.63**	**43.11**	**19.22**	**13.81**	**18.15**	**3.67**	**60.26**	**12.07**	**28.04**	**9.82**
Mean Values for All Programs	**2.54**	**2.43**	**0.14**	**21.15**	**38.66**	**55.31**	**69.42**	**3.06**	**16.22**	**6.17**	**31.26**	**80.03**	**16.98**	**30.26**	**15.07**	**2.58**	**60.49**	**32.30**	**23.53**	**8.68**

Sources: 1. National Survey of Graduate Faculty
2. Institutional Coordinator Response Data
3. Doctorate Records File
4. Federal Agencies
5. Institute for Scientific Information

Notes: *a.* Program in Decision Sciences, Wharton School
b. Program in Computer and Information Science

* The Doctorate Recipient information cannot be separated for two programs at the same institution in the same field and therefore the total for the combined programs is given.

Appendix Table L - 4 Selected Characteristics of Research-Doctorate Programs in Geosciences

Institution	1993 Ratings[1] 93Q	93E	93C	Faculty Tot Fac[2]	% Full[2]	% Supp[2]	% Pub[5]	Pub/ Fac[5]	Gini Pub[5]	Cite/ Fac[5]	Gini Cite[5]	Students[2] Tot Stu	% Fem	Rpt PhDs	Doctorate Recipients[3] % Fem	% Min	% US	% RA	% TA	MYD
California Institute Technology	4.87	4.63	0.05	30	93	93	90	13.9	4.8	99.2	6.0	74	31	62	30	0	77	79	5	7.8
Massachusetts Inst of Technology	4.67	4.52	0.17	41	66	83	88	8.5	3.8	64.2	5.4	161	32	126	26	0	83	69	2	7.1
University of California-Berkeley	4.45	4.09	0.03	17	94	88	94	11.9	9.5	80.5	15.7	35	31	40	23	4	86	58	14	7.8
Columbia University	4.38	4.14	0.09	37	41	86	97	8.4	4.1	79.8	5.6	107	36	70	31	5	78	74	0	8.1
Stanford University [a]	4.33	3.96	0.08	12	50	75	92	9.3	14.2	55.6	20.2	32	16	33	25*	5*	77*	53*	11*	7.6*
Univ of California-San Diego	4.23	4.06	0.16	40	65	80	85	7.1	4.2	36.8	5.7	43	33	34	30	6	80	77	0	7.3
University of Chicago	4.22	4.03	0.16	25	64	80	92	7.6	7.3	43.6	11.4	37	27	28	25	5	78	40	15	8.6
Harvard University	4.20	3.80	-0.32	24	71	67	92	11.3	7.5	90.8	12.6	37	32	36	21	3	83	45	23	6.9
Stanford University	4.15	4.06	-0.09	16	75	88	94	9.7	8.1	70.1	12.8	41	29	44	25*	5*	77*	53*	11*	7.6*
Cornell University	4.15	3.71	0.04	30	70	87	97	11.1	5.6	49.1	5.5	35	17	37	18	5	84	63	14	8.6
Univ of California-Los Angeles	4.11	3.67	0.06	62	79	68	82	9.5	4.8	54.9	5.7	134	28	85	18	4	82	46	24	8.2
Pennsylvania State University	4.11	3.85	0.28	72	61	64	88	6.4	2.4	29.0	5.4	229	21	115	27	2	80	56	11	9.0
Brown University	4.11	3.96	0.03	19	74	89	100	9.3	10.9	71.0	18.1	46	48	40	18	0	88	82	7	7.4
Princeton University	4.01	3.78	-0.25	17	82	76	82	8.2	12.2	48.1	13.5	42	31	61	22	0	67	60	9	7.0
University of Texas at Austin	3.96	3.64	0.33	120	42	43	73	2.9	2.0	9.8	3.5	75	27	55	16	2	80	23	20	9.0
Stanford University [b]	3.96	3.86	-0.14	11	82	45	82	5.9	13.9	23.1	20.3	26	27	22	25*	5*	77*	53*	11*	7.6*
Johns Hopkins University	3.95	3.94	-0.14	13	92	92	92	9.1	15.6	120.2	38.7	32	34	47	26	3	83	45	8	7.6
University of Michigan	3.94	3.89	0.34	29	66	83	97	10.8	6.2	52.1	8.0	74	31	41	22	5	83	67	23	7.9
University of Arizona	3.87	3.62	0.31	33	67	76	94	6.1	5.8	34.0	10.2	130	18	56	26	2	85	36	18	9.9
Univ of California-Santa Barbara	3.70	3.47	0.14	27	67	81	85	5.4	6.9	30.2	10.2	48	33	39	20	0	87	29	27	8.9
Northwestern University	3.63	3.60	-0.07	16	75	81	81	7.4	13.8	42.7	17.0	18	33	21	21	3	91	52	26	6.8
University of Wisconsin-Madison	3.56	3.65	0.37	22	68	64	95	5.6	8.7	26.1	12.7	35	23	41	27	2	91	54	19	7.6
University of Washington	3.55	3.36	0.10	18	72	89	100	4.6	10.4	25.4	13.0	55	25	23	18	0	87	76	14	8.3
Univ of California-Santa Cruz	3.54	3.33	0.40	15	80	87	93	6.3	9.8	39.3	15.8	68	31	35	25	8	83	46	27	8.1
Rice University	3.53	3.46	0.47	17	65	65	94	4.8	9.0	23.2	15.7	55	24	25	23	0	77	26	0	9.9
Mean Values for the Top Quarter	**4.05**	**3.84**	**0.10**	**30.52**	**70.44**	**77.20**	**90.36**	**8.04**	**8.06**	**51.95**	**12.35**	**66.76**	**28.74**	**48.64**	**23.52**	**2.96**	**81.76**	**54.48**	**13.56**	**8.02**
Arizona State University	3.48	3.30	0.48	16	56	88	94	7.5	14.5	37.7	19.6	31	29	17	15	0	100	58	16	7.5
Virginia Polytech Inst & State U	3.47	3.33	0.15	21	86	38	67	4.0	9.1	12.5	10.0	46	22	38	24	0	82	21	46	8.7

Institution	1993 Ratings[1]			Faculty								Students[2]			Doctorate Recipients[3]					
	93Q	93E	93C	Tot Fac[2]	% Full[2]	% Supp[2]	% Pub[5]	Pub/ Fac[5]	Gini Pub[5]	Cite/ Fac[5]	Gini Cite[5]	Tot Stu	% Fem	Rpt PhDs	% Fem	% Min	% US	% RA	% TA	MYD
University of Southern California	3.46	3.33	0.25	18	72	72	89	6.6	9.8	28.2	11.1	70	23	61	22	5	73	41	24	8.6
University of Hawaii at Manoa	3.40	3.38	0.64	42	60	74	83	5.0	4.0	17.5	6.9	48	31	39	26	3	79	78	0	8.7
State U of New York-Stony Brook	3.40	3.30	-0.11	19	68	74	84	6.2	9.2	40.2	16.5	52	31	23	20	0	65	69	0	8.9
University of Minnesota	3.35	3.42	0.19	19	68	84	84	6.6	15.6	33.4	18.6	60	35	26	14	0	91	41	30	8.5
Washington University	3.26	3.37	0.44	17	65	82	76	7.4	10.2	42.1	11.0	28	32	19	30	0	85	58	11	8.3
University of California-Davis	3.25	3.07	0.28	16	38	81	94	5.3	9.7	13.9	13.4	19	21	16	18	0	95	35	41	8.3
U of Illinois at Urbana-Champaign	3.22	3.01	0.00	21	67	76	76	6.2	9.6	32.6	12.2	41	32	19	25	0	86	47	18	7.4
University of Oregon	3.21	3.07	0.42	22	64	64	77	3.6	7.9	16.2	12.4	27	22	10	15	0	77	70	20	7.8
University of Colorado	3.20	3.20	0.12	24	75	83	96	6.4	7.9	64.9	30.7	61	34	56	27	3	89	33	9	10.2
Texas A&M University [a]	3.20	3.18	0.19	13	85	46	85	2.3	11.3	4.8	25.6	30	17	15	7*	5*	80*	35*	28*	8.8*
Colorado School of Mines	3.13	3.12	0.00	52	54	19	52	1.5	7.2	3.2	15.1	80	15	78	14	2	72	29	13	9.6
University of Wyoming	3.12	3.17	0.09	16	81	75	88	5.2	9.6	31.5	15.0	30	20	33	13	0	82	44	16	8.7
Dartmouth College	3.08	3.28	0.15	10	50	40	100	3.9	27.4	20.9	28.9	20	40	10	36	0	93	20	60	6.7
Purdue University	3.08	3.15	0.29	26	54	65	88	5.2	6.2	19.5	10.0	49	14	26	5	0	56	36	29	10.6
Rensselaer Polytechnic Inst	3.03	3.19	0.30	9	67	56	89	7.2	18.9	40.6	37.6	16	31	11	17	0	100	40	20	8.4
Duke University	2.99	2.86	0.42	18	61	72	94	5.2	10.2	24.3	18.8	19	11	10	0	0	75	50	0	9.2
University of Utah	2.97	2.95	0.00	14	71	79	86	5.9	11.5	33.1	15.3	25	12	26	13	4	89	33	10	10.7
Ohio State University	2.97	2.83	0.12	27	41	59	74	3.3	8.4	9.1	12.3	45	24	16	13*	4*	83*	43*	33*	7.9*
Indiana University	2.97	2.97	-0.02	25	52	48	64	3.1	10.6	12.4	19.3	38	11	19	16	5	80	19	24	7.9
U of Massachusetts at Amherst	2.95	3.02	-0.11	17	71	76	100	3.6	8.7	17.2	10.4	15	20	22	17	0	89	28	32	10.7
University of Miami	2.92	3.02	0.00	11	36	82	82	4.5	17.6	13.0	23.8	22	27	14	31	0	92	45	9	8.9
Texas A&M University [c]	2.86	2.94	-0.02	22	41	50	82	2.6	8.7	7.8	15.6	59	15	28	7*	5*	80*	35*	28*	8.8*
Louisiana State U & A&M College	2.83	2.76	0.16	29	62	55	79	4.6	5.8	14.8	10.0	44	25	27	26	0	82	14	36	11.0
Mean Values for the 2nd Quarter	**3.15**	**3.13**	**0.18**	**20.96**	**61.80**	**65.52**	**83.32**	**4.92**	**10.78**	**23.66**	**16.80**	**39.00**	**23.76**	**26.36**	**18.04**	**1.44**	**83.00**	**40.88**	**22.12**	**8.83**
University of Kansas	2.82	2.76	0.03	16	56	63	81	2.8	13.6	10.3	30.4	29	17	10	8	0	77	33	33	8.7
University of Oklahoma	2.77	2.83	0.09	42	45	40	50	1.6	10.5	5.8	18.1	58	28	31	7	0	79	55	9	8.6
U of North Carolina-Chapel Hill	2.75	2.92	0.11	15	53	53	87	4.9	15.1	20.0	30.9	17	12	11	18	0	82	14	36	8.8
University of South Carolina	2.74	2.53	0.08	24	79	67	75	6.4	13.9	18.3	13.7	47	21	52	24	6	73	47	19	7.9

Appendix Table L - 4 Geosciences (Continued)

Institution	1993 Ratings[1] 93Q	93E	93C	Faculty Tot Fac[2]	% Full[2]	% Supp[2]	% Pub[5]	Pub/ Fac[5]	Gini Pub[5]	Cite/ Fac[5]	Gini Cite[5]	Students[2] Tot Stu	% Fem	Rpt PhDs	Doctorate Recipients[3] % Fem	% Min	% US	% RA	% TA	MYD
Southern Methodist University	2.74	3.08	0.02	13	69	54	77	3.2	16.2	11.7	22.6	22	32	11	43	0	93	22	33	11.0
New Mexico Inst of Mining & Tech	2.74	2.72	0.19	16	44	44	81	3.5	14.7	9.2	22.1	22	32	26	20	0	95	33	22	8.4
Saint Louis University	2.73	3.00	0.06	14	50	43	64	2.7	17.5	6.0	23.1	17	18	25	10	0	33	50	6	11.0
Univ of California-Riverside	2.69	2.56	0.14	15	47	60	100	3.8	9.5	16.7	15.0	30	30	7	50	0	50	50	50	10.0
Oregon State University	2.69	2.90	-0.05	20	20	65	65	3.4	10.1	19.3	15.8	23	9	18	9	0	64	47	16	11.0
Lehigh University	2.69	2.90	0.50	14	36	79	57	1.9	19.8	6.2	30.3	10	20	8	13	0	63	17	33	9.9
University of Tennessee-Knoxville	2.65	2.84	0.18	14	43	50	93	5.1	12.6	15.3	18.8	21	24	13	7	0	86	9	55	7.9
University of Nevada, Reno	2.64	2.47	0.22	14	50	50	71	2.9	15.6	7.1	25.6	44	14	15	18	7	94	47	0	11.8
Colorado State University	2.60	2.73	0.29	17	53	41	41	1.0	16.9	1.4	34.2	13	15	22	0	0	89	17	0	8.8
University of Alaska	2.58	2.50	0.14	24	46	46	71	2.6	7.9	9.5	11.4	24	29	12	21	0	83	25	8	11.7
University of Houston	2.58	2.68	0.09	18	50	44	61	1.2	12.0	2.8	18.8	20	20	20	18	0	65	25	19	10.2
Florida State University [d]	2.50	3.23	0.00	16	69	63	69	5.8	14.0	16.4	24.2	24	8	17	17*	0*	76*	27*	20*	9.7*
University of Texas at Dallas	2.47	2.29	0.05	15	73	60	67	5.7	20.7	22.2	23.5	48	17	30	16	8	65	43	29	9.8
University of Iowa	2.46	2.87	-0.11	15	60	60	93	2.9	14.1	18.7	34.2	24	29	13	18	0	88	21	36	8.8
University of Florida	2.45	2.50	0.17	19	68	53	89	5.6	10.5	27.1	17.2	12	8	3	0	0	60	60	20	7.7
University of Cincinnati	2.45	2.53	-0.28	11	73	36	82	2.5	17.8	14.0	24.8	16	6	21	17	6	82	6	69	8.4
State Univ of New York-Binghamton	2.44	2.38	-0.09	13	54	62	77	2.5	14.4	10.3	16.3	28	11	7	20	10	100	67	33	8.7
Syracuse University	2.43	2.30	-0.26	9	56	89	100	9.7	31.6	55.9	46.0	15	20	9	23	13	62	0	56	9.0
University of Rochester	2.42	2.50	-0.08	7	57	86	86	3.6	21.9	11.7	25.0	19	53	11	9	0	82	40	30	9.7
State Univ of New York-Albany	2.42	2.72	-0.62	5	40	100	100	5.6	23.9	24.2	23.1	8	13	9	9	0	64	9	73	6.8
University of Pittsburgh	2.41	2.80	0.05	12	67	42	92	2.0	13.1	7.1	19.5	16	31	10	23	0	92	31	46	10.7
Mean Values for the 3rd Quarter	**2.59**	**2.70**	**0.04**	**15.92**	**54.32**	**58.00**	**77.16**	**3.72**	**15.52**	**14.69**	**23.38**	**24.28**	**20.68**	**16.44**	**16.72**	**2.00**	**75.88**	**31.80**	**30.04**	**9.40**
Georgia Institute of Technology	2.36	2.75	0.07	22	50	64	86	5.3	10.2	40.6	12.8	48	19	28	0	20	56	25	0	8.9
University of Georgia	2.36	2.22	0.70	19	21	58	74	3.7	34.6	11.9	51.4	9	0	15	13	11	60	18	55	9.4
Ohio State University [e]	2.35	2.57	-0.23	10	50	20	50	0.9	35.8	2.2	60.3	44	11	7	13*	4*	83*	43*	33*	7.9*
University of Pennsylvania	2.34	2.44	0.21	24	21	38	63	2.6	14.8	10.1	35.3	14	36	9	50	0	90	30	40	8.7
Case Western Reserve Univ	2.33	2.42	-0.32	6	50	50	83	2.5	27.1	10.5	45.9	4	25	4	33	50	33	50	17	9.1
CUNY - Grad Sch & Univ Center	2.33	2.04	-0.21	16	69	38	56	1.3	13.0	3.8	24.3	28	39	10	29	0	57	0	25	7.9
Michigan State University	2.31	2.53	0.08	13	69	46	62	3.2	18.0	10.6	28.3	9	0	14	18	0	77	25	8	11.8
University of Kentucky	2.25	2.05	0.13	14	36	21	64	3.5	23.6	7.6	27.9	18	17	10	18	0	94	25	31	8.2

Institution	1993 Ratings[1] 93Q	93E	93C	Faculty Tot Fac[2]	% Full[2]	% Supp[2]	% Pub[5]	Pub/ Fac[5]	Gini Pub[5]	Cite/ Fac[5]	Gini Cite[5]	Students[2] Tot Stu	% Fem	Rpt PhDs	Doctorate Recipients[3] % Fem	% Min	% US	% RA	% TA	MYD
State Univ of New York-Buffalo	2.24	2.08	0.00	11	64	64	73	2.6	20.0	4.4	30.6	15	13	4	50	0	83	75	25	10.9
University of Texas-El Paso	2.16	1.90	0.26	14	43	57	64	3.5	19.9	11.4	33.6	23	26	10	8	0	69	10	30	9.8
Michigan Technological University	2.14	2.44	0.27	11	45	64	82	2.6	18.1	10.4	19.4	12	0	8	0	0	88	43	14	8.6
Washington State University	2.08	2.27	-0.19	13	54	31	77	2.6	14.8	5.4	31.6	38	26	16	5	6	90	6	71	7.8
Florida State University [c]	2.07	2.36	-0.03	14	50	29	79	2.6	11.1	5.7	15.0	16	25	12	17*	0*	76*	27*	20*	9.7*
Iowa State University	2.05	2.07	-0.08	10	40	40	80	1.9	16.8	6.9	21.7	11	9	11	9	0	70	29	57	9.2
Northern Illinois University	2.02	2.17	-0.12	17	24	47	65	1.9	10.7	5.6	16.7	16	6	8	14	20	71	0	75	8.1
Texas Tech University	1.97	1.85	0.09	16	63	19	63	1.3	17.0	2.0	26.1	18	11	17	18	0	53	25	42	8.8
University of Alabama	1.92	2.04	0.11	13	46	15	77	2.0	13.3	9.5	25.3	6	17	5	0	0	80	20	40	8.7
University of Nebraska-Lincoln	1.82	1.98	0.09	15	40	40	73	1.5	13.2	1.3	23.5	23	9	9	17	0	92	25	50	8.7
South Dakota Sch of Mines & Tech	1.80	1.99	-0.61	10	70	20	30	0.6	50.0	4.0	52.0	12	17	12	20	0	80	17	0	10.8
Kent State University	1.78	1.45	-0.06	14	57	21	86	2.5	16.4	1.9	20.7	11	27	6	11	0	89	13	38	11.7
University of Idaho	1.71	1.61	0.00	15	47	27	73	2.0	11.3	2.4	20.6	16	19	21	9	0	79	7	13	10.6
University of Wisconsin-Milwaukee	1.64	1.67	0.08	18	33	22	44	1.6	21.2	4.4	57.4	9	0	3	33	0	67	60	20	9.6
West Virginia University	1.57	1.49	-0.14	14	50	29	64	2.1	15.7	3.4	15.3	13	8	9	33	0	78	60	20	6.8
University of Missouri-Rolla	1.22	1.21	-0.63	6	50	33	50	2.3	43.8	5.5	88.6	7	14	2	50	0	50	0	0	11.0
George Washington University	1.16	0.63	-0.33	8	75	50	50	2.6	54.1	13.8	77.3	12	58	6	50	0	100	0	20	15.5
Mean Values for the 4th Quarter	**2.00**	**2.01**	**-0.03**	**13.72**	**48.68**	**37.72**	**66.72**	**2.37**	**21.78**	**7.81**	**34.46**	**17.28**	**17.28**	**10.24**	**20.72**	**4.44**	**74.60**	**25.32**	**29.76**	**9.53**
Mean Values for All Programs	**2.88**	**2.85**	**0.04**	**20.05**	**57.81**	**57.64**	**78.08**	**4.71**	**15.12**	**24.82**	**23.40**	**36.11**	**22.23**	**25.11**	**20.32**	**3.13**	**77.41**	**37.20**	**24.45**	**8.98**

Sources: 1. National Survey of Graduate Faculty
2. Institutional Coordinator Response Data
3. Doctorate Records File
4. Federal Agencies
5. Institute for Scientific Information

Notes: *a.* Program in Geophysics
b. Program in Applied Earth Sciences
c. Program in Geology
d. Program in Meteorology
e. Program in Geodetic Science and Surveying

* The Doctorate Recipient information cannot be separated for two programs at the same institution in the same field and therefore the total for the combined programs is given.

Appendix Table L - 5 Selected Characteristics of Research-Doctorate Programs in Mathematics

Institution	1993 Ratings[1] 93Q	93E	93C	Faculty Tot Fac[2]	% Full[2]	% Supp[2]	% Pub[5]	Pub/ Fac[5]	Gini Pub[5]	Cite/ Fac[5]	Gini Cite[5]	Students[2] Tot Stu	% Fem	Rpt PhDs	Doctorate Recipients[3] % Fem	% Min	% US	% RA	% TA	MYD
University of California-Berkeley	4.94	4.37	0.19	58	91	74	78	4.2	2.9	10.5	4.9	241	15	159	11	6	57	8	58	7.1
Princeton University	4.94	4.69	0.06	37	65	57	81	4.4	6.3	24.5	19.3	67	15	54	10	0	57	27	25	5.2
Massachusetts Inst of Technology	4.92	4.57	0.26	46	76	76	87	5.0	3.7	15.0	8.4	117	15	126	13	6	52	17	52	6.3
Harvard University	4.90	4.58	0.11	27	56	70	78	4.6	7.8	21.3	16.4	54	17	45	4	3	54	45	11	6.4
University of Chicago	4.69	4.64	-0.02	58	57	47	55	2.9	5.9	10.7	22.5	96	16	52	13	5	66	8	52	6.9
Stanford University	4.68	4.41	0.09	24	79	75	92	7.0	9.0	23.1	21.1	68	24	41	15	3	60	29	47	6.6
Yale University	4.55	4.11	0.08	32	53	47	66	3.8	7.8	9.1	11.7	5	20	38	19	11	37	8	27	7.0
New York University	4.49	4.26	-0.09	46	74	65	85	7.2	4.1	20.8	5.9	106	13	88	14	2	49	18	42	6.3
University of Michigan	4.23	3.84	0.17	51	67	59	80	4.0	6.2	9.7	27.1	137	20	67	13	0	62	0	83	8.3
Columbia University	4.23	3.94	-0.16	13	92	85	77	3.8	13.6	14.5	29.7	43	12	37	12	6	55	16	24	6.8
California Institute Technology	4.19	3.90	0.07	13	92	77	54	5.8	24.6	11.8	37.4	30	17	23	14	0	53	9	64	6.2
Univ of California-Los Angeles	4.14	3.91	0.33	84	75	61	86	5.5	2.3	16.0	4.2	203	28	76	11	7	51	21	54	7.0
University of Wisconsin-Madison	4.10	3.82	-0.04	70	84	56	71	4.3	3.0	8.5	4.6	199	22	92	9	2	61	3	83	7.8
University of Minnesota	4.08	3.65	0.21	52	88	56	81	5.2	6.0	9.8	16.9	84	15	82	14	4	32	5	88	7.3
Cornell University	4.05	3.96	0.14	44	84	77	89	5.9	4.8	25.2	8.4	62	16	46	21	0	60	23	56	7.0
Brown University [a]	4.04	4.06	-0.11	21	86	71	81	5.1	10.7	13.7	15.6	47	15	57	13*	5*	56*	26*	45*	6.1*
Univ of California-San Diego	4.02	3.58	0.31	45	82	60	82	5.5	3.8	16.3	7.7	71	18	67	19	11	76	18	69	6.4
University of Maryland College Park	3.97	3.64	0.28	96	71	45	72	3.9	2.4	11.0	8.9	107	34	32	15	8	66	10	59	7.9
Rutgers State Univ-New Brunswick	3.96	3.62	0.49	89	83	58	72	4.6	3.1	10.7	11.5	148	26	48	23	4	35	10	72	7.7
State U of New York-Stony Brook	3.94	3.61	0.38	29	72	52	79	3.1	6.9	5.8	27.0	85	25	40	23	7	40	7	76	7.2
U of Illinois at Urbana-Champaign	3.93	3.63	-0.07	94	81	49	66	2.6	2.9	2.9	9.7	195	24	59	12	0	55	7	77	8.1
University of Pennsylvania	3.87	3.52	0.16	29	79	69	83	3.3	6.2	7.7	26.9	40	28	24	15	0	50	3	72	6.4
University of Texas at Austin	3.85	3.46	0.65	72	71	47	68	3.9	3.9	18.0	16.3	87	15	58	22	3	64	4	80	7.9
Purdue University	3.82	3.54	0.22	54	85	81	91	5.6	3.2	10.4	6.1	87	20	59	11	0	32	4	84	8.3
Rice University [b]	3.82	3.84	0.20	12	83	83	100	5.3	14.1	7.1	23.2	47	49	17	23*	8*	60*	45*	15*	7.5*
University of Washington	3.76	3.47	0.12	46	70	59	78	4.3	4.7	9.7	9.0	88	32	27	11*	2*	66*	24*	57*	7.5*
Brown University	3.73	3.56	-0.37	23	70	70	61	3.3	10.0	8.6	38.7	44	18	24	13*	5*	56*	26*	45*	6.1*
Northwestern University	3.71	3.42	0.13	46	67	63	76	7.7	6.0	18.7	8.7	79	30	36	19	2	75	18	58	6.6
Ohio State University	3.66	3.13	0.38	94	54	53	68	3.7	3.5	7.0	9.9	177	18	60	11	4	30	3	85	8.7
Johns Hopkins University	3.65	3.24	0.04	18	72	56	72	3.3	15.2	2.9	17.2	34	21	23	18*	0*	49*	7*	70*	6.8*

Institution	1993 Ratings[1] 93Q	93E	93C	Faculty Tot Fac[2]	% Full[2]	% Supp[2]	% Pub[5]	Pub/ Fac[5]	Gini Pub[5]	Cite/ Fac[5]	Gini Cite[5]	Students[2] Tot Stu	% Fem	Rpt PhDs	Doctorate Recipients[3] % Fem	% Min	% US	% RA	% TA	MYD
CUNY - Grad Sch & Univ Center	3.65	3.08	-0.03	20	95	60	60	2.1	11.4	1.0	24.5	90	23	23	18	7	58	13	33	8.5
Brandeis University	3.64	3.50	-0.12	19	84	58	84	3.3	9.2	4.4	9.7	52	15	24	14	0	34	6	42	7.9
University of Illinois at Chicago	3.58	3.29	0.39	52	77	77	87	4.6	3.2	6.4	5.3	70	30	48	16	7	44	8	71	9.7
Mean Values for the Top Quarter	**4.11**	**3.81**	**0.13**	**45.88**	**76.21**	**63.42**	**76.97**	**4.51**	**6.92**	**11.90**	**15.59**	**92.73**	**21.39**	**53.09**	**14.82**	**3.88**	**53.09**	**14.42**	**56.85**	**7.20**
Indiana University	3.53	3.33	0.20	44	64	45	82	4.1	5.8	4.8	8.6	90	21	25	24	0	39	0	89	8.5
Duke University	3.53	3.37	0.30	18	61	78	89	3.1	10.3	3.8	13.5	37	22	28	23	8	43	15	73	6.6
University of Utah	3.52	3.19	0.49	41	85	59	68	2.9	6.9	8.3	22.9	73	27	28	16	0	59	9	61	7.1
Pennsylvania State University	3.50	3.37	0.65	59	66	47	73	3.9	3.9	6.0	6.5	103	25	44	16	6	33	5	84	8.4
Rice University	3.49	3.33	-0.03	13	62	92	69	2.3	18.8	2.2	46.7	26	19	12	23*	8*	60*	45*	15*	7.5*
Washington University	3.42	3.49	0.04	26	62	54	81	3.9	9.1	12.3	28.3	49	29	28	13	8	30	3	63	6.9
Carnegie Mellon University	3.41	3.48	0.39	26	73	77	96	6.1	6.5	9.9	10.1	42	17	34	29	10	53	25	75	6.5
University of Washington [a]	3.39	3.24	0.31	10	70	60	80	6.7	28.7	32.9	45.9	44	36	17	11*	2*	66*	24*	57*	7.5*
U of North Carolina-Chapel Hill	3.24	3.01	0.10	34	79	50	71	3.1	5.7	5.4	11.8	51	37	14	17	16	67	19	46	7.4
University of Southern California	3.23	3.07	0.24	42	64	62	71	4.7	4.9	11.3	10.2	38	24	19	20	0	46	0	92	6.4
Georgia Institute of Technology	3.19	3.07	0.71	53	43	42	62	2.7	5.1	3.6	14.8	52	38	20	14	7	71	6	65	8.0
University of Virginia	3.18	3.18	0.04	32	69	63	91	4.2	6.9	7.8	8.7	44	36	28	19	0	85	34	52	6.4
University of Notre Dame	3.11	3.17	0.36	29	59	69	79	4.0	8.2	3.3	11.2	40	33	34	23	0	38	0	93	6.1
University of Oregon	3.06	2.95	0.06	29	72	31	62	3.1	8.9	3.5	13.9	41	24	24	16	4	77	0	78	7.4
Michigan State University	3.05	2.95	0.37	39	67	36	74	4.4	10.9	6.6	20.1	84	18	30	8	0	23	0	87	9.1
Univ of California-Santa Barbara	3.04	2.85	0.40	35	83	49	77	3.7	5.9	3.8	9.5	11	36	25	14	8	46	16	60	6.9
Johns Hopkins University [c]	3.04	2.98	-0.25	9	67	56	78	4.2	22.5	8.0	40.9	26	35	16	18*	0*	49*	7*	70*	6.8*
Boston University	3.03	2.93	0.54	27	44	52	70	4.0	16.4	15.2	45.3	34	71	27	21	0	74	6	47	9.3
Rensselaer Polytechnic Inst	3.02	3.07	-0.20	26	58	73	73	4.3	7.7	7.3	13.1	88	22	24	15	3	67	27	27	7.6
Dartmouth College	2.97	3.09	0.03	22	73	23	45	1.5	14.7	1.4	22.6	24	33	11	38	0	77	0	33	5.8
University of Arizona	2.96	2.72	0.08	57	47	51	75	4.3	4.9	13.6	11.4	64	22	15	14	17	48	39	47	7.7
University of Florida	2.95	2.63	0.33	48	63	48	83	3.4	3.6	3.8	8.6	52	12	18	17	9	67	0	83	7.7
Univ of California-Santa Cruz	2.92	2.07	0.04	13	92	54	77	2.7	13.3	3.8	15.7	43	19	10	33	8	80	0	64	9.3
U of Massachusetts at Amherst	2.90	3.08	-0.22	37	89	62	84	2.9	6.1	5.1	20.0	48	38	32	25	10	50	12	79	8.4

Appendix Table L - 5 Mathematics (Continued)

Institution	1993 Ratings[1] 93Q	93E	93C	Faculty Tot Fac[2]	% Full[2]	% Supp[2]	% Pub[5]	Pub/ Fac[5]	Gini Pub[5]	Cite/ Fac[5]	Gini Cite[5]	Students[2] Tot Stu	% Fem	Rpt PhDs	Doctorate Recipients[3] % Fem	% Min	% US	% RA	% TA	MYD
North Carolina State University	2.90	2.86	0.44	39	59	59	77	4.0	4.6	6.8	8.6	66	24	32	16	4	56	13	66	8.7
University of Georgia	2.90	2.38	0.54	35	49	66	69	2.1	6.7	1.7	12.0	47	36	7	18	0	45	0	100	10.1
University of Rochester	2.90	2.76	0.28	25	64	60	80	2.2	8.3	5.9	27.6	40	28	23	18	0	43	0	27	7.7
University of Pittsburgh	2.88	2.58	0.17	36	44	31	72	3.8	5.9	10.9	29.5	40	20	17	25	0	35	13	75	9.9
University of Iowa	2.85	2.71	0.13	48	65	48	81	4.9	4.4	6.8	7.1	71	25	40	24	4	44	2	81	9.3
University of California-Irvine	2.84	2.78	0.56	25	64	40	68	3.4	8.1	6.8	13.8	55	31	16	7	7	93	0	80	7.5
Texas A&M University	2.84	2.58	0.30	64	58	50	64	4.1	4.0	5.1	5.1	33	9	15	18	0	18	13	75	9.7
University of Colorado	2.83	3.06	0.00	27	70	56	85	3.5	7.4	4.5	12.4	27	48	28	20	0	80	13	63	8.1
State Univ of New York-Buffalo	2.79	2.55	0.08	40	57	40	65	2.5	5.8	2.4	11.6	55	16	24	18	0	15	0	95	7.5
Virginia Polytech Inst & State U	2.79	2.80	0.27	42	67	48	83	5.0	4.7	6.1	8.3	73	32	24	17	0	48	0	78	6.9
University of Houston	2.78	3.01	0.52	31	65	48	61	2.4	7.9	6.6	21.3	88	28	21	14	0	53	8	58	8.9
Mean Values for the 2nd Quarter	**3.09**	**2.96**	**0.24**	**33.74**	**64.97**	**53.69**	**74.71**	**3.66**	**8.67**	**7.07**	**17.65**	**51.40**	**28.30**	**23.14**	**18.91**	**3.97**	**53.66**	**10.11**	**66.80**	**7.82**
State Univ of New York-Binghamton	2.74	2.56	0.17	23	52	35	57	2.1	9.7	1.1	14.8	48	10	12	20	0	100	0	100	7.4
Louisiana State U & A&M College	2.74	2.69	0.22	48	46	35	71	2.4	5.3	1.7	9.8	61	21	23	42	19	67	5	65	8.8
University of Kentucky	2.72	2.47	0.09	43	63	53	63	2.8	5.5	4.4	11.2	47	26	20	24	0	70	25	67	8.9
Temple University	2.67	2.58	0.18	34	56	26	56	1.3	7.8	1.0	23.5	44	20	15	29	0	55	0	50	6.3
Syracuse University	2.62	2.76	0.12	34	59	32	74	2.6	5.5	1.6	12.9	42	31	18	17	8	59	10	86	9.0
Claremont Graduate School	2.61	2.54	0.08	5	60	20	40	1.0	52.0	0.2	100.0	33	30	9	22	0	56	0	17	8.8
University of South Carolina	2.60	2.61	0.63	30	53	47	67	3.9	6.6	4.2	8.2	46	15	20	27	0	27	0	91	6.5
Tulane University	2.59	2.65	-0.20	25	60	56	80	3.4	7.7	3.4	9.3	46	9	17	41	0	50	0	80	7.4
University of Tennessee-Knoxville	2.59	2.53	0.11	33	76	42	67	4.4	7.4	4.7	9.3	43	16	16	11	0	68	0	93	8.9
Iowa State University	2.59	2.82	0.22	35	63	43	91	5.7	5.6	14.5	18.8	41	27	31	6	0	37	7	71	7.8
Univ of California-Riverside	2.55	2.50	0.40	28	64	46	79	3.8	8.0	4.0	15.5	43	42	8	17	0	75	0	45	6.8
University of Delaware	2.54	2.29	0.19	28	61	57	86	5.6	6.7	10.9	12.8	38	29	21	21	0	50	0	88	7.9
Northeastern University	2.52	2.80	0.23	17	47	41	88	4.2	10.0	12.9	51.6	33	6	17	39	0	39	0	65	8.9
Florida State University	2.49	2.41	0.24	35	49	34	74	4.1	6.3	5.5	11.8	51	25	11	14	33	43	11	56	8.6
University of California-Davis	2.48	2.17	0.33	22	64	45	77	3.8	8.0	4.8	14.0	21	14	16	21	5	65	9	73	7.6
State Univ of New York-Albany	2.48	2.45	-0.05	27	56	22	59	1.8	8.9	3.1	24.1	75	20	15	27	0	73	0	71	6.2

Institution	1993 Ratings[1] 93Q	93E	93C	Faculty Tot Fac[2]	% Full[2]	% Supp[2]	% Pub[5]	Pub/ Fac[5]	Gini Pub[5]	Cite/ Fac[5]	Gini Cite[5]	Students[2] Tot Stu	% Fem	Rpt PhDs	Doctorate Recipients[3] % Fem	% Min	% US	% RA	% TA	MYD
Arizona State University	2.43	2.32	0.35	31	58	55	87	4.3	5.2	8.3	14.5	48	17	13	17	0	33	0	86	9.7
Kent State University	2.41	2.40	0.33	25	68	36	60	1.3	10.9	1.2	40.4	37	16	10	6	0	25	8	42	9.7
University of Nebraska-Lincoln	2.40	2.72	0.40	34	35	44	74	2.5	5.6	2.6	8.2	36	28	13	6	9	61	0	77	8.6
Vanderbilt University	2.39	2.46	0.19	23	52	39	74	3.0	7.2	1.9	14.2	29	41	18	19	5	74	0	82	8.6
Case Western Reserve Univ	2.38	1.95	-0.19	18	50	56	83	3.4	13.0	3.5	11.4	2	100	0	0	0	33	23	8	8.5
Oregon State University	2.37	2.26	-0.06	16	44	63	75	3.3	11.5	3.1	18.4	24	25	11	35	0	71	15	46	9.7
Kansas State University	2.35	2.29	0.19	30	37	33	50	2.5	32.8	7.1	72.8	36	11	14	14	0	38	11	67	9.8
Clemson University	2.34	2.59	0.24	40	63	25	68	1.8	5.4	0.7	13.2	54	35	20	25	0	96	10	71	6.4
Auburn University	2.31	2.25	0.32	55	49	18	85	4.4	3.1	3.1	5.0	41	29	19	13	0	83	0	88	7.6
Wayne State University	2.30	2.07	0.35	40	65	28	70	3.1	6.2	3.0	10.7	23	35	11	0	0	0	0	100	6.6
University of Missouri-Columbia	2.30	2.40	0.18	30	57	40	77	3.8	6.4	3.5	9.1	20	25	6	30	0	70	0	50	8.8
Colorado State University	2.28	2.46	0.13	26	65	38	62	2.4	10.3	3.1	17.7	22	32	15	19	0	52	7	80	7.8
Lehigh University	2.22	2.06	0.07	23	52	26	61	3.1	12.5	3.0	15.6	30	57	13	20	0	56	5	65	6.9
University of Hawaii at Manoa	2.20	2.43	0.08	34	71	26	88	2.9	5.3	5.7	28.9	11	27	7	0	0	33	0	71	7.3
Polytechnic University	2.18	2.50	0.18	14	64	36	50	1.3	19.1	4.2	59.2	29	14	16	6	27	83	0	20	13.0
University of Oklahoma	2.18	2.12	0.19	31	39	55	74	3.1	6.8	4.0	15.6	54	31	10	22	0	44	14	71	11.5
University of Connecticut	2.16	2.19	0.00	28	71	43	86	4.4	6.5	4.4	9.9	53	34	23	24	0	24	0	89	8.6
University of Miami	2.12	2.33	0.27	24	50	38	67	2.9	10.3	3.0	20.1	16	31	4	13	0	13	0	29	9.1
Wesleyan University	2.12	2.67	0.08	17	53	29	53	1.8	19.2	0.9	27.3	24	38	13	25	13	67	0	90	6.7
Washington State University	2.10	2.54	0.00	34	71	44	82	3.2	6.1	7.4	24.5	37	24	27	24	0	66	4	85	6.9
Mean Values for the 3rd Quarter	**2.42**	**2.44**	**0.17**	**28.89**	**56.75**	**39.06**	**70.97**	**3.09**	**10.12**	**4.21**	**21.79**	**37.17**	**27.53**	**14.78**	**19.33**	**3.31**	**54.33**	**4.56**	**67.64**	**8.27**
University of North Texas	2.06	1.99	0.32	28	39	14	54	1.8	11.5	0.9	34.0	33	27	19	32	0	73	0	75	7.8
University of Cincinnati	2.06	1.96	0.15	30	83	33	73	2.9	6.7	7.4	44.9	31	35	12	29	50	17	0	60	9.4
Texas Tech University	2.03	2.26	0.15	41	46	24	68	3.4	7.3	6.5	60.9	42	29	17	23	0	15	9	82	7.2
University of Texas at Arlington	2.02	1.97	0.21	22	45	14	68	3.5	13.2	1.3	29.8	38	26	32	21	0	42	0	74	9.2
Southern Illinois University	1.98	1.58	0.25	33	64	27	76	2.8	6.7	2.0	12.0	8	38	18	14	0	14	0	95	8.9

Appendix Table L - 5 Mathematics (Continued)

Institution	1993 Ratings[1] 93Q	93E	93C	Faculty Tot Fac[2]	% Full[2]	% Supp[2]	% Pub[5]	Pub/ Fac[5]	Gini Pub[5]	Cite/ Fac[5]	Gini Cite[5]	Students[2] Tot Stu	% Fem	Rpt PhDs	Doctorate Recipients[3] % Fem	% Min	% US	% RA	% TA	MYD
Drexel University	1.97	1.55	0.00	17	41	47	59	3.4	18.8	11.2	57.5	8	50	6	44	0	80	0	67	9.7
New Mexico State University	1.95	2.55	-0.08	31	55	29	52	1.5	9.3	0.6	20.0	29	52	16	20	0	42	0	62	10.9
University of South Florida	1.90	2.08	0.00	22	68	36	73	5.2	15.6	5.6	47.5	30	10	19	18	0	38	0	75	7.0
Western Michigan University	1.86	2.65	0.31	28	75	29	50	1.3	9.2	1.3	12.3	27	41	18	23	0	37	13	67	6.7
Bowling Green State University	1.85	1.78	0.22	30	60	13	53	2.6	10.3	2.2	10.9	26	35	17	18	0	45	0	88	8.0
University of Wisconsin-Milwaukee	1.84	1.54	0.00	32	22	6	78	3.0	6.9	2.2	10.4	45	20	12	17	0	61	0	88	8.3
Southern Methodist University	1.83	2.11	0.25	7	71	43	100	5.4	25.4	8.1	24.2	13	46	9	22	20	56	14	57	5.8
Howard University	1.82	1.25	0.10	16	69	50	69	2.5	20.3	2.1	32.0	33	36	6	17	100	100	0	50	11.0
Northern Illinois University	1.72	1.31	0.29	49	35	16	76	3.2	4.4	2.8	9.7	39	28	8	20	0	80	0	100	7.7
U of Maryland Baltimore County	1.69	1.92	0.50	17	76	35	88	4.2	10.3	5.1	19.9	44	20	9	0	0	0	13	63	8.6
Clarkson University	1.68	1.79	-0.50	14	29	50	79	6.7	16.7	22.1	31.5	15	20	11	8	50	17	22	56	9.4
Saint Louis University	1.63	1.21	0.00	15	27	7	67	2.1	13.8	1.1	18.3	5	60	3	20	0	100	0	50	9.7
Stevens Inst of Technology	1.62	1.67	0.00	10	70	20	60	1.5	20.8	1.0	34.0	31	13	7	25	0	100	0	33	10.7
University of Rhode Island	1.57	1.25	0.07	12	75	25	75	4.6	24.2	5.5	24.0	25	32	4	29	0	71	7	36	11.5
Ohio University	1.57	1.55	0.00	18	56	17	72	3.2	13.2	2.5	19.8	22	23	14	6	0	33	0	93	7.8
University of Wyoming	1.53	1.59	-0.50	13	46	8	54	2.9	19.6	5.9	25.4	13	31	14	8	0	58	20	80	8.4
University of Alabama	1.47	1.28	0.09	32	41	16	84	2.8	5.7	2.3	17.5	24	17	7	27	0	18	0	60	11.7
Illinois Institute of Technology	1.45	1.67	0.00	13	31	0	54	1.4	17.9	1.6	32.4	7	29	7	27	10	91	22	56	10.7
Old Dominion University	1.39	1.54	0.25	24	33	17	67	4.4	7.7	4.6	14.9	28	32	19	19	14	88	33	33	7.8
University of Missouri-Rolla	1.33	0.94	-0.11	20	40	0	60	1.2	11.1	0.6	23.6	15	53	6	33	0	83	0	100	7.7
University of Alabama-Huntsville	1.28	1.25	0.50	15	20	27	80	1.9	11.0	0.6	35.8	9	44	2	100	0	100	0	0	4.0
George Washington University	1.26	0.79	0.20	15	27	33	53	2.1	23.8	18.8	93.7	10	20	2	33	0	50	0	40	13.0
Colorado School of Mines	1.26	0.63	0.00	22	41	41	55	1.4	12.7	1.0	24.3	22	23	5	0	0	83	40	20	12.0
Adelphi University	1.24	0.67	-0.14	11	64	0	36	0.5	33.3	0.3	55.5	8	50	7	38	0	100	0	14	13.0
Univ of Southwestern Louisiana	1.13	0.91	-0.09	15	53	13	67	3.5	18.1	4.0	33.7	26	31	16	33	14	47	0	60	5.9
Florida Institute of Technology	1.09	0.72	0.25	9	44	11	78	2.8	25.7	0.2	50.0	14	43	3	50	0	25	0	33	7.6
University of Mississippi	0.97	0.56	0.13	14	57	21	29	1.1	31.5	0.5	55.1	7	29	5	17	33	50	0	40	8.5
University of Texas at Dallas	0.76	0.48	0.00	6	67	33	100	2.5	24.4	0.8	36.0	20	5	10	27	22	82	0	75	9.7

Institution	1993 Ratings[1]			Faculty								Students[2]			Doctorate Recipients[3]					
	93Q	93E	93C	Tot Fac[2]	% Full[2]	% Supp[2]	% Pub[5]	Pub/ Fac[5]	Gini Pub[5]	Cite/ Fac[5]	Gini Cite[5]	Tot Stu	% Fem	Rpt PhDs	% Fem	% Min	% US	% RA	% TA	MYD
Idaho State University	0.69	0.42	0.00	15	13	20	53	1.8	19.3	2.7	35.3	14	14	4	33	14	88	0	20	11.0
Illinois State University	0.40	0.40	0.00	5	80	100	20	0.4	100.0	0.6	100.0	10	80	0	60	0	80	0	56	17.0
Mean Values for the 4th Quarter	**1.54**	**1.42**	**0.08**	**20.03**	**50.37**	**25.00**	**65.14**	**2.73**	**17.90**	**3.89**	**33.91**	**22.03**	**32.63**	**10.40**	**26.03**	**9.34**	**58.97**	**5.51**	**58.80**	**9.24**
Mean Values for All Programs	**2.77**	**2.64**	**0.16**	**31.91**	**61.83**	**44.99**	**71.87**	**3.48**	**10.95**	**6.67**	**22.32**	**50.13**	**27.55**	**24.88**	**19.84**	**5.17**	**55.04**	**8.54**	**62.64**	**8.14**

Sources: 1. National Survey of Graduate Faculty
2. Institutional Coordinator Response Data
3. Doctorate Records File
4. Federal Agencies
5. Institute for Scientific Information

Notes: a. Program in Applied Mathematics
b. Program in Computational and Applied Mathematics
c. Program in Mathematical Sciences

* The Doctorate Recipient information cannot be separated for two programs at the same institution in the same field and therefore the total for the combined programs is given.

Appendix Table L - 6 Selected Characteristics of Research-Doctorate Programs in Oceanography

Institution	1993 Ratings[1] 93Q	93E	93C	Faculty Tot Fac[2]	% Full[2]	% Supp[2]	% Pub[5]	Pub/ Fac[5]	Gini Pub[5]	Cite/ Fac[5]	Gini Cite[5]	Students[2] Tot Stu	% Fem	Rpt PhDs	Doctorate Recipients[3] % Fem	% Min	% US	% RA	% TA	MYD
Univ of California-San Diego	4.69	4.21	-0.11	112	65	69	85	6.4	2.0	31.6	2.7	174	37	84	22	5	77	74	0	7.9
Massachusetts Inst of Technology	4.62	4.31	0.02	34	71	79	94	10.5	4.2	69.5	6.6	144	36	85	31	5	86	82	0	7.4
University of Washington	4.31	4.07	0.33	43	56	84	98	6.6	4.0	43.0	4.9	95	43	42	26	2	89	82	2	8.7
Columbia University	4.30	4.00	0.07	19	42	95	100	8.4	7.4	84.1	10.5	59	39	34	43	0	71	83	0	7.8
Oregon State University	3.88	3.46	0.27	45	53	80	89	6.6	4.4	32.9	5.5	63	29	19	8	0	77	77	0	9.3
University of Rhode Island	3.68	3.53	-0.13	28	71	75	93	6.0	5.5	30.8	8.4	103	43	65	33	6	88	65	3	10.5
University of Hawaii at Manoa	3.50	3.11	0.58	34	50	76	79	5.2	6.0	24.9	10.3	50	20	10	17	0	63	77	0	9.4
Mean Values for the Top Quarter	**4.14**	**3.81**	**0.15**	**45.00**	**58.29**	**79.71**	**91.14**	**7.10**	**4.79**	**45.26**	**6.99**	**98.29**	**35.29**	**48.43**	**25.71**	**2.57**	**78.71**	**77.14**	**0.71**	**8.71**
State U of New York-Stony Brook	3.49	3.28	0.50	43	47	60	88	5.4	4.1	23.6	10.3	51	22	33	24	0	55	57	4	8.8
Florida State University	3.48	3.28	0.28	18	72	78	94	7.0	7.7	27.6	11.1	23	26	16	14	0	48	71	0	8.9
University of Maryland College Park	3.42	3.17	0.46	70	60	44	56	3.5	5.0	11.0	7.5	82	43	25	14	0	77	31	0	12.7
University of Miami	3.29	3.05	-0.10	14	43	86	93	4.4	11.7	20.4	16.7	19	53	10	18	5	52	39	7	10.3
Texas A&M University	3.26	3.09	0.19	40	75	53	83	3.9	6.2	15.0	12.8	49	16	42	17	17	81	69	6	9.9
Mean Values for the 2nd Quarter	**3.39**	**3.17**	**0.27**	**37.00**	**59.40**	**64.20**	**82.80**	**4.84**	**6.94**	**19.52**	**11.68**	**44.80**	**32.00**	**25.20**	**17.40**	**4.40**	**62.60**	**53.40**	**3.40**	**10.12**
U of North Carolina-Chapel Hill	3.22	3.13	0.27	18	56	83	67	3.3	14.3	13.9	19.7	18	44	5	30	0	60	67	22	8.7
Duke University	3.22	3.11	-0.03	12	67	83	92	9.9	15.0	22.9	16.4	19	47	14	n/a	n/a	n/a	n/a	n/a	n/a
University of South Florida	3.07	2.83	0.49	22	73	64	91	5.7	9.0	23.3	11.6	52	27	15	22	0	94	36	0	12.4
University of Wisconsin-Madison	3.04	3.06	-0.08	20	95	65	90	8.2	7.7	47.3	9.6	14	43	9	14	20	100	100	0	10.0
Old Dominion University	3.01	3.05	0.72	15	60	67	80	4.3	10.2	11.9	14.7	28	36	10	13	0	63	78	0	9.2
Stanford University	2.98	2.20	0.05	4	50	75	50	0.5	50.0	3.8	100.0	n/a	n/a	4	n/a	n/a	n/a	n/a	n/a	n/a
North Carolina State University	2.86	2.80	0.05	13	46	92	77	5.4	17.6	13.8	25.6	25	24	13	0	0	75	71	0	9.7
Mean Values for the 3rd Quarter	**3.06**	**2.88**	**0.21**	**14.86**	**63.86**	**75.57**	**78.14**	**5.33**	**17.69**	**19.56**	**28.23**	**26.00**	**36.83**	**10.00**	**15.80**	**4.00**	**78.40**	**70.40**	**4.40**	**10.00**
University of South Carolina	2.85	2.87	0.24	25	48	68	88	5.8	6.5	16.2	13.7	20	45	14	20	10	67	42	17	8.9
University of Alaska	2.71	3.02	0.16	21	57	71	81	3.0	8.3	10.0	14.9	15	53	12	19	0	81	86	0	10.7

Institution	1993 Ratings[1]			Faculty								Students[2]			Doctorate Recipients[3]					
	93Q	93E	93C	Tot Fac[2]	% Full[2]	% Supp[2]	% Pub[5]	Pub/ Fac[5]	Gini Pub[5]	Cite/ Fac[5]	Gini Cite[5]	Tot Stu	% Fem	Rpt PhDs	% Fem	% Min	% US	% RA	% TA	MYD
Naval Postgraduate School	2.54	2.11	0.00	10	50	40	80	2.3	17.9	7.6	31.4	9	0	8	10	0	50	29	0	6.6
Louisiana State U & A&M College	2.42	2.65	0.12	23	57	26	87	6.5	16.2	7.9	10.4	43	21	25	25	5	68	62	0	9.3
U of Massachusetts at Amherst	1.77	1.95	0.00	12	50	25	67	4.4	19.5	7.7	26.9	19	47	13	n/a	n/a	n/a	n/a	n/a	n/a
Florida Institute of Technology	1.65	1.83	0.00	7	57	29	86	2.7	22.9	9.9	58.7	5	40	6	10	0	70	25	38	7.1
Northeastern University	1.50	1.91	-0.12	6	17	33	83	2.7	32.0	12.8	39.1	6	33	4	n/a	n/a	n/a	n/a	n/a	n/a
Mean Values for the 4th Quarter	**2.21**	**2.33**	**0.06**	**14.86**	**48.00**	**41.71**	**81.71**	**3.91**	**17.61**	**10.30**	**27.87**	**16.71**	**34.14**	**11.71**	**16.80**	**3.00**	**67.20**	**48.80**	**11.00**	**8.52**
Mean Values for All Programs	**3.18**	**3.04**	**0.16**	**27.23**	**57.23**	**65.38**	**83.50**	**5.33**	**12.13**	**23.98**	**19.23**	**47.40**	**34.68**	**23.73**	**19.55**	**3.41**	**72.36**	**63.77**	**4.50**	**9.28**

Sources: 1. National Survey of Graduate Faculty
2. Institutional Coordinator Response Data
3. Doctorate Records File
4. Federal Agencies
5. Institute for Scientific Information

Appendix Table L - 7 Selected Characteristics of Research-Doctorate Programs in Physics

Institution	1993 Ratings[1] 93Q	93E	93C	Faculty Tot Fac[2]	% Full[2]	% Supp[2]	% Pub[5]	Pub/ Fac[5]	Gini Pub[5]	Cite/ Fac[5]	Gini Cite[5]	Students[2] Tot Stu	% Fem	Rpt PhDs	Doctorate Recipients[3] % Fem	% Min	% US	% RA	% TA	MYD
Harvard University	4.91	4.71	-0.03	32	88	81	97	15.6	4.7	170.7	6.9	149	13	105	14	2	72	56	15	6.4
Princeton University	4.89	4.69	0.23	47	53	45	79	7.8	4.2	110.0	8.3	110	13	81	3	0	71	46	18	6.1
Massachusetts Inst of Technology	4.87	4.64	0.06	83	71	52	90	11.3	2.5	121.2	7.2	315	10	196	12	7	62	79	3	6.9
University of California-Berkeley	4.87	4.49	-0.03	67	88	58	88	13.4	3.7	84.7	4.9	283	9	169	8	4	86	80	5	7.3
California Institute Technology	4.81	4.61	-0.03	39	79	54	90	10.5	5.2	116.1	11.4	154	18	92	8	1	66	50	27	6.7
Cornell University	4.75	4.54	-0.02	54	74	63	83	9.2	3.8	69.6	4.4	182	18	142	12	2	82	70	5	7.3
University of Chicago	4.69	4.55	0.19	40	77	65	93	10.4	4.1	84.2	5.4	154	14	100	6	0	68	85	0	6.9
U of Illinois at Urbana-Champaign	4.66	4.39	0.02	98	76	65	90	13.7	2.9	86.2	3.1	295	8	174	7	2	79	86	7	7.2
Stanford University	4.53	4.35	0.04	25	76	60	84	8.4	6.0	73.8	15.2	135	13	102	12	6	78	83	2	6.9
Univ of California-Santa Barbara	4.43	3.91	0.60	45	78	64	87	14.2	6.2	178.1	6.7	117	13	68	5	0	72	72	12	6.3
University of Texas at Austin	4.33	3.84	0.60	85	76	46	85	10.4	2.6	60.4	3.7	239	12	156	8	5	61	50	20	7.7
Columbia University	4.25	3.87	-0.31	34	50	32	88	8.1	5.1	68.6	7.9	97	10	64	6	4	61	76	5	7.4
Yale University	4.21	4.03	-0.03	61	49	41	87	7.2	3.4	63.1	6.0	99	11	67	9	0	58	77	5	6.8
University of Washington	4.20	3.81	0.38	48	85	54	94	9.0	3.6	60.8	4.5	178	13	70	5	2	58	84	7	7.6
Univ of California-Los Angeles	4.18	3.77	0.35	67	79	49	88	11.9	3.0	70.9	5.0	163	8	130	7	5	66	58	16	8.1
Univ of California-San Diego	4.10	3.82	0.38	61	70	66	92	11.6	4.7	88.2	8.2	155	14	70	7	3	49	84	4	7.5
University of Pennsylvania	4.09	3.77	-0.10	46	74	35	80	8.8	4.5	66.2	6.5	140	11	69	6	4	60	82	2	6.7
University of Maryland College Park	4.02	3.66	0.11	88	75	56	85	10.0	2.5	50.0	3.1	204	13	90	6	5	58	70	15	7.7
University of Michigan	3.96	3.74	0.43	61	64	49	89	7.6	3.0	37.4	4.4	157	20	77	9	6	61	68	15	7.2
Rutgers State Univ-New Brunswick	3.82	3.33	0.64	59	71	63	80	6.2	4.1	69.8	7.7	100	15	47	12	9	40	54	12	7.5
University of Wisconsin-Madison	3.79	3.81	0.13	49	78	57	86	9.1	5.1	49.8	7.0	190	13	120	10	2	77	83	7	7.2
State U of New York-Stony Brook	3.76	3.71	0.06	39	69	69	82	9.0	5.0	65.1	5.5	204	12	108	11	5	45	60	31	6.7
University of Minnesota	3.76	3.54	0.42	48	88	46	96	13.0	6.1	92.8	10.1	142	15	63	10	0	64	76	12	6.5
Ohio State University	3.75	3.70	0.72	50	64	54	80	9.8	7.0	57.4	6.7	164	12	89	8	0	42	58	31	7.5
University of Rochester [a]	3.65	3.91	0.10	18	61	78	94	17.2	6.9	82.9	10.9	85	18	55	11*	1*	67*	70*	4*	7.5*
Brown University	3.60	3.64	0.11	28	75	61	86	6.7	7.7	47.4	10.2	80	6	60	10	2	50	85	5	6.9
University of Rochester	3.60	3.63	0.10	35	57	54	91	9.7	5.1	54.7	8.4	131	15	66	11*	1*	67*	70*	4*	7.5*
Carnegie Mellon University	3.56	3.35	-0.05	33	70	45	85	5.9	5.6	35.9	8.4	61	10	36	14	0	56	79	7	6.7
Johns Hopkins University	3.51	3.65	0.23	32	81	69	94	13.3	5.9	89.1	9.5	104	12	55	6	3	68	60	20	7.5
Rockefeller University	3.46	2.50	-0.64	5	60	0	60	4.6	58.4	30.8	42.8	135	33	7	0	0	58	9	0	7.4

Institution	1993 Ratings[1] 93Q	93E	93C	Faculty Tot Fac[2]	% Full[2]	% Supp[2]	% Pub[5]	Pub/ Fac[5]	Gini Pub[5]	Cite/ Fac[5]	Gini Cite[5]	Students[2] Tot Stu	% Fem	Rpt PhDs	Doctorate Recipients[3] % Fem	% Min	% US	% RA	% TA	MYD
Purdue University	3.44	3.50	-0.02	55	75	36	84	8.1	3.6	48.4	8.1	152	19	85	13	2	49	57	24	6.9
Michigan State University	3.43	3.37	0.31	55	67	64	85	9.2	3.9	46.5	5.6	141	12	51	9	0	42	88	5	7.0
University of California-Irvine	3.37	3.54	0.40	34	74	56	88	6.8	7.2	27.7	8.1	81	9	49	10	0	71	74	6	7.3
Indiana University	3.37	3.33	0.17	47	81	43	81	6.8	4.1	43.6	6.4	95	9	46	14	0	52	82	7	7.5
CUNY - Grad Sch & Univ Center	3.36	3.27	-0.02	56	80	50	73	7.9	7.0	37.5	8.1	136	15	74	15	14	25	57	34	8.8
University of Florida	3.35	3.25	0.66	43	56	58	95	8.7	4.1	34.0	6.3	80	8	27	8	6	49	56	32	8.3
Mean Values for the Top Quarter	**4.04**	**3.84**	**0.17**	**49.08**	**71.92**	**53.83**	**86.36**	**9.75**	**6.18**	**71.49**	**8.13**	**150.19**	**13.17**	**85.00**	**8.94**	**2.86**	**60.83**	**68.72**	**11.78**	**7.21**
Northwestern University	3.31	3.47	0.09	30	70	57	80	15.0	9.5	88.5	9.2	109	19	51	11	0	39	82	5	7.3
University of Colorado	3.30	3.41	0.40	41	73	54	90	10.1	5.4	46.9	7.0	147	9	86	7	0	86	87	3	7.3
Boston University	3.28	3.29	0.63	35	63	51	83	8.7	6.7	77.0	11.5	100	5	42	20	4	60	47	44	7.7
University of Pittsburgh	3.27	3.29	0.11	37	76	78	92	6.3	4.9	31.3	6.0	92	11	54	5	0	29	78	13	6.9
Duke University	3.25	3.45	0.39	32	53	28	78	6.4	6.5	26.8	7.1	71	11	38	4	5	87	75	7	6.8
Florida State University	3.25	3.23	0.66	44	73	34	91	8.2	4.5	34.4	6.7	102	10	34	5	14	68	79	6	7.3
Rice University	3.25	3.35	0.19	23	78	61	96	9.2	7.1	77.2	30.5	58	2	33	13	7	67	73	0	7.2
Brandeis University	3.25	3.21	-0.27	20	80	65	90	8.5	7.5	83.3	16.7	36	14	38	21	7	62	61	11	8.3
University of Arizona	3.23	3.39	0.48	42	74	48	74	9.6	7.2	80.2	17.1	118	4	52	10	4	73	71	4	7.3
University of Virginia	3.23	3.23	0.33	41	73	54	80	6.7	5.5	28.3	6.5	72	11	49	9	5	63	38	44	7.4
Texas A&M University	3.22	3.29	0.60	45	78	44	87	9.2	4.7	43.6	9.0	111	15	36	12	11	67	52	28	7.4
Univ of California-Santa Cruz	3.22	3.33	0.17	18	72	61	89	9.4	9.1	78.6	11.1	52	21	22	14	11	68	50	33	8.2
Iowa State University	3.17	3.42	0.12	38	79	26	89	10.7	5.0	77.2	9.4	90	9	69	10	0	42	80	14	6.8
University of Southern California	3.17	3.00	0.20	32	66	59	78	12.2	5.8	79.2	6.3	62	8	29	8	0	54	83	11	6.8
North Carolina State University	3.16	3.20	0.57	38	71	45	76	13.6	6.2	61.4	8.4	65	26	37	8	3	63	66	24	7.8
Washington University	3.15	3.31	0.35	31	74	71	81	8.7	5.5	38.9	7.2	73	18	40	4	0	79	52	10	8.3
New York University	3.14	3.15	-0.08	29	83	59	79	6.7	8.8	34.7	12.3	34	12	43	11	0	39	27	38	7.5
U of North Carolina-Chapel Hill	3.14	3.27	0.26	28	68	29	75	6.5	8.8	20.3	12.9	55	15	33	10	6	76	56	26	7.4
Pennsylvania State University	3.08	3.08	0.31	32	63	56	78	9.3	6.9	31.0	9.3	67	21	51	11	5	55	57	27	7.9
University of Notre Dame	3.06	3.27	0.34	36	67	78	92	9.7	7.4	47.9	11.7	89	13	47	13	6	55	54	37	8.0
Syracuse University	3.04	3.25	0.08	26	73	73	96	11.1	6.2	56.0	6.7	70	14	35	23	7	34	53	44	7.2

Appendix Table L - 7 Physics (Continued)

Institution	1993 Ratings[1] 93Q	93E	93C	Faculty Tot Fac[2]	% Full[2]	% Supp[2]	% Pub[5]	Pub/ Fac[5]	Gini Pub[5]	Cite/ Fac[5]	Gini Cite[5]	Students[2] Tot Stu	% Fem	Rpt PhDs	Doctorate Recipients[3] % Fem	% Min	% US	% RA	% TA	MYD
Vanderbilt University	3.04	3.14	0.30	25	56	40	88	6.9	8.0	18.3	9.0	52	23	24	8	0	67	55	20	7.3
University of Utah	3.04	3.02	0.11	30	73	53	83	11.1	10.3	54.4	18.7	47	17	27	0	0	53	35	39	7.9
University of Oregon	3.03	3.24	0.32	31	74	61	87	9.6	6.1	64.9	18.3	125	12	46	9	0	51	66	17	6.7
University of Houston	3.02	2.78	0.47	30	70	33	67	7.9	8.5	30.7	11.0	74	18	17	10	8	38	71	17	8.3
Georgia Institute of Technology	3.02	3.09	0.29	26	58	58	81	9.0	8.5	68.9	21.7	90	11	29	17	11	60	49	30	6.1
College of William & Mary	3.00	3.11	0.55	38	55	29	68	4.6	8.5	29.2	17.9	63	17	27	8	0	62	74	26	6.6
U of Massachusetts at Amherst	2.97	3.12	0.15	33	76	52	91	5.9	6.4	26.1	9.6	75	13	29	11	8	71	60	23	7.8
Case Western Reserve Univ	2.96	3.04	-0.15	21	71	57	100	7.7	8.7	54.0	25.7	31	10	31	12	3	68	73	10	7.0
Northeastern University	2.91	3.01	0.16	31	81	65	81	8.5	7.6	45.9	10.5	85	15	33	15	6	46	41	44	8.3
University of California-Davis	2.89	3.01	0.29	31	61	35	90	9.3	9.3	40.5	15.7	86	3	40	8	4	90	33	29	7.6
Rensselaer Polytechnic Inst	2.88	3.11	0.16	27	67	59	78	7.6	10.5	29.0	16.6	18	0	34	13	0	40	44	46	6.9
Univ of California-Riverside	2.88	3.13	0.15	32	59	16	72	3.7	7.8	10.7	16.8	50	6	36	3	14	60	61	7	7.5
Arizona State University	2.87	3.27	0.37	39	49	69	90	10.6	5.2	47.4	7.4	85	16	48	16	0	44	69	19	7.0
Virginia Polytech Inst & State U	2.86	3.01	0.08	35	66	43	69	3.9	6.7	18.0	7.8	44	7	26	13	8	46	39	48	6.6
University of Tennessee-Knoxville	2.83	2.78	0.18	36	89	47	81	8.6	6.1	35.3	8.7	66	18	31	9	0	58	62	24	6.9
University of Iowa	2.79	3.07	0.00	28	68	64	86	9.2	8.3	44.4	12.4	71	6	31	7	0	61	78	9	7.7
Mean Values for the 2nd Quarter	**3.09**	**3.18**	**0.25**	**32.19**	**69.73**	**51.68**	**83.41**	**8.65**	**7.18**	**47.58**	**12.17**	**73.92**	**12.43**	**38.59**	**10.49**	**4.24**	**58.95**	**60.30**	**22.62**	**7.38**
University of Delaware	2.76	2.86	0.23	43	53	35	86	7.0	4.4	33.1	6.6	54	11	27	20	0	57	39	36	7.2
University of Georgia	2.73	2.90	0.12	25	60	48	64	7.4	12.7	29.0	16.6	24	17	15	6	0	41	20	60	7.7
Oregon State University	2.69	2.71	-0.06	19	74	47	74	4.0	10.0	14.1	20.0	56	20	13	19	13	50	85	15	8.3
Tufts University	2.66	2.92	-0.15	20	80	50	90	6.8	8.8	39.3	17.9	55	16	20	18	0	45	31	44	7.5
Kent State University	2.65	3.03	0.15	16	63	75	100	9.6	9.2	35.8	18.2	73	14	32	9	11	43	54	31	6.6
Louisiana State U & A&M College	2.64	2.92	0.07	32	66	56	91	8.9	6.3	47.0	7.6	65	15	29	15	0	26	41	37	8.4
University of Nebraska-Lincoln	2.64	2.96	0.24	28	71	50	82	7.3	10.2	29.0	13.2	35	3	18	19	0	43	67	33	7.7
Drexel University	2.62	2.94	0.04	25	80	52	92	6.6	8.7	42.4	13.4	29	28	28	11	0	67	11	78	7.4
University of Hawaii at Manoa	2.61	2.29	0.20	19	79	37	89	7.5	8.3	28.2	13.3	25	12	14	5	0	61	67	13	7.2
Dartmouth College	2.60	3.26	0.07	19	79	53	74	5.9	12.1	41.4	23.0	35	14	18	18	5	86	27	36	6.7
Ohio University	2.60	2.88	0.32	21	67	43	86	5.7	8.2	19.8	12.1	50	12	21	6	0	28	54	42	7.9

Institution	1993 Ratings[1] 93Q	93E	93C	Faculty Tot Fac[2]	% Full[2]	% Supp[2]	% Pub[5]	Pub/ Fac[5]	Gini Pub[5]	Cite/ Fac[5]	Gini Cite[5]	Students[2] Tot Stu	% Fem	Rpt PhDs	Doctorate Recipients[3] % Fem	% Min	% US	% RA	% TA	MYD
University of South Carolina	2.58	2.69	0.34	24	71	46	83	6.5	6.6	29.4	18.2	31	16	17	14	7	68	12	76	9.2
State Univ of New York-Albany	2.58	2.73	0.43	16	69	25	81	10.9	12.4	27.4	12.7	52	25	32	8	31	46	41	41	7.6
Illinois Institute of Technology	2.56	2.47	0.22	13	62	0	77	3.8	12.6	15.6	43.4	32	22	14	13	0	60	21	57	7.0
University of Illinois at Chicago	2.56	2.53	-0.04	27	59	44	74	8.7	9.1	53.7	12.5	71	13	21	6	0	50	48	15	8.6
University of Alaska	2.50	2.22	0.00	24	71	79	75	6.3	9.9	25.8	14.2	43	12	12	9	0	27	89	0	7.7
University of Wisconsin-Milwaukee	2.49	2.74	0.17	18	61	28	94	9.2	12.3	54.7	13.3	22	14	12	10	0	29	46	23	7.5
University of Kentucky	2.48	2.92	0.26	31	55	61	87	5.4	6.9	21.1	9.5	74	12	17	11	0	37	78	17	8.0
University of Texas at Dallas	2.48	3.00	0.39	17	76	59	82	8.1	13.8	30.8	19.6	79	11	39	2	0	74	32	32	7.9
University of Kansas	2.46	2.68	0.05	24	67	42	88	7.0	6.8	41.0	11.1	39	10	16	10	0	65	60	27	9.3
Temple University	2.43	2.59	-0.37	19	58	21	68	4.0	18.8	17.6	43.1	40	18	24	8	0	27	43	48	8.7
University of Oklahoma	2.42	2.53	0.14	27	48	52	74	3.4	8.6	14.3	19.9	50	12	16	15	0	70	50	33	8.8
University of New Hampshire	2.41	2.56	0.19	30	57	53	77	5.2	7.5	28.1	12.0	31	23	15	12	9	65	60	20	8.1
University of Akron	2.40	3.13	0.00	18	67	56	72	14.0	20.2	44.2	24.5	209	28	96	38	0	56	46	15	7.9
Lehigh University	2.39	2.75	0.22	22	50	55	64	4.7	11.3	19.5	14.5	58	16	22	13	0	41	50	21	8.0
University of Missouri-Columbia	2.38	2.80	0.05	21	52	48	95	8.7	6.7	40.0	11.3	38	8	23	23	0	42	43	43	6.8
Catholic University of America	2.33	2.33	0.00	12	75	50	83	6.9	19.0	17.3	20.6	49	18	17	12	10	81	35	20	9.7
University of Connecticut	2.33	2.18	0.05	26	69	38	88	7.0	11.5	30.2	25.9	58	19	34	16	0	67	39	32	7.8
Kansas State University	2.33	2.86	0.00	24	58	46	88	11.1	9.3	43.5	10.0	35	11	24	12	0	35	83	13	7.4
University of Cincinnati	2.33	2.50	0.00	17	94	53	71	3.9	11.2	14.2	13.6	43	16	32	15	7	42	18	68	7.6
Colorado State University	2.30	2.35	0.24	14	71	43	93	7.0	11.2	15.7	12.8	46	24	20	11	16	78	55	10	8.7
University of North Texas	2.30	2.83	0.11	20	40	35	85	7.6	10.6	20.0	15.7	46	20	24	16	0	48	47	13	8.6
Montana State University	2.27	2.62	-0.25	14	64	50	86	9.4	13.4	35.0	14.7	57	19	24	4	0	40	62	33	7.4
Colorado School of Mines	2.25	2.45	0.47	14	57	36	71	6.6	23.0	36.0	32.8	17	12	9	9	0	45	63	0	6.7
State Univ of New York-Buffalo	2.24	2.30	0.00	15	67	67	100	14.6	11.2	45.7	11.6	98	12	23	6	0	26	30	48	7.5
Stevens Inst of Technology	2.23	1.95	0.00	19	84	32	58	4.9	16.2	13.9	19.1	61	10	21	5	0	44	14	64	8.3
Brigham Young University	2.21	2.92	0.08	29	66	7	76	2.6	6.9	57.3	21.2	24	13	35	0	0	46	50	50	6.7
Mean Values for the 3rd Quarter	**2.47**	**2.68**	**0.11**	**21.68**	**65.95**	**45.19**	**81.57**	**7.14**	**10.97**	**31.11**	**17.29**	**51.46**	**15.57**	**23.62**	**12.00**	**2.95**	**50.16**	**46.24**	**33.62**	**7.84**
New Mexico State University	2.19	2.22	0.14	15	67	47	87	4.9	15.0	17.6	24.6	50	4	12	21	0	57	58	25	8.4

Appendix Table L - 7 Physics (Continued)

Institution	1993 Ratings[1] 93Q	93E	93C	Faculty Tot Fac[2]	% Full[2]	% Supp[2]	% Pub[5]	Pub/ Fac[5]	Gini Pub[5]	Cite/ Fac[5]	Gini Cite[5]	Students[2] Tot Stu	% Fem	Rpt PhDs	Doctorate Recipients[3] % Fem	% Min	% US	% RA	% TA	MYD
University of Maine	2.18	2.38	0.00	15	60	20	87	4.4	9.6	9.5	18.6	22	14	10	7	0	38	29	57	8.0
Clarkson University	2.13	1.85	0.13	11	55	45	91	10.7	14.8	52.8	24.9	14	7	13	26	0	37	41	47	9.3
University of Alabama-Huntsville	2.13	1.92	-0.09	21	62	57	90	9.2	9.0	35.2	9.2	35	9	21	17	0	65	41	0	9.4
Tulane University	2.12	1.53	0.10	12	83	33	92	6.3	12.3	24.5	20.5	18	0	4	20	33	60	20	40	9.4
Univ of Arkansas-Fayetteville	2.12	2.57	0.17	15	60	33	93	6.7	17.8	146.5	63.8	24	13	26	3	6	62	42	50	8.1
University of Texas at Arlington	2.11	1.92	0.77	15	53	27	87	7.1	11.2	29.9	11.8	22	23	12	29	0	56	33	17	9.5
Washington State University	2.10	1.80	0.17	21	52	43	81	8.0	12.5	16.9	13.2	56	16	17	4	0	75	63	19	6.9
Texas Tech University	2.10	2.62	0.15	26	50	15	69	6.4	11.3	24.3	22.6	39	15	21	5	0	43	33	33	8.0
University of Alabama	2.08	1.82	0.55	24	58	29	79	6.7	7.1	20.9	10.9	25	8	12	15	0	38	11	44	12.7
Oklahoma State University	2.07	1.78	-0.07	15	87	47	87	7.1	11.6	20.1	14.5	62	13	13	4	14	65	29	18	6.9
University of Miami	2.03	1.83	0.39	11	45	27	73	4.1	16.9	20.1	23.3	16	13	14	20	0	47	33	33	8.5
American University	2.00	1.45	0.00	11	73	36	91	4.5	13.5	34.5	18.9	28	14	11	21	18	86	31	15	8.6
University of Missouri-Rolla	2.00	2.17	-0.27	19	63	63	95	8.5	13.7	28.6	27.4	24	8	15	5	7	71	72	22	8.4
University of Mass-Lowell	1.92	2.41	-0.12	22	77	9	77	2.4	8.8	4.0	18.8	89	11	26	3	0	39	11	63	8.1
Polytechnic University	1.91	1.97	-0.21	12	67	33	83	5.6	16.9	11.8	17.8	25	4	7	0	0	31	60	10	8.0
University of Alabama-Birmingham	1.90	1.11	0.00	20	45	45	75	6.4	16.3	24.0	20.2	26	15	10	0	0	25	0	20	9.4
Auburn University	1.88	1.48	0.00	15	60	13	87	8.5	13.8	22.0	23.5	43	7	12	13	14	44	92	0	7.6
University of Rhode Island	1.85	1.06	-0.23	10	90	50	90	4.6	16.4	14.5	17.9	31	19	10	10	0	30	0	75	7.8
Clark University	1.82	1.67	0.06	8	63	50	75	3.9	29.8	12.1	33.9	16	25	8	20	0	70	100	0	8.7
Boston College	1.80	1.83	0.00	10	60	50	90	5.2	14.8	21.0	17.4	28	25	18	43	0	35	18	71	8.5
Old Dominion University	1.70	0.94	0.53	19	53	32	58	1.6	15.0	2.3	29.4	46	17	5	20	0	40	60	0	8.4
University of Denver	1.61	1.67	0.00	12	67	50	83	7.1	25.8	35.9	38.1	13	15	9	18	0	64	75	0	7.7
Oakland University	1.60	n/s	n/s	23	22	0	65	8.6	9.5	36.0	14.6	17	18	10	17	0	80	75	0	6.4
Howard University	1.60	1.67	0.00	13	77	38	62	4.9	30.1	16.6	61.1	18	11	8	0	83	55	25	75	12.3
New Mexico Inst of Mining & Tech	1.57	1.19	0.00	13	46	54	85	3.2	13.0	15.2	20.5	11	64	4	n/a	n/a	n/a	n/a	n/a	n/a
Bryn Mawr College	1.48	1.77	-0.11	4	75	50	100	7.5	45.7	29.5	47.1	8	13	8	42	0	67	0	89	11.7
Worcester Polytechnic Inst	1.48	1.46	-0.21	11	64	9	73	7.1	21.6	30.9	24.5	13	8	5	20	0	0	0	0	8.0
Michigan Technological University	1.47	1.43	0.00	12	42	58	83	5.2	15.4	11.3	22.5	23	4	8	20	0	44	50	0	6.7
George Washington University	1.45	1.21	0.16	9	22	22	78	6.0	26.3	26.3	30.6	20	20	2	40	25	80	40	20	9.7
University of Mississippi	1.42	1.62	0.15	13	54	38	69	4.5	15.1	8.8	16.1	26	8	11	0	9	85	90	0	6.4

Institution	1993 Ratings[1]			Faculty								Students[2]			Doctorate Recipients[3]					
	93Q	93E	93C	Tot Fac[2]	% Full[2]	% Supp[2]	% Pub[5]	Pub/ Fac[5]	Gini Pub[5]	Cite/ Fac[5]	Gini Cite[5]	Tot Stu	% Fem	Rpt PhDs	% Fem	% Min	% US	% RA	% TA	MYD
University of Nevada, Reno	1.31	0.83	0.29	17	47	41	47	1.8	26.8	3.3	40.6	28	18	14	0	0	13	25	50	12.0
Oregon Graduate Inst Sci & Tech	1.27	1.00	0.00	11	45	45	82	6.5	14.8	16.7	20.5	15	13	11	10	7	70	89	0	7.0
Univ of Puerto Rico-Rio Piedras	1.22	0.67	0.00	13	69	46	100	6.5	23.9	21.0	41.4	13	23	6	0	67	100	0	0	13.7
Baylor University	1.13	1.46	0.00	10	70	10	50	2.7	27.0	9.9	36.3	21	38	7	11	0	44	14	71	7.4
Texas Christian University	0.67	0.72	0.00	7	57	14	71	8.4	22.8	26.7	29.0	14	14	10	6	10	56	8	23	7.6
Florida Institute of Technology	0.46	0.28	0.00	10	50	50	80	2.4	15.2	3.3	32.2	3	33	4	50	0	75	25	75	8.5
Mean Values for the 4th Quarter	**1.73**	**1.59**	**0.07**	**14.19**	**59.19**	**35.92**	**80.14**	**5.82**	**17.33**	**23.91**	**25.90**	**26.54**	**15.68**	**11.19**	**15.00**	**8.14**	**54.08**	**38.69**	**29.50**	**8.71**
Mean Values for All Programs	**2.82**	**2.83**	**0.15**	**29.15**	**66.66**	**46.61**	**82.84**	**7.83**	**10.44**	**43.33**	**15.92**	**75.02**	**14.22**	**39.29**	**11.60**	**4.53**	**55.99**	**53.49**	**24.43**	**7.78**

Sources: 1. National Survey of Graduate Faculty
2. Institutional Coordinator Response Data
3. Doctorate Records File
4. Federal Agencies
5. Institute for Scientific Information

Notes: *a*. Program in Optics

n/s After trimming no cases remained

* The Doctorate Recipient information cannot be separated for two programs at the same institution in the same field and therefore the total for the combined programs is given.

Appendix Table L - 8 Selected Characteristics of Research-Doctorate Programs in Statistics and Biostatistics

Institution	1993 Ratings[1] 93Q	93E	93C	Faculty Tot Fac[2]	% Full[2]	% Supp[2]	% Pub[5]	Pub/ Fac[5]	Gini Pub[5]	Cite/ Fac[5]	Gini Cite[5]	Students[2] Tot Stu	% Fem	Rpt PhDs	Doctorate Recipients[3] % Fem	% Min	% US	% RA	% TA	MYD
Stanford University	4.76	4.44	0.08	16	56	69	94	9.2	8.2	53.3	15.2	49	29	29	22	0	44	9	55	7.4
University of California-Berkeley [a]	4.76	4.33	0.01	24	75	75	92	6.5	5.9	19.3	16.1	39	18	46	21*	15*	48*	10*	47*	8.2*
University of California-Berkeley [b]	4.43	4.01	0.00	18	89	67	94	7.4	9.0	54.2	18.9	13	46	15	21*	15*	48*	10*	47*	8.2*
Cornell University	4.37	4.06	0.22	31	65	58	94	7.2	5.0	17.3	9.3	26	23	13	19	0	53	15	59	7.9
University of Chicago	4.34	4.09	0.08	13	54	31	77	4.3	15.6	9.6	26.6	30	17	18	11	0	56	27	45	6.6
University of Washington [b]	4.21	4.08	0.40	26	69	38	96	13.3	6.8	119.5	15.1	36	42	28	33*	3*	61*	49*	13*	8.7*
Harvard University	4.17	3.80	-0.01	7	57	43	100	7.9	30.3	61.1	72.2	15	13	18	40	0	70	27	3	6.6
University of Wisconsin-Madison	4.06	4.07	-0.20	25	56	44	96	7.4	6.3	30.4	21.1	52	33	50	27	0	39	40	42	8.4
University of Washington [a]	4.01	3.85	0.41	18	56	67	83	5.8	10.6	57.1	24.5	27	22	16	33*	3*	61*	49*	13*	8.7*
Purdue University	4.00	3.61	0.02	18	61	83	94	5.0	9.6	9.1	20.4	27	22	25	7	0	11	5	60	9.0
U of North Carolina-Chapel Hill [a]	3.98	3.69	-0.08	18	67	50	100	7.2	11.0	18.3	19.6	33	24	26	39*	2*	70*	17*	28*	8.5*
Univ of California-Los Angeles	3.93	3.80	0.40	41	68	41	88	8.8	4.7	56.9	14.7	57	49	44	33	0	58	15	33	9.6
University of Minnesota [a]	3.91	3.65	0.26	19	79	74	89	5.8	7.7	12.6	13.4	30	33	20	9*	0*	55*	19*	48*	8.3*
Iowa State University	3.89	3.99	-0.05	27	70	37	93	4.4	6.2	7.5	9.9	48	17	49	19	0	61	42	30	7.6
Texas A&M University	3.78	3.44	0.55	27	48	26	78	5.3	8.6	12.4	18.5	31	32	26	26	13	63	13	63	8.2
Carnegie Mellon University	3.77	3.84	0.21	15	47	67	80	5.7	12.9	19.9	26.2	28	36	23	36	10	71	8	67	5.4
Mean Values for the Top Quarter	**4.15**	**3.92**	**0.14**	**21.44**	**63.56**	**54.38**	**90.50**	**6.95**	**9.90**	**34.91**	**21.36**	**33.81**	**28.50**	**27.88**	**24.75**	**3.81**	**54.31**	**22.19**	**40.81**	**7.96**
Rutgers State Univ-New Brunswick	3.76	3.16	0.16	20	65	65	70	3.4	14.4	4.6	15.9	46	48	10	27	0	36	0	29	11.4
U of North Carolina-Chapel Hill [b]	3.70	3.58	0.11	28	54	18	79	7.3	9.6	32.5	10.8	42	43	30	39*	2*	70*	17*	28*	8.5*
Pennsylvania State University	3.65	3.53	0.52	19	63	53	68	4.3	12.6	6.3	16.5	47	45	22	26	0	42	6	89	8.8
Yale University	3.62	3.39	-0.19	5	60	80	60	3.0	36.8	16.2	65.5	20	30	12	33	0	57	15	8	8.8
Johns Hopkins University	3.55	3.58	0.38	13	46	31	69	9.4	22.2	86.8	23.5	37	54	11	17	0	36	43	14	9.0
North Carolina State University	3.54	3.36	0.31	29	72	41	93	5.6	4.8	13.4	8.5	78	26	30	13	14	58	33	24	9.4
Florida State University	3.47	3.44	-0.09	16	69	25	81	2.7	15.1	4.9	23.0	20	30	17	10	0	40	7	73	9.6
Columbia University	3.44	3.36	-0.14	20	60	55	70	5.6	19.0	48.9	42.8	23	43	39	24	0	35	24	24	7.8
University of Michigan [a]	3.44	3.36	0.05*	12	58	67	83	3.3	15.3	7.1	44.3	19	37	17	27*	8*	66*	24*	24*	8.4*
U of Illinois at Urbana-Champaign	3.35	3.16	-0.09	19	68	53	84	4.5	8.2	11.1	11.9	38	37	21	15	0	16	21	74	7.7
University of Florida	3.31	3.11	0.34	27	52	15	85	9.8	7.9	25.1	22.6	27	44	16	13	20	73	36	43	6.9

Institution	1993 Ratings[1] 93Q	93E	93C	Faculty Tot Fac[2]	% Full[2]	% Supp[2]	% Pub[5]	Pub/ Fac[5]	Gini Pub[5]	Cite/ Fac[5]	Gini Cite[5]	Students[2] Tot Stu	% Fem	Rpt PhDs	Doctorate Recipients[3] % Fem	% Min	% US	% RA	% TA	MYD
University of Pennsylvania	3.22	3.00	0.52	18	61	39	72	3.4	14.0	8.1	14.6	14	36	13	57	0	33	0	20	7.8
Ohio State University	3.21	3.23	0.34	22	45	55	82	5.0	8.5	5.9	15.1	57	42	38	29	0	33	5	76	8.1
Michigan State University	3.14	2.94	-0.14	16	81	25	69	2.0	11.9	1.9	26.1	21	10	23	15	0	32	8	83	9.7
Colorado State University	3.13	3.06	0.09	13	54	46	92	8.1	12.3	18.2	37.2	27	41	17	5	0	59	12	59	8.6
University of Rochester	3.09	3.18	0.16	11	64	36	82	5.1	13.8	17.5	23.2	16	50	12	25	11	56	0	33	9.6
Mean Values for the 2nd Quarter	**3.41**	**3.28**	**0.15**	**18.00**	**60.75**	**44.00**	**77.44**	**5.16**	**14.15**	**19.28**	**25.09**	**33.25**	**38.50**	**20.50**	**23.44**	**3.44**	**46.38**	**15.69**	**43.81**	**8.76**
Northwestern University	3.05	2.92	0.34	15	80	53	80	6.5	13.5	42.9	30.5	9	44	5	30	14	70	0	67	6.7
University of Michigan [b]	3.02	3.02	-0.19	11	45	45	82	12.2	20.2	73.8	31.6	28	50	23	27*	8*	66*	24*	24*	8.4*
University of Iowa [a]	3.00	3.09	-0.14	15	27	40	80	3.9	11.1	8.0	26.1	20	30	9	29*	0*	65*	36*	36*	11.6*
George Washington University	2.91	2.83	0.00	13	46	46	62	5.1	16.1	9.4	22.9	17	29	8	42	9	92	0	8	16.0
University of Pittsburgh [a]	2.85	2.79	-0.31	9	56	67	78	5.4	17.2	14.8	28.7	17	18	8	26*	0*	37*	30*	39*	9.4*
Oregon State University	2.85	2.86	-0.02	15	60	33	87	4.2	12.5	11.9	15.0	28	29	15	23	0	58	36	27	11.0
Southern Methodist University	2.75	2.68	-0.13	11	64	9	64	2.4	19.5	2.4	27.8	25	24	12	55	0	78	0	57	7.4
Univ of California-Riverside	2.75	2.65	0.03	11	73	36	82	5.7	18.1	7.9	25.0	25	40	16	29	0	64	0	11	9.8
Virginia Polytech Inst & State U	2.74	2.92	-0.28	13	62	0	92	5.7	13.5	7.7	15.6	35	31	24	12	0	80	0	69	8.7
U of Massachusetts at Amherst	2.68	2.78	0.12	13	69	15	100	6.9	12.6	27.7	30.4	12	58	8	44	0	67	0	89	9.4
University of Connecticut	2.62	2.43	0.22	8	75	50	100	7.9	18.3	17.4	61.2	37	30	12	29	0	50	0	60	6.6
Univ of California-Santa Barbara	2.54	2.35	0.15	11	36	36	82	4.1	17.2	1.5	22.4	18	28	4	33	0	42	0	100	6.6
University of Minnesota [b]	2.52	2.72	0.47	5	80	40	100	7.8	33.0	32.4	26.9	12	58	3	9*	0*	55*	19*	48*	8.3*
Temple University	2.50	2.25	0.08	17	41	12	82	2.6	8.9	2.2	28.9	41	34	13	27	10	67	0	50	12.8
Boston University	2.46	2.43	0.07	13	23	38	69	8.8	20.7	68.0	26.5	11	55	0	60	0	100	13	63	9.7
University of Iowa [b]	2.39	2.32	0.00	9	33	22	89	15.2	14.1	73.7	15.2	20	50	7	29*	0*	65*	36*	36*	11.6*
Mean Values for the 3rd Quarter	**2.73**	**2.69**	**0.03**	**11.81**	**54.38**	**33.88**	**83.06**	**6.53**	**16.66**	**25.11**	**27.17**	**22.19**	**38.00**	**10.44**	**31.50**	**2.56**	**66.00**	**12.13**	**49.00**	**9.63**
University of Kentucky	2.27	2.34	-0.24	14	43	43	100	5.5	18.9	12.7	57.2	24	46	12	23	0	46	8	58	7.2
Kansas State University	2.24	2.46	0.00	12	67	0	92	8.0	12.3	9.3	19.2	35	26	15	18	0	27	0	80	9.7
Emory University	2.20	2.46	0.33	9	44	11	78	8.1	22.0	49.9	30.7	14	43	7	50	0	88	14	14	10.9

Appendix Table L - 8 Statistics and Biostatistics (Continued)

Institution	1993 Ratings[1]			Faculty								Students[2]			Doctorate Recipients[3]					
	93Q	93E	93C	Tot Fac[2]	% Full[2]	% Supp[2]	% Pub[5]	Pub/ Fac[5]	Gini Pub[5]	Cite/ Fac[5]	Gini Cite[5]	Tot Stu	% Fem	Rpt PhDs	% Fem	% Min	% US	% RA	% TA	MYD
University of Pittsburgh [b]	2.19	2.63	0.11	12	42	0	92	10.9	12.5	165.8	34.1	50	52	15	26*	0*	37*	30*	39*	9.4*
University of Illinois at Chicago	2.16	2.03	-0.15	7	57	43	86	3.0	28.7	3.3	37.6	29	45	7	0	50	29	14	86	7.6
University of South Carolina	2.16	2.24	0.07	14	36	29	86	5.9	12.7	10.4	16.5	19	58	8	57	0	0	43	43	6.7
University of Colorado	2.15	2.45	0.13	10	30	10	100	7.6	12.8	44.1	13.8	11	36	5	22	13	89	11	0	9.4
State Univ of New York-Buffalo	1.97	1.94	-0.50	5	40	20	100	4.6	21.7	3.4	26.6	7	14	8	29	50	29	0	75	9.3
University of Texas at Dallas	1.94	1.95	-0.10	5	80	0	80	2.0	42.0	1.8	55.5	11	18	4	40	50	40	0	67	7.7
Medical University South Carolina	1.92	1.95	0.00	15	33	13	87	5.9	11.1	11.0	19.8	37	30	18	56	14	88	15	8	11.7
University of Wyoming	1.82	1.74	-0.16	8	63	13	75	3.6	22.7	17.0	38.3	11	36	13	20	0	53	25	25	9.8
University of Alabama	1.70	1.96	0.15	11	55	9	91	3.1	13.8	4.8	19.0	14	21	12	0	0	67	0	75	13.4
American University	1.69	1.59	0.00	9	44	11	78	0.9	15.6	0.4	62.5	18	33	5	40	0	40	0	33	11.6
University of Alabama-Birmingham	1.63	1.30	0.07	16	38	6	81	7.6	19.9	25.1	28.6	17	53	2	50	0	100	50	0	13.0
State U of New York-Stony Brook	1.33	1.52	-0.30	5	0	40	100	6.4	20.8	29.4	37.4	134	29	25	33	0	33	20	40	7.0
Univ of Southwestern Louisiana	0.92	1.37	-0.13	7	14	0	57	2.3	38.2	0.6	62.5	16	31	18	26	0	68	0	44	7.8
University of Northern Colorado	0.75	0.69	0.00	4	50	25	0	0.0		0.0		14	14	21	30	0	70	0	0	17.4
Mean Values for the 4th Quarter	**1.83**	**1.92**	**-0.04**	**9.59**	**43.29**	**16.06**	**81.35**	**5.02**	**20.36**	**22.88**	**34.96**	**27.12**	**34.41**	**11.47**	**30.59**	**10.41**	**53.18**	**13.53**	**40.41**	**9.98**
Mean Values for All Programs	**3.01**	**2.94**	**0.07**	**15.12**	**55.31**	**36.75**	**83.06**	**5.90**	**15.27**	**25.50**	**27.14**	**29.06**	**34.85**	**17.48**	**27.62**	**5.14**	**54.94**	**15.85**	**43.46**	**9.09**

Sources: 1. National Survey of Graduate Faculty
2. Institutional Coordinator Response Data
3. Doctorate Records File
4. Federal Agencies
5. Institute for Scientific Information

Notes: *a.* Program in Statistics
b. Program in Biostatistics

* The Doctorate Recipient information cannot be separated for two programs at the same institution in the same field and therefore the total for the combined programs is given.

APPENDIX M

Selected Characteristics of Research-Doctorate Programs in the Social and Behavioral Sciences

In the tables that follow, information from the National Survey of Graduate Faculty is linked to a variety of statistics depicting participating doctoral programs. The tables have been designed to present information about each program in a field in rank order by the average rating of the scholarly quality of program faculty (93Q), with the top-rated institutions appearing at the beginning of the list. A key to the variables in the table is presented below.

Institution

Institution: U.S. Universities participating in the 1993 NRC Study, ranked in descending order based on the scholarly rating of the program faculty (93Q).

1993 Ratings

93Q: 1993 trimmed mean for scholarly quality of program faculty. The trimmed mean is obtained by dropping the two highest and two lowest scores on the survey before computing the average. For purposes of analysis, scores were converted to a scale of 0 to 5, with 0 denoting "Not sufficient for doctoral education" and 5 denoting "Distinguished." Source: NRC National Survey of Graduate Faculty.

93E: 1993 trimmed mean for program effectiveness in educating research scholars and scientists. The trimmed mean is obtained by dropping the two highest and two lowest scores on the survey before computing the average. For purposes of analysis, scores were converted to a scale of 0 to 5 with 0 denoting "Not Effective" and 5 denoting "Extremely Effective." Source: NRC National Survey of Graduate Faculty.

93C: 1993 trimmed mean for change in program quality in the last five years. The trimmed mean is obtained by dropping the two highest and two lowest scores on the survey before computing the average. For purposes of analysis, scores were converted to a scale of –1 to 1 with –1 denoting "Poorer than 5 years ago" and 1 denoting "Better than 5 years ago." Source: NRC National Survey of Graduate Faculty.

Faculty

Tot Fac: Total number of faculty participating in the program. Source: Institutional Coordinators.

%Full: Percentage of full professors participating in the program. Source: Institutional Coordinators.

%Supp Percentage of program faculty (Tot Fac) with research support (1986-1992). Source: Federal Agencies.

%Pub: Percentage of program faculty (Tot Fac) publishing in the period 1988 to 1992. Source: Institute of Scientific Information.

Pub/Fac: The ratio of the total number of program publications in the period 1988-1992 to the number of program faculty (Tot Fac). Source: Institute of Scientific Information.

Gini Pub: Gini coefficient for program publications, 1988-1992. The Gini coefficient is an indicator of the concentration of publications on a small number of the program faculty during the period 1988-1992. The largest possible value, or maximum concentration, is 100 (only one individual in the program registered a positive count); the smallest value, or minimum concentration, is 100/Fac (All the faculty (Tot Fac) in the program contribute equally). Source: Institute of Scientific Information.

Cite/Fac: The ratio of the total number of program citations in the period 1988-1992 to the number of program faculty (Tot Fac). Source: Institute of Scientific Information.

Gini Cite: Gini coefficient for program citations, 1988-1992. The Gini coefficient is an indicator of the concentration of citations on a small number of the program faculty during the period 1988-1992. The largest possible value, or maximum concentration, is 100 (only one individual in the program registered a positive count); the smallest value, or minimum concentration, is 100/Fac (All the faculty (Tot Fac) in the program contribute equally). Source: Institute of Scientific Information.

Students

Tot Stu:	The number of full and part time graduate students enrolled in the Fall of 1992. Source: Institutional Coordinators.
%Fem:	The percentage of full and part time female graduate students enrolled in the Fall of 1992. Source: Institutional Coordinators.
Rpt PhDs:	The number of PhDs produced by that program for the period academic year 1987-1988 to 1991-1992. Source: Institutional Coordinators.

Doctoral Recipients

%Fem:	The percentage of Ph.D.s awarded to women during the period July 1986-June 1992. Source: Doctorate Records File.
%Min:	The percentage of Ph.D.s known to be awarded to underrepresented minorities (only U.S. Citizens or Permanent Residents) during the period July 1986-June 1992. Source: Doctorate Records File.
%US:	The percentage of Ph.D.s known to be awarded to U.S. Citizens and Permanent Residents during the period July 1986-June 1992. Source: Doctorate Records File.
%RA:	The percentage of Ph.D.s having research assistantships who reported their primary form of support. Source: Doctorate Records File.
%TA:	The percentage of Ph.D.s having teaching assistantships who reported their primary form of support. Source: Doctorate Records File.
MYD:	Median time lapse from entering graduate school to receipt of Ph.D. in years. This is a distributed median with multiple degrees awarded in the median year proportioned over the year. Source: Doctorate Records File.

NOTICE: **n/a** denotes a case where information was not provided by the Institutional Coordinators or was not available from the Doctorate Records File.

Appendix Table M - 1 Selected Characteristics of Research-Doctorate Programs in Anthropology

Institution	1993 Ratings[1] 93Q	93E	93C	Faculty Tot Fac[2]	% Full[2]	% Supp[2]	% Pub[5]	Pub/ Fac[5]	Gini Pub[5]	Cite/ Fac[5]	Gini Cite[5]	Students[2] Tot Stu	% Fem	Rpt PhDs	Doctorate Recipients[3] % Fem	% Min	% US	% RA	% TA	MYD
University of Michigan	4.77	4.40	0.22	41	61	32	68	2.4	6.1	5.2	9.6	94	53	41	51	3	91	16	25	10.2
University of Chicago	4.77	4.19	0.02	29	90	31	69	2.6	9.5	11.9	29.8	203	45	52	38	9	93	3	0	11.5
University of California-Berkeley	4.51	3.93	-0.12	27	81	37	67	2.3	9.5	6.4	19.0	110	60	80	54	12	85	0	18	9.9
Harvard University	4.43	3.67	0.11	28	68	43	71	3.3	8.6	11.8	15.8	144	56	62	27	7	91	0	29	9.6
University of Arizona	4.11	3.60	0.21	47	53	26	66	2.0	6.1	3.7	12.5	181	62	33	50	10	91	13	13	10.5
University of Pennsylvania	3.94	3.68	0.13	36	56	39	47	2.2	10.6	8.0	15.6	120	70	32	56	0	87	3	5	11.5
Stanford University	3.71	3.63	-0.08	14	64	36	29	0.5	30.6	0.3	100.0	61	70	27	50	13	86	6	3	9.4
Yale University	3.67	3.43	-0.14	19	58	47	58	1.3	11.0	4.7	37.8	68	53	32	43	8	88	0	9	9.6
Univ of California-Los Angeles	3.67	3.50	0.15	41	56	44	66	2.4	5.5	10.7	10.5	142	62	96	63	11	92	3	5	11.4
Univ of California-San Diego	3.67	3.44	0.34	25	44	16	76	1.9	13.0	7.8	64.5	36	47	18	52	5	91	10	57	8.7
University of Florida	3.65	3.40	0.19	22	64	18	59	1.5	12.0	0.5	26.3	77	48	43	47	9	94	17	12	9.9
University of Texas at Austin	3.62	3.38	0.24	34	65	21	56	1.8	12.6	2.0	15.9	50	60	43	61	6	97	3	10	11.9
New York University	3.60	3.36	0.46	18	39	33	61	1.5	13.0	2.6	24.1	23	78	16	83	13	96	0	6	12.7
U of Illinois at Urbana-Champaign	3.59	3.47	0.10	28	64	25	64	1.4	7.7	2.8	19.3	100	59	27	40	3	74	18	38	12.5
University of California-Davis	3.51	3.26	0.63	24	58	21	50	1.0	10.4	1.0	17.7	35	60	11	56	13	100	0	29	12.4
Columbia University	3.49	3.21	-0.25	29	34	10	45	1.2	12.9	2.4	21.7	75	59	48	55	12	89	5	2	13.4
Washington University	3.42	3.18	0.44	17	65	53	82	3.8	13.4	7.8	13.1	64	61	11	53	0	88	0	9	12.8
Mean Values for the Top Quarter	**3.89**	**3.57**	**0.16**	**28.18**	**60.00**	**31.29**	**60.82**	**1.95**	**11.32**	**5.27**	**26.66**	**93.12**	**59.00**	**39.53**	**51.71**	**7.88**	**90.18**	**5.71**	**15.88**	**11.05**
Duke University	3.41	3.12	0.04	24	38	33	67	2.9	13.7	12.5	22.8	51	69	9	50	0	100	25	25	8.0
University of Wisconsin-Madison	3.41	3.22	0.46	24	50	21	75	1.3	8.2	4.0	21.7	103	48	25	50	4	100	5	18	11.2
Univ of California-Santa Barbara	3.40	3.26	0.33	19	74	32	68	1.7	11.4	6.9	28.3	63	56	16	56	8	93	5	27	10.9
Johns Hopkins University	3.39	3.44	-0.08	6	83	33	83	1.8	23.9	1.7	30.0	39	62	9	64	38	100	0	0	11.1
CUNY - Grad Sch & Univ Center	3.39	3.27	-0.23	14	64	57	43	0.4	16.6	0.2	100.0	143	65	32	69	11	90	3	0	11.8
University of Virginia	3.38	3.14	0.36	24	29	13	38	1.0	21.9	3.6	95.4	43	42	18	46	0	79	0	5	11.9
Rutgers State Univ-New Brunswick	3.38	3.08	0.33	26	73	12	65	1.8	9.7	4.8	21.5	53	72	25	56	14	88	0	28	12.5
University of Pittsburgh	3.34	2.99	0.26	34	59	32	56	1.8	11.8	3.8	23.8	118	48	17	52	8	86	4	35	12.7
Arizona State University	3.31	3.22	0.61	24	63	33	58	1.9	12.0	4.8	21.1	171	57	23	45	4	96	4	17	12.6
Princeton University	3.30	3.15	-0.02	10	60	20	50	1.2	23.6	1.2	26.3	22	68	10	60	0	84	0	0	10.0

Institution	1993 Ratings[1]			Faculty								Students[2]			Doctorate Recipients[3]					
	93Q	93E	93C	Tot Fac[2]	% Full[2]	% Supp[2]	% Pub[5]	Pub/ Fac[5]	Gini Pub[5]	Cite/ Fac[5]	Gini Cite[5]	Tot Stu	% Fem	Rpt PhDs	% Fem	% Min	% US	% RA	% TA	MYD
Indiana University	3.24	3.16	0.22	27	44	11	37	0.7	13.5	0.7	24.0	141	65	48	51	5	83	7	33	10.9
University of Washington	3.24	3.25	0.04	26	50	31	46	1.9	11.1	4.5	25.1	94	74	36	63	2	91	2	14	11.4
U of North Carolina-Chapel Hill	3.24	2.94	0.38	18	50	33	50	0.6	12.0	0.4	46.8	52	65	12	69	0	100	5	25	12.4
Cornell University	3.21	3.39	-0.07	20	65	15	50	1.8	19.3	6.5	28.2	42	57	38	63	5	78	0	10	11.4
Pennsylvania State University	3.18	3.21	0.27	15	40	53	100	3.6	12.2	15.9	18.7	53	49	18	41	5	91	25	15	10.9
Southern Methodist University	3.10	3.04	0.45	17	59	35	47	1.4	18.3	1.5	39.3	67	54	22	44	4	84	14	23	10.5
Northwestern University	3.09	3.11	-0.05	21	38	33	67	1.8	10.9	9.3	29.9	35	60	29	56	7	98	0	13	9.2
Mean Values for the 2nd Quarter	**3.29**	**3.18**	**0.19**	**20.53**	**55.24**	**29.24**	**58.82**	**1.62**	**14.71**	**4.84**	**35.46**	**75.88**	**59.47**	**22.76**	**55.00**	**6.76**	**90.65**	**5.82**	**16.94**	**11.14**
U of Massachusetts at Amherst	3.04	3.17	-0.21	14	64	7	36	1.1	29.7	4.0	44.6	86	0	32	56	10	95	0	27	12.4
State Univ of New York-Binghamton	3.02	2.94	-0.20	23	26	30	35	0.4	13.5	0.2	68.0	94	51	29	46	0	92	6	26	12.4
State Univ of New York-Buffalo	3.01	2.68	0.19	21	62	19	43	1.0	17.7	0.9	43.4	96	44	13	57	0	100	6	25	11.0
State U of New York-Stony Brook	2.97	3.14	0.17	23	35	61	78	4.5	11.4	21.3	25.4	51	59	25	55	7	90	0	58	10.3
State Univ of New York-Albany	2.82	2.68	0.19	19	37	32	89	2.6	16.7	4.0	26.9	54	61	13	56	18	81	0	57	8.9
University of Connecticut	2.80	2.93	0.12	18	44	11	56	1.3	19.4	2.9	50.8	85	56	27	56	11	85	0	8	11.8
University of Hawaii at Manoa	2.78	2.63	0.07	16	63	19	56	1.4	13.7	0.9	29.7	45	71	16	37	0	77	5	5	12.4
Southern Illinois University	2.76	2.81	0.40	14	43	21	50	1.5	25.6	3.1	54.3	23	48	13	35	0	82	31	31	13.7
Brown University	2.73	2.59	-0.15	12	67	17	58	1.3	18.2	0.3	62.5	36	64	17	57	0	87	5	68	9.0
University of Iowa	2.73	2.62	0.40	16	38	13	56	1.6	13.2	0.9	16.4	53	70	7	38	0	100	0	57	11.7
University of Oregon	2.66	2.68	0.23	23	52	9	39	0.7	12.8	0.5	32.2	27	30	24	38	4	88	14	14	10.2
Michigan State University	2.58	2.75	0.08	23	57	13	39	0.6	13.2	0.7	52.9	59	34	37	37	6	94	20	0	12.1
Tulane University	2.56	2.61	-0.06	10	50	10	30	0.5	44.0	0.8	62.5	67	48	10	41	7	94	0	0	11.1
University of Utah	2.56	2.14	0.16	15	53	27	67	3.0	20.7	17.1	31.6	46	59	7	50	7	100	0	0	12.0
University of Kentucky	2.51	2.57	0.18	20	35	40	40	1.1	13.8	2.5	26.3	39	59	9	79	8	93	30	10	11.0
University of Minnesota	2.49	2.35	-0.26	12	58	17	50	0.9	20.6	0.4	52.0	45	76	12	67	5	88	5	29	13.0
Boston University	2.44	2.27	0.07	13	15	23	23	0.3	37.5	0.6	78.1	29	69	6	53	6	94	0	29	9.8
Mean Values for the 3rd Quarter	**2.73**	**2.68**	**0.08**	**17.18**	**47.00**	**21.71**	**49.71**	**1.40**	**20.10**	**3.59**	**44.56**	**55.00**	**52.88**	**17.47**	**50.47**	**5.24**	**90.59**	**7.18**	**26.12**	**11.34**

Appendix Table M - 1 Anthropology (Continued)

Institution	1993 Ratings[1] 93Q	93E	93C	Faculty Tot Fac[2]	% Full[2]	% Supp[2]	% Pub[5]	Pub/ Fac[5]	Gini Pub[5]	Cite/ Fac[5]	Gini Cite[5]	Students[2] Tot Stu	% Fem	Rpt PhDs	Doctorate Recipients[3] % Fem	% Min	% US	% RA	% TA	MYD
University of Tennessee-Knoxville	2.42	2.86	0.00	13	23	23	38	1.5	30.7	0.9	33.3	31	48	21	24	7	100	5	18	9.8
University of Missouri-Columbia	2.40	2.07	0.09	23	39	30	83	2.4	8.4	7.1	44.9	44	39	11	37	0	100	5	5	14.4
Temple University	2.40	2.30	-0.15	16	44	25	50	1.4	14.8	7.1	63.2	14	n/a	12	42	0	100	0	25	12.7
University of Colorado	2.39	2.43	-0.06	15	53	13	73	1.9	13.4	2.1	24.6	42	69	22	64	0	94	4	8	11.6
Univ of California-Riverside	2.39	2.33	-0.07	18	56	17	50	0.9	13.2	0.6	24.0	49	69	6	40	7	93	22	0	10.8
Vanderbilt University	2.35	2.32	0.38	13	46	15	23	0.4	44.0	0.1	100.0	18	56	1	0	0	100	0	0	6.0
University of Kansas	2.35	2.56	-0.08	16	75	25	44	1.4	30.1	1.4	56.6	15	60	9	53	0	74	13	19	11.7
Brandeis University	2.28	2.08	-0.50	9	33	33	56	0.6	20.0	1.2	100.0	27	63	10	85	0	92	0	0	15.6
University of South Florida	2.17	1.99	0.07	14	43	7	50	1.5	16.5	1.0	29.5	44	75	12	67	27	92	10	0	12.8
Syracuse University	2.09	1.89	0.18	22	27	9	41	0.8	14.8	2.3	38.0	35	66	8	62	0	69	0	38	13.8
University of Wisconsin-Milwaukee	2.08	1.31	0.04	12	33	0	42	0.5	22.2	1.7	68.0	20	55	10	40	14	100	0	8	11.9
Washington State University	2.00	1.97	-0.05	14	43	14	57	1.1	16.4	2.1	29.6	39	41	18	40	0	90	9	26	14.4
Wayne State University	1.98	1.67	-0.31	11	55	0	45	1.0	25.6	3.5	54.1	17	94	8	89	14	100	0	20	12.7
University of Oklahoma	1.89	1.67	0.05	12	17	33	58	1.3	23.5	1.9	44.8	56	68	9	31	0	100	0	13	11.7
University of Rochester	1.89	2.20	-0.46	7	43	0	57	0.7	28.0	1.4	54.0	31	52	8	73	0	91	0	0	10.8
Ohio State University	1.89	1.81	-0.24	13	23	15	54	3.2	27.3	6.7	30.6	57	67	9	44	9	87	0	63	13.4
American University	1.86	2.37	-0.13	9	44	0	22	0.3	55.5	0.6	52.0	39	67	21	60	9	92	0	24	12.6
Catholic University of America	1.21	1.50	-0.50	6	33	33	50	0.7	37.5	0.5	100.0	25	84	8	38	0	100	0	0	17.4
Mean Values for the 4th Quarter	**2.11**	**2.07**	**-0.10**	**13.50**	**40.56**	**16.22**	**49.61**	**1.20**	**24.55**	**2.34**	**52.62**	**33.50**	**63.12**	**11.28**	**49.39**	**4.83**	**93.00**	**3.78**	**14.83**	**12.45**
Mean Values for All Programs	**2.99**	**2.86**	**0.08**	**19.75**	**50.55**	**24.49**	**54.67**	**1.54**	**17.77**	**3.99**	**40.01**	**63.93**	**58.62**	**22.59**	**51.61**	**6.16**	**91.13**	**5.59**	**18.39**	**11.51**

Sources: 1. National Survey of Graduate Faculty
2. Institutional Coordinator Response Data
3. Doctorate Records File
4. Federal Agencies
5. Institute for Scientific Information

Appendix Table M - 2 Selected Characteristics of Research-Doctorate Programs in Economics

Institution	1993 Ratings[1]			Faculty								Students[2]			Doctorate Recipients[3]					
	93Q	93E	93C	Tot Fac[2]	% Full[2]	% Supp[2]	% Pub[5]	Pub/ Fac[5]	Gini Pub[5]	Cite/ Fac[5]	Gini Cite[5]	Tot Stu	% Fem	Rpt PhDs	% Fem	% Min	% US	% RA	% TA	MYD
University of Chicago	4.95	4.63	0.04	31	81	23	71	3.4	6.7	23.7	11.3	216	18	130	14	4	57	5	1	7.8
Harvard University	4.95	4.33	0.30	44	66	23	75	6.3	4.4	23.2	5.2	148	24	137	17	9	58	3	19	6.5
Massachusetts Inst of Technology	4.93	4.71	-0.11	28	68	25	82	5.0	7.0	22.5	11.6	161	29	122	13	4	60	7	20	5.8
Stanford University	4.92	4.58	0.35	36	67	28	78	4.4	5.3	16.1	9.4	146	20	94	19	1	64	49	16	7.1
Princeton University	4.84	4.69	0.05	41	61	39	73	3.9	5.3	12.9	10.2	91	29	86	18	5	55	1	10	6.6
Yale University	4.70	4.01	0.12	44	68	34	82	4.0	5.2	13.3	14.6	130	15	90	16	7	60	1	15	8.3
University of California-Berkeley	4.55	4.05	0.32	41	71	32	88	4.2	4.0	15.4	8.1	150	31	102	26	7	69	12	41	7.6
University of Pennsylvania	4.43	3.91	0.33	51	61	45	76	4.5	4.1	13.0	6.8	178	23	107	16	2	42	22	24	6.9
Northwestern University	4.39	4.04	0.52	47	68	51	85	4.2	3.6	14.2	7.3	103	30	50	14	2	62	19	33	6.7
University of Minnesota	4.22	4.08	-0.22	18	78	33	72	2.9	10.5	4.3	15.3	108	18	77	20	2	47	17	61	7.9
Univ of California-Los Angeles	4.12	3.55	0.13	64	53	23	73	4.2	3.2	9.7	4.5	101	13	92	18	0	64	8	41	7.5
Columbia University	4.07	3.43	-0.04	36	56	6	72	2.4	6.5	2.6	18.4	141	27	74	24	13	61	1	17	8.5
University of Michigan	4.03	3.65	0.24	46	59	28	89	3.9	3.3	12.3	10.1	115	31	79	32	2	85	15	35	8.1
University of Rochester	4.01	3.96	-0.01	27	56	52	89	4.6	6.2	15.6	10.5	121	14	53	14	0	28	5	14	7.6
University of Wisconsin-Madison	3.93	3.79	-0.14	28	64	50	71	3.0	7.5	7.8	13.0	175	26	118	16	2	75	18	43	7.5
Univ of California-San Diego	3.80	3.83	0.66	30	57	37	83	3.8	6.6	19.0	14.8	61	30	59	22	8	36	6	66	7.5
New York University	3.62	3.22	0.55	37	49	27	78	2.5	6.2	7.5	13.7	54	33	65	20	10	57	18	11	9.2
Cornell University	3.56	3.36	0.06	30	70	33	83	3.1	5.0	6.6	14.4	75	25	59	26	6	51	22	47	7.4
California Institute Technology	3.54	3.81	0.07	23	65	22	65	2.7	10.3	6.5	14.9	14	50	12	0	0	75	86	14	6.0
University of Maryland College Park	3.46	2.99	0.40	47	72	11	68	2.8	5.6	32.3	74.7	168	37	55	40	5	85	17	36	8.8
Boston University	3.39	2.76	0.79	36	67	25	81	4.6	7.7	17.3	38.2	112	39	57	18	17	30	8	23	11.4
Duke University	3.36	3.29	0.29	32	69	19	69	2.9	6.5	7.8	11.5	81	25	52	20	5	70	7	39	6.8
Brown University	3.34	3.38	0.23	30	50	7	60	2.7	8.9	6.3	12.4	60	18	39	15	0	50	6	75	7.9
University of Virginia	3.20	3.26	-0.20	26	54	23	69	3.3	11.4	6.2	26.3	67	25	29	19	5	85	0	50	7.6
U of North Carolina-Chapel Hill	3.16	3.16	0.10	33	52	12	79	2.5	7.2	3.5	22.2	99	21	36	19	2	83	10	40	7.4
University of Washington	3.15	3.17	0.12	24	50	4	83	2.9	7.8	14.7	48.6	112	24	53	25	2	71	0	57	8.3
Michigan State University	3.09	3.09	0.18	44	55	11	73	3.3	8.7	12.2	27.6	88	19	41	13	0	55	6	50	8.0
Mean Values for the Top Quarter	**3.99**	**3.73**	**0.19**	**36.07**	**62.48**	**26.78**	**76.56**	**3.63**	**6.47**	**12.83**	**17.61**	**113.89**	**25.70**	**72.89**	**19.04**	**4.44**	**60.56**	**13.67**	**33.26**	**7.66**
U of Illinois at Urbana-Champaign	3.07	2.94	0.17	55	71	18	67	2.2	4.6	2.6	13.2	216	25	87	13	7	50	20	51	6.9

Appendix Table M - 2 Economics (Continued)

Institution	1993 Ratings[1]			Faculty								Students[2]			Doctorate Recipients[3]					
	93Q	93E	93C	Tot Fac[2]	% Full[2]	% Supp[2]	% Pub[5]	Pub/ Fac[5]	Gini Pub[5]	Cite/ Fac[5]	Gini Cite[5]	Tot Stu	% Fem	Rpt PhDs	% Fem	% Min	% US	% RA	% TA	MYD
Washington University	3.00	2.82	0.15	22	50	5	95	2.3	8.2	3.8	18.3	68	25	42	25	3	62	30	45	7.4
University of Iowa	2.97	2.92	0.14	20	60	50	75	3.4	10.3	6.9	26.0	59	24	21	11	0	38	6	88	7.6
University of Texas at Austin	2.91	2.66	0.52	40	55	8	48	2.3	9.5	2.3	15.4	68	24	63	24	16	59	6	49	8.8
Johns Hopkins University	2.87	3.00	-0.54	11	45	18	64	2.9	24.8	2.5	34.4	70	24	42	27	4	47	0	36	9.6
Texas A&M University	2.83	2.69	0.26	27	52	4	81	3.2	7.5	4.5	12.5	93	22	40	18	5	67	22	47	6.9
University of Pittsburgh	2.83	2.71	0.23	29	59	24	62	2.1	7.6	4.8	13.8	58	28	61	19	13	48	2	67	9.3
Ohio State University	2.83	2.69	0.15	35	57	17	66	2.0	7.3	2.9	10.8	102	16	52	24	5	29	13	74	7.7
University of Arizona	2.78	2.44	0.30	19	47	32	68	2.7	12.0	5.2	17.8	35	29	17	15	13	88	18	18	9.4
Iowa State University	2.78	2.90	0.32	57	61	5	63	2.9	5.0	3.0	10.4	84	12	67	19	0	35	45	28	8.0
University of California-Davis	2.75	2.34	0.31	24	54	25	75	3.5	8.4	5.1	12.0	55	24	30	21	11	72	6	49	9.6
State U of New York-Stony Brook	2.73	2.59	-0.06	18	61	22	72	1.7	10.2	2.9	24.4	70	23	27	13	0	34	0	75	8.2
University of Southern California	2.66	2.57	-0.30	23	48	17	65	4.1	9.5	9.3	14.3	76	33	0	13	0	23	8	58	9.4
University of Florida	2.65	2.57	0.19	21	52	5	71	3.3	8.9	4.6	17.1	20	20	31	21	7	36	47	33	7.5
North Carolina State University	2.61	2.43	0.18	36	75	3	89	4.1	5.4	5.8	12.1	96	28	42	32	8	55	29	26	9.3
Boston College	2.53	2.47	0.21	21	43	14	67	2.4	13.3	2.9	22.6	76	32	29	33	4	79	5	45	7.9
Indiana University	2.51	2.68	-0.04	29	52	17	76	3.2	7.3	4.8	15.1	68	29	43	4	4	48	14	52	8.5
Pennsylvania State University	2.49	2.60	0.12	42	33	12	71	3.0	6.1	5.0	15.3	113	29	42	27	4	48	0	72	9.5
Rice University	2.47	2.21	0.12	15	53	13	53	1.8	18.7	10.5	81.2	39	23	12	31	14	44	0	7	8.4
George Mason University	2.46	2.14	0.21	22	45	0	95	5.2	9.3	7.2	10.6	165	29	28	14	13	89	7	7	8.4
Vanderbilt University	2.40	2.48	-0.20	21	43	10	76	4.0	14.4	14.6	46.4	60	28	29	16	0	33	3	54	8.7
Univ of California-Santa Barbara	2.38	2.46	-0.25	27	74	7	63	2.4	18.5	2.6	19.5	46	22	36	12	7	71	0	79	7.5
U of Massachusetts at Amherst	2.37	2.55	-0.07	28	61	7	79	2.4	5.8	2.9	12.4	48	52	38	25	10	85	2	50	9.9
Purdue University	2.37	2.68	-0.32	16	44	6	56	2.3	13.8	2.5	24.5	59	24	44	20	6	65	12	68	6.6
Rutgers State Univ-New Brunswick	2.36	2.29	0.21	29	45	7	72	2.1	6.3	3.1	18.5	44	48	34	14	8	61	3	65	8.4
CUNY - Grad Sch & Univ Center	2.26	2.28	0.06	22	59	14	59	1.7	9.8	3.3	28.9	108	33	48	15	2	67	3	10	8.4
University of Colorado	2.25	2.59	0.27	28	50	14	71	3.2	7.7	4.7	12.9	71	27	53	17	0	63	8	19	8.2
Georgetown University	2.25	1.93	0.25	15	40	0	80	2.9	9.7	2.7	20.8	56	32	26	20	6	46	0	36	9.2
Mean Values for the 2nd Quarter	**2.62**	**2.56**	**0.09**	**26.86**	**53.18**	**13.36**	**70.68**	**2.83**	**10.00**	**4.75**	**20.76**	**75.82**	**27.32**	**38.71**	**19.39**	**6.07**	**55.07**	**11.04**	**46.71**	**8.40**
Syracuse University	2.21	2.13	0.51	26	50	8	65	2.2	8.0	2.9	22.1	42	36	21	28	4	62	40	10	10.0

Institution	1993 Ratings[1] 93Q	93E	93C	Faculty Tot Fac[2]	% Full[2]	% Supp[2]	% Pub[5]	Pub/ Fac[5]	Gini Pub[5]	Cite/ Fac[5]	Gini Cite[5]	Students[2] Tot Stu	% Fem	Rpt PhDs	Doctorate Recipients[3] % Fem	% Min	% US	% RA	% TA	MYD
University of Houston	2.14	2.02	0.06	25	32	16	44	1.6	11.1	1.2	14.8	54	31	17	14	6	61	11	39	6.7
State Univ of New York-Buffalo	2.09	1.86	-0.36	16	50	0	88	2.1	9.2	1.7	26.2	37	30	29	5	8	35	7	70	7.9
Southern Methodist University	2.04	1.81	-0.18	16	31	0	75	5.3	13.8	4.4	28.8	3	0	16	10	0	32	0	60	8.1
Claremont Graduate School	2.02	1.90	-0.29	3	67	0	33	2.3	100.0	2.3	100.0	56	32	16	15	10	53	17	0	11.0
University of Oregon	1.98	1.59	0.17	19	47	16	84	3.3	8.1	2.0	15.6	31	10	26	18	0	63	0	63	8.0
Florida State University	1.97	1.92	0.15	30	57	3	77	3.5	7.2	4.1	11.3	40	25	36	20	19	80	22	22	9.3
University of Georgia	1.95	1.77	0.00	18	44	6	94	4.5	13.0	3.9	16.0	20	20	19	20	0	44	35	30	9.6
University of Kentucky	1.90	1.87	0.20	19	53	11	79	3.7	8.0	6.6	20.0	46	24	23	18	5	75	0	57	7.7
University of South Carolina	1.89	1.50	0.00	17	47	12	76	2.5	16.6	4.5	39.3	23	35	22	30	0	52	28	40	6.4
State Univ of New York-Binghamton	1.88	1.86	0.06	20	40	0	30	0.5	30.0	0.4	28.3	59	20	37	14	10	47	38	28	8.4
Arizona State University	1.85	1.81	-0.03	18	78	0	89	3.7	9.0	3.6	14.8	22	50	20	17	18	58	33	33	7.7
George Washington University	1.83	1.78	0.11	26	50	4	62	1.8	9.7	1.1	22.9	84	31	47	29	10	76	0	16	12.1
Georgia State University	1.77	1.67	0.27	25	64	0	56	1.6	10.5	1.3	30.3	33	33	18	4	16	79	19	25	9.4
Univ of California-Riverside	1.72	1.32	0.35	30	53	7	70	1.9	6.7	2.2	15.7	54	31	14	18	0	82	7	27	8.4
University of Illinois at Chicago	1.72	1.38	0.13	18	50	22	78	3.5	10.8	3.9	28.1	36	33	28	37	6	57	18	14	7.8
American University	1.72	1.53	-0.11	22	55	0	73	1.9	9.2	1.0	16.0	96	35	27	31	3	74	3	23	11.7
University of Kansas	1.71	1.72	-0.10	18	28	0	67	1.8	13.1	3.7	45.4	30	37	14	5	0	63	17	58	8.5
Auburn University	1.68	1.27	0.00	15	47	0	100	5.1	10.4	3.3	15.9	33	30	7	10	13	80	0	60	7.7
Clemson University	1.67	1.95	0.40	39	72	3	46	1.5	8.6	1.4	13.2	33	27	19	33	13	67	14	43	10.7
Southern Illinois University	1.65	1.30	-0.04	13	62	0	69	5.5	17.0	2.8	31.7	54	20	15	17	14	30	38	15	10.9
University of Wyoming	1.65	1.48	-0.64	13	54	0	85	3.0	10.8	3.0	14.3	20	30	7	15	0	92	50	30	6.8
State Univ of New York-Albany	1.65	1.44	-0.11	20	25	5	50	1.5	13.6	0.7	29.5	57	28	35	16	8	30	13	55	7.6
University of Tennessee-Knoxville	1.62	1.30	-0.03	19	79	5	79	3.1	11.3	1.9	15.4	48	19	27	22	6	76	31	36	8.4
Tulane University	1.54	1.30	-0.64	14	29	0	86	1.1	10.2	0.6	28.1	34	24	14	18	10	59	15	46	7.8
Mean Values for the 3rd Quarter	**1.83**	**1.66**	**0.00**	**19.96**	**50.56**	**4.72**	**70.20**	**2.74**	**15.04**	**2.58**	**25.75**	**41.80**	**27.64**	**22.16**	**18.56**	**7.16**	**61.08**	**18.24**	**36.00**	**8.74**
University of Notre Dame	1.53	1.47	0.00	24	42	0	58	1.3	9.8	1.0	24.0	90	39	27	30	7	69	13	35	8.8
Louisiana State U & A&M College	1.53	1.74	0.23	23	70	0	78	4.3	9.2	5.2	13.9	21	48	14	26	10	53	33	27	8.6
Washington State University	1.42	1.54	-0.32	19	26	11	42	1.5	17.4	1.8	19.0	58	29	20	13	0	63	4	75	8.2
University of Connecticut	1.40	1.30	0.13	22	45	5	68	2.3	12.7	2.7	22.8	118	32	25	13	12	60	9	65	11.8
University of Hawaii at Manoa	1.38	0.99	0.00	22	64	9	86	2.3	7.6	1.7	19.3	55	35	37	21	8	25	2	9	9.7
Oklahoma State University	1.23	1.04	-0.11	17	71	0	65	2.0	11.2	0.5	18.7	54	31	20	8	0	32	0	19	9.7

Appendix Table M - 2 Economics (Continued)

Institution	1993 Ratings[1] 93Q	93E	93C	Faculty Tot Fac[2]	% Full[2]	% Supp[2]	% Pub[5]	Pub/ Fac[5]	Gini Pub[5]	Cite/ Fac[5]	Gini Cite[5]	Students[2] Tot Stu	% Fem	Rpt PhDs	Doctorate Recipients[3] % Fem	% Min	% US	% RA	% TA	MYD
University of Nebraska-Lincoln	1.19	0.45	-0.10	20	65	0	65	2.1	14.1	1.9	45.8	41	15	23	16	5	68	0	38	10.0
University of Wisconsin-Milwaukee	1.17	1.31	0.00	23	26	4	43	2.3	21.9	1.6	33.0	27	26	14	26	6	59	4	40	9.6
Lehigh University	1.16	1.11	0.00	30	37	0	47	1.1	9.3	0.9	20.4	21	33	17	71	0	71	0	60	10.8
University of Utah	1.15	1.00	-0.25	20	40	0	45	0.8	13.2	0.8	36.7	54	22	26	21	0	78	8	24	8.7
Temple University	1.11	0.90	-0.17	32	38	0	63	1.3	9.0	1.7	38.0	43	16	18	8	0	71	6	24	10.8
West Virginia University	1.06	1.35	0.07	20	50	5	50	1.2	22.8	0.5	30.0	35	26	20	16	11	47	13	22	9.5
University of Missouri-Columbia	1.04	0.91	-0.37	14	43	0	50	1.0	20.4	1.1	47.5	37	19	24	8*	0*	38*	5*	30*	11.8*
Northern Illinois University	1.02	0.69	0.00	26	54	0	58	1.6	8.6	0.8	17.4	45	29	27	19	9	42	24	29	8.9
University of Alabama	0.99	0.69	-0.05	14	57	0	64	2.9	20.6	2.6	19.7	21	14	4	0	0	63	25	25	9.6
Fordham University	0.93	0.94	0.00	16	38	0	44	1.1	19.7	0.8	38.8	145	23	26	26	30	81	15	15	10.3
University of Cincinnati	0.90	0.75	-0.20	10	80	0	30	0.3	33.3	0.1	100.0	16	19	13	17	17	29	0	47	8.6
University of Texas at Dallas	0.89	0.57	-0.06	12	50	17	58	2.1	17.1	4.8	39.3	34	32	24	9	29	64	18	27	11.4
Howard University	0.83	0.56	0.00	13	62	0	38	0.8	24.0	0.5	100.0	53	28	25	16	76	50	29	5	10.7
Colorado State University	0.81	0.45	-0.10	14	57	14	71	2.0	15.8	1.3	27.7	57	28	19	8	20	42	5	38	8.6
University of New Hampshire	0.74	0.61	0.00	15	20	0	40	0.7	18.0	0.0		13	31	11	29	8	76	14	21	10.6
Rensselaer Polytechnic Inst	0.70	0.83	0.00	8	63	13	63	2.8	25.6	1.1	35.8	19	32	15	26	25	42	21	29	9.7
University of Missouri-Columbia [a]	0.70	1.31	-0.18	12	67	8	67	1.0	18.0	0.3	55.5	77	31	12	8*	0*	38*	5*	30*	11.8*
Colorado School of Mines	0.65	0.67	n/s	9	33	0	33	1.2	48.7	1.0	62.9	18	6	37	23	12	71	5	5	8.9
Utah State University	0.64	0.79	0.00	13	69	0	92	2.9	9.8	0.7	28.3	20	10	15	20	0	39	17	8	12.1
Clark University	0.59	0.42	0.00	11	55	0	45	0.8	28.3	0.6	55.1	3	33	21	29	17	41	10	48	7.4
Northeastern University	0.47	0.14	0.00	10	20	0	60	1.6	22.6	0.7	51.0	34	38	21	31	8	46	0	58	9.3
Mean Values for the 4th Quarter	**1.01**	**0.91**	**-0.06**	**17.37**	**49.70**	**3.19**	**56.41**	**1.68**	**18.10**	**1.36**	**38.48**	**44.78**	**26.85**	**20.56**	**19.93**	**11.48**	**54.00**	**10.56**	**31.59**	**9.85**
Mean Values for All Programs	**2.38**	**2.23**	**0.06**	**25.18**	**54.04**	**12.16**	**68.45**	**2.72**	**12.33**	**5.43**	**25.48**	**69.64**	**26.87**	**38.89**	**19.24**	**7.28**	**57.59**	**13.26**	**37.00**	**8.66**

Sources: 1. National Survey of Graduate Faculty
2. Institutional Coordinator Response Data
3. Doctorate Records File
4. Federal Agencies
5. Institute for Scientific Information

Note: *a.* Program in Agricultural Economics

n/s After trimming no cases remained

* The Doctorate Recipient information cannot be separated for two programs at the same institution in the same field and therefore the total for the combined programs is given.

Appendix Table M - 3 Selected Characteristics of Research-Doctorate Programs in Geography

Institution	1993 Ratings[1] 93Q	93E	93C	Faculty Tot Fac[2]	% Full[2]	% Supp[2]	% Pub[5]	Pub/ Fac[5]	Gini Pub[5]	Cite/ Fac[5]	Gini Cite[5]	Students[2] Tot Stu	% Fem	Rpt PhDs	Doctorate Recipients[3] % Fem	% Min	% US	% RA	% TA	MYD
Pennsylvania State University	4.59	4.18	0.34	21	48	43	76	2.5	8.2	4.0	14.7	38	37	19	28	7	56	10	40	9.7
University of Wisconsin-Madison	4.40	4.14	0.11	22	55	32	73	1.9	9.1	3.1	17.9	51	37	18	17	0	86	10	45	10.4
University of Minnesota	4.22	3.95	-0.24	25	64	16	64	2.0	8.8	4.1	16.8	72	36	28	37	13	82	10	24	10.8
Univ of California-Santa Barbara	4.16	3.95	0.52	20	55	70	80	6.0	8.5	17.9	15.0	79	25	22	25	0	67	47	12	9.8
Ohio State University	4.07	3.95	-0.06	20	70	35	90	3.5	9.2	12.1	32.1	45	31	25	36	6	63	4	78	7.5
University of California-Berkeley	3.99	3.73	-0.25	14	64	29	50	1.4	21.3	7.6	41.2	50	48	25	44	4	94	0	17	10.5
Syracuse University	3.99	3.78	0.32	18	67	22	67	1.6	11.7	2.8	14.0	38	45	22	64	0	55	5	45	9.9
Univ of California-Los Angeles	3.95	3.50	0.18	20	45	15	80	4.0	12.0	12.3	24.6	44	43	11	41	0	88	0	50	10.7
Clark University	3.82	3.63	0.00	16	50	56	88	3.5	10.9	13.3	18.1	60	40	34	29	3	67	22	16	11.4
Mean Values for the Top Quarter	**4.13**	**3.87**	**0.10**	**19.56**	**57.56**	**35.33**	**74.22**	**2.93**	**11.08**	**8.58**	**21.60**	**53.00**	**38.00**	**22.67**	**35.67**	**3.67**	**73.11**	**12.00**	**36.33**	**10.08**
University of Washington	3.66	3.55	0.01	14	57	21	86	5.0	13.6	14.4	22.4	37	35	23	22	0	81	10	26	9.8
State Univ of New York-Buffalo	3.63	3.51	0.48	17	47	29	88	3.0	11.2	4.9	17.6	30	17	13	13	10	63	8	67	7.0
University of Colorado	3.57	3.61	0.43	17	41	59	82	4.5	12.3	12.5	15.8	61	39	31	29	3	77	23	29	9.5
Rutgers State Univ-New Brunswick	3.39	3.17	0.50	25	44	28	80	3.6	9.0	5.2	16.8	23	52	7	33	15	93	45	27	9.4
University of Texas at Austin	3.38	2.88	0.13	22	64	27	55	2.2	12.9	3.5	32.5	19	47	10	25	0	92	11	44	12.4
Arizona State University	3.35	3.22	0.50	15	47	33	100	5.2	11.3	11.7	39.9	36	25	7	19	0	50	17	33	11.8
U of Illinois at Urbana-Champaign	3.30	3.24	-0.21	17	53	29	82	4.3	9.7	6.4	8.5	50	42	13	26	10	63	60	10	7.8
University of Iowa	3.23	3.33	-0.08	14	50	50	71	5.9	20.8	15.7	49.4	42	33	11	14	0	71	33	11	13.6
Louisiana State U & A&M College	3.19	3.14	0.29	17	41	18	65	1.4	13.5	2.6	56.8	49	35	14	33	0	90	29	29	9.8
Mean Values for the 2nd Quarter	**3.41**	**3.29**	**0.23**	**17.56**	**49.33**	**32.67**	**78.78**	**3.90**	**12.70**	**8.54**	**28.86**	**38.56**	**36.11**	**14.33**	**23.78**	**4.22**	**75.56**	**26.22**	**30.67**	**10.12**
University of Arizona	3.17	2.97	0.51	23	39	13	43	1.7	12.5	3.4	19.0	17	24	11	9	0	80	0	29	8.6
University of Kentucky	3.10	3.05	0.57	12	58	33	58	2.1	18.4	2.5	24.2	15	33	9	27	0	64	0	56	8.7
University of Georgia	3.02	3.08	-0.02	13	54	62	100	4.9	9.3	7.1	13.8	20	40	17	18	0	71	40	47	7.7
U of North Carolina-Chapel Hill	2.89	2.92	0.14	12	50	17	67	3.0	18.5	12.3	69.6	26	54	15	25	0	63	29	29	9.4
Johns Hopkins University	2.87	3.11	-0.56	6	67	83	67	2.7	35.1	17.5	64.1	20	30	6	33	0	67	25	0	9.7
University of Florida	2.86	2.76	0.29	11	55	36	82	3.0	13.6	5.3	16.2	30	20	9	27	14	70	0	17	19.4

Appendix Table M - 3 Geography (Continued)

Institution	1993 Ratings[1]			Faculty								Students[2]			Doctorate Recipients[3]					
	93Q	93E	93C	Tot Fac[2]	% Full[2]	% Supp[2]	% Pub[5]	Pub/ Fac[5]	Gini Pub[5]	Cite/ Fac[5]	Gini Cite[5]	Tot Stu	% Fem	Rpt PhDs	% Fem	% Min	% US	% RA	% TA	MYD
Indiana University	2.77	2.85	0.01	12	33	33	67	1.8	17.4	1.5	52.4	15	40	11	17	0	33	0	25	7.7
University of Kansas	2.69	2.93	-0.43	12	33	17	42	0.9	25.6	1.0	70.8	30	23	15	11	0	83	27	33	10.7
Boston University	2.67	2.74	-0.21	17	24	12	53	1.6	15.8	7.8	41.0	15	60	12	38	0	46	38	25	11.1
Mean Values for the 3rd Quarter	**2.89**	**2.93**	**0.03**	**13.11**	**45.89**	**34.00**	**64.33**	**2.41**	**18.47**	**6.49**	**41.23**	**20.89**	**36.00**	**11.67**	**22.78**	**1.56**	**64.11**	**17.67**	**29.00**	**10.33**
University of Oregon	2.61	2.60	0.15	11	64	45	45	1.5	33.5	10.1	50.7	17	29	8	21	0	86	11	44	8.8
University of Maryland College Park	2.40	2.37	-0.26	16	25	25	69	2.1	13.3	4.1	21.7	21	29	4	33	17	100	20	20	16.0
University of Hawaii at Manoa	2.36	2.63	-0.13	13	31	23	69	2.3	19.7	2.2	26.0	35	20	23	39	8	50	6	0	10.8
University of Wisconsin-Milwaukee	2.35	2.21	-0.26	12	42	17	33	0.5	33.3	0.3	37.5	20	25	9	18	20	88	8	17	10.4
University of Nebraska-Lincoln	2.32	2.34	-0.29	9	56	33	56	1.1	32.0	2.3	45.1	26	31	12	38	0	81	13	25	8.8
Oregon State University	2.03	2.29	-0.20	11	55	18	82	2.1	16.4	10.0	91.2	16	44	7	50	0	83	0	0	17.7
University of Utah	1.96	1.76	-0.12	10	60	10	70	1.7	19.7	2.4	40.9	21	19	12	8	0	100	0	43	8.8
Kent State University	1.95	2.13	0.15	10	20	0	40	1.7	37.0	1.1	57.0	17	18	19	22	10	43	0	41	13.9
University of Cincinnati	1.39	1.43	-0.63	7	43	29	57	1.7	27.7	2.1	30.6	15	33	3	33	0	17	0	40	10.7
Mean Values for the 4th Quarter	**2.15**	**2.20**	**-0.18**	**11.00**	**44.00**	**22.22**	**57.89**	**1.63**	**25.84**	**3.84**	**44.52**	**20.89**	**27.56**	**10.78**	**29.11**	**6.11**	**72.00**	**6.44**	**25.56**	**11.77**
Mean Values for All Programs	**3.15**	**3.07**	**0.05**	**15.31**	**49.19**	**31.06**	**68.81**	**2.72**	**17.02**	**6.86**	**34.05**	**33.33**	**34.42**	**14.86**	**27.83**	**3.89**	**71.19**	**15.58**	**30.39**	**10.58**

Sources: 1. National Survey of Graduate Faculty
2. Institutional Coordinator Response Data
3. Doctorate Records File
4. Federal Agencies
5. Institute for Scientific Information

Appendix Table M - 4 Selected Characteristics of Research-Doctorate Programs in History

Institution	1993 Ratings[1] 93Q	93E	93C	Faculty Tot Fac[2]	% Full[2]	% Supp[2]	% Pub[5]	Pub/ Fac[5]	Gini Pub[5]	Cite/ Fac[5]	Gini Cite[5]	Students[2] Tot Stu	% Fem	Rpt PhDs	Doctorate Recipients[3] % Fem	% Min	% US	% RA	% TA	MYD
Yale University	4.89	4.55	0.08	51	71	0	55	1.0	5.1	1.2	25.5	188	39	75	46	8	87	1	13	9.6
University of California-Berkeley	4.79	4.50	0.07	58	74	5	45	0.8	7.5	3.1	76.5	206	51	108	38	4	95	1	43	9.3
Princeton University	4.75	4.48	0.16	37	57	11	46	1.1	10.0	0.9	28.1	68	44	50	37	8	81	1	4	9.2
Harvard University	4.71	4.02	-0.17	43	70	0	47	1.2	7.6	7.5	75.5	146	40	80	34	4	84	0	37	9.6
Columbia University	4.63	4.29	0.32	55	73	2	38	0.9	7.4	0.6	12.9	334	43	96	35	6	87	2	3	12.0
Univ of California-Los Angeles	4.59	4.07	0.35	89	71	4	53	1.2	3.2	2.2	12.5	316	44	118	38	13	87	4	11	11.0
Stanford University	4.56	4.44	0.28	39	69	8	31	1.3	38.1	22.8	92.5	141	40	55	38	7	93	3	4	9.5
University of Chicago	4.49	4.20	0.12	45	76	13	47	1.1	6.4	1.5	22.8	251	37	71	27	4	93	0	1	9.8
Johns Hopkins University	4.42	4.37	0.16	22	91	9	64	1.4	10.8	2.5	73.1	98	45	68	38	4	89	7	14	8.6
University of Wisconsin-Madison	4.37	4.33	0.31	61	66	0	34	0.8	7.8	2.4	27.9	312	39	77	35	9	95	4	21	10.6
University of Michigan	4.30	4.09	0.25	53	64	0	57	1.4	6.0	3.3	22.4	137	44	67	34	7	94	1	19	12.4
University of Pennsylvania	4.24	4.05	0.31	55	69	7	51	1.2	5.5	1.3	16.4	113	52	41	45	5	85	5	32	9.2
Cornell University	4.22	3.87	0.15	42	60	5	36	0.7	8.6	0.3	16.3	85	49	32	39	0	76	0	54	9.9
Brown University	3.96	3.86	0.12	28	68	4	57	1.2	7.9	2.9	59.3	105	47	20	45	7	97	0	60	9.3
Duke University	3.93	3.84	0.42	38	66	5	47	0.9	8.3	1.6	50.2	103	50	44	23	5	94	4	4	8.4
Northwestern University	3.85	3.69	0.33	38	63	5	42	1.1	15.9	0.8	24.8	73	44	27	45	3	95	0	47	9.5
U of North Carolina-Chapel Hill	3.84	3.83	0.43	47	68	0	43	0.9	7.2	1.2	33.6	163	41	52	18	6	94	0	35	11.6
CUNY - Grad Sch & Univ Center	3.73	3.24	0.02	47	91	2	28	0.7	15.4	0.8	94.7	173	39	32	29	14	94	0	0	16.4
University of Virginia	3.68	3.67	0.26	43	53	2	35	0.5	8.0	0.5	39.5	132	33	42	39	3	97	5	23	9.5
Rutgers State Univ-New Brunswick	3.67	3.74	0.42	52	58	4	40	0.8	6.6	0.7	22.1	166	54	46	41	5	97	3	26	11.2
University of Minnesota	3.66	3.83	0.33	46	78	7	52	1.1	5.9	1.1	18.3	72	51	38	34	2	89	2	37	12.2
University of Texas at Austin	3.66	3.63	0.22	64	56	3	28	0.4	7.9	0.2	33.3	64	34	38	24	9	88	0	42	11.0
New York University	3.63	3.60	0.56	36	64	0	31	0.6	11.1	0.2	34.3	57	60	59	46	3	90	0	14	17.0
Indiana University	3.57	3.46	0.12	42	45	5	57	1.1	8.1	2.4	44.9	296	39	35	34	7	88	3	29	10.9
U of Illinois at Urbana-Champaign	3.50	3.67	0.39	52	67	4	27	0.5	9.0	0.3	40.4	138	28	32	21	6	85	0	47	11.6
Univ of California-San Diego	3.46	3.41	0.60	42	52	5	45	0.6	6.5	2.0	45.2	75	39	22	41	18	92	0	60	10.5
University of Rochester	3.45	3.13	-0.15	25	52	0	36	1.1	20.9	0.2	38.8	80	50	22	39	0	97	4	15	10.7
Mean Values for the Top Quarter	**4.09**	**3.92**	**0.24**	**46.30**	**66.37**	**4.07**	**43.41**	**0.95**	**9.73**	**2.39**	**40.07**	**151.56**	**43.56**	**53.59**	**35.67**	**6.19**	**90.48**	**1.85**	**25.74**	**10.76**

Appendix Table M - 4 History (Continued)

Institution	1993 Ratings[1] 93Q	93E	93C	Faculty Tot Fac[2]	% Full[2]	% Supp[2]	% Pub[5]	Pub/ Fac[5]	Gini Pub[5]	Cite/ Fac[5]	Gini Cite[5]	Students[2] Tot Stu	% Fem	Rpt PhDs	Doctorate Recipients[3] % Fem	% Min	% US	% RA	% TA	MYD
Brandeis University	3.41	3.28	0.05	17	53	0	47	0.8	14.7	1.5	51.3	56	63	24	38	0	89	0	29	10.5
University of Iowa	3.40	3.28	0.30	30	60	7	40	1.2	18.1	4.2	36.3	113	35	24	29	0	89	5	60	11.6
University of Maryland College Park	3.40	3.29	0.23	55	47	2	38	0.8	7.4	1.1	22.4	109	38	22	39	9	94	0	19	16.2
Emory University	3.39	3.33	0.58	27	37	0	37	0.8	11.9	0.9	36.9	83	46	17	50	0	100	0	5	11.0
Univ of California-Santa Barbara	3.34	3.08	0.26	43	60	2	23	0.3	11.2	0.0	100.0	105	39	49	28	9	89	0	34	10.2
University of Washington	3.31	3.30	0.22	41	51	10	32	0.8	9.3	3.1	44.3	121	42	33	44	6	95	6	31	11.4
Rice University	3.21	3.00	0.15	20	65	5	40	0.9	19.7	1.9	73.3	30	43	12	38	0	94	7	0	8.3
University of California-Davis	3.19	3.11	0.31	31	71	3	29	1.0	27.7	2.4	75.8	71	44	12	36	18	86	0	33	18.4
Vanderbilt University	3.17	3.05	0.34	26	38	0	46	0.8	10.0	0.3	28.3	28	29	15	26	0	100	0	48	10.2
Ohio State University	3.15	3.11	0.21	71	42	1	24	0.4	7.2	1.2	41.7	90	33	37	21	8	94	3	58	9.0
University of Pittsburgh	3.15	3.25	0.05	35	60	6	60	1.5	7.3	2.1	10.5	84	23	13	40	5	95	0	71	11.7
University of Kansas	3.13	3.11	0.36	35	66	0	37	0.5	9.2	0.4	28.5	53	32	16	17	0	91	0	35	18.4
University of Florida	3.09	3.12	0.47	36	56	8	53	1.1	8.6	1.5	24.8	79	18	12	39	7	83	6	44	12.6
Carnegie Mellon University	3.09	3.26	0.15	21	52	24	48	1.3	12.4	1.4	18.4	47	43	32	43	3	95	0	6	10.8
State Univ of New York-Binghamton	3.04	3.11	0.28	25	36	0	24	0.4	20.9	0.0		101	59	27	50	11	88	0	72	9.4
University of California-Irvine	2.99	2.94	0.30	26	42	0	54	1.4	18.1	1.8	14.0	65	32	19	52	4	100	0	50	11.7
Washington University	2.96	2.72	-0.05	18	50	0	33	0.7	24.2	5.8	64.0	47	40	6	38	13	100	0	40	9.4
State U of New York-Stony Brook	2.90	3.22	0.00	23	39	9	43	0.9	14.2	5.7	89.7	104	44	24	63	9	81	0	36	13.1
College of William & Mary	2.89	2.87	0.14	10	70	0	50	0.8	25.0	0.2	100.0	34	41	15	35	4	100	21	21	8.8
University of Connecticut	2.89	2.67	0.17	28	68	4	32	0.4	12.5	0.1	37.5	124	32	18	24	15	87	0	13	12.4
Michigan State University	2.88	2.81	0.07	48	58	0	31	0.6	9.1	0.8	26.5	58	38	24	20	26	87	0	45	16.6
University of Arizona	2.88	2.78	0.10	23	43	4	43	0.6	11.2	0.1	55.5	94	39	6	46	0	77	17	50	12.4
Georgetown University	2.84	3.12	0.32	33	18	0	30	0.6	15.2	2.7	58.8	69	45	27	28	7	77	0	10	12.3
University of Missouri-Columbia	2.81	2.66	-0.03	27	63	0	37	0.6	11.7	0.0	100.0	59	41	18	43	25	93	0	20	13.9
University of Illinois at Chicago	2.79	2.70	0.00	24	54	4	38	0.7	14.1	1.7	55.5	71	55	11	28	6	94	0	62	14.2
Ohio University	2.79	3.00	0.23	24	58	0	21	0.3	26.5	0.2	68.0	28	21	8	0	0	60	0	43	10.0
Northern Illinois University	2.79	2.57	0.04	35	63	0	34	0.5	10.1	1.0	36.8	37	35	16	39	0	74	0	33	12.6
University of Colorado	2.77	2.42	0.23	29	38	3	45	0.8	10.0	0.7	39.6	55	44	17	52	0	91	0	17	12.8
Syracuse University	2.75	2.54	0.00	26	62	0	31	0.7	15.5	1.8	48.2	36	44	15	29	0	81	0	30	10.2

Institution	1993 Ratings[1] 93Q	93E	93C	Faculty Tot Fac[2]	% Full[2]	% Supp[2]	% Pub[5]	Pub/ Fac[5]	Gini Pub[5]	Cite/ Fac[5]	Gini Cite[5]	Students[2] Tot Stu	% Fem	Rpt PhDs	Doctorate Recipients[3] % Fem	% Min	% US	% RA	% TA	MYD
George Washington University	2.75	2.90	0.03	19	58	0	32	0.6	33.8	0.3	52.0	29	31	13	17	6	94	0	7	16.6
University of Georgia	2.75	2.89	0.36	26	69	0	23	0.3	18.7	0.1	100.0	11	45	10	33	0	100	0	50	12.4
Mean Values for the 2nd Quarter	**3.03**	**2.98**	**0.19**	**30.06**	**53.13**	**2.97**	**37.26**	**0.75**	**15.02**	**1.45**	**51.29**	**67.45**	**39.16**	**19.10**	**35.00**	**6.16**	**89.61**	**2.10**	**34.58**	**12.23**
University of Notre Dame	2.74	2.84	0.37	47	40	2	38	0.6	7.9	0.2	28.3	72	31	25	19	6	90	0	40	10.6
State Univ of New York-Buffalo	2.71	2.64	0.15	19	74	0	32	0.5	20.9	0.3	44.0	77	27	19	32	5	80	0	50	13.7
U of Massachusetts at Amherst	2.68	2.70	-0.21	22	68	5	45	0.5	11.1	0.0		35	51	15	53	13	94	0	38	10.7
Boston University	2.67	2.65	-0.28	26	50	4	42	0.8	12.9	0.4	30.5	45	53	18	36	4	86	0	11	13.3
Univ of California-Riverside	2.62	2.53	0.52	27	52	11	37	0.8	14.7	0.6	35.9	35	49	10	25	9	92	0	22	9.0
University of Houston	2.62	2.38	0.57	38	42	3	11	0.1	28.0	0.0		125	41	19	27	5	90	0	25	16.4
University of Oregon	2.58	2.65	-0.27	24	46	0	42	0.6	11.2	0.1	50.0	17	41	15	33	0	89	8	58	14.5
Boston College	2.57	2.46	0.04	28	32	0	36	0.6	15.6	0.2	68.0	81	51	11	37	6	95	0	24	14.4
Tulane University	2.53	3.03	0.00	23	39	4	39	0.7	12.8	1.3	87.7	78	44	18	44	12	93	0	32	12.7
Purdue University	2.52	2.61	0.07	26	31	0	35	0.4	12.3	0.2	37.5	29	21	10	31	30	91	0	45	12.4
University of Hawaii at Manoa	2.51	3.15	-0.08	30	63	0	27	0.4	15.7	0.2	38.8	45	29	26	42	0	68	4	33	14.6
University of New Hampshire	2.48	2.35	0.50	19	47	0	42	0.8	14.8	0.4	30.6	27	59	9	50	0	100	0	55	13.8
University of Southern California	2.48	2.35	-0.10	20	35	0	60	1.0	10.2	2.7	28.0	58	48	18	25	10	91	0	39	11.6
University of Kentucky	2.48	2.60	0.10	26	46	4	58	1.0	8.1	0.8	25.5	54	35	14	21	5	100	0	42	10.8
Pennsylvania State University	2.46	2.32	0.09	23	35	4	52	0.9	13.3	0.7	43.7	62	29	8	33	0	83	10	30	11.6
Louisiana State U & A&M College	2.46	2.61	0.15	28	57	7	32	0.8	18.1	0.3	48.1	64	30	17	25	16	95	12	24	12.2
University of Oklahoma	2.39	2.24	0.09	25	52	0	24	0.3	18.3	0.1	33.3	28	36	11	43	8	86	9	18	14.4
Temple University	2.37	2.38	0.00	32	44	0	28	0.5	15.5	1.3	54.4	116	34	31	15	0	92	6	12	16.1
Arizona State University	2.37	2.66	0.44	25	44	0	48	1.0	10.9	0.3	42.8	59	31	9	62	8	100	0	14	17.5
Catholic University of America	2.36	2.64	0.08	17	41	0	53	1.1	14.8	0.2	33.3	24	46	14	29	13	100	0	0	19.0
Miami University	2.34	2.18	0.32	25	44	0	28	0.3	15.6	0.1	50.0	27	30	19	17	20	75	0	79	9.6
Loyola University of Chicago	2.34	2.69	0.27	21	48	0	0	0.0		0.0		32	34	12	30	0	80	0	17	16.3
University of South Carolina	2.33	2.39	0.15	33	39	0	24	0.3	15.7	0.2	55.5	53	23	11	33	7	100	0	14	13.7
Claremont Graduate School	2.25	2.32	-0.14	3	67	0	33	0.7	100.0	0.3	100.0	43	37	15	25	0	95	0	0	14.3

Appendix Table M - 4 History (Continued)

Institution	1993 Ratings[1] 93Q	93E	93C	Faculty Tot Fac[2]	% Full[2]	% Supp[2]	% Pub[5]	Pub/ Fac[5]	Gini Pub[5]	Cite/ Fac[5]	Gini Cite[5]	Students[2] Tot Stu	% Fem	Rpt PhDs	Doctorate Recipients[3] % Fem	% Min	% US	% RA	% TA	MYD
Florida State University	2.20	2.47	0.04	23	78	0	35	0.7	14.6	0.9	31.0	113	27	19	20	4	100	0	28	10.0
Mean Values for the 3rd Quarter	**2.48**	**2.55**	**0.11**	**25.20**	**48.56**	**1.76**	**36.04**	**0.62**	**18.04**	**0.47**	**45.31**	**55.96**	**37.48**	**15.72**	**32.28**	**7.24**	**90.60**	**1.96**	**30.00**	**13.33**
University of Nebraska-Lincoln	2.19	2.07	-0.08	23	61	0	35	0.5	13.8	0.0		31	32	4	17	0	100	0	0	16.7
Kent State University	2.19	2.18	0.00	21	57	0	33	0.6	19.4	0.2	100.0	41	39	14	23	16	91	0	29	14.0
University of Cincinnati	2.18	2.24	0.00	17	65	0	35	0.6	30.0	0.9	78.1	15	7	20	41	4	92	0	42	12.8
Texas A&M University	2.15	2.08	0.26	41	24	2	49	0.8	6.1	0.3	25.5	42	26	13	18	13	100	0	9	11.4
American University	2.14	2.05	-0.10	14	57	0	57	1.1	13.7	3.3	60.6	33	36	11	29	0	100	0	17	14.6
Jewish Theological Seminary	2.07	3.33	0.00	5	40	0	60	0.8	37.5	0.0		18	44	6	29	0	100	0	0	17.7
Case Western Reserve Univ	2.05	1.96	-0.35	10	40	0	50	0.5	20.0	0.9	100.0	44	43	14	60	0	100	8	0	17.7
University of Tennessee-Knoxville	1.89	2.14	-0.07	16	63	0	13	0.3	62.5	0.1	100.0	47	23	12	17	0	100	0	43	11.6
University of Alabama	1.88	2.00	-0.25	17	47	0	29	0.5	25.0	0.3	36.0	22	18	9	20	0	100	13	13	11.7
Howard University	1.81	2.26	0.10	12	50	0	33	0.6	30.6	0.2	100.0	22	50	14	37	86	82	20	0	12.8
Washington State University	1.78	1.77	0.14	19	53	0	26	0.3	22.2	0.5	33.3	53	45	10	41	12	100	0	64	10.6
University of Akron	1.76	1.36	0.06	21	57	0	33	0.5	17.3	0.0		16	38	8	50	0	80	0	38	11.5
Univ of Arkansas-Fayetteville	1.70	2.14	0.09	20	40	0	45	0.9	16.0	1.1	34.2	29	31	14	31	6	100	0	42	16.8
Bowling Green State University	1.66	1.45	-0.15	15	67	7	47	0.5	15.6	0.2	55.5	20	25	0	11	0	100	0	33	11.6
Texas Tech University	1.61	1.37	-0.14	27	33	4	33	0.5	12.4	0.1	37.5	32	28	13	21	0	100	0	14	10.0
Brigham Young University	1.56	2.00	-0.10	16	56	0	38	0.4	16.6	0.3	44.0	6	17	60	27	8	87	0	11	13.7
University of North Texas	1.48	1.67	0.00	32	38	0	22	0.3	22.0	0.0	100.0	47	38	8	50	10	100	0	0	13.7
Texas Christian University	1.40	1.67	0.00	12	50	0	17	0.3	55.5	0.0		30	33	13	25	19	100	0	23	10.0
West Virginia University	1.37	1.56	-0.14	14	36	7	50	0.6	15.6	0.0		31	32	11	38	15	100	0	42	10.8
Northern Arizona University	1.29	1.67	0.25	22	41	0	41	0.6	13.6	0.3	38.8	26	50	7	23	0	77	0	11	16.5
University of Texas at Dallas	1.28	1.37	0.00	15	33	0	20	0.2	33.3	0.3	62.5	40	70	11	100	0	100	0	0	16.0
Auburn University	1.22	1.80	0.25	18	44	0	11	0.2	55.5	0.3	68.0	49	31	7	21	7	100	0	33	9.9
Fordham University	1.13	0.83	-0.20	8	50	0	25	0.3	50.0	0.6	68.0	61	33	8	50	9	92	0	0	17.6
Mississippi State University	0.88	0.56	0.00	14	64	0	57	0.8	14.0	0.0		13	38	12	29	8	86	0	73	10.9
Illinois State University	0.67	0.77	-0.36	8	88	0	13	0.1	100.0	0.0		20	20	22	27	0	77	5	25	17.6

Institution	1993 Ratings[1]			Faculty								Students[2]			Doctorate Recipients[3]					
	93Q	93E	93C	Tot Fac[2]	% Full[2]	% Supp[2]	% Pub[5]	Pub/ Fac[5]	Gini Pub[5]	Cite/ Fac[5]	Gini Cite[5]	Tot Stu	% Fem	Rpt PhDs	% Fem	% Min	% US	% RA	% TA	MYD
Univ of Southern Mississippi	0.66	0.51	0.00	5	60	0	80	0.8	25.0	0.0		10	70	4	0	0	100	0	25	15.5
University of North Dakota	0.62	0.64	0.00	10	50	0	10	0.1	100.0	0.0		38	21	4	9	0	100	0	50	19.7
Univ of Puerto Rico-Rio Piedras	0.50	1.67	n/s	14	50	0	0	0.0		0.0		25	52	0	n/a	n/a	n/a	n/a	n/a	n/a
Mean Values for the 4th Quarter	**1.54**	**1.68**	**-0.03**	**16.64**	**50.50**	**0.71**	**34.36**	**0.49**	**31.23**	**0.35**	**63.44**	**30.75**	**35.36**	**11.75**	**31.26**	**7.89**	**94.96**	**1.70**	**23.59**	**13.83**
Mean Values for All Programs	**2.79**	**2.79**	**0.13**	**29.59**	**54.60**	**2.42**	**37.77**	**0.70**	**18.43**	**1.19**	**49.06**	**76.47**	**38.95**	**25.06**	**33.78**	**6.90**	**91.28**	**1.93**	**28.94**	**12.47**

Sources: 1. National Survey of Graduate Faculty
2. Institutional Coordinator Response Data
3. Doctorate Records File
4. Federal Agencies
5. Institute for Scientific Information

n/s After trimming no cases remained

Appendix Table M - 5 Selected Characteristics of Research-Doctorate Programs in Political Science

Institution	1993 Ratings[1] 93Q	93E	93C	Faculty Tot Fac[2]	% Full[2]	% Supp[2]	% Pub[5]	Pub/ Fac[5]	Gini Pub[5]	Cite/ Fac[5]	Gini Cite[5]	Students[2] Tot Stu	% Fem	Rpt PhDs	Doctorate Recipients[3] % Fem	% Min	% US	% RA	% TA	MYD
Harvard University	4.88	4.17	0.35	48	46	15	73	2.7	5.1	12.3	17.8	172	30	111	24	2	84	2	30	9.1
University of California-Berkeley	4.66	4.13	0.06	41	66	10	61	2.0	10.2	1.6	9.9	143	41	97	30	5	85	17	30	10.3
Yale University	4.60	4.24	-0.26	29	62	10	59	2.3	9.2	12.3	28.4	69	36	70	31	13	71	0	0	8.7
University of Michigan	4.60	4.31	0.14	44	59	25	75	1.6	4.2	5.6	10.1	173	28	55	28	11	84	22	25	10.3
Stanford University	4.50	4.02	-0.03	28	68	4	68	1.8	6.8	4.9	15.3	89	29	41	31	9	78	2	2	9.7
University of Chicago	4.41	3.83	-0.11	28	54	21	71	2.6	9.5	11.9	23.6	191	28	74	17	11	82	2	0	10.1
Princeton University	4.39	3.91	0.23	49	57	6	57	1.8	5.0	3.0	14.9	59	41	55	27	6	79	0	5	9.4
Univ of California-Los Angeles	4.25	3.62	0.53	57	70	28	74	2.8	6.2	8.4	20.7	177	32	35	38	5	76	9	52	11.5
Univ of California-San Diego	4.13	3.70	0.80	36	61	14	69	1.9	5.4	4.8	18.1	57	21	10	25	11	75	0	78	8.4
University of Wisconsin-Madison	4.09	3.86	0.21	49	57	6	53	1.2	4.8	1.5	27.8	145	32	54	23	2	85	5	24	9.3
University of Rochester	4.01	4.00	-0.10	18	67	22	72	3.7	13.2	10.7	20.0	31	26	27	25	4	74	4	8	8.6
Massachusetts Inst of Technology	3.96	3.74	-0.04	24	63	8	67	2.1	9.2	5.5	33.9	155	34	60	23	0	87	22	3	9.6
University of Minnesota	3.95	3.92	0.26	30	57	13	53	1.3	9.5	3.1	21.0	87	56	33	25	0	88	9	56	8.5
Duke University	3.94	3.68	0.38	29	45	17	59	2.5	7.2	7.8	13.9	89	29	19	23	6	73	0	0	9.7
Cornell University	3.85	3.61	-0.04	39	62	3	69	1.5	6.6	1.7	17.8	86	40	47	30	9	77	0	56	9.2
Columbia University	3.84	3.22	0.19	48	56	2	60	2.1	6.1	5.0	12.0	355	37	83	37	8	79	1	5	10.5
Ohio State University	3.69	3.40	0.44	33	58	27	64	2.7	8.0	5.9	18.4	148	31	54	25	22	67	30	32	10.2
U of North Carolina-Chapel Hill	3.54	3.54	0.02	28	50	7	57	2.1	10.3	4.0	21.0	103	2	33	31	18	91	3	37	10.5
University of Texas at Austin	3.49	3.22	0.12	53	57	4	51	1.4	4.8	1.5	14.3	89	28	52	15	15	66	2	52	10.7
Indiana University	3.45	3.45	0.02	27	56	19	63	1.7	7.3	2.6	14.8	100	26	50	23	5	78	7	58	11.2
Johns Hopkins University	3.37	3.14	-0.02	19	74	5	47	0.7	13.6	0.7	22.4	59	31	32	29	5	83	1	10	10.2
Northwestern University	3.35	3.14	-0.10	20	70	15	60	1.4	11.2	3.5	27.1	70	43	25	26	10	62	11	19	9.0
University of Washington	3.34	3.02	0.34	30	50	20	63	1.1	6.4	2.0	20.1	70	43	21	25	15	84	0	60	10.8
Washington University	3.29	3.38	-0.32	18	44	28	39	0.9	19.7	1.7	39.5	45	31	21	19	0	77	21	21	7.5
University of Iowa	3.25	3.31	-0.16	22	45	23	59	1.8	16.1	1.6	50.6	30	50	19	10	7	83	0	75	6.4
Mean Values for the Top Quarter	**3.95**	**3.66**	**0.12**	**33.88**	**58.16**	**14.08**	**61.72**	**1.91**	**8.62**	**4.94**	**21.34**	**111.68**	**32.99**	**47.12**	**25.60**	**7.96**	**78.72**	**6.80**	**29.52**	**9.58**
University of Virginia	3.24	2.72	0.05	34	59	0	53	1.4	10.0	3.5	61.0	107	25	48	16	4	84	2	10	7.8
Rutgers State Univ-New Brunswick	3.24	3.14	0.31	30	60	3	53	1.1	8.3	0.6	23.4	103	40	14	30	0	95	0	24	8.9

Institution	1993 Ratings[1] 93Q	93E	93C	Faculty Tot Fac[2]	% Full[2]	% Supp[2]	% Pub[5]	Pub/ Fac[5]	Gini Pub[5]	Cite/ Fac[5]	Gini Cite[5]	Students[2] Tot Stu	% Fem	Rpt PhDs	Doctorate Recipients[3] % Fem	% Min	% US	% RA	% TA	MYD
Michigan State University	3.24	3.31	-0.09	28	46	11	64	2.3	9.1	4.9	14.9	41	29	16	31	13	89	0	33	11.7
University of Maryland College Park	3.23	3.13	0.42	40	52	8	60	1.2	6.0	0.8	18.0	139	39	43	41	11	81	4	36	10.4
U of Illinois at Urbana-Champaign	3.20	3.04	0.02	33	64	6	67	1.9	8.4	0.7	16.1	74	32	26	26	0	79	7	41	8.2
University of Pittsburgh	3.15	2.90	0.25	29	48	7	48	0.9	9.4	0.8	23.1	53	26	8	13	11	62	0	45	8.4
University of California-Irvine	3.14	2.83	0.46	23	52	9	43	2.8	26.6	13.7	53.4	34	24	8	25	0	71	0	71	8.7
University of Houston	2.96	2.69	0.27	28	54	7	25	0.3	18.5	0.0		42	40	21	13	7	93	7	21	11.7
State U of New York-Stony Brook	2.92	2.88	0.31	18	50	44	78	2.7	11.2	7.7	14.7	38	24	12	20	9	73	17	42	8.7
University of Arizona	2.89	2.50	0.26	20	40	15	65	2.2	12.6	3.8	30.2	75	36	11	6	0	67	11	33	10.8
Emory University	2.88	2.69	0.50	22	45	5	64	2.1	10.0	3.4	24.3	45	53	6	36	11	82	33	11	7.4
Georgetown University	2.85	2.49	0.28	31	48	3	58	1.1	8.9	0.9	30.3	100	47	25	19	3	84	0	9	10.6
Florida State University	2.82	2.97	0.02	19	53	0	79	1.9	9.2	2.5	17.5	44	14	27	23	15	67	24	24	8.6
University of Colorado	2.78	2.71	0.30	26	38	15	62	2.2	8.2	3.7	21.2	51	37	12	44	7	94	33	17	7.7
Syracuse University	2.77	2.84	0.08	28	75	7	46	1.1	17.1	0.8	27.4	40	38	17	20	14	60	4	35	9.7
Univ of California-Santa Barbara	2.74	2.55	-0.05	22	59	18	64	2.0	9.0	1.6	19.4	79	35	22	11	28	83	0	37	9.4
University of Pennsylvania	2.68	2.41	-0.16	23	70	0	48	1.6	12.1	3.9	40.8	65	26	14	29	16	61	0	50	10.8
Arizona State University	2.67	2.33	0.18	16	50	0	69	2.2	11.6	3.7	16.1	36	14	9	20	0	56	0	50	9.7
University of Georgia	2.66	2.71	0.14	30	60	3	63	2.4	9.1	2.4	9.0	48	29	45	21	5	70	14	28	11.4
University of Notre Dame	2.66	2.36	0.26	33	58	0	52	1.1	8.5	1.0	23.8	60	38	18	28	11	75	0	68	10.2
University of California-Davis	2.61	2.60	0.49	21	52	5	67	1.9	11.0	2.3	17.0	18	39	4	55	13	89	0	50	12.5
CUNY - Grad Sch & Univ Center	2.57	2.13	-0.15	30	73	0	53	0.8	9.3	0.9	20.1	155	40	23	24	26	80	13	6	10.6
George Washington University	2.57	2.50	0.48	30	60	7	53	1.7	11.4	1.3	20.2	103	29	29	27	7	60	0	12	13.8
Tufts University	2.51	2.33	-0.10	26	50	4	58	1.2	9.5	3.8	86.6	81	25	59	27	0	71	0	0	8.9
Mean Values for the 2nd Quarter	**2.87**	**2.70**	**0.19**	**26.67**	**54.83**	**7.38**	**58.00**	**1.67**	**11.04**	**2.86**	**27.33**	**67.96**	**32.46**	**21.54**	**25.21**	**8.79**	**76.08**	**7.04**	**31.38**	**9.86**
University of Hawaii at Manoa	2.49	2.07	0.00	26	65	0	54	1.3	8.8	0.6	16.4	131	36	50	32	0	56	7	12	11.8
University of Florida	2.48	2.33	0.08	28	50	4	61	1.2	7.9	2.5	30.3	51	43	7	30	0	80	13	50	9.7
University of Wisconsin-Milwaukee	2.48	2.50	0.46	20	60	5	70	1.9	18.1	0.9	48.4	16	38	7	58	0	92	13	63	10.1
Rice University	2.43	2.55	-0.16	12	67	17	75	1.8	14.4	1.6	37.3	18	50	11	50	0	71	0	0	7.0
University of Kentucky	2.42	2.58	-0.43	17	41	18	65	1.8	11.5	4.2	20.9	45	11	12	33	6	89	0	56	9.3

Appendix Table M - 5 Political Science (Continued)

Institution	1993 Ratings[1] 93Q	93E	93C	Faculty Tot Fac[2]	% Full[2]	% Supp[2]	% Pub[5]	Pub/ Fac[5]	Gini Pub[5]	Cite/ Fac[5]	Gini Cite[5]	Students[2] Tot Stu	% Fem	Rpt PhDs	Doctorate Recipients[3] % Fem	% Min	% US	% RA	% TA	MYD
Brandeis University	2.41	2.08	-0.28	12	50	0	50	1.0	26.3	0.3	55.5	32	47	9	43	0	79	0	0	10.1
New York University	2.40	2.56	-0.44	21	48	10	57	1.9	15.1	2.3	23.4	16	69	23	35	9	82	5	23	11.7
University of South Carolina	2.39	2.52	0.21	15	40	13	73	2.5	15.4	3.1	28.2	32	28	11	24	11	65	8	34	9.2
Purdue University	2.38	2.24	0.23	29	38	7	48	0.8	10.0	0.2	18.3	38	45	10	36	38	62	17	42	8.8
U of Massachusetts at Amherst	2.37	2.27	-0.18	21	52	5	52	1.4	18.1	2.0	34.4	55	33	23	30	12	89	3	34	10.3
American University	2.37	2.17	0.15	22	55	0	55	1.5	10.5	1.3	20.9	60	33	16	29*	4*	81*	7*	11*	11.2*
Univ of California-Riverside	2.36	2.13	0.02	19	37	0	53	1.2	14.0	0.6	20.6	27	30	17	21	25	96	0	31	9.3
University of Southern California	2.33	2.15	-0.37	18	39	0	56	1.3	14.9	1.2	26.4	66	29	22	22	12	84	3	24	9.9
University of Kansas	2.33	2.50	0.33	19	74	5	58	1.1	15.1	0.9	34.2	39	18	18	4	0	65	0	20	10.2
University of Nebraska-Lincoln	2.33	2.22	-0.22	18	72	17	61	1.6	16.0	1.4	38.2	19	42	16	32	8	68	7	27	10.6
Vanderbilt University	2.32	2.30	-0.35	14	50	7	36	1.1	50.0	0.4	36.0	23	39	7	27	0	64	0	38	8.7
State Univ of New York-Albany	2.32	2.31	0.03	22	41	0	73	1.6	9.2	1.3	17.3	49	20	9	7	13	57	0	13	13.1
University of Connecticut	2.31	2.43	0.08	26	77	4	46	0.7	11.4	0.2	44.0	98	36	19	26	6	59	5	16	10.2
State Univ of New York-Binghamton	2.27	2.36	-0.20	17	41	0	41	0.8	19.3	0.9	29.7	83	34	21	35	11	79	0	42	7.9
Pennsylvania State University	2.25	2.38	0.02	19	53	0	42	1.2	18.3	0.9	43.2	58	24	17	30	0	52	0	61	11.4
University of Denver	2.23	2.33	-0.20	19	32	11	26	0.5	32.0	0.4	38.7	79	28	54	26	24	65	0	0	11.6
University of Oregon	2.21	2.11	-0.31	18	61	11	56	2.0	18.2	4.2	51.6	34	29	8	22	0	50	0	40	11.9
State Univ of New York-Buffalo	2.06	2.50	-0.28	16	38	6	44	0.8	20.8	0.8	45.5	34	38	17	19	0	50	0	25	10.2
Wayne State University	2.04	2.19	0.24	24	54	13	38	0.7	14.8	1.0	17.5	42	33	16	20	18	92	0	36	12.4
Mean Values for the 3rd Quarter	**2.33**	**2.32**	**-0.07**	**19.67**	**51.46**	**6.38**	**53.75**	**1.32**	**17.09**	**1.38**	**32.37**	**47.71**	**34.71**	**17.50**	**28.79**	**8.21**	**71.96**	**3.67**	**29.08**	**10.28**
Louisiana State U & A&M College	2.02	1.99	-0.06	19	47	0	63	2.0	15.6	1.5	48.7	30	30	11	25	20	83	0	13	8.9
Boston College	2.00	1.29	0.03	16	44	0	38	0.6	22.0	0.1	50.0	47	43	10	43	0	91	0	45	10.6
American University [a]	1.94	1.85	-0.03	18	50	0	39	0.8	29.5	0.3	27.7	44	48	40	29*	4*	81*	7*	11*	11.2*
University of Oklahoma	1.94	2.03	-0.04	24	25	4	46	1.5	23.4	1.7	39.7	58	34	22	24	8	90	16	21	11.3
Claremont Graduate School	1.80	1.74	-0.14	9	33	0	56	0.8	26.5	0.8	34.6	132	31	40	14	17	62	0	0	10.9
University of Missouri-Columbia	1.79	1.43	-0.26	15	47	0	73	1.4	10.6	0.7	35.5	63	11	32	16	11	47	0	38	10.0
Northern Illinois University	1.77	1.98	0.07	30	43	7	60	1.1	6.7	0.7	18.5	57	26	27	27	9	60	7	43	11.6
University of Utah	1.74	1.67	0.00	27	37	7	33	0.6	13.2	0.3	30.6	62	23	7	38	0	100	0	0	23.7

Institution	1993 Ratings[1] 93Q	93E	93C	Faculty Tot Fac[2]	% Full[2]	% Supp[2]	% Pub[5]	Pub/ Fac[5]	Gini Pub[5]	Cite/ Fac[5]	Gini Cite[5]	Students[2] Tot Stu	% Fem	Rpt PhDs	Doctorate Recipients[3] % Fem	% Min	% US	% RA	% TA	MYD
Boston University	1.69	1.14	-0.37	12	50	0	58	0.8	16.0	0.1	100.0	50	40	22	32	17	75	0	39	11.4
University of Cincinnati	1.65	1.02	-0.18	14	50	0	86	1.6	15.2	2.1	27.2	27	30	11	31	22	69	13	50	11.7
University of North Texas	1.64	1.73	0.41	22	27	0	36	1.0	24.0	0.8	46.7	39	26	18	9	21	61	0	0	10.7
Howard University	1.62	2.05	-0.17	18	56	0	50	1.2	16.9	2.4	37.3	69	41	20	4	87	76	0	27	10.8
Temple University	1.54	1.30	-0.28	19	42	0	26	0.4	25.0	0.2	55.5	71	31	17	26	8	75	25	0	11.0
Tulane University	1.49	1.60	-0.33	14	21	0	21	0.4	38.8	0.5	100.0	42	36	10	42	9	92	0	11	8.0
University of New Orleans	1.45	1.67	-0.41	11	82	9	64	1.9	18.8	2.0	22.3	33	39	9	27	0	91	0	44	11.7
Washington State University	1.39	1.04	-0.16	13	46	0	69	3.0	19.6	1.5	22.5	35	31	16	45	0	80	0	69	8.4
University of Tennessee-Knoxville	1.36	1.49	0.06	17	53	0	47	0.9	17.1	0.5	34.3	45	29	16	26	0	76	8	46	10.4
Texas Tech University	1.20	0.88	-0.27	18	50	0	28	0.7	26.3	0.7	38.8	24	46	13	23	44	69	13	25	10.6
University of Texas at Dallas	1.18	1.29	0.47	16	31	0	56	1.1	13.5	0.6	28.3	32	31	9	20	33	60	20	0	8.7
Northern Arizona University	1.17	1.37	0.56	18	39	0	17	0.2	37.5	0.1	100.0	33	39	8	20	0	70	0	0	14.8
Kent State University	1.14	1.17	-0.05	14	50	0	43	0.8	22.3	0.4	38.8	27	33	11	31	38	62	0	50	8.5
Fordham University	1.12	1.07	-0.42	14	36	0	50	0.6	18.5	0.7	52.0	67	36	11	36	10	91	14	14	12.8
Catholic University of America	0.95	0.95	-0.21	12	33	0	25	0.3	37.5	0.1	100.0	41	29	16	8	0	89	0	6	16.5
Clark Atlanta University	0.60	0.79	-0.14	9	33	0	11	0.1	100.0	0.0		50	26	44	16	93	67	0	0	10.5
Idaho State University	0.33	0.28	0.00	7	14	0	14	0.1	100.0	0.6	100.0	20	30	11	25	0	83	0	0	5.7
Mean Values for the 4th Quarter	**1.46**	**1.39**	**-0.08**	**16.24**	**41.56**	**1.08**	**44.36**	**0.96**	**27.78**	**0.78**	**49.54**	**47.92**	**32.76**	**18.04**	**25.48**	**18.04**	**76.00**	**4.92**	**22.08**	**11.22**
Mean Values for All Programs	**2.66**	**2.52**	**0.04**	**24.13**	**51.47**	**7.23**	**54.43**	**1.46**	**16.18**	**2.50**	**32.58**	**69.04**	**33.22**	**26.18**	**26.26**	**10.80**	**75.72**	**5.61**	**27.97**	**10.23**

Sources: 1. National Survey of Graduate Faculty
2. Institutional Coordinator Response Data
3. Doctorate Records File
4. Federal Agencies
5. Institute for Scientific Information

Notes: *a*. Program in International Relations

* The Doctorate Recipient information cannot be separated for two programs at the same institution in the same field and therefore the total for the combined programs is given.

Appendix Table M - 6 Selected Characteristics of Research-Doctorate Programs in Psychology

Institution	1993 Ratings[1]			Faculty								Students[2]			Doctorate Recipients[3]					
	93Q	93E	93C	Tot Fac[2]	% Full[2]	% Supp[2]	% Pub[5]	Pub/ Fac[5]	Gini Pub[5]	Cite/ Fac[5]	Gini Cite[5]	Tot Stu	% Fem	Rpt PhDs	% Fem	% Min	% US	% RA	% TA	MYD
Stanford University	4.82	4.64	0.00	26	73	69	96	6.2	6.1	39.2	10.8	68	46	57	56	14	87	21	2	7.2
University of Michigan	4.63	4.40	0.06	79	66	39	77	4.9	2.6	30.0	8.1	237	65	149	55	14	97	17	23	7.8
Yale University	4.62	4.31	0.02	43	56	44	86	9.0	5.2	49.6	6.2	91	62	68	60	10	94	7	7	7.7
Univ of California-Los Angeles	4.61	4.05	0.24	85	73	42	84	5.7	2.9	24.1	5.3	188	64	143	61	14	94	14	27	7.9
U of Illinois at Urbana-Champaign	4.58	4.36	0.14	73	58	40	84	5.5	2.4	25.4	5.0	229	52	104	43	6	85	30	31	8.3
Harvard University	4.48	4.09	-0.18	25	60	48	92	8.0	8.1	34.8	14.2	68	60	46	56	4	89	7	24	6.5
University of Minnesota	4.46	4.33	0.02	55	67	36	91	6.5	3.1	34.1	6.5	132	63	130	60	3	94	17	13	9.7
University of Pennsylvania	4.35	4.18	-0.02	30	80	43	80	5.6	7.3	21.5	12.2	46	59	36	73	1	94	2	15	8.3
University of California-Berkeley	4.33	4.03	-0.07	39	82	56	92	5.2	5.3	20.3	6.9	130	61	73	60	9	96	21	22	8.6
Univ of California-San Diego	4.32	4.12	0.13	46	72	46	91	9.8	5.3	60.6	11.4	57	46	31	50	2	89	13	42	6.9
Carnegie Mellon University	4.29	4.13	0.13	19	63	74	100	7.3	7.7	39.1	10.4	35	40	17	37	0	79	23	0	5.6
University of Washington	4.24	3.89	0.31	43	60	56	86	6.6	4.4	28.8	5.9	153	61	91	60	8	99	32	17	9.2
Princeton University	4.22	4.10	0.11	21	67	62	86	7.5	8.4	37.4	15.2	46	59	40	48	15	85	17	49	5.4
Cornell University	4.15	4.04	0.15	40	67	48	83	4.3	4.9	18.0	8.4	33	45	27	63	7	86	25	34	7.6
University of Wisconsin-Madison	4.09	3.99	0.10	35	54	51	89	7.2	4.3	28.6	6.3	77	49	43	53	8	94	21	19	9.7
Columbia University	4.04	3.60	0.07	25	64	68	88	5.9	6.8	29.2	10.6	32	56	28	66	8	95	3	5	10.3
University of Texas at Austin	4.04	3.96	0.14	50	58	36	76	4.5	5.2	16.8	5.8	119	50	69	51	9	96	9	15	8.8
University of Chicago	3.98	3.75	0.03	44	77	48	77	4.5	4.8	22.0	8.9	131	67	76	58	3	94	13	0	9.9
Indiana University	3.97	4.08	0.26	43	58	58	84	5.6	4.3	21.4	6.2	97	62	42	54	6	92	24	39	7.1
University of Virginia	3.97	3.78	0.29	33	42	45	88	6.8	5.6	26.1	10.2	106	25	62	62	9	97	11	12	8.7
Ohio State University	3.95	3.70	0.59	67	45	19	81	4.8	3.7	14.8	5.0	231	65	194	58	11	96	11	47	8.1
University of Oregon	3.94	3.83	0.05	29	62	41	76	4.3	6.0	20.8	10.0	53	55	44	51	5	91	11	25	9.7
University of Colorado	3.94	3.67	0.05	48	58	46	88	8.0	4.9	31.0	6.5	127	65	81	50	10	98	12	13	7.9
Northwestern University	3.91	3.64	0.08	37	68	35	76	4.3	5.9	21.2	13.3	32	53	36	63	9	97	4	11	10.3
U of North Carolina-Chapel Hill	3.90	3.90	0.03	66	45	26	79	4.7	3.5	18.6	7.1	150	64	97	57	13	95	13	20	8.3
University of California-Irvine	3.85	3.68	0.49	34	65	26	74	2.6	6.9	7.6	8.4	32	34	28	49	4	92	8	41	9.8
U of Massachusetts at Amherst	3.78	3.59	0.05	47	83	43	85	5.2	4.4	18.3	8.2	105	39	36	63	13	90	17	22	7.7
Rutgers State Univ-New Brunswick	3.76	3.70	0.37	67	57	40	82	5.4	3.1	16.5	5.1	135	57	67	59	3	95	14	41	7.4
University of Southern California	3.74	3.71	0.33	31	55	48	90	7.5	6.5	29.0	11.2	100	71	66	64	6	97	8	19	8.1
Purdue University	3.74	3.70	-0.06	51	41	33	75	3.9	4.2	10.7	8.1	131	59	54	59	5	90	15	37	8.0

Appendix Table M - 6 Psychology (Continued)

Institution	1993 Ratings[1] 93Q	93E	93C	Faculty Tot Fac[2]	% Full[2]	% Supp[2]	% Pub[5]	Pub/ Fac[5]	Gini Pub[5]	Cite/ Fac[5]	Gini Cite[5]	Students[2] Tot Stu	% Fem	Doctorate Recipients[3] Rpt PhDs	% Fem	% Min	% US	% RA	% TA	MYD
University of Rochester	3.73	3.73	0.13	28	79	68	89	6.4	5.5	31.6	8.4	84	49	53	54	4	97	16	21	7.6
Pennsylvania State University	3.72	3.53	0.30	90	59	22	73	4.6	3.9	13.7	7.9	259	76	195	59	11	94	20	24	8.7
Duke University	3.69	3.49	0.09	40	60	45	90	7.5	5.6	39.2	10.6	69	68	36	66	16	98	19	7	7.5
Johns Hopkins University	3.68	3.79	-0.50	11	45	82	100	7.6	19.1	42.9	32.0	21	38	19	52	3	97	13	17	5.8
New York University	3.68	3.45	0.09	50	48	34	78	4.3	3.8	17.5	6.4	120	61	119	62	11	94	9	12	12.8
University of Iowa	3.64	3.63	-0.03	33	76	27	70	4.3	9.1	14.7	11.8	71	65	33	60	7	95	35	9	8.1
Brown University	3.62	3.57	-0.03	23	52	52	74	4.7	9.0	25.0	23.2	17	59	18	58	0	94	4	69	6.1
University of Florida	3.60	3.59	0.30	63	75	30	86	6.1	4.2	14.6	7.3	206	62	116	58	8	96	21	16	7.6
State U of New York-Stony Brook	3.59	3.69	-0.05	33	58	39	76	3.7	6.1	10.4	7.4	178	61	100	66	10	90	8	55	7.8
Vanderbilt University	3.55	3.51	0.19	28	61	50	79	6.7	6.8	28.1	12.4	52	54	46	65	10	94	17	12	7.7
Uniformed Services U of Hlth Sci	3.54	3.33	0.00	5	80	0	100	10.4	22.8	65.8	53.1	27	70	8	67	0	100	36	7	8.6
CUNY - Grad Sch & Univ Center	3.48	3.23	-0.03	109	71	23	57	2.2	3.2	7.8	5.7	455	69	249	66	12	96	4	9	10.6
University of Arizona	3.47	3.29	0.55	38	53	29	84	4.2	4.8	8.0	7.3	110	64	61	55	7	94	12	17	10.7
Emory University	3.46	3.38	0.36	26	54	42	81	4.9	7.7	10.7	9.4	88	60	54	64	7	97	17	0	8.0
Peabody Col at Vanderbilt Univ	3.44	3.33	0.28	28	54	25	57	2.6	9.4	6.6	16.3	115	61	79	48	15	100	22	0	11.7
Michigan State University	3.43	3.45	0.50	48	63	27	63	2.8	4.9	8.0	8.5	160	64	92	49	11	96	19	14	9.6
Mean Values for the Top Quarter	**3.96**	**3.80**	**0.13**	**43.13**	**62.26**	**42.63**	**82.46**	**5.66**	**6.08**	**24.78**	**10.55**	**113.11**	**57.28**	**72.02**	**57.57**	**7.85**	**93.67**	**15.48**	**20.89**	**8.38**
University of California-Davis	3.42	3.42	0.39	28	71	25	89	5.6	6.0	10.8	12.5	34	47	22	69	13	96	0	36	9.4
University of Pittsburgh	3.38	3.33	-0.03	28	71	54	79	4.7	9.0	29.1	14.8	105	70	49	63	10	98	22	13	10.0
Arizona State University	3.35	3.49	0.60	37	70	30	86	6.6	5.2	19.1	7.0	112	65	52	50	13	99	13	9	9.1
Clark University	3.30	3.44	-0.04	19	63	32	89	2.2	8.2	4.6	22.4	57	79	31	59	3	95	15	33	9.1
Univ of California-Santa Barbara	3.28	3.37	-0.07	25	52	48	92	6.5	6.7	23.8	9.2	46	43	35	50	16	91	19	28	7.4
University of Connecticut	3.28	3.45	-0.11	40	70	23	78	4.4	7.5	15.9	12.8	152	66	80	51	4	95	10	26	8.1
University of Maryland College Park	3.28	3.41	0.13	44	61	30	84	4.8	4.3	16.9	6.5	126	69	80	67	12	96	11	19	10.2
University of Utah	3.23	3.29	0.24	29	59	21	83	5.0	8.4	19.6	17.6	78	60	42	51	6	97	5	8	9.5
University of South Florida	3.22	2.91	0.21	24	79	17	83	4.8	7.7	12.6	11.8	142	57	82	51	8	97	8	12	7.6
University of Kansas	3.22	3.46	0.16	28	64	4	82	3.1	6.2	8.7	15.5	136	67	59	52	4	95	8	9	9.3
University of Miami	3.18	3.11	0.18	27	59	26	100	7.8	7.2	26.7	8.6	105	73	80	59	11	98	18	11	8.0

Institution	1993 Ratings[1] 93Q	93E	93C	Faculty Tot Fac[2]	% Full[2]	% Supp[2]	% Pub[5]	Pub/ Fac[5]	Gini Pub[5]	Cite/ Fac[5]	Gini Cite[5]	Students[2] Tot Stu	% Fem	Rpt PhDs	Doctorate Recipients[3] % Fem	% Min	% US	% RA	% TA	MYD
University of Delaware	3.18	3.21	0.20	26	58	35	88	4.3	8.9	17.3	12.8	70	64	41	56	8	98	10	13	7.6
Univ of California-Santa Cruz	3.16	3.04	-0.20	16	63	31	81	4.6	14.6	10.4	22.3	60	45	27	63	17	95	0	52	9.2
State Univ of New York-Albany	3.16	3.26	0.33	31	48	39	77	7.0	12.5	24.2	15.4	121	64	62	59	3	99	48	10	7.3
State Univ of New York-Buffalo	3.15	3.49	-0.06	32	44	44	75	3.7	11.6	13.5	19.6	118	59	82	59	3	94	24	11	8.8
University of Denver	3.14	3.18	-0.17	18	72	39	72	3.6	15.5	12.7	16.7	68	74	37	66	13	99	13	15	9.7
Temple University	3.12	3.28	0.23	40	60	18	63	2.8	7.1	10.5	11.8	77	90	81	53	5	97	7	11	10.8
Washington University	3.12	3.19	-0.13	19	58	26	89	7.7	10.4	50.7	19.8	67	63	39	70	7	99	3	5	7.3
University of Georgia	3.10	3.30	0.14	36	42	31	92	8.0	9.1	16.4	10.4	184	65	107	56	7	95	23	20	7.5
Rice University	3.08	3.16	0.45	12	67	33	75	3.4	16.3	15.9	30.8	43	63	27	61	0	92	9	0	7.0
University of Missouri-Columbia	3.07	3.29	0.00	36	39	19	89	5.2	5.4	15.9	10.8	113	64	62	57	4	98	10	17	8.5
University of Illinois at Chicago	3.05	2.93	0.00	36	53	36	78	2.3	5.8	5.8	7.1	106	76	63	61	6	97	40	17	8.1
University of Houston	3.04	3.16	0.03	33	64	12	67	3.2	7.1	9.2	7.7	186	72	93	48	8	98	8	17	8.6
Univ of California-Riverside	3.02	2.92	0.27	23	52	43	87	3.0	9.3	11.0	17.4	64	75	36	53	14	97	0	37	7.7
Texas A&M University	2.94	2.88	0.50	40	35	20	83	4.6	8.4	10.5	14.6	108	56	31	53	11	99	6	22	9.4
Brandeis University	2.93	3.45	-0.30	14	57	50	86	4.9	11.1	8.1	13.7	25	72	22	74	0	96	0	20	7.9
Northeastern University	2.92	2.85	0.38	17	47	18	76	5.5	22.1	32.1	44.3	35	66	26	38	0	78	18	46	7.9
State Univ of New York-Binghamton	2.91	3.01	0.18	25	44	36	88	7.4	9.5	20.3	20.7	103	63	46	50	2	91	30	23	7.0
University of Alabama-Birmingham	2.91	2.89	0.77	27	37	41	74	3.7	7.5	11.7	9.8	54	69	29	62	0	97	21	0	6.9
Syracuse University	2.88	2.83	0.10	30	40	27	87	3.8	7.7	10.8	11.4	110	70	59	60	4	96	7	23	8.8
Georgia Institute of Technology	2.87	3.06	0.54	20	35	25	70	4.7	12.5	29.3	14.2	84	46	23	46	0	96	29	19	7.4
University of Hawaii at Manoa	2.87	2.84	-0.08	28	68	21	68	3.3	13.3	8.9	21.4	56	54	32	59	4	93	4	6	10.5
Iowa State University	2.82	3.41	0.44	26	62	15	77	3.4	8.7	8.1	14.4	79	62	47	66	2	92	28	16	7.5
Wayne State University	2.81	3.03	0.07	38	61	18	79	4.2	7.6	13.2	12.9	234	62	77	58	10	98	8	23	8.1
Dartmouth College	2.80	2.99	-0.53	15	53	27	80	5.5	11.0	10.4	12.2	14	43	18	50	0	77	13	20	6.4
Colorado State University	2.79	2.83	0.25	29	55	24	83	4.2	5.9	8.5	9.8	95	66	59	53	7	100	6	24	7.5
Florida State University	2.78	2.95	-0.32	17	35	12	76	2.3	14.2	6.2	13.5	63	70	63	48	8	97	9	2	9.3
University of Vermont	2.78	2.78	0.00	23	52	39	78	4.1	8.1	14.3	14.1	93	66	65	63	7	100	26	14	8.2
Case Western Reserve Univ	2.77	2.96	-0.05	16	44	19	100	7.3	10.1	20.8	13.4	49	78	43	66	7	100	0	2	7.5
Bowling Green State University	2.76	3.03	-0.09	29	59	7	83	3.3	7.0	5.8	11.0	127	65	70	43	3	97	33	17	6.5
University of Notre Dame	2.70	2.54	0.12	22	27	9	73	3.3	11.5	5.0	14.1	63	65	26	58	7	100	15	21	7.4

Appendix Table M - 6 Psychology (Continued)

Institution	1993 Ratings[1] 93Q	93E	93C	Faculty Tot Fac[2]	% Full[2]	% Supp[2]	% Pub[5]	Pub/ Fac[5]	Gini Pub[5]	Cite/ Fac[5]	Gini Cite[5]	Students[2] Tot Stu	% Fem	Rpt PhDs	Doctorate Recipients[3] % Fem	% Min	% US	% RA	% TA	MYD
West Virginia University	2.70	2.90	0.04	22	45	5	82	3.3	9.2	5.9	16.0	69	71	63	57	3	94	11	26	7.2
University of Kentucky	2.69	2.76	0.00	30	17	33	97	5.4	6.2	18.4	13.0	84	62	38	59	6	98	9	14	9.6
U of Texas-Southwestern Med Ctr	2.69	3.13	0.20	24	25	21	71	4.7	10.6	39.8	15.2	57	77	33	53	6	100	5	5	8.8
Mean Values for the 2nd Quarter	**3.02**	**3.12**	**0.11**	**26.80**	**53.11**	**26.89**	**81.57**	**4.62**	**9.37**	**15.67**	**14.80**	**90.27**	**64.84**	**50.89**	**56.82**	**6.41**	**95.77**	**13.68**	**17.55**	**8.31**
University of South Carolina	2.67	3.18	0.28	36	56	33	78	2.9	5.8	6.7	10.3	130	74	67	54	10	99	21	10	8.6
Virginia Polytech Inst & State U	2.67	2.85	0.29	24	29	21	83	5.2	8.4	11.4	12.0	86	58	55	57	0	99	13	23	7.0
U of North Carolina-Greensboro	2.67	2.90	0.04	22	68	41	82	4.0	8.0	8.6	11.6	44	64	42	68	8	100	20	15	9.4
University of Tennessee-Knoxville	2.66	2.76	-0.21	23	83	17	70	4.0	13.6	9.3	20.3	97	61	80	52	6	99	11	9	9.3
Boston University	2.65	2.78	0.00	25	44	16	76	2.2	8.4	6.5	16.0	120	68	103	60	10	92	5	13	9.3
University of Nebraska-Lincoln	2.65	2.90	0.06	26	38	12	73	2.4	11.0	6.5	33.2	87	62	64	48	9	97	3	12	9.1
Virginia Commonwealth University	2.63	2.73	0.11	24	46	4	79	3.5	7.4	9.5	14.7	150	61	89	56	7	100	3	12	7.9
Kent State University	2.61	2.83	-0.05	28	54	25	79	3.2	6.0	8.3	8.7	145	59	68	63	7	97	12	7	10.4
Southern Illinois University	2.58	2.90	0.24	32	44	13	81	3.9	6.2	5.6	8.6	100	67	82	55	21	98	33	10	8.1
University of Rhode Island	2.57	2.87	0.07	23	70	17	74	3.4	11.9	19.3	22.8	114	76	73	53	8	100	10	11	10.5
University of New Hampshire	2.56	2.95	0.07	19	21	37	95	3.6	10.1	8.9	27.2	36	58	20	31	3	100	9	74	7.4
University of Texas at Arlington	2.55	2.26	-0.07	12	67	33	75	2.8	14.8	7.5	26.3	23	39	11	47	8	71	8	33	6.7
Georgia State University	2.53	2.41	0.00	29	45	34	66	3.6	10.9	10.8	19.2	137	67	113	52	5	99	4	3	12.2
George Washington University	2.52	2.43	0.33	24	50	13	58	1.9	10.3	2.7	12.0	111	86	77	77	10	100	1	1	10.1
Loyola University of Chicago	2.50	2.69	0.13	36	39	11	61	2.3	5.6	3.9	9.1	115	62	65	56	8	99	17	6	9.3
George Mason University	2.49	2.22	0.71	28	21	14	68	2.6	7.7	4.2	10.3	126	71	18	73	0	100	10	0	9.0
University of Cincinnati	2.46	2.78	0.00	32	63	6	66	2.0	7.9	2.2	14.4	86	70	58	68	6	96	5	9	9.4
Tufts University	2.45	2.85	-0.19	14	50	43	100	6.1	14.1	14.4	21.1	30	57	16	76	0	93	13	26	10.8
University of Louisville	2.41	2.43	0.00	19	63	5	79	2.7	9.4	4.6	25.0	91	56	54	49	7	100	21	11	8.9
Miami University	2.40	2.47	0.07	25	48	12	56	1.4	8.7	3.0	14.7	72	71	58	56	5	98	32	12	8.9
Yeshiva University	2.40	2.03	0.23	27	33	7	44	1.0	11.6	3.0	27.0	107	77	115	69	18	100	0	0	9.9
University of Alabama	2.39	2.50	0.00	20	40	10	90	3.0	8.4	3.8	19.1	31	n/a	47	52	8	97	6	14	8.9
University of Tulsa	2.38	2.61	0.17	16	25	13	56	2.8	14.2	19.8	17.7	49	49	27	50	0	95	48	0	7.7
U of Maryland Baltimore County	2.38	2.19	0.00	23	35	30	74	2.5	8.1	7.8	17.9	108	86	23	89	0	96	4	38	8.9

Institution	1993 Ratings[1] 93Q	93E	93C	Faculty Tot Fac[2]	% Full[2]	% Supp[2]	% Pub[5]	Pub/ Fac[5]	Gini Pub[5]	Cite/ Fac[5]	Gini Cite[5]	Students[2] Tot Stu	% Fem	Rpt PhDs	Doctorate Recipients[3] % Fem	% Min	% US	% RA	% TA	MYD
University of Oklahoma	2.37	2.58	0.22	19	53	26	63	3.5	13.9	6.9	24.3	33	61	20	47	12	97	8	14	10.7
Washington State University	2.37	2.56	0.00	23	48	22	78	4.4	11.5	9.6	34.5	52	60	49	56	3	100	10	52	9.0
Ohio University	2.35	2.78	0.20	25	52	4	88	4.8	6.2	7.0	11.9	101	61	63	49	3	95	9	25	7.3
University of Maine	2.35	2.43	0.10	17	41	6	65	2.4	13.8	4.5	18.2	42	64	31	51	0	100	4	15	9.2
Howard University	2.35	2.33	-0.10	13	85	8	77	2.3	17.1	6.2	34.1	86	70	39	63	76	92	9	9	10.2
Texas Tech University	2.35	2.02	-0.08	28	50	4	57	1.9	9.3	5.0	20.1	125	58	80	42	8	98	10	3	7.8
Bryn Mawr College	2.34	2.17	-0.37	7	71	29	86	3.3	23.2	11.3	28.6	42	76	40	82	4	96	2	10	12.2
North Carolina State University	2.33	2.63	0.28	28	39	11	71	2.1	6.0	3.0	10.2	124	70	59	53	9	100	5	8	13.3
Brigham Young University	2.31	2.44	0.00	28	68	4	57	2.3	11.0	2.5	23.7	70	37	105	33	0	94	9	5	7.9
Louisiana State U & A&M College	2.28	2.55	-0.31	34	35	15	85	4.9	5.9	11.9	7.7	129	59	62	59	5	96	11	22	7.4
American University	2.28	2.03	0.00	14	50	21	79	6.1	11.8	11.7	19.9	65	72	30	59	11	96	4	17	10.6
Catholic University of America	2.27	2.69	0.00	17	47	12	82	2.9	9.4	7.2	15.6	85	62	56	64	10	97	6	4	9.9
Georgetown University	2.27	2.67	0.00	11	45	9	73	3.2	14.9	6.8	21.7	13	62	5	80	0	100	0	0	12.7
New Mexico State University	2.23	2.73	0.13	14	43	29	71	1.4	18.0	3.6	13.7	18	44	16	57	4	100	19	19	10.4
University of Texas at Dallas	2.23	1.88	0.00	26	42	19	54	1.3	12.1	3.0	21.5	77	73	20	87	0	87	20	10	9.8
Texas Christian University	2.23	2.50	0.33	12	50	33	58	5.5	21.1	7.9	20.5	41	49	20	46	3	97	11	11	5.6
Tulane University	2.23	2.62	-0.09	18	39	11	61	3.2	27.5	6.3	41.7	68	68	44	53	10	96	2	52	7.7
Claremont Graduate School	2.22	2.33	-0.19	7	86	14	71	2.3	22.6	4.9	29.5	110	61	55	57	4	96	4	0	10.6
University of Nevada, Reno	2.21	2.38	0.25	13	62	38	69	2.8	16.8	6.8	49.7	67	43	22	53	12	93	6	10	8.9
University of Mississippi	2.18	2.11	0.00	14	50	21	57	2.1	17.7	3.1	42.1	68	51	39	54	6	98	8	1	8.3
Univ of Health Sc/Chicago Med Sch	2.17	2.38	0.00	8	25	25	75	2.3	21.6	4.5	28.7	66	77	48	59	0	96	2	0	8.5
Kansas State University	2.15	2.11	0.00	17	76	12	76	3.1	11.2	3.8	17.6	54	43	17	48	10	95	6	25	9.9
Hahnemann University	2.13	2.04	-0.37	11	36	9	64	1.9	18.3	3.5	43.9	82	71	24	67	0	100	0	8	8.4
Saint Louis University	2.13	1.80	-0.11	20	60	0	80	3.0	10.4	3.1	13.3	92	62	60	58	7	97	0	0	8.6
Mean Values for the 3rd Quarter	**2.40**	**2.51**	**0.05**	**21.06**	**49.69**	**17.69**	**72.08**	**3.04**	**12.08**	**6.93**	**21.08**	**81.35**	**62.83**	**50.60**	**58.08**	**7.52**	**96.69**	**9.88**	**13.94**	**9.22**
University of Wisconsin-Milwaukee	2.12	3.33	0.00	21	38	29	67	2.0	12.9	2.8	18.7	68	72	26	60	5	95	0	47	8.4
University of Akron	2.07	2.22	0.00	24	29	0	67	3.2	11.0	7.9	16.0	171	49	64	47	1	99	19	27	8.8
Univ of Missouri-Saint Louis	2.07	2.67	0.00	16	38	13	69	2.2	12.0	2.1	21.7	94	68	44	59	0	100	2	5	8.7

Appendix Table M - 6 Psychology (Continued)

Institution	1993 Ratings[1] 93Q	93E	93C	Faculty Tot Fac[2]	% Full[2]	% Supp[2]	% Pub[5]	Pub/ Fac[5]	Gini Pub[5]	Cite/ Fac[5]	Gini Cite[5]	Students[2] Tot Stu	% Fem	Rpt PhDs	Doctorate Recipients[3] % Fem	% Min	% US	% RA	% TA	MYD
Northern Illinois University	2.06	2.26	0.06	30	37	7	63	1.9	8.2	3.0	16.9	58	62	28	60	7	95	16	24	7.9
St. John's University	2.05	2.12	0.00	20	45	15	55	1.8	13.1	1.1	18.7	113	74	67	52	1	100	7	1	10.9
Adelphi University	2.04	1.72	-0.14	14	43	7	43	1.2	19.7	3.0	29.3	150	77	139	62	12	98	3	5	9.1
Boston College	2.00	2.33	0.00	16	38	25	50	1.1	16.0	4.0	40.3	20	55	9	65	5	99	5	2	14.2
University of Toledo	2.00	2.22	0.00	18	61	17	72	3.2	11.5	6.0	15.2	51	57	25	63	4	100	22	4	11.4
Lehigh University	1.95	2.00	0.33	16	38	38	75	1.8	11.2	3.8	19.3	23	52	8	57	5	90	21	5	11.4
Fordham University	1.92	2.19	0.00	18	33	0	56	2.5	12.5	1.7	18.2	201	64	69	59	6	98	5	5	12.5
Ball State University	1.92	1.50	0.00	32	59	3	53	2.7	14.8	2.5	21.5	76	59	88	40	1	99	4	4	10.2
Univ of Missouri-Kansas City	1.90	2.12	0.00	12	42	0	75	2.6	37.3	2.2	50.2	22	77	10	60	4	99	0	1	11.6
University of Wyoming	1.90	1.67	0.00	10	60	10	50	1.1	25.6	1.9	34.0	39	69	23	41	0	97	6	38	7.9
Univ of Arkansas-Fayetteville	1.89	1.67	0.11	19	42	11	79	1.6	10.0	3.9	28.3	36	56	42	43	4	100	18	2	7.9
Western Michigan University	1.87	1.79	0.00	19	63	11	58	2.1	25.1	3.8	17.6	48	56	43	39	18	92	4	8	9.8
Auburn University	1.85	2.04	-0.27	22	50	9	59	2.4	14.8	3.2	25.0	107	62	79	57	4	98	8	32	7.6
Hofstra University	1.82	1.67	0.00	12	25	0	75	2.4	15.8	2.3	23.7	143	55	168	48	7	99	0	0	6.9
Old Dominion University	1.81	2.33	0.00	10	60	0	80	1.8	29.6	11.1	83.4	24	67	29	46	0	100	16	26	7.4
Illinois Institute of Technology	1.79	2.08	-0.20	15	27	0	60	1.7	24.8	3.3	71.2	106	58	55	35	9	95	6	6	9.5
University of North Texas	1.76	1.67	-0.09	35	26	6	51	2.7	13.9	4.9	28.0	159	64	73	52	6	98	0	2	9.9
Fuller Theological Seminary	1.73	1.50	0.33	15	53	7	47	1.5	22.8	4.1	43.2	165	61	128	38	7	99	0	0	8.1
University of Montana	1.73	2.41	-0.33	30	47	3	27	0.6	16.9	0.3	25.0	52	58	65	57	4	100	2	20	7.1
Univ of Southern Mississippi	1.72	2.33	0.00	30	57	0	57	3.3	13.3	2.5	14.7	110	65	135	45	6	98	6	3	7.5
Utah State University	1.64	1.67	n/s	17	41	0	71	2.1	10.8	2.5	20.0	54	48	43	46	7	100	12	16	10.9
University of New Orleans	1.64	2.50	1.00	17	59	18	76	3.1	15.2	4.2	20.1	34	68	12	64	7	100	9	18	7.7
Univ of California-San Francisco	1.60	2.22	-1.00	3	67	67	67	8.7	52.6	100.0	50.0	8	75	7	64	9	100	32	0	9.8
Baylor University	1.58	1.67	-0.14	10	70	0	50	1.4	26.5	0.6	100.0	7	57	3	0	0	100	50	0	6.0
Duquesne University	1.55	1.82	-0.12	7	86	0	0	0.0		0.0		110	47	35	36	6	98	0	8	12.5
Oklahoma State University	1.55	1.85	0.00	13	69	8	85	2.0	11.8	1.8	17.5	38	71	50	57	11	98	4	9	9.4
University of North Dakota	1.50	2.08	0.00	13	54	0	69	2.0	16.2	2.3	32.0	53	58	42	46	0	99	4	38	7.6
Univ of Puerto Rico-Rio Piedras	1.40	n/s	n/s	31	48	3	26	0.5	15.5	0.3	28.3	249	74	10	100	100	100	0	0	17.7
Fairleigh Dickinson University	1.40	1.78	0.00	16	63	0	56	1.1	19.0	2.1	24.5	82	73	56	56	9	100	0	0	7.9
Cal Sch Prof Psych-Alameda	1.30	0.69	0.09	38	45	0	11	0.2	27.7	0.3	26.0	528	74	303	62	3	97	0	0	7.9

Institution	1993 Ratings[1] 93Q	93E	93C	Faculty Tot Fac[2]	% Full[2]	% Supp[2]	% Pub[5]	Pub/ Fac[5]	Gini Pub[5]	Cite/ Fac[5]	Gini Cite[5]	Students[2] Tot Stu	% Fem	Rpt PhDs	Doctorate Recipients[3] % Fem	% Min	% US	% RA	% TA	MYD
University of Northern Colorado	1.22	1.67	0.00	18	56	6	50	1.4	14.2	1.6	26.0	47	53	62	50	0	96	5	0	13.8
Saybrook Institute	1.08	0.67	n/s	42	31	0	12	0.2	22.4	0.0	100.0	171	49	78	45	1	98	0	0	15.4
Pacific Grad Sch of Psychology	1.06	0.72	0.00	22	27	0	14	0.2	36.0	0.1	100.0	65	72	70	72	2	100	0	0	16.3
East Texas State University	1.04	0.83	n/s	10	50	0	30	0.7	34.6	0.0		59	54	12	20	0	100	0	24	12.8
Cal Sch Prof Psych-Los Angeles	1.04	0.88	0.57	32	28	3	3	0.1	100.0	0.0	100.0	408	86	344	71	11	98	0	0	6.8
Cal Sch Prof Psych-San Diego	1.04	0.65	0.00	26	54	0	23	0.4	24.0	0.2	100.0	631	72	240	59	9	96	0	0	8.2
Cal Sch Prof Psych-Fresno	0.91	0.46	0.00	20	40	0	20	0.7	51.4	0.3	100.0	144	n/a	137	43	7	99	0	0	7.8
Biola University	0.86	0.19	0.00	21	19	0	10	0.1	50.0	0.0		9	78	36	39	6	94	0	0	8.6
University of Detroit Mercy	0.86	0.56	n/s	15	20	0	0	0.0		0.0		126	69	47	50	2	95	0	0	11.2
Fielding Institute	0.84	0.98	-0.20	29	0	0	3	0.1	100.0	0.4	100.0	430	69	121	71	3	99	0	0	15.5
Mississippi State University	0.80	1.11	n/s	6	50	0	67	1.3	43.7	1.0	72.2	29	55	33	36	4	96	11	5	9.1
Rutgers State Univ-Newark	0.74	0.67	-0.20	5	40	20	40	0.8	62.5	3.4	79.2	34	50	15	52	13	97	9	17	11.7
Texas Woman's University	0.73	0.56	n/s	15	47	7	20	0.2	33.3	0.0		78	77	38	75	6	98	0	1	13.6
Stevens Inst of Technology	0.20	0.00	-1.00	4	50	0	50	2.0	62.5	8.8	54.9	22	41	10	33	8	93	23	8	8.0
Mean Values for the 4th Quarter	**1.52**	**1.61**	**-0.03**	**18.81**	**45.21**	**7.30**	**47.68**	**1.63**	**27.17**	**4.50**	**43.59**	**116.00**	**63.20**	**68.53**	**51.74**	**7.23**	**97.85**	**7.00**	**8.74**	**10.02**
Mean Values for All Programs	**2.71**	**2.75**	**0.07**	**27.34**	**52.49**	**23.44**	**70.72**	**3.71**	**13.63**	**12.83**	**22.10**	**100.17**	**62.01**	**60.55**	**56.04**	**7.26**	**96.02**	**11.44**	**15.21**	**9.00**

Sources: 1. National Survey of Graduate Faculty
2. Institutional Coordinator Response Data
3. Doctorate Records File
4. Federal Agencies
5. Institute for Scientific Information

n/s After trimming no cases remained

Appendix Table M - 7 Selected Characteristics of Research-Doctorate Programs in Sociology

Institution	1993 Ratings[1]			Faculty								Students[2]			Doctorate Recipients[3]					
	93Q	93E	93C	Tot Fac[2]	% Full[2]	% Supp[2]	% Pub[5]	Pub/ Fac[5]	Gini Pub[5]	Cite/ Fac[5]	Gini Cite[5]	Tot Stu	% Fem	Rpt PhDs	% Fem	% Min	% US	% RA	% TA	MYD
University of Chicago	4.77	4.26	0.38	25	68	36	76	3.8	10.6	17.2	18.0	155	39	47	43	14	77	13	0	9.7
University of Wisconsin-Madison	4.74	4.61	0.06	69	71	30	74	2.6	2.8	9.6	8.7	221	0	75	31	9	66	42	15	10.1
University of California-Berkeley	4.56	3.60	-0.02	33	79	21	52	1.1	8.4	2.3	28.0	109	51	62	44	24	87	14	20	10.3
University of Michigan	4.39	4.08	-0.14	36	50	36	78	4.4	9.2	15.1	15.5	163	63	73	53	29	74	17	17	10.2
Univ of California-Los Angeles	4.36	3.79	0.47	73	75	38	75	3.1	4.0	10.0	15.3	139	58	45	58	13	76	14	17	11.8
U of North Carolina-Chapel Hill	4.31	4.00	0.13	25	52	32	72	3.5	8.0	11.1	13.8	78	50	30	57	6	86	15	26	8.7
Harvard University	4.18	3.58	-0.02	17	59	29	71	2.4	12.7	7.3	19.2	81	47	44	37	16	77	7	31	9.6
Stanford University	4.08	3.77	0.03	15	67	53	80	2.4	11.5	9.5	24.9	76	62	38	52	10	82	61	0	9.1
Northwestern University	4.07	3.61	0.38	25	60	8	68	2.5	15.1	7.8	29.9	71	48	35	57	11	88	27	17	8.7
University of Washington	4.03	3.73	0.38	30	60	23	77	3.0	6.9	8.8	13.5	75	57	36	50	9	85	19	35	10.7
University of Pennsylvania	4.02	3.66	0.43	31	68	16	77	2.9	6.7	10.6	11.0	59	64	26	47	4	84	0	52	8.7
Indiana University	3.94	3.85	0.00	30	50	20	73	2.1	5.9	6.6	7.5	74	53	25	37	0	83	23	42	9.8
Princeton University	3.79	3.29	0.27	18	67	28	67	1.7	12.2	2.5	44.8	26	38	19	56	0	84	5	0	8.6
University of Arizona	3.78	3.41	0.15	19	63	37	68	1.7	8.7	4.2	15.5	59	49	19	55	18	89	23	38	10.2
Columbia University	3.76	3.25	-0.31	19	68	16	68	1.6	11.3	3.8	22.6	79	51	23	43	11	76	3	3	13.0
University of Texas at Austin	3.64	3.56	0.22	38	61	26	79	2.4	4.6	7.7	36.9	58	59	49	49	24	77	24	22	9.2
Johns Hopkins University	3.56	3.51	0.00	11	73	45	73	3.3	18.5	10.2	18.7	32	59	11	56	0	79	8	0	10.9
Pennsylvania State University	3.51	3.47	0.70	27	41	33	74	3.1	7.4	7.1	12.2	32	56	18	45	8	88	35	19	11.4
Yale University	3.49	3.04	-0.64	18	56	11	78	2.2	12.0	16.7	35.7	50	44	28	45	17	81	8	0	10.3
Duke University	3.42	3.43	0.35	19	63	47	89	4.6	17.0	25.8	54.5	50	66	18	52	15	87	21	29	8.7
New York University	3.34	2.93	0.18	21	52	29	67	1.5	13.2	1.8	23.2	50	58	22	58	21	94	8	8	14.6
Univ of California-San Diego	3.31	3.01	-0.06	34	44	6	53	1.1	7.5	2.0	18.2	48	46	30	63	9	89	0	41	11.8
Univ of California-Santa Barbara	3.30	3.06	0.09	25	40	12	64	2.8	13.3	11.2	26.0	66	56	19	48	4	86	9	41	9.7
Mean Values for the Top Quarter	**3.93**	**3.59**	**0.13**	**28.61**	**60.30**	**27.48**	**71.87**	**2.60**	**9.89**	**9.08**	**22.33**	**80.48**	**51.04**	**34.43**	**49.39**	**11.83**	**82.39**	**17.22**	**20.57**	**10.25**
University of Minnesota	3.29	3.20	0.02	25	60	40	80	2.4	9.6	7.2	19.9	42	60	36	44	9	80	10	42	11.8
State U of New York-Stony Brook	3.28	3.29	-0.25	23	52	26	74	1.6	7.3	3.5	21.2	74	61	24	45	13	76	7	56	10.7
Ohio State University	3.28	3.24	0.46	32	47	13	75	2.8	7.6	6.9	14.4	88	64	40	41	5	72	17	40	10.4
Vanderbilt University	3.27	2.87	0.36	17	47	24	59	1.6	13.5	3.8	24.9	29	55	12	53	13	84	7	40	11.8

Institution	1993 Ratings[1]			Faculty								Students[2]			Doctorate Recipients[3]					
	93Q	93E	93C	Tot Fac[2]	% Full[2]	% Supp[2]	% Pub[5]	Pub/ Fac[5]	Gini Pub[5]	Cite/ Fac[5]	Gini Cite[5]	Tot Stu	% Fem	Rpt PhDs	% Fem	% Min	% US	% RA	% TA	MYD
Univ of California-Riverside	3.27	2.87	0.38	18	61	0	72	3.3	10.5	4.6	16.0	39	64	17	54	14	88	28	22	8.3
U of Illinois at Urbana-Champaign	3.26	3.07	-0.20	35	60	23	60	2.6	8.0	8.4	12.8	50	62	19	34	8	79	29	33	8.9
State Univ of New York-Albany	3.22	3.18	0.20	24	29	33	79	4.4	9.2	10.1	12.1	80	50	22	36	0	64	29	14	9.4
Rutgers State Univ-New Brunswick	3.09	2.78	0.28	29	34	21	72	2.6	9.7	7.3	15.3	85	72	22	71	15	87	4	33	12.7
Washington State University	3.08	3.04	-0.06	26	50	8	81	3.1	6.6	5.5	11.4	64	63	25	49	9	84	10	69	8.4
University of Maryland College Park	3.06	2.97	0.25	29	55	17	69	3.0	7.8	7.9	12.0	50	60	19	62	13	81	7	37	10.8
State Univ of New York-Binghamton	3.03	2.80	-0.17	13	54	8	46	2.2	23.9	1.5	26.8	104	29	27	30	53	73	38	14	12.8
Cornell University	3.02	3.10	-0.48	12	75	67	50	1.5	22.8	6.8	24.1	23	65	17	45	2	72	13	33	10.1
Florida State University	2.96	2.95	0.44	22	68	9	64	2.4	9.3	4.0	14.4	47	45	9	53	0	87	15	31	10.6
CUNY - Grad Sch & Univ Center	2.86	2.62	0.00	23	57	22	74	1.3	9.5	0.8	17.4	215	50	50	51	25	94	5	2	14.7
Brown University	2.84	3.22	-0.10	23	48	22	74	2.6	7.3	7.0	9.1	62	50	31	54	5	49	0	43	10.5
U of Massachusetts at Amherst	2.83	2.85	-0.40	23	74	13	74	2.3	8.5	3.8	13.8	67	54	24	53	8	81	21	33	9.8
University of Southern California	2.80	2.67	0.09	19	63	11	63	1.5	11.7	3.6	37.8	80	61	38	55	3	89	7	7	10.8
University of Iowa	2.80	2.88	-0.28	17	35	18	65	2.4	14.2	6.4	25.9	33	48	21	44	0	80	58	8	10.6
Michigan State University	2.72	2.70	0.00	26	62	15	69	2.3	8.9	3.9	28.3	101	57	46	37	8	49	15	27	11.7
University of Florida	2.68	2.68	0.39	35	54	20	66	3.6	5.6	6.5	6.9	21	71	20	72	41	88	13	31	10.0
Boston University	2.67	2.63	0.00	23	78	4	61	2.5	14.0	26.8	70.6	57	67	44	61	7	83	0	5	13.9
University of Illinois at Chicago	2.66	2.35	0.28	27	44	15	70	2.6	6.9	5.7	13.9	25	72	16	80	0	55	12	41	14.4
University of Notre Dame	2.63	2.55	0.26	23	30	17	70	1.9	10.4	3.4	13.4	47	53	12	23	20	73	32	16	9.7
Mean Values for the 2nd Quarter	**2.98**	**2.89**	**0.06**	**23.65**	**53.78**	**19.39**	**68.13**	**2.46**	**10.56**	**6.32**	**20.10**	**64.48**	**57.96**	**25.70**	**49.87**	**11.78**	**76.87**	**16.39**	**29.43**	**10.99**
University of Virginia	2.60	2.46	-0.04	14	43	0	50	1.4	21.3	3.0	40.0	34	44	11	50	8	93	0	50	8.7
University of Georgia	2.60	2.62	0.32	20	40	20	70	2.9	9.1	3.8	14.0	26	77	18	45	13	85	43	21	12.7
University of Connecticut	2.54	2.24	0.26	26	73	12	50	0.8	9.5	0.9	15.2	64	61	15	48	11	78	0	40	11.8
Univ of California-San Francisco	2.47	2.57	0.00	17	47	35	82	6.5	30.6	25.7	36.8	30	77	24	85	8	100	11	0	16.8
Texas A&M University	2.47	2.69	0.70	25	52	24	76	3.2	8.6	4.5	11.9	44	55	8	45	27	100	0	13	11.7
Purdue University	2.44	2.42	0.02	33	36	6	48	1.3	8.7	1.9	27.4	70	64	17	36	8	93	9	55	8.6
Univ of California-Santa Cruz	2.41	2.40	-0.24	11	91	0	45	1.1	22.2	1.0	20.6	45	51	16	43	12	81	0	81	9.8
University of Kentucky	2.40	2.36	0.03	26	46	23	81	2.1	6.4	2.4	12.6	52	60	28	44	13	75	18	18	11.3

Appendix Table M - 7 Sociology (Continued)

Institution	1993 Ratings[1] 93Q	93E	93C	Faculty Tot Fac[2]	% Full[2]	% Supp[2]	% Pub[5]	Pub/ Fac[5]	Gini Pub[5]	Cite/ Fac[5]	Gini Cite[5]	Students[2] Tot Stu	% Fem	Rpt PhDs	Doctorate Recipients[3] % Fem	% Min	% US	% RA	% TA	MYD
Boston College	2.32	2.45	0.09	17	53	6	41	1.1	17.4	14.8	58.4	63	51	15	37	14	100	4	7	13.8
University of Oregon	2.29	2.15	-0.05	21	38	0	81	1.8	9.7	2.7	16.6	47	51	27	62	12	90	5	48	11.6
University of Colorado	2.29	2.30	0.33	22	41	9	50	1.7	15.2	4.7	29.8	71	61	20	61	0	96	17	4	12.2
Syracuse University	2.22	2.47	-0.19	19	63	0	37	1.0	23.5	1.8	25.8	43	65	9	59	7	88	0	36	14.4
University of Pittsburgh	2.21	2.17	-0.10	17	71	18	59	2.5	17.9	3.5	30.8	45	40	25	35	6	53	12	52	12.7
Brandeis University	2.19	2.31	-0.36	11	45	9	55	1.5	18.3	2.5	46.1	58	64	12	41	4	93	5	14	11.5
Iowa State University	2.15	2.81	0.19	35	54	9	77	3.2	8.1	6.4	17.1	48	56	42	31	9	61	38	10	8.8
Temple University	2.15	2.02	0.03	25	32	8	36	0.6	14.6	2.9	70.8	62	55	18	36	13	78	0	27	12.8
University of Missouri-Columbia	2.14	2.07	-0.09	17	65	6	71	1.6	12.5	1.9	19.1	35	49	16	22	22	67	15	35	9.5
North Carolina State University	2.13	2.38	0.27	28	29	14	71	2.3	6.8	3.8	9.5	57	56	14	80	26	95	29	29	15.0
Louisiana State U & A&M College	2.12	2.16	0.22	24	21	17	71	1.9	8.1	1.9	21.1	27	44	12	59	21	82	33	40	8.7
University of Kansas	2.10	2.07	-0.17	16	25	0	69	1.3	10.6	2.8	31.4	21	52	13	30	7	79	0	31	12.1
University of Nebraska-Lincoln	2.04	2.56	-0.12	18	44	39	78	2.8	12.1	7.9	19.1	24	67	21	59	0	82	6	35	9.7
Loyola University of Chicago	2.02	1.97	0.05	10	50	0	20	0.3	55.5	0.5	68.0	52	50	16	54	19	70	29	6	16.8
University of Delaware	2.00	1.86	0.00	25	44	20	48	1.1	16.0	4.2	23.0	13	62	7	43	5	90	0	59	7.8
University of New Hampshire	1.99	1.98	-0.09	13	54	8	62	1.5	38.5	2.6	60.2	13	69	15	52	4	100	6	22	10.4
Northeastern University	1.98	2.03	0.18	24	42	4	79	2.3	11.2	11.3	39.1	34	74	12	57	11	83	0	25	10.8
Mean Values for the 3rd Quarter	**2.25**	**2.30**	**0.05**	**20.56**	**47.96**	**11.48**	**60.28**	**1.91**	**16.50**	**4.78**	**30.58**	**43.12**	**58.20**	**17.24**	**48.56**	**11.20**	**84.48**	**11.20**	**30.32**	**11.60**
Tulane University	1.91	1.72	-0.03	13	15	0	62	2.8	19.2	3.9	21.0	34	68	5	80	0	80	0	50	16.7
Arizona State University	1.87	1.74	-0.24	15	27	7	80	1.7	10.4	3.2	37.9	51	67	6	75	0	80	0	50	13.4
State Univ of New York-Buffalo	1.78	1.73	-0.10	12	33	8	75	2.3	17.8	4.5	22.0	40	63	30	62	6	79	3	17	12.3
Bowling Green State University	1.59	1.62	0.00	20	70	5	70	2.0	10.1	1.0	18.0	23	52	16	44	15	72	0	31	11.8
Howard University	1.59	1.80	-0.05	14	29	7	36	1.1	30.4	1.4	37.3	33	67	17	35	100	63	20	0	11.7
University of Hawaii at Manoa	1.59	1.18	0.00	19	42	5	37	0.7	20.4	0.5	50.6	33	48	25	58	0	59	0	27	11.9
Southern Illinois University	1.56	1.37	-0.28	11	27	0	64	1.7	18.0	1.6	70.9	18	56	11	47	9	73	7	64	12.9
University of Tennessee-Knoxville	1.55	1.17	-0.06	13	62	0	46	0.9	26.3	1.3	40.4	19	42	7	60	0	90	20	50	11.1
American University	1.52	1.39	-0.14	13	46	0	31	0.5	26.5	0.6	43.7	57	60	31	37	17	67	0	3	11.4
Colorado State University	1.40	1.45	0.00	14	43	14	50	2.0	31.1	1.4	64.5	19	68	16	17	0	78	0	11	12.6

Institution	1993 Ratings[1]			Faculty								Students[2]			Doctorate Recipients[3]					
	93Q	93E	93C	Tot Fac[2]	% Full[2]	% Supp[2]	% Pub[5]	Pub/ Fac[5]	Gini Pub[5]	Cite/ Fac[5]	Gini Cite[5]	Tot Stu	% Fem	Rpt PhDs	% Fem	% Min	% US	% RA	% TA	MYD
Fordham University	1.36	1.17	-0.23	12	50	25	58	2.0	23.9	2.1	65.1	61	49	33	46	18	94	7	0	15.2
University of Utah	1.34	1.47	-0.14	15	40	7	33	0.7	22.3	0.1	100.0	36	58	9	27	0	56	20	40	9.8
University of Akron	1.30	1.57	-0.17	17	59	12	65	2.2	12.1	2.2	16.0	20	35	15	48	0	68	0	55	9.9
Western Michigan University	1.29	1.46	-0.05	18	50	0	22	0.2	25.0	0.4	38.7	28	57	9	31	22	82	0	14	11.7
Mississippi State University	1.27	1.45	-0.04	16	63	6	44	0.8	21.8	0.8	62.1	33	48	13	21	40	79	7	14	8.9
University of Cincinnati	1.25	0.86	-0.17	9	67	11	67	1.7	20.0	1.1	50.0	21	86	17	45	5	100	8	17	15.0
Kent State University	1.18	1.09	-0.23	13	54	23	69	2.2	18.6	2.8	41.8	50	60	16	68	19	84	0	36	10.8
University of Oklahoma	1.15	1.13	-0.18	11	9	18	82	4.0	12.9	7.7	21.1	25	72	6	60	0	89	0	33	11.0
University of Denver	1.14	1.04	-0.23	8	25	25	63	1.4	25.6	1.8	35.7	9	78	8	53	0	87	7	29	12.7
Utah State University	1.12	1.25	0.00	15	60	0	67	1.7	15.0	1.7	25.1	10	80	8	17	14	58	43	0	11.1
University of North Texas	1.12	1.21	0.09	18	33	0	39	0.5	16.0	0.3	68.0	33	48	18	25	5	96	0	6	11.7
Catholic University of America	1.12	0.99	-0.07	7	43	57	71	2.1	29.7	3.4	35.0	10	60	8	56	13	89	33	0	16.3
Georgia State University	1.11	0.99	-0.05	10	50	20	70	2.4	19.7	3.0	35.3	17	59	9	100	0	100	0	14	23.5
Oklahoma State University	0.60	0.73	-0.09	10	70	0	30	0.6	38.8	0.2	100.0	70	50	6	50	22	100	0	14	9.5
Mean Values for the 4th Quarter	**1.36**	**1.32**	**-0.10**	**13.46**	**44.46**	**10.42**	**55.46**	**1.59**	**21.32**	**1.96**	**45.84**	**31.25**	**59.63**	**14.13**	**48.42**	**12.71**	**80.13**	**7.29**	**23.96**	**12.62**
Mean Values for All Programs	**2.61**	**2.51**	**0.04**	**21.54**	**51.56**	**17.18**	**63.91**	**2.14**	**14.61**	**5.51**	**29.79**	**54.55**	**56.91**	**22.79**	**49.03**	**11.91**	**80.90**	**13.06**	**25.88**	**11.41**

Sources: 1. National Survey of Graduate Faculty
2. Institutional Coordinator Response Data
3. Doctorate Records File
4. Federal Agencies
5. Institute for Scientific Information

APPENDIX N

Selected Characteristics of Research-Doctorate Programs in the Biological Sciences

In the tables that follow, information from the National Survey of Graduate Faculty is linked to a variety of statistics depicting participating doctoral programs. The tables have been designed to present information about each program in a field in rank order by the average rating of the scholarly quality of program faculty (93Q), with the top-rated institutions appearing at the beginning of the list. A key to the variables in the table is presented below.

Institution

Institution: U.S. Universities participating in the 1993 NRC Study, ranked in descending order based on the scholarly rating of the program faculty (93Q).

1993 Ratings

93Q: 1993 trimmed mean for scholarly quality of program faculty. The trimmed mean is obtained by dropping the two highest and two lowest scores on the survey before computing the average. For purposes of analysis, scores were converted to a scale of 0 to 5, with 0 denoting "Not sufficient for doctoral education" and 5 denoting "Distinguished." Source: NRC National Survey of Graduate Faculty.

93E: 1993 trimmed mean for program effectiveness in educating research scholars and scientists. The trimmed mean is obtained by dropping the two highest and two lowest scores on the survey before computing the average. For purposes of analysis, scores were converted to a scale of 0 to 5 with 0 denoting "Not Effective" and 5 denoting "Extremely Effective." Source: NRC National Survey of Graduate Faculty.

93C: 1993 trimmed mean for change in program quality in the last five years. The trimmed mean is obtained by dropping the two highest and two lowest scores on the survey before computing the average. For purposes of analysis, scores were converted to a scale of –1 to 1 with –1 denoting "Poorer than 5 years ago" and 1 denoting "Better than 5 years ago." Source: NRC National Survey of Graduate Faculty.

Faculty

Tot Fac: Total number of faculty participating in the program. Source: Institutional Coordinators.

%Full: Percentage of full professors participating in the program. Source: Institutional Coordinators.

%Supp Percentage of program faculty (Tot Fac) with research support (1986-1992). Source: Federal Agencies.

%Pub: Percentage of program faculty (Tot Fac) publishing in the period 1988 to 1992. Source: Institute of Scientific Information.

Pub/Fac: The ratio of the total number of program publications in the period 1988-1992 to the number of program faculty (Tot Fac). Source: Institute of Scientific Information.

Gini Pub: Gini coefficient for program publications, 1988-1992. The Gini coefficient is an indicator of the concentration of publications on a small number of the program faculty during the period 1988-1992. The largest possible value, or maximum concentration, is 100 (only one individual in the program registered a positive count); the smallest value, or minimum concentration, is 100/Fac (All the faculty (Tot Fac) in the program contribute equally). Source: Institute of Scientific Information.

Cite/Fac: The ratio of the total number of program citations in the period 1988-1992 to the number of program faculty (Tot Fac). Source: Institute of Scientific Information.

Gini Cite: Gini coefficient for program citations, 1988-1992. The Gini coefficient is an indicator of the concentration of citations on a small number of the program faculty during the period 1988-1992. The largest possible value, or maximum concentration, is 100 (only one individual in the program registered a positive count); the smallest value, or minimum concentration, is 100/Fac (All the faculty (Tot Fac) in the program contribute equally). Source: Institute of Scientific Information.

Students

Tot Stu:	The number of full and part time graduate students enrolled in the Fall of 1992. Source: Institutional Coordinators.
%Fem:	The percentage of full and part time female graduate students enrolled in the Fall of 1992. Source: Institutional Coordinators.
Rpt PhDs:	The number of Ph.D.s produced by that program for the period academic year 1987-1988 to 1991-1992. Source: Institutional Coordinators.

Doctoral Recipients

%Fem:	The percentage of Ph.D.s awarded to women during the period July 1986-June 1992. Source: Doctorate Records File.
%Min:	The percentage of Ph.D.s known to be awarded to underrepresented minorities (only U.S. Citizens or Permanent Residents) during the period July 1986-June 1992. Source: Doctorate Records File.
%US:	The percentage of Ph.D.s known to be awarded to U.S. Citizens and Permanent Residents during the period July 1986-June 1992. Source: Doctorate Records File.
%RA:	The percentage of Ph.D.s having research assistantships who reported their primary form of support. Source: Doctorate Records File.
%TA:	The percentage of Ph.D.s having teaching assistantships who reported their primary form of support. Source: Doctorate Records File.
MYD:	Median time lapse from entering graduate school to receipt of Ph.D. in years. This is a distributed median with multiple degrees awarded in the median year proportioned over the year. Source: Doctorate Records File.

NOTICE: **n/a** denotes a case where information was not provided by the Institutional Coordinators or was not available from the Doctorate Records File.

Appendix Table N - 1 Selected Characteristics of Research-Doctorate Programs in Biochemistry and Molecular Biology

Institution	1993 Ratings[1]			Faculty								Students[2]			Doctorate Recipients[3]					
	93Q	93E	93C	Tot Fac[2]	% Full[2]	% Supp[2]	% Pub[5]	Pub/ Fac[5]	Gini Pub[5]	Cite/ Fac[5]	Gini Cite[5]	Tot Stu	% Fem	Rpt PhDs	% Fem	% Min	% US	% RA	% TA	MYD
Univ of California-San Francisco	4.84	4.73	0.56	45	53	82	93	17.3	3.2	463.9	4.8	102	48	27	37	0	98	18	3	7.5
Massachusetts Inst of Technology	4.83	4.68	0.30	54	65	70	98	19.4	3.0	421.5	4.7	n/a	n/a	n/a	46	1	89	29	0	6.8
Stanford University	4.83	4.59	0.11	14	57	86	93	15.1	11.8	350.5	10.8	37	30	17	30	2	93	19	2	7.4
University of California-Berkeley	4.81	4.66	0.22	34	79	88	97	17.9	4.2	360.8	11.6	130	43	118	41	4	87	49	1	6.4
Harvard University	4.80	4.44	0.04	14	79	79	79	21.3	14.2	584.0	13.5	64	45	45	31	2	86	31	0	7.7
Yale University	4.59	4.32	0.25	33	67	85	94	13.9	5.5	205.2	7.4	91	43	68	43	1	87	26	0	7.3
California Institute Technology	4.57	4.41	0.20	30	70	93	97	16.7	5.3	270.7	7.2	85	27	57	23	0	77	32	2	7.5
University of Wisconsin-Madison	4.55	4.30	0.19	173	49	79	84	10.8	1.1	104.2	1.6	275	43	190	33	2	87	59	1	6.9
Univ of California-San Diego	4.53	4.37	0.68	142	67	73	93	16.0	1.5	272.2	2.7	152	34	71	26	7	83	38	10	7.2
Johns Hopkins University	4.38	4.26	0.22	56	57	84	91	10.2	3.0	112.3	5.5	127	41	122	36	3	90	26	0	7.4
Columbia University	4.38	4.25	0.37	62	55	82	92	11.9	3.1	198.6	4.5	47	30	37	45	2	81	39	5	7.1
University of Colorado	4.26	4.01	0.69	34	44	76	85	9.2	5.9	118.7	8.5	68	47	n/a	34	2	92	53	0	7.6
Washington University	4.22	4.15	0.39	139	42	75	91	12.9	1.3	157.7	1.8	100	49	83	30	1	87	19	0	7.2
Univ of California-Los Angeles	4.20	3.93	0.38	56	70	84	88	12.0	2.7	163.2	3.9	139	42	81	38	3	88	47	7	6.8
Duke University	4.18	4.16	0.43	46	59	80	96	15.5	4.8	272.2	9.5	69	52	35	34	0	86	18	0	7.0
University of Pennsylvania	4.11	3.94	0.37	187	49	56	93	12.1	1.0	106.1	1.5	135	39	n/a	42	1	88	35	4	7.5
Brandeis University	4.06	3.92	0.10	20	70	85	95	11.7	7.8	101.1	11.8	48	40	38	37	5	83	21	0	7.4
University of Washington	4.05	4.05	0.21	21	76	81	95	14.6	7.4	326.1	10.4	48	33	28	37	0	90	33	5	6.9
Baylor College of Medicine	4.04	3.88	0.56	103	48	78	90	15.1	2.0	178.2	3.4	101	36	30	36	6	61	51	2	7.7
U of Texas-Southwestern Med Ctr	4.00	3.79	0.58	60	40	77	90	11.9	2.9	163.9	3.9	34	21	31	40	5	81	46	2	7.0
Rockefeller University	3.92	3.91	0.04	7	29	71	100	10.4	24.9	99.6	36.0	n/a	n/a	n/a	36	3	78	5	0	6.8
Cornell University	3.91	3.94	0.14	36	61	83	92	11.7	8.9	115.3	6.8	77	52	40	41	2	64	57	3	7.3
University of Michigan [b]	3.89	3.96	0.45	44	59	77	98	10.3	3.7	96.2	10.3	69	33	56	33*	5*	82*	48*	0*	7.2*
University of Chicago	3.89	3.93	0.00	30	80	73	87	16.0	6.6	220.2	15.2	63	41	33	29	4	92	13	3	6.5
University of Oregon	3.88	3.68	0.20	25	52	72	80	9.9	8.3	110.7	12.4	96	33	54	29	5	84	32	5	7.3
University of Michigan [a]	3.87	3.86	0.53	80	47	96	98	13.6	2.0	178.5	7.1	45	42	24	33*	5*	82*	48*	0*	7.2*
U of North Carolina-Chapel Hill	3.83	3.80	0.63	102	51	81	94	11.0	1.6	109.7	2.6	75	48	42	42	2	82	69	5	7.2
Albert Einstein College of Med	3.79	3.88	0.35	108	56	70	90	9.0	1.7	84.5	3.2	16	50	28	43	6	71	28	0	7.1
University of Utah	3.72	3.45	0.46	25	48	76	76	5.8	10.3	76.5	18.3	48(1)	40(1)	36	58	0	85	30	17	6.9
Vanderbilt University	3.68	3.63	0.38	116	49	64	88	10.7	2.2	129.1	3.3	41	59	46	39	4	98	12	6	6.5

Institution	1993 Ratings[1] 93Q	93E	93C	Faculty Tot Fac[2]	% Full[2]	% Supp[2]	% Pub[5]	Pub/ Fac[5]	Gini Pub[5]	Cite/ Fac[5]	Gini Cite[5]	Students[2] Tot Stu	% Fem	Rpt PhDs	Doctorate Recipients[3] % Fem	% Min	% US	% RA	% TA	MYD
Northwestern University	3.59	3.70	0.35	55	45	82	93	9.5	3.1	102.3	4.9	73	47	44	56	2	84	31	9	6.5
State U of New York-Stony Brook	3.58	3.60	0.44	78	42	76	88	9.3	3.0	77.6	4.0	114	45	51	49	2	74	77	10	7.2
University of Texas at Austin	3.57	3.59	0.16	73	55	63	77	6.8	2.5	40.8	3.4	151	58	89	35	3	71	69	6	6.8
U of Illinois at Urbana-Champaign	3.55	3.59	-0.12	17	65	100	100	13.5	11.0	125.9	13.7	104	39	58	36	1	79	73	9	7.1
University of California-Davis	3.52	3.65	0.10	62	63	87	90	10.6	3.3	76.6	3.9	63	33	48	29	3	76	51	5	7.1
New York University	3.47	3.50	0.32	183	47	64	90	9.2	1.1	110.8	2.1	n/a	n/a	n/a	38	4	75	34	16	8.5
Rutgers State Univ-New Brunswick	3.47	3.48	0.54	87	48	44	86	8.7	3.0	61.1	5.8	98	• 42	39	45	8	76	39	31	7.9
University of Southern California	3.46	3.51	0.54	43	58	58	88	9.1	5.4	105.3	9.6	53	49	39	38	5	80	78	9	6.8
Oregon State University	3.46	3.33	0.43	53	55	75	89	8.8	3.2	45.0	6.0	78	35	79	26	0	57	73	5	7.9
University of Minnesota	3.46	3.52	0.12	41	71	90	100	11.9	3.5	91.3	4.3	115	38	53	27	1	86	68	4	6.9
Carnegie Mellon University	3.45	3.61	0.34	28	46	79	86	8.9	6.3	58.7	7.1	12	33	15	50	5	85	42	4	6.7
Indiana University	3.42	3.40	0.24	31	42	74	81	7.7	7.9	58.6	10.6	27	67	18	35	2	73	49	13	6.8
U of Tex-Health Sci Ctr-Houston	3.42	3.28	0.45	50	66	82	100	15.4	2.9	154.1	4.5	117	48	55	42	0	80	38	0	7.1
Purdue University [a]	3.39	3.33	0.10	19	58	84	95	11.5	9.0	92.3	11.3	37	38	12	34*	4*	76*	69*	13*	6.8*
Rice University	3.39	3.65	0.38	15	73	100	93	10.0	12.6	51.5	15.1	43	53	33	28	0	89	23	0	7.0
Pennsylvania State University	3.39	3.44	0.51	46	52	74	74	7.2	4.2	42.7	5.0	82	54	51	40	0	71	48	33	6.8
University of Iowa	3.36	3.53	0.35	55	58	78	87	9.1	4.1	91.3	10.0	71	37	44	36	0	76	68	8	6.9
Case Western Reserve Univ	3.35	3.24	0.17	40	45	75	88	8.6	4.2	78.3	8.0	63	27	39	29	7	86	31	0	6.8
Mean Values for the Top Quarter	**3.94**	**3.87**	**0.32**	**59.83**	**56.60**	**77.94**	**90.46**	**11.87**	**5.25**	**158.66**	**7.78**	**84.09**	**41.79**	**52.86**	**36.98**	**2.71**	**81.79**	**41.50**	**5.38**	**7.12**
University of Alabama-Birmingham	3.34	3.54	0.49	133	45	71	92	10.4	1.4	85.5	2.4	47	40	18	32	0	81	8	0	7.4
Mayo Graduate School	3.34	3.08	0.33	55	40	0	89	15.5	3.7	155.5	6.3	52	52	12	13	0	88	0	0	6.3
Michigan State University	3.33	3.43	0.17	33	73	76	94	11.2	5.5	97.1	6.5	67	34	49	42	7	79	57	12	7.7
Univ of California-Santa Cruz	3.33	3.38	0.38	20	55	90	80	8.2	13.7	95.6	17.4	83	45	33	20	11	90	33	67	6.8
University of California-Irvine	3.31	3.30	0.42	27	63	81	93	9.1	8.6	97.9	17.1	13	46	14	27	4	91	26	17	6.6
U of Massachusetts Med Center	3.30	3.33	0.55	29	48	55	90	8.8	5.9	94.2	10.7	23	52	9	50	0	100	75	0	7.5
University of Rochester	3.29	3.54	0.28	38	50	84	92	10.6	4.4	75.3	6.5	109	43	53	48	0	87	22	16	6.9

Appendix Table N - 1 Biochemistry and Molecular Biology (Continued)

Institution	1993 Ratings[1]			Faculty								Students[2]			Doctorate Recipients[3]					
	93Q	93E	93C	Tot Fac[2]	% Full[2]	% Supp[2]	% Pub[5]	Pub/ Fac[5]	Gini Pub[5]	Cite/ Fac[5]	Gini Cite[5]	Tot Stu	% Fem	Rpt PhDs	% Fem	% Min	% US	% RA	% TA	MYD
Purdue University [c]	3.24	3.33	0.00	16	69	69	88	8.9	12.5	61.9	14.3	43	28	51	34*	4*	76*	69*	13*	6.8*
University of Arizona	3.23	3.49	0.33	32	69	94	91	16.1	7.7	119.5	7.6	35	51	26	39	6	77	60	8	7.5
Univ of California-Santa Barbara	3.23	3.42	0.13	28	57	82	82	8.1	7.9	50.5	10.9	19	37	13	28	6	80	67	18	7.0
Ohio State University	3.16	3.22	0.45	131	46	65	90	7.5	1.5	39.5	2.0	113	37	49	29	3	63	39	43	7.0
University of Virginia	3.16	3.33	-0.04	23	57	87	100	9.9	6.4	148.2	26.9	66	45	50	39	0	96	38	2	7.5
Brown University	3.09	3.39	0.17	34	44	59	85	7.4	5.4	74.0	9.3	53(2)	53(2)	31	47	7	91	58	21	7.2
Tufts University	3.09	3.33	0.12	30	50	83	93	9.2	5.4	114.6	8.1	38	53	19	53	0	74	47	6	8.5
North Carolina State University	3.09	3.10	0.42	54	50	59	89	7.0	3.4	36.3	5.4	32	59	22	53	10	88	58	13	7.8
U of Tex-Hlth Sci Ct-San Antonio	3.08	3.12	0.27	20	60	75	80	10.8	11.2	62.6	12.2	37	49	13	35	11	82	0	89	9.4
Washington State University	3.05	3.28	0.35	23	65	74	91	9.4	8.6	74.5	11.9	46	35	32	29	6	77	70	6	6.5
University of Georgia	3.03	2.96	0.39	29	69	66	83	12.4	7.3	92.9	7.1	49	27	46	25	3	60	67	5	8.2
Dartmouth College	3.02	3.23	0.24	31	61	77	90	6.3	6.0	55.8	9.9	55	58	42	48	0	79	33	10	6.7
Iowa State University	3.00	3.33	0.05	29	59	72	90	7.6	6.1	37.0	8.3	60	40	43	36	3	70	82	8	7.6
Univ of California-Riverside	2.96	3.29	0.11	24	54	71	79	9.0	11.0	56.3	13.6	80	44	51	37	18	83	68	3	6.9
Texas A&M University [c]	2.95	3.24	0.43	39	59	59	69	10.3	10.6	74.0	10.2	66	24	38	31*	4*	85*	54*	12*	7.6*
University of Missouri-Columbia	2.92	3.13	0.59	49	41	78	88	7.4	4.5	55.8	7.3	43	37	43	29	4	74	61	7	7.3
Saint Louis University	2.91	2.93	0.26	42	50	62	86	7.5	5.0	63.5	7.3	63	51	27	38	5	81	38	4	7.5
University of Connecticut	2.90	2.92	0.11	17	59	24	82	4.9	8.9	43.5	17.2	36	47	19	36	0	86	24	22	7.1
University of Florida	2.88	3.21	0.24	39	69	77	82	11.5	5.0	70.0	6.4	58	41	32	27	8	95	43	27	6.9
Emory University	2.86	3.03	0.55	31	39	90	87	12.0	5.7	136.2	9.4	27	56	13	50	0	83	40	12	6.0
University of Tennessee - Memphis	2.86	3.02	0.56	40	45	55	83	6.6	5.3	68.5	8.6	25	40	10	21	11	64	9	55	8.2
University of Louisville	2.86	2.82	0.50	29	48	62	83	6.4	7.9	36.5	8.6	32	41	13	33	0	85	29	18	6.8
University of Nebraska-Lincoln	2.84	3.05	0.60	27	52	67	89	7.0	7.2	30.7	11.9	25	40	27	43	0	64	65	14	6.9
University of South Carolina	2.84	2.78	0.14	37	41	84	81	5.7	5.1	29.1	7.6	84	42	68	44	6	77	73	23	5.9
University of Cincinnati	2.81	3.00	0.22	16	38	81	94	7.3	10.3	86.1	19.6	57	53	33	45	2	85	45	25	7.7
University of Delaware	2.78	3.00	-0.10	8	75	63	88	11.3	23.8	52.8	31.0	21	33	15	33	0	78	47	53	6.7
Boston University [b]	2.78	2.74	0.27	31	48	68	94	11.6	4.6	94.8	9.1	64	53	41	48*	0*	83*	35*	7*	7.3*
U of Massachusetts at Amherst	2.78	2.72	0.20	24	46	79	83	6.2	9.0	36.6	7.7	35	46	44	46	8	76	70	10	6.7

Institution	1993 Ratings[1] 93Q	93E	93C	Faculty Tot Fac[2]	% Full[2]	% Supp[2]	% Pub[5]	Pub/ Fac[5]	Gini Pub[5]	Cite/ Fac[5]	Gini Cite[5]	Students[2] Tot Stu	% Fem	Rpt PhDs	Doctorate Recipients[3] % Fem	% Min	% US	% RA	% TA	MYD
University of Maryland College Park	2.74	3.06	-0.12	11	73	64	82	6.1	16.8	45.3	24.4	37	51	23	46	3	77	64	19	6.3
University of Illinois at Chicago	2.72	3.11	0.22	16	56	50	88	4.3	10.8	25.6	16.7	24	54	16	30	0	73	24	51	7.2
Georgetown University	2.70	2.95	0.09	17	35	59	71	5.9	19.7	71.8	27.9	26	50	13	48	5	76	17	4	7.2
Thomas Jefferson University	2.69	2.67	0.57	27	44	70	89	12.7	12.3	130.4	17.4	40	58	12	31	0	100	0	14	7.6
Texas A&M University [a]	2.69	3.06	0.56	29	28	69	90	6.7	6.9	69.0	11.5	60	28	21	31*	4*	85*	54*	12*	7.6*
Wayne State University	2.68	2.89	0.33	31	35	55	71	4.1	7.2	19.5	11.0	45	47	14	25	2	88	36	23	7.9
University of Pittsburgh [a]	2.68	3.11	0.00	10	50	70	70	5.2	17.6	102.9	43.7	52(2)	46(2)	7	42*	0*	72*	61*	18*	7.8*
State Univ of New York-Buffalo [a]	2.67	2.45	-0.19	13	69	85	100	8.9	11.2	59.2	16.8	25	40	22	39*	3*	69*	68*	10*	7*
Colorado State University	2.67	2.72	0.39	20	60	65	75	5.1	12.3	32.0	13.5	17	29	17	25	0	84	82	0	7.4
University of Kentucky	2.64	2.76	0.29	13	62	62	69	6.1	17.7	38.6	40.1	21	43	17	52	0	80	62	5	6.5
University of Pittsburgh [b]	2.64	2.99	0.14	28	18	57	82	6.5	7.0	33.0	9.1	n/a	n/a	n/a	42*	0*	72*	61*	18*	7.8*
University of Houston	2.61	2.89	0.39	12	58	100	92	5.1	13.6	17.8	26.2	29	28	18	18	25	53	45	27	6.8
University of New Hampshire	2.60	2.78	n/s	13	38	46	77	4.3	16.1	32.5	26.2	14	21	7	25	0	100	50	13	5.6
Medical College of Pensylvania	2.57	2.71	0.00	18	44	56	89	8.8	9.1	62.7	11.6	17	65	8	64	0	80	14	14	8.7
Mean Values for the 2nd Quarter	**2.94**	**3.08**	**0.27**	**31.14**	**52.33**	**68.31**	**85.61**	**8.34**	**8.87**	**68.23**	**13.72**	**45.06**	**43.58**	**26.96**	**36.86**	**3.86**	**80.35**	**45.88**	**17.84**	**7.22**
University of Kansas [a]	2.56	2.50	-0.12	20	70	60	70	7.4	18.2	36.3	21.8	50	46	38	40*	4*	60*	41*	21*	7.5*
U of Texas, Medical Br-Galveston	2.55	2.80	0.33	54	59	56	89	10.8	4.1	54.0	5.2	56	41	26	28	0	56	56	13	7.9
University of New Mexico	2.53	3.00	0.31	39	33	49	79	5.3	7.2	45.9	11.6	13	31	15	31	7	88	46	8	7.4
State Univ of New York-Buffalo [b]	2.52	2.50	0.00	16	19	0	81	8.4	16.4	44.6	14.1	12	25	10	39*	3*	69*	68*	10*	7*
CUNY - Grad Sch & Univ Center	2.51	2.87	0.15	37	49	73	76	4.5	5.2	28.2	6.8	63	46	41	43	9	69	27	32	8.5
Univ of Missouri-Kansas City	2.50	2.59	0.54	24	38	79	83	4.8	8.3	27.8	12.0	9	56	5	0	0	67	50	50	5.7
University of Nevada, Reno	2.50	2.57	0.58	48	48	54	71	6.3	6.0	32.8	7.9	47	40	23	37	4	86	53	0	7.8
University of Miami	2.49	3.03	-0.19	26	69	58	92	5.3	5.7	48.8	9.6	38	42	20	24	23	76	46	18	7.1
Arizona State University	2.47	2.78	0.32	39	49	77	82	5.2	4.7	25.1	8.0	56	34	27	25	0	88	33	33	6.3
University of Kansas [b]	2.45	2.71	0.07	17	59	76	35	0.9	36.7	2.5	91.0	19	42	14	40*	4*	60*	41*	21*	7.5*
Univ of Maryland at Baltimore	2.43	2.72	0.07	19	58	84	84	10.1	11.8	110.6	12.7	32	59	9	38	13	62	57	0	7.6

Appendix Table N - 1 Biochemistry and Molecular Biology (Continued)

Institution	1993 Ratings[1] 93Q	93E	93C	Faculty Tot Fac[2]	% Full[2]	% Supp[2]	% Pub[5]	Pub/ Fac[5]	Gini Pub[5]	Cite/ Fac[5]	Gini Cite[5]	Students[2] Tot Stu	% Fem	Rpt PhDs	Doctorate Recipients[3] % Fem	% Min	% US	% RA	% TA	MYD
Syracuse University	2.42	2.67	0.29	10	70	90	60	3.5	22.1	34.1	39.9	10	50	3	40	0	90	20	70	7.0
Kansas State University	2.41	2.78	0.22	21	57	62	100	9.6	8.3	36.7	8.2	27	48	19	32	0	54	50	10	8.5
SUNY Health Science Ctr-Syracuse	2.41	3.02	0.15	11	64	91	73	6.8	22.2	48.6	19.3	4	0	7	33	14	78	33	33	6.8
Georgia Institute of Technology	2.39	2.69	0.14	12	50	75	83	8.8	16.2	39.6	15.7	52	48	19	45	13	73	20	50	7.6
University of Vermont	2.38	2.50	0.38	25	40	76	88	7.4	11.1	46.0	10.3	66	33	56	29	8	89	52	9	6.7
U of Arkansas for Medical Sci	2.38	2.17	0.29	20	45	45	85	4.9	7.9	21.5	11.3	17	53	5	21	0	86	38	8	8.0
University of Wisconsin-Milwaukee	2.37	2.75	0.18	30	43	50	63	3.2	10.2	11.3	18.0	49	45	13	45	0	50	57	29	7.7
Florida State University	2.35	2.50	0.17	13	54	69	92	3.6	11.5	22.7	37.5	4	50	5	20	0	64	76	10	6.9
Univ of Health Sc/Chicago Med Sch	2.33	2.59	0.00	14	36	57	93	3.4	12.6	7.0	25.1	11	45	3	25	0	75	33	0	7.1
Wake Forest University	2.33	2.89	0.25	19	16	63	84	4.7	10.1	47.2	25.1	28	46	17	61	0	100	39	0	6.2
U of Maryland Baltimore County	2.31	2.33	0.27	14	50	50	93	9.7	12.3	37.3	15.8	5	40	4	22	0	74	40	40	8.7
George Washington University	2.31	2.59	0.00	14	50	57	50	6.1	30.4	34.8	27.4	21	67	18	50	7	93	33	7	7.8
Univ of Arkansas-Fayetteville	2.30	2.50	0.00	23	61	57	87	8.6	8.6	36.7	9.5	n/a	n/a	n/a	43	0	86	71	14	4.9
Albany Medical College	2.28	2.43	0.22	23	57	30	78	6.2	13.1	34.2	16.7	11	45	8	27	0	100	17	50	6.6
Temple University	2.27	2.83	-0.45	15	53	73	87	7.9	11.4	47.3	17.6	23	17	10	41	6	73	26	17	6.8
Uniformed Services U of Hlth Sci	2.21	2.45	-0.27	13	15	0	77	4.8	15.4	32.3	17.3	7	14	4	33	14	78	13	25	9.9
Louisiana State U & A&M College	2.17	2.53	0.00	68	40	44	78	7.2	3.6	29.9	5.9	68	40	59	26	0	43	56	16	8.3
Texas Tech University	2.16	2.31	0.00	42	33	36	74	3.5	6.1	24.0	31.1	49	31	33	26	0	47	29	43	9.0
Wesleyan University	2.15	2.55	-0.13	8	50	63	75	1.9	21.7	4.0	33.7	21	57	20	33	0	89	38	19	7.4
West Virginia University	2.15	1.98	-0.17	14	50	29	57	2.6	23.1	6.5	31.5	10	10	11	14	8	86	36	27	6.6
University of Texas at Dallas	2.13	2.29	0.25	12	25	67	92	4.0	18.1	25.3	18.0	49	45	36	38	20	63	19	57	7.2
Virginia Polytech Inst & State U	2.13	2.46	0.05	28	36	61	96	5.8	5.0	17.0	7.7	30	53	30	57	18	46	71	0	6.8
Louisiana State U Medical Center	2.12	2.22	0.00	12	58	75	83	7.5	12.6	38.7	15.5	20	40	10	27	0	82	25	50	7.9
Univ of Med & Dent of NJ	2.12	2.33	-0.50	11	55	55	91	10.2	14.8	57.5	25.8	23	35	16	47	8	69	27	17	8.4
Illinois State University	2.10	2.71	0.00	13	54	69	92	5.2	11.2	23.8	16.2	n/a	n/a	n/a	0	n/a	0	0	100	8.5
Medical College of Wisconsin	2.07	1.98	0.06	12	33	83	83	5.5	13.2	36.8	24.6	18	33	9	44	0	78	43	0	6.6
University of North Dakota	2.04	2.41	0.00	12	50	25	58	2.6	21.5	8.7	25.2	17	18	7	36	0	100	33	67	6.8
University of Oklahoma	2.04	2.57	0.10	11	45	82	91	5.5	12.0	28.1	15.4	6	50	5	53	9	77	25	20	6.9

Institution	1993 Ratings[1] 93Q	93E	93C	Faculty Tot Fac[2]	% Full[2]	% Supp[2]	% Pub[5]	Pub/ Fac[5]	Gini Pub[5]	Cite/ Fac[5]	Gini Cite[5]	Students[2] Tot Stu	% Fem	Rpt PhDs	Doctorate Recipients[3] % Fem	% Min	% US	% RA	% TA	MYD
Oklahoma State University	2.00	2.69	-0.14	15	87	53	80	5.9	13.2	25.5	12.9	18	44	14	38	0	64	70	0	8.8
Tulane University	2.00	2.45	-0.10	11	82	45	64	5.4	18.0	37.8	20.8	8	25	2	86	0	43	60	0	9.6
University of Wyoming	2.00	2.78	0.00	20	55	35	75	5.3	9.2	19.9	12.2	21	43	11	29	0	50	64	9	6.8
Northeastern University	2.00	2.08	0.00	22	36	45	77	2.4	9.0	12.6	19.9	18	72	8	33	0	67	0	50	9.7
SUNY-Health Science Ctr-Brooklyn	2.00	2.08	0.00	14	57	50	79	5.1	12.2	22.9	16.2	18	56	13	33	17	38	25	44	8.1
East Carolina U Sch Medicine	2.00	2.67	0.50	22	41	55	86	4.9	8.4	38.3	20.6	25	40	8	29	0	71	0	0	5.7
Utah State University	1.94	2.19	-0.14	25	24	52	80	8.1	8.1	39.0	10.3	36	36	12	5	0	74	53	6	6.6
Old Dominion University	1.91	1.67	n/s	94	38	7	76	4.6	4.5	18.3	6.3	59	53	25	100	0	100	0	0	17.0
Rutgers State Univ-Newark	1.88	1.91	-0.22	18	50	67	83	6.6	8.1	28.3	13.4	65	49	14	33	0	67	0	33	9.7
Mean Values for the 3rd Quarter	**2.25**	**2.51**	**0.07**	**22.92**	**48.15**	**56.44**	**79.27**	**5.79**	**12.53**	**32.02**	**18.72**	**28.46**	**41.15**	**16.57**	**35.40**	**4.45**	**70.79**	**37.71**	**23.67**	**7.71**
University of Idaho	1.87	1.98	0.22	11	45	45	73	4.4	21.8	15.0	34.1	28	18	15	36	0	70	57	14	7.6
Rush University	1.86	1.67	0.00	13	38	15	85	7.1	14.0	40.8	14.6	30	30	10	54	8	92	36	0	8.7
University of South Florida	1.85	2.18	0.30	11	64	64	82	5.4	14.5	28.8	17.9	n/a	n/a	6	50	0	100	57	0	7.9
Lehigh University	1.85	1.67	0.00	8	38	13	25	0.6	68.0	1.8	54.0	22[(2)]	68[(2)]	8	37	0	77	39	35	6.1
Bowling Green State University	1.83	1.67	0.00	11	27	45	82	3.0	12.2	6.2	15.7	7	29	4	40	25	80	0	100	6.7
Montana State University	1.80	2.73	0.29	16	63	56	81	6.8	16.0	30.9	18.1	n/a	n/a	n/a	0	0	50	100	0	7.0
Brigham Young University	1.79	1.67	0.00	17	47	18	76	3.1	9.9	17.0	22.4	13	8	9	0	0	71	36	36	6.1
University of North Texas	1.78	2.05	0.18	16	38	38	75	3.8	13.7	13.4	24.5	30	27	24	31	8	48	67	17	9.4
Medical College of Ohio	1.78	1.82	0.00	10	40	60	70	8.3	29.1	67.2	24.5	40	45	17	30	0	59	6	0	8.4
Loyola University of Chicago	1.77	2.08	0.00	10	50	30	70	4.6	17.2	27.6	21.7	18	44	14	52	6	86	25	19	7.4
Hahnemann University	1.76	1.83	-0.08	16	63	44	75	5.1	16.8	20.5	27.3	19	53	10	54	0	100	0	22	6.0
Creighton University	1.74	2.04	0.17	36	39	8	61	3.0	15.9	6.8	23.8	25	56	5	20	0	75	33	33	7.7
U of Mississippi-Medical Center	1.73	1.39	0.00	12	42	75	92	6.0	14.7	33.2	19.9	18	44	6	0	20	56	71	0	10.6
North Dakota State University	1.69	1.83	0.00	33	24	36	82	3.8	6.2	9.6	10.4	23	48	10	14	0	79	80	10	5.7
Kent State University	1.69	2.29	0.00	16	44	25	81	5.0	10.3	16.4	13.5	26	69	16	30	25	40	11	67	8.6
Univ of Puerto Rico-Rio Piedras	1.67	1.67	0.00	8	50	25	50	1.5	36.1	1.1	50.6	2	0	2	67	100	100	0	0	14.7

Appendix Table N - 1 Biochemistry and Molecular Biology (Continued)

Institution	1993 Ratings[1] 93Q	93E	93C	Faculty Tot Fac[2]	% Full[2]	% Supp[2]	% Pub[5]	Pub/ Fac[5]	Gini Pub[5]	Cite/ Fac[5]	Gini Cite[5]	Students[2] Tot Stu	% Fem	Rpt PhDs	Doctorate Recipients[3] % Fem	% Min	% US	% RA	% TA	MYD
New Mexico State University	1.67	2.00	0.00	11	64	73	91	4.2	14.1	11.5	14.8	19	37	11	40	13	75	40	33	7.4
Howard University	1.67	2.41	0.00	15	27	27	73	2.3	18.3	10.5	33.3	8	38	3	40	33	100	n/a	n/a	6.5
Miami University	1.65	2.03	0.00	12	42	42	67	1.8	26.0	6.3	82.7	43	42	49	33	0	50	0	75	7.0
University of Tennessee-Knoxville	1.64	2.17	0.00	13	69	69	92	7.2	13.7	22.5	17.2	68	34	37	29	6	76	22	35	6.6
Oregon Graduate Inst Sci & Tech	1.57	1.25	0.00	7	29	57	100	7.0	45.1	67.3	71.7	18	39	5	67	0	67	100	0	14.5
University of Hawaii at Manoa	1.57	2.00	0.25	12	58	42	75	3.5	19.1	13.3	42.0	16	25	10	35	0	76	75	8	9.6
Medical College of Georgia	1.56	1.50	-0.12	17	35	47	88	15.5	22.1	115.2	23.1	10	40	12	33	0	57	15	77	6.8
Louisiana St U-Sch Med Shreveport	1.48	2.33	-0.14	8	13	38	88	3.3	20.7	18.1	28.2	18	56	8	43	0	71	86	14	7.7
University of Alabama	1.48	1.50	-0.20	11	27	27	73	2.7	14.6	5.8	19.1	22	50	19	36	0	27	22	78	8.3
Loma Linda University	1.47	1.25	0.00	19	47	26	89	11.0	15.1	100.5	21.8	12	42	15	15	16	95	6	0	7.1
New York Medical College	1.47	1.67	0.00	8	75	63	88	7.1	23.0	22.5	25.0	11	45	8	36	0	80	10	30	10.6
Drexel University	1.46	1.67	n/s	9	33	56	89	2.1	13.5	20.8	44.7	n/a	n/a	9	20	0	100	0	25	10.0
Southern Methodist University	1.43	1.25	n/s	11	45	55	82	4.9	18.0	15.4	23.3	20	55	5	n/a	n/a	n/a	n/a	n/a	n/a
Clemson University	1.41	1.85	0.00	8	63	50	75	2.9	19.4	8.5	37.1	11	45	7	0	0	67	50	50	7.7
Ball State University	1.33	2.22	0.00	17	41	29	29	1.3	35.9	1.0	88.9	11	18	10	n/a	n/a	n/a	n/a	n/a	n/a
Georgia State University	1.32	1.33	0.00	7	71	71	100	3.0	23.3	21.0	31.6	25	44	6	30	25	40	50	0	8.4
Medical University South Carolina	1.32	1.67	0.00	14	57	71	86	9.2	18.3	45.8	23.2	56	43	30	35	0	82	43	0	7.2
University of Montana	1.15	1.67	n/s	4	100	50	75	3.3	45.5	21.8	33.8	5	40	3	33	17	100	60	40	10.0
Clark Atlanta University	1.08	2.08	0.67	12	8	0	50	1.2	22.4	0.8	36.0	28[(2)]	64[(2)]	n/a	46	100	100	22	0	8.8
Catholic University of America	0.93	1.67	n/s	9	33	44	89	2.6	16.8	8.2	32.3	17	53	7	33	17	100	0	25	7.4
Texas Woman's University	0.86	1.48	0.00	5	40	40	60	3.4	69.5	5.6	100.0	11	82	4	73	14	64	29	29	9.6
University of Notre Dame	0.84	0.74	-0.25	6	0	50	67	2.7	39.8	19.0	34.3	13	23	4	24	6	59	22	52	7.5
University of Tulsa	0.69	0.37	0.00	5	20	20	60	2.6	47.9	12.0	82.0	6	50	1	n/a	n/a	n/a	n/a	n/a	n/a
Ohio University	0.63	0.67	n/s	3	100	33	100	16.0	51.6	66.0	67.0	15	20	5	23	0	31	43	43	7.4
Clark University	0.56	0.93	n/s	5	80	40	100	3.8	32.4	11.8	31.6	3	67	8	33	20	83	40	60	7.2
Boston University [a]	0.53	0.00	n/s	2	0	100	100	10.0	50.5	88.5	54.8	5	60	5	48*	0*	83*	35*	7*	7.3*
Univ of Southern Mississippi	0.52	0.42	0.00	7	29	71	57	0.9	33.3	1.0	55.1	12	33	4	25	67	75	0	33	9.6
University of South Dakota	0.50	0.95	0.50	7	57	14	43	1.0	42.8	1.4	82.0	11	55	4	17	0	67	80	0	7.0

Institution	1993 Ratings[1] 93Q	93E	93C	Faculty Tot Fac[2]	% Full[2]	% Supp[2]	% Pub[5]	Pub/ Fac[5]	Gini Pub[5]	Cite/ Fac[5]	Gini Cite[5]	Students[2] Tot Stu	% Fem	Rpt PhDs	Doctorate Recipients[3] % Fem	% Min	% US	% RA	% TA	MYD
Univ of Missouri-Saint Louis	0.46	0.77	0.00	2	0	50	50	2.5	100.0	6.0	100.0	1	100	0	n/a	n/a	n/a	n/a	n/a	n/a
University of Mass-Lowell	0.44	0.56	n/s	5	100	20	60	8.6	56.3	19.8	83.0	0	0	20	55	6	85	8	67	6.4
State Univ of New York-Binghamton	0.41	1.00	0.00	4	50	75	75	4.3	33.5	7.5	34.0	9	56	3	0	0	100	33	33	6.8
Northern Arizona University	0.21	0.17	n/s	4	25	0	50	1.3	68.0	5.5	70.2	0	0	0	n/a	n/a	n/a	n/a	n/a	n/a
University of Alaska	0.15	0.00	n/s	3	67	0	33	1.7	100.0	1.3	100.0	n/a	n/a	n/a	n/a	n/a	n/a	n/a	n/a	n/a
Mean Values for the 4th Quarter	**1.30**	**1.51**	**0.05**	**10.73**	**45.24**	**41.78**	**73.76**	**4.62**	**30.34**	**22.83**	**41.16**	**17.89**	**42.12**	**10.17**	**32.95**	**12.37**	**74.26**	**35.93**	**27.79**	**8.12**
Mean Values for All Programs	**2.60**	**2.74**	**0.18**	**31.05**	**50.56**	**61.05**	**82.25**	**7.64**	**14.31**	**70.18**	**20.42**	**44.03**	**42.18**	**26.36**	**35.62**	**5.67**	**76.88**	**40.42**	**18.37**	**7.52**

Sources: 1. National Survey of Graduate Faculty
2. Institutional Coordinator Response Data
3. Doctorate Records File
4. Federal Agencies
5. Institute for Scientific Information

Notes: *a.* School of Arts and Sciences
b. School of Medicine
c. School of Agriculture

n/s After trimming no cases remained

(1) Combined enrollment for programs in Biochemistry and Molecular Biology and Ecology, Evolution, and Behavior
(2) Combined enrollment for programs in Biochemistry and Molecular Biology and Cell and Developmental Biology

* The Doctorate Recipient information cannot be separated for multiple programs at the same institution in the same field and therefore the total for the combined programs is given.

Appendix Table N - 2 Selected Characteristics of Research-Doctorate Programs in Cell and Developmental Biology

Institution	1993 Ratings[1] 93Q	93E	93C	Faculty Tot Fac[2]	% Full[2]	% Supp[2]	% Pub[5]	Pub/ Fac[5]	Gini Pub[5]	Cite/ Fac[5]	Gini Cite[5]	Students[2] Tot Stu	% Fem	Rpt PhDs	Doctorate Recipients[3] % Fem	% Min	% US	% RA	% TA	MYD
Massachusetts Inst of Technology	4.86	4.66	0.28	54	65	70	98	19.4	3.0	421.5	4.7	n/a	n/a	n/a	38	0	96	8	0	7.2
Rockefeller University	4.77	4.54	0.20	30	50	70	93	19.7	7.1	416.2	11.1	270	33	0	46	4	88	9	0	6.5
Univ of California-San Francisco	4.76	4.57	0.62	55	56	84	95	15.7	2.6	363.1	4.3	36	36	11	60	0	93	25	0	8.4
California Institute Technology	4.73	4.68	0.06	23	70	91	91	13.0	8.8	224.5	12.1	37	35	20	17	0	100	40	0	7.9
Harvard University	4.70	4.33	0.13	37	57	65	92	12.6	4.2	235.5	5.7	98	40	52	36	4	94	15	0	7.3
Stanford University [b]	4.55	4.39	0.16	24	58	79	92	22.3	6.3	338.6	7.3	35	43	27	41*	7*	87*	33*	4*	6.9*
Univ of California-San Diego	4.50	4.15	0.67	109	68	71	96	17.9	1.9	314.0	3.1	65	45	28	33	6	94	18	0	6.8
University of Washington	4.48	4.23	0.76	174	59	71	90	13.2	1.0	185.8	1.9	40	45	0	53	10	91	33	6	7.3
Washington University	4.39	4.24	0.36	117	44	83	94	13.8	1.5	179.9	2.2	72	54	43	46	2	91	21	0	6.8
Yale University	4.37	4.22	0.31	40	45	80	93	13.7	4.0	220.0	5.1	36	50	24	45	0	89	6	0	7.2
Princeton University	4.36	4.45	0.40	27	52	74	81	9.5	7.6	198.2	10.6	86	58	46	50	0	100	17	0	7.5
Stanford University [a]	4.36	4.08	0.02	15	67	67	80	14.9	12.1	154.2	12.1	n/a	n/a	33	41*	7*	87*	33*	4*	6.9*
University of California-Berkeley	4.16	4.19	0.11	42	71	79	95	11.6	4.0	106.2	6.1	95	52	78	47	6	93	30	9	6.8
Duke University	4.11	3.91	0.59	89	45	80	83	14.4	2.8	216.3	5.5	107	41	67	48	0	95	7	0	7.1
University of Chicago	4.10	4.03	0.20	70	57	70	91	11.9	2.8	129.1	4.3	113	47	71	33	0	90	16	0	6.5
University of Wisconsin-Madison	4.05	4.06	0.28	75	65	72	85	10.5	2.0	93.7	4.1	101	63	41	41	2	96	66	7	7.7
Univ of California-Los Angeles	3.99	3.86	0.45	82	56	80	88	10.9	2.2	150.5	4.3	167	47	135	44	6	94	31	7	6.8
U of Texas-Southwestern Med Ctr	3.98	3.77	0.55	55	40	67	89	12.9	4.5	137.3	5.7	57	49	42	49	4	95	34	3	7.5
Columbia University	3.94	3.89	0.20	41	37	68	88	10.5	4.4	138.1	5.9	59	41	53	45	3	81	68	5	7.4
Johns Hopkins University	3.91	3.79	0.19	15	60	93	93	11.3	10.0	111.9	9.7	51	51	36	39	4	88	9	0	7.8
New York University	3.86	3.77	0.43	183	47	64	90	9.2	1.1	110.8	2.1	n/a	n/a	n/a	46	4	81	14	12	7.8
University of Colorado [b]	3.85	3.40	0.35	29	52	55	97	8.6	6.1	272.0	15.6	36	56	15	45*	2*	98*	38*	5*	7.3*
University of Pennsylvania	3.81	3.74	0.06	128	48	66	97	13.7	1.3	135.7	2.0	51	59	33	52	1	91	15	1	7.2
Baylor College of Medicine	3.80	3.58	0.44	76	34	68	91	13.0	2.7	153.5	4.8	113	35	36	34	7	80	47	2	7.7
U of North Carolina-Chapel Hill	3.79	3.78	0.41	77	61	81	92	13.4	2.2	149.5	3.6	307	12	36	48	1	91	47	16	7.6
Albert Einstein College of Med	3.76	3.64	0.20	77	51	70	90	9.9	2.3	103.5	4.1	43	40	61	47	0	84	19	0	7.7
U of Illinois at Urbana-Champaign	3.74	3.62	0.18	50	48	66	78	8.8	4.1	72.7	6.7	60	35	47	38	7	85	42	25	7.8
Brandeis University	3.73	3.57	0.10	21	67	95	86	11.1	9.6	100.9	15.3	48(3)	56(3)	40	67	0	100	0	0	6.7
Vanderbilt University	3.69	3.53	0.57	118	44	59	86	10.2	2.2	129.0	3.4	42	38	15	32	0	96	36	0	6.5
University of Michigan	3.66	3.55	0.30	22	41	95	86	8.3	10.4	87.2	19.8	36	53	28	46	5	93	31	11	7.5

Institution	1993 Ratings[1] 93Q	93E	93C	Faculty Tot Fac[2]	% Full[2]	% Supp[2]	% Pub[5]	Pub/ Fac[5]	Gini Pub[5]	Cite/ Fac[5]	Gini Cite[5]	Students[2] Tot Stu	% Fem	Rpt PhDs	Doctorate Recipients[3] % Fem	% Min	% US	% RA	% TA	MYD
Northwestern University	3.64	3.62	0.45	66	48	80	88	9.0	2.8	97.5	4.2	65	52	67	41	3	95	38	0	6.6
Indiana University	3.59	3.63	0.30	33	42	79	85	7.6	5.8	73.1	7.7	1	0	8	29	0	71	37	26	7.5
University of California-Davis	3.55	3.63	0.34	94	61	76	90	11.3	2.2	74.0	4.2	112	51	81	29	13	70	39	13	8.6
University of Minnesota [b]	3.54	3.45	0.43	28	46	86	93	11.1	6.2	92.7	7.7	43	44	47	36*	1*	78*	53*	3*	7.9*
Cornell University	3.53	3.75	0.29	22	55	50	95	11.6	8.4	53.8	8.8	37	46	21	44	4	81	56	16	8.4
State U of New York-Stony Brook	3.53	3.55	0.46	98	37	66	86	8.7	2.4	80.3	3.1	38	55	71	51	0	87	64	13	7.4
University of Minnesota [a]	3.49	3.41	0.47	48	56	85	92	10.9	4.3	100.5	6.0	38	58	17	36*	1*	78*	53*	3*	7.9*
U of Tex-Health Sci Ctr-Houston	3.46	3.54	0.68	63	56	75	90	16.1	3.4	136.5	3.9	80	38	46	40	0	79	38	0	8.3
University of California-Irvine	3.44	3.33	0.15	20	55	65	90	6.3	11.1	50.9	21.4	46	48	24	24	5	84	36	14	7.4
Michigan State University	3.41	3.55	0.22	80	67	63	89	8.8	2.7	52.7	5.3	72	40	44	26	0	67	68	18	7.7
University of Virginia	3.39	3.69	0.45	55	45	65	93	8.4	3.3	76.3	5.7	66	38	31	41	0	88	11	5	7.6
Case Western Reserve Univ	3.38	3.40	0.17	28	32	86	100	11.2	5.8	153.7	7.7	n/a	n/a	0	47	0	100	8	0	8.1
University of Texas at Austin	3.37	3.56	0.31	66	48	65	71	4.6	3.1	25.4	5.0	113	36	71	45	6	83	38	34	8.3
University of Rochester	3.35	3.14	0.42	42	33	69	83	7.3	4.0	48.7	6.0	91	40	44	45	3	90	21	3	7.2
Mean Values for the Top Quarter	**3.94**	**3.85**	**0.33**	**61.32**	**52.18**	**73.70**	**89.66**	**11.79**	**4.55**	**153.76**	**6.82**	**76.58**	**44.00**	**40.24**	**41.84**	**2.91**	**88.45**	**31.09**	**6.02**	**7.43**
U of Massachusetts Med Center	3.33	3.40	0.48	59	53	64	88	10.3	3.4	100.3	4.4	42	45	14	30	0	60	60	0	7.7
Purdue University	3.33	3.44	0.32	28	43	75	89	6.1	5.7	56.0	9.5	43	51	38	48	13	92	27	45	8.0
University of Miami	3.33	3.33	0.62	49	39	67	86	8.2	5.5	67.7	7.9	29	41	19	54	13	93	19	14	7.5
University of Alabama-Birmingham	3.31	3.39	0.53	142	43	60	85	9.1	1.6	72.1	2.5	24	42	11	35	10	81	17	5	7.9
University of Southern California	3.31	3.00	0.00	34	29	35	88	6.5	5.9	80.0	14.8	51	49	16	35	0	84	50	14	7.4
University of Iowa	3.28	3.50	0.37	53	72	72	91	9.6	3.3	56.8	4.5	93	32	62	42	0	79	32	32	7.4
U of Massachusetts at Amherst	3.21	3.43	0.04	28	71	79	86	7.1	6.1	35.4	8.0	43	47	31	49	3	82	65	10	7.0
Oregon State University	3.20	3.19	0.47	47	60	70	85	6.3	3.8	29.9	9.8	45	40	70	27	7	82	57	4	8.4
Emory University	3.20	3.19	0.35	46	41	89	83	7.6	4.3	74.4	7.7	13	46	6	46	8	89	43	0	6.4
Tufts University [b]	3.16	3.07	0.08	34	29	74	94	5.6	5.4	50.7	9.0	22	64	12	53*	0*	79*	62*	0*	7.8*
University of Illinois at Chicago [b]	3.11	3.14	0.25	11	45	82	100	9.9	14.4	98.6	19.2	39	38	23	39*	0*	82*	24*	20*	8*
Pennsylvania State University	3.10	3.22	0.20	46	48	80	87	6.5	4.2	37.3	5.6	11	64	0	32	0	89	52	24	7.4
Thomas Jefferson University	3.09	2.96	0.65	64	34	34	78	7.9	4.7	58.5	6.5	19	47	12	42	8	100	11	22	6.6

Appendix Table N - 2 Cell and Developmental Biology (Continued)

Institution	1993 Ratings[1] 93Q	93E	93C	Faculty Tot Fac[2]	% Full[2]	% Supp[2]	% Pub[5]	Pub/ Fac[5]	Gini Pub[5]	Cite/ Fac[5]	Gini Cite[5]	Students[2] Tot Stu	% Fem	Rpt PhDs	Doctorate Recipients[3] % Fem	% Min	% US	% RA	% TA	MYD
U of Tex-Hlth Sci Ct-San Antonio	3.09	3.24	0.56	79	41	48	82	8.5	6.0	50.6	4.6	82	52	27	41	4	86	5	55	8.3
Brown University	3.08	3.26	-0.11	15	67	73	73	2.9	15.8	14.5	30.6	53(1)	53(1)	n/a	63	13	100	0	60	7.0
Rutgers State Univ-New Brunswick	3.07	3.07	0.42	46	43	35	83	7.7	4.7	39.4	7.5	65	51	19	39	4	94	18	13	7.3
Ohio State University	3.06	3.38	0.45	140	44	54	88	7.7	1.4	34.4	1.9	66	38	50	33	3	80	37	41	6.9
Iowa State University	3.05	3.33	0.72	62	45	63	94	7.5	2.6	30.5	3.7	114	42	50	32	2	84	44	8	7.7
University of Arizona	3.00	3.25	0.26	40	52	73	85	10.1	5.1	54.5	5.7	40	38	53	35	9	77	29	16	7.1
Tufts University [a]	2.97	3.07	0.00	19	32	47	68	5.6	12.3	37.8	14.8	16	44	14	53*	0*	79*	62*	0*	7.8*
Texas A&M University	2.97	2.96	0.57	19	21	63	79	6.6	11.5	74.4	19.5	18	50	8	36	14	85	43	17	8.6
University of Illinois at Chicago [a]	2.97	2.92	0.31	34	50	47	76	3.7	5.7	17.3	8.9	83	40	53	39*	0*	82*	24*	20*	8*
Univ of Maryland at Baltimore	2.96	3.11	0.46	61	41	75	84	10.4	3.8	93.6	5.4	51	51	6	48	0	90	30	0	10.0
University of Kansas [b]	2.95	2.69	0.29	16	69	63	56	2.5	32.8	25.2	66.3	19	37	9	31*	7*	72*	17*	57*	6.9*
University of Pittsburgh [a]	2.93	3.08	0.16	22	32	82	82	4.8	8.2	79.7	19.0	52(1)	46(1)	20	52*	0*	90*	67*	7*	8.2*
University of Colorado [a]	2.93	3.22	0.33	21	43	81	81	5.7	8.4	40.8	9.0	17	59	2	45*	2*	98*	38*	5*	7.3*
U of Maryland Baltimore County	2.92	3.33	0.69	38	37	68	76	5.7	5.3	28.2	6.4	20	50	4	33	0	100	0	33	8.0
Medical College of Wisconsin	2.88	2.92	0.00	15	27	47	93	5.5	12.9	37.0	13.0	20	40	6	36	11	100	75	0	7.1
University of Missouri-Columbia	2.88	3.08	0.50	46	41	80	87	6.5	3.7	42.5	4.9	51	43	31	36	0	85	32	16	7.6
North Carolina State University	2.88	3.22	0.47	59	39	36	83	6.9	3.6	23.6	4.7	86	55	41	27	14	88	67	12	7.4
Univ of California-Riverside	2.87	2.99	-0.03	22	41	64	77	6.6	7.6	35.8	11.6	50	40	22	46	0	92	30	10	7.6
University of Kentucky [b]	2.82	2.94	0.31	36	31	56	72	4.0	6.6	20.7	9.9	34	47	14	35*	5*	91*	18*	29*	7*
University of Tennessee-Knoxville	2.77	3.08	0.60	12	75	67	83	13.1	15.6	59.2	16.3	27	48	22	31	7	77	41	28	7.8
Uniformed Services U of Hlth Sci	2.77	2.80	0.24	12	58	0	83	10.2	13.9	112.9	18.4	16	50	12	36	0	100	0	25	6.7
University of Florida	2.77	2.94	0.06	43	47	65	91	7.6	4.3	41.6	7.2	48	56	27	21	5	88	45	12	7.1
State Univ of New York-Buffalo [a]	2.75	2.50	-0.14	17	47	82	82	4.9	9.9	30.5	15.6	34	35	15	31*	8*	65*	54*	4*	8.2*
University of Tennessee - Memphis	2.73	2.74	0.82	28	29	46	75	4.8	9.1	20.6	15.3	50	40	14	29	8	93	17	8	7.6
Colorado State University	2.72	2.82	0.17	15	60	60	100	12.1	15.7	71.7	33.3	43	63	25	26	11	82	48	4	8.3
University of Georgia [a]	2.72	3.08	0.08	12	50	83	83	9.3	11.3	60.2	13.7	35	57	19	30*	17*	72*	52*	8*	7.8*
University of Vermont	2.70	3.02	0.60	32	28	63	75	3.5	7.2	25.7	11.1	79	33	36	42	3	91	28	21	5.9
University of Cincinnati	2.68	2.86	-0.18	12	75	42	92	11.8	10.7	100.0	16.7	24	63	20	56	0	70	26	22	7.9
University of New Mexico	2.67	2.95	0.25	42	48	62	88	7.3	5.6	42.8	7.7	21	43	12	57	25	95	19	31	8.7
University of Maryland College Park	2.67	2.88	0.00	19	47	42	79	6.7	12.8	22.8	14.8	46	52	23	54	3	83	38	15	9.4

Institution	1993 Ratings[1]			Faculty								Students[2]			Doctorate Recipients[3]					
	93Q	93E	93C	Tot Fac[2]	% Full[2]	% Supp[2]	% Pub[5]	Pub/ Fac[5]	Gini Pub[5]	Cite/ Fac[5]	Gini Cite[5]	Tot Stu	% Fem	Rpt PhDs	% Fem	% Min	% US	% RA	% TA	MYD
Univ of California-Santa Barbara	2.67	2.74	0.05	11	55	73	64	7.2	17.7	34.1	19.1	n/a	n/a	n/a	18	0	82	44	22	8.6
Rice University	2.65	2.92	0.17	7	43	100	100	4.4	25.2	19.1	31.0	18	83	10	100	0	100	0	0	4.0
Mean Values for the 2nd Quarter	**2.97**	**3.08**	**0.30**	**37.62**	**45.89**	**62.69**	**83.42**	**7.17**	**8.56**	**49.76**	**12.82**	**42.09**	**47.84**	**22.74**	**40.51**	**5.27**	**85.84**	**34.82**	**17.53**	**7.58**
Texas Tech University	2.64	2.74	0.20	22	32	41	73	3.2	8.3	8.9	13.3	18	28	9	47	0	71	9	45	8.8
State Univ of New York-Buffalo [b]	2.64	3.08	0.00	31	65	39	90	9.3	5.8	33.7	9.5	38	53	30	31*	8*	65*	54*	4*	8.2*
Univ of California-Santa Cruz	2.60	2.65	0.19	13	54	100	69	6.8	27.4	93.4	24.4	18	50	12	50	0	100	0	50	16.0
University of Oklahoma	2.59	2.89	0.50	33	39	61	73	5.3	6.3	30.1	9.4	73	49	34	42	7	85	12	20	6.5
Wake Forest University	2.59	2.64	0.50	14	43	50	57	5.1	15.8	85.1	36.6	16	63	10	50	0	94	17	28	7.1
Albany Medical College	2.59	3.33	0.29	38	50	45	82	9.5	7.3	49.8	8.4	37	49	37	43	0	100	31	19	7.3
University of Houston	2.57	2.82	0.00	13	31	31	62	1.9	18.7	4.7	22.7	13	38	9	0	0	67	0	100	8.7
SUNY Health Science Ctr-Syracuse	2.57	2.29	0.00	19	26	32	79	5.8	21.3	85.7	61.9	13	54	7	55	0	73	13	38	7.7
Georgetown University	2.54	2.86	0.00	13	77	85	92	10.3	13.4	77.5	20.7	11	45	13	50	20	67	0	19	5.9
Temple University	2.54	2.78	0.00	18	56	61	72	4.1	9.7	21.7	37.1	31	39	19	29	0	80	17	13	7.2
Louisiana State U & A&M College	2.53	3.18	0.25	58	53	38	84	6.1	3.5	15.1	4.3	23	30	29	42	4	75	22	22	6.6
Arizona State University	2.52	2.67	0.14	17	53	71	82	4.5	11.3	22.0	18.2	16	19	9	50	0	100	20	60	6.7
Washington State University	2.50	3.00	0.00	37	59	65	84	8.2	4.3	51.4	6.9	39	28	24	18	4	93	23	32	6.9
University of Connecticut	2.48	2.90	-0.10	16	56	38	69	3.0	13.1	14.1	16.6	27	74	4	39	3	88	11	20	6.7
University of Pittsburgh [b]	2.47	2.64	0.13	9	33	78	89	6.9	18.7	33.3	23.0	n/a	n/a	n/a	52*	0*	90*	67*	7*	8.2*
Univ of Missouri-Kansas City	2.45	2.78	0.00	15	27	80	73	4.3	17.2	30.9	21.3	9	44	4	n/a	n/a	n/a	n/a	n/a	n/a
University of Kansas [a]	2.43	2.08	0.00	9	44	44	67	3.1	22.4	8.2	25.8	7	57	5	31*	7*	72*	17*	57*	6.9*
Wayne State University	2.43	3.02	0.27	47	49	51	94	7.3	3.7	30.5	6.3	66	47	30	41	5	75	26	22	7.0
University of Nebraska-Lincoln	2.42	2.82	0.31	14	29	50	79	4.1	15.6	22.9	22.4	15	33	14	25	0	83	27	36	5.8
Wesleyan University	2.41	2.90	0.00	12	58	58	67	2.6	31.3	12.6	32.9	20	40	13	33	0	67	33	33	7.9
Univ of Med & Dent of NJ	2.39	2.73	0.13	13	38	54	69	4.0	14.5	29.8	28.6	25	48	15	50	0	67	0	25	7.7
U of Texas, Medical Br-Galveston	2.38	2.80	-0.03	20	50	65	95	9.5	7.5	38.4	9.5	34	35	16	29	4	82	47	5	6.6
Saint Louis University	2.35	2.45	-0.11	9	67	56	78	7.1	28.8	91.9	37.5	8	63	6	53	0	71	25	17	7.2
Tulane University [a]	2.32	2.56	0.09	12	33	17	58	2.3	16.3	5.8	28.2	45(2)	42(2)	n/a	44*	38*	44*	7*	7*	9.3*
University of Kentucky [a]	2.31	2.08	-0.55	9	56	56	78	2.3	17.9	8.9	26.7	18	44	7	35*	5*	91*	18*	29*	7*

Appendix Table N - 2 Cell and Developmental Biology (Continued)

Institution	1993 Ratings[1] 93Q	93E	93C	Faculty Tot Fac[2]	% Full[2]	% Supp[2]	% Pub[5]	Pub/ Fac[5]	Gini Pub[5]	Cite/ Fac[5]	Gini Cite[5]	Students[2] Tot Stu	% Fem	Rpt PhDs	Doctorate Recipients[3] % Fem	% Min	% US	% RA	% TA	MYD
West Virginia University	2.31	3.10	0.00	20	45	25	70	4.0	9.8	16.4	19.8	13	46	12	33	8	72	20	40	7.5
University of South Carolina	2.31	2.72	0.00	47	40	66	77	4.8	4.7	23.3	8.5	116	39	93	33	10	71	33	8	6.4
CUNY - Grad Sch & Univ Center	2.30	2.41	0.50	17	18	71	71	3.1	11.6	17.9	18.8	53	60	n/a	50	12	94	13	0	8.8
Univ of Health Sc/Chicago Med Sch	2.30	2.50	0.38	22	32	36	82	4.3	8.9	26.5	13.7	28	50	13	31	0	81	0	8	7.0
Tulane University [b]	2.28	2.74	0.33	9	67	67	89	5.4	14.6	29.6	35.5	6	67	4	44*	38*	44*	7*	7*	9.3*
Florida State University	2.27	3.33	0.00	12	67	100	100	4.4	9.5	32.5	23.5	10	50	10	46	0	77	20	40	8.3
State Univ of New York-Albany	2.25	2.36	-0.22	10	60	80	100	6.5	20.6	56.1	33.6	15	67	8	43	0	86	50	33	8.4
New York Medical College	2.25	2.26	0.38	25	52	48	84	10.9	14.1	121.6	37.2	31	55	19	77	0	67	9	9	8.7
University of South Florida	2.22	2.03	0.00	9	56	89	56	11.9	28.2	91.1	41.0	n/a	n/a	8	55	18	100	33	11	6.8
Hahnemann University	2.21	2.38	0.00	18	22	44	83	3.3	9.4	13.2	14.6	25	44	14	56	11	100	0	25	6.6
Brigham Young University	2.20	1.67	n/s	12	58	17	67	2.5	17.3	8.2	35.7	11	45	19	17	0	83	0	0	10.4
Clemson University	2.14	2.50	0.00	17	65	24	65	2.8	17.6	4.8	24.9	29	59	9	40	0	100	19	69	5.8
Loyola University of Chicago	2.11	2.45	0.23	10	50	40	70	3.3	37.0	16.7	83.2	19	37	15	39	0	89	13	0	8.7
Medical University South Carolina	2.09	1.95	0.00	29	55	34	72	6.7	7.8	49.4	17.5	22	59	16	48	4	84	33	0	8.0
University of Georgia [c]	2.00	2.67	0.00	20	75	15	95	13.5	11.0	33.2	10.4	83	51	57	30*	17*	72*	52*	8*	7.8*
University of New Hampshire	2.00	2.22	0.00	8	75	50	100	5.4	19.9	15.9	29.7	9	56	10	30	0	100	50	38	7.3
Kansas State University	2.00	2.08	-0.28	6	33	67	83	11.8	47.0	26.8	42.3	5	80	4	29	0	90	26	17	8.1
Georgia State University	2.00	1.43	0.14	13	54	54	85	4.1	16.4	17.7	17.5	17	29	8	20	0	20	100	0	7.4
Creighton University	2.00	2.22	n/s	17	29	12	76	6.2	21.6	28.9	23.3	6	50	8	43	0	100	0	0	11.7
Louisiana State U Medical Center	2.00	2.50	0.13	15	40	13	80	3.5	12.3	23.0	18.6	10	30	4	33	17	100	17	33	8.6
Mean Values for the 3rd Quarter	**2.34**	**2.58**	**0.09**	**18.82**	**48.24**	**51.51**	**78.22**	**5.67**	**15.54**	**34.65**	**24.48**	**26.23**	**47.60**	**16.36**	**39.45**	**5.45**	**80.23**	**22.52**	**23.95**	**7.85**
University of Notre Dame	1.95	2.45	-0.25	10	40	60	80	2.7	17.6	10.6	23.6	14	29	8	27	0	82	0	64	6.4
University of Wyoming	1.90	1.97	0.00	14	50	36	86	5.9	14.3	20.6	22.7	7	57	4	0	n/a	0	0	0	10.0
Southern Illinois University	1.83	1.89	0.00	16	50	69	69	3.6	17.3	11.7	26.8	33	52	11	8	0	60	50	25	8.7
Illinois State University	1.82	2.29	0.00	12	75	83	100	4.6	11.7	19.8	17.1	n/a	n/a	n/a	40	0	20	0	100	7.7
Medical College of Pensylvania	1.79	1.67	0.00	10	20	60	100	6.6	14.1	64.0	24.2	21	43	11	60	0	89	50	17	7.6
Louisiana St U-Sch Med Shreveport	1.75	1.92	0.11	21	38	71	90	8.1	10.3	55.8	20.4	37	43	19	44	0	69	77	0	6.7
University of North Texas	1.75	n/s	n/s	13	23	15	54	2.1	17.6	6.9	33.0	15	20	9	6	14	39	27	18	8.8

Institution	1993 Ratings[1] 93Q	93E	93C	Faculty Tot Fac[2]	% Full[2]	% Supp[2]	% Pub[5]	Pub/ Fac[5]	Gini Pub[5]	Cite/ Fac[5]	Gini Cite[5]	Students[2] Tot Stu	% Fem	Rpt PhDs	Doctorate Recipients[3] % Fem	% Min	% US	% RA	% TA	MYD
Montana State University [d]	1.75	1.67	n/s	14	50	71	93	5.2	13.6	28.1	19.3	n/a	n/a	n/a	36*	0*	82*	64*	36*	8.5*
University of South Alabama	1.74	1.67	0.00	9	44	67	78	5.1	17.1	24.9	19.4	18	39	10	44	0	78	29	14	6.5
Ohio University	1.71	1.50	0.00	11	18	18	82	1.9	13.3	5.1	23.5	11	27	4	75	25	100	33	33	9.0
Boston University	1.69	2.08	0.00	6	33	83	67	3.5	32.4	31.3	49.7	28	50	9	51	3	87	24	24	7.5
U of Arkansas for Medical Sci	1.68	1.67	0.00	9	22	33	67	3.8	31.3	11.7	41.7	11	55	8	38	0	88	0	33	10.6
SUNY-Health Science Ctr-Brooklyn	1.67	1.67	0.00	6	33	50	83	3.2	30.7	18.7	43.3	29	41	11	21	0	67	44	33	8.8
Montana State University [a]	1.67	1.43	-0.33	9	56	78	89	6.8	16.5	39.0	23.7	14	29	8	36*	0*	82*	64*	36*	8.5*
East Carolina U Sch Medicine	1.67	1.67	0.00	14	36	21	86	4.6	14.5	25.1	29.9	8	25	6	0	0	100	0	50	6.7
Kent State University	1.64	1.33	0.00	10	40	30	100	5.6	16.1	27.3	26.0	7	57	3	29	0	71	0	86	9.7
University of Hawaii at Manoa	1.63	1.67	n/s	9	44	44	89	4.3	21.3	12.8	38.0	12	42	11	35	0	88	58	33	10.3
St. John's University	1.63	1.67	0.00	15	47	33	67	2.7	12.8	20.3	28.0	22	55	17	30	0	100	0	22	13.8
Miami University	1.63	2.78	n/s	5	60	80	100	4.8	33.6	8.0	33.7	31	42	31	36	11	69	0	80	6.7
Univ of Puerto Rico-Rio Piedras [b]	1.62	1.25	0.00	15	27	0	47	0.9	21.4	1.0	25.3	2	50	0	29*	100*	86*	0*	33*	12.6*
George Washington University	1.50	1.67	-0.14	6	83	67	67	2.3	41.8	10.3	54.2	26	62	7	33	0	67	18	0	9.4
Loma Linda University	1.50	1.67	0.00	20	50	20	85	4.5	8.8	15.3	11.8	25	44	9	67	0	67	0	33	9.0
Catholic University of America	1.50	1.67	0.00	9	33	44	78	2.3	19.2	8.2	32.3	17	53	7	38	0	100	0	38	12.7
Auburn University [c]	1.50	1.67	0.00	17	18	29	94	9.0	8.6	18.2	10.0	7	57	6	18*	13*	73*	56*	0*	11*
University of Idaho	1.44	1.67	0.00	8	25	38	50	2.9	48.2	8.9	84.3	2	0	5	22	0	63	86	0	6.8
Clark University	1.43	2.08	n/s	5	80	40	100	3.4	31.4	9.6	31.8	0	0	3	50	0	100	0	100	6.0
Auburn University [a]	1.38	1.00	0.00	9	22	22	56	2.9	23.6	5.0	36.0	16	31	4	18*	13*	73*	56*	0*	11*
University of Louisville	1.33	0.72	0.00	5	60	80	60	8.8	49.8	38.2	50.1	22	32	14	52	5	87	15	20	8.6
Lehigh University	1.33	1.33	1.00	8	38	13	25	0.6	68.0	1.8	54.0	22[(1)]	68[(1)]	n/a	0	0	100	0	50	9.5
Fordham University	1.16	0.91	-0.33	8	50	25	75	2.5	23.0	5.6	33.1	64[(2)]	59[(2)]	n/a	33	0	83	0	67	6.7
University of Montana	1.07	1.67	0.00	8	38	38	63	4.1	30.9	13.0	44.6	3	33	6	42	0	73	38	38	7.4
Bowling Green State University	1.00	1.67	0.00	9	22	56	78	2.4	16.5	5.2	22.8	6	0	2	40	25	80	0	20	9.8
Oklahoma State University	0.94	0.97	-0.67	4	75	50	50	2.5	58.0	2.3	80.2	110	30	3	40	0	80	0	67	8.1
Univ of Puerto Rico-Rio Piedras [a]	0.94	0.95	0.00	9	0	33	67	2.2	29.0	2.9	42.3	8	38	9	29*	100*	86*	0*	33*	12.6*
University of Dayton	0.93	0.83	0.00	7	29	57	57	2.4	33.5	5.3	46.6	4	25	2	0	100	100	0	0	6.0
Northern Arizona University	0.86	1.11	n/s	5	60	40	60	2.6	47.9	9.4	84.4	1	100	4	0	n/a	0	100	0	9.0
Drexel University	0.81	0.95	0.00	4	0	75	100	2.3	28.3	7.3	65.0	n/a	n/a	n/a	0	0	100	0	0	19.0

Appendix Table N - 2 Cell and Developmental Biology (Continued)

Institution	1993 Ratings[1]			Faculty								Students[2]			Doctorate Recipients[3]					
	93Q	93E	93C	Tot Fac[2]	% Full[2]	% Supp[2]	% Pub[5]	Pub/ Fac[5]	Gini Pub[5]	Cite/ Fac[5]	Gini Cite[5]	Tot Stu	% Fem	Rpt PhDs	% Fem	% Min	% US	% RA	% TA	MYD
University of Tulsa	0.80	0.83	n/s	6	33	17	67	2.5	37.7	10.2	79.3	4	50	1	0	0	100	0	0	16.0
Clark Atlanta University	0.72	n/s	n/s	17	24	0	18	0.4	50.0	3.8	96.9	28(1)	64(1)	23	38	100	88	20	0	9.1
University of South Dakota	0.69	0.83	n/s	4	25	25	100	3.3	32.5	14.5	66.9	1	0	6	40	0	100	20	0	5.7
Univ of Arkansas-Fayetteville	0.60	0.83	0.00	4	50	25	75	0.8	33.3	1.8	100.0	2	50	5	10	0	100	14	14	9.9
Utah State University	0.50	0.00	n/s	4	25	50	75	2.5	36.0	6.3	41.7	3	67	0	0	0	83	40	0	8.4
State Univ of New York-Binghamton	0.33	1.67	n/s	5	20	60	60	4.0	35.5	9.6	44.5	4	25	1	n/a	n/a	n/a	n/a	n/a	n/a
Georgia Institute of Technology	0.16	0.00	n/s	2	0	100	100	3.5	59.1	25.5	50.9	3	0	2	50	n/a	0	100	0	10.0
Univ of Southern Mississippi	0.13	0.00	n/s	7	29	71	57	0.9	33.3	1.0	55.1	14	50	4	17	0	33	0	67	10.4
Mean Values for the 4th Quarter	**1.31**	**1.42**	**-0.02**	**9.29**	**37.67**	**46.16**	**74.31**	**3.59**	**28.03**	**15.15**	**41.96**	**16.95**	**40.35**	**7.58**	**29.14**	**12.41**	**74.84**	**24.61**	**29.18**	**9.25**
Mean Values for All Programs	**2.63**	**2.74**	**0.19**	**31.60**	**45.96**	**58.43**	**81.36**	**7.03**	**14.23**	**62.83**	**21.60**	**39.97**	**45.01**	**21.90**	**37.75**	**6.40**	**82.36**	**28.30**	**19.16**	**8.03**

Sources: 1. National Survey of Graduate Faculty
2. Institutional Coordinator Response Data
3. Doctorate Records File
4. Federal Agencies
5. Institute for Scientific Information

Notes: *a.* School of Arts and Sciences
b. School of Medicine
c. School of Veterinary Medicine
d. School of Agriculture

n/s After trimming no cases remained

(1) Combined enrollment for programs in Biochemistry and Molecular Biology and Cell and Developmental Biology
(2) Combined enrollment for programs in Cell and Developmental Biology and Ecology, Evolution, and Behavior
(3) Combined enrollment for programs in Cell and Developmental Biology and Molecular and General Genetics

* The Doctorate Recipient information cannot be separated for multiple programs at the same institution in the same field and therefore the total for the combined programs is given.

Appendix Table N - 3 Selected Characteristics of Research-Doctorate Programs in Ecology, Evolution, and Behavior

Institution	1993 Ratings[1] 93Q	93E	93C	Faculty Tot Fac[2]	% Full[2]	% Supp[2]	% Pub[5]	Pub/ Fac[5]	Gini Pub[5]	Cite/ Fac[5]	Gini Cite[5]	Students[2] Tot Stu	% Fem	Rpt PhDs	Doctorate Recipients[3] % Fem	% Min	% US	% RA	% TA	MYD
Stanford University	4.51	4.23	0.07	10	80	80	90	16.1	13.3	96.1	19.2	n/a	n/a	26	47	0	100	36	7	7.3
University of Chicago	4.51	4.31	0.31	30	57	80	87	6.9	5.4	31.1	8.0	39	38	23	38	15	100	0	8	7.2
Duke University	4.49	4.33	0.33	62	63	73	89	6.5	2.7	35.2	4.2	171	50	91	35	1	92	12	55	7.4
Cornell University	4.44	4.24	0.39	92	53	70	87	8.8	2.0	54.2	4.9	7	57	80	34	4	72	35	23	8.3
University of California-Davis	4.42	4.12	0.49	197	57	42	87	7.2	0.9	27.4	1.6	288	47	206	30	5	79	39	15	8.8
Princeton University	4.34	3.96	0.16	11	64	36	73	3.4	18.0	8.5	16.4	26	50	28	55	0	91	13	0	6.8
University of Washington	4.30	4.20	0.33	41	80	83	85	6.4	5.1	35.5	7.8	119	51	55	32	0	89	18	18	7.7
University of California-Berkeley	4.29	4.15	0.05	57	67	60	91	7.4	3.4	32.5	5.2	283	48	172	33	10	91	29	41	8.0
University of Wisconsin-Madison	4.18	4.13	0.43	90	63	49	91	7.4	1.8	39.2	4.2	123	37	100	29	6	78	51	17	7.7
State U of New York-Stony Brook	4.12	3.86	0.10	29	52	76	86	7.6	14.6	34.2	12.5	46	52	25	33	5	78	17	48	8.8
University of Texas at Austin	4.12	3.77	0.19	54	56	56	70	5.4	5.0	19.1	6.9	89	36	57	28	1	82	8	60	8.6
University of Michigan	4.10	3.98	-0.11	52	69	71	87	6.0	3.5	29.5	8.1	100	38	95	36	3	90	12	65	8.9
Washington University	3.94	3.69	0.37	24	54	58	88	8.5	9.5	35.8	11.2	35	40	20	33	0	67	55	0	6.8
University of Pennsylvania	3.90	3.67	0.21	55	33	62	87	7.2	3.1	50.3	6.5	58	41	43	11	0	84	0	50	7.9
University of Minnesota	3.88	3.77	0.33	66	65	58	88	6.5	2.6	23.5	4.2	91	45	59	31	0	79	51	15	7.8
University of Georgia	3.87	3.72	0.46	84	52	55	80	6.7	2.3	31.0	3.4	137	40	73	33	2	70	34	28	9.2
Yale University	3.83	3.66	-0.11	59	61	78	86	11.6	3.6	165.4	4.6	122	48	60	46	9	85	18	0	7.8
Univ of California-Los Angeles	3.82	3.67	0.00	41	68	61	93	9.1	7.0	39.0	7.4	73	44	261	32	5	86	0	67	9.0
Univ of California-San Diego	3.82	3.50	0.41	39	67	51	90	6.8	4.7	33.7	6.9	15	33	8	60	0	100	60	0	8.7
Univ of California-Santa Barbara	3.81	3.63	0.22	28	79	61	89	7.9	6.2	35.0	8.4	77	39	43	17	0	100	39	35	9.6
University of Arizona	3.80	3.77	0.44	26	46	54	85	4.5	5.7	31.4	14.3	61	48	25	22	6	84	26	38	9.0
University of California-Irvine	3.77	3.63	0.54	21	62	57	90	7.2	8.7	34.2	12.9	28	43	9	70	10	100	29	57	8.7
Oregon State University	3.74	3.64	0.37	127	57	35	85	4.8	1.5	12.5	3.2	124	42	80	24	0	66	42	18	9.1
University of Utah	3.65	3.56	0.20	16	63	50	88	5.3	21.2	16.9	22.1	48(1)	40(1)	n/a	10	0	90	17	17	10.0
Rutgers State Univ-New Brunswick	3.60	3.24	0.36	39	49	38	74	8.8	10.7	21.8	7.1	62	52	35	26	0	80	19	38	8.6
Univ of California-Riverside	3.60	3.51	0.48	26	46	73	96	6.6	6.8	26.1	8.8	35	46	21	27	7	67	54	3	8.2
Pennsylvania State University [b]	3.60	3.55	0.67	93	47	37	84	6.6	2.8	25.9	6.2	7	0	1	31*	3*	75*	52*	15*	8.5*
University of Florida	3.57	3.43	0.17	45	76	56	87	6.8	4.0	30.0	7.1	57	37	45	26	5	73	32	38	9.8
U of Illinois at Urbana-Champaign	3.52	3.62	-0.09	74	49	36	82	5.6	2.5	22.0	3.9	58	45	57	35	1	77	49	18	8.4
Indiana University	3.49	3.49	0.54	27	41	70	81	5.7	8.9	39.6	15.9	0	0	15	25	0	92	5	71	8.6

Appendix Table N - 3 Ecology, Evolution, and Behavior (Continued)

Institution	1993 Ratings[1] 93Q	93E	93C	Faculty Tot Fac[2]	% Full[2]	% Supp[2]	% Pub[5]	Pub/ Fac[5]	Gini Pub[5]	Cite/ Fac[5]	Gini Cite[5]	Students[2] Tot Stu	% Fem	Rpt PhDs	Doctorate Recipients[3] % Fem	% Min	% US	% RA	% TA	MYD
University of Kansas	3.46	3.62	0.35	46	43	52	78	3.7	4.2	8.2	6.7	67	25	54	30	0	89	22	30	8.4
University of Colorado	3.46	3.37	0.51	38	53	68	82	6.1	5.0	32.1	15.9	86	49	29	33	0	92	9	36	8.8
Mean Values for the Top Quarter	**3.94**	**3.78**	**0.29**	**53.09**	**58.50**	**58.94**	**85.50**	**7.03**	**6.15**	**36.15**	**8.62**	**81.68**	**42.10**	**61.16**	**32.88**	**3.06**	**84.31**	**27.59**	**29.09**	**8.39**
Florida State University	3.41	3.29	0.08	16	75	56	81	4.1	12.9	20.9	17.8	15	13	14	33	0	72	20	33	8.2
Michigan State University	3.41	3.45	0.09	39	67	44	87	7.5	5.5	39.3	11.5	n/a	n/a	10	28	4	80	46	16	8.7
Arizona State University	3.41	3.33	0.42	32	59	53	88	5.7	4.7	14.1	7.1	58	29	21	29	4	89	18	27	11.2
U of Massachusetts at Amherst	3.39	3.43	-0.02	65	49	34	77	5.4	3.7	14.2	5.2	105	47	58	49	0	81	30	38	8.6
Utah State University	3.39	3.41	0.61	70	34	19	79	4.2	3.3	10.9	9.1	17	24	29	27	0	66	28	16	10.0
Washington State University	3.37	3.44	0.34	84	43	45	82	7.9	2.8	37.7	4.3	47	30	49	19	2	71	47	26	8.3
University of Connecticut	3.35	3.46	0.30	28	57	46	79	3.2	6.5	8.4	9.6	35	29	16	32	3	85	17	41	8.8
University of Tennessee-Knoxville	3.35	3.26	0.26	61	77	41	69	4.6	5.5	15.8	9.0	56	27	46	32	3	81	30	40	8.5
Northern Arizona University	3.35	3.45	0.64	22	55	55	77	5.8	13.9	24.2	28.3	21	43	33	30	5	89	28	15	9.4
U of North Carolina-Chapel Hill	3.33	3.43	0.04	28	68	54	79	4.0	7.0	13.9	16.9	44	36	13	32	0	96	5	43	7.8
Pennsylvania State University	3.31	3.47	0.54	109	50	18	83	5.6	1.9	14.6	3.4	17	24	17	31*	3*	75*	52*	15*	8.5*
Brown University	3.30	3.25	0.33	11	36	82	82	4.1	16.5	16.7	28.7	16	63	4	50	0	100	0	50	5.6
University of Maryland College Park	3.28	3.37	0.27	70	34	39	74	4.5	3.0	19.4	4.9	103	48	55	32	5	83	27	30	8.7
Ohio State University	3.27	3.11	0.16	105	45	38	71	4.1	2.7	12.8	4.0	94	38	44	25	0	74	28	48	9.5
University of New Mexico	3.24	3.40	0.59	30	40	73	80	5.2	5.7	23.0	7.8	65	32	31	21	0	100	25	50	10.4
North Carolina State University	3.20	3.30	0.17	75	56	29	85	5.9	2.7	23.8	4.6	10	50	16	30	8	79	54	11	8.4
University of Virginia	3.14	3.24	0.57	42	43	62	79	5.3	4.7	23.7	11.0	47	26	24	22	0	89	11	33	9.7
University of Oklahoma	3.11	3.11	0.31	41	51	51	83	3.6	5.1	8.7	7.3	56	30	24	23	4	83	24	64	8.6
State Univ of New York-Albany	3.10	3.12	-0.07	8	63	38	88	4.6	19.7	14.4	31.3	14	43	12	0	0	80	0	75	7.0
Purdue University	3.10	3.25	0.16	34	56	41	79	5.3	6.3	23.6	16.2	46	41	37	23	0	74	52	7	8.3
Syracuse University	3.09	2.96	-0.21	7	86	57	100	8.0	21.6	30.0	32.3	14	43	10	13	0	63	25	25	11.0
University of Kentucky [a]	3.04	2.95	0.46	17	53	35	94	7.0	10.8	16.9	14.0	22	27	7	27*	5*	51*	52*	4*	7.7*
University of Vermont	3.04	2.89	0.33	27	37	52	74	4.1	8.6	18.0	18.1	21	33	13	27	0	86	13	63	8.6
Iowa State University	3.00	3.00	0.27	25	44	32	84	5.1	6.5	11.8	14.3	34	29	18	20	6	61	48	8	7.5
University of Wyoming	3.00	3.18	0.43	39	46	21	90	5.3	5.7	8.2	12.1	34	29	30	12	3	93	40	14	9.5
Colorado State University	2.99	2.91	0.34	17	71	47	65	5.9	13.3	24.6	16.1	53	45	35	35	2	72	39	18	9.3

Institution	1993 Ratings[1] 93Q	93E	93C	Faculty Tot Fac[2]	% Full[2]	% Supp[2]	% Pub[5]	Pub/ Fac[5]	Gini Pub[5]	Cite/ Fac[5]	Gini Cite[5]	Students[2] Tot Stu	% Fem	Rpt PhDs	Doctorate Recipients[3] % Fem	% Min	% US	% RA	% TA	MYD
University of Nebraska-Lincoln	2.96	2.69	0.40	17	88	41	71	4.0	10.5	6.1	17.6	15	20	9	27	14	81	41	5	8.4
University of Rochester	2.95	2.87	-0.33	12	58	67	92	7.4	11.7	44.2	18.6	23	39	5	0	0	100	0	100	5.0
University of Iowa	2.94	3.14	-0.41	33	55	76	85	7.0	7.6	38.3	11.6	4	50	5	42	6	84	20	67	8.8
University of Hawaii at Manoa	2.94	3.05	0.33	64	55	33	78	3.4	4.2	10.0	6.2	56	39	40	31	0	82	26	26	11.3
Univ of California-Santa Cruz	2.93	2.93	-0.05	11	82	64	91	6.3	15.5	24.3	23.7	31	48	15	33	25	67	67	0	9.5
Louisiana State U & A&M College	2.91	3.03	0.18	74	51	23	85	6.5	3.4	16.4	4.7	84	26	66	20	5	63	48	24	9.4
Mean Values for the 2nd Quarter	**3.18**	**3.19**	**0.24**	**41.03**	**55.75**	**45.81**	**81.59**	**5.33**	**7.92**	**19.65**	**13.35**	**40.55**	**35.52**	**25.19**	**26.72**	**3.34**	**79.69**	**30.03**	**32.25**	**8.76**
CUNY - Grad Sch & Univ Center	2.87	2.99	0.05	36	64	19	56	1.7	8.2	4.8	15.0	56	54	46	46	9	86	0	26	10.3
University of South Carolina	2.87	3.14	0.33	23	39	65	91	4.4	7.6	12.8	18.6	24	33	20	36	0	71	57	21	8.6
State Univ of New York-Binghamton	2.86	2.81	0.48	10	20	60	90	5.7	18.8	16.4	20.2	9	56	3	0	0	100	0	0	11.0
Johns Hopkins University	2.83	3.15	-0.14	14	36	64	86	8.1	12.2	28.3	16.0	n/a	n/a	11	n/a	n/a	n/a	n/a	n/a	n/a
University of Alaska	2.83	3.16	0.35	23	39	39	83	4.3	8.4	8.7	22.9	n/a	n/a	n/a	40	0	80	0	67	9.8
Virginia Polytech Inst & State U	2.80	2.87	0.04	17	53	35	88	7.7	19.3	19.1	27.1	11	27	19	26	0	73	50	22	7.5
University of Missouri-Columbia	2.79	2.78	0.47	8	50	88	88	4.5	20.0	16.6	27.0	12	42	7	11	5	63	43	0	9.6
Texas Tech University	2.79	2.96	0.45	26	23	31	73	3.7	9.5	11.1	16.5	38	24	28	17	0	67	31	31	8.6
University of Kentucky [b]	2.79	2.92	0.00	33	39	30	91	10.2	5.0	37.2	6.2	56	21	28	27*	5*	51*	52*	4*	7.7*
University of Nevada, Reno	2.74	2.83	0.68	25	44	12	60	2.8	9.6	4.3	9.8	25	48	6	0	0	100	n/a	n/a	17.0
Vanderbilt University	2.73	2.57	0.26	13	38	38	77	4.5	12.3	12.4	25.8	15	40	9	0	0	100	0	100	6.8
Miami University	2.67	2.98	0.38	13	54	54	77	6.2	18.9	13.4	20.0	31	42	31	40	0	86	5	58	8.0
Dartmouth College	2.65	2.73	0.04	5	40	60	80	6.4	31.4	35.4	34.9	10	30	7	25	0	88	25	50	8.7
Univ of Southwestern Louisiana	2.64	2.44	0.62	22	18	50	77	3.8	9.8	11.6	18.2	19	37	8	100	0	100	0	100	8.0
Rutgers State Univ-Newark	2.61	3.10	-0.31	13	69	54	69	6.6	16.3	24.4	20.7	20	55	11	36	10	91	0	50	11.4
Texas A&M University	2.61	2.80	0.12	36	36	64	81	6.2	6.1	51.1	12.7	25	32	18	19	10	67	29	19	9.9
Clemson University	2.61	2.81	0.00	26	54	27	50	1.6	9.6	2.5	13.1	38	39	20	38	9	83	31	53	10.8
Idaho State University	2.60	2.71	0.50	41	46	10	46	1.2	8.4	2.0	12.2	8	88	21	0	0	80	25	25	6.6
Tulane University	2.58	2.57	0.17	9	33	33	78	2.4	20.6	6.9	21.8	45(2)	42(2)	n/a	33	0	67	0	100	7.7
University of Alabama	2.57	2.62	0.57	15	60	47	80	3.3	11.2	7.9	20.6	17	24	6	33	0	100	0	67	8.7
Kansas State University	2.57	3.00	-0.10	14	43	29	79	4.8	10.3	10.6	13.0	9	44	11	30	8	63	51	15	7.8
Wake Forest University	2.56	2.73	0.13	16	38	50	75	3.9	14.9	10.1	16.5	28	43	13	0	0	100	0	0	11.0

Appendix Table N - 3 Ecology, Evolution, and Behavior (Continued)

Institution	1993 Ratings[1]			Faculty								Students[2]			Doctorate Recipients[3]					
	93Q	93E	93C	Tot Fac[2]	% Full[2]	% Supp[2]	% Pub[5]	Pub/ Fac[5]	Gini Pub[5]	Cite/ Fac[5]	Gini Cite[5]	Tot Stu	% Fem	Rpt PhDs	% Fem	% Min	% US	% RA	% TA	MYD
Claremont Graduate School	2.54	3.24	0.22	5	40	0	100	7.2	26.8	17.4	56.1	7	14	8	0	0	86	60	0	8.8
Boston University	2.54	2.75	0.11	9	44	67	100	6.2	13.5	15.2	18.7	24	67	23	42	11	100	13	20	10.3
University of South Florida	2.54	2.65	0.08	12	75	25	100	6.4	11.9	10.6	20.0	n/a	n/a	6	17	0	100	0	20	11.9
University of Maine	2.52	2.63	0.00	40	55	35	83	4.2	3.9	13.7	5.8	29	34	22	36	0	73	44	6	9.3
University of Montana	2.51	2.82	0.15	21	62	43	76	2.5	11.5	8.6	27.0	14	36	5	17	0	72	13	33	9.2
University of Pittsburgh	2.42	2.38	0.06	11	36	36	55	2.5	22.9	8.9	37.3	52	46	4	25	33	75	33	33	6.6
George Mason University	2.41	2.67	0.22	38	37	34	53	3.2	10.6	4.2	9.6	87	45	8	0	0	100	0	0	23.5
Bowling Green State University	2.40	2.50	-0.27	12	58	25	83	3.0	15.2	8.5	28.6	10	20	8	25	0	100	0	71	8.9
Mean Values for the 3rd Quarter	**2.65**	**2.81**	**0.19**	**19.53**	**44.77**	**40.80**	**77.50**	**4.64**	**13.49**	**14.49**	**20.40**	**26.63**	**40.12**	**14.54**	**24.79**	**3.45**	**83.52**	**20.07**	**35.39**	**9.79**
Southern Illinois University	2.39	2.65	0.04	33	61	18	85	3.0	8.4	2.1	17.3	41	27	44	29	0	91	29	24	10.4
Wayne State University	2.39	2.26	0.00	27	52	26	67	3.7	10.9	13.1	32.3	55	51	53	0	25	100	0	75	11.0
Oklahoma State University	2.39	2.87	-0.05	21	67	29	95	4.8	11.5	13.7	20.6	66	26	23	22	6	68	35	14	8.1
University of Notre Dame	2.37	2.87	-0.19	7	29	71	86	5.9	20.9	13.7	28.2	17	35	10	0	0	60	0	100	10.7
California Institute Technology	2.35	2.00	0.00	4	100	50	75	9.8	40.1	87.3	45.4	0	0	0	n/a	n/a	n/a	n/a	n/a	n/a
Univ of Missouri-Saint Louis	2.33	2.35	0.22	10	0	30	50	1.8	22.8	3.0	75.7	17	35	1	n/a	n/a	n/a	n/a	n/a	n/a
SUNY Col Environ Sci & Forestry	2.27	2.87	-0.18	12	83	8	75	6.6	14.4	24.8	27.7	26	38	19	22	6	78	35	20	8.8
University of Houston	2.24	2.12	-0.27	6	33	67	100	4.3	26.0	9.3	27.7	6	50	6	25	0	75	75	0	10.6
State Univ of New York-Buffalo	2.17	2.08	-0.13	8	50	50	63	3.4	28.1	12.8	30.1	9	33	4	25	0	75	50	50	9.4
Old Dominion University	2.16	2.31	0.00	14	71	21	79	4.1	10.7	4.2	13.9	15	20	8	14	0	60	60	0	8.7
Brigham Young University	2.14	2.22	0.06	14	71	21	86	4.6	16.6	11.2	24.3	8	63	61	21	0	86	0	40	10.3
University of Idaho	2.14	1.67	0.32	8	13	13	75	2.1	25.2	8.3	39.0	2	0	0	17	8	67	22	11	10.2
Ohio University	2.13	2.33	0.33	20	55	40	95	3.6	9.7	6.1	12.9	14	43	14	30	0	72	0	69	9.4
Univ of Arkansas-Fayetteville	2.12	2.03	0.41	22	36	41	59	2.6	17.0	3.5	19.2	25	32	15	20	0	72	30	24	10.3
University of Cincinnati	2.11	2.33	0.20	20	50	25	75	3.1	8.4	13.4	18.4	12	50	21	33	0	100	0	50	9.8
Saint Louis University	2.06	1.25	0.00	13	54	31	62	1.9	16.4	2.4	26.5	17	65	9	0	0	100	0	50	9.5
New Mexico State University	2.00	2.05	-0.17	24	38	13	71	2.1	8.6	2.9	20.2	41	20	38	0	7	83	23	38	10.0
Mississippi State University	2.00	1.96	-0.12	15	53	13	80	3.7	13.5	7.5	14.9	6	100	16	28	31	78	47	13	8.6
Illinois State University	1.91	2.02	-0.12	14	57	36	93	5.3	13.1	14.9	19.4	n/a	n/a	n/a	50	0	100	0	0	11.5
University of New Hampshire	1.88	1.95	-0.50	6	67	17	100	4.3	19.5	8.0	22.5	n/a	n/a	n/a	32	0	79	58	21	9.6

Institution	1993 Ratings[1] 93Q	93E	93C	Faculty Tot Fac[2]	% Full[2]	% Supp[2]	% Pub[5]	Pub/ Fac[5]	Gini Pub[5]	Cite/ Fac[5]	Gini Cite[5]	Students[2] Tot Stu	% Fem	Rpt PhDs	Doctorate Recipients[3] % Fem	% Min	% US	% RA	% TA	MYD
Kent State University	1.88	2.31	-0.18	8	75	25	50	4.3	28.8	10.1	39.4	11	55	5	29	0	100	0	83	10.6
Drexel University	1.83	0.83	0.25	3	33	33	33	0.3	100.0	1.7	100.0	n/a	n/a	n/a	n/a	n/a	n/a	n/a	n/a	n/a
Howard University	1.80	1.33	0.20	29	52	31	76	2.4	6.2	7.4	9.8	22	64	7	67	75	67	25	25	14.0
University of North Texas	1.72	2.22	0.14	11	55	9	91	4.7	16.0	7.2	16.4	47	34	26	0	0	80	0	0	10.7
University of Alabama-Birmingham	1.68	2.22	1.00	19	42	21	74	4.7	14.1	8.1	12.7	n/a	n/a	n/a	0	0	100	n/a	n/a	15.0
Montana State University	1.63	2.08	-0.18	12	58	17	75	3.8	20.3	7.8	39.6	11	9	13	22	0	68	50	11	8.7
North Dakota State University	1.61	1.67	0.00	17	53	41	82	2.8	11.8	6.8	32.4	31	32	18	22	5	62	44	4	9.6
Univ of Southern Mississippi	1.50	1.88	0.00	12	75	42	58	2.1	17.7	3.4	31.7	47	34	3	50	0	50	50	50	8.5
Fordham University	1.45	0.63	-0.28	10	20	20	50	1.5	24.4	2.1	51.0	64(2)	59(2)	n/a	33	0	100	0	0	11.8
Univ of Puerto Rico-Rio Piedras	1.31	1.67	0.29	9	0	33	33	1.6	47.9	3.9	89.0	n/a	n/a	n/a	n/a	n/a	n/a	n/a	n/a	n/a
Clark University	1.20	0.95	0.00	6	50	67	83	3.3	25.5	7.2	86.8	5	60	0	n/a	n/a	n/a	n/a	n/a	n/a
Loma Linda University	1.17	2.08	1.00	12	67	8	58	2.5	24.8	8.1	26.3	15	27	7	n/a	n/a	n/a	n/a	n/a	n/a
University of Dayton	1.16	1.25	0.00	6	50	33	50	2.8	61.2	9.2	77.3	1	100	0	0	n/a	0	n/a	n/a	9.0
New York Medical College	0.50	n/s	n/s	8	25	38	88	10.1	25.8	31.9	23.9	6	33	4	n/a	n/a	n/a	n/a	n/a	n/a
University of Tulsa	0.47	0.00	0.00	2	50	0	0	0.0		0.0		1	0	0	n/a	n/a	n/a	n/a	n/a	n/a
Mean Values for the 4th Quarter	**1.84**	**1.92**	**0.06**	**13.20**	**49.86**	**29.66**	**70.63**	**3.65**	**22.54**	**10.77**	**34.49**	**21.27**	**39.85**	**14.66**	**21.89**	**6.27**	**76.70**	**25.32**	**30.88**	**10.18**
Mean Values for All Programs	**2.88**	**2.91**	**0.19**	**31.47**	**52.28**	**43.52**	**78.64**	**5.14**	**12.67**	**20.14**	**19.43**	**43.24**	**39.32**	**29.45**	**26.81**	**3.93**	**81.18**	**25.97**	**31.85**	**9.23**

Sources: 1. National Survey of Graduate Faculty
2. Institutional Coordinator Response Data
3. Doctorate Records File
4. Federal Agencies
5. Institute for Scientific Information

Notes: *a.* School of Arts and Sciences
b. School of Agriculture

n/s After trimming no cases remained

(1) Combined enrollment for programs in Biochemistry and Molecular Biology and Ecology, Evolution, and Behavior
(2) Combined enrollment for programs in Cell and Developmental Biology and Ecology, Evolution, and Behavior

* The Doctorate Recipient information cannot be separated for multiple programs at the same institution in the same field and therefore the total for the combined programs is given.

Appendix Table N - 4 Selected Characteristics of Research-Doctorate Programs in Molecular and General Genetics

Institution	1993 Ratings[1] 93Q	93E	93C	Faculty Tot Fac[2]	% Full[2]	% Supp[2]	% Pub[5]	Pub/ Fac[5]	Gini Pub[5]	Cite/ Fac[5]	Gini Cite[5]	Students[2] Tot Stu	% Fem	Rpt PhDs	Doctorate Recipients[3] % Fem	% Min	% US	% RA	% TA	MYD
Massachusetts Inst of Technology	4.88	4.75	0.34	54	65	70	98	19.4	3.0	421.5	4.7	n/a	n/a	n/a	25	0	100	25	0	7.7
Univ of California-San Francisco	4.87	4.80	0.57	51	51	84	94	16.3	2.9	448.3	4.3	13	23	10	18	0	80	0	0	6.7
Harvard University	4.77	4.55	0.34	34	38	24	94	20.6	5.2	499.0	5.5	80	55	32	38	0	87	30	0	6.6
California Institute Technology	4.51	4.47	0.00	6	67	100	100	17.2	35.2	375.7	41.5	0	0	2	n/a	n/a	n/a	n/a	n/a	n/a
Stanford University	4.48	4.44	0.31	11	73	91	91	23.0	14.1	260.5	16.1	32	56	10	33	0	78	29	0	7.6
Univ of California-San Diego	4.44	4.17	0.67	78	62	64	92	16.9	3.2	329.8	4.6	57	33	23	0	0	100	0	0	6.0
University of Wisconsin-Madison	4.33	4.40	0.35	56	66	84	88	11.3	2.6	129.2	4.4	46	48	35	60	4	85	38	0	7.3
Yale University	4.32	4.29	0.08	41	56	78	90	14.4	4.4	212.8	5.4	40	55	30	42	4	88	4	0	7.2
Johns Hopkins University	4.26	4.01	0.33	49	49	73	94	14.0	3.6	302.3	11.9	80	56	41	45	0	100	13	0	6.4
University of California-Berkeley	4.21	4.18	0.33	15	60	87	93	11.7	14.9	178.5	18.3	48	50	44	48	5	92	5	5	6.6
University of Chicago	4.17	4.25	0.43	52	60	69	90	12.5	5.8	162.5	11.5	81	46	57	30	0	89	6	0	7.8
Columbia University	4.14	3.93	0.32	37	57	78	86	12.0	5.7	173.7	7.1	44	52	4	53	0	94	39	0	7.7
University of Utah	4.08	3.80	0.59	21	19	57	81	10.3	12.4	257.8	16.4	32	41	7	40	0	75	100	0	9.7
Baylor College of Medicine	4.07	4.05	0.83	49	24	63	92	11.9	4.4	155.8	11.0	44	34	5	50	0	100	100	0	7.0
Duke University	4.01	3.83	0.54	46	46	78	87	9.1	3.9	140.6	7.8	34	50	25	100	0	100	0	0	5.0
Washington University	3.98	3.86	0.57	47	26	70	96	11.8	3.4	185.3	5.5	39	44	1	50	0	63	38	0	9.0
University of Washington	3.93	4.02	0.05	16	63	94	94	6.7	8.4	92.1	14.3	47	53	31	35	0	100	6	0	7.5
U of Texas-Southwestern Med Ctr	3.91	3.78	0.64	31	35	58	87	10.2	8.3	135.0	16.4	40	23	5	n/a	n/a	n/a	n/a	n/a	n/a
University of Pennsylvania	3.81	3.72	0.32	130	45	52	93	11.7	1.4	117.1	2.2	91	44	62	52	0	95	20	0	7.7
U of North Carolina-Chapel Hill	3.78	3.66	0.65	63	33	78	97	9.0	3.0	85.3	4.1	39	46	24	50	5	95	22	0	6.4
University of Michigan	3.75	3.93	0.31	21	48	86	95	12.3	9.7	263.0	37.4	34	59	14	76	0	93	36	0	6.7
State U of New York-Stony Brook	3.73	3.62	0.53	62	23	45	87	7.1	3.1	119.0	6.4	45	49	15	41	6	82	56	0	8.6
Cornell University	3.68	3.92	0.13	28	57	89	96	10.2	5.9	115.0	9.2	37	59	16	55	0	82	38	38	8.3
Indiana University	3.64	3.78	0.24	25	36	88	88	8.3	7.0	96.7	8.2	7	57	12	45	0	97	38	4	6.9
Albert Einstein College of Med	3.53	3.60	0.24	46	52	76	87	8.8	4.1	102.1	7.5	22	41	40	57	14	100	14	0	7.6
Mean Values for the Top Quarter	**4.13**	**4.07**	**0.39**	**42.76**	**48.44**	**73.44**	**91.60**	**12.67**	**7.02**	**214.34**	**11.27**	**43.00**	**44.75**	**22.71**	**45.35**	**1.65**	**90.22**	**28.57**	**2.04**	**7.30**
U of Tex-Health Sci Ctr-Houston	3.49	3.44	0.61	47	49	70	98	13.8	3.4	158.5	5.2	37	46	6	36	13	73	33	0	6.7
Brandeis University	3.48	3.49	-0.05	21	67	95	86	11.1	9.6	100.9	15.3	48(1)	56(1)	n/a	0	0	100	100	0	7.8

Institution	1993 Ratings[1] 93Q	93E	93C	Faculty Tot Fac[2]	% Full[2]	% Supp[2]	% Pub[5]	Pub/ Fac[5]	Gini Pub[5]	Cite/ Fac[5]	Gini Cite[5]	Students[2] Tot Stu	% Fem	Rpt PhDs	Doctorate Recipients[3] % Fem	% Min	% US	% RA	% TA	MYD
University of Texas at Austin	3.47	3.56	0.39	57	58	74	81	6.7	3.2	36.9	4.5	77	35	79	83	0	50	25	50	11.5
University of Rochester	3.44	3.43	0.37	55	33	80	89	9.6	3.0	71.9	4.1	35	37	11	n/a	n/a	n/a	n/a	n/a	n/a
North Carolina State University	3.36	3.64	0.28	28	64	68	89	6.9	5.5	35.6	7.8	30	40	16	40	0	80	75	0	6.7
Rutgers State Univ-New Brunswick	3.35	3.38	0.56	96	53	32	77	6.6	3.4	39.0	8.6	153	52	74	25	0	75	0	33	11.6
Pennsylvania State University	3.34	3.71	0.44	83	52	59	88	7.8	2.8	41.1	4.7	45	51	17	69	0	56	56	13	8.6
Emory University	3.34	3.28	0.67	51	35	71	78	8.6	4.1	109.4	7.2	62	56	18	33	0	100	0	0	6.7
University of Arizona	3.32	3.26	0.70	33	39	67	85	5.7	4.7	27.0	7.0	8	75	3	25	0	86	0	33	9.9
U of Illinois at Urbana-Champaign	3.30	3.33	0.50	50	38	64	90	8.8	3.7	49.6	4.9	n/a	n/a	n/a	57	17	86	17	33	7.3
Michigan State University	3.26	3.58	0.55	87	60	60	85	7.6	2.6	47.9	4.6	75	44	56	31	0	55	40	20	6.7
Vanderbilt University	3.26	3.21	0.37	33	27	67	73	7.6	6.4	127.4	8.9	n/a	n/a	n/a	n/a	n/a	n/a	n/a	n/a	n/a
Texas A&M University	3.24	3.15	0.61	53	42	45	83	7.5	3.6	33.8	6.0	55	31	26	26	0	96	43	7	6.8
University of Minnesota	3.23	3.39	0.23	54	46	76	85	8.0	3.2	55.9	4.9	46	50	23	55	7	67	78	11	8.5
University of Georgia	3.22	3.40	0.27	16	63	88	94	9.2	11.6	77.3	16.9	50	42	30	39	6	89	40	0	10.1
Case Western Reserve Univ	3.22	3.33	0.72	13	23	69	85	4.9	15.2	49.4	58.5	23	57	7	33	13	89	25	0	7.7
University of California-Davis	3.21	3.56	0.21	44	45	50	82	9.3	4.4	74.2	10.8	93	30	95	32	11	72	32	13	8.4
University of Iowa	3.21	3.46	0.35	41	54	78	90	9.9	4.5	72.1	7.0	33	52	10	43	0	71	38	0	7.7
Univ of California-Riverside	3.17	3.33	0.35	51	45	71	90	7.6	3.9	38.6	4.7	21	52	29	0	0	100	0	100	8.0
University of Alabama-Birmingham	3.15	3.33	0.33	56	59	48	89	10.3	3.4	79.4	6.9	23	70	21	50	0	83	20	0	5.7
University of Pittsburgh [a]	3.11	3.33	0.73	19	37	42	79	5.3	10.9	20.4	15.4	n/a	n/a	n/a	64*	0*	71*	67*	0*	7.4*
Univ of California-Santa Barbara	3.09	2.99	0.15	9	67	89	78	5.4	20.1	43.6	18.7	n/a	n/a	n/a	n/a	n/a	n/a	n/a	n/a	n/a
University of California-Irvine	3.09	3.33	0.08	10	70	90	90	11.6	16.4	151.2	17.1	36	31	17	0	0	100	0	0	8.5
University of Colorado	3.07	3.39	-0.04	8	38	75	88	5.8	21.6	39.0	30.3	n/a	n/a	n/a	57	0	100	14	0	7.7
University of Florida	3.07	3.45	0.79	34	41	68	74	5.0	7.3	35.5	9.6	37	46	26	0	0	100	n/a	n/a	19.0
U of Massachusetts Med Center	3.07	3.21	0.43	34	41	68	94	7.9	4.9	80.6	6.4	18	61	16	n/a	n/a	n/a	n/a	n/a	n/a
Mean Values for the 2nd Quarter	**3.25**	**3.38**	**0.41**	**41.65**	**47.92**	**67.85**	**85.38**	**8.02**	**7.05**	**65.24**	**11.38**	**47.86**	**48.29**	**29.00**	**36.27**	**3.05**	**81.77**	**33.48**	**14.90**	**8.59**
New York University	3.04	3.33	0.55	25	60	64	88	5.3	7.0	31.0	21.2	46	50	47	33	0	100	0	0	10.4
Oregon State University	3.00	3.03	0.22	50	58	48	80	6.6	3.8	33.3	8.8	33	52	22	25	0	75	50	0	10.0
Ohio State University	2.98	3.14	0.27	29	48	79	93	7.5	6.0	56.2	8.0	67	45	27	40	0	60	0	40	8.1
University of Cincinnati	2.97	3.33	0.12	16	38	81	94	7.3	10.3	86.1	19.6	57	53	33	50	0	100	50	0	7.1
Univ of California-Santa Cruz	2.97	3.06	0.40	12	42	100	75	5.4	24.8	73.3	37.2	13	46	2	0	100	100	0	0	9.0

Appendix Table N - 4 Molecular and General Genetics (Continued)

Institution	1993 Ratings[1] 93Q	93E	93C	Faculty Tot Fac[2]	% Full[2]	% Supp[2]	% Pub[5]	Pub/ Fac[5]	Gini Pub[5]	Cite/ Fac[5]	Gini Cite[5]	Students[2] Tot Stu	% Fem	Rpt PhDs	Doctorate Recipients[3] % Fem	% Min	% US	% RA	% TA	MYD
State Univ of New York-Buffalo	2.94	3.33	0.50	45	49	82	89	7.8	4.4	44.6	5.0	7	57	0	0	0	100	n/a	n/a	8.0
Kansas State University	2.90	2.78	0.00	16	38	50	94	6.1	13.8	26.7	15.9	18	17	14	100	0	100	100	0	7.0
University of Connecticut	2.88	3.24	0.00	15	53	60	80	3.3	14.3	19.1	17.9	19	58	9	42	0	73	11	78	7.4
University of Pittsburgh[b]	2.85	3.03	0.38	12	33	33	92	13.3	26.2	119.9	45.1	43	79	12	64*	0*	71*	67*	0*	7.4*
Temple University	2.84	3.33	0.38	27	52	63	81	7.0	6.9	30.1	8.9	9	22	0	100	0	67	67	33	5.8
University of Virginia	2.83	2.64	0.08	7	57	86	86	4.0	23.2	21.0	32.2	41	54	32	0	0	100	50	0	8.8
Iowa State University	2.82	2.87	0.31	43	44	47	86	7.0	4.5	30.0	5.7	22	41	11	71	0	83	20	40	6.4
University of Illinois at Chicago	2.81	3.06	0.14	12	17	67	92	5.4	15.7	68.2	40.3	30	20	9	44	0	89	43	14	6.8
Wayne State University	2.77	3.20	0.45	18	33	61	94	10.8	11.2	69.4	12.3	19	32	9	n/a	n/a	n/a	n/a	n/a	n/a
University of Kansas	2.67	2.50	0.00	22	50	55	91	4.6	7.7	15.5	18.9	22	36	6	n/a	n/a	n/a	n/a	n/a	n/a
Louisiana State U & A&M College	2.67	2.22	0.25	38	34	24	68	4.2	5.3	12.0	8.7	18	22	15	0	0	100	100	0	5.0
State Univ of New York-Albany	2.59	2.74	0.00	13	46	85	77	6.5	16.4	59.5	25.0	10	60	15	n/a	n/a	n/a	n/a	n/a	n/a
Louisiana State U Medical Center	2.54	3.06	0.00	11	27	36	82	8.9	20.9	55.8	24.0	18	50	9	n/a	n/a	n/a	n/a	n/a	n/a
University of Hawaii at Manoa	2.52	2.41	0.00	15	73	73	87	5.7	13.8	47.2	25.9	19	53	4	60	0	100	20	40	7.4
Arizona State University	2.50	2.33	0.13	12	42	42	58	3.7	17.3	12.2	24.0	6	17	5	n/a	n/a	n/a	n/a	n/a	n/a
University of Missouri-Columbia	2.44	2.50	0.00	19	42	37	89	7.8	7.6	20.6	8.2	14	57	20	100	0	80	50	25	6.8
University of Notre Dame	2.43	3.33	0.00	8	50	63	63	5.0	33.3	23.9	30.2	11	18	7	50	0	50	0	100	6.0
Syracuse University	2.40	2.82	0.00	10	70	100	80	4.8	16.4	37.1	34.4	10	40	13	n/a	n/a	n/a	n/a	n/a	n/a
SUNY-Health Science Ctr-Brooklyn	2.40	1.67	0.00	13	46	69	77	3.6	17.1	22.7	22.2	29	55	6	n/a	n/a	n/a	n/a	n/a	n/a
Montana State University	2.30	3.00	0.20	15	53	27	80	4.7	13.6	9.9	23.8	n/a	n/a	n/a	0	n/a	0	100	0	13.0
Wake Forest University	2.29	3.33	0.00	25	12	44	60	2.6	10.9	39.5	43.1	2	0	0	n/a	n/a	n/a	n/a	n/a	n/a
Mean Values for the 3rd Quarter	**2.71**	**2.90**	**0.17**	**20.31**	**44.88**	**60.62**	**82.15**	**6.11**	**13.55**	**40.95**	**21.79**	**23.32**	**41.36**	**13.08**	**43.28**	**5.88**	**80.44**	**42.82**	**21.76**	**7.80**
Albany Medical College	2.13	3.33	n/s	13	46	38	85	5.8	17.4	26.6	17.9	19	53	18	n/a	n/a	n/a	n/a	n/a	n/a
University of New Hampshire	2.08	2.50	0.00	14	50	36	86	4.3	13.9	15.8	42.8	6	50	5	0	0	100	0	100	4.0
Florida State University	2.00	3.13	0.13	12	58	75	100	3.7	9.9	27.6	30.8	9	44	14	0	0	100	0	100	11.0
Hahnemann University	2.00	2.71	-0.20	12	33	42	100	7.4	12.5	25.3	17.9	14	43	3	n/a	n/a	n/a	n/a	n/a	n/a
University of Nebraska-Lincoln	2.00	3.00	0.00	13	54	54	92	3.8	12.0	32.8	30.8	9	56	2	n/a	n/a	n/a	n/a	n/a	n/a
West Virginia University	2.00	2.22	0.00	18	44	22	67	3.7	15.9	11.8	18.1	13	62	14	50	0	60	11	11	7.1
Medical College of Wisconsin	1.92	1.67	0.00	12	33	75	75	4.2	18.4	28.7	23.9	20	55	3	n/a	n/a	n/a	n/a	n/a	n/a
Univ of Maryland at Baltimore	1.86	1.67	0.00	6	33	33	83	9.5	25.9	22.0	37.2	12	58	7	86	0	100	50	0	7.8
University of Oklahoma	1.73	1.67	0.00	7	29	71	100	4.9	20.2	29.0	24.5	6	50	4	n/a	n/a	n/a	n/a	n/a	n/a

Institution	1993 Ratings[1] 93Q	93E	93C	Faculty Tot Fac[2]	% Full[2]	% Supp[2]	% Pub[5]	Pub/ Fac[5]	Gini Pub[5]	Cite/ Fac[5]	Gini Cite[5]	Students[2] Tot Stu	% Fem	Rpt PhDs	Doctorate Recipients[3] % Fem	% Min	% US	% RA	% TA	MYD
University of New Mexico	1.73	1.67	0.00	10	30	70	90	13.1	21.5	111.3	22.0	n/a	n/a	0	50	50	100	100	0	10.0
University of Houston	1.62	1.11	-0.20	5	20	60	80	2.4	31.9	7.8	43.1	4	50	1	0	0	100	n/a	n/a	14.0
Howard University	1.56	2.29	0.00	7	71	29	86	4.3	24.8	5.0	28.4	26	65	7	40	63	89	11	11	8.8
Georgia Institute of Technology	1.55	1.67	n/s	5	40	80	80	3.2	31.2	17.2	30.5	16	38	19	50	0	100	50	0	9.5
Clemson University	1.45	1.19	0.00	9	56	33	89	3.8	16.6	8.0	29.9	7	57	8	n/a	n/a	n/a	n/a	n/a	n/a
Miami University	1.33	2.14	0.00	7	57	29	43	0.6	37.5	0.3	50.0	40	40	40	n/a	n/a	n/a	n/a	n/a	n/a
University of Louisville	1.27	3.33	n/s	7	57	71	86	4.4	23.2	27.6	31.0	n/a	n/a	n/a	n/a	n/a	n/a	n/a	n/a	n/a
Illinois State University	1.25	1.00	0.00	5	60	80	100	4.4	29.7	27.2	33.8	n/a	n/a	n/a	100	0	100	0	0	19.0
University of Tennessee-Knoxville	1.11	1.11	0.00	3	67	67	67	4.3	50.2	24.0	55.5	27	52	21	60	0	90	13	0	6.7
Boston University	1.05	1.43	-0.33	3	67	33	67	5.7	51.5	27.3	50.4	1	0	1	n/a	n/a	n/a	n/a	n/a	n/a
Drexel University	0.93	1.67	n/s	5	20	80	80	2.2	25.6	8.4	45.0	n/a	n/a	3	n/a	n/a	n/a	n/a	n/a	n/a
University of Tulsa	0.75	0.56	-0.33	4	25	0	50	1.3	68.0	1.5	100.0	3	33	0	n/a	n/a	n/a	n/a	n/a	n/a
Bowling Green State University	0.69	n/s	0.00	4	75	75	100	4.5	35.1	11.5	80.2	2	50	2	40	0	100	25	50	7.6
Ohio University	0.47	0.33	n/s	2	50	0	100	5.0	68.0	5.0	52.0	1	0	0	n/a	n/a	n/a	n/a	n/a	n/a
Clark University	0.30	n/s	n/s	3	67	67	100	5.7	39.7	18.0	36.8	2	100	2	n/a	n/a	n/a	n/a	n/a	n/a
University of Idaho	0.24	0.00	-0.75	1	0	100	100	5.0	100.0	2.0	100.0	0	0	0	n/a	n/a	n/a	n/a	n/a	n/a
Northern Arizona University	0.17	0.83	n/s	3	33	67	0	0.0		0.0		0	0	0	n/a	n/a	n/a	n/a	n/a	n/a
Mean Values for the 4th Quarter	**1.35**	**1.76**	**-0.09**	**7.31**	**45.19**	**53.35**	**81.00**	**4.51**	**32.02**	**20.07**	**41.30**	**10.77**	**43.45**	**7.25**	**43.27**	**10.27**	**94.45**	**26.00**	**27.20**	**9.59**
Mean Values for All Programs	**2.85**	**3.04**	**0.24**	**27.86**	**46.59**	**63.72**	**84.97**	**7.78**	**14.82**	**83.90**	**21.34**	**31.05**	**44.33**	**17.48**	**41.84**	**4.36**	**85.96**	**33.07**	**14.11**	**8.15**

Sources: 1. National Survey of Graduate Faculty
2. Institutional Coordinator Response Data
3. Doctorate Records File
4. Federal Agencies
5. Institute for Scientific Information

Notes: *a.* School of Medicine
b. School of Public Health

n/s After trimming no cases remained

(1) Combined enrollment for programs in Cell and Developmental Biology and Molecular and General Genetics

* The Doctorate Recipient information cannot be separated for multiple programs at the same institution in the same field and therefore the total for the combined programs is given.

Appendix Table N - 5 Selected Characteristics of Research-Doctorate Programs in Neurosciences

Institution	1993 Ratings[1]			Faculty								Students[2]			Doctorate Recipients[3]					
	93Q	93E	93C	Tot Fac[2]	% Full[2]	% Supp[2]	% Pub[5]	Pub/ Fac[5]	Gini Pub[5]	Cite/ Fac[5]	Gini Cite[5]	Tot Stu	% Fem	Rpt PhDs	% Fem	% Min	% US	% RA	% TA	MYD
Univ of California-San Diego	4.82	4.48	0.72	97	72	63	96	19.2	2.0	242.4	3.3	89	40	35	33	5	88	47	0	7.0
Yale University	4.76	4.44	0.43	75	47	77	92	13.5	2.5	148.2	3.2	35	40	6	26	6	95	25	0	7.6
Harvard University	4.73	4.33	0.32	110	30	32	100	13.3	1.7	213.6	2.9	60	48	16	39	0	87	15	0	7.3
Univ of California-San Francisco	4.66	4.45	0.41	34	62	85	100	15.7	4.9	306.4	10.0	34	44	20	28	4	90	25	0	7.6
Stanford University	4.64	4.56	0.35	44	55	89	95	15.3	3.7	175.1	5.6	43	44	24	35	0	91	22	2	7.5
Columbia University	4.58	4.29	0.17	33	52	70	88	14.9	4.5	222.9	8.5	62	45	16	31	0	63	33	8	7.7
Johns Hopkins University	4.47	4.33	0.39	61	48	79	87	14.5	3.7	191.6	7.2	n/a	n/a	20	32	5	90	7	0	7.4
Washington University	4.43	4.42	-0.08	66	45	92	92	10.9	2.4	138.9	4.3	36	47	47	33	0	92	23	0	7.5
University of California-Berkeley	4.32	4.12	0.54	18	83	94	89	9.7	10.1	155.1	30.4	27	22	19	27	0	67	5	20	7.0
California Institute Technology	4.30	4.22	0.06	17	65	94	88	11.6	11.0	146.8	18.3	35	31	17	6	0	88	27	0	7.6
University of Pennsylvania	4.30	4.17	0.53	67	64	79	88	11.1	3.1	107.2	4.8	48	44	12	33	0	95	21	5	6.8
University of Washington	4.28	4.11	0.43	47	74	96	98	14.6	3.5	164.1	5.9	24	46	0	25	0	83	25	17	9.0
Rockefeller University	4.23	4.26	0.08	11	91	45	55	3.7	20.1	48.1	26.0	135	33	0	40	0	80	0	0	6.8
Massachusetts Inst of Technology	4.21	4.07	0.08	28	79	86	93	9.5	8.6	73.5	12.0	55	24	39	33	14	85	14	0	7.0
Univ of California-Los Angeles	3.91	3.69	-0.03	73	56	71	89	11.2	2.7	86.9	3.5	46	46	27	28	9	79	33	0	7.8
Duke University	3.83	3.86	0.78	27	41	78	70	10.2	11.0	59.0	12.6	24	29	3	29	0	86	14	0	7.7
Case Western Reserve Univ	3.83	3.69	0.73	19	47	79	84	8.2	8.4	129.0	13.7	36	42	8	55	9	100	22	0	6.6
University of Michigan	3.79	3.75	0.15	60	43	82	97	11.7	2.6	87.2	4.1	24	46	21	29	5	81	30	5	6.6
Baylor College of Medicine	3.75	3.48	0.66	38	42	50	68	11.0	8.0	117.8	15.4	32	28	16	10	0	80	41	0	7.6
Brandeis University	3.75	3.88	0.26	12	83	92	92	17.2	11.5	189.7	16.7	35	54	33	14	33	57	14	14	7.6
University of California-Irvine [a]	3.72	3.72	-0.02	13	77	92	92	19.8	13.2	197.0	18.4	45	42	16	41*	4*	93*	19*	15*	6.2*
University of Chicago	3.63	3.60	-0.09	33	58	85	91	9.5	4.6	64.0	7.3	25	48	14	30	0	95	6	0	6.9
Northwestern University	3.60	3.59	0.46	81	54	69	90	7.9	2.3	57.7	3.3	52	42	21	44	3	95	40	7	6.9
Cornell University	3.59	3.74	0.04	30	63	90	90	8.0	5.5	42.7	7.3	35	37	20	24	6	86	11	32	8.4
University of Wisconsin-Madison	3.58	3.53	0.33	49	51	80	80	7.0	3.5	47.9	4.7	29	52	17	44	3	83	62	3	7.3
Mean Values for the Top Quarter	**4.15**	**4.03**	**0.31**	**45.72**	**59.28**	**77.96**	**88.16**	**11.97**	**6.20**	**136.51**	**9.98**	**44.42**	**40.59**	**18.68**	**30.76**	**4.24**	**85.16**	**23.24**	**5.12**	**7.34**
U of North Carolina-Chapel Hill	3.57	3.57	0.32	55	55	89	95	11.8	3.0	110.7	5.3	30	53	26	43	7	100	18	4	6.9
Albert Einstein College of Med	3.57	3.61	0.07	46	61	74	89	12.2	3.7	108.8	6.8	25	28	28	40	0	84	5	0	8.3

Institution	1993 Ratings[1] 93Q	93E	93C	Faculty Tot Fac[2]	% Full[2]	% Supp[2]	% Pub[5]	Pub/ Fac[5]	Gini Pub[5]	Cite/ Fac[5]	Gini Cite[5]	Students[2] Tot Stu	% Fem	Rpt PhDs	Doctorate Recipients[3] % Fem	% Min	% US	% RA	% TA	MYD
State U of New York-Stony Brook	3.54	3.41	-0.04	17	41	88	88	5.2	10.5	38.6	15.3	25	44	10	44	0	94	40	13	7.3
Vanderbilt University	3.49	3.44	0.37	39	62	62	82	6.5	5.4	39.5	7.7	0	0	n/a	50	0	100	50	0	5.4
University of Iowa	3.46	3.45	0.35	42	60	81	90	12.8	4.4	103.1	11.4	18	22	7	11	0	56	86	0	8.8
University of Virginia	3.46	3.45	0.29	43	47	86	86	12.6	3.8	99.7	4.7	22	41	17	27	4	88	36	4	7.5
University of Oregon	3.46	3.65	0.50	18	56	78	89	6.3	8.9	50.6	18.2	29	41	12	38	0	100	9	0	7.8
Emory University	3.45	3.46	0.58	60	45	72	92	7.7	3.0	40.9	4.9	32	47	8	29	0	86	17	17	6.7
University of Minnesota	3.43	3.37	0.48	36	56	69	89	8.6	5.1	56.5	8.3	35	46	1	14	0	100	33	17	8.6
Mayo Graduate School	3.42	3.27	0.31	50	44	0	88	14.5	3.7	95.3	5.4	10	20	0	n/a	n/a	n/a	n/a	n/a	n/a
University of Southern California	3.41	3.35	0.53	18	50	89	89	9.7	13.3	54.7	16.5	40	50	0	17	0	83	20	40	7.8
U of Texas-Southwestern Med Ctr	3.41	3.05	0.65	17	18	76	82	7.6	14.9	129.1	28.3	16	25	2	67	0	67	33	17	7.2
University of Colorado	3.40	3.33	0.17	31	58	87	90	12.4	5.6	106.9	6.9	17	59	0	18	10	91	36	27	6.8
University of California-Irvine [b]	3.38	3.41	-0.02	10	90	100	100	14.1	15.6	138.4	20.0	11	64	7	41*	4*	93*	19*	15*	6.2*
University of Pittsburgh [a]	3.36	3.33	0.40	15	27	80	93	11.7	13.4	72.5	17.6	28	57	10	46*	5*	92*	27*	13*	7.1*
U of Illinois at Urbana-Champaign	3.33	3.37	0.19	54	41	74	91	8.4	3.4	38.5	5.1	27	33	12	20	0	80	47	16	7.8
U of Texas, Medical Br-Galveston	3.31	3.43	0.09	39	62	72	87	11.0	4.9	70.7	6.2	25	24	12	25	0	83	64	0	8.7
University of Rochester	3.30	3.40	-0.28	60	38	82	97	8.2	2.3	49.0	3.8	30	33	17	37	4	90	11	4	7.2
University of Pittsburgh [b]	3.28	3.33	0.14	19	32	89	95	9.5	8.4	55.6	9.8	n/a	n/a	n/a	46*	5*	92*	27*	13*	7.1*
Colorado State University	3.25	3.47	0.71	13	38	85	77	4.7	30.2	52.3	73.4	11	9	5	29	0	71	20	20	11.7
Rutgers State Univ-New Brunswick	3.22	3.38	0.61	48	46	29	79	7.8	5.6	26.8	5.7	43	58	13	20	11	90	29	57	7.4
University of Arizona	3.20	3.21	0.75	28	43	71	89	6.0	6.8	30.4	10.3	16	75	0	17	0	83	0	0	11.7
University of Connecticut [a]	3.14	3.26	-0.02	13	62	23	92	7.6	11.1	38.7	15.7	6	50	7	50*	0*	88*	7*	27*	7.6*
University of Texas at Austin	3.08	3.25	0.19	50	66	68	92	8.8	3.3	38.6	3.9	n/a	n/a	64	78	0	100	13	75	7.4
Georgetown University	3.08	3.15	0.28	41	41	63	93	10.0	5.3	104.3	10.2	0	0	0	57	0	100	0	0	6.8
U of Tex-Health Sci Ctr-Houston	3.05	3.14	0.32	27	56	74	96	6.4	6.7	54.3	12.1	32	31	14	25	0	92	56	0	8.3
Mean Values for the 2nd Quarter	**3.35**	**3.37**	**0.31**	**34.19**	**49.81**	**71.58**	**89.62**	**9.31**	**7.78**	**69.40**	**12.83**	**22.00**	**37.92**	**11.33**	**35.56**	**2.00**	**88.12**	**28.12**	**15.16**	**7.76**
Medical College of Pensylvania	3.04	2.89	-0.06	19	47	63	79	3.8	9.7	22.9	17.3	17	41	11	100	0	100	0	25	6.8
University of Tennessee - Memphis	3.03	3.01	0.54	34	38	62	94	5.8	5.0	50.0	6.7	19	21	9	50	0	50	0	33	8.0
Brown University	2.98	3.38	0.03	14	29	79	100	5.8	9.4	41.9	17.2	n/a	n/a	n/a	36	0	91	14	71	7.4
Ohio State University	2.97	3.10	0.33	64	47	55	84	10.3	2.9	41.0	3.5	18	56	2	0	0	100	50	0	7.5

Appendix Table N - 5 Neurosciences (Continued)

Institution	1993 Ratings[1] 93Q	93E	93C	Faculty Tot Fac[2]	% Full[2]	% Supp[2]	% Pub[5]	Pub/ Fac[5]	Gini Pub[5]	Cite/ Fac[5]	Gini Cite[5]	Students[2] Tot Stu	% Fem	Rpt PhDs	Doctorate Recipients[3] % Fem	% Min	% US	% RA	% TA	MYD
New York University	2.96	3.33	0.21	23	48	65	91	6.6	6.4	28.7	8.6	11	9	0	36	14	100	8	17	9.0
Rutgers State Univ-Newark	2.93	3.06	0.72	24	25	50	67	4.2	9.2	18.7	15.7	28	36	0	80	20	100	25	0	6.8
University of Connecticut [b]	2.89	3.10	0.26	33	42	76	85	5.8	4.4	41.1	7.4	20	45	7	50*	0*	88*	7*	27*	7.6*
Tufts University	2.88	2.94	-0.12	11	18	91	100	11.1	16.6	92.2	15.1	12	58	4	50	0	100	75	0	6.7
University of Florida	2.84	3.04	-0.03	30	40	80	97	7.1	6.0	27.0	9.9	27	33	13	30	0	95	29	0	8.2
U of Massachusetts at Amherst	2.80	2.93	0.39	27	63	59	78	5.1	8.4	21.8	13.3	30	37	6	75	0	75	60	40	6.8
Wake Forest University	2.79	2.68	0.25	13	31	62	77	1.6	12.4	0.9	43.0	15	40	0	25	0	100	0	50	7.0
Florida State University	2.70	2.90	0.14	22	82	86	91	4.7	6.4	16.0	10.8	28	50	12	22	17	78	44	11	7.1
Hahnemann University	2.64	2.90	0.57	24	17	58	75	5.4	9.8	21.8	14.2	17	29	1	0	0	100	0	100	10.0
Michigan State University	2.64	2.70	-0.25	25	72	80	96	10.2	6.3	38.1	8.5	20	50	15	44	0	93	54	15	6.9
State Univ of New York-Buffalo [b]	2.51	2.89	-0.19	25	60	52	92	6.9	7.7	24.9	11.1	76	29	47	0*	0*	100*	100*	0*	9*
Pennsylvania State University	2.50	2.88	0.08	31	65	61	81	6.6	7.0	33.3	9.5	3	33	2	100	0	75	100	0	7.7
Wayne State University	2.47	2.58	0.35	40	55	70	95	9.7	3.7	47.3	4.8	15	40	0	0	0	67	100	0	12.7
SUNY-Health Science Ctr-Brooklyn	2.47	2.57	-0.05	27	44	63	70	4.1	7.5	22.2	13.1	10	50	4	20	20	100	0	100	8.7
CUNY - Grad Sch & Univ Center	2.43	2.58	0.18	31	61	48	71	5.8	8.7	34.4	11.5	16	56	4	31	10	77	9	0	8.3
Syracuse University	2.38	2.50	-0.07	10	60	100	100	6.3	10.7	28.1	12.1	14	21	3	33	0	100	100	0	8.0
Purdue University	2.31	2.50	-0.28	8	50	75	75	3.8	27.7	57.0	35.9	22	18	6	31	10	77	38	23	7.1
State Univ of New York-Buffalo [a]	2.24	2.78	0.00	26	42	73	85	4.2	6.6	24.2	11.5	48	29	26	0*	0*	100*	100*	0*	9*
Uniformed Services U of Hlth Sci	2.23	2.29	0.00	36	36	0	86	6.9	5.5	33.0	10.4	4	50	0	n/a	n/a	n/a	n/a	n/a	n/a
State Univ of New York-Albany	2.21	2.08	-0.52	7	29	57	86	4.0	22.7	18.7	45.8	8	38	3	25	0	25	33	33	6.8
University of Miami	2.14	2.31	-0.16	9	56	78	89	9.9	23.6	135.8	45.1	6	33	0	0	0	100	n/a	n/a	5.0
Mean Values for the 3rd Quarter	**2.64**	**2.80**	**0.09**	**24.52**	**46.28**	**65.72**	**85.76**	**6.23**	**9.77**	**36.84**	**16.08**	**20.17**	**37.58**	**7.29**	**34.92**	**3.79**	**87.13**	**41.13**	**23.70**	**7.84**
Albany Medical College	2.08	2.17	-0.43	19	53	74	100	9.1	7.6	38.5	12.2	21	52	6	50	0	100	25	25	9.0
University of New Mexico	2.08	1.67	0.00	16	31	75	81	4.2	13.0	15.1	16.3	2	0	5	n/a	n/a	n/a	n/a	n/a	n/a
Kent State University	2.03	2.00	0.07	28	39	14	75	5.8	9.8	24.3	13.4	19	47	15	33	0	72	38	38	8.0
George Washington University	2.00	2.92	0.13	10	60	80	40	5.0	44.5	33.1	48.9	2	100	0	n/a	n/a	n/a	n/a	n/a	n/a
Oregon State University	1.96	2.36	0.00	10	40	60	90	5.9	26.1	19.5	33.5	24	33	5	43	0	100	43	43	7.1
University of Oklahoma	1.93	1.81	0.00	37	38	32	78	6.6	6.7	18.1	9.5	18	83	11	n/a	n/a	n/a	n/a	n/a	n/a
University of Missouri-Columbia	1.92	1.67	0.31	12	58	100	92	7.3	17.6	35.0	24.3	7	71	7	33	0	33	29	29	10.6
Medical College of Ohio	1.86	1.95	0.67	33	55	42	85	6.4	7.5	22.2	11.9	3	0	0	50	0	50	0	0	7.0

Institution	1993 Ratings[1] 93Q	93E	93C	Faculty Tot Fac[2]	% Full[2]	% Supp[2]	% Pub[5]	Pub/ Fac[5]	Gini Pub[5]	Cite/ Fac[5]	Gini Cite[5]	Students[2] Tot Stu	% Fem	Rpt PhDs	Doctorate Recipients[3] % Fem	% Min	% US	% RA	% TA	MYD
Ohio University	1.77	2.14	0.25	10	0	60	70	3.4	16.2	15.7	21.8	6	50	3	0	n/a	0	0	100	8.5
University of Louisville	1.69	1.11	0.22	14	43	57	86	3.4	11.1	9.4	21.2	26	46	4	50	0	50	50	0	6.0
Louisiana State U & A&M College	1.47	1.67	0.33	27	41	30	93	6.4	6.8	18.6	14.4	14	71	3	0	0	100	0	100	8.0
Georgia State University	1.45	2.22	0.00	5	20	100	100	8.4	29.1	22.4	37.1	11	64	2	50	0	100	100	0	6.5
University of Wyoming	1.42	2.00	0.25	12	42	50	83	5.3	13.3	19.6	15.2	5	40	5	50	0	100	0	100	6.5
East Carolina U Sch Medicine	1.21	1.19	0.00	8	50	25	75	6.9	21.3	45.4	30.0	4	0	5	0	0	100	0	0	8.0
Loma Linda University	1.17	1.00	0.09	7	29	14	71	5.4	24.7	21.3	32.9	2	0	3	n/a	n/a	n/a	n/a	n/a	n/a
Montana State University	1.04	0.83	0.00	6	33	50	83	1.8	22.3	3.5	34.6	n/a	n/a	n/a	n/a	n/a	n/a	n/a	n/a	n/a
Kansas State University	0.91	1.19	0.00	7	43	29	29	1.6	50.4	2.3	88.2	3	33	2	29	0	29	86	0	5.8
Univ of California-Santa Cruz	0.89	1.00	-0.25	3	100	67	100	7.3	52.4	38.3	67.6	4	50	4	0	0	100	0	100	10.5
Univ of California-Santa Barbara	0.84	1.19	-0.33	3	33	100	100	9.7	56.4	56.7	55.9	n/a	n/a	n/a	50	0	100	0	100	7.6
Texas Woman's University	0.72	0.00	0.00	4	25	50	75	4.8	59.0	8.5	70.9	3	100	3	100	50	100	0	0	6.0
Clark University	0.72	1.17	-0.50	5	60	60	100	3.6	33.3	16.8	27.6	2	50	1	100	0	100	0	100	6.0
Boston University	0.67	0.56	-1.00	3	0	100	100	6.0	41.3	16.7	33.8	4	75	1	33	6	94	40	13	7.3
University of Idaho	0.59	0.00	n/s	2	100	100	100	3.0	55.5	15.0	100.0	1	0	0	n/a	n/a	n/a	n/a	n/a	n/a
Univ of Puerto Rico-Rio Piedras	0.58	0.24	-0.50	3	33	33	33	0.3	100.0	0.0		1	0	0	n/a	n/a	n/a	n/a	n/a	n/a
Northern Arizona University	0.48	0.00	0.00	2	50	100	100	6.5	52.6	10.0	58.0	2	0	0	n/a	n/a	n/a	n/a	n/a	n/a
Miami University	0.39	0.00	n/s	3	0	33	67	1.3	50.0	0.7	100.0	12	33	14	0	0	100	0	0	5.0
Mean Values for the 4th Quarter	**1.30**	**1.31**	**-0.03**	**11.12**	**41.38**	**59.04**	**81.00**	**5.21**	**31.87**	**20.26**	**39.17**	**8.17**	**41.58**	**4.13**	**37.28**	**3.29**	**79.33**	**22.83**	**41.56**	**7.41**
Mean Values for All Programs	**2.85**	**2.87**	**0.17**	**28.76**	**49.12**	**68.51**	**86.12**	**8.16**	**14.02**	**65.34**	**19.45**	**23.69**	**39.42**	**10.44**	**34.42**	**3.33**	**85.34**	**29.02**	**19.78**	**7.60**

Sources: 1. National Survey of Graduate Faculty
2. Institutional Coordinator Response Data
3. Doctorate Records File
4. Federal Agencies
5. Institute for Scientific Information

Notes: *a*. School of Arts and Sciences
b. School of Medicine

n/s After trimming no cases remained

* The Doctorate Recipient information cannot be separated for multiple programs at the same institution in the same field and therefore the total for the combined programs is given.

Appendix Table N - 6 Selected Characteristics of Research-Doctorate Programs in Pharmacology

Institution	1993 Ratings[1] 93Q	93E	93C	Faculty Tot Fac[2]	% Full[2]	% Supp[2]	% Pub[5]	Pub/ Fac[5]	Gini Pub[5]	Cite/ Fac[5]	Gini Cite[5]	Students[2] Tot Stu	% Fem	Rpt PhDs	Doctorate Recipients[3] % Fem	% Min	% US	% RA	% TA	MYD
Yale University	4.45	4.32	0.35	34	53	79	94	15.8	5.3	126.3	5.6	36	42	32	47	0	86	10	0	7.3
U of Texas-Southwestern Med Ctr	4.39	4.04	0.48	39	54	87	92	17.4	4.6	293.4	5.9	34	44	9	50	0	75	0	0	9.7
Univ of California-San Diego	4.36	3.87	0.56	31	84	77	97	26.5	6.3	348.5	12.5	24	50	22	42	9	96	42	0	6.9
Johns Hopkins University	4.21	4.22	0.46	35	63	77	94	16.0	7.5	322.1	21.5	34	56	27	24	0	90	3	0	6.4
Duke University	4.18	4.03	0.44	41	46	56	80	14.5	5.5	100.0	6.9	52	40	31	43	0	91	3	0	6.3
Vanderbilt University	4.17	4.15	0.56	35	49	51	89	12.8	7.5	110.7	7.5	20	35	23	35	0	84	18	0	5.8
Harvard University	4.14	4.00	0.39	42	43	57	100	16.4	4.3	216.7	5.2	58	43	32	38	0	94	0	0	7.7
U of North Carolina-Chapel Hill [a]	4.03	3.99	0.50	33	55	58	85	12.0	8.6	101.9	10.0	30	47	22	46*	2*	92*	41*	0*	7.1*
University of Washington	4.02	4.01	0.32	10	70	80	90	18.1	14.8	242.3	23.2	40	50	34	43	0	94	24	0	6.3
University of Pennsylvania	4.02	4.02	0.58	40	35	78	95	18.0	4.8	191.1	7.2	45	51	18	41	0	91	26	0	6.9
Massachusetts Inst of Technology	3.90	3.69	0.13	7	71	86	100	22.0	20.4	191.1	20.4	28	36	16	76	0	83	71	0	6.8
University of Wisconsin-Madison	3.89	3.93	0.21	57	67	68	96	12.4	2.8	68.2	3.7	41	49	27	31	6	87	54	0	6.7
University of Michigan [b]	3.85	3.82	0.17	23	65	96	96	15.1	6.5	123.7	10.0	36	44	25	31*	0*	90*	29*	0*	7.3*
New York University	3.84	3.75	0.30	158	45	65	91	9.8	1.3	123.4	2.2	100	43	107	43	0	81	30	5	7.9
Emory University	3.83	3.81	0.56	48	52	85	90	9.4	3.3	64.8	5.0	20	55	12	20	0	100	17	0	5.6
U of North Carolina-Chapel Hill [f]	3.82	4.14	0.58	52	29	31	90	15.8	4.2	100.4	5.0	31	45	25	46*	2*	92*	41*	0*	7.1*
Stanford University	3.81	3.75	0.00	12	50	100	100	22.5	10.6	330.0	13.8	20	55	16	47	0	100	14	0	6.9
University of Colorado	3.81	3.86	0.46	44	55	64	91	14.6	4.0	140.3	9.5	30	53	18	25	4	93	8	4	6.6
University of Rochester	3.79	3.81	0.56	49	51	80	94	12.6	3.1	71.4	4.2	42	43	34	38	0	100	27	0	7.3
University of Iowa	3.79	3.97	-0.03	22	64	68	82	15.9	11.2	100.1	13.3	24	67	29	27	13	78	15	0	7.0
University of Minnesota	3.76	3.61	0.50	22	50	86	100	11.5	6.9	60.0	15.1	31	48	27	32	0	76	35	6	8.3
University of Arizona	3.71	3.60	0.41	34	56	65	91	11.9	4.6	73.3	9.6	49	35	25	32	3	84	32	7	6.8
University of Kansas [b]	3.70	3.56	0.35	15	80	40	80	9.1	22.6	34.4	20.3	26	38	21	21*	3*	90*	18*	12*	6.7*
University of Virginia	3.65	3.61	-0.03	17	53	82	94	19.5	10.7	155.5	9.3	16	38	12	47	0	93	8	0	7.6
Columbia University	3.65	3.33	0.16	21	62	81	100	18.1	7.5	179.2	8.7	11	55	10	38	0	69	18	0	6.9
University of Chicago	3.64	3.53	0.14	28	54	75	93	9.6	5.7	85.5	7.3	35	49	16	44	0	100	25	0	6.9
State U of New York-Stony Brook	3.62	3.33	0.39	39	41	59	92	9.9	7.0	86.5	6.8	26	50	15	27	8	80	50	8	6.8
University of Texas at Austin	3.61	3.49	0.60	31	68	58	94	9.8	4.6	48.0	7.2	64	59	27	20	10	100	0	29	7.7
University of Michigan [a]	3.60	3.49	0.10	27	63	59	89	9.7	6.5	95.4	13.4	24	54	21	31*	0*	90*	29*	0*	7.3*
Albert Einstein College of Med	3.59	3.44	0.22	25	68	80	96	12.0	6.2	121.4	9.8	19	58	33	50	11	75	0	0	8.4

Appendix Table N - 6 Pharmacology (Continued)

Institution	1993 Ratings[1] 93Q	93E	93C	Faculty Tot Fac[2]	% Full[2]	% Supp[2]	% Pub[5]	Pub/ Fac[5]	Gini Pub[5]	Cite/ Fac[5]	Gini Cite[5]	Students[2] Tot Stu	% Fem	Rpt PhDs	Doctorate Recipients[3] % Fem	% Min	% US	% RA	% TA	MYD
University of Kentucky [a]	3.56	3.64	0.75	48	46	58	92	11.0	3.0	37.3	4.1	50	36	16	26*	9*	85*	46*	11*	6.9*
Mean Values for the Top Quarter	**3.88**	**3.80**	**0.36**	**36.10**	**56.19**	**70.52**	**92.48**	**14.51**	**7.16**	**140.09**	**9.81**	**35.35**	**47.35**	**25.23**	**37.45**	**2.58**	**88.35**	**23.68**	**2.65**	**7.09**
North Carolina State University	3.53	3.30	0.48	35	23	23	86	10.9	4.6	47.6	7.1	8	63	4	29	12	95	27	3	8.6
Mayo Graduate School	3.53	3.50	0.40	16	56	0	88	10.4	10.9	83.1	14.3	17	53	9	33	25	67	0	0	7.7
Georgetown University	3.52	3.64	0.34	21	76	48	100	14.6	9.5	158.5	17.9	20	35	14	45	6	80	8	0	6.9
University of California-Davis	3.51	3.75	0.30	42	55	48	90	15.1	4.4	51.1	5.8	50	54	29	25	0	86	48	0	7.0
Michigan State University	3.50	3.81	0.42	19	58	79	95	12.4	8.2	41.6	9.0	24	42	23	34	3	94	52	4	6.4
Rutgers State Univ-New Brunswick	3.49	3.69	0.76	54	65	31	87	13.8	3.9	54.4	5.0	21	57	8	40	0	96	41	5	7.8
U of Tex-Health Sci Ctr-Houston	3.47	3.47	0.20	35	60	83	91	12.2	8.2	99.6	7.8	17	35	6	23	6	82	48	0	6.6
University of Miami	3.42	3.11	0.24	18	44	72	78	6.7	11.4	54.3	24.6	20	50	11	35	8	75	23	0	8.4
Medical University South Carolina	3.41	3.39	0.55	23	48	57	87	8.3	10.8	55.6	14.5	15	27	6	8	9	92	33	11	8.0
Univ of California-Los Angeles	3.40	3.07	-0.04	19	58	53	95	18.4	9.7	183.4	10.7	20	50	8	79	0	93	42	0	7.4
University of Utah	3.37	3.49	0.23	25	56	64	84	8.8	7.5	38.5	10.1	32	41	29	52	0	83	28	0	5.8
SUNY-Health Science Ctr-Brooklyn	3.36	3.15	-0.09	13	38	62	62	4.1	16.4	23.2	26.0	11	18	2	0	n/a	0	n/a	n/a	5.0
Baylor College of Medicine	3.36	3.29	0.00	11	55	45	91	13.7	15.4	110.5	22.3	3	33	15	13	0	50	29	0	8.4
University of Pittsburgh	3.36	3.21	0.70	23	35	61	96	10.5	8.4	46.7	14.1	16	44	3	31	7	94	18	18	9.6
Oregon State University	3.36	3.39	0.30	40	52	38	73	7.4	6.4	32.3	9.8	92	32	47	42	0	83	15	8	8.9
University of Cincinnati	3.34	3.03	0.23	29	55	59	97	9.5	5.3	47.0	14.6	69	39	40	26	4	87	24	8	7.8
Saint Louis University	3.33	3.40	0.28	21	48	62	86	6.1	9.7	44.0	11.9	9	67	13	56	0	81	14	0	6.6
Cornell University [e]	3.33	3.46	0.30	33	61	42	97	14.3	5.2	53.9	9.0	33	42	17	44*	4*	96*	43*	4*	7*
West Virginia University	3.32	3.54	0.12	14	79	36	86	6.5	11.5	27.6	18.3	18	50	16	50	5	88	6	6	5.5
University of Florida	3.32	3.25	0.47	25	60	76	80	11.7	6.7	54.5	8.7	27	48	22	41	6	82	74	5	7.3
Thomas Jefferson University	3.30	3.21	0.32	29	52	38	93	5.1	6.5	17.9	9.9	14	50	14	30	0	100	6	19	7.7
Ohio State University	3.26	3.33	0.33	26	38	38	85	11.0	7.0	36.0	9.4	17	41	11	29	12	74	36	24	6.7
Medical College of Wisconsin	3.26	3.18	0.19	13	38	62	85	11.2	17.9	67.8	21.9	6	33	8	45	0	100	29	14	7.4
University of Tennessee - Memphis	3.25	3.23	0.11	29	55	38	97	7.8	6.8	40.0	10.2	12	42	4	40	0	100	0	33	6.8
Dartmouth College	3.24	3.33	0.25	14	57	64	86	7.5	10.1	32.0	13.4	27	48	9	45	10	91	11	0	9.7
Wake Forest University	3.20	3.33	0.31	15	33	53	60	1.3	22.4	3.0	87.3	10	40	8	43	0	100	40	20	6.7

Institution	1993 Ratings[1] 93Q	93E	93C	Faculty Tot Fac[2]	% Full[2]	% Supp[2]	% Pub[5]	Pub/ Fac[5]	Gini Pub[5]	Cite/ Fac[5]	Gini Cite[5]	Students[2] Tot Stu	% Fem	Rpt PhDs	Doctorate Recipients[3] % Fem	% Min	% US	% RA	% TA	MYD
University of Illinois at Chicago	3.18	3.33	0.00	14	57	71	86	6.8	10.6	47.4	22.0	26	50	27	40	11	80	14	34	7.8
Utah State University	3.18	3.33	0.30	18	50	39	100	9.2	10.7	36.5	16.5	28	36	11	20	0	86	27	0	10.0
Brown University	3.17	3.33	0.00	11	45	64	82	3.5	13.4	12.9	17.1	1	0	5	50	0	83	0	20	8.0
University of Vermont	3.17	3.40	0.06	12	50	67	75	9.7	14.4	142.7	23.6	9	33	2	50	0	100	100	0	14.5
Washington State University	3.16	3.16	0.54	40	45	53	78	7.4	5.7	36.8	16.5	29	52	19	21	10	88	67	10	5.9
Texas A&M University	3.16	3.27	0.43	21	62	57	95	16.5	12.7	66.1	16.4	38	47	18	43	5	73	50	5	6.0
Mean Values for the 2nd Quarter	**3.34**	**3.36**	**0.28**	**23.69**	**52.00**	**52.59**	**86.59**	**9.76**	**9.76**	**57.70**	**16.43**	**23.09**	**42.25**	**14.31**	**36.31**	**4.61**	**83.72**	**30.74**	**8.10**	**7.62**
Cornell University [d]	3.12	3.07	0.20	8	25	88	100	12.8	16.2	111.9	22.7	21	43	13	44*	4*	96*	43*	4*	7*
Univ of Maryland at Baltimore	3.12	3.10	-0.11	12	25	92	100	12.6	12.0	76.8	14.9	12	58	7	44	10	81	15	35	7.3
U of Texas, Medical Br-Galveston	3.12	3.21	0.11	18	67	67	83	11.2	10.5	75.2	13.9	18	39	13	40	7	70	50	6	7.7
University of Louisville	3.10	3.00	0.13	21	76	19	90	7.2	9.2	28.7	10.3	14	71	10	33	8	87	45	0	5.9
Medical College of Georgia	3.09	3.26	0.67	14	64	57	71	7.3	17.6	26.0	20.4	14	57	6	50	33	75	43	29	6.7
Uniformed Services U of Hlth Sci	3.08	3.13	-0.14	12	83	0	92	8.6	13.7	66.8	20.4	6	33	9	55	13	89	33	0	7.1
Temple University	3.08	2.87	0.00	16	69	50	100	7.0	9.7	40.5	18.3	19	42	14	17	0	90	15	15	8.4
U of Tex-Hlth Sci Ct-San Antonio	3.07	2.99	0.05	13	23	38	85	6.8	20.2	35.8	34.8	13	54	7	50	10	100	0	75	7.4
Wayne State University	3.06	3.06	0.28	24	38	50	88	6.2	9.2	36.5	13.4	18	50	13	18	7	88	30	40	8.2
Tufts University	3.06	3.27	0.24	12	50	75	92	23.6	19.7	158.8	21.2	3	0	0	n/a	n/a	n/a	n/a	n/a	n/a
University of Connecticut [b]	3.06	3.12	0.00	10	50	80	100	6.1	15.0	38.7	18.0	5	20	2	41*	4*	97*	35*	0*	6.9*
Pennsylvania State University	3.05	2.81	0.06	9	56	67	89	7.2	23.7	24.4	31.2	20	75	12	35	10	100	37	0	6.3
University of Alabama-Birmingham	3.04	3.05	0.19	34	38	74	97	11.4	4.5	70.1	6.2	33	42	8	29	11	64	9	0	7.5
University of California-Irvine	3.04	2.99	0.19	7	43	86	100	8.0	21.0	32.6	31.6	12	42	10	53	6	95	43	0	5.7
Albany Medical College	3.04	3.33	0.36	19	53	74	100	9.1	7.6	38.5	12.2	21	52	6	63	0	100	0	33	5.6
University of Kansas [a]	3.03	3.20	0.13	7	71	71	100	6.7	18.6	27.0	49.9	11	36	9	21*	3*	90*	18*	12*	6.7*
State Univ of New York-Buffalo	3.03	3.13	0.22	17	41	65	94	7.7	8.1	38.6	9.7	16	25	10	37	0	83	26	21	7.2
George Washington University	3.03	2.99	0.04	10	70	50	90	5.7	16.0	35.2	38.3	13	38	10	45	10	91	0	10	6.9
Tulane University	3.02	3.09	0.13	11	73	45	100	14.4	16.1	72.3	16.8	13	31	10	20	0	93	0	0	6.5
U of Massachusetts Med Center	3.00	3.33	0.40	25	52	48	80	8.1	6.9	50.9	12.2	7	57	4	33	0	100	33	0	6.0
Iowa State University	3.00	2.92	0.12	17	94	29	94	9.2	9.7	26.0	11.3	18	44	10	20	0	70	50	25	8.7

Appendix Table N - 6 Pharmacology (Continued)

Institution	1993 Ratings[1] 93Q	93E	93C	Faculty Tot Fac[2]	% Full[2]	% Supp[2]	% Pub[5]	Pub/ Fac[5]	Gini Pub[5]	Cite/ Fac[5]	Gini Cite[5]	Students[2] Tot Stu	% Fem	Rpt PhDs	Doctorate Recipients[3] % Fem	% Min	% US	% RA	% TA	MYD
SUNY Health Science Ctr-Syracuse	3.00	3.33	0.45	17	24	53	82	5.4	9.7	30.0	12.0	8	63	2	20	0	100	75	0	5.7
Medical College of Pensylvania	2.97	3.25	0.00	13	46	38	92	6.5	14.3	31.0	20.3	14	29	4	25	0	60	25	0	6.8
Case Western Reserve Univ	2.94	3.00	0.10	10	60	50	90	8.8	15.8	88.0	30.2	11	45	13	20	0	100	21	0	6.7
University of Georgia	2.92	3.13	0.20	16	6	19	75	6.8	11.6	24.1	14.1	17	59	8	29	0	65	33	17	8.3
New York Medical College	2.91	2.95	-0.08	11	27	45	100	11.5	14.9	79.9	21.0	15	47	12	29	0	87	30	0	6.8
Purdue University	2.89	3.10	0.00	10	70	30	80	8.2	17.2	19.5	17.3	14	43	16	29	0	80	20	25	6.1
University of Kentucky [b]	2.87	3.00	0.27	9	44	78	89	6.8	15.3	29.8	25.0	12	33	4	26*	9*	85*	46*	11*	6.9*
State Univ of New York-Albany	2.87	3.21	0.46	29	31	10	48	1.8	9.5	5.6	12.9	34	47	3	n/a	n/a	n/a	n/a	n/a	n/a
Loyola University of Chicago	2.85	2.94	0.21	9	56	56	89	9.6	20.2	52.4	26.1	12	50	10	44	0	100	0	0	7.8
University of Connecticut [c]	2.82	2.84	0.27	11	64	0	100	6.4	15.1	31.2	22.9	17	53	12	41*	4*	97*	35*	0*	6.9*
Univ of Med & Dent of NJ	2.79	3.18	0.00	11	55	45	73	5.8	17.9	20.5	30.1	19	37	8	36	14	73	0	13	6.3
Mean Values for the 3rd Quarter	**3.00**	**3.09**	**0.16**	**14.44**	**51.38**	**51.53**	**89.47**	**8.58**	**13.96**	**47.60**	**20.61**	**15.00**	**44.22**	**8.59**	**34.90**	**5.43**	**86.87**	**27.00**	**12.37**	**6.93**
Louisiana State U Medical Center	2.76	3.04	0.15	13	15	46	77	2.1	14.6	6.2	28.3	10	50	6	36	10	100	0	89	5.5
University of Oklahoma	2.76	3.22	0.10	25	56	24	76	6.1	9.0	11.2	11.1	24	46	9	33	14	78	0	22	8.8
Louisiana State U & A&M College	2.75	3.21	0.00	23	48	39	78	8.6	8.6	30.8	16.2	4	75	3	80	25	80	0	40	6.7
University of South Carolina	2.75	2.98	0.13	10	20	70	80	3.8	19.3	19.1	27.2	10	50	6	0	0	100	0	0	6.1
U of Mississippi-Medical Center	2.68	2.98	-0.39	10	40	60	90	12.8	20.8	35.9	18.9	17	47	16	25	0	56	40	0	9.7
East Carolina U Sch Medicine	2.58	2.67	0.31	11	55	55	91	8.5	15.1	29.7	16.4	7	71	8	20	0	89	13	13	5.7
University of Missouri-Columbia	2.57	2.88	0.00	13	38	85	92	7.5	11.0	52.0	14.0	13	23	7	25	0	88	17	0	6.0
Northeast Louisiana University	2.55	2.50	0.60	25	32	0	0	0.0		0.0		45	20	23	27	0	82	57	0	7.7
University of South Florida	2.50	2.57	0.43	8	50	25	50	1.9	27.1	12.3	46.9	n/a	n/a	5	17	17	100	0	0	6.6
Medical College of Ohio	2.48	2.36	0.00	12	42	50	92	7.2	12.3	47.1	12.1	38	34	15	53	11	59	7	0	8.0
University of Mississippi	2.47	2.67	-0.28	6	50	50	100	12.2	24.7	30.7	27.3	8	25	n/a	40	0	60	75	0	7.8
Louisiana St U-Sch Med Shreveport	2.47	2.50	-0.11	14	50	29	86	5.6	11.2	10.5	24.2	16	38	2	50	0	100	50	0	7.4
St. John's University	2.46	2.59	-0.25	11	36	9	91	4.0	18.6	10.8	57.3	41	41	45	26	10	96	0	20	10.9
University of Southern California	2.46	2.56	-0.54	10	50	10	70	3.7	18.9	6.7	31.1	1	0	3	55	0	82	17	0	9.8
Clemson University	2.40	2.67	0.00	8	38	0	63	1.3	22.0	2.3	100.0	22	23	0	n/a	n/a	n/a	n/a	n/a	n/a
University of Houston	2.38	2.54	-0.29	8	38	25	88	6.9	22.9	18.4	32.9	16	56	11	0	13	67	11	56	10.5
University of Hawaii at Manoa	2.35	2.92	-0.08	7	86	0	86	6.1	51.2	13.6	78.9	15	20	3	43	0	83	25	0	7.7

Institution	1993 Ratings[1]			Faculty								Students[2]			Doctorate Recipients[3]					
	93Q	93E	93C	Tot Fac[2]	% Full[2]	% Supp[2]	% Pub[5]	Pub/ Fac[5]	Gini Pub[5]	Cite/ Fac[5]	Gini Cite[5]	Tot Stu	% Fem	Rpt PhDs	% Fem	% Min	% US	% RA	% TA	MYD
Phila Col of Pharmacy & Science	2.33	2.26	-0.33	9	33	44	78	2.7	22.5	5.7	30.7	15	47	9	27	7	100	8	23	7.0
Loma Linda University	2.31	2.38	-0.09	9	67	11	67	5.9	29.4	11.4	28.4	7	43	3	33	0	100	0	0	7.7
Univ of Health Sc/Chicago Med Sch	2.23	2.08	0.22	9	33	44	89	3.2	22.9	5.1	41.2	10	80	3	0	0	100	n/a	n/a	5.8
Texas Tech University	2.23	2.40	-0.31	9	56	56	78	2.7	21.5	7.8	34.8	4	25	2	0	0	50	100	0	6.1
Kent State University	2.22	2.17	0.00	7	29	0	71	7.6	49.2	19.7	55.3	1	100	4	50	0	100	25	0	7.1
Southern Illinois University	2.16	2.44	0.08	8	75	63	75	8.5	17.7	49.5	19.4	8	63	14	18	11	82	0	0	8.5
Univ of California-Santa Barbara	2.13	3.00	0.33	3	67	67	100	10.7	41.9	52.7	43.5	n/a	n/a	n/a	25	0	100	0	0	6.4
Howard University	2.08	2.22	-0.67	6	33	0	50	1.7	38.0	2.0	43.0	3	67	5	29	83	86	20	0	7.4
University of South Dakota	2.00	2.62	0.00	11	18	36	73	2.3	18.4	5.0	27.6	4	50	3	0	0	50	100	0	5.0
Indiana University	1.89	1.82	0.00	5	20	40	60	5.2	35.7	16.0	40.4	4	100	5	18	0	100	13	0	7.8
Hahnemann University	1.80	1.84	-0.25	6	33	17	67	4.0	28.8	9.8	30.0	1	100	0	n/a	n/a	n/a	n/a	n/a	n/a
Univ of Puerto Rico-Rio Piedras	1.79	1.39	-0.20	8	13	38	50	2.4	32.4	4.1	32.9	6	83	1	n/a	n/a	n/a	n/a	n/a	n/a
Ohio University	1.63	2.38	0.00	3	0	33	67	1.3	62.5	1.0	100.0	5	60	0	n/a	n/a	n/a	n/a	n/a	n/a
University of Idaho	1.53	1.16	0.00	1	100	100	100	7.0	100.0	15.0	100.0	0	0	0	100	0	100	0	100	10.0
Univ of California-Santa Cruz	0.25	0.33	n/s	1	0	0	100	9.0	100.0	8.0	100.0	2	50	1	n/a	n/a	n/a	n/a	n/a	n/a
Mean Values for the 4th Quarter	**2.25**	**2.42**	**-0.05**	**9.66**	**41.28**	**35.19**	**76.09**	**5.39**	**29.94**	**17.19**	**40.97**	**11.90**	**49.57**	**7.07**	**30.74**	**7.44**	**84.74**	**22.23**	**13.96**	**7.54**
Mean Values for All Programs	**3.11**	**3.16**	**0.19**	**20.85**	**50.17**	**52.31**	**86.11**	**9.52**	**15.15**	**65.06**	**21.90**	**21.38**	**45.78**	**13.82**	**35.00**	**4.93**	**85.93**	**26.06**	**9.04**	**7.30**

Sources: 1. National Survey of Graduate Faculty
2. Institutional Coordinator Response Data
3. Doctorate Records File
4. Federal Agencies
5. Institute for Scientific Information

Notes: *a.* School of Arts and Sciences
b. School of Medicine
c. School of Pharmacology
d. School of Veterinary Medicine
e. School of Engineering
f. Interdisciplinary with the Schools of Medicine, Pharmacology, and Public Health

n/s After trimming no cases remained

* The Doctorate Recipient information cannot be separated for multiple programs at the same institution in the same field and therefore the total for the combined programs is given.

Appendix Table N - 7 Selected Characteristics of Research-Doctorate Programs in Physiology

Institution	1993 Ratings[1] 93Q	93E	93C	Faculty Tot Fac[2]	% Full[2]	% Supp[2]	% Pub[5]	Pub/ Fac[5]	Gini Pub[5]	Cite/ Fac[5]	Gini Cite[5]	Students[2] Tot Stu	% Fem	Rpt PhDs	Doctorate Recipients[3] % Fem	% Min	% US	% RA	% TA	MYD
Yale University	4.48	4.38	0.06	28	64	71	89	11.6	7.2	115.7	10.2	24	25	19	14	0	100	20	0	7.0
Univ of California-San Diego	4.47	4.25	0.61	55	69	76	91	17.8	4.6	178.7	7.9	12	50	15	33	5	95	38	0	6.5
University of Pennsylvania	4.27	3.95	0.16	36	92	83	100	14.0	5.0	128.6	10.6	10	50	8	33	0	90	5	0	7.6
Univ of California-Los Angeles	4.23	4.02	0.15	41	80	83	100	13.5	4.6	87.9	5.0	36	50	42	28	4	75	37	11	7.4
Univ of California-San Francisco	4.21	4.00	0.28	20	65	80	95	20.2	7.9	248.1	17.4	17	47	11	50	18	85	36	0	7.0
Baylor College of Medicine	4.21	3.84	0.57	34	62	76	88	19.1	5.5	207.0	7.9	20	50	8	75	0	75	0	0	14.7
University of Washington	4.20	4.10	-0.02	29	90	72	86	9.1	6.2	93.0	9.4	34	32	20	42	0	95	47	0	7.2
Stanford University	4.20	4.17	0.52	7	14	100	86	15.7	23.3	330.3	27.7	3	33	10	64	0	100	73	0	7.2
University of Virginia	4.19	3.83	0.35	23	48	70	96	11.8	6.4	126.1	9.0	17	65	9	33	0	87	0	0	7.6
Columbia University	4.19	3.83	0.20	21	62	71	95	13.6	7.9	196.2	11.0	18	39	8	17	0	50	50	0	5.7
University of Chicago	4.00	3.86	0.41	45	51	71	89	7.6	4.1	58.6	6.3	52	48	22	50	25	100	25	0	9.0
University of Iowa	3.99	3.81	0.42	23	48	74	87	11.3	10.2	179.2	20.1	28	29	18	8	0	88	33	0	7.9
California Institute Technology	3.98	3.70	-0.08	4	100	75	100	15.3	40.6	218.0	63.9	0	0	0	n/a	n/a	n/a	n/a	n/a	n/a
New York University	3.91	3.64	0.22	183	47	64	90	9.2	1.1	110.8	2.1	n/a	n/a	n/a	60	0	100	25	0	12.5
University of Michigan	3.89	3.65	0.11	30	57	83	90	15.5	4.9	104.5	6.8	24	46	19	50	0	84	20	5	6.6
Vanderbilt University	3.89	3.77	0.39	29	38	72	93	13.7	5.5	162.3	7.0	22	41	17	41	7	88	27	0	6.6
Albert Einstein College of Med	3.88	3.57	0.23	37	62	65	95	10.4	4.3	82.1	7.0	10	30	13	29	0	57	33	0	12.0
Mayo Graduate School	3.87	3.68	0.10	25	64	0	92	22.6	6.7	107.2	8.5	8	50	5	0	25	80	0	0	7.8
Johns Hopkins University	3.86	3.77	0.22	22	32	77	95	8.0	7.7	69.9	14.9	1	100	3	58	0	64	13	0	10.0
U of Illinois at Urbana-Champaign	3.81	3.92	0.36	51	61	76	84	9.5	3.9	59.5	5.3	53	38	83	32	0	73	38	26	7.6
University of Alabama-Birmingham	3.81	3.70	0.63	45	62	82	100	11.8	4.4	72.7	7.2	32	31	12	22	0	89	13	0	8.7
Emory University	3.71	3.49	0.67	48	52	79	83	8.9	3.5	62.6	5.3	20	55	9	40	0	50	20	10	6.7
U of Tex-Health Sci Ctr-Houston	3.69	3.57	0.36	30	60	67	100	11.5	6.8	69.2	12.5	12	8	10	22	0	67	57	0	8.4
University of Arizona	3.69	3.60	0.43	49	53	65	90	9.1	3.2	46.5	5.0	26	38	11	40	11	83	11	22	8.5
University of Wisconsin-Madison	3.68	3.64	0.43	67	54	67	93	11.3	3.2	58.5	6.0	89	42	43	35	0	82	25	44	8.0
Northwestern University	3.67	3.61	0.27	24	38	79	83	7.8	9.3	45.6	12.0	9	56	21	50	0	100	25	0	6.6
Duke University	3.67	3.49	-0.13	17	41	71	94	12.1	8.3	82.8	10.5	7	29	8	27	0	87	0	8	7.4
University of California-Davis	3.64	3.64	0.30	64	64	59	97	10.3	2.5	34.4	3.7	48	38	29	47	15	90	26	17	8.6
U of Massachusetts Med Center	3.63	3.44	0.39	37	38	59	84	8.9	5.5	62.8	7.6	7	29	8	60	0	100	75	0	6.8
Dartmouth College	3.61	3.56	0.23	27	59	63	70	5.4	8.4	43.9	14.2	17	24	5	42	0	83	20	0	10.2

Institution	1993 Ratings[1] 93Q	93E	93C	Faculty Tot Fac[2]	% Full[2]	% Supp[2]	% Pub[5]	Pub/ Fac[5]	Gini Pub[5]	Cite/ Fac[5]	Gini Cite[5]	Students[2] Tot Stu	% Fem	Rpt PhDs	Doctorate Recipients[3] % Fem	% Min	% US	% RA	% TA	MYD
Cornell University	3.59	3.76	0.22	35	60	66	91	11.4	5.2	54.0	5.9	20	50	17	45	0	73	33	33	8.4
Case Western Reserve Univ	3.55	3.56	0.62	27	26	48	78	8.5	7.3	58.0	9.1	43	30	5	0	0	80	60	0	6.1
U of North Carolina-Chapel Hill	3.55	3.45	0.21	22	64	100	95	9.5	6.5	106.8	18.4	21	52	15	38	8	81	79	0	8.3
U of Texas, Medical Br-Galveston	3.52	3.68	0.29	20	30	60	75	5.0	8.0	30.3	11.4	13	15	6	0	0	90	44	0	9.5
University of Texas at Austin	3.52	3.39	0.53	42	60	60	74	6.4	5.6	28.4	5.5	37	41	41	14	0	100	0	60	8.6
Mean Values for the Top Quarter	**3.89**	**3.75**	**0.31**	**37.06**	**56.20**	**70.40**	**89.94**	**11.64**	**7.29**	**106.29**	**11.21**	**23.24**	**40.03**	**16.76**	**35.26**	**3.47**	**83.56**	**29.65**	**6.94**	**8.20**
Rutgers State Univ-New Brunswick	3.47	3.33	0.50	48	46	29	79	7.8	5.6	26.8	5.7	n/a	n/a	n/a	50	0	88	15	38	7.9
Harvard University	3.45	3.52	-0.47	8	50	50	100	12.6	16.8	114.3	23.2	10	50	18	38	0	89	20	0	7.8
Pennsylvania State University [f]	3.45	3.39	0.50	44	48	36	93	7.5	3.6	30.4	6.2	56	34	22	31*	7*	96*	32*	11*	6.9*
State Univ of New York-Buffalo	3.40	3.40	-0.05	24	79	58	79	5.5	7.2	14.4	10.0	16	31	16	12	0	73	64	14	8.8
Colorado State University	3.38	3.62	0.46	16	50	63	100	15.3	10.7	87.5	18.1	24	58	21	32	4	96	25	8	8.5
U of Tex-Hlth Sci Ct-San Antonio	3.37	3.39	0.50	23	52	74	96	8.8	6.5	46.1	9.5	20	45	7	40	0	90	0	89	9.7
Ohio State University	3.37	3.33	0.37	36	47	53	86	11.4	6.3	41.3	6.3	15	47	10	56	11	79	39	11	8.2
University of Vermont	3.35	3.30	0.20	18	50	72	89	7.3	8.2	37.2	8.9	7	29	9	38	0	75	0	75	5.7
Albany Medical College	3.34	3.33	0.00	26	50	50	81	11.3	9.9	60.8	11.3	19	42	19	23	0	94	0	8	7.4
Univ of Maryland at Baltimore	3.33	3.38	0.13	16	69	81	100	12.2	9.3	125.8	14.9	18	44	10	69	0	77	46	0	7.8
Michigan State University	3.31	3.41	0.03	34	65	68	88	10.1	6.1	45.6	8.3	34	44	21	42	0	85	35	22	8.6
University of Tennessee - Memphis	3.31	3.47	0.57	20	60	55	75	9.8	13.9	48.3	17.8	9	56	4	50	40	83	0	75	6.1
University of Pittsburgh	3.31	3.60	-0.11	13	46	54	85	8.7	12.3	45.7	14.7	15	40	5	29	0	71	33	17	7.7
State U of New York-Stony Brook	3.28	3.50	0.29	18	50	72	83	7.6	9.6	49.0	18.8	20	45	13	50	0	50	63	13	7.5
Thomas Jefferson University	3.28	2.96	0.28	13	62	46	85	13.7	23.6	82.4	28.5	6	100	12	36	0	100	0	23	5.5
University of Rochester	3.28	3.33	-0.33	14	21	79	93	8.1	11.8	47.4	24.5	8	50	3	67	0	100	20	0	7.5
Medical College of Wisconsin	3.27	3.50	0.52	24	67	67	96	18.6	8.3	89.9	8.0	16	50	11	33	0	86	17	0	6.8
University of Miami	3.26	3.23	0.00	18	83	78	83	5.8	10.1	48.2	10.4	4	25	4	8	0	75	9	9	8.1
University of Southern California	3.25	3.28	0.10	27	52	59	81	10.4	10.1	45.4	14.0	16	31	12	45	0	75	100	0	7.4
Pennsylvania State University [c]	3.24	3.16	0.50	33	45	30	97	7.3	5.1	31.2	9.2	13	62	9	31*	7*	96*	32*	11*	6.9*
University of Connecticut	3.22	3.41	0.13	16	50	38	88	4.8	9.0	20.5	23.1	26	54	12	62	0	69	0	57	7.8
University of Kansas [b]	3.22	3.33	0.29	17	71	71	88	7.8	12.5	41.2	22.7	16	56	11	42*	8*	100*	0*	40*	10.3*

Appendix Table N - 7 Physiology (Continued)

Institution	1993 Ratings[1] 93Q	93E	93C	Faculty Tot Fac[2]	% Full[2]	% Supp[2]	% Pub[5]	Pub/ Fac[5]	Gini Pub[5]	Cite/ Fac[5]	Gini Cite[5]	Students[2] Tot Stu	% Fem	Rpt PhDs	Doctorate Recipients[3] % Fem	% Min	% US	% RA	% TA	MYD
University of Florida	3.21	3.49	0.17	22	73	68	100	16.6	7.3	73.4	10.5	17	24	13	41	0	77	35	6	7.9
Pennsylvania State University [e]	3.20	3.18	0.50	57	44	30	86	6.9	3.1	23.2	7.9	53	75	21	31*	7*	96*	32*	11*	6.9*
Georgetown University	3.19	3.33	-0.20	20	40	45	80	9.0	9.7	66.0	12.2	15	47	15	33	17	87	0	0	9.4
Saint Louis University	3.19	3.27	0.36	21	48	62	86	6.1	9.7	44.0	11.9	4	25	7	33	0	78	14	0	7.8
University of Cincinnati	3.17	3.18	0.00	9	67	100	100	12.6	33.2	55.7	33.5	21	48	18	26	6	100	15	0	8.1
SUNY-Health Science Ctr-Brooklyn	3.17	3.04	-0.15	21	57	48	90	9.4	8.7	44.5	13.2	13	15	1	n/a	n/a	n/a	n/a	n/a	n/a
University of Illinois at Chicago	3.15	3.18	0.21	21	52	76	86	6.6	9.7	39.5	11.5	27	44	13	63	5	88	35	30	7.6
Arizona State University	3.13	3.33	0.50	16	69	69	94	5.8	8.7	16.9	11.8	14	57	15	33	0	100	33	33	14.7
Tufts University	3.10	3.23	0.07	9	44	78	89	7.7	16.7	114.8	14.8	22	55	6	40	0	100	50	0	8.7
Wake Forest University	3.10	3.25	0.65	19	42	53	63	1.4	22.9	2.0	46.3	6	17	7	13	0	100	57	14	6.8
University of California-Irvine	3.05	2.97	0.00	10	60	90	90	11.5	13.9	103.4	14.5	13	8	7	33	15	93	31	38	7.8
University of Missouri-Columbia	3.02	3.22	0.31	24	46	71	88	8.1	6.9	30.3	9.3	24	33	27	35	0	74	12	24	8.9
Brown University	3.02	3.33	0.29	15	53	67	93	7.4	8.4	36.3	10.1	9	33	6	67	0	100	20	40	9.5
Mean Values for the 2nd Quarter	**3.25**	**3.32**	**0.20**	**22.00**	**54.51**	**61.14**	**88.29**	**9.19**	**10.73**	**52.27**	**14.90**	**17.82**	**43.35**	**11.91**	**39.18**	**3.74**	**86.47**	**26.00**	**21.09**	**8.03**
Louisiana St U-Sch Med Shreveport	3.00	2.92	0.78	8	50	88	100	24.5	23.1	239.4	34.8	11	36	5	40	0	60	0	0	6.7
North Carolina State University	3.00	3.33	0.83	30	50	33	80	8.2	5.8	21.5	7.9	28	50	19	15	0	80	67	0	7.8
University of Kentucky	3.00	3.23	0.46	25	68	52	88	4.7	6.3	12.3	10.4	18	44	13	38	0	82	43	14	7.6
University of Minnesota	3.00	3.14	0.25	24	46	63	75	5.3	7.0	21.3	11.1	16	38	15	26	0	79	57	11	8.7
Tulane University	2.97	2.98	0.50	10	20	40	80	7.1	17.3	33.1	20.9	13	23	2	50	0	100	0	0	6.6
Uniformed Services U of Hlth Sci	2.96	3.10	-0.09	23	35	0	91	7.0	6.7	24.7	7.9	9	56	12	67	0	94	9	18	8.7
Boston University	2.96	3.10	0.00	9	67	89	100	15.4	20.0	93.4	37.2	19	74	12	41	0	91	39	6	7.9
University of Louisville	2.94	3.10	0.15	17	41	41	88	7.7	10.8	24.6	12.6	21	57	10	33	0	100	14	0	6.8
Washington State University	2.92	3.14	0.38	18	61	61	83	8.9	9.9	37.3	11.9	3	0	3	20	0	90	44	11	6.4
Temple University	2.90	3.21	0.11	19	37	47	74	8.1	15.1	48.7	21.2	11	55	16	32	0	100	27	0	6.8
SUNY Health Science Ctr-Syracuse	2.90	3.04	0.08	23	39	52	74	3.7	9.2	17.5	11.5	2	0	6	22	0	67	71	0	11.7
Oregon State University	2.90	3.15	0.67	29	48	38	86	6.1	6.1	14.0	10.5	32	34	32	0	0	100	0	0	11.0
Louisiana State U Medical Center	2.87	2.78	-0.07	26	46	50	88	8.5	9.6	32.6	13.7	10	30	12	39	7	78	13	33	8.4
University of Oklahoma	2.83	2.56	0.11	15	40	40	87	4.3	13.1	12.2	19.4	3	100	3	33	0	83	0	67	7.6

Institution	1993 Ratings[1] 93Q	93E	93C	Faculty Tot Fac[2]	% Full[2]	% Supp[2]	% Pub[5]	Pub/ Fac[5]	Gini Pub[5]	Cite/ Fac[5]	Gini Cite[5]	Students[2] Tot Stu	% Fem	Rpt PhDs	Doctorate Recipients[3] % Fem	% Min	% US	% RA	% TA	MYD
West Virginia University	2.80	3.10	-0.06	21	52	52	76	6.0	9.4	22.5	11.3	8	38	8	41	8	71	25	33	7.4
University of Georgia	2.80	3.01	0.45	15	47	33	87	8.5	10.9	23.7	17.4	24	58	16	55	10	91	33	0	10.8
Wayne State University	2.76	2.94	0.27	23	57	57	87	12.3	7.8	49.0	11.4	33	42	21	32	9	71	21	57	8.1
Florida State University	2.75	3.33	0.00	17	65	71	82	3.9	9.4	10.2	13.1	19	47	7	50	50	100	0	0	5.0
University of Hawaii at Manoa	2.75	3.13	0.00	12	58	17	58	3.4	19.4	10.3	19.9	13	46	14	27	0	85	55	0	9.4
Loyola University of Chicago	2.73	3.26	0.00	7	43	57	100	8.9	18.4	32.0	23.5	8	38	7	80	0	80	30	10	9.4
University of Colorado	2.73	3.13	0.17	9	44	89	78	5.4	19.6	29.6	21.7	7	43	2	17	0	100	25	50	7.6
New York Medical College	2.72	2.92	-0.14	12	42	58	75	9.1	14.1	58.1	17.7	12	25	6	14	17	86	60	0	6.6
Iowa State University	2.72	3.06	0.20	15	80	47	87	7.2	17.4	29.4	51.1	20	30	5	0	0	75	22	22	8.8
Medical College of Georgia	2.71	2.58	0.00	25	40	40	80	7.3	13.3	19.6	28.9	13	54	18	13	17	88	14	57	7.4
Louisiana State U & A&M College	2.70	3.11	0.33	49	55	27	90	7.8	4.5	18.6	10.1	39	33	26	8	0	75	25	42	9.7
Kent State University	2.62	2.78	0.38	24	33	17	88	4.0	6.9	11.4	8.4	11	55	13	36	0	82	0	86	12.4
Hahnemann University	2.58	2.50	0.14	11	27	64	82	4.7	15.6	21.2	25.5	6	67	1	50	0	100	0	0	9.5
Univ of Health Sc/Chicago Med Sch	2.56	2.57	-0.11	9	67	89	89	4.2	24.3	16.2	39.1	12	33	6	25	25	100	0	0	7.0
University of North Texas	2.55	3.00	0.17	36	19	17	42	2.1	12.9	5.1	17.7	43	37	28	0	0	100	25	0	7.7
Kansas State University	2.50	2.95	0.27	17	53	29	41	4.2	27.3	9.0	50.3	5	40	3	33	0	83	50	25	9.7
University of Kansas [a]	2.50	3.33	0.00	9	78	33	78	2.8	23.8	6.0	29.6	8	50	1	42*	8*	100*	0*	40*	10.3*
University of Alaska	2.43	3.33	0.00	6	33	50	83	4.3	32.8	8.0	34.9	n/a	n/a	n/a	0	0	100	n/a	n/a	14.5
Loma Linda University	2.42	2.80	0.00	17	53	47	76	8.4	12.0	52.0	35.5	15	20	5	57	0	100	33	0	8.0
Texas Tech University	2.40	2.59	0.00	13	54	38	77	3.8	13.7	10.5	19.9	11	55	3	17	0	83	40	20	11.7
Auburn University	2.38	3.33	0.00	12	50	25	67	7.1	19.7	16.9	38.4	8	25	6	43	0	71	50	17	7.8
Mean Values for the 3rd Quarter	**2.75**	**3.02**	**0.18**	**18.14**	**48.51**	**47.17**	**80.49**	**7.00**	**14.09**	**31.20**	**21.61**	**15.03**	**42.14**	**10.47**	**31.31**	**4.31**	**87.00**	**26.24**	**18.21**	**8.61**
Medical College of Pensylvania	2.36	2.83	0.36	7	57	29	57	4.0	34.4	34.9	39.0	2	50	3	33	0	100	0	0	8.0
University of Wyoming	2.36	2.88	0.14	11	55	27	91	7.7	18.1	34.1	28.7	16	31	9	0	0	67	0	67	9.4
University of South Carolina	2.35	2.58	0.00	8	50	38	100	5.4	15.5	18.1	20.0	6	33	5	14	0	57	83	0	8.7
Texas A&M University	2.32	2.78	0.00	12	67	17	83	6.8	14.7	9.4	22.1	15	33	12	31	0	86	20	20	8.7

Appendix Table N - 7 Physiology (Continued)

Institution	1993 Ratings[1] 93Q	93E	93C	Faculty Tot Fac[2]	% Full[2]	% Supp[2]	% Pub[5]	Pub/ Fac[5]	Gini Pub[5]	Cite/ Fac[5]	Gini Cite[5]	Students[2] Tot Stu	% Fem	Rpt PhDs	Doctorate Recipients[3] % Fem	% Min	% US	% RA	% TA	MYD
University of New Mexico	2.27	2.71	0.00	11	45	55	100	5.3	13.7	10.4	23.5	4	50	5	14	0	100	33	17	8.4
Univ of Med & Dent of NJ	2.20	2.17	-0.33	8	50	50	100	6.4	20.7	27.6	17.1	9	22	9	46	0	77	9	0	8.4
Clemson University	2.15	2.62	0.00	13	77	31	85	6.8	12.6	14.3	15.7	4	50	9	43	29	100	71	0	7.8
Oklahoma State University	2.10	2.33	0.00	9	56	11	78	7.1	20.6	8.4	24.8	10	50	6	33	0	100	0	40	8.8
Howard University	2.00	2.17	0.00	10	60	0	80	3.5	18.6	4.4	37.8	14	50	13	38	89	69	13	13	8.8
University of Notre Dame	1.93	2.67	0.00	5	60	80	100	9.8	25.0	33.4	28.9	11	45	4	75	0	75	0	100	7.6
Virginia Polytech Inst & State U [c]	1.85	2.22	0.00	6	67	17	83	8.3	22.8	10.8	40.3	6	50	3	0*	0*	100*	50*	0*	9*
Univ of Puerto Rico-Rio Piedras	1.85	1.67	n/s	13	23	8	54	0.6	15.6	1.4	23.4	1	100	5	n/a	n/a	n/a	n/a	n/a	n/a
East Carolina U Sch Medicine	1.82	2.36	0.11	9	44	22	67	4.3	21.7	16.4	35.7	5	40	7	43	0	71	20	0	8.4
Ohio University	1.80	n/s	n/s	10	30	10	80	3.0	16.8	6.3	18.3	6	33	6	0	0	100	0	100	10.0
Illinois State University	1.78	3.33	0.00	9	78	44	78	2.8	24.1	4.7	44.1	n/a	n/a	n/a	0	0	100	0	0	6.0
Univ of California-Santa Cruz	1.69	2.50	0.00	5	80	80	100	9.2	27.9	58.8	29.0	13	46	13	0	0	100	0	0	7.5
Northern Arizona University	1.67	2.29	0.20	8	13	38	63	1.6	23.0	3.3	40.8	0	0	1	n/a	n/a	n/a	n/a	n/a	n/a
Virginia Polytech Inst & State U [a]	1.63	3.33	n/s	10	50	10	80	4.9	17.7	13.5	24.6	6	50	5	0*	0*	100*	50*	0*	9*
University of Houston	1.59	1.67	-0.60	4	50	25	50	2.5	58.0	1.8	59.1	1	0	3	0	50	67	0	67	6.7
Medical College of Ohio	1.56	1.91	-0.17	7	43	29	86	5.7	21.6	20.0	23.3	7	14	7	40	14	78	0	0	7.4
Virginia Polytech Inst & State U	1.56	1.67	0.00	11	45	55	91	10.7	12.1	17.9	13.5	52	62	12	0*	0*	100*	50*	0*	9*
State Univ of New York-Binghamton	1.50	3.33	n/s	5	40	20	60	5.8	52.6	13.0	73.9	6	33	3	n/a	n/a	n/a	n/a	n/a	n/a
Univ of California-Riverside	1.50	1.67	n/s	6	67	50	83	5.7	22.6	15.2	26.4	6	33	5	0	0	100	100	0	9.5
Bowling Green State University	1.50	2.50	n/s	6	67	33	83	2.8	24.5	3.7	51.6	2	0	3	0	0	100	0	100	8.0
Indiana University	1.47	2.00	-0.75	5	60	20	100	3.6	29.0	7.6	80.4	5	20	9	38	4	86	33	33	7.9
University of South Dakota	1.45	1.67	n/s	11	18	36	73	2.3	18.4	5.0	27.6	4	50	3	0	0	50	100	0	6.0
University of Nebraska-Lincoln	1.38	1.67	0.00	6	100	50	100	4.8	21.9	6.7	38.2	0	0	0	30	0	80	33	11	8.6
Utah State University	1.33	n/s	n/s	6	50	67	83	5.7	24.2	26.7	27.6	0	0	4	0	0	80	0	25	9.0
Miami University	1.18	1.91	0.00	6	67	50	83	5.5	33.7	18.2	48.4	12	33	14	25	0	75	0	100	7.0
Montana State University	0.91	1.67	0.00	8	50	13	50	2.1	40.4	3.5	50.5	n/a	n/a	n/a	n/a	n/a	n/a	n/a	n/a	n/a
North Dakota State University	0.88	1.11	0.00	4	75	25	75	4.3	54.3	16.8	85.9	1	100	2	n/a	n/a	n/a	n/a	n/a	n/a
Univ of California-Santa Barbara	0.80	1.67	n/s	3	33	100	67	8.0	78.1	45.7	80.4	n/a	n/a	n/a	80	0	80	67	33	7.7

Institution	1993 Ratings[1] 93Q	93E	93C	Faculty Tot Fac[2]	% Full[2]	% Supp[2]	% Pub[5]	Pub/ Fac[5]	Gini Pub[5]	Cite/ Fac[5]	Gini Cite[5]	Students[2] Tot Stu	% Fem	Rpt PhDs	Doctorate Recipients[3] % Fem	% Min	% US	% RA	% TA	MYD
University of New Hampshire	0.67	n/s	n/s	5	60	20	60	3.6	46.2	11.8	55.1	n/a	n/a	n/a	100	0	100	100	0	6.0
University of Idaho	0.42	0.00	n/s	2	50	50	100	5.0	52.0	5.0	68.0	1	0	2	0	0	100	50	0	10.4
Univ of Southern Mississippi	0.38	0.83	n/s	6	67	67	50	1.7	46.0	2.7	57.0	n/a	n/a	1	0	0	100	0	0	8.0
Mean Values for the 4th Quarter	**1.61**	**2.15**	**-0.05**	**7.57**	**54.40**	**36.49**	**79.23**	**5.07**	**28.55**	**15.19**	**39.45**	**7.50**	**35.93**	**5.90**	**22.77**	**6.20**	**86.60**	**29.40**	**24.20**	**8.19**
Mean Values for All Programs	**2.87**	**3.08**	**0.18**	**21.29**	**53.43**	**53.55**	**84.37**	**8.11**	**15.11**	**49.88**	**21.70**	**16.19**	**40.53**	**11.43**	**32.35**	**4.41**	**86.09**	**27.98**	**17.54**	**8.27**

Sources: 1. National Survey of Graduate Faculty
2. Institutional Coordinator Response Data
3. Doctorate Records File
4. Federal Agencies
5. Institute for Scientific Information

Notes: *a.* School of Arts and Sciences
b. School of Medicine
c. School of Agriculture
d. School of Veterinary Medicine
e. Interdisciplinary with the Schools of Agriculture and Arts and Sciences
f. Interdisciplinary with the Schools of Agriculture, Arts and Sciences, and Medicine

n/s After trimming no cases remained

* The Doctorate Recipient information cannot be separated for multiple programs at the same institution in the same field and therefore the total for the combined programs is given.

APPENDIX O

Correlation Tables for Selected Characteristics of Research-Doctorate Programs

The following tables give the intercorrelations between the selected characteristics of programs provided in Appendixes J-N. The mean (Mean) for the measures and their standard deviations (S.D.) are given on the first two lines of the tables. The number of observations (No.) used in computing the means, standard deviations, and correlations are given on line three. The correlations are the Pearson product-moment correlations.

Appendix Table O - 1 Correlation Table for Selected Characteristics of Programs in Aerospace Engineering

	1993 Ratings			Faculty								Students			Doctorate Recipients					
	93Q	93E	93C	Tot Fac	% Full	% Supp	% Pub	Pub/ Fac	Gini Pub	Cite/ Fac	Gini Cite	Tot Stu	% Fem Stu	Rpt PhDs	% Fem	% Min	% US	% RA	% TA	MYD
Mean	3.19	3.16	0.10	18.73	0.56	51.07	72.24	4.05	15.79	7.58	28.16	57.42	7.56	28.06	3.60	5.03	55.73	51.45	9.34	8.05
S. D.	0.77	0.68	0.19	7.28	0.18	20.49	14.93	1.83	9.24	6.97	15.08	49.80	4.87	25.20	6.12	9.42	22.66	23.48	14.56	1.56
No.	33	33	33	33	33	33	33	33	33	33	33	33	33	33	33	33	33	33	33	33
93Q	1.00	0.98	0.24	0.41	0.47	0.54	0.54	0.62	-0.58	0.62	-0.53	0.53	-0.14	0.69	0.08	-0.29	-0.17	0.55	-0.15	-0.54
93E		1.00	0.24	0.39	0.42	0.56	0.59	0.60	-0.62	0.56	-0.54	0.49	-0.18	0.64	0.04	-0.23	-0.23	0.56	-0.10	-0.63
93C			1.00	0.65	-0.09	0.13	0.15	0.29	-0.52	0.10	-0.44	0.44	-0.09	0.32	-0.14	-0.16	-0.16	-0.10	-0.01	-0.19
Tot Fac				1.00	0.13	0.05	-0.04	0.19	-0.65	0.04	-0.57	0.49	-0.22	0.52	0.18	-0.06	-0.12	0.22	-0.17	-0.10
% Full					1.00	0.19	0.30	0.33	-0.46	0.54	-0.48	0.07	-0.13	0.06	0.21	-0.13	-0.14	0.49	-0.20	-0.19
% Supp						1.00	0.63	0.52	-0.33	0.49	-0.48	0.34	0.12	0.30	0.05	-0.34	-0.31	0.45	-0.05	-0.43
% Pub							1.00	0.65	-0.44	0.50	-0.33	0.19	-0.06	0.28	-0.07	0.05	-0.35	0.33	0.30	-0.70
Pub/Fac								1.00	-0.42	0.63	-0.45	0.38	-0.21	0.52	-0.01	-0.01	-0.11	0.19	-0.12	-0.43
Gini-Pub									1.00	-0.21	0.76	-0.41	0.19	-0.37	-0.16	0.05	0.37	-0.50	0.04	0.48
Cite/Fac										1.00	-0.18	0.21	-0.06	0.20	0.11	-0.20	-0.21	0.32	-0.05	-0.30
Gini-Cite											1.00	-0.41	0.00	-0.39	-0.11	0.19	0.13	-0.45	0.38	0.28
Tot Stu												1.00	0.16	0.72	0.17	-0.25	-0.10	0.15	-0.24	-0.20
% Fem Stu													1.00	0.00	0.15	-0.53	0.10	-0.07	-0.17	0.21
Rpt PhDs														1.00	0.07	-0.15	-0.14	0.23	-0.16	-0.30
% Fem															1.00	-0.20	-0.12	0.10	-0.15	0.06
% Min																1.00	-0.08	-0.16	0.26	-0.09
% Citz																	1.00	-0.25	-0.45	0.33
% RA																		1.00	-0.23	-0.49
% TA																			1.00	-0.17
MYD																				1.00

Note: The data from which these correlations are produced are given in Appendix Table K - 1.

Appendix Table O - 2 Correlation Table for Selected Characteristics of Programs in Anthropology

	1993 Ratings			Faculty								Students			Doctorate Recipients					
	93Q	93E	93C	Tot Fac	% Full	% Supp	% Pub	Pub/ Fac	Gini Pub	Cite/ Fac	Gini Cite	Tot Stu	% Fem Stu	Rpt PhDs	% Fem	% Min	% US	% RA	% TA	MYD
Mean	2.99	2.86	0.08	19.75	0.51	24.52	54.69	1.54	17.77	3.99	40.01	63.93	59.37	22.59	51.52	6.13	91.18	5.58	18.36	11.51
S. D.	0.73	0.64	0.25	8.40	0.16	13.80	16.02	0.89	9.78	4.38	24.41	42.08	15.01	17.29	14.47	6.70	7.30	7.81	17.04	1.76
No.	69	69	69	69	69	69	69	69	69	69	69	69	69	69	69	69	69	69	69	69
93Q	1.00	0.95	0.38	0.70	0.56	0.43	0.34	0.38	-0.58	0.32	-0.42	0.64	-0.19	0.64	0.02	0.15	-0.12	0.08	-0.01	-0.38
93E		1.00	0.34	0.63	0.55	0.43	0.28	0.34	-0.47	0.28	-0.41	0.59	-0.24	0.64	0.02	0.14	-0.17	0.13	-0.01	-0.40
93C			1.00	0.40	0.09	0.14	0.21	0.25	-0.36	0.14	-0.39	0.16	-0.18	-0.01	-0.22	-0.04	0.02	0.19	0.19	-0.24
Tot Fac				1.00	0.22	0.23	0.22	0.35	-0.67	0.30	-0.53	0.64	-0.15	0.63	-0.04	-0.04	-0.15	0.19	0.08	-0.16
% Full					1.00	0.13	0.22	0.15	-0.25	0.06	-0.26	0.38	-0.11	0.37	0.08	0.24	-0.15	0.02	-0.15	-0.15
% Supp						1.00	0.45	0.52	-0.37	0.50	-0.13	0.32	0.08	0.23	0.00	-0.02	0.04	0.09	-0.03	-0.12
% Pub							1.00	0.77	-0.58	0.60	-0.51	0.16	-0.01	0.13	0.06	0.14	0.06	0.06	0.17	-0.04
Pub/Fac								1.00	-0.44	0.84	-0.59	0.24	-0.01	0.23	-0.07	0.07	-0.03	0.04	0.25	-0.14
Gini-Pub									1.00	-0.35	0.60	-0.43	0.03	-0.42	-0.13	0.01	0.08	-0.23	-0.11	0.01
Cite/Fac										1.00	-0.37	0.22	-0.04	0.25	-0.05	0.00	0.07	0.00	0.14	-0.15
Gini-Cite											1.00	-0.33	0.06	-0.34	-0.06	-0.15	0.05	-0.18	-0.17	0.10
Tot Stu												1.00	-0.20	0.64	-0.08	0.07	-0.07	0.01	-0.04	-0.08
% Fem Stu													1.00	-0.18	0.28	0.05	0.06	-0.20	0.01	0.13
Rpt PhDs														1.00	0.00	0.14	-0.15	-0.02	-0.09	-0.15
% Fem															1.00	0.27	-0.06	-0.13	-0.04	0.24
% Min																1.00	0.12	-0.13	-0.12	-0.08
% Citz																	1.00	-0.12	-0.19	-0.04
% RA																		1.00	0.00	-0.11
% TA																			1.00	-0.14
MYD																				1.00

Note: The data from which these correlations are produced are given in Appendix Table M - 1.

Appendix Table O - 3 Correlation Table for Selected Characteristics of Programs in Art History

	1993 Ratings			Faculty					Students			Doctorate Recipients					
	93Q	93E	93C	Tot Fac	% Full	% Supp	No. Awd	Awd Fac	Tot Stu	% Fem Stu	Rpt PhDs	% Fem	% Min	% US	% RA	% TA	MYD
Mean	3.15	3.01	0.04	14.39	0.52	0.94	4.00	0.24	48.76	72.81	18.24	68.62	3.41	93.30	2.08	18.07	12.71
S. D.	0.88	0.79	0.24	6.09	0.18	2.81	3.36	0.18	46.05	10.06	14.12	14.40	4.95	7.12	3.97	18.18	2.14
No.	38	38	38	38	38	38	38	38	38	38	38	38	38	38	38	38	38
93Q	1.00	0.97	0.28	0.59	0.67	-0.14	0.64	0.32	0.48	-0.33	0.77	-0.08	-0.02	-0.20	-0.03	-0.22	-0.29
93E		1.00	0.21	0.54	0.68	-0.16	0.58	0.27	0.48	-0.35	0.73	-0.03	-0.10	-0.18	0.06	-0.23	-0.35
93C			1.00	0.42	0.02	0.17	0.40	0.12	0.08	-0.01	0.11	-0.05	0.16	0.15	0.06	0.10	0.17
Tot Fac				1.00	0.11	-0.18	0.50	-0.12	0.53	-0.19	0.71	0.10	0.09	0.19	-0.15	-0.14	0.17
% Full					1.00	-0.11	0.43	0.39	0.30	-0.23	0.44	0.10	-0.16	-0.15	0.09	-0.20	-0.31
% Supp						1.00	0.07	0.17	-0.18	0.01	-0.20	-0.20	0.01	0.14	0.14	0.36	-0.17
No. Awd							1.00	0.72	0.49	-0.08	0.62	-0.19	-0.01	-0.01	0.07	-0.19	-0.09
Awd Fac								1.00	0.08	-0.07	0.17	-0.37	-0.13	-0.24	0.16	-0.15	-0.35
Tot Stu									1.00	-0.02	0.51	-0.08	0.06	0.03	-0.08	-0.22	0.04
% Fem Stu										1.00	-0.17	0.20	0.18	0.30	-0.07	-0.12	0.34
Rpt PhDs											1.00	0.02	0.09	-0.17	-0.13	-0.35	-0.04
% Fem												1.00	-0.13	0.45	-0.22	-0.13	0.19
% Min													1.00	-0.02	-0.16	-0.11	0.31
% Citz														1.00	-0.22	0.11	0.30
% RA															1.00	-0.14	-0.18
% TA																1.00	-0.11
MYD																	1.00

Note: The data from which these correlations are produced are given in Appendix Table J - 1.

Appendix Table O - 4 Correlation Table for Selected Characteristics of Programs in Astrophysics and Astronomy

	1993 Ratings			Faculty								Students			Doctorate Recipients					
	93Q	93E	93C	Tot Fac	% Full	% Supp	% Pub	Pub/ Fac	Gini Pub	Cite/ Fac	Gini Cite	Tot Stu	% Fem Stu	Rpt PhDs	% Fem	% Min	% US	% RA	% TA	MYD
Mean	3.27	3.15	0.14	15.82	0.67	74.08	92.24	10.26	11.95	69.14	16.50	25.39	21.93	13.88	14.49	2.74	77.04	59.86	19.58	7.42
S. D.	0.88	0.75	0.22	6.73	0.14	14.74	8.53	3.50	5.44	39.36	7.89	10.32	11.01	8.70	8.81	4.28	15.48	20.45	17.30	0.99
No.	33	33	33	33	33	33	33	33	33	33	33	33	33	33	33	33	33	33	33	33
93Q	1.00	0.97	-0.08	0.66	0.48	0.14	0.04	0.75	-0.74	0.73	-0.74	0.74	0.12	0.65	-0.27	0.07	0.13	0.30	-0.48	-0.52
93E		1.00	-0.18	0.56	0.48	0.16	0.05	0.81	-0.67	0.80	-0.69	0.71	0.15	0.63	-0.25	0.07	0.15	0.26	-0.45	-0.44
93C			1.00	0.17	-0.15	-0.35	-0.25	-0.34	-0.04	-0.31	-0.12	0.01	-0.21	-0.08	0.26	-0.07	0.07	0.11	-0.04	0.11
Tot Fac				1.00	0.11	0.04	-0.14	0.34	-0.85	0.26	-0.79	0.55	0.16	0.42	-0.06	0.07	0.03	0.27	-0.25	-0.32
% Full					1.00	0.34	0.43	0.58	-0.35	0.44	-0.18	0.47	0.04	0.39	-0.08	-0.07	0.04	0.29	-0.30	-0.41
% Supp						1.00	0.56	0.33	-0.15	0.30	-0.04	-0.05	-0.06	-0.02	-0.06	0.04	-0.08	0.22	0.06	-0.06
% Pub							1.00	0.29	-0.15	0.29	-0.09	0.03	-0.07	-0.13	0.03	0.28	0.04	0.23	-0.20	-0.23
Pub/Fac								1.00	-0.53	0.88	-0.58	0.51	0.03	0.46	-0.26	0.03	0.13	0.31	-0.40	-0.27
Gini-Pub									1.00	-0.45	0.83	-0.58	-0.17	-0.45	-0.04	-0.08	0.08	-0.39	0.29	0.51
Cite/Fac										1.00	-0.45	0.47	0.13	0.37	-0.20	0.05	0.05	0.31	-0.36	-0.30
Gini-Cite											1.00	-0.65	0.11	-0.53	0.02	-0.10	-0.14	-0.33	0.43	0.29
Tot Stu												1.00	0.01	0.75	-0.08	0.07	0.00	0.34	-0.48	-0.43
% Fem Stu													1.00	-0.05	-0.14	0.17	0.17	0.07	-0.05	-0.11
Rpt PhDs														1.00	-0.07	0.00	0.08	0.21	-0.24	-0.35
% Fem															1.00	-0.09	-0.33	0.02	0.18	0.35
% Min																1.00	0.12	-0.10	0.15	0.03
% Citz																	1.00	-0.45	0.07	0.18
% RA																		1.00	-0.67	-0.31
% TA																			1.00	0.35
MYD																				1.00

Note: The data from which these correlations are produced are given in Appendix Table L - 1.

Appendix Table O - 5 Correlation Table for Selected Characteristics of Programs in Biochemistry and Molecular Biology

	1993 Ratings			Faculty								Students			Doctorate Recipients					
	93Q	93E	93C	Tot Fac	% Full	% Supp	% Pub	Pub/ Fac	Gini Pub	Cite/ Fac	Gini Cite	Tot Stu	% Fem Stu	Rpt PhDs	% Fem	% Min	% US	% RA	% TA	MYD
Mean	2.60	2.74	0.18	31.05	0.51	61.06	82.22	7.64	14.31	70.17	20.42	43.01	42.49	26.36	35.62	5.66	76.84	40.43	18.36	7.53
S. D.	1.04	0.96	0.23	32.11	0.17	22.74	13.74	4.08	15.30	82.63	20.13	38.08	13.43	25.58	13.98	12.49	15.82	22.95	21.32	1.38
No.	194	194	182	194	194	194	194	194	194	194	194	184	180	184	188	187	188	187	187	188
93Q	1.00	0.97	0.47	0.55	0.27	0.58	0.49	0.72	-0.68	0.71	-0.67	0.67	-0.10	0.65	0.07	-0.26	0.25	0.09	-0.40	-0.26
93E		1.00	0.47	0.52	0.29	0.58	0.46	0.65	-0.70	0.64	-0.67	0.64	-0.09	0.61	0.07	-0.24	0.22	0.12	-0.38	-0.30
93C			1.00	0.47	0.04	0.28	0.19	0.30	-0.38	0.27	-0.34	0.31	0.06	0.25	-0.02	-0.04	0.26	0.11	-0.24	-0.19
Tot Fac				1.00	0.01	0.19	0.26	0.38	-0.47	0.29	-0.47	0.66	0.01	0.60	0.06	-0.14	0.10	0.02	-0.25	-0.03
% Full					1.00	0.29	0.19	0.39	-0.12	0.28	-0.14	0.19	-0.13	0.23	-0.03	-0.15	0.01	0.12	-0.03	-0.09
% Supp						1.00	0.55	0.50	-0.42	0.41	-0.42	0.40	0.04	0.40	-0.01	-0.20	0.08	0.16	-0.23	-0.26
% Pub							1.00	0.61	-0.61	0.40	-0.63	0.32	0.00	0.31	-0.06	-0.26	0.01	0.10	-0.24	-0.13
Pub/Fac								1.00	-0.42	0.83	-0.49	0.54	-0.06	0.49	0.02	-0.27	0.16	0.00	-0.34	-0.19
Gini-Pub									1.00	-0.31	0.89	-0.46	0.20	-0.43	0.07	0.21	-0.10	-0.10	0.28	0.20
Cite/Fac										1.00	-0.33	0.49	-0.04	0.44	0.03	-0.17	0.25	-0.08	-0.34	-0.14
Gini-Cite											1.00	-0.46	0.11	-0.41	0.06	0.19	-0.13	-0.11	0.26	0.20
Tot Stu												1.00	-0.01	0.90	0.04	-0.16	0.10	0.12	-0.28	-0.14
% Fem Stu													1.00	-0.04	0.17	-0.21	0.00	-0.09	0.04	-0.04
Rpt PhDs														1.00	0.05	-0.14	0.09	0.15	-0.28	-0.19
% Fem															1.00	0.09	0.19	-0.03	-0.21	0.32
% Min																1.00	0.07	-0.20	0.06	0.31
% Citz																	1.00	-0.17	-0.29	-0.11
% RA																		1.00	-0.37	-0.14
% TA																			1.00	-0.01
MYD																				1.00

Note: The data from which these correlations are produced are given in Appendix Table N - 1.

Appendix Table O - 6 Correlation Table for Selected Characteristics of Programs in Biomedical Engineering

	1993 Ratings			Faculty								Students			Doctorate Recipients					
	93Q	93E	93C	Tot Fac	% Full	% Supp	% Pub	Pub/ Fac	Gini Pub	Cite/ Fac	Gini Cite	Tot Stu	% Fem Stu	Rpt PhDs	% Fem	% Min	% US	% RA	% TA	MYD
Mean	3.43	3.25	0.23	25.24	0.51	51.27	84.40	7.74	11.76	28.46	18.38	36.80	24.33	20.51	18.86	4.89	70.40	46.85	4.59	7.64
S. D.	0.71	0.63	0.32	16.70	0.20	23.67	9.36	4.08	7.88	22.87	11.82	26.42	13.49	20.90	13.38	8.49	16.74	19.80	7.77	1.03
No.	38	38	38	38	38	38	38	38	38	38	38	35	35	35	38	38	38	38	38	38
93Q	1.00	0.96	0.64	0.60	0.39	0.30	0.18	0.66	-0.71	0.65	-0.72	0.65	0.02	0.54	0.10	-0.33	0.31	0.08	-0.23	-0.48
93E		1.00	0.62	0.51	0.40	0.41	0.17	0.67	-0.64	0.65	-0.65	0.60	0.06	0.50	0.13	-0.35	0.32	0.02	-0.22	-0.44
93C			1.00	0.43	0.22	0.09	0.25	0.38	-0.63	0.38	-0.55	0.32	0.05	0.06	0.17	-0.30	0.05	0.01	-0.01	-0.41
Tot Fac				1.00	0.16	-0.03	0.18	0.38	-0.78	0.44	-0.76	0.69	-0.20	0.62	-0.06	-0.20	0.32	0.11	-0.15	-0.19
% Full					1.00	0.17	0.11	0.59	-0.16	0.47	-0.31	0.32	-0.05	0.40	-0.27	0.04	0.09	-0.11	-0.03	-0.03
% Supp						1.00	0.47	0.43	0.07	0.45	0.00	0.14	-0.04	0.15	0.05	-0.10	-0.04	-0.04	0.06	-0.11
% Pub							1.00	0.43	-0.20	0.37	-0.24	0.06	-0.39	0.02	-0.26	-0.05	-0.05	-0.10	0.09	0.12
Pub/Fac								1.00	-0.34	0.92	-0.50	0.56	-0.06	0.46	-0.14	-0.17	0.21	-0.01	-0.27	-0.22
Gini-Pub									1.00	-0.38	0.86	-0.48	0.00	-0.36	-0.08	0.25	-0.27	-0.01	0.17	0.38
Cite/Fac										1.00	-0.48	0.59	-0.02	0.47	0.06	-0.15	0.33	-0.09	-0.32	-0.27
Gini-Cite											1.00	-0.49	0.12	-0.44	-0.08	0.08	-0.27	0.12	0.17	0.19
Tot Stu												1.00	-0.04	0.79	0.24	-0.26	0.26	0.15	-0.29	-0.21
% Fem Stu													1.00	-0.31	0.29	-0.27	0.06	0.11	-0.02	-0.37
Rpt PhDs														1.00	0.02	-0.02	0.12	0.10	-0.14	-0.05
% Fem															1.00	-0.12	0.14	-0.04	-0.15	-0.15
% Min																1.00	-0.04	-0.35	0.22	0.25
% Citz																	1.00	-0.20	-0.15	-0.10
% RA																		1.00	0.04	-0.34
% TA																			1.00	0.22
MYD																				1.00

Note: The data from which these correlations are produced are given in Appendix Table K - 2.

Appendix Table O - 7 Correlation Table for Selected Characteristics of Programs in Cell and Developmental Biology

	1993 Ratings			Faculty								Students			Doctorate Recipients					
	93Q	93E	93C	Tot Fac	% Full	% Supp	% Pub	Pub/ Fac	Gini Pub	Cite/ Fac	Gini Cite	Tot Stu	% Fem Stu	Rpt PhDs	% Fem	% Min	% US	% RA	% TA	MYD
Mean	2.63	2.74	0.19	31.60	0.46	58.42	81.33	7.03	14.23	62.82	21.60	38.79	44.76	21.90	37.73	6.39	82.37	28.29	19.20	8.03
S. D.	1.02	0.98	0.26	31.90	0.16	22.27	13.82	4.09	12.83	74.37	19.87	41.62	14.42	21.34	15.13	15.80	17.89	23.06	21.49	1.81
No.	179	177	164	179	179	179	179	179	179	179	179	167	161	167	177	174	177	177	177	177
93Q	1.00	0.96	0.50	0.61	0.36	0.46	0.44	0.76	-0.73	0.74	-0.72	0.50	0.11	0.51	0.32	-0.24	0.30	0.09	-0.33	-0.39
93E		1.00	0.51	0.58	0.38	0.44	0.44	0.71	-0.74	0.66	-0.73	0.49	0.12	0.53	0.33	-0.20	0.29	0.06	-0.27	-0.42
93C			1.00	0.55	-0.08	0.17	0.13	0.34	-0.42	0.32	-0.44	0.30	-0.02	0.33	0.07	-0.07	0.19	0.03	-0.28	-0.12
Tot Fac				1.00	0.13	0.21	0.29	0.49	-0.58	0.41	-0.56	0.47	0.01	0.50	0.15	-0.09	0.15	0.08	-0.25	-0.22
% Full					1.00	0.24	0.23	0.39	-0.17	0.26	-0.18	0.23	0.26	0.27	0.11	-0.26	-0.03	0.00	0.11	-0.31
% Supp						1.00	0.44	0.43	-0.26	0.38	-0.34	0.25	0.00	0.27	0.31	-0.26	0.03	0.21	-0.19	-0.22
% Pub							1.00	0.54	-0.55	0.39	-0.54	0.22	0.03	0.25	0.27	-0.37	0.07	0.20	-0.16	-0.21
Pub/Fac								1.00	-0.52	0.83	-0.56	0.46	0.09	0.40	0.25	-0.20	0.18	0.15	-0.41	-0.27
Gini-Pub									1.00	-0.41	0.88	-0.40	-0.04	-0.48	-0.26	0.19	-0.21	-0.10	0.24	0.30
Cite/Fac										1.00	-0.39	0.44	0.03	0.25	0.24	-0.15	0.23	0.00	-0.37	-0.21
Gini-Cite											1.00	-0.38	-0.01	-0.45	-0.27	0.19	-0.18	-0.13	0.15	0.34
Tot Stu												1.00	-0.10	0.60	0.13	-0.11	0.14	0.07	-0.18	-0.21
% Fem Stu													1.00	0.02	0.11	-0.03	0.03	-0.05	-0.09	0.08
Rpt PhDs														1.00	0.11	-0.09	0.12	0.15	-0.22	-0.23
% Fem															1.00	-0.10	0.25	-0.07	-0.06	-0.30
% Min																1.00	-0.01	-0.15	-0.05	0.16
% Citz																	1.00	-0.28	-0.06	-0.08
% RA																		1.00	-0.36	-0.14
% TA																			1.00	0.00
MYD																				1.00

Note: The data from which these correlations are produced are given in Appendix Table N - 2.

Appendix Table O - 8 Correlation Table for Selected Characteristics of Programs in Chemical Engineering

	1993 Ratings			Faculty									Students			Doctorate Recipients					
	93Q	93E	93C	Tot Fac	% Full	% Supp	% Pub	Pub/ Fac	Gini Pub	Cite/ Fac	Gini Cite	Tot Stu	% Fem Stu	Rpt PhDs	% Fem	% Min	% US	% RA	% TA	MYD
Mean	2.70	2.68	0.05	13.81	0.61	54.55	80.64	8.04	18.35	25.50	27.17	43.90	18.15	34.38	11.27	4.18	57.71	57.76	15.24	6.93
S. D.	0.92	0.89	0.24	5.87	0.15	23.45	14.54	4.47	9.88	23.49	15.29	35.01	10.31	29.64	7.53	6.76	18.40	22.02	16.81	1.01
No.	93	93	93	93	93	93	93	93	93	93	93	93	92	93	92	92	92	92	92	92
93Q	1.00	0.98	0.41	0.63	0.17	0.58	0.38	0.80	-0.61	0.75	-0.60	0.73	0.16	0.80	0.25	0.00	0.39	0.35	-0.41	-0.50
93E		1.00	0.41	0.61	0.19	0.57	0.37	0.78	-0.62	0.72	-0.60	0.71	0.13	0.79	0.20	-0.01	0.37	0.35	-0.44	-0.52
93C			1.00	0.56	0.11	0.17	0.14	0.22	-0.52	0.21	-0.39	0.33	-0.01	0.36	0.13	0.04	0.29	0.09	-0.07	-0.22
Tot Fac				1.00	0.15	0.23	0.17	0.47	-0.66	0.45	-0.58	0.63	-0.07	0.67	0.06	0.06	0.26	0.24	-0.26	-0.26
% Full					1.00	-0.08	-0.03	0.13	-0.16	0.14	-0.17	0.08	-0.01	0.14	0.02	0.14	0.04	-0.04	0.06	-0.04
% Supp						1.00	0.48	0.61	-0.37	0.57	-0.35	0.42	0.30	0.41	0.29	0.00	0.21	0.15	-0.31	-0.39
% Pub							1.00	0.47	-0.58	0.40	-0.51	0.29	0.29	0.26	0.07	0.03	0.08	0.05	-0.05	-0.12
Pub/Fac								1.00	-0.42	0.93	-0.50	0.62	0.21	0.70	0.11	-0.02	0.22	0.36	-0.34	-0.35
Gini-Pub									1.00	-0.37	0.80	-0.47	-0.08	-0.47	-0.08	-0.08	-0.31	-0.15	0.21	0.29
Cite/Fac										1.00	-0.38	0.57	0.21	0.62	0.16	-0.08	0.28	0.30	-0.33	-0.33
Gini-Cite											1.00	-0.46	-0.13	-0.50	-0.03	-0.08	-0.25	-0.22	0.18	0.25
Tot Stu												1.00	0.13	0.88	0.07	-0.02	0.28	0.30	-0.34	-0.29
% Fem Stu													1.00	0.13	0.05	0.08	0.20	-0.09	0.08	0.05
Rpt PhDs														1.00	0.08	0.01	0.34	0.29	-0.34	-0.34
% Fem															1.00	0.17	0.33	-0.07	0.06	-0.20
% Min																1.00	0.06	-0.21	0.05	0.00
% Citz																	1.00	0.11	-0.17	-0.19
% RA																		1.00	-0.71	-0.48
% TA																			1.00	0.55
MYD																				1.00

Note: The data from which these correlations are produced are given in Appendix Table K - 3.

Appendix Table O - 9 Correlation Table for Selected Characteristics of Programs in Chemistry

	1993 Ratings			Faculty								Students			Doctorate Recipients					
	93Q	93E	93C	Tot Fac	% Full	% Supp	% Pub	Pub/ Fac	Gini Pub	Cite/ Fac	Gini Cite	Tot Stu	% Fem Stu	Rpt PhDs	% Fem	% Min	% US	% RA	% TA	MYD
Mean	2.60	2.71	0.06	23.10	0.61	54.98	82.76	10.49	12.43	55.69	17.28	87.20	32.17	60.62	22.72	6.28	70.33	40.70	34.74	7.04
S. D.	1.03	0.95	0.23	10.45	0.13	21.22	11.46	5.34	7.22	48.57	10.85	69.82	9.19	56.80	9.17	10.85	15.66	21.22	20.26	1.25
No.	168	168	168	168	168	168	168	168	168	168	168	167	166	167	168	168	168	168	168	168
93Q	1.00	0.97	0.48	0.71	0.47	0.72	0.48	0.82	-0.71	0.81	-0.69	0.82	-0.04	0.81	0.12	-0.18	0.30	0.62	-0.50	-0.57
93E		1.00	0.46	0.69	0.47	0.69	0.46	0.78	-0.71	0.76	-0.71	0.78	-0.04	0.78	0.15	-0.19	0.28	0.58	-0.46	-0.57
93C			1.00	0.47	0.05	0.24	0.18	0.36	-0.43	0.34	-0.41	0.44	0.08	0.36	0.00	-0.08	0.26	0.24	-0.25	-0.35
Tot Fac				1.00	0.34	0.39	0.23	0.49	-0.69	0.42	-0.65	0.79	0.01	0.73	0.09	-0.06	0.15	0.29	-0.22	-0.41
% Full					1.00	0.43	0.30	0.46	-0.30	0.39	-0.34	0.38	-0.08	0.41	0.06	-0.10	0.12	0.30	-0.26	-0.16
% Supp						1.00	0.53	0.67	-0.46	0.67	-0.48	0.56	0.05	0.55	0.13	-0.15	0.21	0.50	-0.42	-0.34
% Pub							1.00	0.52	-0.56	0.42	-0.51	0.34	0.05	0.34	0.06	-0.14	0.15	0.29	-0.23	-0.24
Pub/Fac								1.00	-0.48	0.88	-0.51	0.67	-0.09	0.69	-0.03	-0.14	0.17	0.58	-0.46	-0.45
Gini-Pub									1.00	-0.41	0.90	-0.61	0.03	-0.55	-0.10	0.06	-0.17	-0.25	0.17	0.39
Cite/Fac										1.00	-0.41	0.64	-0.07	0.66	0.02	-0.15	0.26	0.61	-0.53	-0.39
Gini-Cite											1.00	-0.59	0.00	-0.54	-0.12	0.01	-0.14	-0.25	0.19	0.39
Tot Stu												1.00	-0.08	0.89	0.04	-0.13	0.24	0.48	-0.39	-0.40
% Fem Stu													1.00	-0.07	0.38	0.01	-0.08	-0.19	0.11	0.08
Rpt PhDs														1.00	0.05	-0.12	0.24	0.51	-0.40	-0.40
% Fem															1.00	0.10	0.10	-0.07	0.01	0.02
% Min																1.00	-0.01	-0.19	-0.01	0.07
% Citz																	1.00	0.22	-0.40	-0.29
% RA																		1.00	-0.75	-0.45
% TA																			1.00	0.29
MYD																				1.00

Note: The data from which these correlations are produced are given in Appendix Table L - 2.

Appendix Table O - 10 Correlation Table for Selected Characteristics of Programs in Civil Engineering

	1993 Ratings			Faculty								Students			Doctorate Recipients					
	93Q	93E	93C	Tot Fac	% Full	% Supp	% Pub	Pub/ Fac	Gini Pub	Cite/ Fac	Gini Cite	Tot Stu	% Fem Stu	Rpt PhDs	% Fem	% Min	% US	% RA	% TA	MYD
Mean	2.85	2.84	0.09	21.45	0.53	40.12	68.49	3.54	15.61	6.39	26.35	47.34	11.91	34.32	6.93	6.03	45.89	40.83	14.68	8.22
S. D.	0.80	0.77	0.23	14.24	0.14	19.64	16.02	2.14	8.90	7.11	15.92	38.73	8.30	33.69	6.42	8.31	14.64	20.30	14.40	1.18
No.	86	86	86	86	86	86	86	86	86	86	85	85	83	85	86	86	86	86	86	86
93Q	1.00	0.97	0.35	0.64	0.34	0.41	0.43	0.56	-0.64	0.56	-0.58	0.57	0.23	0.67	0.08	-0.03	-0.06	0.49	-0.26	-0.33
93E		1.00	0.35	0.60	0.29	0.38	0.44	0.54	-0.66	0.55	-0.57	0.52	0.24	0.64	0.11	-0.02	-0.05	0.50	-0.21	-0.34
93C			1.00	0.39	-0.15	0.03	0.05	0.10	-0.47	0.05	-0.46	0.12	0.06	0.12	-0.03	0.12	0.11	0.23	-0.04	-0.10
Tot Fac				1.00	0.14	-0.03	0.08	0.11	-0.60	0.18	-0.48	0.64	0.00	0.69	-0.07	0.05	-0.01	0.28	-0.26	-0.10
% Full					1.00	0.12	0.07	0.19	0.10	0.29	-0.05	0.25	0.12	0.20	0.09	0.06	0.01	0.14	-0.19	0.06
% Supp						1.00	0.51	0.56	-0.16	0.52	-0.24	0.03	0.08	0.16	0.03	-0.05	-0.13	0.31	-0.12	-0.38
% Pub							1.00	0.63	-0.56	0.49	-0.48	0.13	0.25	0.24	-0.05	-0.24	-0.10	0.35	-0.06	-0.19
Pub/Fac								1.00	-0.31	0.82	-0.33	0.20	0.19	0.28	0.12	-0.03	-0.13	0.41	-0.03	-0.29
Gini-Pub									1.00	-0.25	0.75	-0.36	-0.10	-0.46	0.02	0.10	0.01	-0.38	0.15	0.12
Cite/Fac										1.00	-0.21	0.18	0.28	0.32	0.16	-0.04	0.02	0.55	-0.13	-0.18
Gini-Cite											1.00	-0.35	0.01	-0.39	0.22	-0.09	0.06	-0.42	0.29	0.31
Tot Stu												1.00	0.09	0.61	-0.01	0.05	-0.11	0.17	-0.14	-0.09
% Fem Stu													1.00	0.21	0.38	-0.15	0.20	0.12	0.03	-0.12
Rpt PhDs														1.00	0.04	-0.05	-0.01	0.28	-0.28	-0.21
% Fem															1.00	0.12	0.04	-0.13	0.34	-0.07
% Min																1.00	-0.16	-0.02	0.09	-0.15
% Citz																	1.00	0.00	-0.03	0.36
% RA																		1.00	-0.48	-0.33
% TA																			1.00	0.04
MYD																				1.00

Note: The data from which these correlations are produced are given in Appendix Table K - 4.

Appendix Table O - 11 Correlation Table for Selected Characteristics of Programs in Classics

	1993 Ratings			Faculty					Students			Doctorate Recipients					
	93Q	93E	93C	Tot Fac	% Full	% Supp	No. Awd	Awd Fac	Tot Stu	% Fem Stu	Rpt PhDs	% Fem	% Min	% US	% RA	% TA	MYD
Mean	3.27	2.83	0.05	13.14	0.59	0.65	4.00	0.23	22.45	46.66	9.34	42.86	3.78	93.71	0.99	36.88	10.46
S. D.	0.93	0.93	0.33	6.57	0.18	2.06	3.98	0.18	10.49	15.57	5.85	21.74	18.55	11.26	4.00	30.39	2.96
No.	29	29	29	29	29	29	29	29	29	29	29	29	29	29	28	28	29
93Q	1.00	0.95	0.26	0.63	0.55	0.20	0.69	0.41	0.48	-0.01	0.73	-0.25	-0.11	0.20	0.06	0.08	-0.61
93E		1.00	0.24	0.57	0.56	0.26	0.57	0.35	0.55	-0.02	0.78	-0.27	-0.17	0.12	0.05	0.07	-0.60
93C			1.00	0.41	-0.11	-0.30	0.32	0.21	-0.16	-0.38	-0.01	-0.28	-0.06	0.25	0.15	0.16	0.17
Tot Fac				1.00	0.15	0.14	0.62	0.14	0.18	-0.15	0.40	-0.13	-0.14	-0.01	-0.07	0.34	-0.49
% Full					1.00	0.07	0.41	0.33	0.30	0.06	0.37	-0.21	0.06	-0.10	-0.03	-0.03	-0.63
% Supp						1.00	0.07	0.00	0.18	0.32	0.08	0.13	-0.05	-0.16	-0.08	-0.13	-0.22
No. Awd							1.00	0.76	0.37	-0.11	0.47	0.02	-0.10	0.09	-0.11	0.17	-0.44
Awd Fac								1.00	0.26	-0.17	0.30	0.11	-0.09	0.13	-0.09	-0.07	-0.16
Tot Stu									1.00	0.01	0.57	0.20	-0.17	0.04	-0.13	-0.01	-0.37
% Fem Stu										1.00	-0.06	-0.15	-0.07	-0.03	0.17	-0.09	-0.15
Rpt PhDs											1.00	-0.09	-0.24	0.08	0.03	0.20	-0.41
% Fem												1.00	-0.38	0.07	-0.18	-0.47	0.24
% Min													1.00	0.11	-0.07	0.15	-0.10
% Citz														1.00	0.15	-0.42	0.18
% RA															1.00	-0.24	0.01
% TA																1.00	-0.17
MYD																	1.00

Note: The data from which these correlations are produced are given in Appendix Table J - 2.

Appendix Table O - 12 Correlation Table for Selected Characteristics of Programs in Comparative Literature

	1993 Ratings			Faculty					Students			Doctorate Recipients					
	93Q	93E	93C	Tot Fac	% Full	% Supp	No. Awd	Awd Fac	Tot Stu	% Fem Stu	Rpt PhDs	% Fem	% Min	% US	% RA	% TA	MYD
Mean	3.04	2.99	0.04	20.20	0.57	0.99	4.89	0.19	38.61	62.46	14.52	57.07	7.90	78.58	1.03	46.97	10.45
S. D.	0.85	0.62	0.31	13.67	0.16	2.73	4.78	0.13	23.29	12.11	9.16	18.36	12.24	17.69	2.96	27.53	1.92
No.	44	44	44	44	44	44	44	44	44	43	44	44	44	44	43	43	44
93Q	1.00	0.96	0.53	0.28	0.42	-0.02	0.62	0.60	0.32	-0.05	0.41	-0.28	-0.09	0.31	-0.17	0.00	-0.42
93E		1.00	0.37	0.17	0.46	-0.03	0.52	0.57	0.35	-0.02	0.50	-0.34	-0.17	0.37	-0.17	0.07	-0.30
93C			1.00	0.43	0.14	0.08	0.44	0.26	0.06	-0.25	-0.03	0.05	0.04	0.17	-0.29	-0.04	-0.33
Tot Fac				1.00	-0.16	0.20	0.66	0.08	0.14	-0.06	-0.04	-0.10	-0.01	0.08	-0.16	-0.13	-0.20
% Full					1.00	0.03	0.15	0.30	0.15	-0.14	0.34	0.02	-0.12	0.11	0.00	0.24	-0.07
% Supp						1.00	0.26	0.26	-0.14	-0.05	-0.07	-0.18	-0.24	0.03	-0.03	-0.03	0.02
No. Awd							1.00	0.69	0.15	0.02	0.07	-0.26	-0.03	0.14	-0.21	-0.03	-0.43
Awd Fac								1.00	0.01	0.07	0.09	-0.26	-0.15	0.16	-0.27	0.13	-0.47
Tot Stu									1.00	-0.17	0.43	-0.10	-0.10	0.03	0.03	0.20	0.12
% Fem Stu										1.00	0.23	-0.06	0.08	-0.09	-0.16	-0.17	-0.05
Rpt PhDs											1.00	-0.10	-0.16	0.25	-0.03	0.02	0.10
% Fem												1.00	-0.10	-0.02	0.10	-0.22	-0.03
% Min													1.00	-0.14	-0.03	-0.06	-0.18
% Citz														1.00	-0.29	-0.09	0.02
% RA															1.00	0.05	0.10
% TA																1.00	-0.02
MYD																	1.00

Note: The data from which these correlations are produced are given in Appendix Table J - 3.

Appendix Table O - 13 Correlation Table for Selected Characteristics of Programs in Computer Sciences

	1993 Ratings			Faculty								Students			Doctorate Recipients					
	93Q	93E	93C	Tot Fac	% Full	% Supp	% Pub	Pub/ Fac	Gini Pub	Cite/ Fac	Gini Cite	Tot Stu	% Fem Stu	Rpt PhDs	% Fem	% Min	% US	% RA	% TA	MYD
Mean	2.54	2.43	0.14	21.15	0.39	55.31	69.42	3.06	16.22	6.17	31.26	80.03	17.00	30.26	15.06	2.58	60.49	32.29	23.50	8.68
S. D.	1.02	1.03	0.26	11.80	0.14	22.87	17.11	1.68	13.21	6.43	22.80	79.12	7.48	28.08	10.51	4.30	15.48	23.26	20.02	1.63
No.	108	108	108	108	108	108	108	108	108	108	104	107	107	107	108	108	108	108	108	108
93Q	1.00	0.98	0.35	0.63	0.41	0.66	0.53	0.62	-0.59	0.61	-0.58	0.32	-0.12	0.66	-0.24	-0.08	0.17	0.72	-0.40	-0.51
93E		1.00	0.34	0.60	0.41	0.66	0.54	0.62	-0.61	0.59	-0.57	0.34	-0.14	0.67	-0.25	-0.07	0.16	0.73	-0.40	-0.53
93C			1.00	0.25	-0.03	0.29	0.22	0.17	-0.44	0.14	-0.29	0.02	0.08	-0.03	-0.01	0.07	0.19	0.31	-0.27	-0.28
Tot Fac				1.00	0.33	0.16	0.22	0.36	-0.59	0.24	-0.54	0.44	-0.15	0.68	-0.08	0.01	0.09	0.30	-0.14	-0.19
% Full					1.00	0.21	0.31	0.31	-0.35	0.25	-0.29	0.20	-0.21	0.36	-0.14	-0.07	0.05	0.23	-0.20	-0.27
% Supp						1.00	0.57	0.60	-0.36	0.55	-0.48	0.07	-0.14	0.24	-0.25	-0.13	0.01	0.64	-0.25	-0.50
% Pub							1.00	0.81	-0.57	0.52	-0.57	0.21	-0.13	0.38	-0.29	0.08	-0.16	0.46	-0.14	-0.52
Pub/Fac								1.00	-0.47	0.70	-0.53	0.26	0.00	0.47	-0.23	-0.06	-0.18	0.49	-0.07	-0.45
Gini-Pub									1.00	-0.28	0.70	-0.27	0.11	-0.40	0.33	-0.01	0.03	-0.40	0.27	0.60
Cite/Fac										1.00	-0.19	0.15	0.07	0.41	-0.21	-0.12	0.01	0.52	-0.18	-0.37
Gini-Cite											1.00	-0.29	0.23	-0.42	0.14	-0.04	0.08	-0.44	0.03	0.47
Tot Stu												1.00	-0.06	0.55	-0.03	0.04	-0.06	0.16	0.00	-0.18
% Fem Stu													1.00	-0.12	0.05	0.15	-0.01	0.01	-0.12	0.09
Rpt PhDs														1.00	-0.17	0.03	0.03	0.39	-0.22	-0.30
% Fem															1.00	0.17	0.22	-0.24	0.16	0.44
% Min																1.00	0.01	0.03	-0.18	0.03
% Citz																	1.00	0.06	-0.40	0.11
% RA																		1.00	-0.47	-0.41
% TA																			1.00	0.23
MYD																				1.00

Note: The data from which these correlations are produced are given in Appendix Table L - 3.

Appendix Table O - 14 Correlation Table for Selected Characteristics of Programs in Ecology, Evolution, and Behavior

	1993 Ratings			Faculty								Students			Doctorate Recipients					
	93Q	93E	93C	Tot Fac	% Full	% Supp	% Pub	Pub/ Fac	Gini Pub	Cite/ Fac	Gini Cite	Tot Stu	% Fem Stu	Rpt PhDs	% Fem	% Min	% US	% RA	% TA	MYD
Mean	2.88	2.91	0.19	31.47	0.52	43.50	78.59	5.14	12.67	20.13	19.43	41.58	39.46	29.45	26.85	3.93	81.15	25.97	31.84	9.23
S. D.	0.84	0.79	0.27	29.05	0.17	19.75	14.91	2.36	12.17	19.92	17.14	46.62	16.06	37.20	15.97	8.82	15.02	20.29	26.02	2.08
No.	129	128	128	129	129	129	129	129	128	129	128	120	114	120	120	119	120	117	117	120
93Q	1.00	0.94	0.26	0.55	0.26	0.55	0.45	0.53	-0.55	0.47	-0.60	0.50	0.04	0.50	0.26	-0.12	0.20	0.06	-0.03	-0.36
93E		1.00	0.28	0.53	0.24	0.50	0.54	0.62	-0.62	0.46	-0.67	0.48	-0.01	0.48	0.21	-0.19	0.17	0.09	-0.03	-0.33
93C			1.00	0.29	-0.21	0.04	-0.03	-0.03	-0.19	-0.07	-0.22	0.12	-0.14	0.05	0.04	-0.10	0.10	0.03	-0.09	0.06
Tot Fac				1.00	0.05	0.05	0.16	0.22	-0.53	0.20	-0.54	0.66	-0.03	0.61	0.12	-0.03	-0.08	0.22	-0.12	-0.08
% Full					1.00	0.10	0.24	0.31	-0.17	0.26	-0.26	0.13	0.07	0.18	0.15	0.05	0.03	0.13	-0.09	-0.13
% Supp						1.00	0.39	0.49	-0.14	0.52	-0.17	0.18	0.19	0.15	0.25	-0.05	0.13	-0.12	0.16	-0.25
% Pub							1.00	0.61	-0.46	0.33	-0.46	0.12	-0.03	0.21	0.09	-0.08	0.04	0.22	-0.17	-0.25
Pub/Fac								1.00	-0.27	0.79	-0.36	0.18	0.01	0.28	0.14	-0.08	0.05	0.20	-0.16	-0.26
Gini-Pub									1.00	-0.17	0.86	-0.46	0.20	-0.42	-0.26	-0.05	-0.25	-0.12	0.07	0.08
Cite/Fac										1.00	-0.23	0.19	0.07	0.22	0.19	0.01	0.08	0.05	-0.09	-0.26
Gini-Cite											1.00	-0.43	0.11	-0.41	-0.26	-0.02	-0.20	-0.14	0.10	0.02
Tot Stu												1.00	0.07	0.76	0.11	0.00	0.06	0.01	-0.02	-0.03
% Fem Stu													1.00	0.10	0.03	0.29	0.01	-0.23	0.08	0.05
Rpt PhDs														1.00	0.10	-0.02	0.06	-0.03	0.04	-0.10
% Fem															1.00	0.21	0.11	0.06	0.05	-0.23
% Min																1.00	-0.14	0.10	-0.10	0.10
% Citz																	1.00	-0.59	0.27	0.18
% RA																		1.00	-0.57	-0.19
% TA																			1.00	-0.17
MYD																				1.00

Note: The data from which these correlations are produced are given in Appendix Table N - 3.

Appendix Table O - 15 Correlation Table for Selected Characteristics of Programs in Economics

	1993 Ratings			Faculty								Students			Doctorate Recipients					
	93Q	93E	93C	Tot Fac	% Full	% Supp	% Pub	Pub/ Fac	Gini Pub	Cite/ Fac	Gini Cite	Tot Stu	% Fem Stu	Rpt PhDs	% Fem	% Min	% US	% RA	% TA	MYD
Mean	2.38	2.23	0.06	25.18	0.54	12.13	68.51	2.72	12.33	5.43	25.48	69.64	26.85	38.89	19.24	7.25	57.60	13.21	36.99	8.66
S. D.	1.17	1.13	0.25	11.44	0.14	13.33	15.38	1.22	11.09	5.95	19.13	45.89	8.78	28.57	9.31	9.31	16.99	14.19	20.38	1.44
No.	107	107	106	107	107	107	107	107	107	107	106	107	107	107	107	107	107	107	107	107
93Q	1.00	0.98	0.37	0.67	0.39	0.73	0.44	0.60	-0.41	0.75	-0.46	0.67	-0.09	0.81	-0.04	-0.28	0.06	0.03	0.00	-0.56
93E		1.00	0.34	0.64	0.38	0.72	0.40	0.56	-0.40	0.72	-0.46	0.65	-0.06	0.77	-0.05	-0.31	0.05	0.05	0.04	-0.56
93C			1.00	0.55	0.22	0.31	0.18	0.28	-0.36	0.38	-0.27	0.24	0.12	0.30	0.21	0.07	0.08	0.09	-0.13	-0.06
Tot Fac				1.00	0.27	0.43	0.24	0.34	-0.55	0.50	-0.49	0.59	-0.07	0.66	0.12	-0.22	0.12	0.01	0.03	-0.30
% Full					1.00	0.31	0.27	0.30	-0.12	0.35	-0.08	0.32	0.02	0.38	-0.09	0.09	-0.07	0.20	-0.21	-0.12
% Supp						1.00	0.32	0.43	-0.32	0.56	-0.36	0.47	-0.06	0.59	-0.08	-0.19	-0.08	-0.04	0.05	-0.41
% Pub							1.00	0.70	-0.57	0.38	-0.53	0.24	0.05	0.25	-0.09	-0.29	0.05	0.07	0.06	-0.28
Pub/Fac								1.00	-0.33	0.61	-0.46	0.34	-0.11	0.41	-0.11	-0.21	-0.04	0.09	-0.05	-0.34
Gini-Pub									1.00	-0.31	0.69	-0.31	-0.06	-0.34	-0.05	0.23	-0.12	-0.01	-0.19	0.28
Cite/Fac										1.00	-0.13	0.60	-0.01	0.65	0.03	-0.17	0.02	-0.04	-0.11	-0.36
Gini-Cite											1.00	-0.26	-0.01	-0.37	0.04	0.42	-0.16	-0.12	-0.16	0.35
Tot Stu												1.00	-0.08	0.78	0.01	-0.09	0.11	-0.12	-0.12	-0.23
% Fem Stu													1.00	-0.17	0.16	0.17	0.18	0.15	-0.03	0.07
Rpt PhDs														1.00	0.03	-0.11	0.02	-0.07	-0.12	-0.40
% Fem															1.00	0.03	0.18	-0.10	-0.02	0.14
% Min																1.00	0.00	0.07	-0.24	0.28
% Citz																	1.00	0.04	-0.13	-0.07
% RA																		1.00	-0.29	-0.17
% TA																			1.00	-0.24
MYD																				1.00

Note: The data from which these correlations are produced are given in Appendix Table M - 2.

Appendix Table O - 16 Correlation Table for Selected Characteristics of Programs in Electrical Engineering

	1993 Ratings			Faculty								Students			Doctorate Recipients					
	93Q	93E	93C	Tot Fac	% Full	% Supp	% Pub	Pub/ Fac	Gini Pub	Cite/ Fac	Gini Cite	Tot Stu	% Fem Stu	Rpt PhDs	% Fem	% Min	% US	% RA	% TA	MYD
Mean	2.63	2.60	0.12	27.33	0.49	43.23	71.33	5.03	13.37	13.71	25.03	88.32	10.63	50.29	5.71	4.98	50.48	39.67	21.30	7.75
S. D.	0.93	0.92	0.22	16.13	0.15	21.58	17.12	3.53	9.81	17.64	17.76	90.52	5.91	58.85	5.02	9.80	18.40	21.30	18.24	1.34
No.	126	126	126	126	126	126	126	126	126	126	126	125	124	126	126	125	126	126	126	126
93Q	1.00	0.98	0.37	0.73	0.35	0.69	0.59	0.76	-0.58	0.67	-0.60	0.69	0.07	0.76	0.12	-0.16	0.03	0.59	-0.50	-0.33
93E		1.00	0.38	0.70	0.32	0.69	0.56	0.73	-0.58	0.65	-0.59	0.66	0.08	0.73	0.14	-0.16	0.02	0.58	-0.50	-0.30
93C			1.00	0.57	0.08	0.30	0.15	0.24	-0.40	0.17	-0.36	0.34	-0.14	0.29	0.05	0.02	0.08	0.23	-0.25	-0.04
Tot Fac				1.00	0.19	0.39	0.32	0.45	-0.59	0.34	-0.56	0.74	-0.09	0.73	0.01	-0.13	0.09	0.41	-0.36	-0.20
% Full					1.00	0.27	0.14	0.28	-0.13	0.28	-0.17	0.31	0.10	0.32	0.11	-0.05	0.05	0.25	-0.18	-0.16
% Supp						1.00	0.70	0.65	-0.48	0.55	-0.47	0.43	0.18	0.51	0.18	-0.03	-0.05	0.62	-0.36	-0.22
% Pub							1.00	0.70	-0.54	0.53	-0.58	0.37	0.20	0.41	0.12	0.01	-0.15	0.51	-0.24	-0.21
Pub/Fac								1.00	-0.29	0.93	-0.42	0.58	0.16	0.60	0.18	-0.02	0.04	0.61	-0.41	-0.21
Gini-Pub									1.00	-0.20	0.81	-0.38	0.03	-0.42	-0.02	0.27	0.16	-0.35	0.14	0.38
Cite/Fac										1.00	-0.29	0.50	0.20	0.51	0.18	-0.08	0.10	0.53	-0.37	-0.23
Gini-Cite											1.00	-0.41	-0.05	-0.42	-0.12	0.18	0.17	-0.40	0.22	0.28
Tot Stu												1.00	0.06	0.80	0.08	-0.05	0.12	0.39	-0.31	-0.16
% Fem Stu													1.00	0.00	0.05	0.01	-0.06	0.18	-0.12	-0.02
Rpt PhDs														1.00	0.01	-0.07	0.11	0.42	-0.38	-0.18
% Fem															1.00	-0.04	-0.14	0.09	-0.03	-0.12
% Min																1.00	0.10	-0.10	-0.12	0.11
% Citz																	1.00	0.03	-0.42	0.12
% RA																		1.00	-0.58	-0.38
% TA																			1.00	0.05
MYD																				1.00

Note: The data from which these correlations are produced are given in Appendix Table K - 5.

Appendix Table O - 17 Correlation Table for Selected Characteristics of Programs in English Language and Literature

	1993 Ratings			Faculty					Students			Doctorate Recipients					
	93Q	93E	93C	Tot Fac	% Full	% Supp	No. Awd	Awd Fac	Tot Stu	% Fem Stu	Rpt PhDs	% Fem	% Min	% US	% RA	% TA	MYD
Mean	2.70	2.77	0.15	32.14	0.51	3.70	4.72	0.12	85.06	61.38	33.27	58.77	5.40	92.47	0.75	41.25	12.20
S. D.	0.98	0.84	0.24	15.40	0.15	3.96	4.89	0.11	59.75	11.56	24.99	12.02	8.59	7.16	2.63	20.41	2.81
No.	127	127	127	127	127	127	127	127	127	126	127	126	126	126	126	126	126
93Q	1.00	0.97	0.41	0.57	0.31	0.07	0.75	0.60	0.59	-0.18	0.58	-0.19	-0.15	0.08	0.00	0.24	-0.57
93E		1.00	0.38	0.57	0.28	0.11	0.70	0.54	0.58	-0.16	0.58	-0.25	-0.14	0.07	0.03	0.29	-0.57
93C			1.00	0.45	0.02	0.01	0.28	0.04	0.29	-0.02	0.18	0.10	-0.01	0.21	0.11	0.15	-0.13
Tot Fac				1.00	-0.03	0.00	0.54	0.07	0.65	-0.09	0.61	-0.16	-0.13	-0.03	-0.08	0.34	-0.30
% Full					1.00	-0.06	0.31	0.34	0.14	-0.15	0.19	-0.08	-0.13	0.02	0.03	0.09	-0.37
% Supp						1.00	0.10	0.07	0.02	-0.03	-0.07	-0.15	-0.07	0.04	0.15	0.06	-0.12
No. Awd							1.00	0.77	0.53	-0.10	0.48	-0.20	-0.09	-0.01	-0.08	0.11	-0.44
Awd Fac								1.00	0.23	-0.09	0.22	-0.19	-0.09	0.01	-0.06	-0.03	-0.42
Tot Stu									1.00	-0.07	0.70	-0.23	-0.14	-0.01	-0.06	0.18	-0.35
% Fem Stu										1.00	-0.08	0.29	0.14	0.07	0.14	-0.18	0.16
Rpt PhDs											1.00	-0.22	-0.10	-0.04	-0.04	0.26	-0.37
% Fem												1.00	0.07	0.21	0.07	-0.28	0.17
% Min													1.00	-0.04	-0.04	-0.14	0.26
% Citz														1.00	0.02	-0.14	0.05
% RA															1.00	-0.15	0.12
% TA																1.00	-0.46
MYD																	1.00

Note: The data from which these correlations are produced are given in Appendix Table J-4.

Appendix Table O - 18 Correlation Table for Selected Characteristics of Programs in French Language and Literature

	1993 Ratings			Faculty					Students			Doctorate Recipients					
	93Q	93E	93C	Tot Fac	% Full	% Supp	No. Awd	Awd Fac	Tot Stu	% Fem Stu	Rpt PhDs	% Fem	% Min	% US	% RA	% TA	MYD
Mean	3.09	2.90	0.03	12.84	0.51	0.86	1.76	0.13	29.64	73.70	11.34	73.89	7.40	87.65	1.01	55.52	11.69
S. D.	0.81	0.74	0.26	4.63	0.18	2.88	1.71	0.13	21.15	22.05	7.23	15.03	10.95	11.41	5.26	30.19	3.24
No.	45	45	45	45	45	45	45	45	44	43	44	45	45	45	44	44	45
93Q	1.00	0.94	0.40	0.25	0.55	0.18	0.63	0.41	0.27	0.18	0.63	-0.22	-0.27	0.04	-0.16	-0.07	-0.52
93E		1.00	0.32	0.36	0.52	0.26	0.64	0.37	0.35	0.22	0.77	-0.25	-0.28	-0.10	-0.20	0.00	-0.57
93C			1.00	0.35	0.19	0.14	0.32	0.02	0.15	0.02	0.01	-0.08	-0.12	0.19	-0.04	-0.02	-0.11
Tot Fac				1.00	-0.02	0.18	0.15	-0.24	0.54	0.26	0.33	-0.08	0.06	-0.14	-0.07	0.29	-0.19
% Full					1.00	0.06	0.20	0.17	0.00	-0.05	0.26	-0.23	-0.03	0.06	-0.11	-0.04	-0.43
% Supp						1.00	0.22	0.05	0.07	-0.17	0.32	-0.14	-0.15	0.04	-0.06	0.14	-0.17
No. Awd							1.00	0.80	0.13	0.33	0.51	0.09	-0.31	0.06	0.00	-0.04	-0.22
Awd Fac								1.00	-0.07	0.09	0.20	0.12	-0.30	-0.09	-0.06	-0.08	-0.18
Tot Stu									1.00	-0.04	0.31	-0.15	0.02	0.04	-0.15	0.28	-0.14
% Fem Stu										1.00	0.40	0.09	-0.06	0.18	-0.05	-0.10	-0.11
Rpt PhDs											1.00	-0.27	-0.07	0.00	-0.20	-0.19	-0.44
% Fem												1.00	0.24	-0.10	0.24	-0.01	0.31
% Min													1.00	-0.09	-0.09	0.06	0.11
% Citz														1.00	0.18	-0.24	0.30
% RA															1.00	-0.27	0.60
% TA																1.00	-0.34
MYD																	1.00

Note: The data from which these correlations are produced are given in Appendix Table J - 5.

Appendix Table O - 19 Correlation Table for Selected Characteristics of Programs in Geography

	1993 Ratings			Faculty								Students			Doctorate Recipients					
	93Q	93E	93C	Tot Fac	% Full	% Supp	% Pub	Pub/ Fac	Gini Pub	Cite/ Fac	Gini Cite	Tot Stu	% Fem Stu	Rpt PhDs	% Fem	% Min	% US	% RA	% TA	MYD
Mean	3.15	3.07	0.05	15.31	0.49	31.09	68.78	2.72	17.02	6.87	34.05	33.33	34.44	14.86	27.82	3.89	71.19	15.54	30.35	10.57
S. D.	0.77	0.66	0.32	4.89	0.13	17.91	16.79	1.44	8.48	5.14	20.01	17.15	10.72	7.70	11.92	5.91	19.12	16.02	17.85	2.70
No.	36	36	36	36	36	36	36	36	36	36	36	36	36	36	36	36	36	36	36	36
93Q	1.00	0.98	0.46	0.74	0.41	0.28	0.40	0.39	-0.67	0.33	-0.52	0.71	0.26	0.56	0.12	-0.02	0.18	0.15	0.23	-0.27
93E		1.00	0.41	0.66	0.37	0.35	0.43	0.43	-0.63	0.40	-0.43	0.72	0.25	0.61	0.13	-0.06	0.11	0.21	0.16	-0.27
93C			1.00	0.48	0.02	0.05	0.29	0.34	-0.49	0.08	-0.38	0.17	-0.05	0.12	-0.15	-0.03	0.04	0.00	0.35	-0.13
Tot Fac				1.00	0.07	-0.11	0.21	0.21	-0.75	0.01	-0.55	0.49	0.30	0.32	0.07	0.19	0.28	0.20	0.23	-0.16
% Full					1.00	0.37	0.25	0.15	-0.14	0.33	-0.11	0.26	0.12	0.16	0.20	-0.24	0.27	-0.09	0.18	-0.20
% Supp						1.00	0.41	0.51	-0.06	0.60	-0.19	0.29	-0.02	0.14	-0.05	-0.19	-0.09	0.37	-0.18	-0.15
% Pub							1.00	0.75	-0.68	0.49	-0.36	0.37	0.09	0.21	0.06	-0.04	-0.08	0.26	0.08	-0.02
Pub/Fac								1.00	-0.48	0.73	-0.34	0.44	0.06	0.20	-0.15	-0.11	-0.09	0.49	-0.08	-0.03
Gini-Pub									1.00	-0.15	0.59	-0.49	-0.31	-0.33	-0.09	-0.03	-0.10	-0.24	-0.18	0.07
Cite/Fac										1.00	0.07	0.39	0.20	0.20	0.07	-0.31	0.03	0.35	-0.22	0.02
Gini-Cite											1.00	-0.40	0.03	-0.32	0.00	-0.33	0.01	-0.12	-0.23	0.23
Tot Stu												1.00	0.04	0.72	0.16	0.04	0.15	0.28	-0.13	-0.10
% Fem Stu													1.00	0.09	0.47	-0.22	0.03	0.32	-0.07	-0.08
Rpt PhDs														1.00	0.17	-0.02	0.00	0.02	0.03	-0.22
% Fem															1.00	0.02	-0.07	-0.10	-0.17	0.22
% Min																1.00	0.15	0.03	-0.13	0.26
% Citz																	1.00	0.06	-0.06	0.11
% RA																		1.00	-0.30	-0.19
% TA																			1.00	-0.42
MYD																				1.00

Note: The data from which these correlations are produced are given in Appendix Table M - 3.

Appendix Table O - 20 Correlation Table for Selected Characteristics of Programs in Geosciences

	1993 Ratings			Faculty								Students			Doctorate Recipients					
	93Q	93E	93C	Tot Fac	% Full	% Supp	% Pub	Pub/ Fac	Gini Pub	Cite/ Fac	Gini Cite	Tot Stu	% Fem Stu	Rpt PhDs	% Fem	% Min	% US	% RA	% TA	MYD
Mean	2.95	2.92	0.07	20.28	0.59	59.59	79.39	4.76	14.03	24.53	21.75	35.53	22.66	25.42	19.72	2.68	78.80	38.10	23.83	8.95
S. D.	0.80	0.74	0.24	14.78	0.16	21.25	15.04	2.82	8.96	23.61	14.40	32.22	10.96	22.18	11.09	6.10	13.04	20.76	17.71	1.41
No.	100	100	100	100	100	100	100	100	100	100	100	100	99	100	100	100	100	100	100	100
93Q	1.00	0.97	0.30	0.45	0.47	0.66	0.56	0.79	-0.62	0.74	-0.61	0.57	0.38	0.70	0.09	-0.02	0.18	0.59	-0.37	-0.48
93E		1.00	0.30	0.40	0.44	0.65	0.56	0.73	-0.62	0.70	-0.61	0.52	0.32	0.65	0.02	-0.02	0.17	0.56	-0.34	-0.50
93C			1.00	0.31	-0.11	0.19	0.21	0.10	-0.45	-0.01	-0.39	0.20	-0.01	0.17	-0.16	-0.15	0.18	0.26	-0.14	-0.06
Tot Fac				1.00	-0.01	0.06	0.02	0.17	-0.50	0.13	-0.45	0.66	0.11	0.64	0.00	-0.05	0.04	0.20	-0.23	-0.10
% Full					1.00	0.35	0.29	0.51	-0.16	0.51	-0.19	0.22	0.35	0.36	0.15	-0.08	0.17	0.29	-0.31	-0.11
% Supp						1.00	0.65	0.75	-0.33	0.69	-0.38	0.26	0.35	0.35	0.08	0.04	0.12	0.47	-0.23	-0.27
% Pub							1.00	0.63	-0.47	0.56	-0.48	0.19	0.29	0.24	-0.01	0.08	0.18	0.32	0.09	-0.34
Pub/Fac								1.00	-0.36	0.90	-0.38	0.38	0.36	0.52	0.14	0.04	0.12	0.49	-0.27	-0.42
Gini-Pub									1.00	-0.30	0.89	-0.45	-0.08	-0.49	0.19	0.10	-0.11	-0.42	0.17	0.35
Cite/Fac										1.00	-0.26	0.36	0.40	0.53	0.16	0.06	0.11	0.45	-0.32	-0.39
Gini-Cite											1.00	-0.42	-0.10	-0.48	0.22	0.10	-0.14	-0.43	0.12	0.36
Tot Stu												1.00	0.23	0.85	0.07	-0.01	0.07	0.36	-0.27	-0.21
% Fem Stu													1.00	0.24	0.38	-0.10	0.29	0.16	-0.17	-0.06
Rpt PhDs														1.00	0.08	-0.03	0.06	0.36	-0.36	-0.24
% Fem															1.00	0.03	0.05	0.16	-0.10	0.13
% Min																1.00	-0.35	0.01	0.06	-0.09
% Citz																	1.00	0.06	0.03	-0.08
% RA																		1.00	-0.52	-0.37
% TA																			1.00	-0.11
MYD																				1.00

Note: The data from which these correlations are produced are given in Appendix Table L - 4.

Appendix Table O - 21 Correlation Table for Selected Characteristics of Programs in German Language and Literature

	1993 Ratings			Faculty					Students			Doctorate Recipients					
	93Q	93E	93C	Tot Fac	% Full	% Supp	No. Awd	Awd Fac	Tot Stu	% Fem Stu	Rpt PhDs	% Fem	% Min	% US	% RA	% TA	MYD
Mean	3.16	2.93	-0.07	11.16	0.58	0.39	1.38	0.10	24.41	57.30	10.72	60.31	0.00	81.99	2.38	59.96	10.90
S. D.	0.75	0.71	0.21	4.36	0.20	2.21	1.76	0.10	13.95	15.92	6.27	18.89	0.00	16.40	5.15	27.94	2.49
No.	32	32	32	32	32	32	32	32	32	31	32	32	32	32	32	32	32
93Q	1.00	0.98	0.10	0.35	0.32	0.02	0.57	0.60	0.41	-0.21	0.38	-0.53		-0.03	0.08	0.23	-0.64
93E		1.00	0.06	0.37	0.29	0.02	0.55	0.60	0.46	-0.17	0.42	-0.49		0.04	0.09	0.23	-0.63
93C			1.00	0.07	-0.12	0.04	0.20	0.14	-0.27	0.23	-0.20	-0.12		-0.09	-0.02	-0.02	0.03
Tot Fac				1.00	0.04	-0.13	0.33	0.02	0.40	0.06	0.47	-0.07		0.22	-0.07	0.09	-0.13
% Full					1.00	0.16	0.20	0.22	0.04	-0.22	0.22	-0.26		-0.35	0.43	0.12	-0.31
% Supp						1.00	-0.04	0.04	0.03	-0.02	0.01	0.06		0.05	0.56	-0.15	0.07
No. Awd							1.00	0.84	0.40	-0.21	0.19	-0.40		0.03	0.04	0.18	-0.41
Awd Fac								1.00	0.40	-0.21	0.15	-0.44		0.01	0.13	0.19	-0.47
Tot Stu									1.00	0.15	0.60	-0.23		0.22	0.19	0.16	-0.24
% Fem Stu										1.00	-0.13	0.06		0.07	-0.02	-0.02	0.39
Rpt PhDs											1.00	-0.20		0.16	0.00	-0.11	-0.23
% Fem												1.00		-0.19	-0.23	-0.17	0.15
% Min																	
% Citz														1.00	0.20	-0.13	0.25
% RA															1.00	0.02	-0.09
% TA																1.00	-0.03
MYD																	1.00

Note: The data from which these correlations are produced are given in Appendix Table J - 6.

Appendix Table O - 22 Correlation Table for Selected Characteristics of Programs in History

	1993 Ratings			Faculty								Students			Doctorate Recipients					
	93Q	93E	93C	Tot Fac	% Full	% Supp	% Pub	Pub/ Fac	Gini Pub	Cite/ Fac	Gini Cite	Tot Stu	% Fem Stu	Rpt PhDs	% Fem	% Min	% US	% RA	% TA	MYD
Mean	2.79	2.79	0.13	29.53	0.55	2.40	37.73	0.70	18.39	1.18	49.06	76.06	38.89	24.87	33.59	6.80	91.37	1.90	28.67	12.51
S. D.	1.00	0.90	0.21	15.02	0.14	3.71	13.59	0.33	17.39	2.45	25.52	64.86	11.08	22.30	13.52	9.82	8.06	4.02	19.66	2.80
No.	111	111	110	111	111	111	111	111	109	111	97	111	111	111	110	110	110	110	110	110
93Q	1.00	0.96	0.42	0.73	0.39	0.37	0.31	0.60	-0.52	0.38	-0.26	0.68	0.22	0.73	0.16	-0.05	-0.16	0.03	-0.02	-0.45
93E		1.00	0.45	0.69	0.35	0.37	0.27	0.57	-0.49	0.37	-0.26	0.64	0.20	0.70	0.15	-0.02	-0.16	0.05	-0.03	-0.41
93C			1.00	0.48	-0.01	0.17	-0.02	0.18	-0.33	0.06	-0.34	0.29	0.15	0.22	0.02	0.04	-0.06	-0.09	0.13	-0.19
Tot Fac				1.00	0.22	0.22	0.07	0.29	-0.53	0.18	-0.41	0.72	0.06	0.71	0.00	0.03	-0.15	-0.08	0.06	-0.29
% Full					1.00	0.16	0.07	0.23	0.07	0.15	0.08	0.32	-0.01	0.44	-0.14	-0.07	-0.15	0.06	-0.01	-0.13
% Supp						1.00	0.28	0.46	-0.24	0.23	-0.20	0.23	0.08	0.23	0.10	-0.04	-0.04	0.07	-0.05	-0.36
% Pub							1.00	0.78	-0.48	0.12	-0.35	0.15	0.22	0.20	0.08	-0.06	0.16	0.08	0.01	-0.19
Pub/Fac								1.00	-0.41	0.44	-0.34	0.37	0.20	0.40	0.17	-0.06	0.11	0.06	-0.04	-0.28
Gini-Pub									1.00	-0.03	0.51	-0.30	-0.22	-0.30	-0.16	-0.04	0.10	0.01	-0.11	0.32
Cite/Fac										1.00	0.17	0.27	0.07	0.30	0.11	-0.02	-0.01	-0.01	-0.05	-0.22
Gini-Cite											1.00	-0.22	0.03	-0.19	0.07	0.20	0.07	0.16	-0.17	0.11
Tot Stu												1.00	0.12	0.77	0.08	0.00	-0.05	0.02	-0.11	-0.26
% Fem Stu													1.00	0.15	0.38	0.02	0.06	-0.03	-0.11	-0.05
Rpt PhDs														1.00	0.07	0.00	-0.14	0.00	-0.16	-0.32
% Fem															1.00	0.01	0.05	0.08	-0.09	0.00
% Min																1.00	-0.06	0.24	-0.03	-0.02
% Citz																	1.00	-0.10	-0.16	0.05
% RA																		1.00	-0.13	-0.11
% TA																			1.00	-0.25
MYD																				1.00

Note: The data from which these correlations are produced are given in Appendix Table M - 4.

Appendix Table O - 23 Correlation Table for Selected Characteristics of Programs in Industrial Engineering

	1993 Ratings			Faculty								Students			Doctorate Recipients					
	93Q	93E	93C	Tot Fac	% Full	% Supp	% Pub	Pub/ Fac	Gini Pub	Cite/ Fac	Gini Cite	Tot Stu	% Fem Stu	Rpt PhDs	% Fem	% Min	% US	% RA	% TA	MYD
Mean	2.88	2.84	0.09	15.41	0.46	36.73	68.33	3.68	22.19	4.85	40.75	42.81	18.69	22.42	11.00	6.13	44.09	26.50	28.44	8.27
S. D.	0.85	0.80	0.26	9.35	0.17	20.23	16.32	2.24	12.33	6.85	27.83	31.99	8.21	16.80	9.24	9.53	19.73	22.63	20.82	1.40
No.	37	37	37	37	37	37	37	37	37	37	35	36	36	36	37	36	37	37	37	37
93Q	1.00	0.98	0.63	0.74	0.50	0.31	0.42	0.20	-0.77	0.45	-0.56	0.53	0.28	0.79	0.23	0.11	-0.12	0.54	-0.35	-0.40
93E		1.00	0.61	0.70	0.45	0.37	0.46	0.27	-0.79	0.48	-0.57	0.50	0.34	0.77	0.22	0.11	-0.14	0.53	-0.32	-0.44
93C			1.00	0.76	0.12	0.04	0.11	-0.22	-0.67	0.06	-0.39	0.49	0.29	0.53	0.14	0.16	-0.07	0.43	-0.25	-0.22
Tot Fac				1.00	0.07	0.19	0.21	-0.03	-0.74	0.15	-0.50	0.55	0.24	0.65	0.06	0.04	-0.11	0.63	-0.31	-0.27
% Full					1.00	-0.05	0.16	-0.05	-0.28	0.45	-0.15	-0.02	-0.02	0.31	0.11	0.14	0.07	0.10	-0.21	-0.33
% Supp						1.00	0.50	0.61	-0.26	0.34	-0.30	0.05	0.18	0.15	-0.04	0.16	-0.05	-0.01	0.17	-0.21
% Pub							1.00	0.67	-0.60	0.30	-0.66	0.16	0.12	0.29	0.07	0.11	-0.09	0.20	-0.15	-0.26
Pub/Fac								1.00	-0.09	0.49	-0.42	-0.08	0.10	0.13	0.07	-0.14	-0.06	-0.06	0.10	-0.01
Gini-Pub									1.00	-0.20	0.72	-0.46	-0.29	-0.63	-0.02	-0.25	0.26	-0.51	0.34	0.40
Cite/Fac										1.00	-0.13	-0.10	0.27	0.17	-0.04	-0.16	0.12	-0.08	0.23	-0.08
Gini-Cite											1.00	-0.39	-0.04	-0.54	-0.05	0.07	0.29	-0.40	0.38	0.27
Tot Stu												1.00	-0.01	0.57	0.00	-0.10	0.01	0.35	-0.27	-0.12
% Fem Stu													1.00	0.20	0.02	0.31	-0.13	0.00	0.04	0.19
Rpt PhDs														1.00	0.22	0.01	-0.13	0.36	-0.47	-0.09
% Fem															1.00	-0.20	0.22	0.18	-0.15	-0.07
% Min																1.00	-0.13	0.03	-0.14	0.02
% Citz																	1.00	-0.38	0.35	0.22
% RA																		1.00	-0.55	-0.53
% TA																			1.00	0.00
MYD																				1.00

Note: The data from which these correlations are produced are given in Appendix Table K - 6.

Appendix Table O - 24 Correlation Table for Selected Characteristics of Programs in Linguistics

	1993 Ratings			Faculty					Students			Doctorate Recipients					
	93Q	93E	93C	Tot Fac	% Full	% Supp	No. Awd	Awd Fac	Tot Stu	% Fem Stu	Rpt PhDs	% Fem	% Min	% US	% RA	% TA	MYD
Mean	2.97	2.79	0.15	15.15	0.53	21.07	1.88	0.10	39.85	57.28	22.93	50.69	8.63	64.88	8.94	31.38	10.64
S. D.	0.96	0.94	0.29	9.52	0.18	16.97	2.04	0.09	25.73	16.88	18.91	14.01	10.33	18.30	15.90	24.42	2.88
No.	41	41	40	41	41	41	41	41	40	40	40	41	41	41	41	41	41
93Q	1.00	0.97	0.14	0.32	0.38	0.49	0.36	0.35	0.29	0.00	0.29	-0.13	-0.18	-0.10	0.25	0.34	-0.56
93E		1.00	0.12	0.26	0.32	0.48	0.29	0.31	0.25	0.02	0.21	-0.15	-0.13	-0.08	0.25	0.39	-0.62
93C			1.00	0.09	-0.22	0.44	-0.01	0.00	-0.02	0.13	-0.05	-0.21	0.09	-0.07	-0.34	0.36	0.05
Tot Fac				1.00	0.24	-0.06	0.51	0.03	0.37	-0.10	0.43	0.09	-0.02	-0.06	-0.15	0.10	-0.04
% Full					1.00	0.03	0.30	0.23	0.30	-0.33	0.28	0.10	-0.34	-0.04	0.27	-0.17	-0.10
% Supp						1.00	0.04	0.27	-0.08	-0.10	-0.13	-0.14	0.00	0.29	0.16	0.25	-0.10
No. Awd							1.00	0.69	0.18	0.07	0.12	0.01	-0.17	0.13	-0.05	-0.06	-0.08
Awd Fac								1.00	0.04	-0.03	0.02	-0.21	-0.19	0.16	0.02	0.16	-0.02
Tot Stu									1.00	-0.14	0.83	0.03	-0.21	-0.08	-0.11	-0.16	0.06
% Fem Stu										1.00	-0.30	0.16	0.24	-0.01	-0.35	0.17	-0.11
Rpt PhDs											1.00	-0.03	-0.19	-0.17	-0.03	-0.10	-0.01
% Fem												1.00	0.31	0.17	0.09	-0.30	0.04
% Min													1.00	0.12	-0.04	-0.05	0.15
% Citz														1.00	-0.04	-0.15	0.33
% RA															1.00	-0.22	-0.23
% TA																1.00	-0.40
MYD																	1.00

Note: The data from which these correlations are produced are given in Appendix Table J - 7.

Appendix Table O - 25 Correlation Table for Selected Characteristics of Programs in Materials Science

	1993 Ratings			Faculty								Students			Doctorate Recipients					
	93Q	93E	93C	Tot Fac	% Full	% Supp	% Pub	Pub/ Fac	Gini Pub	Cite/ Fac	Gini Cite	Tot Stu	% Fem Stu	Rpt PhDs	% Fem	% Min	% US	% RA	% TA	MYD
Mean	3.07	2.96	0.08	18.28	0.63	58.14	84.96	11.84	16.14	47.48	25.44	48.64	16.47	33.39	11.13	3.05	49.82	68.49	4.26	7.62
S. D.	0.78	0.74	0.31	12.88	0.15	20.76	14.58	8.02	10.51	45.00	18.11	35.84	9.09	32.65	9.67	6.37	19.84	18.67	7.92	1.38
No.	65	65	65	65	65	65	65	65	65	65	65	64	62	64	62	61	62	62	62	62
93Q	1.00	0.94	0.29	0.47	0.34	0.57	0.51	0.60	-0.52	0.55	-0.51	0.63	0.35	0.68	-0.03	0.15	0.26	0.44	-0.17	-0.34
93E		1.00	0.28	0.40	0.36	0.54	0.35	0.54	-0.40	0.51	-0.41	0.58	0.33	0.69	-0.07	0.13	0.19	0.38	-0.10	-0.38
93C			1.00	0.41	0.16	0.35	0.19	0.21	-0.43	0.23	-0.38	0.24	0.10	0.02	0.18	0.01	0.12	-0.13	0.21	-0.23
Tot Fac				1.00	0.09	0.24	0.16	0.19	-0.62	0.17	-0.55	0.61	0.14	0.51	0.16	0.01	0.13	0.12	-0.06	-0.10
% Full					1.00	0.14	0.23	0.36	-0.16	0.27	-0.14	0.26	0.00	0.33	-0.08	0.00	0.06	0.16	-0.05	-0.25
% Supp						1.00	0.49	0.60	-0.38	0.55	-0.49	0.31	0.37	0.13	-0.01	0.24	0.24	0.31	-0.17	-0.31
% Pub							1.00	0.58	-0.52	0.49	-0.43	0.27	0.18	0.14	0.18	0.24	0.42	0.24	-0.10	-0.02
Pub/Fac								1.00	-0.34	0.91	-0.38	0.36	0.23	0.27	-0.11	0.20	0.22	0.45	-0.09	-0.28
Gini-Pub									1.00	-0.22	0.86	-0.50	-0.33	-0.31	-0.16	-0.07	-0.27	-0.12	0.12	0.09
Cite/Fac										1.00	-0.22	0.29	0.19	0.22	-0.09	0.20	0.26	0.43	-0.07	-0.27
Gini-Cite											1.00	-0.48	-0.32	-0.24	-0.08	-0.10	-0.26	-0.19	0.05	0.24
Tot Stu												1.00	0.37	0.72	0.12	-0.07	0.19	0.22	-0.06	-0.10
% Fem Stu													1.00	0.30	0.28	0.16	0.46	0.09	-0.29	-0.07
Rpt PhDs														1.00	0.04	-0.06	0.11	0.22	-0.16	-0.11
% Fem															1.00	0.05	0.47	-0.27	-0.05	0.28
% Min																1.00	0.01	0.34	-0.07	-0.04
% Citz																	1.00	-0.07	-0.12	-0.07
% RA																		1.00	-0.37	-0.16
% TA																			1.00	-0.16
MYD																				1.00

Note: The data from which these correlations are produced are given in Appendix Table K - 7.

Appendix Table O - 26 Correlation Table for Selected Characteristics of Programs in Mathematics

	1993 Ratings			Faculty								Students			Doctorate Recipients					
	93Q	93E	93C	Tot Fac	% Full	% Supp	% Pub	Pub/ Fac	Gini Pub	Cite/ Fac	Gini Cite	Tot Stu	% Fem Stu	Rpt PhDs	% Fem	% Min	% US	% RA	% TA	MYD
Mean	2.77	2.64	0.16	31.91	0.62	44.98	71.85	3.48	10.95	6.67	22.32	49.83	27.61	24.88	19.82	5.22	55.02	8.59	62.62	8.15
S. D.	0.99	0.96	0.21	18.12	0.16	20.32	13.61	1.40	10.72	5.98	17.81	40.54	13.71	22.99	11.89	11.73	21.98	10.99	22.91	1.76
No.	139	139	139	139	139	139	139	139	139	139	139	139	138	139	139	137	139	139	139	139
93Q	1.00	0.97	0.12	0.50	0.55	0.67	0.35	0.51	-0.43	0.56	-0.40	0.63	-0.31	0.73	-0.36	-0.14	-0.12	0.36	-0.02	-0.50
93E		1.00	0.12	0.47	0.55	0.65	0.36	0.51	-0.44	0.54	-0.40	0.58	-0.30	0.69	-0.37	-0.16	-0.15	0.36	0.00	-0.54
93C			1.00	0.35	-0.01	0.04	0.13	0.07	-0.24	0.01	-0.19	0.17	-0.02	0.09	0.00	-0.09	-0.12	-0.20	0.22	-0.09
Tot Fac				1.00	0.19	0.18	0.17	0.27	-0.55	0.21	-0.51	0.75	-0.21	0.57	-0.26	-0.11	-0.18	0.00	0.35	-0.18
% Full					1.00	0.56	0.24	0.30	-0.05	0.23	-0.19	0.39	-0.13	0.45	-0.25	0.01	-0.13	0.13	0.04	-0.23
% Supp						1.00	0.38	0.49	-0.04	0.48	-0.16	0.35	-0.10	0.45	-0.15	0.00	-0.11	0.44	-0.11	-0.16
% Pub							1.00	0.67	-0.52	0.37	-0.49	0.19	-0.16	0.29	-0.16	0.00	-0.23	0.22	0.14	-0.38
Pub/Fac								1.00	-0.34	0.73	-0.38	0.30	-0.21	0.45	-0.29	0.00	-0.25	0.35	0.12	-0.39
Gini-Pub									1.00	-0.14	0.78	-0.37	0.33	-0.35	0.33	0.08	0.19	-0.09	-0.29	0.48
Cite/Fac										1.00	-0.03	0.29	-0.21	0.46	-0.24	0.01	-0.11	0.42	-0.12	-0.25
Gini-Cite											1.00	-0.36	0.14	-0.35	0.32	0.09	0.07	-0.13	-0.35	0.42
Tot Stu												1.00	-0.29	0.79	-0.26	-0.08	-0.08	0.08	0.16	-0.19
% Fem Stu													1.00	-0.31	0.20	-0.02	0.17	-0.01	-0.15	0.16
Rpt PhDs														1.00	-0.26	-0.08	-0.10	0.17	0.09	-0.32
% Fem															1.00	-0.06	0.30	-0.25	-0.15	0.09
% Min																1.00	0.09	0.05	-0.14	0.14
% Citz																	1.00	0.07	-0.24	0.09
% RA																		1.00	-0.45	-0.18
% TA																			1.00	-0.10
MYD																				1.00

Note: The data from which these correlations are produced are given in Appendix Table L - 5.

Appendix Table O - 27 Correlation Table for Selected Characteristics of Programs in Mechanical Engineering

	1993 Ratings			Faculty								Students			Doctorate Recipients					
	93Q	93E	93C	Tot Fac	% Full	% Supp	% Pub	Pub/ Fac	Gini Pub	Cite/ Fac	Gini Cite	Tot Stu	% Fem Stu	Rpt PhDs	% Fem	% Min	% US	% RA	% TA	MYD
Mean	2.75	2.74	0.09	23.12	0.54	45.65	70.88	4.38	15.05	8.65	27.17	61.61	8.85	35.75	4.51	3.22	47.35	43.24	18.45	7.99
S. D.	0.84	0.81	0.21	14.64	0.16	19.56	16.21	2.72	9.47	11.02	18.68	60.71	5.74	36.56	4.24	6.73	16.82	20.33	16.76	1.25
No.	110	110	110	110	110	110	110	110	109	110	106	109	108	109	110	110	110	110	110	110
93Q	1.00	0.98	0.34	0.62	0.31	0.68	0.63	0.66	-0.69	0.47	-0.66	0.63	-0.05	0.73	0.11	0.00	-0.06	0.54	-0.22	-0.29
93E		1.00	0.37	0.59	0.31	0.66	0.62	0.62	-0.69	0.44	-0.65	0.61	-0.04	0.72	0.14	0.07	-0.09	0.50	-0.18	-0.30
93C			1.00	0.55	-0.09	0.16	0.13	0.24	-0.33	0.16	-0.26	0.26	-0.02	0.27	0.03	-0.06	-0.04	0.17	-0.08	-0.18
Tot Fac				1.00	0.06	0.22	0.26	0.27	-0.63	0.18	-0.45	0.66	-0.15	0.65	0.02	-0.06	-0.01	0.31	-0.06	-0.17
% Full					1.00	0.18	0.10	0.15	-0.11	0.13	-0.25	0.15	-0.10	0.16	-0.14	-0.03	-0.12	0.22	-0.13	0.07
% Supp						1.00	0.65	0.67	-0.37	0.53	-0.37	0.31	0.03	0.38	0.07	0.01	-0.01	0.52	-0.26	-0.20
% Pub							1.00	0.64	-0.59	0.44	-0.53	0.36	-0.04	0.37	0.07	0.05	-0.05	0.49	-0.13	-0.29
Pub/Fac								1.00	-0.33	0.84	-0.40	0.36	0.00	0.41	0.09	-0.10	-0.01	0.51	-0.21	-0.32
Gini-Pub									1.00	-0.15	0.80	-0.49	0.14	-0.52	-0.04	-0.02	0.05	-0.36	0.13	0.20
Cite/Fac										1.00	-0.12	0.21	0.07	0.25	0.05	-0.09	0.01	0.40	-0.20	-0.21
Gini-Cite											1.00	-0.46	0.14	-0.50	0.05	0.04	0.15	-0.35	0.17	0.28
Tot Stu												1.00	-0.13	0.84	-0.01	-0.05	0.08	0.34	-0.21	-0.06
% Fem Stu													1.00	-0.12	0.22	-0.09	-0.10	0.00	0.07	-0.02
Rpt PhDs														1.00	-0.01	0.00	-0.02	0.36	-0.20	-0.16
% Fem															1.00	0.08	0.00	0.06	0.02	-0.04
% Min																1.00	-0.18	-0.09	0.01	0.03
% Citz																	1.00	-0.20	-0.23	0.05
% RA																		1.00	-0.30	-0.30
% TA																			1.00	-0.19
MYD																				1.00

Note: The data from which these correlations are produced are given in Appendix Table K - 8.

Appendix Table O - 28 Correlation Table for Selected Characteristics of Programs in Molecular and General Genetics

	1993 Ratings			Faculty								Students			Doctorate Recipients					
	93Q	93E	93C	Tot Fac	% Full	% Supp	% Pub	Pub/ Fac	Gini Pub	Cite/ Fac	Gini Cite	Tot Stu	% Fem Stu	Rpt PhDs	% Fem	% Min	% US	% RA	% TA	MYD
Mean	2.85	3.04	0.24	27.86	0.47	63.70	84.95	7.78	14.82	83.89	21.34	30.20	45.68	17.48	41.89	4.32	85.93	33.05	14.12	8.15
S. D.	1.08	0.99	0.28	23.58	0.15	21.48	13.60	4.21	15.69	99.01	18.99	26.05	16.18	18.47	26.88	14.98	17.57	30.61	26.61	2.50
No.	103	101	96	103	103	103	103	103	102	103	102	93	88	93	74	73	74	71	71	74
93Q	1.00	0.92	0.67	0.60	0.12	0.32	0.35	0.74	-0.72	0.71	-0.70	0.55	0.04	0.38	-0.06	-0.17	-0.01	-0.06	-0.31	-0.29
93E		1.00	0.65	0.53	0.26	0.33	0.37	0.67	-0.73	0.64	-0.67	0.49	0.14	0.37	-0.10	-0.17	-0.11	-0.12	-0.12	-0.32
93C			1.00	0.60	-0.05	0.07	0.16	0.36	-0.69	0.32	-0.61	0.46	0.09	0.26	-0.10	-0.05	-0.08	-0.01	-0.24	-0.01
Tot Fac				1.00	0.03	-0.01	0.17	0.39	-0.61	0.30	-0.64	0.68	0.00	0.55	-0.03	-0.16	-0.14	-0.09	-0.09	-0.13
% Full					1.00	0.20	0.15	0.18	-0.12	0.11	-0.16	0.16	0.18	0.27	-0.09	-0.04	-0.03	-0.34	0.13	-0.01
% Supp						1.00	0.28	0.25	-0.15	0.25	-0.14	0.00	0.20	0.02	-0.07	0.08	0.33	-0.23	-0.09	0.06
% Pub							1.00	0.48	-0.19	0.32	-0.23	0.14	0.28	0.05	0.13	-0.11	0.27	-0.08	-0.11	-0.05
Pub/Fac								1.00	-0.36	0.87	-0.44	0.37	0.11	0.18	0.01	-0.07	0.06	0.00	-0.36	-0.27
Gini-Pub									1.00	-0.29	0.88	-0.45	-0.16	-0.35	0.06	0.21	0.12	-0.03	0.07	0.19
Cite/Fac										1.00	-0.30	0.31	0.03	0.11	-0.08	-0.07	0.12	-0.10	-0.33	-0.22
Gini-Cite											1.00	-0.46	-0.10	-0.36	-0.03	0.16	0.17	-0.05	0.15	0.11
Tot Stu												1.00	0.07	0.81	-0.01	-0.16	-0.22	-0.15	-0.21	0.10
% Fem Stu													1.00	0.03	0.01	0.07	0.06	-0.24	-0.06	0.09
Rpt PhDs														1.00	0.01	-0.15	-0.16	-0.23	-0.07	0.14
% Fem															1.00	-0.13	-0.11	0.12	-0.13	-0.14
% Min																1.00	0.11	-0.05	-0.11	0.07
% Citz																	1.00	-0.21	-0.13	-0.08
% RA																		1.00	-0.33	0.01
% TA																			1.00	-0.04
MYD																				1.00

Note: The data from which these correlations are produced are given in Appendix Table N - 4.

Appendix Table O - 29 Correlation Table for Selected Characteristics of Programs in Music

	1993 Ratings			Faculty					Students			Doctorate Recipients					
	93Q	93E	93C	Tot Fac	% Full	% Supp	No. Awd	Awd Fac	Tot Stu	% Fem Stu	Rpt PhDs	% Fem	% Min	% US	% RA	% TA	MYD
Mean	3.11	2.87	0.06	21.85	0.49	0.67	1.58	0.09	52.49	57.94	28.92	36.07	4.78	90.88	0.62	24.84	11.43
S. D.	0.79	0.75	0.21	16.50	0.17	2.17	2.16	0.14	55.29	64.22	29.17	13.19	6.16	8.30	1.58	19.06	1.77
No.	65	65	65	65	65	65	65	65	65	65	65	65	65	65	65	65	65
93Q	1.00	0.97	0.25	0.17	0.26	0.07	0.73	0.62	0.34	-0.26	0.27	-0.12	-0.01	-0.29	0.10	0.15	-0.52
93E		1.00	0.24	0.13	0.24	0.08	0.69	0.61	0.29	-0.20	0.27	-0.14	0.02	-0.27	0.06	0.11	-0.53
93C			1.00	0.21	-0.08	0.06	0.10	0.06	0.09	-0.04	0.18	0.09	0.25	-0.01	0.12	0.21	-0.35
Tot Fac				1.00	0.16	-0.02	0.13	-0.21	0.69	-0.18	0.70	-0.05	-0.03	0.03	0.15	-0.07	-0.07
% Full					1.00	-0.10	0.26	0.13	0.23	0.06	0.31	0.00	-0.10	-0.02	0.12	0.02	0.04
% Supp						1.00	0.01	0.01	0.05	-0.08	0.01	0.17	0.05	0.12	0.02	0.18	-0.25
No. Awd							1.00	0.85	0.27	-0.18	0.24	-0.14	-0.02	-0.25	-0.01	0.14	-0.37
Awd Fac								1.00	-0.05	-0.16	-0.09	-0.14	0.00	-0.19	-0.08	0.20	-0.29
Tot Stu									1.00	-0.18	0.75	-0.02	-0.07	-0.07	0.09	0.09	-0.17
% Fem Stu										1.00	0.04	0.15	-0.03	0.18	0.08	-0.03	0.20
Rpt PhDs											1.00	-0.02	-0.10	0.02	0.13	0.04	-0.20
% Fem												1.00	0.11	0.03	-0.03	0.36	0.01
% Min													1.00	0.06	0.25	0.01	-0.14
% Citz														1.00	-0.12	-0.27	0.34
% RA															1.00	0.05	-0.05
% TA																1.00	-0.31
MYD																	1.00

Note: The data from which these correlations are produced are given in Appendix Table J - 8.

Appendix Table O - 30 Correlation Table for Selected Characteristics of Programs in Neurosciences

	1993 Ratings			Faculty								Students			Doctorate Recipients					
	93Q	93E	93C	Tot Fac	% Full	% Supp	% Pub	Pub/ Fac	Gini Pub	Cite/ Fac	Gini Cite	Tot Stu	% Fem Stu	Rpt PhDs	% Fem	% Min	% US	% RA	% TA	MYD
Mean	2.85	2.87	0.17	28.76	0.49	68.52	86.12	8.16	14.02	65.33	19.45	23.05	40.15	10.44	34.43	3.32	85.31	29.03	19.79	7.59
S. D.	1.12	1.12	0.32	21.64	0.19	22.88	13.07	3.92	16.28	60.37	20.34	20.78	18.51	11.75	22.72	7.48	18.88	27.72	29.77	1.29
No.	102	102	100	102	102	102	102	102	102	102	101	97	91	97	92	91	92	91	91	92
93Q	1.00	0.97	0.51	0.65	0.30	0.28	0.24	0.67	-0.71	0.71	-0.65	0.58	0.03	0.43	-0.06	-0.05	0.05	-0.05	-0.42	0.02
93E		1.00	0.49	0.61	0.30	0.29	0.23	0.64	-0.73	0.65	-0.68	0.56	0.03	0.43	-0.08	-0.10	0.09	0.00	-0.35	0.06
93C			1.00	0.39	0.06	-0.04	-0.07	0.23	-0.46	0.28	-0.29	0.22	-0.13	0.00	-0.08	-0.01	-0.11	-0.12	-0.16	0.17
Tot Fac				1.00	0.10	-0.06	0.22	0.52	-0.61	0.45	-0.62	0.40	0.09	0.43	-0.07	-0.07	0.09	0.05	-0.30	0.03
% Full					1.00	0.26	0.20	0.33	-0.13	0.30	-0.10	0.28	-0.12	0.25	-0.03	0.02	0.06	0.03	-0.12	0.08
% Supp						1.00	0.47	0.32	-0.06	0.29	-0.03	0.06	0.04	0.18	0.00	0.00	0.10	0.13	-0.16	0.08
% Pub							1.00	0.48	-0.40	0.31	-0.32	0.07	0.13	0.24	0.03	-0.13	0.31	0.03	0.02	0.13
Pub/Fac								1.00	-0.44	0.85	-0.46	0.32	0.14	0.38	-0.13	0.03	0.11	0.03	-0.30	-0.01
Gini-Pub									1.00	-0.34	0.92	-0.35	-0.06	-0.34	0.09	0.19	-0.04	-0.10	0.27	-0.14
Cite/Fac										1.00	-0.30	0.39	0.04	0.36	-0.10	0.02	0.02	-0.07	-0.31	-0.10
Gini-Cite											1.00	-0.32	-0.17	-0.31	-0.03	0.10	-0.13	-0.10	0.18	-0.13
Tot Stu												1.00	0.03	0.39	-0.13	-0.02	0.08	0.10	-0.31	-0.07
% Fem Stu													1.00	0.02	0.15	0.35	0.12	-0.08	0.16	-0.08
Rpt PhDs														1.00	-0.03	0.05	0.11	0.05	-0.15	-0.06
% Fem															1.00	0.18	0.12	-0.08	-0.01	-0.38
% Min																1.00	0.05	-0.17	-0.06	-0.13
% Citz																	1.00	-0.09	0.00	-0.15
% RA																		1.00	-0.39	0.08
% TA																			1.00	0.13
MYD																				1.00

Note: The data from which these correlations are produced are given in Appendix Table N - 5.

Appendix Table O - 31 Correlation Table for Selected Characteristics of Programs in Oceanography

	1993 Ratings			Faculty								Students			Doctorate Recipients					
	93Q	93E	93C	Tot Fac	% Full	% Supp	% Pub	Pub/ Fac	Gini Pub	Cite/ Fac	Gini Cite	Tot Stu	% Fem Stu	Rpt PhDs	% Fem	% Min	% US	% RA	% TA	MYD
Mean	3.18	3.04	0.16	27.23	0.57	65.41	83.44	5.33	12.13	23.97	19.23	45.58	34.68	23.73	19.51	3.43	72.36	63.65	4.47	9.28
S. D.	0.82	0.67	0.24	22.94	0.15	20.74	12.15	2.36	10.46	19.17	20.46	43.44	12.78	22.93	9.56	5.68	14.46	21.14	9.39	1.50
No.	26	26	26	26	26	26	26	26	26	26	26	26	25	26	22	22	22	22	22	22
93Q	1.00	0.95	0.15	0.62	0.34	0.70	0.34	0.57	-0.60	0.70	-0.51	0.77	0.04	0.70	0.51	0.01	0.23	0.50	-0.49	-0.07
93E		1.00	0.14	0.61	0.35	0.66	0.47	0.67	-0.73	0.74	-0.67	0.79	0.17	0.74	0.58	0.06	0.32	0.61	-0.46	-0.04
93C			1.00	0.14	0.04	0.09	-0.13	-0.09	-0.32	-0.12	-0.26	-0.01	-0.23	-0.20	-0.12	-0.39	-0.18	-0.02	-0.14	0.31
Tot Fac				1.00	0.23	0.07	0.02	0.21	-0.57	0.20	-0.49	0.81	-0.01	0.67	0.11	0.08	0.23	0.11	-0.27	0.10
% Full					1.00	0.12	0.18	0.42	-0.42	0.22	-0.32	0.28	0.04	0.32	0.00	0.61	0.59	0.30	-0.15	0.25
% Supp						1.00	0.29	0.41	-0.28	0.52	-0.23	0.22	0.24	0.18	0.25	-0.12	0.07	0.55	-0.27	0.03
% Pub							1.00	0.68	-0.55	0.61	-0.56	0.27	0.00	0.34	0.38	0.19	0.16	0.29	-0.13	-0.31
Pub/Fac								1.00	-0.58	0.75	-0.63	0.47	0.15	0.49	0.44	0.26	0.38	0.57	-0.40	-0.14
Gini-Pub									1.00	-0.47	0.94	-0.57	-0.06	-0.50	-0.37	-0.22	-0.33	-0.44	0.51	-0.26
Cite/Fac										1.00	-0.43	0.52	0.14	0.54	0.60	0.13	0.35	0.53	-0.28	-0.26
Gini-Cite											1.00	-0.52	-0.05	-0.44	-0.40	-0.21	-0.29	-0.53	0.73	-0.36
Tot Stu												1.00	0.02	0.93	0.43	0.03	0.40	0.24	-0.35	-0.05
% Fem Stu													1.00	0.01	0.30	0.09	0.30	0.16	0.28	0.27
Rpt PhDs														1.00	0.51	0.19	0.38	0.27	-0.28	-0.18
% Fem															1.00	0.04	0.17	0.23	-0.04	-0.11
% Min																1.00	0.43	0.26	-0.01	0.09
% Citz																	1.00	0.36	-0.18	0.38
% RA																		1.00	-0.45	-0.09
% TA																			1.00	-0.30
MYD																				1.00

Note: The data from which these correlations are produced are given in Appendix Table L - 6.

Appendix Table O - 32 Correlation Table for Selected Characteristics of Programs in Pharmacology

	1993 Ratings			Faculty								Students			Doctorate Recipients					
	93Q	93E	93C	Tot Fac	% Full	% Supp	% Pub	Pub/ Fac	Gini Pub	Cite/ Fac	Gini Cite	Tot Stu	% Fem Stu	Rpt PhDs	% Fem	% Min	% US	% RA	% TA	MYD
Mean	3.11	3.16	0.19	20.85	0.50	52.29	86.04	9.51	15.15	65.06	21.90	21.31	46.32	13.82	34.99	4.90	85.88	26.08	9.03	7.30
S. D.	0.66	0.61	0.26	17.54	0.18	24.75	14.18	5.01	14.71	67.92	19.79	16.94	16.58	13.09	16.27	9.40	14.63	22.68	17.05	1.32
No.	127	127	126	127	127	127	127	127	126	127	126	125	123	125	120	119	120	118	118	120
93Q	1.00	0.94	0.58	0.55	0.34	0.49	0.35	0.63	-0.76	0.65	-0.68	0.51	-0.18	0.49	0.14	-0.18	0.05	-0.01	-0.27	-0.09
93E		1.00	0.59	0.53	0.31	0.43	0.32	0.58	-0.76	0.57	-0.65	0.48	-0.23	0.45	0.09	-0.17	0.03	0.02	-0.30	-0.15
93C			1.00	0.49	0.09	0.24	0.12	0.32	-0.44	0.27	-0.40	0.41	0.01	0.26	-0.02	-0.19	0.25	0.06	-0.10	-0.18
Tot Fac				1.00	0.05	0.16	0.12	0.28	-0.49	0.28	-0.49	0.70	-0.02	0.73	0.02	-0.11	0.04	0.06	-0.13	-0.02
% Full					1.00	0.19	0.33	0.34	-0.14	0.25	-0.19	0.12	-0.21	0.18	0.25	-0.06	0.04	-0.07	-0.07	0.03
% Supp						1.00	0.48	0.50	-0.26	0.50	-0.33	0.18	-0.11	0.21	0.15	-0.26	0.05	0.03	-0.01	-0.11
% Pub							1.00	0.58	-0.19	0.39	-0.31	0.13	-0.09	0.18	0.18	-0.29	0.12	-0.09	0.00	-0.01
Pub/Fac								1.00	-0.31	0.83	-0.45	0.29	-0.06	0.30	0.28	-0.21	0.05	0.05	-0.29	0.00
Gini-Pub									1.00	-0.31	0.84	-0.44	0.16	-0.36	0.17	0.10	0.08	-0.11	0.33	0.13
Cite/Fac										1.00	-0.34	0.27	-0.04	0.30	0.23	-0.17	0.08	-0.04	-0.29	0.03
Gini-Cite											1.00	-0.39	0.03	-0.34	0.07	0.09	0.11	-0.10	0.32	0.11
Tot Stu												1.00	-0.12	0.82	0.04	-0.14	0.02	0.00	-0.15	0.08
% Fem Stu													1.00	-0.04	-0.03	0.22	0.25	-0.10	0.07	-0.14
Rpt PhDs														1.00	0.04	-0.12	0.02	-0.04	-0.16	0.06
% Fem															1.00	0.00	0.25	-0.12	0.19	0.14
% Min																1.00	-0.12	-0.12	0.13	0.02
% Citz																	1.00	-0.25	0.10	0.00
% RA																		1.00	-0.27	-0.04
% TA																			1.00	0.12
MYD																				1.00

Note: The data from which these correlations are produced are given in Appendix Table N - 6.

Appendix Table O - 33 Correlation Table for Selected Characteristics of Programs in Philosophy

	1993 Ratings			Faculty					Students			Doctorate Recipients					
	93Q	93E	93C	Tot Fac	% Full	% Supp	No. Awd	Awd Fac	Tot Stu	% Fem Stu	Rpt PhDs	% Fem	% Min	% US	% RA	% TA	MYD
Mean	2.84	2.79	0.07	17.15	0.56	6.45	2.92	0.14	44.00	25.86	15.38	22.85	4.07	84.02	2.41	44.55	9.94
S. D.	0.95	0.80	0.29	6.85	0.16	10.02	2.82	0.13	21.73	8.30	7.84	10.75	5.69	15.53	11.93	26.36	1.66
No.	72	72	72	72	72	72	72	72	72	72	72	72	71	72	72	72	72
93Q	1.00	0.94	0.22	0.39	0.31	0.30	0.80	0.72	0.17	0.15	0.35	0.24	-0.10	-0.06	-0.06	0.30	-0.50
93E		1.00	0.23	0.38	0.29	0.22	0.74	0.68	0.19	0.14	0.39	0.30	-0.10	0.03	-0.15	0.31	-0.45
93C			1.00	0.45	0.16	0.03	0.14	0.05	0.14	-0.12	-0.08	0.20	-0.09	0.12	0.01	0.23	-0.07
Tot Fac				1.00	-0.05	0.11	0.34	0.05	0.48	0.04	0.39	0.17	-0.06	0.13	-0.08	0.34	-0.01
% Full					1.00	-0.02	0.29	0.26	-0.01	0.12	0.07	0.15	0.15	0.14	-0.27	0.18	-0.10
% Supp						1.00	0.17	0.12	-0.09	-0.05	-0.08	-0.10	-0.14	-0.49	0.62	-0.09	-0.40
No. Awd							1.00	0.91	0.15	0.13	0.42	0.14	-0.13	0.01	-0.10	0.26	-0.36
Awd Fac								1.00	0.01	0.13	0.31	0.13	-0.11	-0.08	-0.09	0.19	-0.38
Tot Stu									1.00	0.09	0.44	0.12	-0.06	0.23	-0.14	-0.03	0.15
% Fem Stu										1.00	0.26	0.24	-0.10	0.08	-0.15	-0.14	-0.05
Rpt PhDs											1.00	0.31	-0.05	0.16	-0.16	0.05	-0.12
% Fem												1.00	-0.28	0.15	-0.24	0.03	-0.04
% Min													1.00	0.01	-0.07	-0.03	0.09
% Citz														1.00	-0.67	0.16	0.22
% RA															1.00	-0.24	-0.28
% TA																1.00	-0.22
MYD																	1.00

Note: The data from which these correlations are produced are given in Appendix Table J - 9.

Appendix Table O - 34 Correlation Table for Selected Characteristics of Programs in Physics

	1993 Ratings			Faculty								Students			Doctorate Recipients					
	93Q	93E	93C	Tot Fac	% Full	% Supp	% Pub	Pub/ Fac	Gini Pub	Cite/ Fac	Gini Cite	Tot Stu	% Fem Stu	Rpt PhDs	% Fem	% Min	% US	% RA	% TA	MYD
Mean	2.82	2.83	0.15	29.15	0.67	46.62	82.82	7.83	10.44	43.33	15.92	73.73	14.20	39.29	11.52	4.54	55.97	53.51	24.45	7.78
S. D.	0.92	0.91	0.23	17.05	0.12	16.81	9.90	2.92	7.66	30.16	10.88	58.83	7.47	36.18	8.32	10.17	17.17	23.80	20.74	1.18
No.	147	146	146	147	147	147	147	147	147	147	147	147	146	147	147	145	146	146	146	146
93Q	1.00	0.95	0.20	0.78	0.41	0.40	0.30	0.55	-0.59	0.70	-0.62	0.78	-0.22	0.81	-0.26	-0.18	0.22	0.48	-0.35	-0.46
93E		1.00	0.20	0.72	0.37	0.40	0.30	0.57	-0.64	0.67	-0.61	0.71	-0.24	0.77	-0.23	-0.24	0.21	0.50	-0.28	-0.53
93C			1.00	0.32	-0.06	0.09	0.00	0.15	-0.38	0.12	-0.30	0.14	-0.10	0.11	-0.03	-0.02	0.11	0.18	-0.07	-0.04
Tot Fac				1.00	0.27	0.28	0.17	0.42	-0.64	0.47	-0.62	0.80	-0.22	0.82	-0.23	-0.12	0.14	0.45	-0.29	-0.32
% Full					1.00	0.33	0.26	0.27	-0.22	0.30	-0.22	0.34	-0.16	0.36	-0.17	0.10	0.08	0.02	0.11	-0.10
% Supp						1.00	0.46	0.47	-0.37	0.37	-0.39	0.32	-0.11	0.35	0.05	-0.09	0.08	0.32	-0.13	-0.12
% Pub							1.00	0.49	-0.36	0.38	-0.30	0.19	-0.19	0.24	0.10	0.00	0.23	0.20	-0.14	-0.10
Pub/Fac								1.00	-0.37	0.70	-0.45	0.54	-0.17	0.55	-0.07	-0.09	0.15	0.34	-0.31	-0.27
Gini-Pub									1.00	-0.37	0.79	-0.41	0.29	-0.49	0.17	0.21	-0.08	-0.46	0.21	0.44
Cite/Fac										1.00	-0.27	0.55	-0.17	0.61	-0.11	-0.12	0.21	0.32	-0.26	-0.35
Gini-Cite											1.00	-0.49	0.19	-0.50	0.13	0.33	-0.03	-0.43	0.31	0.45
Tot Stu												1.00	-0.12	0.88	-0.17	-0.11	0.17	0.38	-0.32	-0.33
% Fem Stu													1.00	-0.16	0.09	0.02	0.06	-0.26	0.21	0.13
Rpt PhDs														1.00	-0.14	-0.12	0.25	0.40	-0.30	-0.33
% Fem															1.00	-0.09	-0.01	-0.17	0.22	0.17
% Min																1.00	0.22	-0.19	0.06	0.47
% Citz																	1.00	0.21	-0.28	-0.07
% RA																		1.00	-0.70	-0.48
% TA																			1.00	0.30
MYD																				1.00

Note: The data from which these correlations are produced are given in Appendix Table L - 7.

Appendix Table O - 35 Correlation Table for Selected Characteristics of Programs in Physiology

	1993 Ratings			Faculty								Students			Doctorate Recipients					
	93Q	93E	93C	Tot Fac	% Full	% Supp	% Pub	Pub/ Fac	Gini Pub	Cite/ Fac	Gini Cite	Tot Stu	% Fem Stu	Rpt PhDs	% Fem	% Min	% US	% RA	% TA	MYD
Mean	2.87	3.08	0.18	21.19	0.53	53.78	84.48	8.22	15.16	51.23	21.79	15.98	41.76	11.38	32.41	4.37	85.86	27.81	17.40	8.26
S. D.	0.90	0.70	0.27	19.28	0.16	23.49	12.61	4.31	12.51	55.14	17.25	14.02	19.11	10.32	21.02	11.53	13.19	25.31	25.55	1.69
No.	140	137	128	140	140	140	140	140	140	140	140	133	127	133	133	133	133	132	132	133
93Q	1.00	0.91	0.44	0.51	0.07	0.48	0.42	0.61	-0.73	0.61	-0.71	0.39	0.07	0.37	0.23	-0.05	-0.10	-0.05	-0.21	-0.05
93E		1.00	0.44	0.43	0.08	0.40	0.30	0.51	-0.65	0.53	-0.63	0.36	0.01	0.36	0.26	-0.11	-0.03	-0.03	-0.16	-0.05
93C			1.00	0.37	-0.13	0.20	0.03	0.26	-0.45	0.23	-0.43	0.34	0.13	0.23	0.04	-0.18	0.01	0.07	-0.04	0.04
Tot Fac				1.00	0.00	0.14	0.15	0.21	-0.53	0.17	-0.52	0.71	0.04	0.62	0.14	-0.04	-0.01	-0.01	-0.09	0.13
% Full					1.00	0.19	0.30	0.23	0.02	0.11	0.09	0.03	-0.06	0.08	-0.09	0.10	-0.02	-0.08	0.01	-0.01
% Supp						1.00	0.45	0.48	-0.17	0.55	-0.24	0.15	-0.07	0.16	0.24	-0.17	-0.04	0.04	-0.15	-0.12
% Pub							1.00	0.57	-0.40	0.40	-0.35	0.17	0.05	0.13	0.16	-0.10	-0.08	-0.11	-0.05	0.06
Pub/Fac								1.00	-0.31	0.80	-0.33	0.22	0.08	0.19	0.22	-0.05	-0.13	-0.05	-0.23	-0.16
Gini-Pub									1.00	-0.19	0.91	-0.49	-0.08	-0.41	-0.08	0.07	0.13	0.03	0.12	-0.05
Cite/Fac										1.00	-0.20	0.07	0.03	0.07	0.24	-0.07	-0.10	0.03	-0.29	-0.14
Gini-Cite											1.00	-0.46	-0.06	-0.40	-0.11	0.07	0.10	0.04	0.13	-0.06
Tot Stu												1.00	0.05	0.72	0.01	0.00	0.03	0.04	-0.04	-0.04
% Fem Stu													1.00	0.04	0.27	0.00	0.11	-0.17	-0.02	0.01
Rpt PhDs														1.00	0.00	-0.03	-0.01	0.01	0.01	-0.03
% Fem															1.00	0.04	-0.03	0.02	-0.02	-0.05
% Min																1.00	-0.03	-0.16	0.05	-0.15
% Citz																	1.00	-0.14	-0.09	0.04
% RA																		1.00	-0.38	-0.06
% TA																			1.00	0.07
MYD																				1.00

Note: The data from which these correlations are produced are given in Appendix Table N - 7.

Appendix Table O - 36 Correlation Table for Selected Characteristics of Programs in Political Science

	1993 Ratings			Faculty								Students			Doctorate Recipients					
	93Q	93E	93C	Tot Fac	% Full	% Supp	% Pub	Pub/ Fac	Gini Pub	Cite/ Fac	Gini Cite	Tot Stu	% Fem Stu	Rpt PhDs	% Fem	% Min	% US	% RA	% TA	MYD
Mean	2.66	2.52	0.04	24.13	0.51	7.21	54.42	1.46	16.18	2.49	32.58	68.72	33.31	26.18	26.23	10.74	75.78	5.57	27.96	10.23
S. D.	0.98	0.89	0.27	10.09	0.13	8.44	15.03	0.72	14.70	2.90	20.79	50.41	9.83	20.62	10.05	14.76	11.99	8.14	21.07	2.15
No.	98	98	98	98	98	98	98	98	98	98	96	98	97	98	98	98	98	98	98	98
93Q	1.00	0.97	0.33	0.74	0.48	0.52	0.52	0.57	-0.59	0.62	-0.54	0.52	0.01	0.59	0.03	-0.28	0.15	0.11	0.10	-0.24
93E		1.00	0.31	0.69	0.47	0.56	0.49	0.56	-0.57	0.59	-0.55	0.44	0.00	0.54	-0.01	-0.26	0.14	0.11	0.10	-0.25
93C			1.00	0.48	0.08	0.18	0.16	0.22	-0.25	0.19	-0.27	0.18	-0.06	0.03	0.00	-0.09	0.00	0.16	0.16	-0.01
Tot Fac				1.00	0.35	0.25	0.28	0.28	-0.53	0.32	-0.46	0.64	0.02	0.59	0.02	-0.14	0.14	0.09	0.12	0.01
% Full					1.00	0.20	0.41	0.32	-0.47	0.20	-0.39	0.22	0.11	0.21	0.09	-0.16	-0.09	-0.01	0.18	-0.05
% Supp						1.00	0.37	0.51	-0.25	0.53	-0.31	0.13	0.02	0.15	-0.04	-0.15	0.09	0.25	0.17	-0.16
% Pub							1.00	0.75	-0.68	0.43	-0.58	0.20	-0.11	0.18	0.14	-0.20	-0.04	0.19	0.29	-0.21
Pub/Fac								1.00	-0.46	0.75	-0.49	0.17	-0.15	0.23	0.12	-0.21	0.00	0.17	0.23	-0.24
Gini-Pub									1.00	-0.26	0.65	-0.31	0.00	-0.19	-0.08	0.29	-0.03	-0.17	-0.24	-0.04
Cite/Fac										1.00	-0.23	0.30	-0.19	0.39	-0.01	-0.13	0.04	0.06	0.04	-0.20
Gini-Cite											1.00	-0.28	0.05	-0.26	-0.03	-0.11	0.01	-0.20	-0.23	0.05
Tot Stu												1.00	-0.06	0.72	-0.01	-0.05	0.10	0.10	-0.18	0.05
% Fem Stu													1.00	-0.05	0.27	-0.02	0.22	0.12	-0.06	-0.11
Rpt PhDs														1.00	-0.08	-0.01	0.05	0.05	-0.23	-0.06
% Fem															1.00	-0.24	0.31	0.12	0.12	-0.02
% Min																1.00	-0.13	0.01	-0.08	-0.02
% Citz																	1.00	0.07	-0.02	0.08
% RA																		1.00	-0.10	-0.15
% TA																			1.00	-0.16
MYD																				1.00

Note: The data from which these correlations are produced are given in Appendix Table M - 5.

Appendix Table O - 37 Correlation Table for Selected Characteristics of Programs in Psychology

	1993 Ratings			Faculty								Students			Doctorate Recipients					
	93Q	93E	93C	Tot Fac	% Full	% Supp	% Pub	Pub/ Fac	Gini Pub	Cite/ Fac	Gini Cite	Tot Stu	% Fem Stu	Rpt PhDs	% Fem	% Min	% US	% RA	% TA	MYD
Mean	2.71	2.75	0.07	27.34	0.52	23.42	70.68	3.71	13.63	12.83	22.10	100.17	63.18	60.55	56.02	7.28	96.07	11.43	15.22	9.00
S. D.	0.95	0.92	0.25	15.79	0.16	18.32	20.62	2.15	13.70	13.62	20.68	84.10	15.53	48.73	11.42	9.68	4.36	10.16	14.29	1.97
No.	185	184	178	185	185	185	185	185	183	185	180	185	185	185	185	185	185	185	185	185
93Q	1.00	0.96	0.26	0.57	0.44	0.74	0.70	0.74	-0.65	0.60	-0.65	-0.04	-0.21	0.02	0.15	0.02	-0.35	0.33	0.34	-0.36
93E		1.00	0.24	0.50	0.42	0.72	0.76	0.74	-0.68	0.58	-0.69	-0.10	-0.21	-0.08	0.19	0.09	-0.30	0.35	0.37	-0.36
93C			1.00	0.30	-0.06	0.06	0.11	0.07	-0.28	-0.10	-0.25	0.13	0.02	0.14	0.05	0.02	0.05	0.09	0.05	-0.09
Tot Fac				1.00	0.16	0.25	0.15	0.26	-0.39	0.17	-0.39	0.51	0.00	0.53	0.12	0.11	-0.11	0.15	0.18	-0.06
% Full					1.00	0.33	0.33	0.33	-0.32	0.31	-0.26	-0.10	-0.18	-0.05	-0.02	0.16	-0.22	0.18	0.09	-0.15
% Supp						1.00	0.57	0.69	-0.36	0.65	-0.42	-0.18	-0.24	-0.18	0.19	-0.01	-0.36	0.32	0.29	-0.29
% Pub							1.00	0.75	-0.65	0.49	-0.64	-0.35	-0.17	-0.29	0.09	-0.05	-0.22	0.33	0.35	-0.44
Pub/Fac								1.00	-0.42	0.83	-0.46	-0.18	-0.20	-0.15	0.10	-0.05	-0.25	0.36	0.26	-0.42
Gini-Pub									1.00	-0.17	0.80	0.15	0.18	0.14	-0.08	-0.03	0.14	-0.20	-0.24	0.21
Cite/Fac										1.00	-0.22	-0.15	-0.14	-0.13	0.09	-0.03	-0.21	0.36	0.12	-0.29
Gini-Cite											1.00	0.15	0.18	0.10	-0.19	-0.04	0.15	-0.17	-0.22	0.23
Tot Stu												1.00	0.17	0.84	0.16	0.17	0.11	-0.13	-0.14	0.09
% Fem Stu													1.00	0.24	0.21	0.07	0.28	-0.18	-0.17	0.08
Rpt PhDs														1.00	0.05	0.05	0.12	-0.14	-0.15	-0.05
% Fem															1.00	0.26	0.09	-0.17	-0.07	0.27
% Min																1.00	0.02	-0.09	-0.06	0.26
% Citz																	1.00	-0.16	-0.30	0.28
% RA																		1.00	0.05	-0.32
% TA																			1.00	-0.34
MYD																				1.00

Note: The data from which these correlations are produced are given in Appendix Table M - 6.

Appendix Table O - 38 Correlation Table for Selected Characteristics of Programs in Religion

	1993 Ratings			Faculty					Students			Doctorate Recipients					
	93Q	93E	93C	Tot Fac	% Full	% Supp	No. Awd	Awd Fac	Tot Stu	% Fem Stu	Rpt PhDs	% Fem	% Min	% US	% RA	% TA	MYD
Mean	3.15	2.92	0.07	24.34	0.59	0.20	3.26	0.10	81.82	30.38	35.37	21.55	4.71	88.34	1.03	8.76	13.24
S. D.	0.84	0.66	0.30	12.08	0.18	0.69	5.08	0.12	55.05	12.17	33.14	12.63	6.03	15.35	2.47	14.90	2.44
No.	38	38	38	38	38	38	38	38	38	37	38	38	38	38	38	38	38
93Q	1.00	0.97	0.36	0.36	0.10	0.21	0.56	0.58	0.07	0.64	0.09	0.15	0.05	0.33	-0.04	0.00	-0.13
93E		1.00	0.38	0.32	0.16	0.19	0.51	0.54	0.06	0.59	0.07	0.13	-0.03	0.37	0.01	0.00	-0.14
93C			1.00	0.30	0.09	-0.19	0.13	0.03	0.01	0.14	-0.02	-0.06	0.06	0.05	0.31	-0.14	0.11
Tot Fac				1.00	0.11	0.38	0.50	0.09	0.27	-0.04	0.35	0.01	-0.14	0.00	0.15	-0.01	-0.11
% Full					1.00	0.17	0.21	0.13	-0.06	-0.07	0.03	-0.44	-0.19	-0.09	0.04	0.08	0.09
% Supp						1.00	0.42	0.26	-0.03	0.32	-0.22	0.25	0.00	0.10	0.03	0.02	-0.04
No. Awd							1.00	0.81	-0.12	0.42	-0.05	0.26	-0.01	0.10	-0.07	0.26	-0.30
Awd Fac								1.00	-0.11	0.53	-0.07	0.21	0.23	0.22	-0.06	0.15	-0.37
Tot Stu									1.00	-0.10	0.75	0.05	0.07	0.00	0.03	-0.30	-0.01
% Fem Stu										1.00	-0.21	0.52	0.15	0.37	0.07	0.02	0.02
Rpt PhDs											1.00	-0.21	0.00	0.00	0.00	-0.28	-0.22
% Fem												1.00	0.04	0.04	0.14	0.23	-0.09
% Min													1.00	-0.05	-0.10	0.13	-0.22
% Citz														1.00	0.18	0.00	-0.12
% RA															1.00	-0.06	0.03
% TA																1.00	-0.12
MYD																	1.00

Note: The data from which these correlations are produced are given in Appendix Table J - 10.

Appendix Table O - 39 Correlation Table for Selected Characteristics of Programs in Sociology

	1993 Ratings			Faculty								Students			Doctorate Recipients					
	93Q	93E	93C	Tot Fac	% Full	% Supp	% Pub	Pub/ Fac	Gini Pub	Cite/ Fac	Gini Cite	Tot Stu	% Fem Stu	Rpt PhDs	% Fem	% Min	% US	% RA	% TA	MYD
Mean	2.61	2.51	0.03	21.46	0.51	17.01	63.74	2.13	14.68	5.48	29.90	53.88	56.66	22.66	49.01	11.86	81.02	12.92	26.18	11.38
S. D.	0.99	0.89	0.24	10.32	0.16	14.19	15.08	1.04	8.68	5.32	19.74	38.11	11.78	14.06	14.79	13.37	11.76	13.68	18.33	2.42
No.	95	95	95	95	95	95	95	95	95	95	95	95	94	95	95	95	95	95	95	95
93Q	1.00	0.97	0.34	0.59	0.38	0.46	0.43	0.41	-0.55	0.47	-0.51	0.59	-0.28	0.63	0.02	-0.01	-0.04	0.29	-0.02	-0.36
93E		1.00	0.35	0.61	0.36	0.48	0.45	0.46	-0.57	0.51	-0.55	0.57	-0.28	0.61	-0.02	0.00	-0.08	0.33	-0.02	-0.40
93C			1.00	0.43	0.02	0.13	0.22	0.32	-0.34	0.18	-0.29	0.13	0.04	0.08	0.12	0.06	0.13	0.19	-0.09	-0.12
Tot Fac				1.00	0.20	0.18	0.28	0.27	-0.62	0.26	-0.43	0.58	-0.24	0.60	-0.03	0.04	-0.14	0.20	0.07	-0.27
% Full					1.00	0.19	-0.01	-0.02	-0.05	0.16	-0.06	0.27	-0.24	0.35	-0.13	0.01	-0.04	0.01	-0.08	-0.19
% Supp						1.00	0.47	0.48	-0.20	0.41	-0.31	0.21	0.04	0.28	0.14	-0.06	0.02	0.29	-0.20	-0.06
% Pub							1.00	0.74	-0.62	0.47	-0.57	0.19	0.14	0.29	0.29	-0.19	0.02	0.21	0.05	-0.11
Pub/Fac								1.00	-0.35	0.71	-0.44	0.17	0.18	0.26	0.31	-0.09	0.01	0.24	-0.07	-0.07
Gini-Pub									1.00	-0.21	0.66	-0.34	0.10	-0.38	-0.03	0.13	0.11	-0.12	-0.24	0.34
Cite/Fac										1.00	-0.10	0.23	0.11	0.34	0.21	-0.10	0.08	0.10	-0.19	-0.09
Gini-Cite											1.00	-0.22	0.05	-0.23	-0.17	0.01	0.11	-0.24	-0.23	0.18
Tot Stu												1.00	-0.42	0.78	-0.10	0.15	-0.09	0.16	-0.19	-0.12
% Fem Stu													1.00	-0.30	0.24	-0.06	0.17	-0.13	0.01	0.19
Rpt PhDs														1.00	-0.10	0.12	-0.22	0.21	-0.22	-0.16
% Fem															1.00	-0.18	0.36	-0.20	0.12	0.45
% Min																1.00	-0.05	0.14	-0.25	-0.02
% Citz																	1.00	-0.19	-0.11	0.18
% RA																		1.00	-0.27	-0.17
% TA																			1.00	-0.25
MYD																				1.00

Note: The data from which these correlations are produced are given in Appendix Table M - 7.

Appendix Table O - 40 Correlation Table for Selected Characteristics of Programs in Spanish and Portuguese Language and Literature

	1993 Ratings			Faculty					Students			Doctorate Recipients					
	93Q	93E	93C	Tot Fac	% Full	% Supp	No. Awd	Awd Fac	Tot Stu	% Fem Stu	Rpt PhDs	% Fem	% Min	% US	% RA	% TA	MYD
Mean	2.95	2.92	0.01	12.96	0.51	0.17	1.00	0.08	33.08	63.10	14.49	60.71	51.83	78.07	0.63	58.67	10.97
S. D.	0.63	0.56	0.26	6.46	0.18	1.24	1.23	0.10	16.87	11.66	7.96	14.59	18.79	15.04	1.89	25.23	2.43
No.	54	54	54	54	54	54	54	54	53	52	53	54	54	54	54	54	54
93Q	1.00	0.94	0.46	0.26	0.31	-0.01	0.40	0.37	0.39	-0.11	0.37	-0.16	-0.13	0.26	0.16	0.21	-0.21
93E		1.00	0.41	0.34	0.26	0.01	0.40	0.36	0.41	-0.04	0.44	-0.06	-0.10	0.16	0.17	0.26	-0.27
93C			1.00	0.16	0.13	0.05	0.06	-0.04	0.24	-0.18	0.03	-0.03	-0.01	0.22	-0.13	-0.02	0.15
Tot Fac				1.00	-0.03	-0.04	0.08	-0.15	0.50	-0.03	0.67	-0.11	0.00	-0.09	0.11	0.08	0.05
% Full					1.00	-0.11	0.04	0.09	0.01	0.03	0.17	-0.09	-0.09	0.12	-0.05	-0.07	0.06
% Supp						1.00	0.11	0.02	-0.08	-0.08	-0.06	0.01	-0.01	-0.01	-0.05	-0.25	-0.07
No. Awd							1.00	0.85	0.15	0.20	0.01	-0.11	-0.21	0.09	0.23	0.10	-0.31
Awd Fac								1.00	-0.08	0.13	-0.14	-0.10	-0.10	0.13	0.15	-0.09	-0.31
Tot Stu									1.00	0.00	0.42	-0.04	-0.37	-0.11	0.00	0.35	-0.03
% Fem Stu										1.00	-0.11	-0.22	-0.04	-0.17	-0.04	0.35	-0.21
Rpt PhDs											1.00	0.03	0.01	0.03	0.22	0.03	0.16
% Fem												1.00	0.10	0.10	-0.10	-0.03	0.16
% Min													1.00	0.05	-0.06	-0.35	0.30
% Citz														1.00	-0.13	-0.26	0.31
% RA															1.00	-0.02	-0.21
% TA																1.00	-0.52
MYD																	1.00

Note: The data from which these correlations are produced are given in Appendix Table J - 11.

Appendix Table O - 41 Correlation Table for Selected Characteristics of Programs in Statistics and Biostatistics

	1993 Ratings			Faculty								Students			Doctorate Recipients					
	93Q	93E	93C	Tot Fac	% Full	% Supp	% Pub	Pub/ Fac	Gini Pub	Cite/ Fac	Gini Cite	Tot Stu	% Fem Stu	Rpt PhDs	% Fem	% Min	% US	% RA	% TA	MYD
Mean	3.01	2.93	0.07	15.12	0.55	36.76	83.03	5.90	15.27	25.51	27.14	28.66	35.04	17.48	27.56	5.21	54.95	15.83	43.44	9.09
S. D.	0.92	0.82	0.22	7.36	0.17	22.14	15.15	2.84	8.02	30.18	14.92	19.69	12.47	11.37	13.84	11.32	20.48	15.08	25.40	2.16
No.	65	65	65	65	65	65	65	65	64	65	64	65	64	65	65	64	65	65	65	65
93Q	1.00	0.98	0.30	0.63	0.51	0.66	0.28	0.25	-0.50	0.17	-0.36	0.12	-0.08	0.51	-0.21	-0.14	-0.12	0.23	0.00	-0.40
93E		1.00	0.30	0.62	0.47	0.60	0.32	0.30	-0.50	0.24	-0.38	0.14	-0.04	0.54	-0.23	-0.17	-0.11	0.26	0.01	-0.44
93C			1.00	0.42	0.22	0.11	-0.01	0.24	-0.30	0.23	-0.33	0.01	0.36	0.00	0.05	-0.18	0.13	0.07	-0.05	-0.07
Tot Fac				1.00	0.28	0.24	0.19	0.22	-0.74	0.10	-0.58	0.29	0.11	0.63	-0.08	-0.14	-0.01	0.26	0.00	-0.14
% Full					1.00	0.30	0.12	-0.08	-0.17	-0.09	-0.15	-0.19	-0.11	0.21	-0.33	0.07	-0.19	-0.13	0.16	-0.16
% Supp						1.00	0.08	0.04	-0.21	-0.02	-0.08	0.12	-0.05	0.29	-0.18	-0.11	-0.26	0.08	-0.02	-0.28
% Pub							1.00	0.46	-0.31	0.20	-0.15	0.21	0.12	0.10	-0.20	0.12	-0.14	0.19	0.22	-0.46
Pub/Fac								1.00	-0.22	0.77	-0.23	0.14	0.47	0.08	0.05	-0.13	0.18	0.44	-0.18	-0.18
Gini-Pub									1.00	-0.07	0.72	-0.29	0.00	-0.48	0.14	0.26	0.05	-0.17	-0.07	-0.09
Cite/Fac										1.00	-0.02	0.11	0.42	0.05	0.10	-0.14	0.11	0.45	-0.30	-0.09
Gini-Cite											1.00	-0.19	-0.10	-0.29	0.13	0.08	0.02	-0.16	-0.09	-0.15
Tot Stu												1.00	-0.04	0.54	-0.10	-0.14	-0.22	0.18	0.00	-0.16
% Fem Stu													1.00	-0.24	0.16	-0.12	0.07	0.15	-0.04	-0.06
Rpt PhDs														1.00	-0.21	-0.18	-0.16	0.19	-0.05	-0.20
% Fem															1.00	-0.07	0.31	0.00	-0.31	0.09
% Min																1.00	-0.10	-0.15	0.19	-0.11
% Citz																	1.00	0.02	-0.40	0.33
% RA																		1.00	-0.44	-0.09
% TA																			1.00	-0.36
MYD																				1.00

Note: The data from which these correlations are produced are given in Appendix Table L - 8.

APPENDIX P

Relative Rankings of Research-Doctorate Programs Along Selected Dimensions

In the tables that follow, programs in each field have been ranked by the mean rating of the "scholarly quality of program faculty" on the 1993 NRC National Survey of Graduate Faculty. The ranking numbers for the measures used in these appendix tables were calculated by taking an average of the rank order of the program. For example, if a program has the 10th. highest value for a measure and is the only program with that value, it is given a ranking of 10. However, if four programs have the 10th. highest value for the measure, then the average of the 10th, 11th, 12th, and 13th positions which they occupy is calculated and each is given a ranking of 11.5.

To show the relationship of those rankings to rankings in other domains, ratings/measures are provided with rankings given in **bold** type and the values given in parentheses. Where information is available, ratings from the 1982 study have been ranked ordered.

Institution:	U.S. universities participating in the 1993 NRC Study.
93Q:	Rank order of "scholarly quality of program faculty" trimmed means for 1993 NRC Study. (Average score on a scale of 0 to 5 with 5 representing "Distinguished.") Source: NRC National Survey of Graduate Faculty.
93E:	Rank order of "program effectiveness in educating research scholars and scientists" trimmed means for the 1993 NRC Study. (Average score on a scale of 0 to 5 with 5 representing "Extremely Effective.") Source: NRC National Survey of Graduate Faculty.
% D:	Rank order of "Distinguished" ratings. (Percentage of useable questionnaires where the program was rated Distinguished.) Source: NRC National Survey of Graduate Faculty.

% D-S:	Rank order of "Distinguished" or "Strong" ratings. (Percentage of the useable questionnaires where the program was rated Distinguished or Strong.) Source: NRC National Survey of Graduate Faculty.
93QT:	Rank order of "scholarly quality of program" faculty trimmed means by faculty from institutions with top-rated programs in their corresponding fields in the 1993 NRC Study. (Average of "scholarly quality of program faculty" on a scale of 0 to 5 as rated by faculty from institutions that were from the upper-half of all programs in this field in the overall Faculty Quality ratings.) Source: NRC National Survey of Graduate Faculty.
93ET:	Rank order of "program effectiveness in educating research scholars and scientists" trimmed means by faculty from insitutions with top-rated programs in their corresponding fields in the 1993 NRC Study. (Average of "program effectiveness in education research scholars and scientists on a scale of 0 to 5, as rated by faculty from institutions from the upper-half of all programs in this field in the overall Faculty Quality ratings.) Source: NRC National Survey of Graduate Faculty.
VIS:	Rank order of visibility of the doctoral program. (Percentage of the questionnaires which reported some knowledge of the program by an answer other than "Don't know well enough to evaluate" or "Little or no familiarity" to one or more of the five questions.) Source: NRC National Survey of Graduate Faculty.
FA:	Rank order of the total number of awards and honors attributed to program faculty. (Total number of awards and honors attributed to program faculty.) Source: See Appendix G for award organizations. [For programs in the Arts and Humanities only.]
TC:	Rank order of the total number of citations attributed to program faculty. (Total number of citations attributed to program faculty.) Source: Institute of Scientific Information. [For programs in Engineering, the Physical Sciences, the Social and Behavioral Sciences, and the Biological Sciences only.]
C/F:	Rank order of the citation density for the program faculty. (Total number of citations (TC) divided by the number of program faculty (TF).) Source: Institute of Scientific Information. [For programs in Engineering, the Physical Sciences, the Social and Behavioral Sciences, and the Biological Sciences only.]

82Q:	Rank order of Faculty Quality Score for 1982 Study. (Average score on a scale of 0 to 5 with 5 representing "Distinguished.") Source: 1982 *An Assessment of Research-Doctorate Programs in the United States.*
82E:	Rank order of Program Effectiveness measure for the 1982 Study. (Average score on a scale of 0 to 5 with 5 representing "Extremely Effective.") Source: Source: 1982 *An Assessment of Research-Doctorate Programs in the United States.*
TF:	Number of Program Faculty in Fall 1992. Source: Institutional Coordinators.
TG:	Number of Graduate students in Fall 1992. Source: Institutional Coordinators.

NOTICE: **n/a** denotes a case where information was not provided by the Institutional Coordinators.

Appendix Table P - 1 Relative Rankings for Research-Doctorate Programs in Aerospace Engineering

Institution	93Q[1]	93E[1]	% D[1]	% D-S[1]	93Q T[1]	93E T[1]	VIS[1]	TC[2]	C/F[2]	82Q[3]	82E[3]	TF[4]	TG[4]
California Institute Technology	1 (4.61)	1 (4.43)	2 (59)	3 (84)	1 (4.65)	1 (4.38)	3 (95)	12 (189)	5 (12.6)			15	54
Massachusetts Inst of Technology	2 (4.54)	2 (4.31)	1 (60)	1.5 (87)	2.5 (4.53)	2 (4.33)	2 (97)	15 (125)	20 (4.5)			28	127
Stanford University	3 (4.50)	3 (4.26)	3 (55)	1.5 (87)	2.5 (4.53)	3 (4.26)	1 (98)	7 (283)	3 (18.9)			15	163
Princeton University	4 (4.30)	4 (4.03)	4 (36)	4 (77)	4 (4.40)	4 (4.00)	4 (90)	1 (422)	2 (19.2)			22	93
University of Michigan	5 (4.05)	5 (3.80)	6 (20)	5 (71)	5 (4.06)	5 (3.76)	5.5 (88)	9 (241)	8.5 (10.0)			24	94
Cornell University	6 (3.93)	6 (3.75)	5 (22)	9.5 (49)	6 (3.90)	6 (3.59)	13.5 (77)	3 (320)	1 (35.6)			9	23
Purdue University	7 (3.71)	9 (3.46)	10 (9)	8 (52)	8 (3.69)	11 (3.33)	9 (84)	10 (203)	11 (8.8)			23	61
University of Texas at Austin	8 (3.67)	7 (3.64)	8.5 (10)	7 (53)	10 (3.57)	7 (3.58)	8 (86)	2 (350)	10 (9.2)			38	57
Georgia Institute of Technology	9 (3.66)	8 (3.49)	8.5 (10)	9.5 (49)	11 (3.51)	8 (3.43)	7 (87)	13 (142)	17 (4.9)			29	157
Univ of California-San Diego	10.5 (3.62)	15 (3.27)	7 (11)	11 (40)	7 (3.72)	16 (3.22)	13.5 (77)	11 (199)	8.5 (10.0)			20	16
Univ of California-Los Angeles	10.5 (3.62)	10 (3.44)	11 (6)	6 (54)	9 (3.67)	9 (3.38)	5.5 (88)	5 (289)	4 (14.5)			20	46
University of Minnesota	12 (3.40)	12 (3.33)	12.5 (3)	14 (28)	12 (3.42)	14 (3.28)	21.5 (68)	4 (295)	7 (10.9)			27	50
University of Colorado	13 (3.35)	17 (3.17)	14.5 (2)	12.5 (33)	13 (3.31)	15 (3.23)	13.5 (77)	8 (246)	12.5 (8.2)			30	204
U of Illinois at Urbana-Champaign	14 (3.34)	13 (3.31)	12.5 (3)	12.5 (33)	14 (3.29)	13 (3.29)	13.5 (77)	6 (286)	6 (12.4)			23	69
Virginia Polytech Inst & State U	15 (3.24)	14 (3.30)	26 (0)	15 (26)	15 (3.17)	11 (3.33)	20 (70)	17 (110)	16 (5.5)			20	47
North Carolina State University	16 (3.19)	21 (3.10)	17 (1)	17 (22)	20 (2.92)	25 (2.84)	29 (60)	20 (92)	23 (4.0)			23	64
Texas A&M University	17.5 (3.12)	19.5 (3.11)	14.5 (2)	16 (25)	17 (3.08)	20.5 (3.04)	17.5 (74)	22.5 (70)	21 (4.4)			16	27
Pennsylvania State University	17.5 (3.12)	11 (3.37)	26 (0)	18 (21)	16 (3.13)	11 (3.33)	10.5 (78)	26 (42)	27 (2.5)			17	85
University of Washington	19 (3.08)	18 (3.13)	26 (0)	19 (20)	18 (3.05)	17 (3.11)	16 (75)	21 (77)	24 (3.9)			20	27
University of Maryland College Park	20 (3.05)	19.5 (3.11)	26 (0)	20 (18)	23 (2.85)	22 (3.02)	10.5 (78)	19 (99)	14 (7.6)			13	124
Iowa State University	21.5 (2.96)	22 (3.08)	26 (0)	22 (15)	22 (2.87)	19 (3.05)	26 (64)	22.5 (70)	19 (4.7)			15	16
Rensselaer Polytechnic Inst	21.5 (2.96)	16 (3.20)	26 (0)	22 (15)	21 (2.89)	18 (3.08)	27 (63)	30 (18)	29.5 (1.5)			12	18
University of Cincinnati	23 (2.94)	25 (2.80)	26 (0)	22 (15)	19 (2.97)	24 (2.92)	17.5 (74)	18 (106)	12.5 (8.2)			13	54
Ohio State University	24 (2.84)	23 (3.03)	17 (1)	24 (14)	24 (2.77)	20.5 (3.04)	19 (73)	25 (57)	22 (4.1)			14	27
University of Notre Dame	25 (2.76)	24 (2.99)	26 (0)	25.5 (12)	25 (2.70)	23 (2.99)	24 (67)	28 (24)	26 (3.4)			7	18
University of Kansas	26 (2.63)	27 (2.68)	17 (1)	25.5 (12)	26 (2.65)	26 (2.81)	28 (61)	31 (11)	31 (1.2)			9	14
University of Florida	27 (2.50)	28 (2.47)	26 (0)	28 (6)	27.5 (2.44)	29.5 (2.32)	30 (53)	16 (116)	18 (4.8)			24	52
Air Force Inst of Technology	28 (2.45)	29 (2.45)	26 (0)	27 (7)	30 (2.30)	29.5 (2.32)	24 (67)	24 (61)	25 (3.6)			17	18
State Univ of New York-Buffalo	29 (2.43)	26 (2.76)	26 (0)	29.5 (5)	29 (2.35)	27 (2.75)	24 (67)	14 (140)	15 (6.4)			22	11
Naval Postgraduate School	30 (2.42)	30 (2.43)	26 (0)	32 (3)	27.5 (2.44)	31 (2.29)	21.5 (68)	32 (7)	33 (0.4)			16	7

Institution	93Q [1]	93E [1]	% D [1]	% D-S [1]	93Q T [1]	93E T [1]	VIS [1]	TC [2]	C/F [2]	82Q [3]	82E [3]	TF [4]	TG [4]
University of Tennessee-Knoxville	**31** (2.17)	**32** (2.26)	**26** (0)	**31** (4)	**32** (2.00)	**32** (1.92)	**31** (52)	**27** (34)	**29.5** (1.5)			22	57
Auburn University	**32** (2.15)	**31** (2.36)	**26** (0)	**29.5** (5)	**31** (2.20)	**28** (2.35)	**32** (49)	**29** (21)	**28** (2.1)			10	4
University of Dayton	**33** (1.07)	**33** (0.95)	**26** (0)	**33** (1)	**33** (0.92)	**33** (0.37)	**33** (43)	**33** (4)	**32** (0.8)			5	11

Sources: 1. National Survey of Graduate Faculty
2. Institute for Scientific Information
3. 1982 Survey of Graduate Faculty
4. Institutional Coordinator Data

Appendix Table P - 2 Relative Rankings for Research-Doctorate Programs in Anthropology

Institution	93Q [1]	93E [1]	% D [1]	% D-S [1]	93Q T [1]	93E T [1]	VIS [1]	TC [2]	C/F [2]	82Q [3]	82E [3]	TF [4]	TG [4]
University of Michigan	1.5* (4.77)	1 (4.40)	1 (78)	2 (96)	2 (4.74)	1 (4.45)	2.5 (100)	9 (212)	18 (5.2)	3 (4.54)	1 (4.30)	41	94
University of Chicago	1.5* (4.77)	2 (4.19)	2 (77)	1 (97)	1 (4.87)	2 (4.31)	2.5 (100)	3 (345)	5 (11.9)	2 (4.58)	2 (4.05)	29	203
University of California-Berkeley	3 (4.51)	3 (3.93)	3 (60)	3 (89)	3 (4.48)	4 (3.89)	2.5 (100)	12.5 (174)	17 (6.4)	1 (4.63)	3 (3.95)	27	110
Harvard University	4 (4.43)	5 (3.67)	4 (53)	4 (87)	4 (4.38)	5 (3.71)	2.5 (100)	4 (329)	6 (11.8)	7 (3.81)	9 (3.47)	28	144
University of Arizona	5 (4.11)	7 (3.60)	5 (29)	5 (77)	5 (4.16)	6 (3.59)	8 (97)	12.5 (174)	27 (3.7)	5 (4.01)	5.5 (3.75)	47	181
University of Pennsylvania	6 (3.94)	4 (3.68)	6 (23)	6 (74)	7 (3.80)	7 (3.58)	6 (98)	6 (287)	9 (8.0)	4 (4.12)	5.5 (3.75)	36	120
Stanford University	7 (3.71)	6 (3.63)	7 (18)	12 (55)	6 (3.84)	3 (3.92)	18 (89)	65.5 (4)	65.5 (0.3)	9 (3.75)	4 (3.80)	14	61
Yale University	9 (3.67)	12 (3.43)	8.5 (16)	11 (57)	9.5 (3.67)	12.5 (3.46)	9.5 (96)	24 (89)	21 (4.7)	6 (3.90)	7 (3.60)	19	68
Univ of California-Los Angeles	9 (3.67)	8 (3.50)	8.5 (16)	7.5 (59)	9.5 (3.67)	9 (3.50)	6 (98)	2 (437)	7 (10.7)	8 (3.80)	8 (3.57)	41	142
Univ of California-San Diego	9 (3.67)	10.5 (3.44)	10 (15)	14 (49)	8 (3.70)	10 (3.49)	28.5 (85)	10.5 (195)	10.5 (7.8)	17 (3.31)	15.5 (3.18)	25	36
University of Florida	11 (3.65)	13 (3.40)	11 (14)	9.5 (58)	19.5 (3.44)	21 (3.26)	9.5 (96)	52 (12)	61 (0.5)	16 (3.34)	26.5 (2.90)	22	77
University of Texas at Austin	12 (3.62)	15 (3.38)	13 (11)	7.5 (59)	11.5 (3.61)	12.5 (3.46)	6 (98)	30 (69)	39 (2.0)	15 (3.45)	11 (3.43)	34	50
New York University	13 (3.60)	16 (3.36)	22 (7)	9.5 (58)	11.5 (3.61)	19.5 (3.29)	11 (95)	35 (46)	33.5 (2.6)	36 (2.53)	40 (2.48)	18	23
U of Illinois at Urbana-Champaign	14 (3.59)	9 (3.47)	19 (8)	13 (51)	13 (3.59)	8 (3.56)	22.5 (88)	27 (78)	32 (2.8)	14 (3.51)	15.5 (3.18)	28	100
University of California-Davis	15 (3.51)	18.5 (3.26)	22 (7)	18 (44)	14 (3.58)	17 (3.33)	22.5 (88)	41 (24)	48.5 (1.0)	40 (2.48)	33 (2.72)	24	35
Columbia University	16 (3.49)	23.5 (3.21)	16.5 (9)	15 (46)	15.5 (3.48)	28.5 (3.14)	12 (94)	29 (70)	35 (2.4)	12 (3.55)	17 (3.12)	29	75
Washington University	17 (3.42)	25 (3.18)	19 (8)	26 (38)	28.5 (3.18)	35.5 (3.00)	32 (81)	15 (133)	10.5 (7.8)	42 (2.41)	38.5 (2.50)	17	64
Duke University	18.5 (3.41)	31 (3.12)	14.5 (10)	22.5 (41)	18 (3.45)	33 (3.06)	22.5 (88)	5 (299)	4 (12.5)	22 (3.03)	24.5 (2.93)	24	51
University of Wisconsin-Madison	18.5 (3.41)	21.5 (3.22)	32.5 (3)	16.5 (45)	19.5 (3.44)	19.5 (3.29)	14.5 (91)	23 (96)	24 (4.0)	24 (3.00)	20 (3.07)	24	103
Univ of California-Santa Barbara	20 (3.40)	18.5 (3.26)	29.5 (4)	19.5 (43)	24.5 (3.32)	28.5 (3.14)	26 (87)	16.5 (131)	14 (6.9)	13 (3.52)	18.5 (3.10)	19	63
Johns Hopkins University	21.5 (3.39)	10.5 (3.44)	12 (13)	16.5 (45)	15.5 (3.48)	14 (3.45)	28.5 (85)	57 (10)	41.5 (1.7)			6	39
CUNY - Grad Sch & Univ Center	21.5 (3.39)	17 (3.27)	14.5 (10)	24.5 (39)	22.5 (3.38)	15 (3.43)	22.5 (88)	67.5 (3)	67.5 (0.2)	10 (3.73)	18.5 (3.10)	14	143
University of Virginia	23.5 (3.38)	29.5 (3.14)	25 (6)	22.5 (41)	22.5 (3.38)	17 (3.33)	27 (86)	25.5 (87)	28 (3.6)	25 (2.99)	35 (2.60)	24	43
Rutgers State Univ-New Brunswick	23.5 (3.38)	33 (3.08)	32.5 (3)	21 (42)	21 (3.40)	33 (3.06)	13 (93)	19 (124)	19.5 (4.8)	19 (3.20)	31 (2.75)	26	53
University of Pittsburgh	25 (3.34)	35 (2.99)	25 (6)	19.5 (43)	28.5 (3.18)	40 (2.80)	14.5 (91)	18 (128)	26 (3.8)	23 (3.02)	23 (2.97)	34	118
Arizona State University	26 (3.31)	21.5 (3.22)	27.5 (5)	28 (34)	27 (3.22)	26 (3.18)	38 (77)	21 (114)	19.5 (4.8)	33 (2.61)	28 (2.83)	24	171
Princeton University	27 (3.30)	28 (3.15)	19 (8)	24.5 (39)	17 (3.47)	22.5 (3.24)	32 (81)	52 (12)	46.5 (1.2)	38 (2.50)	42 (2.43)	10	22
Indiana University	29 (3.24)	27 (3.16)	27.5 (5)	31 (32)	31 (3.16)	24 (3.22)	30 (82)	44.5 (20)	55.5 (0.7)	30 (2.80)	22 (3.00)	27	141
University of Washington	29 (3.24)	20 (3.25)	29.5 (4)	27 (35)	26 (3.30)	17 (3.33)	18 (89)	20 (118)	22 (4.5)	20 (3.13)	13.5 (3.23)	26	94
U of North Carolina-Chapel Hill	29 (3.24)	36.5 (2.94)	44 (1)	29.5 (33)	24.5 (3.32)	38 (2.88)	22.5 (88)	60 (8)	63.5 (0.4)	27 (2.85)	26.5 (2.90)	18	52

Appendix Table P - 2 Anthropology (Continued)

Institution	93Q[1]	93E[1]	% D[1]	% D-S[1]	93Q T[1]	93E T[1]	VIS[1]	TC[2]	C/F[2]	82Q[3]	82E[3]	TF[4]	TG[4]
Cornell University	**31** (3.21)	**14** (3.39)	**37** (2)	**32** (31)	**30** (3.17)	**11** (3.48)	**16** (90)	**16.5** (131)	**16** (6.6)	**18** (3.31)	**12** (3.37)	20	42
Pennsylvania State University	**32** (3.18)	**23.5** (3.21)	**25** (6)	**29.5** (33)	**33** (3.08)	**41** (2.78)	**39** (76)	**8** (238)	**3** (15.9)	**26** (2.97)	**21** (3.03)	15	53
Southern Methodist University	**33** (3.10)	**34** (3.04)	**22** (7)	**33.5** (29)	**35** (2.99)	**33** (3.06)	**35** (80)	**40** (26)	**43** (1.5)	**44** (2.37)	**45** (2.38)	17	67
Northwestern University	**34** (3.09)	**32** (3.11)	**44** (1)	**33.5** (29)	**33** (3.08)	**31** (3.10)	**22.5** (88)	**10.5** (195)	**8** (9.3)	**11** (3.59)	**10** (3.45)	21	35
U of Massachusetts at Amherst	**35** (3.04)	**26** (3.17)	**37** (2)	**35** (24)	**34** (3.02)	**25** (3.21)	**35** (80)	**31** (56)	**24** (4.0)	**21** (3.08)	**13.5** (3.23)	14	86
State Univ of New York-Binghamton	**36** (3.02)	**36.5** (2.94)	**37** (2)	**38** (21)	**40** (2.83)	**39** (2.86)	**37** (78)	**63** (5)	**67.5** (0.2)	**32** (2.61)	**30** (2.77)	23	94
State Univ of New York-Buffalo	**37** (3.01)	**43** (2.68)	**59** (0)	**36** (23)	**36** (2.97)	**49** (2.53)	**18** (89)	**46** (19)	**51.5** (0.9)	**28** (2.84)	**32** (2.73)	21	96
State U of New York-Stony Brook	**38** (2.97)	**29.5** (3.14)	**16.5** (9)	**37** (22)	**37** (2.89)	**23** (3.24)	**43.5** (72)	**1** (490)	**1** (21.3)	**43** (2.38)	**55** (2.12)	23	51
State Univ of New York-Albany	**39** (2.82)	**43** (2.68)	**59** (0)	**46** (12)	**44** (2.73)	**52** (2.50)	**54** (66)	**28** (76)	**24** (4.0)	**55** (2.06)	**59.5** (1.82)	19	54
University of Connecticut	**40** (2.80)	**38** (2.93)	**44** (1)	**40.5** (18)	**38** (2.88)	**27** (3.17)	**32** (81)	**32** (52)	**31** (2.9)	**34** (2.59)	**43.5** (2.42)	18	85
University of Hawaii at Manoa	**41** (2.78)	**45** (2.63)	**59** (0)	**46** (12)	**39** (2.85)	**44** (2.71)	**54** (66)	**48.5** (15)	**51.5** (0.9)	**29** (2.82)	**24.5** (2.93)	16	45
Southern Illinois University	**42** (2.76)	**40** (2.81)	**37** (2)	**40.5** (18)	**44** (2.73)	**36** (3.00)	**48** (69)	**36** (43)	**30** (3.1)	**54** (2.09)	**53** (2.22)	14	23
Brown University	**43.5** (2.73)	**48** (2.59)	**59** (0)	**39** (19)	**41** (2.76)	**47** (2.65)	**35** (80)	**65.5** (4)	**65.5** (0.3)	**45** (2.33)	**47** (2.37)	12	36
University of Iowa	**43.5** (2.73)	**46** (2.62)	**59** (0)	**42** (15)	**42** (2.75)	**46** (2.67)	**42** (73)	**48.5** (15)	**51.5** (0.9)			16	53
University of Oregon	**45** (2.66)	**43** (2.68)	**32.5** (3)	**51** (9)	**46** (2.67)	**45** (2.68)	**51.5** (67)	**54.5** (11)	**61** (0.5)	**48** (2.29)	**38.5** (2.50)	23	27
Michigan State University	**46** (2.58)	**41** (2.75)	**44** (1)	**50** (10)	**49** (2.52)	**30** (3.12)	**49.5** (68)	**47** (17)	**55.5** (0.7)	**35** (2.58)	**29** (2.78)	23	59
Tulane University	**47.5** (2.56)	**47** (2.61)	**37** (2)	**43.5** (14)	**45** (2.68)	**42** (2.75)	**40.5** (74)	**60** (8)	**54** (0.8)	**39** (2.49)	**36** (2.53)	10	67
University of Utah	**47.5** (2.56)	**59** (2.14)	**44** (1)	**43.5** (14)	**47** (2.63)	**52** (2.50)	**51.5** (67)	**7** (257)	**2** (17.1)	**52** (2.16)	**52** (2.23)	15	46
University of Kentucky	**49** (2.51)	**49** (2.57)	**59** (0)	**48.5** (11)	**57** (2.27)	**55** (2.38)	**46.5** (70)	**33.5** (51)	**33.5** (2.6)	**57.5** (2.03)	**56.5** (2.03)	20	39
University of Minnesota	**50** (2.49)	**53** (2.35)	**44** (1)	**53.5** (8)	**51** (2.42)	**57** (2.28)	**46.5** (70)	**63** (5)	**63.5** (0.4)	**41** (2.48)	**50.5** (2.25)	12	45
Boston University	**51** (2.44)	**57** (2.27)	**44** (1)	**48.5** (11)	**50** (2.49)	**56** (2.33)	**49.5** (68)	**60** (8)	**58** (0.6)	**53** (2.15)	**56.5** (2.03)	13	29
University of Tennessee-Knoxville	**52** (2.42)	**39** (2.86)	**44** (1)	**56.5** (7)	**53** (2.35)	**43** (2.74)	**63** (59)	**52** (12)	**51.5** (0.9)	**61** (1.67)	**58** (1.98)	13	31
University of Missouri-Columbia	**53.5** (2.40)	**61** (2.07)	**59** (0)	**53.5** (8)	**59** (2.13)	**64** (1.67)	**67** (50)	**14** (163)	**12.5** (7.1)	**51** (2.23)	**49** (2.33)	23	44
Temple University	**53.5** (2.40)	**56** (2.30)	**59** (0)	**56.5** (7)	**55** (2.31)	**58** (2.26)	**40.5** (74)	**22** (113)	**12.5** (7.1)			16	14
University of Colorado	**55.5** (2.39)	**51** (2.43)	**59** (0)	**59** (5)	**56** (2.30)	**54** (2.43)	**56.5** (65)	**38** (31)	**37.5** (2.1)	**37** (2.52)	**34** (2.62)	15	42
Univ of California-Riverside	**55.5** (2.39)	**54** (2.33)	**59** (0)	**66** (2)	**49** (2.52)	**52** (2.50)	**45** (71)	**57** (10)	**58** (0.6)	**47** (2.30)	**41** (2.47)	18	49
Vanderbilt University	**57.5** (2.35)	**55** (2.32)	**32.5** (3)	**46** (12)	**52** (2.36)	**52** (2.50)	**60** (60)	**69** (1)	**69** (0.1)			13	18
University of Kansas	**57.5** (2.35)	**50** (2.56)	**59** (0)	**58** (6)	**54** (2.34)	**37** (2.95)	**56.5** (65)	**43** (22)	**44.5** (1.4)	**46** (2.30)	**50.5** (2.25)	16	15
Brandeis University	**59** (2.28)	**60** (2.08)	**59** (0)	**53.5** (8)	**60** (2.09)	**62** (1.89)	**43.5** (72)	**54.5** (11)	**46.5** (1.2)	**31** (2.69)	**37** (2.52)	9	27
University of South Florida	**60** (2.17)	**62** (1.99)	**59** (0)	**60.5** (4)	**61** (2.08)	**61** (1.95)	**68** (49)	**50** (14)	**48.5** (1.0)			14	44

Institution	93Q [1]	93E [1]	% D [1]	% D-S [1]	93Q T [1]	93E T [1]	VIS [1]	TC [2]	C/F [2]	82Q [3]	82E [3]	TF [4]	TG [4]
Syracuse University	**61** (2.09)	**64** (1.89)	**59** (0)	**66** (2)	**65** (1.90)	**67** (1.43)	**69** (44)	**33.5** (51)	**36** (2.3)	**60** (1.80)	**61** (1.75)	22	35
University of Wisconsin-Milwaukee	**62** (2.08)	**69** (1.31)	**59** (0)	**60.5** (4)	**58** (2.25)	**69** (1.11)	**60** (60)	**44.5** (20)	**41.5** (1.7)	**49** (2.26)	**54** (2.18)	12	20
Washington State University	**63** (2.00)	**63** (1.97)	**59** (0)	**63** (3)	**63** (2.04)	**59** (2.22)	**60** (60)	**39** (29)	**37.5** (2.1)	**50** (2.24)	**47** (2.37)	14	39
Wayne State University	**64** (1.98)	**66.5** (1.67)	**59** (0)	**66** (2)	**66** (1.88)	**68** (1.41)	**60** (60)	**37** (39)	**29** (3.5)	**57.5** (2.03)	**59.5** (1.82)	11	17
University of Oklahoma	**66** (1.89)	**66.5** (1.67)	**44** (1)	**63** (3)	**65** (1.90)	**64** (1.67)	**66** (51)	**42** (23)	**40** (1.9)	**63** (1.37)	**63** (1.47)	12	56
University of Rochester	**66** (1.89)	**58** (2.20)	**59** (0)	**53.5** (8)	**62** (2.05)	**60** (2.00)	**60** (60)	**57** (10)	**44.5** (1.4)	**56** (2.05)	**43.5** (2.42)	7	31
Ohio State University	**66** (1.89)	**65** (1.81)	**59** (0)	**63** (3)	**68** (1.62)	**66** (1.48)	**54** (66)	**25.5** (87)	**15** (6.7)	**59** (1.97)	**47** (2.37)	13	57
American University	**68** (1.86)	**52** (2.37)	**59** (0)	**68.5** (1)	**67** (1.76)	**48** (2.59)	**64** (53)	**63** (5)	**58** (0.6)	**64** (1.33)	**64** (1.27)	9	39
Catholic University of America	**69** (1.21)	**68** (1.50)	**59** (0)	**68.5** (1)	**69** (1.15)	**65** (1.50)	**65** (52)	**67.5** (3)	**61** (0.5)	**62** (1.43)	**62** (1.48)	6	25

Sources: 1. National Survey of Graduate Faculty
2. Institute for Scientific Information
3. 1982 Survey of Graduate Faculty
4. Institutional Coordinator Data

* Two programs recieved the highest quality rating, and using the standard convention of average rankings, each program was given a rank of 1.5.

Appendix Table P - 3 Relative Rankings for Research-Doctorate Programs in Art History

Institution	93Q [1]	93E [1]	% D [1]	% D-S [1]	93Q T [1]	93E T [1]	VIS [1]	FA [2]	82Q [3]	82E [3]	TF [4]	TG [4]
Columbia University	1.5* (4.79)	3 (4.29)	1 (79)	1.5 (96)	1 (4.87)	5 (4.07)	3 (99)	1 (16)	4 (4.68)	4 (4.22)	35	228
New York University	1.5* (4.79)	2 (4.32)	2 (76)	1.5 (96)	3 (4.75)	3 (4.12)	5.5 (98)	3 (11)	1 (4.90)	1 (4.57)	25	23
University of California-Berkeley	3 (4.67)	4 (4.18)	3 (72)	3.5 (93)	2 (4.79)	2 (4.19)	1.5 (100)	4.5 (7)	6 (4.27)	6 (3.77)	12	42
Harvard University	4 (4.49)	5 (4.11)	4 (55)	3.5 (93)	4 (4.67)	4 (4.08)	1.5 (100)	4.5 (7)	2 (4.85)	3 (4.45)	15	101
Yale University	5 (4.44)	1 (4.36)	5 (49)	5 (89)	5 (4.44)	1 (4.39)	5.5 (98)	28 (2)	3 (4.72)	2 (4.47)	23	68
Princeton University	6 (4.04)	6 (3.78)	6 (30)	6.5 (70)	7 (3.94)	7 (3.62)	8.5 (97)	21.5 (3)	5 (4.47)	5 (4.15)	17	55
Johns Hopkins University	7 (3.93)	12 (3.46)	7 (27)	9.5 (63)	6 (4.04)	11.5 (3.33)	14 (92)	6 (6)	9 (3.54)	11 (3.28)	5	16
Northwestern University	8 (3.83)	8 (3.57)	9.5 (13)	6.5 (70)	8 (3.86)	8 (3.57)	12 (95)	2 (13)	23 (2.47)	25 (2.30)	12	33
University of Pennsylvania	9 (3.80)	9 (3.51)	8 (17)	8 (65)	10 (3.69)	10 (3.43)	5.5 (98)	16.5 (4)	11 (3.48)	10 (3.38)	20	66
University of Chicago	10 (3.74)	10 (3.49)	9.5 (13)	9.5 (63)	9 (3.82)	6 (3.63)	10.5 (96)	10 (5)	14 (3.04)	13 (3.00)	14	105
University of Michigan	11 (3.71)	7 (3.58)	11.5 (9)	11 (61)	11 (3.65)	13 (3.29)	8.5 (97)	10 (5)	8 (3.56)	8 (3.67)	25	41
CUNY - Grad Sch & Univ Center	12 (3.60)	15 (3.38)	11.5 (9)	12.5 (50)	12 (3.51)	14 (3.24)	13 (93)	10 (5)			17	207
Univ of California-Los Angeles	13 (3.52)	12 (3.46)	13.5 (6)	12.5 (50)	13 (3.36)	9 (3.46)	5.5 (98)	10 (5)	12 (3.18)	17 (2.85)	16	72
Stanford University	14 (3.49)	14 (3.45)	13.5 (6)	14 (49)	14 (3.30)	16 (3.07)	10.5 (96)	10 (5)	7 (3.68)	9 (3.57)	17	36
University of Delaware	15 (3.40)	16 (3.33)	16 (5)	15 (40)	16.5 (3.18)	15 (3.14)	15.5 (88)	10 (5)	19 (2.72)	15 (2.92)	14	49
University of Virginia	16 (3.31)	17 (3.07)	16 (5)	17 (33)	19 (3.07)	20 (2.87)	20 (85)	28 (2)	20 (2.63)	20 (2.52)	20	32
Bryn Mawr College	17 (3.28)	12 (3.46)	16 (5)	16 (37)	16.5 (3.18)	11.5 (3.33)	20 (85)	34 (1)	10 (3.52)	7 (3.75)	6	37
Brown University	18 (3.20)	18 (3.05)	19.5 (2)	18 (32)	18 (3.14)	18 (2.92)	15.5 (88)	28 (2)	13 (3.14)	12 (3.13)	9	41
University of Texas at Austin	19 (3.17)	21 (3.03)	19.5 (2)	19 (25)	15 (3.19)	17 (3.03)	22.5 (84)	21.5 (3)	28 (2.13)	29 (1.88)	15	22
Rutgers State Univ-New Brunswick	20 (3.04)	19.5 (3.04)	23 (1)	20.5 (21)	20 (2.95)	21.5 (2.84)	17 (87)	10 (5)	24 (2.42)	23 (2.33)	18	53
Univ of California-Santa Barbara	21 (2.98)	25 (2.78)	23 (1)	20.5 (21)	21 (2.91)	23 (2.80)	25 (83)	16.5 (4)			15	43
University of Pittsburgh	22 (2.90)	19.5 (3.04)	32 (0)	26 (10)	23 (2.78)	19 (2.90)	18 (86)	28 (2)	15 (2.99)	18 (2.73)	12	32
Cornell University	23 (2.87)	23 (2.80)	18 (3)	23 (14)	22 (2.83)	24.5 (2.67)	22.5 (84)	16.5 (4)	17 (2.87)	15 (2.92)	14	23
Indiana University	24.5 (2.85)	22 (2.87)	23 (1)	22 (18)	25 (2.59)	24.5 (2.67)	25 (83)	28 (2)	18 (2.85)	19 (2.70)	14	38
Boston University	24.5 (2.85)	26 (2.73)	23 (1)	24.5 (12)	24 (2.72)	27 (2.58)	20 (85)	16.5 (4)	21 (2.59)	21 (2.35)	13	34
U of Illinois at Urbana-Champaign	26 (2.67)	24 (2.79)	32 (0)	24.5 (12)	26.5 (2.58)	21.5 (2.84)	27 (82)	37 (0)			10	42
University of Kansas	27 (2.56)	27 (2.57)	32 (0)	27 (9)	29 (2.42)	26 (2.61)	29 (75)	37 (0)	27 (2.14)	23 (2.33)	13	26
University of Maryland College Park	28 (2.53)	32 (2.25)	32 (0)	30 (7)	26.5 (2.58)	31 (2.30)	28 (78)	37 (0)	22 (2.55)	23 (2.33)	17	37
Ohio State University	29 (2.48)	36 (1.98)	32 (0)	32.5 (6)	30 (2.34)	34.5 (1.67)	35.5 (66)	21.5 (3)	30 (1.76)	31 (1.73)	20	19
University of Minnesota	30 (2.47)	29 (2.43)	32 (0)	30 (7)	28 (2.43)	32 (2.08)	25 (83)	28 (2)	26 (2.31)	26.5 (2.27)	13	14

Institution	93Q [1]	93E [1]	% D [1]	% D-S [1]	93Q T [1]	93E T [1]	VIS [1]	FA [2]	82Q [3]	82E [3]	TF [4]	TG [4]
University of Washington	**31** (2.39)	**34** (2.15)	**32** (0)	**30** (7)	**32** (2.23)	**35** (1.67)	**31** (70)	**34** (1)	**32** (1.57)	**32** (1.50)	11	19
U of North Carolina-Chapel Hill	**32** (2.33)	**28** (2.46)	**32** (0)	**32.5** (6)	**31** (2.32)	**28** (2.40)	**34** (68)	**16.5** (4)	**16** (2.98)	**15** (2.92)	6	20
Washington University	**33** (2.31)	**33** (2.24)	**32** (0)	**28** (8)	**34** (2.12)	**35** (1.67)	**30** (73)	**28** (2)	**29** (2.06)	**30** (1.77)	9	22
Pennsylvania State University	**34** (2.28)	**31** (2.31)	**32** (0)	**34.5** (4)	**35** (2.06)	**30** (2.33)	**37** (65)	**34** (1)	**25** (2.35)	**26.5** (2.27)	11	46
University of Wisconsin-Madison	**35** (2.14)	**30** (2.35)	**32** (0)	**36.5** (3)	**33** (2.17)	**29** (2.36)	**32.5** (69)	**16.5** (4)	**31** (1.67)	**28** (2.00)	10	69
Florida State University	**36** (2.10)	**37** (1.67)	**32** (0)	**36.5** (3)	**36** (2.03)	**35** (1.67)	**32.5** (69)	**21.5** (3)	**35** (1.18)	**34.5** (1.17)	11	11
Case Western Reserve Univ	**37** (1.79)	**35** (2.08)	**23** (1)	**34.5** (4)	**37** (1.48)	**37** (1.52)	**35.5** (66)	**28** (2)	**33** (1.54)	**33** (1.33)	7	23
University of Georgia	**38** (0.90)	**38** (0.79)	**32** (0)	**38** (1)	**38** (0.70)	**38** (0.28)	**38** (54)	**28** (2)	**34** (1.42)	**34.5** (1.17)	6	8

Sources: 1. National Survey of Graduate Faculty
2. Associations and Organizations Administrating Prestigious Awards and Honors
3. 1982 Survey of Graduate Faculty
4. Institutional Coordinator Data

* Two programs recieved the highest quality rating, and using the standard convention of average rankings, each program was given a rank of 1.5.

Appendix Table P - 4 Relative Rankings for Research-Doctorate Programs in Astrophysics and Astronomy

Institution	93Q [1]	93E [1]	% D [1]	% D-S [1]	93Q T [1]	93E T [1]	VIS [1]	TC [2]	C/F [2]	82Q [3]	82E [3]	TF [4]	TG [4]
California Institute Technology	1 (4.91)	1 (4.75)	1 (89)	1 (100)	1 (4.94)	1 (4.73)	3.5 (100)	1 (4483)	1 (203.8)			22	31
Princeton University	2 (4.79)	3 (4.38)	2 (77)	2.5 (96)	2 (4.80)	3 (4.43)	9.5 (98)	9 (1597)	6 (99.8)			16	56
University of California-Berkeley	3 (4.65)	2 (4.53)	3 (67)	2.5 (96)	3 (4.72)	2 (4.56)	3.5 (100)	2 (2329)	2 (137.0)			17	40
Harvard University	4 (4.49)	6 (3.92)	4 (53)	4 (94)	4 (4.48)	5 (4.06)	3.5 (100)	4 (2002)	5 (100.1)			20	32
University of Chicago	5 (4.36)	7 (3.85)	5 (42)	6 (89)	5 (4.32)	7.5 (3.69)	12 (97)	3 (2010)	12.5 (74.4)			27	33
Univ of California-Santa Cruz	6 (4.31)	4 (4.14)	6 (38)	5 (91)	6 (4.30)	4 (4.08)	7.5 (99)	5 (1963)	4 (115.5)			17	32
University of Arizona	7 (4.10)	8 (3.69)	7 (24)	7 (85)	8 (4.03)	7.5 (3.69)	3.5 (100)	6 (1882)	16 (64.9)			29	32
Massachusetts Inst of Technology	8 (4.00)	9 (3.68)	9 (18)	8 (81)	7 (4.05)	9 (3.65)	3.5 (100)	10 (1590)	7 (88.3)			18	46
Cornell University	9 (3.98)	5 (3.97)	8 (19)	9 (79)	9 (3.95)	6 (3.89)	7.5 (99)	8 (1860)	12.5 (74.4)			25	34
University of Texas at Austin	10 (3.65)	11 (3.39)	13 (5)	10 (60)	11 (3.59)	13 (3.27)	3.5 (100)	12 (1484)	17 (64.5)			23	29
University of Hawaii at Manoa	11 (3.60)	17 (3.09)	10 (8)	11 (56)	10 (3.64)	20 (2.95)	12 (97)	11 (1576)	24 (49.3)			32	30
University of Colorado	12 (3.54)	12 (3.38)	16 (3)	12 (55)	12 (3.52)	11.5 (3.30)	9.5 (98)	13 (1342)	9.5 (83.9)			16	33
U of Illinois at Urbana-Champaign	13 (3.53)	14 (3.24)	11 (6)	13 (50)	14 (3.38)	14 (3.21)	18 (94)	16 (1136)	21 (54.1)			21	20
University of Wisconsin-Madison	14 (3.46)	10 (3.47)	13 (5)	14 (45)	13 (3.40)	11.5 (3.30)	18 (94)	22 (663)	20 (55.3)			12	26
Yale University	15 (3.31)	13 (3.31)	13 (5)	15 (35)	16 (3.23)	15 (3.15)	18 (94)	20 (839)	9.5 (83.9)			10	20
Univ of California-Los Angeles	16 (3.27)	18 (3.05)	18.5 (2)	16 (32)	15 (3.31)	16 (3.11)	14 (96)	17 (1098)	14 (73.2)			15	23
University of Virginia	17 (3.23)	16 (3.16)	18.5 (2)	17 (30)	18 (3.18)	17 (3.04)	21.5 (93)	21 (684)	27 (45.6)			15	13
Columbia University	18 (3.20)	23 (2.90)	16 (3)	18 (29)	17 (3.22)	19 (2.98)	15 (95)	19 (859)	19 (61.4)			14	19
University of Maryland College Park	19 (3.07)	19 (3.02)	28 (0)	20 (22)	20 (3.02)	21 (2.93)	12 (97)	14 (1276)	15 (67.2)			19	31
U of Massachusetts at Amherst	20 (3.04)	15 (3.23)	21 (1)	19 (23)	19 (3.05)	10 (3.31)	25 (91)	7 (1873)	3 (133.8)			14	25
Pennsylvania State University	21 (3.00)	25 (2.75)	21 (1)	22 (17)	21 (3.00)	25 (2.70)	18 (94)	28 (371)	31 (23.2)			16	22
Stanford University	22 (2.96)	22 (2.91)	16 (3)	21 (21)	22 (2.90)	23 (2.86)	23 (92)	25 (432)	18 (61.7)			7	16
Ohio State University	23 (2.91)	24 (2.76)	28 (0)	23 (11)	23 (2.89)	24 (2.72)	18 (94)	18 (911)	22.5 (50.6)			18	18
University of Minnesota	24 (2.89)	21 (2.94)	21 (1)	24 (10)	24 (2.87)	22 (2.90)	25 (91)	15 (1137)	11 (81.2)			14	21
University of Michigan	25 (2.65)	20 (3.00)	28 (0)	26 (7)	26 (2.72)	18 (2.99)	21.5 (93)	26.5 (374)	25 (46.8)			8	13
State U of New York-Stony Brook	26 (2.58)	26 (2.59)	28 (0)	25 (9)	25 (2.73)	26 (2.66)	25 (91)	23 (599)	8 (85.6)			7	17
Boston University	27 (2.40)	27 (2.56)	28 (0)	27 (6)	27 (2.39)	28 (2.56)	27 (88)	24 (452)	30 (23.8)			19	26
Indiana University	28 (2.16)	28 (2.53)	28 (0)	30.5 (2)	28 (2.11)	27 (2.57)	30 (81)	29 (354)	22.5 (50.6)			7	20
Louisiana State U & A&M College	29 (2.06)	31 (2.02)	28 (0)	28.5 (3)	31 (1.91)	31 (2.05)	29 (82)	31 (300)	28 (33.3)			9	12
Iowa State University	30 (2.03)	30 (2.07)	28 (0)	33 (0)	29.5 (2.02)	32 (2.00)	31 (80)	30 (327)	26 (46.7)			7	5

Institution	93Q [1]	93E [1]	% D [1]	% D-S [1]	93Q T [1]	93E T [1]	VIS [1]	TC [2]	C/F [2]	82Q [3]	82E [3]	TF [4]	TG [4]
University of Florida	**31** (1.98)	**32** (1.92)	**28** (0)	**32** (1)	**30** (2.02)	**30** (2.14)	**32** (79)	**26.5** (374)	**29** (26.7)			14	26
New Mexico State University	**32** (1.85)	**33** (1.82)	**28** (0)	**30.5** (2)	**32** (1.84)	**33** (1.83)	**28** (86)	**33** (59)	**33** (7.4)			8	23
Georgia State University	**33** (1.81)	**29** (2.10)	**28** (0)	**28.5** (3)	**33** (1.69)	**29** (2.18)	**33** (73)	**32** (84)	**32** (14.0)			6	14

Sources: 1. National Survey of Graduate Faculty
2. Institute for Scientific Information
3. 1982 Survey of Graduate Faculty
4. Institutional Coordinator Data

Appendix Table P - 5 Relative Rankings for Research-Doctorate Programs in Biochemistry and Molecular Biology

Institution	93Q [1]	93E [1]	% D [1]	% D-S [1]	93Q T [1]	93E T [1]	VIS [1]	TC [2]	C/F [2]	82Q [3]	82E [3]	TF [4]	TG [4]
Univ of California-San Francisco	1 (4.84)	1 (4.73)	3.5 (75)	5 (87)	1 (4.91)	1 (4.84)	12 (89)	4 (20875)	2 (463.9)			45	102
Massachusetts Inst of Technology	2.5 (4.83)	2 (4.68)	1.5 (76)	2 (91)	3 (4.87)	3 (4.67)	4 (93)	2 (22759)	3 (421.5)			54	n/a
Stanford University	2.5 (4.83)	4 (4.59)	3.5 (75)	7 (86)	2 (4.90)	4 (4.60)	12 (89)	32 (4907)	5 (350.5)			14	37
University of California-Berkeley	4 (4.81)	3 (4.66)	1.5 (76)	1 (92)	5 (4.81)	2 (4.68)	1 (96)	13 (12266)	4 (360.8)			34	130
Harvard University	5 (4.80)	5 (4.44)	5 (74)	3 (89)	4 (4.85)	6 (4.42)	6 (92)	20 (8176)	1 (584.0)			14	64
Yale University	6 (4.59)	8 (4.32)	7 (56)	8 (83)	7 (4.69)	7.5 (4.41)	12 (89)	24 (6770)	11 (205.2)			33	91
California Institute Technology	7 (4.57)	6 (4.41)	6 (57)	9 (82)	6 (4.77)	5 (4.51)	7 (91)	21 (8120)	9 (270.7)			30	85
University of Wisconsin-Madison	8 (4.55)	9 (4.30)	8 (53)	5 (87)	9 (4.57)	9 (4.31)	2 (94)	8 (18021)	37 (104.2)			173	275
Univ of California-San Diego	9 (4.53)	7 (4.37)	9 (51)	5 (87)	8 (4.63)	7.5 (4.41)	4 (93)	1 (38659)	7.5 (272.2)			142	152
Johns Hopkins University	10.5 (4.38)	10 (4.26)	10 (40)	10 (80)	12 (4.33)	11 (4.26)	8.5 (90)	26 (6288)	30 (112.3)			56	127
Columbia University	10.5 (4.38)	11 (4.25)	11 (39)	11 (79)	10 (4.41)	10 (4.27)	16 (87)	12 (12312)	12 (198.6)			62	47
University of Colorado	12 (4.26)	15 (4.01)	13 (33)	12.5 (75)	11 (4.39)	12.5 (4.17)	15 (88)	38 (4037)	26 (118.7)			34	68
Washington University	13 (4.22)	13 (4.15)	14 (31)	14 (74)	15 (4.17)	14 (4.09)	12 (89)	3 (21921)	17 (157.7)			139	100
Univ of California-Los Angeles	14 (4.20)	19.5 (3.93)	12 (36)	12.5 (75)	13.5 (4.21)	17 (3.96)	4 (93)	17 (9140)	16 (163.2)			56	139
Duke University	15 (4.18)	12 (4.16)	15 (28)	15 (73)	13.5 (4.21)	12.5 (4.17)	12 (89)	11 (12523)	7.5 (272.2)			46	69
University of Pennsylvania	16 (4.11)	17.5 (3.94)	17 (23)	16.5 (67)	16.5 (4.07)	22.5 (3.88)	21 (83)	6 (19840)	35 (106.1)			187	135
Brandeis University	17 (4.06)	21 (3.92)	20 (18)	16.5 (67)	16.5 (4.07)	20.5 (3.89)	24 (81)	64 (2022)	40 (101.1)			20	48
University of Washington	18 (4.05)	14 (4.05)	18 (22)	18 (66)	20 (4.00)	16 (4.02)	18 (85)	23 (6848)	6 (326.1)			21	48
Baylor College of Medicine	19 (4.04)	23.5 (3.88)	16 (24)	19.5 (64)	20 (4.00)	24 (3.86)	17 (86)	7 (18354)	14 (178.2)			103	101
U of Texas-Southwestern Med Ctr	20 (4.00)	27 (3.79)	19 (19)	21 (59)	18 (4.02)	28.5 (3.73)	27 (80)	16 (9832)	15 (163.9)			60	34
Rockefeller University	21 (3.92)	22 (3.91)	29.5 (8)	47 (28)	20 (4.00)	15 (4.05)	71 (49)	111 (697)	42 (99.6)			7	n/a
Cornell University	22 (3.91)	17.5 (3.94)	21 (17)	22 (58)	23.5 (3.90)'	18 (3.95)	27 (80)	37 (4149)	27 (115.3)			36	77
University of Michigan [b]	23.5 (3.89)	16 (3.96)	24 (13)	27.5 (50)	27 (3.83)	25.5 (3.84)	32 (76)	35 (4232)	45 (96.2)			44	69
University of Chicago	23.5 (3.89)	19.5 (3.93)	25.5 (11)	24.5 (55)	26 (3.88)	20.5 (3.89)	32 (76)	25 (6605)	10 (220.2)			30	63
University of Oregon	25 (3.88)	29 (3.68)	22 (16)	24.5 (55)	23.5 (3.90)	28.5 (3.73)	21 (83)	51 (2767)	32 (110.7)			25	96
University of Michigan [a]	26 (3.87)	25 (3.86)	23 (15)	26 (52)	22 (3.92)	22.5 (3.88)	27 (80)	10 (14283)	13 (178.5)			80	45
U of North Carolina-Chapel Hill	27 (3.83)	26 (3.80)	25.5 (11)	19.5 (64)	25 (3.89)	27 (3.77)	8.5 (90)	15 (11187)	34 (109.7)			102	75
Albert Einstein College of Med	28 (3.79)	23.5 (3.88)	27.5 (10)	23 (57)	28 (3.78)	19 (3.92)	21 (83)	18 (9128)	56 (84.5)			108	16
University of Utah	29 (3.72)	45 (3.45)	27.5 (10)	31.5 (42)	29 (3.73)	53.5 (3.33)	45 (70)	69.5 (1912)	60 (76.5)			25	48[(1)]
Vanderbilt University	30 (3.68)	32 (3.63)	29.5 (8)	27.5 (50)	30 (3.68)	33.5 (3.55)	19 (84)	9 (14974)	23 (129.1)			116	41

Appendix Table P - 5 Biochemistry and Molecular Biology (Continued)

Institution	93Q [1]	93E [1]	% D [1]	% D-S [1]	93Q T [1]	93E T [1]	VIS [1]	TC [2]	C/F [2]	82Q [3]	82E [3]	TF [4]	TG [4]
Northwestern University	**31** (3.59)	**28** (3.70)	**33.5** (6)	**29** (47)	**33** (3.57)	**32** (3.61)	**24** (81)	**28** (5626)	**39** (102.3)			55	73
State U of New York-Stony Brook	**32** (3.58)	**34** (3.60)	**37.5** (5)	**30** (45)	**33** (3.57)	**35** (3.54)	**24** (81)	**27** (6053)	**58** (77.6)			78	114
University of Texas at Austin	**33** (3.57)	**35.5** (3.59)	**33.5** (6)	**36** (36)	**36** (3.48)	**54** (3.33)	**42** (72)	**46** (2975)	**100.5** (40.8)			73	151
U of Illinois at Urbana-Champaign	**34** (3.55)	**35.5** (3.59)	**33.5** (6)	**34.5** (38)	**34** (3.54)	**31** (3.62)	**32** (76)	**61** (2141)	**24** (125.9)			17	104
University of California-Davis	**35** (3.52)	**30.5** (3.65)	**42** (4)	**31.5** (42)	**31** (3.60)	**30** (3.67)	**29.5** (78)	**33** (4752)	**59** (76.6)			62	63
New York University	**36.5** (3.47)	**42** (3.50)	**33.5** (6)	**37** (35)	**35** (3.51)	**34** (3.55)	**42** (72)	**5** (20270)	**31** (110.8)			183	n/a
Rutgers State Univ-New Brunswick	**36.5** (3.47)	**44** (3.48)	**42** (4)	**33** (40)	**41** (3.43)	**45** (3.39)	**29.5** (78)	**29** (5317)	**76** (61.1)			87	98
University of Southern California	**39** (3.46)	**41** (3.51)	**42** (4)	**40** (32)	**40** (3.44)	**41** (3.49)	**34.5** (74)	**34** (4529)	**36** (105.3)			43	53
Oregon State University	**39** (3.46)	**55** (3.33)	**48** (3)	**53.5** (23)	**48** (3.33)	**54** (3.33)	**61** (56)	**60** (2384)	**96** (45.0)			53	78
University of Minnesota	**39** (3.46)	**40** (3.52)	**48** (3)	**40** (32)	**43** (3.39)	**38** (3.51)	**50** (63)	**40** (3743)	**51.5** (91.3)			41	115
Carnegie Mellon University	**41** (3.45)	**33** (3.61)	**33.5** (6)	**40** (32)	**37** (3.46)	**41** (3.49)	**37.5** (73)	**78** (1643)	**78** (58.7)			28	12
Indiana University	**42.5** (3.42)	**49** (3.40)	**48** (3)	**38** (34)	**42** (3.40)	**62** (3.29)	**37.5** (73)	**72** (1818)	**79** (58.6)			31	27
U of Tex-Health Sci Ctr-Houston	**42.5** (3.42)	**61.5** (3.28)	**147** (0)	**34.5** (38)	**46** (3.37)	**66** (3.20)	**37.5** (73)	**22** (7705)	**19** (154.1)			50	117
Purdue University [a]	**45** (3.39)	**55** (3.33)	**33.5** (6)	**43.5** (30)	**57** (3.15)	**82** (3.04)	**46** (67)	**74** (1753)	**50** (92.3)			19	37
Rice University	**45** (3.39)	**30.5** (3.65)	**42** (4)	**50.5** (24)	**38** (3.45)	**26** (3.84)	**67.5** (53)	**104** (772)	**86** (51.5)			15	43
Pennsylvania State University	**45** (3.39)	**46** (3.44)	**82.5** (1)	**45.5** (29)	**45** (3.38)	**39** (3.50)	**47** (66)	**66** (1963)	**99** (42.7)			46	82
University of Iowa	**47** (3.36)	**39** (3.53)	**82.5** (1)	**43.5** (30)	**48** (3.33)	**41** (3.49)	**42** (72)	**31** (5024)	**51.5** (91.3)			55	71
Case Western Reserve Univ	**48** (3.35)	**63.5** (3.24)	**82.5** (1)	**48** (25)	**49** (3.31)	**54** (3.33)	**50** (63)	**45** (3130)	**57** (78.3)			40	63
University of Alabama-Birmingham	**49.5** (3.34)	**37.5** (3.54)	**42** (4)	**45.5** (29)	**51** (3.26)	**36** (3.53)	**42** (72)	**14** (11378)	**55** (85.5)			133	47
Mayo Graduate School	**49.5** (3.34)	**73** (3.08)	**147** (0)	**58.5** (18)	**52** (3.25)	**82** (3.04)	**75** (47)	**19** (8551)	**18** (155.5)			55	52
Michigan State University	**51.5** (3.33)	**47** (3.43)	**37.5** (5)	**55.5** (22)	**55** (3.16)	**63** (3.25)	**58** (58)	**44** (3205)	**44** (97.1)			33	67
Univ of California-Santa Cruz	**51.5** (3.33)	**51** (3.38)	**42** (4)	**57** (19)	**53** (3.23)	**54** (3.33)	**56.5** (59)	**69.5** (1912)	**46** (95.6)			20	83
University of California-Irvine	**53** (3.31)	**59** (3.30)	**82.5** (1)	**42** (31)	**45** (3.38)	**43** (3.43)	**34.5** (74)	**58** (2642)	**43** (97.9)			27	13
U of Massachusetts Med Center	**54** (3.30)	**55** (3.33)	**42** (4)	**50.5** (24)	**40** (3.44)	**54** (3.33)	**52** (62)	**53.5** (2733)	**48** (94.2)			29	23
University of Rochester	**55** (3.29)	**37.5** (3.54)	**58** (2)	**55.5** (22)	**50** (3.30)	**37** (3.52)	**54** (60)	**50** (2862)	**61** (75.3)			38	109
Purdue University [c]	**56** (3.24)	**55** (3.33)	**58** (2)	**60.5** (17)	**57** (3.15)	**54** (3.33)	**63.5** (55)	**94** (991)	**75** (61.9)			16	43
University of Arizona	**57.5** (3.23)	**43** (3.49)	**58** (2)	**53.5** (23)	**60** (3.11)	**66** (3.20)	**42** (72)	**39** (3824)	**25** (119.5)			32	35
Univ of California-Santa Barbara	**57.5** (3.23)	**48** (3.42)	**58** (2)	**50.5** (24)	**54** (3.20)	**44** (3.40)	**54** (60)	**80** (1413)	**87** (50.5)			28	19
Ohio State University	**59.5** (3.16)	**66** (3.22)	**58** (2)	**50.5** (24)	**62** (3.03)	**72** (3.14)	**37.5** (73)	**30** (5177)	**103** (39.5)			131	113
University of Virginia	**59.5** (3.16)	**55** (3.33)	**82.5** (1)	**62.5** (16)	**59** (3.12)	**54** (3.33)	**63.5** (55)	**43** (3408)	**20** (148.2)			23	66

Institution	93Q [1]	93E [1]	% D [1]	% D-S [1]	93Q T [1]	93E T [1]	VIS [1]	TC [2]	C/F [2]	82Q [3]	82E [3]	TF [4]	TG [4]
Brown University	**62** (3.09)	**50** (3.39)	**48** (3)	**60.5** (17)	**64** (2.97)	**54** (3.33)	**65.5** (54)	**59** (2515)	**63.5** (74.0)			34	53(2)
Tufts University	**62** (3.09)	**55** (3.33)	**58** (2)	**66.5** (13)	**59** (3.12)	**54** (3.33)	**48** (64)	**42** (3439)	**29** (114.6)			30	38
North Carolina State University	**62** (3.09)	**72** (3.10)	**58** (2)	**58.5** (18)	**73** (2.85)	**70** (3.16)	**54** (60)	**68** (1958)	**117** (36.3)			54	32
U of Tex-Hlth Sci Ct-San Antonio	**64** (3.08)	**69** (3.12)	**58** (2)	**64.5** (14)	**64** (2.97)	**93** (2.87)	**56.5** (59)	**84** (1253)	**73.5** (62.7)			20	37
Washington State University	**65** (3.05)	**61.5** (3.28)	**48** (3)	**64.5** (14)	**61** (3.05)	**54** (3.33)	**61** (56)	**77** (1713)	**62** (74.5)			23	46
University of Georgia	**66** (3.03)	**85** (2.96)	**82.5** (1)	**71.5** (10)	**73** (2.85)	**92** (2.88)	**73** (48)	**56** (2694)	**49** (92.9)			29	49
Dartmouth College	**67** (3.02)	**65** (3.23)	**58** (2)	**68** (12)	**67** (2.91)	**64** (3.24)	**61** (56)	**75** (1730)	**82.5** (55.8)			31	55
Iowa State University	**68** (3.00)	**55** (3.33)	**82.5** (1)	**66.5** (13)	**71** (2.88)	**54** (3.33)	**67.5** (53)	**89** (1072)	**110** (37.0)			29	60
Univ of California-Riverside	**69** (2.96)	**60** (3.29)	**82.5** (1)	**71.5** (10)	**64** (2.97)	**54** (3.33)	**69** (51)	**82** (1350)	**81** (56.3)			24	80
Texas A&M University [c]	**70** (2.95)	**63.5** (3.24)	**147** (0)	**62.5** (16)	**71** (2.88)	**68** (3.18)	**50** (63)	**49** (2885)	**63.5** (74.0)			39	66
University of Missouri-Columbia	**71** (2.92)	**68** (3.13)	**147** (0)	**69** (11)	**79** (2.74)	**76** (3.08)	**73** (48)	**53.5** (2733)	**82.5** (55.8)			49	43
Saint Louis University	**72** (2.91)	**87** (2.93)	**58** (2)	**71.5** (10)	**66** (2.92)	**90** (2.98)	**65.5** (54)	**57** (2666)	**72** (63.5)			42	63
University of Connecticut	**73** (2.90)	**88** (2.92)	**147** (0)	**78** (8)	**68** (2.90)	**79** (3.06)	**77.5** (45)	**107** (740)	**98** (43.5)			17	36
University of Florida	**74** (2.88)	**67** (3.21)	**147** (0)	**81.5** (7)	**75** (2.84)	**71** (3.15)	**70** (50)	**55** (2729)	**66** (70.0)			39	58
Emory University	**76** (2.86)	**77.5** (3.03)	**82.5** (1)	**75** (9)	**76** (2.81)	**82** (3.04)	**83.5** (43)	**36** (4223)	**21** (136.2)			31	27
University of Tennessee - Memphis	**76** (2.86)	**79.5** (3.02)	**147** (0)	**86.5** (6)	**85** (2.69)	**79** (3.06)	**80** (44)	**52** (2742)	**68** (68.6)			40	25
University of Louisville	**76** (2.86)	**94** (2.82)	**147** (0)	**91** (5)	**94** (2.62)	**107** (2.62)	**142.5** (27)	**90** (1058)	**115** (36.5)			29	32
University of Nebraska-Lincoln	**78.5** (2.84)	**76** (3.05)	**82.5** (1)	**78** (8)	**77** (2.78)	**69** (3.17)	**94.5** (39)	**102** (830)	**128** (30.7)			27	25
University of South Carolina	**78.5** (2.84)	**98** (2.78)	**147** (0)	**86.5** (6)	**102** (2.55)	**117** (2.50)	**120** (31)	**88** (1076)	**130** (29.1)			37	84
University of Cincinnati	**80** (2.81)	**82** (3.00)	**82.5** (1)	**91** (5)	**91** (2.65)	**95** (2.86)	**80** (44)	**81** (1378)	**54** (86.1)			16	57
University of Delaware	**82** (2.78)	**82** (3.00)	**82.5** (1)	**75** (9)	**69** (2.89)	**75** (3.10)	**83.5** (43)	**132.5** (422)	**85** (52.8)			8	21
Boston University [b]	**82** (2.78)	**103** (2.74)	**147** (0)	**71.5** (10)	**89** (2.66)	**105** (2.64)	**86.5** (42)	**47** (2940)	**47** (94.8)			31	64
U of Massachusetts at Amherst	**82** (2.78)	**106** (2.72)	**147** (0)	**75** (9)	**85** (2.69)	**117** (2.50)	**97.5** (38)	**99** (879)	**114** (36.6)			24	35
University of Maryland College Park	**84** (2.74)	**74.5** (3.06)	**147** (0)	**81.5** (7)	**73** (2.85)	**86** (3.00)	**108** (34)	**123** (498)	**95** (45.3)			11	37
University of Illinois at Chicago	**85** (2.72)	**70.5** (3.11)	**147** (0)	**86.5** (6)	**100** (2.57)	**86** (3.00)	**89.5** (41)	**136** (410)	**137** (25.6)			16	24
Georgetown University	**86** (2.70)	**86** (2.95)	**82.5** (1)	**99.5** (4)	**95** (2.61)	**99** (2.78)	**108** (34)	**85** (1221)	**65** (71.8)			17	26
Thomas Jefferson University	**87.5** (2.69)	**114** (2.67)	**82.5** (1)	**81.5** (7)	**107** (2.45)	**102** (2.71)	**89.5** (41)	**41** (3522)	**22** (130.4)			27	40
Texas A&M University [a]	**87.5** (2.69)	**74.5** (3.06)	**147** (0)	**78** (8)	**82** (2.70)	**90** (2.98)	**77.5** (45)	**65** (2002)	**67** (69.0)			29	60
Wayne State University	**89.5** (2.68)	**90** (2.89)	**82.5** (1)	**86.5** (6)	**81** (2.72)	**80** (3.05)	**59** (57)	**117** (603)	**154** (19.5)			31	45
University of Pittsburgh [a]	**89.5** (2.68)	**70.5** (3.11)	**147** (0)	**99.5** (4)	**88** (2.67)	**54** (3.33)	**100** (37)	**92** (1029)	**38** (102.9)			10	52(2)

Appendix Table P - 5 Biochemistry and Molecular Biology (Continued)

Institution	93Q [1]	93E [1]	% D [1]	% D-S [1]	93Q T [1]	93E T [1]	VIS [1]	TC [2]	C/F [2]	82Q [3]	82E [3]	TF [4]	TG [4]
State Univ of New York-Buffalo [a]	91.5 (2.67)	130 (2.45)	147 (0)	86.5 (6)	91 (2.65)	126 (2.41)	114.5 (32)	106 (769)	77 (59.2)			13	25
Colorado State University	91.5 (2.67)	106 (2.72)	147 (0)	99.5 (4)	78 (2.75)	96 (2.83)	86.5 (42)	115 (640)	126 (32.0)			20	17
University of Kentucky	93.5 (2.64)	101 (2.76)	147 (0)	99.5 (4)	81 (2.72)	101 (2.74)	94.5 (39)	122 (502)	106 (38.6)			13	21
University of Pittsburgh [b]	93.5 (2.64)	84 (2.99)	147 (0)	116.5 (3)	92 (2.64)	73 (3.11)	92 (40)	97 (925)	122 (33.0)			28	n/a
University of Houston	95 (2.61)	90 (2.89)	58 (2)	99.5 (4)	85 (2.69)	99 (2.78)	149 (26)	157 (213)	158 (17.8)			12	29
University of New Hampshire	96 (2.60)	98 (2.78)	147 (0)	135 (2)	97 (2.60)	(n/s)	192 (16)	132.5 (422)	124 (32.5)			13	14
Medical College of Pensylvania	97 (2.57)	109 (2.71)	82.5 (1)	81.5 (7)	85 (2.69)	86 (3.00)	105 (35)	87 (1129)	73.5 (62.7)			18	17
University of Kansas [a]	98 (2.56)	125 (2.50)	147 (0)	99.5 (4)	98 (2.59)	117 (2.50)	97.5 (38)	108 (727)	116 (36.4)			20	50
U of Texas, Medical Br-Galveston	99 (2.55)	95 (2.80)	147 (0)	86.5 (6)	87 (2.68)	99 (2.78)	76 (46)	48 (2917)	84 (54.0)			54	56
University of New Mexico	100 (2.53)	82 (3.00)	82.5 (1)	99.5 (4)	103 (2.52)	66 (3.20)	73 (48)	73 (1792)	93 (45.9)			39	13
State Univ of New York-Buffalo [b]	101 (2.52)	125 (2.50)	147 (0)	160.5 (1)	99 (2.58)	117 (2.50)	160.5 (24)	109 (713)	97 (44.6)			16	12
CUNY - Grad Sch & Univ Center	102 (2.51)	92 (2.87)	82.5 (1)	99.5 (4)	108 (2.44)	86 (3.00)	89.5 (41)	91 (1043)	133 (28.2)			37	63
Univ of Missouri-Kansas City	103.5 (2.50)	117 (2.59)	147 (0)	116.5 (3)	114 (2.33)	141 (2.08)	114.5 (32)	113 (668)	135 (27.8)			24	9
University of Nevada, Reno	103.5 (2.50)	119.5 (2.57)	147 (0)	160.5 (1)	97 (2.60)	99 (2.78)	125 (30)	79 (1576)	123 (32.8)			48	47
University of Miami	105 (2.49)	77.5 (3.03)	147 (0)	135 (2)	104 (2.50)	77 (3.07)	83.5 (43)	83 (1268)	88 (48.8)			26	38
Arizona State University	106 (2.47)	98 (2.78)	147 (0)	99.5 (4)	107 (2.45)	110 (2.58)	83.5 (43)	95 (979)	140 (25.1)			39	56
University of Kansas [b]	107 (2.45)	109 (2.71)	147 (0)	160.5 (1)	101 (2.56)	107 (2.62)	125 (30)	182 (43)	187 (2.5)			17	19
Univ of Maryland at Baltimore	108 (2.43)	106 (2.72)	147 (0)	116.5 (3)	111 (2.37)	103 (2.69)	103 (36)	62 (2102)	33 (110.6)			19	32
Syracuse University	109 (2.42)	114 (2.67)	147 (0)	135 (2)	114 (2.33)	107 (2.62)	135.5 (28)	140 (341)	120 (34.1)			10	10
Kansas State University	110.5 (2.41)	98 (2.78)	82.5 (1)	116.5 (3)	120 (2.22)	110 (2.58)	114.5 (32)	105 (771)	112.5 (36.7)			21	27
SUNY Health Science Ctr-Syracuse	110.5 (2.41)	79.5 (3.02)	147 (0)	116.5 (3)	109 (2.41)	54 (3.33)	108 (34)	118 (535)	89 (48.6)			11	4
Georgia Institute of Technology	112 (2.39)	111.5 (2.69)	82.5 (1)	99.5 (4)	117 (2.29)	75 (3.10)	125 (30)	127 (475)	102 (39.6)			12	52
University of Vermont	113.5 (2.38)	125 (2.50)	82.5 (1)	116.5 (3)	116 (2.32)	135 (2.22)	80 (44)	86 (1149)	92 (46.0)			25	66
U of Arkansas for Medical Sci	113.5 (2.38)	145.5 (2.17)	147 (0)	116.5 (3)	110 (2.38)	133 (2.29)	149 (26)	131 (431)	148 (21.6)			20	17
University of Wisconsin-Milwaukee	115 (2.37)	102 (2.75)	58 (2)	99.5 (4)	123 (2.13)	126 (2.41)	135.5 (28)	141 (338)	170 (11.3)			30	49
Florida State University	116 (2.35)	125 (2.50)	147 (0)	116.5 (3)	119 (2.23)	135 (2.22)	142.5 (27)	149 (295)	144 (22.7)			13	4
Univ of Health Sc/Chicago Med Sch	117.5 (2.33)	117 (2.59)	147 (0)	116.5 (3)	105 (2.47)	104 (2.67)	108 (34)	172 (98)	177 (7.0)			14	11
Wake Forest University	117.5 (2.33)	90 (2.89)	147 (0)	160.5 (1)	128 (2.07)	117 (2.50)	135.5 (28)	98 (897)	91 (47.2)			19	28
U of Maryland Baltimore County	119.5 (2.31)	136 (2.33)	147 (0)	116.5 (3)	125 (2.10)	161 (1.67)	129.5 (29)	120 (522)	109 (37.3)			14	5
George Washington University	119.5 (2.31)	117 (2.59)	147 (0)	160.5 (1)	114 (2.33)	130 (2.33)	135.5 (28)	125 (487)	118 (34.8)			14	21

Institution	93Q [1]	93E [1]	% D [1]	% D-S [1]	93Q T [1]	93E T [1]	VIS [1]	TC [2]	C/F [2]	82Q [3]	82E [3]	TF [4]	TG [4]
Univ of Arkansas-Fayetteville	**121** (2.30)	**125** (2.50)	**147** (0)	**116.5** (3)	**134** (2.00)	(n/s)	**193** (14)	**100.5** (843)	**112.5** (36.7)			23	n/a
Albany Medical College	**122** (2.28)	**132** (2.43)	**58** (2)	**116.5** (3)	**93** (2.63)	**86** (3.00)	**175** (21)	**103** (786)	**119** (34.2)			23	11
Temple University	**123** (2.27)	**93** (2.83)	**147** (0)	**116.5** (3)	**114** (2.33)	**92** (2.88)	**94.5** (39)	**110** (709)	**90** (47.3)			15	23
Uniformed Services U of Hlth Sci	**124** (2.21)	**130** (2.45)	**82.5** (1)	**99.5** (4)	**122** (2.14)	**117** (2.50)	**94.5** (39)	**134** (420)	**125** (32.3)			13	7
Louisiana State U & A&M College	**125** (2.17)	**122** (2.53)	**82.5** (1)	**135** (2)	**145** (1.83)	**137** (2.18)	**100** (37)	**63** (2033)	**129** (29.9)			68	68
Texas Tech University	**126** (2.16)	**138** (2.31)	**58** (2)	**116.5** (3)	**125** (2.10)	**138** (2.17)	**100** (37)	**93** (1008)	**141** (24.0)			42	49
Wesleyan University	**127.5** (2.15)	**121** (2.55)	**147** (0)	**135** (2)	**134** (2.00)	**117** (2.50)	**108** (34)	**183** (32)	**186** (4.0)			8	21
West Virginia University	**127.5** (2.15)	**157** (1.98)	**147** (0)	**186** (0)	**134** (2.00)	**150** (1.85)	**125** (30)	**173** (91)	**179** (6.5)			14	10
University of Texas at Dallas	**129.5** (2.13)	**139.5** (2.29)	**147** (0)	**116.5** (3)	**134** (2.00)	**161** (1.67)	**135.5** (28)	**148** (303)	**139** (25.3)			12	49
Virginia Polytech Inst & State U	**129.5** (2.13)	**128** (2.46)	**147** (0)	**135** (2)	**119** (2.23)	**124** (2.45)	**114.5** (32)	**126** (476)	**159.5** (17.0)			28	30
Louisiana State U Medical Center	**131.5** (2.12)	**141.5** (2.22)	**147** (0)	**135** (2)	**134** (2.00)	**161** (1.67)	**155.5** (25)	**129** (464)	**105** (38.7)			12	20
Univ of Med & Dent of NJ	**131.5** (2.12)	**136** (2.33)	**147** (0)	**160.5** (1)	**121** (2.19)	**117** (2.50)	**135.5** (28)	**116** (633)	**80** (57.5)			11	23
Illinois State University	**133** (2.10)	**109** (2.71)	**82.5** (1)	**160.5** (1)	**134** (2.00)	**141** (2.08)	**135.5** (28)	**146** (310)	**142** (23.8)			13	n/a
Medical College of Wisconsin	**134** (2.07)	**157** (1.98)	**147** (0)	**135** (2)	**128** (2.07)	**161** (1.67)	**103** (36)	**130** (441)	**111** (36.8)			12	18
University of North Dakota	**135.5** (2.04)	**133.5** (2.41)	**82.5** (1)	**116.5** (3)	**134** (2.00)	**130** (2.33)	**142.5** (27)	**170** (104)	**173** (8.7)			12	17
University of Oklahoma	**135.5** (2.04)	**119.5** (2.57)	**147** (0)	**160.5** (1)	**134** (2.00)	**117** (2.50)	**135.5** (28)	**147** (309)	**134** (28.1)			11	6
Oklahoma State University	**139.5** (2.00)	**111.5** (2.69)	**147** (0)	**135** (2)	**139** (1.92)	**95** (2.86)	**114.5** (32)	**139** (382)	**138** (25.5)			15	18
Tulane University	**139.5** (2.00)	**130** (2.45)	**147** (0)	**135** (2)	**151** (1.75)	**141** (2.08)	**114.5** (32)	**135** (416)	**108** (37.8)			11	8
University of Wyoming	**139.5** (2.00)	**98** (2.78)	**147** (0)	**160.5** (1)	**134** (2.00)	**54** (3.33)	**135.5** (28)	**137.5** (398)	**152** (19.9)			20	21
Northeastern University	**139.5** (2.00)	**148.5** (2.08)	**147** (0)	**160.5** (1)	**134** (2.00)	**130** (2.33)	**177.5** (20)	**152** (277)	**166** (12.6)			22	18
SUNY-Health Science Ctr-Brooklyn	**139.5** (2.00)	**148.5** (2.08)	**147** (0)	**186** (0)	**140** (1.88)	**161** (1.67)	**167** (23)	**143** (321)	**143** (22.9)			14	18
East Carolina U Sch Medicine	**139.5** (2.00)	**114** (2.67)	**147** (0)	**186** (0)	**153** (1.70)	**117** (2.50)	**181.5** (19)	**100.5** (843)	**107** (38.3)			22	25
Utah State University	**143** (1.94)	**143** (2.19)	**58** (2)	**99.5** (4)	**145** (1.83)	**139** (2.12)	**89.5** (41)	**96** (976)	**104** (39.0)			25	36
Old Dominion University	**144** (1.91)	**169** (1.67)	**147** (0)	**186** (0)	**142** (1.86)	(n/s)	**190** (17)	**76** (1721)	**156** (18.3)			94	59
Rutgers State Univ-Newark	**145** (1.88)	**159** (1.91)	**147** (0)	**186** (0)	**158** (1.63)	**161** (1.67)	**149** (26)	**121** (509)	**132** (28.3)			18	65
University of Idaho	**146** (1.87)	**157** (1.98)	**147** (0)	**91** (5)	**154** (1.67)	**149** (1.88)	**103** (36)	**163** (165)	**163** (15.0)			11	28
Rush University	**147** (1.86)	**169** (1.67)	**147** (0)	**160.5** (1)	**149** (1.78)	**171** (1.39)	**181.5** (19)	**119** (531)	**100.5** (40.8)			13	30
University of South Florida	**148.5** (1.85)	**144** (2.18)	**147** (0)	**160.5** (1)	**143** (1.84)	**133** (2.29)	**114.5** (32)	**144** (317)	**131** (28.8)			11	n/a
Lehigh University	**148.5** (1.85)	**169** (1.67)	**147** (0)	**160.5** (1)	**142** (1.86)	**161** (1.67)	**186** (18)	**188** (14)	**188** (1.8)			8	22(2)
Bowling Green State University	**150** (1.83)	**169** (1.67)	**147** (0)	**186** (0)	**170** (1.40)	(n/s)	**181.5** (19)	**177.5** (68)	**181** (6.2)			11	7

Appendix Table P - 5 Biochemistry and Molecular Biology (Continued)

Institution	93Q [1]	93E [1]	% D [1]	% D-S [1]	93Q T [1]	93E T [1]	VIS [1]	TC [2]	C/F [2]	82Q [3]	82E [3]	TF [4]	TG [4]
Montana State University	151 (1.80)	104 (2.73)	147 (0)	135 (2)	150 (1.77)	117 (2.50)	125 (30)	124 (494)	127 (30.9)			16	n/a
Brigham Young University	152 (1.79)	169 (1.67)	147 (0)	160.5 (1)	163 (1.56)	161 (1.67)	167 (23)	151 (289)	159.5 (17.0)			17	13
University of North Texas	153.5 (1.78)	151 (2.05)	82.5 (1)	116.5 (3)	160 (1.60)	128 (2.38)	167 (23)	156 (215)	164 (13.4)			16	30
Medical College of Ohio	153.5 (1.78)	163 (1.82)	82.5 (1)	99.5 (4)	152 (1.72)	161 (1.67)	125 (30)	112 (672)	70 (67.2)			10	40
Loyola University of Chicago	155 (1.77)	148.5 (2.08)	147 (0)	160.5 (1)	156 (1.64)	117 (2.50)	177.5 (20)	153 (276)	136 (27.6)			10	18
Hahnemann University	156 (1.76)	161.5 (1.83)	147 (0)	160.5 (1)	147 (1.82)	148 (1.91)	114.5 (32)	142 (328)	151 (20.5)			16	19
Creighton University	157 (1.74)	152 (2.04)	147 (0)	186 (0)	164 (1.55)	161 (1.67)	167 (23)	155 (243)	178 (6.8)			36	25
U of Mississippi-Medical Center	158 (1.73)	178 (1.39)	82.5 (1)	160.5 (1)	158 (1.63)	161 (1.67)	120 (31)	137.5 (398)	121 (33.2)			12	18
North Dakota State University	159.5 (1.69)	161.5 (1.83)	147 (0)	135 (2)	162 (1.57)	161 (1.67)	160.5 (24)	145 (316)	172 (9.6)			33	23
Kent State University	159.5 (1.69)	139.5 (2.29)	147 (0)	135 (2)	168 (1.46)	145 (2.00)	167 (23)	154 (263)	161 (16.4)			16	26
Univ of Puerto Rico-Rio Piedras	162 (1.67)	169 (1.67)	147 (0)	116.5 (3)	145 (1.83)	(n/s)	186 (18)	192 (9)	191 (1.1)			8	2
New Mexico State University	162 (1.67)	154.5 (2.00)	147 (0)	160.5 (1)	160 (1.60)	151 (1.83)	129.5 (29)	168 (126)	169 (11.5)			11	19
Howard University	162 (1.67)	133.5 (2.41)	147 (0)	160.5 (1)	167 (1.50)	117 (2.50)	172.5 (22)	165 (158)	171 (10.5)			15	8
Miami University	164 (1.65)	153 (2.03)	147 (0)	135 (2)	125 (2.10)	128 (2.38)	149 (26)	175 (76)	180 (6.3)			12	43
University of Tennessee-Knoxville	165 (1.64)	145.5 (2.17)	147 (0)	160.5 (1)	155 (1.65)	145 (2.00)	125 (30)	150 (292)	145.5 (22.5)			13	68
Oregon Graduate Inst Sci & Tech	166.5 (1.57)	181 (1.25)	82.5 (1)	160.5 (1)	148 (1.79)	161 (1.67)	155.5 (25)	128 (471)	69 (67.3)			7	18
University of Hawaii at Manoa	166.5 (1.57)	154.5 (2.00)	147 (0)	160.5 (1)	171 (1.39)	161 (1.67)	142.5 (27)	164 (160)	165 (13.3)			12	16
Medical College of Georgia	168 (1.56)	175.5 (1.50)	147 (0)	135 (2)	160 (1.60)	172 (1.33)	181.5 (19)	67 (1959)	28 (115.2)			17	10
Louisiana St U-Sch Med Shreveport	169.5 (1.48)	136 (2.33)	147 (0)	160.5 (1)	174 (1.22)	145 (2.00)	149 (26)	167 (145)	157 (18.1)			8	18
University of Alabama	169.5 (1.48)	175.5 (1.50)	147 (0)	186 (0)	165 (1.54)	170 (1.53)	149 (26)	179 (64)	183 (5.8)			11	22
Loma Linda University	171.5 (1.47)	181 (1.25)	147 (0)	160.5 (1)	173 (1.31)	176 (0.83)	172.5 (22)	71 (1910)	41 (100.5)			19	12
New York Medical College	171.5 (1.47)	169 (1.67)	147 (0)	160.5 (1)	180 (0.86)	161 (1.67)	160.5 (24)	160 (180)	145.5 (22.5)			8	11
Drexel University	173 (1.46)	169 (1.67)	147 (0)	186 (0)	172 (1.38)	(n/s)	186 (18)	159 (187)	150 (20.8)			9	n/a
Southern Methodist University	174 (1.43)	181 (1.25)	147 (0)	186 (0)	177 (1.17)	161 (1.67)	186 (18)	162 (169)	162 (15.4)			11	20
Clemson University	175 (1.41)	160 (1.85)	147 (0)	160.5 (1)	169 (1.42)	147 (1.95)	172.5 (22)	177.5 (68)	174 (8.5)			8	11
Ball State University	176 (1.33)	141.5 (2.22)	82.5 (1)	160.5 (1)	179 (1.00)	(n/s)	194 (12)	187 (17)	192.5 (1.0)			17	11
Georgia State University	177.5 (1.32)	179 (1.33)	147 (0)	135 (2)	176 (1.18)	176 (0.83)	155.5 (25)	166 (147)	149 (21.0)			7	25
Medical University South Carolina	177.5 (1.32)	169 (1.67)	147 (0)	186 (0)	175 (1.20)	161 (1.67)	149 (26)	114 (641)	94 (45.8)			14	56
University of Montana	179 (1.15)	169 (1.67)	147 (0)	160.5 (1)	167 (1.50)	(n/s)	186 (18)	174 (87)	147 (21.8)			4	5
Clark Atlanta University	180 (1.08)	148.5 (2.08)	147 (0)	116.5 (3)	178 (1.11)	135 (2.22)	190 (17)	190.5 (10)	194 (0.8)			12	28(2)

Institution	93Q [1]	93E [1]	% D [1]	% D-S [1]	93Q T [1]	93E T [1]	VIS [1]	TC [2]	C/F [2]	82Q [3]	82E [3]	TF [4]	TG [4]
Catholic University of America	**181** (0.93)	**169** (1.67)	**82.5** (1)	**160.5** (1)	**181** (0.83)	**161** (1.67)	**167** (23)	**176** (74)	**175** (8.2)			9	17
Texas Woman's University	**182** (0.86)	**177** (1.48)	**82.5** (1)	**135** (2)	**182** (0.80)	**145** (2.00)	**160.5** (24)	**185** (28)	**184** (5.6)			5	11
University of Notre Dame	**183** (0.84)	**187** (0.74)	**147** (0)	**160.5** (1)	**183** (0.72)	**180** (0.56)	**120** (31)	**169** (114)	**155** (19.0)			6	13
University of Tulsa	**184** (0.69)	**191** (0.37)	**147** (0)	**186** (0)	**187** (0.46)	**182** (0.33)	**149** (26)	**180** (60)	**167** (12.0)			5	6
Ohio University	**185** (0.63)	**188** (0.67)	**147** (0)	**186** (0)	**186** (0.55)	**176** (0.83)	**149** (26)	**158** (198)	**71** (66.0)			3	15
Clark University	**186** (0.56)	**185** (0.93)	**147** (0)	**160.5** (1)	**190** (0.36)	**176** (0.83)	**160.5** (24)	**181** (59)	**168** (11.8)			5	3
Boston University [a]	**187** (0.53)	**193.5** (0.00)	**147** (0)	**160.5** (1)	**184** (0.69)	**185** (0.00)	**160.5** (24)	**161** (177)	**53** (88.5)			2	5
Univ of Southern Mississippi	**188** (0.52)	**190** (0.42)	**147** (0)	**186** (0)	**189** (0.39)	**182** (0.33)	**167** (23)	**193** (7)	**192.5** (1.0)			7	12
University of South Dakota	**189** (0.50)	**184** (0.95)	**147** (0)	**160.5** (1)	**191** (0.29)	**185** (0.00)	**177.5** (20)	**190.5** (10)	**189** (1.4)			7	11
Univ of Missouri-Saint Louis	**190** (0.46)	**186** (0.77)	**82.5** (1)	**116.5** (3)	**185** (0.61)	**173** (0.91)	**135.5** (28)	**189** (12)	**182** (6.0)			2	1
University of Mass-Lowell	**191** (0.44)	**189** (0.56)	**82.5** (1)	**160.5** (1)	**192** (0.25)	**180** (0.56)	**172.5** (22)	**171** (99)	**153** (19.8)			5	0
State Univ of New York-Binghamton	**192** (0.41)	**183** (1.00)	**147** (0)	**186** (0)	**188** (0.40)	**176** (0.83)	**177.5** (20)	**184** (30)	**176** (7.5)			4	9
Northern Arizona University	**193** (0.21)	**192** (0.17)	**147** (0)	**186** (0)	**193** (0.17)	**185** (0.00)	**155.5** (25)	**186** (22)	**185** (5.5)			4	0
University of Alaska	**194** (0.15)	**193.5** (0.00)	**147** (0)	**186** (0)	**194** (0.00)	**185** (0.00)	**190** (17)	**194** (4)	**190** (1.3)			3	n/a

Sources: 1. National Survey of Graduate Faculty
2. Institute for Scientific Information
3. 1982 Survey of Graduate Faculty
4. Institutional Coordinator Data

Notes: *a.* School of Arts and Sciences
b. School of Medicine
c. School of Agriculture

n/s After trimming no cases remained

(1) Combined enrollment for programs in Biochemistry and Molecular Biology and Ecology, Evolution, and Behavior
(2) Combined enrollment for programs in Biochemistry and Molecular Biology and Cell and Developmental Biology

Appendix Table P - 6 Relative Rankings for Research-Doctorate Programs in Biomedical Engineering

Institution	93Q [1]	93E [1]	% D [1]	% D-S [1]	93Q T [1]	93E T [1]	VIS [1]	TC [2]	C/F [2]	82Q [3]	82E [3]	TF [4]	TG [4]
Massachusetts Inst of Technology	1 (4.62)	2 (4.17)	1 (49)	1 (73)	1 (4.74)	2 (4.31)	4 (80)	1 (4891)	3 (71.9)			68	134
Univ of California-San Diego	2 (4.45)	1 (4.43)	2 (34)	7 (55)	2 (4.54)	1 (4.33)	11 (66)	17 (620)	13 (34.4)			18	38
University of Washington	3 (4.35)	6 (3.85)	3 (33)	4 (68)	3 (4.40)	4 (3.96)	5.5 (79)	8 (1408)	10 (41.4)			34	62
Duke University	4 (4.33)	12 (3.63)	4.5 (29)	2 (72)	4 (4.33)	18 (3.50)	5.5 (79)	10 (877)	14 (31.3)			28	54
University of Pennsylvania	5 (4.28)	9 (3.82)	4.5 (29)	3 (70)	6 (4.24)	11.5 (3.68)	1 (86)	5 (2260)	9 (41.9)			54	90
Johns Hopkins University	6 (4.25)	3 (4.09)	6 (28)	5 (65)	5 (4.28)	3 (4.17)	3 (83)	11 (867)	8 (43.4)			20	47
Univ of California-San Francisco	7 (4.19)	5 (3.89)	8 (20)	14 (36)	8 (4.05)	5 (3.89)	15.5 (62)	2 (4204)	1 (100.1)			42	51*
University of California-Berkeley	8 (4.08)	7 (3.84)	7 (25)	8.5 (51)	7 (4.06)	8 (3.78)	7.5 (73)	9 (1324)	6 (49.0)			27	51*
University of Utah	9 (3.97)	10 (3.69)	9 (19)	6 (60)	9 (4.00)	9 (3.73)	2 (84)	7 (1505)	19 (22.5)			67	n/a
Rice University	10 (3.94)	4 (3.95)	11 (13)	12.5 (40)	10 (3.91)	13 (3.67)	20.5 (58)	15 (640)	5 (58.2)			11	54
University of Michigan	11 (3.91)	11 (3.68)	13 (10)	8.5 (51)	12 (3.86)	14 (3.61)	9 (72)	3 (2809)	7 (47.6)			59	70
Stanford University	12 (3.86)	8 (3.83)	10 (16)	11 (41)	14 (3.77)	6.5 (3.83)	15.5 (62)	25 (363)	4 (60.5)			6	n/a
Case Western Reserve Univ	13 (3.84)	13 (3.60)	12 (12)	10 (48)	11 (3.89)	11.5 (3.68)	7.5 (73)	27 (288)	21 (20.6)			14	39
Northwestern University	14 (3.82)	14 (3.54)	14 (8)	12.5 (40)	13 (3.83)	15 (3.60)	17 (61)	19 (442)	23 (16.4)			27	12
University of Rochester	15 (3.67)	15 (3.53)	15 (6)	21.5 (23)	15 (3.67)	6.5 (3.83)	26 (48)	6 (1623)	11 (37.7)			43	20
Vanderbilt University	16 (3.65)	21 (3.30)	20 (3)	19 (28)	18 (3.53)	23 (3.33)	23 (56)	20.5 (439)	16 (29.3)			15	23
University of Minnesota	17.5 (3.49)	17 (3.38)	27.5 (1)	16 (33)	23 (3.40)	23 (3.33)	12.5 (65)	4 (2551)	2 (77.3)			33	28
U of North Carolina-Chapel Hill	17.5 (3.49)	23 (3.24)	27.5 (1)	20 (27)	21 (3.47)	23 (3.33)	22 (57)	16 (623)	22 (20.1)			31	54
University of Texas at Austin	19.5 (3.48)	19 (3.33)	16.5 (4)	23.5 (22)	16 (3.56)	23 (3.33)	29 (47)	20.5 (439)	29 (13.3)			33	21
Pennsylvania State University	19.5 (3.48)	25 (3.13)	20 (3)	15 (35)	19.5 (3.50)	28.5 (3.06)	10 (70)	12 (801)	17 (28.6)			28	30
University of Virginia	21 (3.44)	16 (3.40)	20 (3)	18 (31)	22 (3.44)	19 (3.44)	14 (64)	26 (302)	24 (15.9)			19	47
Drexel University	22 (3.42)	27 (3.04)	27.5 (1)	17 (32)	17 (3.54)	27 (3.14)	12.5 (65)	24 (364)	32 (8.9)			41	25
University of California-Davis	23 (3.37)	24 (3.15)	27.5 (1)	23.5 (22)	19.5 (3.50)	23 (3.33)	26 (48)	18 (596)	20 (22.1)			27	21
University of Iowa	24 (3.35)	19 (3.33)	27.5 (1)	27 (17)	25 (3.20)	16.5 (3.54)	30.5 (44)	30 (137)	27 (13.7)			10	32
University of Alabama-Birmingham	25 (3.27)	19 (3.33)	27.5 (1)	26 (18)	24 (3.25)	10 (3.72)	26 (48)	23 (376)	28 (13.4)			28	34
Ohio State University	26 (3.26)	22 (3.25)	16.5 (4)	21.5 (23)	30.5 (3.00)	23 (3.33)	20.5 (58)	28 (259)	30 (11.8)			22	38
Rutgers State Univ-New Brunswick	27 (3.16)	28 (2.99)	20 (3)	25 (19)	28 (3.10)	28.5 (3.06)	18 (60)	13 (745)	18 (24.8)			30	67
U of Texas-Southwestern Med Ctr	28 (3.13)	31.5 (2.67)	27.5 (1)	29.5 (11)	26.5 (3.14)	30.5 (3.00)	30.5 (44)	14 (736)	12 (36.8)			20	28
Rensselaer Polytechnic Inst	29 (2.97)	29 (2.89)	27.5 (1)	28 (15)	32.5 (2.92)	32 (2.81)	19 (59)	31 (113)	26 (14.1)			8	37
Iowa State University	30 (2.92)	34.5 (2.50)	35.5 (0)	32 (8)	26.5 (3.14)	30.5 (3.00)	37 (31)	33 (58)	36 (3.2)			18	10

Institution	93Q [1]	93E [1]	% D [1]	% D-S [1]	93Q T [1]	93E T [1]	VIS [1]	TC [2]	C/F [2]	82Q [3]	82E [3]	TF [4]	TG [4]
North Carolina State University	**31** (2.86)	**34.5** (2.50)	**35.5** (0)	**35.5** (4)	**31** (3.00)	**34** (2.50)	**38** (24)	**32** (84)	**33** (4.2)			20	26
Dartmouth College	**32** (2.83)	**26** (3.06)	**20** (3)	**31** (10)	**29** (3.08)	**17** (3.54)	**34.5** (41)	**22** (434)	**15** (31.0)			14	9
Clemson University	**33** (2.74)	**30** (2.78)	**27.5** (1)	**29.5** (11)	**33** (2.92)	**33** (2.67)	**33** (42)	**37** (18)	**37** (2.3)			8	18
Texas A&M University	**34** (2.50)	**33** (2.58)	**35.5** (0)	**33** (7)	**36** (2.18)	**37** (1.67)	**34.5** (41)	**35** (32)	**34** (4.0)			8	17
University of Illinois at Chicago	**35** (2.41)	**31.5** (2.67)	**27.5** (1)	**35.5** (4)	**34** (2.33)	**23** (3.33)	**36** (40)	**29** (158)	**25** (14.4)			11	4
University of Miami	**36** (2.11)	**37** (2.03)	**35.5** (0)	**37** (3)	**35** (2.20)	**37** (1.67)	**32** (43)	**36** (23)	**35** (3.3)			7	8
University of Akron	**37** (1.92)	**36** (2.04)	**35.5** (0)	**38** (1)	**38** (1.85)	**37** (1.67)	**26** (48)	**38** (4)	**38** (0.6)			7	39
Worcester Polytechnic Inst	**38** (1.72)	**38** (1.56)	**35.5** (0)	**34** (5)	**37** (1.89)	**37** (1.67)	**26** (48)	**34** (35)	**31** (11.7)			3	1

Sources: 1. National Survey of Graduate Faculty
2. Institute for Scientific Information
3. 1982 Survey of Graduate Faculty
4. Institutional Coordinator Data

* University of California-San Francisco and University of California-Berkeley reported combined enrollments and degree data

Appendix Table P - 7 Relative Rankings for Research-Doctorate Programs in Cell and Developmental Biology

Institution	93Q [1]	93E [1]	% D [1]	% D-S [1]	93Q T [1]	93E T [1]	VIS [1]	TC [2]	C/F [2]	82Q [3]	82E [3]	TF [4]	TG [4]
Massachusetts Inst of Technology	1 (4.86)	2 (4.66)	1 (86)	1 (97)	1 (4.93)	2 (4.75)	1 (100)	3 (22759)	1 (421.5)			54	n/a
Rockefeller University	2 (4.77)	4 (4.54)	2 (75)	3 (93)	3.5 (4.78)	4 (4.53)	5 (96)	10 (12486)	2 (416.2)			30	270
Univ of California-San Francisco	3 (4.76)	3 (4.57)	3 (74)	6 (87)	2 (4.89)	3 (4.71)	7.5 (94)	6 (19972)	3 (363.1)			55	36
California Institute Technology	4 (4.73)	1 (4.68)	5 (65)	9.5 (78)	3.5 (4.78)	1 (4.79)	13 (87)	31 (5164)	8 (224.5)			23	37
Harvard University	5 (4.70)	7 (4.33)	4 (69)	4 (91)	5 (4.77)	7 (4.35)	3.5 (97)	17 (8712)	7 (235.5)			37	98
Stanford University [b]	6 (4.55)	6 (4.39)	6 (52)	7 (85)	7 (4.58)	6 (4.43)	10 (91)	19 (8126)	4 (338.6)			24	35
Univ of California-San Diego	7 (4.50)	12 (4.15)	7.5 (50)	2 (95)	6 (4.62)	10 (4.25)	2 (98)	1 (34224)	5 (314.0)			109	65
University of Washington	8 (4.48)	9 (4.23)	7.5 (50)	5 (89)	8 (4.54)	8.5 (4.26)	3.5 (97)	2 (32327)	12 (185.8)			174	40
Washington University	9 (4.39)	8 (4.24)	9.5 (43)	8 (84)	12.5 (4.29)	12 (4.12)	6 (95)	4 (21053)	13 (179.9)			117	72
Yale University	10 (4.37)	10 (4.22)	9.5 (43)	11 (77)	10 (4.49)	8.5 (4.26)	10 (91)	16 (8801)	9 (220.0)			40	36
Princeton University	11.5 (4.36)	5 (4.45)	11 (39)	15.5 (67)	11 (4.46)	5 (4.46)	20.5 (82)	30 (5352)	11 (198.2)			27	86
Stanford University [a]	11.5 (4.36)	13 (4.08)	12 (35)	9.5 (78)	9 (4.50)	13 (4.11)	15 (85)	48 (2313)	14 (154.2)			15	n/a
University of California-Berkeley	13 (4.16)	11 (4.19)	14 (24)	15.5 (67)	12.5 (4.29)	11 (4.23)	23 (81)	34 (4462)	29 (106.2)			42	95
Duke University	14 (4.11)	16 (3.91)	13 (28)	13 (74)	14 (4.17)	16 (4.01)	7.5 (94)	7 (19254)	10 (216.3)			89	107
University of Chicago	15 (4.10)	15 (4.03)	15 (23)	12 (75)	15 (4.11)	15 (4.02)	12 (90)	15 (9038)	23 (129.1)			70	113
University of Wisconsin-Madison	16 (4.05)	14 (4.06)	16 (20)	14 (73)	16 (4.05)	14 (4.04)	10 (91)	24 (7025)	37 (93.7)			75	101
Univ of California-Los Angeles	17 (3.99)	18 (3.86)	20 (16)	17 (65)	19.5 (4.00)	18.5 (3.81)	17 (84)	11 (12337)	17 (150.5)			82	167
U of Texas-Southwestern Med Ctr	18 (3.98)	21.5 (3.77)	18 (17)	29 (44)	18 (4.03)	21 (3.75)	38 (66)	23 (7553)	20 (137.3)			55	57
Columbia University	19 (3.94)	17 (3.89)	17 (18)	19.5 (56)	17 (4.04)	17 (3.99)	23 (81)	29 (5663)	19 (138.1)			41	59
Johns Hopkins University	20 (3.91)	19 (3.79)	22 (13)	25 (47)	22 (3.90)	23 (3.64)	36 (68)	63 (1679)	27 (111.9)			15	51
New York University	21 (3.86)	21.5 (3.77)	20 (16)	22 (53)	21 (3.96)	20 (3.77)	25 (80)	5 (20270)	28 (110.8)			183	n/a
University of Colorado [b]	22 (3.85)	45 (3.40)	27 (9)	40 (28)	19.5 (4.00)	39.5 (3.43)	68 (45)	21 (7888)	6 (272.0)			29	36
University of Pennsylvania	23 (3.81)	24 (3.74)	23 (11)	19.5 (56)	30.5 (3.64)	25 (3.63)	26 (78)	8 (17371)	22 (135.7)			128	51
Baylor College of Medicine	24 (3.80)	31 (3.58)	20 (16)	23 (52)	23 (3.83)	31 (3.57)	19 (83)	12 (11663)	16 (153.5)			76	113
U of North Carolina-Chapel Hill	25 (3.79)	20 (3.78)	24.5 (10)	21 (55)	27 (3.74)	18.5 (3.81)	14 (86)	13 (11509)	18 (149.5)			77	307
Albert Einstein College of Med	26 (3.76)	26 (3.64)	27 (9)	18 (58)	25 (3.76)	27.5 (3.61)	17 (84)	20 (7967)	30 (103.5)			77	43
U of Illinois at Urbana-Champaign	27 (3.74)	29.5 (3.62)	24.5 (10)	27.5 (45)	25 (3.76)	31 (3.57)	30.5 (72)	40 (3636)	55 (72.7)			50	60
Brandeis University	28 (3.73)	32 (3.57)	29 (8)	24 (48)	25 (3.76)	31 (3.57)	28.5 (74)	50 (2118)	31 (100.9)			21	48[(3)]
Vanderbilt University	29 (3.69)	38 (3.53)	27 (9)	26 (46)	28.5 (3.66)	35 (3.49)	20.5 (82)	9 (15217)	24 (129.0)			118	42
University of Michigan	30 (3.66)	35 (3.55)	31.5 (5)	34 (35)	28.5 (3.66)	33.5 (3.50)	48 (58)	53 (1919)	43 (87.2)			22	36

Appendix Table P - 7 Cell and Developmental Biology (Continued)

Institution	93Q [1]	93E [1]	% D [1]	% D-S [1]	93Q T [1]	93E T [1]	VIS [1]	TC [2]	C/F [2]	82Q [3]	82E [3]	TF [4]	TG [4]
Northwestern University	**31** (3.64)	**29.5** (3.62)	**42** (3)	**27.5** (45)	**31** (3.64)	**26** (3.62)	**28.5** (74)	**26** (6438)	**36** (97.5)			66	65
Indiana University	**32** (3.59)	**27.5** (3.63)	**42** (3)	**30** (43)	**32** (3.63)	**28** (3.61)	**33** (70)	**47** (2413)	**54** (73.1)			33	1
University of California-Davis	**33** (3.55)	**27.5** (3.63)	**30** (7)	**33** (38)	**37** (3.49)	**38** (3.44)	**17** (84)	**25** (6955)	**53** (74.0)			94	112
University of Minnesota [b]	**34** (3.54)	**40** (3.45)	**42** (3)	**45.5** (22)	**36** (3.50)	**38** (3.44)	**66.5** (46)	**46** (2595)	**40** (92.7)			28	43
Cornell University	**35.5** (3.53)	**23** (3.75)	**42** (3)	**51** (20)	**36** (3.50)	**23** (3.64)	**76.5** (41)	**76** (1184)	**68** (53.8)			22	37
State U of New York-Stony Brook	**35.5** (3.53)	**35** (3.55)	**50** (2)	**31.5** (42)	**34** (3.58)	**42** (3.41)	**23** (81)	**22** (7872)	**46** (80.3)			98	38
University of Minnesota [a]	**37** (3.49)	**43** (3.41)	**35** (4)	**35** (32)	**40** (3.42)	**52** (3.33)	**39** (65)	**32** (4825)	**32** (100.5)			48	38
U of Tex-Health Sci Ctr-Houston	**38** (3.46)	**37** (3.54)	**31.5** (5)	**31.5** (42)	**33** (3.60)	**29** (3.60)	**27** (75)	**18** (8600)	**21** (136.5)			63	80
University of California-Irvine	**39** (3.44)	**51.5** (3.33)	**50** (2)	**45.5** (22)	**41** (3.41)	**52** (3.33)	**56** (52)	**83** (1019)	**71** (51.0)			20	46
Michigan State University	**40** (3.41)	**35** (3.55)	**35** (4)	**42** (25)	**39** (3.43)	**36** (3.47)	**51.5** (56)	**36** (4219)	**69** (52.7)			80	72
University of Virginia	**41** (3.39)	**25** (3.69)	**67** (1)	**38** (29)	**42** (3.39)	**23** (3.64)	**34.5** (69)	**37** (4199)	**50** (76.3)			55	66
Case Western Reserve Univ	**42** (3.38)	**45** (3.40)	**50** (2)	**48.5** (21)	**39** (3.43)	**34** (3.50)	**59.5** (50)	**35** (4303)	**15** (153.7)			28	n/a
University of Texas at Austin	**43** (3.37)	**33** (3.56)	**35** (4)	**38** (29)	**43** (3.36)	**40** (3.43)	**41.5** (63)	**64** (1678)	**113** (25.4)			66	113
University of Rochester	**44** (3.35)	**64.5** (3.14)	**42** (3)	**38** (29)	**45** (3.31)	**81** (3.00)	**32** (71)	**51** (2046)	**76** (48.7)			42	91
U of Massachusetts Med Center	**46** (3.33)	**45** (3.40)	**42** (3)	**42** (25)	**44** (3.33)	**62** (3.24)	**37** (67)	**27** (5917)	**33** (100.3)			59	42
Purdue University	**46** (3.33)	**41** (3.44)	**67** (1)	**54** (19)	**48** (3.26)	**52** (3.33)	**54** (54)	**66** (1568)	**65** (56.0)			28	43
University of Miami	**46** (3.33)	**51.5** (3.33)	**130** (0)	**45.5** (22)	**46** (3.29)	**52** (3.33)	**49.5** (57)	**42** (3315)	**58** (67.7)			49	29
University of Alabama-Birmingham	**48.5** (3.31)	**47** (3.39)	**35** (4)	**36** (30)	**49** (3.25)	**74** (3.10)	**30.5** (72)	**14** (10234)	**56** (72.1)			142	24
University of Southern California	**48.5** (3.31)	**78.5** (3.00)	**130** (0)	**42** (25)	**47** (3.28)	**74** (3.10)	**56** (52)	**45** (2721)	**47** (80.0)			34	51
University of Iowa	**50** (3.28)	**39** (3.50)	**35** (4)	**51** (20)	**51** (3.21)	**52** (3.33)	**41.5** (63)	**44** (3011)	**63** (56.8)			53	93
U of Massachusetts at Amherst	**51** (3.21)	**42** (3.43)	**42** (3)	**45.5** (22)	**53** (3.18)	**41** (3.42)	**46** (59)	**86** (990)	**89** (35.4)			28	43
Oregon State University	**52.5** (3.20)	**61.5** (3.19)	**67** (1)	**62.5** (13)	**51** (3.21)	**64** (3.22)	**62** (49)	**70** (1406)	**102** (29.9)			47	45
Emory University	**52.5** (3.20)	**61.5** (3.19)	**130** (0)	**48.5** (21)	**69** (2.97)	**72** (3.14)	**44** (60)	**41** (3422)	**51.5** (74.4)			46	13
Tufts University [b]	**54** (3.16)	**74** (3.07)	**130** (0)	**60.5** (14)	**52** (3.20)	**66** (3.20)	**69.5** (44)	**61** (1725)	**72** (50.7)			34	22
University of Illinois at Chicago [b]	**55** (3.11)	**64.5** (3.14)	**42** (3)	**56.5** (18)	**66** (3.00)	**52** (3.33)	**56** (52)	**79** (1085)	**35** (98.6)			11	39
Pennsylvania State University	**56** (3.10)	**59** (3.22)	**67** (1)	**54** (19)	**56** (3.13)	**52** (3.33)	**53** (55)	**62** (1717)	**86** (37.3)			46	11
Thomas Jefferson University	**57.5** (3.09)	**81.5** (2.96)	**42** (3)	**54** (19)	**55** (3.16)	**94** (2.80)	**49.5** (57)	**39** (3743)	**62** (58.5)			64	19
U of Tex-Hlth Sci Ct-San Antonio	**57.5** (3.09)	**57** (3.24)	**50** (2)	**51** (20)	**54** (3.17)	**69** (3.16)	**41.5** (63)	**38** (3998)	**73** (50.6)			79	82
Brown University	**59** (3.08)	**55** (3.26)	**130** (0)	**65** (12)	**59** (3.08)	**64** (3.22)	**59.5** (50)	**134** (217)	**140.5** (14.5)			15	53[(1)]
Rutgers State Univ-New Brunswick	**60** (3.07)	**74** (3.07)	**67** (1)	**58** (17)	**63** (3.02)	**91** (2.83)	**41.5** (63)	**57** (1813)	**81** (39.4)			46	65

Institution	93Q [1]	93E [1]	% D [1]	% D-S [1]	93Q T [1]	93E T [1]	VIS [1]	TC [2]	C/F [2]	82Q [3]	82E [3]	TF [4]	TG [4]
Ohio State University	**61** (3.06)	**48** (3.38)	**67** (1)	**56.5** (18)	**70** (2.93)	**71** (3.15)	**34.5** (69)	**33** (4810)	**90** (34.4)			140	66
Iowa State University	**62** (3.05)	**51.5** (3.33)	**67** (1)	**59** (15)	**57** (3.12)	**52** (3.33)	**66.5** (46)	**55** (1893)	**99** (30.5)			62	114
University of Arizona	**63** (3.00)	**56** (3.25)	**130** (0)	**60.5** (14)	**62** (3.03)	**52** (3.33)	**46** (59)	**49** (2179)	**67** (54.5)			40	40
Tufts University [a]	**65** (2.97)	**74** (3.07)	**67** (1)	**65** (12)	**60** (3.06)	**85** (2.96)	**76.5** (41)	**96** (719)	**85** (37.8)			19	16
Texas A&M University	**65** (2.97)	**81.5** (2.96)	**67** (1)	**74.5** (9)	**66** (3.00)	**98** (2.71)	**84** (38)	**69** (1413)	**51.5** (74.4)			19	18
University of Illinois at Chicago [a]	**65** (2.97)	**87** (2.92)	**130** (0)	**74.5** (9)	**66** (3.00)	**88** (2.88)	**71.5** (43)	**100** (588)	**134** (17.3)			34	83
Univ of Maryland at Baltimore	**67** (2.96)	**66** (3.11)	**50** (2)	**62.5** (13)	**69** (2.97)	**76** (3.07)	**51.5** (56)	**28** (5712)	**38** (93.6)			61	51
University of Kansas [b]	**68** (2.95)	**109** (2.69)	**67** (1)	**85** (6)	**85** (2.70)	**114** (2.33)	**132.5** (27)	**109** (403)	**114** (25.2)			16	19
University of Pittsburgh [a]	**69.5** (2.93)	**70** (3.08)	**130** (0)	**74.5** (9)	**61** (3.04)	**64** (3.22)	**46** (59)	**60** (1754)	**48** (79.7)			22	52[(1)]
University of Colorado [a]	**69.5** (2.93)	**59** (3.22)	**130** (0)	**81** (7)	**66** (3.00)	**71** (3.15)	**73.5** (42)	**88** (857)	**80** (40.8)			21	17
U of Maryland Baltimore County	**71** (2.92)	**51.5** (3.33)	**67** (1)	**67** (11)	**83** (2.72)	**52** (3.33)	**80** (40)	**81** (1072)	**106** (28.2)			38	20
Medical College of Wisconsin	**73** (2.88)	**87** (2.92)	**67** (1)	**81** (7)	**83** (2.72)	**78** (3.06)	**110.5** (33)	**104** (555)	**87** (37.0)			15	20
University of Missouri-Columbia	**73** (2.88)	**70** (3.08)	**130** (0)	**69.5** (10)	**71** (2.91)	**79** (3.03)	**63** (48)	**52** (1956)	**78** (42.5)			46	51
North Carolina State University	**73** (2.88)	**59** (3.22)	**130** (0)	**74.5** (9)	**73** (2.86)	**78** (3.06)	**64.5** (47)	**71** (1390)	**117** (23.6)			59	86
Univ of California-Riverside	**75** (2.87)	**80** (2.99)	**130** (0)	**69.5** (10)	**87** (2.64)	**93** (2.81)	**73.5** (42)	**92** (788)	**88** (35.8)			22	50
University of Kentucky [b]	**76** (2.82)	**84.5** (2.94)	**130** (0)	**91.5** (5)	**80** (2.73)	**85** (2.96)	**88.5** (37)	**94** (744)	**124** (20.7)			36	34
University of Tennessee-Knoxville	**78** (2.77)	**70** (3.08)	**67** (1)	**99.5** (4)	**80** (2.73)	**52** (3.33)	**103.5** (34)	**97** (710)	**61** (59.2)			12	27
Uniformed Services U of Hlth Sci	**78** (2.77)	**98.5** (2.80)	**130** (0)	**65** (12)	**88** (2.63)	**115** (2.29)	**69.5** (44)	**72** (1355)	**26** (112.9)			12	16
University of Florida	**78** (2.77)	**84.5** (2.94)	**130** (0)	**91.5** (5)	**77** (2.74)	**91** (2.83)	**64.5** (47)	**59** (1787)	**79** (41.6)			43	48
State Univ of New York-Buffalo [a]	**80** (2.75)	**117.5** (2.50)	**130** (0)	**99.5** (4)	**80** (2.73)	**108** (2.50)	**97** (35)	**105** (519)	**99** (30.5)			17	34
University of Tennessee - Memphis	**81** (2.73)	**104.5** (2.74)	**130** (0)	**91.5** (5)	**90** (2.62)	**113** (2.41)	**103.5** (34)	**102** (577)	**125.5** (20.6)			28	50
Colorado State University	**82.5** (2.72)	**96** (2.82)	**67** (1)	**78.5** (8)	**80** (2.73)	**119** (2.22)	**120** (30)	**80** (1076)	**57** (71.7)			15	43
University of Georgia [a]	**82.5** (2.72)	**70** (3.08)	**130** (0)	**69.5** (10)	**59** (3.08)	**52** (3.33)	**97** (35)	**95** (722)	**60** (60.2)			12	35
University of Vermont	**84** (2.70)	**76.5** (3.02)	**130** (0)	**91.5** (5)	**93** (2.60)	**91** (2.83)	**103.5** (34)	**90** (821)	**111** (25.7)			32	79
University of Cincinnati	**85** (2.68)	**93.5** (2.86)	**130** (0)	**78.5** (8)	**73** (2.86)	**67** (3.18)	**80** (40)	**74** (1200)	**34** (100.0)			12	24
University of New Mexico	**87** (2.67)	**83** (2.95)	**67** (1)	**120** (2)	**90** (2.62)	**98** (2.71)	**103.5** (34)	**58** (1799)	**77** (42.8)			42	21
University of Maryland College Park	**87** (2.67)	**92** (2.88)	**67** (1)	**69.5** (10)	**92** (2.61)	**101** (2.69)	**71.5** (43)	**108** (433)	**121** (22.8)			19	46
Univ of California-Santa Barbara	**87** (2.67)	**104.5** (2.74)	**67** (1)	**81** (7)	**75** (2.78)	**83** (2.98)	**59.5** (50)	**114** (375)	**91** (34.1)			11	n/a
Rice University	**89** (2.65)	**87** (2.92)	**67** (1)	**74.5** (9)	**100** (2.50)	**52** (3.33)	**84** (38)	**142** (134)	**129** (19.1)			7	18
Texas Tech University	**90.5** (2.64)	**104.5** (2.74)	**50** (2)	**85** (6)	**76** (2.75)	**52** (3.33)	**110.5** (33)	**135** (196)	**156** (8.9)			22	18

Appendix Table P - 7 Cell and Developmental Biology (Continued)

Institution	93Q [1]	93E [1]	% D [1]	% D-S [1]	93Q T [1]	93E T [1]	VIS [1]	TC [2]	C/F [2]	82Q [3]	82E [3]	TF [4]	TG [4]
State Univ of New York-Buffalo [b]	90.5 (2.64)	70 (3.08)	130 (0)	99.5 (4)	90 (2.62)	74 (3.10)	97 (35)	82 (1045)	92 (33.7)			31	38
Univ of California-Santa Cruz	92 (2.60)	112 (2.65)	130 (0)	85 (6)	83 (2.72)	88 (2.88)	76.5 (41)	73 (1214)	39 (93.4)			13	18
University of Oklahoma	94 (2.59)	91 (2.89)	67 (1)	99.5 (4)	100 (2.50)	104 (2.59)	92.5 (36)	85 (993)	101 (30.1)			33	73
Wake Forest University	94 (2.59)	113.5 (2.64)	130 (0)	99.5 (4)	107 (2.42)	95 (2.78)	110.5 (33)	75 (1192)	45 (85.1)			14	16
Albany Medical College	94 (2.59)	51.5 (3.33)	130 (0)	140 (1)	95 (2.57)	52 (3.33)	125 (29)	56 (1892)	74 (49.8)			38	37
University of Houston	96.5 (2.57)	96 (2.82)	130 (0)	85 (6)	100 (2.50)	119 (2.22)	115.5 (31)	159.5 (61)	172 (4.7)			13	13
SUNY Health Science Ctr-Syracuse	96.5 (2.57)	126.5 (2.29)	130 (0)	107.5 (3)	95 (2.57)	126 (2.00)	167 (19)	65 (1628)	44 (85.7)			19	13
Georgetown University	98.5 (2.54)	93.5 (2.86)	67 (1)	85 (6)	118 (2.27)	124 (2.08)	88.5 (37)	84 (1007)	49 (77.5)			13	11
Temple University	98.5 (2.54)	101 (2.78)	130 (0)	120 (2)	100 (2.50)	98 (2.71)	92.5 (36)	111 (391)	123 (21.7)			18	31
Louisiana State U & A&M College	100 (2.53)	63 (3.18)	130 (0)	120 (2)	110 (2.38)	81 (3.00)	146 (24)	87 (874)	139 (15.1)			58	23
Arizona State University	101 (2.52)	110.5 (2.67)	130 (0)	120 (2)	96 (2.56)	108 (2.50)	97 (35)	115 (374)	122 (22.0)			17	16
Washington State University	102 (2.50)	78.5 (3.00)	130 (0)	120 (2)	97 (2.55)	86 (2.92)	88.5 (37)	54 (1900)	70 (51.4)			37	39
University of Connecticut	103 (2.48)	89.5 (2.90)	67 (1)	74.5 (9)	118 (2.27)	108 (2.50)	59.5 (50)	132 (225)	142 (14.1)			16	27
University of Pittsburgh [b]	104 (2.47)	113.5 (2.64)	67 (1)	107.5 (3)	74 (2.82)	89 (2.86)	140.5 (25)	125 (300)	93 (33.3)			9	n/a
Univ of Missouri-Kansas City	105 (2.45)	101 (2.78)	130 (0)	140 (1)	(n/s)	(n/s)	168.5 (18)	107 (464)	97 (30.9)			15	9
University of Kansas [a]	106.5 (2.43)	133 (2.08)	130 (0)	99.5 (4)	109 (2.39)	140 (1.67)	110.5 (33)	153.5 (74)	159 (8.2)			9	7
Wayne State University	106.5 (2.43)	76.5 (3.02)	130 (0)	140 (1)	120 (2.20)	52 (3.33)	76.5 (41)	67 (1435)	99 (30.5)			47	66
University of Nebraska-Lincoln	108 (2.42)	96 (2.82)	130 (0)	91.5 (5)	114 (2.30)	98 (2.71)	120 (30)	120 (320)	120 (22.9)			14	15
Wesleyan University	109 (2.41)	89.5 (2.90)	130 (0)	91.5 (5)	104 (2.48)	81 (3.00)	84 (38)	141 (151)	146 (12.6)			12	20
Univ of Med & Dent of NJ	110 (2.39)	107 (2.73)	130 (0)	99.5 (4)	104 (2.48)	98 (2.71)	92.5 (36)	113 (387)	103 (29.8)			13	25
U of Texas, Medical Br-Galveston	111 (2.38)	98.5 (2.80)	130 (0)	120 (2)	112 (2.31)	104 (2.59)	80 (40)	93 (768)	83 (38.4)			20	34
Saint Louis University	112 (2.35)	121 (2.45)	130 (0)	107.5 (3)	86 (2.67)	108 (2.50)	103.5 (34)	89 (827)	41 (91.9)			9	8
Tulane University [a]	113 (2.32)	115 (2.56)	130 (0)	107.5 (3)	105 (2.46)	108 (2.50)	97 (35)	156 (70)	165 (5.8)			12	45(2)
University of Kentucky [a]	115 (2.31)	133 (2.08)	130 (0)	120 (2)	116 (2.29)	124 (2.08)	136 (26)	152 (80)	156 (8.9)			9	18
West Virginia University	115 (2.31)	67 (3.10)	130 (0)	140 (1)	124 (2.13)	52 (3.33)	146 (24)	119 (329)	136 (16.5)			20	13
University of South Carolina	115 (2.31)	108 (2.72)	130 (0)	140 (1)	109 (2.39)	68 (3.17)	84 (38)	78 (1093)	118 (23.3)			47	116
CUNY - Grad Sch & Univ Center	117.5 (2.30)	123 (2.41)	130 (0)	107.5 (3)	116 (2.29)	140 (1.67)	140.5 (25)	123.5 (304)	132 (17.9)			17	53
Univ of Health Sc/Chicago Med Sch	117.5 (2.30)	117.5 (2.50)	130 (0)	120 (2)	123 (2.14)	119 (2.22)	88.5 (37)	101 (582)	110 (26.5)			22	28
Tulane University [b]	119 (2.28)	104.5 (2.74)	130 (0)	91.5 (5)	114 (2.30)	52 (3.33)	115.5 (31)	128 (266)	104 (29.6)			9	6
Florida State University	120 (2.27)	51.5 (3.33)	130 (0)	165.5 (0)	106 (2.43)	52 (3.33)	136 (26)	112 (390)	95 (32.5)			12	10

Institution	93Q [1]	93E [1]	% D [1]	% D-S [1]	93Q T [1]	93E T [1]	VIS [1]	TC [2]	C/F [2]	82Q [3]	82E [3]	TF [4]	TG [4]
State Univ of New York-Albany	**121.5** (2.25)	**125** (2.36)	**67** (1)	**99.5** (4)	**126** (2.06)	**119** (2.22)	**103.5** (34)	**103** (561)	**64** (56.1)			10	15
New York Medical College	**121.5** (2.25)	**128** (2.26)	**130** (0)	**120** (2)	**111** (2.35)	**122** (2.14)	**103.5** (34)	**43** (3040)	**25** (121.6)			25	31
University of South Florida	**123** (2.22)	**136** (2.03)	**130** (0)	**120** (2)	**119** (2.22)	**119** (2.22)	**110.5** (33)	**91** (820)	**42** (91.1)			9	n/a
Hahnemann University	**124** (2.21)	**124** (2.38)	**130** (0)	**165.5** (0)	**129** (2.00)	**140** (1.67)	**129.5** (28)	**129** (238)	**143** (13.2)			18	25
Brigham Young University	**125** (2.20)	**149** (1.67)	**130** (0)	**91.5** (5)	**100** (2.50)	(n/s)	**152** (23)	**149** (98)	**159** (8.2)			12	11
Clemson University	**126** (2.14)	**117.5** (2.50)	**130** (0)	**120** (2)	**133** (1.86)	**128** (1.95)	**115.5** (31)	**151** (81)	**171** (4.8)			17	29
Loyola University of Chicago	**127** (2.11)	**121** (2.45)	**67** (1)	**120** (2)	**122** (2.17)	**113** (2.41)	**103.5** (34)	**139** (167)	**135** (16.7)			10	19
Medical University South Carolina	**128** (2.09)	**138** (1.95)	**130** (0)	**140** (1)	**133** (1.86)	**140** (1.67)	**160** (21)	**68** (1433)	**75** (49.4)			29	22
University of Georgia [c]	**131.5** (2.00)	**110.5** (2.67)	**67** (1)	**120** (2)	**148** (1.50)	(n/s)	**164.5** (20)	**98** (664)	**94** (33.2)			20	83
University of New Hampshire	**131.5** (2.00)	**129.5** (2.22)	**130** (0)	**107.5** (3)	**129** (2.00)	**108** (2.50)	**160** (21)	**143** (127)	**137** (15.9)			8	9
Kansas State University	**131.5** (2.00)	**133** (2.08)	**130** (0)	**120** (2)	**125** (2.07)	**108** (2.50)	**120** (30)	**140** (161)	**109** (26.8)			6	5
Georgia State University	**131.5** (2.00)	**159.5** (1.43)	**130** (0)	**140** (1)	**122** (2.17)	**140** (1.67)	**132.5** (27)	**131** (230)	**133** (17.7)			13	17
Creighton University	**131.5** (2.00)	**129.5** (2.22)	**130** (0)	**140** (1)	**140** (1.67)	(n/s)	**176.5** (15)	**106** (491)	**105** (28.9)			17	6
Louisiana State U Medical Center	**131.5** (2.00)	**117.5** (2.50)	**130** (0)	**165.5** (0)	**131** (1.91)	**102** (2.67)	**115.5** (31)	**118** (345)	**119** (23.0)			15	10
University of Notre Dame	**135** (1.95)	**121** (2.45)	**130** (0)	**140** (1)	**133** (1.86)	**140** (1.67)	**120** (30)	**146** (106)	**149** (10.6)			10	14
University of Wyoming	**136** (1.90)	**137** (1.97)	**130** (0)	**165.5** (0)	**135** (1.85)	**128** (1.95)	**125** (29)	**126** (289)	**125.5** (20.6)			14	7
Southern Illinois University	**137** (1.83)	**140** (1.89)	**67** (1)	**120** (2)	**152** (1.36)	**140** (1.67)	**110.5** (33)	**138** (187)	**147.5** (11.7)			16	33
Illinois State University	**138** (1.82)	**126.5** (2.29)	**130** (0)	**165.5** (0)	**143** (1.63)	**126** (2.00)	**156** (22)	**130** (237)	**128** (19.8)			12	n/a
Medical College of Pensylvania	**139** (1.79)	**149** (1.67)	**130** (0)	**165.5** (0)	**146** (1.57)	(n/s)	**146** (24)	**99** (640)	**59** (64.0)			10	21
Louisiana St U-Sch Med Shreveport	**141** (1.75)	**139** (1.92)	**130** (0)	**107.5** (3)	**148** (1.50)	**140** (1.67)	**84** (38)	**77** (1172)	**66** (55.8)			21	37
University of North Texas	**141** (1.75)	(n/s)	**130** (0)	**165.5** (0)	(n/s)	(n/s)	**179** (11)	**150** (90)	**163** (6.9)			13	15
Montana State University [d]	**141** (1.75)	**149** (1.67)	**130** (0)	**165.5** (0)	**138** (1.75)	(n/s)	**160** (21)	**110** (393)	**107** (28.1)			14	n/a
University of South Alabama	**143** (1.74)	**149** (1.67)	**130** (0)	**140** (1)	**154** (1.25)	**158** (0.72)	**120** (30)	**133** (224)	**116** (24.9)			9	18
Ohio University	**144** (1.71)	**158** (1.50)	**130** (0)	**165.5** (0)	**141** (1.64)	**154** (1.11)	**136** (26)	**162** (56)	**169** (5.1)			11	11
Boston University	**145** (1.69)	**133** (2.08)	**130** (0)	**140** (1)	**129** (2.00)	**119** (2.22)	**146** (24)	**137** (188)	**96** (31.3)			6	28
U of Arkansas for Medical Sci	**146** (1.68)	**149** (1.67)	**130** (0)	**140** (1)	**148** (1.50)	**140** (1.67)	**160** (21)	**147** (105)	**147.5** (11.7)			9	11
SUNY-Health Science Ctr-Brooklyn	**148** (1.67)	**149** (1.67)	**130** (0)	**165.5** (0)	**143** (1.63)	**140** (1.67)	**136** (26)	**145** (112)	**130** (18.7)			6	29
Montana State University [a]	**148** (1.67)	**159.5** (1.43)	**130** (0)	**165.5** (0)	**136** (1.83)	**140** (1.67)	**152** (23)	**116.5** (351)	**82** (39.0)			9	14
East Carolina U Sch Medicine	**148** (1.67)	**149** (1.67)	**130** (0)	**165.5** (0)	**138** (1.75)	**140** (1.67)	**176.5** (15)	**116.5** (351)	**115** (25.1)			14	8
Kent State University	**150** (1.64)	**161.5** (1.33)	**130** (0)	**165.5** (0)	**161** (1.00)	**156** (0.83)	**171** (17)	**127** (273)	**108** (27.3)			10	7

Appendix Table P - 7 Cell and Developmental Biology (Continued)

Institution	93Q [1]	93E [1]	% D [1]	% D-S [1]	93Q T [1]	93E T [1]	VIS [1]	TC [2]	C/F [2]	82Q [3]	82E [3]	TF [4]	TG [4]
University of Hawaii at Manoa	**152** (1.63)	**149** (1.67)	**130** (0)	**140** (1)	**161** (1.00)	**140** (1.67)	**146** (24)	**144** (115)	**145** (12.8)			9	12
St. John's University	**152** (1.63)	**149** (1.67)	**130** (0)	**140** (1)	**151** (1.38)	**140** (1.67)	**146** (24)	**123.5** (304)	**127** (20.3)			15	22
Miami University	**152** (1.63)	**101** (2.78)	**130** (0)	**165.5** (0)	**161** (1.00)	(n/s)	**168.5** (18)	**170** (40)	**161** (8.0)			5	31
Univ of Puerto Rico-Rio Piedras [b]	**154** (1.62)	**163** (1.25)	**130** (0)	**165.5** (0)	**143** (1.63)	**152** (1.25)	**164.5** (20)	**175** (15)	**178.5** (1.0)			15	2
George Washington University	**156.5** (1.50)	**149** (1.67)	**50** (2)	**107.5** (3)	**153** (1.33)	**140** (1.67)	**92.5** (36)	**158** (62)	**150** (10.3)			6	26
Loma Linda University	**156.5** (1.50)	**149** (1.67)	**130** (0)	**140** (1)	**140** (1.67)	**140** (1.67)	**152** (23)	**122** (307)	**138** (15.4)			20	25
Catholic University of America	**156.5** (1.50)	**149** (1.67)	**130** (0)	**140** (1)	**151** (1.38)	**140** (1.67)	**140.5** (25)	**153.5** (74)	**159** (8.2)			9	17
Auburn University [c]	**156.5** (1.50)	**149** (1.67)	**130** (0)	**165.5** (0)	**129** (2.00)	**140** (1.67)	**173.5** (16)	**121** (309)	**131** (18.2)			17	7
University of Idaho	**159** (1.44)	**149** (1.67)	**130** (0)	**120** (2)	**155** (1.20)	**140** (1.67)	**125** (29)	**155** (71)	**156** (8.9)			8	2
Clark University	**160** (1.43)	**133** (2.08)	**130** (0)	**165.5** (0)	(n/s)	(n/s)	**176.5** (15)	**164.5** (48)	**152.5** (9.6)			5	0
Auburn University [a]	**161** (1.38)	**165** (1.00)	**130** (0)	**165.5** (0)	**145** (1.60)	**140** (1.67)	**164.5** (20)	**168.5** (45)	**170** (5.0)			9	16
University of Louisville	**162.5** (1.33)	**174** (0.72)	**130** (0)	**165.5** (0)	**156** (1.14)	**156** (0.83)	**156** (22)	**136** (191)	**84** (38.2)			5	22
Lehigh University	**162.5** (1.33)	**161.5** (1.33)	**130** (0)	**165.5** (0)	**157** (1.10)	**140** (1.67)	**129.5** (28)	**176** (14)	**176.5** (1.8)			8	22[(1)]
Fordham University	**164** (1.16)	**169** (0.91)	**130** (0)	**165.5** (0)	**161** (1.00)	**152** (1.25)	**125** (29)	**168.5** (45)	**166** (5.6)			8	64[(2)]
University of Montana	**165** (1.07)	**149** (1.67)	**130** (0)	**140** (1)	**161** (1.00)	**140** (1.67)	**152** (23)	**148** (104)	**144** (13.0)			8	3
Bowling Green State University	**166** (1.00)	**149** (1.67)	**130** (0)	**140** (1)	**166** (0.60)	(n/s)	**156** (22)	**166.5** (47)	**168** (5.2)			9	6
Oklahoma State University	**167.5** (0.94)	**166** (0.97)	**67** (1)	**140** (1)	**165** (0.83)	**154** (1.11)	**129.5** (28)	**177** (9)	**175** (2.3)			4	110
Univ of Puerto Rico-Rio Piedras [a]	**167.5** (0.94)	**167.5** (0.95)	**130** (0)	**140** (1)	**164** (0.88)	**159** (0.56)	**171** (17)	**173** (26)	**174** (2.9)			9	8
University of Dayton	**169** (0.93)	**171.5** (0.83)	**130** (0)	**140** (1)	**161** (1.00)	**156** (0.83)	**125** (29)	**171** (37)	**167** (5.3)			7	4
Northern Arizona University	**170** (0.86)	**164** (1.11)	**130** (0)	**165.5** (0)	**175** (0.00)	(n/s)	**171** (17)	**166.5** (47)	**154** (9.4)			5	1
Drexel University	**171** (0.81)	**167.5** (0.95)	**130** (0)	**140** (1)	**167** (0.50)	**162** (0.00)	**129.5** (28)	**172** (29)	**162** (7.3)			4	n/a
University of Tulsa	**172** (0.80)	**171.5** (0.83)	**130** (0)	**140** (1)	**169** (0.40)	**162** (0.00)	**160** (21)	**159.5** (61)	**151** (10.2)			6	4
Clark Atlanta University	**173** (0.72)	(n/s)	**130** (0)	**165.5** (0)	**171** (0.33)	(n/s)	**173.5** (16)	**157** (64)	**173** (3.8)			17	28[(1)]
University of South Dakota	**174** (0.69)	**171.5** (0.83)	**130** (0)	**165.5** (0)	**168** (0.43)	(n/s)	**146** (24)	**161** (58)	**140.5** (14.5)			4	1
Univ of Arkansas-Fayetteville	**175** (0.60)	**171.5** (0.83)	**130** (0)	**165.5** (0)	**173** (0.13)	(n/s)	**152** (23)	**178.5** (7)	**176.5** (1.8)			4	2
Utah State University	**176** (0.50)	**176** (0.00)	**130** (0)	**165.5** (0)	**172** (0.20)	**162** (0.00)	**136** (26)	**174** (25)	**164** (6.3)			4	3

Institution	93Q [1]	93E [1]	% D [1]	% D-S [1]	93Q T [1]	93E T [1]	VIS [1]	TC [2]	C/F [2]	82Q [3]	82E [3]	TF [4]	TG [4]
State Univ of New York-Binghamton	**177** (0.33)	**149** (1.67)	**130** (0)	**165.5** (0)	**175** (0.00)	(n/s)	**176.5** (15)	**164.5** (48)	**152.5** (9.6)			5	4
Georgia Institute of Technology	**178** (0.16)	**176** (0.00)	**130** (0)	**120** (2)	**170** (0.36)	**162** (0.00)	**140.5** (25)	**163** (51)	**112** (25.5)			2	3
Univ of Southern Mississippi	**179** (0.13)	**176** (0.00)	**130** (0)	**165.5** (0)	**175** (0.00)	(n/s)	**164.5** (20)	**178.5** (7)	**178.5** (1.0)			7	14

Sources: 1. National Survey of Graduate Faculty
2. Institute for Scientific Information
3. 1982 Survey of Graduate Faculty
4. Institutional Coordinator Data

Notes: *a.* School of Arts and Sciences
b. School of Medicine
c. School of Veterinary Medicine
d. School of Agriculture

n/s After trimming no cases remained

(1) Combined enrollment for programs in Biochemistry and Molecular Biology and Cell and Developmental Biology
(2) Combined enrollment for programs in Cell and Developmental Biology and Ecology, Evolution, and Behavior
(3) Combined enrollment for programs in Cell and Developmental Biology and Molecular and General Genetics

Appendix Table P - 8 Relative Rankings for Research-Doctorate Programs in Chemical Engineering

Institution	93Q [1]	93E [1]	% D [1]	% D-S [1]	93Q T [1]	93E T [1]	VIS [1]	TC [2]	C/F [2]	82Q [3]	82E [3]	TF [4]	TG [4]
University of Minnesota	1 (4.86)	1 (4.57)	1 (83)	1 (97)	1 (4.90)	1 (4.66)	4 (97)	1 (3751)	1 (117.2)	1 (4.89)	1 (4.70)	32	142
Massachusetts Inst of Technology	2 (4.73)	2.5 (4.43)	2 (75)	3 (93)	2 (4.84)	2 (4.46)	1 (99)	3 (2438)	5 (78.6)	7 (4.33)	8 (3.97)	31	190
University of California-Berkeley	3 (4.63)	2.5 (4.43)	3 (64)	4 (92)	4 (4.60)	4 (4.39)	4 (97)	4 (1697)	4 (89.3)	4 (4.63)	5 (4.38)	19	95
University of Wisconsin-Madison	4 (4.62)	4 (4.37)	4 (61)	2 (95)	3 (4.63)	5 (4.37)	4 (97)	19 (609)	27.5 (32.1)	2 (4.76)	2 (4.62)	19	95
U of Illinois at Urbana-Champaign	5 (4.42)	6 (4.28)	7.5 (43)	5 (84)	6 (4.49)	6.5 (4.33)	18 (91)	14 (685)	12 (45.7)	9 (4.01)	7 (4.05)	15	74
California Institute Technology	6 (4.41)	7 (4.24)	5 (48)	6 (82)	7 (4.48)	6.5 (4.33)	10.5 (94)	15 (671)	6 (67.1)	3 (4.66)	4 (4.43)	10	63
Stanford University	7 (4.35)	5 (4.31)	6 (44)	8 (80)	5 (4.57)	3 (4.44)	14 (93)	6 (1039)	2 (103.9)	5 (4.53)	3 (4.45)	10	56
University of Delaware	8 (4.34)	8 (4.21)	7.5 (43)	7 (81)	8 (4.31)	9 (4.10)	10.5 (94)	8 (874)	14.5 (43.7)	6 (4.49)	6 (4.18)	20	121
Princeton University	9 (4.14)	9 (4.02)	9 (30)	10 (75)	9 (4.27)	8 (4.13)	7.5 (95)	16 (656)	14.5 (43.7)	10 (3.99)	9 (3.90)	15	62
University of Texas at Austin	10 (4.08)	13 (3.73)	10 (25)	9 (76)	10 (3.98)	14 (3.64)	10.5 (94)	2 (2874)	3 (95.8)	13 (3.74)	14 (3.55)	30	91
University of Pennsylvania	11 (3.97)	10.5 (3.81)	11 (15)	11 (74)	11 (3.95)	10 (3.82)	16.5 (92)	11 (723)	13 (45.2)	11 (3.94)	11 (3.62)	16	53
Carnegie Mellon University	12 (3.87)	12 (3.80)	14 (12)	12 (71)	12 (3.94)	11 (3.79)	7.5 (95)	38 (359)	41 (21.1)	15 (3.60)	13 (3.58)	17	80
Cornell University	13 (3.86)	10.5 (3.81)	16.5 (11)	13 (65)	14 (3.86)	12 (3.78)	23 (88)	12 (714)	21 (37.6)	18 (3.37)	17 (3.28)	19	197
Univ of California-Santa Barbara	14 (3.82)	18 (3.45)	14 (12)	16 (62)	13 (3.89)	15 (3.52)	23 (88)	7 (933)	11 (51.8)			18	45
Northwestern University	15 (3.75)	14 (3.67)	14 (12)	14.5 (63)	15 (3.79)	13 (3.65)	14 (93)	23 (515)	31.5 (30.3)	12 (3.84)	10 (3.80)	17	62
Purdue University	16 (3.67)	15 (3.63)	16.5 (11)	14.5 (63)	16 (3.60)	16 (3.49)	2 (98)	9 (803)	27.5 (32.1)	14 (3.67)	15 (3.53)	25	69
University of Houston	17 (3.66)	21 (3.37)	12 (13)	17 (54)	17 (3.57)	20 (3.39)	6 (96)	52 (198)	67 (11.0)	8 (4.06)	12 (3.60)	18	67
University of Michigan	18 (3.52)	19 (3.43)	22 (4)	18 (51)	19 (3.45)	17 (3.48)	19.5 (89)	13 (707)	20 (39.3)	17 (3.37)	18 (3.23)	18	71
CUNY - Grad Sch & Univ Center	19 (3.46)	27 (3.15)	22 (4)	19 (42)	18 (3.51)	23 (3.16)	30.5 (85)	60 (152)	63 (11.7)	31 (2.73)	33.5 (2.72)	13	22
University of Washington	20 (3.44)	17 (3.48)	18 (6)	20 (39)	22 (3.31)	21 (3.30)	23 (88)	18 (619)	25 (34.4)	16 (3.42)	16 (3.35)	18	62
U of Massachusetts at Amherst	21.5 (3.35)	23 (3.28)	19 (5)	24 (35)	20.5 (3.33)	22 (3.21)	30.5 (85)	26 (455)	24 (35.0)	21 (3.17)	21 (3.17)	13	52
Rice University	21.5 (3.35)	16 (3.54)	22 (4)	22 (37)	23 (3.24)	18 (3.43)	28.5 (86)	27 (454)	31.5 (30.3)	20 (3.19)	22 (3.10)	15	57
Pennsylvania State University	23 (3.34)	22 (3.29)	27 (3)	22 (37)	24 (3.21)	24 (3.15)	19.5 (89)	24 (489)	45 (18.1)	27 (2.95)	25 (2.95)	27	87
University of Notre Dame	24 (3.30)	20 (3.38)	38.5 (1)	22 (37)	20.5 (3.33)	19 (3.40)	16.5 (92)	41 (318)	33 (28.9)	19 (3.24)	20 (3.18)	11	46
North Carolina State University	25 (3.20)	25 (3.21)	27 (3)	25 (33)	25 (3.13)	25 (3.12)	14 (93)	17 (632)	22 (37.2)	33 (2.68)	30 (2.85)	17	53
University of Colorado	26 (3.18)	26 (3.19)	27 (3)	26 (30)	26 (3.06)	29 (3.01)	23 (88)	39 (351)	40 (23.4)	26 (2.96)	29 (2.88)	15	57
Lehigh University	27 (3.13)	24 (3.26)	68.5 (0)	27 (27)	27 (3.04)	26 (3.10)	35 (83)	10 (760)	18 (40.0)	32 (2.70)	28 (2.90)	19	69
University of California-Davis	28 (3.11)	28 (3.12)	22 (4)	29 (23)	29.5 (3.02)	27 (3.03)	23 (88)	20 (593)	23 (37.1)			16	23
State Univ of New York-Buffalo	29 (3.08)	29 (3.09)	31.5 (2)	34.5 (18)	29.5 (3.02)	30.5 (2.97)	26.5 (87)	22 (554)	19 (39.6)	22 (3.10)	31 (2.82)	14	64
University of Virginia	30.5 (3.01)	33 (3.00)	27 (3)	39 (16)	29.5 (3.02)	34 (2.94)	43 (76)	36 (375)	30 (31.3)	43 (2.46)	37.5 (2.63)	12	30

Institution	93Q [1]	93E [1]	% D [1]	% D-S [1]	93Q T [1]	93E T [1]	VIS [1]	TC [2]	C/F [2]	82Q [3]	82E [3]	TF [4]	TG [4]
Georgia Institute of Technology	**30.5** (3.01)	**30.5** (3.07)	**31.5** (2)	**28** (26)	**37** (2.82)	**32** (2.96)	**10.5** (94)	**35** (386)	**53.5** (15.4)	**36** (2.62)	**37.5** (2.63)	25	45
Yale University	**32.5** (2.98)	**43** (2.76)	**27** (3)	**31** (20)	**30** (3.02)	**40** (2.80)	**33** (84)	**28** (450)	**9** (56.3)	**34** (2.67)	**39** (2.62)	8	29
Iowa State University	**32.5** (2.98)	**39.5** (2.85)	**31.5** (2)	**37** (17)	**36** (2.84)	**41** (2.78)	**36.5** (82)	**25** (458)	**34** (28.6)	**23** (3.07)	**19** (3.20)	16	43
University of Florida	**34** (2.97)	**32** (3.03)	**68.5** (0)	**37** (17)	**32** (2.88)	**31** (2.97)	**36.5** (82)	**48.5** (218)	**51** (15.6)	**25** (3.00)	**23** (3.08)	14	28
Rensselaer Polytechnic Inst	**35.5** (2.95)	**34.5** (2.99)	**31.5** (2)	**31** (20)	**35** (2.85)	**37** (2.89)	**26.5** (87)	**37** (370)	**36** (26.4)	**37** (2.59)	**35** (2.68)	14	69
Johns Hopkins University	**35.5** (2.95)	**38** (2.95)	**68.5** (0)	**33** (19)	**35** (2.85)	**36** (2.90)	**38.5** (81)	**32.5** (415)	**10** (51.9)			8	30
Texas A&M University	**37** (2.91)	**41** (2.81)	**22** (4)	**31** (20)	**39** (2.76)	**43** (2.71)	**28.5** (86)	**45.5** (239)	**62** (12.0)	**45** (2.43)	**51.5** (2.42)	20	51
Washington University	**38** (2.89)	**36.5** (2.98)	**38.5** (1)	**37** (17)	**33** (2.86)	**28** (3.02)	**42** (78)	**72** (75)	**75** (6.3)	**28** (2.82)	**24** (2.97)	12	45
Univ of California-Los Angeles	**39** (2.88)	**49.5** (2.68)	**68.5** (0)	**34.5** (18)	**40** (2.74)	**50** (2.52)	**38.5** (81)	**5** (1486)	**7** (64.6)	**38** (2.58)	**55** (2.38)	23	50
University of Rochester	**40** (2.81)	**36.5** (2.98)	**68.5** (0)	**41** (12)	**38** (2.81)	**33** (2.95)	**46** (74)	**34** (411)	**29** (31.6)	**24** (3.03)	**27** (2.92)	13	42
Ohio State University	**41** (2.73)	**30.5** (3.07)	**68.5** (0)	**40** (13)	**42** (2.58)	**38** (2.88)	**33** (84)	**40** (346)	**39** (24.7)	**35** (2.63)	**32** (2.80)	14	60
Virginia Polytech Inst & State U	**42** (2.67)	**49.5** (2.68)	**38.5** (1)	**42** (11)	**46** (2.49)	**47** (2.56)	**41** (79)	**42.5** (300)	**37.5** (25.0)			12	37
Rutgers State Univ-New Brunswick	**43** (2.66)	**34.5** (2.99)	**68.5** (0)	**57.5** (4)	**41** (2.61)	**35** (2.93)	**68.5** (62)	**55** (186)	**58** (13.3)	**62** (1.84)	**63** (1.85)	14	75
University of Pittsburgh	**44** (2.64)	**45** (2.75)	**38.5** (1)	**43.5** (10)	**51** (2.39)	**52** (2.44)	**46** (74)	**48.5** (218)	**68** (9.9)	**55** (2.22)	**44.5** (2.52)	22	35
Michigan State University	**45** (2.60)	**47** (2.74)	**68.5** (0)	**47.5** (7)	**46** (2.49)	**47** (2.56)	**52** (71)	**57** (177)	**60** (12.6)	**61** (1.92)	**68** (1.77)	14	40
Case Western Reserve Univ	**46** (2.59)	**42** (2.77)	**68.5** (0)	**72.5** (2)	**43** (2.57)	**43** (2.71)	**46** (74)	**21** (591)	**8** (59.1)	**30** (2.79)	**26** (2.93)	10	33
Syracuse University	**47.5** (2.57)	**45** (2.75)	**38.5** (1)	**47.5** (7)	**52** (2.38)	**49** (2.53)	**44** (75)	**29** (429)	**16** (42.9)	**44** (2.45)	**40** (2.60)	10	15
Illinois Institute of Technology	**47.5** (2.57)	**52.5** (2.54)	**68.5** (0)	**45** (9)	**47** (2.47)	**51** (2.45)	**33** (84)	**58** (169)	**53.5** (15.4)	**50** (2.36)	**48.5** (2.43)	11	32
Clarkson University	**49** (2.54)	**48** (2.69)	**68.5** (0)	**53.5** (5)	**48** (2.45)	**45** (2.57)	**56** (69)	**50** (216)	**55.5** (14.4)	**41** (2.52)	**36** (2.65)	15	48
Brigham Young University	**50** (2.53)	**39.5** (2.85)	**68.5** (0)	**63** (3)	**49** (2.43)	**40** (2.80)	**76.5** (57)	**51** (206)	**48** (17.2)	**46** (2.40)	**44.5** (2.52)	12	13
University of Connecticut	**51** (2.49)	**54** (2.53)	**68.5** (0)	**47.5** (7)	**44** (2.56)	**44** (2.64)	**48.5** (73)	**42.5** (300)	**37.5** (25.0)	**40** (2.56)	**46** (2.48)	12	45
University of Maryland College Park	**52** (2.48)	**45** (2.75)	**68.5** (0)	**47.5** (7)	**50** (2.41)	**48** (2.55)	**50** (72)	**59** (162)	**61** (12.5)	**47** (2.39)	**48.5** (2.43)	13	47
University of Utah	**53** (2.47)	**52.5** (2.54)	**68.5** (0)	**43.5** (10)	**53** (2.31)	**53** (2.40)	**54.5** (70)	**32.5** (415)	**47** (17.3)	**42** (2.51)	**41** (2.58)	24	66
University of Oklahoma	**54** (2.41)	**51** (2.57)	**68.5** (0)	**53.5** (5)	**55** (2.23)	**56** (2.27)	**61.5** (65)	**44** (295)	**35** (26.8)	**49** (2.37)	**42.5** (2.53)	11	66
Louisiana State U & A&M College	**55** (2.40)	**55.5** (2.47)	**68.5** (0)	**53.5** (5)	**54** (2.25)	**54** (2.35)	**57.5** (68)	**31** (418)	**52** (15.5)	**52** (2.34)	**53.5** (2.40)	27	39
Columbia University	**56** (2.29)	**60** (2.24)	**38.5** (1)	**53.5** (5)	**56** (2.22)	**57** (2.20)	**52** (71)	**76** (69)	**65** (11.5)	**52** (2.34)	**48.5** (2.43)	6	19
University of Southern California	**57** (2.25)	**55.5** (2.47)	**68.5** (0)	**57.5** (4)	**58** (2.17)	**55** (2.32)	**63.5** (64)	**45.5** (239)	**26** (34.1)	**59** (1.97)	**60.5** (1.97)	7	27
University of Missouri-Rolla	**58** (2.22)	**62** (2.14)	**68.5** (0)	**72.5** (2)	**57** (2.20)	**62** (1.99)	**54.5** (70)	**69.5** (83)	**74** (6.4)	**48** (2.37)	**51.5** (2.42)	13	11
Kansas State University	**59.5** (2.18)	**61** (2.21)	**68.5** (0)	**63** (3)	**63** (1.98)	**61** (2.03)	**60** (66)	**83** (39)	**85** (3.9)	**58** (2.06)	**56.5** (2.08)	10	6
University of Tennessee-Knoxville	**59.5** (2.18)	**64** (2.12)	**68.5** (0)	**63** (3)	**61** (2.00)	**65** (1.92)	**76.5** (57)	**91** (19)	**92** (1.3)	**39** (2.57)	**42.5** (2.53)	15	28

Appendix Table P - 8 Chemical Engineering (Continued)

Institution	93Q [1]	93E [1]	% D [1]	% D-S [1]	93Q T [1]	93E T [1]	VIS [1]	TC [2]	C/F [2]	82Q [3]	82E [3]	TF [4]	TG [4]
University of Illinois at Chicago	61 (2.15)	58.5 (2.26)	38.5 (1)	53.5 (5)	70 (1.93)	60 (2.04)	48.5 (73)	53 (194)	46 (17.6)			11	10
Washington State University	62.5 (2.14)	63 (2.13)	68.5 (0)	50 (6)	69 (1.94)	63 (1.96)	73.5 (58)	65 (124)	57 (13.8)			9	22
Polytechnic University	62.5 (2.14)	67 (2.04)	68.5 (0)	72.5 (2)	59 (2.09)	75 (1.73)	66 (63)	54 (188)	43 (20.9)	64 (1.79)	60.5 (1.97)	9	19
Arizona State University	64 (2.12)	58.5 (2.26)	68.5 (0)	82.5 (1)	60 (2.01)	59 (2.06)	57.5 (68)	47 (237)	44 (18.2)			13	20
Colorado School of Mines	65 (2.11)	57 (2.37)	68.5 (0)	53.5 (5)	68 (1.95)	58 (2.10)	76.5 (57)	64 (127)	70 (9.1)			14	9
University of Iowa	66.5 (2.09)	77 (1.84)	68.5 (0)	63 (3)	65 (1.97)	75 (1.73)	76.5 (57)	68 (90)	66 (11.3)			8	32
Wayne State University	66.5 (2.09)	73 (1.96)	68.5 (0)	82.5 (1)	72 (1.91)	69 (1.81)	63.5 (64)	69.5 (83)	73 (6.9)	68 (1.72)	64 (1.83)	12	15
West Virginia University	68 (2.08)	69.5 (2.02)	38.5 (1)	63 (3)	66 (1.96)	70 (1.80)	52 (71)	74 (73)	80 (4.9)	52 (2.34)	48.5 (2.43)	15	11
Worcester Polytechnic Inst	69 (2.07)	71.5 (2.00)	38.5 (1)	72.5 (2)	63 (1.98)	66 (1.87)	61.5 (65)	61 (151)	49 (16.8)	65 (1.74)	69 (1.73)	9	15
Oklahoma State University	70 (2.04)	65 (2.08)	68.5 (0)	63 (3)	72 (1.91)	71 (1.79)	80 (55)	78 (54)	71 (9.0)	54 (2.27)	53.5 (2.40)	6	55
University of Kentucky	71.5 (1.98)	78 (1.82)	68.5 (0)	63 (3)	76 (1.80)	77 (1.67)	66 (63)	66 (117)	69 (9.8)	63 (1.81)	62 (1.92)	12	30
Auburn University	71.5 (1.98)	66 (2.07)	68.5 (0)	63 (3)	73 (1.89)	65 (1.92)	80 (55)	56 (185)	59 (13.2)	74 (1.16)	75 (1.27)	14	53
University of Cincinnati	73.5 (1.97)	68 (2.03)	68.5 (0)	72.5 (2)	78 (1.76)	68 (1.86)	70.5 (60)	63 (131)	50 (16.4)	57 (2.08)	56.5 (2.08)	8	29
University of Tulsa	73.5 (1.97)	71.5 (2.00)	68.5 (0)	72.5 (2)	74 (1.86)	72 (1.78)	68.5 (62)	73 (74)	72 (8.2)	66 (1.74)	65.5 (1.80)	9	18
Vanderbilt University	75.5 (1.94)	82 (1.74)	68.5 (0)	72.5 (2)	77 (1.78)	80 (1.52)	66 (63)	87.5 (26)	89 (2.4)	71 (1.63)	65.5 (1.80)	11	13
University of Kansas	75.5 (1.94)	74 (1.95)	68.5 (0)	82.5 (1)	65 (1.97)	68 (1.86)	85 (50)	89 (24)	91 (2.0)	56 (2.10)	59 (2.02)	12	5
Oregon State University	77 (1.93)	83 (1.73)	38.5 (1)	63 (3)	68 (1.95)	79 (1.58)	40 (80)	75 (72)	55.5 (14.4)	29 (2.81)	33.5 (2.72)	5	18
Tulane University	78 (1.91)	79 (1.81)	68.5 (0)	82.5 (1)	75 (1.83)	77 (1.67)	80 (55)	79 (50)	78 (5.6)	72 (1.56)	71 (1.45)	9	38
University of Arizona	79 (1.86)	69.5 (2.02)	68.5 (0)	82.5 (1)	79 (1.72)	73 (1.74)	70.5 (60)	71 (81)	64 (11.6)			7	23
New Jersey Inst of Technology	80 (1.75)	81 (1.77)	68.5 (0)	72.5 (2)	80 (1.64)	79 (1.58)	59 (67)	84 (32)	87 (3.2)	67 (1.73)	70 (1.53)	10	30
Clemson University	81 (1.74)	84 (1.71)	68.5 (0)	82.5 (1)	83 (1.53)	85 (1.31)	72 (59)	77 (60)	79 (5.5)	70 (1.66)	67 (1.78)	11	41
Stevens Inst of Technology	82 (1.73)	75 (1.89)	68.5 (0)	72.5 (2)	83 (1.53)	83 (1.45)	82.5 (51)	62 (147)	42 (21.0)	73 (1.46)	72 (1.42)	7	6
University of Missouri-Columbia	83 (1.70)	80 (1.78)	68.5 (0)	72.5 (2)	83 (1.53)	82 (1.46)	73.5 (58)	67 (105)	76 (5.8)	60 (1.96)	58 (2.03)	18	18
Duke University	84 (1.63)	90 (1.18)	68.5 (0)	82.5 (1)	81 (1.56)	90 (0.94)	92 (43)	30 (423)	17 (42.3)			10	14
University of Akron	85 (1.62)	85 (1.58)	68.5 (0)	82.5 (1)	86 (1.47)	84 (1.44)	82.5 (51)	81.5 (40)	81.5 (4.4)	76 (0.91)	76 (0.83)	9	49
University of Wyoming	86 (1.55)	76 (1.88)	68.5 (0)	90.5 (0)	86 (1.47)	81 (1.49)	88 (47)	87.5 (26)	86 (3.7)			7	9
University of Maine	87 (1.49)	91 (1.04)	68.5 (0)	90.5 (0)	86 (1.47)	87 (1.00)	85 (50)	80 (45)	83 (4.1)			11	30
University of Rhode Island	88 (1.42)	89 (1.19)	68.5 (0)	82.5 (1)	88 (1.42)	88 (0.99)	85 (50)	85 (31)	81.5 (4.4)	69 (1.71)	73 (1.37)	7	29
Northeastern University	89 (1.38)	86 (1.40)	68.5 (0)	82.5 (1)	89 (1.22)	86 (1.27)	87 (49)	86 (28)	84 (4.0)			7	2
University of Louisville	90.5 (1.33)	87.5 (1.39)	68.5 (0)	90.5 (0)	90 (1.13)	89 (0.97)	90 (45)	93 (9)	93 (1.0)			9	8

Institution	93Q [1]	93E [1]	% D [1]	% D-S [1]	93Q T [1]	93E T [1]	VIS [1]	TC [2]	C/F [2]	82Q [3]	82E [3]	TF [4]	TG [4]
University of Idaho	**90.5** (1.33)	**87.5** (1.39)	**68.5** (0)	**90.5** (0)	**91** (0.95)	**93** (0.64)	**93** (41)	**81.5** (40)	**77** (5.7)	**75** (1.04)	**74** (1.28)	7	12
Ohio University	**92** (0.93)	**92** (0.80)	**68.5** (0)	**90.5** (0)	**92** (0.87)	**91** (0.74)	**91** (44)	**90** (22)	**88** (2.8)			8	9
University of Mississippi	**93** (0.76)	**93** (0.61)	**68.5** (0)	**90.5** (0)	**93** (0.74)	**92** (0.65)	**89** (46)	**92** (14)	**90** (2.3)			6	7

Sources: 1. National Survey of Graduate Faculty
2. Institute for Scientific Information
3. 1982 Survey of Graduate Faculty
4. Institutional Coordinator Data

Appendix Table P - 9 Relative Rankings for Research-Doctorate Programs in Chemistry

Institution	93Q [1]	93E [1]	% D [1]	% D-S [1]	93Q T [1]	93E T [1]	VIS [1]	TC [2]	C/F [2]	82Q [3]	82E [3]	TF [4]	TG [4]
University of California-Berkeley	1 (4.96)	2 (4.72)	2 (90)	3 (96)	1 (4.98)	1 (4.83)	10.5 (96)	2 (8417)	3 (187.0)	1 (4.93)	2 (4.65)	45	298
California Institute Technology	2 (4.94)	1 (4.75)	1 (91)	1 (99)	2 (4.97)	2.5 (4.76)	2.5 (99)	7 (5002)	2 (200.1)	2 (4.89)	1 (4.73)	25	177
Harvard University	3.5 (4.87)	4.5 (4.57)	3.5 (83)	6 (94)	5 (4.86)	4 (4.69)	7.5 (97)	3 (7253)	1 (362.7)	3 (4.88)	4 (4.60)	20	196
Stanford University	3.5 (4.87)	4.5 (4.57)	5 (82)	3 (96)	4 (4.87)	5 (4.65)	7.5 (97)	20 (3629)	4 (172.8)	6 (4.54)	7 (4.33)	21	233
Massachusetts Inst of Technology	5 (4.86)	3 (4.70)	3.5 (83)	3 (96)	3 (4.88)	2.5 (4.76)	4.5 (98)	5 (6063)	5 (168.4)	4 (4.79)	3 (4.63)	36	245
Cornell University	6 (4.55)	6 (4.40)	7 (55)	7 (93)	7 (4.54)	6 (4.47)	4.5 (98)	14 (4100)	14 (124.2)	11 (4.37)	11 (4.22)	33	197
Columbia University	7 (4.54)	8 (4.37)	6 (56)	10 (88)	6 (4.58)	7 (4.41)	10.5 (96)	32 (2504)	10 (147.3)	5 (4.55)	5 (4.53)	17	98
U of Illinois at Urbana-Champaign	8 (4.48)	7 (4.38)	9.5 (48)	5 (95)	10 (4.43)	9 (4.30)	2.5 (99)	15 (3931)	31 (89.3)	7 (4.46)	6 (4.42)	44	277
University of Wisconsin-Madison	10 (4.46)	10 (4.26)	8 (50)	8 (92)	8 (4.48)	10 (4.29)	1 (100)	36 (2291)	66 (54.5)	8 (4.41)	8 (4.25)	42	275
University of Chicago	10 (4.46)	11.5 (4.20)	9.5 (48)	11 (87)	9 (4.47)	11 (4.22)	14.5 (94)	12 (4291)	12 (143.0)	10 (4.39)	9.5 (4.23)	30	135
Univ of California-Los Angeles	10 (4.46)	13 (4.00)	11 (44)	9 (90)	11 (4.39)	13 (4.05)	17 (93)	1 (8517)	8 (163.8)	9 (4.41)	9.5 (4.23)	52	186
Yale University	12 (4.38)	9 (4.31)	12 (42)	12.5 (86)	12 (4.36)	8 (4.35)	12.5 (95)	19 (3642)	6 (165.5)	14 (3.94)	13.5 (3.95)	22	149
University of Texas at Austin	13 (4.28)	19 (3.81)	13.5 (35)	12.5 (86)	13 (4.23)	21.5 (3.71)	7.5 (97)	6 (5883)	16 (117.7)	17 (3.81)	19 (3.67)	50	197
Northwestern University	14 (4.23)	11.5 (4.20)	13.5 (35)	14 (81)	14 (4.15)	12 (4.17)	7.5 (97)	9 (4636)	11 (144.9)	12 (4.05)	12 (3.98)	32	146
Texas A&M University	15 (4.11)	26.5 (3.63)	15 (19)	15 (77)	15.5 (4.00)	27.5 (3.53)	28 (89)	11 (4364)	37 (82.3)	22 (3.65)	30 (3.40)	53	298
Indiana University	16 (3.99)	22 (3.74)	19 (15)	17.5 (73)	19 (3.90)	19 (3.75)	23 (91)	22 (3533)	23 (100.9)	18 (3.73)	21 (3.63)	35	192
U of North Carolina-Chapel Hill	17 (3.97)	14 (3.93)	16 (18)	17.5 (73)	17.5 (3.92)	15 (3.90)	20 (92)	21 (3626)	25 (98.0)	19 (3.73)	16 (3.83)	37	236
Univ of California-San Diego	18.5 (3.95)	18 (3.82)	17 (17)	22 (67)	21.5 (3.86)	21.5 (3.71)	23 (91)	8 (4942)	26 (95.0)	21 (3.69)	27.5 (3.50)	52	95
Pennsylvania State University	18.5 (3.95)	24 (3.70)	20 (14)	16 (74)	17.5 (3.92)	23 (3.68)	14.5 (94)	29 (2685)	53 (68.8)	25 (3.50)	22 (3.57)	39	227
Princeton University	20 (3.92)	16.5 (3.83)	26.5 (8)	20 (71)	21.5 (3.86)	16 (3.86)	35 (87)	33 (2477)	15 (118.0)	13 (3.95)	13.5 (3.95)	21	115
University of Minnesota	21 (3.89)	21 (3.75)	24.5 (11)	19 (72)	20 (3.87)	24 (3.66)	12.5 (95)	13 (4153)	30 (92.3)	23 (3.63)	24 (3.55)	45	256
Ohio State University	22 (3.87)	20 (3.79)	22.5 (12)	21 (68)	23 (3.85)	18 (3.78)	25 (90)	26 (3193)	45 (77.9)	16 (3.86)	17.5 (3.82)	41	291
Univ of California-San Francisco	23 (3.86)	15 (3.91)	22.5 (12)	40 (35)	15.5 (4.00)	14 (4.00)	123.5 (55)	4 (6147)	9 (161.8)			38	83
Purdue University	24 (3.83)	16.5 (3.83)	18 (16)	23.5 (64)	25 (3.71)	17 (3.81)	17 (93)	10 (4487)	28 (93.5)	15 (3.92)	17.5 (3.82)	48	332
University of Pennsylvania	25 (3.78)	23 (3.71)	29.5 (7)	25 (62)	24 (3.73)	20 (3.73)	28 (89)	17 (3845)	17 (113.1)	29 (3.43)	27.5 (3.50)	34	185
Iowa State University	26 (3.76)	25 (3.66)	32 (6)	23.5 (64)	27 (3.65)	29 (3.51)	28 (89)	24 (3414)	20 (106.7)	24 (3.57)	15 (3.85)	32	196
Johns Hopkins University	27 (3.74)	29 (3.57)	24.5 (11)	31 (50)	30 (3.59)	30 (3.49)	52 (80)	60 (1329)	59 (60.4)	40 (3.11)	42 (3.22)	22	84
University of Washington	28.5 (3.70)	35 (3.49)	26.5 (8)	26.5 (54)	26 (3.68)	34 (3.45)	32 (88)	16 (3858)	34 (83.9)	28 (3.45)	37 (3.32)	46	169
Rice University	28.5 (3.70)	30 (3.56)	29.5 (7)	28.5 (53)	28 (3.64)	32.5 (3.46)	45 (83)	38 (2204)	18 (110.2)	34 (3.31)	26 (3.52)	20	76
University of Florida	30 (3.67)	39.5 (3.42)	29.5 (7)	28.5 (53)	34.5 (3.52)	35 (3.44)	35 (87)	18 (3643)	24 (98.5)	36 (3.21)	36 (3.35)	37	189

Institution	93Q [1]	93E [1]	% D [1]	% D-S [1]	93Q T [1]	93E T [1]	VIS [1]	TC [2]	C/F [2]	82Q [3]	82E [3]	TF [4]	TG [4]
University of Utah	**31.5** (3.63)	**28** (3.58)	**29.5** (7)	**26.5** (54)	**29** (3.63)	**25** (3.59)	**17** (93)	**23** (3469)	**13** (138.8)	**20** (3.72)	**24** (3.55)	25	169
University of Rochester	**31.5** (3.63)	**31** (3.54)	**34.5** (5)	**33.5** (49)	**33** (3.55)	**28** (3.53)	**47.5** (82)	**54** (1856)	**40.5** (80.7)	**27** (3.46)	**20** (3.65)	23	116
Univ of California-Santa Barbara	**33** (3.57)	**43.5** (3.39)	**34.5** (5)	**31** (50)	**31** (3.57)	**45** (3.33)	**20** (92)	**25** (3392)	**19** (109.4)	**38** (3.19)	**39** (3.27)	31	107
University of Pittsburgh	**34** (3.56)	**32** (3.52)	**57** (1)	**31** (50)	**33** (3.55)	**33** (3.46)	**20** (92)	**28** (2774)	**22** (102.7)	**37** (3.19)	**35** (3.37)	27	205
University of Michigan	**35** (3.53)	**26.5** (3.63)	**34.5** (5)	**33.5** (49)	**38** (3.44)	**26** (3.58)	**32** (88)	**31** (2541)	**58** (60.5)	**32** (3.32)	**29** (3.43)	42	194
University of California-Irvine	**36** (3.52)	**43.5** (3.39)	**38.5** (3)	**36** (45)	**36** (3.51)	**40** (3.42)	**38** (86)	**40** (2162)	**32** (86.5)	**41.5** (3.09)	**40.5** (3.23)	25	119
Colorado State University	**37** (3.50)	**33.5** (3.50)	**57** (1)	**35** (48)	**37** (3.45)	**31** (3.48)	**28** (89)	**35** (2307)	**35.5** (82.4)	**39** (3.18)	**44.5** (3.18)	28	141
Emory University	**38** (3.37)	**36** (3.47)	**57** (1)	**38** (37)	**40** (3.25)	**41** (3.39)	**52** (80)	**51** (1969)	**21** (103.6)	**80** (2.28)	**77.5** (2.60)	19	119
Michigan State University	**39** (3.35)	**33.5** (3.50)	**45** (2)	**37** (43)	**43** (3.20)	**40** (3.42)	**23** (91)	**39** (2194)	**61** (57.7)	**26** (3.49)	**24** (3.55)	38	185
University of Southern California	**40** (3.34)	**45** (3.38)	**45** (2)	**42** (34)	**39** (3.32)	**48** (3.31)	**38** (86)	**41** (2127)	**29** (92.5)	**30** (3.39)	**38** (3.28)	23	110
University of Oregon	**41** (3.31)	**39.5** (3.42)	**38.5** (3)	**45** (31)	**42** (3.22)	**42** (3.38)	**42.5** (84)	**43** (2100)	**39** (80.8)	**31** (3.37)	**32.5** (3.38)	26	101
University of Colorado	**42** (3.30)	**55** (3.22)	**21** (13)	**46** (30)	**35** (3.52)	**37** (3.43)	**108** (59)	**49.5** (1982)	**7** (165.2)	**33** (3.31)	**32.5** (3.38)	12	n/a
University of Virginia	**43** (3.29)	**41** (3.41)	**45** (2)	**42** (34)	**41** (3.24)	**48** (3.31)	**32** (88)	**55** (1755)	**47** (73.1)	**57** (2.78)	**59** (3.02)	24	85
Duke University	**44** (3.28)	**37.5** (3.43)	**57** (1)	**39** (36)	**44** (3.18)	**37** (3.43)	**45** (83)	**68.5** (1110)	**64** (55.5)	**50** (2.93)	**44.5** (3.18)	20	96
Brandeis University	**45** (3.26)	**47** (3.33)	**38.5** (3)	**47.5** (28)	**48** (3.08)	**45** (3.33)	**64.5** (75)	**67** (1137)	**55** (63.2)	**43** (3.09)	**32.5** (3.38)	18	45
State U of New York-Stony Brook	**46** (3.25)	**42** (3.40)	**57** (1)	**42** (34)	**46** (3.13)	**37** (3.43)	**38** (86)	**42** (2107)	**50** (70.2)	**41.5** (3.09)	**53** (3.08)	30	158
University of South Carolina	**47.5** (3.24)	**47** (3.33)	**57** (1)	**49.5** (25)	**45** (3.17)	**53** (3.22)	**58.5** (78)	**47** (2040)	**44** (78.5)	**60** (2.70)	**56.5** (3.03)	26	126
University of California-Davis	**47.5** (3.24)	**37.5** (3.43)	**57** (1)	**44** (33)	**48** (3.08)	**45** (3.33)	**35** (87)	**45** (2075)	**57** (61.0)	**46** (3.00)	**40.5** (3.23)	34	139
University of Georgia	**49** (3.17)	**65** (3.13)	**34.5** (5)	**47.5** (28)	**52** (3.00)	**67** (3.04)	**28** (89)	**46** (2062)	**43** (79.3)	**45** (3.04)	**50** (3.10)	26	95
University of Houston	**50** (3.16)	**60.5** (3.18)	**45** (2)	**49.5** (25)	**50** (3.07)	**61** (3.12)	**52** (80)	**34** (2446)	**27** (94.1)	**64** (2.63)	**66.5** (2.92)	26	96
Florida State University	**51** (3.11)	**72.5** (3.00)	**116.5** (0)	**54** (22)	**52** (3.00)	**72** (2.94)	**40.5** (85)	**68.5** (1110)	**101** (31.7)	**35** (3.28)	**32.5** (3.38)	35	110
Wayne State University	**52.5** (3.08)	**49.5** (3.30)	**116.5** (0)	**51** (24)	**54** (2.97)	**49** (3.28)	**45** (83)	**58** (1451)	**73** (45.3)	**48** (2.97)	**48** (3.12)	32	143
University of Maryland College Park	**52.5** (3.08)	**63.5** (3.16)	**116.5** (0)	**52.5** (23)	**48** (3.08)	**52** (3.23)	**47.5** (82)	**57** (1533)	**76** (43.8)	**51** (2.92)	**53** (3.08)	35	104
Dartmouth College	**54** (3.07)	**52** (3.28)	**57** (1)	**52.5** (23)	**53** (2.98)	**55** (3.20)	**40.5** (85)	**113** (512)	**107** (30.1)			17	33
Washington University	**55** (3.04)	**51** (3.29)	**45** (2)	**55** (20)	**58** (2.90)	**65** (3.06)	**76** (70)	**62** (1289)	**63** (56.0)	**61** (2.69)	**66.5** (2.92)	23	76
Brown University	**56** (3.02)	**57** (3.20)	**38.5** (3)	**69.5** (13)	**55** (2.96)	**60** (3.13)	**67.5** (74)	**88** (777)	**77** (43.2)	**49** (2.93)	**50** (3.10)	18	70
State Univ of New York-Buffalo	**57** (2.99)	**63.5** (3.16)	**57** (1)	**64.5** (15)	**63** (2.78)	**67** (3.04)	**52** (80)	**52** (1955)	**38** (81.5)	**47** (2.99)	**46.5** (3.17)	24	118
U of Massachusetts at Amherst	**58** (2.98)	**47** (3.33)	**116.5** (0)	**67** (14)	**61** (2.83)	**50** (3.27)	**56.5** (79)	**27** (2826)	**40.5** (80.7)	**65** (2.62)	**46.5** (3.17)	35	98
Rutgers State Univ-New Brunswick	**59.5** (2.97)	**76** (2.89)	**57** (1)	**61** (16)	**58** (2.90)	**78** (2.82)	**58.5** (78)	**49.5** (1982)	**74** (45.0)	**58** (2.73)	**64** (2.97)	44	137
Syracuse University	**59.5** (2.97)	**60.5** (3.18)	**116.5** (0)	**64.5** (15)	**59** (2.86)	**58** (3.14)	**42.5** (84)	**77** (1014)	**70** (48.3)	**78** (2.30)	**76** (2.62)	21	70

Appendix Table P - 9 Chemistry (Continued)

Institution	93Q [1]	93E [1]	% D [1]	% D-S [1]	93Q T [1]	93E T [1]	VIS [1]	TC [2]	C/F [2]	82Q [3]	82E [3]	TF [4]	TG [4]
Oregon State University	**61** (2.96)	**53.5** (3.25)	**116.5** (0)	**69.5** (13)	**56** (2.91)	**45** (3.33)	**76** (70)	**89** (745)	**108** (29.8)	**56** (2.79)	**50** (3.10)	25	79
University of Notre Dame	**62** (2.94)	**49.5** (3.30)	**45** (2)	**56.5** (18)	**73** (2.66)	**55** (3.20)	**52** (80)	**64** (1284)	**71** (47.6)	**62** (2.68)	**71** (2.73)	27	97
University of Illinois at Chicago	**63** (2.93)	**60.5** (3.18)	**45** (2)	**58** (17)	**63** (2.78)	**63** (3.07)	**52** (80)	**70** (1095)	**82** (40.6)	**81** (2.22)	**79** (2.57)	27	81
Georgia Institute of Technology	**64** (2.92)	**56** (3.21)	**116.5** (0)	**56.5** (18)	**72** (2.69)	**56** (3.17)	**64.5** (75)	**86** (811)	**114** (29.0)	**44** (3.07)	**43** (3.20)	28	95
Louisiana State U & A&M College	**65.5** (2.91)	**68** (3.08)	**116.5** (0)	**67** (14)	**66** (2.76)	**68** (3.03)	**67.5** (74)	**76** (1017)	**113** (29.1)	**55** (2.79)	**68** (2.88)	35	100
University of Nebraska-Lincoln	**65.5** (2.91)	**70.5** (3.04)	**116.5** (0)	**71.5** (12)	**66** (2.76)	**65** (3.06)	**76** (70)	**78** (972)	**88** (37.4)	**54** (2.82)	**53** (3.08)	26	114
Virginia Polytech Inst & State U	**67** (2.90)	**53.5** (3.25)	**57** (1)	**71.5** (12)	**68** (2.74)	**51** (3.26)	**84** (66)	**74** (1046)	**92** (34.9)	**74** (2.40)	**70** (2.83)	30	141
University of Kansas	**68** (2.89)	**66** (3.10)	**45** (2)	**61** (16)	**61** (2.83)	**60** (3.13)	**60.5** (77)	**90** (735)	**111** (29.4)	**66** (2.59)	**63** (2.98)	25	76
Arizona State University	**69** (2.88)	**69** (3.07)	**116.5** (0)	**74** (11)	**64** (2.77)	**71** (2.99)	**64.5** (75)	**30** (2575)	**33** (85.8)	**69** (2.53)	**59** (3.02)	30	97
Univ of California-Riverside	**70** (2.86)	**74** (2.95)	**57** (1)	**61** (16)	**70** (2.71)	**79** (2.79)	**56.5** (79)	**56** (1582)	**60** (58.6)	**63** (2.63)	**73.5** (2.67)	27	61
Case Western Reserve Univ	**71** (2.83)	**60.5** (3.18)	**45** (2)	**74** (11)	**76** (2.60)	**62** (3.11)	**64.5** (75)	**61** (1318)	**35.5** (82.4)	**53** (2.83)	**61.5** (3.00)	16	77
University of Cincinnati	**72** (2.82)	**75** (2.94)	**116.5** (0)	**61** (16)	**72** (2.69)	**78** (2.82)	**62** (76)	**53** (1873)	**48** (72.0)	**59** (2.71)	**55** (3.07)	26	76
University of Delaware	**73** (2.80)	**58** (3.19)	**116.5** (0)	**76.5** (10)	**67** (2.75)	**57** (3.16)	**52** (80)	**37** (2213)	**52** (69.2)	**71** (2.48)	**65** (2.93)	32	49
Carnegie Mellon University	**74** (2.79)	**72.5** (3.00)	**116.5** (0)	**67** (14)	**69** (2.72)	**73** (2.90)	**72** (71)	**92** (710)	**91** (35.5)	**52** (2.91)	**61.5** (3.00)	20	45
Washington State University	**75** (2.73)	**88.5** (2.66)	**116.5** (0)	**61** (16)	**81** (2.49)	**82** (2.73)	**70** (72)	**63** (1287)	**87** (37.9)	**68** (2.53)	**56.5** (3.03)	34	48
University of Iowa	**76** (2.72)	**67** (3.09)	**116.5** (0)	**81** (7)	**74** (2.65)	**71** (2.99)	**72** (71)	**72** (1056)	**79** (42.2)	**72** (2.45)	**69** (2.85)	25	104
Kansas State University	**77** (2.66)	**70.5** (3.04)	**116.5** (0)	**81** (7)	**77** (2.55)	**69** (3.00)	**76** (70)	**96.5** (669)	**84** (39.4)	**73** (2.44)	**75** (2.65)	17	48
New York University	**78.5** (2.65)	**85.5** (2.68)	**116.5** (0)	**81** (7)	**75** (2.62)	**83** (2.72)	**102** (60)	**59** (1337)	**83** (40.5)	**75** (2.39)	**82.5** (2.53)	33	69
University of Tennessee-Knoxville	**78.5** (2.65)	**78** (2.85)	**116.5** (0)	**87** (5)	**82** (2.47)	**74** (2.87)	**94.5** (62)	**48** (1983)	**54** (66.1)	**82** (2.22)	**77.5** (2.60)	30	95
North Carolina State University	**80.5** (2.64)	**81** (2.79)	**116.5** (0)	**74** (11)	**78** (2.54)	**75** (2.86)	**60.5** (77)	**65** (1269)	**72** (47.0)	**89** (2.08)	**82.5** (2.53)	27	56
Brigham Young University	**80.5** (2.64)	**88.5** (2.66)	**116.5** (0)	**87** (5)	**83** (2.43)	**92** (2.55)	**114** (57)	**44** (2096)	**42** (80.6)	**90** (2.03)	**93** (2.28)	26	34
Rensselaer Polytechnic Inst	**82** (2.55)	**77** (2.86)	**116.5** (0)	**78** (8)	**80** (2.50)	**76** (2.83)	**76** (70)	**102** (606)	**128** (23.3)	**70** (2.51)	**59** (3.02)	26	121
Univ of California-Santa Cruz	**83** (2.52)	**79.5** (2.81)	**116.5** (0)	**76.5** (10)	**79** (2.51)	**80** (2.75)	**69** (73)	**79** (967)	**62** (56.9)	**76** (2.35)	**73.5** (2.67)	17	78
Lehigh University	**84** (2.48)	**83** (2.74)	**116.5** (0)	**105** (3)	**86** (2.37)	**85** (2.69)	**118** (56)	**109.5** (529)	**126** (24.0)			22	68
University of Connecticut	**85** (2.47)	**85.5** (2.68)	**116.5** (0)	**105** (3)	**93** (2.24)	**106** (2.33)	**94.5** (62)	**71** (1080)	**68** (49.1)	**87** (2.12)	**85** (2.43)	22	95
Vanderbilt University	**86** (2.43)	**79.5** (2.81)	**116.5** (0)	**94** (4)	**84** (2.41)	**85** (2.69)	**79** (68)	**75** (1031)	**46** (73.6)	**67** (2.58)	**72** (2.72)	14	54
Boston College	**87** (2.37)	**95** (2.60)	**116.5** (0)	**94** (4)	**88** (2.33)	**88** (2.58)	**97** (61)	**80** (877)	**65** (54.8)	**114** (1.57)	**118** (1.70)	16	62
CUNY - Grad Sch & Univ Center	**88.5** (2.36)	**96** (2.57)	**116.5** (0)	**81** (7)	**89** (2.31)	**95** (2.50)	**72** (71)	**103** (604)	**156** (11.8)	**77** (2.31)	**89.5** (2.33)	51	128
Boston University	**88.5** (2.36)	**88.5** (2.66)	**116.5** (0)	**128** (1)	**91** (2.25)	**88** (2.58)	**84** (66)	**98** (654)	**104.5** (31.1)	**91** (2.00)	**97.5** (2.23)	21	67
Texas Tech University	**90** (2.35)	**97.5** (2.53)	**116.5** (0)	**87** (5)	**96** (2.13)	**107** (2.28)	**80.5** (67)	**81** (876)	**103** (31.3)	**85** (2.18)	**87** (2.40)	28	75

Institution	93Q [1]	93E [1]	% D [1]	% D-S [1]	93Q T [1]	93E T [1]	VIS [1]	TC [2]	C/F [2]	82Q [3]	82E [3]	TF [4]	TG [4]
Wesleyan University	91.5 (2.34)	93 (2.64)	57 (1)	84 (6)	94 (2.18)	88 (2.58)	87.5 (65)	121 (406)	123 (25.4)			16	35
University of Vermont	91.5 (2.34)	97.5 (2.53)	116.5 (0)	128 (1)	85 (2.40)	86 (2.63)	118 (56)	111 (522)	93 (34.8)	84 (2.18)	88 (2.37)	15	37
University of New Hampshire	93 (2.29)	110.5 (2.32)	116.5 (0)	94 (4)	100 (2.09)	110 (2.22)	108 (59)	133 (307)	133 (20.5)	104 (1.72)	105 (1.97)	15	36
Clemson University	94 (2.28)	103 (2.46)	116.5 (0)	94 (4)	97 (2.11)	102 (2.40)	102 (60)	104 (598)	98 (33.2)	118 (1.45)	118 (1.70)	18	48
University of Oklahoma	96 (2.26)	91.5 (2.65)	57 (1)	87 (5)	98 (2.10)	95 (2.50)	92 (63)	83 (853)	89 (37.1)	79 (2.29)	80 (2.55)	23	118
University of Alabama	96 (2.26)	84 (2.72)	116.5 (0)	115 (2)	90 (2.27)	95 (2.50)	118 (56)	99 (651)	81 (40.7)	103 (1.77)	106 (1.92)	16	45
University of Hawaii at Manoa	96 (2.26)	104 (2.45)	116.5 (0)	128 (1)	87 (2.35)	100 (2.41)	97 (61)	96.5 (669)	96 (33.5)	83 (2.20)	82.5 (2.53)	20	38
University of Nevada, Reno	98 (2.23)	110.5 (2.32)	116.5 (0)	105 (3)	93 (2.24)	104 (2.36)	87.5 (65)	123 (392)	116 (28.0)			14	31
University of Kentucky	99 (2.20)	82 (2.78)	116.5 (0)	94 (4)	101 (2.06)	82 (2.73)	84 (66)	93 (704)	112 (29.3)	100 (1.83)	100 (2.08)	24	73
Oklahoma State University	100 (2.19)	100 (2.50)	116.5 (0)	105 (3)	109 (1.96)	100 (2.41)	151.5 (48)	87 (797)	56 (61.3)	97 (1.92)	95.5 (2.25)	13	49
Georgetown University	101.5 (2.17)	106 (2.43)	116.5 (0)	87 (5)	107 (1.97)	114 (2.13)	84 (66)	101 (640)	78 (42.7)	96 (1.94)	86 (2.42)	15	61
University of New Orleans	101.5 (2.17)	102 (2.47)	116.5 (0)	105 (3)	107 (1.97)	90 (2.57)	111.5 (58)	112 (515)	120 (25.8)	88 (2.10)	93 (2.28)	20	42
Univ of Arkansas-Fayetteville	103 (2.16)	100 (2.50)	116.5 (0)	128 (1)	100 (2.09)	92 (2.55)	137.5 (52)	84 (842)	90 (36.6)	86 (2.13)	95.5 (2.25)	23	58
Northeastern University	104.5 (2.15)	88.5 (2.66)	116.5 (0)	94 (4)	110 (1.94)	95 (2.50)	84 (66)	66 (1209)	49 (71.1)	109 (1.62)	99 (2.12)	17	46
State Univ of New York-Binghamton	104.5 (2.15)	107 (2.40)	116.5 (0)	115 (2)	96 (2.13)	108 (2.27)	128.5 (54)	151 (215)	148 (15.4)	92 (1.99)	97.5 (2.23)	14	33
State Univ of New York-Albany	107 (2.13)	117 (2.26)	116.5 (0)	105 (3)	103 (2.03)	117 (2.08)	92 (63)	91 (712)	80 (41.9)			17	29
University of Missouri-Columbia	107 (2.13)	100 (2.50)	116.5 (0)	105 (3)	103 (2.03)	102 (2.40)	92 (63)	129 (352)	151.5 (13.5)	102 (1.78)	107.5 (1.87)	26	74
Montana State University	107 (2.13)	91.5 (2.65)	116.5 (0)	115 (2)	105 (2.00)	103 (2.37)	128.5 (54)	128 (354)	124 (25.3)	120 (1.40)	122 (1.62)	14	44
Polytechnic University	109 (2.11)	110.5 (2.32)	116.5 (0)	105 (3)	117 (1.82)	117 (2.08)	141.5 (51)	117 (429)	106 (30.6)	93 (1.97)	82.5 (2.53)	14	62
Clarkson University	110 (2.10)	108 (2.39)	116.5 (0)	81 (7)	120 (1.78)	110 (2.22)	97 (61)	140 (268)	143 (16.8)	95 (1.94)	89.5 (2.33)	16	52
University of Missouri-Rolla	111 (2.09)	128.5 (1.97)	116.5 (0)	153 (0)	112 (1.92)	137 (1.67)	145 (50)	100 (643)	121 (25.7)	119 (1.44)	116 (1.73)	25	56
Texas Christian University	112 (2.07)	135.5 (1.81)	116.5 (0)	115 (2)	112 (1.92)	142 (1.54)	123.5 (55)	146 (236)	137 (19.7)			12	20
Miami University	113 (2.06)	94 (2.62)	116.5 (0)	105 (3)	109 (1.96)	97 (2.46)	102 (60)	118 (424)	142 (17.0)			25	38
University of Texas at Arlington	114 (2.05)	120 (2.20)	116.5 (0)	105 (3)	119 (1.81)	106 (2.33)	114 (57)	95 (687)	86 (38.2)			18	25
Univ of Missouri-Saint Louis	116 (2.02)	119 (2.22)	116.5 (0)	115 (2)	117 (1.82)	126 (1.85)	133 (53)	135 (300)	140 (17.6)			17	32
University of Akron	116 (2.02)	110.5 (2.32)	116.5 (0)	128 (1)	113 (1.89)	115 (2.11)	102 (60)	131 (312)	138 (18.4)	115 (1.55)	112.5 (1.78)	17	86
University of Wyoming	116 (2.02)	125.5 (2.03)	116.5 (0)	128 (1)	105 (2.00)	127 (1.84)	102 (60)	116 (446)	109 (29.7)	123 (1.39)	131 (1.35)	15	44
Drexel University	118 (1.99)	127 (1.98)	116.5 (0)	94 (4)	132 (1.66)	125 (1.95)	123.5 (55)	114 (473)	110 (29.6)	117 (1.49)	109 (1.85)	16	33
University of Wisconsin-Milwaukee	119 (1.94)	118 (2.24)	116.5 (0)	128 (1)	126 (1.73)	117 (2.08)	89.5 (64)	108 (535)	97 (33.4)	98 (1.88)	91 (2.30)	16	59
New Mexico State University	120 (1.91)	122 (2.12)	116.5 (0)	128 (1)	114 (1.85)	123 (1.96)	133 (53)	85 (832)	69 (48.9)			17	49

Appendix Table P - 9 Chemistry (Continued)

Institution	93Q [1]	93E [1]	% D [1]	% D-S [1]	93Q T [1]	93E T [1]	VIS [1]	TC [2]	C/F [2]	82Q [3]	82E [3]	TF [4]	TG [4]
Tulane University	**121.5** (1.90)	**116** (2.27)	**116.5** (0)	**128** (1)	**115** (1.84)	**112** (2.17)	**80.5** (67)	**139** (274)	**141** (17.1)	**111** (1.58)	**112.5** (1.78)	16	44
University of South Florida	**121.5** (1.90)	**141** (1.77)	**116.5** (0)	**153** (0)	**122** (1.77)	**154** (1.30)	**156** (46)	**147** (232)	**146.5** (15.5)	**129** (1.29)	**129** (1.40)	15	52
Auburn University	**123** (1.88)	**134** (1.82)	**116.5** (0)	**153** (0)	**126** (1.73)	**137** (1.67)	**133** (53)	**115** (470)	**134** (20.4)	**122** (1.40)	**120** (1.67)	23	61
University of North Texas	**124** (1.84)	**141** (1.77)	**116.5** (0)	**153** (0)	**127** (1.72)	**154** (1.30)	**137.5** (52)	**106** (577)	**118.5** (26.2)	**116** (1.50)	**127** (1.48)	22	33
Southern Illinois University	**126** (1.82)	**113.5** (2.29)	**116.5** (0)	**128** (1)	**129** (1.69)	**119** (2.06)	**89.5** (64)	**126** (374)	**127** (23.4)	**107** (1.67)	**110** (1.83)	16	25
Univ of Puerto Rico-Rio Piedras	**126** (1.82)	**121** (2.19)	**116.5** (0)	**153** (0)	**129** (1.69)	**98** (2.44)	**164.5** (40)	**132** (308)	**153** (13.4)			23	39
University of Alabama-Birmingham	**126** (1.82)	**137** (1.80)	**116.5** (0)	**153** (0)	**124** (1.75)	**122** (1.97)	**137.5** (52)	**82** (861)	**95** (34.4)			25	22
Kent State University	**128** (1.81)	**115** (2.28)	**116.5** (0)	**128** (1)	**124** (1.75)	**110** (2.22)	**151.5** (48)	**125** (383)	**135** (20.2)	**99** (1.84)	**93** (2.28)	19	27
University of Mass-Lowell	**130** (1.80)	**105** (2.44)	**116.5** (0)	**115** (2)	**136** (1.52)	**113** (2.16)	**161** (43)	**120** (414)	**144** (15.9)			26	114
University of Idaho	**130** (1.80)	**138** (1.79)	**116.5** (0)	**128** (1)	**117** (1.82)	**129** (1.79)	**108** (59)	**124** (385)	**117** (27.5)	**110** (1.61)	**114.5** (1.77)	14	40
West Virginia University	**130** (1.80)	**130** (1.95)	**116.5** (0)	**153** (0)	**122** (1.77)	**125** (1.95)	**128.5** (54)	**109.5** (529)	**104.5** (31.1)			17	34
Rutgers State Univ-Newark	**132.5** (1.78)	**123** (2.08)	**116.5** (0)	**94** (4)	**129** (1.69)	**130** (1.78)	**108** (59)	**122** (399)	**131** (21.0)	**106** (1.68)	**104** (1.98)	19	50
Northern Illinois University	**132.5** (1.78)	**125.5** (2.03)	**116.5** (0)	**153** (0)	**132** (1.66)	**121** (1.98)	**128.5** (54)	**73** (1055)	**75** (44.0)	**124** (1.38)	**121** (1.63)	24	27
Oregon Graduate Inst Sci & Tech	**134** (1.77)	**149.5** (1.58)	**116.5** (0)	**94** (4)	**142** (1.44)	**137** (1.67)	**158.5** (45)	**107** (556)	**51** (69.5)			8	13
Temple University	**135** (1.73)	**132** (1.86)	**116.5** (0)	**153** (0)	**134** (1.57)	**132** (1.77)	**123.5** (55)	**130** (336)	**136** (19.8)	**108** (1.65)	**111** (1.82)	17	55
Virginia Commonwealth University	**136.5** (1.69)	**133** (1.85)	**116.5** (0)	**153** (0)	**138** (1.50)	**144** (1.52)	**141.5** (51)	**148** (230)	**149** (15.3)			15	45
Tufts University	**136.5** (1.69)	**149.5** (1.58)	**116.5** (0)	**153** (0)	**145** (1.35)	**137** (1.67)	**151.5** (48)	**157** (162)	**151.5** (13.5)			12	40
University of Miami	**138** (1.67)	**145** (1.67)	**116.5** (0)	**105** (3)	**133** (1.65)	**129** (1.79)	**133** (53)	**105** (595)	**67** (54.1)	**130** (1.20)	**128** (1.42)	11	34
University of Rhode Island	**139.5** (1.65)	**113.5** (2.29)	**116.5** (0)	**128** (1)	**138** (1.50)	**120** (2.05)	**151.5** (48)	**119** (419)	**118.5** (26.2)	**105** (1.68)	**101.5** (2.03)	16	40
University of Toledo	**139.5** (1.65)	**155** (1.40)	**116.5** (0)	**153** (0)	**140** (1.48)	**156** (1.07)	**111.5** (58)	**143.5** (251)	**150** (14.8)			17	38
Baylor University	**141** (1.64)	**151** (1.54)	**116.5** (0)	**128** (1)	**140** (1.48)	**148** (1.41)	**114** (57)	**136** (287)	**139** (17.9)	**127** (1.31)	**123** (1.58)	16	33
North Dakota State University	**142** (1.62)	**153** (1.48)	**116.5** (0)	**128** (1)	**135** (1.53)	**150** (1.37)	**137.5** (52)	**153** (201)	**146.5** (15.5)	**128** (1.29)	**125.5** (1.50)	13	36
University of Maine	**143** (1.60)	**143** (1.72)	**116.5** (0)	**153** (0)	**144** (1.37)	**151** (1.36)	**147.5** (49)	**155** (188)	**145** (15.7)			12	13
University of Louisville	**144** (1.59)	**128.5** (1.97)	**116.5** (0)	**153** (0)	**141** (1.45)	**132** (1.77)	**123.5** (55)	**94** (701)	**85** (38.9)	**126** (1.35)	**124** (1.53)	18	76
Loyola University of Chicago	**145** (1.56)	**139** (1.78)	**116.5** (0)	**105** (3)	**147** (1.28)	**146** (1.49)	**145** (50)	**158** (127)	**159** (7.9)	**125** (1.36)	**114.5** (1.77)	16	46
Howard University	**146** (1.46)	**148** (1.60)	**116.5** (0)	**153** (0)	**143** (1.39)	**137** (1.67)	**118** (56)	**154** (190)	**158** (9.5)	**101** (1.80)	**103** (2.00)	20	45
Ohio University	**147** (1.42)	**147** (1.62)	**116.5** (0)	**128** (1)	**148** (1.23)	**152** (1.33)	**102** (60)	**149** (226)	**154** (13.3)	**112** (1.58)	**118** (1.70)	17	33
Seton Hall University	**148** (1.41)	**152** (1.53)	**116.5** (0)	**128** (1)	**149** (1.22)	**137** (1.67)	**123.5** (55)	**160** (75)	**164.5** (5.0)			15	58
SUNY Col Environ Sci & Forestry	**149** (1.35)	**124** (2.04)	**57** (1)	**105** (3)	**157** (0.89)	**137** (1.67)	**168** (29)	**152** (207)	**94** (34.5)	**94** (1.96)	**101.5** (2.03)	6	15
Bryn Mawr College	**150** (1.33)	**141** (1.77)	**116.5** (0)	**115** (2)	**146** (1.29)	**143** (1.53)	**108** (59)	**163** (54)	**157** (10.8)	**131** (1.16)	**130** (1.37)	5	15

Institution	93Q [1]	93E [1]	% D [1]	% D-S [1]	93Q T [1]	93E T [1]	VIS [1]	TC [2]	C/F [2]	82Q [3]	82E [3]	TF [4]	TG [4]
University of Texas at Dallas	**151** (1.32)	**145** (1.67)	**116.5** (0)	**153** (0)	**153** (1.08)	**149** (1.39)	**145** (50)	**137** (285)	**115** (28.5)			10	31
University of North Dakota	**152** (1.31)	**131** (1.88)	**116.5** (0)	**153** (0)	**150** (1.17)	**137** (1.67)	**163** (41)	**167** (30)	**167** (2.0)	**121** (1.40)	**132** (1.33)	15	25
Wake Forest University	**153** (1.23)	**145** (1.67)	**116.5** (0)	**153** (0)	**152** (1.12)	**146** (1.49)	**102** (60)	**138** (283)	**130** (21.8)			13	25
Univ of Southern Mississippi	**154** (1.22)	**157** (1.11)	**116.5** (0)	**153** (0)	**155** (1.00)	**159** (0.74)	**156** (46)	**127** (371)	**132** (20.6)	**134** (0.75)	**134** (0.93)	18	39
Stevens Inst of Technology	**155** (1.21)	**154** (1.44)	**116.5** (0)	**153** (0)	**151** (1.16)	**148** (1.41)	**151.5** (48)	**143.5** (251)	**102** (31.4)			8	1
American University	**156** (1.14)	**135.5** (1.81)	**116.5** (0)	**153** (0)	**159** (0.86)	**137** (1.67)	**158.5** (45)	**165** (39)	**166** (3.9)	**133** (0.93)	**133** (1.12)	10	35
University of Mississippi	**157** (1.13)	**158** (1.09)	**116.5** (0)	**153** (0)	**156** (0.90)	**161** (0.67)	**160** (44)	**134** (306)	**122** (25.5)			12	22
Mississippi State University	**158.5** (1.12)	**156** (1.28)	**116.5** (0)	**153** (0)	**158** (0.88)	**155** (1.11)	**166** (38)	**156** (176)	**155** (12.6)			14	52
Colorado School of Mines	**158.5** (1.12)	**163** (0.87)	**116.5** (0)	**153** (0)	**155** (1.00)	**166** (0.45)	**147.5** (49)	**159** (99)	**161** (6.2)			16	18
Univ of Missouri-Kansas City	**160.5** (1.08)	**159.5** (1.02)	**116.5** (0)	**128** (1)	**162** (0.76)	**161** (0.67)	**156** (46)	**141** (264)	**129** (22.0)	**113** (1.58)	**107.5** (1.87)	12	8
Catholic University of America	**160.5** (1.08)	**164.5** (0.80)	**116.5** (0)	**128** (1)	**161** (0.80)	**164** (0.52)	**133** (53)	**150** (223)	**99.5** (31.9)	**132** (1.16)	**125.5** (1.50)	7	23
University of Montana	**162** (0.98)	**164.5** (0.80)	**116.5** (0)	**153** (0)	**164** (0.70)	**163** (0.56)	**141.5** (51)	**142** (255)	**99.5** (31.9)			8	8
George Washington University	**163** (0.93)	**159.5** (1.02)	**116.5** (0)	**153** (0)	**160** (0.83)	**158** (0.78)	**151.5** (48)	**145** (247)	**125** (24.7)			10	21
Worcester Polytechnic Inst	**164.5** (0.81)	**166** (0.65)	**116.5** (0)	**153** (0)	**165** (0.59)	**165** (0.48)	**118** (56)	**161** (62)	**162.5** (5.2)			12	14
Wichita State University	**164.5** (0.81)	**161** (0.93)	**116.5** (0)	**153** (0)	**164** (0.70)	**157** (0.91)	**141.5** (51)	**164** (52)	**162.5** (5.2)			10	18
Phila Col of Pharmacy & Science	**166** (0.50)	**168** (0.30)	**116.5** (0)	**153** (0)	**166** (0.56)	**168** (0.00)	**167** (30)	**162** (60)	**164.5** (5.0)			12	8
University of Detroit Mercy	**167** (0.44)	**162** (0.89)	**116.5** (0)	**153** (0)	**167** (0.32)	**161** (0.67)	**164.5** (40)	**168** (7)	**168** (0.8)			9	4
New Mexico Inst of Mining & Tech	**168** (0.37)	**167** (0.42)	**116.5** (0)	**153** (0)	**168** (0.28)	**167** (0.13)	**162** (42)	**166** (38)	**160** (7.6)			5	9

Sources:
1. National Survey of Graduate Faculty
2. Institute for Scientific Information
3. 1982 Survey of Graduate Faculty
4. Institutional Coordinator Data

Appendix Table P - 10 Relative Rankings for Research-Doctorate Programs in Civil Engineering

Institution	93Q [1]	93E [1]	% D [1]	% D-S [1]	93Q T [1]	93E T [1]	VIS [1]	TC [2]	C/F [2]	82Q [3]	82E [3]	TF [4]	TG [4]
Massachusetts Inst of Technology	1 (4.61)	1 (4.47)	2 (58)	3.5 (86)	2 (4.53)	1.5 (4.43)	7 (92)	2 (1036)	3 (25.9)	2 (4.74)	3 (4.33)	40	78
University of California-Berkeley	2 (4.56)	6 (4.22)	1 (59)	1 (91)	1 (4.65)	5 (4.20)	1 (98)	3 (633)	9 (14.7)	1 (4.83)	1 (4.55)	43	138
Stanford University	3 (4.44)	3 (4.29)	3 (52)	6 (76)	3 (4.41)	3 (4.24)	6 (93)	6 (530)	6 (23.0)	6 (4.13)	5 (4.18)	23	106
University of Texas at Austin	4 (4.42)	4 (4.27)	5 (47)	2 (88)	6 (4.29)	4 (4.23)	3 (97)	1 (1407)	8 (15.1)	5 (4.15)	7.5 (3.82)	93	79
U of Illinois at Urbana-Champaign	5 (4.41)	5 (4.23)	4 (48)	3.5 (86)	7 (4.25)	7 (4.11)	3 (97)	11 (388)	32 (5.5)	3 (4.53)	2 (4.37)	71	250
Cornell University	6 (4.30)	7 (4.08)	6 (34)	5 (79)	4.5 (4.33)	6 (4.12)	10 (88)	8 (451)	11 (13.7)	7 (4.06)	6 (3.92)	33	62
California Institute Technology	7 (4.27)	2 (4.42)	7 (31)	8 (68)	4.5 (4.33)	1.5 (4.43)	21 (80)	10 (409)	1 (34.1)	4 (4.49)	4 (4.30)	12	35
Princeton University	8 (3.99)	8 (3.89)	10.5 (18)	11 (59)	8 (4.00)	8 (3.83)	22.5 (79)	14 (299)	10 (14.2)	12 (3.62)	12 (3.43)	21	62
Northwestern University	9 (3.96)	11.5 (3.73)	8.5 (22)	10 (60)	9 (3.92)	9 (3.78)	18.5 (82)	4 (596)	5 (23.8)	8 (3.87)	7.5 (3.82)	25	73
University of Michigan	10 (3.90)	9 (3.82)	8.5 (22)	9 (63)	10.5 (3.86)	10 (3.73)	8 (89)	18 (243)	16.5 (10.6)	10 (3.65)	10 (3.57)	23	80
Purdue University	11 (3.89)	11.5 (3.73)	10.5 (18)	7 (71)	10.5 (3.86)	13 (3.63)	3 (97)	28.5 (124)	57 (2.2)	9 (3.86)	9 (3.68)	56	110
Carnegie Mellon University	12 (3.85)	10 (3.79)	12 (10)	13 (56)	12 (3.78)	11 (3.72)	24 (78)	25 (148)	24 (8.7)	18 (3.25)	19 (3.05)	17	42
University of Minnesota	13 (3.76)	14 (3.62)	16.5 (7)	12 (57)	13 (3.62)	14 (3.62)	16 (83)	13 (338)	16.5 (10.6)	29 (2.71)	31.5 (2.63)	32	72
University of Washington	14 (3.67)	13 (3.66)	16.5 (7)	14 (55)	14 (3.60)	12 (3.68)	10 (88)	12 (386)	15 (11.4)	11 (3.63)	13 (3.38)	34	42
U of North Carolina-Chapel Hill	15 (3.58)	16 (3.50)	13.5 (8)	21 (34)	16 (3.48)	17 (3.40)	51 (59)	21 (198)	20.5 (9.9)			20	44
University of California-Davis	16 (3.54)	15 (3.51)	19.5 (5)	15 (44)	15 (3.49)	15.5 (3.53)	12.5 (86)	32 (112)	38.5 (4.1)	21 (3.09)	20.5 (2.98)	27	50
Texas A&M University	17.5 (3.40)	23.5 (3.27)	13.5 (8)	17 (42)	25 (3.17)	26 (3.12)	5 (94)	15 (267)	37 (4.2)	20 (3.19)	20.5 (2.98)	63	100
Georgia Institute of Technology	17.5 (3.40)	25 (3.26)	38 (1)	16 (43)	18 (3.28)	27.5 (3.10)	10 (88)	33 (109)	50.5 (2.7)	19 (3.25)	18 (3.12)	41	99
Virginia Polytech Inst & State U	19.5 (3.39)	19 (3.36)	16.5 (7)	18 (39)	21 (3.21)	21 (3.25)	12.5 (86)	26 (135)	40.5 (4.0)	24 (2.81)	30 (2.65)	34	54
Lehigh University	19.5 (3.39)	18 (3.37)	22 (4)	21 (34)	23.5 (3.18)	23 (3.22)	25.5 (76)	66 (23)	77 (1.0)	15 (3.43)	16 (3.20)	22	31
Univ of California-Los Angeles	21 (3.37)	21.5 (3.28)	38 (1)	19 (38)	20 (3.23)	27.5 (3.10)	16 (83)	17 (249)	22 (9.6)	16 (3.32)	17 (3.18)	26	93
University of Wisconsin-Madison	22 (3.34)	23.5 (3.27)	22 (4)	23 (33)	23.5 (3.18)	37 (3.01)	27.5 (74)	9 (431)	12 (13.1)	14 (3.43)	15 (3.30)	33	59
Rice University	23 (3.28)	26 (3.24)	22 (4)	30 (23)	28 (3.10)	35.5 (3.02)	53 (58)	61.5 (30)	43 (3.8)	25 (2.80)	35.5 (2.53)	8	20
University of Colorado	24 (3.27)	20 (3.33)	19.5 (5)	21 (34)	22 (3.20)	20 (3.29)	16 (83)	28.5 (124)	46.5 (3.4)	23 (2.89)	22 (2.90)	36	93
Colorado State University	25 (3.23)	21.5 (3.28)	25 (3)	24 (31)	26 (3.15)	18.5 (3.33)	20 (81)	39.5 (76)	54 (2.5)	13 (3.60)	11 (3.53)	30	120
Johns Hopkins University	26 (3.22)	17 (3.44)	16.5 (7)	27 (26)	19 (3.26)	15.5 (3.53)	46.5 (61)	53 (42)	29 (6.0)	62 (1.36)	63 (1.30)	7	25
Duke University	27.5 (3.21)	30 (3.12)	28.5 (2)	25 (29)	29 (3.07)	31.5 (3.04)	18.5 (82)	47.5 (58)	45 (3.6)	35 (2.64)	34 (2.55)	16	63
Columbia University	27.5 (3.21)	28 (3.16)	66 (0)	34.5 (17)	17 (3.31)	18.5 (3.33)	71.5 (47)	51 (46)	43 (3.8)	17 (3.30)	14 (3.37)	12	17
University of Iowa	29 (3.19)	27 (3.23)	66 (0)	31 (22)	27 (3.11)	24.5 (3.14)	39 (65)	19 (211)	13 (11.7)	32 (2.69)	26 (2.78)	18	45
North Carolina State University	30 (3.17)	29 (3.13)	25 (3)	28 (25)	32 (3.00)	22 (3.24)	22.5 (79)	41 (71)	63.5 (2.0)	22 (2.97)	26 (2.78)	35	70

Institution	93Q [1]	93E [1]	% D [1]	% D-S [1]	93Q T [1]	93E T [1]	VIS [1]	TC [2]	C/F [2]	82Q [3]	82E [3]	TF [4]	TG [4]
State Univ of New York-Buffalo	**31** (3.14)	**31** (3.11)	**28.5** (2)	**29** (24)	**31** (3.04)	**30** (3.09)	**25.5** (76)	**7** (504)	**7** (16.8)	**43** (2.30)	**44.5** (2.32)	30	72
Pennsylvania State University	**32** (3.12)	**39.5** (2.95)	**38** (1)	**26** (28)	**35** (2.93)	**47** (2.80)	**14** (85)	**44** (65)	**55** (2.4)	**37** (2.50)	**31.5** (2.63)	27	102
University of California-Irvine	**33** (3.04)	**44.5** (2.88)	**66** (0)	**33** (18)	**30** (3.06)	**44** (2.92)	**51** (59)	**70.5** (19)	**75** (1.1)			17	47
University of Arizona	**34** (3.03)	**32.5** (3.09)	**28.5** (2)	**34.5** (17)	**39** (2.85)	**38** (2.99)	**27.5** (74)	**22** (181)	**23** (9.1)	**48** (2.17)	**49** (2.10)	20	93
Rensselaer Polytechnic Inst	**35** (2.97)	**34** (3.04)	**38** (1)	**32** (21)	**34** (2.96)	**34** (3.03)	**29.5** (72)	**16** (265)	**4** (24.1)	**26** (2.76)	**33** (2.62)	11	33
University of Florida	**36.5** (2.93)	**39.5** (2.95)	**28.5** (2)	**36.5** (16)	**34** (2.96)	**36** (3.02)	**43** (64)	**79** (14)	**83.5** (0.6)	**44** (2.28)	**43** (2.35)	25	49
University of Notre Dame	**36.5** (2.93)	**35.5** (3.03)	**66** (0)	**36.5** (16)	**37** (2.89)	**32** (3.04)	**45** (63)	**27** (129)	**20.5** (9.9)	**54** (1.91)	**52** (1.95)	13	17
University of Maryland College Park	**38** (2.92)	**32.5** (3.09)	**38** (1)	**41.5** (13)	**42** (2.76)	**30** (3.09)	**34** (68)	**39.5** (76)	**52.5** (2.6)	**40** (2.34)	**40** (2.45)	29	82
University of Virginia	**39** (2.91)	**42.5** (2.90)	**38** (1)	**38** (15)	**36** (2.91)	**40** (2.97)	**51** (.59)	**42** (69)	**33** (4.6)	**39** (2.39)	**54** (1.80)	15	16
Ohio State University	**40** (2.88)	**35.5** (3.03)	**38** (1)	**53.5** (6)	**40** (2.79)	**25** (3.14)	**39** (65)	**38** (79)	**35.5** (4.4)	**27** (2.74)	**26** (2.78)	18	47
Michigan State University	**41** (2.85)	**38** (2.99)	**66** (0)	**39.5** (14)	**43** (2.72)	**34** (3.03)	**34** (68)	**61.5** (30)	**68.5** (1.6)	**38** (2.44)	**38** (2.48)	19	43
Vanderbilt University	**42.5** (2.84)	**42.5** (2.90)	**66** (0)	**47** (11)	**44** (2.70)	**46** (2.82)	**36** (67)	**20** (207)	**14** (11.5)	**61** (1.43)	**61.5** (1.38)	18	37
Clarkson University	**42.5** (2.84)	**46** (2.85)	**66** (0)	**47** (11)	**38** (2.86)	**44** (2.92)	**46.5** (61)	**34** (106)	**28** (6.2)			17	35
University of Kansas	**44** (2.82)	**51.5** (2.70)	**66** (0)	**41.5** (13)	**46** (2.63)	**52** (2.67)	**39** (65)	**45** (64)	**49** (2.8)	**31** (2.69)	**35.5** (2.53)	23	36
Iowa State University	**45.5** (2.80)	**41** (2.92)	**25** (3)	**44** (12)	**45** (2.68)	**44** (2.92)	**39** (65)	**54** (41)	**70** (1.5)	**28** (2.73)	**28** (2.68)	28	26
University of Delaware	**45.5** (2.80)	**37** (3.01)	**66** (0)	**44** (12)	**42** (2.76)	**41** (2.96)	**48.5** (60)	**24** (174)	**19** (10.2)			17	34
U of Massachusetts at Amherst	**47** (2.77)	**57** (2.64)	**66** (0)	**39.5** (14)	**50** (2.49)	**62** (2.41)	**31** (70)	**30** (120)	**25** (8.0)	**30** (2.70)	**24** (2.80)	15	19
Utah State University	**48** (2.70)	**47** (2.84)	**66** (0)	**52** (7)	**54** (2.44)	**53** (2.63)	**67** (49)	**23** (178)	**30.5** (5.7)	**33** (2.69)	**23** (2.83)	31	64
Washington University	**49** (2.66)	**51.5** (2.70)	**66** (0)	**49** (10)	**48** (2.56)	**39** (2.98)	**63** (52)	**72.5** (17)	**60.5** (2.1)	**34** (2.65)	**29** (2.67)	8	16
University of Pittsburgh	**50** (2.65)	**50** (2.75)	**66** (0)	**53.5** (6)	**49** (2.55)	**49** (2.72)	**29.5** (72)	**50** (52)	**48** (3.1)	**42** (2.31)	**47** (2.18)	17	22
University of Houston	**51** (2.62)	**65** (2.39)	**66** (0)	**50.5** (8)	**47** (2.57)	**64** (2.37)	**39** (65)	**47.5** (58)	**38.5** (4.1)	**50** (2.06)	**51** (2.02)	14	57
Oregon State University	**52** (2.61)	**44.5** (2.88)	**66** (0)	**44** (12)	**52** (2.47)	**42** (2.94)	**59** (53)	**37** (81)	**26** (7.4)	**36** (2.52)	**37** (2.50)	11	30
University of Kentucky	**53** (2.58)	**49** (2.76)	**38** (1)	**47** (11)	**51** (2.48)	**51** (2.69)	**43** (64)	**47.5** (58)	**46.5** (3.4)			17	31
Auburn University	**54** (2.55)	**54** (2.67)	**38** (1)	**50.5** (8)	**53** (2.46)	**48** (2.73)	**32** (69)	**35** (101)	**35.5** (4.4)			23	20
University of Cincinnati	**55** (2.44)	**55.5** (2.65)	**66** (0)	**58.5** (5)	**64** (2.19)	**60** (2.46)	**34** (68)	**47.5** (58)	**34** (4.5)	**58** (1.63)	**56** (1.72)	13	56
University of Oklahoma	**56** (2.43)	**59** (2.56)	**66** (0)	**68.5** (3)	**55** (2.42)	**50** (2.71)	**63** (52)	**60** (31)	**68.5** (1.6)	**51** (2.05)	**44.5** (2.32)	20	28
Brigham Young University	**57** (2.42)	**55.5** (2.65)	**66** (0)	**63.5** (4)	**65** (2.17)	**56** (2.50)	**83.5** (35)	**68** (22)	**66.5** (1.7)			13	10
Arizona State University	**58** (2.41)	**53** (2.69)	**66** (0)	**58.5** (5)	**63** (2.21)	**61** (2.45)	**48.5** (60)	**56** (35)	**50.5** (2.7)			13	39
Texas Tech University	**60** (2.40)	**61** (2.47)	**38** (1)	**58.5** (5)	**57** (2.36)	**66** (2.32)	**69** (48)	**76** (15)	**80** (0.8)	**56** (1.74)	**58** (1.62)	19	24
University of Missouri-Rolla	**60** (2.40)	**64** (2.40)	**66** (0)	**58.5** (5)	**67** (2.09)	**68** (2.22)	**43** (64)	**81** (12)	**80** (0.8)	**41** (2.34)	**39** (2.47)	15	24

Appendix Table P - 10 Civil Engineering (Continued)

Institution	93Q [1]	93E [1]	% D [1]	% D-S [1]	93Q T [1]	93E T [1]	VIS [1]	TC [2]	C/F [2]	82Q [3]	82E [3]	TF [4]	TG [4]
Syracuse University	**60** (2.40)	**60** (2.50)	**66** (0)	**58.5** (5)	**56** (2.41)	**58** (2.47)	**59** (53)	**5** (543)	**2** (31.9)	**55** (1.85)	**50** (2.07)	17	13
Clemson University	**62** (2.39)	**48** (2.82)	**38** (1)	**58.5** (5)	**61** (2.27)	**56** (2.50)	**54** (57)	**64** (27)	**60.5** (2.1)	**52** (2.00)	**57** (1.67)	13	18
Washington State University	**63.5** (2.35)	**63** (2.43)	**38** (1)	**68.5** (3)	**59** (2.33)	**60** (2.46)	**63** (52)	**63** (29)	**66.5** (1.7)			17	49
University of Illinois at Chicago	**63.5** (2.35)	**67** (2.30)	**66** (0)	**63.5** (4)	**59** (2.33)	**56** (2.50)	**81.5** (37)	**31** (113)	**18** (10.3)			11	28
University of Tennessee-Knoxville	**65** (2.33)	**58** (2.62)	**66** (0)	**76.5** (2)	**59** (2.33)	**56** (2.50)	**74.5** (43)	**72.5** (17)	**78** (0.9)	**47** (2.19)	**46** (2.20)	18	38
West Virginia University	**66** (2.26)	**68** (2.29)	**66** (0)	**76.5** (2)	**66** (2.13)	**72** (1.98)	**56** (55)	**83** (6)	**85** (0.3)	**49** (2.16)	**48** (2.17)	19	25
Louisiana State U &-A&M College	**67** (2.23)	**66** (2.36)	**66** (0)	**68.5** (3)	**73** (2.00)	**65** (2.33)	**55** (56)	**36** (93)	**40.5** (4.0)			23	46
University of Connecticut	**68** (2.22)	**77** (1.79)	**66** (0)	**76.5** (2)	**69** (2.07)	**76** (1.85)	**57** (54)	**52** (45)	**52.5** (2.6)	**53** (1.92)	**53** (1.83)	17	13
Oklahoma State University	**70** (2.21)	**72.5** (2.11)	**38** (1)	**76.5** (2)	**71** (2.04)	**68** (2.22)	**63** (52)	**82** (11)	**80** (0.8)	**45** (2.26)	**41** (2.40)	14	140
Illinois Institute of Technology	**70** (2.21)	**62** (2.45)	**66** (0)	**58.5** (5)	**71** (2.04)	**64** (2.37)	**63** (52)	**76** (15)	**60.5** (2.1)	**57** (1.69)	**55** (1.78)	7	17
University of Wisconsin-Milwaukee	**70** (2.21)	**76** (1.91)	**66** (0)	**76.5** (2)	**62** (2.26)	**73** (1.95)	**79** (40)	**74** (16)	**75** (1.1)			14	n/a
University of Nebraska-Lincoln	**72** (2.15)	**70** (2.18)	**66** (0)	**82** (1)	**73** (2.00)	**69** (2.16)	**69** (48)	**55** (40)	**63.5** (2.0)			20	13
University of New Hampshire	**73** (2.14)	**71** (2.13)	**38** (1)	**58.5** (5)	**69** (2.07)	**70** (2.08)	**69** (48)	**65** (26)	**65** (1.9)			14	6
University of Missouri-Columbia	**75** (1.95)	**72.5** (2.11)	**66** (0)	**68.5** (3)	**75** (1.79)	**74** (1.93)	**66** (50)	**68** (22)	**57** (2.2)	**46** (2.22)	**42** (2.37)	10	15
Kansas State University	**75** (1.95)	**74** (1.99)	**66** (0)	**68.5** (3)	**80** (1.53)	**77** (1.67)	**73** (45)	**76** (15)	**72.5** (1.3)			12	15
George Washington University	**75** (1.95)	**79** (1.67)	**66** (0)	**68.5** (3)	**76** (1.76)	**81** (1.33)	**74.5** (43)	**57.5** (34)	**43** (3.8)			9	18
New Mexico State University	**77** (1.94)	**69** (2.22)	**66** (0)	**76.5** (2)	**74** (1.84)	**71** (2.05)	**80** (38)	**70.5** (19)	**75** (1.1)			18	14
University of Akron	**78** (1.77)	**80** (1.60)	**66** (0)	**82** (1)	**83** (1.30)	**80** (1.37)	**76.5** (42)	**43** (67)	**27** (6.7)			10	47
University of Miami	**79** (1.68)	**78** (1.74)	**66** (0)	**76.5** (2)	**78** (1.60)	**79** (1.39)	**71.5** (47)	**79** (14)	**72.5** (1.3)			11	12
Northeastern University	**80** (1.67)	**82** (1.48)	**38** (1)	**68.5** (3)	**77** (1.62)	**84** (1.19)	**59** (53)	**59** (32)	**60.5** (2.1)			15	10
Catholic University of America	**81** (1.65)	**85** (1.11)	**66** (0)	**68.5** (3)	**79** (1.54)	**83** (1.25)	**86** (29)	**84.5** (5)	**82** (0.7)			7	n/a
University of Rhode Island	**82** (1.60)	**83** (1.43)	**66** (0)	**76.5** (2)	**81** (1.40)	**83** (1.25)	**85** (33)	**57.5** (34)	**30.5** (5.7)	**60** (1.45)	**59.5** (1.40)	6	64
Tulane University	**83** (1.43)	**84** (1.37)	**66** (0)	**85** (0)	**84** (1.27)	**85** (0.93)	**78** (41)	**79** (14)	**71** (1.4)	**59** (1.50)	**59.5** (1.40)	10	41
University of Alabama	**84.5** (1.41)	**81** (1.59)	**66** (0)	**82** (1)	**85** (1.24)	**79** (1.39)	**76.5** (42)	**84.5** (5)	**83.5** (0.6)			9	18
Wayne State University	**84.5** (1.41)	**75** (1.93)	**66** (0)	**85** (0)	**82** (1.31)	**75** (1.88)	**81.5** (37)	**68** (22)	**57** (2.2)	**63** (1.14)	**61.5** (1.38)	10	32
University of Mississippi	**86** (1.22)	**86** (1.08)	**66** (0)	**85** (0)	**86** (0.88)	**86** (0.83)	**83.5** (35)	**86** (0)	**86** (0.0)			7	4

Sources: 1. National Survey of Graduate Faculty
2. Institute for Scientific Information
3. 1982 Survey of Graduate Faculty
4. Institutional Coordinator Data

Appendix Table P - 11 Relative Rankings for Research-Doctorate Programs in Classics

Institution	93Q [1]	93E [1]	% D [1]	% D-S [1]	93Q T [1]	93E T [1]	VIS [1]	FA [2]	82Q [3]	82E [3]	TF [4]	TG [4]
Harvard University	1 (4.79)	4 (3.86)	1 (80)	2 (96)	1 (4.84)	4 (3.75)	4 (100)	1 (17)	1 (4.92)	1 (4.42)	19	41
University of California-Berkeley	2 (4.77)	1 (4.41)	2 (77)	1 (97)	2 (4.76)	1 (4.32)	4 (100)	6.5 (7)	2 (4.63)	2 (4.05)	18	25
University of Michigan	3 (4.54)	2 (4.26)	3 (59)	3 (93)	3 (4.53)	2 (4.21)	4 (100)	4.5 (8)	5 (4.06)	3 (3.83)	22	34
Princeton University	4 (4.16)	3 (4.15)	4 (42)	6 (76)	4 (4.14)	3 (4.10)	9 (99)	16 (2)	4 (4.12)	4 (3.78)	8	24
Yale University	5 (4.12)	6 (3.52)	5 (32)	5 (81)	5 (4.11)	7 (3.43)	4 (100)	22.5 (1)	3 (4.38)	7 (3.63)	17	35
Brown University	6 (4.10)	8 (3.46)	6 (27)	4 (83)	6 (4.03)	8 (3.40)	4 (100)	2 (11)	7 (3.84)	10.5 (3.27)	10	23
University of Chicago	7 (4.00)	14 (3.09)	7 (25)	8 (73)	7 (3.89)	16 (2.90)	13.5 (97)	13 (4)	12 (3.63)	17 (2.80)	12	23
University of Texas at Austin	8 (3.92)	9 (3.40)	8 (23)	9 (71)	10 (3.84)	10 (3.30)	11.5 (98)	6.5 (7)	9 (3.76)	8.5 (3.33)	31	13
Univ of California-Los Angeles	9 (3.89)	11 (3.23)	10 (16)	7 (74)	8 (3.88)	9 (3.38)	9 (99)	8.5 (6)	16 (3.14)	21 (2.38)	19	22
Columbia University	10 (3.86)	13 (3.15)	9 (22)	11.5 (67)	9 (3.87)	12 (3.20)	4 (100)	8.5 (6)	10 (3.72)	12 (3.25)	13	21
U of North Carolina-Chapel Hill	11 (3.81)	5 (3.57)	11 (14)	11.5 (67)	12 (3.77)	5 (3.48)	11.5 (98)	11 (5)	6 (3.94)	5 (3.77)	15	25
Cornell University	12 (3.73)	10 (3.38)	12 (11)	10 (69)	11 (3.80)	11 (3.27)	4 (100)	4.5 (8)	13 (3.54)	10.5 (3.27)	24	16
University of Pennsylvania	13 (3.62)	18 (2.65)	14 (8)	13 (59)	13 (3.52)	18 (2.54)	9 (99)	3 (9)	11 (3.65)	13 (3.23)	24	22
Bryn Mawr College	14 (3.48)	7 (3.48)	13 (9)	14 (50)	14 (3.47)	6 (3.47)	15.5 (95)	11 (5)	8 (3.77)	6 (3.73)	10	55
Duke University	15 (3.37)	15 (3.01)	15 (7)	15 (44)	15 (3.31)	13 (3.07)	15.5 (95)	22.5 (1)	18 (2.78)	16 (2.92)	11	16
Stanford University	16 (3.32)	12 (3.17)	20 (1)	16 (43)	16 (3.23)	14 (3.03)	13.5 (97)	16 (2)	14 (3.39)	8.5 (3.33)	11	36
U of Illinois at Urbana-Champaign	17 (3.02)	19 (2.60)	20 (1)	17 (30)	17 (2.97)	21 (2.43)	19.5 (92)	11 (5)	15 (3.21)	14 (2.95)	15	20
University of Virginia	18 (2.98)	20 (2.57)	17 (2)	18 (28)	19.5 (2.90)	19 (2.50)	18 (93)	16 (2)	26 (1.93)	26 (1.60)	6	15
University of Wisconsin-Madison	19 (2.92)	17 (2.76)	26 (0)	21 (18)	19.5 (2.90)	17 (2.83)	21 (91)	22.5 (1)	20 (2.57)	18 (2.52)	11	13
University of Washington	20 (2.89)	16 (2.87)	26 (0)	19 (24)	18 (2.93)	15 (2.93)	22.5 (90)	22.5 (1)	24 (2.15)	22 (2.33)	11	20
Ohio State University	21 (2.60)	21 (2.38)	26 (0)	23 (10)	21.5 (2.54)	22 (2.40)	25.5 (88)	16 (2)	19 (2.60)	19.5 (2.48)	16	26
Univ of California-Santa Barbara	22 (2.59)	24 (1.91)	20 (1)	22 (12)	21.5 (2.54)	25 (1.85)	19.5 (92)	22.5 (1)			8	12
Johns Hopkins University	23 (2.52)	28 (1.33)	16 (4)	20 (22)	24 (2.40)	28 (1.13)	17 (94)	28 (0)	21 (2.48)	23 (2.02)	9	8
University of Minnesota	24 (2.43)	22 (2.33)	26 (0)	25 (9)	23 (2.42)	20 (2.45)	24 (89)	22.5 (1)	22 (2.37)	19.5 (2.48)	13	29
New York University	25 (2.33)	25 (1.84)	26 (0)	25 (9)	25 (2.39)	23 (2.03)	22.5 (90)	22.5 (1)	25 (2.09)	27 (1.48)	8	8
Boston University	26 (2.31)	26 (1.78)	20 (1)	25 (9)	26 (2.23)	26 (1.79)	25.5 (88)	28 (0)	23 (2.35)	24 (1.85)	5	27
University of Cincinnati	27 (2.10)	23 (1.96)	26 (0)	27 (4)	27 (2.06)	24 (1.91)	27 (86)	28 (0)	17 (2.91)	15 (2.93)	5	16
Fordham University	28 (1.83)	27 (1.38)	20 (1)	28.5 (2)	28 (1.87)	27 (1.49)	28 (80)	22.5 (1)	28 (1.30)	28 (1.20)	5	17
Catholic University of America	29 (0.93)	29 (0.56)	26 (0)	28.5 (2)	29 (0.60)	29 (0.00)	29 (46)	16 (2)	27 (1.38)	25 (1.72)	5	9

Sources: 1. National Survey of Graduate Faculty
2. Associations and Organizations Administrating Prestigious Awards and Honors
3. 1982 Survey of Graduate Faculty
4. Institutional Coordinator Data

Appendix Table P - 12 Relative Rankings for Research-Doctorate Programs in Comparative Literature

Institution	93Q [1]	93E [1]	% D [1]	% D-S [1]	93Q T [1]	93E T [1]	VIS [1]	FA [2]	82Q [3]	82E [3]	TF [4]	TG [4]
Yale University	1 (4.70)	1 (4.30)	1 (74)	1 (91)	1 (4.79)	1 (4.57)	6 (99)	8 (9)			18	32
Duke University	2 (4.51)	7 (3.80)	2 (62)	4 (83)	2 (4.55)	4 (3.95)	9.5 (97)	3 (12)			25	60
Columbia University	3 (4.44)	5 (3.82)	3 (52)	2 (89)	3 (4.53)	8 (3.80)	2 (100)	1.5 (21)			75	55
Harvard University	4 (4.37)	6 (3.81)	4 (50)	3 (84)	5 (4.32)	9 (3.68)	2 (100)	4.5 (11)			21	63
Princeton University	5 (4.32)	3 (3.96)	5 (46)	6 (80)	4 (4.42)	3 (4.07)	6 (99)	9.5 (7)			17	33
Cornell University	6 (4.31)	8 (3.78)	6 (41)	5 (82)	7 (4.29)	7 (3.84)	6 (99)	9.5 (7)			27	25
Johns Hopkins University	7 (4.18)	2 (4.12)	7 (39)	10.5 (70)	6 (4.31)	2 (4.30)	11 (94)	15 (5)			13	25
University of California-Irvine	8 (4.06)	10 (3.63)	10 (26)	7 (79)	10 (4.13)	11 (3.64)	2 (100)	20.5 (4)			13	40
Stanford University	9 (4.05)	9 (3.75)	8.5 (28)	9 (72)	8 (4.20)	5 (3.92)	6 (99)	6.5 (10)			11	32
University of California-Berkeley	10 (4.00)	4 (3.83)	8.5 (28)	10.5 (70)	11 (3.97)	6 (3.91)	9.5 (97)	27 (3)			20	95
University of Pennsylvania	11 (3.99)	11 (3.57)	11 (22)	8 (77)	9 (4.16)	10 (3.66)	6 (99)	1.5 (21)			35	52
University of Chicago	12 (3.56)	12.5 (3.29)	13 (10)	12 (52)	12 (3.65)	14 (3.33)	13 (90)	20.5 (4)			22	38
New York University	13 (3.49)	15 (3.19)	12 (11)	13 (49)	13 (3.61)	17 (3.20)	13 (90)	20.5 (4)			18	13
University of Washington	14 (3.37)	14 (3.21)	18.5 (3)	14 (39)	14 (3.53)	14 (3.33)	13 (90)	32.5 (2)			25	81
University of Michigan	15 (3.23)	16 (3.17)	18.5 (3)	15.5 (32)	16 (3.20)	18 (3.18)	15 (88)	32.5 (2)			9	57
Univ of California-Los Angeles	16 (3.22)	12.5 (3.29)	18.5 (3)	15.5 (32)	18 (3.12)	14 (3.33)	17.5 (85)	12 (6)			28	49
Northwestern University	17 (3.20)	18.5 (3.01)	18.5 (3)	17 (31)	15 (3.30)	14 (3.33)	16 (86)	4.5 (11)			29	24
Univ of California-San Diego	18 (3.17)	18.5 (3.01)	14 (5)	19 (27)	19 (3.11)	24 (2.86)	21 (78)	12 (6)			18	33
Indiana University	19 (3.08)	21 (2.97)	15 (4)	18 (28)	21 (3.02)	23 (2.96)	23 (77)	20.5 (4)			24	120
Brown University	20 (2.98)	20 (2.99)	33 (0)	21.5 (19)	22 (3.00)	21 (3.02)	23 (77)	32.5 (2)			8	18
University of Texas at Austin	21 (2.96)	17 (3.14)	33 (0)	20 (21)	17 (3.15)	14 (3.33)	19 (82)	20.5 (4)			44	40
Rutgers State Univ-New Brunswick	22 (2.92)	22.5 (2.92)	33 (0)	25 (13)	20 (3.05)	19 (3.13)	33 (65)	37.5 (1)			21	38
University of Southern California	23 (2.86)	27.5 (2.72)	33 (0)	21.5 (19)	24 (2.72)	29 (2.64)	17.5 (85)	37.5 (1)			13	20
Emory University	24 (2.72)	27.5 (2.72)	33 (0)	23 (18)	25 (2.69)	32 (2.43)	20 (81)	27 (3)			19	31
Washington University	25 (2.70)	31.5 (2.65)	33 (0)	27 (12)	23 (2.75)	27.5 (2.71)	30 (68)	15 (5)			21	48
Univ of California-Riverside	26 (2.66)	34 (2.56)	18.5 (3)	27 (12)	26 (2.50)	30 (2.62)	40 (58)	32.5 (2)			35	17
Pennsylvania State University	27 (2.65)	35 (2.55)	33 (0)	27 (12)	36 (2.19)	40 (2.00)	40 (58)	27 (3)			25	43
University of Minnesota	28 (2.53)	26 (2.75)	33 (0)	33.5 (8)	27 (2.46)	26 (2.73)	23 (77)	42 (0)			7	46
State U of New York-Stony Brook	29 (2.49)	33 (2.57)	33 (0)	33.5 (8)	30.5 (2.31)	38 (2.08)	31 (66)	12 (6)			16	45
University of Iowa	30 (2.48)	24 (2.79)	33 (0)	36.5 (6)	28 (2.45)	22 (3.00)	35 (63)	37.5 (1)			11	30

Institution	93Q [1]	93E [1]	% D [1]	% D-S [1]	93Q T [1]	93E T [1]	VIS [1]	FA [2]	82Q [3]	82E [3]	TF [4]	TG [4]
University of Rochester	**31** (2.47)	**42** (2.14)	**33** (0)	**29** (11)	**33** (2.27)	**42** (1.67)	**25.5** (74)	**20.5** (4)			19	21
U of North Carolina-Chapel Hill	**32** (2.44)	**25** (2.76)	**33** (0)	**30.5** (9)	**31** (2.31)	**25** (2.74)	**27.5** (73)	**20.5** (4)			7	41
U of Illinois at Urbana-Champaign	**33** (2.39)	**36.5** (2.50)	**33** (0)	**36.5** (6)	**29** (2.33)	**36** (2.17)	**33** (65)	**27** (3)			9	34
State Univ of New York-Binghamton	**34** (2.36)	**22.5** (2.92)	**33** (0)	**24** (14)	**35** (2.23)	**20** (3.06)	**25.5** (74)	**42** (0)			8	64
U of Massachusetts at Amherst	**35** (2.35)	**36.5** (2.50)	**33** (0)	**42.5** (3)	**37** (2.16)	**39** (2.04)	**37** (62)	**42** (0)			10	29
University of Arizona	**36** (2.32)	**40.5** (2.26)	**33** (0)	**33.5** (8)	**32** (2.29)	**36** (2.17)	**29** (69)	**15** (5)			35	21
University of Wisconsin-Madison	**37** (2.25)	**29** (2.68)	**33** (0)	**38** (5)	**39** (1.98)	**33** (2.36)	**33** (65)	**32.5** (2)			8	38
University of California-Davis	**38** (2.23)	**38** (2.46)	**33** (0)	**33.5** (8)	**35** (2.23)	**36** (2.17)	**27.5** (73)	**32.5** (2)			8	17
University of Maryland College Park	**39** (2.21)	**40.5** (2.26)	**33** (0)	**40** (4)	**38** (2.13)	**34** (2.33)	. **40** (58)	**6.5** (10)			58	31
CUNY - Grad Sch & Univ Center	**40** (2.18)	**30** (2.66)	**33** (0)	**30.5** (9)	**40** (1.96)	**28** (2.71)	**37** (62)	**42** (0)			6	72
University of Oregon	**41** (2.10)	**31.5** (2.65)	**33** (0)	**40** (4)	**41** (1.85)	**31** (2.50)	**42** (55)	**20.5** (4)			14	28
University of Connecticut	**42** (1.93)	**39** (2.33)	**33** (0)	**42.5** (3)	**42** (1.66)	**42** (1.67)	**37** (62)	**27** (3)			16	21
Catholic University of America	**43** (1.60)	**43** (1.95)	**18.5** (3)	**40** (4)	**43** (1.47)	**42** (1.67)	**43** (49)	**42** (0)			8	3
University of South Carolina	**44** (1.55)	**44** (1.50)	**33** (0)	**44** (0)	**44** (1.17)	**44** (0.56)	**44** (35)	**37.5** (1)			15	14

Sources: 1. National Survey of Graduate Faculty
2. Associations and Organizations Administrating Prestigious Awards and Honors
3. 1982 Survey of Graduate Faculty
4. Institutional Coordinator Data

Appendix Table P - 13 Relative Rankings for Research-Doctorate Programs in Computer Sciences

Institution	93Q [1]	93E [1]	% D [1]	% D-S [1]	93Q T [1]	93E T [1]	VIS [1]	TC [2]	C/F [2]	82Q [3]	82E [3]	TF [4]	TG [4]
Stanford University	1 (4.97)	2 (4.60)	1 (95)	1 (99)	1 (4.99)	1 (4.63)	1.5 (100)	6 (508)	8 (16.4)	1 (4.95)	1 (4.70)	31	133
Massachusetts Inst of Technology	2 (4.91)	1 (4.62)	2 (86)	4 (95)	3 (4.90)	3 (4.58)	6 (97)	3 (611)	9 (15.7)	2 (4.88)	2 (4.63)	39	170
University of California-Berkeley	3 (4.88)	3 (4.58)	3 (85)	2.5 (96)	2 (4.92)	2 (4.61)	5 (98)	4 (582)	12 (14.6)	4 (4.49)	4 (4.32)	40	169
Carnegie Mellon University	4 (4.76)	5 (4.38)	4 (75)	2.5 (96)	4 (4.75)	5 (4.32)	3.5 (99)	14 (354)	28 (8.4)	3 (4.79)	3 (4.45)	42	163
Cornell University	5 (4.64)	4 (4.47)	5 (65)	5 (94)	5 (4.60)	4 (4.52)	3.5 (99)	8 (462)	15 (12.8)	5 (4.30)	5 (4.18)	36	91
Princeton University	6 (4.31)	10 (3.84)	6 (40)	6 (81)	6 (4.29)	10 (3.81)	8.5 (96)	11 (391)	5 (21.7)	14 (2.99)	14 (3.15)	18	45
University of Texas at Austin	7 (4.18)	11 (3.81)	7.5 (32)	7 (80)	7 (4.10)	11 (3.78)	12.5 (95)	13 (360)	40 (6.4)	11 (3.22)	9 (3.42)	56	92
U of Illinois at Urbana-Champaign	8 (4.09)	8 (3.93)	7.5 (32)	8 (77)	9 (4.02)	9 (3.87)	1.5 (100)	2 (686)	19 (11.6)	7 (3.76)	6 (3.75)	59	398
University of Washington	9 (4.04)	6 (4.05)	9 (29)	10 (73)	8 (4.07)	6 (4.20)	8.5 (96)	17.5 (333)	20 (11.5)	9 (3.42)	10 (3.33)	29	100
University of Wisconsin-Madison	10 (4.00)	9 (3.87)	12 (20)	9 (74)	10.5 (4.01)	7 (3.99)	16 (93)	15 (343)	25 (9.8)	10 (3.23)	11.5 (3.23)	35	142
Harvard University	11 (3.94)	17.5 (3.47)	10 (23)	12 (69)	12 (3.97)	20.5 (3.38)	12.5 (95)	27 (242)	13 (14.2)			17	46
California Institute Technology	12 (3.93)	7 (3.97)	11 (22)	14 (63)	10.5 (4.01)	8 (3.98)	21 (90)	44 (110)	22 (11.0)	27 (2.49)	29 (2.50)	10	25
Brown University	13 (3.86)	12 (3.75)	18 (10)	11 (71)	13.5 (3.77)	12 (3.72)	16 (93)	56.5 (66)	57 (3.9)	15 (2.90)	20 (2.83)	17	49
Univ of California-Los Angeles	14.5 (3.73)	16 (3.48)	13 (14)	13 (64)	15 (3.69)	18 (3.41)	8.5 (96)	20 (317)	36 (6.7)	6 (3.77)	7 (3.58)	47	145
Yale University	14.5 (3.73)	20 (3.44)	14 (13)	16 (56)	13.5 (3.77)	15.5 (3.45)	18 (92)	25 (249)	10 (15.6)	8 (3.53)	8 (3.50)	16	68
University of Maryland College Park	16 (3.69)	19 (3.45)	15.5 (11)	15 (57)	18 (3.51)	24 (3.21)	8.5 (96)	10 (429)	26.5 (9.1)	13 (3.06)	11.5 (3.23)	47	207
New York University	17 (3.60)	17.5 (3.47)	15.5 (11)	18.5 (49)	17 (3.56)	15.5 (3.45)	19.5 (91)	1 (816)	2 (25.5)	16 (2.85)	21 (2.82)	32	99
U of Massachusetts at Amherst	18 (3.59)	23.5 (3.36)	18 (10)	17 (51)	19 (3.46)	23 (3.22)	24 (88)	16 (339)	21 (11.3)	18 (2.76)	22 (2.75)	30	139
Rice University	19 (3.55)	14 (3.51)	22.5 (5)	21 (45)	16 (3.57)	14 (3.52)	33 (82)	54.5 (69)	51 (4.6)	28 (2.45)	25.5 (2.58)	15	48
University of Southern California	20 (3.52)	26 (3.19)	21 (7)	18.5 (49)	22 (3.33)	31 (3.03)	16 (93)	21 (307)	35 (6.8)	12 (3.21)	16 (3.05)	45	133
University of Michigan	21 (3.49)	14 (3.51)	25 (4)	23 (41)	23 (3.29)	20.5 (3.38)	24 (88)	32 (195)	38.5 (6.5)			30	242
Columbia University	22.5 (3.45)	23.5 (3.36)	20 (8)	22 (43)	20 (3.43)	22 (3.37)	12.5 (95)	40 (139)	41 (6.3)	26 (2.53)	38.5 (2.05)	22	67
Univ of California-San Diego	22.5 (3.45)	28 (3.11)	22.5 (5)	20 (47)	21 (3.34)	29.5 (3.05)	12.5 (95)	26 (246)	32.5 (7.2)	25 (2.56)	38.5 (2.05)	34	72
University of Chicago	24.5 (3.31)	43.5 (2.88)	18 (10)	25.5 (35)	24 (3.26)	29.5 (3.05)	39 (78)	51 (84)	38.5 (6.5)			13	39
University of Pennsylvania [a]	24.5 (3.31)	21 (3.42)	33.5 (2)	25.5 (35)	25 (3.20)	17 (3.42)	29 (84)	5 (534)	4 (22.3)	20 (2.72)	17 (2.92)	24	199
Purdue University	26 (3.28)	25 (3.31)	46 (1)	24 (36)	27 (3.11)	25.5 (3.08)	22 (89)	29 (223)	31 (7.4)			30	120
Rutgers State Univ-New Brunswick	27 (3.25)	31.5 (3.05)	27 (3)	27 (31)	28 (3.09)	32 (2.98)	35.5 (81)	17.5 (333)	32.5 (7.2)	31 (2.43)	34 (2.27)	46	125
Duke University	28 (3.17)	30 (3.08)	33.5 (2)	28 (28)	29 (3.08)	36 (2.88)	33 (82)	12 (371)	6 (19.5)	29 (2.43)	27 (2.57)	19	48
U of North Carolina-Chapel Hill	29 (3.16)	22 (3.40)	25 (4)	30.5 (24)	30 (3.04)	19 (3.39)	24 (88)	41 (124)	34 (6.9)	21 (2.71)	18.5 (2.90)	18	118
University of Rochester	30 (3.13)	14 (3.51)	25 (4)	30.5 (24)	26 (3.17)	13 (3.59)	37.5 (80)	35 (172)	14 (13.2)	22 (2.71)	18.5 (2.90)	13	41

Institution	93Q [1]	93E [1]	% D [1]	% D-S [1]	93Q T [1]	93E T [1]	VIS [1]	TC [2]	C/F [2]	82Q [3]	82E [3]	TF [4]	TG [4]
State U of New York-Stony Brook	31 (3.12)	29 (3.10)	33.5 (2)	33.5 (22)	35 (2.93)	26 (3.08)	33 (82)	23 (277)	17 (12.0)	23.5 (2.68)	15 (3.07)	23	120
Georgia Institute of Technology	32 (3.10)	34 (3.00)	80.5 (0)	33.5 (22)	31 (3.02)	35 (2.92)	26.5 (85)	47 (105)	63.5 (2.9)	19 (2.72)	25.5 (2.58)	36	127
University of Arizona	33 (3.05)	35 (2.99)	46 (1)	29 (25)	35 (2.93)	42 (2.71)	31 (83)	9 (449)	1 (34.5)	35 (2.35)	32 (2.30)	13	35
University of California-Irvine	34 (3.03)	36 (2.98)	33.5 (2)	35.5 (21)	33 (2.95)	39 (2.84)	29 (84)	38 (159)	42 (6.1)	30 (2.43)	33 (2.28)	26	132
University of Virginia	35 (3.02)	31.5 (3.05)	46 (1)	32 (23)	39 (2.82)	34 (2.94)	35.5 (81)	49 (92)	46.5 (5.1)	44 (1.73)	41 (1.98)	18	60
Indiana University	36 (3.00)	27 (3.17)	33.5 (2)	39 (17)	33 (2.95)	28 (3.07)	29 (84)	61.5 (56)	72 (2.3)	36 (2.32)	36 (2.12)	24	66
Johns Hopkins University	37 (2.96)	37 (2.96)	33.5 (2)	37 (20)	37 (2.89)	34 (2.94)	52 (65)	56.5 (66)	37 (6.6)			10	38
Northwestern University	38 (2.93)	40 (2.92)	46 (1)	35.5 (21)	41 (2.73)	40 (2.83)	26.5 (85)	34 (173)	29 (7.9)	32 (2.40)	28 (2.52)	22	99
Ohio State University	39 (2.92)	38 (2.94)	33.5 (2)	38 (18)	43 (2.68)	43 (2.68)	19.5 (91)	19 (318)	26.5 (9.1)	33 (2.37)	24 (2.63)	35	106
University of Colorado	40.5 (2.90)	39 (2.93)	33.5 (2)	43.5 (14)	36 (2.91)	39 (2.84)	45 (72)	24 (271)	23 (10.8)			25	164
University of Utah	40.5 (2.90)	33 (3.04)	46 (1)	43.5 (14)	38 (2.85)	28 (3.07)	56.5 (63)	75 (32)	77 (2.0)	17 (2.84)	13 (3.20)	16	57
Oregon Graduate Inst Sci & Tech	42 (2.83)	47 (2.80)	46 (1)	46.5 (12)	40 (2.79)	41 (2.72)	49.5 (66)	76 (28)	81 (1.6)			17	47
University of Pittsburgh	43 (2.81)	49 (2.72)	33.5 (2)	45 (13)	42 (2.71)	51 (2.45)	37.5 (80)	42.5 (117)	44 (5.6)	41 (1.92)	40 (2.03)	21	54
Syracuse University	44 (2.80)	41 (2.91)	33.5 (2)	40.5 (16)	46 (2.48)	46 (2.58)	40 (77)	28 (229)	43 (5.7)	34 (2.36)	31 (2.38)	40	71
University of Pennsylvania [b]	45 (2.72)	43.5 (2.88)	33.5 (2)	50.5 (9)	54 (2.33)	52 (2.41)	99 (37)	22 (301)	16 (12.5)			24	39
University of Florida	46 (2.70)	53.5 (2.48)	80.5 (0)	40.5 (16)	47 (2.46)	60 (2.02)	45 (72)	48 (103)	54.5 (4.3)			24	53
University of Minnesota	47 (2.67)	45 (2.87)	33.5 (2)	42 (15)	52 (2.34)	45 (2.62)	41 (76)	52.5 (80)	48.5 (5.0)	23.5 (2.68)	23 (2.73)	16	77
Univ of California-Santa Barbara	48 (2.65)	63 (2.18)	80.5 (0)	50.5 (9)	50 (2.36)	63 (1.88)	56.5 (63)	31 (209)	11 (14.9)	38 (2.12)	42 (1.92)	14	42
Rensselaer Polytechnic Inst	49 (2.63)	42 (2.90)	80.5 (0)	50.5 (9)	45 (2.53)	37 (2.87)	49.5 (66)	67 (44)	67 (2.6)			17	71
Univ of California-Santa Cruz	50 (2.59)	61.5 (2.24)	80.5 (0)	53.5 (8)	48 (2.40)	55 (2.20)	52 (65)	36 (164)	18 (11.7)			14	44
University of Illinois at Chicago	51 (2.56)	46 (2.86)	80.5 (0)	58.5 (6)	56 (2.27)	44 (2.67)	59 (61)	37 (161)	53 (4.4)			37	n/a
Washington University	52 (2.54)	52 (2.53)	46 (1)	46.5 (12)	54 (2.33)	49 (2.50)	75 (50)	50 (87)	46.5 (5.1)	50 (1.44)	46.5 (1.67)	17	31
Michigan State University	53 (2.53)	48 (2.74)	80.5 (0)	48 (10)	57 (2.22)	47 (2.56)	52 (65)	59 (61)	65 (2.8)	49 (1.46)	50 (1.48)	22	79
Pennsylvania State University	54.5 (2.52)	50 (2.59)	80.5 (0)	50.5 (9)	52 (2.34)	51 (2.45)	42 (75)	7 (465)	3 (24.5)	39 (2.11)	35 (2.15)	19	77
CUNY - Grad Sch & Univ Center	54.5 (2.52)	57 (2.33)	80.5 (0)	53.5 (8)	64 (2.04)	63 (1.88)	65 (56)	58 (64)	86 (1.1)			56	149
Dartmouth College	56 (2.45)	56 (2.40)	80.5 (0)	55.5 (7)	44 (2.54)	53 (2.33)	48 (67)	88.5 (13)	90 (0.9)			14	26
Boston University	58 (2.42)	55 (2.44)	46 (1)	62 (5)	50 (2.36)	58 (2.08)	59 (61)	81 (23)	72 (2.3)			10	42
University of California-Davis	58 (2.42)	51 (2.58)	80.5 (0)	55.5 (7)	59 (2.14)	54 (2.32)	45 (72)	45.5 (108)	56 (4.0)			27	41
State Univ of New York-Buffalo	58 (2.42)	53.5 (2.48)	80.5 (0)	58.5 (6)	55 (2.29)	49 (2.50)	43 (74)	74 (33)	79.5 (1.7)	37 (2.28)	30 (2.40)	20	123
North Carolina State University	60 (2.36)	67 (1.96)	80.5 (0)	62 (5)	64 (2.04)	67 (1.67)	64 (57)	68 (41)	79.5 (1.7)			24	47

Appendix Table P - 13 Computer Sciences (Continued)

Institution	93Q [1]	93E [1]	% D [1]	% D-S [1]	93Q T [1]	93E T [1]	VIS [1]	TC [2]	C/F [2]	82Q [3]	82E [3]	TF [4]	TG [4]
Arizona State University	61 (2.33)	59 (2.26)	46 (1)	62 (5)	60 (2.10)	67 (1.67)	47 (71)	88.5 (13)	95 (0.5)			27	48
University of Iowa	62 (2.31)	61.5 (2.24)	80.5 (0)	67 (3)	58 (2.18)	59 (2.06)	62 (59)	45.5 (108)	52 (4.5)	45 (1.67)	44 (1.83)	24	32
Texas A&M University	63 (2.30)	58 (2.30)	46 (1)	58.5 (6)	62 (2.07)	61 (1.96)	54.5 (64)	65 (51)	75 (2.1)	54 (1.07)	54 (1.20)	24	110
University of Oregon	64 (2.20)	66 (2.01)	80.5 (0)	75.5 (2)	61 (2.09)	65 (1.75)	54.5 (64)	54.5 (69)	45 (5.3)			13	22
University of Kentucky	65 (2.12)	78.5 (1.67)	80.5 (0)	67 (3)	65 (2.00)	56 (2.17)	59 (61)	72.5 (35)	72 (2.3)			15	35
Virginia Polytech Inst & State U	66 (2.10)	78.5 (1.67)	80.5 (0)	75.5 (2)	69 (1.82)	76 (1.33)	73 (51)	61.5 (56)	60 (3.5)			16	31
Case Western Reserve Univ	67.5 (2.04)	64 (2.10)	46 (1)	64 (4)	72 (1.74)	64 (1.76)	61 (60)	78.5 (26)	70 (2.4)	51 (1.26)	53 (1.27)	11	31
George Washington University	67.5 (2.04)	60 (2.25)	80.5 (0)	75.5 (2)	70 (1.81)	57 (2.14)	66.5 (55)	96.5 (5)	97.5 (0.4)			13	116
University of South Florida	69 (2.03)	74 (1.75)	80.5 (0)	58.5 (6)	73 (1.65)	73 (1.37)	82 (47)	78.5 (26)	78 (1.9)			14	8
Temple University	70.5 (2.00)	92 (1.45)	80.5 (0)	67 (3)	69 (1.82)	76 (1.33)	97 (38)	100.5 (3)	101.5 (0.2)			18	36
Oregon State University	70.5 (2.00)	84 (1.57)	80.5 (0)	75.5 (2)	66 (1.96)	70 (1.50)	70.5 (52)	78.5 (26)	54.5 (4.3)			6	47
Univ of Southwestern Louisiana	72 (1.92)	65 (2.08)	80.5 (0)	75.5 (2)	76 (1.59)	71 (1.47)	63 (58)	78.5 (26)	86 (1.1)			23	60
Vanderbilt University	73 (1.90)	75 (1.74)	80.5 (0)	102 (0)	67 (1.83)	76 (1.33)	73 (51)	33 (180)	7 (18.0)	42 (1.83)	45 (1.82)	10	42
University of Nebraska-Lincoln	74 (1.89)	69 (1.89)	80.5 (0)	75.5 (2)	79 (1.50)	76 (1.33)	87.5 (43)	60 (58)	61 (3.4)			17	13
University of Houston	75 (1.85)	86 (1.54)	80.5 (0)	102 (0)	75 (1.62)	80 (1.22)	73 (51)	92 (9)	95 (0.5)			18	70
University of Texas at Dallas	76 (1.84)	68 (1.92)	80.5 (0)	88.5 (1)	83 (1.38)	95 (0.72)	85.5 (44)	71 (38)	66 (2.7)			14	534
Louisiana State U & A&M College	77.5 (1.81)	70 (1.87)	80.5 (0)	67 (3)	88 (1.25)	96 (0.63)	66.5 (55)	30 (221)	30 (7.6)			29	66
Iowa State University	77.5 (1.81)	72 (1.80)	80.5 (0)	75.5 (2)	74 (1.64)	79 (1.25)	70.5 (52)	39 (149)	24 (9.9)	43 (1.73)	37 (2.07)	15	28
New Mexico State University	79.5 (1.80)	73 (1.77)	80.5 (0)	75.5 (2)	71 (1.78)	72 (1.43)	87.5 (43)	96.5 (5)	97.5 (0.4)			12	25
Wayne State University	79.5 (1.80)	78.5 (1.67)	80.5 (0)	88.5 (1)	87 (1.31)	102 (0.37)	84 (45)	66 (50)	59 (3.6)			14	369
Washington State University	81 (1.78)	91 (1.46)	80.5 (0)	75.5 (2)	77 (1.56)	87 (0.95)	80.5 (48)	42.5 (117)	63.5 (2.9)	48 (1.52)	48.5 (1.62)	41	26
Kansas State University	82 (1.75)	82.5 (1.58)	80.5 (0)	75.5 (2)	86 (1.33)	99 (0.48)	80.5 (48)	86 (15)	82.5 (1.4)	55 (0.85)	55 (0.95)	11	54
University of Central Florida	83 (1.71)	88 (1.52)	80.5 (0)	75.5 (2)	84 (1.35)	87 (0.95)	77.5 (49)	69.5 (40)	68.5 (2.5)			16	28
Naval Postgraduate School	84 (1.67)	93 (1.40)	80.5 (0)	67 (3)	83 (1.38)	83 (1.07)	77.5 (49)	86 (15)	75 (2.1)			7	13
University of Texas at Arlington	85 (1.65)	78.5 (1.67)	80.5 (0)	102 (0)	85 (1.34)	82 (1.19)	85.5 (44)	100.5 (3)	101.5 (0.2)			19	36
University of Kansas	86 (1.62)	71 (1.83)	80.5 (0)	102 (0)	81 (1.45)	78 (1.30)	69 (53)	64 (52)	50 (4.7)	40 (1.93)	43 (1.90)	11	14
University of Alabama-Huntsville	87 (1.61)	94 (1.39)	80.5 (0)	102 (0)	102 (0.89)	91 (0.83)	100.5 (36)	52.5 (80)	48.5 (5.0)			16	22
Old Dominion University	88 (1.55)	90 (1.48)	80.5 (0)	75.5 (2)	91 (1.22)	104 (0.33)	90.5 (42)	63 (55)	58 (3.7)			15	28
U of Maryland Baltimore County	89.5 (1.54)	87 (1.53)	80.5 (0)	88.5 (1)	78 (1.55)	69 (1.54)	68 (54)	86 (15)	88.5 (1.0)			15	126
Southern Methodist University	89.5 (1.54)	78.5 (1.67)	80.5 (0)	102 (0)	97 (1.05)	87 (0.95)	77.5 (49)	90.5 (11)	82.5 (1.4)	47 (1.62)	48.5 (1.62)	8	57

Institution	93Q [1]	93E [1]	% D [1]	% D-S [1]	93Q T [1]	93E T [1]	VIS [1]	TC [2]	C/F [2]	82Q [3]	82E [3]	TF [4]	TG [4]
Illinois Institute of Technology	**91** (1.52)	**82.5** (1.58)	**80.5** (0)	**88.5** (1)	**93** (1.16)	**84** (1.00)	**90.5** (42)	**93** (8)	**91** (0.7)			11	182
University of Connecticut	**92** (1.47)	**85** (1.56)	**80.5** (0)	**88.5** (1)	**80** (1.47)	**82** (1.19)	**97** (38)	**84** (16)	**86** (1.1)	**46** (1.65)	**46.5** (1.67)	15	42
University of South Carolina	**93** (1.36)	**89** (1.49)	**80.5** (0)	**88.5** (1)	**99** (1.00)	**87** (0.95)	**93.5** (41)	**69.5** (40)	**62** (3.3)			12	29
University of North Texas	**94.5** (1.35)	**98.5** (1.04)	**46** (1)	**88.5** (1)	**91** (1.22)	**94** (0.74)	**77.5** (49)	**72.5** (35)	**75** (2.1)			17	39
Florida State University	**94.5** (1.35)	**103.5** (0.83)	**80.5** (0)	**102** (0)	**95** (1.10)	**91** (0.83)	**107** (30)	**94** (7)	**92.5** (0.6)			12	36
Lehigh University	**96** (1.32)	**78.5** (1.67)	**80.5** (0)	**88.5** (1)	**92** (1.20)	**67** (1.67)	**108** (27)	**106.5** (0)	**106.5** (0.0)			11	26
University of Mass-Lowell	**97.5** (1.29)	**97** (1.16)	**80.5** (0)	**102** (0)	**103** (0.85)	**91** (0.83)	**97** (38)	**104** (1)	**103.5** (0.1)			15	52
University of Alabama-Birmingham	**97.5** (1.29)	**101** (0.91)	**80.5** (0)	**102** (0)	**94** (1.12)	**102** (0.37)	**100.5** (36)	**83** (18)	**84** (1.2)			15	22
Mississippi State University	**99** (1.26)	**95** (1.28)	**46** (1)	**88.5** (1)	**101** (0.91)	**108** (0.00)	**102.5** (35)	**103** (2)	**103.5** (0.1)			16	18
Kent State University	**100** (1.25)	**106** (0.52)	**80.5** (0)	**88.5** (1)	**89** (1.23)	**100** (0.46)	**90.5** (42)	**100.5** (3)	**99.5** (0.3)			11	28
University of Oklahoma	**101** (1.17)	**98.5** (1.04)	**80.5** (0)	**88.5** (1)	**105** (0.75)	**98** (0.56)	**105.5** (32)	**96.5** (5)	**92.5** (0.6)	**56** (0.78)	**56** (0.53)	9	24
Tulane University	**102** (1.14)	**105** (0.63)	**80.5** (0)	**102** (0)	**101** (0.91)	**104** (0.33)	**83** (46)	**82** (20)	**68.5** (2.5)			8	46
Stevens Inst of Technology	**103.5** (1.13)	**96** (1.23)	**80.5** (0)	**88.5** (1)	**99** (1.00)	**91** (0.83)	**104** (33)	**90.5** (11)	**88.5** (1.0)	**53** (1.17)	**51** (1.43)	11	50
Worcester Polytechnic Inst	**103.5** (1.13)	**103.5** (0.83)	**80.5** (0)	**102** (0)	**96** (1.07)	**91** (0.83)	**105.5** (32)	**100.5** (3)	**99.5** (0.3)			12	14
University of Missouri-Rolla	**105.5** (1.10)	**100** (1.03)	**80.5** (0)	**88.5** (1)	**106** (0.74)	**105** (0.28)	**90.5** (42)	**96.5** (5)	**95** (0.5)	**52** (1.21)	**52** (1.35)	10	18
State Univ of New York-Binghamton	**105.5** (1.10)	**102** (0.88)	**80.5** (0)	**88.5** (1)	**104** (0.82)	**98** (0.56)	**95** (39)	**106.5** (0)	**106.5** (0.0)			8	33
New Mexico Inst of Mining & Tech	**107** (0.52)	**108** (0.00)	**80.5** (0)	**102** (0)	**107** (0.13)	**108** (0.00)	**93.5** (41)	**106.5** (0)	**106.5** (0.0)			5	11
Oklahoma State University	**108** (0.21)	**107** (0.11)	**80.5** (0)	**102** (0)	**108** (0.07)	**106** (0.24)	**102.5** (35)	**106.5** (0)	**106.5** (0.0)			3	116

Sources: 1. National Survey of Graduate Faculty
2. Institute for Scientific Information
3. 1982 Survey of Graduate Faculty
4. Institutional Coordinator Data

Notes: *a.* Program in Decision Sciences, Wharton School
b. Program in Computer and Information Science

Appendix Table P - 14 Relative Rankings for Research-Doctorate Programs in Ecology, Evolution, and Behavior

Institution	93Q [1]	93E [1]	% D [1]	% D-S [1]	93Q T [1]	93E T [1]	VIS [1]	TC [2]	C/F [2]	82Q [3]	82E [3]	TF [4]	TG [4]
Stanford University	**1.5*** (4.51)	**4** (4.23)	**1** (55)	**3** (86)	**3** (4.49)	**4.5** (4.27)	**1.5** (96)	**34.5** (961)	**2** (96.1)			10	n/a
University of Chicago	**1.5*** (4.51)	**2** (4.31)	**2.5** (47)	**12** (61)	**1** (4.61)	**1** (4.37)	**34** (73)	**36** (932)	**27** (31.1)			30	39
Duke University	**3** (4.49)	**1** (4.33)	**4** (46)	**4** (83)	**2** (4.52)	**2.5** (4.31)	**6** (89)	**9** (2180)	**18** (35.2)			62	171
Cornell University	**4** (4.44)	**3** (4.24)	**2.5** (47)	**2** (87)	**4** (4.48)	**2.5** (4.31)	**1.5** (96)	**3** (4983)	**4** (54.2)			92	7
University of California-Davis	**5** (4.42)	**8** (4.12)	**5** (43)	**1** (88)	**5** (4.44)	**7** (4.23)	**3** (94)	**2** (5393)	**33** (27.4)			197	288
Princeton University	**6** (4.34)	**10** (3.96)	**6.5** (38)	**10** (67)	**6** (4.37)	**9** (3.97)	**21** (79)	**106.5** (93)	**95.5** (8.5)			11	26
University of Washington	**7** (4.30)	**5** (4.20)	**6.5** (38)	**5** (77)	**8** (4.28)	**6** (4.24)	**6** (89)	**20** (1457)	**16** (35.5)			41	119
University of California-Berkeley	**8** (4.29)	**6** (4.15)	**8** (36)	**6** (76)	**7** (4.30)	**8** (4.10)	**8** (88)	**10** (1855)	**23** (32.5)			57	283
University of Wisconsin-Madison	**9** (4.18)	**7** (4.13)	**9** (29)	**7.5** (71)	**10** (4.23)	**4.5** (4.27)	**10** (86)	**4** (3532)	**10** (39.2)			90	123
State U of New York-Stony Brook	**10.5** (4.12)	**11** (3.86)	**11** (24)	**7.5** (71)	**9** (4.27)	**10** (3.93)	**10** (86)	**32** (991)	**20.5** (34.2)			29	46
University of Texas at Austin	**10.5** (4.12)	**13** (3.77)	**12** (23)	**14.5** (58)	**11** (4.22)	**11.5** (3.92)	**27.5** (76)	**30** (1029)	**50.5** (19.1)			54	89
University of Michigan	**12** (4.10)	**9** (3.98)	**10** (27)	**9** (70)	**12** (4.05)	**11.5** (3.92)	**4** (91)	**19** (1532)	**31** (29.5)			52	100
Washington University	**13** (3.94)	**16** (3.69)	**13** (19)	**14.5** (58)	**13** (4.02)	**17** (3.73)	**16.5** (81)	**38** (858)	**15** (35.8)			24	35
University of Pennsylvania	**14** (3.90)	**17.5** (3.67)	**15.5** (17)	**16.5** (56)	**20** (3.84)	**19** (3.67)	**18.5** (80)	**6** (2767)	**6** (50.3)			55	58
University of Minnesota	**15** (3.88)	**13** (3.77)	**19.5** (12)	**13** (59)	**18** (3.88)	**14** (3.86)	**21** (79)	**17** (1551)	**44** (23.5)			66	91
University of Georgia	**16** (3.87)	**15** (3.72)	**15.5** (17)	**11** (66)	**15.5** (3.91)	**15** (3.80)	**6** (89)	**7** (2603)	**28** (31.0)			84	137
Yale University	**17** (3.83)	**19** (3.66)	**15.5** (17)	**18.5** (55)	**22** (3.78)	**18** (3.72)	**16.5** (81)	**1** (9758)	**1** (165.4)			59	122
Univ of California-Los Angeles	**18.5** (3.82)	**17.5** (3.67)	**15.5** (17)	**18.5** (55)	**23** (3.77)	**21** (3.63)	**14** (83)	**14** (1597)	**11** (39.0)			41	73
Univ of California-San Diego	**18.5** (3.82)	**28** (3.50)	**18** (14)	**20.5** (53)	**17** (3.89)	**34.5** (3.44)	**23** (78)	**24** (1313)	**22** (33.7)			39	15
Univ of California-Santa Barbara	**20** (3.81)	**21.5** (3.63)	**21** (11)	**24** (46)	**15.5** (3.91)	**16** (3.76)	**37** (71)	**33** (979)	**19** (35.0)			28	77
University of Arizona	**21** (3.80)	**13** (3.77)	**24.5** (7)	**16.5** (56)	**14** (3.96)	**13** (3.87)	**24.5** (77)	**40** (817)	**26** (31.4)			26	61
University of California-Irvine	**22** (3.77)	**21.5** (3.63)	**22.5** (8)	**22** (51)	**19** (3.86)	**20** (3.64)	**27.5** (76)	**43** (718)	**20.5** (34.2)			21	28
Oregon State University	**23** (3.74)	**20** (3.64)	**19.5** (12)	**20.5** (53)	**24.5** (3.65)	**22** (3.59)	**12.5** (84)	**16** (1582)	**77** (12.5)			127	124
University of Utah	**24** (3.65)	**25** (3.56)	**27.5** (6)	**26** (41)	**21** (3.81)	**26** (3.54)	**45.5** (66)	**69** (270)	**54.5** (16.9)			16	48(1)
Rutgers State Univ-New Brunswick	**26** (3.60)	**49** (3.24)	**31.5** (5)	**25** (43)	**24.5** (3.65)	**53** (3.20)	**24.5** (77)	**39** (850)	**47** (21.8)			39	62
Univ of California-Riverside	**26** (3.60)	**27** (3.51)	**44** (3)	**28** (37)	**26** (3.61)	**24** (3.57)	**40.5** (69)	**45** (679)	**34** (26.1)			26	35
Pennsylvania State University [b]	**26** (3.60)	**26** (3.55)	**44** (3)	**39.5** (28)	**27** (3.58)	**33** (3.45)	**77** (49)	**8** (2409)	**35** (25.9)			93	7
University of Florida	**28** (3.57)	**36** (3.43)	**31.5** (5)	**23** (48)	**29** (3.51)	**38** (3.37)	**10** (86)	**22** (1352)	**29.5** (30.0)			45	57
U of Illinois at Urbana-Champaign	**29** (3.52)	**23.5** (3.62)	**22.5** (8)	**30** (35)	**30** (3.47)	**23** (3.58)	**18.5** (80)	**13** (1626)	**46** (22.0)			74	58
Indiana University	**30** (3.49)	**29** (3.49)	**31.5** (5)	**32** (33)	**28** (3.57)	**47** (3.27)	**40.5** (69)	**29** (1069)	**8** (39.6)			27	0

Appendix Table P - 14 Ecology, Evolution, and Behavior (Continued)

Institution	93Q[1]	93E[1]	% D[1]	% D-S[1]	93Q T[1]	93E T[1]	VIS[1]	TC[2]	C/F[2]	82Q[3]	82E[3]	TF[4]	TG[4]
University of Kansas	**31.5** (3.46)	**23.5** (3.62)	**27.5** (6)	**29** (36)	**34** (3.42)	**25** (3.55)	**21** (79)	**55** (379)	**99.5** (8.2)			46	67
University of Colorado	**31.5** (3.46)	**40.5** (3.37)	**31.5** (5)	**31** (34)	**32** (3.43)	**37** (3.38)	**34** (73)	**27** (1218)	**24** (32.1)			38	86
Florida State University	**34** (3.41)	**44** (3.29)	**24.5** (7)	**37** (29)	**36** (3.38)	**49** (3.26)	**50** (64)	**59** (334)	**48** (20.9)			16	15
Michigan State University	**34** (3.41)	**32.5** (3.45)	**36** (4)	**39.5** (28)	**41** (3.31)	**31** (3.50)	**50** (64)	**18** (1533)	**9** (39.3)			39	n/a
Arizona State University	**34** (3.41)	**42** (3.33)	**36** (4)	**27** (39)	**43** (3.25)	**43** (3.33)	**30** (75)	**51** (451)	**66** (14.1)			32	58
U of Massachusetts at Amherst	**36.5** (3.39)	**36** (3.43)	**27.5** (6)	**35.5** (30)	**41** (3.31)	**43** (3.33)	**15** (82)	**37** (926)	**65** (14.2)			65	105
Utah State University	**36.5** (3.39)	**38** (3.41)	**53.5** (2)	**39.5** (28)	**38** (3.36)	**43** (3.33)	**43** (68)	**42** (764)	**83** (10.9)			70	17
Washington State University	**38** (3.37)	**34** (3.44)	**36** (4)	**42.5** (27)	**35** (3.39)	**29** (3.51)	**38** (70)	**5** (3165)	**13** (37.7)			84	47
University of Connecticut	**40** (3.35)	**31** (3.46)	**44** (3)	**44.5** (26)	**32** (3.43)	**28** (3.53)	**34** (73)	**74** (236)	**97** (8.4)			28	35
University of Tennessee-Knoxville	**40** (3.35)	**45** (3.26)	**44** (3)	**35.5** (30)	**37** (3.37)	**49** (3.26)	**40.5** (69)	**34.5** (961)	**60** (15.8)			61	56
Northern Arizona University	**40** (3.35)	**32.5** (3.45)	**44** (3)	**39.5** (28)	**32** (3.43)	**31** (3.50)	**54.5** (58)	**48** (532)	**40** (24.2)			22	21
U of North Carolina-Chapel Hill	**42** (3.33)	**36** (3.43)	**44** (3)	**42.5** (27)	**46** (3.23)	**35** (3.44)	**31.5** (74)	**54** (388)	**67** (13.9)			28	44
Pennsylvania State University	**43** (3.31)	**30** (3.47)	**36** (4)	**44.5** (26)	**41** (3.31)	**36** (3.40)	**40.5** (69)	**15** (1586)	**63** (14.6)			109	17
Brown University	**44** (3.30)	**46.5** (3.25)	**53.5** (2)	**47** (25)	**39** (3.35)	**51** (3.22)	**58.5** (56)	**79** (184)	**56** (16.7)			11	16
University of Maryland College Park	**45** (3.28)	**40.5** (3.37)	**69.5** (1)	**33.5** (31)	**45** (3.24)	**28** (3.53)	**12.5** (84)	**21** (1356)	**49** (19.4)			70	103
Ohio State University	**46** (3.27)	**57.5** (3.11)	**36** (4)	**33.5** (31)	**48** (3.13)	**63** (3.04)	**27.5** (76)	**23** (1346)	**75** (12.8)			105	94
University of New Mexico	**47** (3.24)	**39** (3.40)	**44** (3)	**47** (25)	**47** (3.19)	**32** (3.48)	**31.5** (74)	**44** (690)	**45** (23.0)			30	65
North Carolina State University	**48** (3.20)	**43** (3.30)	**44** (3)	**49** (24)	**50** (3.11)	**54** (3.18)	**45.5** (66)	**12** (1783)	**41** (23.8)			75	10
University of Virginia	**49** (3.14)	**49** (3.24)	**53.5** (2)	**50** (22)	**53** (3.03)	**43** (3.33)	**47.5** (65)	**31** (994)	**42** (23.7)			42	47
University of Oklahoma	**50** (3.11)	**57.5** (3.11)	**105.5** (0)	**47** (25)	**51** (3.09)	**56** (3.12)	**27.5** (76)	**56** (355)	**92.5** (8.7)			41	56
State Univ of New York-Albany	**51.5** (3.10)	**56** (3.12)	**69.5** (1)	**60** (13)	**49** (3.12)	**43** (3.33)	**85.5** (45)	**97** (115)	**64** (14.4)			8	14
Purdue University	**51.5** (3.10)	**46.5** (3.25)	**105.5** (0)	**52** (18)	**58** (2.97)	**55** (3.14)	**44** (67)	**41** (801)	**43** (23.6)			34	46
Syracuse University	**53** (3.09)	**66.5** (2.96)	**44** (3)	**56** (14)	**45** (3.24)	**65** (2.96)	**67.5** (54)	**76** (210)	**29.5** (30.0)			7	14
University of Kentucky[a]	**54.5** (3.04)	**68** (2.95)	**69.5** (1)	**63** (12)	**53** (3.03)	**75** (2.82)	**56** (57)	**67** (288)	**54.5** (16.9)			17	22
University of Vermont	**54.5** (3.04)	**72** (2.89)	**69.5** (1)	**60** (13)	**55** (3.00)	**69** (2.92)	**52.5** (62)	**50** (487)	**52** (18.0)			27	21
Iowa State University	**56.5** (3.00)	**62.5** (3.00)	**105.5** (0)	**56** (14)	**58** (2.97)	**61** (3.06)	**74** (50)	**64** (296)	**79** (11.8)			25	34
University of Wyoming	**56.5** (3.00)	**51** (3.18)	**105.5** (0)	**56** (14)	**61** (2.93)	**51** (3.22)	**58.5** (56)	**61** (321)	**99.5** (8.2)			39	34
Colorado State University	**58** (2.99)	**71** (2.91)	**53.5** (2)	**51** (19)	**66** (2.82)	**70** (2.90)	**36** (72)	**52** (418)	**37** (24.6)			17	53
University of Nebraska-Lincoln	**59** (2.96)	**88** (2.69)	**53.5** (2)	**72** (9)	**60** (2.94)	**79** (2.72)	**67.5** (54)	**100** (103)	**113** (6.1)			17	15
University of Rochester	**60** (2.95)	**75** (2.87)	**105.5** (0)	**79** (7)	**55** (3.00)	**64** (2.98)	**79.5** (48)	**49** (530)	**7** (44.2)			12	23

Institution	93Q [1]	93E [1]	% D [1]	% D-S [1]	93Q T [1]	93E T [1]	VIS [1]	TC [2]	C/F [2]	82Q [3]	82E [3]	TF [4]	TG [4]
University of Iowa	**61.5** (2.94)	**54.5** (3.14)	**44** (3)	**67.5** (10)	**64** (2.84)	**58** (3.10)	**74** (50)	**25** (1264)	**12** (38.3)			33	4
University of Hawaii at Manoa	**61.5** (2.94)	**60** (3.05)	**53.5** (2)	**67.5** (10)	**62** (2.88)	**58** (3.10)	**67.5** (54)	**46** (638)	**88** (10.0)			64	56
Univ of California-Santa Cruz	**63** (2.93)	**69** (2.93)	**69.5** (1)	**60** (13)	**56** (2.98)	**58** (3.10)	**47.5** (65)	**71** (267)	**39** (24.3)			11	31
Louisiana State U & A&M College	**64** (2.91)	**61** (3.03)	**69.5** (1)	**56** (14)	**64** (2.84)	**71** (2.89)	**54.5** (58)	**28** (1210)	**58.5** (16.4)			74	84
CUNY - Grad Sch & Univ Center	**65.5** (2.87)	**64** (2.99)	**69.5** (1)	**63** (12)	**72** (2.67)	**82** (2.67)	**77** (49)	**83** (171)	**114** (4.8)			36	56
University of South Carolina	**65.5** (2.87)	**54.5** (3.14)	**69.5** (1)	**76** (8)	**71** (2.68)	**51** (3.22)	**77** (49)	**65** (294)	**75** (12.8)			23	24
State Univ of New York-Binghamton	**67** (2.86)	**80.5** (2.81)	**105.5** (0)	**67.5** (10)	**58** (2.97)	**73** (2.86)	**79.5** (48)	**84** (164)	**58.5** (16.4)			10	9
Johns Hopkins University	**68.5** (2.83)	**53** (3.15)	**69.5** (1)	**72** (9)	**74** (2.65)	**60** (3.08)	**94.5** (39)	**53** (396)	**32** (28.3)			14	n/a
University of Alaska	**68.5** (2.83)	**52** (3.16)	**105.5** (0)	**67.5** (10)	**64** (2.84)	**43** (3.33)	**62** (55)	**78** (199)	**92.5** (8.7)			23	n/a
Virginia Polytech Inst & State U	**70** (2.80)	**75** (2.87)	**69.5** (1)	**53** (16)	**75** (2.63)	**80** (2.68)	**52.5** (62)	**60** (325)	**50.5** (19.1)			17	11
University of Missouri-Columbia	**72** (2.79)	**83** (2.78)	**69.5** (1)	**72** (9)	**68** (2.71)	**77** (2.78)	**81.5** (47)	**92** (133)	**57** (16.6)			8	12
Texas Tech University	**72** (2.79)	**66.5** (2.96)	**69.5** (1)	**76** (8)	**69** (2.70)	**73** (2.86)	**74** (50)	**66** (289)	**82** (11.1)			26	38
University of Kentucky [b]	**72** (2.79)	**70** (2.92)	**105.5** (0)	**91** (5)	**82** (2.50)	**43** (3.33)	**124** (21)	**26** (1226)	**14** (37.2)			33	56
University of Nevada, Reno	**74** (2.74)	**78** (2.83)	**69.5** (1)	**63** (12)	**68** (2.71)	**77** (2.78)	**50** (64)	**99** (107)	**115** (4.3)			25	25
Vanderbilt University	**75** (2.73)	**94.5** (2.57)	**105.5** (0)	**91** (5)	**74** (2.65)	**84** (2.62)	**85.5** (45)	**85.5** (161)	**78** (12.4)			13	15
Miami University	**76** (2.67)	**65** (2.98)	**105.5** (0)	**65** (11)	**79** (2.57)	**69** (2.92)	**67.5** (54)	**82** (174)	**71.5** (13.4)			13	31
Dartmouth College	**77** (2.65)	**85.5** (2.73)	**69.5** (1)	**72** (9)	**70** (2.69)	**88** (2.55)	**67.5** (54)	**81** (177)	**17** (35.4)			5	10
Univ of Southwestern Louisiana	**78** (2.64)	**97** (2.44)	**105.5** (0)	**101** (3)	**77** (2.60)	**99** (2.29)	**111** (31)	**72.5** (255)	**80** (11.6)			22	19
Rutgers State Univ-Newark	**80** (2.61)	**59** (3.10)	**69.5** (1)	**83.5** (6)	**79** (2.57)	**77** (2.78)	**94.5** (39)	**62** (317)	**38** (24.4)			13	20
Texas A&M University	**80** (2.61)	**82** (2.80)	**69.5** (1)	**76** (8)	**90** (2.36)	**88** (2.55)	**58.5** (56)	**11** (1839)	**5** (51.1)			36	25
Clemson University	**80** (2.61)	**80.5** (2.81)	**105.5** (0)	**107** (2)	**80** (2.53)	**82** (2.67)	**72** (51)	**116** (65)	**123** (2.5)			26	38
Idaho State University	**82** (2.60)	**87** (2.71)	**105.5** (0)	**79** (7)	**93** (2.32)	**95** (2.43)	**89** (44)	**109** (83)	**127** (2.0)			41	8
Tulane University	**83** (2.58)	**94.5** (2.57)	**69.5** (1)	**83.5** (6)	**87** (2.45)	**97** (2.36)	**62** (55)	**117** (62)	**110** (6.9)			9	45[(2)]
University of Alabama	**84.5** (2.57)	**93** (2.62)	**105.5** (0)	**83.5** (6)	**91** (2.35)	**102** (2.22)	**94.5** (39)	**95** (118)	**104** (7.9)			15	17
Kansas State University	**84.5** (2.57)	**62.5** (3.00)	**105.5** (0)	**91** (5)	**84** (2.48)	**63** (3.04)	**67.5** (54)	**90** (148)	**84.5** (10.6)			14	9
Wake Forest University	**86** (2.56)	**85.5** (2.73)	**105.5** (0)	**91** (5)	**108** (2.00)	**102** (2.22)	**122.5** (23)	**85.5** (161)	**86.5** (10.1)			16	28
Claremont Graduate School	**88** (2.54)	**49** (3.24)	**27.5** (6)	**56** (14)	**82** (2.50)	**43** (3.33)	**81.5** (47)	**108** (87)	**53** (17.4)			5	7
Boston University	**88** (2.54)	**84** (2.75)	**69.5** (1)	**91** (5)	**87** (2.45)	**82** (2.67)	**85.5** (45)	**91** (137)	**61** (15.2)			9	24
University of South Florida	**88** (2.54)	**90.5** (2.65)	**105.5** (0)	**101** (3)	**85** (2.47)	**92** (2.50)	**67.5** (54)	**93** (127)	**84.5** (10.6)			12	n/a
University of Maine	**90** (2.52)	**92** (2.63)	**105.5** (0)	**83.5** (6)	**76** (2.62)	**86** (2.59)	**67.5** (54)	**47** (548)	**69** (13.7)			40	29

Appendix Table P - 14 Ecology, Evolution, and Behavior (Continued)

Institution	93Q [1]	93E [1]	% D [1]	% D-S [1]	93Q T [1]	93E T [1]	VIS [1]	TC [2]	C/F [2]	82Q [3]	82E [3]	TF [4]	TG [4]
University of Montana	**91** (2.51)	**79** (2.82)	**105.5** (0)	**101** (3)	**84** (2.48)	**67** (2.94)	**62** (55)	**80** (180)	**94** (8.6)			21	14
University of Pittsburgh	**92** (2.42)	**98** (2.38)	**105.5** (0)	**91** (5)	**103** (2.10)	**117** (1.67)	**94.5** (39)	**103** (98)	**91** (8.9)			11	52
George Mason University	**93** (2.41)	**89** (2.67)	**105.5** (0)	**97** (4)	**95** (2.30)	**92** (2.50)	**106.5** (33)	**87** (159)	**116.5** (4.2)			38	87
Bowling Green State University	**94** (2.40)	**96** (2.50)	**105.5** (0)	**97** (4)	**97** (2.25)	**96** (2.41)	**104** (35)	**101.5** (102)	**95.5** (8.5)			12	10
Southern Illinois University	**96** (2.39)	**90.5** (2.65)	**69.5** (1)	**107** (2)	**98** (2.24)	**92** (2.50)	**58.5** (56)	**114** (68)	**125.5** (2.1)			33	41
Wayne State University	**96** (2.39)	**104** (2.26)	**105.5** (0)	**107** (2)	**100** (2.22)	**106** (2.12)	**94.5** (39)	**57** (354)	**73** (13.1)			27	55
Oklahoma State University	**96** (2.39)	**75** (2.87)	**105.5** (0)	**116.5** (1)	**88** (2.40)	**86** (2.59)	**99.5** (38)	**68** (287)	**69** (13.7)			21	66
University of Notre Dame	**98** (2.37)	**75** (2.87)	**53.5** (2)	**79** (7)	**100** (2.22)	**73** (2.86)	**85.5** (45)	**105** (96)	**69** (13.7)			7	17
California Institute Technology	**99** (2.35)	**115** (2.00)	**44** (3)	**72** (9)	**102** (2.11)	**102** (2.22)	**106.5** (33)	**58** (349)	**3** (87.3)			4	0
Univ of Missouri-Saint Louis	**100** (2.33)	**99** (2.35)	**69.5** (1)	**97** (4)	**89** (2.38)	**99** (2.29)	**99.5** (38)	**126** (30)	**121** (3.0)			10	17
SUNY Col Environ Sci & Forestry	**101** (2.27)	**75** (2.87)	**105.5** (0)	**83.5** (6)	**93** (2.32)	**66** (2.95)	**103** (36)	**63** (298)	**36** (24.8)			12	26
University of Houston	**102** (2.24)	**108** (2.12)	**53.5** (2)	**91** (5)	**93** (2.32)	**102** (2.22)	**102** (37)	**119** (56)	**89** (9.3)			6	6
State Univ of New York-Buffalo	**103** (2.17)	**110** (2.08)	**105.5** (0)	**116.5** (1)	**108** (2.00)	**110** (1.88)	**115** (29)	**101.5** (102)	**75** (12.8)			8	9
Old Dominion University	**104** (2.16)	**102.5** (2.31)	**69.5** (1)	**107** (2)	**100** (2.22)	**107** (2.08)	**113.5** (30)	**118** (59)	**116.5** (4.2)			14	15
Brigham Young University	**105.5** (2.14)	**106** (2.22)	**105.5** (0)	**91** (5)	**110** (1.92)	**104** (2.18)	**94.5** (39)	**88** (157)	**81** (11.2)			14	8
University of Idaho	**105.5** (2.14)	**120** (1.67)	**105.5** (0)	**116.5** (1)	**106** (2.05)	**117** (1.67)	**90** (42)	**115** (66)	**98** (8.3)			8	2
Ohio University	**107** (2.13)	**100.5** (2.33)	**105.5** (0)	**107** (2)	**104** (2.07)	**92** (2.50)	**85.5** (45)	**94** (123)	**112** (6.2)			20	14
Univ of Arkansas-Fayetteville	**108** (2.12)	**113** (2.03)	**105.5** (0)	**107** (2)	**113** (1.78)	**109** (2.04)	**99.5** (38)	**112** (76)	**119** (3.5)			22	25
University of Cincinnati	**109** (2.11)	**100.5** (2.33)	**105.5** (0)	**101** (3)	**96** (2.26)	**92** (2.50)	**108.5** (32)	**70** (268)	**71.5** (13.4)			20	12
Saint Louis University	**110** (2.06)	**123.5** (1.25)	**69.5** (1)	**116.5** (1)	**108** (2.00)	**117** (1.67)	**125** (20)	**125** (31)	**124** (2.4)			13	17
New Mexico State University	**111.5** (2.00)	**112** (2.05)	**105.5** (0)	**91** (5)	**115** (1.72)	**111** (1.81)	**85.5** (45)	**113** (70)	**122** (2.9)			24	41
Mississippi State University	**111.5** (2.00)	**116** (1.96)	**105.5** (0)	**116.5** (1)	**106** (2.05)	**106** (2.12)	**105** (34)	**98** (113)	**106** (7.5)			15	6
Illinois State University	**113** (1.91)	**114** (2.02)	**105.5** (0)	**126** (0)	**111** (1.88)	**108** (2.05)	**99.5** (38)	**77** (208)	**62** (14.9)			14	n/a
University of New Hampshire	**114.5** (1.88)	**117** (1.95)	**105.5** (0)	**101** (3)	**117** (1.62)	**117** (1.67)	**113.5** (30)	**121** (48)	**103** (8.0)			6	n/a
Kent State University	**114.5** (1.88)	**102.5** (2.31)	**105.5** (0)	**116.5** (1)	**117** (1.62)	**92** (2.50)	**108.5** (32)	**110** (81)	**86.5** (10.1)			8	11
Drexel University	**116** (1.83)	**126** (0.83)	**69.5** (1)	**83.5** (6)	**114** (1.74)	**125** (0.83)	**91** (40)	**128** (5)	**128** (1.7)			3	n/a
Howard University	**117** (1.80)	**122** (1.33)	**105.5** (0)	**116.5** (1)	**112** (1.86)	**125** (0.83)	**126** (19)	**75** (214)	**107** (7.4)			29	22
University of North Texas	**118** (1.72)	**106** (2.22)	**105.5** (0)	**116.5** (1)	**118** (1.56)	**117** (1.67)	**111** (31)	**111** (79)	**108.5** (7.2)			11	47
University of Alabama-Birmingham	**119** (1.68)	**106** (2.22)	**105.5** (0)	**107** (2)	**124** (1.25)	**117** (1.67)	**128** (17)	**89** (153)	**101.5** (8.1)			19	n/a
Montana State University	**120** (1.63)	**110** (2.08)	**105.5** (0)	**126** (0)	**125** (1.10)	**117** (1.67)	**121** (24)	**106.5** (93)	**105** (7.8)			12	11

Institution	93Q [1]	93E [1]	% D [1]	% D-S [1]	93Q T [1]	93E T [1]	VIS [1]	TC [2]	C/F [2]	82Q [3]	82E [3]	TF [4]	TG [4]
North Dakota State University	**121** (1.61)	**120** (1.67)	**69.5** (1)	**116.5** (1)	**120** (1.37)	**123** (1.11)	**111** (31)	**96** (116)	**111** (6.8)			17	31
Univ of Southern Mississippi	**122** (1.50)	**118** (1.88)	**105.5** (0)	**126** (0)	**121** (1.36)	**117** (1.67)	**120** (25)	**123** (41)	**120** (3.4)			12	47
Fordham University	**123** (1.45)	**127** (0.63)	**105.5** (0)	**116.5** (1)	**123** (1.27)	**127** (0.28)	**116** (28)	**127** (21)	**125.5** (2.1)			10	64(2)
Univ of Puerto Rico-Rio Piedras	**124** (1.31)	**120** (1.67)	**105.5** (0)	**126** (0)	**119** (1.40)	**117** (1.67)	**122.5** (23)	**124** (35)	**118** (3.9)			9	n/a
Clark University	**125** (1.20)	**125** (0.95)	**105.5** (0)	**116.5** (1)	**122** (1.33)	**122** (1.33)	**118.5** (26)	**122** (43)	**108.5** (7.2)			6	5
Loma Linda University	**126** (1.17)	**110** (2.08)	**105.5** (0)	**126** (0)	**126** (1.00)	**117** (1.67)	**127** (18)	**104** (97)	**101.5** (8.1)			12	15
University of Dayton	**127** (1.16)	**123.5** (1.25)	**105.5** (0)	**116.5** (1)	**127** (0.83)	**125** (0.83)	**117** (27)	**120** (55)	**90** (9.2)			6	1
New York Medical College	**128** (0.50)	(n/s)	**105.5** (0)	**126** (0)	**128** (0.33)	(n/s)	**129** (9)	**72.5** (255)	**25** (31.9)			8	6
University of Tulsa	**129** (0.47)	**128** (0.00)	**105.5** (0)	**126** (0)	**129** (0.25)	**128** (0.00)	**118.5** (26)	**129** (0)	**129** (0.0)			2	1

Sources:
1. National Survey of Graduate Faculty
2. Institute for Scientific Information
3. 1982 Survey of Graduate Faculty
4. Institutional Coordinator Data

Notes: *a.* School of Arts and Sciences
b. School of Agriculture

n/s After trimming no cases remained

(1) Combined enrollment for programs in Biochemistry and Molecular Biology and Ecology, Evolution, and Behavior
(2) Combined enrollment for programs in Cell and Developmental Biology and Ecology, Evolution, and Behavior

* Two programs recieved the highest quality rating, and using the standard convention of average rankings, each program was given a rank of 1.5.

Appendix Table P - 15 Relative Rankings for Research-Doctorate Programs in Economics

Institution	93Q [1]	93E [1]	% D [1]	% D-S [1]	93Q T [1]	93E T [1]	VIS [1]	TC [2]	C/F [2]	82Q [3]	82E [3]	TF [4]	TG [4]
University of Chicago	1.5* (4.95)	3 (4.63)	1 (94)	4 (98)	1 (5.00)	1 (4.73)	5.5 (100)	3 (734)	2 (23.7)	4 (4.83)	2 (4.52)	31	216
Harvard University	1.5* (4.95)	5 (4.33)	2 (92)	2 (99)	2 (4.99)	5 (4.27)	5.5 (100)	2 (1022)	3 (23.2)	2 (4.90)	7 (3.97)	44	148
Massachusetts Inst of Technology	3 (4.93)	1 (4.71)	3 (91)	4 (98)	3 (4.96)	3 (4.70)	5.5 (100)	7 (629)	4 (22.5)	1 (4.99)	1 (4.77)	28	161
Stanford University	4 (4.92)	4 (4.58)	4 (90)	1 (100)	4 (4.91)	4 (4.49)	5.5 (100)	11 (581)	7 (16.1)	3 (4.84)	3.5 (4.32)	36	146
Princeton University	5 (4.84)	2 (4.69)	5 (83)	4 (98)	5 (4.82)	2 (4.71)	5.5 (100)	15 (530)	15 (12.9)	5 (4.79)	3.5 (4.32)	41	91
Yale University	6 (4.70)	9 (4.01)	6 (68)	6 (97)	6 (4.77)	11 (3.89)	12.5 (99)	10 (587)	13 (13.3)	6 (4.73)	6 (4.08)	44	130
University of California-Berkeley	7 (4.55)	7 (4.05)	7 (59)	7 (95)	7 (4.56)	8 (3.97)	5.5 (100)	6 (631)	9 (15.4)	11 (4.07)	10 (3.80)	41	150
University of Pennsylvania	8 (4.43)	11 (3.91)	8 (47)	8 (93)	8.5 (4.39)	13 (3.81)	12.5 (99)	5 (663)	14 (13.0)	8 (4.27)	11 (3.70)	51	178
Northwestern University	9 (4.39)	8 (4.04)	9 (43)	9 (90)	8.5 (4.39)	9 (3.92)	21.5 (96)	4 (668)	12 (14.2)	10 (4.09)	12 (3.68)	47	103
University of Minnesota	10 (4.22)	6 (4.08)	10 (33)	11 (85)	10 (4.21)	7 (4.06)	15.5 (98)	51 (78)	44 (4.3)	7 (4.36)	5 (4.12)	18	108
Univ of California-Los Angeles	11 (4.12)	16 (3.55)	12.5 (22)	10 (89)	11 (4.05)	16 (3.43)	12.5 (99)	9 (622)	19 (9.7)	13 (4.05)	14 (3.52)	64	101
Columbia University	12 (4.07)	17 (3.43)	11 (28)	13 (80)	14 (3.90)	21 (3.16)	5.5 (100)	46 (94)	66.5 (2.6)	9 (4.18)	15 (3.45)	36	141
University of Michigan	13 (4.03)	15 (3.65)	12.5 (22)	12 (82)	12.5 (3.95)	15 (3.48)	5.5 (100)	13 (567)	16 (12.3)	15 (3.86)	13 (3.55)	46	115
University of Rochester	14 (4.01)	10 (3.96)	14 (21)	15 (76)	15 (3.89)	10 (3.91)	18.5 (97)	16 (420)	8 (15.6)	14 (3.89)	9 (3.82)	27	121
University of Wisconsin-Madison	15 (3.93)	14 (3.79)	15 (18)	14 (78)	12.5 (3.95)	14 (3.71)	5.5 (100)	21 (219)	21.5 (7.8)	12 (4.06)	8 (3.90)	28	175
Univ of California-San Diego	16 (3.80)	12 (3.83)	16 (13)	16 (65)	16 (3.79)	12 (3.82)	27 (93)	12 (570)	5 (19.0)	18 (3.18)	20 (3.00)	30	61
New York University	17 (3.62)	22 (3.22)	27 (2)	17 (61)	18 (3.65)	20 (3.23)	5.5 (100)	19 (276)	23 (7.5)	16 (3.42)	30.5 (2.60)	37	54
Cornell University	18 (3.56)	19 (3.36)	20.5 (4)	18 (55)	19 (3.54)	18 (3.30)	18.5 (97)	25 (199)	26.5 (6.6)	20 (3.16)	22 (2.97)	30	75
California Institute Technology	19 (3.54)	13 (3.81)	17 (7)	19 (50)	17 (3.67)	6 (4.11)	31.5 (88)	31 (149)	28 (6.5)	24 (2.95)	18 (3.12)	23	14
University of Maryland College Park	20 (3.46)	27 (2.99)	18.5 (5)	20 (49)	21 (3.39)	30 (2.75)	18.5 (97)	1 (1516)	1 (32.3)	19 (3.18)	28 (2.67)	47	168
Boston University	21 (3.39)	32 (2.76)	20.5 (4)	21 (48)	20 (3.46)	31.5 (2.70)	24.5 (94)	8 (624)	6 (17.3)	37 (2.30)	36.5 (2.25)	36	112
Duke University	22 (3.36)	20 (3.29)	18.5 (5)	22 (39)	23 (3.19)	25 (2.91)	18.5 (97)	20 (251)	21.5 (7.8)	23 (2.98)	19 (3.02)	32	81
Brown University	23 (3.34)	18 (3.38)	23.5 (3)	23 (38)	22 (3.30)	19 (3.29)	12.5 (99)	26 (188)	29 (6.3)	17 (3.38)	16 (3.32)	30	60
University of Virginia	24 (3.20)	21 (3.26)	75 (0)	24 (32)	24 (3.14)	17 (3.33)	27 (93)	28 (162)	30 (6.2)	22 (2.99)	25 (2.83)	26	67
U of North Carolina-Chapel Hill	25 (3.16)	24 (3.16)	27 (2)	27 (24)	25.5 (3.02)	22 (3.08)	31.5 (88)	42 (115)	51 (3.5)	28 (2.78)	26 (2.80)	33	99
University of Washington	26 (3.15)	23 (3.17)	75 (0)	25 (30)	27.5 (3.00)	24 (2.99)	27 (93)	17 (352)	10 (14.7)	25 (2.94)	21 (2.98)	24	112
Michigan State University	27 (3.09)	25 (3.09)	35.5 (1)	28 (23)	25.5 (3.02)	27 (2.87)	29 (92)	14 (535)	17 (12.2)	26 (2.90)	24 (2.88)	44	88
U of Illinois at Urbana-Champaign	28 (3.07)	28 (2.94)	35.5 (1)	26 (27)	27.5 (3.00)	29 (2.80)	15.5 (98)	32 (142)	66.5 (2.6)	27 (2.81)	30.5 (2.60)	55	216
Washington University	29 (3.00)	31 (2.82)	27 (2)	29.5 (21)	31.5 (2.93)	37 (2.59)	21.5 (96)	49 (83)	48 (3.8)	30 (2.65)	27 (2.68)	22	68
University of Iowa	30 (2.97)	29 (2.92)	75 (0)	29.5 (21)	30 (2.95)	27 (2.87)	30 (90)	34 (138)	25 (6.9)	43 (2.11)	39.5 (2.22)	20	59

Institution	93Q [1]	93E [1]	% D [1]	% D-S [1]	93Q T [1]	93E T [1]	VIS [1]	TC [2]	C/F [2]	82Q [3]	82E [3]	TF [4]	TG [4]
University of Texas at Austin	**31** (2.91)	**38** (2.66)	**75** (0)	**32.5** (17)	**33** (2.90)	**36** (2.60)	**23** (95)	**47.5** (90)	**71.5** (2.3)	**41** (2.20)	**48** (1.97)	40	68
Johns Hopkins University	**32** (2.87)	**26** (3.00)	**75** (0)	**36** (13)	**32** (2.93)	**23** (3.02)	**46** (80)	**83.5** (28)	**69.5** (2.5)	**21** (3.12)	**17** (3.17)	11	70
Texas A&M University	**34** (2.83)	**34.5** (2.69)	**35.5** (1)	**38** (12)	**36** (2.74)	**39** (2.54)	**37** (86)	**40** (121)	**41.5** (4.5)	**31** (2.52)	**32** (2.53)	27	93
University of Pittsburgh	**34** (2.83)	**33** (2.71)	**35.5** (1)	**40.5** (11)	**34** (2.89)	**33** (2.65)	**44.5** (81)	**34** (138)	**37** (4.8)	**44** (2.10)	**38** (2.23)	29	58
Ohio State University	**34** (2.83)	**34.5** (2.69)	**75** (0)	**40.5** (11)	**37** (2.69)	**36** (2.60)	**33.5** (87)	**43** (101)	**59** (2.9)	**36** (2.33)	**35** (2.28)	35	102
University of Arizona	**36.5** (2.78)	**48** (2.44)	**35.5** (1)	**32.5** (17)	**40** (2.62)	**50** (2.18)	**24.5** (94)	**44** (99)	**32.5** (5.2)			19	35
Iowa State University	**36.5** (2.78)	**30** (2.90)	**75** (0)	**34** (14)	**38** (2.65)	**32** (2.70)	**44.5** (81)	**27** (169)	**55.5** (3.0)	**33** (2.42)	**23** (2.93)	57	84
University of California-Davis	**38** (2.75)	**50** (2.34)	**75** (0)	**36** (13)	**35** (2.77)	**45** (2.32)	**40** (85)	**38.5** (122)	**34** (5.1)	**35** (2.39)	**39.5** (2.22)	24	55
State U of New York-Stony Brook	**39** (2.73)	**40.5** (2.59)	**23.5** (3)	**31** (20)	**29** (2.98)	**27** (2.87)	**42.5** (83)	**67** (53)	**59** (2.9)	**38** (2.27)	**36.5** (2.25)	18	70
University of Southern California	**40** (2.66)	**42.5** (2.57)	**35.5** (1)	**43.5** (10)	**43** (2.51)	**44** (2.35)	**37** (86)	**22** (214)	**20** (9.3)	**29** (2.72)	**34** (2.33)	23	76
University of Florida	**41** (2.65)	**42.5** (2.57)	**75** (0)	**46** (8)	**41** (2.53)	**43** (2.38)	**41** (84)	**45** (97)	**40** (4.6)	**40** (2.21)	**50.5** (1.92)	21	20
North Carolina State University	**42** (2.61)	**49** (2.43)	**75** (0)	**43.5** (10)	**39** (2.64)	**53** (2.08)	**47** (79)	**24** (207)	**31** (5.8)	**47** (1.89)	**41** (2.20)	36	96
Boston College	**43** (2.53)	**46** (2.47)	**75** (0)	**49** (7)	**42** (2.52)	**46** (2.29)	**49** (76)	**62** (60)	**59** (2.9)	**50** (1.81)	**52.5** (1.88)	21	76
Indiana University	**44** (2.51)	**36.5** (2.68)	**35.5** (1)	**49** (7)	**44** (2.44)	**34** (2.61)	**33.5** (87)	**34** (138)	**37** (4.8)	**48.5** (1.88)	**46** (2.03)	29	68
Pennsylvania State University	**45** (2.49)	**39** (2.60)	**75** (0)	**40.5** (11)	**47** (2.35)	**42** (2.46)	**50.5** (75)	**23** (212)	**35** (5.0)	**46** (1.99)	**49** (1.95)	42	113
Rice University	**46** (2.47)	**53** (2.21)	**75** (0)	**53.5** (5)	**45** (2.40)	**48** (2.22)	**58.5** (72)	**30** (157)	**18** (10.5)	**56** (1.70)	**50.5** (1.92)	15	39
George Mason University	**47** (2.46)	**54** (2.14)	**23.5** (3)	**36** (13)	**50** (2.23)	**58** (1.76)	**37** (86)	**29** (158)	**24** (7.2)			22	165
Vanderbilt University	**48** (2.40)	**45** (2.48)	**75** (0)	**46** (8)	**54** (2.13)	**52** (2.12)	**37** (86)	**18** (306)	**11** (14.6)	**34** (2.40)	**33** (2.37)	21	60
Univ of California-Santa Barbara	**49** (2.38)	**47** (2.46)	**75** (0)	**67** (2)	**47** (2.35)	**48** (2.22)	**48** (77)	**57.5** (70)	**66.5** (2.6)	**42** (2.15)	**42** (2.13)	27	46
U of Massachusetts at Amherst	**50.5** (2.37)	**44** (2.55)	**23.5** (3)	**40.5** (11)	**48** (2.30)	**39** (2.54)	**37** (86)	**50** (81)	**59** (2.9)	**39** (2.25)	**47** (1.98)	28	48
Purdue University	**50.5** (2.37)	**36.5** (2.68)	**75** (0)	**53.5** (5)	**49** (2.28)	**42** (2.46)	**56** (73)	**70** (40)	**69.5** (2.5)	**32** (2.46)	**29** (2.65)	16	59
Rutgers State Univ-New Brunswick	**52** (2.36)	**51** (2.29)	**35.5** (1)	**59.5** (3)	**52** (2.20)	**55** (2.00)	**42.5** (83)	**47.5** (90)	**54** (3.1)	**51** (1.79)	**59.5** (1.58)	29	44
CUNY - Grad Sch & Univ Center	**53** (2.26)	**52** (2.28)	**75** (0)	**53.5** (5)	**54** (2.13)	**49** (2.19)	**60** (71)	**54** (73)	**52.5** (3.3)	**59** (1.57)	**61** (1.43)	22	108
University of Colorado	**54.5** (2.25)	**40.5** (2.59)	**75** (0)	**53.5** (5)	**55** (2.10)	**40** (2.50)	**53** (74)	**36** (132)	**39** (4.7)	**57** (1.61)	**54** (1.75)	28	71
Georgetown University	**54.5** (2.25)	**58** (1.93)	**75** (0)	**67** (2)	**51** (2.21)	**57** (1.78)	**63.5** (68)	**69** (41)	**63.5** (2.7)	**78** (1.02)	**74** (1.12)	15	56
Syracuse University	**56** (2.21)	**55** (2.13)	**75** (0)	**49** (7)	**58** (2.05)	**56** (1.88)	**53** (74)	**52.5** (76)	**59** (2.9)	**53** (1.76)	**43.5** (2.08)	26	42
University of Houston	**57** (2.14)	**56** (2.02)	**75** (0)	**59.5** (3)	**60** (2.00)	**52** (2.12)	**56** (73)	**81** (31)	**85** (1.2)			25	54
State Univ of New York-Buffalo	**58** (2.09)	**62.5** (1.86)	**75** (0)	**59.5** (3)	**58** (2.05)	**67** (1.46)	**56** (73)	**85** (27)	**79** (1.7)			16	37
Southern Methodist University	**59** (2.04)	**64.5** (1.81)	**75** (0)	**67** (2)	**56** (2.09)	**64** (1.50)	**70** (66)	**57.5** (70)	**43** (4.4)	**48.5** (1.88)	**52.5** (1.88)	16	3
Claremont Graduate School	**60** (2.02)	**60** (1.90)	**75** (0)	**46** (8)	**60** (2.00)	**54** (2.04)	**75** (62)	**102.5** (7)	**71.5** (2.3)	**45** (2.01)	**43.5** (2.08)	3	56

Appendix Table P - 15 Economics (Continued)

Institution	93Q [1]	93E [1]	% D [1]	% D-S [1]	93Q T [1]	93E T [1]	VIS [1]	TC [2]	C/F [2]	82Q [3]	82E [3]	TF [4]	TG [4]
University of Oregon	**61** (1.98)	**71** (1.59)	**75** (0)	**79** (1)	**61** (1.83)	**73** (1.17)	**71** (64)	**72.5** (38)	**74** (2.0)	**55** (1.70)	**45** (2.05)	19	31
Florida State University	**62** (1.97)	**59** (1.92)	**75** (0)	**59.5** (3)	**70** (1.61)	**70** (1.30)	**76** (61)	**38.5** (122)	**45** (4.1)	**61** (1.52)	**55.5** (1.70)	30	40
University of Georgia	**63** (1.95)	**67** (1.77)	**75** (0)	**67** (2)	**62** (1.82)	**64** (1.50)	**73** (63)	**55.5** (71)	**46.5** (3.9)			18	20
University of Kentucky	**64** (1.90)	**61** (1.87)	**75** (0)	**79** (1)	**63** (1.81)	**69** (1.31)	**67.5** (67)	**37** (125)	**26.5** (6.6)	**60** (1.54)	**67** (1.28)	19	46
University of South Carolina	**65** (1.89)	**74** (1.50)	**75** (0)	**79** (1)	**65** (1.75)	**78** (1.08)	**50.5** (75)	**52.5** (76)	**41.5** (4.5)	**69** (1.32)	**76** (1.05)	17	23
State Univ of New York-Binghamton	**66** (1.88)	**62.5** (1.86)	**35.5** (1)	**59.5** (3)	**64** (1.76)	**61** (1.58)	**67.5** (67)	**96.5** (9)	**102.5** (0.5)	**58** (1.60)	**59.5** (1.58)	20	59
Arizona State University	**67** (1.85)	**64.5** (1.81)	**75** (0)	**79** (1)	**69** (1.66)	**62** (1.54)	**78** (59)	**61** (64)	**50** (3.6)			18	22
George Washington University	**68** (1.83)	**66** (1.78)	**75** (0)	**79** (1)	**68** (1.67)	**60** (1.67)	**58.5** (72)	**82** (29)	**87** (1.1)	**54** (1.71)	**57** (1.67)	26	84
Georgia State University	**69** (1.77)	**70** (1.67)	**75** (0)	**67** (2)	**74** (1.53)	**90** (0.83)	**67.5** (67)	**80** (33)	**83.5** (1.3)	**70** (1.22)	**73** (1.15)	25	33
Univ of California-Riverside	**71** (1.72)	**80** (1.32)	**35.5** (1)	**56** (4)	**72** (1.60)	**76** (1.11)	**63.5** (68)	**60** (66)	**73** (2.2)	**74** (1.06)	**80** (0.85)	30	54
University of Illinois at Chicago	**71** (1.72)	**78** (1.38)	**35.5** (1)	**79** (1)	**66** (1.68)	**82** (1.04)	**53** (74)	**55.5** (71)	**46.5** (3.9)			18	36
American University	**71** (1.72)	**73** (1.53)	**75** (0)	**59.5** (3)	**76** (1.50)	**78** (1.08)	**61** (69)	**86.5** (23)	**90** (1.0)	**67.5** (1.33)	**70.5** (1.18)	22	96
University of Kansas	**73** (1.71)	**69** (1.72)	**35.5** (1)	**79** (1)	**72** (1.60)	**64** (1.50)	**73** (63)	**59** (67)	**49** (3.7)	**65** (1.40)	**65** (1.35)	18	30
Auburn University	**74** (1.68)	**87** (1.27)	**75** (0)	**79** (1)	**77** (1.47)	**93** (0.74)	**63.5** (68)	**68** (49)	**52.5** (3.3)			15	33
Clemson University	**75** (1.67)	**57** (1.95)	**75** (0)	**67** (2)	**76** (1.50)	**60** (1.67)	**93** (49)	**65** (56)	**82** (1.4)			39	33
Southern Illinois University	**77** (1.65)	**84.5** (1.30)	**75** (0)	**67** (2)	**80** (1.30)	**84** (0.97)	**63.5** (68)	**76** (37)	**62** (2.8)	**83** (0.58)	**83** (0.55)	13	54
University of Wyoming	**77** (1.65)	**75** (1.48)	**75** (0)	**79** (1)	**79** (1.32)	**85** (0.95)	**81.5** (56)	**71** (39)	**55.5** (3.0)			13	20
State Univ of New York-Albany	**77** (1.65)	**77** (1.44)	**75** (0)	**97** (0)	**68** (1.67)	**71** (1.25)	**80** (58)	**92** (14)	**97** (0.7)	**73** (1.08)	**67** (1.28)	20	57
University of Tennessee-Knoxville	**79** (1.62)	**84.5** (1.30)	**75** (0)	**67** (2)	**83** (1.19)	**97** (0.61)	**78** (59)	**76** (37)	**75.5** (1.9)			19	48
Tulane University	**80** (1.54)	**84.5** (1.30)	**75** (0)	**97** (0)	**74** (1.53)	**72** (1.19)	**73** (63)	**99.5** (8)	**99.5** (0.6)	**52** (1.76)	**55.5** (1.70)	14	34
University of Notre Dame	**81.5** (1.53)	**76** (1.47)	**35.5** (1)	**51** (6)	**84** (1.15)	**74** (1.15)	**67.5** (67)	**86.5** (23)	**90** (1.0)	**80** (0.88)	**77** (1.03)	24	90
Louisiana State U & A&M College	**81.5** (1.53)	**68** (1.74)	**75** (0)	**79** (1)	**85** (1.09)	**90** (0.83)	**83** (54)	**41** (119)	**32.5** (5.2)			23	21
Washington State University	**83** (1.42)	**72** (1.54)	**75** (0)	**97** (0)	**78** (1.36)	**67** (1.46)	**85** (52)	**79** (34)	**77** (1.8)	**76.5** (1.05)	**78** (0.98)	19	58
University of Connecticut	**84** (1.40)	**84.5** (1.30)	**75** (0)	**79** (1)	**83** (1.19)	**82** (1.04)	**81.5** (56)	**63** (59)	**63.5** (2.7)	**63** (1.42)	**63** (1.40)	22	118
University of Hawaii at Manoa	**85** (1.38)	**91** (0.99)	**75** (0)	**79** (1)	**81** (1.20)	**94** (0.72)	**90** (50)	**76** (37)	**79** (1.7)	**76.5** (1.05)	**75** (1.07)	22	55
Oklahoma State University	**86** (1.23)	**89** (1.04)	**75** (0)	**97** (0)	**93** (0.95)	**76** (1.11)	**87** (51)	**99.5** (8)	**102.5** (0.5)	**64** (1.42)	**58** (1.62)	17	54
University of Nebraska-Lincoln	**87** (1.19)	**104.5** (0.45)	**75** (0)	**97** (0)	**89** (1.00)	**102** (0.24)	**96** (46)	**72.5** (38)	**75.5** (1.9)	**72** (1.16)	**72** (1.17)	20	41
University of Wisconsin-Milwaukee	**88** (1.17)	**81.5** (1.31)	**75** (0)	**97** (0)	**87** (1.04)	**80** (1.06)	**90** (50)	**76** (37)	**81** (1.6)	**62** (1.42)	**67** (1.28)	23	27
Lehigh University	**89** (1.16)	**88** (1.11)	**75** (0)	**97** (0)	**89** (1.00)	**90** (0.83)	**102** (41)	**83.5** (28)	**92** (0.9)			30	21
University of Utah	**90** (1.15)	**90** (1.00)	**75** (0)	**97** (0)	**92** (0.96)	**68** (1.39)	**85** (52)	**90** (16)	**94** (0.8)	**66** (1.38)	**64** (1.37)	20	54

Institution	93Q [1]	93E [1]	% D [1]	% D-S [1]	93Q T [1]	93E T [1]	VIS [1]	TC [2]	C/F [2]	82Q [3]	82E [3]	TF [4]	TG [4]
Temple University	**91** (1.11)	**94** (0.90)	**75** (0)	**97** (0)	**89** (1.00)	**86** (0.91)	**78** (59)	**66** (55)	**79** (1.7)			32	43
West Virginia University	**92** (1.06)	**79** (1.35)	**35.5** (1)	**67** (2)	**94** (0.85)	**80** (1.06)	**90** (50)	**94** (10)	**102.5** (0.5)	**75** (1.05)	**69** (1.23)	20	35
University of Missouri-Columbia	**93** (1.04)	**93** (0.91)	**75** (0)	**97** (0)	**92** (0.96)	**90** (0.83)	**90** (50)	**91** (15)	**87** (1.1)	**67.5** (1.33)	**62** (1.42)	14	37
Northern Illinois University	**94** (1.02)	**98.5** (0.69)	**75** (0)	**97** (0)	**86** (1.07)	**100** (0.50)	**85** (52)	**88** (21)	**94** (0.8)	**81** (0.69)	**84** (0.53)	26	45
University of Alabama	**95** (0.99)	**98.5** (0.69)	**75** (0)	**97** (0)	**95** (0.84)	**90** (0.83)	**94.5** (48)	**76** (37)	**66.5** (2.6)			14	21
Fordham University	**96** (0.93)	**92** (0.94)	**75** (0)	**97** (0)	**98** (0.72)	**90** (0.83)	**94.5** (48)	**93** (12)	**94** (0.8)	**84** (0.55)	**82** (0.65)	16	145
University of Cincinnati	**97** (0.90)	**97** (0.75)	**75** (0)	**97** (0)	**100** (0.68)	**95** (0.67)	**98** (44)	**106** (1)	**106** (0.1)	**79** (0.98)	**79** (0.97)	10	16
University of Texas at Dallas	**98** (0.89)	**102** (0.57)	**75** (0)	**79** (1)	**98** (0.72)	**96** (0.63)	**99.5** (43)	**64** (57)	**37** (4.8)			12	34
Howard University	**99** (0.83)	**103** (0.56)	**75** (0)	**97** (0)	**96** (0.73)	**99** (0.56)	**105** (38)	**102.5** (7)	**102.5** (0.5)			13	53
Colorado State University	**100** (0.81)	**104.5** (0.45)	**75** (0)	**97** (0)	**98** (0.72)	**105** (0.00)	**97** (45)	**89** (18)	**83.5** (1.3)	**71** (1.18)	**70.5** (1.18)	14	57
University of New Hampshire	**101** (0.74)	**101** (0.61)	**75** (0)	**97** (0)	**107** (0.38)	**105** (0.00)	**104** (39)	**107** (0)	**107** (0.0)			15	13
Rensselaer Polytechnic Inst	**102.5** (0.70)	**95** (0.83)	**75** (0)	**97** (0)	**105** (0.44)	**99** (0.56)	**99.5** (43)	**96.5** (9)	**87** (1.1)			8	19
University of Missouri-Columbia [a]	**102.5** (0.70)	**81.5** (1.31)	**75** (0)	**97** (0)	**101** (0.59)	**82** (1.04)	**106** (32)	**105** (3)	**105** (0.3)			12	77
Colorado School of Mines	**104** (0.65)	**100** (0.67)	**75** (0)	**79** (1)	**106** (0.42)	**105** (0.00)	**107** (30)	**96.5** (9)	**90** (1.0)			9	18
Utah State University	**105** (0.64)	**96** (0.79)	**75** (0)	**79** (1)	**103** (0.48)	**101** (0.42)	**103** (40)	**96.5** (9)	**97** (0.7)			13	20
Clark University	**106** (0.59)	**106** (0.42)	**75** (0)	**97** (0)	**102** (0.52)	**105** (0.00)	**90** (50)	**102.5** (7)	**99.5** (0.6)	**82** (0.62)	**81** (0.77)	11	3
Northeastern University	**107** (0.47)	**107** (0.14)	**75** (0)	**97** (0)	**105** (0.44)	**105** (0.00)	**101** (42)	**102.5** (7)	**97** (0.7)			10	34

Sources: 1. National Survey of Graduate Faculty
2. Institute for Scientific Information
3. 1982 Survey of Graduate Faculty
4. Institutional Coordinator Data

Note: *a.* Program in Agriculural Economics

* Two programs recieved the highest quality rating, and using the standard convention of average rankings, each program was given a rank of 1.5.

Appendix Table P - 16 Relative Rankings for Research-Doctorate Programs in Electrical Engineering

Institution	93Q [1]	93E [1]	% D [1]	% D-S [1]	93Q T [1]	93E T [1]	VIS [1]	TC [2]	C/F [2]	82Q [3]	82E [3]	TF [4]	TG [4]
Stanford University	1 (4.83)	1 (4.68)	1 (81)	1 (93)	1 (4.88)	1 (4.77)	1.5 (97)	3 (3606)	3 (80.1)	3 (4.77)	3 (4.52)	45	357
Massachusetts Inst of Technology	2 (4.79)	2 (4.61)	2 (76)	2 (92)	2 (4.79)	2 (4.64)	3 (96)	1 (4144)	5 (57.6)	1 (4.85)	2 (4.57)	72	400
U of Illinois at Urbana-Champaign	3 (4.70)	3 (4.57)	4 (67)	4 (88)	3 (4.72)	3 (4.60)	5 (94)	2 (4133)	9 (44.4)	4 (4.57)	4 (4.37)	93	472
University of California-Berkeley	4 (4.69)	4 (4.46)	3 (69)	3 (90)	4 (4.69)	4 (4.44)	1.5 (97)	4 (2640)	8 (48.9)	2 (4.78)	1 (4.58)	54	345
California Institute Technology	5 (4.46)	5 (4.34)	5 (47)	5 (86)	5 (4.46)	5 (4.30)	4 (95)	13 (1403)	1 (93.5)	10 (3.72)	9 (3.68)	15	74
University of Michigan	6 (4.38)	6 (4.17)	6 (42)	6 (81)	7 (4.31)	6 (4.10)	7 (90)	8 (1891)	15 (29.5)	9 (3.79)	13 (3.53)	64	388
Cornell University	7 (4.35)	7 (4.08)	7 (37)	7 (80)	6 (4.37)	7 (4.05)	8.5 (89)	11 (1569)	14 (33.4)	7 (3.96)	6 (3.85)	47	133
Purdue University	8 (4.02)	10 (3.94)	8 (28)	8 (70)	10 (3.96)	9 (3.90)	6 (93)	10 (1653)	17 (28.0)	8 (3.91)	7 (3.78)	59	250
Princeton University	9 (4.01)	9 (4.00)	9 (24)	14.5 (56)	8 (4.07)	8 (3.97)	17 (79)	7 (1913)	2 (91.1)	11 (3.70)	10 (3.67)	21	114
University of Southern California	10.5 (4.00)	15 (3.71)	10 (23)	12 (61)	11 (3.85)	12 (3.70)	16 (81)	32 (473)	46.5 (12.1)	5 (4.09)	8 (3.77)	39	1282
Univ of California-Los Angeles	10.5 (4.00)	11 (3.79)	12 (19)	9 (69)	9 (4.00)	11 (3.79)	10 (88)	16 (1237)	20 (24.7)	6 (4.08)	5 (3.93)	50	302
Carnegie Mellon University	12 (3.94)	8 (4.05)	11 (21)	13 (60)	12.5 (3.81)	10 (3.82)	14 (84)	27 (606)	35 (15.9)	12 (3.61)	11 (3.60)	38	140
Georgia Institute of Technology	13 (3.93)	14 (3.72)	13.5 (15)	10 (68)	14 (3.75)	16 (3.53)	11 (87)	33 (472)	70 (6.0)	22 (3.18)	21.5 (3.15)	79	383
University of Texas at Austin	14 (3.88)	13 (3.74)	13.5 (15)	11 (62)	15 (3.67)	14 (3.61)	8.5 (89)	9 (1699)	22 (23.3)	14 (3.48)	14 (3.37)	73	114
Columbia University	15 (3.79)	12 (3.75)	18.5 (9)	14.5 (56)	12.5 (3.81)	13 (3.65)	18.5 (78)	17 (1177)	6 (56.0)	19 (3.23)	15 (3.27)	21	95
University of Wisconsin-Madison	16 (3.77)	17 (3.62)	18.5 (9)	18.5 (47)	18 (3.60)	22.5 (3.43)	24.5 (74)	21 (922)	28 (18.8)	25 (3.11)	25 (3.10)	49	161
University of Maryland College Park	17 (3.75)	18.5 (3.59)	15 (13)	16 (53)	19 (3.59)	18 (3.48)	15 (82)	14 (1401)	21 (23.4)	17 (3.29)	17 (3.20)	60	236
University of Minnesota	18 (3.73)	18.5 (3.59)	16 (10)	18.5 (47)	17 (3.62)	19.5 (3.47)	23 (75)	22 (906)	27 (19.3)	20 (3.22)	23.5 (3.13)	47	96
Univ of California-Santa Barbara	19 (3.71)	20 (3.58)	22 (6)	17 (48)	16 (3.64)	17 (3.51)	24.5 (74)	5 (2393)	4 (70.4)	23 (3.17)	23.5 (3.13)	34	221
Univ of California-San Diego	20 (3.57)	25 (3.37)	22 (6)	21 (44)	20 (3.56)	24 (3.38)	21.5 (76)	12 (1423)	10 (36.5)	18 (3.29)	34.5 (2.90)	39	141
North Carolina State University	21 (3.54)	23 (3.43)	25 (5)	20 (45)	21 (3.51)	21 (3.44)	12 (86)	6 (2031)	16 (28.6)	42 (2.52)	44 (2.67)	71	146
Ohio State University	22 (3.53)	16 (3.63)	18.5 (9)	23 (38)	25 (3.32)	22.5 (3.43)	33.5 (67)	44 (318)	63 (7.8)	15 (3.31)	20 (3.17)	41	94
Rensselaer Polytechnic Inst	23 (3.44)	21 (3.46)	29.5 (3)	22 (40)	23 (3.38)	19.5 (3.47)	13 (85)	29 (513)	45 (12.2)	16 (3.30)	29 (3.03)	42	124
Polytechnic University	24.5 (3.42)	27 (3.33)	18.5 (9)	24.5 (35)	24 (3.35)	27 (3.28)	27.5 (72)	80 (84)	99 (2.3)	13 (3.56)	12 (3.55)	36	79
University of Washington	24.5 (3.42)	27 (3.33)	27.5 (4)	24.5 (35)	26 (3.31)	29 (3.25)	21.5 (76)	23 (759)	32.5 (16.5)	30.5 (3.00)	31 (2.97)	46	188
Rice University	26 (3.36)	22 (3.45)	27.5 (4)	32 (26)	22 (3.47)	15 (3.57)	46.5 (59)	38 (399)	24 (22.2)	28 (3.04)	16 (3.23)	18	80
Virginia Polytech Inst & State U	27 (3.30)	24 (3.41)	22 (6)	32 (26)	44 (2.90)	32.5 (3.18)	36.5 (65)	55 (243)	68.5 (6.4)	39 (2.60)	41.5 (2.72)	38	93
Pennsylvania State University	28.5 (3.28)	29 (3.31)	25 (5)	26 (29)	30 (3.19)	25 (3.29)	18.5 (78)	20 (932)	26 (19.4)	35 (2.80)	32 (2.95)	48	258
U of Massachusetts at Amherst	28.5 (3.28)	34 (3.21)	35.5 (2)	28 (27)	27 (3.26)	34.5 (3.14)	27.5 (72)	43 (321)	54 (10.7)	36 (2.70)	38 (2.75)	30	124
Yale University	30.5 (3.26)	37 (3.15)	25 (5)	28 (27)	29 (3.21)	40.5 (3.05)	36.5 (65)	48 (306)	25 (20.4)	32 (2.94)	30 (2.98)	15	54

Institution	93Q [1]	93E [1]	% D [1]	% D-S [1]	93Q T [1]	93E T [1]	VIS [1]	TC [2]	C/F [2]	82Q [3]	82E [3]	TF [4]	TG [4]
University of Florida	30.5 (3.26)	33 (3.22)	48 (1)	32 (26)	40 (2.96)	41 (3.05)	50 (57)	25 (670)	31 (17.6)	24 (3.15)	28 (3.05)	38	99
Texas A&M University	32 (3.25)	27 (3.33)	35.5 (2)	32 (26)	35 (3.10)	36 (3.12)	30 (69)	30 (496)	53 (10.8)	62.5 (2.14)	64.5 (2.22)	46	8
University of California-Davis	33 (3.24)	43 (3.02)	91 (0)	35 (25)	36 (3.08)	44 (3.00)	35 (66)	37 (402)	51 (11.2)	44 (2.48)	54 (2.45)	36	69
Johns Hopkins University	34 (3.23)	31 (3.26)	29.5 (3)	36.5 (23)	28 (3.23)	27 (3.28)	40 (63)	51 (296)	30 (18.5)	26.5 (3.11)	18.5 (3.18)	16	53
Brown University	35 (3.22)	32 (3.24)	35.5 (2)	38 (22)	38 (3.04)	33 (3.18)	63.5 (52)	42 (341)	18 (26.2)	29 (3.02)	26.5 (3.07)	13	54
Arizona State University	37 (3.17)	41 (3.09)	35.5 (2)	32 (26)	37 (3.05)	37 (3.10)	26 (73)	36 (414)	49 (11.5)	56.5 (2.25)	63 (2.23)	36	109
Washington University	37 (3.17)	39 (3.11)	48 (1)	39.5 (21)	31 (3.17)	35 (3.14)	46.5 (59)	49.5 (298)	62 (8.5)	46 (2.42)	39.5 (2.73)	35	206
University of Colorado	37 (3.17)	38 (3.14)	91 (0)	28 (27)	32 (3.16)	31 (3.19)	20 (77)	24 (693)	29 (18.7)	21 (3.19)	36 (2.88)	37	158
Northwestern University	39 (3.16)	30 (3.27)	48 (1)	39.5 (21)	34 (3.15)	27 (3.28)	31.5 (68)	19 (992)	13 (34.2)	26.5 (3.11)	18.5 (3.18)	29	101
University of Arizona	40 (3.12)	35 (3.20)	35.5 (2)	41 (20)	42 (2.94)	30 (3.21)	31.5 (68)	49.5 (298)	64 (7.5)	34 (2.85)	26.5 (3.07)	40	101
University of Pennsylvania	41 (3.11)	45 (2.95)	91 (0)	44.5 (15)	34 (3.15)	44 (3.00)	41.5 (61)	26 (613)	11 (36.1)	30.5 (3.00)	21.5 (3.15)	17	67
Case Western Reserve Univ	42 (3.05)	48 (2.86)	35.5 (2)	42 (18)	47 (2.82)	54 (2.70)	63.5 (52)	66 (144)	52 (11.1)	37 (2.70)	37 (2.83)	13	33
University of Utah	43 (3.02)	53 (2.80)	48 (1)	44.5 (15)	39 (3.00)	47 (2.86)	57 (54)	54 (256)	58 (10.2)	56.5 (2.25)	53 (2.47)	25	38
Michigan State University	44 (3.00)	36 (3.16)	91 (0)	52 (12)	50 (2.79)	39 (3.06)	63.5 (52)	45 (317)	41 (13.2)	40 (2.57)	34.5 (2.90)	24	52
University of Notre Dame	45 (2.98)	51 (2.83)	91 (0)	36.5 (23)	43 (2.92)	51 (2.80)	29 (70)	47 (307)	34 (16.2)	38 (2.65)	45.5 (2.62)	19	63
University of Rochester	46.5 (2.96)	42 (3.06)	48 (1)	48.5 (14)	46 (2.85)	45 (2.98)	44 (60)	28 (550)	19 (25.0)	55 (2.26)	59 (2.35)	22	61
University of California-Irvine	46.5 (2.96)	40 (3.10)	91 (0)	44.5 (15)	41 (2.95)	38 (3.09)	55 (55)	61 (184)	61 (8.8)	64 (2.13)	66 (2.18)	21	72
Drexel University	48 (2.90)	47 (2.90)	35.5 (2)	44.5 (15)	48 (2.80)	49 (2.82)	53 (56)	31 (482)	43.5 (12.4)	68 (1.90)	67.5 (2.15)	39	40
Syracuse University	49 (2.86)	57 (2.73)	35.5 (2)	48.5 (14)	53 (2.67)	56 (2.69)	38.5 (64)	59 (218)	46.5 (12.1)	33 (2.92)	33 (2.93)	18	76
Rutgers State Univ-New Brunswick	50 (2.83)	50 (2.84)	48 (1)	48.5 (14)	50 (2.79)	49 (2.82)	44 (60)	35 (426)	48 (11.8)	75 (1.76)	76 (1.82)	36	91
CUNY - Grad Sch & Univ Center	51 (2.79)	46 (2.92)	91 (0)	64 (7)	45 (2.86)	42 (3.02)	104.5 (37)	18 (997)	12 (34.4)	61 (2.18)	50.5 (2.50)	29	83
Iowa State University	52 (2.78)	60 (2.68)	48 (1)	48.5 (14)	62 (2.50)	73 (2.25)	59.5 (53)	73 (106)	93.5 (2.7)	41 (2.55)	43 (2.70)	40	54
University of Iowa	53 (2.73)	44 (3.00)	48 (1)	59 (8)	53 (2.67)	46 (2.88)	84.5 (43)	52 (281)	37.5 (14.1)	67 (1.92)	69.5 (2.05)	20	41
Duke University	54.5 (2.71)	58 (2.71)	35.5 (2)	51 (13)	57 (2.61)	57 (2.68)	50 (57)	41 (363)	32.5 (16.5)	49 (2.37)	45.5 (2.62)	22	52
University of Virginia	54.5 (2.71)	54 (2.78)	91 (0)	53.5 (11)	58 (2.60)	52 (2.78)	41.5 (61)	60 (212)	55.5 (10.6)	60 (2.20)	60 (2.27)	20	145
Northeastern University	56 (2.70)	55 (2.76)	91 (0)	56 (9)	55 (2.65)	56 (2.69)	33.5 (67)	39 (383)	60 (9.3)	66 (1.95)	74 (1.88)	41	73
University of Rhode Island	57 (2.66)	67 (2.57)	91 (0)	56 (9)	51 (2.75)	61 (2.56)	90 (41)	96 (52)	83 (4.0)	62.5 (2.14)	69.5 (2.05)	13	109
State U of New York-Stony Brook	58 (2.63)	49 (2.85)	48 (1)	69.5 (6)	59 (2.56)	49 (2.82)	48 (58)	85 (73)	84 (3.7)	45 (2.42)	52 (2.48)	20	128
Auburn University	59 (2.61)	65 (2.60)	91 (0)	69.5 (6)	75 (2.28)	85 (2.11)	68 (51)	58 (226)	59 (9.4)	71 (1.79)	61.5 (2.25)	24	34
State Univ of New York-Buffalo	60.5 (2.60)	52 (2.81)	91 (0)	64 (7)	66 (2.41)	58 (2.65)	82.5 (44)	15 (1315)	7 (50.6)	53.5 (2.27)	55 (2.43)	26	58

Appendix Table P - 16 Electrical Engineering (Continued)

Institution	93Q [1]	93E [1]	% D [1]	% D-S [1]	93Q T [1]	93E T [1]	VIS [1]	TC [2]	C/F [2]	82Q [3]	82E [3]	TF [4]	TG [4]
Colorado State University	60.5 (2.60)	82 (2.35)	91 (0)	69.5 (6)	56 (2.64)	65 (2.47)	57 (54)	34 (432)	23 (22.7)	51 (2.35)	58 (2.37)	19	17
Oregon State University	63 (2.59)	62.5 (2.62)	48 (1)	56 (9)	63 (2.48)	53 (2.71)	44 (60)	67 (138)	55.5 (10.6)	73 (1.77)	67.5 (2.15)	13	29
University of Texas at Arlington	63 (2.59)	74 (2.47)	91 (0)	64 (7)	76 (2.26)	76 (2.22)	59.5 (53)	63 (162)	72 (5.4)	76 (1.72)	75 (1.87)	30	98
University of Pittsburgh	63 (2.59)	59 (2.69)	91 (0)	73.5 (5)	62 (2.50)	59 (2.62)	63.5 (52)	76 (99)	74.5 (5.2)	47 (2.41)	57 (2.38)	19	165
University of Illinois at Chicago	65 (2.58)	64 (2.61)	91 (0)	64 (7)	60 (2.53)	64 (2.50)	50 (57)	46 (308)	50 (11.4)	59 (2.21)	56 (2.42)	27	173
University of Tennessee-Knoxville	66 (2.57)	61 (2.64)	91 (0)	64 (7)	80 (2.18)	80 (2.19)	77.5 (47)	88.5 (68)	96 (2.5)	52 (2.32)	48.5 (2.53)	27	35
Lehigh University	67 (2.54)	56 (2.74)	91 (0)	53.5 (11)	53 (2.67)	60 (2.61)	74.5 (49)	78 (95)	73 (5.3)			18	31
Naval Postgraduate School	68 (2.53)	86.5 (2.22)	91 (0)	73.5 (5)	69 (2.35)	91 (1.99)	53 (56)	112 (20)	118 (0.7)			29	5
Texas Tech University	69 (2.47)	66 (2.59)	91 (0)	73.5 (5)	64 (2.46)	63 (2.55)	82.5 (44)	83 (80)	86.5 (3.3)	50 (2.36)	41.5 (2.72)	24	22
George Washington University	70.5 (2.46)	71 (2.50)	91 (0)	64 (7)	77 (2.23)	70 (2.32)	68 (51)	104.5 (32)	108 (1.6)			20	96
Vanderbilt University	70.5 (2.46)	71 (2.50)	91 (0)	79 (4)	71 (2.32)	63 (2.55)	53 (56)	72 (111)	78 (4.6)	81 (1.37)	82 (1.35)	24	83
University of Kansas	72 (2.45)	88 (2.20)	91 (0)	79 (4)	71 (2.32)	95 (1.83)	87 (42)	87 (69)	82 (4.1)	53.5 (2.27)	48.5 (2.53)	17	14
Clemson University	73 (2.44)	77.5 (2.40)	91 (0)	64 (7)	67 (2.38)	73 (2.25)	38.5 (64)	90 (64)	104 (2.1)			31	36
Clarkson University	74.5 (2.41)	74 (2.47)	91 (0)	79 (4)	66 (2.41)	83 (2.17)	80.5 (45)	75 (103)	68.5 (6.4)	84 (1.32)	83.5 (1.32)	16	49
New Mexico State University	74.5 (2.41)	71 (2.50)	91 (0)	85.5 (3)	80 (2.18)	69 (2.36)	96.5 (39)	106 (27)	113 (1.2)			22	42
Southern Methodist University	76 (2.40)	77.5 (2.40)	91 (0)	59 (8)	78 (2.21)	76 (2.22)	57 (54)	97 (50)	91 (2.9)	48 (2.39)	47 (2.57)	17	76
University of Central Florida	77 (2.39)	74 (2.47)	48 (1)	59 (8)	85 (2.12)	88 (2.00)	80.5 (45)	53 (257)	65 (6.9)			37	100
University of Delaware	78.5 (2.37)	76 (2.43)	48 (1)	73.5 (5)	68 (2.36)	68 (2.41)	96.5 (39)	104.5 (32)	104 (2.1)			15	27
University of Connecticut	78.5 (2.37)	84 (2.27)	91 (0)	85.5 (3)	82 (2.15)	86 (2.08)	71.5 (50)	57 (235)	43.5 (12.4)	58 (2.23)	50.5 (2.50)	19	63
Washington State University	80.5 (2.32)	62.5 (2.62)	91 (0)	85.5 (3)	86 (2.06)	66 (2.44)	90 (41)	70 (117)	91 (2.9)			41	81
University of Missouri-Rolla	80.5 (2.32)	85 (2.26)	91 (0)	85.5 (3)	73 (2.29)	80 (2.19)	71.5 (50)	109 (23)	113 (1.2)	43 (2.52)	39.5 (2.73)	19	19
Boston University	82.5 (2.29)	96 (1.88)	91 (0)	85.5 (3)	73 (2.29)	94 (1.84)	63.5 (52)	40 (376)	57 (10.4)			36	n/a
University of Missouri-Columbia	82.5 (2.29)	69 (2.54)	91 (0)	120 (0)	84 (2.14)	76 (2.22)	108.5 (35)	93.5 (58)	101.5 (2.2)	65 (2.11)	64.5 (2.22)	26	78
Illinois Institute of Technology	84 (2.23)	80 (2.38)	91 (0)	79 (4)	75 (2.28)	71 (2.26)	74.5 (49)	81.5 (82)	71 (5.9)	72 (1.79)	71 (2.02)	14	64
Ohio University	85 (2.22)	86.5 (2.22)	91 (0)	94.5 (2)	82 (2.15)	76 (2.22)	96.5 (39)	120 (6)	122 (0.3)	85 (1.06)	85 (1.15)	22	24
Air Force Inst of Technology	86 (2.21)	94 (1.93)	91 (0)	79 (4)	84 (2.14)	92 (1.98)	93 (40)	93.5 (58)	106.5 (1.7)	79.5 (1.49)	79 (1.67)	34	20
University of Cincinnati	87 (2.16)	83 (2.31)	91 (0)	79 (4)	90 (2.00)	84 (2.12)	76 (48)	62 (170)	42 (13.1)	74 (1.77)	72.5 (1.97)	13	73
West Virginia University	88 (2.15)	100 (1.81)	91 (0)	107 (1)	94 (1.85)	101 (1.52)	96.5 (39)	74 (105)	67 (6.6)	78 (1.54)	78 (1.73)	16	23
Wayne State University	89.5 (2.14)	89 (2.18)	48 (1)	79 (4)	93 (1.93)	91 (1.99)	68 (51)	71 (112)	79 (4.3)	70 (1.81)	77 (1.77)	26	40
University of Houston	89.5 (2.14)	92 (2.10)	91 (0)	107 (1)	90 (2.00)	88 (2.00)	79 (46)	65 (145)	74.5 (5.2)	79.5 (1.49)	72.5 (1.97)	28	58

Institution	93Q [1]	93E [1]	% D [1]	% D-S [1]	93Q T [1]	93E T [1]	VIS [1]	TC [2]	C/F [2]	82Q [3]	82E [3]	TF [4]	TG [4]
Worcester Polytechnic Inst	**91** (2.12)	**80** (2.38)	**35.5** (2)	**69.5** (6)	**91** (1.97)	**80** (2.19)	**77.5** (47)	**79** (92)	**80.5** (4.2)			22	5
Brigham Young University	**92** (2.10)	**68** (2.55)	**91** (0)	**120** (0)	**87** (2.05)	**67** (2.43)	**112.5** (34)	**123** (4)	**124** (0.2)			21	1
Stevens Inst of Technology	**93** (2.09)	**97** (1.87)	**48** (1)	**85.5** (3)	**88** (2.04)	**93** (1.91)	**63.5** (52)	**113** (19)	**110.5** (1.4)			14	28
University of Oklahoma	**94** (2.06)	**80** (2.38)	**91** (0)	**94.5** (2)	**97** (1.79)	**82** (2.18)	**90** (41)	**102** (38)	**101.5** (2.2)	**77** (1.56)	**80** (1.62)	17	25
University of Alabama-Huntsville	**95** (2.03)	**93** (2.07)	**91** (0)	**107** (1)	**96** (1.82)	**96** (1.77)	**84.5** (43)	**86** (72)	**80.5** (4.2)			17	53
University of Wisconsin-Milwaukee	**96** (2.00)	**90.5** (2.16)	**91** (0)	**94.5** (2)	**92** (1.94)	**88** (2.00)	**118.5** (31)	**88.5** (68)	**88.5** (3.2)			21	61
University of Kentucky	**97** (1.85)	**99** (1.83)	**91** (0)	**120** (0)	**98** (1.72)	**104** (1.46)	**71.5** (50)	**103** (36)	**106.5** (1.7)			21	24
Univ of Southwestern Louisiana	**98** (1.81)	**111** (1.41)	**91** (0)	**107** (1)	**96** (1.82)	**113** (1.28)	**93** (40)	**107** (25)	**115.5** (1.1)			23	30
University of Miami	**99** (1.77)	**104.5** (1.60)	**91** (0)	**94.5** (2)	**99** (1.62)	**107** (1.43)	**87** (42)	**100** (40)	**91** (2.9)			14	27
Louisiana State U & A&M College	**100** (1.75)	**98** (1.84)	**91** (0)	**120** (0)	**113** (1.28)	**104** (1.46)	**87** (42)	**84** (78)	**85** (3.4)			23	57
University of South Florida	**101** (1.72)	**95** (1.91)	**91** (0)	**107** (1)	**111** (1.31)	**107** (1.43)	**101** (38)	**118** (10)	**117** (0.8)			13	52
Mississippi State University	**102** (1.67)	**107** (1.57)	**91** (0)	**94.5** (2)	**111** (1.31)	**112** (1.30)	**112.5** (34)	**125** (2)	**125.5** (0.1)	**82** (1.34)	**83.5** (1.32)	21	28
New Jersey Inst of Technology	**103** (1.66)	**104.5** (1.60)	**91** (0)	**94.5** (2)	**103** (1.46)	**98** (1.67)	**71.5** (50)	**110.5** (21)	**109** (1.5)	**83** (1.34)	**81** (1.40)	14	48
Oklahoma State University	**104** (1.63)	**108** (1.54)	**91** (0)	**120** (0)	**101** (1.55)	**98** (1.67)	**108.5** (35)	**117** (12)	**113** (1.2)	**69** (1.90)	**61.5** (2.25)	10	245
University of Alabama	**105** (1.59)	**101** (1.77)	**91** (0)	**107** (1)	**117** (1.22)	**107** (1.43)	**112.5** (34)	**121** (5)	**122** (0.3)			15	62
University of South Carolina	**106.5** (1.58)	**102** (1.74)	**91** (0)	**94.5** (2)	**107** (1.42)	**100** (1.53)	**101** (38)	**98** (48)	**97** (2.4)			20	35
Kansas State University	**106.5** (1.58)	**103** (1.67)	**91** (0)	**107** (1)	**106** (1.43)	**98** (1.67)	**108.5** (35)	**91** (63)	**88.5** (3.2)			20	22
Florida Institute of Technology	**108.5** (1.56)	**90.5** (2.16)	**48** (1)	**94.5** (2)	**115** (1.23)	**76** (2.22)	**108.5** (35)	**123** (4)	**122** (0.3)			16	36
Univ of Arkansas-Fayetteville	**108.5** (1.56)	**109** (1.49)	**91** (0)	**120** (0)	**112** (1.29)	**120** (1.00)	**116.5** (32)	**95** (53)	**86.5** (3.3)			16	14
University of Toledo	**110** (1.55)	**115** (1.25)	**91** (0)	**120** (0)	**121** (1:08)	**116** (1.11)	**121** (30)	**99** (43)	**99** (2.3)			19	32
University of Dayton	**111** (1.52)	**116.5** (1.23)	**91** (0)	**107** (1)	**114** (1.27)	**123** (0.93)	**93** (40)	**68** (126)	**39** (14.0)			9	28
Howard University	**112** (1.43)	**110** (1.48)	**91** (0)	**107** (1)	**100** (1.57)	**102** (1.50)	**101** (38)	**108** (24)	**93.5** (2.7)			9	53
Old Dominion University	**113** (1.41)	**106** (1.58)	**91** (0)	**94.5** (2)	**104** (1.45)	**111** (1.37)	**101** (38)	**69** (123)	**66** (6.8)			18	70
University of Akron	**114** (1.40)	**118** (1.17)	**91** (0)	**94.5** (2)	**102** (1.47)	**114** (1.22)	**106** (36)	**56** (240)	**37.5** (14.1)			17	96
Oregon Graduate Inst Sci & Tech	**115** (1.39)	**112.5** (1.39)	**91** (0)	**120** (0)	**108** (1.41)	**110** (1.39)	**118.5** (31)	**64** (147)	**36** (14.7)			10	21
University of Wyoming	**116** (1.38)	**122** (0.95)	**91** (0)	**94.5** (2)	**106** (1.43)	**122** (0.95)	**112.5** (34)	**110.5** (21)	**104** (2.1)			10	7
University of New Hampshire	**117** (1.31)	**124.5** (0.83)	**91** (0)	**107** (1)	**119** (1.13)	**122** (0.95)	**126** (21)	**81.5** (82)	**76** (5.1)			16	4
Florida Atlantic University	**118** (1.25)	**119** (1.11)	**91** (0)	**120** (0)	**121** (1.08)	**116** (1.11)	**123** (29)	**123** (4)	**119** (0.6)			7	26
Wichita State University	**119** (1.24)	**124.5** (0.83)	**91** (0)	**94.5** (2)	**126** (0.57)	**125** (0.56)	**125** (27)	**119** (7)	**120** (0.5)			14	23
Portland State University	**120** (1.19)	**116.5** (1.23)	**91** (0)	**107** (1)	**118** (1.14)	**118** (1.03)	**101** (38)	**92** (60)	**77** (5.0)			12	31

Appendix Table P - 16 Electrical Engineering (Continued)

Institution	93Q [1]	93E [1]	% D [1]	% D-S [1]	93Q T [1]	93E T [1]	VIS [1]	TC [2]	C/F [2]	82Q [3]	82E [3]	TF [4]	TG [4]
State Univ of New York-Binghamton	**121** (1.16)	**120** (1.03)	**91** (0)	**120** (0)	**123** (0.80)	**124** (0.74)	**124** (28)	**114.5** (18)	**110.5** (1.4)			13	43
University of Mass-Lowell	**122** (1.15)	**121** (1.02)	**91** (0)	**120** (0)	**117** (1.22)	**117** (1.06)	**116.5** (32)	**101** (39)	**99** (2.3)			17	46
University of Vermont	**123** (1.05)	**114** (1.31)	**91** (0)	**107** (1)	**109** (1.33)	**110** (1.39)	**121** (30)	**77** (96)	**40** (13.7)			7	16
University of Idaho	**124** (1.00)	**112.5** (1.39)	**91** (0)	**120** (0)	**121** (1.08)	**107** (1.43)	**121** (30)	**116** (15)	**115.5** (1.1)			14	14
Tennessee Technological Univ	**125** (0.94)	**123** (0.91)	**91** (0)	**120** (0)	**125** (0.68)	**120** (1.00)	**115** (33)	**114.5** (18)	**95** (2.6)			7	19
Tulane University	**126** (0.84)	**126** (0.50)	**91** (0)	**107** (1)	**124** (0.71)	**126** (0.49)	**104.5** (37)	**126** (1)	**125.5** (0.1)			8	27

Sources:
1. National Survey of Graduate Faculty
2. Institute for Scientific Information
3. 1982 Survey of Graduate Faculty
4. Institutional Coordinator Data

Appendix Table P - 17 Relative Rankings for Research-Doctorate Programs in English Language and Literature

Institution	93Q [1]	93E [1]	% D [1]	% D-S [1]	93Q T [1]	93E T [1]	VIS [1]	FA [2]	82Q [3]	82E [3]	TF [4]	TG [4]
Yale University	**2*** (4.77)	**2.5** (4.43)	**1** (75)	**1** (97)	**1.5** (4.83)	**3** (4.45)	**1** (99)	**4.5** (17)	**1** (4.91)	**1** (4.43)	50	90
University of California-Berkeley	**2*** (4.77)	**1** (4.53)	**2.5** (74)	**2** (94)	**1.5** (4.83)	**1** (4.68)	**2.5** (97)	**3** (18)	**2** (4.69)	**2** (4.27)	62	220
Harvard University	**2*** (4.77)	**8** (4.14)	**2.5** (74)	**3** (91)	**3** (4.80)	**9** (4.04)	**6.5** (95)	**1.5** (21)	**4** (4.48)	**4** (4.15)	34	134
University of Virginia	**4** (4.58)	**5** (4.27)	**4** (60)	**6** (87)	**4** (4.72)	**4** (4.33)	**4.5** (96)	**20.5** (9)	**3** (4.60)	**9** (4.00)	71	204
Duke University	**5.5** (4.55)	**10** (3.98)	**5** (58)	**4** (89)	**6** (4.59)	**11.5** (3.91)	**2.5** (97)	**9.5** (15)	**28** (3.17)	**28** (3.15)	35	141
Stanford University	**5.5** (4.55)	**4** (4.30)	**6** (56)	**6** (87)	**5** (4.63)	**5** (4.22)	**4.5** (96)	**15.5** (12)	**10** (4.20)	**5** (4.12)	41	99
Cornell University	**7** (4.49)	**2.5** (4.43)	**8** (49)	**8** (86)	**7** (4.54)	**2** (4.49)	**14.5** (93)	**20.5** (9)	**7** (4.28)	**3** (4.25)	48	83
University of Pennsylvania	**8.5** (4.47)	**6** (4.24)	**7** (50)	**9.5** (85)	**11** (4.40)	**6** (4.19)	**10** (94)	**1.5** (21)	**11** (3.98)	**12** (3.70)	49	123
Columbia University	**8.5** (4.47)	**13** (3.91)	**9** (48)	**6** (87)	**8** (4.49)	**13** (3.89)	**10** (94)	**7** (16)	**6** (4.38)	**10** (3.80)	48	290
University of Chicago	**10** (4.41)	**7** (4.20)	**10** (47)	**9.5** (85)	**10** (4.43)	**8** (4.06)	**6.5** (95)	**82** (2)	**5** (4.39)	**7.5** (4.03)	34	193
Johns Hopkins University	**11** (4.33)	**9** (3.99)	**11** (39)	**11** (80)	**9** (4.48)	**7** (4.10)	**17.5** (92)	**15.5** (12)	**8** (4.25)	**6** (4.08)	11	49
Univ of California-Los Angeles	**12** (4.10)	**11** (3.97)	**14** (23)	**12** (78)	**12** (4.08)	**10** (3.93)	**14.5** (93)	**7** (16)	**12** (3.97)	**11** (3.72)	66	139
Princeton University	**13** (4.05)	**12** (3.94)	**12** (28)	**15** (68)	**13** (4.00)	**11.5** (3.91)	**17.5** (92)	**13** (13)	**9** (4.23)	**7.5** (4.03)	22	53
Brown University	**14** (3.99)	**15** (3.76)	**13** (24)	**16.5** (65)	**16** (3.88)	**19** (3.55)	**10** (94)	**22.5** (8)	**13** (3.91)	**13.5** (3.65)	30	79
University of California-Irvine	**15** (3.95)	**22** (3.60)	**16** (18)	**16.5** (65)	**15** (3.92)	**16** (3.68)	**19** (90)	**52.5** (4)	**26** (3.25)	**29** (3.12)	24	90
University of Michigan	**16** (3.93)	**14** (3.87)	**17** (17)	**13** (70)	**17** (3.87)	**14** (3.82)	**10** (94)	**9.5** (15)	**16** (3.60)	**13.5** (3.65)	50	156
Rutgers State Univ-New Brunswick	**17** (3.92)	**16** (3.71)	**15** (21)	**14** (69)	**14** (3.97)	**15** (3.74)	**14.5** (93)	**11.5** (14)	**15** (3.78)	**18.5** (3.43)	51	233
CUNY - Grad Sch & Univ Center	**18.5** (3.78)	**20.5** (3.62)	**18** (16)	**20** (50)	**19** (3.66)	**30** (3.29)	**33** (82)	**11.5** (14)	**14** (3.88)	**22** (3.37)	41	280
Indiana University	**18.5** (3.78)	**20.5** (3.62)	**20** (11)	**18** (59)	**20** (3.59)	**23.5** (3.44)	**26.5** (86)	**31.5** (6)	**17** (3.56)	**15** (3.62)	71	273
New York University	**20** (3.77)	**19** (3.63)	**19** (15)	**19** (51)	**18** (3.76)	**18** (3.60)	**24.5** (87)	**18.5** (11)	**21** (3.51)	**25.5** (3.23)	31	109
University of Texas at Austin	**21** (3.54)	**30** (3.36)	**22.5** (8)	**21** (48)	**23** (3.42)	**34** (3.23)	**14.5** (93)	**7** (16)	**23** (3.38)	**18.5** (3.43)	76	103
University of Wisconsin-Madison	**22** (3.53)	**17** (3.69)	**22.5** (8)	**25** (39)	**23** (3.42)	**20** (3.54)	**22.5** (88)	**31.5** (6)	**19** (3.52)	**17** (3.48)	46	127
University of Washington	**23** (3.48)	**24** (3.48)	**32** (4)	**23** (44)	**23** (3.42)	**21** (3.53)	**20.5** (89)	**82** (2)	**24** (3.35)	**24** (3.30)	57	183
U of North Carolina-Chapel Hill	**24** (3.43)	**25** (3.47)	**21** (10)	**24** (40)	**33.5** (3.27)	**36** (3.18)	**26.5** (86)	**18.5** (11)	**20** (3.52)	**20** (3.40)	55	245
University of Southern California	**25** (3.41)	**27** (3.40)	**39.5** (3)	**22** (47)	**26** (3.35)	**22** (3.45)	**10** (94)	**65.5** (3)	**32** (3.05)	**39** (2.90)	23	143
University of Pittsburgh	**26.5** (3.40)	**32.5** (3.33)	**32** (4)	**29** (35)	**25** (3.39)	**27** (3.33)	**31.5** (83)	**103.5** (1)	**70** (1.99)	**67.5** (2.20)	32	64
State Univ of New York-Buffalo	**26.5** (3.40)	**23** (3.51)	**53** (2)	**27** (36)	**21** (3.49)	**23.5** (3.44)	**24.5** (87)	**31.5** (6)	**18** (3.56)	**27** (3.22)	40	200
U of Illinois at Urbana-Champaign	**28** (3.38)	**26** (3.41)	**28** (5)	**36** (29)	**29** (3.30)	**27** (3.33)	**34** (81)	**31.5** (6)	**25** (3.28)	**23** (3.35)	72	147
Northwestern University	**29** (3.37)	**28.5** (3.37)	**28** (5)	**27** (36)	**29** (3.30)	**31** (3.28)	**28** (85)	**31.5** (6)	**22** (3.48)	**21** (3.38)	25	43
Vanderbilt University	**30.5** (3.33)	**42.5** (3.13)	**25** (7)	**27** (36)	**31.5** (3.29)	**55** (2.87)	**31.5** (83)	**40.5** (5)	**46.5** (2.56)	**45.5** (2.72)	29	11

Appendix Table P - 17 English Language and Literature (Continued)

Institution	93Q [1]	93E [1]	% D [1]	% D-S [1]	93Q T [1]	93E T [1]	VIS [1]	FA [2]	82Q [3]	82E [3]	TF [4]	TG [4]
Emory University	**30.5** (3.33)	**41** (3.15)	**73** (1)	**30.5** (33)	**27** (3.33)	**38** (3.13)	**38** (79)	**82** (2)	**43** (2.67)	**33.5** (2.98)	26	91
University of Wisconsin-Milwaukee	**32** (3.31)	**38** (3.23)	**28** (5)	**33** (31)	**29** (3.30)	**27** (3.33)	**45** (75)	**65.5** (3)	**41** (2.69)	**41** (2.83)	47	95
Ohio State University	**33** (3.28)	**32.5** (3.33)	**25** (7)	**38** (27)	**36** (3.20)	**44** (3.04)	**35.5** (80)	**82** (2)	**38** (2.86)	**37** (2.93)	65	201
Univ of California-Santa Barbara	**34.5** (3.27)	**28.5** (3.37)	**39.5** (3)	**30.5** (33)	**34** (3.27)	**27** (3.33)	**35.5** (80)	**52.5** (4)	**37** (2.86)	**50** (2.57)	33	81
Univ of California-Riverside	**34.5** (3.27)	**45** (3.08)	**39.5** (3)	**33** (31)	**32** (3.29)	**47** (3.00)	**47** (73)	**25.5** (7)	**57** (2.33)	**64** (2.28)	31	105
University of Minnesota	**36** (3.24)	**18** (3.68)	**32** (4)	**42** (23)	**40** (3.15)	**17** (3.62)	**43.5** (76)	**40.5** (5)	**42** (2.68)	**39** (2.90)	38	104
Univ of California-San Diego	**37** (3.21)	**35.5** (3.26)	**39.5** (3)	**41** (24)	**35** (3.23)	**33** (3.24)	**49** (72)	**65.5** (3)	**31** (3.06)	**32** (3.02)	22	43
Boston University	**38** (3.20)	**32.5** (3.33)	**32** (4)	**39.5** (26)	**45** (3.00)	**41** (3.10)	**47** (73)	**4.5** (17)	**39** (2.82)	**56.5** (2.40)	38	76
University of Florida	**39** (3.19)	**35.5** (3.26)	**39.5** (3)	**35** (30)	**39** (3.18)	**32** (3.25)	**22.5** (88)	**52.5** (4)	**62** (2.22)	**65** (2.23)	30	104
University of Maryland College Park	**40.5** (3.18)	**32.5** (3.33)	**53** (2)	**33** (31)	**45** (3.00)	**27** (3.33)	**20.5** (89)	**15.5** (12)	**29** (3.16)	**31** (3.05)	73	142
U of Massachusetts at Amherst	**40.5** (3.18)	**44** (3.09)	**53** (2)	**37** (28)	**39** (3.18)	**47** (3.00)	**29.5** (84)	**15.5** (12)	**35** (2.87)	**35** (2.97)	57	161
Pennsylvania State University	**42** (3.14)	**40** (3.16)	**39.5** (3)	**39.5** (26)	**42** (3.03)	**41** (3.10)	**43.5** (76)	**31.5** (6)	**40** (2.78)	**36** (2.95)	44	100
Univ of California-Santa Cruz	**43** (3.10)	**58** (2.97)	**53** (2)	**44** (22)	**37** (3.19)	**60** (2.80)	**62** (66)	**103.5** (1)			14	4
Brandeis University	**44** (3.09)	**46.5** (3.05)	**106** (0)	**44** (22)	**41** (3.08)	**45** (3.02)	**58** (67)	**52.5** (4)	**55** (2.36)	**44** (2.73)	12	76
University of Iowa	**45** (3.07)	**42.5** (3.13)	**53** (2)	**49.5** (19)	**54** (2.90)	**62** (2.78)	**52.5** (69)	**40.5** (5)	**27** (3.25)	**16** (3.60)	44	132
University of Rochester	**46** (3.05)	**58** (2.97)	**73** (1)	**48** (20)	**48** (2.95)	**43** (3.06)	**41** (77)	**40.5** (5)	**33** (2.97)	**30** (3.07)	18	85
University of Kentucky	**47.5** (3.04)	**49** (3.03)	**53** (2)	**56** (15)	**53** (2.91)	**41** (3.10)	**75** (61)	**52.5** (4)	**52.5** (2.39)	**59** (2.37)	29	73
University of California-Davis	**47.5** (3.04)	**70** (2.79)	**53** (2)	**44** (22)	**51** (2.92)	**56** (2.86)	**38** (79)	**25.5** (7)	**46.5** (2.56)	**54** (2.45)	25	80
State U of New York-Stony Brook	**49** (3.03)	**51.5** (3.01)	**53** (2)	**46.5** (21)	**47** (2.98)	**53** (2.90)	**29.5** (84)	**65.5** (3)	**30** (3.10)	**25.5** (3.23)	32	164
Washington University	**50** (3.02)	**39** (3.18)	**73** (1)	**52.5** (17)	**45** (3.00)	**57** (2.83)	**47** (73)	**52.5** (4)	**44** (2.64)	**43** (2.77)	22	97
Carnegie Mellon University	**51.5** (2.97)	**37** (3.25)	**25** (7)	**46.5** (21)	**67** (2.57)	**51** (2.94)	**58** (67)	**82** (2)			16	45
University of Colorado	**51.5** (2.97)	**58** (2.97)	**106** (0)	**49.5** (19)	**45** (3.00)	**35** (3.22)	**38** (79)	**40.5** (5)	**49** (2.49)	**45.5** (2.72)	35	75
Rice University	**53** (2.95)	**56** (2.98)	**106** (0)	**52.5** (17)	**51** (2.92)	**71** (2.62)	**55.5** (68)	**25.5** (7)	**48** (2.55)	**48.5** (2.67)	21	57
University of Georgia	**54** (2.91)	**63** (2.92)	**106** (0)	**58.5** (14)	**49** (2.94)	**62** (2.78)	**41** (77)	**40.5** (5)	**77** (1.62)	**75** (1.92)	32	81
University of South Carolina	**55** (2.90)	**50** (3.02)	**39.5** (3)	**54** (16)	**56** (2.81)	**58** (2.82)	**55.5** (68)	**22.5** (8)	**34** (2.90)	**42** (2.82)	43	99
Texas A&M University	**56** (2.89)	**66** (2.83)	**73** (1)	**61.5** (13)	**68** (2.56)	**79** (2.33)	**79.5** (59)	**25.5** (7)	**78** (1.62)	**78** (1.77)	55	80
Purdue University	**57** (2.83)	**46.5** (3.05)	**32** (4)	**66** (11)	**61** (2.71)	**66** (2.71)	**69.5** (63)	**65.5** (3)	**60** (2.28)	**56.5** (2.40)	49	157
University of Arizona	**58** (2.81)	**54.5** (2.99)	**73** (1)	**61.5** (13)	**57** (2.80)	**54** (2.88)	**41** (77)	**65.5** (3)	**67** (2.09)	**60.5** (2.33)	32	63
Michigan State University	**60** (2.80)	**73** (2.72)	**39.5** (3)	**56** (15)	**64** (2.65)	**76** (2.38)	**52.5** (69)	**52.5** (4)	**36** (2.87)	**39** (2.90)	46	133
Louisiana State U & A&M College	**60** (2.80)	**54.5** (2.99)	**53** (2)	**61.5** (13)	**55** (2.82)	**41** (3.10)	**52.5** (69)	**40.5** (5)	**63** (2.21)	**62.5** (2.30)	47	111

Institution	93Q [1]	93E [1]	% D [1]	% D-S [1]	93Q T [1]	93E T [1]	VIS [1]	FA [2]	82Q [3]	82E [3]	TF [4]	TG [4]
University of Missouri-Columbia	**60** (2.80)	**69** (2.80)	**53** (2)	**61.5** (13)	**63** (2.70)	**49** (2.96)	**67.5** (64)	**52.5** (4)	**68** (2.08)	**70** (2.15)	34	84
Temple University	**62** (2.79)	**68** (2.81)	**53** (2)	**58.5** (14)	**60** (2.73)	**68** (2.67)	**50** (70)	**40.5** (5)	**65** (2.17)	**71** (2.08)	42	71
University of Notre Dame	**63** (2.78)	**63** (2.92)	**39.5** (3)	**56** (15)	**58** (2.77)	**59** (2.81)	**52.5** (69)	**52.5** (4)	**72** (1.90)	**66** (2.22)	38	54
University of Illinois at Chicago	**64** (2.75)	**76** (2.58)	**106** (0)	**66** (11)	**59** (2.74)	**86** (2.14)	**62** (66)	**31.5** (6)			29	81
Boston College	**65** (2.72)	**61** (2.94)	**73** (1)	**75** (8)	**51** (2.92)	**37** (3.15)	**82** (55)	**103.5** (1)	**75** (1.69)	**86** (1.52)	34	27
University of Oregon	**66** (2.71)	**60** (2.95)	**106** (0)	**79** (7)	**65** (2.64)	**51** (2.94)	**71.5** (62)	**65.5** (3)	**59** (2.30)	**60.5** (2.33)	37	90
State Univ of New York-Binghamton	**67** (2.67)	**48** (3.04)	**73** (1)	**66** (11)	**66** (2.60)	**64** (2.74)	**69.5** (63)	**103.5** (1)	**45** (2.58)	**48.5** (2.67)	31	50
University of Tennessee-Knoxville	**68** (2.66)	**65** (2.84)	**53** (2)	**69** (10)	**73** (2.45)	**86** (2.14)	**75** (61)	**40.5** (5)	**51** (2.43)	**52.5** (2.48)	35	73
University of Kansas	**69** (2.65)	**51.5** (3.01)	**53** (2)	**75** (8)	**72** (2.49)	**68** (2.67)	**67.5** (64)	**103.5** (1)	**52.5** (2.39)	**51** (2.53)	41	104
Tufts University	**70** (2.64)	**53** (3.00)	**106** (0)	**64** (12)	**63** (2.70)	**65** (2.73)	**65.5** (65)	**103.5** (1)	**56** (2.36)	**47** (2.70)	16	48
University of Miami	**71** (2.57)	**74.5** (2.61)	**73** (1)	**71.5** (9)	**70** (2.55)	**52** (2.92)	**62** (66)	**82** (2)			17	16
Saint Louis University	**72** (2.56)	**77** (2.55)	**53** (2)	**75** (8)	**74** (2.38)	**86** (2.14)	**58** (67)	**82** (2)	**66** (2.10)	**69** (2.17)	15	22
University of New Hampshire	**73** (2.55)	**85** (2.37)	**73** (1)	**69** (10)	**70** (2.55)	**90** (2.04)	**79.5** (59)	**82** (2)			40	24
University of Nebraska-Lincoln	**74** (2.53)	**71** (2.78)	**39.5** (3)	**82.5** (6)	**79** (2.27)	**62** (2.78)	**81** (57)	**103.5** (1)	**54** (2.37)	**52.5** (2.48)	55	94
Miami University	**75** (2.49)	**67** (2.82)	**73** (1)	**69** (10)	**75** (2.37)	**81** (2.26)	**62** (66)	**65.5** (3)			34	30
Syracuse University	**76** (2.47)	**91.5** (2.29)	**73** (1)	**71.5** (9)	**78** (2.29)	**94** (1.88)	**62** (66)	**103.5** (1)	**58** (2.32)	**55** (2.42)	27	16
Wayne State University	**77** (2.39)	**82** (2.47)	**106** (0)	**82.5** (6)	**76** (2.36)	**74** (2.40)	**71.5** (62)	**82** (2)	**69** (2.04)	**67.5** (2.20)	39	39
Arizona State University	**79** (2.38)	**72** (2.76)	**73** (1)	**75** (8)	**87** (2.04)	**70** (2.64)	**75** (61)	**82** (2)	**73** (1.75)	**73** (2.00)	28	58
George Washington University	**79** (2.38)	**105** (2.10)	**106** (0)	**79** (7)	**83** (2.08)	**103** (1.53)	**93.5** (47)	**52.5** (4)			23	44
University of Alabama	**79** (2.38)	**74.5** (2.61)	**106** (0)	**92** (4)	**77** (2.32)	**76** (2.38)	**89.5** (48)	**82** (2)			38	89
Claremont Graduate School	**81.5** (2.31)	**86** (2.35)	**73** (1)	**51** (18)	**71** (2.54)	**83** (2.22)	**75** (61)	**82** (2)	**50** (2.45)	**33.5** (2.98)	3	53
University of Connecticut	**81.5** (2.31)	**63** (2.92)	**106** (0)	**107** (2)	**80** (2.16)	**47** (3.00)	**78** (60)	**40.5** (5)	**64** (2.20)	**62.5** (2.30)	33	137
Tulane University	**83** (2.26)	**89** (2.31)	**73** (1)	**75** (8)	**89** (2.00)	**92** (1.95)	**75** (61)	**52.5** (4)	**61** (2.25)	**58** (2.38)	23	80
University of Oklahoma	**84** (2.25)	**100** (2.15)	**73** (1)	**92** (4)	**82** (2.12)	**91** (1.98)	**65.5** (65)	**52.5** (4)	**71** (1.91)	**74** (1.98)	26	27
Florida State University	**85** (2.23)	**97** (2.25)	**106** (0)	**92** (4)	**87** (2.04)	**95** (1.85)	**85.5** (51)	**31.5** (6)	**83.5** (1.33)	**89** (1.45)	33	90
Univ of Southern Mississippi	**86.5** (2.19)	**96** (2.26)	**73** (1)	**86.5** (5)	**100** (1.62)	**112** (1.25)	**102.5** (44)	**121** (0)			24	35
Washington State University	**86.5** (2.19)	**80** (2.50)	**106** (0)	**124** (0)	**85** (2.07)	**72** (2.50)	**116.5** (35)	**121** (0)	**83.5** (1.33)	**84.5** (1.55)	26	61
University of Houston	**88** (2.15)	**80** (2.50)	**106** (0)	**86.5** (5)	**81** (2.14)	**68** (2.67)	**85.5** (51)	**82** (2)			35	93
Texas Christian University	**89** (2.13)	**94.5** (2.27)	**53** (2)	**82.5** (6)	**109** (1.45)	**117** (1.04)	**110.5** (40)	**121** (0)			14	39
Loyola University of Chicago	**90.5** (2.11)	**78** (2.54)	**73** (1)	**79** (7)	**91** (1.86)	**90** (2.04)	**93.5** (47)	**82** (2)	**89** (1.26)	**80.5** (1.67)	28	44

Appendix Table P - 17 English Language and Literature (Continued)

Institution	93Q [1]	93E [1]	% D [1]	% D-S [1]	93Q T [1]	93E T [1]	VIS [1]	FA [2]	82Q [3]	82E [3]	TF [4]	TG [4]
Case Western Reserve Univ	**90.5** (2.11)	**87** (2.33)	**106** (0)	**98.5** (3)	**89** (2.00)	**88** (2.08)	**89.5** (48)	**121** (0)	**80** (1.51)	**83** (1.58)	14	58
Auburn University	**92.5** (2.08)	**103** (2.11)	**53** (2)	**86.5** (5)	**104** (1.56)	**109** (1.33)	**102.5** (44)	**82** (2)	**94** (1.00)	**96** (1.12)	32	30
Kent State University	**92.5** (2.08)	**94.5** (2.27)	**106** (0)	**107** (2)	**85** (2.07)	**76** (2.38)	**106** (43)	**65.5** (3)	**76** (1.67)	**84.5** (1.55)	30	75
University of North Texas	**94** (2.05)	**107** (2.05)	**53** (2)	**82.5** (6)	**94** (1.77)	**99** (1.67)	**87.5** (50)	**103.5** (1)			43	77
University of Tulsa	**95** (2.02)	**83** (2.46)	**106** (0)	**98.5** (3)	**89** (2.00)	**73** (2.43)	**84** (52)	**103.5** (1)	**91** (1.21)	**92** (1.37)	13	28
University of Mississippi	**96** (1.95)	**108** (2.02)	**106** (0)	**107** (2)	**97** (1.71)	**119** (1.00)	**93.5** (47)	**121** (0)	**87.5** (1.28)	**88** (1.47)	25	51
U of North Carolina-Greensboro	**97** (1.94)	**98** (2.19)	**73** (1)	**98.5** (3)	**111** (1.42)	**112** (1.25)	**106** (43)	**103.5** (1)			28	56
Northern Illinois University	**98** (1.87)	**103** (2.11)	**73** (1)	**107** (2)	**107** (1.50)	**107** (1.39)	**108** (42)	**65.5** (3)	**90** (1.21)	**87** (1.48)	40	64
University of Texas at Arlington	**99** (1.83)	**91.5** (2.29)	**106** (0)	**92** (4)	**98** (1.70)	**83** (2.22)	**93.5** (47)	**103.5** (1)			18	87
Bowling Green State University	**100** (1.82)	**84** (2.38)	**106** (0)	**107** (2)	**108** (1.47)	**99** (1.67)	**109** (41)	**103.5** (1)	**85** (1.32)	**82** (1.62)	29	37
University of Texas at Dallas	**101** (1.81)	**118** (1.36)	**106** (0)	**86.5** (5)	**107** (1.50)	**110** (1.30)	**93.5** (47)	**52.5** (4)			15	45
University of Rhode Island	**102** (1.80)	**80** (2.50)	**106** (0)	**107** (2)	**96** (1.72)	**79** (2.33)	**126.5** (29)	**103.5** (1)	**92** (1.19)	**93** (1.30)	20	120
University of Toledo	**103** (1.74)	**120.5** (1.28)	**106** (0)	**92** (4)	**103** (1.57)	**124** (0.42)	**99** (45)	**82** (2)			22	31
Illinois State University	**104** (1.72)	**113.5** (1.76)	**106** (0)	**107** (2)	**100** (1.62)	**107** (1.39)	**112** (38)	**121** (0)			36	59
Ohio University	**105.5** (1.69)	**103** (2.11)	**73** (1)	**98.5** (3)	**105** (1.53)	**109** (1.33)	**116.5** (35)	**103.5** (1)	**82** (1.46)	**80.5** (1.67)	15	23
Univ of Southwestern Louisiana	**105.5** (1.69)	**112** (1.78)	**106** (0)	**107** (2)	**102** (1.59)	**99** (1.67)	**97** (46)	**65.5** (3)			28	52
Texas Tech University	**107.5** (1.67)	**101** (2.12)	**106** (0)	**92** (4)	**120** (0.95)	**119** (1.00)	**102.5** (44)	**52.5** (4)	**95** (0.87)	**94** (1.23)	30	46
University of Denver	**107.5** (1.67)	**88** (2.32)	**106** (0)	**107** (2)	**94** (1.77)	**93** (1.91)	**99** (45)	**103.5** (1)	**93** (1.17)	**90.5** (1.43)	21	27
University of Cincinnati	**109** (1.66)	**99** (2.17)	**106** (0)	**116.5** (1)	**110** (1.43)	**99** (1.67)	**99** (45)	**121** (0)			17	32
Fordham University	**110.5** (1.64)	**113.5** (1.76)	**73** (1)	**98.5** (3)	**92** (1.80)	**104** (1.48)	**83** (53)	**103.5** (1)	**79** (1.62)	**72** (2.02)	17	109
Southern Illinois University	**110.5** (1.64)	**106** (2.08)	**73** (1)	**116.5** (1)	**102** (1.59)	**99** (1.67)	**106** (43)	**82** (2)	**74** (1.73)	**78** (1.77)	13	0
Howard University	**112** (1.60)	**91.5** (2.29)	**106** (0)	**116.5** (1)	**95** (1.75)	**79** (2.33)	**124** (31)	**103.5** (1)			12	27
West Virginia University	**113** (1.58)	**116** (1.57)	**106** (0)	**116.5** (1)	**112** (1.38)	**115** (1.11)	**93.5** (47)	**65.5** (3)			30	29
Lehigh University	**114** (1.56)	**91.5** (2.29)	**106** (0)	**116.5** (1)	**113** (1.35)	**99** (1.67)	**119** (34)	**82** (2)	**86** (1.30)	**76** (1.85)	16	54
Ball State University	**115** (1.49)	**110.5** (1.85)	**106** (0)	**124** (0)	**118** (1.06)	**83** (2.22)	**110.5** (40)	**103.5** (1)	**87.5** (1.28)	**90.5** (1.43)	21	18
Univ of Arkansas-Fayetteville	**116** (1.47)	**110.5** (1.85)	**106** (0)	**116.5** (1)	**115** (1.27)	**99** (1.67)	**113.5** (37)	**82** (2)	**81** (1.47)	**78** (1.77)	19	23
University of South Florida	**117** (1.38)	**120.5** (1.28)	**106** (0)	**17** (2)	**116** (1.22)	**120** (0.93)	**119** (34)	**103.5** (1)			24	82
University of North Dakota	**118** (1.24)	**109** (1.95)	**106** (0)	**124** (0)	**114** (1.30)	(n/s)	**124** (31)	**103.5** (1)	**97** (0.71)	**98** (0.78)	23	49
Baylor University	**119** (1.19)	**119** (1.31)	**106** (0)	**124** (0)	**122** (0.83)	**115** (1.11)	**113.5** (37)	**121** (0)			13	13
Catholic University of America	**120.5** (1.14)	**117** (1.47)	**73** (1)	**92** (4)	**117** (1.18)	**105** (1.43)	**87.5** (50)	**121** (0)	**98** (0.57)	**97** (1.05)	10	39

Institution	93Q [1]	93E [1]	% D [1]	% D-S [1]	93Q T [1]	93E T [1]	VIS [1]	FA [2]	82Q [3]	82E [3]	TF [4]	TG [4]
St. John's University	**120.5** (1.14)	**124** (0.93)	**106** (0)	**107** (2)	**119** (1.00)	**122** (0.83)	**122** (32)	**121** (0)			11	35
Oklahoma State University	**122** (1.13)	**115** (1.58)	**106** (0)	**98.5** (3)	**121** (0.88)	**117** (1.04)	**102.5** (44)	**82** (2)	**96** (0.82)	**95** (1.18)	15	153
Indiana Univ of Pennsylvania	**123** (0.89)	**122** (1.21)	**106** (0)	**124** (0)	**123** (0.65)	**113** (1.19)	**119** (34)	**121** (0)			16	84
Drew University	**124** (0.84)	**126** (0.83)	**106** (0)	**116.5** (1)	**125** (0.46)	**122** (0.83)	**126.5** (29)	**121** (0)			12	45
Texas Woman's University	**125** (0.80)	**126** (0.83)	**106** (0)	**116.5** (1)	**126** (0.42)	**126** (0.00)	**121** (33)	**121** (0)			11	28
Idaho State University	**126** (0.72)	**126** (0.83)	**106** (0)	**124** (0)	**124** (0.61)	**122** (0.83)	**124** (31)	**82** (2)			23	12
Middle Tennessee State University	**127** (0.61)	**123** (1.00)	**106** (0)	**124** (0)	**127** (0.08)	**125** (0.33)	**115** (36)	**103.5** (1)			22	12

Sources: 1. National Survey of Graduate Faculty
2. Associations and Organizations Administrating Prestigious Awards and Honors
3. 1982 Survey of Graduate Faculty
4. Institutional Coordinator Data

n/s After trimming no cases remained

* Three programs recieved the highest quality rating, and using the standard convention of average rankings, each program was given a rank of 2.

Appendix Table P - 18 Relative Rankings for Research-Doctorate Programs in French Language and Literature

Institution	93Q [1]	93E [1]	% D [1]	% D-S [1]	93Q T [1]	93E T [1]	VIS [1]	FA [2]	82Q [3]	82E [3]	TF [4]	TG [4]
Yale University	1 (4.68)	1 (4.49)	1 (68)	1 (94)	1 (4.74)	1 (4.65)	6.5 (99)	1 (6)	1 (4.75)	1 (4.57)	18	20
Princeton University	2 (4.55)	2 (4.35)	2 (60)	2.5 (91)	2 (4.48)	2 (4.49)	1.5 (100)	10.5 (3)	2 (4.70)	2 (4.30)	13	26
Duke University	3 (4.43)	8 (3.78)	3 (49)	4 (89)	3 (4.42)	8 (3.73)	11 (98)	3.5 (5)	14.5 (3.20)	16 (3.18)	16	31
Columbia University	4 (4.40)	5.5 (3.90)	4.5 (45)	2.5 (91)	5 (4.37)	6 (3.94)	6.5 (99)	6.5 (4)	3 (4.43)	4 (3.87)	13	90
University of Pennsylvania	5 (4.37)	4 (3.98)	4.5 (45)	5 (87)	4 (4.40)	4 (4.10)	6.5 (99)	3.5 (5)	7 (3.65)	9 (3.43)	11	36
Stanford University	6 (4.20)	12 (3.52)	6 (37)	7 (77)	7 (4.13)	11.5 (3.50)	12 (97)	18 (2)	13 (3.47)	7 (3.52)	12	35
University of California-Berkeley	7 (4.19)	5.5 (3.90)	7 (34)	6 (82)	6 (4.34)	7 (3.90)	6.5 (99)	10.5 (3)	8 (3.60)	12 (3.37)	13	27
Cornell University	8 (4.08)	3 (4.03)	8 (31)	8.5 (76)	8 (4.12)	3 (4.15)	1.5 (100)	10.5 (3)	10 (3.55)	5 (3.68)	17	20
University of Michigan	9 (3.97)	9 (3.73)	10 (20)	8.5 (76)	9 (4.08)	5 (3.96)	6.5 (99)	18 (2)	9 (3.58)	10 (3.42)	14	29
University of California-Irvine	10 (3.78)	27.5 (2.71)	9 (23)	11 (64)	10 (3.77)	28 (2.61)	16.5 (95)	27 (1)	16 (3.19)	19 (3.08)	9	16
University of Wisconsin-Madison	11 (3.74)	7 (3.79)	13.5 (10)	10 (66)	11 (3.68)	10 (3.59)	6.5 (99)	6.5 (4)	14.5 (3.20)	13.5 (3.35)	22	94
New York University	12 (3.66)	11 (3.53)	12 (12)	12 (53)	12 (3.64)	11.5 (3.50)	14 (96)	10.5 (3)	4 (4.25)	3 (3.92)	12	17
University of Virginia	13 (3.60)	10 (3.61)	13.5 (10)	13 (51)	13 (3.47)	9 (3.64)	14 (96)	10.5 (3)	5 (3.70)	13.5 (3.35)	17	46
CUNY - Grad Sch & Univ Center	14 (3.48)	13 (3.28)	16 (9)	14 (48)	15 (3.28)	13 (3.24)	16.5 (95)	18 (2)	6 (3.68)	8 (3.45)	13	43
Emory University	15 (3.38)	27.5 (2.71)	11 (14)	15 (44)	14 (3.44)	22 (2.83)	18.5 (93)	38.5 (0)	42 (1.07)	42 (1.20)	10	25
University of Chicago	16 (3.30)	14.5 (3.11)	16 (9)	16 (40)	16 (3.27)	14 (3.17)	18.5 (93)	18 (2)	18 (3.13)	18 (3.17)	6	59*
Harvard University	17 (3.19)	19 (2.92)	18 (8)	18 (38)	19 (3.11)	18 (2.97)	6.5 (99)	18 (2)	17 (3.16)	25 (2.70)	7	34
Johns Hopkins University	18.5 (3.13)	26 (2.72)	16 (9)	17 (39)	18 (3.16)	21 (2.85)	6.5 (99)	18 (2)	26 (2.50)	22.5 (2.75)	5	7
Univ of California-Los Angeles	18.5 (3.13)	21 (2.87)	32.5 (1)	23 (23)	17 (3.18)	15 (3.03)	24.5 (88)	27 (1)	29 (2.41)	26 (2.68)	12	38
Louisiana State U & A&M College	20 (3.08)	25 (2.73)	21 (3)	21 (26)	20 (3.10)	26 (2.73)	23 (89)	27 (1)			15	21
Brown University	21 (3.07)	14.5 (3.11)	26 (2)	19 (28)	21 (2.93)	18 (2.97)	30.5 (84)	27 (1)	22 (2.73)	16 (3.18)	12	24
Rutgers State Univ-New Brunswick	22 (3.03)	33 (2.62)	21 (3)	24 (22)	22 (2.91)	29 (2.57)	33.5 (82)	38.5 (0)	24 (2.62)	31 (2.50)	18	46
University of Texas at Austin	23 (2.97)	17 (2.96)	21 (3)	21 (26)	30.5 (2.62)	23 (2.82)	27.5 (86)	27 (1)	21 (2.89)	20 (3.02)	25	18
Washington University	24 (2.93)	35 (2.55)	19 (4)	21 (26)	27 (2.79)	35 (2.33)	14 (96)	38.5 (0)	33 (2.32)	29 (2.53)	10	32
Indiana University	25 (2.89)	16 (3.07)	26 (2)	25 (20)	28 (2.69)	18 (2.97)	29 (85)	27 (1)	12 (3.49)	6 (3.65)	23	75
University of Minnesota	26.5 (2.88)	20 (2.91)	26 (2)	28 (18)	26 (2.82)	24 (2.76)	24.5 (88)	27 (1)	32 (2.33)	32.5 (2.48)	12	34
University of Iowa	26.5 (2.88)	31 (2.69)	40.5 (0)	26 (19)	25 (2.83)	27 (2.67)	32 (83)	38.5 (0)	35 (2.26)	37 (2.32)	12	17
University of California-Davis	28 (2.82)	22 (2.83)	26 (2)	28 (18)	23 (2.87)	16 (2.99)	21 (91)	18 (2)	20 (2.90)	24 (2.72)	8	2
Northwestern University	29 (2.71)	24 (2.75)	32.5 (1)	32 (14)	30.5 (2.62)	25 (2.75)	30.5 (84)	3.5 (5)	30 (2.38)	30 (2.52)	12	11
Ohio State University	30.5 (2.70)	23 (2.77)	32.5 (1)	28 (18)	32.5 (2.55)	32 (2.46)	27.5 (86)	38.5 (0)	25 (2.60)	27.5 (2.63)	20	60

Institution	93Q [1]	93E [1]	% D [1]	% D-S [1]	93Q T [1]	93E T [1]	VIS [1]	FA [2]	82Q [3]	82E [3]	TF [4]	TG [4]
U of Illinois at Urbana-Champaign	**30.5** (2.70)	**18** (2.94)	**32.5** (1)	**32** (14)	**33** (2.55)	**20** (2.86)	**33.5** (82)	**38.5** (0)	**11** (3.53)	**11** (3.40)	17	60
Rice University	**32** (2.68)	**34** (2.59)	**26** (2)	**32** (14)	**24** (2.85)	**30** (2.55)	**26** (87)	**10.5** (3)	**27** (2.47)	**22.5** (2.75)	9	11
Pennsylvania State University	**33** (2.66)	**29** (2.70)	**40.5** (0)	**34** (12)	**36** (2.36)	**34** (2.40)	**20** (92)	**18** (2)	**23** (2.64)	**21** (2.90)	18	42
U of North Carolina-Chapel Hill	**34** (2.63)	**31** (2.69)	**32.5** (1)	**35** (11)	**34** (2.40)	**34** (2.40)	**36.5** (79)	**38.5** (0)	**19** (2.95)	**16** (3.18)	10	44
University of Washington	**35** (2.60)	**40** (2.08)	**26** (2)	**30** (15)	**29** (2.64)	**37** (2.13)	**22** (90)	**27** (1)	**34** (2.32)	**27.5** (2.63)	8	20
Tulane University	**36.5** (2.41)	**38** (2.12)	**40.5** (0)	**36.5** (8)	**35** (2.38)	**39** (1.96)	**35** (80)	**3.5** (5)	**39** (2.09)	**36** (2.35)	12	38
University of Florida	**36.5** (2.41)	**36.5** (2.13)	**40.5** (0)	**39** (7)	**41** (2.13)	**43** (1.67)	**38** (76)	**38.5** (0)			8	9
U of Massachusetts at Amherst	**38** (2.39)	**42** (1.88)	**40.5** (0)	**39** (7)	**37** (2.34)	**41** (1.77)	**39** (75)	**38.5** (0)	**31** (2.35)	**34** (2.45)	15	14
Michigan State University	**39** (2.33)	**31** (2.69)	**40.5** (0)	**39** (7)	**39** (2.27)	**31** (2.50)	**36.5** (79)	**38.5** (0)	**37** (2.22)	**38** (2.22)	12	31
University of Pittsburgh	**40** (2.21)	**41** (2.01)	**40.5** (0)	**41** (5)	**38** (2.30)	**36** (2.29)	**40** (72)	**18** (2)	**28** (2.45)	**35** (2.37)	10	12
University of Maryland College Park	**41** (2.18)	**43** (1.87)	**26** (2)	**36.5** (8)	**41** (2.13)	**44** (1.54)	**42** (67)	**27** (1)	**40** (1.94)	**40** (1.90)	18	14
University of Kansas	**42** (2.12)	**39** (2.10)	**40.5** (0)	**42** (3)	**43** (1.93)	**40** (1.78)	**41** (69)	**38.5** (0)	**36** (2.26)	**32.5** (2.48)	9	12
University of Oregon	**43** (1.92)	**36.5** (2.13)	**32.5** (1)	**43** (2)	**42** (2.07)	**38** (2.08)	**43.5** (59)	**38.5** (0)	**38** (2.11)	**39** (2.03)	10	4
University of Cincinnati	**44** (1.66)	**44** (1.83)	**40.5** (0)	**45** (0)	**44** (1.61)	**43** (1.67)	**43.5** (59)	**38.5** (0)			10	19
Catholic University of America	**45** (1.13)	**45** (1.09)	**40.5** (0)	**44** (1)	**45** (1.04)	**45** (1.03)	**45** (56)	**38.5** (0)	**41** (1.21)	**41** (1.62)	5	15**

Sources: 1. National Survey of Graduate Faculty
2. Associations and Organizations Administrating Prestigious Awards and Honors
3. 1982 Survey of Graduate Faculty
4. Institutional Coordinator Data

* Enrollment data is for the Romance Language Department which includes French, Spanish, and Portuguese Language and Literature programs

** Enrollment data is for the Modern Language Department which includes French, Spanish, and Portuguese Language and Literature programs

Appendix Table P - 19 Relative Rankings for Research-Doctorate Programs in Geography

Institution	93Q [1]	93E [1]	% D [1]	% D-S [1]	93Q T [1]	93E T [1]	VIS [1]	TC [2]	C/F [2]	82Q [3]	82E [3]	TF [4]	TG [4]
Pennsylvania State University	1 (4.59)	1 (4.18)	1 (61)	1 (92)	1 (4.58)	1 (4.21)	2.5 (98)	19.5 (83)	22 (4.0)	2 (4.30)	4 (3.97)	21	38
University of Wisconsin-Madison	2 (4.40)	2 (4.14)	2 (52)	2 (84)	2 (4.37)	2 (4.11)	2.5 (98)	23 (69)	25 (3.1)	4 (4.13)	2 (4.12)	22	51
University of Minnesota	3 (4.22)	4 (3.95)	3 (38)	3 (83)	3 (4.21)	4 (3.84)	2.5 (98)	17 (102)	20.5 (4.1)	1 (4.56)	1 (4.25)	25	72
Univ of California-Santa Barbara	4 (4.16)	4 (3.95)	5 (29)	4 (78)	4 (4.10)	5 (3.79)	7 (94)	1 (359)	1 (18.0)			20	79
Ohio State University	5 (4.07)	4 (3.95)	6 (26)	5 (77)	5 (4.09)	3 (3.91)	9.5 (93)	3 (242)	9 (12.1)	6 (3.86)	5 (3.93)	20	45
University of California-Berkeley	6.5 (3.99)	7 (3.73)	4 (31)	8 (69)	7 (4.04)	6 (3.67)	6 (96)	15 (106)	14 (7.6)	3 (4.18)	3 (4.02)	14	50
Syracuse University	6.5 (3.99)	6 (3.78)	8 (21)	7 (72)	8 (3.95)	9 (3.58)	12 (92)	26 (51)	26 (2.8)	8 (3.58)	11 (3.38)	18	38
Univ of California-Los Angeles	8 (3.95)	12 (3.50)	7 (22)	6 (74)	6 (4.07)	11 (3.46)	5 (97)	2 (247)	7 (12.4)	5 (3.97)	6 (3.73)	20	44
Clark University	9 (3.82)	8 (3.63)	9 (16)	9 (67)	9 (3.90)	7 (3.65)	2.5 (98)	5.5 (213)	5 (13.3)	7 (3.81)	7.5 (3.63)	16	60
University of Washington	10 (3.66)	10 (3.55)	10.5 (10)	11 (54)	10 (3.59)	10 (3.54)	15.5 (89)	7 (201)	4 (14.4)	9 (3.56)	7.5 (3.63)	14	37
State Univ of New York-Buffalo	11 (3.63)	11 (3.51)	10.5 (10)	10 (57)	11 (3.56)	13 (3.33)	13.5 (90)	19.5 (83)	19 (4.9)	15 (3.18)	20 (2.83)	17	30
University of Colorado	12 (3.57)	9 (3.61)	12 (8)	12 (48)	12 (3.49)	8 (3.61)	9.5 (93)	5.5 (213)	6 (12.5)	17.5 (2.97)	18 (3.00)	17	61
Rutgers State Univ-New Brunswick	13 (3.39)	16 (3.17)	16.5 (3)	13 (43)	14 (3.35)	19 (3.07)	18 (88)	11 (129)	18 (5.2)	21 (2.86)	23 (2.63)	25	23
University of Texas at Austin	14 (3.38)	24 (2.88)	13 (6)	15.5 (36)	13 (3.36)	25.5 (2.74)	21.5 (84)	22 (78)	23 (3.5)	25 (2.53)	29 (2.27)	22	19
Arizona State University	15 (3.35)	15 (3.22)	14.5 (4)	14 (41)	15 (3.28)	17 (3.11)	9.5 (93)	8 (176)	10 (11.7)			15	36
U of Illinois at Urbana-Champaign	16 (3.30)	14 (3.24)	20 (2)	15.5 (36)	16.5 (3.23)	14 (3.27)	15.5 (89)	14 (109)	16 (6.4)	11 (3.43)	10 (3.40)	17	50
University of Iowa	17 (3.23)	13 (3.33)	14.5 (4)	17 (34)	16.5 (3.23)	12 (3.40)	18 (88)	4 (220)	3 (15.7)	12 (3.33)	9 (3.48)	14	42
Louisiana State U & A&M College	18 (3.19)	17 (3.14)	30.5 (0)	20 (28)	19 (3.10)	18 (3.08)	21.5 (84)	27 (45)	27 (2.6)	14 (3.24)	13 (3.23)	17	49
University of Arizona	19 (3.17)	21 (2.97)	20 (2)	18.5 (30)	18 (3.19)	22 (2.86)	18 (88)	21 (79)	24 (3.4)	26 (2.40)	30 (2.23)	23	17
University of Kentucky	20 (3.10)	20 (3.05)	16.5 (3)	18.5 (30)	21 (3.02)	20 (2.96)	13.5 (90)	28 (30)	28 (2.5)	30 (2.07)	32 (1.95)	12	15
University of Georgia	21 (3.02)	19 (3.08)	20 (2)	21 (20)	20 (3.04)	16 (3.16)	9.5 (93)	18 (92)	15 (7.1)	16 (3.15)	15 (3.10)	13	20
U of North Carolina-Chapel Hill	22 (2.89)	23 (2.92)	30.5 (0)	24 (16)	25 (2.78)	21 (2.87)	20 (86)	9 (148)	8 (12.3)	23 (2.62)	22 (2.72)	12	26
Johns Hopkins University	23 (2.87)	18 (3.11)	20 (2)	22 (19)	22 (2.95)	15 (3.20)	25 (79)	16 (105)	2 (17.5)	10 (3.53)	14 (3.17)	6	20
University of Florida	24 (2.86)	26 (2.76)	20 (2)	23 (17)	23 (2.94)	24 (2.75)	23 (82)	25 (58)	17 (5.3)	32 (1.95)	31 (2.07)	11	30
Indiana University	25 (2.77)	25 (2.85)	23.5 (1)	27 (10)	24 (2.79)	27 (2.73)	30.5 (73)	32 (18)	33 (1.5)	20 (2.89)	16 (3.03)	12	15
University of Kansas	26 (2.69)	22 (2.93)	30.5 (0)	27 (10)	27 (2.61)	23 (2.83)	28.5 (76)	34 (12)	35 (1.0)	13 (3.30)	12 (3.30)	12	30
Boston University	27 (2.67)	27 (2.74)	23.5 (1)	25 (12)	26 (2.65)	25.5 (2.74)	27 (77)	10 (133)	13 (7.8)	24 (2.58)	24 (2.40)	17	15
University of Oregon	28 (2.61)	29 (2.60)	30.5 (0)	27 (10)	28 (2.53)	29 (2.46)	26 (78)	12 (111)	11 (10.1)	27.5 (2.29)	25 (2.35)	11	17
University of Maryland College Park	29 (2.40)	30 (2.37)	30.5 (0)	29.5 (6)	29 (2.35)	30 (2.25)	32 (69)	24 (65)	20.5 (4.1)	27.5 (2.29)	27.5 (2.30)	16	21
University of Hawaii at Manoa	30 (2.36)	28 (2.63)	30.5 (0)	29.5 (6)	30 (2.32)	28 (2.63)	33 (67)	29 (28)	31 (2.2)	19 (2.92)	17 (3.02)	13	35

Institution	93Q [1]	93E [1]	% D [1]	% D-S [1]	93Q T [1]	93E T [1]	VIS [1]	TC [2]	C/F [2]	82Q [3]	82E [3]	TF [4]	TG [4]
University of Wisconsin-Milwaukee	**31** (2.35)	**33** (2.21)	**30.5** (0)	**31.5** (5)	**31** (2.31)	**34** (2.07)	**24** (80)	**36** (4)	**36** (0.3)	**17.5** (2.97)	**19** (2.92)	12	20
University of Nebraska-Lincoln	**32** (2.32)	**31** (2.34)	**30.5** (0)	**33** (4)	**32** (2.23)	**31** (2.21)	**30.5** (73)	**31** (21)	**30** (2.3)	**22** (2.70)	**21** (2.78)	9	26
Oregon State University	**33** (2.03)	**32** (2.29)	**30.5** (0)	**31.5** (5)	**35** (1.87)	**33** (2.11)	**35** (65)	**13** (110)	**12** (10.0)	**31** (2.01)	**26** (2.33)	11	16
University of Utah	**34** (1.96)	**35** (1.76)	**30.5** (0)	**34.5** (2)	**33** (2.05)	**35** (1.81)	**36** (58)	**30** (24)	**29** (2.4)	**33** (1.69)	**33.5** (1.72)	10	21
Kent State University	**35** (1.95)	**34** (2.13)	**30.5** (0)	**34.5** (2)	**34** (1.94)	**33** (2.11)	**28.5** (76)	**35** (11)	**34** (1.1)	**34** (1.63)	**33.5** (1.72)	10	17
University of Cincinnati	**36** (1.39)	**36** (1.43)	**30.5** (0)	**36** (1)	**36** (1.45)	**36** (1.36)	**34** (66)	**33** (15)	**32** (2.1)	**29** (2.09)	**27.5** (2.30)	7	15

Sources:
1. National Survey of Graduate Faculty
2. Institute for Scientific Information
3. 1982 Survey of Graduate Faculty
4. Institutional Coordinator Data

Appendix Table P - 20 Relative Rankings for Research-Doctorate Programs in Geosciences

Institution	93Q [1]	93E [1]	% D [1]	% D-S [1]	93Q T [1]	93E T [1]	VIS [1]	TC [2]	C/F [2]	82Q [3]	82E [3]	TF [4]	TG [4]
California Institute Technology	1 (4.87)	1 (4.63)	1 (81)	1.5 (91)	1 (4.90)	1 (4.59)	8 (94)	2 (2976)	2 (99.2)	1 (4.87)	1 (4.62)	30	74
Massachusetts Inst of Technology	2 (4.67)	2 (4.52)	2 (62)	1.5 (91)	2 (4.69)	2 (4.52)	8 (94)	4 (2632)	9 (64.2)	2 (4.75)	2 (4.50)	41	161
University of California-Berkeley	3 (4.45)	4 (4.09)	3 (49)	3 (86)	4 (4.33)	4 (4.07)	5 (95)	12 (1369)	4 (80.5)	8 (4.08)	12 (3.70)	17	35
Columbia University	4 (4.38)	3 (4.14)	4 (46)	4 (83)	3 (4.40)	3 (4.17)	5 (95)	3 (2954)	5 (79.8)	4 (4.28)	4.5 (4.03)	37	107
Stanford University [a]	5 (4.33)	8.5 (3.96)	5.5 (35)	8.5 (76)	5 (4.32)	10 (3.90)	18 (86)	26 (667)	11 (55.6)	6 (4.20)	3 (4.12)	12	32
Univ of California-San Diego	6 (4.23)	5.5 (4.06)	7.5 (33)	12.5 (70)	8 (4.22)	6 (4.04)	15.5 (87)	11 (1471)	24 (36.8)			40	43
University of Chicago	7 (4.22)	7 (4.03)	7.5 (33)	14 (69)	7 (4.24)	8 (3.99)	21 (85)	17 (1091)	16 (43.6)	5 (4.25)	11 (3.75)	25	37
Harvard University	8 (4.20)	14 (3.80)	5.5 (35)	6 (78)	6 (4.30)	11 (3.84)	1 (98)	5 (2180)	3 (90.8)	7 (4.13)	6 (3.97)	24	37
Stanford University	9.5 (4.15)	5.5 (4.06)	9 (32)	6 (78)	12 (4.06)	5 (4.05)	2.5 (96)	16 (1121)	7 (70.1)	13 (3.71)	10 (3.78)	16	41
Cornell University	9.5 (4.15)	16 (3.71)	11.5 (25)	6 (78)	10 (4.10)	16 (3.62)	10 (92)	10 (1474)	14 (49.1)	9 (4.01)	8.5 (3.80)	30	35
Univ of California-Los Angeles	12 (4.11)	17 (3.67)	10 (26)	8.5 (76)	9 (4.14)	15 (3.68)	5 (95)	1 (3406)	12 (54.9)	3 (4.48)	4.5 (4.03)	62	134
Pennsylvania State University	12 (4.11)	13 (3.85)	11.5 (25)	12.5 (70)	14.5 (3.91)	17 (3.57)	11.5 (90)	6 (2087)	31 (29.0)	26 (3.26)	25 (3.30)	72	229
Brown University	12 (4.11)	8.5 (3.96)	14 (23)	10 (74)	11 (4.09)	9 (3.94)	11.5 (90)	13 (1349)	6 (71.0)	15.5 (3.65)	16.5 (3.57)	19	46
Princeton University	14 (4.01)	15 (3.78)	16 (21)	17 (66)	14.5 (3.91)	13 (3.82)	13.5 (89)	19 (817)	15 (48.1)	10 (3.97)	7 (3.82)	17	42
University of Texas at Austin	15.5 (3.96)	19 (3.64)	14 (23)	11 (72)	19 (3.67)	31 (3.21)	2.5 (96)	14 (1177)	70 (9.8)	11 (3.78)	13.5 (3.63)	120	75
Stanford University [b]	15.5 (3.96)	12 (3.86)	18 (14)	19 (55)	13 (3.97)	14 (3.69)	34 (77)	52 (254)	39 (23.1)	23 (3.39)	22 (3.42)	11	26
Johns Hopkins University	17 (3.95)	10 (3.94)	17 (19)	18 (63)	16 (3.83)	7 (4.02)	15.5 (87)	7 (1563)	1 (120.2)	19 (3.62)	16.5 (3.57)	13	32
University of Michigan	18 (3.94)	11 (3.89)	14 (23)	15 (68)	17 (3.79)	12 (3.83)	8 (94)	9 (1512)	13 (52.1)	21 (3.50)	18 (3.55)	29	74
University of Arizona	19 (3.87)	20 (3.62)	19 (11)	16 (67)	18 (3.76)	18.5 (3.50)	13.5 (89)	15 (1123)	25 (34.0)	18 (3.65)	15 (3.62)	33	130
Univ of California-Santa Barbara	20 (3.70)	22 (3.47)	20 (9)	20 (50)	21 (3.55)	22 (3.38)	18 (86)	20 (816)	30 (30.2)	14 (3.68)	13.5 (3.63)	27	48
Northwestern University	21 (3.63)	21 (3.60)	27 (4)	24 (45)	20 (3.57)	18.5 (3.50)	32 (78)	25 (683)	17 (42.7)	20 (3.56)	21 (3.43)	16	18
University of Wisconsin-Madison	22 (3.56)	18 (3.65)	21.5 (7)	22.5 (46)	26 (3.35)	20 (3.44)	24 (84)	30 (574)	34 (26.1)	12 (3.71)	8.5 (3.80)	22	35
University of Washington	23 (3.55)	27 (3.36)	30 (3)	22.5 (46)	23 (3.49)	29 (3.23)	24 (84)	37 (457)	35 (25.4)	24 (3.33)	24 (3.38)	18	55
Univ of California-Santa Cruz	24 (3.54)	29 (3.33)	36 (2)	25.5 (44)	22 (3.51)	27 (3.25)	29.5 (79)	29 (589)	22 (39.3)	34 (3.08)	32.5 (3.12)	15	68
Rice University	25 (3.53)	23 (3.46)	36 (2)	21 (49)	24.5 (3.44)	21 (3.39)	21 (85)	41 (395)	38 (23.2)	50 (2.64)	53.5 (2.72)	17	55
Arizona State University	26 (3.48)	31.5 (3.30)	25 (5)	29.5 (35)	24.5 (3.44)	32.5 (3.20)	51.5 (69)	28 (603)	23 (37.7)	32 (3.13)	32.5 (3.12)	16	31
Virginia Polytech Inst & State U	27 (3.47)	29 (3.33)	21.5 (7)	27 (40)	30 (3.29)	37 (3.11)	37.5 (76)	51 (262)	58 (12.5)	17 (3.65)	20 (3.47)	21	46
University of Southern California	28 (3.46)	29 (3.33)	50 (1)	25.5 (44)	27 (3.34)	29 (3.23)	26.5 (81)	32 (508)	32 (28.2)	33 (3.09)	28 (3.22)	18	70
University of Hawaii at Manoa	29.5 (3.40)	25 (3.38)	27 (4)	29.5 (35)	28 (3.33)	24 (3.33)	47.5 (71)	22 (737)	47 (17.5)	43 (2.91)	53.5 (2.72)	42	48
State U of New York-Stony Brook	29.5 (3.40)	31.5 (3.30)	50 (1)	28 (36)	31 (3.28)	26 (3.28)	37.5 (76)	21 (763)	21 (40.2)	15.5 (3.65)	19 (3.52)	19	52

Institution	93Q [1]	93E [1]	% D [1]	% D-S [1]	93Q T [1]	93E T [1]	VIS [1]	TC [2]	C/F [2]	82Q [3]	82E [3]	TF [4]	TG [4]
University of Minnesota	**31** (3.35)	**24** (3.42)	**23.5** (6)	**33** (31)	**29** (3.30)	**29** (3.23)	**24** (84)	**27** (635)	**26** (33.4)	**25** (3.27)	**26** (3.28)	19	60
Washington University	**32** (3.26)	**26** (3.37)	**36** (2)	**37.5** (25)	**33** (3.19)	**24** (3.33)	**57** (65)	**23** (716)	**18** (42.1)	**49** (2.66)	**40** (2.95)	17	28
University of California-Davis	**33** (3.25)	**42.5** (3.07)	**36** (2)	**35** (29)	**33** (3.19)	**44** (2.95)	**34** (77)	**59** (222)	**55** (13.9)	**44** (2.91)	**36.5** (3.07)	16	19
U of Illinois at Urbana-Champaign	**34** (3.22)	**46** (3.01)	**80** (0)	**31.5** (32)	**36** (3.12)	**49** (2.85)	**18** (86)	**24** (684)	**28** (32.6)	**29** (3.18)	**29** (3.18)	21	41
University of Oregon	**35** (3.21)	**42.5** (3.07)	**50** (1)	**37.5** (25)	**35** (3.13)	**42** (3.02)	**29.5** (79)	**44** (356)	**51** (16.2)	**38** (2.96)	**32.5** (3.12)	22	27
University of Colorado	**36.5** (3.20)	**35** (3.20)	**30** (3)	**34** (30)	**39** (3.04)	**45** (2.92)	**21** (85)	**8** (1558)	**8** (64.9)	**35** (3.06)	**27** (3.25)	24	61
Texas A&M University [a]	**36.5** (3.20)	**37** (3.18)	**50** (1)	**41.5** (22)	**37** (3.09)	**40** (3.03)	**58.5** (63)	**88** (62)	**87** (4.8)	**30** (3.14)	**41.5** (2.93)	13	30
Colorado School of Mines	**38** (3.13)	**40** (3.12)	**23.5** (6)	**31.5** (32)	**45** (2.85)	**49** (2.85)	**29.5** (79)	**64** (164)	**93** (3.2)			52	80
University of Wyoming	**39** (3.12)	**38** (3.17)	**80** (0)	**37.5** (25)	**38** (3.06)	**39** (3.08)	**26.5** (81)	**34** (504)	**29** (31.5)	**48** (2.77)	**43.5** (2.92)	16	30
Dartmouth College	**40.5** (3.08)	**33** (3.28)	**27** (4)	**37.5** (25)	**40** (3.03)	**36** (3.16)	**34** (77)	**61** (209)	**41** (20.9)			10	20
Purdue University	**40.5** (3.08)	**39** (3.15)	**36** (2)	**45** (19)	**41** (3.02)	**33** (3.20)	**29.5** (79)	**33** (506)	**43** (19.5)	**46** (2.81)	**46.5** (2.87)	26	49
Rensselaer Polytechnic Inst	**42** (3.03)	**36** (3.19)	**50** (1)	**46** (18)	**34** (3.16)	**35** (3.17)	**64.5** (59)	**43** (365)	**19.5** (40.6)	**59.5** (2.44)	**62** (2.40)	9	16
Duke University	**43** (2.99)	**55** (2.86)	**36** (2)	**40** (23)	**43** (2.88)	**56** (2.70)	**47.5** (71)	**39** (437)	**36** (24.3)			18	19
University of Utah	**45** (2.97)	**49** (2.95)	**36** (2)	**41.5** (22)	**49** (2.78)	**52** (2.78)	**42.5** (73)	**36** (463)	**27** (33.1)	**36** (3.05)	**32.5** (3.12)	14	25
Ohio State University	**45** (2.97)	**57.5** (2.83)	**36** (2)	**47** (17)	**47** (2.83)	**60** (2.65)	**50** (70)	**54.5** (245)	**74** (9.1)	**42** (2.92)	**39** (3.02)	27	45
Indiana University	**45** (2.97)	**48** (2.97)	**36** (2)	**43.5** (20)	**42** (2.95)	**55** (2.75)	**37.5** (76)	**46** (311)	**59** (12.4)	**28** (3.19)	**23** (3.40)	25	38
U of Massachusetts at Amherst	**47** (2.95)	**44.5** (3.02)	**50** (1)	**50** (15)	**51** (2.68)	**46** (2.88)	**47.5** (71)	**48** (293)	**48** (17.2)	**37** (3.03)	**36.5** (3.07)	17	15
University of Miami	**48** (2.92)	**44.5** (3.02)	**80** (0)	**48.5** (16)	**47** (2.83)	**43** (2.97)	**47.5** (71)	**69** (143)	**57** (13.0)	**31** (3.13)	**35** (3.08)	11	22
Texas A&M University [c]	**49** (2.86)	**50** (2.94)	**50** (1)	**43.5** (20)	**56** (2.63)	**68** (2.43)	**42.5** (73)	**62** (172)	**75** (7.8)	**39** (2.95)	**43.5** (2.92)	22	59
Louisiana State U & A&M College	**50** (2.83)	**60.5** (2.76)	**30** (3)	**54** (12)	**53** (2.66)	**69** (2.41)	**55** (66)	**40** (429)	**53** (14.8)	**57** (2.47)	**51** (2.75)	29	44
University of Kansas	**51** (2.82)	**60.5** (2.76)	**80** (0)	**48.5** (16)	**58** (2.61)	**65** (2.50)	**37.5** (76)	**63** (165)	**67.5** (10.3)	**45** (2.88)	**41.5** (2.93)	16	29
University of Oklahoma	**52** (2.77)	**57.5** (2.83)	**50** (1)	**61** (10)	**50** (2.70)	**59** (2.67)	**53** (67)	**54.5** (245)	**82** (5.8)	**53** (2.59)	**61** (2.42)	42	58
U of North Carolina-Chapel Hill	**53** (2.75)	**51** (2.92)	**80** (0)	**54** (12)	**54** (2.65)	**65** (2.50)	**40.5** (74)	**47** (300)	**42** (20.0)	**41** (2.94)	**30** (3.13)	15	17
University of South Carolina	**55** (2.74)	**70** (2.53)	**50** (1)	**51** (14)	**56** (2.63)	**73** (2.35)	**55** (66)	**38** (440)	**46** (18.3)	**40** (2.94)	**45** (2.88)	24	47
Southern Methodist University	**55** (2.74)	**41** (3.08)	**80** (0)	**58** (11)	**59** (2.59)	**38** (3.10)	**44.5** (72)	**67** (152)	**61.5** (11.7)	**56** (2.54)	**56.5** (2.62)	13	22
New Mexico Inst of Mining & Tech	**55** (2.74)	**64.5** (2.72)	**80** (0)	**65.5** (8)	**49** (2.78)	**50** (2.81)	**60.5** (62)	**68** (147)	**73** (9.2)	**58** (2.46)	**55** (2.68)	16	22
Saint Louis University	**57** (2.73)	**47** (3.00)	**50** (1)	**70** (7)	**44** (2.86)	**35** (3.17)	**96** (38)	**81** (84)	**81** (6.0)	**72** (2.06)	**58.5** (2.53)	14	17
Univ of California-Riverside	**59** (2.69)	**68** (2.56)	**50** (1)	**58** (11)	**52** (2.67)	**59** (2.67)	**64.5** (59)	**53** (251)	**49** (16.7)	**74** (1.95)	**65** (2.28)	15	30
Oregon State University	**59** (2.69)	**52.5** (2.90)	**80** (0)	**52** (13)	**62** (2.53)	**53** (2.76)	**44.5** (72)	**42** (386)	**44** (19.3)	**54** (2.55)	**52** (2.73)	20	23
Lehigh University	**59** (2.69)	**52.5** (2.90)	**80** (0)	**62.5** (9)	**62** (2.53)	**55** (2.75)	**69** (57)	**79** (87)	**80** (6.2)	**68** (2.09)	**71** (2.02)	14	10

Appendix Table P - 20 Geosciences (Continued)

Institution	93Q [1]	93E [1]	% D [1]	% D-S [1]	93Q T [1]	93E T [1]	VIS [1]	TC [2]	C/F [2]	82Q [3]	82E [3]	TF [4]	TG [4]
University of Tennessee-Knoxville	**61** (2.65)	**56** (2.84)	**50** (1)	**58** (11)	**65** (2.52)	**47** (2.87)	**55** (66)	**60** (214)	**52** (15.3)	**73** (2.03)	**70** (2.17)	14	21
University of Nevada, Reno	**62** (2.64)	**75** (2.47)	**80** (0)	**65.5** (8)	**56** (2.63)	**73** (2.35)	**60.5** (62)	**77** (100)	**77.5** (7.1)			14	44
Colorado State University	**63** (2.60)	**63** (2.73)	**80** (0)	**75** (6)	**74** (2.32)	**65** (2.50)	**75** (53)	**98** (23)	**99** (1.4)			17	13
University of Alaska	**64.5** (2.58)	**73** (2.50)	**50** (1)	**70** (7)	**69** (2.42)	**71** (2.38)	**64.5** (59)	**57.5** (227)	**71.5** (9.5)	**55** (2.54)	**66** (2.25)	24	24
University of Houston	**64.5** (2.58)	**66** (2.68)	**50** (1)	**65.5** (8)	**62** (2.53)	**61** (2.56)	**40.5** (74)	**90** (50)	**94** (2.8)	**64** (2.23)	**73** (1.90)	18	20
Florida State University [d]	**66** (2.50)	**34** (3.23)	**80** (0)	**84.5** (4)	**60** (2.56)	**24** (3.33)	**100** (24)	**50** (263)	**50** (16.4)			16	24
University of Texas at Dallas	**67** (2.47)	**82** (2.29)	**80** (0)	**75** (6)	**68** (2.46)	**76** (2.26)	**75** (53)	**45** (333)	**40** (22.2)	**51** (2.62)	**48** (2.85)	15	48
University of Iowa	**68** (2.46)	**54** (2.87)	**80** (0)	**75** (6)	**78** (2.26)	**42** (3.02)	**72.5** (54)	**49** (280)	**45** (18.7)	**61** (2.41)	**50** (2.77)	15	24
University of Florida	**69.5** (2.45)	**73** (2.50)	**80** (0)	**58** (11)	**65** (2.52)	**65** (2.50)	**67.5** (58)	**31** (514)	**33** (27.1)			19	12
University of Cincinnati	**69.5** (2.45)	**70** (2.53)	**80** (0)	**70** (7)	**76** (2.29)	**79** (2.11)	**64.5** (59)	**66** (154)	**54** (14.0)	**47** (2.80)	**49** (2.80)	11	16
State Univ of New York-Binghamton	**71** (2.44)	**79** (2.38)	**80** (0)	**84.5** (4)	**74** (2.32)	**77** (2.15)	**51.5** (69)	**71** (134)	**67.5** (10.3)	**52** (2.62)	**56.5** (2.62)	13	28
Syracuse University	**72** (2.43)	**81** (2.30)	**80** (0)	**70** (7)	**80** (2.18)	**82** (2.00)	**78** (52)	**35** (503)	**10** (55.9)	**62** (2.27)	**60** (2.45)	9	15
University of Rochester	**73.5** (2.42)	**73** (2.50)	**50** (1)	**54** (12)	**67** (2.50)	**65** (2.50)	**62** (60)	**82** (82)	**61.5** (11.7)			7	19
State Univ of New York-Albany	**73.5** (2.42)	**64.5** (2.72)	**80** (0)	**58** (11)	**65** (2.52)	**57** (2.68)	**58.5** (63)	**73** (121)	**37** (24.2)	**22** (3.47)	**38** (3.03)	5	8
University of Pittsburgh	**75** (2.41)	**59** (2.80)	**80** (0)	**89** (3)	**74** (2.32)	**65** (2.50)	**81** (50)	**80** (85)	**77.5** (7.1)	**63** (2.26)	**63** (2.35)	12	16
Georgia Institute of Technology	**76.5** (2.36)	**62** (2.75)	**50** (1)	**75** (6)	**72** (2.35)	**52** (2.78)	**91** (43)	**18** (893)	**19.5** (40.6)			22	48
University of Georgia	**76.5** (2.36)	**84** (2.22)	**80** (0)	**75** (6)	**77** (2.28)	**83** (1.95)	**78** (52)	**57.5** (227)	**60** (11.9)			19	9
Ohio State University [e]	**78** (2.35)	**67** (2.57)	**50** (1)	**80** (5)	**82** (2.14)	**82** (2.00)	**98** (32)	**99** (22)	**96** (2.2)	**27** (3.21)	**46.5** (2.87)	10	44
University of Pennsylvania	**79** (2.34)	**76.5** (2.44)	**80** (0)	**65.5** (8)	**79** (2.24)	**74** (2.31)	**83** (49)	**56** (243)	**69** (10.1)			24	14
Case Western Reserve Univ	**80.5** (2.33)	**78** (2.42)	**80** (0)	**62.5** (9)	**71** (2.39)	**71** (2.38)	**81** (50)	**87** (63)	**65** (10.5)	**66** (2.18)	**67** (2.23)	6	4
CUNY - Grad Sch & Univ Center	**80.5** (2.33)	**89.5** (2.04)	**80** (0)	**80** (5)	**71** (2.39)	**85** (1.83)	**70.5** (55)	**89** (61)	**91** (3.8)			16	28
Michigan State University	**82** (2.31)	**70** (2.53)	**80** (0)	**70** (7)	**85** (2.00)	**78** (2.14)	**67.5** (58)	**70** (138)	**64** (10.6)	**59.5** (2.44)	**58.5** (2.53)	13	9
University of Kentucky	**83** (2.25)	**88** (2.05)	**50** (1)	**80** (5)	**87** (1.86)	**96** (1.11)	**75** (53)	**76** (107)	**76** (7.6)	**70** (2.07)	**77** (1.67)	14	18
State Univ of New York-Buffalo	**84** (2.24)	**86** (2.08)	**80** (0)	**80** (5)	**81** (2.16)	**88** (1.67)	**93** (42)	**91.5** (48)	**88.5** (4.4)			11	15
University of Texas-El Paso	**85** (2.16)	**93** (1.90)	**80** (0)	**89** (3)	**85** (2.00)	**90** (1.37)	**70.5** (55)	**65** (160)	**63** (11.4)			14	23
Michigan Technological University	**86** (2.14)	**76.5** (2.44)	**80** (0)	**84.5** (4)	**92** (1.70)	**88** (1.67)	**78** (52)	**74** (114)	**66** (10.4)			11	12
Washington State University	**87** (2.08)	**83** (2.27)	**80** (0)	**80** (5)	**88** (1.85)	**86** (1.82)	**89.5** (44)	**85** (70)	**86** (5.4)	**71** (2.07)	**68** (2.20)	13	38
Florida State University [c]	**88** (2.07)	**80** (2.36)	**80** (0)	**89** (3)	**83** (2.04)	**76** (2.26)	**72.5** (54)	**83** (80)	**83** (5.7)	**67** (2.16)	**64** (2.32)	14	16
Iowa State University	**89** (2.05)	**87** (2.07)	**80** (0)	**95.5** (1)	**86** (1.96)	**80** (2.08)	**81** (50)	**86** (69)	**79** (6.9)	**65** (2.20)	**72** (1.93)	10	11
Northern Illinois University	**90** (2.02)	**85** (2.17)	**80** (0)	**95.5** (1)	**90** (1.76)	**84** (1.88)	**84.5** (48)	**78** (96)	**84** (5.6)			17	16

Institution	93Q [1]	93E [1]	% D [1]	% D-S [1]	93Q T [1]	93E T [1]	VIS [1]	TC [2]	C/F [2]	82Q [3]	82E [3]	TF [4]	TG [4]
Texas Tech University	**91** (1.97)	**94** (1.85)	**80** (0)	**89** (3)	**89** (1.83)	**96** (1.11)	**95** (40)	**96** (32)	**97** (2.0)			16	18
University of Alabama	**92** (1.92)	**89.5** (2.04)	**80** (0)	**95.5** (1)	**93** (1.64)	**91** (1.33)	**87.5** (45)	**72** (123)	**71.5** (9.5)			13	6
University of Nebraska-Lincoln	**93** (1.82)	**92** (1.98)	**80** (0)	**89** (3)	**91** (1.74)	**88** (1.67)	**84.5** (48)	**100** (20)	**100** (1.3)			15	23
South Dakota Sch of Mines & Tech	**94** (1.80)	**91** (1.99)	**80** (0)	**95.5** (1)	**94** (1.59)	**92** (1.30)	**93** (42)	**93** (40)	**90** (4.0)			10	12
Kent State University	**95** (1.78)	**98** (1.45)	**80** (0)	**84.5** (4)	**97** (1.35)	**98** (0.90)	**89.5** (44)	**97** (26)	**98** (1.9)			14	11
University of Idaho	**96** (1.71)	**96** (1.61)	**80** (0)	**92** (2)	**96** (1.50)	**97** (1.06)	**87.5** (45)	**94** (36)	**95** (2.4)	**76** (1.58)	**75** (1.83)	15	16
University of Wisconsin-Milwaukee	**97** (1.64)	**95** (1.67)	**50** (1)	**95.5** (1)	**96** (1.50)	**93** (1.25)	**97** (36)	**84** (79)	**88.5** (4.4)			18	9
West Virginia University	**98** (1.57)	**97** (1.49)	**80** (0)	**99.5** (0)	**99** (1.19)	**94** (1.21)	**93** (42)	**91.5** (48)	**92** (3.4)	**69** (2.08)	**69** (2.18)	14	13
University of Missouri-Rolla	**99** (1.22)	**99** (1.21)	**80** (0)	**95.5** (1)	**100** (1.10)	**99** (0.83)	**86** (46)	**95** (33)	**85** (5.5)	**75** (1.77)	**74** (1.85)	6	7
George Washington University	**100** (1.16)	**100** (0.63)	**80** (0)	**99.5** (0)	**98** (1.22)	**100** (0.00)	**99** (27)	**75** (110)	**56** (13.8)	**77** (1.56)	**76** (1.73)	8	12

Sources: 1. National Survey of Graduate Faculty
2. Institute for Scientific Information
3. 1982 Survey of Graduate Faculty
4. Institutional Coordinator Data

Notes: *a.* Program in Geophysics
b. Program in Applied Earth Sciences
c. Program in Geology
d. Program in Meteorology
e. Program in Geodetic Science and Surveying

Appendix Table P - 21 Relative Rankings for Research-Doctorate Programs in German Language and Literature

Institution	93Q [1]	93E [1]	% D [1]	% D-S [1]	93Q T [1]	93E T [1]	VIS [1]	FA [2]	82Q [3]	82E [3]	TF [4]	TG [4]
University of California-Berkeley	1 (4.32)	2 (3.88)	1.5 (42)	1 (84)	1 (4.33)	3 (3.73)	5 (97)	4.5 (3)	4 (4.35)	6 (4.07)	16	33
Princeton University	2 (4.22)	1 (3.91)	1.5 (42)	2.5 (76)	2.5 (4.29)	1 (3.79)	7.5 (96)	8.5 (2)	3 (4.47)	3.5 (4.18)	11	22
Cornell University	3 (4.19)	4 (3.73)	3 (41)	4 (74)	2.5 (4.29)	2 (3.75)	7.5 (96)	1 (8)	8 (4.09)	8 (3.73)	20	27
Harvard University	4 (4.01)	3 (3.78)	5 (29)	2.5 (76)	4 (4.06)	4 (3.71)	2.5 (99)	16 (1)	10 (3.75)	11.5 (3.45)	10	22
Yale University	5 (3.95)	5 (3.68)	4 (31)	5 (71)	6 (3.83)	9 (3.43)	1 (100)	16 (1)	2 (4.52)	1 (4.33)	9	17
Stanford University	6 (3.83)	7 (3.61)	7 (23)	8 (63)	5 (3.85)	5 (3.69)	4 (98)	4.5 (3)	7 (4.10)	7 (4.00)	7	30
Washington University	7 (3.81)	8 (3.55)	10 (15)	6 (67)	10 (3.78)	10 (3.40)	11.5 (95)	8.5 (2)	17 (3.35)	17.5 (3.28)	10	49
University of Virginia	8 (3.77)	9 (3.54)	9 (16)	8 (63)	7 (3.82)	8 (3.53)	15.5 (94)	8.5 (2)	9 (3.99)	10 (3.58)	11	23
Johns Hopkins University	9 (3.75)	11 (3.33)	6 (24)	11 (58)	8.5 (3.80)	11 (3.25)	15.5 (94)	16 (1)	24 (2.72)	21 (2.97)	5	17
University of Wisconsin-Madison	10 (3.74)	6 (3.65)	8 (21)	10 (62)	11 (3.69)	7 (3.64)	7.5 (96)	8.5 (2)	1 (4.54)	2 (4.30)	13	66
University of Minnesota	11 (3.68)	10 (3.48)	12 (11)	8 (63)	8.5 (3.80)	6 (3.68)	2.5 (99)	16 (1)	23 (3.01)	20 (3.17)	12	27
University of Washington	12 (3.60)	13 (3.17)	13.5 (6)	12 (56)	12 (3.62)	14 (3.10)	15.5 (94)	2 (5)	12 (3.54)	14 (3.42)	13	37
University of Texas at Austin	13 (3.40)	12 (3.26)	11 (12)	13 (43)	13 (3.33)	12 (3.22)	15.5 (94)	26.5 (0)	6 (4.15)	5 (4.10)	25	22
Indiana University	14.5 (3.28)	16 (3.02)	15 (5)	15.5 (39)	16.5 (3.15)	19 (2.86)	7.5 (96)	16 (1)	5 (4.29)	3.5 (4.18)	15	48
University of California-Irvine	14.5 (3.28)	14 (3.10)	17 (4)	15.5 (39)	15 (3.22)	13 (3.14)	19.5 (91)	8.5 (2)	22 (3.02)	22.5 (2.95)	8	12
University of Pennsylvania	16 (3.26)	17 (2.99)	13.5 (6)	15.5 (39)	18 (3.14)	22 (2.67)	11.5 (95)	16 (1)	18 (3.33)	17.5 (3.28)	8	27
Ohio State University	17 (3.25)	19 (2.97)	17 (4)	15.5 (39)	14 (3.32)	15 (2.96)	11.5 (95)	8.5 (2)	20 (3.19)	15.5 (3.38)	15	34
U of North Carolina-Chapel Hill	18 (3.21)	20 (2.91)	30.5 (0)	19.5 (31)	16.5 (3.15)	18 (2.90)	18 (93)	26.5 (0)	21 (3.09)	19 (3.18)	11	20
U of Massachusetts at Amherst	19 (3.18)	21.5 (2.88)	17 (4)	19.5 (31)	19 (3.11)	20 (2.79)	19.5 (91)	26.5 (0)	14 (3.50)	15.5 (3.38)	10	24
U of Illinois at Urbana-Champaign	20 (3.11)	15 (3.05)	21 (2)	18 (33)	20 (3.07)	16 (2.94)	22.5 (89)	3 (4)	11 (3.54)	9 (3.62)	13	40
University of Michigan	21 (3.04)	18 (2.98)	25.5 (1)	22 (27)	21 (2.96)	17 (2.91)	21 (90)	16 (1)	15 (3.42)	11.5 (3.45)	13	26
Univ of California-Los Angeles	22 (2.94)	21.5 (2.88)	19 (3)	21 (30)	24 (2.72)	23 (2.61)	11.5 (95)	26.5 (0)	13 (3.52)	13 (3.43)	18	35
University of California-Davis	23 (2.90)	23 (2.65)	25.5 (1)	23 (20)	22 (2.91)	24 (2.56)	22.5 (89)	16 (1)	28 (2.27)	28.5 (2.33)	7	15
Univ of California-Santa Barbara	24 (2.77)	24 (2.60)	25.5 (1)	24 (18)	23 (2.75)	21 (2.68)	24.5 (88)	26.5 (0)	16 (3.36)	22.5 (2.95)	10	12
State Univ of New York-Albany	25 (2.59)	28 (1.96)	21 (2)	25 (14)	25 (2.49)	28 (1.82)	24.5 (88)	26.5 (0)	19 (3.21)	24 (2.83)	7	9
New York University	26 (2.37)	29 (1.89)	25.5 (1)	29.5 (4)	26 (2.36)	29 (1.81)	28 (81)	26.5 (0)	27 (2.57)	26 (2.63)	11	15
Pennsylvania State University	27 (2.31)	27 (2.03)	30.5 (0)	27.5 (6)	27.5 (2.26)	27 (1.87)	26 (84)	26.5 (0)	29 (2.24)	28.5 (2.33)	13	22
Georgetown University	28 (2.15)	25 (2.14)	21 (2)	26 (7)	27.5 (2.26)	26 (2.14)	27 (83)	16 (1)			8	17
University of Cincinnati	29 (1.99)	26 (2.09)	30.5 (0)	29.5 (4)	29 (1.94)	25 (2.18)	29 (79)	26.5 (0)	26 (2.61)	25 (2.77)	6	5
University of Pittsburgh	30 (1.89)	32 (1.57)	25.5 (1)	27.5 (6)	30 (1.91)	32 (1.43)	31 (73)	26.5 (0)	30 (2.11)	31 (1.88)	7	12

Institution	93Q [1]	93E [1]	% D [1]	% D-S [1]	93Q T [1]	93E T [1]	VIS [1]	FA [2]	82Q [3]	82E [3]	TF [4]	TG [4]
State Univ of New York-Buffalo	**31** (1.80)	**31** (1.63)	**30.5** (0)	**31** (3)	**31** (1.67)	**31** (1.48)	**32** (70)	**26.5** (0)	**25** (2.72)	**27** (2.43)	7	6
Rutgers State Univ-New Brunswick	**32** (1.69)	**30** (1.76)	**25.5** (1)	**32** (2)	**32** (1.64)	**30** (1.55)	**30** (74)	**26.5** (0)	**31** (1.79)	**30** (1.97)	8	30

Sources: 1. National Survey of Graduate Faculty
2. Associations and Organizations Administrating Prestigious Awards and Honors
3. 1982 Survey of Graduate Faculty
4. Institutional Coordinator Data

Appendix Table P - 22 Relative Rankings for Research-Doctorate Programs in History

Institution	93Q [1]	93E [1]	% D [1]	% D-S [1]	93Q T [1]	93E T [1]	VIS [1]	TC [2]	C/F [2]	82Q [3]	82E [3]	TF [4]	TG [4]
Yale University	1 (4.89)	1 (4.55)	1 (86)	1 (97)	1 (4.90)	2 (4.53)	1.5 (99)	20.5 (60)	33.5 (1.2)	1 (4.83)	1 (4.43)	51	188
University of California-Berkeley	2 (4.79)	2 (4.50)	3.5 (74)	4.5 (93)	2 (4.84)	3 (4.50)	8 (97)	4 (181)	8.5 (3.1)	2 (4.79)	2 (4.25)	58	206
Princeton University	3 (4.75)	3 (4.48)	2 (76)	2.5 (94)	3 (4.80)	1 (4.58)	1.5 (99)	38.5 (33)	41 (0.9)	4 (4.65)	3 (4.18)	37	68
Harvard University	4 (4.71)	12 (4.02)	3.5 (74)	8 (90)	4 (4.76)	14 (3.94)	4.5 (98)	2 (324)	2 (7.5)	3 (4.75)	7 (4.02)	43	146
Columbia University	5 (4.63)	7 (4.29)	5 (64)	2.5 (94)	7 (4.62)	9 (4.15)	4.5 (98)	38.5 (33)	52 (0.6)	7 (4.47)	8 (4.00)	55	334
Univ of California-Los Angeles	6 (4.59)	10 (4.07)	6 (57)	4.5 (93)	5 (4.69)	10 (4.08)	4.5 (98)	3 (198)	17 (2.2)	11 (4.05)	17 (3.58)	89	316
Stanford University	7 (4.56)	4 (4.44)	7 (56)	6.5 (91)	6 (4.65)	4 (4.47)	10.5 (96)	1 (891)	1 (22.8)	8 (4.36)	4 (4.15)	39	141
University of Chicago	8 (4.49)	8 (4.20)	8 (53)	6.5 (91)	8 (4.57)	7 (4.23)	4.5 (98)	19 (67)	26 (1.5)	6 (4.47)	9 (3.90)	45	251
Johns Hopkins University	9 (4.42)	5 (4.37)	9 (44)	12.5 (82)	9 (4.46)	5 (4.43)	16 (93)	25.5 (54)	13 (2.5)	9 (4.25)	5.5 (4.07)	22	98
University of Wisconsin-Madison	10 (4.37)	6 (4.33)	10 (43)	10.5 (83)	11 (4.31)	6 (4.27)	8 (97)	6 (144)	15 (2.4)	10 (4.21)	10 (3.83)	61	312
University of Michigan	11 (4.30)	9 (4.09)	11 (39)	9 (86)	10 (4.37)	8 (4.20)	8 (97)	5 (173)	6.5 (3.3)	5 (4.51)	5.5 (4.07)	53	137
University of Pennsylvania	12 (4.24)	11 (4.05)	12 (35)	10.5 (83)	13 (4.24)	11 (4.05)	10.5 (96)	18 (71)	30 (1.3)	12 (4.03)	15 (3.63)	55	113
Cornell University	13 (4.22)	13 (3.87)	13 (29)	12.5 (82)	12 (4.25)	13 (3.95)	14 (94)	56 (14)	65.5 (0.3)	15 (3.90)	13 (3.70)	42	85
Brown University	14 (3.96)	14 (3.86)	15 (17)	14 (72)	14 (4.05)	15 (3.92)	12 (95)	15 (80)	10 (2.9)	16 (3.86)	14 (3.67)	28	105
Duke University	15 (3.93)	15 (3.84)	14 (23)	16 (66)	15 (4.00)	16 (3.90)	14 (94)	20.5 (60)	24 (1.6)	21.5 (3.66)	21 (3.43)	38	103
Northwestern University	16 (3.85)	19 (3.69)	20 (10)	15 (67)	16 (3.93)	19 (3.69)	22 (89)	40 (32)	45.5 (0.8)	18 (3.76)	19 (3.52)	38	73
U of North Carolina-Chapel Hill	17 (3.84)	16.5 (3.83)	16 (16)	17 (64)	17 (3.80)	18 (3.74)	17.5 (91)	23 (56)	33.5 (1.2)	17 (3.82)	12 (3.72)	47	163
CUNY - Grad Sch & Univ Center	18 (3.73)	34 (3.24)	22 (9)	18 (63)	19.5 (3.68)	37 (3.17)	22 (89)	34 (37)	45.5 (0.8)	13 (3.97)	27.5 (3.25)	47	173
University of Virginia	19 (3.68)	20.5 (3.67)	19 (11)	24 (49)	23 (3.60)	22 (3.53)	32 (82)	47.5 (20)	54.5 (0.5)	21.5 (3.66)	16 (3.60)	43	132
Rutgers State Univ-New Brunswick	20 (3.67)	18 (3.74)	18 (12)	21 (54)	18 (3.72)	12 (3.97)	19 (90)	36 (35)	49 (0.7)	27 (3.36)	25.5 (3.30)	52	166
University of Minnesota	21.5 (3.66)	16.5 (3.83)	17 (13)	23 (51)	21.5 (3.65)	17 (3.79)	22 (89)	27 (52)	36.5 (1.1)	26 (3.38)	23.5 (3.33)	46	72
University of Texas at Austin	21.5 (3.66)	22 (3.63)	22 (9)	19.5 (55)	21.5 (3.65)	21 (3.54)	17.5 (91)	53.5 (15)	79.5 (0.2)	23 (3.53)	23.5 (3.33)	64	64
New York University	23 (3.63)	23 (3.60)	24 (8)	19.5 (55)	19.5 (3.68)	24 (3.46)	22 (89)	64 (8)	79.5 (0.2)	32 (3.06)	31 (3.07)	36	57
Indiana University	24 (3.57)	24 (3.46)	26 (6)	22 (52)	24 (3.54)	23 (3.49)	14 (94)	11 (102)	15 (2.4)	14 (3.94)	11 (3.73)	42	296
U of Illinois at Urbana-Champaign	25 (3.50)	20.5 (3.67)	25 (7)	25 (44)	30 (3.32)	20 (3.60)	27.5 (86)	53.5 (15)	65.5 (0.3)	30 (3.27)	27.5 (3.25)	52	138
Univ of California-San Diego	26 (3.46)	25 (3.41)	22 (9)	29 (36)	25 (3.50)	29 (3.33)	25.5 (87)	14 (82)	19.5 (2.0)	29 (3.29)	30 (3.08)	42	75
University of Rochester	27 (3.45)	37 (3.13)	33.5 (3)	26 (43)	26 (3.48)	32 (3.28)	25.5 (87)	68.5 (6)	79.5 (0.2)	19 (3.74)	18 (3.53)	25	80
Brandeis University	28 (3.41)	30.5 (3.28)	33.5 (3)	28 (37)	29 (3.39)	34 (3.25)	29.5 (85)	43.5 (25)	26 (1.5)	20 (3.71)	20 (3.45)	17	56
University of Iowa	29.5 (3.40)	30.5 (3.28)	28 (4)	31 (32)	28 (3.42)	26 (3.36)	36.5 (77)	9 (126)	5 (4.2)	25 (3.40)	25.5 (3.30)	30	113
University of Maryland College Park	29.5 (3.40)	29 (3.29)	33.5 (3)	27 (40)	27 (3.43)	25 (3.39)	29.5 (85)	22 (59)	36.5 (1.1)	33 (3.05)	41 (2.80)	55	109

Institution	93Q [1]	93E [1]	% D [1]	% D-S [1]	93Q T [1]	93E T [1]	VIS [1]	TC [2]	C/F [2]	82Q [3]	82E [3]	TF [4]	TG [4]
Emory University	**31** (3.39)	**26.5** (3.33)	**33.5** (3)	**30** (35)	**31** (3.31)	**39** (3.16)	**33.5** (81)	**43.5** (25)	**41** (0.9)	**44** (2.78)	**32.5** (3.00)	27	83
Univ of California-Santa Barbara	**32** (3.34)	**44** (3.08)	**27** (5)	**32.5** (29)	**33** (3.26)	**49** (2.92)	**36.5** (77)	**91** (2)	**103** (0.0)	**28** (3.34)	**29** (3.23)	43	105
University of Washington	**33** (3.31)	**28** (3.30)	**33.5** (3)	**36** (25)	**32** (3.29)	**39** (3.16)	**39** (75)	**8** (128)	**8.5** (3.1)	**24** (3.41)	**22** (3.40)	41	121
Rice University	**34** (3.21)	**47.5** (3.00)	**90** (0)	**34.5** (28)	**36** (3.15)	**29** (3.33)	**42.5** (73)	**33** (39)	**19.5** (2.0)	**40** (2.86)	**36.5** (2.95)	20	30
University of California-Davis	**35** (3.19)	**41.5** (3.11)	**41** (2)	**32.5** (29)	**34** (3.18)	**35** (3.22)	**22** (89)	**16** (75)	**15** (2.4)	**37** (2.91)	**34.5** (2.97)	31	71
Vanderbilt University	**36** (3.17)	**45** (3.05)	**56** (1)	**37** (24)	**35** (3.16)	**42** (3.11)	**31** (83)	**61** (9)	**65.5** (0.3)	**31** (3.09)	**32.5** (3.00)	26	28
Ohio State University	**37.5** (3.15)	**41.5** (3.11)	**33.5** (3)	**34.5** (28)	**42** (2.98)	**47** (2.98)	**27.5** (86)	**13** (87)	**33.5** (1.2)	**39** (2.86)	**38** (2.88)	71	90
University of Pittsburgh	**37.5** (3.15)	**33** (3.25)	**56** (1)	**40** (21)	**38** (3.13)	**29** (3.33)	**40.5** (74)	**17** (72)	**18** (2.1)	**42** (2.82)	**34.5** (2.97)	35	84
University of Kansas	**39** (3.13)	**41.5** (3.11)	**33.5** (3)	**43** (18)	**38** (3.13)	**42** (3.11)	**50** (71)	**56** (14)	**57** (0.4)	**38** (2.87)	**42** (2.78)	35	53
University of Florida	**40.5** (3.09)	**38.5** (3.12)	**33.5** (3)	**38** (23)	**39** (3.12)	**33** (3.26)	**45.5** (72)	**24** (55)	**26** (1.5)	**67** (2.07)	**65** (2.10)	36	79
Carnegie Mellon University	**40.5** (3.09)	**32** (3.26)	**56** (1)	**41** (20)	**41** (3.08)	**36** (3.18)	**38** (76)	**42** (30)	**28** (1.4)	**63** (2.16)	**58** (2.37)	21	47
State Univ of New York-Binghamton	**42** (3.04)	**41.5** (3.11)	**41** (2)	**39** (22)	**40** (3.11)	**45** (3.07)	**33.5** (81)	**104.5** (0)	**103** (0.0)	**50** (2.48)	**49.5** (2.48)	25	101
University of California-Irvine	**43** (2.99)	**49** (2.94)	**90** (0)	**45.5** (16)	**46** (2.92)	**50** (2.90)	**50** (71)	**28** (47)	**21.5** (1.8)	**68** (2.03)	**76** (1.87)	26	65
Washington University	**44** (2.96)	**56** (2.72)	**41** (2)	**42** (19)	**44** (2.94)	**58** (2.68)	**50** (71)	**10** (104)	**3** (5.8)	**43** (2.78)	**39** (2.85)	18	47
State U of New York-Stony Brook	**45** (2.90)	**35** (3.22)	**90** (0)	**48** (15)	**46** (2.92)	**29** (3.33)	**45.5** (72)	**7** (132)	**4** (5.7)	**35** (2.92)	**40** (2.82)	23	104
College of William & Mary	**46.5** (2.89)	**52** (2.87)	**56** (1)	**45.5** (16)	**48** (2.87)	**56** (2.78)	**68** (59)	**91** (2)	**79.5** (0.2)			10	34
University of Connecticut	**46.5** (2.89)	**60** (2.67)	**90** (0)	**48** (15)	**51** (2.76)	**64** (2.61)	**61** (65)	**81** (4)	**90.5** (0.1)	**45** (2.63)	**45** (2.60)	28	124
Michigan State University	**48.5** (2.88)	**54** (2.81)	**56** (1)	**44** (17)	**47** (2.91)	**51** (2.86)	**35** (78)	**35** (36)	**45.5** (0.8)	**49** (2.49)	**44** (2.63)	48	58
University of Arizona	**48.5** (2.88)	**55** (2.78)	**56** (1)	**59** (11)	**49** (2.85)	**52** (2.84)	**55.5** (67)	**85.5** (3)	**90.5** (0.1)	**51** (2.48)	**47** (2.55)	23	94
Georgetown University	**50** (2.84)	**38.5** (3.12)	**33.5** (3)	**50.5** (14)	**43** (2.95)	**40** (3.13)	**58.5** (66)	**12** (90)	**11.5** (2.7)	**82** (1.41)	**67** (2.07)	33	69
University of Missouri-Columbia	**51** (2.81)	**61.5** (2.66)	**90** (0)	**61.5** (10)	**53** (2.74)	**67** (2.56)	**64** (63)	**96** (1)	**103** (0.0)	**36** (2.92)	**36.5** (2.95)	27	59
University of Illinois at Chicago	**53** (2.79)	**57.5** (2.70)	**33.5** (3)	**48** (15)	**52** (2.75)	**53** (2.81)	**45.5** (72)	**32** (40)	**23** (1.7)	**34** (2.93)	**43** (2.72)	24	71
Ohio University	**53** (2.79)	**47.5** (3.00)	**90** (0)	**53.5** (13)	**50** (2.83)	**43** (3.08)	**55.5** (67)	**74.5** (5)	**79.5** (0.2)			24	28
Northern Illinois University	**53** (2.79)	**70** (2.57)	**90** (0)	**59** (11)	**56** (2.71)	**71** (2.50)	**62** (64)	**37** (34)	**38** (1.0)			35	37
University of Colorado	**55** (2.77)	**75** (2.42)	**41** (2)	**53.5** (13)	**57** (2.70)	**80** (2.22)	**54** (69)	**49** (19)	**49** (0.7)	**66** (2.09)	**69** (2.05)	29	55
Syracuse University	**57** (2.75)	**71** (2.54)	**56** (1)	**66.5** (8)	**59** (2.68)	**76** (2.38)	**75.5** (56)	**29.5** (46)	**21.5** (1.8)	**52** (2.42)	**55** (2.40)	26	36
George Washington University	**57** (2.75)	**50** (2.90)	**56** (1)	**50.5** (14)	**61** (2.66)	**56** (2.78)	**64** (63)	**74.5** (5)	**65.5** (0.3)	**75** (1.80)	**73** (1.98)	19	29
University of Georgia	**57** (2.75)	**51** (2.89)	**56** (1)	**56.5** (12)	**63** (2.61)	**66** (2.58)	**77** (55)	**91** (2)	**90.5** (0.1)	**46** (2.59)	**53** (2.42)	26	11
University of Notre Dame	**59** (2.74)	**53** (2.84)	**56** (1)	**56.5** (12)	**55** (2.72)	**45** (3.07)	**45.5** (72)	**61** (9)	**79.5** (0.2)	**74** (1.84)	**67** (2.07)	47	72
State Univ of New York-Buffalo	**60** (2.71)	**65.5** (2.64)	**90** (0)	**61.5** (10)	**64** (2.60)	**64** (2.61)	**50** (71)	**74.5** (5)	**65.5** (0.3)	**57** (2.34)	**58** (2.37)	19	77

Appendix Table P - 22 History (Continued)

Institution	93Q [1]	93E [1]	% D [1]	% D-S [1]	93Q T [1]	93E T [1]	VIS [1]	TC [2]	C/F [2]	82Q [3]	82E [3]	TF [4]	TG [4]
U of Massachusetts at Amherst	61 (2.68)	57.5 (2.70)	41 (2)	53.5 (13)	59 (2.68)	54 (2.80)	42.5 (73)	104.5 (0)	103 (0.0)	61 (2.26)	55 (2.40)	22	35
Boston University	62 (2.67)	63.5 (2.65)	56 (1)	53.5 (13)	62 (2.63)	68 (2.54)	40.5 (74)	58 (11)	57 (0.4)	41 (2.83)	47 (2.55)	26	45
Univ of California-Riverside	63.5 (2.62)	72 (2.53)	90 (0)	59 (11)	54 (2.73)	71 (2.50)	53 (70)	51 (16)	52 (0.6)	78 (1.64)	79.5 (1.67)	27	35
University of Houston	63.5 (2.62)	77.5 (2.38)	90 (0)	70.5 (7)	65 (2.58)	66 (2.58)	80 (53)	104.5 (0)	103 (0.0)			38	125
University of Oregon	65 (2.58)	63.5 (2.65)	56 (1)	82 (5)	61 (2.66)	59 (2.67)	58.5 (66)	91 (2)	90.5 (0.1)	64 (2.14)	55 (2.40)	24	17
Boston College	66 (2.57)	74 (2.46)	90 (0)	64 (9)	72 (2.46)	78 (2.33)	58.5 (66)	74.5 (5)	79.5 (0.2)	83 (1.41)	81 (1.62)	28	81
Tulane University	67 (2.53)	46 (3.03)	56 (1)	70.5 (7)	67 (2.50)	46 (3.00)	75.5 (56)	41 (31)	30 (1.3)	56 (2.36)	63 (2.28)	23	78
Purdue University	68 (2.52)	67.5 (2.61)	90 (0)	76.5 (6)	68 (2.49)	71 (2.50)	66.5 (61)	81 (4)	79.5 (0.2)			26	29
University of Hawaii at Manoa	69 (2.51)	36 (3.15)	90 (0)	64 (9)	76 (2.31)	49 (2.92)	102 (40)	68.5 (6)	79.5 (0.2)	65 (2.12)	72 (2.00)	30	45
University of New Hampshire	71 (2.48)	79.5 (2.35)	56 (1)	70.5 (7)	73 (2.43)	88 (2.00)	71 (58)	65.5 (7)	57 (0.4)	71 (1.89)	82 (1.58)	19	27
University of Southern California	71 (2.48)	79.5 (2.35)	56 (1)	66.5 (8)	69 (2.48)	75 (2.39)	50 (71)	25.5 (54)	11.5 (2.7)	69 (2.03)	70 (2.03)	20	58
University of Kentucky	71 (2.48)	69 (2.60)	90 (0)	76.5 (6)	74 (2.39)	74 (2.41)	58.5 (66)	47.5 (20)	45.5 (0.8)	53 (2.38)	51 (2.47)	26	54
Pennsylvania State University	73.5 (2.46)	81.5 (2.32)	90 (0)	70.5 (7)	78 (2.28)	82 (2.19)	74 (57)	51 (16)	49 (0.7)	76 (1.78)	78 (1.72)	23	62
Louisiana State U & A&M College	73.5 (2.46)	67.5 (2.61)	90 (0)	86 (4)	78 (2.28)	77 (2.36)	93 (44)	61 (9)	65.5 (0.3)	62 (2.20)	47 (2.55)	28	64
University of Oklahoma	75 (2.39)	84.5 (2.24)	90 (0)	82 (5)	75 (2.33)	82 (2.19)	66.5 (61)	85.5 (3)	90.5 (0.1)	55 (2.37)	58 (2.37)	25	28
Temple University	76.5 (2.37)	77.5 (2.38)	56 (1)	82 (5)	78 (2.28)	71 (2.50)	80 (53)	31 (42)	30 (1.3)	47 (2.57)	52 (2.45)	32	116
Arizona State University	76.5 (2.37)	61.5 (2.66)	90 (0)	70.5 (7)	82 (2.17)	61 (2.64)	78 (54)	65.5 (7)	65.5 (0.3)			25	59
Catholic University of America	78 (2.36)	65.5 (2.64)	90 (0)	76.5 (6)	70 (2.47)	61 (2.64)	71 (58)	85.5 (3)	79.5 (0.2)	72 (1.87)	74 (1.97)	17	24
Miami University	79.5 (2.34)	86.5 (2.18)	90 (0)	76.5 (6)	83 (2.14)	85 (2.03)	80 (53)	91 (2)	90.5 (0.1)	90 (1.07)	77 (1.75)	25	27
Loyola University of Chicago	79.5 (2.34)	59 (2.69)	90 (0)	89 (3)	72 (2.46)	56 (2.78)	83 (51)	104.5 (0)	103 (0.0)	84 (1.33)	85 (1.48)	21	32
University of South Carolina	81 (2.33)	76 (2.39)	56 (1)	86 (4)	81 (2.21)	74 (2.41)	82 (52)	68.5 (6)	79.5 (0.2)	54 (2.38)	60 (2.33)	33	53
Claremont Graduate School	82 (2.25)	81.5 (2.32)	56 (1)	64 (9)	87 (2.03)	88 (2.00)	84.5 (50)	96 (1)	65.5 (0.3)	48 (2.52)	61 (2.32)	3	43
Florida State University	83 (2.20)	73 (2.47)	56 (1)	76.5 (6)	92 (1.84)	88 (2.00)	99 (41)	46 (21)	41 (0.9)	73 (1.85)	67 (2.07)	23	113
University of Nebraska-Lincoln	84.5 (2.19)	91 (2.07)	90 (0)	76.5 (6)	85 (2.13)	92 (1.95)	64 (63)	104.5 (0)	103 (0.0)	58 (2.29)	49.5 (2.48)	23	31
Kent State University	84.5 (2.19)	86.5 (2.18)	90 (0)	89 (3)	85 (2.13)	88 (2.00)	71 (58)	81 (4)	79.5 (0.2)	60 (2.26)	71 (2.02)	21	41
University of Cincinnati	86 (2.18)	84.5 (2.24)	90 (0)	82 (5)	88 (1.97)	79 (2.29)	71 (58)	51 (16)	41 (0.9)	59 (2.28)	62 (2.30)	17	15
Texas A&M University	87 (2.15)	90 (2.08)	90 (0)	89 (3)	86 (2.04)	95 (1.80)	84.5 (50)	56 (14)	65.5 (0.3)			41	42
American University	88 (2.14)	92 (2.05)	90 (0)	70.5 (7)	80 (2.22)	83 (2.14)	71 (58)	29.5 (46)	6.5 (3.3)	79 (1.59)	79.5 (1.67)	14	33
Jewish Theological Seminary	89 (2.07)	26.5 (3.33)	56 (1)	86 (4)	66 (2.55)	29 (3.33)	110 (21)	104.5 (0)	103 (0.0)			5	18
Case Western Reserve Univ	90 (2.05)	95 (1.96)	56 (1)	93 (2)	90 (1.92)	84 (2.04)	88.5 (47)	61 (9)	41 (0.9)	77 (1.77)	64 (2.12)	10	44

Institution	93Q [1]	93E [1]	% D [1]	% D-S [1]	93Q T [1]	93E T [1]	VIS [1]	TC [2]	C/F [2]	82Q [3]	82E [3]	TF [4]	TG [4]
University of Tennessee-Knoxville	**91** (1.89)	**88.5** (2.14)	**90** (0)	**82** (5)	**96** (1.63)	**104** (1.25)	**99** (41)	**91** (2)	**90.5** (0.1)	**70** (1.92)	**75** (1.95)	16	47
University of Alabama	**92** (1.88)	**93.5** (2.00)	**90** (0)	**100** (1)	**91** (1.91)	**92** (1.95)	**87** (48)	**74.5** (5)	**65.5** (0.3)			17	22
Howard University	**93** (1.81)	**83** (2.26)	**56** (1)	**100** (1)	**89** (1.95)	**62** (2.62)	**90** (46)	**91** (2)	**79.5** (0.2)	**87** (1.14)	**88** (1.30)	12	22
Washington State University	**94** (1.78)	**97** (1.77)	**90** (0)	**93** (2)	**94** (1.81)	**94** (1.83)	**99** (41)	**61** (9)	**54.5** (0.5)	**89** (1.09)	**86** (1.43)	19	53
University of Akron	**95** (1.76)	**106** (1.36)	**90** (0)	**93** (2)	**93** (1.82)	**98** (1.67)	**88.5** (47)	**104.5** (0)	**103** (0.0)			21	16
Univ of Arkansas-Fayetteville	**96** (1.70)	**88.5** (2.14)	**90** (0)	**93** (2)	**98** (1.57)	**88** (2.00)	**96.5** (42)	**45** (23)	**33.5** (1.2)	**81** (1.41)	**83** (1.57)	20	29
Bowling Green State University	**97** (1.66)	**103** (1.45)	**90** (0)	**100** (1)	**95** (1.69)	**108** (1.11)	**93** (44)	**85.5** (3)	**79.5** (0.2)			15	20
Texas Tech University	**98** (1.61)	**104.5** (1.37)	**90** (0)	**100** (1)	**99** (1.53)	**108** (1.11)	**107** (37)	**81** (4)	**90.5** (0.1)	**92** (0.83)	**91** (1.15)	27	32
Brigham Young University	**99** (1.56)	**93.5** (2.00)	**56** (1)	**100** (1)	**97** (1.61)	**93** (1.91)	**95** (43)	**74.5** (5)	**65.5** (0.3)			16	6
University of North Texas	**100** (1.48)	**99.5** (1.67)	**90** (0)	**100** (1)	**100** (1.43)	**104** (1.25)	**109** (30)	**96** (1)	**103** (0.0)	**85** (1.29)	**87** (1.38)	32	47
Texas Christian University	**101** (1.40)	**99.5** (1.67)	**90** (0)	**108** (0)	**103** (1.33)	**101** (1.48)	**86** (49)	**104.5** (0)	**103** (0.0)	**91** (0.96)	**92** (1.12)	12	30
West Virginia University	**102** (1.37)	**102** (1.56)	**56** (1)	**100** (1)	**101** (1.42)	**98** (1.67)	**102** (40)	**104.5** (0)	**103** (0.0)	**86** (1.27)	**89** (1.28)	14	31
Northern Arizona University	**103** (1.29)	**99.5** (1.67)	**90** (0)	**108** (0)	**104** (1.21)	**98** (1.67)	**102** (40)	**68.5** (6)	**65.5** (0.3)			22	26
University of Texas at Dallas	**104** (1.28)	**104.5** (1.37)	**90** (0)	**108** (0)	**102** (1.39)	**98** (1.67)	**104** (39)	**81** (4)	**65.5** (0.3)			15	40
Auburn University	**105** (1.22)	**96** (1.80)	**90** (0)	**108** (0)	**105** (1.16)	**104** (1.25)	**91** (45)	**74.5** (5)	**65.5** (0.3)	**88** (1.10)	**93** (1.07)	18	49
Fordham University	**106** (1.13)	**107** (0.83)	**90** (0)	**93** (2)	**106** (1.12)	**106** (1.17)	**93** (44)	**74.5** (5)	**52** (0.6)	**80** (1.51)	**84** (1.52)	8	61
Mississippi State University	**107** (0.88)	**110** (0.56)	**90** (0)	**108** (0)	**107** (0.75)	**111** (0.00)	**107** (37)	**104.5** (0)	**103** (0.0)	**93** (0.81)	**90** (1.17)	14	13
Illinois State University	**108** (0.67)	**108** (0.77)	**56** (1)	**100** (1)	**108** (0.62)	**102** (1.39)	**96.5** (42)	**104.5** (0)	**103** (0.0)			8	20
Univ of Southern Mississippi	**109** (0.66)	**111** (0.51)	**90** (0)	**108** (0)	**110** (0.36)	**111** (0.00)	**105** (38)	**104.5** (0)	**103** (0.0)			5	10
University of North Dakota	**110** (0.62)	**109** (0.64)	**90** (0)	**100** (1)	**109** (0.57)	**109** (0.83)	**107** (37)	**104.5** (0)	**103** (0.0)			10	38
Univ of Puerto Rico-Rio Piedras	**111** (0.50)	**99.5** (1.67)	**90** (0)	**108** (0)	**111** (0.33)	**98** (1.67)	**111** (14)	**104.5** (0)	**103** (0.0)			14	25

Sources: 1. National Survey of Graduate Faculty
2. Institute for Scientific Information
3. 1982 Survey of Graduate Faculty
4. Institutional Coordinator Data

Appendix Table P - 23 Relative Rankings for Research-Doctorate Programs in Industrial Engineering

Institution	93Q [1]	93E [1]	% D [1]	% D-S [1]	93Q T [1]	93E T [1]	VIS [1]	TC [2]	C/F [2]	82Q [3]	82E [3]	TF [4]	TG [4]
Georgia Institute of Technology	**1** (4.71)	**2** (4.30)	**1** (68)	**1** (96)	**1** (4.69)	**2** (4.30)	**1.5** (99)	**6** (168)	**14** (3.7)			46	121
University of California-Berkeley	**2** (4.44)	**1** (4.31)	**4** (45)	**4** (80)	**2** (4.57)	**1** (4.46)	**8.5** (90)	**3** (273)	**4** (18.2)			15	47
Purdue University	**3** (4.43)	**4** (4.07)	**2** (50)	**3** (85)	**3** (4.48)	**4** (4.04)	**3.5** (96)	**8** (109)	**15** (3.5)			31	66
University of Michigan	**4** (4.36)	**3** (4.19)	**3** (47)	**2** (88)	**4** (4.47)	**3** (4.17)	**1.5** (99)	**4** (203)	**5** (9.2)			22	84
Texas A&M University	**5** (3.81)	**10** (3.44)	**6.5** (16)	**5** (65)	**5.5** (3.78)	**10** (3.41)	**3.5** (96)	**11** (76)	**20.5** (2.5)			31	91
Northwestern University	**6** (3.73)	**6** (3.62)	**8** (14)	**6** (60)	**5.5** (3.78)	**5** (3.75)	**8.5** (90)	**1** (667)	**2** (24.7)			27	18
Stanford University	**7** (3.68)	**7** (3.60)	**6.5** (16)	**10** (46)	**9** (3.50)	**8** (3.56)	**12** (83)	**5** (201)	**3** (22.3)			9	29
Virginia Polytech Inst & State U	**8** (3.66)	**5** (3.68)	**5** (17)	**7** (52)	**7** (3.56)	**6.5** (3.61)	**5** (94)	**19** (39)	**23** (1.6)			24	70
Pennsylvania State University	**9** (3.50)	**8** (3.52)	**9** (9)	**8** (49)	**11** (3.39)	**6.5** (3.61)	**6.5** (92)	**14** (68)	**17** (3.1)			22	135
University of Wisconsin-Madison	**10** (3.48)	**9** (3.48)	**10.5** (5)	**11** (43)	**10** (3.43)	**9** (3.47)	**12** (83)	**7** (112)	**7** (6.6)			17	58
North Carolina State University	**11** (3.46)	**11** (3.36)	**10.5** (5)	**9** (47)	**8** (3.51)	**11** (3.37)	**6.5** (92)	**16** (54)	**19** (2.6)			21	36
Ohio State University	**12** (3.24)	**12** (3.33)	**16.5** (1)	**12** (34)	**12** (3.24)	**12** (3.30)	**10** (86)	**10** (93)	**11** (4.4)			21	51
U of Illinois at Urbana-Champaign	**13** (3.13)	**13** (3.25)	**13** (2)	**15** (26)	**14** (3.05)	**14.5** (3.16)	**21** (75)	**2** (456)	**1** (26.8)			17	26
Rensselaer Polytechnic Inst	**14** (3.12)	**16** (3.02)	**16.5** (1)	**13** (32)	**13** (3.20)	**16** (3.03)	**16** (80)	**9** (105)	**18** (2.9)			36	39
Lehigh University	**15** (3.03)	**14** (3.18)	**12** (3)	**16** (23)	**15** (3.00)	**13** (3.20)	**14** (82)	**32** (4)	**33.5** (0.3)			14	23
Oklahoma State University	**16** (2.99)	**20** (2.78)	**28.5** (0)	**14** (29)	**16** (2.85)	**20.5** (2.68)	**18** (78)	**29.5** (5)	**30.5** (0.5)			10	112
Arizona State University	**17** (2.97)	**17** (3.01)	**28.5** (0)	**17** (22)	**19** (2.77)	**18** (2.83)	**12** (83)	**25** (15)	**24** (1.5)			10	52
State Univ of New York-Buffalo	**18** (2.86)	**15** (3.15)	**16.5** (1)	**19.5** (11)	**18** (2.78)	**14.5** (3.16)	**26** (70)	**13** (69)	**9.5** (4.6)			15	26
University of Florida	**19** (2.82)	**18** (2.87)	**16.5** (1)	**18** (17)	**17** (2.83)	**17** (2.87)	**18** (78)	**17** (51)	**6** (7.3)			7	22
Auburn University	**20** (2.73)	**21** (2.71)	**28.5** (0)	**21.5** (10)	**20** (2.66)	**19** (2.74)	**18** (78)	**28** (7)	**30.5** (0.5)			14	19
Iowa State University	**21** (2.69)	**19** (2.83)	**16.5** (1)	**23** (9)	**21.5** (2.53)	**20.5** (2.68)	**22.5** (74)	**15** (65)	**12.5** (4.3)			15	19
University of Southern California	**22** (2.64)	**26** (2.42)	**28.5** (0)	**19.5** (11)	**23** (2.51)	**26** (2.21)	**15** (81)	**27** (10)	**26** (1.3)			8	24
University of Pittsburgh	**23** (2.61)	**22** (2.67)	**28.5** (0)	**27** (4)	**21.5** (2.53)	**22** (2.65)	**28** (65)	**24** (17)	**27** (1.2)			14	36
University of Iowa	**24** (2.49)	**23** (2.49)	**28.5** (0)	**30** (3)	**24** (2.43)	**24** (2.42)	**22.5** (74)	**18** (43)	**8** (5.4)			8	34
U of Massachusetts at Amherst	**25** (2.42)	**25** (2.46)	**28.5** (0)	**30** (3)	**25** (2.33)	**27** (2.20)	**29** (64)	**21** (24)	**16** (3.4)			7	24
University of Oklahoma	**26** (2.37)	**24** (2.47)	**16.5** (1)	**21.5** (10)	**28** (2.15)	**25** (2.33)	**20** (76)	**20** (34)	**12.5** (4.3)			8	15
Univ of Arkansas-Fayetteville	**27** (2.33)	**29** (2.15)	**28.5** (0)	**24** (7)	**27** (2.19)	**30** (1.87)	**27** (68)	**32** (4)	**32** (0.4)			9	14
University of Nebraska-Lincoln	**28** (2.28)	**30** (2.14)	**28.5** (0)	**27** (4)	**26** (2.22)	**28.5** (1.96)	**33.5** (51)	**22** (22)	**22** (2.2)			10	11
Kansas State University	**29** (2.27)	**31** (2.07)	**28.5** (0)	**27** (4)	**30.5** (1.97)	**33** (1.58)	**30** (62)	**29.5** (5)	**28.5** (0.6)			9	13
Northeastern University	**30** (2.17)	**27** (2.28)	**28.5** (0)	**25** (5)	**29** (2.14)	**23** (2.47)	**24** (73)	**12** (73)	**9.5** (4.6)			16	26

Institution	93Q [1]	93E [1]	% D [1]	% D-S [1]	93Q T [1]	93E T [1]	VIS [1]	TC [2]	C/F [2]	82Q [3]	82E [3]	TF [4]	TG [4]
Wayne State University	**31.5** (2.08)	**32** (2.00)	**28.5** (0)	**32.5** (2)	**31** (1.97)	**32** (1.67)	**31** (58)	**26** (13)	**25** (1.4)			9	36
Clemson University	**31.5** (2.08)	**28** (2.20)	**28.5** (0)	**32.5** (2)	**32** (1.95)	**29** (1.96)	**25** (72)	**34** (3)	**33.5** (0.3)			9	9
University of Missouri-Columbia	**33** (1.78)	**34** (1.72)	**28.5** (0)	**35** (1)	**33** (1.73)	**36** (1.39)	**32** (54)	**32** (4)	**28.5** (0.6)			7	17
University of Wisconsin-Milwaukee	**34** (1.77)	**37** (1.44)	**28.5** (0)	**30** (3)	**35** (1.54)	**37** (1.36)	**37** (46)	**23** (20)	**20.5** (2.5)			8	n/a
University of Alabama-Huntsville	**35** (1.71)	**36** (1.52)	**28.5** (0)	**37** (0)	**34** (1.67)	**34** (1.48)	**33.5** (51)	**35** (1)	**35** (0.1)			12	38
University of Houston	**36** (1.61)	**33** (1.83)	**28.5** (0)	**35** (1)	**36** (1.45)	**31** (1.86)	**35.5** (49)	**36.5** (0)	**36.5** (0.0)			9	69
Oregon State University	**37** (1.28)	**35** (1.56)	**28.5** (0)	**35** (1)	**37** (1.04)	**35** (1.42)	**35.5** (49)	**36.5** (0)	**36.5** (0.0)			3	31

Sources:
1. National Survey of Graduate Faculty
2. Institute for Scientific Information
3. 1982 Survey of Graduate Faculty
4. Institutional Coordinator Data

Appendix Table P - 24 Relative Rankings for Research-Doctorate Programs in Linguistics

Institution	93Q [1]	93E [1]	% D [1]	% D-S [1]	93Q T [1]	93E T [1]	VIS [1]	FA [2]	82Q [3]	82E [3]	TF [4]	TG [4]
Massachusetts Inst of Technology	1 (4.79)	2 (4.39)	1 (84)	2.5 (91)	1 (4.82)	2 (4.55)	2 (100)	9 (3)	1 (4.74)	1 (4.28)	13	29
Stanford University	2 (4.59)	4 (4.01)	2 (61)	2.5 (91)	2 (4.66)	4 (4.07)	8 (98)	9 (3)	9 (3.62)	8 (3.50)	13	44
Univ of California-Los Angeles	3 (4.56)	3 (4.17)	3 (60)	1 (92)	4 (4.56)	3 (4.10)	5.5 (99)	25 (1)	2 (4.44)	2 (4.02)	42	85
U of Massachusetts at Amherst	4 (4.44)	1 (4.44)	4 (54)	5 (85)	3 (4.64)	1 (4.62)	5.5 (99)	15.5 (2)	8 (3.75)	3 (3.97)	12	45
University of Pennsylvania	5 (4.16)	7 (3.68)	7 (27)	4 (87)	5 (4.09)	9 (3.61)	5.5 (99)	2 (7)	6 (3.88)	11 (3.35)	28	61
University of Chicago	6.5 (3.97)	8 (3.64)	5 (31)	8 (70)	7 (3.97)	10 (3.60)	5.5 (99)	1 (9)	4 (3.94)	4.5 (3.72)	25	48
University of California-Berkeley	6.5 (3.97)	13 (3.40)	6 (30)	6 (72)	7 (3.97)	14 (3.33)	2 (100)	9 (3)	5 (3.88)	10 (3.40)	15	53
Ohio State University	8 (3.80)	12 (3.46)	11 (10)	7 (71)	7 (3.97)	8 (3.63)	10.5 (96)	5.5 (4)	11 (3.44)	9 (3.42)	15	20
Cornell University	9 (3.78)	5 (3.89)	10 (11)	9 (66)	9 (3.84)	5 (4.06)	13 (95)	25 (1)	18.5 (2.77)	17 (2.77)	26	51
Univ of California-Santa Cruz	10 (3.66)	6 (3.80)	9 (13)	10.5 (57)	10 (3.79)	6 (3.83)	20 (87)	25 (1)			5	26
University of Texas at Austin	11 (3.61)	11 (3.48)	8 (18)	10.5 (57)	11 (3.65)	12 (3.56)	2 (100)	3 (6)	3 (4.09)	4.5 (3.72)	50	46
University of Southern California	12.5 (3.58)	14 (3.39)	12.5 (8)	12 (55)	13 (3.56)	13 (3.38)	13 (95)	25 (1)	13 (2.93)	16 (2.87)	18	56
University of Arizona	12.5 (3.58)	9.5 (3.51)	16.5 (5)	13 (54)	12 (3.64)	7 (3.67)	13 (95)	36 (0)	20 (2.71)	18.5 (2.73)	17	34
Univ of California-San Diego	14 (3.43)	16 (3.08)	14.5 (6)	14 (47)	16 (3.44)	17 (3.08)	10.5 (96)	15.5 (2)	7 (3.80)	6 (3.60)	16	40
CUNY - Grad Sch & Univ Center	15 (3.41)	17.5 (2.99)	18.5 (4)	15 (44)	15 (3.45)	16 (3.09)	9 (97)	9 (3)	16 (2.91)	18.5 (2.73)	15	71
University of Connecticut	16 (3.36)	9.5 (3.51)	12.5 (8)	16 (32)	14 (3.52)	11 (3.58)	29.5 (80)	36 (0)	18.5 (2.77)	12 (3.08)	7	41
University of Washington	17 (3.16)	19 (2.92)	34 (0)	17.5 (30)	17 (3.22)	18 (3.01)	16.5 (92)	15.5 (2)	17 (2.84)	15 (2.90)	8	26
U of Illinois at Urbana-Champaign	18 (3.10)	15 (3.22)	22 (2)	17.5 (30)	18 (3.13)	15 (3.31)	16.5 (92)	15.5 (2)	10 (3.51)	7 (3.58)	13	93
Georgetown University	19 (3.00)	27 (2.55)	14.5 (6)	19 (26)	24 (2.80)	28.5 (2.50)	29.5 (80)	15.5 (2)	24 (2.38)	22 (2.55)	17	132
Brown University	20 (2.94)	22 (2.69)	22 (2)	21 (20)	19 (3.04)	20.5 (2.92)	24.5 (83)	36 (0)	21 (2.57)	23 (2.52)	7	12
Harvard University	21 (2.92)	17.5 (2.99)	16.5 (5)	20 (25)	20 (3.02)	19 (2.94)	15 (94)	9 (3)	12 (3.26)	13 (3.02)	6	19
State Univ of New York-Buffalo	22 (2.87)	25 (2.56)	25 (1)	22 (19)	21 (2.94)	25 (2.71)	18 (91)	25 (1)	27 (2.01)	26 (2.05)	9	33
University of Pittsburgh	23 (2.83)	31.5 (2.26)	18.5 (4)	23.5 (18)	23 (2.87)	28.5 (2.50)	21.5 (84)	36 (0)	29 (1.82)	29 (1.62)	10	7
State U of New York-Stony Brook	24 (2.82)	21 (2.78)	25 (1)	23.5 (18)	22 (2.90)	22 (2.86)	27 (82)	36 (0)			8	3
University of Hawaii at Manoa	25 (2.79)	20 (2.81)	20 (3)	25.5 (17)	26 (2.72)	20.5 (2.92)	21.5 (84)	25 (1)	14.5 (2.93)	14 (2.97)	23	63
University of Oregon	26 (2.68)	27 (2.55)	22 (2)	27 (15)	30 (2.58)	32 (2.38)	28 (81)	15.5 (2)			17	14
Indiana University	27 (2.66)	29 (2.50)	34 (0)	29 (10)	25 (2.77)	24 (2.74)	19 (88)	15.5 (2)	23 (2.53)	21 (2.57)	14	69
Boston University	28.5 (2.60)	23 (2.60)	34 (0)	28 (14)	29 (2.63)	23 (2.81)	24.5 (83)	36 (0)			9	47
University of Delaware	28.5 (2.60)	27 (2.55)	34 (0)	30.5 (8)	28 (2.67)	26 (2.58)	33.5 (71)	25 (1)			12	31
Yale University	30 (2.57)	24 (2.59)	25 (1)	25.5 (17)	27 (2.70)	27 (2.56)	24.5 (83)	36 (0)	14.5 (2.93)	24 (2.32)	7	19

Institution	93Q [1]	93E [1]	% D [1]	% D-S [1]	93Q T [1]	93E T [1]	VIS [1]	FA [2]	82Q [3]	82E [3]	TF [4]	TG [4]
University of Michigan	**31** (2.37)	**33** (2.10)	**34** (0)	**30.5** (8)	**31** (2.45)	**33** (2.37)	**24.5** (83)	**25** (1)	**22** (2.56)	**20** (2.58)	16	34
University of Wisconsin-Madison	**32** (2.20)	**31.5** (2.26)	**34** (0)	**34.5** (3)	**33** (2.23)	**30** (2.42)	**31** (78)	**36** (0)	**25** (2.22)	**25** (2.15)	10	44
University of Colorado	**33** (2.15)	**30** (2.36)	**34** (0)	**37.5** (2)	**32** (2.24)	**31** (2.40)	**32** (74)	**25** (1)			7	36
University of South Carolina	**34.5** (1.91)	**40** (1.21)	**34** (0)	**34.5** (3)	**34** (2.00)	**40** (1.33)	**40** (57)	**5.5** (4)			28	31
University of Kansas	**34.5** (1.91)	**34** (2.02)	**34** (0)	**37.5** (2)	**36** (1.90)	**34** (2.22)	**39** (59)	**15.5** (2)	**28** (1.96)	**27** (2.03)	11	15
New York University	**36** (1.84)	**36** (1.73)	**34** (0)	**34.5** (3)	**35** (1.95)	**36** (1.86)	**33.5** (71)	**25** (1)	**26** (2.05)	**28** (2.00)	7	14
University of Florida	**37** (1.78)	**35** (1.91)	**34** (0)	**34.5** (3)	**37** (1.85)	**35** (2.17)	**36** (63)	**4** (5)	**30** (0.87)	**30** (1.02)	18	22
Michigan State University	**38** (1.76)	**37** (1.57)	**34** (0)	**40.5** (0)	**38** (1.66)	**38** (1.48)	**37** (61)	**36** (0)			23	15
Rice University	**39** (1.72)	**38** (1.47)	**34** (0)	**32** (4)	**39** (1.65)	**37** (1.67)	**35** (67)	**36** (0)			6	15
University of Texas at Arlington	**40** (1.26)	**39** (1.25)	**34** (0)	**39** (1)	**40** (1.30)	**39** (1.46)	**38** (60)	**36** (0)			5	n/a
Indiana Univ of Pennsylvania	**41** (0.55)	**41** (0.00)	**34** (0)	**40.5** (0)	**41** (0.67)	**41** (0.00)	**41** (28)	**25** (1)			13	50

Sources: 1. National Survey of Graduate Faculty

2. Associations and Organizations Administrating Prestigious Awards and Honors

3. 1982 Survey of Graduate Faculty

4. Institutional Coordinator Data

Appendix Table P - 25 Relative Rankings for Research-Doctorate Programs in Materials Science

Institution	93Q [1]	93E [1]	% D [1]	% D-S [1]	93Q T [1]	93E T [1]	VIS [1]	TC [2]	C/F [2]	82Q [3]	82E [3]	TF [4]	TG [4]
Massachusetts Inst of Technology	1 (4.61)	1 (4.22)	1 (58)	1 (92)	1 (4.65)	1 (4.26)	1.5 (96)	14 (1747)	25.5 (48.5)			36	125
Northwestern University	2 (4.47)	4.5 (4.08)	2 (48)	2 (82)	2 (4.54)	3 (4.22)	3 (95)	4 (3512)	10 (100.3)			35	124
Cornell University	3 (4.35)	3 (4.10)	4.5 (35)	3 (78)	4 (4.41)	4 (4.16)	5 (88)	11 (2170)	13 (83.5)			26	82
University of California-Berkeley	4 (4.33)	4.5 (4.08)	4.5 (35)	5 (76)	5 (4.40)	5 (4.03)	7.5 (86)	7 (2906)	6 (116.2)			25	95
U of Illinois at Urbana-Champaign	5 (4.29)	7 (3.93)	3 (38)	4 (77)	3 (4.44)	6.5 (4.00)	4 (92)	12 (2134)	25.5 (48.5)			44	117
Stanford University	6 (4.24)	6 (4.00)	6 (32)	6 (71)	6 (4.27)	6.5 (4.00)	7.5 (86)	27 (539)	17 (67.4)			8	114
U of Massachusetts at Amherst	7 (4.20)	2 (4.21)	8 (24)	16.5 (42)	7 (4.21)	2 (4.24)	37 (57)	8 (2316)	3 (154.4)			15	82
Univ of California-Santa Barbara	8 (4.18)	10.5 (3.65)	7 (28)	7 (69)	8 (4.20)	9 (3.73)	9.5 (85)	2 (5083)	1 (188.3)			27	71
Pennsylvania State University	9 (3.97)	8 (3.83)	9 (23)	8 (68)	9 (3.97)	8 (3.82)	1.5 (96)	1 (5306)	20 (62.4)			85	168
University of Pennsylvania	10 (3.79)	12 (3.62)	13.5 (9)	10 (53)	10 (3.81)	11.5 (3.64)	17 (78)	16 (1574)	15 (78.7)			20	62
Carnegie Mellon University	11.5 (3.75)	9 (3.72)	10 (11)	13 (51)	13 (3.71)	10 (3.66)	12.5 (82)	35 (394)	42 (21.9)			18	24
California Institute Technology	11.5 (3.75)	17 (3.44)	11.5 (10)	23 (32)	11 (3.76)	14 (3.54)	41.5 (55)	17 (1339)	2 (167.4)			8	17
Rensselaer Polytechnic Inst	13 (3.68)	10.5 (3.65)	13.5 (9)	10 (53)	15.5 (3.69)	11.5 (3.64)	6 (87)	34 (406)	44 (19.3)			21	47
University of Wisconsin-Madison	14.5 (3.66)	21 (3.33)	15 (7)	14 (46)	15.5 (3.69)	21 (3.29)	18 (77)	5 (3147)	19 (62.9)			50	76
University of Michigan	14.5 (3.66)	15 (3.47)	18.5 (5)	10 (53)	14 (3.70)	16 (3.49)	11 (84)	22 (755)	28 (36.0)			21	67
University of Florida	16 (3.65)	19 (3.36)	21 (4)	12 (52)	17 (3.66)	20 (3.30)	14.5 (81)	24 (645)	36 (23.9)			27	95
University of Minnesota	17 (3.64)	14 (3.53)	11.5 (10)	15 (45)	12 (3.72)	15 (3.53)	12.5 (82)	3 (3753)	4 (144.3)			26	79
Case Western Reserve Univ	18 (3.56)	13 (3.56)	18.5 (5)	19 (39)	19 (3.54)	13 (3.55)	19 (75)	47 (226)	40 (22.6)			10	46
University of Wisconsin-Madison [a]	19 (3.52)	25 (3.22)	31 (2)	21 (35)	18 (3.58)	22 (3.28)	24 (68)	15 (1625)	7 (116.1)			14	31
University of Texas at Austin	20 (3.50)	26.5 (3.19)	16.5 (6)	22 (33)	20 (3.52)	23 (3.23)	20 (73)	6 (3077)	14 (81.0)			38	36
Ohio State University	21 (3.48)	19 (3.36)	21 (4)	16.5 (42)	22 (3.45)	18.5 (3.33)	9.5 (85)	42 (265)	54 (10.2)			26	83
University of Virginia	23 (3.44)	19 (3.36)	21 (4)	24.5 (29)	21 (3.48)	18.5 (3.33)	24 (68)	20 (874)	27 (43.7)			20	72
Lehigh University	23 (3.44)	16 (3.45)	25.5 (3)	19 (39)	24 (3.40)	17 (3.46)	16 (79)	25 (608)	29 (32.0)			19	53
North Carolina State University	23 (3.44)	22 (3.27)	25.5 (3)	19 (39)	23 (3.41)	24 (3.20)	14.5 (81)	9 (2286)	5 (134.5)			17	93
Rutgers State Univ-New Brunswick [b]	25 (3.36)	28 (3.15)	25.5 (3)	28 (25)	25 (3.37)	27 (3.08)	39 (56)	32 (449)	41 (22.5)			20	57
Univ of California-Los Angeles	26 (3.34)	24 (3.23)	25.5 (3)	26.5 (26)	26 (3.30)	25 (3.16)	21.5 (72)	10 (2264)	9 (102.9)			22	93
Arizona State University [c]	27 (3.27)	49 (2.64)	16.5 (6)	26.5 (26)	28 (3.26)	51 (2.50)	28 (64)	13 (1952)	23 (54.2)			36	24
University of Arizona	28 (3.25)	29 (3.08)	39 (1)	24.5 (29)	27 (3.29)	31.5 (2.98)	21.5 (72)	46 (229)	50 (14.3)			16	77
Columbia University	29 (3.20)	26.5 (3.19)	31 (2)	30 (21)	30 (3.19)	28 (3.07)	26.5 (66)	37 (300)	38 (23.1)			13	12
Brown University	30 (3.18)	30 (3.05)	31 (2)	29 (22)	29 (3.24)	26 (3.13)	39 (56)	33 (419)	16 (69.8)			6	23

Institution	93Q [1]	93E [1]	% D [1]	% D-S [1]	93Q T [1]	93E T [1]	VIS [1]	TC [2]	C/F [2]	82Q [3]	82E [3]	TF [4]	TG [4]
University of Akron	**31** (3.14)	**40** (2.92)	**39** (1)	**44** (9)	**36** (2.92)	**47** (2.59)	**64** (26)	**26** (543)	**21** (60.3)			9	48
Purdue University	**32** (3.05)	**41** (2.91)	**31** (2)	**31** (18)	**31** (3.05)	**40** (2.83)	**24** (68)	**29** (522)	**18** (65.3)			8	10
Johns Hopkins University	**33** (3.02)	**36** (2.96)	**31** (2)	**34** (14)	**34** (2.98)	**40** (2.83)	**29.5** (63)	**48** (223)	**45.5** (18.6)			12	66
Vanderbilt University	**34** (2.98)	**54** (2.47)	**39** (1)	**41** (10)	**33** (3.00)	**53** (2.26)	**49.5** (48)	**49** (205)	**56** (9.8)			21	25
Arizona State University [d]	**35** (2.97)	**46** (2.78)	**39** (1)	**32** (17)	**38** (2.90)	**45** (2.68)	**34.5** (59)	**36** (354)	**35** (25.3)			14	16
University of Utah	**36.5** (2.94)	**31** (3.03)	**39** (1)	**35.5** (12)	**39** (2.89)	**32** (2.98)	**39** (56)	**19** (1111)	**8** (111.1)			10	81
University of Rochester	**36.5** (2.94)	**32** (3.02)	**55** (0)	**46.5** (8)	**36** (2.92)	**30** (3.00)	**53** (41)	**40** (276)	**30** (30.7)			9	19
Virginia Polytech Inst & State U	**38** (2.92)	**39** (2.93)	**25.5** (3)	**33** (16)	**43** (2.80)	**38** (2.85)	**29.5** (63)	**51** (179)	**51** (13.8)			13	53
Drexel University	**39.5** (2.91)	**43** (2.81)	**55** (0)	**38** (11)	**32** (3.03)	**44** (2.72)	**32** (62)	**39** (287)	**34** (26.1)			11	55
Rutgers State Univ-New Brunswick [d]	**39.5** (2.91)	**42** (2.85)	**55** (0)	**41** (10)	**38** (2.90)	**44** (2.72)	**34.5** (59)	**50** (182)	**48** (16.5)			11	47
State U of New York-Stony Brook	**41** (2.90)	**36** (2.96)	**55** (0)	**38** (11)	**45** (2.74)	**38** (2.85)	**45** (53)	**38** (290)	**33** (26.4)			11	47
University of Washington	**42.5** (2.88)	**33** (2.99)	**55** (0)	**38** (11)	**40** (2.88)	**36** (2.88)	**32** (62)	**18** (1158)	**12** (89.1)			13	35
University of Mass-Lowell	**42.5** (2.88)	**23** (3.24)	**55** (0)	**48.5** (6)	**41** (2.87)	**30** (3.00)	**60.5** (29)	**63** (20)	**64** (1.7)			12	35
Georgia Institute of Technology	**44** (2.87)	**36** (2.96)	**25.5** (3)	**41** (10)	**43** (2.80)	**33** (2.94)	**41.5** (55)	**57** (97)	**57** (6.5)			15	34
University of Pittsburgh	**45.5** (2.80)	**51** (2.61)	**39** (1)	**35.5** (12)	**43** (2.80)	**48** (2.58)	**26.5** (66)	**41** (267)	**43** (20.5)			13	20
University of Missouri-Rolla	**45.5** (2.80)	**34** (2.97)	**55** (0)	**44** (9)	**47** (2.69)	**35** (2.89)	**36** (58)	**53** (148)	**55** (9.9)			15	22
University of Delaware	**47** (2.77)	**47** (2.73)	**39** (1)	**46.5** (8)	**47** (2.69)	**49** (2.57)	**47.5** (50)	**44** (260)	**37** (23.6)			11	16
University of Southern California	**48** (2.73)	**38** (2.94)	**55** (0)	**44** (9)	**49** (2.63)	**34** (2.93)	**32** (62)	**23** (653)	**22** (54.4)			12	41
Colorado School of Mines	**49** (2.64)	**52.5** (2.59)	**55** (0)	**53** (4)	**48** (2.64)	**52** (2.47)	**52** (45)	**30** (504)	**31** (28.0)			18	22
Michigan State University	**50** (2.58)	**44.5** (2.80)	**55** (0)	**55** (3)	**50** (2.53)	**42** (2.76)	**43.5** (54)	**55** (127)	**61** (5.5)			23	18
University of Maryland College Park	**51** (2.43)	**56** (2.03)	**39** (1)	**51** (5)	**53** (2.28)	**56** (1.83)	**46** (52)	**56** (121)	**49** (15.1)			8	42
Stevens Inst of Technology	**52** (2.40)	**44.5** (2.80)	**55** (0)	**51** (5)	**51** (2.44)	**40** (2.83)	**43.5** (54)	**61** (53)	**59** (5.9)			9	24
Duke University	**53** (2.23)	**50** (2.63)	**55** (0)	**48.5** (6)	**52** (2.43)	**46** (2.61)	**56** (34)	**28** (536)	**11** (89.3)			6	10
University of Cincinnati	**54** (2.22)	**48** (2.67)	**55** (0)	**55** (3)	**54** (2.20)	**50** (2.56)	**49.5** (48)	**52** (161)	**39** (23.0)			7	32
University of Alabama-Birmingham	**55** (2.18)	**55** (2.22)	**39** (1)	**57.5** (2)	**55** (2.06)	**55** (1.96)	**54** (36)	**21** (803)	**32** (27.7)			29	40
South Dakota Sch of Mines & Tech	**56** (2.08)	**52.5** (2.59)	**55** (0)	**60.5** (1)	**59** (1.78)	**54** (2.22)	**65** (23)	**65** (11)	**65** (0.8)			13	12
Illinois Institute of Technology	**57** (2.06)	**61** (1.48)	**55** (0)	**55** (3)	**56** (1.89)	**61** (1.33)	**51** (46)	**64** (16)	**63** (2.3)			7	26
Oregon Graduate Inst Sci & Tech	**58** (2.00)	**57** (2.00)	**55** (0)	**60.5** (1)	**58** (1.79)	**57** (1.67)	**60.5** (29)	**62** (37)	**62** (3.7)			10	29
University of Houston	**59** (1.90)	**65** (1.11)	**55** (0)	**60.5** (1)	**57** (1.82)	**63** (1.16)	**57.5** (33)	**59** (67)	**60** (5.6)			12	25
University of Notre Dame	**60** (1.88)	**58** (1.84)	**39** (1)	**51** (5)	**63** (1.62)	**58** (1.49)	**47.5** (50)	**45** (254)	**24** (50.8)			5	14

Appendix Table P - 25 Materials Science (Continued)

Institution	93Q [1]	93E [1]	% D [1]	% D-S [1]	93Q T [1]	93E T [1]	VIS [1]	TC [2]	C/F [2]	82Q [3]	82E [3]	TF [4]	TG [4]
University of Alabama-Huntsville	**61** (1.85)	**60** (1.67)	**55** (0)	**57.5** (2)	**64** (1.58)	**65** (0.97)	**57.5** (33)	**31** (488)	**47** (17.4)			28	23
University of Kentucky	**62** (1.71)	**63** (1.42)	**55** (0)	**64** (0)	**60** (1.68)	**61** (1.33)	**55** (35)	**58** (91)	**52** (13.0)			7	12
University of Wisconsin-Milwaukee	**63** (1.68)	**64** (1.37)	**55** (0)	**64** (0)	**61** (1.65)	**62** (1.28)	**59** (32)	**54** (130)	**45.5** (18.6)			7	n/a
Auburn University	**64** (1.65)	**59** (1.80)	**55** (0)	**64** (0)	**62** (1.63)	**59** (1.43)	**62** (28)	**60** (58)	**58** (6.4)			9	92
University of Vermont	**65** (1.43)	**62** (1.46)	**39** (1)	**60.5** (1)	**65** (1.32)	**64** (1.11)	**63** (27)	**43** (263)	**53** (12.5)			21	11

Sources: 1. National Survey of Graduate Faculty
2. Institute for Scientific Information
3. 1982 Survey of Graduate Faculty
4. Institutional Coordinator Data

Notes: *a.* Program in Metallurgial Engineering
b. Program in Ceramic Science and Engineering
c. Program in Science and Engineering of Materials
d. Program in Materials Science and Engineering

Appendix Table P - 26 Relative Rankings for Research-Doctorate Programs in Mathematics

Institution	93Q [1]	93E [1]	% D [1]	% D-S [1]	93Q T [1]	93E T [1]	VIS [1]	TC [2]	C/F [2]	82Q [3]	82E [3]	TF [4]	TG [4]
University of California-Berkeley	**1.5*** (4.94)	**6** (4.37)	**1** (90)	**1** (98)	**4** (4.95)	**6** (4.42)	**1** (98)	**14** (607)	**29** (10.5)	**2** (4.91)	**2.5** (4.52)	58	241
Princeton University	**1.5*** (4.94)	**1** (4.69)	**2** (88)	**3.5** (94)	**1.5** (4.98)	**1** (4.85)	**8** (95)	**7** (906)	**3** (24.5)	**1** (4.92)	**1** (4.73)	37	67
Massachusetts Inst of Technology	**3** (4.92)	**4** (4.57)	**3** (86)	**2** (95)	**3** (4.97)	**4** (4.66)	**2.5** (97)	**11** (689)	**14** (15.0)	**3** (4.90)	**4** (4.47)	46	117
Harvard University	**4** (4.90)	**3** (4.58)	**4** (84)	**5** (91)	**1.5** (4.98)	**2** (4.70)	**8** (95)	**16** (574)	**6** (21.3)	**4.5** (4.80)	**2.5** (4.52)	27	54
University of Chicago	**5** (4.69)	**2** (4.64)	**5** (65)	**7.5** (86)	**5.5** (4.72)	**3** (4.69)	**15** (91)	**13** (620)	**27.5** (10.7)	**4.5** (4.80)	**5** (4.43)	58	96
Stanford University	**6** (4.68)	**5** (4.41)	**6** (63)	**3.5** (94)	**5.5** (4.72)	**7** (4.39)	**4.5** (96)	**18** (555)	**4** (23.1)	**6** (4.61)	**6** (4.37)	24	68
Yale University	**7** (4.55)	**8** (4.11)	**7** (55)	**6** (89)	**8** (4.59)	**8** (4.32)	**8** (95)	**35** (291)	**35** (9.1)	**7** (4.55)	**8** (4.13)	32	5
New York University	**8** (4.49)	**7** (4.26)	**8** (51)	**9** (85)	**7** (4.60)	**5** (4.51)	**13.5** (93)	**5** (958)	**7** (20.8)	**8** (4.52)	**7** (4.30)	46	106
University of Michigan	**9.5** (4.23)	**14.5** (3.84)	**10** (28)	**7.5** (86)	**9** (4.32)	**12** (3.93)	**8** (95)	**21** (497)	**33.5** (9.7)	**11** (4.10)	**10** (4.02)	51	137
Columbia University	**9.5** (4.23)	**11** (3.94)	**11** (26)	**16** (72)	**10** (4.28)	**15** (3.84)	**29.5** (81)	**61** (188)	**15.5** (14.5)	**9** (4.38)	**15** (3.80)	13	43
California Institute Technology	**11** (4.19)	**13** (3.90)	**9** (29)	**14.5** (75)	**12** (4.14)	**16** (3.81)	**17.5** (89)	**68** (153)	**21** (11.8)	**17** (3.84)	**16** (3.73)	13	30
Univ of California-Los Angeles	**12** (4.14)	**12** (3.91)	**13** (23)	**10** (84)	**11** (4.16)	**14** (3.86)	**8** (95)	**1** (1343)	**12** (16.0)	**15** (3.95)	**12.5** (3.87)	84	203
University of Wisconsin-Madison	**13** (4.10)	**16** (3.82)	**12** (24)	**11** (78)	**18** (4.03)	**13** (3.88)	**11.5** (94)	**15** (596)	**37** (8.5)	**10** (4.18)	**9** (4.07)	70	199
University of Minnesota	**14** (4.08)	**17** (3.65)	**14.5** (21)	**13** (76)	**15** (4.08)	**17** (3.72)	**16** (90)	**19** (512)	**32** (9.8)	**16** (3.90)	**17** (3.67)	52	84
Cornell University	**15** (4.05)	**10** (3.96)	**14.5** (21)	**12** (77)	**16.5** (4.04)	**10** (4.02)	**13.5** (93)	**3** (1109)	**2** (25.2)	**13** (4.01)	**12.5** (3.87)	44	62
Brown University [a]	**16** (4.04)	**9** (4.06)	**19** (17)	**26** (55)	**22** (3.90)	**11** (3.99)	**39** (74)	**36** (288)	**17** (13.7)	**12** (4.09)	**11** (3.92)	21	47
Univ of California-San Diego	**17** (4.02)	**22** (3.58)	**17** (19)	**20.5** (64)	**14** (4.09)	**21** (3.61)	**26.5** (83)	**10** (734)	**11** (16.3)	**29** (3.40)	**26** (3.33)	45	71
University of Maryland College Park	**18** (3.97)	**18** (3.64)	**21** (13)	**19** (67)	**19** (3.95)	**23.5** (3.57)	**23** (86)	**4** (1058)	**24** (11.0)	**25** (3.47)	**27** (3.30)	96	107
Rutgers State Univ-New Brunswick	**19** (3.96)	**20** (3.62)	**20** (15)	**14.5** (75)	**16.5** (4.04)	**18** (3.69)	**11.5** (94)	**6** (955)	**27.5** (10.7)	**21** (3.60)	**24** (3.38)	89	148
State U of New York-Stony Brook	**20** (3.94)	**21** (3.61)	**18** (18)	**22** (62)	**13** (4.10)	**20** (3.65)	**28** (82)	**66** (167)	**61** (5.8)	**19** (3.72)	**22** (3.40)	29	85
U of Illinois at Urbana-Champaign	**21** (3.93)	**19** (3.63)	**16** (20)	**18** (68)	**23** (3.82)	**27** (3.55)	**4.5** (96)	**38** (272)	**100.5** (2.9)	**14** (4.00)	**14** (3.83)	94	195
University of Pennsylvania	**22** (3.87)	**25** (3.52)	**22** (11)	**23** (61)	**21** (3.92)	**23.5** (3.57)	**26.5** (83)	**48** (222)	**43** (7.7)	**20** (3.69)	**20** (3.42)	29	40
University of Texas at Austin	**23** (3.85)	**30** (3.46)	**24.5** (10)	**20.5** (64)	**24** (3.80)	**30** (3.41)	**20** (88)	**2** (1297)	**10** (18.0)	**31** (3.27)	**33.5** (3.03)	72	87
Purdue University	**24.5** (3.82)	**24** (3.54)	**24.5** (10)	**17** (71)	**25.5** (3.75)	**22** (3.60)	**2.5** (97)	**17** (561)	**30** (10.4)	**27** (3.44)	**19** (3.45)	54	87
Rice University [b]	**24.5** (3.82)	**14.5** (3.84)	**27.5** (9)	**37** (34)	**20** (3.94)	**9** (4.09)	**76.5** (56)	**87.5** (85)	**47.5** (7.1)			12	47
University of Washington	**26** (3.76)	**29** (3.47)	**27.5** (9)	**24** (59)	**31** (3.61)	**36** (3.27)	**17.5** (89)	**23** (444)	**33.5** (9.7)	**22** (3.59)	**22** (3.40)	46	88
Brown University	**27** (3.73)	**23** (3.56)	**24.5** (10)	**27.5** (54)	**33** (3.57)	**29** (3.44)	**24** (85)	**53** (198)	**36** (8.6)			23	44
Northwestern University	**28** (3.71)	**31** (3.42)	**31.5** (7)	**27.5** (54)	**30** (3.65)	**33** (3.33)	**25** (84)	**8** (861)	**9** (18.7)	**24** (3.48)	**28** (3.27)	46	79
Ohio State University	**29** (3.66)	**42** (3.13)	**33** (6)	**25** (56)	**34.5** (3.55)	**50** (2.93)	**20** (88)	**12** (656)	**49** (7.0)	**37** (2.98)	**33.5** (3.03)	94	177
Johns Hopkins University	**30.5** (3.65)	**37.5** (3.24)	**29.5** (8)	**32** (43)	**27** (3.74)	**33** (3.33)	**38** (75)	**109** (52)	**100.5** (2.9)	**28** (3.40)	**39** (2.88)	18	34

Appendix Table P - 26 Mathematics (Continued)

Institution	93Q [1]	93E [1]	% D [1]	% D-S [1]	93Q T [1]	93E T [1]	VIS [1]	TC [2]	C/F [2]	82Q [3]	82E [3]	TF [4]	TG [4]
CUNY - Grad Sch & Univ Center	**30.5** (3.65)	**44.5** (3.08)	**34** (5)	**29** (51)	**26** (3.75)	**44** (3.03)	**29.5** (81)	**127.5** (20)	**125.5** (1.0)	**23** (3.51)	**30** (3.18)	20	90
Brandeis University	**32** (3.64)	**26** (3.50)	**31.5** (7)	**33.5** (42)	**28** (3.70)	**26** (3.56)	**41** (72)	**90** (83)	**76** (4.4)	**18** (3.78)	**18** (3.47)	19	52
University of Illinois at Chicago	**33** (3.58)	**36** (3.29)	**29.5** (8)	**31** (46)	**37** (3.51)	**41** (3.14)	**22** (87)	**28** (332)	**56** (6.4)	**34** (3.01)	**47** (2.78)	52	70
Indiana University	**34.5** (3.53)	**34.5** (3.33)	**36.5** (4)	**36** (38)	**36** (3.53)	**28** (3.47)	**37** (77)	**50** (213)	**70.5** (4.8)	**26** (3.47)	**25** (3.37)	44	90
Duke University	**34.5** (3.53)	**32.5** (3.37)	**42** (3)	**30** (47)	**29** (3.69)	**31** (3.40)	**32** (80)	**99** (69)	**84.5** (3.8)	**42** (2.84)	**59** (2.50)	18	37
University of Utah	**36** (3.52)	**39** (3.19)	**36.5** (4)	**35** (41)	**32** (3.58)	**40** (3.17)	**36** (78)	**27** (341)	**38.5** (8.3)	**32** (3.15)	**44** (2.82)	41	73
Pennsylvania State University	**37** (3.50)	**32.5** (3.37)	**36.5** (4)	**33.5** (42)	**38** (3.48)	**35** (3.28)	**20** (88)	**26** (355)	**58** (6.0)	**35.5** (3.00)	**31** (3.07)	59	103
Rice University	**38** (3.49)	**34.5** (3.33)	**42** (3)	**38** (31)	**35** (3.55)	**33** (3.33)	**42** (70)	**120** (29)	**109** (2.2)	**30** (3.40)	**22** (3.40)	13	26
Washington University	**39** (3.42)	**27** (3.49)	**42** (3)	**39** (30)	**39** (3.36)	**19** (3.67)	**50.5** (66)	**32** (320)	**20** (12.3)	**33** (3.13)	**33.5** (3.03)	26	49
Carnegie Mellon University	**40** (3.41)	**28** (3.48)	**24.5** (10)	**43** (22)	**43** (3.21)	**26** (3.56)	**71.5** (59)	**41.5** (257)	**31** (9.9)	**35.5** (3.00)	**29** (3.23)	26	42
University of Washington [a]	**41** (3.39)	**37.5** (3.24)	**47** (2)	**46.5** (19)	**40** (3.33)	**52** (2.86)	**98** (46)	**29** (329)	**1** (32.9)			10	44
U of North Carolina-Chapel Hill	**42** (3.24)	**50.5** (3.01)	**56.5** (1)	**40** (28)	**42** (3.23)	**45** (3.01)	**34.5** (79)	**63** (183)	**66** (5.4)	**39** (2.95)	**41** (2.85)	34	51
University of Southern California	**43** (3.23)	**47** (3.07)	**42** (3)	**41** (25)	**41** (3.26)	**47** (2.98)	**34.5** (79)	**22** (473)	**22** (11.3)	**43** (2.83)	**52** (2.68)	42	38
Georgia Institute of Technology	**44** (3.19)	**47** (3.07)	**56.5** (1)	**43** (22)	**50** (2.97)	**56** (2.75)	**59** (63)	**57.5** (190)	**87** (3.6)	**71.5** (2.19)	**70** (2.23)	53	52
University of Virginia	**45** (3.18)	**40** (3.18)	**42** (3)	**49.5** (16)	**45** (3.12)	**37** (3.24)	**47.5** (67)	**46** (251)	**42** (7.8)	**38** (2.96)	**33.5** (3.03)	32	44
University of Notre Dame	**46** (3.11)	**41** (3.17)	**47** (2)	**48** (17)	**44** (3.14)	**39** (3.21)	**65.5** (61)	**84** (95)	**92** (3.3)	**46** (2.72)	**42.5** (2.83)	29	40
University of Oregon	**47** (3.06)	**53.5** (2.95)	**102** (0)	**51** (15)	**47** (3.01)	**42** (3.07)	**54** (64)	**82** (101)	**89** (3.5)	**40** (2.94)	**37** (2.95)	29	41
Michigan State University	**48** (3.05)	**53.5** (2.95)	**56.5** (1)	**43** (22)	**52** (2.92)	**53** (2.83)	**32** (80)	**41.5** (257)	**53.5** (6.6)	**49** (2.68)	**50.5** (2.75)	39	84
Univ of California-Santa Barbara	**49.5** (3.04)	**57** (2.85)	**102** (0)	**45** (20)	**46** (3.05)	**58** (2.73)	**44.5** (69)	**71** (133)	**84.5** (3.8)	**52** (2.66)	**48.5** (2.77)	35	11
Johns Hopkins University [c]	**49.5** (3.04)	**52** (2.98)	**102** (0)	**70** (9)	**73** (2.50)	**80** (2.22)	**121** (36)	**95.5** (72)	**41** (8.0)			9	26
Boston University	**51** (3.03)	**55** (2.93)	**102** (0)	**53** (14)	**50** (2.97)	**49** (2.95)	**50.5** (66)	**24** (410)	**13** (15.2)	**91** (1.69)	**100** (1.27)	27	34
Rensselaer Polytechnic Inst	**52** (3.02)	**47** (3.07)	**102** (0)	**57.5** (12)	**52** (2.92)	**49** (2.95)	**82.5** (51)	**59.5** (189)	**46** (7.3)	**45** (2.72)	**45.5** (2.80)	26	88
Dartmouth College	**53** (2.97)	**43** (3.09)	**36.5** (4)	**46.5** (19)	**56** (2.83)	**51** (2.88)	**44.5** (69)	**118.5** (30)	**118** (1.4)	**55.5** (2.62)	**55** (2.60)	22	24
University of Arizona	**54** (2.96)	**64.5** (2.72)	**56.5** (1)	**62** (11)	**54** (2.85)	**63** (2.50)	**44.5** (69)	**9** (774)	**18** (13.6)	**55.5** (2.62)	**55** (2.60)	57	64
University of Florida	**55** (2.95)	**71** (2.63)	**102** (0)	**49.5** (16)	**59** (2.78)	**78** (2.26)	**44.5** (69)	**62** (184)	**84.5** (3.8)	**68** (2.28)	**68** (2.25)	48	52
Univ of California-Santa Cruz	**56** (2.92)	**106.5** (2.07)	**102** (0)	**53** (14)	**48** (3.00)	**100** (1.79)	**65.5** (61)	**110.5** (50)	**84.5** (3.8)			13	43
U of Massachusetts at Amherst	**58.5** (2.90)	**44.5** (3.08)	**56.5** (1)	**57.5** (12)	**53** (2.87)	**47** (2.98)	**32** (80)	**59.5** (189)	**68** (5.1)	**51** (2.66)	**50.5** (2.75)	37	48
North Carolina State University	**58.5** (2.90)	**56** (2.86)	**102** (0)	**53** (14)	**60** (2.76)	**59** (2.69)	**81** (52)	**40** (264)	**51** (6.8)	**75** (2.08)	**75.5** (2.05)	39	66
University of Georgia	**58.5** (2.90)	**93** (2.38)	**102** (0)	**66** (10)	**58** (2.80)	**82** (2.19)	**47.5** (67)	**104** (61)	**114.5** (1.7)	**69** (2.25)	**71** (2.20)	35	47
University of Rochester	**58.5** (2.90)	**62.5** (2.76)	**102** (0)	**66** (10)	**55** (2.84)	**56** (2.75)	**65.5** (61)	**69** (147)	**59.5** (5.9)	**47** (2.71)	**40** (2.87)	25	40

Institution	93Q [1]	93E [1]	% D [1]	% D-S [1]	93Q T [1]	93E T [1]	VIS [1]	TC [2]	C/F [2]	82Q [3]	82E [3]	TF [4]	TG [4]
University of Pittsburgh	**61** (2.88)	**75** (2.58)	**102** (0)	**57.5** (12)	**64** (2.69)	**67** (2.38)	**71.5** (59)	**25** (391)	**25.5** (10.9)	**58** (2.48)	**45.5** (2.80)	36	40
University of Iowa	**62** (2.85)	**66** (2.71)	**102** (0)	**57.5** (12)	**65** (2.67)	**69** (2.35)	**65.5** (61)	**30** (328)	**51** (6.8)	**70** (2.20)	**61** (2.45)	48	71
University of California-Irvine	**63.5** (2.84)	**61** (2.78)	**47** (2)	**70** (9)	**57** (2.81)	**63** (2.50)	**59** (63)	**65** (170)	**51** (6.8)			25	55
Texas A&M University	**63.5** (2.84)	**75** (2.58)	**102** (0)	**57.5** (12)	**66** (2.63)	**74** (2.31)	**59** (63)	**31** (324)	**68** (5.1)			64	33
University of Colorado	**65** (2.83)	**49** (3.06)	**102** (0)	**62** (11)	**61** (2.75)	**38** (3.23)	**59** (63)	**76** (122)	**74** (4.5)	**41** (2.86)	**38** (2.93)	27	27
State Univ of New York-Buffalo	**66.5** (2.79)	**78.5** (2.55)	**102** (0)	**66** (10)	**69** (2.60)	**80** (2.22)	**76.5** (56)	**83** (98)	**105.5** (2.5)	**48** (2.71)	**48.5** (2.77)	40	55
Virginia Polytech Inst & State U	**66.5** (2.79)	**59.5** (2.80)	**102** (0)	**66** (10)	**70** (2.58)	**61** (2.56)	**54** (64)	**44** (255)	**57** (6.1)	**64** (2.31)	**65.5** (2.33)	42	73
University of Houston	**68** (2.78)	**50.5** (3.01)	**56.5** (1)	**57.5** (12)	**64** (2.69)	**43** (3.06)	**59** (63)	**52** (204)	**53.5** (6.6)	**85** (1.86)	**79** (2.02)	31	88
State Univ of New York-Binghamton	**69.5** (2.74)	**77** (2.56)	**42** (3)	**70** (9)	**62** (2.72)	**69** (2.35)	**54** (64)	**123** (25)	**122.5** (1.1)	**89.5** (1.70)	**86** (1.77)	23	48
Louisiana State U & A&M College	**69.5** (2.74)	**67** (2.69)	**102** (0)	**62** (11)	**76** (2.44)	**69** (2.35)	**40** (73)	**92** (80)	**114.5** (1.7)	**53** (2.65)	**53** (2.65)	48	61
University of Kentucky	**71** (2.72)	**85** (2.47)	**102** (0)	**73** (8)	**71** (2.53)	**91** (1.97)	**71.5** (59)	**56** (191)	**76** (4.4)	**44** (2.82)	**36** (3.02)	43	47
Temple University	**72** (2.67)	**75** (2.58)	**102** (0)	**85.5** (5)	**67** (2.62)	**65** (2.43)	**50.5** (66)	**116.5** (33)	**125.5** (1.0)	**62** (2.35)	**73** (2.10)	34	44
Syracuse University	**73** (2.62)	**62.5** (2.76)	**102** (0)	**77** (7)	**74** (2.46)	**58** (2.73)	**71.5** (59)	**108** (53)	**116.5** (1.6)	**65** (2.30)	**68** (2.25)	34	42
Claremont Graduate School	**74** (2.61)	**80.5** (2.54)	**102** (0)	**81** (6)	**78** (2.43)	**66** (2.41)	**121** (36)	**139** (1)	**138.5** (0.2)	**66** (2.30)	**65.5** (2.33)	5	33
University of South Carolina	**75** (2.60)	**72** (2.61)	**102** (0)	**73** (8)	**84** (2.31)	**76** (2.27)	**85** (50)	**72** (126)	**78.5** (4.2)	**88** (1.77)	**92** (1.57)	30	46
Tulane University	**77** (2.59)	**69.5** (2.65)	**102** (0)	**66** (10)	**89** (2.23)	**78** (2.26)	**50.5** (66)	**89** (84)	**91** (3.4)	**50** (2.68)	**42.5** (2.83)	25	46
University of Tennessee-Knoxville	**77** (2.59)	**82** (2.53)	**102** (0)	**73** (8)	**81** (2.33)	**83** (2.17)	**59** (63)	**67** (154)	**72** (4.7)	**76** (2.07)	**68** (2.25)	33	43
Iowa State University	**77** (2.59)	**58** (2.82)	**102** (0)	**81** (6)	**86** (2.29)	**63** (2.50)	**63** (62)	**20** (509)	**15.5** (14.5)	**74** (2.10)	**75.5** (2.05)	35	41
Univ of California-Riverside	**79** (2.55)	**83.5** (2.50)	**102** (0)	**77** (7)	**78** (2.43)	**74** (2.31)	**74.5** (57)	**78** (113)	**81** (4.0)	**63** (2.33)	**55** (2.60)	28	43
University of Delaware	**80** (2.54)	**96.5** (2.29)	**102** (0)	**77** (7)	**81** (2.33)	**85** (2.14)	**68.5** (60)	**34** (306)	**25.5** (10.9)	**71.5** (2.19)	**72** (2.18)	28	38
Northeastern University	**81** (2.52)	**59.5** (2.80)	**102** (0)	**111** (2)	**68** (2.61)	**60** (2.64)	**79.5** (53)	**49** (220)	**19** (12.9)	**57** (2.49)	**64** (2.37)	17	33
Florida State University	**82** (2.49)	**90** (2.41)	**56.5** (1)	**85.5** (5)	**99** (2.00)	**112** (1.46)	**74.5** (57)	**55** (192)	**64.5** (5.5)	**61** (2.38)	**60** (2.47)	35	51
University of California-Davis	**83.5** (2.48)	**102** (2.17)	**102** (0)	**77** (7)	**81** (2.33)	**94** (1.84)	**68.5** (60)	**80** (105)	**70.5** (4.8)	**67** (2.29)	**63** (2.38)	22	21
State Univ of New York-Albany	**83.5** (2.48)	**88** (2.45)	**102** (0)	**94** (4)	**72** (2.52)	**87** (2.08)	**98** (46)	**87.5** (85)	**94.5** (3.1)	**59** (2.44)	**57.5** (2.57)	27	75
Arizona State University	**85** (2.43)	**95** (2.32)	**102** (0)	**81** (6)	**95** (2.08)	**87** (2.08)	**88.5** (49)	**43** (256)	**38.5** (8.3)			31	48
Kent State University	**86** (2.41)	**91.5** (2.40)	**102** (0)	**85.5** (5)	**91** (2.20)	**98** (1.81)	**79.5** (53)	**118.5** (30)	**121** (1.2)	**87** (1.79)	**84** (1.87)	25	37
University of Nebraska-Lincoln	**87** (2.40)	**64.5** (2.72)	**102** (0)	**94** (4)	**87** (2.28)	**54** (2.78)	**85** (50)	**85** (89)	**104** (2.6)	**86** (1.84)	**88** (1.72)	34	36
Vanderbilt University	**88** (2.39)	**86.5** (2.46)	**56.5** (1)	**85.5** (5)	**96** (2.04)	**105** (1.67)	**95** (47)	**113** (44)	**113** (1.9)	**79** (2.02)	**75.5** (2.05)	23	29
Case Western Reserve Univ	**89** (2.38)	**112** (1.95)	**56.5** (1)	**77** (7)	**76** (2.44)	**105** (1.67)	**92.5** (48)	**103** (63)	**89** (3.5)	**54** (2.62)	**57.5** (2.57)	18	2
Oregon State University	**90** (2.37)	**98.5** (2.26)	**102** (0)	**122.5** (1)	**79** (2.41)	**93** (1.91)	**98** (46)	**110.5** (50)	**94.5** (3.1)	**60** (2.39)	**62** (2.43)	16	24

Appendix Table P - 26 Mathematics (Continued)

Institution	93Q[1]	93E[1]	% D[1]	% D-S[1]	93Q T[1]	93E T[1]	VIS[1]	TC[2]	C/F[2]	82Q[3]	82E[3]	TF[4]	TG[4]
Kansas State University	91 (2.35)	96.5 (2.29)	56.5 (1)	103 (3)	85 (2.30)	87 (2.08)	85 (50)	51 (212)	47.5 (7.1)			30	36
Clemson University	92 (2.34)	73 (2.59)	102 (0)	111 (2)	99 (2.00)	85 (2.14)	109 (41)	121.5 (28)	131 (0.7)	93 (1.68)	82 (1.90)	40	54
Auburn University	93 (2.31)	100 (2.25)	102 (0)	111 (2)	93 (2.12)	96 (1.82)	92.5 (48)	64 (171)	94.5 (3.1)	84 (1.86)	85 (1.78)	55	41
Wayne State University	94.5 (2.30)	106.5 (2.07)	102 (0)	94 (4)	90 (2.21)	96 (1.82)	59 (63)	77 (121)	98 (3.0)	73 (2.18)	75.5 (2.05)	40	23
University of Missouri-Columbia	94.5 (2.30)	91.5 (2.40)	102 (0)	111 (2)	88 (2.26)	72 (2.33)	92.5 (48)	81 (104)	89 (3.5)	89.5 (1.70)	93.5 (1.52)	30	20
Colorado State University	96 (2.28)	86.5 (2.46)	102 (0)	94 (4)	99 (2.00)	105 (1.67)	102 (45)	91 (81)	94.5 (3.1)	82 (1.89)	90 (1.67)	26	22
Lehigh University	97 (2.22)	108 (2.06)	102 (0)	103 (3)	94 (2.09)	105 (1.67)	104 (44)	97.5 (70)	98 (3.0)			23	30
University of Hawaii at Manoa	98 (2.20)	89 (2.43)	42 (3)	94 (4)	107 (1.75)	105 (1.67)	92.5 (48)	54 (193)	62 (5.7)			34	11
Polytechnic University	99.5 (2.18)	83.5 (2.50)	102 (0)	111 (2)	83 (2.32)	72 (2.33)	113.5*(40)	106 (59)	78.5 (4.2)	77 (2.05)	80 (2.00)	14	29
University of Oklahoma	99.5 (2.18)	103 (2.12)	102 (0)	134.5 (0)	92 (2.13)	99 (1.80)	88.5 (49)	73.5 (124)	81 (4.0)	78 (2.02)	81 (1.97)	31	54
University of Connecticut	101 (2.16)	101 (2.19)	102 (0)	122.5 (1)	101 (1.97)	98 (1.81)	98 (46)	75 (123)	76 (4.4)	80 (1.96)	88 (1.72)	28	53
University of Miami	102.5 (2.12)	94 (2.33)	102 (0)	103 (3)	103 (1.87)	89 (2.00)	109 (41)	95.5 (72)	98 (3.0)			24	16
Wesleyan University	102.5 (2.12)	68 (2.67)	102 (0)	103 (3)	99 (2.00)	80 (2.22)	88.5 (49)	130 (16)	128.5 (0.9)	83 (1.87)	83 (1.88)	17	24
Washington State University	104 (2.10)	80.5 (2.54)	102 (0)	122.5 (1)	108 (1.72)	91 (1.97)	102 (45)	45 (252)	44.5 (7.4)			34	37
University of North Texas	105.5 (2.06)	109 (1.99)	102 (0)	94 (4)	114 (1.61)	115 (1.37)	82.5 (51)	124 (24)	128.5 (0.9)			28	33
University of Cincinnati	105.5 (2.06)	111 (1.96)	102 (0)	103 (3)	102 (1.94)	105 (1.67)	78 (55)	47 (223)	44.5 (7.4)	81 (1.89)	78 (2.03)	30	31
Texas Tech University	107 (2.03)	98.5 (2.26)	102 (0)	122.5 (1)	110 (1.71)	113 (1.39)	117.5 (39)	39 (265)	55 (6.5)	92 (1.68)	91 (1.60)	41	42
University of Texas at Arlington	108 (2.02)	110 (1.97)	102 (0)	94 (4)	105 (1.79)	110 (1.50)	88.5 (49)	121.5 (28)	119.5 (1.3)	94 (1.67)	93.5 (1.52)	22	38
Southern Illinois University	109 (1.98)	119 (1.58)	102 (0)	94 (4)	110 (1.71)	115 (1.37)	102 (45)	102 (65)	112 (2.0)	97 (1.51)	99 (1.28)	33	8
Drexel University	110 (1.97)	120.5 (1.55)	102 (0)	122.5 (1)	105 (1.79)	119 (1.25)	113.5 (40)	57.5 (190)	23 (11.2)			17	8
New Mexico State University	111 (1.95)	78.5 (2.55)	102 (0)	134.5 (0)	116 (1.53)	105 (1.67)	113.5 (40)	127.5 (20)	133.5 (0.6)			31	29
University of South Florida	112 (1.90)	105 (2.08)	102 (0)	134.5 (0)	112 (1.67)	105 (1.67)	126 (35)	73.5 (124)	63 (5.6)	98 (1.48)	95 (1.50)	22	30
Western Michigan University	113 (1.86)	69.5 (2.65)	102 (0)	103 (3)	118 (1.48)	75 (2.29)	109 (41)	115 (36)	119.5 (1.3)	102 (1.13)	103 (0.98)	28	27
Bowling Green State University	114 (1.85)	115 (1.78)	56.5 (1)	85.5 (5)	113 (1.65)	111 (1.48)	113.5 (40)	100.5 (66)	109 (2.2)	99 (1.33)	102 (1.05)	30	26
University of Wisconsin-Milwaukee	115 (1.84)	122.5 (1.54)	56.5 (1)	111 (2)	115 (1.58)	120 (1.19)	105 (43)	97.5 (70)	109 (2.2)	95 (1.64)	88 (1.72)	32	45
Southern Methodist University	116 (1.83)	104 (2.11)	102 (0)	94 (4)	122 (1.31)	123 (1.11)	126 (35)	107 (57)	40 (8.1)			7	13
Howard University	117 (1.82)	127 (1.25)	102 (0)	122.5 (1)	107 (1.75)	128 (0.70)	109 (41)	116.5 (33)	111 (2.1)			16	33
Northern Illinois University	118 (1.72)	124 (1.31)	56.5 (1)	111 (2)	117 (1.52)	124 (1.04)	117.5 (39)	70 (137)	102 (2.8)			49	39
U of Maryland Baltimore County	119 (1.69)	113 (1.92)	102 (0)	94 (4)	119 (1.43)	109 (1.54)	106 (42)	86 (86)	68 (5.1)			17	44
Clarkson University	120 (1.68)	114 (1.79)	56.5 (1)	103 (3)	112 (1.67)	93 (1.91)	133 (32)	33 (309)	5 (22.1)	96 (1.53)	97 (1.42)	14	15

Institution	93Q [1]	93E [1]	% D [1]	% D-S [1]	93Q T [1]	93E T [1]	VIS [1]	TC [2]	C/F [2]	82Q [3]	82E [3]	TF [4]	TG [4]
Saint Louis University	**121** (1.63)	**129** (1.21)	**102** (0)	**85.5** (5)	**122** (1.31)	**127** (0.74)	**126** (35)	**129** (17)	**122.5** (1.1)	**107** (0.72)	**106** (0.83)	15	5
Stevens Inst of Technology	**122** (1.62)	**116.5** (1.67)	**102** (0)	**111** (2)	**124** (1.14)	**117** (1.33)	**130.5** (33)	**132** (10)	**125.5** (1.0)	**101** (1.15)	**98** (1.40)	10	31
University of Rhode Island	**123.5** (1.57)	**127** (1.25)	**102** (0)	**111** (2)	**126** (1.09)	**125** (0.83)	**117.5** (39)	**100.5** (66)	**64.5** (5.5)			12	25
Ohio University	**123.5** (1.57)	**120.5** (1.55)	**102** (0)	**122.5** (1)	**123** (1.30)	**121** (1.17)	**133** (32)	**112** (45)	**105.5** (2.5)	**100** (1.31)	**104** (0.93)	18	22
University of Wyoming	**125** (1.53)	**118** (1.59)	**102** (0)	**122.5** (1)	**126** (1.09)	**123** (1.11)	**126** (35)	**93** (77)	**59.5** (5.9)			13	13
University of Alabama	**126** (1.47)	**125** (1.28)	**56.5** (1)	**122.5** (1)	**120** (1.35)	**126** (0.76)	**126** (35)	**94** (74)	**107** (2.3)	**105** (1.05)	**107** (0.73)	32	24
Illinois Institute of Technology	**127** (1.45)	**116.5** (1.67)	**102** (0)	**94** (4)	**128** (1.00)	**119** (1.25)	**133** (32)	**126** (21)	**116.5** (1.6)	**104** (1.07)	**105** (0.90)	13	7
Old Dominion University	**128** (1.39)	**122.5** (1.54)	**102** (0)	**122.5** (1)	**128** (1.00)	**117** (1.33)	**135.5** (30)	**79** (111)	**73** (4.6)			24	28
University of Missouri-Rolla	**129** (1.33)	**130** (0.94)	**102** (0)	**134.5** (0)	**129** (0.95)	**137** (0.00)	**109** (41)	**131** (12)	**133.5** (0.6)	**103** (1.12)	**96** (1.45)	20	15
University of Alabama-Huntsville	**130** (1.28)	**127** (1.25)	**102** (0)	**122.5** (1)	**135** (0.67)	**137** (0.00)	**121** (36)	**133** (9)	**133.5** (0.6)			15	9
George Washington University	**131.5** (1.26)	**132** (0.79)	**56.5** (1)	**122.5** (1)	**136** (0.65)	**133** (0.21)	**130.5** (33)	**37** (282)	**8** (18.8)			15	10
Colorado School of Mines	**131.5** (1.26)	**135** (0.63)	**102** (0)	**134.5** (0)	**130** (0.92)	**129** (0.56)	**138** (28)	**125** (23)	**125.5** (1.0)			22	22
Adelphi University	**133** (1.24)	**134** (0.67)	**102** (0)	**122.5** (1)	**133** (0.73)	**137** (0.00)	**135.5** (30)	**136.5** (3)	**137** (0.3)	**106** (0.93)	**101** (1.18)	11	8
Univ of Southwestern Louisiana	**134** (1.13)	**131** (0.91)	**102** (0)	**134.5** (0)	**131** (0.86)	**130** (0.50)	**98** (46)	**105** (60)	**81** (4.0)			15	26
Florida Institute of Technology	**135** (1.09)	**133** (0.72)	**102** (0)	**122.5** (1)	**134** (0.71)	**137** (0.00)	**126** (35)	**138** (2)	**138.5** (0.2)			9	14
University of Mississippi	**136** (0.97)	**136** (0.56)	**102** (0)	**134.5** (0)	**132** (0.85)	**132** (0.30)	**126** (35)	**134** (7)	**136** (0.5)			14	7
University of Texas at Dallas	**137** (0.76)	**137** (0.48)	**102** (0)	**134.5** (0)	**137** (0.57)	**131** (0.33)	**139** (26)	**135** (5)	**130** (0.8)			6	20
Idaho State University	**138** (0.69)	**138** (0.42)	**102** (0)	**134.5** (0)	**138** (0.44)	**137** (0.00)	**137** (29)	**114** (40)	**103** (2.7)			15	14
Illinois State University	**139** (0.40)	**139** (0.40)	**102** (0)	**134.5** (0)	**139** (0.11)	**137** (0.00)	**117.5** (39)	**136.5** (3)	**133.5** (0.6)			5	10

Sources: 1. National Survey of Graduate Faculty
2. Institute for Scientific Information
3. 1982 Survey of Graduate Faculty
4. Institutional Coordinator Data

Notes: *a.* Program in Applied Mathematics
b. Program in Computational and Applied Mathematics
c. Program in Mathematical Sciences

* Two programs recieved the highest quality rating, and using the standard convention of average rankings, each program was given a rank of 1.5.

Appendix Table P - 27 Relative Rankings for Research-Doctorate Programs in Mechanical Engineering

Institution	93Q [1]	93E [1]	% D [1]	% D-S [1]	93Q T [1]	93E T [1]	VIS [1]	TC [2]	C/F [2]	82Q [3]	82E [3]	TF [4]	TG [4]
Stanford University	**1** (4.77)	**1.5** (4.50)	**1** (73)	**2** (91)	**1** (4.75)	**2** (4.52)	**2** (96)	**4** (1191)	**4** (38.4)	**2** (4.62)	**1** (4.50)	31	219
Massachusetts Inst of Technology	**2** (4.65)	**3** (4.45)	**2** (66)	**1** (92)	**3** (4.56)	**3** (4.47)	**1** (98)	**6** (922)	**17** (15.6)	**1** (4.76)	**2** (4.43)	59	412
University of California-Berkeley	**3** (4.54)	**1.5** (4.50)	**3** (57)	**3** (84)	**2** (4.68)	**1** (4.58)	**4.5** (93)	**11** (606)	**18.5** (14.8)	**3** (4.60)	**3** (4.35)	41	235
California Institute Technology	**4** (4.35)	**4** (4.30)	**4** (46)	**4** (77)	**4** (4.35)	**4** (4.36)	**4.5** (93)	**18** (409)	**10** (22.7)	**4** (4.27)	**4** (4.10)	18	41
University of Michigan	**5** (4.22)	**8** (4.00)	**5** (32)	**5** (76)	**5** (4.27)	**9** (4.01)	**6.5** (92)	**17** (424)	**35** (8.8)	**7** (3.95)	**12** (3.67)	48	175
Princeton University	**6** (4.19)	**5** (4.09)	**6** (31)	**10** (59)	**6** (4.25)	**5** (4.15)	**18** (78)	**16** (440)	**11** (20.0)	**6** (4.00)	**5** (4.07)	22	93
Cornell University	**7** (4.15)	**9** (3.99)	**7** (28)	**8** (71)	**7** (4.21)	**6** (4.09)	**8.5** (91)	**10** (611)	**12** (19.7)	**11** (3.81)	**9** (3.77)	31	49
University of Minnesota	**8** (4.09)	**11** (3.85)	**9.5** (23)	**9** (68)	**12** (3.98)	**12** (3.66)	**10** (87)	**15** (482)	**22** (12.7)	**5** (4.13)	**6** (3.95)	38	109
U of Illinois at Urbana-Champaign	**9** (4.07)	**6** (4.02)	**8** (24)	**7** (74)	**8** (4.05)	**7** (4.06)	**8.5** (91)	**20** (388)	**42** (7.3)	**12** (3.78)	**10** (3.73)	53	230
Univ of California-San Diego	**10.5** (4.04)	**13.5** (3.59)	**9.5** (23)	**13** (56)	**10.5** (4.00)	**16.5** (3.45)	**20** (77)	**14** (492)	**23** (12.6)			39	34
Purdue University	**10.5** (4.04)	**7** (4.01)	**11** (22)	**6** (75)	**10.5** (4.00)	**8** (4.03)	**3** (95)	**19** (407)	**40** (7.5)	**8** (3.90)	**7** (3.90)	54	109
Northwestern University	**12** (3.98)	**10** (3.87)	**12** (21)	**11.5** (58)	**9** (4.04)	**10** (3.94)	**16** (81)	**9** (699)	**7** (26.9)	**14** (3.49)	**15** (3.35)	26	85
Brown University	**13** (3.79)	**12** (3.80)	**13.5** (14)	**19** (45)	**13** (3.79)	**11** (3.90)	**26.5** (73)	**8** (804)	**3** (44.7)	**9** (3.88)	**8** (3.83)	18	54
Univ of California-Los Angeles	**14** (3.76)	**17.5** (3.51)	**16** (8)	**18** (47)	**14** (3.75)	**13** (3.51)	**20** (77)	**7** (832)	**9** (25.2)	**10** (3.88)	**11** (3.68)	33	94
University of Texas at Austin	**15** (3.73)	**13.5** (3.59)	**13.5** (14)	**14** (52)	**18** (3.58)	**14.5** (3.47)	**11** (86)	**1** (2384)	**6** (28.0)	**17** (3.32)	**16** (3.33)	85	92
Rensselaer Polytechnic Inst	**16** (3.69)	**17.5** (3.51)	**24** (4)	**15.5** (49)	**15** (3.74)	**16.5** (3.45)	**20** (77)	**38** (185)	**56** (5.4)	**16** (3.38)	**14** (3.45)	34	99
Pennsylvania State University	**17** (3.68)	**15** (3.55)	**15** (11)	**11.5** (58)	**17** (3.59)	**20** (3.38)	**6.5** (92)	**3** (1350)	**14.5** (17.3)	**31** (2.91)	**20** (3.13)	78	259
Georgia Institute of Technology	**18** (3.62)	**16** (3.54)	**17** (6)	**17** (48)	**16** (3.61)	**14.5** (3.47)	**13.5** (84)	**28** (232)	**61** (4.1)	**24** (3.02)	**22.5** (3.12)	57	172
Carnegie Mellon University	**19** (3.59)	**19** (3.46)	**24** (4)	**15.5** (49)	**19** (3.51)	**18** (3.42)	**13.5** (84)	**57** (115)	**57.5** (4.8)	**22** (3.10)	**20** (3.13)	24	45
Case Western Reserve Univ	**20.5** (3.48)	**20** (3.41)	**19** (5)	**21** (35)	**22** (3.36)	**22** (3.33)	**30.5** (70)	**80** (38)	**79** (2.4)	**21** (3.10)	**20** (3.13)	16	34
University of Wisconsin-Madison	**20.5** (3.48)	**22** (3.33)	**24** (4)	**20** (42)	**20** (3.50)	**22** (3.33)	**12** (85)	**72** (55)	**89.5** (1.7)	**15** (3.49)	**13** (3.57)	32	76
University of Pennsylvania	**22** (3.40)	**25** (3.27)	**24** (4)	**26.5** (28)	**21** (3.47)	**19** (3.40)	**37** (65)	**49** (154)	**21** (12.8)	**20** (3.14)	**18** (3.18)	12	50
Lehigh University	**23** (3.38)	**23** (3.30)	**19** (5)	**23** (31)	**26** (3.21)	**31.5** (3.17)	**30.5** (70)	**32** (206)	**52** (5.9)	**18** (3.24)	**17** (3.30)	35	109
North Carolina State University	**24** (3.33)	**27.5** (3.24)	**24** (4)	**26.5** (28)	**23** (3.27)	**25** (3.26)	**35** (68)	**22** (353)	**48.5** (6.3)	**29** (2.97)	**33** (2.95)	56	106
Ohio State University	**25** (3.32)	**24** (3.28)	**29.5** (3)	**22** (33)	**24** (3.26)	**27** (3.21)	**15** (83)	**25** (276)	**32.5** (9.2)	**25.5** (3.00)	**27** (3.07)	30	86
University of California-Davis	**26** (3.28)	**21** (3.36)	**36** (2)	**24** (30)	**28** (3.16)	**22** (3.33)	**24** (75)	**26** (247)	**43.5** (6.7)	**28** (2.97)	**22.5** (3.12)	37	81
Rice University	**27.5** (3.22)	**34.5** (3.16)	**46** (1)	**30** (25)	**33.5** (3.08)	**34.5** (3.11)	**35** (68)	**58** (113)	**40** (7.5)	**27** (2.97)	**30** (3.02)	15	75
Texas A&M University	**27.5** (3.22)	**26** (3.25)	**81** (0)	**28** (27)	**32** (3.10)	**29** (3.20)	**17** (80)	**33** (205)	**64** (3.8)	**50.5** (2.43)	**56.5** (2.50)	54	111
Columbia University	**29.5** (3.18)	**42** (3.07)	**29.5** (3)	**29** (26)	**27** (3.19)	**44** (2.90)	**35** (68)	**39** (173)	**14.5** (17.3)	**19** (3.18)	**27** (3.07)	10	34
Virginia Polytech Inst & State U	**29.5** (3.18)	**32** (3.18)	**46** (1)	**25** (29)	**30** (3.13)	**24** (3.28)	**22.5** (76)	**52** (136)	**54.5** (5.7)	**30** (2.96)	**24** (3.10)	24	51

Institution	93Q [1]	93E [1]	% D [1]	% D-S [1]	93Q T [1]	93E T [1]	VIS [1]	TC [2]	C/F [2]	82Q [3]	82E [3]	TF [4]	TG [4]
Rutgers State Univ-New Brunswick	31 (3.16)	30 (3.21)	81 (0)	44 (17)	41 (3.00)	26 (3.25)	48 (60)	34.5 (202)	36.5 (8.4)	47 (2.48)	49.5 (2.60)	24	41
University of Washington	32 (3.13)	29 (3.22)	36 (2)	32 (23)	41 (3.00)	41 (2.98)	28 (72)	36 (199)	34 (9.0)	23 (3.07)	34.5 (2.92)	22	71
University of Maryland College Park	34 (3.11)	39.5 (3.10)	24 (4)	35.5 (20)	31 (3.11)	45 (2.89)	29 (71)	5 (1104)	13 (19.0)	38 (2.67)	34.5 (2.92)	58	86
University of Arizona	34 (3.11)	37.5 (3.11)	81 (0)	35.5 (20)	37 (3.03)	29 (3.20)	45.5 (61)	41.5 (168)	45 (6.5)	57 (2.30)	51 (2.57)	26	42
University of California-Irvine	34 (3.11)	47 (3.01)	81 (0)	38 (19)	29 (3.14)	47 (2.88)	53 (58)	24 (312)	20 (14.2)			22	59
University of Notre Dame	37 (3.08)	43 (3.06)	36 (2)	44 (17)	37 (3.03)	50 (2.83)	38.5 (64)	65.5 (75)	66.5 (3.1)	36 (2.70)	36 (2.90)	24	24
University of Houston	37 (3.08)	39.5 (3.10)	46 (1)	40.5 (18)	37 (3.03)	39 (3.05)	26.5 (73)	70 (58)	79 (2.4)	32 (2.87)	38 (2.85)	24	67
Arizona State University	37 (3.08)	48 (2.98)	81 (0)	40.5 (18)	43 (2.95)	50 (2.83)	41 (63)	46.5 (157)	38 (7.9)	40 (2.65)	53.5 (2.53)	20	52
Univ of California-Santa Barbara	40 (3.07)	34.5 (3.16)	24 (4)	35.5 (20)	34 (3.08)	29 (3.20)	43.5 (62)	2 (1406)	1 (63.9)			22	86
State Univ of New York-Buffalo	40 (3.07)	31 (3.19)	81 (0)	40.5 (18)	44 (2.94)	37 (3.08)	22.5 (76)	51 (142)	54.5 (5.7)	44 (2.56)	45.5 (2.70)	25	77
University of Virginia	40 (3.07)	44.5 (3.04)	81 (0)	40.5 (18)	41 (3.00)	42 (2.93)	48 (60)	76 (46)	85 (2.1)	41 (2.64)	25 (3.08)	22	132
Duke University	42 (3.06)	33 (3.17)	29.5 (3)	35.5 (20)	35 (3.05)	32 (3.17)	32.5 (69)	45 (160)	25.5 (12.3)			13	40
Michigan State University	43 (3.02)	36 (3.12)	81 (0)	32 (23)	39 (3.02)	37 (3.08)	25 (74)	30 (211)	32.5 (9.2)	39 (2.65)	43 (2.75)	23	29
Illinois Institute of Technology	44 (2.98)	44.5 (3.04)	46 (1)	44 (17)	46 (2.90)	40 (3.01)	48 (60)	63 (80)	60 (4.4)	34 (2.77)	37 (2.87)	18	23
University of Illinois at Chicago	45 (2.97)	46 (3.03)	36 (2)	32 (23)	50 (2.81)	47 (2.88)	32.5 (69)	41.5 (168)	53 (5.8)	35 (2.71)	29 (3.05)	29	74
Iowa State University	46 (2.96)	41 (3.08)	81 (0)	47.5 (14)	45 (2.92)	39 (3.05)	53 (58)	84 (35)	83 (2.2)	25.5 (3.00)	27 (3.07)	16	54
Johns Hopkins University	47.5 (2.94)	54 (2.79)	19 (5)	46 (15)	25 (3.23)	51 (2.80)	60.5 (54)	21 (368)	2 (61.3)	13 (3.67)	39.5 (2.78)	6	34
University of Delaware	47.5 (2.94)	27.5 (3.24)	29.5 (3)	47.5 (14)	55 (2.72)	35 (3.11)	58 (56)	40 (171)	29.5 (10.1)	55.5 (2.37)	47 (2.65)	17	78
Washington State University	49 (2.92)	49 (2.96)	81 (0)	49.5 (13)	48 (2.84)	48 (2.86)	43.5 (62)	23 (346)	28 (10.2)			34	57
University of Missouri-Rolla	50 (2.88)	56.5 (2.76)	46 (1)	56 (9)	47 (2.86)	55 (2.68)	41 (63)	37 (188)	48.5 (6.3)	52 (2.40)	55 (2.52)	30	57
University of Colorado	51 (2.86)	60 (2.72)	81 (0)	51 (11)	50 (2.81)	60 (2.57)	56.5 (57)	31 (209)	25.5 (12.3)			17	38
University of Florida	52 (2.83)	37.5 (3.11)	81 (0)	59 (8)	53 (2.77)	33 (3.15)	53 (58)	89 (25)	85 (2.1)	55.5 (2.37)	49.5 (2.60)	12	33
State U of New York-Stony Brook	53.5 (2.82)	51 (2.89)	46 (1)	53 (10)	56 (2.67)	52 (2.78)	53 (58)	12 (555)	5 (29.2)	33 (2.85)	32 (2.98)	19	51
University of Iowa	53.5 (2.82)	52 (2.85)	81 (0)	49.5 (13)	52 (2.78)	43 (2.92)	45.5 (61)	59 (96)	46.5 (6.4)	45 (2.55)	31 (3.00)	15	46
Washington University	55 (2.78)	53 (2.80)	81 (0)	56 (9)	58 (2.61)	56 (2.67)	88 (40)	53 (132)	31 (9.4)	53 (2.39)	56.5 (2.50)	14	33
CUNY - Grad Sch & Univ Center	56 (2.76)	58.5 (2.73)	36 (2)	53 (10)	57 (2.63)	62 (2.56)	77 (44)	44 (161)	29.5 (10.1)			16	27
University of Southern California	57 (2.73)	62.5 (2.63)	36 (2)	56 (9)	59 (2.60)	70 (2.42)	66.5 (52)	43 (163)	18.5 (14.8)	54 (2.38)	53.5 (2.53)	11	21
University of Rochester	58 (2.72)	75.5 (2.47)	81 (0)	61 (7)	54 (2.76)	72 (2.38)	88 (40)	13 (512)	8 (25.6)	42 (2.64)	43 (2.75)	20	34
University of Cincinnati	59 (2.71)	50 (2.91)	36 (2)	53 (10)	62 (2.56)	53 (2.72)	41 (63)	74.5 (47)	74.5 (2.5)	62 (2.13)	41 (2.77)	19	82
U of Massachusetts at Amherst	60.5 (2.70)	65 (2.61)	81 (0)	59 (8)	52 (2.78)	57 (2.65)	66.5 (52)	55 (119)	50.5 (6.0)	48 (2.44)	58.5 (2.48)	20	44

Appendix Table P - 27 Mechanical Engineering (Continued)

Institution	93Q [1]	93E [1]	% D [1]	% D-S [1]	93Q T [1]	93E T [1]	VIS [1]	TC [2]	C/F [2]	82Q [3]	82E [3]	TF [4]	TG [4]
University of Utah	**60.5** (2.70)	**61** (2.70)	**81** (0)	**59** (8)	**60** (2.59)	**60** (2.57)	**59** (55)	**48** (155)	**43.5** (6.7)			23	68
University of Rhode Island	**62** (2.59)	**72.5** (2.50)	**46** (1)	**62.5** (6)	**64** (2.43)	**81** (2.04)	**63** (53)	**78.5** (40)	**74.5** (2.5)	**61** (2.19)	**66** (2.22)	16	55
Clemson University	**63** (2.54)	**67** (2.57)	**36** (2)	**65** (5)	**61** (2.57)	**66** (2.50)	**50** (59)	**69** (64)	**70** (2.7)			24	33
George Washington University	**64** (2.52)	**55** (2.78)	**81** (0)	**62.5** (6)	**65** (2.41)	**54** (2.71)	**80.5** (43)	**91** (21)	**95.5** (1.3)			16	45
Colorado State University	**65** (2.51)	**58.5** (2.73)	**81** (0)	**65** (5)	**66** (2.39)	**58** (2.58)	**69.5** (51)	**56** (116)	**57.5** (4.8)	**46** (2.52)	**39.5** (2.78)	24	33
University of Oklahoma	**66** (2.43)	**56.5** (2.76)	**81** (0)	**73** (4)	**72** (2.28)	**66** (2.50)	**66.5** (52)	**68** (69)	**59** (4.6)	**49** (2.43)	**66** (2.22)	15	30
Michigan Technological University	**67** (2.40)	**65** (2.61)	**81** (0)	**91.5** (2)	**70** (2.30)	**63** (2.53)	**38.5** (64)	**50** (143)	**65** (3.6)			40	29
Clarkson University	**68** (2.39)	**72.5** (2.50)	**81** (0)	**73** (4)	**68** (2.33)	**74** (2.26)	**60.5** (54)	**27** (236)	**24** (12.4)			19	66
University of Pittsburgh	**69** (2.36)	**62.5** (2.63)	**81** (0)	**73** (4)	**73** (2.26)	**66** (2.50)	**72.5** (49)	**61** (84)	**50.5** (6.0)	**71** (1.76)	**68** (2.15)	14	42
Old Dominion University	**70** (2.35)	**69.5** (2.53)	**81** (0)	**83** (3)	**71** (2.29)	**66** (2.50)	**72.5** (49)	**81.5** (37)	**89.5** (1.7)	**70** (1.84)	**71** (2.02)	22	117
University of Kentucky	**71** (2.33)	**78.5** (2.38)	**81** (0)	**83** (3)	**63** (2.47)	**75** (2.25)	**56.5** (57)	**54** (122)	**46.5** (6.4)	**50.5** (2.43)	**60** (2.40)	19	32
University of Connecticut	**72** (2.32)	**85.5** (2.07)	**81** (0)	**73** (4)	**74** (2.25)	**87** (1.88)	**80.5** (43)	**81.5** (37)	**85** (2.1)	**60** (2.20)	**58.5** (2.48)	18	46
Vanderbilt University	**73** (2.31)	**69.5** (2.53)	**81** (0)	**83** (3)	**67** (2.37)	**62** (2.56)	**66.5** (52)	**87.5** (28)	**82** (2.3)	**65.5** (2.03)	**52** (2.55)	12	46
Auburn University	**75** (2.29)	**74** (2.48)	**81** (0)	**73** (4)	**81** (2.04)	**76** (2.13)	**71** (50)	**94** (19)	**98** (1.1)	**67** (1.94)	**66** (2.22)	18	32
Wayne State University	**75** (2.29)	**71** (2.52)	**81** (0)	**83** (3)	**75** (2.21)	**71** (2.41)	**63** (53)	**65.5** (75)	**66.5** (3.1)	**59** (2.24)	**61** (2.37)	24	64
Kansas State University	**75** (2.29)	**87.5** (2.06)	**81** (0)	**101.5** (1)	**76** (2.20)	**81** (2.04)	**93** (38)	**92.5** (20)	**95.5** (1.3)	**68** (1.88)	**64** (2.23)	16	13
University of Tennessee-Knoxville	**77** (2.23)	**78.5** (2.38)	**81** (0)	**73** (4)	**91** (1.86)	**82** (2.02)	**74** (48)	**85** (34)	**91.5** (1.5)	**64** (2.09)	**62** (2.28)	22	34
Oklahoma State University	**78** (2.21)	**80** (2.37)	**81** (0)	**73** (4)	**78** (2.14)	**77** (2.12)	**53** (58)	**83** (36)	**69** (2.8)	**37** (2.68)	**43** (2.75)	13	181
University of Toledo	**79** (2.17)	**93.5** (1.92)	**81** (0)	**91.5** (2)	**96** (1.70)	**92** (1.67)	**107** (29)	**77** (42)	**71.5** (2.6)			16	26
University of Kansas	**80** (2.16)	**68** (2.54)	**81** (0)	**83** (3)	**90** (1.87)	**66** (2.50)	**88** (40)	**87.5** (28)	**87** (2.0)			14	14
Worcester Polytechnic Inst	**81.5** (2.14)	**77** (2.43)	**46** (1)	**91.5** (2)	**80** (2.05)	**84** (1.95)	**80.5** (43)	**73** (54)	**88** (1.9)			28	12
Oregon State University	**81.5** (2.14)	**75.5** (2.47)	**81** (0)	**73** (4)	**69** (2.32)	**69** (2.45)	**77** (44)	**100** (11)	**93.5** (1.4)	**58** (2.26)	**45.5** (2.70)	8	27
University of Texas at Arlington	**83.5** (2.12)	**81** (2.19)	**81** (0)	**73** (4)	**83** (2.00)	**79** (2.06)	**80.5** (43)	**74.5** (47)	**74.5** (2.5)			19	50
University of Missouri-Columbia	**83.5** (2.12)	**85.5** (2.07)	**81** (0)	**101.5** (1)	**85** (1.94)	**92** (1.67)	**103.5** (34)	**60** (88)	**62** (4.0)	**72** (1.74)	**72** (1.98)	22	40
West Virginia University	**85** (2.10)	**92** (1.93)	**81** (0)	**83** (3)	**77** (2.16)	**87** (1.88)	**69.5** (51)	**62** (82)	**79** (2.4)			34	35
University of Akron	**86** (2.08)	**90.5** (1.95)	**81** (0)	**83** (3)	**92** (1.84)	**104** (1.25)	**83.5** (42)	**71** (56)	**68** (2.9)	**76** (1.43)	**75** (1.67)	19	125
University of Wisconsin-Milwaukee	**87** (2.06)	**65** (2.61)	**81** (0)	**91.5** (2)	**89** (1.88)	**73** (2.33)	**85.5** (41)	**86** (31)	**79** (2.4)			13	n/a
Tulane University	**89** (2.03)	**98** (1.85)	**46** (1)	**73** (4)	**84** (1.95)	**97** (1.48)	**96** (37)	**92.5** (20)	**74.5** (2.5)	**69** (1.88)	**70** (2.03)	8	30
Northeastern University	**89** (2.03)	**96** (1.90)	**81** (0)	**101.5** (1)	**93** (1.79)	**99** (1.45)	**77** (44)	**65.5** (75)	**63** (3.9)			19	16
Syracuse University	**89** (2.03)	**97** (1.86)	**81** (0)	**101.5** (1)	**95** (1.77)	**94** (1.54)	**83.5** (42)	**95** (16)	**100** (1.0)	**63** (2.11)	**63** (2.27)	16	21

Institution	93Q [1]	93E [1]	% D [1]	% D-S [1]	93Q T [1]	93E T [1]	VIS [1]	TC [2]	C/F [2]	82Q [3]	82E [3]	TF [4]	TG [4]
Catholic University of America	**91** (2.00)	**82.5** (2.14)	**81** (0)	**101.5** (1)	**86** (1.93)	**85** (1.92)	**99.5** (36)	**90** (23)	**71.5** (2.6)	**73** (1.64)	**73** (1.90)	9	32
Southern Methodist University	**92** (1.98)	**87.5** (2.06)	**81** (0)	**73** (4)	**89** (1.88)	**89** (1.84)	**63** (53)	**98.5** (12)	**98** (1.1)			11	35
University of South Carolina	**93** (1.94)	**95** (1.91)	**81** (0)	**73** (4)	**83** (2.00)	**92** (1.67)	**93** (38)	**78.5** (40)	**79** (2.4)			17	18
University of Alabama-Huntsville	**94** (1.90)	**84** (2.08)	**81** (0)	**91.5** (2)	**100** (1.59)	**99** (1.45)	**75** (45)	**34.5** (202)	**36.5** (8.4)			24	56
Tennessee Technological Univ	**95** (1.89)	**99** (1.81)	**36** (2)	**65** (5)	**99** (1.61)	**96** (1.50)	**85.5** (41)	**102** (6)	**102** (0.7)			9	27
University of Alabama	**96** (1.88)	**89** (2.00)	**81** (0)	**101.5** (1)	**87** (1.89)	**87** (1.88)	**103.5** (34)	**104** (3)	**104.5** (0.3)	**75** (1.45)	**76** (1.53)	12	8
Stevens Inst of Technology	**97** (1.79)	**104.5** (1.44)	**81** (0)	**101.5** (1)	**95** (1.77)	**101** (1.37)	**96** (37)	**96.5** (15)	**98** (1.1)	**65.5** (2.03)	**69** (2.07)	14	24
Louisiana State U & A&M College	**98** (1.78)	**100.5** (1.67)	**81** (0)	**91.5** (2)	**98** (1.62)	**103** (1.30)	**103.5** (34)	**29** (218)	**16** (16.8)			13	38
New Jersey Inst of Technology	**99** (1.77)	**93.5** (1.92)	**81** (0)	**91.5** (2)	**102** (1.53)	**100** (1.41)	**90.5** (39)	**108.5** (0)	**108.5** (0.0)	**74** (1.56)	**74** (1.85)	12	34
University of Miami	**100** (1.72)	**82.5** (2.14)	**81** (0)	**101.5** (1)	**97** (1.63)	**92** (1.67)	**90.5** (39)	**101** (8)	**101** (0.9)	**77** (0.97)	**77** (1.42)	9	14
University of Vermont	**101** (1.70)	**100.5** (1.67)	**81** (0)	**73** (4)	**79** (2.07)	**78** (2.08)	**99.5** (36)	**105.5** (2)	**106** (0.2)			9	4
University of Nebraska-Lincoln	**102** (1.68)	**102** (1.60)	**81** (0)	**108.5** (0)	**104** (1.40)	**106** (1.06)	**93** (38)	**46.5** (157)	**27** (11.2)			14	10
University of Wyoming	**103** (1.57)	**90.5** (1.95)	**81** (0)	**91.5** (2)	**101** (1.54)	**84** (1.95)	**109.5** (27)	**96.5** (15)	**93.5** (1.4)			11	5
Wichita State University	**104** (1.48)	**106** (1.39)	**81** (0)	**101.5** (1)	**106** (1.20)	**105** (1.11)	**106** (32)	**108.5** (0)	**108.5** (0.0)			11	21
Howard University	**105** (1.41)	**104.5** (1.44)	**81** (0)	**108.5** (0)	**105** (1.39)	**96** (1.50)	**96** (37)	**98.5** (12)	**91.5** (1.5)			8	27
Polytechnic University	**106** (1.36)	**103** (1.49)	**81** (0)	**101.5** (1)	**103** (1.47)	**103** (1.30)	**103.5** (34)	**105.5** (2)	**104.5** (0.3)	**43** (2.60)	**48** (2.63)	6	18
Florida Institute of Technology	**107** (1.35)	**107** (1.14)	**46** (1)	**91.5** (2)	**107** (1.10)	**107** (0.91)	**99.5** (36)	**65.5** (75)	**40** (7.5)			10	5
Montana State University	**108** (1.24)	**108** (0.97)	**46** (1)	**91.5** (2)	**108** (0.91)	**108** (0.56)	**109.5** (27)	**103** (5)	**103** (0.6)			9	2
University of Tulsa	**109** (0.83)	**109** (0.59)	**81** (0)	**108.5** (0)	**110** (0.75)	**109** (0.46)	**99.5** (36)	**108.5** (0)	**108.5** (0.0)			9	7
University of Detroit Mercy	**110** (0.76)	**110** (0.51)	**81** (0)	**108.5** (0)	**109** (0.90)	**110** (0.33)	**108** (28)	**108.5** (0)	**108.5** (0.0)			7	8

Sources: 1. National Survey of Graduate Faculty
2. Institute for Scientific Information
3. 1982 Survey of Graduate Faculty
4. Institutional Coordinator Data

Appendix Table P - 28 Relative Rankings for Research-Doctorate Programs in Molecular and General Genetics

Institution	93Q [1]	93E [1]	% D [1]	% D-S [1]	93Q T [1]	93E T [1]	VIS [1]	TC [2]	C/F [2]	82Q [3]	82E [3]	TF [4]	TG [4]
Massachusetts Inst of Technology	1 (4.88)	2 (4.75)	1 (79)	2.5 (89)	2 (4.92)	2 (4.83)	3 (92)	3 (22759)	3 (421.5)			54	n/a
Univ of California-San Francisco	2 (4.87)	1 (4.80)	3 (71)	5 (81)	1 (4.94)	1 (4.96)	13.5 (83)	2 (22865)	2 (448.3)			51	13
Harvard University	3 (4.77)	3 (4.55)	2 (72)	1 (93)	3 (4.88)	3 (4.62)	1.5 (94)	4 (16967)	1 (499.0)			34	80
California Institute Technology	4 (4.51)	4 (4.47)	5 (45)	11 (73)	4 (4.60)	4 (4.60)	17.5 (80)	37 (2254)	4 (375.7)			6	0
Stanford University	5 (4.48)	5 (4.44)	4 (49)	2.5 (89)	5 (4.55)	7 (4.33)	1.5 (94)	32 (2865)	8 (260.5)			11	32
Univ of California-San Diego	6 (4.44)	10 (4.17)	6 (44)	7.5 (79)	6 (4.46)	10 (4.23)	9 (87)	1 (25726)	5 (329.8)			78	57
University of Wisconsin-Madison	7 (4.33)	6 (4.40)	7 (36)	4 (83)	9.5 (4.28)	6 (4.37)	4.5 (91)	13 (7236)	20 (129.2)			56	46
Yale University	8 (4.32)	7 (4.29)	8.5 (34)	6 (80)	7 (4.36)	8 (4.29)	7.5 (88)	7 (8724)	10 (212.8)			41	40
Johns Hopkins University	9 (4.26)	13 (4.01)	8.5 (34)	7.5 (79)	9.5 (4.28)	11.5 (4.19)	6 (90)	6 (14811)	6 (302.3)			49	80
University of California-Berkeley	10 (4.21)	9 (4.18)	10 (29)	15 (68)	8 (4.31)	5 (4.38)	15.5 (82)	34 (2677)	12 (178.5)			15	48
University of Chicago	11 (4.17)	8 (4.25)	11 (28)	9.5 (76)	11 (4.23)	11.5 (4.19)	4.5 (91)	9 (8451)	14 (162.5)			52	81
Columbia University	12 (4.14)	14.5 (3.93)	14.5 (17)	9.5 (76)	12 (4.18)	19 (3.83)	13.5 (83)	15 (6428)	13 (173.7)			37	44
University of Utah	13 (4.08)	19 (3.80)	13 (21)	13 (70)	13 (4.17)	14 (3.98)	10.5 (85)	18 (5413)	9 (257.8)			21	32
Baylor College of Medicine	14 (4.07)	11 (4.05)	12 (22)	22 (48)	16.5 (4.05)	13 (4.08)	25 (71)	10 (7633)	16 (155.8)			49	44
Duke University	15 (4.01)	18 (3.83)	14.5 (17)	14 (69)	18 (3.95)	23 (3.71)	10.5 (85)	14 (6469)	18 (140.6)			46	34
Washington University	16 (3.98)	17 (3.86)	16.5 (15)	12 (72)	16.5 (4.05)	16 (3.95)	7.5 (88)	8 (8710)	11 (185.3)			47	39
University of Washington	17 (3.93)	12 (4.02)	18 (14)	16 (61)	14 (4.11)	9 (4.26)	17.5 (80)	46 (1473)	31 (92.1)			16	47
U of Texas-Southwestern Med Ctr	18 (3.91)	20.5 (3.78)	19 (11)	21 (49)	15 (4.08)	17.5 (3.89)	34.5 (66)	23 (4186)	19 (135.0)			31	40
University of Pennsylvania	19 (3.81)	22 (3.72)	16.5 (15)	18 (54)	19 (3.80)	21.5 (3.72)	12 (84)	5 (15220)	24 (117.1)			130	91
U of North Carolina-Chapel Hill	20 (3.78)	24 (3.66)	22 (7)	17 (56)	21 (3.77)	24.5 (3.68)	15.5 (82)	19 (5371)	33 (85.3)			63	39
University of Michigan	21 (3.75)	14.5 (3.93)	20 (9)	20 (51)	20 (3.79)	17.5 (3.89)	20 (76)	17 (5524)	7 (263.0)			21	34
State U of New York-Stony Brook	22 (3.73)	26 (3.62)	22 (7)	19 (52)	22.5 (3.70)	28 (3.56)	19 (79)	12 (7375)	23 (119.0)			62	45
Cornell University	23 (3.68)	16 (3.92)	26 (5)	23 (42)	24 (3.68)	15 (3.97)	26 (69)	29 (3221)	25 (115.0)			28	37
Indiana University	24 (3.64)	20.5 (3.78)	26 (5)	24 (41)	22.5 (3.70)	24.5 (3.68)	28 (68)	36 (2417)	30 (96.7)			25	7
Albert Einstein College of Med	25 (3.53)	27 (3.60)	31 (3)	25 (40)	27 (3.49)	27 (3.57)	23 (74)	20 (4698)	28 (102.1)			46	22
U of Tex-Health Sci Ctr-Houston	26 (3.49)	34 (3.44)	29 (4)	26.5 (34)	28.5 (3.40)	32 (3.50)	28 (68)	11 (7450)	15 (158.5)			47	37
Brandeis University	27 (3.48)	31 (3.49)	35 (2)	28 (33)	25 (3.60)	31 (3.51)	31.5 (67)	38 (2118)	29 (100.9)			21	48[(1)]
University of Texas at Austin	28 (3.47)	29.5 (3.56)	26 (5)	34 (24)	32 (3.27)	29.5 (3.54)	39 (56)	39 (2102)	59 (36.9)			57	77
University of Rochester	29 (3.44)	35 (3.43)	78 (0)	26.5 (34)	26 (3.50)	46.5 (3.33)	21.5 (75)	25 (3953)	40 (71.9)			55	35
North Carolina State University	30 (3.36)	25 (3.64)	22 (7)	41.5 (19)	47.5 (3.08)	26 (3.61)	48.5 (46)	54 (997)	60 (35.6)			28	30

Institution	93Q [1]	93E [1]	% D [1]	% D-S [1]	93Q T [1]	93E T [1]	VIS [1]	TC [2]	C/F [2]	82Q [3]	82E [3]	TF [4]	TG [4]
Rutgers State Univ-New Brunswick	**31** (3.35)	**39** (3.38)	**31** (3)	**30** (27)	**30** (3.38)	**60** (3.17)	**31.5** (67)	**26** (3742)	**55.5** (39.0)			96	153
Pennsylvania State University	**32.5** (3.34)	**23** (3.71)	**26** (5)	**31.5** (25)	**33** (3.26)	**22** (3.72)	**24** (72)	**27** (3415)	**53** (41.1)			83	45
Emory University	**32.5** (3.34)	**54** (3.28)	**78** (0)	**29** (32)	**39** (3.18)	**62** (3.11)	**21.5** (75)	**16** (5579)	**27** (109.4)			51	62
University of Arizona	**34** (3.32)	**55** (3.26)	**45** (1)	**34** (24)	**31** (3.29)	**47** (3.33)	**37** (58)	**56** (890)	**74** (27.0)			33	8
U of Illinois at Urbana-Champaign	**35** (3.30)	**46.5** (3.33)	**78** (0)	**38.5** (20)	**45** (3.09)	**47** (3.33)	**41.5** (55)	**35** (2481)	**47** (49.6)			50	n/a
Michigan State University	**36.5** (3.26)	**28** (3.58)	**26** (5)	**38.5** (20)	**36** (3.22)	**20** (3.75)	**41.5** (55)	**24** (4163)	**49** (47.9)			87	75
Vanderbilt University	**36.5** (3.26)	**57.5** (3.21)	**78** (0)	**34** (24)	**37** (3.21)	**47** (3.33)	**31.5** (67)	**22** (4205)	**21** (127.4)			33	n/a
Texas A&M University	**38** (3.24)	**60** (3.15)	**78** (0)	**45.5** (15)	**38** (3.20)	**61** (3.14)	**46.5** (47)	**42** (1793)	**62** (33.8)			53	55
University of Minnesota	**39** (3.23)	**37.5** (3.39)	**45** (1)	**31.5** (25)	**56** (2.97)	**47** (3.33)	**34.5** (66)	**30** (3019)	**45** (55.9)			54	46
University of Georgia	**40.5** (3.22)	**36** (3.40)	**35** (2)	**41.5** (19)	**34** (3.25)	**47** (3.33)	**43.5** (54)	**51** (1237)	**36** (77.3)			16	50
Case Western Reserve Univ	**40.5** (3.22)	**46.5** (3.33)	**45** (1)	**47** (14)	**49** (3.07)	**47** (3.33)	**60.5** (39)	**63** (642)	**48** (49.4)			13	23
University of California-Davis	**42.5** (3.21)	**29.5** (3.56)	**31** (3)	**36** (23)	**45** (3.09)	**33** (3.49)	**31.5** (67)	**28** (3265)	**37** (74.2)			44	93
University of Iowa	**42.5** (3.21)	**32** (3.46)	**35** (2)	**37** (21)	**42** (3.13)	**47** (3.33)	**28** (68)	**31** (2956)	**39** (72.1)			41	33
Univ of California-Riverside	**44** (3.17)	**46.5** (3.33)	**45** (1)	**45.5** (15)	**41** (3.14)	**47** (3.33)	**51** (44)	**41** (1970)	**57** (38.6)			51	21
University of Alabama-Birmingham	**45** (3.15)	**46.5** (3.33)	**45** (1)	**53** (10)	**29** (3.40)	**47** (3.33)	**62.5** (37)	**21** (4445)	**35** (79.4)			56	23
University of Pittsburgh [a]	**46** (3.11)	**46.5** (3.33)	**78** (0)	**49** (12)	**52** (3.05)	**47** (3.33)	**51** (44)	**70** (387)	**84** (20.4)			19	n/a
Univ of California-Santa Barbara	**47.5** (3.09)	**70** (2.99)	**45** (1)	**41.5** (19)	**50** (3.06)	**68** (2.98)	**36** (59)	**68.5** (392)	**52** (43.6)			9	n/a
University of California-Irvine	**47.5** (3.09)	**46.5** (3.33)	**78** (0)	**44** (18)	**36** (3.22)	**35** (3.44)	**45** (51)	**45** (1512)	**17** (151.2)			10	36
University of Colorado	**50** (3.07)	**37.5** (3.39)	**35** (2)	**41.5** (19)	**40** (3.16)	**34** (3.48)	**43.5** (54)	**76** (312)	**55.5** (39.0)			8	n/a
University of Florida	**50** (3.07)	**33** (3.45)	**45** (1)	**58** (8)	**54** (3.00)	**30** (3.54)	**57** (40)	**52** (1207)	**61** (35.5)			34	37
U of Massachusetts Med Center	**50** (3.07)	**57.5** (3.21)	**78** (0)	**56** (9)	**43** (3.10)	**47** (3.33)	**51** (44)	**33** (2740)	**34** (80.6)			34	18
New York University	**52** (3.04)	**46.5** (3.33)	**78** (0)	**64** (5)	**48** (3.08)	**47** (3.33)	**64** (36)	**60** (776)	**65** (31.0)			25	46
Oregon State University	**53** (3.00)	**66.5** (3.03)	**78** (0)	**50** (11)	**54** (3.00)	**68** (2.98)	**39** (56)	**43** (1666)	**63** (33.3)			50	33
Ohio State University	**54** (2.98)	**61** (3.14)	**45** (1)	**48** (13)	**58** (2.96)	**58** (3.21)	**39** (56)	**44** (1631)	**44** (56.2)			29	67
University of Cincinnati	**55.5** (2.97)	**46.5** (3.33)	**78** (0)	**53** (10)	**45** (3.09)	**47** (3.33)	**53.5** (43)	**48** (1378)	**32** (86.1)			16	57
Univ of California-Santa Cruz	**55.5** (2.97)	**64** (3.06)	**78** (0)	**58** (8)	**60** (2.89)	**63** (3.10)	**60.5** (39)	**57** (880)	**38** (73.3)			12	13
State Univ of New York-Buffalo	**57** (2.94)	**46.5** (3.33)	**78** (0)	**53** (10)	**52** (3.05)	**47** (3.33)	**46.5** (47)	**40** (2007)	**51** (44.6)			45	7
Kansas State University	**58** (2.90)	**73** (2.78)	**45** (1)	**64** (5)	**68** (2.67)	**73** (2.78)	**74** (25)	**66.5** (427)	**75** (26.7)			16	18
University of Connecticut	**59** (2.88)	**56** (3.24)	**45** (1)	**53** (10)	**62** (2.80)	**59** (3.18)	**53.5** (43)	**79** (287)	**85** (19.1)			15	19
University of Pittsburgh [b]	**60** (2.85)	**66.5** (3.03)	**78** (0)	**64** (5)	**61** (2.87)	**65** (3.06)	**65.5** (35)	**47** (1439)	**22** (119.9)			12	43

Appendix Table P - 28 Molecular and General Genetics (Continued)

Institution	93Q [1]	93E [1]	% D [1]	% D-S [1]	93Q T [1]	93E T [1]	VIS [1]	TC [2]	C/F [2]	82Q [3]	82E [3]	TF [4]	TG [4]
Temple University	61 (2.84)	46.5 (3.33)	78 (0)	64 (5)	64 (2.75)	47 (3.33)	67 (31)	59 (812)	66 (30.1)			27	9
University of Virginia	62 (2.83)	76 (2.64)	78 (0)	67.5 (4)	60 (2.89)	71 (2.83)	70.5 (28)	86 (147)	82 (21.0)			7	41
Iowa State University	63 (2.82)	71 (2.87)	45 (1)	61 (6)	66 (2.69)	69 (2.96)	62.5 (37)	49 (1288)	67 (30.0)			43	22
University of Illinois at Chicago	64 (2.81)	64 (3.06)	35 (2)	53 (10)	58 (2.96)	65 (3.06)	48.5 (46)	58 (818)	42 (68.2)			12	30
Wayne State University	65 (2.77)	59 (3.20)	78 (0)	58 (8)	65 (2.70)	47 (3.33)	57 (40)	50 (1250)	41 (69.4)			18	19
University of Kansas	66.5 (2.67)	78 (2.50)	78 (0)	74.5 (2)	64 (2.75)	78 (1.67)	74 (25)	74 (341)	89 (15.5)			22	22
Louisiana State U & A&M College	66.5 (2.67)	83.5 (2.22)	78 (0)	96 (0)	54 (3.00)	47 (3.33)	103 (13)	65 (455)	91 (12.0)			38	18
State Univ of New York-Albany	68 (2.59)	74 (2.74)	78 (0)	60 (7)	69 (2.64)	70 (2.86)	57 (40)	61 (774)	43 (59.5)			13	10
Louisiana State U Medical Center	69 (2.54)	64 (3.06)	78 (0)	64 (5)	80 (1.83)	74 (2.50)	91 (19)	64 (614)	46 (55.8)			11	18
University of Hawaii at Manoa	70 (2.52)	80 (2.41)	78 (0)	74.5 (2)	71 (2.55)	75 (2.22)	65.5 (35)	62 (708)	50 (47.2)			15	19
Arizona State University	71 (2.50)	81 (2.33)	78 (0)	69.5 (3)	74 (2.45)	76 (1.85)	57 (40)	87 (146)	90 (12.2)			12	6
University of Missouri-Columbia	72 (2.44)	78 (2.50)	78 (0)	83.5 (1)	73 (2.50)	73 (2.78)	77.5 (24)	68.5 (392)	83 (20.6)			19	14
University of Notre Dame	73 (2.43)	46.5 (3.33)	78 (0)	67.5 (4)	68 (2.67)	(n/s)	82.5 (21)	84 (191)	79 (23.9)			8	11
Syracuse University	74.5 (2.40)	72 (2.82)	45 (1)	74.5 (2)	72 (2.53)	65 (3.06)	57 (40)	71 (371)	58 (37.1)			10	10
SUNY-Health Science Ctr-Brooklyn	74.5 (2.40)	89 (1.67)	78 (0)	83.5 (1)	70 (2.60)	(n/s)	70.5 (28)	78 (295)	80 (22.7)			13	29
Montana State University	76 (2.30)	68.5 (3.00)	78 (0)	83.5 (1)	75 (2.25)	47 (3.33)	97 (17)	85 (148)	94 (9.9)			15	n/a
Wake Forest University	77 (2.29)	46.5 (3.33)	78 (0)	96 (0)	78 (2.00)	(n/s)	101.5 (15)	55 (988)	54 (39.5)			25	2
Albany Medical College	78 (2.13)	46.5 (3.33)	78 (0)	96 (0)	78 (2.00)	47 (3.33)	93.5 (18)	72 (346)	76 (26.6)			13	19
University of New Hampshire	79 (2.08)	78 (2.50)	78 (0)	96 (0)	76 (2.20)	47 (3.33)	87.5 (20)	80 (221)	88 (15.8)			14	6
Florida State University	81.5 (2.00)	62 (3.13)	45 (1)	69.5 (3)	80 (1.83)	47 (3.33)	87.5 (20)	75 (331)	70.5 (27.6)			12	9
Hahnemann University	81.5 (2.00)	75 (2.71)	78 (0)	74.5 (2)	85 (1.46)	78 (1.67)	68 (30)	77 (304)	77 (25.3)			12	14
University of Nebraska-Lincoln	81.5 (2.00)	68.5 (3.00)	78 (0)	83.5 (1)	93 (1.00)	(n/s)	82.5 (21)	66.5 (427)	64 (32.8)			13	9
West Virginia University	81.5 (2.00)	83.5 (2.22)	78 (0)	96 (0)	84 (1.50)	(n/s)	101.5 (15)	81 (212)	92 (11.8)			18	13
Medical College of Wisconsin	84 (1.92)	89 (1.67)	78 (0)	96 (0)	82 (1.67)	(n/s)	87.5 (20)	73 (344)	69 (28.7)			12	20
Univ of Maryland at Baltimore	85 (1.86)	89 (1.67)	78 (0)	83.5 (1)	82 (1.67)	(n/s)	87.5 (20)	89 (132)	81 (22.0)			6	12
University of Oklahoma	86.5 (1.73)	89 (1.67)	78 (0)	96 (0)	90 (1.25)	(n/s)	97 (17)	82 (203)	68 (29.0)			7	6
University of New Mexico	86.5 (1.73)	89 (1.67)	78 (0)	96 (0)	87 (1.33)	(n/s)	93.5 (18)	53 (1113)	26 (111.3)			10	n/a
University of Houston	88 (1.62)	95.5 (1.11)	78 (0)	74.5 (2)	83 (1.57)	82 (0.56)	93.5 (18)	97 (39)	97 (7.8)			5	4
Howard University	89 (1.56)	82 (2.29)	78 (0)	83.5 (1)	86 (1.40)	78 (1.67)	77.5 (24)	98 (35)	98.5 (5.0)			7	26
Georgia Institute of Technology	90 (1.55)	89 (1.67)	78 (0)	96 (0)	90 (1.25)	(n/s)	93.5 (18)	90 (86)	87 (17.2)			5	16

Institution	93Q[1]	93E[1]	% D[1]	% D-S[1]	93Q T[1]	93E T[1]	VIS[1]	TC[2]	C/F[2]	82Q[3]	82E[3]	TF[4]	TG[4]
Clemson University	**91** (1.45)	**94** (1.19)	**78** (0)	**96** (0)	**93** (1.00)	**81** (0.83)	**99.5** (16)	**92.5** (72)	**96** (8.0)			9	7
Miami University	**92** (1.33)	**85** (2.14)	**78** (0)	**83.5** (1)	**100** (0.20)	(n/s)	**82.5** (21)	**101.5** (2)	**102** (0.3)			7	40
University of Louisville	**93** (1.27)	**46.5** (3.33)	**78** (0)	**96** (0)	**93** (1.00)	(n/s)	**80** (22)	**83** (193)	**70.5** (27.6)			7	n/a
Illinois State University	**94** (1.25)	**97** (1.00)	**78** (0)	**83.5** (1)	**91** (1.08)	**85** (0.00)	**87.5** (20)	**88** (136)	**73** (27.2)			5	n/a
University of Tennessee-Knoxville	**95** (1.11)	**95.5** (1.11)	**45** (1)	**74.5** (2)	**88** (1.30)	(n/s)	**72** (26)	**92.5** (72)	**78** (24.0)			3	27
Boston University	**96** (1.05)	**93** (1.43)	**78** (0)	**83.5** (1)	**95** (0.92)	**80** (1.25)	**69** (29)	**91** (82)	**72** (27.3)			3	1
Drexel University	**97** (0.93)	**89** (1.67)	**78** (0)	**96** (0)	**98** (0.33)	(n/s)	**87.5** (20)	**96** (42)	**95** (8.4)			5	n/a
University of Tulsa	**98** (0.75)	**99** (0.56)	**45** (1)	**74.5** (2)	**97** (0.50)	**85** (0.00)	**82.5** (21)	**100** (6)	**101** (1.5)			4	3
Bowling Green State University	**99** (0.69)	(n/s)	**78** (0)	**83.5** (1)	**97** (0.50)	(n/s)	**77.5** (24)	**95** (46)	**93** (11.5)			4	2
Ohio University	**100** (0.47)	**100** (0.33)	**78** (0)	**96** (0)	**99** (0.27)	**83** (0.42)	**77.5** (24)	**99** (10)	**98.5** (5.0)			2	1
Clark University	**101** (0.30)	(n/s)	**78** (0)	**96** (0)	**102** (0.14)	(n/s)	**99.5** (16)	**94** (54)	**86** (18.0)			3	2
University of Idaho	**102** (0.24)	**101** (0.00)	**78** (0)	**74.5** (2)	**102** (0.14)	**85** (0.00)	**74** (25)	**101.5** (2)	**100** (2.0)			1	0
Northern Arizona University	**103** (0.17)	**98** (0.83)	**78** (0)	**96** (0)	**103** (0.00)	(n/s)	**97** (17)	**103** (0)	**103** (0.0)			3	0

Sources: 1. National Survey of Graduate Faculty
2. Institute for Scientific Information
3. 1982 Survey of Graduate Faculty
4. Institutional Coordinator Data

Notes: *a.* School of Medicine
b. School of Public Health

n/s After trimming no cases remained

(1) Combined enrollment for programs in Cell and Developmental Biology and Molecular and General Genetics

Appendix Table P - 29 Relative Rankings for Research-Doctorate Programs in Music

Institution	93Q [1]	93E [1]	% D [1]	% D-S [1]	93Q T [1]	93E T [1]	VIS [1]	FA [2]	82Q [3]	82E [3]	TF [4]	TG [4]
Harvard University	1 (4.59)	2 (4.26)	1 (57)	2 (80)	1 (4.67)	2 (4.24)	5 (88)	3 (7)			11	44
University of Chicago	2 (4.53)	1 (4.32)	3 (50)	3.5 (76)	2 (4.63)	1 (4.60)	10.5 (84)	1 (9)	3 (4.46)	3 (4.25)	12	56
University of California-Berkeley	3 (4.51)	4.5 (4.11)	4 (48)	6.5 (74)	3 (4.57)	5 (4.14)	6 (86)	7 (5)	1 (4.54)	1 (4.33)	18	35
CUNY - Grad Sch & Univ Center	4 (4.41)	9.5 (3.79)	8 (36)	3.5 (76)	7 (4.24)	11 (3.63)	12.5 (81)	5 (6)	6 (4.02)	14 (3.40)	38	145
Yale University	5 (4.40)	4.5 (4.11)	2 (51)	1 (81)	4 (4.45)	3 (4.17)	2.5 (95)	51.5 (0)	4 (4.40)	4 (4.15)	12	55
Princeton University	6 (4.39)	3 (4.18)	5.5 (44)	11 (61)	5 (4.40)	4 (4.15)	15.5 (79)	7 (5)	2 (4.53)	2 (4.27)	11	32
University of Pennsylvania	7 (4.35)	9.5 (3.79)	5.5 (44)	9 (67)	6 (4.26)	9 (3.87)	8 (85)	3 (7)	8 (3.97)	10 (3.62)	15	34
University of Rochester	8 (4.24)	6.5 (4.03)	7 (39)	6.5 (74)	10 (4.07)	8 (3.95)	4 (94)	3 (7)	16 (3.63)	15 (3.37)	50	119
University of Michigan	9 (4.16)	6.5 (4.03)	9 (31)	5 (75)	11 (3.98)	6.5 (3.99)	2.5 (95)	13 (3)	7 (4.02)	8 (3.68)	22	21
U of Illinois at Urbana-Champaign	10 (4.11)	12 (3.60)	10.5 (28)	8 (71)	12 (3.89)	18 (3.29)	1 (96)	10 (4)	5 (4.05)	7 (3.72)	74	288
Columbia University	11.5 (4.05)	13 (3.56)	10.5 (28)	10 (66)	9 (4.10)	13 (3.60)	8 (85)	10 (4)	10 (3.89)	6 (3.75)	18	107
Cornell University	11.5 (4.05)	8 (3.90)	12 (25)	12 (59)	8 (4.11)	6.5 (3.99)	12.5 (81)	10 (4)	9 (3.96)	5 (3.88)	17	17
Brandeis University	13 (3.85)	11 (3.73)	20 (10)	17 (43)	14.5 (3.84)	10 (3.77)	33.5 (65)	18.5 (2)	17 (3.56)	17 (3.17)	8	13
State U of New York-Stony Brook	14 (3.80)	16 (3.45)	14.5 (13)	14 (48)	13 (3.88)	12 (3.61)	20 (76)	30 (1)			32	153
Stanford University	15 (3.79)	14.5 (3.52)	17 (12)	15 (47)	14.5 (3.84)	15 (3.45)	22.5 (74)	7 (5)	14 (3.73)	9 (3.65)	14	26
U of North Carolina-Chapel Hill	16 (3.72)	14.5 (3.52)	13 (15)	16 (45)	16 (3.61)	16 (3.40)	26.5 (72)	30 (1)	12.5 (3.80)	13 (3.48)	9	35
University of Texas at Austin	17 (3.69)	18 (3.37)	14.5 (13)	13 (49)	17 (3.49)	19 (3.13)	8 (85)	51.5 (0)	18 (3.16)	20.5 (2.80)	21	103
Univ of California-Los Angeles	18 (3.56)	25 (3.12)	21.5 (9)	20 (38)	19.5 (3.43)	25.5 (2.95)	15.5 (79)	18.5 (2)	11 (3.81)	12 (3.53)	26	93
New York University	19 (3.53)	17 (3.41)	23.5 (8)	21 (36)	18 (3.45)	17 (3.30)	26.5 (72)	30 (1)	12.5 (3.80)	11 (3.55)	10	2
Indiana University	20 (3.47)	27 (3.04)	27 (6)	32 (22)	35.5 (2.78)	36 (2.59)	54.5 (46)	51.5 (0)	15 (3.67)	16 (3.30)	6	6
University of North Texas	21 (3.43)	22 (3.20)	19 (11)	19 (39)	22.5 (3.22)	24 (2.97)	19 (77)	18.5 (2)	25 (2.85)	23 (2.70)	83	118
Duke University	22 (3.42)	19 (3.33)	28 (5)	26.5 (29)	21 (3.26)	25.5 (2.95)	40.5 (61)	30 (1)			12	40
Northwestern University	23.5 (3.41)	20 (3.30)	17 (12)	18 (42)	29.5 (2.97)	20 (3.11)	10.5 (84)	51.5 (0)	22 (3.00)	22 (2.72)	35	25
Univ of California-Santa Barbara	23.5 (3.41)	29.5 (2.89)	32 (3)	24 (32)	19.5 (3.43)	29.5 (2.78)	40.5 (61)	30 (1)	29 (2.62)	30.5 (2.40)	10	28
Univ of California-San Diego	25 (3.32)	40 (2.61)	23.5 (8)	29.5 (27)	22.5 (3.22)	35 (2.62)	36.5 (64)	30 (1)	41 (1.92)	40.5 (1.85)	24	35
University of Iowa	26 (3.31)	24 (3.13)	21.5 (9)	26.5 (29)	33 (2.91)	28 (2.86)	24.5 (73)	30 (1)	23 (2.96)	18 (2.93)	43	121
Florida State University	27 (3.26)	21 (3.29)	17 (12)	22 (33)	26 (3.05)	14 (3.54)	28.5 (70)	30 (1)	32 (2.50)	26.5 (2.53)	47	136
Ohio State University	28 (3.23)	34 (2.74)	41.5 (1)	28 (28)	27.5 (3.00)	40 (2.50)	24.5 (73)	13 (3)	24 (2.85)	24 (2.65)	50	202
University of Washington	29 (3.22)	29.5 (2.89)	25.5 (7)	24 (32)	24 (3.16)	27 (2.90)	17.5 (78)	30 (1)	26 (2.80)	28 (2.48)	28	31
Rutgers State Univ-New Brunswick	30.5 (3.16)	28 (3.03)	29.5 (4)	33 (21)	31 (2.96)	31 (2.74)	31 (68)	30 (1)	19 (3.08)	20.5 (2.80)	13	45

Appendix Table P - 29 Music (Continued)

Institution	93Q [1]	93E [1]	% D [1]	% D-S [1]	93Q T [1]	93E T [1]	VIS [1]	FA [2]	82Q [3]	82E [3]	TF [4]	TG [4]
University of Minnesota	**30.5** (3.16)	**34** (2.74)	**34.5** (2)	**24** (32)	**28** (3.00)	**32** (2.73)	**17.5** (78)	**51.5** (0)	**31** (2.58)	**30.5** (2.40)	15	19
University of Wisconsin-Madison	**32** (3.13)	**26** (3.07)	**41.5** (1)	**29.5** (27)	**30** (2.97)	**22** (3.06)	**22.5** (74)	**30** (1)	**28** (2.63)	**32** (2.27)	15	28
Washington University	**33** (3.08)	**23** (3.14)	**41.5** (1)	**34.5** (20)	**25** (3.11)	**22** (3.06)	**42** (58)	**30** (1)	**44** (1.81)	**44.5** (1.67)	9	27
University of Cincinnati	**34** (3.02)	**31** (2.81)	**25.5** (7)	**31** (24)	**38** (2.77)	**23** (2.98)	**28.5** (70)	**30** (1)	**35** (2.10)	**37** (1.95)	22	210
University of Maryland College Park	**35** (2.95)	**32** (2.79)	**29.5** (4)	**34.5** (20)	**36** (2.78)	**34** (2.68)	**14** (80)	**30** (1)	**30** (2.58)	**26.5** (2.53)	45	103
University of Southern California	**36.5** (2.91)	**37** (2.66)	**41.5** (1)	**36.5** (19)	**45** (2.56)	**46** (2.31)	**38.5** (63)	**18.5** (2)	**21** (3.04)	**19** (2.82)	7	9
State Univ of New York-Buffalo	**36.5** (2.91)	**36** (2.67)	**41.5** (1)	**38** (18)	**32** (2.92)	**30** (2.78)	**21** (75)	**18.5** (2)	**20** (3.06)	**29** (2.45)	20	61
Temple University	**38** (2.90)	**41** (2.58)	**34.5** (2)	**36.5** (19)	**45** (2.56)	**42** (2.46)	**36.5** (64)	**30** (1)			38	47
University of Arizona	**39** (2.87)	**44.5** (2.53)	**56.5** (0)	**39** (16)	**40** (2.74)	**45** (2.38)	**30** (69)	**18.5** (2)			47	87
University of Pittsburgh	**40** (2.83)	**38.5** (2.64)	**41.5** (1)	**45.5** (12)	**38** (2.77)	**40** (2.50)	**47.5** (51)	**13** (3)	**37** (2.05)	**33** (2.10)	11	38
Louisiana State U & A&M College	**41** (2.81)	**34** (2.74)	**56.5** (0)	**40** (14)	**43** (2.61)	**40** (2.50)	**38.5** (63)	**51.5** (0)	**50** (0.83)	**50** (0.93)	41	21
University of Miami	**42** (2.79)	**44.5** (2.53)	**56.5** (0)	**45.5** (12)	**34** (2.87)	**38** (2.57)	**47.5** (51)	**51.5** (0)	**47** (1.43)	**48** (1.38)	41	60
Catholic University of America	**43** (2.78)	**42.5** (2.54)	**56.5** (0)	**42.5** (13)	**39** (2.75)	**37** (2.58)	**47.5** (51)	**51.5** (0)	**39** (1.96)	**42** (1.75)	6	29
Brown University	**44** (2.73)	**42.5** (2.54)	**56.5** (0)	**42.5** (13)	**41** (2.72)	**43** (2.44)	**45** (52)	**51.5** (0)			5	10
Michigan State University	**45** (2.69)	**38.5** (2.64)	**41.5** (1)	**47.5** (10)	**42** (2.70)	**33** (2.71)	**57** (43)	**51.5** (0)	**43** (1.84)	**34** (2.05)	12	16
University of Kansas	**46** (2.65)	**46.5** (2.50)	**32** (3)	**42.5** (13)	**54** (2.14)	**54** (1.67)	**44** (54)	**51.5** (0)	**34** (2.26)	**35.5** (2.00)	11	34
University of Oregon	**47** (2.55)	**50** (2.26)	**56.5** (0)	**47.5** (10)	**46** (2.41)	**49** (1.91)	**33.5** (65)	**51.5** (0)	**36** (2.08)	**38** (1.92)	36	49
Case Western Reserve Univ	**48** (2.52)	**49** (2.33)	**56.5** (0)	**52** (5)	**49** (2.29)	**51** (1.85)	**43** (55)	**51.5** (0)	**42** (1.87)	**39** (1.90)	7	14
Wesleyan University	**49** (2.50)	**54** (2.14)	**32** (3)	**42.5** (13)	**47** (2.32)	**49** (1.91)	**54.5** (46)	**51.5** (0)	**27** (2.69)	**25** (2.55)	10	24
Boston University	**50** (2.48)	**46.5** (2.50)	**41.5** (1)	**50** (7)	**51** (2.22)	**47** (2.26)	**33.5** (65)	**51.5** (0)	**33** (2.35)	**35.5** (2.00)	14	7
University of Georgia	**51** (2.45)	**53** (2.16)	**56.5** (0)	**56** (4)	**55** (2.08)	**58** (1.43)	**56** (45)	**51.5** (0)			11	38
University of Hartford	**52** (2.44)	**51** (2.21)	**41.5** (1)	**49** (9)	**54** (2.14)	**50** (1.88)	**47.5** (51)	**51.5** (0)			28	14
University of Colorado	**53** (2.36)	**48** (2.35)	**56.5** (0)	**56** (4)	**49** (2.29)	**44** (2.41)	**52.5** (47)	**18.5** (2)	**38** (1.98)	**40.5** (1.85)	12	14
University of Kentucky	**54** (2.33)	**52** (2.18)	**56.5** (0)	**60.5** (3)	**58** (2.00)	**54** (1.67)	**33.5** (65)	**51.5** (0)	**40** (1.92)	**43** (1.73)	14	22
West Virginia University	**55** (2.27)	**64** (1.45)	**56.5** (0)	**56** (4)	**50** (2.25)	**54** (1.67)	**58** (42)	**18.5** (2)	**46** (1.71)	**47** (1.60)	10	5
Claremont Graduate School	**56** (2.23)	**61** (1.82)	**56.5** (0)	**56** (4)	**58** (2.00)	**64** (1.11)	**61** (39)	**51.5** (0)			3	52
Texas Tech University	**57** (2.22)	**62.5** (1.67)	**56.5** (0)	**63** (2)	**52** (2.17)	**62** (1.25)	**64** (35)	**51.5** (0)			33	43
Kent State University	**58** (2.20)	**56** (2.10)	**41.5** (1)	**52** (5)	**56** (2.06)	**52** (1.80)	**52.5** (47)	**51.5** (0)			11	36
University of South Carolina	**59** (2.13)	**55** (2.11)	**56.5** (0)	**52** (5)	**60** (1.79)	**57** (1.48)	**50.5** (49)	**51.5** (0)			20	9
Ball State University	**60** (2.06)	**62.5** (1.67)	**56.5** (0)	**56** (4)	**59** (1.82)	**62** (1.25)	**50.5** (49)	**51.5** (0)	**45** (1.71)	**44.5** (1.67)	36	34

Institution	93Q [1]	93E [1]	% D [1]	% D-S [1]	93Q T [1]	93E T [1]	VIS [1]	FA [2]	82Q [3]	82E [3]	TF [4]	TG [4]
University of Alabama	**61** (2.02)	**59** (1.91)	**41.5** (1)	**64.5** (1)	**62** (1.75)	**56** (1.53)	**59.5** (40)	**51.5** (0)			15	28
Southern Baptist Theological Sem	**62** (1.95)	**60** (1.85)	**56.5** (0)	**60.5** (3)	**65** (0.83)	**65** (0.67)	**63** (36)	**51.5** (0)			15	20
University of Northern Colorado	**63** (1.86)	**58** (1.93)	**41.5** (1)	**60.5** (3)	**62** (1.75)	**60** (1.33)	**59.5** (40)	**51.5** (0)			21	35
University of Oklahoma	**64** (1.84)	**57** (2.00)	**56.5** (0)	**64.5** (1)	**63** (1.60)	**59** (1.39)	**62** (38)	**51.5** (0)	**48** (1.42)	**46** (1.62)	6	3
Univ of Missouri-Kansas City	**65** (1.40)	**65** (1.37)	**56.5** (0)	**60.5** (3)	**64** (0.89)	**64** (1.11)	**65** (33)	**51.5** (0)	**49** (1.20)	**49** (1.32)	4	1

Sources: 1. National Survey of Graduate Faculty
2. Associations and Organizations Administrating Prestigious Awards and Honors
3. 1982 Survey of Graduate Faculty
4. Institutional Coordinator Data

Appendix Table P - 30 Relative Rankings for Research-Doctorate Programs in Neurosciences

Institution	93Q [1]	93E [1]	% D [1]	% D-S [1]	93Q T [1]	93E T [1]	VIS [1]	TC [2]	C/F [2]	82Q [3]	82E [3]	TF [4]	TG [4]
Univ of California-San Diego	1 (4.82)	2 (4.48)	1 (81)	1 (97)	2 (4.82)	2.5 (4.48)	1 (100)	1 (23508)	2 (242.4)			97	89
Yale University	2 (4.76)	4 (4.44)	3 (72)	2 (94)	4.5 (4.74)	7 (4.39)	5.5 (97)	4 (11116)	11 (148.2)			75	35
Harvard University	3 (4.73)	6.5 (4.33)	2 (73)	3.5 (92)	1 (4.85)	2.5 (4.48)	5.5 (97)	2 (23497)	4 (213.6)			110	60
Univ of California-San Francisco	4 (4.66)	3 (4.45)	4 (68)	3.5 (92)	3 (4.75)	5 (4.44)	2.5 (98)	5 (10416)	1 (306.4)			34	34
Stanford University	5 (4.64)	1 (4.56)	5 (62)	7.5 (84)	4.5 (4.74)	1 (4.66)	11.5 (91)	8 (7705)	8 (175.1)			44	43
Columbia University	6 (4.58)	8 (4.29)	6 (60)	5 (89)	6 (4.67)	8 (4.33)	2.5 (98)	9 (7355)	3 (222.9)			33	62
Johns Hopkins University	7 (4.47)	6.5 (4.33)	7 (51)	6 (88)	7 (4.59)	6 (4.42)	5.5 (97)	3 (11685)	6 (191.6)			61	n/a
Washington University	8 (4.43)	5 (4.42)	8 (49)	7.5 (84)	8 (4.49)	4 (4.47)	8 (96)	6 (9165)	13 (138.9)			66	36
University of California-Berkeley	9 (4.32)	12 (4.12)	9 (40)	14 (75)	10 (4.35)	13 (4.06)	17.5 (88)	23 (2791)	10 (155.1)			18	27
California Institute Technology	10.5 (4.30)	10 (4.22)	10 (38)	12.5 (77)	9 (4.36)	9 (4.32)	17.5 (88)	27 (2495)	12 (146.8)			17	35
University of Pennsylvania	10.5 (4.30)	11 (4.17)	13 (32)	9 (83)	11 (4.33)	11 (4.17)	14 (90)	10 (7180)	21 (107.2)			67	48
University of Washington	12 (4.28)	13 (4.11)	11 (36)	10 (82)	12 (4.32)	12 (4.09)	9.5 (93)	7 (7714)	9 (164.1)			47	24
Rockefeller University	13 (4.23)	9 (4.26)	12 (34)	11 (79)	14 (4.17)	10 (4.23)	5.5 (97)	71 (529)	46 (48.1)			11	135
Massachusetts Inst of Technology	14 (4.21)	14 (4.07)	14 (30)	12.5 (77)	13 (4.23)	14 (4.02)	11.5 (91)	35 (2057)	30 (73.5)			28	55
Univ of California-Los Angeles	15 (3.91)	20.5 (3.69)	15 (19)	15 (64)	16 (3.83)	23.5 (3.59)	9.5 (93)	11 (6345)	29 (86.9)			73	46
Duke University	16.5 (3.83)	16 (3.86)	17 (13)	16 (62)	15 (3.90)	17 (3.85)	14 (90)	40 (1593)	34 (59.0)			27	24
Case Western Reserve Univ	16.5 (3.83)	20.5 (3.69)	20.5 (10)	18 (56)	19 (3.78)	18 (3.72)	25 (82)	29 (2451)	17 (129.0)			19	36
University of Michigan	18 (3.79)	17 (3.75)	16 (16)	17 (57)	20 (3.74)	15 (3.89)	14 (90)	13 (5233)	28 (87.2)			60	24
Baylor College of Medicine	19.5 (3.75)	28 (3.48)	18 (12)	20 (50)	17.5 (3.80)	20 (3.65)	26.5 (81)	17 (4476)	18 (117.8)			38	32
Brandeis University	19.5 (3.75)	15 (3.88)	24.5 (8)	26.5 (42)	17.5 (3.80)	16 (3.87)	48 (66)	31 (2276)	7 (189.7)			12	35
University of California-Irvine [a]	21 (3.72)	19 (3.72)	19 (11)	19 (53)	21 (3.62)	19 (3.69)	24 (83)	26 (2561)	5 (197.0)			13	45
University of Chicago	22 (3.63)	24 (3.60)	22 (9)	23 (44)	22 (3.60)	23.5 (3.59)	30.5 (79)	33 (2111)	33 (64.0)			33	25
Northwestern University	23 (3.60)	25 (3.59)	24.5 (8)	21 (47)	25 (3.56)	31.5 (3.48)	19 (86)	16 (4674)	35 (57.7)			81	52
Cornell University	24 (3.59)	18 (3.74)	24.5 (8)	30.5 (39)	26 (3.51)	22 (3.61)	38 (73)	46 (1280)	50 (42.7)			30	35
University of Wisconsin-Madison	25 (3.58)	27 (3.53)	46.5 (3)	28 (41)	23.5 (3.57)	33 (3.47)	33 (76)	30 (2345)	47 (47.9)			49	29
U of North Carolina-Chapel Hill	26.5 (3.57)	26 (3.57)	20.5 (10)	22 (46)	27 (3.50)	25 (3.57)	16 (89)	12 (6088)	19 (110.7)			55	30
Albert Einstein College of Med	26.5 (3.57)	23 (3.61)	24.5 (8)	30.5 (39)	23.5 (3.57)	30 (3.50)	32 (77)	14 (5007)	20 (108.8)			46	25
State U of New York-Stony Brook	28 (3.54)	35.5 (3.41)	30.5 (5)	26.5 (42)	28 (3.49)	34 (3.45)	40.5 (72)	65 (657)	57.5 (38.6)			17	25
Vanderbilt University	29 (3.49)	33 (3.44)	30.5 (5)	36.5 (31)	30 (3.46)	42 (3.33)	44.5 (69)	41 (1539)	55 (39.5)			39	0
University of Iowa	31 (3.46)	31.5 (3.45)	28 (6)	29 (40)	29 (3.48)	27 (3.55)	21 (85)	18 (4332)	24 (103.1)			42	18

Institution	93Q [1]	93E [1]	% D [1]	% D-S [1]	93Q T [1]	93E T [1]	VIS [1]	TC [2]	C/F [2]	82Q [3]	82E [3]	TF [4]	TG [4]
University of Virginia	31 (3.46)	31.5 (3.45)	38 (4)	24.5 (43)	34 (3.40)	32 (3.48)	21 (85)	19 (4288)	25 (99.7)			43	22
University of Oregon	31 (3.46)	22 (3.65)	54.5 (2)	32 (37)	31 (3.44)	21 (3.62)	46.5 (68)	56 (910)	43 (50.6)			18	29
Emory University	33 (3.45)	30 (3.46)	30.5 (5)	24.5 (43)	32 (3.43)	26 (3.56)	21 (85)	28 (2456)	54 (40.9)			60	32
University of Minnesota	34 (3.43)	40.5 (3.37)	38 (4)	35 (33)	38 (3.37)	49 (3.17)	34.5 (75)	36 (2034)	38 (56.5)			36	35
Mayo Graduate School	35 (3.42)	47 (3.27)	38 (4)	46.5 (24)	38 (3.37)	42 (3.33)	65.5 (52)	15 (4765)	26 (95.3)			50	10
University of Southern California	36.5 (3.41)	42 (3.35)	27 (7)	34 (34)	35 (3.39)	29 (3.51)	26.5 (81)	54 (984)	40 (54.7)			18	40
U of Texas-Southwestern Med Ctr	36.5 (3.41)	56 (3.05)	46.5 (3)	36.5 (31)	33 (3.42)	54 (3.12)	44.5 (69)	32 (2194)	16 (129.1)			17	16
University of Colorado	38 (3.40)	44.5 (3.33)	38 (4)	33 (35)	36 (3.38)	35 (3.44)	30.5 (79)	21 (3313)	22 (106.9)			31	17
University of California-Irvine [b]	39 (3.38)	35.5 (3.41)	38 (4)	42.5 (28)	39 (3.33)	29 (3.51)	42.5 (70)	43 (1384)	14 (138.4)			10	11
University of Pittsburgh [a]	40 (3.36)	44.5 (3.33)	30.5 (5)	46.5 (24)	43 (3.24)	46 (3.26)	56.5 (58)	49 (1087)	31 (72.5)			15	28
U of Illinois at Urbana-Champaign	41 (3.33)	40.5 (3.37)	38 (4)	40.5 (29)	42 (3.25)	42 (3.33)	38 (73)	34 (2077)	59.5 (38.5)			54	27
U of Texas, Medical Br-Galveston	42 (3.31)	34 (3.43)	46.5 (3)	38.5 (30)	41 (3.29)	38 (3.39)	34.5 (75)	24 (2756)	32 (70.7)			39	25
University of Rochester	43 (3.30)	37 (3.40)	38 (4)	38.5 (30)	40 (3.30)	36 (3.43)	28.5 (80)	22 (2938)	45 (49.0)			60	30
University of Pittsburgh [b]	44 (3.28)	44.5 (3.33)	63.5 (1)	42.5 (28)	45 (3.16)	42 (3.33)	40.5 (72)	51 (1057)	39 (55.6)			19	n/a
Colorado State University	45 (3.25)	29 (3.47)	54.5 (2)	48 (23)	44 (3.21)	42 (3.33)	42.5 (70)	61 (680)	42 (52.3)			13	11
Rutgers State Univ-New Brunswick	46 (3.22)	38.5 (3.38)	38 (4)	45 (26)	46 (3.10)	37 (3.41)	38 (73)	45 (1285)	72 (26.8)			48	43
University of Arizona	47 (3.20)	50 (3.21)	38 (4)	44 (27)	48 (3.02)	51 (3.15)	23 (84)	57 (850)	68 (30.4)			28	16
University of Connecticut [a]	48 (3.14)	48 (3.26)	38 (4)	40.5 (29)	50 (2.97)	55 (3.11)	28.5 (80)	73 (503)	56 (38.7)			13	6
University of Texas at Austin	49.5 (3.08)	49 (3.25)	38 (4)	53 (17)	49 (2.98)	47 (3.21)	59 (57)	37 (1931)	57.5 (38.6)			50	n/a
Georgetown University	49.5 (3.08)	51 (3.15)	46.5 (3)	49.5 (20)	47 (3.04)	49 (3.17)	51 (62)	20 (4277)	23 (104.3)			41	0
U of Tex-Health Sci Ctr-Houston	51 (3.05)	52 (3.14)	54.5 (2)	49.5 (20)	51 (2.96)	52 (3.13)	46.5 (68)	42 (1466)	41 (54.3)			27	32
Medical College of Pensylvania	52 (3.04)	64.5 (2.89)	63.5 (1)	58.5 (14)	59 (2.81)	67 (2.63)	65.5 (52)	77 (435)	76 (22.9)			19	17
University of Tennessee - Memphis	53 (3.03)	58 (3.01)	46.5 (3)	52 (18)	54 (2.88)	64 (2.78)	53 (61)	39 (1700)	44 (50.0)			34	19
Brown University	54 (2.98)	38.5 (3.38)	54.5 (2)	58.5 (14)	52 (2.94)	49 (3.17)	59 (57)	70 (586)	51 (41.9)			14	n/a
Ohio State University	55 (2.97)	53.5 (3.10)	54.5 (2)	54.5 (16)	59 (2.81)	61 (2.97)	50 (63)	25 (2622)	53 (41.0)			64	18
New York University	56 (2.96)	44.5 (3.33)	85 (0)	56.5 (15)	55 (2.86)	42 (3.33)	53 (61)	64 (660)	69 (28.7)			23	11
Rutgers State Univ-Newark	57 (2.93)	55 (3.06)	63.5 (1)	56.5 (15)	54 (2.88)	58 (3.09)	59 (57)	76 (449)	85.5 (18.7)			24	28
University of Connecticut [b]	58 (2.89)	53.5 (3.10)	54.5 (2)	51 (19)	56 (2.85)	54 (3.12)	36 (74)	44 (1357)	52 (41.1)			33	20
Tufts University	59 (2.88)	59 (2.94)	85 (0)	54.5 (16)	57 (2.82)	58 (3.09)	49 (65)	53 (1014)	27 (92.2)			11	12
University of Florida	60 (2.84)	57 (3.04)	46.5 (3)	62 (10)	60 (2.73)	60 (3.00)	53 (61)	58 (810)	71 (27.0)			30	27

Appendix Table P - 30 Neurosciences (Continued)

Institution	93Q [1]	93E [1]	% D [1]	% D-S [1]	93Q T [1]	93E T [1]	VIS [1]	TC [2]	C/F [2]	82Q [3]	82E [3]	TF [4]	TG [4]
U of Massachusetts at Amherst	**61** (2.80)	**60** (2.93)	**85** (0)	**61** (11)	**63** (2.62)	**62** (2.92)	**64** (53)	**69** (588)	**80.5** (21.8)			27	30
Wake Forest University	**62** (2.79)	**69** (2.68)	**54.5** (2)	**65** (8)	**62** (2.63)	**68** (2.62)	**62** (54)	**100** (12)	**100** (0.9)			13	15
Florida State University	**63** (2.70)	**62.5** (2.90)	**54.5** (2)	**60** (12)	**65** (2.45)	**69** (2.61)	**55** (60)	**80** (351)	**91** (16.0)			22	28
Hahnemann University	**64.5** (2.64)	**62.5** (2.90)	**54.5** (2)	**63.5** (9)	**62** (2.63)	**59** (3.06)	**71.5** (46)	**72** (524)	**80.5** (21.8)			24	17
Michigan State University	**64.5** (2.64)	**68** (2.70)	**63.5** (1)	**67** (7)	**64** (2.54)	**70** (2.58)	**56.5** (58)	**55** (952)	**62** (38.1)			25	20
State Univ of New York-Buffalo [b]	**66** (2.51)	**64.5** (2.89)	**85** (0)	**63.5** (9)	**67** (2.42)	**56** (3.10)	**67** (50)	**67** (622)	**73** (24.9)			25	76
Pennsylvania State University	**67** (2.50)	**66** (2.88)	**85** (0)	**70** (6)	**71** (2.23)	**66** (2.67)	**68.5** (48)	**52** (1031)	**65** (33.3)			31	3
Wayne State University	**68.5** (2.47)	**70.5** (2.58)	**54.5** (2)	**67** (7)	**68** (2.41)	**72** (2.56)	**68.5** (48)	**38** (1893)	**48** (47.3)			40	15
SUNY-Health Science Ctr-Brooklyn	**68.5** (2.47)	**72** (2.57)	**85** (0)	**70** (6)	**69** (2.33)	**75** (2.26)	**62** (54)	**68** (600)	**78.5** (22.2)			27	10
CUNY - Grad Sch & Univ Center	**70** (2.43)	**70.5** (2.58)	**85** (0)	**72** (5)	**67** (2.42)	**64** (2.78)	**75** (43)	**50** (1066)	**64** (34.4)			31	16
Syracuse University	**71** (2.38)	**73.5** (2.50)	**85** (0)	**67** (7)	**70** (2.29)	**74** (2.33)	**71.5** (46)	**82** (281)	**70** (28.1)			10	14
Purdue University	**72** (2.31)	**73.5** (2.50)	**63.5** (1)	**74** (4)	**72** (2.22)	**72** (2.56)	**62** (54)	**75** (456)	**36** (57.0)			8	22
State Univ of New York-Buffalo [a]	**73** (2.24)	**67** (2.78)	**63.5** (1)	**82** (2)	**73** (2.18)	**42** (3.33)	**101.5** (22)	**66** (630)	**75** (24.2)			26	48
Uniformed Services U of Hlth Sci	**74** (2.23)	**77** (2.29)	**85** (0)	**76.5** (3)	**76** (2.06)	**79** (1.91)	**73** (45)	**48** (1189)	**67** (33.0)			36	4
State Univ of New York-Albany	**75** (2.21)	**81** (2.08)	**85** (0)	**74** (4)	**75** (2.11)	**76** (2.19)	**76** (42)	**89.5** (131)	**85.5** (18.7)			7	8
University of Miami	**76** (2.14)	**76** (2.31)	**85** (0)	**70** (6)	**78** (1.92)	**65** (2.76)	**70** (47)	**47** (1222)	**15** (135.8)			9	6
Albany Medical College	**77.5** (2.08)	**79** (2.17)	**85** (0)	**82** (2)	**74** (2.12)	**73** (2.50)	**95** (28)	**59.5** (731)	**59.5** (38.5)			19	21
University of New Mexico	**77.5** (2.08)	**87** (1.67)	**85** (0)	**91** (1)	**77** (1.94)	**85** (1.67)	**97** (27)	**83** (241)	**93** (15.1)			16	2
Kent State University	**79** (2.03)	**82.5** (2.00)	**85** (0)	**91** (1)	**81** (1.76)	**79** (1.91)	**79** (38)	**62** (679)	**74** (24.3)			28	19
George Washington University	**80** (2.00)	**61** (2.92)	**85** (0)	**76.5** (3)	**83** (1.65)	**85** (1.67)	**79** (38)	**81** (331)	**66** (33.1)			10	2
Oregon State University	**81** (1.96)	**75** (2.36)	**85** (0)	**74** (4)	**84** (1.53)	**77** (2.00)	**97** (27)	**85** (195)	**84** (19.5)			10	24
University of Oklahoma	**82** (1.93)	**85** (1.81)	**85** (0)	**91** (1)	**79** (1.87)	**79** (1.91)	**88.5** (31)	**63** (671)	**88** (18.1)			37	18
University of Missouri-Columbia	**83** (1.92)	**87** (1.67)	**85** (0)	**82** (2)	**80** (1.85)	**85** (1.67)	**77** (41)	**78** (420)	**63** (35.0)			12	7
Medical College of Ohio	**84** (1.86)	**84** (1.95)	**85** (0)	**82** (2)	**82** (1.72)	**81** (1.85)	**74** (44)	**59.5** (731)	**78.5** (22.2)			33	3
Ohio University	**85** (1.77)	**80** (2.14)	**85** (0)	**82** (2)	**92** (0.93)	(n/s)	**81** (36)	**87** (157)	**92** (15.7)			10	6
University of Louisville	**86** (1.69)	**93** (1.11)	**85** (0)	**91** (1)	**85** (1.47)	**85** (1.67)	**92** (30)	**89.5** (131)	**96** (9.4)			14	26
Louisiana State U & A&M College	**87** (1.47)	**87** (1.67)	**85** (0)	**91** (1)	**86** (1.39)	**85** (1.67)	**101.5** (22)	**74** (501)	**87** (18.6)			27	14
Georgia State University	**88** (1.45)	**78** (2.22)	**85** (0)	**82** (2)	**88** (1.05)	**85** (1.67)	**92** (30)	**92** (112)	**77** (22.4)			5	11
University of Wyoming	**89** (1.42)	**82.5** (2.00)	**63.5** (1)	**82** (2)	**90** (0.95)	**85** (1.67)	**97** (27)	**84** (235)	**83** (19.6)			12	5
East Carolina U Sch Medicine	**90** (1.21)	**90** (1.19)	**85** (0)	**99** (0)	**87** (1.11)	**93** (0.83)	**100** (23)	**79** (363)	**49** (45.4)			8	4

Institution	93Q [1]	93E [1]	% D [1]	% D-S [1]	93Q T [1]	93E T [1]	VIS [1]	TC [2]	C/F [2]	82Q [3]	82E [3]	TF [4]	TG [4]
Loma Linda University	**91** (1.17)	**94.5** (1.00)	**85** (0)	**82** (2)	**89** (0.96)	**92** (1.11)	**79** (38)	**88** (149)	**82** (21.3)			7	2
Montana State University	**92** (1.04)	**96** (0.83)	**85** (0)	**99** (0)	**93** (0.72)	**94** (0.67)	**86** (32)	**97** (21)	**98** (3.5)			6	n/a
Kansas State University	**93** (0.91)	**90** (1.19)	**85** (0)	**99** (0)	**92** (0.93)	**90** (1.25)	**99** (24)	**99** (16)	**99** (2.3)			7	3
Univ of California-Santa Cruz	**94** (0.89)	**94.5** (1.00)	**63.5** (1)	**91** (1)	**95** (0.63)	**98** (0.00)	**83.5** (33)	**91** (115)	**61** (38.3)			3	4
Univ of California-Santa Barbara	**95** (0.84)	**90** (1.19)	**85** (0)	**82** (2)	**94** (0.70)	**91** (1.19)	**92** (30)	**86** (170)	**37** (56.7)			3	n/a
Texas Woman's University	**96.5** (0.72)	**100.5** (0.00)	**85** (0)	**91** (1)	**98** (0.39)	**98** (0.00)	**82** (34)	**95** (34)	**97** (8.5)			4	3
Clark University	**96.5** (0.72)	**92** (1.17)	**85** (0)	**99** (0)	**96** (0.57)	**90** (1.25)	**88.5** (31)	**93** (84)	**89** (16.8)			5	2
Boston University	**98** (0.67)	**97** (0.56)	**85** (0)	**91** (1)	**99** (0.38)	**98** (0.00)	**86** (32)	**94** (50)	**90** (16.7)			3	4
University of Idaho	**99** (0.59)	**100.5** (0.00)	**85** (0)	**91** (1)	**100** (0.29)	**98** (0.00)	**92** (30)	**96** (30)	**94** (15.0)			2	1
Univ of Puerto Rico-Rio Piedras	**100** (0.58)	**98** (0.24)	**85** (0)	**99** (0)	**97** (0.46)	**98** (0.00)	**83.5** (33)	**102** (0)	**102** (0.0)			3	1
Northern Arizona University	**101** (0.48)	**100.5** (0.00)	**85** (0)	**99** (0)	**102** (0.15)	**98** (0.00)	**86** (32)	**98** (20)	**95** (10.0)			2	2
Miami University	**102** (0.39)	**100.5** (0.00)	**85** (0)	**99** (0)	**101** (0.19)	**98** (0.00)	**92** (30)	**101** (2)	**101** (0.7)			3	12

Sources: 1. National Survey of Graduate Faculty
2. Institute for Scientific Information
3. 1982 Survey of Graduate Faculty
4. Institutional Coordinator Data

Notes: *a.* School of Arts and Sciences
b. School of Medicine

n/s After trimming no cases remained

Appendix Table P - 31 Relative Rankings for Research-Doctorate Programs in Oceanography

Institution	93Q [1]	93E [1]	% D [1]	% D-S [1]	93Q T [1]	93E T [1]	VIS [1]	TC [2]	C/F [2]	82Q [3]	82E [3]	TF [4]	TG [4]
Univ of California-San Diego	1 (4.69)	2 (4.21)	1 (66)	1 (96)	1 (4.73)	2 (4.22)	1.5 (97)	1 (3534)	6 (31.6)			112	174
Massachusetts Inst of Technology	2 (4.62)	1 (4.31)	2 (55)	2 (88)	2 (4.64)	1 (4.37)	5 (90)	2 (2364)	2 (69.5)			34	144
University of Washington	3 (4.31)	3 (4.07)	3 (39)	3 (80)	3.5 (4.32)	3 (4.07)	3 (93)	3 (1848)	4 (43.0)			43	95
Columbia University	4 (4.30)	4 (4.00)	4 (34)	4 (75)	3.5 (4.32)	4 (4.04)	9 (84)	4 (1597)	1 (84.1)			19	59
Oregon State University	5 (3.88)	6 (3.46)	5 (12)	5 (62)	5 (3.85)	6 (3.39)	7 (87)	5 (1481)	5 (32.9)			45	63
University of Rhode Island	6 (3.68)	5 (3.53)	6 (11)	6 (56)	6 (3.63)	5 (3.47)	1.5 (97)	8 (863)	7 (30.8)			28	103
University of Hawaii at Manoa	7 (3.50)	11.5 (3.11)	16.5 (2)	7 (48)	7 (3.45)	16 (2.94)	6 (88)	9 (848)	9 (24.9)			34	50
State U of New York-Stony Brook	8 (3.49)	7.5 (3.28)	7 (6)	8 (45)	9 (3.36)	8.5 (3.12)	8 (85)	6 (1014)	10 (23.6)			43	51
Florida State University	9 (3.48)	7.5 (3.28)	9 (5)	9 (41)	8 (3.42)	7 (3.19)	10 (81)	13 (497)	8 (27.6)			18	23
University of Maryland College Park	10 (3.42)	9 (3.17)	9 (5)	10 (33)	10 (3.33)	12 (3.04)	11 (76)	10 (773)	20 (11.0)			70	82
University of Miami	11 (3.29)	15.5 (3.05)	14 (3)	12.5 (28)	11 (3.32)	8.5 (3.12)	19 (63)	15 (286)	13 (20.4)			14	19
Texas A&M University	12 (3.26)	13 (3.09)	11.5 (4)	11 (32)	14 (3.13)	17 (2.92)	4 (91)	11 (600)	15 (15.0)			40	49
U of North Carolina-Chapel Hill	13.5 (3.22)	10 (3.13)	11.5 (4)	14 (27)	13 (3.15)	11 (3.05)	16.5 (73)	17 (251)	16 (13.9)			18	18
Duke University	13.5 (3.22)	11.5 (3.11)	14 (3)	12.5 (28)	15 (3.09)	13.5 (3.01)	12.5 (75)	16 (275)	12 (22.9)			12	19
University of South Florida	15 (3.07)	19 (2.83)	23.5 (0)	15 (24)	16.5 (2.98)	19 (2.72)	14.5 (74)	12 (512)	11 (23.3)			22	52
University of Wisconsin-Madison	16 (3.04)	14 (3.06)	19 (1)	19.5 (13)	12 (3.20)	10 (3.08)	24 (44)	7 (946)	3 (47.3)			20	14
Old Dominion University	17 (3.01)	15.5 (3.05)	16.5 (2)	16.5 (19)	16.5 (2.98)	15 (2.97)	12.5 (75)	21 (178)	19 (11.9)			15	28
Stanford University	18 (2.98)	22 (2.20)	9 (5)	16.5 (19)	18 (2.88)	23 (2.03)	20 (54)	26 (15)	26 (3.8)			4	n/a
North Carolina State University	19 (2.86)	20 (2.80)	19 (1)	18 (17)	19 (2.85)	18 (2.85)	14.5 (74)	20 (179)	17 (13.8)			13	25
University of South Carolina	20 (2.85)	18 (2.87)	14 (3)	19.5 (13)	21 (2.63)	20 (2.69)	18 (65)	14 (404)	14 (16.2)			25	20
University of Alaska	21 (2.71)	17 (3.02)	23.5 (0)	21 (7)	20 (2.69)	13.5 (3.01)	16.5 (73)	18 (210)	21 (10.0)			21	15
Naval Postgraduate School	22 (2.54)	23 (2.11)	23.5 (0)	22.5 (4)	22 (2.54)	22 (2.05)	22 (49)	24 (76)	25 (7.6)			10	9
Louisiana State U & A&M College	23 (2.42)	21 (2.65)	23.5 (0)	22.5 (4)	23 (2.27)	21 (2.53)	21 (53)	19 (181)	23 (7.9)			23	43
U of Massachusetts at Amherst	24 (1.77)	24 (1.95)	23.5 (0)	26 (0)	24 (1.72)	24 (1.83)	26 (28)	22 (92)	24 (7.7)			12	19
Florida Institute of Technology	25 (1.65)	26 (1.83)	23.5 (0)	25 (1)	25 (1.57)	25 (1.82)	23 (48)	25 (69)	22 (9.9)			7	5
Northeastern University	26 (1.50)	25 (1.91)	19 (1)	24 (3)	26 (1.37)	26 (1.67)	25 (30)	23 (77)	18 (12.8)			6	6

Sources: 1. National Survey of Graduate Faculty
2. Institute for Scientific Information
3. 1982 Survey of Graduate Faculty
4. Institutional Coordinator Data

Appendix Table P - 32 Relative Rankings for Research-Doctorate Programs in Pharmacology

Institution	93Q [1]	93E [1]	% D [1]	% D-S [1]	93Q T [1]	93E T [1]	VIS [1]	TC [2]	C/F [2]	82Q [3]	82E [3]	TF [4]	TG [4]
Yale University	1 (4.45)	1 (4.32)	2.5 (40)	1 (77)	1 (4.47)	1 (4.17)	1 (86)	9 (4295)	16 (126.3)			34	36
U of Texas-Southwestern Med Ctr	2 (4.39)	5 (4.04)	1 (42)	4 (67)	2 (4.43)	4 (4.07)	4 (80)	2 (11442)	4 (293.4)			39	34
Univ of California-San Diego	3 (4.36)	13 (3.87)	2.5 (40)	3 (68)	3 (4.41)	14 (3.88)	4 (80)	4 (10804)	1 (348.5)			31	24
Johns Hopkins University	4 (4.21)	2 (4.22)	4 (33)	5.5 (62)	4 (4.40)	2.5 (4.09)	4 (80)	3 (11275)	3 (322.1)			35	34
Duke University	5 (4.18)	6 (4.03)	8 (22)	5.5 (62)	8 (4.10)	5 (4.06)	8.5 (76)	10 (4098)	26 (100.0)			41	52
Vanderbilt University	6 (4.17)	3 (4.15)	5 (25)	2 (69)	6.5 (4.11)	6 (4.04)	2 (85)	13 (3873)	21 (110.7)			35	20
Harvard University	7 (4.14)	9 (4.00)	6 (24)	9.5 (49)	5 (4.12)	9 (3.96)	21.5 (67)	5 (9102)	6 (216.7)			42	58
U of North Carolina-Chapel Hill [a]	8 (4.03)	10 (3.99)	9 (20)	7 (58)	10.5 (3.88)	15 (3.82)	7 (77)	19 (3364)	23 (101.9)			33	30
University of Washington	9.5 (4.02)	8 (4.01)	7 (23)	9.5 (49)	6.5 (4.11)	7 (4.00)	10 (74)	28 (2423)	5 (242.3)			10	40
University of Pennsylvania	9.5 (4.02)	7 (4.02)	10 (18)	11 (47)	9 (3.97)	8 (3.98)	18.5 (68)	6 (7645)	7.5 (191.1)			40	45
Massachusetts Inst of Technology	11 (3.90)	22.5 (3.69)	17.5 (11)	37 (27)	13 (3.86)	12.5 (3.89)	78.5 (43)	44 (1338)	7.5 (191.1)			7	28
University of Wisconsin-Madison	12 (3.89)	12 (3.93)	11 (15)	16 (43)	10.5 (3.88)	2.5 (4.09)	24 (66)	12 (3889)	40 (68.2)			57	41
University of Michigan [b]	13 (3.85)	15 (3.82)	13 (13)	8 (51)	14.5 (3.81)	17.5 (3.67)	8.5 (76)	24 (2846)	17 (123.7)			23	36
New York University	14 (3.84)	20 (3.75)	13 (13)	14.5 (45)	17 (3.77)	19 (3.66)	14.5 (69)	1 (19494)	18 (123.4)			158	100
Emory University	15 (3.83)	17 (3.81)	19.5 (10)	14.5 (45)	20.5 (3.69)	31 (3.45)	14.5 (69)	21 (3108)	44 (64.8)			48	20
U of North Carolina-Chapel Hill [f]	16 (3.82)	4 (4.14)	15.5 (12)	21.5 (39)	20.5 (3.69)	10 (3.95)	35.5 (59)	8 (5219)	24 (100.4)			52	31
Stanford University	17.5 (3.81)	20 (3.75)	13 (13)	12.5 (46)	12 (3.87)	11 (3.91)	11 (71)	11 (3960)	2 (330.0)			12	20
University of Colorado	17.5 (3.81)	14 (3.86)	21 (9)	18 (41)	18 (3.76)	21.5 (3.64)	32.5 (62)	7 (6174)	15 (140.3)			44	30
University of Rochester	19.5 (3.79)	17 (3.81)	15.5 (12)	17 (42)	23 (3.67)	16 (3.73)	18.5 (68)	15 (3500)	38 (71.4)			49	42
University of Iowa	19.5 (3.79)	11 (3.97)	17.5 (11)	19.5 (40)	14.5 (3.81)	12.5 (3.89)	18.5 (68)	31 (2203)	25 (100.1)			22	24
University of Minnesota	21 (3.76)	26.5 (3.61)	23.5 (8)	26.5 (35)	20.5 (3.69)	28.5 (3.54)	41 (57)	46 (1319)	45 (60.0)			22	31
University of Arizona	22 (3.71)	28 (3.60)	23.5 (8)	12.5 (46)	25.5 (3.63)	23 (3.63)	6 (79)	27 (2492)	36 (73.3)			34	49
University of Kansas [b]	23 (3.70)	29 (3.56)	26.5 (7)	23 (38)	25.5 (3.63)	30 (3.51)	27 (65)	76 (516)	79 (34.4)			15	26
University of Virginia	24.5 (3.65)	26.5 (3.61)	19.5 (10)	24.5 (37)	16 (3.78)	20 (3.65)	14.5 (69)	25 (2644)	13 (155.5)			17	16
Columbia University	24.5 (3.65)	48 (3.33)	31.5 (5)	21.5 (39)	35.5 (3.47)	50.5 (3.33)	27 (65)	14 (3764)	10 (179.2)			21	11
University of Chicago	26 (3.64)	31 (3.53)	28.5 (6)	24.5 (37)	30 (3.56)	50.5 (3.33)	32.5 (62)	29 (2395)	31 (85.5)			28	35
State U of New York-Stony Brook	27 (3.62)	48 (3.33)	37 (4)	26.5 (35)	20.5 (3.69)	50.5 (3.33)	34 (61)	18 (3373)	30 (86.5)			39	26
University of Texas at Austin	28 (3.61)	34 (3.49)	31.5 (5)	32 (29)	32.5 (3.52)	50.5 (3.33)	53.5 (53)	38 (1487)	57 (48.0)			31	64
University of Michigan [a]	29 (3.60)	34 (3.49)	37 (4)	19.5 (40)	24 (3.64)	28.5 (3.54)	12 (70)	26 (2577)	28 (95.4)			27	24
Albert Einstein College of Med	30 (3.59)	38 (3.44)	37 (4)	31 (31)	32.5 (3.52)	50.5 (3.33)	38 (58)	22 (3036)	19 (121.4)			25	19

Appendix Table P - 32 Pharmacology (Continued)

Institution	93Q [1]	93E [1]	% D [1]	% D-S [1]	93Q T [1]	93E T [1]	VIS [1]	TC [2]	C/F [2]	82Q [3]	82E [3]	TF [4]	TG [4]
University of Kentucky [a]	**31** (3.56)	**24.5** (3.64)	**85** (1)	**37** (27)	**29** (3.59)	**51** (3.33)	**53.5** (53)	**34** (1790)	**71** (37.3)			48	50
North Carolina State University	**32.5** (3.53)	**54** (3.30)	**31.5** (5)	**52** (19)	**27** (3.61)	**51** (3.33)	**76** (44)	**37** (1665)	**58** (47.6)			35	8
Mayo Graduate School	**32.5** (3.53)	**32** (3.50)	**37** (4)	**33.5** (28)	**29** (3.59)	**26** (3.56)	**41** (57)	**45** (1330)	**32** (83.1)			16	17
Georgetown University	**34** (3.52)	**24.5** (3.64)	**23.5** (8)	**28.5** (34)	**46** (3.36)	**51** (3.33)	**21.5** (67)	**20** (3328)	**12** (158.5)			21	20
University of California-Davis	**35** (3.51)	**20** (3.75)	**23.5** (8)	**40.5** (26)	**31** (3.54)	**18** (3.67)	**29** (64)	**32** (2145)	**54** (51.1)			42	50
Michigan State University	**36** (3.50)	**17** (3.81)	**37** (4)	**30** (33)	**44** (3.38)	**22** (3.64)	**14.5** (69)	**65** (790)	**64** (41.6)			19	24
Rutgers State Univ-New Brunswick	**37** (3.49)	**22.5** (3.69)	**26.5** (7)	**28.5** (34)	**36** (3.47)	**27** (3.55)	**18.5** (68)	**23** (2939)	**48** (54.4)			54	21
U of Tex-Health Sci Ctr-Houston	**38** (3.47)	**36** (3.47)	**45.5** (3)	**33.5** (28)	**40** (3.40)	**51** (3.33)	**24** (66)	**16** (3486)	**27** (99.6)			35	17
University of Miami	**39** (3.42)	**77** (3.11)	**85** (1)	**42.5** (25)	**42** (3.39)	**68** (3.23)	**66** (49)	**53** (977)	**49** (54.3)			18	20
Medical University South Carolina	**40** (3.41)	**41.5** (3.39)	**45.5** (3)	**42.5** (25)	**39** (3.41)	**70** (3.22)	**44** (56)	**48** (1279)	**46** (55.6)			23	15
Univ of California-Los Angeles	**41** (3.40)	**81.5** (3.07)	**45.5** (3)	**44** (24)	**38** (3.42)	**80** (3.11)	**47** (55)	**17** (3485)	**9** (183.4)			19	20
University of Utah	**42** (3.37)	**34** (3.49)	**60** (2)	**37** (27)	**55** (3.23)	**51** (3.33)	**35.5** (59)	**54** (962)	**69.5** (38.5)			25	32
SUNY-Health Science Ctr-Brooklyn	**44.5** (3.36)	**72** (3.15)	**28.5** (6)	**45.5** (22)	**53** (3.24)	**90** (2.95)	**47** (55)	**92** (301)	**97** (23.2)			13	11
Baylor College of Medicine	**44.5** (3.36)	**55** (3.29)	**31.5** (5)	**37** (27)	**42** (3.39)	**33** (3.43)	**30.5** (63)	**50** (1216)	**22** (110.5)			11	3
University of Pittsburgh	**44.5** (3.36)	**65** (3.21)	**45.5** (3)	**48** (21)	**37** (3.43)	**51** (3.33)	**38** (58)	**52** (1074)	**62** (46.7)			23	16
Oregon State University	**44.5** (3.36)	**41.5** (3.39)	**60** (2)	**50** (20)	**34** (3.48)	**25** (3.58)	**66** (49)	**47** (1290)	**81** (32.3)			40	92
University of Cincinnati	**47** (3.34)	**86** (3.03)	**85** (1)	**37** (27)	**46** (3.36)	**93** (2.92)	**27** (65)	**41.5** (1363)	**61** (47.0)			29	69
Saint Louis University	**48.5** (3.33)	**39.5** (3.40)	**60** (2)	**48** (21)	**44** (3.38)	**51** (3.33)	**44** (56)	**56** (924)	**63** (44.0)			21	9
Cornell University [e]	**48.5** (3.33)	**37** (3.46)	**85** (1)	**66.5** (14)	**49** (3.28)	**51** (3.33)	**94.5** (38)	**35** (1779)	**50** (53.9)			33	33
West Virginia University	**50.5** (3.32)	**30** (3.54)	**45.5** (3)	**45.5** (22)	**48** (3.29)	**34** (3.41)	**38** (58)	**84.5** (387)	**91** (27.6)			14	18
University of Florida	**50.5** (3.32)	**59.5** (3.25)	**60** (2)	**40.5** (26)	**51** (3.25)	**85** (3.08)	**24** (66)	**41.5** (1363)	**47** (54.5)			25	27
Thomas Jefferson University	**52** (3.30)	**65** (3.21)	**85** (1)	**48** (21)	**47** (3.33)	**83** (3.10)	**58** (52)	**75** (520)	**103** (17.9)			29	14
Ohio State University	**53.5** (3.26)	**48** (3.33)	**114** (0)	**59.5** (16)	**75** (3.05)	**51** (3.33)	**53.5** (53)	**55** (936)	**75** (36.0)			26	17
Medical College of Wisconsin	**53.5** (3.26)	**69.5** (3.18)	**114** (0)	**63** (15)	**55** (3.23)	**73** (3.18)	**70** (47)	**59** (881)	**41** (67.8)			13	6
University of Tennessee - Memphis	**55** (3.25)	**61** (3.23)	**85** (1)	**55.5** (18)	**61** (3.17)	**77** (3.13)	**49** (54)	**51** (1160)	**66** (40.0)			29	12
Dartmouth College	**56** (3.24)	**48** (3.33)	**60** (2)	**52** (19)	**61** (3.17)	**33** (3.43)	**53.5** (53)	**80** (448)	**82** (32.0)			14	27
Wake Forest University	**57** (3.20)	**48** (3.33)	**85** (1)	**70.5** (13)	**63** (3.16)	**51** (3.33)	**94.5** (38)	**120** (45)	**123** (3.0)			15	10
University of Illinois at Chicago	**58.5** (3.18)	**48** (3.33)	**45.5** (3)	**70.5** (13)	**75** (3.05)	**51** (3.33)	**76** (44)	**69** (664)	**59** (47.4)			14	26
Utah State University	**58.5** (3.18)	**48** (3.33)	**85** (1)	**70.5** (13)	**53** (3.24)	**51** (3.33)	**104** (34)	**70.5** (657)	**73.5** (36.5)			18	28
Brown University	**60.5** (3.17)	**48** (3.33)	**45.5** (3)	**87** (9)	**65** (3.15)	**83** (3.10)	**114.5** (29)	**106** (142)	**107** (12.9)			11	1

Institution	93Q [1]	93E [1]	% D [1]	% D-S [1]	93Q T [1]	93E T [1]	VIS [1]	TC [2]	C/F [2]	82Q [3]	82E [3]	TF [4]	TG [4]
University of Vermont	**60.5** (3.17)	**39.5** (3.40)	**60** (2)	**55.5** (18)	**51** (3.25)	**51** (3.33)	**53.5** (53)	**36** (1712)	**14** (142.7)			12	9
Washington State University	**62.5** (3.16)	**71** (3.16)	**60** (2)	**59.5** (16)	**78** (3.00)	**77** (3.13)	**53.5** (53)	**39** (1470)	**72** (36.8)			40	29
Texas A&M University	**62.5** (3.16)	**56.5** (3.27)	**85** (1)	**55.5** (18)	**63** (3.16)	**70** (3.22)	**62.5** (50)	**40** (1388)	**43** (66.1)			21	38
Cornell University [d]	**65** (3.12)	**81.5** (3.07)	**60** (2)	**74** (12)	**72** (3.06)	**93** (2.92)	**104** (34)	**58** (895)	**20** (111.9)			8	21
Univ of Maryland at Baltimore	**65** (3.12)	**78.5** (3.10)	**60** (2)	**52** (19)	**66** (3.14)	**88** (2.96)	**30.5** (63)	**57** (921)	**34** (76.8)			12	12
U of Texas, Medical Br-Galveston	**65** (3.12)	**65** (3.21)	**85** (1)	**66.5** (14)	**69** (3.11)	**51** (3.33)	**72.5** (46)	**43** (1353)	**35** (75.2)			18	18
University of Louisville	**67** (3.10)	**88.5** (3.00)	**85** (1)	**82** (10)	**72** (3.06)	**77** (3.13)	**86** (40)	**73** (603)	**90** (28.7)			21	14
Medical College of Georgia	**68** (3.09)	**58** (3.26)	**85** (1)	**74** (12)	**89** (2.80)	**75** (3.15)	**78.5** (43)	**87** (364)	**93.5** (26.0)			14	14
Uniformed Services U of Hlth Sci	**69.5** (3.08)	**74** (3.13)	**45.5** (3)	**63** (15)	**69** (3.11)	**73** (3.18)	**44** (56)	**63** (801)	**42** (66.8)			12	6
Temple University	**69.5** (3.08)	**101** (2.87)	**114** (0)	**82** (10)	**57** (3.22)	**97** (2.83)	**72.5** (46)	**72** (648)	**65** (40.5)			16	19
U of Tex-Hlth Sci Ct-San Antonio	**71** (3.07)	**92** (2.99)	**85** (1)	**66.5** (14)	**87** (2.87)	**88** (2.96)	**62.5** (50)	**79** (465)	**77** (35.8)			13	13
Wayne State University	**73** (3.06)	**83** (3.06)	**37** (4)	**63** (15)	**55** (3.23)	**83** (3.10)	**41** (57)	**62** (875)	**73.5** (36.5)			24	18
Tufts University	**73** (3.06)	**56.5** (3.27)	**37** (4)	**59.5** (16)	**82** (2.95)	**51** (3.33)	**59.5** (51)	**33** (1906)	**11** (158.8)			12	3
University of Connecticut [b]	**73** (3.06)	**76** (3.12)	**60** (2)	**77** (11)	**58** (3.21)	**51** (3.33)	**86** (40)	**84.5** (387)	**67** (38.7)			10	5
Pennsylvania State University	**75** (3.05)	**103** (2.81)	**60** (2)	**59.5** (16)	**94** (2.72)	**106** (2.62)	**47** (55)	**97** (220)	**95** (24.4)			9	20
University of Alabama-Birmingham	**77** (3.04)	**84** (3.05)	**60** (2)	**70.5** (13)	**88** (2.86)	**95** (2.89)	**70** (47)	**30** (2382)	**39** (70.1)			34	33
University of Caiifornia-Irvine	**77** (3.04)	**92** (2.99)	**60** (2)	**55.5** (18)	**69** (3.11)	**80** (3.11)	**53.5** (53)	**95** (228)	**80** (32.6)			7	12
Albany Medical College	**77** (3.04)	**48** (3.33)	**85** (1)	**82** (10)	**65** (3.15)	**51** (3.33)	**98.5** (37)	**66** (731)	**69.5** (38.5)			19	21
University of Kansas [a]	**80** (3.03)	**68** (3.20)	**85** (1)	**74** (12)	**59** (3.19)	**51** (3.33)	**68** (48)	**100** (189)	**92** (27.0)			7	11
State Univ of New York-Buffalo	**80** (3.03)	**74** (3.13)	**85** (1)	**82** (10)	**85** (2.88)	**75** (3.15)	**74** (45)	**70.5** (657)	**68** (38.6)			17	16
George Washington University	**80** (3.03)	**92** (2.99)	**114** (0)	**66.5** (14)	**80** (2.98)	**97** (2.83)	**53.5** (53)	**89** (352)	**78** (35.2)			10	13
Tulane University	**82** (3.02)	**80** (3.09)	**45.5** (3)	**77** (11)	**81** (2.96)	**67** (3.24)	**62.5** (50)	**64** (795)	**37** (72.3)			11	13
U of Massachusetts Med Center	**84** (3.00)	**48** (3.33)	**85** (1)	**82** (10)	**85** (2.88)	**51** (3.33)	**83** (41)	**49** (1273)	**55** (50.9)			25	7
Iowa State University	**84** (3.00)	**98.5** (2.92)	**85** (1)	**91** (8)	**72** (3.06)	**86** (3.00)	**94.5** (38)	**81** (442)	**93.5** (26.0)			17	18
SUNY Health Science Ctr-Syracuse	**84** (3.00)	**48** (3.33)	**85** (1)	**95.5** (7)	**104** (2.50)	**51** (3.33)	**122.5** (25)	**77** (510)	**87** (30.0)			17	8
Medical College of Pensylvania	**86** (2.97)	**59.5** (3.25)	**114** (0)	**82** (10)	**67** (3.13)	**71** (3.21)	**70** (47)	**82** (403)	**84** (31.0)			13	14
Case Western Reserve Univ	**87** (2.94)	**88.5** (3.00)	**114** (0)	**91** (8)	**83** (2.92)	**51** (3.33)	**90** (39)	**60** (880)	**29** (88.0)			10	11
University of Georgia	**88** (2.92)	**74** (3.13)	**60** (2)	**87** (9)	**96** (2.69)	**102** (2.71)	**90** (39)	**86** (385)	**96** (24.1)			16	17
New York Medical College	**89** (2.91)	**96** (2.95)	**60** (2)	**82** (10)	**78** (3.00)	**51** (3.33)	**94.5** (38)	**61** (879)	**33** (79.9)			11	15
Purdue University	**90** (2.89)	**78.5** (3.10)	**114** (0)	**91** (8)	**90** (2.75)	**98** (2.82)	**59.5** (51)	**98** (195)	**100** (19.5)			10	14

Appendix Table P - 32 Pharmacology (Continued)

Institution	93Q [1]	93E [1]	% D [1]	% D-S [1]	93Q T [1]	93E T [1]	VIS [1]	TC [2]	C/F [2]	82Q [3]	82E [3]	TF [4]	TG [4]
University of Kentucky [b]	91.5 (2.87)	88.5 (3.00)	114 (0)	77 (11)	96 (2.69)	88 (2.96)	66 (49)	94 (268)	88 (29.8)			9	12
State Univ of New York-Albany	91.5 (2.87)	65 (3.21)	114 (0)	99.5 (6)	85 (2.88)	(n/s)	114.5 (29)	102 (162)	119 (5.6)			29	34
Loyola University of Chicago	93 (2.85)	97 (2.94)	114 (0)	91 (8)	94 (2.72)	102 (2.71)	62.5 (50)	78 (472)	52 (52.4)			9	12
University of Connecticut [c]	94 (2.82)	102 (2.84)	114 (0)	91 (8)	78 (3.00)	104 (2.67)	100.5 (35)	90 (343)	83 (31.2)			11	17
Univ of Med & Dent of NJ	95 (2.79)	69.5 (3.18)	85 (1)	87 (9)	106 (2.47)	93 (2.92)	86 (40)	96 (226)	98 (20.5)			11	19
Louisiana State U Medical Center	96.5 (2.76)	85 (3.04)	45.5 (3)	104 (5)	98 (2.65)	104 (2.67)	86 (40)	112.5 (80)	117 (6.2)			13	10
University of Oklahoma	96.5 (2.76)	62 (3.22)	114 (0)	95.5 (7)	104 (2.50)	51 (3.33)	86 (40)	93 (281)	110 (11.2)			25	24
Louisiana State U & A&M College	98.5 (2.75)	65 (3.21)	85 (1)	95.5 (7)	108 (2.40)	51 (3.33)	116.5 (28)	67 (708)	85 (30.8)			23	4
University of South Carolina	98.5 (2.75)	94.5 (2.98)	114 (0)	99.5 (6)	99 (2.64)	93 (2.92)	94.5 (38)	99 (191)	101 (19.1)			10	10
U of Mississippi-Medical Center	100 (2.68)	94.5 (2.98)	85 (1)	95.5 (7)	100 (2.61)	100 (2.78)	76 (44)	88 (359)	76 (35.9)			10	17
East Carolina U Sch Medicine	101 (2.58)	105 (2.67)	60 (2)	99.5 (6)	119 (2.10)	121 (1.67)	100.5 (35)	91 (327)	89 (29.7)			11	7
University of Missouri-Columbia	102 (2.57)	100 (2.88)	114 (0)	111 (4)	110 (2.33)	104 (2.67)	98.5 (37)	68 (676)	53 (52.0)			13	13
Northeast Louisiana University	103 (2.55)	112.5 (2.50)	85 (1)	99.5 (6)	97 (2.67)	114 (2.08)	110.5 (31)	127 (0)	127 (0.0)			25	45
University of South Florida	104 (2.50)	109 (2.57)	114 (0)	118 (3)	111 (2.26)	109 (2.38)	81 (42)	110 (98)	108 (12.3)			8	n/a
Medical College of Ohio	105 (2.48)	118 (2.36)	85 (1)	122 (2)	101 (2.54)	116 (2.00)	104 (34)	74 (565)	60 (47.1)			12	38
University of Mississippi	106.5 (2.47)	105 (2.67)	60 (2)	104 (5)	104 (2.50)	108 (2.50)	118 (27)	101 (184)	86 (30.7)			6	8
Louisiana St U-Sch Med Shreveport	106.5 (2.47)	112.5 (2.50)	85 (1)	111 (4)	108 (2.40)	100 (2.78)	81 (42)	104.5 (147)	112 (10.5)			14	16
St. John's University	108.5 (2.46)	108 (2.59)	60 (2)	118 (3)	122 (2.00)	121 (1.67)	125 (22)	108 (119)	111 (10.8)			11	41
University of Southern California	108.5 (2.46)	110 (2.56)	114 (0)	125.5 (1)	92 (2.73)	83 (3.10)	104 (34)	115 (67)	116 (6.7)			10	1
Clemson University	110 (2.40)	105 (2.67)	114 (0)	122 (2)	78 (3.00)	(n/s)	127 (17)	122 (18)	124 (2.3)			8	22
University of Houston	111 (2.38)	111 (2.54)	85 (1)	111 (4)	114 (2.18)	110 (2.35)	104 (34)	104.5 (147)	102 (18.4)			8	16
University of Hawaii at Manoa	112 (2.35)	98.5 (2.92)	60 (2)	104 (5)	116 (2.17)	51 (3.33)	107.5 (33)	111 (95)	106 (13.6)			7	15
Phila Col of Pharmacy & Science	113 (2.33)	119 (2.26)	85 (1)	104 (5)	92 (2.73)	114 (2.08)	112.5 (30)	118 (51)	118 (5.7)			9	15
Loma Linda University	114 (2.31)	116.5 (2.38)	85 (1)	111 (4)	117 (2.14)	111 (2.33)	112.5 (30)	109 (103)	109 (11.4)			9	7
Univ of Health Sc/Chicago Med Sch	115.5 (2.23)	122 (2.08)	114 (0)	111 (4)	120 (2.09)	116 (2.00)	110.5 (31)	119 (46)	120 (5.1)			9	10
Texas Tech University	115.5 (2.23)	115 (2.40)	114 (0)	118 (3)	113 (2.25)	108 (2.50)	81 (42)	114 (70)	115 (7.8)			9	4
Kent State University	117 (2.22)	121 (2.17)	114 (0)	111 (4)	118 (2.12)	112 (2.17)	107.5 (33)	107 (138)	99 (19.7)			7	1
Southern Illinois University	118 (2.16)	114 (2.44)	85 (1)	125.5 (1)	116 (2.17)	116 (2.00)	94.5 (38)	83 (396)	56 (49.5)			8	8
Univ of California-Santa Barbara	119 (2.13)	88.5 (3.00)	114 (0)	104 (5)	104 (2.50)	24 (3.61)	120 (26)	103 (158)	51 (52.7)			3	n/a
Howard University	120 (2.08)	120 (2.22)	114 (0)	125.5 (1)	113 (2.25)	121 (1.67)	126 (21)	124 (12)	125 (2.0)			6	3

Institution	93Q [1]	93E [1]	% D [1]	% D-S [1]	93Q T [1]	93E T [1]	VIS [1]	TC [2]	C/F [2]	82Q [3]	82E [3]	TF [4]	TG [4]
University of South Dakota	**121** (2.00)	**107** (2.62)	**85** (1)	**125.5** (1)	**122** (2.00)	**51** (3.33)	**124** (23)	**117** (55)	**121** (5.0)			11	4
Indiana University	**122** (1.89)	**124** (1.82)	**114** (0)	**111** (4)	**124** (1.78)	**121** (1.67)	**116.5** (28)	**112.5** (80)	**104** (16.0)			5	4
Hahnemann University	**123** (1.80)	**123** (1.84)	**114** (0)	**118** (3)	**124** (1.78)	**118** (1.82)	**90** (39)	**116** (59)	**113** (9.8)			6	1
Univ of Puerto Rico-Rio Piedras	**124** (1.79)	**125** (1.39)	**114** (0)	**118** (3)	**125** (1.57)	**123** (1.11)	**122.5** (25)	**121** (33)	**122** (4.1)			8	6
Ohio University	**125** (1.63)	**116.5** (2.38)	**114** (0)	**111** (4)	**109** (2.38)	**51** (3.33)	**120** (26)	**126** (3)	**126** (1.0)			3	5
University of Idaho	**126** (1.53)	**126** (1.16)	**85** (1)	**111** (4)	**126** (1.25)	**124** (0.00)	**109** (32)	**123** (15)	**105** (15.0)			1	0
Univ of California-Santa Cruz	**127** (0.25)	**127** (0.33)	**114** (0)	**122** (2)	**127** (0.20)	**(n/s)** (*)	**120** (26)	**125** (8)	**114** (8.0)			1	2

Sources: 1. National Survey of Graduate Faculty
2. Institute for Scientific Information
3. 1982 Survey of Graduate Faculty
4. Institutional Coordinator Data

Notes: *a.* School of Arts and Sciences
b. School of Medicine
c. School of Pharmacology
d. School of Veterinary Medicine
e. School of Engineering
f. Interdisciplinary with the Schools of Medicine, Pharmacology, and Public Health

n/s After trimming no cases remained

Appendix Table P - 33 Relative Rankings for Research-Doctorate Programs in Philosophy

Institution	93Q [1]	93E [1]	% D [1]	% D-S [1]	93Q T [1]	93E T [1]	VIS [1]	FA [2]	82Q [3]	82E [3]	TF [4]	TG [4]
Princeton University	**1** (4.93)	**1** (4.56)	**1** (91)	**1** (97)	**1** (5.00)	**2** (4.67)	**6** (99)	**8.5** (7)	**2** (4.70)	**1** (4.52)	16	34
University of Pittsburgh	**2** (4.73)	**2** (4.43)	**2** (75)	**2.5** (95)	**2** (4.86)	**1** (4.69)	**2.5** (100)	**3.5** (9)	**3** (4.63)	**2** (4.40)	30	60
Harvard University	**3** (4.69)	**9** (3.77)	**3** (73)	**4** (94)	**3** (4.82)	**7** (3.99)	**2.5** (100)	**1** (11)	**1** (4.73)	**3** (4.18)	14	44
University of California-Berkeley	**4** (4.66)	**11** (3.66)	**4** (69)	**2.5** (95)	**4** (4.67)	**10** (3.76)	**2.5** (100)	**8.5** (7)	**4** (4.48)	**7** (3.78)	16	34
University of Pittsburgh [a]	**5** (4.47)	**3** (4.26)	**6** (49)	**5** (92)	**6** (4.38)	**5** (4.12)	**9** (98)	**12** (6)	**6** (4.37)	**4** (3.90)	17	38
Univ of California-Los Angeles	**6** (4.42)	**6** (4.01)	**5** (50)	**6** (83)	**5** (4.61)	**4** (4.15)	**20** (95)	**16.5** (5)	**5** (4.41)	**5** (3.87)	25	46
Stanford University	**7** (4.20)	**5** (4.02)	**7** (32)	**7.5** (81)	**9** (4.19)	**6** (4.04)	**17** (96)	**29.5** (3)	**8** (4.13)	**6** (3.82)	18	52
University of Michigan	**8** (4.15)	**8** (3.88)	**8** (31)	**9** (79)	**7** (4.33)	**8** (3.94)	**13** (97)	**8.5** (7)	**9** (4.02)	**8** (3.72)	19	48
Cornell University	**9** (4.11)	**4** (4.14)	**9** (27)	**7.5** (81)	**9** (4.19)	**3** (4.35)	**13** (97)	**3.5** (9)	**11** (3.77)	**11** (3.62)	15	31
Massachusetts Inst of Technology	**10** (4.01)	**7** (3.91)	**10** (24)	**11** (76)	**9** (4.19)	**9** (3.88)	**17** (96)	**16.5** (5)	**10** (3.97)	**9.5** (3.65)	11	29
University of Arizona	**11** (3.99)	**10** (3.74)	**11** (21)	**10** (77)	**11** (4.04)	**11** (3.72)	**9** (98)	**29.5** (3)	**12** (3.63)	**25.5** (2.90)	19	36
University of Chicago	**12** (3.88)	**17.5** (3.41)	**13.5** (16)	**12** (74)	**13** (3.87)	**19** (3.38)	**6** (99)	**3.5** (9)	**7** (4.25)	**9.5** (3.65)	20	59
Rutgers State Univ-New Brunswick	**13.5** (3.82)	**16** (3.44)	**13.5** (16)	**14** (68)	**12** (3.93)	**20** (3.33)	**13** (97)	**29.5** (3)	**37** (2.48)	**44** (2.22)	28	59
Brown University	**13.5** (3.82)	**12** (3.62)	**16** (12)	**13** (70)	**16** (3.71)	**13** (3.61)	**2.5** (100)	**12** (6)	**13** (3.61)	**12** (3.53)	13	26
Univ of California-San Diego	**15** (3.79)	**15** (3.47)	**12** (18)	**15** (65)	**15** (3.72)	**14** (3.53)	**13** (97)	**22** (4)	**34** (2.58)	**31** (2.67)	18	40
University of Notre Dame	**16** (3.69)	**13** (3.61)	**15** (14)	**17** (57)	**18** (3.58)	**12** (3.63)	**6** (99)	**3.5** (9)	**30** (2.80)	**24** (2.92)	33	67
U of North Carolina-Chapel Hill	**17** (3.67)	**17.5** (3.41)	**20.5** (5)	**16** (61)	**17** (3.61)	**17.5** (3.41)	**24** (93)	**29.5** (3)	**23** (3.12)	**16** (3.25)	20	48
University of Illinois at Chicago	**18** (3.51)	**20** (3.33)	**20.5** (5)	**18** (50)	**14** (3.73)	**15** (3.48)	**17** (96)	**8.5** (7)	**16** (3.34)	**17** (3.20)	17	38
CUNY - Grad Sch & Univ Center	**19** (3.45)	**35** (2.84)	**17** (7)	**20** (43)	**20** (3.39)	**26.5** (2.92)	**20** (95)	**22** (4)	**21** (3.18)	**36** (2.50)	32	108
U of Massachusetts at Amherst	**20** (3.44)	**19** (3.37)	**26** (3)	**19** (46)	**19** (3.46)	**17.5** (3.41)	**9** (98)	**16.5** (5)	**14** (3.54)	**13** (3.48)	15	62
University of California-Irvine	**21** (3.30)	**31** (2.96)	**18** (6)	**21.5** (37)	**21** (3.34)	**26.5** (2.92)	**29.5** (91)	**38** (2)	**24** (3.11)	**18** (3.08)	12	32
University of Wisconsin-Madison	**22.5** (3.28)	**21** (3.11)	**26** (3)	**21.5** (37)	**22** (3.26)	**30** (2.85)	**22.5** (94)	**29.5** (3)	**19** (3.21)	**21.5** (2.98)	26	126
Syracuse University	**22.5** (3.28)	**14** (3.52)	**26** (3)	**23.5** (35)	**23** (3.21)	**16** (3.42)	**26.5** (92)	**16.5** (5)	**27** (2.96)	**29** (2.73)	20	46
Ohio State University	**24** (3.21)	**22** (3.07)	**60.5** (0)	**27** (31)	**24** (3.18)	**22** (3.14)	**32** (90)	**29.5** (3)	**29** (2.80)	**23** (2.95)	36	55
Northwestern University	**25** (3.18)	**27.5** (2.99)	**31** (2)	**23.5** (35)	**29** (3.00)	**31** (2.84)	**26.5** (92)	**6** (8)	**36** (2.54)	**39** (2.37)	21	35
University of Pennsylvania	**27** (3.15)	**24.5** (3.04)	**26** (3)	**29** (27)	**28** (3.02)	**29** (2.86)	**26.5** (92)	**22** (4)	**31** (2.76)	**32** (2.65)	15	36
University of Texas at Austin	**27** (3.15)	**27.5** (2.99)	**31** (2)	**26** (33)	**34** (2.84)	**42** (2.45)	**29.5** (91)	**12** (6)	**25** (3.04)	**20** (3.02)	37	61
Columbia University	**27** (3.15)	**34** (2.87)	**31** (2)	**25** (34)	**25** (3.16)	**34** (2.70)	**20** (95)	**16.5** (5)	**15** (3.52)	**14.5** (3.27)	17	75
Boston University	**29** (3.12)	**33** (2.91)	**20.5** (5)	**28** (29)	**33** (2.85)	**39** (2.54)	**13** (97)	**22** (4)	**20** (3.19)	**21.5** (2.98)	22	57
Indiana University	**30** (3.11)	**23** (3.06)	**20.5** (5)	**30.5** (24)	**26** (3.08)	**23.5** (3.00)	**39.5** (84)	**16.5** (5)	**17** (3.32)	**14.5** (3.27)	17	51

Institution	93Q [1]	93E [1]	% D [1]	% D-S [1]	93Q T [1]	93E T [1]	VIS [1]	FA [2]	82Q [3]	82E [3]	TF [4]	TG [4]
Johns Hopkins University	**31** (3.03)	**30** (2.97)	**40.5** (1)	**32** (23)	**27** (3.07)	**25** (2.94)	**26.5** (92)	**49** (1)	**28** (2.81)	**28** (2.83)	9	38
University of Minnesota	**32** (3.01)	**29** (2.98)	**40.5** (1)	**33** (20)	**30** (2.98)	**24** (3.00)	**39.5** (84)	**49** (1)	**26** (3.02)	**19** (3.07)	22	41
University of Rochester	**33** (2.95)	**24.5** (3.04)	**40.5** (1)	**30.5** (24)	**35** (2.79)	**41** (2.50)	**32** (90)	**64.5** (0)	**32** (2.75)	**30** (2.70)	13	31
University of Southern California	**34** (2.89)	**39** (2.73)	**60.5** (0)	**36.5** (13)	**32** (2.91)	**36** (2.62)	**47** (75)	**49** (1)	**22** (3.15)	**27** (2.88)	13	30
University of Maryland College Park	**35** (2.86)	**42** (2.67)	**40.5** (1)	**34** (19)	**32** (2.91)	**41** (2.50)	**32** (90)	**49** (1)			22	26
U of Illinois at Urbana-Champaign	**36** (2.77)	**38** (2.78)	**40.5** (1)	**43** (8)	**36** (2.76)	**32** (2.82)	**36.5** (85)	**49** (1)	**33** (2.69)	**33** (2.62)	22	46
Rice University	**37** (2.72)	**37** (2.80)	**60.5** (0)	**35** (14)	**37** (2.62)	**21** (3.15)	**34** (88)	**29.5** (3)	**49** (2.05)	**58** (1.58)	11	18
Vanderbilt University	**38** (2.61)	**32** (2.95)	**26** (3)	**38** (12)	**44** (2.19)	**38** (2.58)	**44.5** (78)	**49** (1)	**47** (2.12)	**40.5** (2.33)	15	58
Univ of California-Riverside	**39** (2.57)	**43** (2.61)	**40.5** (1)	**49.5** (5)	**38** (2.60)	**37** (2.59)	**42.5** (82)	**49** (1)	**62** (1.40)	**62** (1.23)	19	40
Emory University	**40** (2.54)	**26** (3.00)	**40.5** (1)	**36.5** (13)	**47** (2.09)	**43** (2.38)	**56** (65)	**22** (4)	**58** (1.64)	**59** (1.57)	14	46
Georgetown University	**41** (2.51)	**36** (2.83)	**60.5** (0)	**49.5** (5)	**42** (2.41)	**35** (2.67)	**36.5** (85)	**38** (2)	**50** (2.04)	**43** (2.25)	26	49
Univ of California-Santa Barbara	**42** (2.46)	**60** (2.04)	**60.5** (0)	**41.5** (9)	**40** (2.48)	**51** (2.00)	**49** (74)	**49** (1)	**41** (2.28)	**47.5** (2.15)	11	44
University of Virginia	**43** (2.38)	**51** (2.42)	**60.5** (0)	**62.5** (2)	**42** (2.41)	**45** (2.29)	**44.5** (78)	**64.5** (0)	**51** (2.00)	**50** (2.02)	11	34
Duke University	**44** (2.37)	**44** (2.58)	**60.5** (0)	**49.5** (5)	**43** (2.38)	**33** (2.71)	**42.5** (82)	**29.5** (3)	**46** (2.12)	**56** (1.87)	11	21
Washington University	**45** (2.35)	**48** (2.47)	**60.5** (0)	**58.5** (3)	**45** (2.11)	**47** (2.22)	**49** (74)	**29.5** (3)	**39** (2.42)	**40.5** (2.33)	14	37
State U of New York-Stony Brook	**46** (2.33)	**50** (2.43)	**40.5** (1)	**39.5** (10)	**49** (2.03)	**53** (1.82)	**53** (71)	**38** (2)			24	54
Temple University	**47.5** (2.31)	**52** (2.36)	**40.5** (1)	**44.5** (6)	**50** (2.01)	**52** (1.85)	**35** (86)	**38** (2)	**35** (2.57)	**37** (2.47)	14	46
Carnegie Mellon University	**47.5** (2.31)	**66** (1.67)	**40.5** (1)	**39.5** (10)	**39** (2.50)	**51** (2.00)	**68.5** (52)	**64.5** (0)			13	13
Loyola University of Chicago	**49** (2.28)	**47** (2.50)	**40.5** (1)	**55.5** (4)	**53** (1.87)	**58** (1.67)	**57** (64)	**64.5** (0)			29	75
State Univ of New York-Buffalo	**50** (2.24)	**55** (2.22)	**60.5** (0)	**49.5** (5)	**52** (1.97)	**54** (1.80)	**46** (76)	**64.5** (0)	**44** (2.21)	**46** (2.17)	19	54
University of Iowa	**51** (2.23)	**41** (2.68)	**60.5** (0)	**49.5** (5)	**51** (2.00)	**28** (2.88)	**54** (70)	**38** (2)	**42** (2.25)	**35** (2.53)	11	44
University of Miami	**52** (2.22)	**46** (2.56)	**40.5** (1)	**49.5** (5)	**46** (2.10)	**58** (1.67)	**39.5** (84)	**64.5** (0)	**59** (1.61)	**61** (1.43)	8	18
Catholic University of America	**53** (2.16)	**45** (2.57)	**26** (3)	**49.5** (5)	**56** (1.83)	**49** (2.14)	**58** (62)	**49** (1)	**38** (2.44)	**34** (2.60)	15	66
University of Kansas	**54** (2.10)	**40** (2.69)	**60.5** (0)	**58.5** (3)	**55** (1.84)	**58** (1.67)	**51.5** (72)	**49** (1)	**56** (1.71)	**51** (1.98)	16	36
Pennsylvania State University	**55** (2.09)	**57** (2.17)	**40.5** (1)	**44.5** (6)	**58** (1.73)	**64** (1.37)	**55** (68)	**29.5** (3)	**43** (2.23)	**42** (2.28)	14	38
University of Nebraska-Lincoln	**56** (2.07)	**53.5** (2.35)	**60.5** (0)	**62.5** (2)	**48** (2.06)	**45** (2.29)	**39.5** (84)	**64.5** (0)	**55** (1.80)	**53** (1.95)	10	33
Boston College	**57** (2.05)	**53.5** (2.35)	**26** (3)	**41.5** (9)	**64** (1.50)	**62** (1.39)	**66.5** (53)	**64.5** (0)	**60** (1.60)	**45** (2.18)	22	73
Florida State University	**58** (1.95)	**63** (1.86)	**60.5** (0)	**62.5** (2)	**55** (1.84)	**62** (1.39)	**49** (74)	**64.5** (0)	**45** (2.19)	**52** (1.97)	10	28
Michigan State University	**59.5** (1.91)	**58** (2.15)	**40.5** (1)	**62.5** (2)	**57** (1.79)	**47** (2.22)	**59** (61)	**49** (1)	**54** (1.81)	**55** (1.90)	25	25
Yale University	**59.5** (1.91)	**62** (1.92)	**60.5** (0)	**55.5** (4)	**60** (1.67)	**62** (1.39)	**22.5** (94)	**49** (1)	**18** (3.28)	**25.5** (2.90)	14	33

Appendix Table P - 33 Philosophy (Continued)

Institution	93Q [1]	93E [1]	% D [1]	% D-S [1]	93Q T [1]	93E T [1]	VIS [1]	FA [2]	82Q [3]	82E [3]	TF [4]	TG [4]
Tulane University	61.5 (1.86)	59 (2.14)	60.5 (0)	62.5 (2)	59 (1.70)	65 (1.33)	51.5 (72)	49 (1)	61 (1.49)	54 (1.93)	11	41
University of Georgia	61.5 (1.86)	64 (1.81)	60.5 (0)	67 (1)	62 (1.60)	58 (1.67)	62 (55)	64.5 (0)	64 (1.16)	63 (1.15)	14	26
Saint Louis University	63 (1.84)	49 (2.46)	60.5 (0)	49.5 (5)	63 (1.57)	47 (2.22)	64.5 (54)	49 (1)	52 (1.93)	47.5 (2.15)	17	9
Fordham University	64 (1.81)	56 (2.20)	40.5 (1)	55.5 (4)	70 (1.20)	58 (1.67)	66.5 (53)	49 (1)	40 (2.30)	38 (2.38)	13	124
University of Hawaii at Manoa	65 (1.78)	71.5 (1.11)	60.5 (0)	67 (1)	61 (1.61)	67 (1.25)	72 (42)	38 (2)	57 (1.67)	57 (1.77)	13	34
University of Kentucky	66 (1.59)	66 (1.67)	40.5 (1)	55.5 (4)	69 (1.23)	70 (0.95)	62 (55)	64.5 (0)			16	27
University of Cincinnati	67 (1.56)	61 (1.95)	60.5 (0)	70.5 (0)	65 (1.45)	58 (1.67)	70 (51)	64.5 (0)	53 (1.89)	60 (1.47)	10	17
University of Oregon	68 (1.52)	69 (1.31)	60.5 (0)	70.5 (0)	66 (1.39)	68 (1.19)	62 (55)	64.5 (0)	63 (1.28)	64 (1.13)	9	28
Southern Illinois University	69 (1.41)	70 (1.17)	60.5 (0)	70.5 (0)	67 (1.35)	72 (0.56)	68.5 (52)	38 (2)	66 (0.97)	66 (0.98)	13	14
University of Tennessee-Knoxville	70 (1.32)	71.5 (1.11)	60.5 (0)	70.5 (0)	68 (1.25)	72 (0.56)	71 (47)	64.5 (0)	65 (1.05)	65 (1.07)	11	26
Duquesne University	71 (1.29)	66 (1.67)	60.5 (0)	67 (1)	72 (1.03)	69 (1.00)	64.5 (54)	64.5 (0)			9	54
Claremont Graduate School	72 (1.10)	68 (1.58)	60.5 (0)	62.5 (2)	71 (1.11)	67 (1.25)	60 (57)	64.5 (0)	48 (2.08)	49 (2.07)	3	40

Sources: 1. National Survey of Graduate Faculty
2. Associations and Organizations Administrating Prestigious Awards and Honors
3. 1982 Survey of Graduate Faculty
4. Institutional Coordinator Data

Note: *a*. Program in History and Philosophy of Science

Appendix Table P - 34 Relative Rankings for Research-Doctorate Programs in Physics

Institution	93Q [1]	93E [1]	% D [1]	% D-S [1]	93Q T [1]	93E T [1]	VIS [1]	TC [2]	C/F [2]	82Q [3]	82E [3]	TF [4]	TG [4]
Harvard University	1 (4.91)	1 (4.71)	1 (85)	1.5 (96)	2 (4.91)	1 (4.82)	1.5 (97)	5 (5463)	2 (170.7)	1 (4.93)	2 (4.62)	32	149
Princeton University	2 (4.89)	2 (4.69)	2 (84)	4 (95)	1 (4.92)	2 (4.69)	4.5 (96)	7 (5170)	6 (110.0)	3 (4.88)	3 (4.60)	47	110
Massachusetts Inst of Technology	3.5 (4.87)	3 (4.64)	3.5 (81)	4 (95)	3 (4.88)	3 (4.68)	4.5 (96)	1 (10057)	4 (121.2)	5 (4.84)	5.5 (4.45)	83	315
University of California-Berkeley	3.5 (4.87)	7 (4.49)	3.5 (81)	4 (95)	4 (4.87)	7 (4.41)	4.5 (96)	4 (5676)	12 (84.7)	4 (4.86)	7 (4.42)	67	283
California Institute Technology	5 (4.81)	4 (4.61)	5 (77)	1.5 (96)	5 (4.84)	4.5 (4.66)	1.5 (97)	10 (4526)	5 (116.1)	2 (4.91)	5.5 (4.45)	39	154
Cornell University	6 (4.75)	6 (4.54)	6 (68)	7.5 (91)	7 (4.77)	6 (4.58)	10.5 (94)	15 (3759)	25 (69.6)	6 (4.65)	1 (4.70)	54	182
University of Chicago	7 (4.69)	5 (4.55)	7 (67)	6 (92)	6 (4.78)	4.5 (4.66)	4.5 (96)	17 (3368)	13 (84.2)	7 (4.63)	8 (4.37)	40	154
U of Illinois at Urbana-Champaign	8 (4.66)	8 (4.39)	8 (60)	7.5 (91)	8 (4.61)	9 (4.25)	10.5 (94)	2 (8443)	11 (86.2)	10 (4.32)	9 (4.12)	98	295
Stanford University	9 (4.53)	9 (4.35)	9 (51)	9 (88)	9 (4.56)	8 (4.39)	12 (93)	41 (1844)	22 (73.8)	8 (4.59)	4 (4.50)	25	135
Univ of California-Santa Barbara	10 (4.43)	11.5 (3.91)	10 (45)	12 (83)	10 (4.41)	12 (3.84)	15 (91)	3 (8015)	1 (178.1)	19 (3.77)	20 (3.42)	45	117
University of Texas at Austin	11 (4.33)	14 (3.84)	11 (39)	10 (86)	11 (4.37)	16.5 (3.73)	8 (95)	8 (5132)	34 (60.4)	16 (3.87)	26.5 (3.22)	85	239
Columbia University	12 (4.25)	13 (3.87)	12 (36)	17 (75)	12 (4.25)	11 (3.94)	15 (91)	31 (2334)	27 (68.6)	9 (4.49)	11 (3.83)	34	97
Yale University	13 (4.21)	10 (4.03)	13 (30)	14 (78)	13 (4.20)	10 (3.96)	17 (90)	14 (3849)	31 (63.1)	11 (4.15)	10 (3.98)	61	99
University of Washington	14 (4.20)	16.5 (3.81)	15.5 (22)	13 (81)	14 (4.19)	13 (3.82)	18 (89)	20 (2917)	33 (60.8)	17 (3.86)	16.5 (3.57)	48	178
Univ of California-Los Angeles	15 (4.18)	18.5 (3.77)	14 (29)	11 (84)	17 (4.09)	21 (3.67)	8 (95)	9 (4753)	23 (70.9)	18 (3.83)	15 (3.60)	67	163
Univ of California-San Diego	16 (4.10)	15 (3.82)	17.5 (19)	18 (74)	15 (4.12)	15 (3.74)	22.5 (86)	6 (5379)	10 (88.2)	13 (4.11)	14 (3.63)	61	155
University of Pennsylvania	17 (4.09)	18.5 (3.77)	15.5 (22)	15.5 (77)	16 (4.10)	18.5 (3.71)	13 (92)	18 (3045)	28 (66.2)	14 (4.04)	12 (3.77)	46	140
University of Maryland College Park	18 (4.02)	23 (3.66)	17.5 (19)	15.5 (77)	19 (3.88)	26.5 (3.53)	8 (95)	12 (4397)	44 (50.0)	21 (3.73)	19 (3.50)	88	204
University of Michigan	19 (3.96)	20 (3.74)	20.5 (12)	19 (69)	18 (3.91)	16.5 (3.73)	21 (87)	32 (2279)	68 (37.4)	22 (3.66)	16.5 (3.57)	61	157
Rutgers State Univ-New Brunswick	20 (3.82)	39 (3.33)	19 (14)	21.5 (61)	20 (3.84)	43 (3.29)	19.5 (88)	13 (4116)	24 (69.8)	33 (3.10)	26.5 (3.22)	59	100
University of Wisconsin-Madison	21 (3.79)	16.5 (3.81)	20.5 (12)	23.5 (57)	22.5 (3.78)	14 (3.78)	22.5 (86)	29 (2440)	45 (49.8)	20 (3.77)	18 (3.55)	49	190
State U of New York-Stony Brook	22.5 (3.76)	21 (3.71)	24.5 (6)	20 (64)	22.5 (3.78)	20 (3.70)	15 (91)	27 (2540)	29 (65.1)	12 (4.11)	13 (3.72)	39	204
University of Minnesota	22.5 (3.76)	27.5 (3.54)	26.5 (5)	21.5 (61)	21 (3.80)	26.5 (3.53)	19.5 (88)	11 (4453)	7 (92.8)	23 (3.53)	23 (3.33)	48	142
Ohio State University	24 (3.75)	22 (3.70)	23 (7)	23.5 (57)	24 (3.76)	22 (3.61)	26.5 (83)	21 (2871)	35 (57.4)	39 (2.99)	47 (3.00)	50	164
University of Rochester [a]	25 (3.65)	11.5 (3.91)	40.5 (2)	41.5 (27)	25 (3.59)	23.5 (3.57)	87.5 (46)	50 (1493)	15 (82.9)			18	85
Brown University	26.5 (3.60)	25 (3.64)	26.5 (5)	26 (48)	27.5 (3.54)	18.5 (3.71)	28.5 (82)	57 (1328)	48.5 (47.4)	26 (3.49)	24 (3.27)	28	80
University of Rochester	26.5 (3.60)	26 (3.63)	28.5 (4)	25 (49)	26 (3.58)	23.5 (3.57)	24.5 (85)	39 (1913)	38.5 (54.7)	25 (3.49)	21 (3.38)	35	131
Carnegie Mellon University	28 (3.56)	36.5 (3.35)	28.5 (4)	27 (46)	27.5 (3.54)	37.5 (3.33)	30.5 (81)	62 (1186)	71.5 (35.9)	24 (3.52)	22 (3.37)	33	61
Johns Hopkins University	29 (3.51)	24 (3.65)	24.5 (6)	31.5 (37)	31 (3.45)	25 (3.54)	44.5 (75)	22 (2852)	8 (89.1)	34 (3.10)	25 (3.23)	32	104
Rockefeller University	30 (3.46)	102.5 (2.50)	22 (9)	41.5 (27)	29 (3.47)	77.5 (2.78)	64.5 (60)	135 (154)	85.5 (30.8)	15 (3.91)	37.5 (3.15)	5	135

Appendix Table P - 34 Physics (Continued)

Institution	93Q [1]	93E [1]	% D [1]	% D-S [1]	93Q T [1]	93E T [1]	VIS [1]	TC [2]	C/F [2]	82Q [3]	82E [3]	TF [4]	TG [4]
Purdue University	31 (3.44)	29 (3.50)	110.5 (0)	28.5 (39)	32 (3.44)	31 (3.44)	28.5 (82)	24 (2664)	46 (48.4)			55	152
Michigan State University	32 (3.43)	35 (3.37)	60 (1)	31.5 (37)	30 (3.46)	32 (3.43)	37.5 (78)	26 (2559)	52 (46.5)	27 (3.22)	28.5 (3.18)	55	141
University of California-Irvine	33.5 (3.37)	27.5 (3.54)	32 (3)	34 (33)	38 (3.26)	28 (3.46)	35 (79)	73 (942)	100 (27.7)	38 (3.01)	43 (3.10)	34	81
Indiana University	33.5 (3.37)	39 (3.33)	40.5 (2)	30 (38)	35 (3.33)	50 (3.20)	41.5 (76)	35 (2051)	57.5 (43.6)	32 (3.13)	40 (3.13)	47	95
CUNY - Grad Sch & Univ Center	35 (3.36)	46.5 (3.27)	32 (3)	28.5 (39)	43 (3.18)	58 (3.13)	39.5 (77)	34 (2102)	67 (37.5)	31 (3.15)	45.5 (3.03)	56	136
University of Florida	36 (3.35)	50.5 (3.25)	40.5 (2)	35 (32)	35 (3.33)	38 (3.33)	30.5 (81)	51 (1461)	80 (34.0)	55 (2.57)	55 (2.82)	43	80
Northwestern University	37 (3.31)	30 (3.47)	40.5 (2)	33 (36)	40 (3.24)	34 (3.39)	26.5 (83)	25 (2654)	9 (88.5)	37 (3.02)	32.5 (3.17)	30	109
University of Colorado	38 (3.30)	33 (3.41)	60 (1)	38 (29)	42 (3.19)	31 (3.44)	35 (79)	38 (1922)	51 (46.9)	35 (3.06)	37.5 (3.15)	41	147
Boston University	39 (3.28)	43 (3.29)	40.5 (2)	36.5 (31)	37 (3.28)	49 (3.21)	35 (79)	23 (2694)	21 (77.0)	69.5 (2.33)	77 (2.45)	35	100
University of Pittsburgh	40 (3.27)	43 (3.29)	60 (1)	50 (21)	39 (3.25)	45 (3.26)	50.5 (71)	64 (1158)	82 (31.3)	30 (3.15)	37.5 (3.15)	37	92
Duke University	42.5 (3.25)	31 (3.45)	32 (3)	41.5 (27)	44 (3.17)	34 (3.39)	41.5 (76)	76 (857)	102 (26.8)	40 (2.97)	41.5 (3.12)	32	71
Florida State University	42.5 (3.25)	53.5 (3.23)	40.5 (2)	39 (28)	51 (3.09)	69 (2.98)	47 (74)	48 (1514)	79 (34.4)	41 (2.97)	50 (2.97)	44	102
Rice University	42.5 (3.25)	36.5 (3.35)	40.5 (2)	41.5 (27)	37 (3.28)	41 (3.31)	44.5 (75)	43 (1775)	19.5 (77.2)	46 (2.89)	32.5 (3.17)	23	58
Brandeis University	42.5 (3.25)	55 (3.21)	60 (1)	44.5 (25)	41 (3.20)	58 (3.13)	54 (69)	45 (1667)	14 (83.4)	29 (3.15)	32.5 (3.17)	20	36
University of Arizona	45.5 (3.23)	34 (3.39)	40.5 (2)	44.5 (25)	46 (3.13)	38 (3.33)	24.5 (85)	16 (3369)	16 (80.2)	36 (3.03)	45.5 (3.03)	42	118
University of Virginia	45.5 (3.23)	53.5 (3.23)	60 (1)	36.5 (31)	46 (3.13)	52 (3.18)	32.5 (80)	63 (1160)	97 (28.3)	43 (2.93)	41.5 (3.12)	41	72
Texas A&M University	47.5 (3.22)	43 (3.29)	60 (1)	46.5 (23)	48 (3.11)	47 (3.24)	37.5 (78)	37 (1964)	57.5 (43.6)	54 (2.61)	66.5 (2.62)	45	111
Univ of California-Santa Cruz	47.5 (3.22)	39 (3.33)	110.5 (0)	46.5 (23)	33 (3.36)	38 (3.33)	61 (63)	56 (1414)	18 (78.6)	67 (2.36)	70.5 (2.58)	18	52
Iowa State University	49.5 (3.17)	32 (3.42)	32 (3)	52 (20)	64 (2.89)	54 (3.17)	57.5 (65)	19 (2935)	19.5 (77.2)	45 (2.91)	50 (2.97)	38	90
University of Southern California	49.5 (3.17)	73.5 (3.00)	60 (1)	50 (21)	47 (3.12)	72 (2.94)	55.5 (67)	28 (2534)	17 (79.2)	52 (2.70)	53.5 (2.85)	32	62
North Carolina State University	51 (3.16)	56 (3.20)	60 (1)	48 (22)	52 (3.07)	55 (3.16)	55.5 (67)	30 (2335)	32 (61.4)	75 (2.18)	82 (2.37)	38	65
Washington University	52 (3.15)	41 (3.31)	110.5 (0)	58 (15)	54 (3.05)	38 (3.33)	52.5 (70)	61 (1205)	66 (38.9)	50 (2.76)	48 (2.98)	31	73
New York University	53.5 (3.14)	57 (3.15)	110.5 (0)	50 (21)	50 (3.10)	49 (3.21)	32.5 (80)	69 (1007)	77 (34.7)	28 (3.15)	32.5 (3.17)	29	34
U of North Carolina-Chapel Hill	53.5 (3.14)	46.5 (3.27)	110.5 (0)	53.5 (19)	50 (3.10)	42 (3.30)	52.5 (70)	96 (567)	115 (20.3)	42 (2.96)	32.5 (3.17)	28	55
Pennsylvania State University	55 (3.08)	65 (3.08)	110.5 (0)	55 (18)	54 (3.05)	63 (3.08)	48.5 (72)	70 (993)	83 (31.0)	59 (2.49)	52 (2.93)	32	67
University of Notre Dame	56 (3.06)	46.5 (3.27)	60 (1)	53.5 (19)	56 (3.00)	54 (3.17)	39.5 (77)	44 (1725)	47 (47.9)	65 (2.38)	70.5 (2.58)	36	89
Syracuse University	58 (3.04)	50.5 (3.25)	60 (1)	58 (15)	57 (2.96)	45 (3.26)	48.5 (72)	52 (1456)	37 (56.0)	47 (2.89)	37.5 (3.15)	26	70
Vanderbilt University	58 (3.04)	58 (3.14)	60 (1)	58 (15)	63 (2.90)	64 (3.07)	76.5 (54)	104 (458)	121 (18.3)	73 (2.27)	59 (2.68)	25	52
University of Utah	58 (3.04)	69 (3.02)	110.5 (0)	61.5 (14)	63 (2.90)	71 (2.96)	72.5 (56)	47 (1633)	40 (54.4)	66 (2.37)	63 (2.63)	30	47
University of Oregon	60 (3.03)	52 (3.24)	60 (1)	61.5 (14)	61 (2.92)	46 (3.25)	44.5 (75)	36 (2011)	30 (64.9)	49 (2.78)	57 (2.73)	31	125

Institution	93Q [1]	93E [1]	% D [1]	% D-S [1]	93Q T [1]	93E T [1]	VIS [1]	TC [2]	C/F [2]	82Q [3]	82E [3]	TF [4]	TG [4]
University of Houston	**61.5** (3.02)	**87.5** (2.78)	**40.5** (2)	**61.5** (14)	**66** (2.88)	**87** (2.59)	**61** (63)	**74** (922)	**87** (30.7)	**78** (2.14)	**89** (2.13)	30	74
Georgia Institute of Technology	**61.5** (3.02)	**64** (3.09)	**110.5** (0)	**65.5** (13)	**66** (2.88)	**63** (3.08)	**74.5** (55)	**42** (1792)	**26** (68.9)	**71** (2.33)	**73** (2.55)	26	90
College of William & Mary	**63** (3.00)	**62.5** (3.11)	**110.5** (0)	**65.5** (13)	**60** (2.93)	**66** (3.04)	**69** (58)	**66** (1111)	**92** (29.2)	**68** (2.35)	**63** (2.63)	38	63
U of Massachusetts at Amherst	**64** (2.97)	**61** (3.12)	**110.5** (0)	**61.5** (14)	**55** (3.02)	**58** (3.13)	**50.5** (71)	**75** (860)	**105** (26.1)	**53** (2.65)	**53.5** (2.85)	33	75
Case Western Reserve Univ	**65** (2.96)	**67** (3.04)	**60** (1)	**56** (16)	**72** (2.74)	**69** (2.98)	**57.5** (65)	**65** (1134)	**41** (54.0)	**44** (2.91)	**44** (3.05)	21	31
Northeastern University	**66** (2.91)	**71** (3.01)	**110.5** (0)	**65.5** (13)	**69** (2.77)	**73** (2.86)	**59** (64)	**55** (1422)	**53** (45.9)	**51** (2.71)	**56** (2.78)	31	85
University of California-Davis	**67** (2.89)	**71** (3.01)	**110.5** (0)	**65.5** (13)	**68** (2.85)	**76** (2.81)	**44.5** (75)	**59** (1257)	**63** (40.5)	**60** (2.49)	**59** (2.68)	31	86
Rensselaer Polytechnic Inst	**68.5** (2.88)	**62.5** (3.11)	**110.5** (0)	**72.5** (9)	**58** (2.94)	**66** (3.04)	**61** (63)	**85** (783)	**94** (29.0)	**61** (2.48)	**28.5** (3.18)	27	18
Univ of California-Riverside	**68.5** (2.88)	**59.5** (3.13)	**110.5** (0)	**72.5** (9)	**67** (2.87)	**58** (3.13)	**64.5** (60)	**114** (341)	**140** (10.7)	**64** (2.40)	**68.5** (2.60)	32	50
Arizona State University	**70** (2.87)	**46.5** (3.27)	**40.5** (2)	**68** (12)	**73** (2.73)	**58** (3.13)	**69** (58)	**40** (1849)	**48.5** (47.4)	**98** (1.72)	**94** (2.00)	39	85
Virginia Polytech Inst & State U	**71** (2.86)	**71** (3.01)	**110.5** (0)	**86** (5)	**60** (2.93)	**61** (3.10)	**66** (59)	**92** (629)	**122** (18.0)	**48** (2.86)	**63** (2.63)	35	44
University of Tennessee-Knoxville	**72** (2.83)	**87.5** (2.78)	**40.5** (2)	**71** (10)	**76** (2.68)	**89** (2.56)	**72.5** (56)	**58** (1272)	**74** (35.3)	**56** (2.53)	**63** (2.63)	36	66
University of Iowa	**73** (2.79)	**66** (3.07)	**32** (3)	**69.5** (11)	**71** (2.75)	**69** (2.98)	**69** (58)	**60** (1243)	**55** (44.4)	**57** (2.52)	**50** (2.97)	28	71
University of Delaware	**74** (2.76)	**83.5** (2.86)	**110.5** (0)	**74.5** (8)	**74** (2.72)	**88** (2.58)	**69** (58)	**54** (1425)	**81** (33.1)	**81** (2.03)	**85** (2.18)	43	54
University of Georgia	**75** (2.73)	**81** (2.90)	**110.5** (0)	**106.5** (3)	**78** (2.67)	**79** (2.74)	**95** (43)	**87** (724)	**94** (29.0)			25	24
Oregon State University	**76** (2.69)	**92** (2.71)	**110.5** (0)	**86** (5)	**78** (2.67)	**95** (2.38)	**98** (41)	**121** (267)	**135** (14.1)	**93** (1.81)	**96** (1.97)	19	56
Tufts University	**77** (2.66)	**78.5** (2.92)	**60** (1)	**77.5** (7)	**80** (2.57)	**69** (2.98)	**80.5** (52)	**83** (785)	**65** (39.3)	**77** (2.16)	**72** (2.57)	20	55
Kent State University	**78** (2.65)	**68** (3.03)	**110.5** (0)	**81.5** (6)	**75** (2.70)	**52** (3.18)	**87.5** (46)	**95** (573)	**73** (35.8)	**97** (1.74)	**91** (2.07)	16	73
Louisiana State U & A&M College	**79.5** (2.64)	**78.5** (2.92)	**110.5** (0)	**86** (5)	**91** (2.35)	**74** (2.83)	**76.5** (54)	**49** (1503)	**50** (47.0)	**58** (2.52)	**84** (2.30)	32	65
University of Nebraska-Lincoln	**79.5** (2.64)	**75** (2.96)	**110.5** (0)	**95** (4)	**84** (2.50)	**78** (2.78)	**82** (49)	**80** (812)	**94** (29.0)	**62** (2.42)	**66.5** (2.62)	28	35
Drexel University	**81** (2.62)	**76** (2.94)	**110.5** (0)	**86** (5)	**86** (2.46)	**82** (2.71)	**84** (47)	**67** (1059)	**60** (42.4)	**92** (1.81)	**87.5** (2.15)	25	29
University of Hawaii at Manoa	**82** (2.61)	**111** (2.29)	**110.5** (0)	**95** (4)	**70** (2.76)	**96** (2.31)	**101.5** (40)	**98** (535)	**98** (28.2)			19	25
Dartmouth College	**83.5** (2.60)	**49** (3.26)	**110.5** (0)	**81.5** (6)	**79** (2.63)	**29** (3.45)	**101.5** (40)	**82** (786)	**61** (41.4)	**74** (2.21)	**32.5** (3.17)	19	35
Ohio University	**83.5** (2.60)	**82** (2.88)	**110.5** (0)	**95** (4)	**85** (2.47)	**85** (2.67)	**107** (38)	**109** (415)	**119** (19.8)	**82** (2.02)	**63** (2.63)	21	50
University of South Carolina	**85.5** (2.58)	**93** (2.69)	**60** (1)	**74.5** (8)	**81** (2.55)	**82** (2.71)	**63** (61)	**88** (706)	**91** (29.4)	**101.5** (1.67)	**101** (1.80)	24	31
State Univ of New York-Albany	**85.5** (2.58)	**91** (2.73)	**110.5** (0)	**128** (1)	**82** (2.54)	**100** (2.22)	**121** (34)	**106** (439)	**101** (27.4)	**94** (1.80)	**93** (2.02)	16	52
Illinois Institute of Technology	**87.5** (2.56)	**104** (2.47)	**40.5** (2)	**77.5** (7)	**83** (2.53)	**93** (2.45)	**74.5** (55)	**131** (203)	**130** (15.6)	**99** (1.70)	**100** (1.83)	13	32
University of Illinois at Chicago	**87.5** (2.56)	**100.5** (2.53)	**60** (1)	**69.5** (11)	**95** (2.31)	**100** (2.22)	**80.5** (52)	**53** (1451)	**42** (53.7)	**79** (2.10)	**81** (2.38)	27	71
University of Alaska	**89** (2.50)	**112.5** (2.22)	**60** (1)	**95** (4)	**89** (2.40)	(n/s)	**145** (16)	**93** (620)	**106** (25.8)			24	43
University of Wisconsin-Milwaukee	**90** (2.49)	**90** (2.74)	**60** (1)	**77.5** (7)	**90** (2.38)	**98** (2.29)	**110** (37)	**71** (985)	**38.5** (54.7)	**90** (1.83)	**87.5** (2.15)	18	22

Appendix Table P - 34 Physics (Continued)

Institution	93Q [1]	93E [1]	% D [1]	% D-S [1]	93Q T [1]	93E T [1]	VIS [1]	TC [2]	C/F [2]	82Q [3]	82E [3]	TF [4]	TG [4]
University of Kentucky	91.5 (2.48)	78.5 (2.92)	110.5 (0)	86 (5)	87 (2.44)	75 (2.82)	69 (58)	90 (655)	111 (21.1)	95 (1.77)	97 (1.95)	31	74
University of Texas at Dallas	91.5 (2.48)	73.5 (3.00)	110.5 (0)	117 (2)	104 (2.13)	91 (2.50)	110 (37)	99 (523)	85.5 (30.8)	88 (1.93)	99 (1.85)	17	79
University of Kansas	93 (2.46)	94 (2.68)	110.5 (0)	106.5 (3)	89 (2.40)	86 (2.62)	84 (47)	72 (984)	62 (41.0)	76 (2.16)	77 (2.45)	24	39
Temple University	94 (2.43)	97 (2.59)	110.5 (0)	95 (4)	97 (2.28)	94 (2.41)	107 (38)	116 (335)	123.5 (17.6)	72 (2.29)	77 (2.45)	19	40
University of Oklahoma	95 (2.42)	100.5 (2.53)	110.5 (0)	117 (2)	93 (2.33)	102 (2.18)	91.5 (44)	111 (387)	133 (14.3)	80 (2.07)	83 (2.32)	27	50
University of New Hampshire	96 (2.41)	99 (2.56)	60 (1)	95 (4)	93 (2.33)	104 (2.14)	97 (42)	77 (843)	99 (28.1)	101.5 (1.67)		30	31
University of Akron	97 (2.40)	59.5 (3.13)	110.5 (0)	117 (2)	101 (2.20)	38 (3.33)	138 (24)	81 (795)	56 (44.2)			18	209
Lehigh University	98 (2.39)	89 (2.75)	110.5 (0)	128 (1)	93 (2.33)	80 (2.73)	95 (43)	108 (429)	120 (19.5)			22	58
University of Missouri-Columbia	99 (2.38)	86 (2.80)	110.5 (0)	95 (4)	100 (2.24)	91 (2.50)	95 (43)	78 (840)	64 (40.0)	84.5 (2.00)	86 (2.17)	21	38
Catholic University of America	101.5 (2.33)	109 (2.33)	60 (1)	81.5 (6)	103 (2.14)	115 (1.67)	110 (37)	130 (208)	125 (17.3)	87 (1.96)	74.5 (2.47)	12	49
University of Connecticut	101.5 (2.33)	114 (2.18)	110.5 (0)	95 (4)	96 (2.29)	106 (1.93)	78.5 (53)	84 (784)	88 (30.2)	69.5 (2.33)	68.5 (2.60)	26	58
Kansas State University	101.5 (2.33)	83.5 (2.86)	110.5 (0)	95 (4)	108 (2.10)	82 (2.71)	87.5 (46)	68 (1043)	59 (43.5)	84.5 (2.00)	92 (2.03)	24	35
University of Cincinnati	101.5 (2.33)	102.5 (2.50)	110.5 (0)	95 (4)	102 (2.18)	102 (2.18)	78.5 (53)	124 (242)	134 (14.2)	84.5 (2.00)	79 (2.43)	17	43
Colorado State University	104.5 (2.30)	108 (2.35)	60 (1)	95 (4)	106 (2.12)	102 (2.18)	91.5 (44)	127 (220)	129 (15.7)	103 (1.65)	80 (2.42)	14	46
University of North Texas	104.5 (2.30)	85 (2.83)	110.5 (0)	106.5 (3)	115 (2.00)	91 (2.50)	134 (27)	110 (401)	117 (20.1)	106 (1.27)	110 (1.12)	20	46
Montana State University	106 (2.27)	95.5 (2.62)	60 (1)	106.5 (3)	115 (2.00)	115 (1.67)	91.5 (44)	102 (490)	76 (35.0)	96 (1.76)	90 (2.08)	14	57
Colorado School of Mines	107 (2.25)	105 (2.45)	110.5 (0)	77.5 (7)	123 (1.77)	108 (1.88)	105 (39)	100 (504)	69.5 (36.0)			14	17
State Univ of New York-Buffalo	108 (2.24)	110 (2.30)	60 (1)	106.5 (3)	100 (2.24)	105 (2.00)	87.5 (46)	89 (685)	54 (45.7)	100 (1.68)	103 (1.72)	15	98
Stevens Inst of Technology	109 (2.23)	117 (1.95)	110.5 (0)	117 (2)	98 (2.25)	115 (1.67)	114.5 (36)	122.5 (264)	136 (13.9)	63 (2.41)	74.5 (2.47)	19	61
Brigham Young University	110 (2.21)	78.5 (2.92)	110.5 (0)	106.5 (3)	106 (2.12)	85 (2.67)	121 (34)	46 (1661)	36 (57.3)			29	24
New Mexico State University	111 (2.19)	112.5 (2.22)	110.5 (0)	128 (1)	115 (2.00)	134 (0.83)	129 (29)	122.5 (264)	123.5 (17.6)			15	50
University of Maine	112 (2.18)	107 (2.38)	60 (1)	117 (2)	119 (1.86)	115 (1.67)	136.5 (26)	137 (142)	142 (9.5)			15	22
Clarkson University	113.5 (2.13)	120 (1.85)	110.5 (0)	81.5 (6)	127 (1.63)	122 (1.46)	101.5 (40)	94 (581)	43 (52.8)	112 (1.03)	107 (1.32)	11	14
University of Alabama-Huntsville	113.5 (2.13)	118.5 (1.92)	110.5 (0)	140.5 (0)	110 (2.06)	115 (1.67)	136.5 (26)	86 (740)	75 (35.2)			21	35
Tulane University	115.5 (2.12)	131 (1.53)	110.5 (0)	106.5 (3)	111 (2.05)	126 (1.19)	91.5 (44)	119 (294)	107 (24.5)	108 (1.20)	109 (1.15)	12	18
Univ of Arkansas-Fayetteville	115.5 (2.12)	98 (2.57)	110.5 (0)	128 (1)	121 (1.83)	115 (1.67)	125.5 (32)	33 (2197)	3 (146.5)			15	24
University of Texas at Arlington	117 (2.11)	118.5 (1.92)	110.5 (0)	117 (2)	118 (1.88)	125 (1.25)	114.5 (36)	105 (448)	89 (29.9)			15	22
Washington State University	118.5 (2.10)	124 (1.80)	60 (1)	95 (4)	126 (1.67)	132 (1.00)	127.5 (31)	113 (354)	126 (16.9)	107 (1.24)	102 (1.77)	21	56
Texas Tech University	118.5 (2.10)	95.5 (2.62)	110.5 (0)	140.5 (0)	115 (2.00)	98 (2.29)	101.5 (40)	91 (633)	108 (24.3)			26	39
University of Alabama	120 (2.08)	123 (1.82)	110.5 (0)	117 (2)	115 (2.00)	132 (1.00)	114.5 (36)	101 (501)	114 (20.9)			24	25

Institution	93Q [1]	93E [1]	% D [1]	% D-S [1]	93Q T [1]	93E T [1]	VIS [1]	TC [2]	C/F [2]	82Q [3]	82E [3]	TF [4]	TG [4]
Oklahoma State University	**121** (2.07)	**125** (1.78)	**110.5** (0)	**128** (1)	**110** (2.06)	**123** (1.30)	**114.5** (36)	**118** (301)	**117** (20.1)	**91** (1.82)	**95** (1.98)	15	62
University of Miami	**122** (2.03)	**121.5** (1.83)	**110.5** (0)	**117** (2)	**107** (2.11)	**115** (1.67)	**118.5** (35)	**126** (221)	**117** (20.1)			11	16
American University	**123.5** (2.00)	**135** (1.45)	**110.5** (0)	**95** (4)	**115** (2.00)	**121** (1.52)	**121** (34)	**112** (379)	**78** (34.5)	**105** (1.34)	**104** (1.60)	11	28
University of Missouri-Rolla	**123.5** (2.00)	**115** (2.17)	**110.5** (0)	**117** (2)	**128** (1.56)	**115** (1.67)	**123.5** (33)	**97** (544)	**96** (28.6)	**84.5** (2.00)	**59** (2.68)	19	24
University of Mass-Lowell	**125** (1.92)	**106** (2.41)	**110.5** (0)	**140.5** (0)	**120** (1.85)	**115** (1.67)	**123.5** (33)	**144** (87)	**144** (4.0)			22	89
Polytechnic University	**126** (1.91)	**116** (1.97)	**110.5** (0)	**128** (1)	**124** (1.75)	**115** (1.67)	**107** (38)	**138** (141)	**138** (11.8)	**89** (1.91)	**98** (1.93)	12	25
University of Alabama-Birmingham	**127** (1.90)	**139** (1.11)	**110.5** (0)	**140.5** (0)	**137** (1.29)	**141** (0.00)	**134** (27)	**103** (480)	**109** (24.0)			20	26
Auburn University	**128** (1.88)	**132** (1.48)	**110.5** (0)	**117** (2)	**130** (1.54)	**128** (1.11)	**127.5** (31)	**117** (330)	**110** (22.0)	**109** (1.19)	**106** (1.45)	15	43
University of Rhode Island	**129** (1.85)	**140** (1.06)	**110.5** (0)	**117** (2)	**132** (1.45)	**139** (0.42)	**131** (28)	**136** (145)	**132** (14.5)			10	31
Clark University	**130** (1.82)	**128** (1.67)	**110.5** (0)	**140.5** (0)	**122** (1.79)	**130** (1.04)	**101.5** (40)	**143** (97)	**137** (12.1)			8	16
Boston College	**131** (1.80)	**121.5** (1.83)	**60** (1)	**106.5** (3)	**130** (1.54)	**115** (1.67)	**84** (47)	**129** (210)	**112.5** (21.0)	**110** (1.16)	**111** (1.03)	10	28
Old Dominion University	**132** (1.70)	**142** (0.94)	**110.5** (0)	**140.5** (0)	**125** (1.72)	**134** (0.83)	**118.5** (35)	**146** (44)	**147** (2.3)			19	46
University of Denver	**133** (1.61)	**128** (1.67)	**110.5** (0)	**140.5** (0)	**137** (1.29)	**138** (0.56)	**134** (27)	**107** (431)	**71.5** (35.9)	**104** (1.64)	**108** (1.27)	12	13
Oakland University	**134.5** (1.60)	(n/s)	**60** (1)	**128** (1)	**134** (1.33)	(n/s)	**147** (11)	**79** (828)	**69.5** (36.0)			23	17
Howard University	**134.5** (1.60)	**128** (1.67)	**110.5** (0)	**128** (1)	**137** (1.29)	**128** (1.11)	**131** (28)	**128** (216)	**128** (16.6)	**111** (1.11)	**105** (1.58)	13	18
New Mexico Inst of Mining & Tech	**136** (1.57)	**138** (1.19)	**110.5** (0)	**140.5** (0)	**143** (1.00)	**141** (0.00)	**141** (22)	**132** (198)	**131** (15.2)			13	11
Bryn Mawr College	**137.5** (1.48)	**126** (1.77)	**110.5** (0)	**106.5** (3)	**140** (1.27)	**107** (1.91)	**114.5** (36)	**140** (118)	**90** (29.5)			4	8
Worcester Polytechnic Inst	**137.5** (1.48)	**133.5** (1.46)	**110.5** (0)	**106.5** (3)	**140** (1.27)	**134** (0.83)	**114.5** (36)	**115** (340)	**84** (30.9)			11	13
Michigan Technological University	**139** (1.47)	**136** (1.43)	**110.5** (0)	**140.5** (0)	**134** (1.33)	**115** (1.67)	**141** (22)	**139** (135)	**139** (11.3)			12	23
George Washington University	**140** (1.45)	**137** (1.21)	**110.5** (0)	**128** (1)	**131** (1.48)	**128** (1.11)	**101.5** (40)	**125** (237)	**104** (26.3)			9	20
University of Mississippi	**141** (1.42)	**130** (1.62)	**110.5** (0)	**140.5** (0)	**135** (1.31)	**125** (1.25)	**125.5** (32)	**141** (114)	**143** (8.8)			13	26
University of Nevada, Reno	**142** (1.31)	**143** (0.83)	**110.5** (0)	**140.5** (0)	**141** (1.14)	**138** (0.56)	**139** (23)	**145** (56)	**145.5** (3.3)	**113** (0.91)		17	28
Oregon Graduate Inst Sci & Tech	**143** (1.27)	**141** (1.00)	**110.5** (0)	**128** (1)	**147** (0.00)	(n/s)	**144** (20)	**134** (184)	**127** (16.7)			11	15
Univ of Puerto Rico-Rio Piedras	**144** (1.22)	**145** (0.67)	**110.5** (0)	**140.5** (0)	**144** (0.75)	(n/s)	**146** (15)	**120** (273)	**112.5** (21.0)			13	13
Baylor University	**145** (1.13)	**133.5** (1.46)	**110.5** (0)	**128** (1)	**143** (1.00)	(n/s)	**141** (22)	**142** (99)	**141** (9.9)			10	21
Texas Christian University	**146** (0.67)	**144** (0.72)	**110.5** (0)	**140.5** (0)	**146** (0.43)	**136** (0.67)	**131** (28)	**133** (187)	**103** (26.7)			7	14
Florida Institute of Technology	**147** (0.46)	**146** (0.28)	**110.5** (0)	**140.5** (0)	**145** (0.50)	**141** (0.00)	**143** (21)	**147** (33)	**145.5** (3.3)			10	3

Sources: 1. National Survey of Graduate Faculty
2. Institute for Scientific Information
3. 1982 Survey of Graduate Faculty
4. Institutional Coordinator Data

Note: a. Program in Optics

n/s After trimming no cases remained

Appendix Table P - 35 Relative Rankings for Research-Doctorate Programs in Physiology

Institution	93Q [1]	93E [1]	% D [1]	% D-S [1]	93Q T [1]	93E T [1]	VIS [1]	TC [2]	C/F [2]	82Q [3]	82E [3]	TF [4]	TG [4]
Yale University	1 (4.48)	1 (4.38)	2 (46)	2 (77)	1 (4.71)	1 (4.63)	2 (86)	12 (3240)	13 (115.7)	2 (4.34)	2 (4.15)	28	24
Univ of California-San Diego	2 (4.47)	2 (4.25)	1 (48)	1 (81)	2 (4.48)	3 (4.19)	1 (90)	2 (9831)	8 (178.7)			55	12
University of Pennsylvania	3 (4.27)	7 (3.95)	3 (34)	4 (68)	3.5 (4.43)	7 (4.08)	3 (83)	6 (4629)	10 (128.6)	4 (4.30)	5 (4.08)	36	10
Univ of California-Los Angeles	4 (4.23)	5 (4.02)	7 (29)	3 (70)	6.5 (4.31)	5 (4.14)	7 (81)	10 (3603)	24 (87.9)	5 (4.25)	7 (3.90)	41	36
Univ of California-San Francisco	5.5 (4.21)	6 (4.00)	4 (31)	6 (65)	6.5 (4.31)	4 (4.17)	5 (82)	4 (4963)	2 (248.2)	1 (4.48)	3.5 (4.10)	20	17
Baylor College of Medicine	5.5 (4.21)	10 (3.84)	8.5 (27)	7 (64)	5 (4.37)	14 (3.84)	12.5 (76)	3 (7038)	5 (207.0)			34	20
University of Washington	7.5 (4.20)	4 (4.10)	5.5 (30)	5 (67)	9 (4.24)	6 (4.12)	5 (82)	18 (2697)	22 (93.0)	3 (4.31)	1 (4.25)	29	34
Stanford University	7.5 (4.20)	3 (4.17)	10 (26)	15.5 (50)	3.5 (4.43)	2 (4.35)	28 (65)	23 (2312)	1 (330.3)			7	3
University of Virginia	9.5 (4.19)	11.5 (3.83)	5.5 (30)	8.5 (63)	11 (4.15)	9 (3.91)	9 (78)	17 (2901)	11 (126.1)	12 (3.76)	10.5 (3.78)	23	17
Columbia University	9.5 (4.19)	11.5 (3.83)	8.5 (27)	8.5 (63)	8 (4.28)	11 (3.86)	10.5 (77)	8 (4120)	6 (196.2)	8 (3.96)	17.5 (3.57)	21	18
University of Chicago	11 (4.00)	9 (3.86)	13.5 (15)	11.5 (54)	14 (3.98)	10 (3.87)	21 (70)	20 (2638)	39 (58.6)	16 (3.64)	19.5 (3.53)	45	52
University of Iowa	12 (3.99)	13 (3.81)	12 (17)	11.5 (54)	10 (4.22)	8 (3.97)	18.5 (72)	7 (4122)	7 (179.2)	26 (3.42)	21 (3.52)	23	28
California Institute Technology	13 (3.98)	17.5 (3.70)	11 (18)	31 (34)	12 (4.08)	22 (3.57)	62 (46)	61 (872)	4 (218.0)			4	0
New York University	14 (3.91)	23 (3.64)	15.5 (13)	24 (41)	13 (4.00)	22 (3.57)	30 (63)	1 (20270)	16 (110.8)	32 (3.28)	42.5 (2.95)	183	n/a
University of Michigan	15.5 (3.89)	21 (3.65)	13.5 (15)	10 (57)	17 (3.84)	27 (3.51)	10.5 (77)	13 (3135)	19 (104.5)	7 (4.12)	8 (3.82)	30	24
Vanderbilt University	15.5 (3.89)	14.5 (3.77)	18.5 (11)	27 (36)	15 (3.97)	17 (3.65)	45 (55)	5 (4707)	9 (162.3)	24 (3.48)	27 (3.33)	29	22
Albert Einstein College of Med	17 (3.88)	29.5 (3.57)	15.5 (13)	17 (49)	16 (3.95)	18 (3.64)	18.5 (72)	14 (3036)	28 (82.1)	17 (3.61)	30.5 (3.28)	37	10
Mayo Graduate School	18 (3.87)	19.5 (3.68)	21.5 (10)	14 (51)	21 (3.77)	26 (3.53)	17 (73)	19 (2680)	17 (107.2)	13 (3.74)	22 (3.47)	25	8
Johns Hopkins University	19 (3.86)	14.5 (3.77)	21.5 (10)	23 (43)	18.5 (3.81)	15.5 (3.68)	28 (65)	35 (1538)	31 (69.9)	25 (3.48)	30.5 (3.28)	22	1
U of Illinois at Urbana-Champaign	20.5 (3.81)	8 (3.92)	18.5 (11)	15.5 (50)	22 (3.76)	12.5 (3.85)	12.5 (76)	15 (3032)	37 (59.5)	11 (3.81)	14.5 (3.65)	51	53
University of Alabama-Birmingham	20.5 (3.81)	17.5 (3.70)	18.5 (11)	19 (48)	18.5 (3.81)	15.5 (3.68)	14 (75)	11 (3272)	30 (72.7)	29 (3.35)	27 (3.33)	45	32
Emory University	22 (3.71)	37 (3.49)	26.5 (8)	19 (48)	20 (3.78)	25 (3.54)	15.5 (74)	16 (3003)	35 (62.6)	48 (2.72)	46.5 (2.78)	48	20
U of Tex-Health Sci Ctr-Houston	23.5 (3.69)	29.5 (3.57)	26.5 (8)	22 (45)	23 (3.75)	20 (3.58)	20 (71)	27 (2077)	32 (69.2)	23 (3.50)	25 (3.40)	30	12
University of Arizona	23.5 (3.69)	27.5 (3.60)	26.5 (8)	13 (52)	30.5 (3.54)	29.5 (3.49)	5 (82)	24 (2278)	52 (46.5)	33 (3.28)	30.5 (3.28)	49	26
University of Wisconsin-Madison	25 (3.68)	23 (3.64)	26.5 (8)	25 (39)	28 (3.65)	22 (3.57)	23.5 (68)	9 (3922)	40 (58.5)	38.5 (3.00)	33 (3.27)	67	89
Northwestern University	26.5 (3.67)	26 (3.61)	26.5 (8)	29.5 (35)	26 (3.68)	37.5 (3.42)	34 (61)	47 (1094)	56.5 (45.6)	27 (3.41)	27 (3.33)	24	9
Duke University	26.5 (3.67)	37 (3.49)	30.5 (7)	21 (46)	24 (3.71)	60.5 (3.33)	15.5 (74)	37 (1407)	26 (82.8)	9 (3.94)	6 (3.92)	17	7
University of California-Davis	28 (3.64)	23 (3.64)	18.5 (11)	19 (48)	41 (3.38)	24 (3.56)	8 (80)	25 (2199)	69 (34.4)	14 (3.74)	9 (3.80)	64	48
U of Massachusetts Med Center	29 (3.63)	41 (3.44)	37.5 (4)	27 (36)	25 (3.70)	60.5 (3.33)	42 (56)	22 (2324)	34 (62.8)			37	7
Dartmouth College	30 (3.61)	31.5 (3.56)	30.5 (7)	36.5 (27)	32 (3.50)	60.5 (3.33)	49.5 (52)	45 (1184)	61 (43.9)			27	17

Appendix Table P - 35 Physiology (Continued)

Institution	93Q [1]	93E [1]	% D [1]	% D-S [1]	93Q T [1]	93E T [1]	VIS [1]	TC [2]	C/F [2]	82Q [3]	82E [3]	TF [4]	TG [4]
Cornell University	31 (3.59)	16 (3.76)	23 (9)	29.5 (35)	40 (3.40)	19 (3.63)	23.5 (68)	30 (1890)	44 (54.0)	21 (3.53)	13 (3.67)	35	20
Case Western Reserve Univ	32.5 (3.55)	31.5 (3.56)	26.5 (8)	32 (31)	29 (3.63)	32 (3.47)	28 (65)	33 (1565)	42 (58.0)	49 (2.72)	64 (2.15)	27	43
U of North Carolina-Chapel Hill	32.5 (3.55)	40 (3.45)	45 (3)	27 (36)	33 (3.49)	39 (3.41)	22 (69)	21 (2349)	18 (106.8)	10 (3.82)	19.5 (3.53)	22	21
U of Texas, Medical Br-Galveston	34.5 (3.52)	19.5 (3.68)	37.5 (4)	36.5 (27)	31 (3.54)	13 (3.85)	52.5 (49)	73 (607)	76.5 (30.4)			20	13
University of Texas at Austin	34.5 (3.52)	46 (3.39)	37.5 (4)	44 (23)	46 (3.32)	61 (3.33)	59 (47)	44 (1193)	81 (28.4)			42	37
Rutgers State Univ-New Brunswick	36 (3.47)	56.5 (3.33)	51 (2)	41 (24)	35 (3.46)	61 (3.33)	51 (51)	42 (1285)	83 (26.8)	37 (3.11)	30.5 (3.28)	48	n/a
Harvard University	37.5 (3.45)	33 (3.52)	32 (6)	33.5 (30)	37 (3.45)	28 (3.50)	34 (61)	57 (914)	15 (114.3)	6 (4.13)	3.5 (4.10)	8	10
Pennsylvania State University [f]	37.5 (3.45)	46 (3.39)	107 (0)	51 (18)	38 (3.42)	61 (3.33)	77 (37)	39 (1339)	76.5 (30.4)	22 (3.52)	17.5 (3.57)	44	56
State Univ of New York-Buffalo	39 (3.40)	44 (3.40)	37.5 (4)	38.5 (26)	52 (3.27)	61 (3.33)	39.5 (57)	87 (345)	107 (14.4)	15 (3.73)	10.5 (3.78)	24	16
Colorado State University	40 (3.38)	25 (3.62)	33 (5)	38.5 (26)	42 (3.37)	61 (3.33)	39.5 (57)	38 (1400)	25 (87.5)	34 (3.19)	23.5 (3.42)	16	24
U of Tex-Hlth Sci Ct-San Antonio	41.5 (3.37)	46 (3.39)	37.5 (4)	44 (23)	48 (3.31)	89 (3.10)	34 (61)	49 (1060)	53 (46.1)			23	20
Ohio State University	41.5 (3.37)	56.5 (3.33)	45 (3)	41 (24)	45 (3.33)	61 (3.33)	38 (58)	36 (1486)	62 (41.3)			36	15
University of Vermont	43 (3.35)	65 (3.30)	37.5 (4)	41 (24)	48 (3.31)	82 (3.28)	49.5 (52)	70 (669)	66 (37.2)	41 (2.94)	36 (3.08)	18	7
Albany Medical College	44 (3.34)	56.5 (3.33)	107 (0)	66.5 (13)	53 (3.26)	61 (3.33)	77 (37)	32 (1580)	36 (60.8)	53 (2.63)	38.5 (3.02)	26	19
Univ of Maryland at Baltimore	45 (3.33)	48 (3.38)	51 (2)	35 (28)	39 (3.41)	83 (3.25)	25 (67)	28 (2013)	12 (125.8)			16	18
Michigan State University	47 (3.31)	42.5 (3.41)	45 (3)	33.5 (30)	56 (3.18)	61 (3.33)	26 (66)	34 (1551)	56.5 (45.6)	19 (3.54)	14.5 (3.65)	34	34
University of Tennessee - Memphis	47 (3.31)	39 (3.47)	51 (2)	49 (19)	52 (3.27)	34 (3.46)	52.5 (49)	53 (967)	49 (48.4)	45 (2.80)	53.5 (2.60)	20	9
University of Pittsburgh	47 (3.31)	27.5 (3.60)	63.5 (1)	57.5 (16)	57 (3.16)	61 (3.33)	64.5 (45)	74 (594)	54.5 (45.7)			13	15
State U of New York-Stony Brook	50 (3.28)	34.5 (3.50)	45 (3)	46.5 (21)	44 (3.35)	32 (3.47)	45 (55)	60 (882)	46.5 (49.0)			18	20
Thomas Jefferson University	50 (3.28)	96 (2.96)	63.5 (1)	51 (18)	55 (3.20)	92 (3.00)	69 (42)	48 (1071)	27 (82.4)			13	6
University of Rochester	50 (3.28)	56.5 (3.33)	107 (0)	54.5 (17)	35 (3.46)	38 (3.42)	69 (42)	71 (664)	51 (47.4)	28 (3.41)	16 (3.58)	14	8
Medical College of Wisconsin	52 (3.27)	34.5 (3.50)	37.5 (4)	44 (23)	44 (3.35)	36 (3.44)	45 (55)	26 (2158)	23 (89.9)	64 (2.24)	62 (2.25)	24	16
University of Miami	53 (3.26)	71 (3.23)	63.5 (1)	51 (18)	54 (3.23)	61 (3.33)	59 (47)	62 (868)	50 (48.2)	31 (3.29)	48.5 (2.75)	18	4
University of Southern California	54 (3.25)	66 (3.28)	107 (0)	46.5 (21)	50 (3.28)	61 (3.33)	36.5 (59)	43 (1225)	58 (45.4)	35 (3.13)	37 (3.05)	27	16
Pennsylvania State University [c]	55 (3.24)	78 (3.16)	51 (2)	71 (11)	37 (3.45)	61 (3.33)	90 (30)	52 (1029)	75 (31.2)			33	13
University of Connecticut	56.5 (3.22)	42.5 (3.41)	63.5 (1)	57.5 (16)	66 (3.06)	30 (3.49)	62 (46)	89 (328)	93 (20.5)	60 (2.50)	63 (2.18)	16	26
University of Kansas [b]	56.5 (3.22)	56.5 (3.33)	63.5 (1)	68.5 (12)	59 (3.15)	61 (3.33)	77 (37)	67 (701)	63 (41.2)	46 (2.79)	50 (2.70)	17	16
University of Florida	58 (3.21)	37 (3.49)	107 (0)	48 (20)	62 (3.11)	35 (3.45)	42 (56)	31 (1615)	29 (73.4)	42 (2.88)	40.5 (2.97)	22	17
Pennsylvania State University [e]	59 (3.20)	76 (3.18)	107 (0)	79 (8)	27 (3.67)	(*)	120 (21)	40 (1325)	88 (23.2)			57	53
Georgetown University	60.5 (3.19)	56.5 (3.33)	63.5 (1)	59.5 (15)	61 (3.14)	61 (3.33)	66.5 (44)	41 (1320)	33 (66.0)	43 (2.84)	40.5 (2.97)	20	15

Institution	93Q [1]	93E [1]	% D [1]	% D-S [1]	93Q T [1]	93E T [1]	VIS [1]	TC [2]	C/F [2]	82Q [3]	82E [3]	TF [4]	TG [4]
Saint Louis University	**60.5** (3.19)	**67** (3.27)	**107** (0)	**63** (14)	**75** (2.96)	**61** (3.33)	**59** (47)	**56** (924)	**60** (44.0)			21	4
University of Cincinnati	**62.5** (3.17)	**76** (3.18)	**63.5** (1)	**54.5** (17)	**49** (3.29)	**61** (3.33)	**31.5** (62)	**78** (501)	**43** (55.7)	**50** (2.70)	**42.5** (2.95)	9	21
SUNY-Health Science Ctr-Brooklyn	**62.5** (3.17)	**90.5** (3.04)	**107** (0)	**54.5** (17)	**71** (3.00)	**94** (2.96)	**55.5** (48)	**54** (934)	**59** (44.5)	**44** (2.84)	**48.5** (2.75)	21	13
University of Illinois at Chicago	**64** (3.15)	**76** (3.18)	**45** (3)	**63** (14)	**71** (3.00)	**61** (3.33)	**55.5** (48)	**65** (830)	**64** (39.5)	**40** (2.95)	**38.5** (3.02)	21	27
Arizona State University	**65** (3.13)	**56.5** (3.33)	**51** (2)	**84.5** (6)	**61** (3.14)	**61** (3.33)	**108** (24)	**93** (270)	**101.5** (16.9)			16	14
Tufts University	**66.5** (3.10)	**71** (3.23)	**45** (3)	**74.5** (10)	**59** (3.15)	**32** (3.47)	**80.5** (36)	**51** (1033)	**14** (114.8)	**72** (1.37)	**68** (1.38)	9	22
Wake Forest University	**66.5** (3.10)	**69** (3.25)	**107** (0)	**63** (14)	**71** (3.00)	**61** (3.33)	**55.5** (48)	**132.5** (38)	**138** (2.0)			19	6
University of California-Irvine	**68** (3.05)	**95** (2.97)	**107** (0)	**63** (14)	**67** (3.04)	**96** (2.92)	**64.5** (45)	**50** (1034)	**20** (103.4)	**36** (3.13)	**23.5** (3.42)	10	13
University of Missouri-Columbia	**69.5** (3.02)	**73** (3.22)	**63.5** (1)	**59.5** (15)	**65** (3.08)	**85** (3.22)	**42** (56)	**66** (728)	**78** (30.3)	**18** (3.57)	**12** (3.68)	24	24
Brown University	**69.5** (3.02)	**56.5** (3.33)	**63.5** (1)	**63** (14)	**63** (3.09)	**61** (3.33)	**55.5** (48)	**76** (544)	**67** (36.3)	**30** (3.32)	**35** (3.17)	15	9
Louisiana St U-Sch Med Shreveport	**72.5** (3.00)	**99.5** (2.92)	**37.5** (4)	**74.5** (10)	**83** (2.79)	**92** (3.00)	**74** (38)	**29** (1915)	**3** (239.4)			8	11
North Carolina State University	**72.5** (3.00)	**56.5** (3.33)	**63.5** (1)	**84.5** (6)	**80** (2.88)	**61** (3.33)	**91** (29)	**72** (645)	**90** (21.5)	**51** (2.65)	**46.5** (2.78)	30	28
University of Kentucky	**72.5** (3.00)	**71** (3.23)	**63.5** (1)	**66.5** (13)	**71** (3.00)	**85** (3.22)	**36.5** (59)	**90** (308)	**112** (12.3)			25	18
University of Minnesota	**72.5** (3.00)	**80.5** (3.14)	**63.5** (1)	**54.5** (17)	**76** (2.95)	**87** (3.13)	**31.5** (62)	**77** (510)	**91** (21.3)	**20** (3.54)	**34** (3.23)	24	16
Tulane University	**75** (2.97)	**94** (2.98)	**63.5** (1)	**68.5** (12)	**71** (3.00)	**61** (3.33)	**77** (37)	**88** (331)	**72** (33.1)	**61** (2.48)	**61** (2.37)	10	13
Uniformed Services U of Hlth Sci	**76.5** (2.96)	**86.5** (3.10)	**107** (0)	**74.5** (10)	**82** (2.85)	**86** (3.20)	**47** (54)	**75** (569)	**85** (24.7)			23	9
Boston University	**76.5** (2.96)	**86.5** (3.10)	**107** (0)	**84.5** (6)	**80** (2.88)	**61** (3.33)	**98.5** (27)	**64** (841)	**21** (93.4)			9	19
University of Louisville	**78** (2.94)	**86.5** (3.10)	**63.5** (1)	**77.5** (9)	**84** (2.73)	**89** (3.10)	**72.5** (39)	**82** (419)	**86** (24.6)	**69.5** (2.00)	**67** (1.87)	17	21
Washington State University	**79** (2.92)	**80.5** (3.14)	**107** (0)	**77.5** (9)	**91** (2.58)	**98** (2.88)	**62** (46)	**69** (672)	**65** (37.3)	**62** (2.30)	**45** (2.80)	18	3
Temple University	**81** (2.90)	**74** (3.21)	**63.5** (1)	**92** (5)	**92** (2.57)	**61** (3.33)	**102.5** (26)	**55** (925)	**48** (48.7)	**68** (2.09)	**65.5** (2.08)	19	11
SUNY Health Science Ctr-Syracuse	**81** (2.90)	**90.5** (3.04)	**107** (0)	**74.5** (10)	**71** (3.00)	**61** (3.33)	**69** (42)	**84** (403)	**100** (17.5)	**47** (2.77)	**44** (2.93)	23	2
Oregon State University	**81** (2.90)	**79** (3.15)	**107** (0)	**103.5** (3)	**88** (2.67)	**61** (3.33)	**108** (24)	**83** (406)	**109** (14.0)			29	32
Louisiana State U Medical Center	**83** (2.87)	**105** (2.78)	**63.5** (1)	**80.5** (7)	**80** (2.88)	**102** (2.78)	**83.5** (33)	**63** (848)	**73** (32.6)			26	10
University of Oklahoma	**84** (2.83)	**114** (2.56)	**107** (0)	**103.5** (3)	**77** (2.92)	**99** (2.86)	**82** (34)	**102.5** (183)	**113** (12.2)	**63** (2.27)	**60** (2.38)	15	3
West Virginia University	**85.5** (2.80)	**86.5** (3.10)	**107** (0)	**71** (11)	**96** (2.46)	**61** (3.33)	**48** (53)	**80** (473)	**89** (22.5)	**59** (2.53)		21	8
University of Georgia	**85.5** (2.80)	**92** (3.01)	**107** (0)	**103.5** (3)	**113** (2.00)	(n/s)	**108** (24)	**86** (355)	**87** (23.7)	**69.5** (2.00)		15	24
Wayne State University	**87** (2.76)	**98** (2.94)	**107** (0)	**80.5** (7)	**86** (2.69)	**89** (3.10)	**77** (37)	**46** (1126)	**46.5** (49.0)	**54** (2.60)	**57.5** (2.50)	23	33
Florida State University	**88.5** (2.75)	**56.5** (3.33)	**107** (0)	**97.5** (4)	**85** (2.72)	**61** (3.33)	**94** (28)	**104** (173)	**120** (10.2)			17	19
University of Hawaii at Manoa	**88.5** (2.75)	**82.5** (3.13)	**107** (0)	**121** (1)	**78** (2.90)	**61** (3.33)	**112.5** (23)	**115** (123)	**119** (10.3)	**56** (2.58)	**57.5** (2.50)	12	13
Loyola University of Chicago	**90.5** (2.73)	**68** (3.26)	**45** (3)	**71** (11)	**93** (2.56)	**61** (3.33)	**71** (40)	**97** (224)	**74** (32.0)	**52** (2.64)	**52** (2.63)	7	8

Appendix Table P - 35 Physiology (Continued)

Institution	93Q [1]	93E [1]	% D [1]	% D-S [1]	93Q T [1]	93E T [1]	VIS [1]	TC [2]	C/F [2]	82Q [3]	82E [3]	TF [4]	TG [4]
University of Colorado	90.5 (2.73)	82.5 (3.13)	107 (0)	84.5 (6)	65 (3.08)	61 (3.33)	86.5 (32)	94 (266)	79 (29.6)	38.5 (3.00)	55.5 (2.53)	9	7
New York Medical College	92.5 (2.72)	99.5 (2.92)	107 (0)	84.5 (6)	94 (2.52)	98 (2.88)	72.5 (39)	68 (697)	41 (58.1)			12	12
Iowa State University	92.5 (2.72)	89 (3.06)	107 (0)	92 (5)	91 (2.58)	61 (3.33)	94 (28)	81 (441)	80 (29.4)	55 (2.58)	55.5 (2.53)	15	20
Medical College of Georgia	94 (2.71)	111.5 (2.58)	107 (0)	92 (5)	88 (2.67)	106 (2.50)	83.5 (33)	79 (489)	95 (19.6)			25	13
Louisiana State U & A&M College	95 (2.70)	84 (3.11)	107 (0)	92 (5)	102 (2.29)	61 (3.33)	102.5 (26)	58 (913)	96 (18.6)	73 (1.27)		49	39
Kent State University	96 (2.62)	105 (2.78)	107 (0)	103.5 (3)	95 (2.50)	102 (2.78)	122 (20)	92 (274)	115 (11.4)			24	11
Hahnemann University	97 (2.58)	116 (2.50)	107 (0)	103.5 (3)	71 (3.00)	61 (3.33)	102.5 (26)	96 (233)	92 (21.2)			11	6
Univ of Health Sc/Chicago Med Sch	98 (2.56)	113 (2.57)	63.5 (1)	97.5 (4)	98 (2.35)	109 (2.29)	86.5 (32)	109 (146)	105 (16.2)			9	12
University of North Texas	99 (2.55)	93 (3.00)	107 (0)	103.5 (3)	103 (2.27)	102 (2.78)	98.5 (27)	102.5 (183)	129 (5.1)			36	43
Kansas State University	100.5 (2.50)	97 (2.95)	107 (0)	92 (5)	99 (2.33)	96 (2.92)	86.5 (32)	107 (153)	122 (9.0)	65 (2.18)		17	5
University of Kansas [a]	100.5 (2.50)	56.5 (3.33)	107 (0)	121 (1)	109 (2.13)	61 (3.33)	116.5 (22)	127 (54)	128 (6.0)	66 (2.14)	59 (2.45)	9	8
University of Alaska	102 (2.43)	56.5 (3.33)	107 (0)	103.5 (3)	(n/s)	(n/s)	136.5 (12)	128 (48)	124 (8.0)			6	n/a
Loma Linda University	103 (2.42)	103 (2.80)	107 (0)	92 (5)	100 (2.30)	61 (3.33)	98.5 (27)	59 (884)	45 (52.0)			17	15
Texas Tech University	104 (2.40)	110 (2.59)	107 (0)	92 (5)	108 (2.16)	104 (2.71)	66.5 (44)	112.5 (137)	117 (10.5)			13	11
Auburn University	105 (2.38)	56.5 (3.33)	107 (0)	121 (1)	105 (2.25)	61 (3.33)	120 (21)	99 (203)	101.5 (16.9)			12	8
Medical College of Pensylvania	106.5 (2.36)	102 (2.83)	63.5 (1)	92 (5)	89 (2.64)	92 (3.00)	94 (28)	95 (244)	68 (34.9)			7	2
University of Wyoming	106.5 (2.36)	101 (2.88)	107 (0)	111.5 (2)	97 (2.40)	61 (3.33)	116.5 (22)	85 (375)	70 (34.1)			11	16
University of South Carolina	108 (2.35)	111.5 (2.58)	107 (0)	84.5 (6)	116 (1.90)	61 (3.33)	86.5 (32)	110 (145)	98 (18.1)			8	6
Texas A&M University	109 (2.32)	105 (2.78)	107 (0)	92 (5)	121 (1.80)	102 (2.78)	94 (28)	117 (113)	121 (9.4)			12	15
University of New Mexico	110 (2.27)	107 (2.71)	107 (0)	111.5 (2)	105 (2.25)	106 (2.50)	80.5 (36)	116 (114)	118 (10.4)			11	4
Univ of Med & Dent of NJ	111 (2.20)	122.5 (2.17)	107 (0)	134 (0)	107 (2.20)	115 (1.67)	98.5 (27)	98 (221)	82 (27.6)	57 (2.57)	53.5 (2.60)	8	9
Clemson University	112 (2.15)	109 (2.62)	107 (0)	111.5 (2)	121 (1.80)	115 (1.67)	112.5 (23)	101 (186)	108 (14.3)			13	4
Oklahoma State University	113 (2.10)	119 (2.33)	107 (0)	103.5 (3)	118 (1.88)	(n/s)	94 (28)	120 (76)	123 (8.4)			9	10
Howard University	114 (2.00)	122.5 (2.17)	107 (0)	134 (0)	107 (2.20)	108 (2.38)	105 (25)	129 (44)	133 (4.4)	67 (2.13)	65.5 (2.08)	10	14
University of Notre Dame	115 (1.93)	108 (2.67)	63.5 (1)	111.5 (2)	118 (1.88)	106 (2.50)	120 (21)	105 (167)	71 (33.4)			5	11
Virginia Polytech Inst & State U [c]	116.5 (1.85)	121 (2.22)	107 (0)	121 (1)	113 (2.00)	(n/s)	124 (19)	122.5 (65)	116 (10.8)			6	6
Univ of Puerto Rico-Rio Piedras	116.5 (1.85)	130.5 (1.67)	107 (0)	134 (0)	102 (2.29)	(n/s)	124 (19)	137 (18)	140 (1.4)			13	1
East Carolina U Sch Medicine	118 (1.82)	118 (2.36)	107 (0)	121 (1)	126 (1.30)	112 (2.08)	89 (31)	108 (148)	104 (16.4)			9	5
Ohio University	119 (1.80)	(n/s)	107 (0)	121 (1)	113 (2.00)	(n/s)	139.5 (10)	124 (63)	127 (6.3)			10	6
Illinois State University	120 (1.78)	56.5 (3.33)	107 (0)	103.5 (3)	113 (2.00)	(n/s)	134.5 (14)	130 (42)	132 (4.7)			9	n/a

Institution	93Q [1]	93E [1]	% D [1]	% D-S [1]	93Q T [1]	93E T [1]	VIS [1]	TC [2]	C/F [2]	82Q [3]	82E [3]	TF [4]	TG [4]
Univ of California-Santa Cruz	121 (1.69)	116 (2.50)	107 (0)	111.5 (2)	121 (1.80)	(n/s)	102.5 (26)	91 (294)	38 (58.8)			5	13
Northern Arizona University	122 (1.67)	120 (2.29)	107 (0)	134 (0)	113 (2.00)	110 (2.22)	108 (24)	135 (26)	136 (3.3)			8	0
Virginia Polytech Inst & State U [a]	123 (1.63)	56.5 (3.33)	107 (0)	121 (1)	123 (1.75)	(n/s)	131 (15)	114 (135)	110 (13.5)			10	6
University of Houston	124 (1.59)	130.5 (1.67)	107 (0)	121 (1)	121 (1.80)	(n/s)	108 (24)	140 (7)	139 (1.8)	71 (1.59)		4	1
Medical College of Ohio	125.5 (1.56)	125.5 (1.91)	107 (0)	121 (1)	126 (1.30)	112 (2.08)	112.5 (23)	111 (140)	94 (20.0)			7	7
Virginia Polytech Inst & State U [d]	125.5 (1.56)	130.5 (1.67)	107 (0)	134 (0)	113 (2.00)	(n/s)	131 (15)	100 (197)	99 (17.9)			11	52
State Univ of New York-Binghamton	128 (1.50)	56.5 (3.33)	107 (0)	121 (1)	129 (1.00)	(n/s)	127 (17)	122.5 (65)	111 (13.0)			5	6
Univ of California-Riverside	128 (1.50)	130.5 (1.67)	107 (0)	134 (0)	(n/s)	(n/s)	136.5 (12)	119 (91)	106 (15.2)			6	6
Bowling Green State University	128 (1.50)	116 (2.50)	107 (0)	134 (0)	129 (1.00)	(n/s)	134.5 (14)	136 (22)	134 (3.7)			6	2
Indiana University	130 (1.47)	124 (2.00)	107 (0)	103.5 (3)	124 (1.50)	115 (1.67)	116.5 (22)	132.5 (38)	125 (7.6)	58 (2.55)	51 (2.68)	5	5
University of South Dakota	131 (1.45)	130.5 (1.67)	107 (0)	134 (0)	127 (1.14)	(n/s)	116.5 (22)	126 (55)	130.5 (5.0)			11	4
University of Nebraska-Lincoln	132 (1.38)	130.5 (1.67)	107 (0)	121 (1)	(n/s)	(n/s)	131 (15)	131 (40)	126 (6.7)			6	0
Utah State University	133 (1.33)	(n/s)	107 (0)	134 (0)	(n/s)	(n/s)	139.5 (10)	106 (160)	84 (26.7)			6	0
Miami University	134 (1.18)	125.5 (1.91)	107 (0)	121 (1)	132 (0.60)	115 (1.67)	112.5 (23)	118 (109)	97 (18.2)			6	12
Montana State University	135 (0.91)	130.5 (1.67)	107 (0)	134 (0)	131 (0.75)	(n/s)	128 (16)	134 (28)	135 (3.5)			8	n/a
North Dakota State University	136 (0.88)	135 (1.11)	63.5 (1)	121 (1)	135 (0.33)	(n/s)	131 (15)	121 (67)	103 (16.8)			4	1
Univ of California-Santa Barbara	137 (0.80)	130.5 (1.67)	107 (0)	111.5 (2)	129 (1.00)	(n/s)	131 (15)	112.5 (137)	54.5 (45.7)			3	n/a
University of New Hampshire	138 (0.67)	(n/s)	107 (0)	134 (0)	133 (0.50)	(n/s)	138 (11)	125 (59)	114 (11.8)			5	n/a
University of Idaho	139 (0.42)	137 (0.00)	107 (0)	134 (0)	134 (0.40)	(n/s)	124 (19)	139 (10)	130.5 (5.0)			2	1
Univ of Southern Mississippi	140 (0.38)	136 (0.83)	107 (0)	134 (0)	136 (0.00)	(n/s)	126 (18)	138 (16)	137 (2.7)			6	n/a

Sources: 1. National Survey of Graduate Faculty
2. Institute for Scientific Information
3. 1982 Survey of Graduate Faculty
4. Institutional Coordinator Data

Notes: *a.* School of Arts and Sciences
b. School of Medicine
c. School of Agriculture
d. School of Veterinary Medicine
e. Interdisciplinary with the Schools of Agriculture and Arts and Sciences
f. Interdisciplinary with the Schools of Agriculture, Arts and Sciences, and Medicine

n/s After trimming no cases remained

Appendix Table P - 36 Relative Rankings for Research-Doctorate Programs in Political Science

Institution	93Q [1]	93E [1]	% D [1]	% D-S [1]	93Q T [1]	93E T [1]	VIS [1]	TC [2]	C/F [2]	82Q [3]	82E [3]	TF [4]	TG [4]
Harvard University	1 (4.88)	3 (4.17)	1 (86)	1 (99)	1 (4.95)	3 (4.14)	1.5 (100)	1 (592)	2.5 (12.3)	2 (4.69)	5 (4.02)	48	172
University of California-Berkeley	2 (4.66)	4 (4.13)	2 (67)	2.5 (94)	2.5 (4.64)	4 (4.07)	1.5 (100)	33 (66)	45.5 (1.6)	3 (4.66)	4 (4.03)	41	143
Yale University	3.5 (4.60)	2 (4.24)	3 (64)	4 (92)	4 (4.56)	1 (4.24)	4.5 (99)	3 (356)	2.5 (12.3)	1 (4.81)	1 (4.45)	29	69
University of Michigan	3.5 (4.60)	1 (4.31)	4 (62)	2.5 (94)	2.5 (4.64)	2 (4.20)	4.5 (99)	6 (245)	10 (5.6)	4 (4.55)	2 (4.15)	44	173
Stanford University	5 (4.50)	5 (4.02)	5 (55)	5 (88)	5 (4.52)	5.5 (3.96)	11.5 (97)	13.5 (138)	13.5 (4.9)	7 (4.18)	6.5 (3.98)	28	89
University of Chicago	6 (4.41)	10 (3.83)	7 (50)	6.5 (86)	6 (4.47)	8 (3.79)	7.5 (98)	4 (334)	4 (11.9)	5 (4.54)	3 (4.07)	28	191
Princeton University	7 (4.39)	8 (3.91)	6 (52)	6.5 (86)	7 (4.37)	10 (3.75)	4.5 (99)	12 (146)	29 (3.0)	9 (3.86)	14.5 (3.48)	49	59
Univ of California-Los Angeles	8 (4.25)	14 (3.62)	8 (37)	8 (85)	9 (4.20)	15 (3.48)	4.5 (99)	2 (481)	6 (8.4)	16 (3.46)	17 (3.28)	57	177
Univ of California-San Diego	9 (4.13)	12 (3.70)	10.5 (28)	9 (79)	8 (4.33)	11.5 (3.73)	16 (95)	11 (172)	15 (4.8)	29 (2.88)	30 (2.72)	36	57
University of Wisconsin-Madison	10 (4.09)	9 (3.86)	9 (29)	10 (76)	10 (4.05)	9 (3.78)	7.5 (98)	27 (73)	49.5 (1.5)	8 (4.14)	8 (3.93)	49	145
University of Rochester	11 (4.01)	6 (4.00)	12 (27)	13 (72)	11.5 (4.00)	5.5 (3.96)	15 (96)	10 (192)	5 (10.7)	12 (3.72)	10 (3.77)	18	31
Massachusetts Inst of Technology	12 (3.96)	11 (3.74)	13 (23)	14 (70)	13 (3.90)	14 (3.51)	18.5 (94)	16 (131)	11 (5.5)	6 (4.28)	6.5 (3.98)	24	155
University of Minnesota	13 (3.95)	7 (3.92)	16 (18)	11 (75)	15.5 (3.83)	7 (3.83)	11.5 (97)	21 (92)	27.5 (3.1)	10 (3.76)	9 (3.87)	30	87
Duke University	14 (3.94)	13 (3.68)	14 (20)	12 (74)	11.5 (4.00)	11.5 (3.73)	11.5 (97)	8 (225)	7 (7.8)	18 (3.38)	21 (3.07)	29	89
Cornell University	15 (3.85)	15 (3.61)	16 (18)	15 (67)	15.5 (3.83)	13 (3.66)	11.5 (97)	34 (65)	42 (1.7)	11 (3.75)	11 (3.55)	39	86
Columbia University	16 (3.84)	22.5 (3.22)	10.5 (28)	16 (61)	14 (3.86)	19.5 (3.19)	11.5 (97)	7 (242)	12 (5.0)	15 (3.57)	22 (3.00)	48	355
Ohio State University	17 (3.69)	18 (3.40)	16 (18)	17 (54)	17 (3.53)	21 (3.18)	18.5 (94)	9 (194)	9 (5.9)	19 (3.32)	18.5 (3.23)	33	148
U of North Carolina-Chapel Hill	18 (3.54)	16 (3.54)	19 (9)	19 (47)	18 (3.44)	16 (3.45)	25 (92)	18 (112)	18 (4.0)	14 (3.60)	12 (3.52)	28	103
University of Texas at Austin	19 (3.49)	22.5 (3.22)	21 (8)	18 (49)	19 (3.33)	24 (3.05)	18.5 (94)	23 (78)	49.5 (1.5)	28 (2.97)	27 (2.77)	53	89
Indiana University	20 (3.45)	17 (3.45)	21 (8)	20 (45)	23 (3.17)	19.5 (3.19)	25 (92)	32 (69)	30 (2.6)	17 (3.44)	16 (3.33)	27	100
Johns Hopkins University	21 (3.37)	25 (3.14)	18 (10)	22.5 (40)	23 (3.17)	29 (2.89)	21.5 (93)	73 (14)	73.5 (0.7)	22 (3.22)	23 (2.95)	19	59
Northwestern University	22 (3.35)	25 (3.14)	25.5 (4)	21 (42)	25.5 (3.16)	28 (2.91)	18.5 (94)	30 (71)	24 (3.6)	13 (3.62)	13 (3.50)	20	70
University of Washington	23 (3.34)	29 (3.02)	32 (2)	24 (38)	20 (3.29)	26 (2.99)	33 (87)	35.5 (59)	39 (2.0)	26.5 (3.00)	28.5 (2.73)	30	70
Washington University	24 (3.29)	19 (3.38)	23.5 (6)	25 (37)	23 (3.17)	17 (3.33)	29.5 (90)	49 (30)	42 (1.7)	20 (3.28)	14.5 (3.48)	18	45
University of Iowa	25 (3.25)	20.5 (3.31)	27.5 (3)	28 (34)	28 (3.10)	23 (3.10)	35 (86)	45.5 (36)	45.5 (1.6)	24 (3.10)	20 (3.17)	22	30
University of Virginia	27 (3.24)	35 (2.72)	21 (8)	22.5 (40)	31 (2.96)	37 (2.63)	21.5 (93)	17 (119)	25 (3.5)	35 (2.74)	34 (2.63)	34	107
Rutgers State Univ-New Brunswick	27 (3.24)	25 (3.14)	25.5 (4)	26 (36)	25.5 (3.16)	25 (3.03)	28 (91)	67 (18)	79 (0.6)	26.5 (3.00)	25.5 (2.87)	30	103
Michigan State University	27 (3.24)	20.5 (3.31)	32 (2)	31 (31)	29 (3.08)	18 (3.23)	37 (85)	15 (137)	13.5 (4.9)	32 (2.82)	25.5 (2.87)	28	41
University of Maryland College Park	29 (3.23)	27 (3.13)	48 (1)	27 (35)	21 (3.18)	22 (3.17)	11.5 (97)	47 (33)	67.5 (0.8)	36 (2.73)	33 (2.67)	40	139
U of Illinois at Urbana-Champaign	30 (3.20)	28 (3.04)	23.5 (6)	31 (31)	32 (2.92)	30 (2.87)	25 (92)	61 (22)	73.5 (0.7)	21 (3.25)	18.5 (3.23)	33	74

Institution	93Q [1]	93E [1]	% D [1]	% D-S [1]	93Q T [1]	93E T [1]	VIS [1]	TC [2]	C/F [2]	82Q [3]	82E [3]	TF [4]	TG [4]
University of Pittsburgh	31 (3.15)	31 (2.90)	32 (2)	29 (32)	30 (3.00)	34 (2.72)	25 (92)	61 (22)	67.5 (0.8)	33 (2.78)	24 (2.92)	29	53
University of California-Irvine	32 (3.14)	34 (2.83)	79.5 (0)	31 (31)	27 (3.11)	27 (2.92)	31 (89)	5 (315)	1 (13.7)			23	34
University of Houston	33 (2.96)	38.5 (2.69)	48 (1)	33 (22)	36 (2.73)	35 (2.71)	53.5 (78)	97.5 (0)	97.5 (0.0)			28	42
State U of New York-Stony Brook	34 (2.92)	32 (2.88)	48 (1)	35 (20)	34 (2.83)	32 (2.80)	71.5 (66)	13.5 (138)	8 (7.7)			18	38
University of Arizona	35 (2.89)	48 (2.50)	48 (1)	36.5 (19)	37 (2.72)	61 (2.19)	39.5 (83)	25 (75)	20.5 (3.8)	43 (2.54)	45.5 (2.28)	20	75
Emory University	36 (2.88)	38.5 (2.69)	48 (1)	36.5 (19)	40 (2.64)	46 (2.38)	53.5 (78)	26 (74)	26 (3.4)	71 (1.43)	70 (1.43)	22	45
Georgetown University	37 (2.85)	51 (2.49)	32 (2)	34 (21)	33 (2.89)	40 (2.57)	29.5 (90)	55 (27)	62 (0.9)	59.5 (2.00)	58 (1.90)	31	100
Florida State University	38 (2.82)	30 (2.97)	48 (1)	38.5 (18)	44 (2.53)	32 (2.80)	39.5 (83)	39 (47)	31.5 (2.5)	46 (2.44)	39.5 (2.45)	19	44
University of Colorado	39 (2.78)	36.5 (2.71)	48 (1)	42.5 (14)	35 (2.76)	33 (2.76)	46 (81)	20 (96)	22.5 (3.7)	56 (2.09)	55 (1.95)	26	51
Syracuse University	40 (2.77)	33 (2.84)	32 (2)	42.5 (14)	39 (2.68)	36 (2.67)	42.5 (82)	57.5 (23)	67.5 (0.8)	45 (2.49)	35.5 (2.62)	28	40
Univ of California-Santa Barbara	41 (2.74)	43.5 (2.55)	32 (2)	38.5 (18)	38 (2.71)	41 (2.56)	46 (81)	45.5 (36)	45.5 (1.6)	38 (2.68)	41 (2.40)	22	79
University of Pennsylvania	42 (2.68)	53 (2.41)	48 (1)	40.5 (15)	43 (2.54)	46 (2.38)	25 (92)	22 (90)	19 (3.9)	31 (2.84)	42.5 (2.38)	23	65
Arizona State University	43 (2.67)	58.5 (2.33)	48 (1)	45 (13)	47 (2.41)	71 (2.07)	39.5 (83)	35.5 (59)	22.5 (3.7)			16	36
University of Georgia	44.5 (2.66)	36.5 (2.71)	27.5 (3)	45 (13)	49 (2.35)	38 (2.58)	46 (81)	28.5 (72)	33.5 (2.4)	47 (2.43)	44 (2.37)	30	48
University of Notre Dame	44.5 (2.66)	55.5 (2.36)	48 (1)	47.5 (12)	42 (2.56)	56 (2.25)	46 (81)	48 (32)	58 (1.0)	64 (1.96)	60 (1.88)	33	60
University of California-Davis	46 (2.61)	40 (2.60)	48 (1)	54.5 (9)	41 (2.58)	40 (2.57)	50.5 (80)	37.5 (49)	35.5 (2.3)	49 (2.32)	51 (2.12)	21	18
CUNY - Grad Sch & Univ Center	47.5 (2.57)	69.5 (2.13)	32 (2)	40.5 (15)	46 (2.44)	72 (2.05)	46 (81)	52.5 (28)	62 (0.9)	25 (3.06)	39.5 (2.45)	30	155
George Washington University	47.5 (2.57)	48 (2.50)	79.5 (0)	49 (11)	46 (2.44)	43 (2.40)	32 (88)	44 (38)	54 (1.3)	65 (1.94)	63 (1.85)	30	103
Tufts University	49 (2.51)	58.5 (2.33)	48 (1)	51 (10)	56 (2.22)	52 (2.32)	71.5 (66)	19 (100)	20.5 (3.8)			26	81
University of Hawaii at Manoa	50 (2.49)	73 (2.07)	79.5 (0)	54.5 (9)	48 (2.38)	66 (2.13)	62 (74)	71.5 (15)	79 (0.6)	23 (3.13)	31.5 (2.68)	26	131
University of Florida	51.5 (2.48)	58.5 (2.33)	48 (1)	51 (10)	54 (2.24)	51 (2.33)	35 (86)	31 (70)	31.5 (2.5)	53 (2.16)	56.5 (1.93)	28	51
University of Wisconsin-Milwaukee	51.5 (2.48)	48 (2.50)	48 (1)	45 (13)	63 (2.15)	58 (2.22)	56 (77)	65.5 (19)	58 (1.0)	51 (2.20)	48 (2.22)	20	16
Rice University	53 (2.43)	43.5 (2.55)	48 (1)	51 (10)	53 (2.27)	48 (2.37)	71.5 (66)	65.5 (19)	45.5 (1.6)	69 (1.64)	66 (1.70)	12	18
University of Kentucky	54 (2.42)	41 (2.58)	48 (1)	60 (7)	59 (2.19)	46 (2.38)	39.5 (83)	28.5 (72)	16.5 (4.2)	40 (2.61)	31.5 (2.68)	17	45
Brandeis University	55 (2.41)	72 (2.08)	48 (1)	47.5 (12)	51 (2.33)	69 (2.10)	56 (77)	91.5 (3)	88 (0.3)	41 (2.57)	45.5 (2.28)	12	32
New York University	56 (2.40)	42 (2.56)	79.5 (0)	60 (7)	52 (2.30)	53 (2.30)	35 (86)	37.5 (49)	35.5 (2.3)	39 (2.62)	42.5 (2.38)	21	16
University of South Carolina	57 (2.39)	45 (2.52)	48 (1)	57 (8)	67 (2.08)	61 (2.19)	67.5 (70)	40 (46)	27.5 (3.1)			15	32
Purdue University	58 (2.38)	64 (2.24)	79.5 (0)	64 (6)	60 (2.17)	66 (2.13)	60 (75)	83 (7)	91 (0.2)	57 (2.05)	63 (1.85)	29	38
U of Massachusetts at Amherst	59.5 (2.37)	63 (2.27)	48 (1)	68.5 (4)	50 (2.34)	42 (2.50)	56 (77)	41.5 (43)	39 (2.0)	30 (2.84)	37 (2.58)	21	55
American University	59.5 (2.37)	67 (2.17)	79.5 (0)	54.5 (9)	58 (2.21)	74 (1.97)	42.5 (82)	52.5 (28)	54 (1.3)			22	60

Appendix Table P - 36 Political Science (Continued)

Institution	93Q [1]	93E [1]	% D [1]	% D-S [1]	93Q T [1]	93E T [1]	VIS [1]	TC [2]	C/F [2]	82Q [3]	82E [3]	TF [4]	TG [4]
Univ of California-Riverside	61 (2.36)	69.5 (2.13)	79.5 (0)	60 (7)	63 (2.15)	73 (2.00)	58.5 (76)	76.5 (11)	79 (0.6)	58 (2.03)	67 (1.67)	19	27
University of Southern California	63 (2.33)	68 (2.15)	48 (1)	64 (6)	64 (2.12)	64 (2.16)	65 (73)	61 (22)	56 (1.2)	42 (2.55)	50 (2.13)	18	66
University of Kansas	63 (2.33)	48 (2.50)	79.5 (0)	60 (7)	69 (2.07)	54 (2.28)	58.5 (76)	69 (17)	62 (0.9)	62 (1.97)	65 (1.77)	19	39
University of Nebraska-Lincoln	63 (2.33)	65 (2.22)	79.5 (0)	79.5 (2)	61 (2.16)	75 (1.92)	81.5 (58)	56 (25)	52 (1.4)	66 (1.81)	68 (1.62)	18	19
Vanderbilt University	65.5 (2.32)	62 (2.30)	79.5 (0)	54.5 (9)	67 (2.08)	69 (2.10)	50.5 (80)	88.5 (5)	85 (0.4)	34 (2.76)	35.5 (2.62)	14	23
State Univ of New York-Albany	65.5 (2.32)	61 (2.31)	79.5 (0)	86 (1)	67 (2.08)	64 (2.16)	65 (73)	52.5 (28)	54 (1.3)	61 (1.99)	54 (2.00)	22	49
University of Connecticut	67 (2.31)	52 (2.43)	79.5 (0)	68.5 (4)	70 (2.06)	58 (2.22)	65 (73)	88.5 (5)	91 (0.2)	50 (2.30)	52.5 (2.02)	26	98
State Univ of New York-Binghamton	68 (2.27)	55.5 (2.36)	48 (1)	60 (7)	67 (2.08)	56 (2.25)	62 (74)	71.5 (15)	62 (0.9)	59.5 (2.00)	52.5 (2.02)	17	83
Pennsylvania State University	69 (2.25)	54 (2.38)	79.5 (0)	64 (6)	72 (2.00)	51 (2.33)	50.5 (80)	69 (17)	62 (0.9)	48 (2.33)	47 (2.27)	19	58
University of Denver	70 (2.23)	58.5 (2.33)	79.5 (0)	66 (5)	56 (2.22)	46 (2.38)	78.5 (59)	83 (7)	85 (0.4)			19	79
University of Oregon	71 (2.21)	71 (2.11)	79.5 (0)	73.5 (3)	58 (2.21)	66 (2.13)	69 (68)	24 (76)	16.5 (4.2)	37 (2.70)	28.5 (2.73)	18	34
State Univ of New York-Buffalo	72 (2.06)	48 (2.50)	79.5 (0)	73.5 (3)	74 (1.90)	49 (2.36)	71.5 (66)	74 (13)	67.5 (0.8)	44 (2.52)	38 (2.55)	16	34
Wayne State University	73 (2.04)	66 (2.19)	79.5 (0)	68.5 (4)	79 (1.64)	81 (1.67)	81.5 (58)	57.5 (23)	58 (1.0)			24	42
Louisiana State U & A&M College	74 (2.02)	76 (1.99)	79.5 (0)	73.5 (3)	76 (1.74)	77 (1.81)	67.5 (70)	52.5 (28)	49.5 (1.5)			19	30
Boston College	75 (2.00)	88.5 (1.29)	79.5 (0)	79.5 (2)	72 (2.00)	87 (1.22)	77 (60)	93.5 (2)	94.5 (0.1)			16	47
American University [a]	76.5 (1.94)	78 (1.85)	48 (1)	73.5 (3)	73 (1.94)	78 (1.78)	84 (57)	86.5 (6)	88 (0.3)			18	44
University of Oklahoma	76.5 (1.94)	75 (2.03)	79.5 (0)	94 (0)	77 (1.70)	62 (2.17)	88.5 (53)	43 (41)	42 (1.7)	68 (1.67)	60 (1.88)	24	58
Claremont Graduate School	78 (1.80)	79 (1.74)	48 (1)	73.5 (3)	75 (1.75)	79 (1.73)	50.5 (80)	83 (7)	67.5 (0.8)	54 (2.16)	49 (2.15)	9	132
University of Missouri-Columbia	79 (1.79)	85 (1.43)	79.5 (0)	94 (0)	82 (1.52)	88 (1.19)	74.5 (65)	76.5 (11)	73.5 (0.7)	63 (1.97)	63 (1.85)	15	63
Northern Illinois University	80 (1.77)	77 (1.98)	79.5 (0)	79.5 (2)	85 (1.45)	76 (1.82)	74.5 (65)	61 (22)	73.5 (0.7)	75 (1.26)	75 (1.28)	30	57
University of Utah	81 (1.74)	81.5 (1.67)	79.5 (0)	86 (1)	83 (1.50)	82 (1.48)	93.5 (48)	83 (7)	88 (0.3)	77 (1.14)	77 (0.93)	27	62
Boston University	82 (1.69)	91 (1.14)	48 (1)	68.5 (4)	78 (1.66)	85 (1.33)	62 (74)	95.5 (1)	94.5 (0.1)	52 (2.17)	56.5 (1.93)	12	50
University of Cincinnati	83 (1.65)	94 (1.02)	79.5 (0)	94 (0)	85 (1.45)	93 (1.00)	85.5 (55)	50 (29)	37 (2.1)	70 (1.50)	73 (1.37)	14	27
University of North Texas	84 (1.64)	80 (1.73)	79.5 (0)	79.5 (2)	81 (1.53)	70 (2.08)	78.5 (59)	69 (17)	67.5 (0.8)			22	39
Howard University	85 (1.62)	74 (2.05)	79.5 (0)	79.5 (2)	86 (1.39)	58 (2.22)	85.5 (55)	41.5 (43)	33.5 (2.4)	76 (1.16)	76 (1.12)	18	69
Temple University	86 (1.54)	87 (1.30)	79.5 (0)	86 (1)	80 (1.62)	83 (1.41)	81.5 (58)	91.5 (3)	91 (0.2)	55 (2.12)	60 (1.88)	19	71
Tulane University	87 (1.49)	83 (1.60)	79.5 (0)	94 (0)	87 (1.36)	84 (1.39)	81.5 (58)	83 (7)	82.5 (0.5)	72 (1.42)	71 (1.42)	14	42
University of New Orleans	88 (1.45)	81.5 (1.67)	48 (1)	73.5 (3)	89 (1.24)	86 (1.31)	76 (64)	61 (22)	39 (2.0)			11	33
Washington State University	89 (1.39)	93 (1.04)	79.5 (0)	94 (0)	88 (1.28)	96 (0.76)	92 (50)	64 (20)	49.5 (1.5)			13	35
University of Tennessee-Knoxville	90 (1.36)	84 (1.49)	79.5 (0)	86 (1)	90 (1.08)	91 (1.11)	91 (52)	80 (8)	82.5 (0.5)	67 (1.75)	69 (1.55)	17	45

Institution	93Q [1]	93E [1]	% D [1]	% D-S [1]	93Q T [1]	93E T [1]	VIS [1]	TC [2]	C/F [2]	82Q [3]	82E [3]	TF [4]	TG [4]
Texas Tech University	**91** (1.20)	**96** (0.88)	**79.5** (0)	**94** (0)	**92** (1.04)	**94** (0.83)	**88.5** (53)	**75** (12)	**73.5** (0.7)			18	24
University of Texas at Dallas	**92** (1.18)	**88.5** (1.29)	**79.5** (0)	**79.5** (2)	**95** (0.97)	**91** (1.11)	**88.5** (53)	**79** (9)	**79** (0.6)			16	32
Northern Arizona University	**93** (1.17)	**86** (1.37)	**79.5** (0)	**94** (0)	**92** (1.04)	**81** (1.67)	**96.5** (46)	**93.5** (2)	**94.5** (0.1)			18	33
Kent State University	**94** (1.14)	**90** (1.17)	**79.5** (0)	**86** (1)	**94** (1.00)	**91** (1.11)	**93.5** (48)	**86.5** (6)	**85** (0.4)	**74** (1.27)	**72** (1.40)	14	27
Fordham University	**95** (1.12)	**92** (1.07)	**79.5** (0)	**94** (0)	**92** (1.04)	**91** (1.11)	**95** (47)	**78** (10)	**73.5** (0.7)			14	67
Catholic University of America	**96** (0.95)	**95** (0.95)	**79.5** (0)	**86** (1)	**96** (0.95)	**95** (0.77)	**88.5** (53)	**95.5** (1)	**94.5** (0.1)	**73** (1.40)	**74** (1.30)	12	41
Clark Atlanta University	**97** (0.60)	**97** (0.79)	**79.5** (0)	**86** (1)	**97** (0.30)	**97** (0.30)	**96.5** (46)	**97.5** (0)	**97.5** (0.0)	**78** (0.35)	**78** (0.47)	9	50
Idaho State University	**98** (0.33)	**98** (0.28)	**79.5** (0)	**94** (0)	**98** (0.22)	**98** (0.00)	**98** (45)	**90** (4)	**79** (0.6)			7	20

Sources: 1. National Survey of Graduate Faculty
2. Institute for Scientific Information
3. 1982 Survey of Graduate Faculty
4. Institutional Coordinator Data

Note: *a.* Program in International Relations

Appendix Table P - 37 Relative Rankings for Research-Doctorate Programs in Psychology

Institution	93Q [1]	93E [1]	% D [1]	% D-S [1]	93Q T [1]	93E T [1]	VIS [1]	TC [2]	C/F [2]	82Q [3]	82E [3]	TF [4]	TG [4]
Stanford University	1 (4.82)	1 (4.64)	1 (82)	1 (96)	1 (4.87)	1 (4.66)	1.5 (100)	13 (1019)	8.5 (39.2)	1 (4.75)	1 (4.35)	26	68
University of Michigan	2 (4.63)	2 (4.40)	2 (66)	4 (87)	2 (4.72)	2 (4.47)	3.5 (96)	2 (2373)	17 (30.0)	4 (4.50)	5.5 (4.08)	79	237
Yale University	3 (4.62)	5 (4.31)	3 (61)	3 (88)	3 (4.68)	3 (4.39)	3.5 (96)	3 (2131)	5 (49.6)	3 (4.52)	3 (4.22)	43	91
Univ of California-Los Angeles	4 (4.61)	12 (4.05)	5.5 (57)	2 (91)	4.5 (4.62)	10 (4.06)	7 (94)	4 (2049)	30 (24.1)	7 (4.35)	9 (3.85)	85	188
U of Illinois at Urbana-Champaign	5 (4.58)	3 (4.36)	4 (58)	6 (85)	4.5 (4.62)	4 (4.33)	5 (95)	6 (1854)	27 (25.4)	10 (4.21)	5.5 (4.08)	73	229
Harvard University	6 (4.48)	10 (4.09)	5.5 (57)	5 (86)	6.5 (4.43)	14 (3.96)	1.5 (100)	24 (870)	12 (34.8)	2 (4.57)	11 (3.82)	25	68
University of Minnesota	7 (4.46)	4 (4.33)	7 (51)	7 (83)	6.5 (4.43)	7 (4.17)	7 (94)	5 (1878)	13 (34.1)	8 (4.33)	4 (4.20)	55	132
University of Pennsylvania	8 (4.35)	6 (4.18)	9 (42)	10 (78)	8 (4.42)	5 (4.25)	9.5 (91)	41 (645)	33 (21.5)	6 (4.40)	2 (4.23)	30	46
University of California-Berkeley	9 (4.33)	14 (4.03)	8 (46)	10 (78)	11.5 (4.28)	19 (3.86)	7 (94)	30 (791)	38.5 (20.3)	5 (4.43)	7 (3.88)	39	130
Univ of California-San Diego	10 (4.32)	8 (4.12)	10 (41)	10 (78)	9 (4.40)	8 (4.13)	9.5 (91)	1 (2786)	3 (60.6)	11 (4.19)	13 (3.75)	46	57
Carnegie Mellon University	11 (4.29)	7 (4.13)	11 (39)	18 (66)	10 (4.30)	11.5 (4.05)	21 (86)	36 (743)	10 (39.1)	12 (4.00)	8 (3.87)	19	35
University of Washington	12 (4.24)	18 (3.89)	13.5 (28)	8 (81)	11.5 (4.28)	15 (3.94)	14.5 (89)	9 (1237)	22 (28.8)	17 (3.88)	16.5 (3.67)	43	153
Princeton University	13 (4.22)	9 (4.10)	12 (30)	14 (70)	13 (4.15)	9 (4.07)	26.5 (84)	32 (786)	11 (37.4)	21 (3.84)	22 (3.60)	21	46
Cornell University	14 (4.15)	13 (4.04)	15.5 (25)	12 (75)	14 (4.11)	11.5 (4.05)	17.5 (88)	38 (722)	47 (18.1)	19 (3.86)	24.5 (3.57)	40	33
University of Wisconsin-Madison	15 (4.09)	15 (3.99)	15.5 (25)	13 (73)	15 (4.09)	16 (3.91)	14.5 (89)	14 (1002)	23 (28.6)	15 (3.90)	14.5 (3.70)	35	77
Columbia University	16.5 (4.04)	33 (3.60)	13.5 (28)	25 (56)	17 (4.05)	34 (3.54)	26.5 (84)	37 (730)	19 (29.2)	13 (3.95)	20.5 (3.62)	25	32
University of Texas at Austin	16.5 (4.04)	16 (3.96)	17 (22)	15 (68)	16 (4.08)	13 (3.99)	12 (90)	28 (840)	51 (16.8)	20 (3.84)	26 (3.52)	50	119
University of Chicago	18 (3.98)	22 (3.75)	20 (18)	19.5 (64)	18 (4.04)	21 (3.75)	26.5 (84)	16 (969)	32 (22.0)	9 (4.21)	16.5 (3.67)	44	131
Indiana University	19.5 (3.97)	11 (4.08)	18 (21)	16.5 (67)	22.5 (3.97)	6 (4.21)	12 (90)	19 (921)	34 (21.4)	18 (3.87)	10 (3.83)	43	97
University of Virginia	19.5 (3.97)	21 (3.78)	20 (18)	16.5 (67)	22.5 (3.97)	26 (3.63)	17.5 (88)	25 (860)	26 (26.1)	33 (3.38)	41.5 (3.20)	33	106
Ohio State University	21 (3.95)	26 (3.70)	26.5 (14)	19.5 (64)	21 (3.98)	23 (3.71)	26.5 (84)	15 (989)	57 (14.8)	32 (3.41)	30 (3.40)	67	231
University of Oregon	22.5 (3.94)	19 (3.83)	20 (18)	21.5 (61)	19.5 (4.02)	17.5 (3.89)	21 (86)	43 (602)	36.5 (20.8)	16 (3.89)	12 (3.78)	29	53
University of Colorado	22.5 (3.94)	30 (3.67)	22.5 (17)	27 (55)	24.5 (3.94)	27.5 (3.61)	40 (77)	8 (1487)	16 (31.0)	14 (3.94)	14.5 (3.70)	48	127
Northwestern University	24 (3.91)	31 (3.64)	22.5 (17)	21.5 (61)	19.5 (4.02)	22 (3.73)	17.5 (88)	33 (783)	35 (21.2)	27 (3.63)	18 (3.65)	37	32
U of North Carolina-Chapel Hill	25 (3.90)	17 (3.90)	24 (16)	29.5 (54)	24.5 (3.94)	17.5 (3.89)	32 (81)	11 (1230)	44 (18.6)	23 (3.74)	23 (3.58)	66	150
University of California-Irvine	26 (3.85)	29 (3.68)	29.5 (11)	24 (58)	26 (3.83)	27.5 (3.61)	26.5 (84)	79 (257)	103 (7.6)	46 (3.07)	39.5 (3.22)	34	32
U of Massachusetts at Amherst	27 (3.78)	34.5 (3.59)	34 (10)	29.5 (54)	27.5 (3.80)	20 (3.76)	26.5 (84)	26 (859)	46 (18.3)	40 (3.30)	45.5 (3.12)	47	105
Rutgers State Univ-New Brunswick	28 (3.76)	26 (3.70)	25 (15)	23 (60)	30.5 (3.71)	30 (3.60)	12 (90)	12 (1104)	52 (16.5)	30 (3.54)	35.5 (3.27)	67	135
University of Southern California	29.5 (3.74)	24 (3.71)	34 (10)	27 (55)	29 (3.72)	24 (3.66)	21 (86)	21 (898)	21 (29.0)	37 (3.33)	43.5 (3.18)	31	100
Purdue University	29.5 (3.74)	26 (3.70)	34 (10)	31 (51)	32 (3.67)	25 (3.65)	37 (78)	51 (547)	77.5 (10.7)	31 (3.49)	38 (3.25)	51	131

Appendix Table P - 37 Psychology (Continued)

Institution	93Q [1]	93E [1]	% D [1]	% D-S [1]	93Q T [1]	93E T [1]	VIS [1]	TC [2]	C/F [2]	82Q [3]	82E [3]	TF [4]	TG [4]
University of Rochester	31 (3.73)	23 (3.73)	34 (10)	34 (48)	35 (3.62)	32 (3.59)	37 (78)	22 (886)	15 (31.6)	42 (3.15)	35.5 (3.27)	28	84
Pennsylvania State University	32 (3.72)	37 (3.53)	26.5 (14)	27 (55)	34 (3.63)	45 (3.41)	17.5 (88)	10 (1236)	62 (13.7)	28 (3.62)	24.5 (3.57)	90	259
Duke University	33 (3.69)	40 (3.49)	28 (13)	35 (47)	31 (3.71)	37 (3.50)	23 (85)	7 (1568)	8.5 (39.2)	24 (3.69)	28 (3.43)	40	69
Johns Hopkins University	34.5 (3.68)	20 (3.79)	29.5 (11)	43 (36)	36 (3.61)	30 (3.60)	68 (61)	56 (472)	6 (42.9)	22 (3.75)	27 (3.50)	11	21
New York University	34.5 (3.68)	44.5 (3.45)	42 (7)	32.5 (50)	28 (3.80)	38 (3.49)	37 (78)	23 (876)	48 (17.5)	39 (3.30)	39.5 (3.22)	50	120
University of Iowa	36 (3.64)	32 (3.63)	34 (10)	38 (42)	37 (3.59)	41 (3.44)	40 (77)	55 (484)	58 (14.7)	38 (3.31)	30 (3.40)	33	71
Brown University	37 (3.62)	36 (3.57)	39 (9)	39 (40)	33 (3.64)	33 (3.56)	44.5 (75)	47 (575)	28 (25.0)	26 (3.64)	19 (3.63)	23	17
University of Florida	38 (3.60)	34.5 (3.59)	34 (10)	36 (46)	41 (3.46)	47 (3.39)	30 (82)	20 (919)	59 (14.6)	48 (2.92)	49 (2.98)	63	206
State U of New York-Stony Brook	39 (3.59)	28 (3.69)	42 (7)	32.5 (50)	38 (3.57)	30 (3.60)	32 (81)	64 (343)	82 (10.4)	25 (3.66)	20.5 (3.62)	33	178
Vanderbilt University	40 (3.55)	38 (3.51)	34 (10)	45 (32)	39 (3.51)	52 (3.33)	52 (72)	31 (788)	24 (28.1)	43 (3.11)	35.5 (3.27)	28	52
Uniformed Services U of Hlth Sci	41 (3.54)	54.5 (3.33)	45 (6)	50 (27)	43 (3.42)	75 (2.96)	94 (47)	66.5 (329)	2 (65.8)			5	27
CUNY - Grad Sch & Univ Center	42 (3.48)	63 (3.23)	39 (9)	37 (43)	46 (3.37)	71 (3.06)	35 (79)	27 (850)	101.5 (7.8)	29 (3.61)	35.5 (3.27)	109	455
University of Arizona	43 (3.47)	59 (3.29)	85.5 (1)	41.5 (37)	40 (3.50)	52 (3.33)	32 (81)	72.5 (305)	97.5 (8.0)	75 (2.33)	83.5 (2.40)	38	110
Emory University	44 (3.46)	51 (3.38)	51 (4)	40 (39)	47 (3.36)	52 (3.33)	34 (80)	77 (277)	77.5 (10.7)	74 (2.34)	68.5 (2.55)	26	88
Peabody Col at Vanderbilt Univ	45 (3.44)	54.5 (3.33)	39 (9)	48 (29)	42 (3.44)	56 (3.27)	55 (71)	96 (185)	111 (6.6)			28	115
Michigan State University	46 (3.43)	44.5 (3.45)	51 (4)	41.5 (37)	50 (3.28)	39 (3.48)	55 (71)	63 (382)	97.5 (8.0)	45 (3.10)	41.5 (3.20)	48	160
University of California-Davis	47 (3.42)	48 (3.42)	45 (6)	52 (25)	44 (3.40)	52 (3.33)	60 (67)	74.5 (303)	75 (10.8)	73 (2.34)	77.5 (2.43)	28	34
University of Pittsburgh	48 (3.38)	54.5 (3.33)	47.5 (5)	46.5 (31)	46 (3.37)	46 (3.40)	52 (72)	29 (814)	20 (29.1)	34 (3.37)	33 (3.28)	28	105
Arizona State University	49 (3.35)	40 (3.49)	56 (3)	44 (33)	49 (3.31)	42 (3.43)	47.5 (74)	40 (705)	43 (19.1)	60.5 (2.61)	61 (2.65)	37	112
Clark University	50 (3.30)	47 (3.44)	47.5 (5)	55 (23)	59 (3.08)	75 (2.96)	63 (66)	123.5 (88)	126.5 (4.6)	69 (2.41)	58.5 (2.70)	19	57
Univ of California-Santa Barbara	52 (3.28)	52 (3.37)	42 (7)	52 (25)	51 (3.27)	43 (3.42)	49.5 (73)	44 (595)	31 (23.8)	41 (3.28)	43.5 (3.18)	25	46
University of Connecticut	52 (3.28)	44.5 (3.45)	51 (4)	49 (28)	48 (3.34)	35 (3.52)	40 (77)	42 (635)	55 (15.9)	35.5 (3.36)	32 (3.33)	40	152
University of Maryland College Park	52 (3.28)	49.5 (3.41)	56 (3)	46.5 (31)	53 (3.22)	40 (3.47)	44.5 (75)	35 (744)	50 (16.9)	50 (2.92)	48 (3.05)	44	126
University of Utah	54 (3.23)	59 (3.29)	45 (6)	58 (22)	52 (3.24)	57 (3.25)	63 (66)	49 (567)	41 (19.6)	51 (2.91)	47 (3.08)	29	78
University of South Florida	55.5 (3.22)	83 (2.91)	51 (4)	52 (25)	60 (3.07)	84 (2.81)	44.5 (75)	74.5 (303)	66 (12.6)	58 (2.63)	68.5 (2.55)	24	142
University of Kansas	55.5 (3.22)	42 (3.46)	56 (3)	55 (23)	61 (3.06)	45 (3.41)	42 (76)	83 (244)	91 (8.7)	35.5 (3.36)	30 (3.40)	28	136
University of Miami	57.5 (3.18)	71 (3.11)	64.5 (2)	61 (21)	58 (3.11)	77 (2.94)	65.5 (63)	39 (721)	25 (26.7)	84 (2.27)	96.5 (2.12)	27	105
University of Delaware	57.5 (3.18)	64 (3.21)	64.5 (2)	67.5 (18)	56 (3.12)	58 (3.23)	58 (68)	57 (449)	49 (17.3)	93 (2.04)	93 (2.17)	26	70
Univ of California-Santa Cruz	59.5 (3.16)	73 (3.04)	85.5 (1)	69 (16)	56 (3.12)	73 (3.00)	68 (61)	104 (167)	82 (10.4)			16	60
State Univ of New York-Albany	59.5 (3.16)	62 (3.26)	85.5 (1)	55 (23)	54 (3.15)	66 (3.13)	47.5 (74)	34 (749)	29 (24.2)	57 (2.66)	50 (2.93)	31	121

Institution	93Q [1]	93E [1]	% D [1]	% D-S [1]	93Q T [1]	93E T [1]	VIS [1]	TC [2]	C/F [2]	82Q [3]	82E [3]	TF [4]	TG [4]
State Univ of New York-Buffalo	61 (3.15)	40 (3.49)	64.5 (2)	61 (21)	65 (3.00)	62 (3.20)	60 (67)	59 (433)	63 (13.5)	44 (3.10)	45.5 (3.12)	32	118
University of Denver	62 (3.14)	66.5 (3.18)	85.5 (1)	61 (21)	58 (3.11)	66 (3.13)	65.5 (63)	86 (229)	65 (12.7)	47 (2.98)	51 (2.92)	18	68
Temple University	63.5 (3.12)	61 (3.28)	64.5 (2)	58 (22)	63 (3.03)	69 (3.07)	55 (71)	61 (419)	79.5 (10.5)	59 (2.62)	63 (2.62)	40	77
Washington University	63.5 (3.12)	65 (3.19)	143 (0)	58 (22)	62 (3.05)	64 (3.15)	49.5 (73)	17 (964)	4 (50.7)	55 (2.83)	55.5 (2.77)	19	67
University of Georgia	65 (3.10)	57 (3.30)	51 (4)	65 (19)	73 (2.89)	60 (3.22)	44.5 (75)	45 (592)	53 (16.4)	56 (2.73)	52.5 (2.90)	36	184
Rice University	66 (3.08)	68.5 (3.16)	64.5 (2)	74 (12)	65 (3.00)	71 (3.06)	109 (43)	93 (191)	55 (15.9)	124 (1.39)	122 (1.47)	12	43
University of Missouri-Columbia	67 (3.07)	59 (3.29)	143 (0)	65 (19)	68 (2.98)	52 (3.33)	60 (67)	48 (573)	55 (15.9)	65 (2.53)	62 (2.63)	36	113
University of Illinois at Chicago	68 (3.05)	81 (2.93)	64.5 (2)	67.5 (18)	67 (2.99)	86 (2.78)	70 (59)	91 (210)	119.5 (5.8)	52 (2.88)	57 (2.73)	36	106
University of Houston	69 (3.04)	68.5 (3.16)	143 (0)	63 (20)	70 (2.94)	72 (3.04)	52 (72)	72.5 (305)	87 (9.2)	49 (2.92)	60 (2.68)	33	186
Univ of California-Riverside	70 (3.02)	82 (2.92)	64.5 (2)	65 (19)	74 (2.85)	91 (2.73)	63 (66)	80 (253)	73 (11.0)	88 (2.12)	91 (2.27)	23	64
Texas A&M University	71 (2.94)	89 (2.88)	85.5 (1)	70 (14)	72 (2.90)	93 (2.72)	57 (69)	60 (420)	79.5 (10.5)			40	108
Brandeis University	72 (2.93)	44.5 (3.45)	143 (0)	74 (12)	70 (2.94)	36 (3.51)	73 (56)	114 (114)	95.5 (8.1)	63 (2.56)	76 (2.45)	14	25
Northeastern University	73 (2.92)	92 (2.85)	143 (0)	90 (8)	76 (2.80)	81 (2.86)	82 (51)	52 (546)	14 (32.1)	72 (2.39)	80.5 (2.42)	17	35
State Univ of New York-Binghamton	74.5 (2.91)	76 (3.01)	64.5 (2)	71.5 (13)	77 (2.78)	89 (2.74)	82 (51)	53 (508)	38.5 (20.3)	60.5 (2.61)	66.5 (2.57)	25	103
University of Alabama-Birmingham	74.5 (2.91)	88 (2.89)	143 (0)	71.5 (13)	65 (3.00)	79 (2.92)	79.5 (52)	70 (315)	68.5 (11.7)			27	54
Syracuse University	76 (2.88)	96 (2.83)	85.5 (1)	78 (11)	84 (2.69)	103 (2.59)	76 (54)	68 (325)	75 (10.8)	62 (2.56)	66.5 (2.57)	30	110
Georgia Institute of Technology	77.5 (2.87)	72 (3.06)	85.5 (1)	90 (8)	80 (2.73)	86 (2.78)	117 (39)	46 (585)	18 (29.3)			20	84
University of Hawaii at Manoa	77.5 (2.87)	94 (2.84)	143 (0)	90 (8)	80 (2.73)	119 (2.33)	78 (53)	81 (249)	88.5 (8.9)	64 (2.56)	80.5 (2.42)	28	56
Iowa State University	79 (2.82)	49.5 (3.41)	143 (0)	84.5 (9)	82 (2.72)	52 (3.33)	85 (50)	90 (211)	95.5 (8.1)	91 (2.08)	92 (2.22)	26	79
Wayne State University	80 (2.81)	74.5 (3.03)	56 (3)	78 (11)	95 (2.53)	82 (2.83)	71.5 (57)	54 (503)	64 (13.2)	81 (2.30)	80.5 (2.42)	38	234
Dartmouth College	81 (2.80)	77 (2.99)	143 (0)	84.5 (9)	72 (2.90)	68 (3.10)	100.5 (45)	107 (156)	82 (10.4)			15	14
Colorado State University	82 (2.79)	96 (2.83)	85.5 (1)	90 (8)	78 (2.75)	109 (2.50)	131 (34)	82 (247)	93 (8.5)	110 (1.77)	108.5 (1.95)	29	95
Florida State University	83.5 (2.78)	79.5 (2.95)	85.5 (1)	78 (11)	91 (2.60)	96 (2.71)	112 (42)	119 (106)	115.5 (6.2)	54 (2.83)	54 (2.85)	17	63
University of Vermont	83.5 (2.78)	99.5 (2.78)	85.5 (1)	90 (8)	90 (2.64)	109 (2.50)	85 (50)	66.5 (329)	61 (14.3)	79 (2.32)	73 (2.48)	23	93
Case Western Reserve Univ	85 (2.77)	78 (2.96)	85.5 (1)	81.5 (10)	80 (2.73)	75 (2.96)	68 (61)	65 (332)	36.5 (20.8)	114 (1.69)	106 (2.02)	16	49
Bowling Green State University	86 (2.76)	74.5 (3.03)	143 (0)	84.5 (9)	83 (2.71)	64 (3.15)	82 (51)	102.5 (169)	119.5 (5.8)	70 (2.41)	52.5 (2.90)	29	127
University of Notre Dame	87.5 (2.70)	116 (2.54)	85.5 (1)	84.5 (9)	85 (2.67)	119 (2.33)	104.5 (44)	117 (110)	122.5 (5.0)	119 (1.53)	113 (1.83)	22	63
West Virginia University	87.5 (2.70)	85.5 (2.90)	143 (0)	78 (11)	88 (2.65)	89 (2.74)	94 (47)	111 (129)	118 (5.9)	82 (2.29)	83.5 (2.40)	22	69
University of Kentucky	89.5 (2.69)	102.5 (2.76)	143 (0)	78 (11)	97 (2.52)	119 (2.33)	76 (54)	50 (551)	45 (18.4)	104 (1.85)	105 (2.05)	30	84
U of Texas-Southwestern Med Ctr	89.5 (2.69)	70 (3.13)	143 (0)	101 (6)	104 (2.38)	52 (3.33)	172.5 (21)	18 (956)	7 (39.8)			24	57

Appendix Table P - 37 Psychology (Continued)

Institution	93Q [1]	93E [1]	% D [1]	% D-S [1]	93Q T [1]	93E T [1]	VIS [1]	TC [2]	C/F [2]	82Q [3]	82E [3]	TF [4]	TG [4]
University of South Carolina	92 (2.67)	66.5 (3.18)	85.5 (1)	95.5 (7)	93 (2.55)	60 (3.22)	79.5 (52)	84 (240)	110 (6.7)	98 (1.97)	101 (2.08)	36	130
Virginia Polytech Inst & State U	92 (2.67)	92 (2.85)	85.5 (1)	74 (12)	88 (2.65)	93 (2.72)	88.5 (49)	78 (274)	70 (11.4)	83 (2.29)	96.5 (2.12)	24	86
U of North Carolina-Greensboro	92 (2.67)	85.5 (2.90)	143 (0)	95.5 (7)	75 (2.82)	68 (3.10)	97.5 (46)	94.5 (190)	92 (8.6)	90 (2.08)	65 (2.58)	22	44
University of Tennessee-Knoxville	94 (2.66)	102.5 (2.76)	143 (0)	101 (6)	88 (2.65)	79 (2.92)	85 (50)	89 (215)	86 (9.3)	80 (2.31)	70 (2.52)	23	97
Boston University	95.5 (2.65)	99.5 (2.78)	143 (0)	81.5 (10)	108 (2.33)	98 (2.64)	88.5 (49)	106 (162)	112.5 (6.5)	53 (2.87)	55.5 (2.77)	25	120
University of Nebraska-Lincoln	95.5 (2.65)	85.5 (2.90)	143 (0)	101 (6)	111 (2.31)	87 (2.75)	76 (54)	101 (170)	112.5 (6.5)	89 (2.11)	87 (2.33)	26	87
Virginia Commonwealth University	97 (2.63)	104.5 (2.73)	64.5 (2)	95.5 (7)	93 (2.55)	102 (2.61)	128 (35)	87 (227)	85 (9.5)	96.5 (1.98)	107 (2.00)	24	150
Kent State University	98 (2.61)	96 (2.83)	143 (0)	95.5 (7)	86 (2.66)	84 (2.81)	74 (55)	85 (232)	94 (8.3)	78 (2.32)	77.5 (2.43)	28	145
Southern Illinois University	99 (2.58)	85.5 (2.90)	56 (3)	107 (5)	98 (2.46)	81 (2.86)	88.5 (49)	98 (178)	121 (5.6)	68 (2.42)	58.5 (2.70)	32	100
University of Rhode Island	100 (2.57)	90 (2.87)	143 (0)	118 (4)	100 (2.44)	100 (2.62)	97.5 (46)	58 (445)	42 (19.3)	107 (1.79)	108.5 (1.95)	23	114
University of New Hampshire	101 (2.56)	79.5 (2.95)	143 (0)	118 (4)	108 (2.33)	102 (2.61)	126 (36)	102.5 (169)	88.5 (8.9)	105.5 (1.80)	103 (2.07)	19	36
University of Texas at Arlington	102 (2.55)	134.5 (2.26)	143 (0)	118 (4)	97 (2.52)	123 (2.29)	109 (43)	121 (90)	104 (7.5)			12	23
Georgia State University	103 (2.53)	125.5 (2.41)	64.5 (2)	90 (8)	94 (2.54)	116 (2.36)	71.5 (57)	71 (313)	75 (10.8)	94 (2.00)	96.5 (2.12)	29	137
George Washington University	104 (2.52)	123 (2.43)	85.5 (1)	101 (6)	116 (2.27)	123 (2.29)	137 (32)	143 (65)	154 (2.7)	108 (1.78)	111 (1.88)	24	111
Loyola University of Chicago	105 (2.50)	106.5 (2.69)	85.5 (1)	118 (4)	104 (2.38)	96 (2.71)	94 (47)	108.5 (140)	134.5 (3.9)	85 (2.24)	74.5 (2.47)	36	115
George Mason University	106 (2.49)	137.5 (2.22)	85.5 (1)	107 (5)	99 (2.45)	131 (2.08)	114 (41)	113 (118)	130.5 (4.2)			28	126
University of Cincinnati	107 (2.46)	99.5 (2.78)	143 (0)	101 (6)	106 (2.35)	104 (2.57)	104.5 (44)	142 (70)	161.5 (2.2)	77 (2.32)	80.5 (2.42)	32	86
Tufts University	108 (2.45)	92 (2.85)	85.5 (1)	90 (8)	113 (2.30)	62 (3.20)	91 (48)	92 (201)	60 (14.4)			14	30
University of Louisville	109 (2.41)	123 (2.43)	143 (0)	118 (4)	120 (2.25)	150 (1.67)	145.5 (29)	125 (87)	126.5 (4.6)	101 (1.87)	99.5 (2.10)	19	91
Miami University	110.5 (2.40)	120 (2.47)	143 (0)	131.5 (3)	106 (2.35)	115 (2.40)	109 (43)	134.5 (75)	149.5 (3.0)	92 (2.05)	88.5 (2.32)	25	72
Yeshiva University	110.5 (2.40)	151.5 (2.03)	143 (0)	147 (2)	108 (2.33)	150 (1.67)	94 (47)	127.5 (81)	149.5 (3.0)	116 (1.58)	116 (1.67)	27	107
University of Alabama	112 (2.39)	118 (2.50)	143 (0)	118 (4)	134 (2.08)	150 (1.67)	131 (34)	134.5 (75)	137.5 (3.8)	71 (2.39)	71.5 (2.50)	20	31
University of Tulsa	113.5 (2.38)	112 (2.61)	85.5 (1)	101 (6)	127 (2.20)	105 (2.56)	100.5 (45)	69 (317)	40 (19.8)			16	49
U of Maryland Baltimore County	113.5 (2.38)	140.5 (2.19)	143 (0)	107 (5)	124 (2.22)	132 (2.00)	94 (47)	97 (179)	101.5 (7.8)			23	108
University of Oklahoma	115.5 (2.37)	113 (2.58)	85.5 (1)	107 (5)	130 (2.13)	119 (2.33)	134 (33)	110 (132)	107 (6.9)	111 (1.76)	90 (2.28)	19	33
Washington State University	115.5 (2.37)	114 (2.56)	143 (0)	131.5 (3)	118 (2.26)	114 (2.43)	141.5 (30)	88 (221)	84 (9.6)	86 (2.19)	86 (2.37)	23	52
Ohio University	118.5 (2.35)	99.5 (2.78)	85.5 (1)	131.5 (3)	129 (2.15)	100 (2.62)	109 (43)	99 (174)	106 (7.0)	95 (1.98)	99.5 (2.10)	25	101
University of Maine	118.5 (2.35)	123 (2.43)	143 (0)	118 (4)	141 (1.89)	123 (2.29)	134 (33)	132 (76)	128.5 (4.5)			17	42
Howard University	118.5 (2.35)	131 (2.33)	143 (0)	131.5 (3)	113 (2.30)	126 (2.22)	104.5 (44)	129 (80)	115.5 (6.2)			13	86
Texas Tech University	118.5 (2.35)	153 (2.02)	143 (0)	131.5 (3)	118 (2.26)	138 (1.80)	134 (33)	108.5 (140)	122.5 (5.0)	123 (1.41)	121 (1.48)	28	125

Institution	93Q [1]	93E [1]	% D [1]	% D-S [1]	93Q T [1]	93E T [1]	VIS [1]	TC [2]	C/F [2]	82Q [3]	82E [3]	TF [4]	TG [4]
Bryn Mawr College	121 (2.34)	142 (2.17)	143 (0)	147 (2)	125 (2.21)	150 (1.67)	114 (41)	130 (79)	71 (11.3)	102 (1.87)	74.5 (2.47)	7	42
North Carolina State University	122 (2.33)	110 (2.63)	143 (0)	118 (4)	111 (2.31)	91 (2.73)	104.5 (44)	126 (85)	149.5 (3.0)	112 (1.75)		28	124
Brigham Young University	123 (2.31)	121 (2.44)	85.5 (1)	131.5 (3)	134 (2.08)	129 (2.14)	124 (37)	140.5 (71)	156.5 (2.5)	118 (1.57)		28	70
Louisiana State U & A&M College	124.5 (2.28)	115 (2.55)	143 (0)	131.5 (3)	114 (2.28)	113 (2.44)	128 (35)	62 (404)	67 (11.9)	109 (1.78)	116 (1.67)	34	129
American University	124.5 (2.28)	151.5 (2.03)	143 (0)	147 (2)	132 (2.11)	150 (1.67)	124 (37)	105 (164)	68.5 (11.7)			14	65
Catholic University of America	126.5 (2.27)	106.5 (2.69)	143 (0)	147 (2)	116 (2.27)	109 (2.50)	114 (41)	112 (122)	105 (7.2)	87 (2.19)	85 (2.38)	17	85
Georgetown University	126.5 (2.27)	108.5 (2.67)	143 (0)	147 (2)	102 (2.41)	96 (2.71)	128 (35)	134.5 (75)	108.5 (6.8)			11	13
New Mexico State University	129.5 (2.23)	104.5 (2.73)	64.5 (2)	131.5 (3)	129 (2.15)	131 (2.08)	155 (27)	150 (50)	140 (3.6)			14	18
University of Texas at Dallas	129.5 (2.23)	155 (1.88)	143 (0)	118 (4)	124 (2.22)	150 (1.67)	120.5 (38)	131 (77)	149.5 (3.0)			26	77
Texas Christian University	129.5 (2.23)	118 (2.50)	143 (0)	147 (2)	120 (2.25)	150 (1.67)	169.5 (22)	120 (95)	99.5 (7.9)	99 (1.91)		12	41
Tulane University	129.5 (2.23)	111 (2.62)	143 (0)	147 (2)	122 (2.24)	96 (2.71)	137 (32)	115 (113)	114 (6.3)	103 (1.86)	103 (2.07)	18	68
Claremont Graduate School	132 (2.22)	131 (2.33)	143 (0)	118 (4)	122 (2.24)	121 (2.31)	117 (39)	159 (34)	124.5 (4.9)	67 (2.42)	88.5 (2.32)	7	110
University of Nevada, Reno	133 (2.21)	127.5 (2.38)	85.5 (1)	107 (5)	143 (1.88)	129 (2.14)	100.5 (45)	123.5 (88)	108.5 (6.8)			13	67
University of Mississippi	134 (2.18)	145.5 (2.11)	143 (0)	118 (4)	127 (2.20)	135 (1.88)	141.5 (30)	152 (44)	146 (3.1)	132 (1.10)	130 (1.15)	14	68
Univ of Health Sc/Chicago Med Sch	135 (2.17)	127.5 (2.38)	143 (0)	164 (1)	101 (2.43)	109 (2.50)	141.5 (30)	156 (36)	128.5 (4.5)			8	66
Kansas State University	136 (2.15)	145.5 (2.11)	85.5 (1)	118 (4)	137 (2.00)	139 (1.75)	124 (37)	144.5 (64)	137.5 (3.8)	66 (2.51)	71.5 (2.50)	17	54
Hahnemann University	137.5 (2.13)	149.5 (2.04)	143 (0)	118 (4)	148 (1.82)	150 (1.67)	100.5 (45)	155 (39)	141 (3.5)			11	82
Saint Louis University	137.5 (2.13)	158 (1.80)	143 (0)	147 (2)	146 (1.83)	150 (1.67)	150.5 (28)	146 (63)	144.5 (3.2)	117 (1.58)	124 (1.42)	20	92
University of Wisconsin-Milwaukee	139 (2.12)	54.5 (3.33)	143 (0)	131.5 (3)	132 (2.11)	52 (3.33)	139 (31)	149 (58)	153 (2.8)	96.5 (1.98)	103 (2.07)	21	68
University of Akron	140.5 (2.07)	137.5 (2.22)	143 (0)	118 (4)	151 (1.72)	126 (2.22)	166.5 (23)	94.5 (190)	99.5 (7.9)			24	171
Univ of Missouri-Saint Louis	140.5 (2.07)	108.5 (2.67)	143 (0)	164 (1)	137 (2.00)	(n/s)	172.5 (21)	159 (34)	163.5 (2.1)			16	94
Northern Illinois University	142 (2.06)	134.5 (2.26)	143 (0)	131.5 (3)	140 (1.96)	137 (1.83)	109 (43)	122 (89)	149.5 (3.0)	105.5 (1.80)	94 (2.13)	30	58
St. John's University	143 (2.05)	143.5 (2.12)	143 (0)	147 (2)	137 (2.00)	150 (1.67)	158.5 (26)	166.5 (23)	169 (1.2)			20	113
Adelphi University	144 (2.04)	161 (1.72)	85.5 (1)	101 (6)	148 (1.82)	160 (1.43)	88.5 (49)	153.5 (42)	149.5 (3.0)	129 (1.23)	127.5 (1.25)	14	150
Boston College	145.5 (2.00)	131 (2.33)	143 (0)	147 (2)	137 (2.00)	127 (2.17)	120.5 (38)	144.5 (64)	133 (4.0)			16	20
University of Toledo	145.5 (2.00)	137.5 (2.22)	143 (0)	164 (1)	158 (1.63)	(n/s)	169.5 (22)	118 (108)	117 (6.0)	130 (1.19)		18	51
Lehigh University	147 (1.95)	154 (2.00)	143 (0)	178 (0)	145 (1.85)	150 (n/s)	150.5 (28)	148 (60)	137.5 (3.8)			16	23
Fordham University	148.5 (1.92)	140.5 (2.19)	143 (0)	164 (1)	149 (1.75)	133 (1.97)	145.5 (29)	161.5 (30)	167 (1.7)	113 (1.71)	116 (1.67)	18	201
Ball State University	148.5 (1.92)	169.5 (1.50)	143 (0)	178 (0)	156 (1.67)	163 (1.25)	175.5 (20)	127.5 (81)	156.5 (2.5)			32	76
Univ of Missouri-Kansas City	150.5 (1.90)	143.5 (2.12)	85.5 (1)	164 (1)	159 (1.57)	150 (1.67)	158.5 (26)	165 (26)	161.5 (2.2)			12	22

Appendix Table P - 37 Psychology (Continued)

Institution	93Q [1]	93E [1]	% D [1]	% D-S [1]	93Q T [1]	93E T [1]	VIS [1]	TC [2]	C/F [2]	82Q [3]	82E [3]	TF [4]	TG [4]
University of Wyoming	**150.5** (1.90)	**165** (1.67)	**143** (0)	**178** (0)	**137** (2.00)	**150** (1.67)	**175.5** (20)	**168** (19)	**165** (1.9)	**133** (1.09)	**123** (1.45)	10	39
Univ of Arkansas-Fayetteville	**152** (1.89)	**165** (1.67)	**143** (0)	**164** (1)	**143** (1.88)	**150** (1.67)	**131** (34)	**134.5** (75)	**134.5** (3.9)	**126** (1.35)	**116** (1.67)	19	36
Western Michigan University	**153** (1.87)	**159** (1.79)	**85.5** (1)	**147** (2)	**145** (1.85)	**134** (1.95)	**150.5** (28)	**138.5** (72)	**137.5** (3.8)	**100** (1.91)	**96.5** (2.12)	19	48
Auburn University	**154** (1.85)	**149.5** (2.04)	**143** (0)	**118** (4)	**160** (1.56)	**136** (1.85)	**117** (39)	**140.5** (71)	**144.5** (3.2)	**115** (1.68)	**120** (1.55)	22	107
Hofstra University	**155** (1.82)	**165** (1.67)	**143** (0)	**118** (4)	**158** (1.63)	**150** (1.67)	**120.5** (38)	**164** (28)	**159.5** (2.3)	**140** (0.65)	**131** (0.87)	12	143
Old Dominion University	**156** (1.81)	**131** (2.33)	**143** (0)	**147** (2)	**154** (1.69)	**109** (2.50)	**163.5** (24)	**116** (111)	**72** (11.1)			10	24
Illinois Institute of Technology	**157** (1.79)	**147.5** (2.08)	**85.5** (1)	**147** (2)	**151** (1.72)	**150** (1.67)	**175.5** (20)	**151** (49)	**143** (3.3)	**127** (1.29)	**129** (1.18)	15	106
University of North Texas	**158** (1.76)	**165** (1.67)	**85.5** (1)	**147** (2)	**164** (1.40)	**150** (1.67)	**120.5** (38)	**100** (173)	**124.5** (4.9)	**128** (1.24)	**125.5** (1.33)	35	159
Fuller Theological Seminary	**159.5** (1.73)	**169.5** (1.50)	**143** (0)	**147** (2)	**161** (1.50)	**164** (1.17)	**137** (32)	**147** (61)	**132** (4.1)	**121** (1.45)	**125.5** (1.33)	15	165
University of Montana	**159.5** (1.73)	**125.5** (2.41)	**143** (0)	**164** (1)	**153** (1.70)	**109** (2.50)	**169.5** (22)	**173** (8)	**174.5** (0.3)	**122** (1.43)	**110** (1.92)	30	52
Univ of Southern Mississippi	**161** (1.72)	**131** (2.33)	**143** (0)	**178** (0)	**156** (1.67)	**150** (1.67)	**150.5** (28)	**137** (74)	**156.5** (2.5)	**138** (0.70)		30	110
Utah State University	**162.5** (1.64)	**165** (1.67)	**143** (0)	**164** (1)	**173** (1.00)	(n/s)	**179.5** (18)	**153.5** (42)	**156.5** (2.5)	**125** (1.38)	**119** (1.58)	17	54
University of New Orleans	**162.5** (1.64)	**118** (2.50)	**143** (0)	**164** (1)	**151** (1.72)	(n/s)	**163.5** (24)	**138.5** (72)	**130.5** (4.2)			17	34
Univ of California-San Francisco	**164** (1.60)	**137.5** (2.22)	**64.5** (2)	**118** (4)	**170** (1.22)	**109** (2.50)	**141.5** (30)	**76** (300)	**1** (100.0)			3	8
Baylor University	**165** (1.58)	**165** (1.67)	**143** (0)	**147** (2)	**166** (1.31)	**161** (1.39)	**155** (27)	**174.5** (6)	**171** (0.6)	**134** (1.08)	**127.5** (1.25)	10	7
Duquesne University	**166.5** (1.55)	**157** (1.82)	**143** (0)	**147** (2)	**173** (1.00)	**162** (1.33)	**163.5** (24)	**183** (0)	**182** (0.0)			7	110
Oklahoma State University	**166.5** (1.55)	**156** (1.85)	**143** (0)	**164** (1)	**164** (1.40)	**150** (1.67)	**158.5** (26)	**166.5** (23)	**166** (1.8)	**120** (1.47)	**116** (1.67)	13	38
University of North Dakota	**168** (1.50)	**147.5** (2.08)	**143** (0)	**178** (0)	**162** (1.43)	(n/s)	**166.5** (23)	**161.5** (30)	**159.5** (2.3)	**131** (1.19)	**112** (1.87)	13	53
Univ of Puerto Rico-Rio Piedras	**169.5** (1.40)	(n/s)	**143** (0)	**147** (2)	**173** (1.00)	(n/s)	**183.5** (12)	**172** (9)	**174.5** (0.3)			31	249
Fairleigh Dickinson University	**169.5** (1.40)	**160** (1.78)	**143** (0)	**178** (0)	**167** (1.29)	**150** (1.67)	**163.5** (24)	**159** (34)	**163.5** (2.1)			16	82
Cal Sch Prof Psych-Alameda	**171** (1.30)	**176** (0.69)	**143** (0)	**147** (2)	**176** (0.89)	**171** (0.00)	**150.5** (28)	**171** (10)	**174.5** (0.3)	**135** (1.00)	**132** (0.78)	38	528
University of Northern Colorado	**172** (1.22)	**165** (1.67)	**143** (0)	**178** (0)	**169** (1.25)	(n/s)	**183.5** (12)	**163** (29)	**168** (1.6)			18	47
Saybrook Institute	**173** (1.08)	**177.5** (0.67)	**143** (0)	**178** (0)	**165** (1.33)	(n/s)	**178** (19)	**179.5** (1)	**182** (0.0)			42	171
Pacific Grad Sch of Psychology	**174** (1.06)	**175** (0.72)	**143** (0)	**178** (0)	**173** (1.00)	**166** (0.63)	**145.5** (29)	**178** (2)	**178** (0.1)			22	65
East Texas State University	**176** (1.04)	**174** (0.83)	**85.5** (1)	**147** (2)	**169** (1.25)	(n/s)	**175.5** (20)	**183** (0)	**182** (0.0)			10	59
Cal Sch Prof Psych-Los Angeles	**176** (1.04)	**173** (0.88)	**143** (0)	**147** (2)	**178** (0.80)	**171** (0.00)	**155** (27)	**179.5** (1)	**182** (0.0)			32	408
Cal Sch Prof Psych-San Diego	**176** (1.04)	**179** (0.65)	**143** (0)	**178** (0)	**183** (0.67)	**171** (0.00)	**145.5** (29)	**177** (4)	**177** (0.2)	**139** (0.67)	**133** (0.33)	26	631
Cal Sch Prof Psych-Fresno	**178** (0.91)	**182** (0.46)	**143** (0)	**164** (1)	**183** (0.67)	**171** (0.00)	**161** (25)	**176** (5)	**174.5** (0.3)			20	144
Biola University	**179.5** (0.86)	**183** (0.19)	**143** (0)	**164** (1)	**178** (0.80)	**171** (0.00)	**169.5** (22)	**183** (0)	**182** (0.0)	**137** (0.80)		21	9
University of Detroit Mercy	**179.5** (0.86)	**180.5** (0.56)	**143** (0)	**178** (0)	**173** (1.00)	(n/s)	**185** (11)	**183** (0)	**182** (0.0)	**136** (0.84)		15	126

Institution	93Q [1]	93E [1]	% D [1]	% D-S [1]	93Q T [1]	93E T [1]	VIS [1]	TC [2]	C/F [2]	82Q [3]	82E [3]	TF [4]	TG [4]
Fielding Institute	**181** (0.84)	**172** (0.98)	**143** (0)	**178** (0)	**180** (0.75)	**166** (0.63)	**150.5** (28)	**170** (11)	**172** (0.4)			29	430
Mississippi State University	**182** (0.80)	**171** (1.11)	**143** (0)	**178** (0)	**183** (0.67)	(n/s)	**181.5** (17)	**174.5** (6)	**170** (1.0)			6	29
Rutgers State Univ-Newark	**183** (0.74)	**177.5** (0.67)	**143** (0)	**164** (1)	**179** (0.79)	**171** (0.00)	**158.5** (26)	**169** (17)	**142** (3.4)	**76** (2.33)	**64** (2.60)	5	34
Texas Woman's University	**184** (0.73)	**180.5** (0.56)	**143** (0)	**178** (0)	**183** (0.67)	**171** (0.00)	**179.5** (18)	**183** (0)	**182** (0.0)	**141** (0.44)		15	78
Stevens Inst of Technology	**185** (0.20)	**184** (0.00)	**143** (0)	**178** (0)	**185** (0.25)	**171** (0.00)	**181.5** (17)	**157** (35)	**90** (8.8)			4	22

Sources: 1. National Survey of Graduate Faculty
2. Institute for Scientific Information
3. 1982 Survey of Graduate Faculty
4. Institutional Coordinator Data

n/s After trimming no cases remained

Appendix Table P - 38 Relative Rankings for Research-Doctorate Programs in Religion

Institution	93Q [1]	93E [1]	% D [1]	% D-S [1]	93Q T [1]	93E T [1]	VIS [1]	FA [2]	82Q [3]	82E [3]	TF [4]	TG [4]
University of Chicago	**1** (4.76)	**2** (4.01)	**1.5** (72)	**1** (93)	**1** (4.80)	**3** (3.99)	**3** (96)	**7** (8)			26	224
Harvard University	**2** (4.73)	**1** (4.10)	**1.5** (72)	**2** (92)	**2** (4.77)	**1** (4.25)	**1** (98)	**3** (14)			39	59
Princeton University	**3** (4.33)	**4** (3.89)	**3** (41)	**4.5** (75)	**3** (4.45)	**2** (4.00)	**7** (89)	**5.5** (9)			12	28
Duke University	**4** (4.25)	**3** (3.90)	**4** (40)	**3** (80)	**4** (4.34)	**4** (3.82)	**2** (97)	**8** (7)			33	102
Emory University	**5** (4.05)	**6** (3.59)	**6** (20)	**4.5** (75)	**5** (4.00)	**5** (3.53)	**5** (92)	**4** (10)			43	118
University of Virginia	**6** (3.96)	**9** (3.46)	**8** (16)	**6** (63)	**7** (3.89)	**9** (3.33)	**9.5** (84)	**9** (4)			29	81
Vanderbilt University	**7** (3.85)	**8** (3.50)	**7** (17)	**7** (60)	**9** (3.81)	**12** (3.28)	**6** (90)	**14** (2)			27	133
Princeton Theological Seminary	**8** (3.84)	**5** (3.61)	**5** (22)	**8** (58)	**10** (3.76)	**6** (3.42)	**4** (93)	**32** (0)			37	126
Univ of California-Santa Barbara	**9** (3.82)	**11** (3.33)	**9** (15)	**10.5** (51)	**13** (3.64)	**13** (3.23)	**16** (77)	**32** (0)			18	60
Jewish Theological Seminary	**10.5** (3.74)	**12.5** (3.26)	**14** (7)	**18** (28)	**6** (3.90)	**9** (3.33)	**33** (48)	**5.5** (9)			37	99
University of Pennsylvania	**10.5** (3.74)	**15** (3.22)	**14** (7)	**10.5** (51)	**8** (3.84)	**14** (3.21)	**16** (77)	**1.5** (19)			47	28
University of Notre Dame	**12** (3.73)	**14** (3.24)	**10** (14)	**9** (52)	**11** (3.75)	**9** (3.33)	**8** (88)	**20.5** (1)			30	83
Hebrew Union College	**13** (3.71)	**7** (3.53)	**14** (7)	**16** (30)	**12** (3.74)	**9** (3.33)	**31** (50)	**32** (0)			28	47
Columbia University	**14** (3.57)	**10** (3.40)	**17** (3)	**12** (44)	**14** (3.60)	**9** (3.33)	**13.5** (78)	**11** (3)			23	55
Brown University	**15** (3.55)	**12.5** (3.26)	**17** (3)	**13.5** (42)	**15** (3.46)	**15** (3.19)	**13.5** (78)	**1.5** (19)			42	19
Southern Methodist University	**16** (3.53)	**16** (3.13)	**11** (9)	**15** (38)	**17** (3.24)	**17** (2.99)	**9.5** (84)	**32** (0)			24	25
Boston College	**17** (3.42)	**17** (3.12)	**17** (3)	**13.5** (42)	**16** (3.34)	**16** (3.11)	**12** (80)	**20.5** (1)			31	73
Union Theological Seminary in VA	**18** (3.08)	**18** (3.10)	**12** (8)	**19** (26)	**24** (2.83)	**20** (2.83)	**16** (77)	**32** (0)			20	49
Stanford University	**19** (3.05)	**19** (3.00)	**21** (2)	**17** (29)	**18** (3.03)	**19** (2.84)	**21** (71)	**14** (2)			10	30
Claremont Graduate School	**20.5** (3.02)	**21** (2.78)	**21** (2)	**21** (22)	**22** (2.86)	**21** (2.81)	**18** (74)	**20.5** (1)			5	106
Drew University	**20.5** (3.02)	**22** (2.76)	**25** (1)	**20** (24)	**19.5** (2.91)	**22** (2.76)	**11** (83)	**11** (3)			35	191
Boston University	**22** (2.93)	**20** (2.90)	**32.5** (0)	**23.5** (15)	**19.5** (2.91)	**18** (2.90)	**21** (71)	**14** (2)			11	137
Northwestern University	**23** (2.91)	**24** (2.73)	**32.5** (0)	**23.5** (15)	**25** (2.80)	**26** (2.62)	**19** (73)	**11** (3)			13	15
Catholic University of America	**24** (2.90)	**23** (2.74)	**25** (1)	**25** (14)	**23** (2.85)	**27** (2.61)	**26** (63)	**20.5** (1)			35	130
Temple University	**25** (2.84)	**30** (2.55)	**32.5** (0)	**22** (16)	**21** (2.89)	**23** (2.75)	**23** (66)	**20.5** (1)			17	92
University of Iowa	**26.5** (2.83)	**29** (2.58)	**32.5** (0)	**26** (13)	**28** (2.72)	**28** (2.50)	**21** (71)	**32** (0)			13	35
Syracuse University	**26.5** (2.83)	**25.5** (2.65)	**32.5** (0)	**28.5** (11)	**26** (2.79)	**24** (2.74)	**26** (63)	**20.5** (1)			12	58
Fordham University	**28** (2.73)	**27.5** (2.61)	**32.5** (0)	**27** (12)	**29** (2.68)	**29** (2.35)	**24** (64)	**32** (0)			20	207
University of Denver	**29** (2.65)	**27.5** (2.61)	**32.5** (0)	**31.5** (9)	**27** (2.73)	**25** (2.73)	**28** (59)	**20.5** (1)			30	78
Rice University	**30** (2.56)	**31** (2.41)	**32.5** (0)	**30** (10)	**32** (2.26)	**33.5** (2.08)	**26** (63)	**20.5** (1)			7	25

Institution	93Q [1]	93E [1]	% D [1]	% D-S [1]	93Q T [1]	93E T [1]	VIS [1]	FA [2]	82Q [3]	82E [3]	TF [4]	TG [4]
Baylor University	**31** (2.50)	**25.5** (2.65)	**21** (2)	**28.5** (11)	**33** (2.10)	**31** (2.22)	**34** (47)	**32** (0)			36	73
University of Southern California	**32** (2.49)	**32** (2.22)	**32.5** (0)	**31.5** (9)	**30** (2.48)	**32** (2.14)	**29.5** (54)	**20.5** (1)			7	58
University of Pittsburgh	**33** (2.15)	**35** (1.95)	**32.5** (0)	**37** (2)	**31** (2.39)	**34** (2.08)	**35** (45)	**20.5** (1)			16	18
Southern Baptist Theological Sem	**34** (1.96)	**33** (2.14)	**21** (2)	**33** (6)	**36** (1.71)	**35** (2.00)	**29.5** (54)	**32** (0)			33	171
Andrews University	**35** (1.86)	**38** (1.39)	**21** (2)	**35.5** (3)	**35** (1.75)	**37** (1.11)	**36** (33)	**32** (0)			41	125
Duquesne University	**36** (1.83)	**36** (1.91)	**32.5** (0)	**35.5** (3)	**34** (1.91)	**31** (2.22)	**37** (32)	**32** (0)			10	85
Fuller Theological Seminary	**37** (1.74)	**34** (2.04)	**25** (1)	**34** (4)	**37** (1.19)	**37** (1.11)	**32** (49)	**32** (0)			4	63
New Orleans Baptist Theo Seminary	**38** (1.24)	**37** (1.56)	**32.5** (0)	**38** (0)	**38** (0.78)	**38** (0.67)	**38** (29)	**32** (0)			24	61

Sources:
1. National Survey of Graduate Faculty
2. Associations and Organizations Administrating Prestigious Awards and Honors
3. 1982 Survey of Graduate Faculty
4. Institutional Coordinator Data

Appendix Table P - 39 Relative Rankings for Research-Doctorate Programs in Sociology

Institution	93Q [1]	93E [1]	% D [1]	% D-S [1]	93Q T [1]	93E T [1]	VIS [1]	TC [2]	C/F [2]	82Q [3]	82E [3]	TF [4]	TG [4]
University of Chicago	1 (4.77)	2 (4.26)	1 (79)	1 (95)	1 (4.85)	2 (4.33)	2 (100)	7 (429)	4 (17.2)	1 (4.66)	4 (4.00)	25	155
University of Wisconsin-Madison	2 (4.74)	1 (4.61)	2 (75)	2 (94)	2 (4.76)	1 (4.61)	5.5 (99)	2 (660)	15 (9.6)	2 (4.58)	1 (4.52)	69	221
University of California-Berkeley	3 (4.56)	11 (3.60)	3 (62)	3.5 (91)	3 (4.63)	18 (3.30)	5.5 (99)	48 (77)	67 (2.3)	3 (4.49)	8 (3.78)	33	109
University of Michigan	4 (4.39)	3 (4.08)	4 (45)	5.5 (90)	4 (4.43)	3 (4.08)	10 (98)	4 (542)	6 (15.1)	4 (4.47)	2 (4.35)	36	163
Univ of California-Los Angeles	5 (4.36)	6 (3.79)	5 (43)	3.5 (91)	6 (4.25)	9 (3.66)	5.5 (99)	1 (728)	14 (10.0)	9 (4.09)	10 (3.70)	73	139
U of North Carolina-Chapel Hill	6 (4.31)	4 (4.00)	6 (41)	5.5 (90)	5 (4.36)	4 (3.99)	5.5 (99)	13 (278)	10 (11.1)	6 (4.27)	3 (4.18)	25	78
Harvard University	7 (4.18)	12 (3.58)	7 (37)	7 (83)	7 (4.22)	11 (3.52)	2 (100)	32 (124)	24.5 (7.3)	5 (4.32)	9 (3.77)	17	81
Stanford University	8 (4.08)	7 (3.77)	8 (28)	9 (75)	8 (4.18)	6 (3.81)	10 (98)	30.5 (142)	16 (9.5)	7 (4.20)	5 (3.90)	15	76
Northwestern University	9 (4.07)	10 (3.61)	9 (26)	10.5 (74)	9 (4.04)	12.5 (3.51)	19.5 (95)	24 (195)	21 (7.8)	22 (3.34)	24 (3.10)	25	71
University of Washington	10 (4.03)	8 (3.73)	11 (21)	8 (81)	12 (3.95)	8 (3.69)	2 (100)	15 (265)	17 (8.8)	11 (3.96)	7 (3.85)	30	75
University of Pennsylvania	11 (4.02)	9 (3.66)	10 (22)	10.5 (74)	10 (4.03)	7 (3.71)	13.5 (97)	8 (328)	11 (10.6)	12 (3.87)	12.5 (3.42)	31	59
Indiana University	12 (3.94)	5 (3.85)	12 (19)	12 (69)	11 (4.01)	5 (3.91)	19.5 (95)	23 (198)	31 (6.6)	13 (3.87)	6 (3.88)	30	74
Princeton University	13 (3.79)	18.5 (3.29)	14 (13)	13 (68)	13 (3.88)	20 (3.23)	16 (96)	63.5 (45)	64.5 (2.5)	16 (3.56)	20.5 (3.27)	18	26
University of Arizona	14 (3.78)	17 (3.41)	16 (10)	14 (65)	14 (3.86)	15 (3.40)	23 (94)	46 (80)	41.5 (4.2)	10 (4.06)	12.5 (3.42)	19	59
Columbia University	15 (3.76)	20 (3.25)	13 (17)	15.5 (61)	15 (3.83)	19 (3.24)	10 (98)	50 (73)	48 (3.8)	8 (4.15)	11 (3.60)	19	79
University of Texas at Austin	16 (3.64)	13 (3.56)	17 (9)	15.5 (61)	18 (3.54)	10 (3.54)	10 (98)	11 (293)	22.5 (7.7)	18 (3.52)	14 (3.38)	38	58
Johns Hopkins University	17 (3.56)	14 (3.51)	15 (11)	17 (56)	17 (3.55)	12.5 (3.51)	13.5 (97)	34 (112)	12 (10.2)	36 (2.72)	30.5 (2.92)	11	32
Pennsylvania State University	18 (3.51)	15 (3.47)	19.5 (6)	18 (49)	16 (3.57)	14 (3.42)	34 (88)	25 (192)	27 (7.1)	53 (2.22)	39 (2.58)	27	32
Yale University	19 (3.49)	28.5 (3.04)	24 (4)	19 (48)	19 (3.44)	31.5 (2.86)	19.5 (95)	9 (300)	5 (16.7)	15 (3.71)	23 (3.20)	18	50
Duke University	20 (3.42)	16 (3.43)	18 (7)	20 (47)	23 (3.27)	16.5 (3.37)	16 (96)	5 (491)	2 (25.8)	28 (3.16)	20.5 (3.27)	19	50
New York University	21 (3.34)	33 (2.93)	19.5 (6)	29 (33)	26.5 (3.21)	33 (2.82)	38 (87)	66.5 (38)	75 (1.8)	26 (3.25)	26 (3.02)	21	50
Univ of California-San Diego	22 (3.31)	30 (3.01)	27 (3)	22 (40)	28 (3.16)	38 (2.64)	25.5 (93)	52.5 (68)	70 (2.0)	24 (3.29)	33 (2.87)	34	48
Univ of California-Santa Barbara	23 (3.30)	27 (3.06)	24 (4)	22 (40)	26.5 (3.21)	30 (2.87)	28 (91)	12 (280)	9 (11.2)	27 (3.20)	32 (2.88)	25	66
University of Minnesota	24 (3.29)	23 (3.20)	30.5 (2)	25 (37)	25 (3.25)	22 (3.17)	19.5 (95)	26 (179)	26 (7.2)	23 (3.31)	16 (3.33)	25	42
State U of New York-Stony Brook	25.5 (3.28)	18.5 (3.29)	27 (3)	26 (36)	20 (3.30)	16.5 (3.37)	10 (98)	45 (81)	52.5 (3.5)	14 (3.72)	16 (3.33)	23	74
Ohio State University	25.5 (3.28)	21 (3.24)	30.5 (2)	22 (40)	24 (3.26)	21 (3.19)	16 (96)	21 (221)	29 (6.9)	45.5 (2.40)	46 (2.48)	32	88
Vanderbilt University	27.5 (3.27)	35.5 (2.87)	21.5 (5)	27.5 (34)	21.5 (3.29)	34 (2.81)	25.5 (93)	54 (64)	48 (3.8)	32.5 (2.82)	36 (2.75)	17	29
Univ of California-Riverside	27.5 (3.27)	35.5 (2.87)	30.5 (2)	27.5 (34)	21.5 (3.29)	37 (2.68)	30.5 (90)	43 (83)	38 (4.6)	44 (2.42)	52 (2.32)	18	39
U of Illinois at Urbana-Champaign	29 (3.26)	26 (3.07)	38.5 (1)	24 (38)	30 (3.09)	28 (2.96)	23 (94)	10 (294)	18 (8.4)	17 (3.54)	20.5 (3.27)	35	50
State Univ of New York-Albany	30 (3.22)	24 (3.18)	70 (0)	30 (31)	29 (3.10)	24 (3.08)	41.5 (84)	17 (242)	13 (10.1)	29 (3.12)	29 (2.95)	24	80

Institution	93Q [1]	93E [1]	% D [1]	% D-S [1]	93Q T [1]	93E T [1]	VIS [1]	TC [2]	C/F [2]	82Q [3]	82E [3]	TF [4]	TG [4]
Rutgers State Univ-New Brunswick	31 (3.09)	40 (2.78)	38.5 (1)	32.5 (27)	33 (2.94)	41 (2.56)	34 (88)	22 (212)	24.5 (7.3)	30 (3.11)	35 (2.78)	29	85
Washington State University	32 (3.08)	28.5 (3.04)	38.5 (1)	32.5 (27)	35 (2.90)	27 (2.97)	46.5 (82)	29 (143)	36 (5.5)	31 (3.09)	18 (3.28)	26	64
University of Maryland College Park	33 (3.06)	31 (2.97)	70 (0)	31 (30)	36 (2.83)	29 (2.93)	23 (94)	18 (230)	19.5 (7.9)	37 (2.70)	38 (2.65)	29	50
State Univ of New York-Binghamton	34 (3.03)	39 (2.80)	21.5 (5)	36 (22)	34 (2.92)	39 (2.62)	49 (81)	80.5 (19)	79 (1.5)	38 (2.70)	41 (2.52)	13	104
Cornell University	35 (3.02)	25 (3.10)	70 (0)	35 (24)	31 (3.02)	25 (3.07)	28 (91)	44 (82)	30 (6.8)	19 (3.46)	16 (3.33)	12	23
Florida State University	36 (2.96)	32 (2.95)	70 (0)	37 (21)	32 (2.95)	32 (2.86)	30.5 (90)	40 (89)	43 (4.0)	52 (2.24)	50 (2.33)	22	47
CUNY - Grad Sch & Univ Center	37 (2.86)	46.5 (2.62)	30.5 (2)	34 (26)	41 (2.65)	50 (2.29)	38 (87)	80.5 (19)	87.5 (0.8)	25 (3.26)	30.5 (2.92)	23	215
Brown University	38 (2.84)	22 (3.22)	27 (3)	44.5 (14)	38 (2.75)	23 (3.10)	40 (86)	27 (161)	28 (7.0)	32.5 (2.82)	27 (2.98)	23	62
U of Massachusetts at Amherst	39 (2.83)	37 (2.85)	38.5 (1)	44.5 (14)	39 (2.74)	35 (2.72)	34 (88)	41 (87)	48 (3.8)	20 (3.37)	20.5 (3.27)	23	67
University of Southern California	40.5 (2.80)	44 (2.67)	70 (0)	38.5 (19)	44 (2.56)	46 (2.40)	28 (91)	52.5 (68)	51 (3.6)	21 (3.36)	25 (3.08)	19	80
University of Iowa	40.5 (2.80)	34 (2.88)	70 (0)	41 (16)	37 (2.79)	26 (2.98)	52 (79)	35 (109)	33.5 (6.4)	49 (2.28)	52 (2.32)	17	33
Michigan State University	42 (2.72)	41 (2.70)	70 (0)	40 (18)	46 (2.48)	48 (2.39)	41.5 (84)	39 (102)	44.5 (3.9)	34 (2.81)	28 (2.97)	26	101
University of Florida	43 (2.68)	43 (2.68)	70 (0)	38.5 (19)	50 (2.35)	44 (2.42)	44 (83)	19 (227)	32 (6.5)	61 (1.85)	63 (1.82)	35	21
Boston University	44 (2.67)	45 (2.63)	70 (0)	44.5 (14)	47 (2.44)	48 (2.39)	38 (87)	3 (616)	1 (26.8)	35 (2.73)	34 (2.82)	23	57
University of Illinois at Chicago	45 (2.66)	58 (2.35)	38.5 (1)	47.5 (11)	40 (2.66)	49 (2.37)	46.5 (82)	28 (154)	35 (5.7)	41 (2.66)	40 (2.55)	27	25
University of Notre Dame	46 (2.63)	50 (2.55)	70 (0)	58 (6)	42 (2.63)	43 (2.47)	49 (81)	47 (79)	54.5 (3.4)	64 (1.79)	61 (1.98)	23	47
University of Virginia	47.5 (2.60)	52 (2.46)	38.5 (1)	52.5 (8)	44 (2.56)	45 (2.41)	34 (88)	65 (42)	57.5 (3.0)	39 (2.69)	43 (2.50)	14	34
University of Georgia	47.5 (2.60)	46.5 (2.62)	70 (0)	47.5 (11)	45 (2.55)	42 (2.50)	34 (88)	49 (76)	48 (3.8)	54 (2.16)	54 (2.30)	20	26
University of Connecticut	49 (2.54)	61 (2.24)	70 (0)	58 (6)	48 (2.42)	63 (1.97)	44 (83)	76.5 (24)	86 (0.9)	43 (2.45)	43 (2.50)	26	64
Univ of California-San Francisco	50.5 (2.47)	48 (2.57)	24 (4)	44.5 (14)	50 (2.35)	36 (2.71)	49 (81)	6 (437)	3 (25.7)			17	30
Texas A&M University	50.5 (2.47)	42 (2.69)	70 (0)	49 (10)	50 (2.35)	40 (2.61)	54.5 (76)	33 (113)	39.5 (4.5)			25	44
Purdue University	52 (2.44)	54 (2.42)	70 (0)	50 (9)	53 (2.29)	56 (2.14)	59 (73)	55.5 (62)	72 (1.9)	50 (2.25)	48 (2.45)	33	70
Univ of California-Santa Cruz	53 (2.41)	55 (2.40)	38.5 (1)	42 (15)	52 (2.31)	52 (2.27)	51 (80)	87 (11)	84.5 (1.0)			11	45
University of Kentucky	54 (2.40)	57 (2.36)	70 (0)	52.5 (8)	55 (2.14)	62 (2.00)	54.5 (76)	55.5 (62)	66 (2.4)	57 (2.03)	49 (2.35)	26	52
Boston College	55 (2.32)	53 (2.45)	70 (0)	58 (6)	57 (2.11)	51 (2.28)	57 (74)	16 (252)	7 (14.8)			17	63
University of Oregon	56.5 (2.29)	64 (2.15)	70 (0)	52.5 (8)	58 (2.10)	65 (1.84)	61.5 (72)	58 (57)	62 (2.7)	48 (2.29)	46 (2.48)	21	47
University of Colorado	56.5 (2.29)	60 (2.30)	70 (0)	63.5 (4)	54 (2.15)	60 (2.04)	44 (83)	38 (103)	37 (4.7)	60 (1.86)	60 (2.08)	22	71
Syracuse University	58 (2.22)	51 (2.47)	70 (0)	55.5 (7)	60 (2.02)	58 (2.06)	53 (77)	69 (35)	75 (1.8)	51 (2.25)	57.5 (2.15)	19	43
University of Pittsburgh	59 (2.21)	62 (2.17)	38.5 (1)	63.5 (4)	56 (2.13)	64 (1.96)	76 (63)	57 (60)	52.5 (3.5)	42 (2.51)	37 (2.70)	17	45
Brandeis University	60 (2.19)	59 (2.31)	70 (0)	52.5 (8)	61 (1.98)	57 (2.12)	63.5 (71)	73 (28)	64.5 (2.5)	40 (2.66)	43 (2.50)	11	58

Appendix Table P - 39 Sociology (Continued)

Institution	93Q [1]	93E [1]	% D [1]	% D-S [1]	93Q T [1]	93E T [1]	VIS [1]	TC [2]	C/F [2]	82Q [3]	82E [3]	TF [4]	TG [4]
Iowa State University	**61.5** (2.15)	**38** (2.81)	**38.5** (1)	**55.5** (7)	**69** (1.77)	**55** (2.19)	**78.5** (62)	**20** (224)	**33.5** (6.4)	**62** (1.83)	**52** (2.32)	35	48
Temple University	**61.5** (2.15)	**68** (2.02)	**70** (0)	**70.5** (3)	**64** (1.94)	**72** (1.58)	**61.5** (72)	**51** (72)	**59** (2.9)	**55** (2.14)	**56** (2.17)	25	62
University of Missouri-Columbia	**63** (2.14)	**65.5** (2.07)	**70** (0)	**60** (5)	**71** (1.74)	**73** (1.48)	**56** (75)	**71** (33)	**72** (1.9)	**45.5** (2.40)	**46** (2.48)	17	35
North Carolina State University	**64** (2.13)	**56** (2.38)	**70** (0)	**70.5** (3)	**62** (1.97)	**53** (2.24)	**66** (70)	**36** (107)	**48** (3.8)	**71** (1.40)	**66.5** (1.62)	28	57
Louisiana State U & A&M College	**65** (2.12)	**63** (2.16)	**70** (0)	**63.5** (4)	**59** (2.05)	**61** (2.02)	**59** (73)	**62** (46)	**72** (1.9)	**78** (0.94)	**73** (1.47)	24	27
University of Kansas	**66** (2.10)	**65.5** (2.07)	**70** (0)	**63.5** (4)	**65** (1.92)	**68** (1.77)	**63.5** (71)	**63.5** (45)	**60.5** (2.8)	**58** (2.00)	**59** (2.10)	16	21
University of Nebraska-Lincoln	**67** (2.04)	**49** (2.56)	**70** (0)	**63.5** (4)	**67** (1.81)	**54** (2.22)	**76** (63)	**30.5** (142)	**19.5** (7.9)	**56** (2.12)	**57.5** (2.15)	18	24
Loyola University of Chicago	**68** (2.02)	**70** (1.97)	**70** (0)	**70.5** (3)	**73** (1.73)	**60** (2.04)	**74** (64)	**92.5** (5)	**90.5** (0.5)	**69** (1.55)	**74** (1.42)	10	52
University of Delaware	**69** (2.00)	**71** (1.86)	**70** (0)	**70.5** (3)	**73** (1.73)	**74** (1.47)	**66** (70)	**37** (106)	**41.5** (4.2)			25	13
University of New Hampshire	**70** (1.99)	**69** (1.98)	**70** (0)	**63.5** (4)	**66** (1.85)	**66** (1.83)	**59** (73)	**70** (34)	**63** (2.6)	**59** (1.86)	**69.5** (1.58)	13	13
Northeastern University	**71** (1.98)	**67** (2.03)	**70** (0)	**89** (0)	**70** (1.75)	**67** (1.81)	**70.5** (67)	**14** (270)	**8** (11.3)			24	34
Tulane University	**72** (1.91)	**75** (1.72)	**38.5** (1)	**70.5** (3)	**63** (1.95)	**69** (1.76)	**66** (70)	**60** (51)	**44.5** (3.9)	**77** (1.02)	**78** (1.12)	13	34
Arizona State University	**73** (1.87)	**73** (1.74)	**70** (0)	**70.5** (3)	**69** (1.77)	**77** (1.30)	**70.5** (67)	**61** (48)	**56** (3.2)			15	51
State Univ of New York-Buffalo	**74** (1.78)	**74** (1.73)	**70** (0)	**76** (2)	**75** (1.55)	**79** (1.07)	**81.5** (60)	**59** (54)	**39.5** (4.5)	**47** (2.37)	**55** (2.23)	12	40
Bowling Green State University	**76** (1.59)	**76** (1.62)	**70** (0)	**80** (1)	**74** (1.57)	**76** (1.35)	**81.5** (60)	**78** (20)	**84.5** (1.0)	**70** (1.44)	**66.5** (1.62)	20	23
Howard University	**76** (1.59)	**72** (1.80)	**70** (0)	**80** (1)	**79** (1.31)	**71** (1.67)	**83** (57)	**80.5** (19)	**80.5** (1.4)			14	33
University of Hawaii at Manoa	**76** (1.59)	**86** (1.18)	**70** (0)	**89** (0)	**76** (1.52)	**80** (1.06)	**94** (45)	**89** (9)	**90.5** (0.5)	**63** (1.82)	**68** (1.60)	19	33
Southern Illinois University	**78** (1.56)	**83** (1.37)	**70** (0)	**70.5** (3)	**78** (1.37)	**86** (0.95)	**68** (69)	**83** (18)	**78** (1.6)	**66** (1.61)	**69.5** (1.58)	11	18
University of Tennessee-Knoxville	**79** (1.55)	**87.5** (1.17)	**38.5** (1)	**76** (2)	**77** (1.41)	**83** (0.98)	**73** (65)	**84** (17)	**82** (1.3)	**67** (1.60)	**65** (1.70)	13	19
American University	**80** (1.52)	**82** (1.39)	**70** (0)	**70.5** (3)	**81** (1.26)	**86** (0.95)	**80** (61)	**90** (8)	**89** (0.6)	**75** (1.29)	**75** (1.28)	13	57
Colorado State University	**81** (1.40)	**80.5** (1.45)	**70** (0)	**89** (0)	**84** (1.16)	**78** (1.11)	**84.5** (56)	**80.5** (19)	**80.5** (1.4)			14	19
Fordham University	**82** (1.36)	**87.5** (1.17)	**70** (0)	**89** (0)	**80** (1.27)	**86** (0.95)	**90.5** (52)	**75** (25)	**69** (2.1)	**65** (1.75)	**62** (1.87)	12	61
University of Utah	**83** (1.34)	**78** (1.47)	**70** (0)	**89** (0)	**83** (1.22)	**71** (1.67)	**89** (53)	**95** (1)	**95** (0.1)	**73** (1.35)	**71** (1.52)	15	36
University of Akron	**84** (1.30)	**77** (1.57)	**70** (0)	**89** (0)	**82** (1.25)	**75** (1.46)	**72** (66)	**66.5** (38)	**68** (2.2)	**68** (1.55)	**64** (1.75)	17	20
Western Michigan University	**85** (1.29)	**79** (1.46)	**70** (0)	**89** (0)	**85** (1.14)	**84** (0.97)	**86.5** (55)	**91** (7)	**92** (0.4)	**76** (1.27)	**76** (1.27)	18	28
Mississippi State University	**86** (1.27)	**80.5** (1.45)	**70** (0)	**89** (0)	**91** (0.97)	**88** (0.94)	**88** (54)	**86** (13)	**87.5** (0.8)	**81** (0.77)	**80** (1.02)	16	33
University of Cincinnati	**87** (1.25)	**94** (0.86)	**70** (0)	**89** (0)	**88** (1.05)	**92** (0.56)	**69** (68)	**88** (10)	**83** (1.1)			9	21
Kent State University	**88** (1.18)	**90** (1.09)	**70** (0)	**80** (1)	**90** (1.00)	**94** (0.33)	**90.5** (52)	**68** (36)	**60.5** (2.8)	**72** (1.40)	**72** (1.50)	13	50
University of Oklahoma	**89** (1.15)	**89** (1.13)	**70** (0)	**80** (1)	**87** (1.06)	**93** (0.42)	**76** (63)	**42** (85)	**22.5** (7.7)			11	25
University of Denver	**90** (1.14)	**91** (1.04)	**70** (0)	**76** (2)	**93** (0.79)	**95** (0.28)	**78.5** (62)	**85** (14)	**75** (1.8)	**74** (1.34)	**77** (1.22)	8	9

Institution	93Q [1]	93E [1]	% D [1]	% D-S [1]	93Q T [1]	93E T [1]	VIS [1]	TC [2]	C/F [2]	82Q [3]	82E [3]	TF [4]	TG [4]
Utah State University	**92** (1.12)	**84** (1.25)	**70** (0)	**89** (0)	**94** (0.76)	**90** (0.76)	**93** (47)	**74** (26)	**77** (1.7)			15	10
University of North Texas	**92** (1.12)	**85** (1.21)	**70** (0)	**89** (0)	**92** (0.91)	**81** (1.05)	**84.5** (56)	**92.5** (5)	**93** (0.3)	**82** (0.47)	**82** (0.45)	18	33
Catholic University of America	**92** (1.12)	**92.5** (0.99)	**70** (0)	**89** (0)	**86** (1.09)	**82** (1.00)	**86.5** (55)	**76.5** (24)	**54.5** (3.4)	**80** (0.88)	**80** (1.02)	7	10
Georgia State University	**94** (1.11)	**92.5** (0.99)	**70** (0)	**89** (0)	**89** (1.03)	**89** (0.77)	**92** (50)	**72** (30)	**57.5** (3.0)			10	17
Oklahoma State University	**95** (0.60)	**95** (0.73)	**38.5** (1)	**80** (1)	**95** (0.59)	**91** (0.61)	**95** (43)	**94** (2)	**94** (0.2)	**79** (0.91)	**80** (1.02)	10	70

Sources: 1. National Survey of Graduate Faculty
2. Institute for Scientific Information
3. 1982 Survey of Graduate Faculty
4. Institutional Coordinator Data

Appendix Table P - 40 Relative Rankings for Research-Doctorate Programs in Spanish and Portuguese Language and Literature

Institution	93Q [1]	93E [1]	% D [1]	% D-S [1]	93Q T [1]	93E T [1]	VIS [1]	FA [2]	82Q [3]	82E [3]	TF [4]	TG [4]
Columbia University	**1** (4.31)	**10** (3.46)	**1** (45)	**1** (80)	**1** (4.48)	**11** (3.55)	**3** (97)	**12.5** (2)	**13** (3.39)	**19.5** (3.10)	11	47
Duke University	**2** (3.87)	**24.5** (3.10)	**7.5** (19)	**2.5** (65)	**2** (3.98)	**23.5** (3.16)	**12** (93)	**22.5** (1)	**18** (3.15)	**22** (3.07)	9	22
Brown University	**3** (3.83)	**1.5** (3.76)	**5** (20)	**4.5** (61)	**4** (3.93)	**7** (3.71)	**12** (93)	**12.5** (2)	**14** (3.39)	**11.5** (3.43)	14	32
Princeton University	**4** (3.80)	**5** (3.65)	**2** (24)	**6** (59)	**5.5** (3.90)	**2** (3.83)	**12** (93)	**12.5** (2)	**16** (3.33)	**14** (3.27)	7	21
University of Virginia	**5** (3.76)	**7** (3.55)	**3** (22)	**9.5** (54)	**3** (3.96)	**4.5** (3.81)	**20** (91)	**2** (4)	**25** (2.86)	**23** (3.05)	17	31
University of Pennsylvania	**6** (3.75)	**11** (3.41)	**10** (15)	**4.5** (61)	**7** (3.87)	**10** (3.58)	**7** (95)	**41** (0)	**2** (4.32)	**1** (4.07)	9	44
University of Wisconsin-Madison	**7** (3.74)	**4** (3.66)	**11.5** (13)	**8** (56)	**10** (3.72)	**3** (3.82)	**12** (93)	**5.5** (3)	**7** (3.66)	**6** (3.67)	23	49
Cornell University	**8** (3.73)	**3** (3.69)	**11.5** (13)	**2.5** (65)	**9** (3.78)	**6** (3.78)	**2** (98)	**22.5** (1)	**12** (3.40)	**13** (3.40)	9	15
University of California-Berkeley	**9** (3.70)	**6** (3.61)	**5** (20)	**7** (58)	**5.5** (3.90)	**4.5** (3.81)	**5** (96)	**2** (4)	**4** (3.97)	**3** (3.87)	13	33
Harvard University	**10** (3.63)	**12** (3.40)	**5** (20)	**13.5** (46)	**8** (3.82)	**9** (3.62)	**23** (90)	**22.5** (1)	**1** (4.49)	**3** (3.87)	8	41
University of Kansas	**11** (3.60)	**1.5** (3.76)	**7.5** (19)	**11.5** (49)	**12** (3.57)	**1** (3.97)	**26** (88)	**12.5** (2)	**10** (3.52)	**5** (3.70)	15	38
University of Texas at Austin	**12** (3.54)	**9** (3.51)	**9** (17)	**9.5** (54)	**11** (3.60)	**8** (3.64)	**1** (100)	**41** (0)	**3** (4.12)	**3** (3.87)	44	49
University of Michigan	**13** (3.46)	**8** (3.53)	**17.5** (7)	**13.5** (46)	**14** (3.46)	**12** (3.52)	**5** (96)	**22.5** (1)	**5** (3.84)	**7.5** (3.57)	11	44
University of California-Davis	**14** (3.43)	**20** (3.20)	**17.5** (7)	**16** (43)	**13** (3.53)	**15** (3.38)	**20** (91)	**22.5** (1)	**34** (2.43)	**34** (2.47)	8	24
University of California-Irvine	**15** (3.41)	**13.5** (3.33)	**17.5** (7)	**11.5** (49)	**15** (3.42)	**23.5** (3.16)	**8** (94)	**41** (0)	**21** (3.05)	**17** (3.17)	12	36
Univ of California-Los Angeles	**16** (3.37)	**15** (3.31)	**22.5** (5)	**15** (44)	**16** (3.37)	**15** (3.38)	**17** (92)	**5.5** (3)	**8** (3.65)	**7.5** (3.57)	21	65
Stanford University	**17** (3.30)	**20** (3.20)	**14** (8)	**18** (40)	**18.5** (3.33)	**27** (3.11)	**12** (93)	**2** (4)	**6** (3.68)	**9** (3.53)	10	35
Univ of California-San Diego	**18.5** (3.27)	**27.5** (3.07)	**17.5** (7)	**17** (42)	**17** (3.35)	**26** (3.12)	**23** (90)	**22.5** (1)	**9** (3.58)	**21** (3.08)	7	14
CUNY - Grad Sch & Univ Center	**18.5** (3.27)	**22.5** (3.16)	**22.5** (5)	**19** (36)	**20.5** (3.32)	**18** (3.28)	**30** (86)	**41** (0)	**28** (2.82)	**31.5** (2.58)	22	58
Indiana University	**20.5** (3.23)	**17** (3.24)	**17.5** (7)	**21.5** (33)	**25** (3.15)	**20** (3.24)	**17** (92)	**22.5** (1)	**11** (3.51)	**11.5** (3.43)	21	90
Univ of California-Santa Barbara	**20.5** (3.23)	**18** (3.23)	**21** (6)	**20** (34)	**20.5** (3.32)	**15** (3.38)	**12** (93)	**41** (0)	**23** (2.91)	**25** (2.88)	17	36
U of Illinois at Urbana-Champaign	**22** (3.22)	**13.5** (3.33)	**25.5** (4)	**24.5** (31)	**26** (3.12)	**17** (3.30)	**5** (96)	**12.5** (2)	**15** (3.36)	**10** (3.48)	22	62
New York University	**23** (3.19)	**27.5** (3.07)	**29.5** (3)	**21.5** (33)	**18.5** (3.33)	**28** (3.08)	**28.5** (87)	**41** (0)	**31** (2.68)	**28** (2.78)	14	8
Pennsylvania State University	**24.5** (3.12)	**20** (3.20)	**13** (9)	**24.5** (31)	**31** (2.91)	**29** (2.97)	**17** (92)	**41** (0)	**30** (2.72)	**26.5** (2.87)	22	46
Univ of Puerto Rico-Rio Piedras	**24.5** (3.12)	**16** (3.30)	**29.5** (3)	**30** (21)	**23.5** (3.17)	**13** (3.46)	**52** (69)	**41** (0)	**38** (2.28)	**37** (2.40)	19	18
University of Pittsburgh	**26** (3.11)	**24.5** (3.10)	**17.5** (7)	**27** (27)	**23.5** (3.17)	**22** (3.18)	**26** (88)	**41** (0)	**17** (3.16)	**18** (3.15)	10	46
Washington University	**27.5** (3.06)	**22.5** (3.16)	**25.5** (4)	**26** (29)	**27** (3.09)	**21** (3.23)	**28.5** (87)	**12.5** (2)	**45** (1.96)	**45** (2.22)	11	26
University of Minnesota	**27.5** (3.06)	**30** (3.00)	**34** (2)	**23** (32)	**22** (3.19)	**19** (3.25)	**20** (91)	**41** (0)	**22** (3.01)	**16** (3.22)	9	32
University of Kentucky	**29** (2.94)	**26** (3.09)	**34** (2)	**30** (21)	**29** (2.95)	**25** (3.15)	**44.5** (77)	**22.5** (1)	**19** (3.08)	**15** (3.23)	11	55
Georgetown University	**30** (2.92)	**31** (2.95)	**40.5** (1)	**28** (23)	**28** (2.96)	**31** (2.88)	**23** (90)	**12.5** (2)	**43** (2.07)	**43** (2.23)	11	23

Institution	93Q [1]	93E [1]	% D [1]	% D-S [1]	93Q T [1]	93E T [1]	VIS [1]	FA [2]	82Q [3]	82E [3]	TF [4]	TG [4]
U of North Carolina-Chapel Hill	**31** (2.91)	**29** (3.01)	**25.5** (4)	**30** (21)	**32** (2.80)	**30** (2.93)	**26** (88)	**41** (0)	**20** (3.06)	**19.5** (3.10)	14	49
University of Maryland College Park	**32** (2.84)	**34** (2.75)	**25.5** (4)	**32** (16)	**30** (2.94)	**35** (2.80)	**32** (84)	**41** (0)	**24** (2.88)	**31.5** (2.58)	12	32
Ohio State University	**33** (2.83)	**32** (2.80)	**34** (2)	**34** (14)	**33** (2.79)	**34** (2.81)	**12** (93)	**12.5** (2)	**46** (1.95)	**43** (2.23)	18	56
U of Massachusetts at Amherst	**34** (2.63)	**37** (2.67)	**34** (2)	**37.5** (11)	**34** (2.68)	**39** (2.67)	**34.5** (83)	**5.5** (3)	**33** (2.44)	**29.5** (2.72)	15	39
Rutgers State Univ-New Brunswick	**35** (2.61)	**36** (2.72)	**40.5** (1)	**36** (13)	**35** (2.65)	**32** (2.86)	**36.5** (82)	**41** (0)	**32** (2.54)	**29.5** (2.72)	12	28
University of Colorado	**36.5** (2.59)	**38.5** (2.61)	**29.5** (3)	**34** (14)	**39** (2.46)	**43** (2.50)	**32** (84)	**41** (0)	**48** (1.83)	**49** (1.95)	13	33
Michigan State University	**36.5** (2.59)	**33** (2.77)	**40.5** (1)	**34** (14)	**36** (2.61)	**33** (2.82)	**39.5** (80)	**41** (0)	**36** (2.30)	**35.5** (2.42)	10	43
Arizona State University	**38** (2.58)	**35** (2.73)	**34** (2)	**37.5** (11)	**37** (2.57)	**36** (2.78)	**38** (81)	**12.5** (2)	**39** (2.26)	**40** (2.32)	13	28
State Univ of New York-Buffalo	**39** (2.43)	**42** (2.48)	**29.5** (3)	**46.5** (5)	**40** (2.45)	**45** (2.46)	**44.5** (77)	**41** (0)	**26** (2.85)	**24** (2.98)	8	40
Tulane University	**40** (2.34)	**43** (2.47)	**49.5** (0)	**39** (10)	**42** (2.34)	**46** (2.44)	**42.5** (78)	**41** (0)	**41** (2.16)	**43** (2.23)	12	22
State U of New York-Stony Brook	**41** (2.33)	**41** (2.50)	**40.5** (1)	**40** (9)	**43** (2.32)	**40** (2.55)	**36.5** (82)	**22.5** (1)			9	41
University of Chicago	**42** (2.32)	**38.5** (2.61)	**40.5** (1)	**43.5** (7)	**39** (2.46)	**38** (2.73)	**42.5** (78)	**12.5** (2)			5	59*
State Univ of New York-Albany	**43** (2.29)	**45.5** (2.38)	**40.5** (1)	**51** (4)	**45** (2.23)	**44** (2.47)	**47.5** (73)	**41** (0)	**29** (2.77)	**41** (2.28)	10	27
University of Washington	**44** (2.25)	**44** (2.46)	**49.5** (0)	**46.5** (5)	**41** (2.37)	**37** (2.74)	**41** (79)	**41** (0)	**27** (2.83)	**26.5** (2.87)	11	16
Syracuse University	**45** (2.18)	**47.5** (2.19)	**40.5** (1)	**41.5** (8)	**44** (2.31)	**47** (2.35)	**46** (74)	**41** (0)	**42** (2.15)	**47.5** (2.05)	7	5
University of Missouri-Columbia	**46** (2.17)	**47.5** (2.19)	**49.5** (0)	**46.5** (5)	**46** (2.19)	**49** (2.32)	**49.5** (70)	**41** (0)	**40** (2.20)	**35.5** (2.42)	12	25
University of Florida	**47** (2.15)	**50** (2.10)	**49.5** (0)	**41.5** (8)	**47** (2.17)	**52** (1.85)	**39.5** (80)	**5.5** (3)	**49** (1.77)	**47.5** (2.05)	9	21
University of Connecticut	**48** (2.13)	**51** (2.01)	**49.5** (0)	**51** (4)	**50** (2.08)	**50** (1.98)	**47.5** (73)	**41** (0)	**37** (2.29)	**38** (2.38)	6	26
Boston University	**49** (2.12)	**40** (2.57)	**49.5** (0)	**43.5** (7)	**53** (1.98)	**41** (2.54)	**34.5** (83)	**41** (0)			5	9
University of Georgia	**50.5** (2.08)	**45.5** (2.38)	**49.5** (0)	**46.5** (5)	**51** (2.03)	**43** (2.50)	**52** (69)	**22.5** (1)	**35** (2.33)	**33** (2.52)	23	20
Florida State University	**50.5** (2.08)	**49** (2.13)	**49.5** (0)	**54** (2)	**49** (2.12)	**49** (2.32)	**52** (69)	**41** (0)	**50** (1.67)	**51** (1.87)	9	19
Catholic University of America	**52** (2.06)	**53** (1.70)	**49.5** (0)	**51** (4)	**49** (2.12)	**53** (1.73)	**32** (84)	**41** (0)	**44** (2.01)	**39** (2.33)	7	15**
Temple University	**53** (1.83)	**52** (1.82)	**49.5** (0)	**51** (4)	**52** (2.00)	**51** (1.93)	**49.5** (70)	**41** (0)	**51** (1.59)	**46** (2.13)	12	20
Texas Tech University	**54** (1.80)	**54** (1.59)	**40.5** (1)	**51** (4)	**54** (1.74)	**54** (1.54)	**54** (61)	**41** (0)	**47** (1.91)	**50** (1.90)	11	14

Sources:
1. National Survey of Graduate Faculty
2. Associations and Organizations Administrating Prestigious Awards and Honors
3. 1982 Survey of Graduate Faculty
4. Institutional Coordinator Data

* Enrollment data is for the Romance Language Department which includes French, Spanish, and Portuguese Language and Literature programs

** Enrollment data is for the Modern Language Department which includes French, Spanish, and Portuguese Language and Literature programs

Appendix Table P - 41 Relative Rankings for Research-Doctorate Programs in Statistics and Biostatistics

Institution	93Q [1]	93E [1]	% D [1]	% D-S [1]	93Q T [1]	93E T [1]	VIS [1]	TC [2]	C/F [2]	82Q [3]	82E [3]	TF [4]	TG [4]
Stanford University	**1.5*** (4.76)	**1** (4.44)	**1.5** (77)	**1** (93)	**1** (4.92)	**1** (4.47)	**1** (99)	**10** (853)	**11** (53.3)	**2** (4.87)	**1** (4.65)	16	49
University of California-Berkeley [a]	**1.5*** (4.76)	**2** (4.33)	**1.5** (77)	**2** (90)	**2** (4.84)	**2** (4.30)	**2** (97)	**17** (463)	**24** (19.3)	**1** (4.88)	**2** (4.37)	24	39
University of California-Berkeley [b]	**3** (4.43)	**7** (4.01)	**3** (51)	**4.5** (84)	**4.5** (4.41)	**6** (3.99)	**4** (96)	**7** (976)	**10** (54.2)			18	13
Cornell University	**4** (4.37)	**6** (4.06)	**4** (44)	**4.5** (84)	**3** (4.43)	**3** (4.11)	**7.5** (95)	**16** (537)	**29** (17.3)	**6** (3.98)	**7** (3.70)	31	26
University of Chicago	**5** (4.34)	**3** (4.09)	**5** (40)	**3** (88)	**4.5** (4.41)	**5** (4.02)	**4** (96)	**44** (125)	**41** (9.6)	**3** (4.68)	**4** (3.88)	13	30
University of Washington [b]	**6** (4.21)	**4** (4.08)	**6** (33)	**12.5** (70)	**6** (4.20)	**4** (4.06)	**22** (86)	**1** (3106)	**2** (119.5)	**10** (3.83)	**9** (3.68)	26	36
Harvard University	**7** (4.17)	**11.5** (3.80)	**7** (32)	**6** (80)	**7** (4.13)	**9** (3.88)	**7.5** (95)	**20** (428)	**7** (61.1)	**7** (3.97)	**18** (3.15)	7	15
University of Wisconsin-Madison	**8** (4.06)	**5** (4.07)	**8** (27)	**7** (77)	**8.5** (4.06)	**7** (3.98)	**7.5** (95)	**12** (760)	**18** (30.4)	**4** (4.31)	**3** (4.07)	25	52
University of Washington [a]	**9** (4.01)	**9** (3.85)	**9** (21)	**12.5** (70)	**8.5** (4.06)	**10** (3.83)	**13** (93)	**5** (1027)	**8** (57.1)			18	27
Purdue University	**10** (4.00)	**15** (3.61)	**11** (18)	**10** (72)	**10** (4.03)	**15** (3.48)	**16.5** (91)	**35** (163)	**44** (9.1)	**9** (3.86)	**12** (3.48)	18	27
U of North Carolina-Chapel Hill [a]	**11** (3.98)	**13** (3.69)	**13.5** (16)	**8** (76)	**12** (3.94)	**13** (3.60)	**13** (93)	**25** (330)	**25** (18.3)	**5** (3.99)	**10** (3.65)	18	33
Univ of California-Los Angeles	**12** (3.93)	**11.5** (3.80)	**10** (19)	**10** (72)	**13** (3.85)	**14** (3.55)	**4** (96)	**2** (2334)	**9** (56.9)	**16** (3.65)	**13** (3.35)	41	57
University of Minnesota [a]	**13** (3.91)	**14** (3.65)	**13.5** (16)	**10** (72)	**11** (3.95)	**11.5** (3.76)	**10.5** (94)	**27** (239)	**35** (12.6)	**14** (3.71)	**11** (3.50)	19	30
Iowa State University	**14** (3.89)	**8** (3.99)	**12** (17)	**14.5** (68)	**14.5** (3.78)	**8** (3.90)	**10.5** (94)	**30** (202)	**49** (7.5)	**8** (3.97)	**5** (3.80)	27	48
Texas A&M University	**15** (3.78)	**19.5** (3.44)	**19** (9)	**14.5** (68)	**17.5** (3.67)	**24** (3.23)	**7.5** (95)	**24** (336)	**36** (12.4)	**24** (3.06)	**21** (3.03)	27	31
Carnegie Mellon University	**16** (3.77)	**10** (3.84)	**16.5** (12)	**16** (62)	**14.5** (3.78)	**11.5** (3.76)	**16.5** (91)	**26** (299)	**23** (19.9)	**17** (3.49)	**15** (3.28)	15	28
Rutgers State Univ-New Brunswick	**17** (3.76)	**27.5** (3.16)	**15** (13)	**17.5** (55)	**17.5** (3.67)	**25** (3.21)	**23.5** (85)	**50** (92)	**55** (4.6)	**19** (3.19)	**24.5** (2.92)	20	46
U of North Carolina-Chapel Hill [b]	**18** (3.70)	**16.5** (3.58)	**16.5** (12)	**17.5** (55)	**19** (3.57)	**19** (3.37)	**13** (93)	**8** (910)	**16** (32.5)	**13** (3.71)	**7** (3.70)	28	42
Pennsylvania State University	**19** (3.65)	**18** (3.53)	**20** (8)	**19** (53)	**20** (3.50)	**18** (3.38)	**19.5** (89)	**46.5** (120)	**51** (6.3)	**31** (2.72)	**29** (2.73)	19	47
Yale University	**20** (3.62)	**21** (3.39)	**18** (11)	**20.5** (49)	**16** (3.69)	**17** (3.41)	**25** (84)	**53** (81)	**31** (16.2)	**15** (3.70)	**16** (3.25)	5	20
Johns Hopkins University	**21** (3.55)	**16.5** (3.58)	**21.5** (7)	**25.5** (39)	**26** (3.28)	**20** (3.30)	**38** (75)	**4** (1128)	**3** (86.8)	**29** (2.84)	**26** (2.88)	13	37
North Carolina State University	**22** (3.54)	**23** (3.36)	**21.5** (7)	**20.5** (49)	**22** (3.42)	**27** (3.18)	**19.5** (89)	**22** (390)	**33** (13.4)	**25** (3.05)	**17** (3.22)	29	78
Florida State University	**23** (3.47)	**19.5** (3.44)	**23.5** (6)	**25.5** (39)	**23** (3.40)	**16** (3.42)	**21** (87)	**54** (78)	**53** (4.9)	**12** (3.80)	**7** (3.70)	16	20
Columbia University	**24.5** (3.44)	**23** (3.36)	**23.5** (6)	**22** (45)	**24** (3.35)	**22.5** (3.25)	**16.5** (91)	**6** (979)	**13** (49.0)	**11** (3.82)	**14** (3.32)	20	23
University of Michigan [a]	**24.5** (3.44)	**23** (3.36)	**27** (3)	**23** (41)	**21** (3.45)	**21** (3.29)	**23.5** (85)	**52** (85)	**50** (7.1)	**21** (3.12)	**20** (3.05)	12	19
U of Illinois at Urbana-Champaign	**26** (3.35)	**27.5** (3.16)	**35** (1)	**27** (36)	**25** (3.32)	**28** (3.13)	**29** (80)	**29** (211)	**38** (11.1)	**18** (3.44)	**31** (2.63)	19	38
University of Florida	**27** (3.31)	**29** (3.11)	**25.5** (4)	**24** (40)	**28** (3.21)	**29.5** (3.04)	**16.5** (91)	**13** (677)	**21.5** (25.1)	**38** (2.36)	**35** (2.35)	27	27
University of Pennsylvania	**28** (3.22)	**33** (3.00)	**25.5** (4)	**28.5** (24)	**30** (3.16)	**34** (2.87)	**32.5** (77)	**39** (145)	**45** (8.1)	**35** (2.55)	**33** (2.38)	18	14
Ohio State University	**29** (3.21)	**25** (3.23)	**52.5** (0)	**30** (21)	**27** (3.22)	**22.5** (3.25)	**26.5** (83)	**43** (130)	**52** (5.9)	**36** (2.53)	**32** (2.58)	22	57
Michigan State University	**30** (3.14)	**34** (2.94)	**52.5** (0)	**31.5** (20)	**29** (3.20)	**32** (2.90)	**38** (75)	**57** (31)	**60** (1.9)	**23** (3.06)	**23** (2.98)	16	21

Institution	93Q [1]	93E [1]	% D [1]	% D-S [1]	93Q T [1]	93E T [1]	VIS [1]	TC [2]	C/F [2]	82Q [3]	82E [3]	TF [4]	TG [4]
Colorado State University	**31** (3.13)	**31** (3.06)	**35** (1)	**28.5** (24)	**31** (3.08)	**31** (2.97)	**26.5** (83)	**28** (237)	**26** (18.2)	**20** (3.15)	**19** (3.12)	13	27
University of Rochester	**32** (3.09)	**26** (3.18)	**29** (2)	**31.5** (20)	**32** (3.07)	**26** (3.20)	**35** (76)	**31** (192)	**27** (17.5)	**27** (3.00)	**27** (2.87)	11	16
Northwestern University	**33** (3.05)	**35.5** (2.92)	**52.5** (0)	**33** (18)	**33** (3.02)	**33** (2.89)	**38** (75)	**15** (643)	**15** (42.9)			15	9
University of Michigan [b]	**34** (3.02)	**32** (3.02)	**52.5** (0)	**34** (16)	**34** (2.95)	**35** (2.85)	**44** (69)	**11** (812)	**4** (73.8)			11	28
University of Iowa [a]	**35** (3.00)	**30** (3.09)	**52.5** (0)	**39** (12)	**35** (2.86)	**30** (3.04)	**30.5** (79)	**46.5** (120)	**46** (8.0)	**26** (3.03)	**22** (3.02)	15	20
George Washington University	**36** (2.91)	**38** (2.83)	**52.5** (0)	**36** (15)	**36** (2.80)	**36** (2.73)	**28** (81)	**45** (122)	**42** (9.4)	**34** (2.56)	**37** (2.20)	13	17
University of Pittsburgh [a]	**37.5** (2.85)	**39** (2.79)	**35** (1)	**40** (11)	**39** (2.73)	**41** (2.60)	**35** (76)	**42** (133)	**32** (14.8)	**22** (3.12)	**38** (2.15)	9	17
Oregon State University	**37.5** (2.85)	**37** (2.86)	**52.5** (0)	**38** (13)	**37** (2.79)	**39** (2.67)	**41.5** (72)	**32** (179)	**37** (11.9)	**30** (2.81)	**28** (2.83)	15	28
Southern Methodist University	**39.5** (2.75)	**42** (2.68)	**29** (2)	**36** (15)	**42** (2.63)	**44** (2.47)	**35** (76)	**58** (26)	**58** (2.4)	**33** (2.61)	**30** (2.72)	11	25
Univ of California-Riverside	**39.5** (2.75)	**43** (2.65)	**35** (1)	**42** (10)	**40** (2.67)	**43** (2.54)	**47** (67)	**51** (87)	**47** (7.9)	**37** (2.40)	**36** (2.22)	11	25
Virginia Polytech Inst & State U	**41** (2.74)	**35.5** (2.92)	**35** (1)	**36** (15)	**44** (2.62)	**38** (2.69)	**30.5** (79)	**49** (100)	**48** (7.7)	**28** (2.93)	**24.5** (2.92)	13	35
U of Massachusetts at Amherst	**42** (2.68)	**40** (2.78)	**29** (2)	**42** (10)	**38** (2.76)	**40** (2.61)	**43** (70)	**23** (360)	**20** (27.7)			13	12
University of Connecticut	**43** (2.62)	**48.5** (2.43)	**52.5** (0)	**44** (9)	**44** (2.62)	**46** (2.35)	**45.5** (68)	**40** (139)	**28** (17.4)	**41** (2.10)	**41** (1.88)	8	37
Univ of California-Santa Barbara	**44** (2.54)	**50** (2.35)	**52.5** (0)	**48** (5)	**41** (2.65)	**42** (2.58)	**45.5** (68)	**60.5** (17)	**62** (1.5)			11	18
University of Minnesota [b]	**45** (2.52)	**41** (2.72)	**52.5** (0)	**42** (10)	**45** (2.50)	**38** (2.69)	**50.5** (60)	**36** (162)	**17** (32.4)	**40** (2.17)	**39** (2.03)	5	12
Temple University	**46** (2.50)	**53** (2.25)	**52.5** (0)	**48** (5)	**47** (2.40)	**52** (2.05)	**40** (73)	**56** (38)	**59** (2.2)	**46** (1.76)	**45** (1.80)	17	41
Boston University	**47** (2.46)	**48.5** (2.43)	**52.5** (0)	**45** (8)	**46** (2.49)	**48** (2.17)	**32.5** (77)	**9** (884)	**6** (68.0)	**47** (1.39)	**47** (1.40)	13	11
University of Iowa [b]	**48** (2.39)	**52** (2.32)	**52.5** (0)	**48** (5)	**53** (2.00)	**51** (2.08)	**60.5** (46)	**14** (663)	**5** (73.7)			9	20
University of Kentucky	**49** (2.27)	**51** (2.34)	**52.5** (0)	**50** (4)	**48** (2.18)	**45** (2.42)	**41.5** (72)	**33** (178)	**34** (12.7)	**32** (2.64)	**34** (2.37)	14	24
Kansas State University	**50** (2.24)	**45.5** (2.46)	**52.5** (0)	**52.5** (3)	**51** (2.05)	**47** (2.33)	**49** (65)	**48** (112)	**43** (9.3)	**45** (1.82)	**40** (1.98)	12	35
Emory University	**51** (2.20)	**45.5** (2.46)	**52.5** (0)	**52.5** (3)	**53** (2.00)	**51** (2.08)	**56** (55)	**18** (449)	**12** (49.9)			9	14
University of Pittsburgh [b]	**52** (2.19)	**44** (2.63)	**52.5** (0)	**52.5** (3)	**55** (1.86)	**58** (1.67)	**60.5** (46)	**3** (1990)	**1** (165.8)	**44** (1.86)	**46** (1.62)	12	50
University of Illinois at Chicago	**53.5** (2.16)	**55** (2.03)	**52.5** (0)	**56** (2)	**50** (2.08)	**53** (1.98)	**55** (56)	**59** (23)	**57** (3.3)			7	29
University of South Carolina	**53.5** (2.16)	**54** (2.24)	**52.5** (0)	**59.5** (1)	**49** (2.17)	**49** (2.14)	**48** (66)	**38** (146)	**40** (10.4)			14	19
University of Colorado	**55** (2.15)	**47** (2.45)	**52.5** (0)	**46** (6)	**57** (1.73)	**58** (1.67)	**58** (48)	**19** (441)	**14** (44.1)			10	11
State Univ of New York-Buffalo	**56** (1.97)	**59** (1.94)	**35** (1)	**52.5** (3)	**56** (1.82)	**60** (1.56)	**50.5** (60)	**60.5** (17)	**56** (3.4)	**43** (1.88)	**42** (1.87)	5	7
University of Texas at Dallas	**57** (1.94)	**57.5** (1.95)	**52.5** (0)	**63.5** (0)	**54** (1.98)	**54** (1.86)	**53.5** (57)	**62** (9)	**61** (1.8)			5	11
Medical University South Carolina	**58** (1.92)	**57.5** (1.95)	**52.5** (0)	**59.5** (1)	**58** (1.72)	**58** (1.67)	**62** (45)	**34** (165)	**39** (11.0)			15	37
University of Wyoming	**59** (1.82)	**60** (1.74)	**35** (1)	**56** (2)	**61** (1.59)	**61** (1.22)	**59** (47)	**41** (136)	**30** (17.0)	**42** (1.89)	**44** (1.83)	8	11
University of Alabama	**60** (1.70)	**56** (1.96)	**52.5** (0)	**59.5** (1)	**61** (1.59)	**55** (1.81)	**52** (58)	**55** (53)	**54** (4.8)			11	14

Appendix Table P - 41 Statistics and Biostatistics (Continued)

Institution	93Q [1]	93E [1]	% D [1]	% D-S [1]	93Q T [1]	93E T [1]	VIS [1]	TC [2]	C/F [2]	82Q [3]	82E [3]	TF [4]	TG [4]
American University	**61** (1.69)	**61** (1.59)	**52.5** (0)	**63.5** (0)	**59** (1.66)	**56** (1.80)	**53.5** (57)	**63.5** (4)	**64** (0.4)	**48** (0.91)	**48** (0.65)	9	18
University of Alabama-Birmingham	**62** (1.63)	**64** (1.30)	**52.5** (0)	**63.5** (0)	**62** (1.42)	**64** (0.56)	**65** (39)	**21** (402)	**21.5** (25.1)			16	17
State U of New York-Stony Brook	**63** (1.33)	**62** (1.52)	**52.5** (0)	**63.5** (0)	**63** (1.25)	**62** (1.16)	**57** (52)	**37** (147)	**19** (29.4)	**39** (2.19)	**43** (1.85)	5	134
Univ of Southwestern Louisiana	**64** (0.92)	**63** (1.37)	**35** (1)	**56** (2)	**64** (0.64)	**63** (0.83)	**63** (42)	**63.5** (4)	**63** (0.6)			7	16
University of Northern Colorado	**65** (0.75)	**65** (0.69)	**35** (1)	**59.5** (1)	**65** (0.48)	**65** (0.00)	**64** (41)	**65** (0)	**65** (0.0)			4	14

Sources:
1. National Survey of Graduate Faculty
2. Institute for Scientific Information
3. 1982 Survey of Graduate Faculty
4. Institutional Coordinator Data

Notes: *a.* Program in Statistics
b. Program in Biostatistics

* Two programs recieved the highest quality rating, and using the standard convention of average rankings, each program was given a rank of 1.5.

APPENDIX Q

Mean Scores with Confidence Intervals for the Scholarly Quality of Program Faculty

This section includes 41 charts which illustrate the mean score and confidence interval for each program on a field-by-field basis. Scores are presented in descending order from the program rated first in that field. Ratings ranged from 5 to 0, with five representing, "Distinguished." The horizontal line through the mean indicates a confidence interval of ±1.5 standard errors around that mean.

In comparing the mean ratings of two programs, if their reported confidence intervals do not overlap, one may safely conclude that the program ratings are significantly different (at the .05 level of significance)—i.e., the observed difference in mean ratings is too large to be plausibly attributed to sampling error.

Note: This confidence interval is computed under procedural rules that with a probability of about 86 percent will yield an interval with the following property: It will include the average score that would have arisen if an indefinitely large number of independent raters drawn at random from the same pool were to rate the program In this sense we are 86 percent confident that the interval includes the rating that would have been granted were the universe of raters to be surveyed. The choice of 1.5 standard errors (and hence an 86 percent interval) is motivated here, as it was when the same intervals were used in 1982, because it permits the easy performance of pairwise significance tests. The given rule for comparing non-overlapping intervals is valid as long as the ratio of the two estimated standard error does not exceed 2.41. (The exact statistical significance of this criterion then lies between .050 and .034.) In addition, it requires for its validity that the two mean rankings be uncorrelated. Because each rater rated fifty programs, the trimmed means for different programs will be positively correlated, and the reliability of the ranking will exceed that inferred from considering the standard errors of these means separately. Thus these intervals, and test derived from them, should only be considered a rough guide, probably a conservative one at that.

Appendix Figure Q - 1 Means and Confidence Intervals for the Scholarly Quality of Program Faculty Ratings of the 33 Programs in Aerospace Engineering

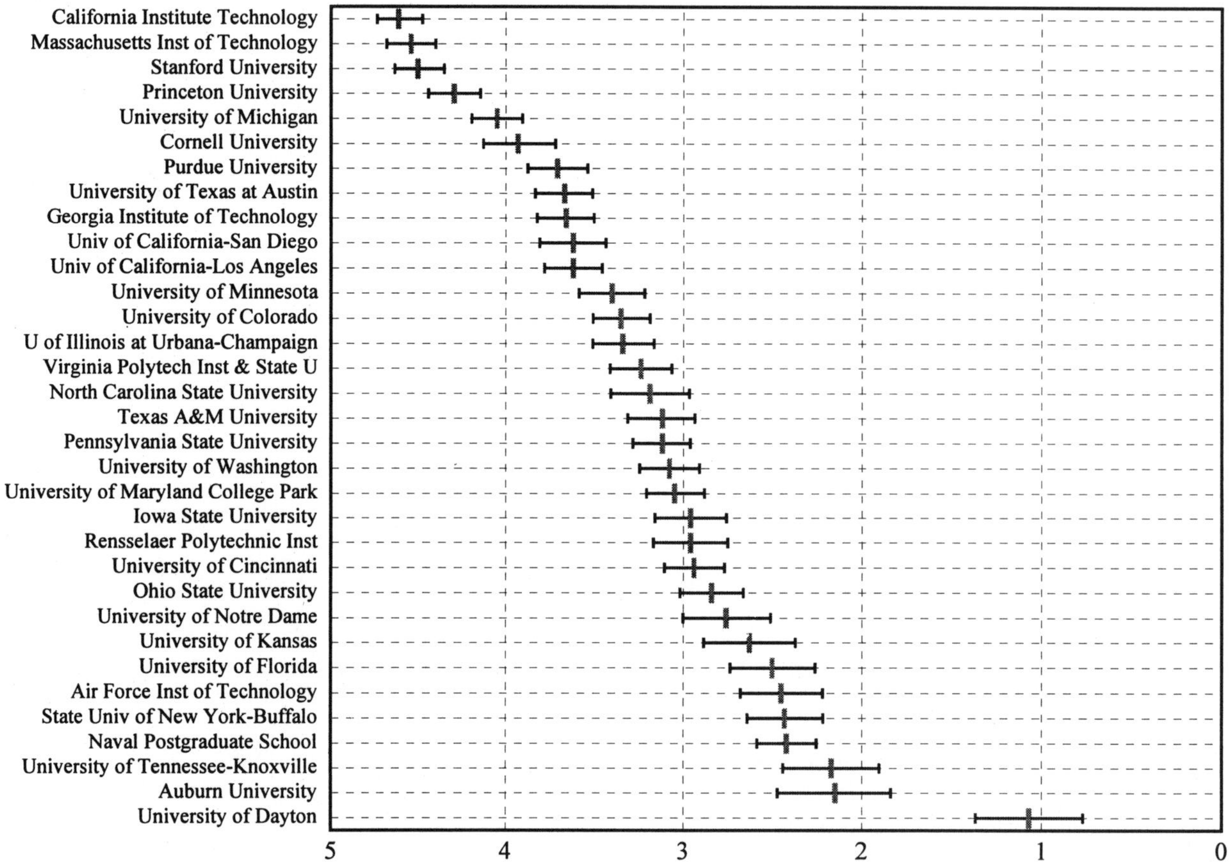

Source: National Survey of Graduate Faculty

Appendix Figure Q - 2 Means and Confidence Intervals for the Scholarly Quality of Program Faculty Ratings of the 69 Programs in Anthropology

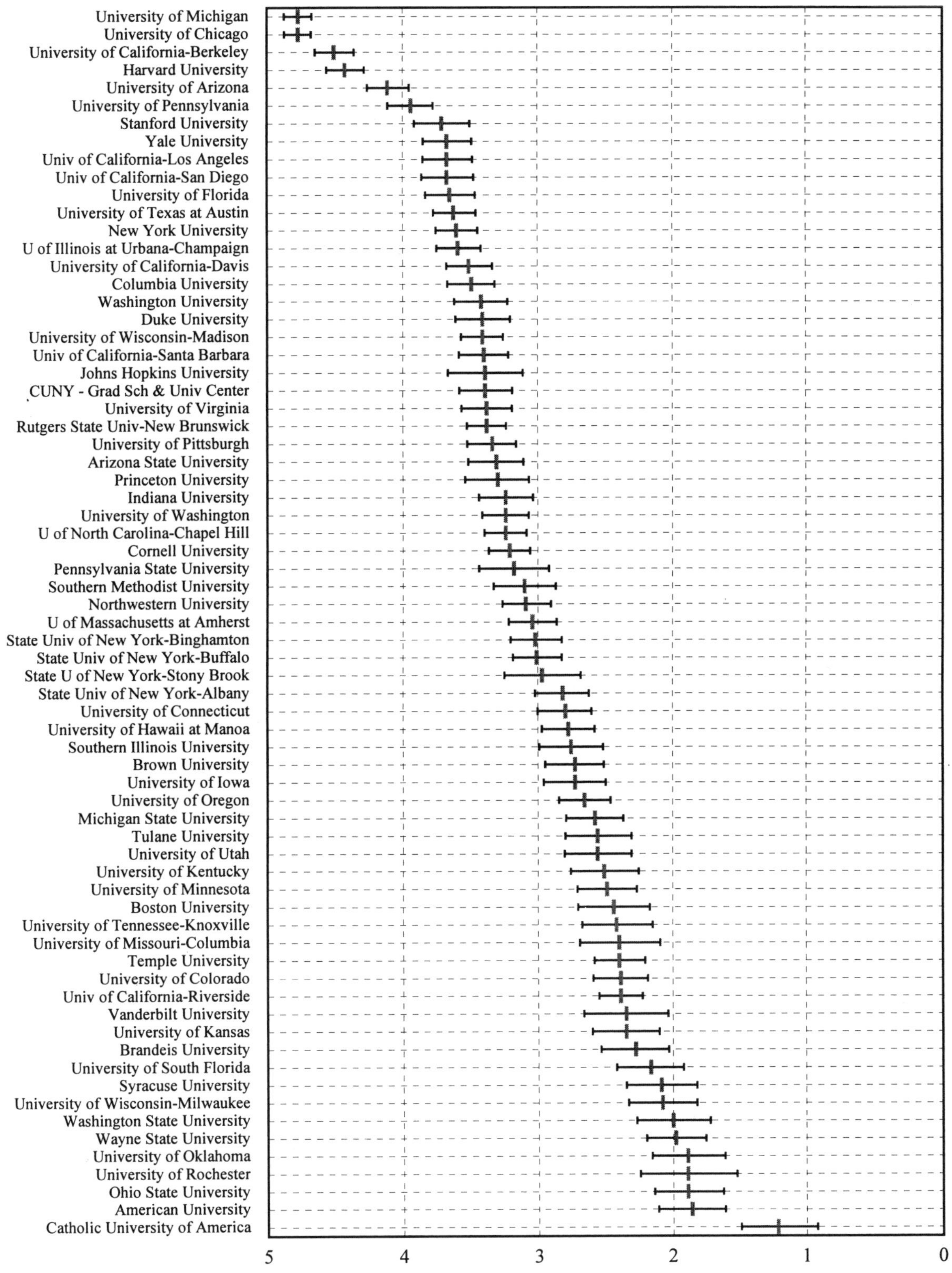

Source: National Survey of Graduate Faculty

Appendix Figure Q - 3 Means and Confidence Intervals for the Scholarly Quality of Program Faculty Ratings of the 38 Programs in Art History

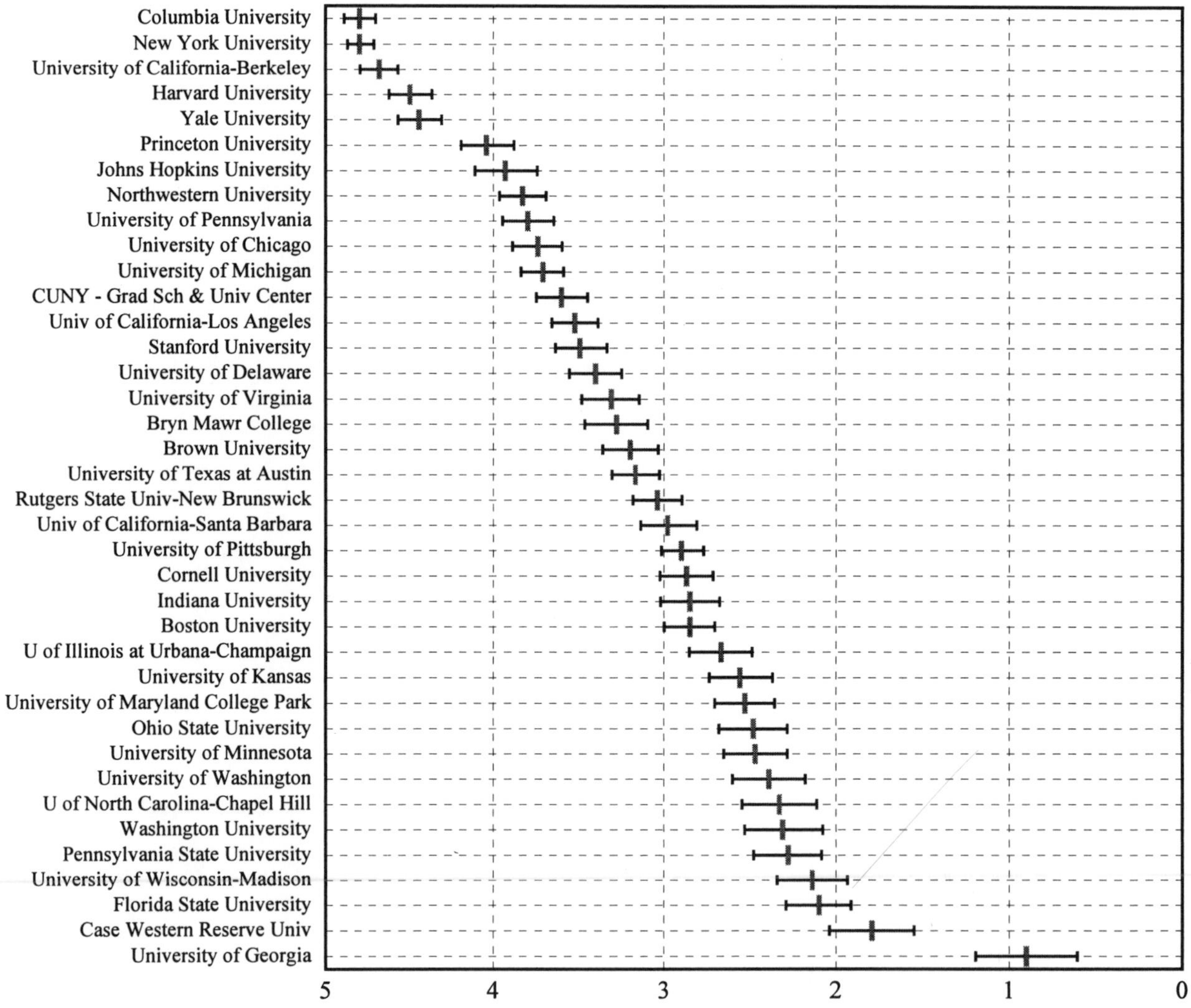

Source: National Survey of Graduate Faculty

Appendix Figure Q - 4 Means and Confidence Intervals for the Scholarly Quality of Program Faculty Ratings of the 33 Programs in Astrophysics and Astronomy

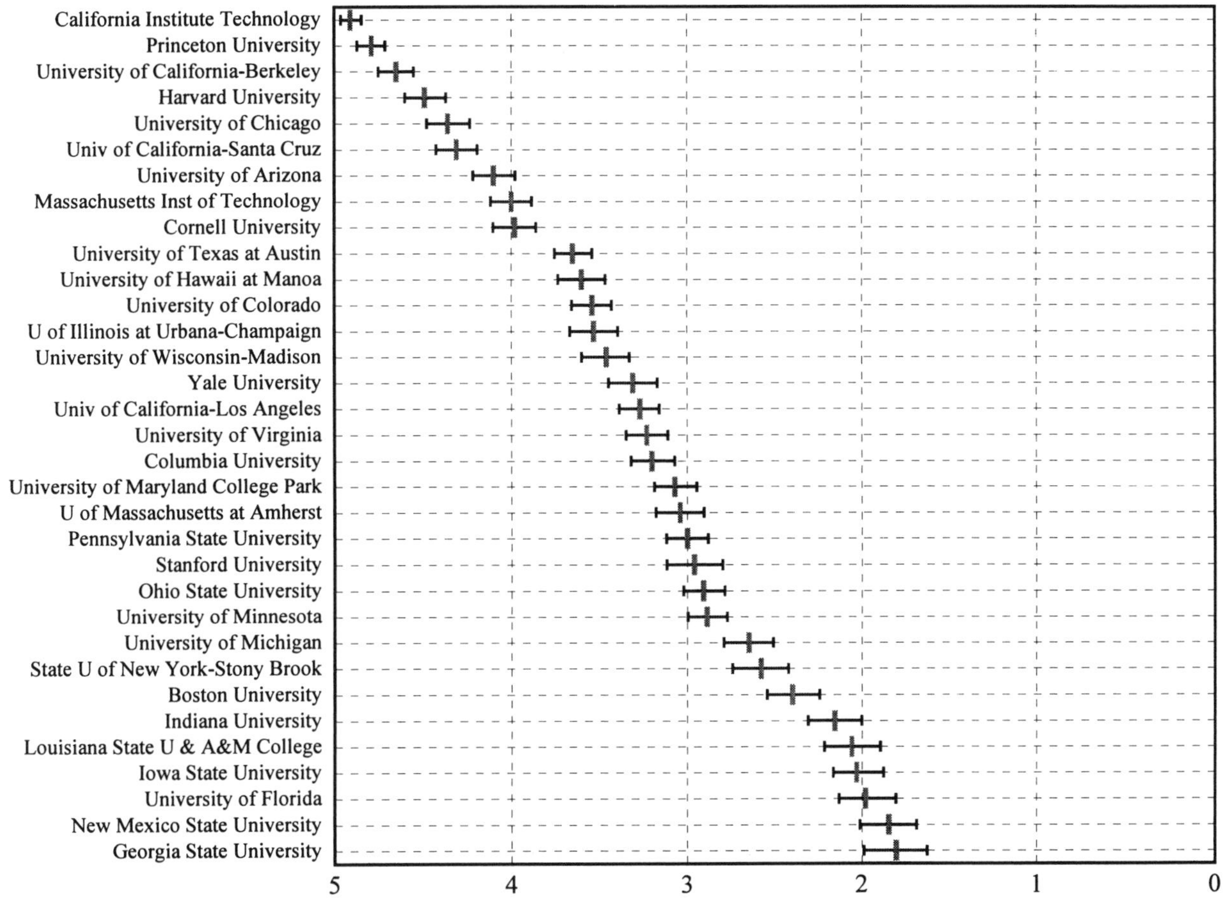

Source: National Survey of Graduate Faculty

Appendix Figure Q - 5 Means and Confidence Intervals for the Scholarly Quality of Program Faculty Ratings of the 194 Programs in Biochemistry and Molecular Biology

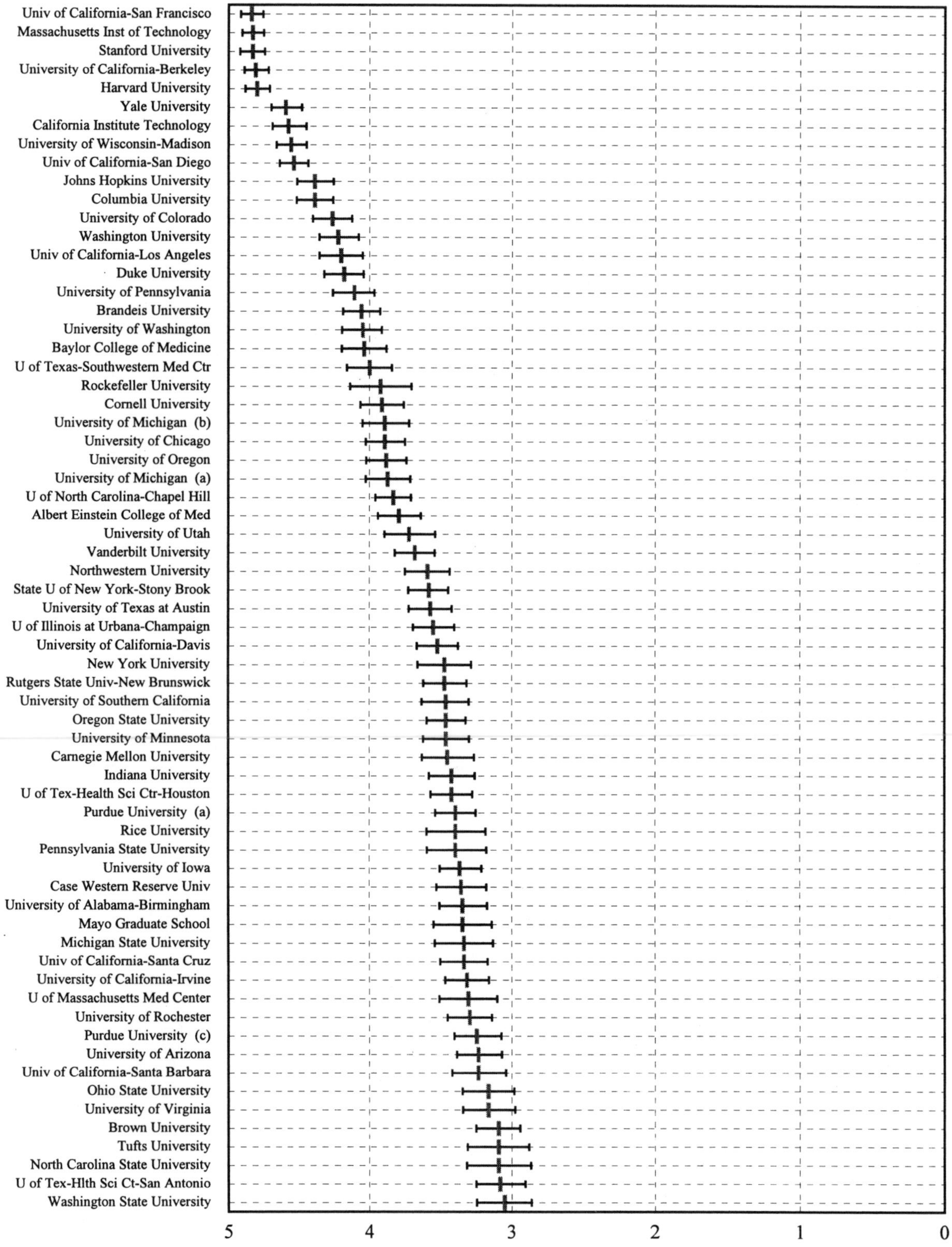

Appendix Figure Q - 5 Biochemistry and Molecular Biology (Continued)

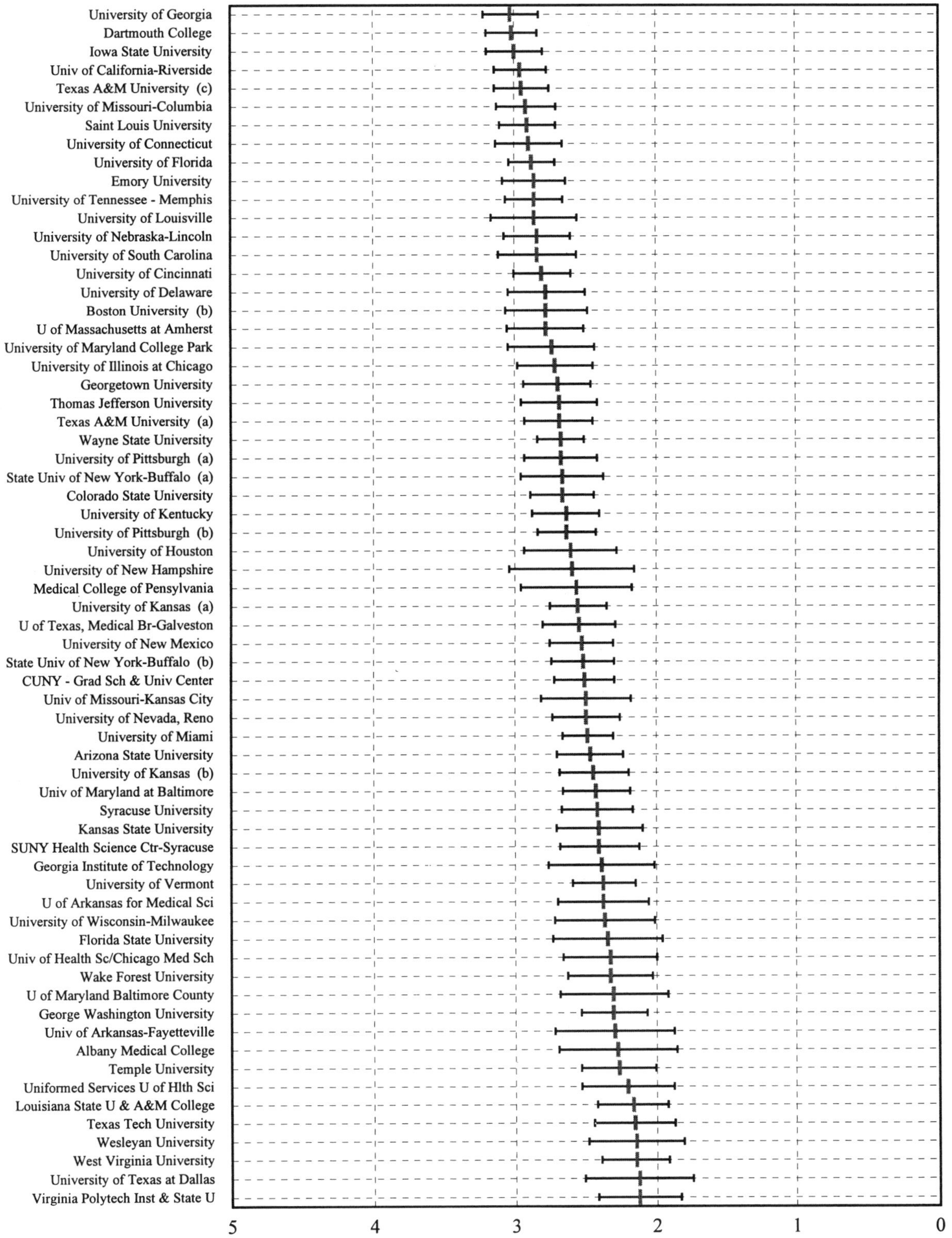

Appendix Figure Q - 5 Biochemistry and Molecular Biology (Continued)

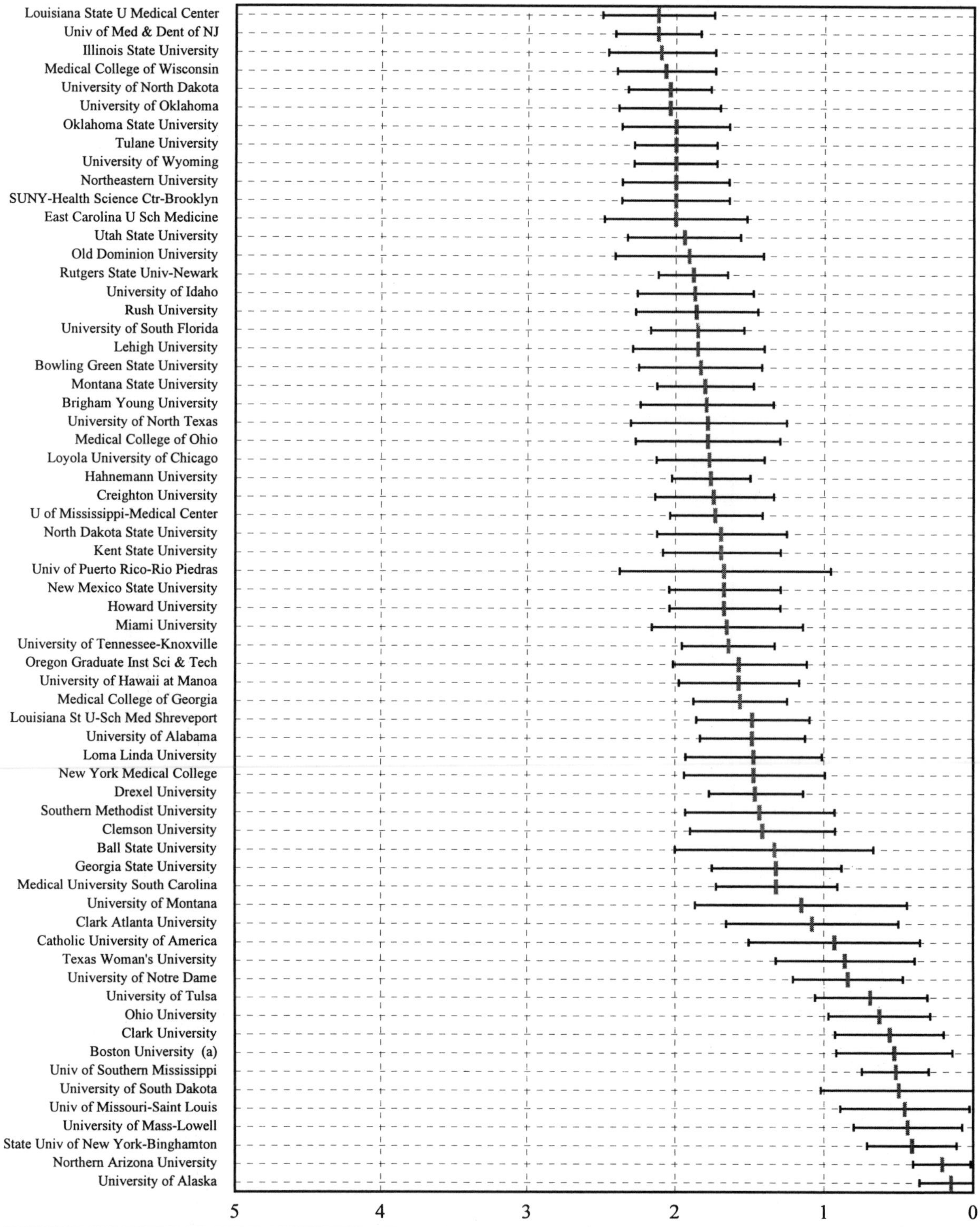

Source: National Survey of Graduate Faculty

Note: (a) School of Arts and Sciences
(b) School of Medicine
(c) School of Agriculture

Appendix Figure Q - 6 Means and Confidence Intervals for the Scholarly Quality of Program Faculty Ratings of the 38 Programs in Biomedical Engineering

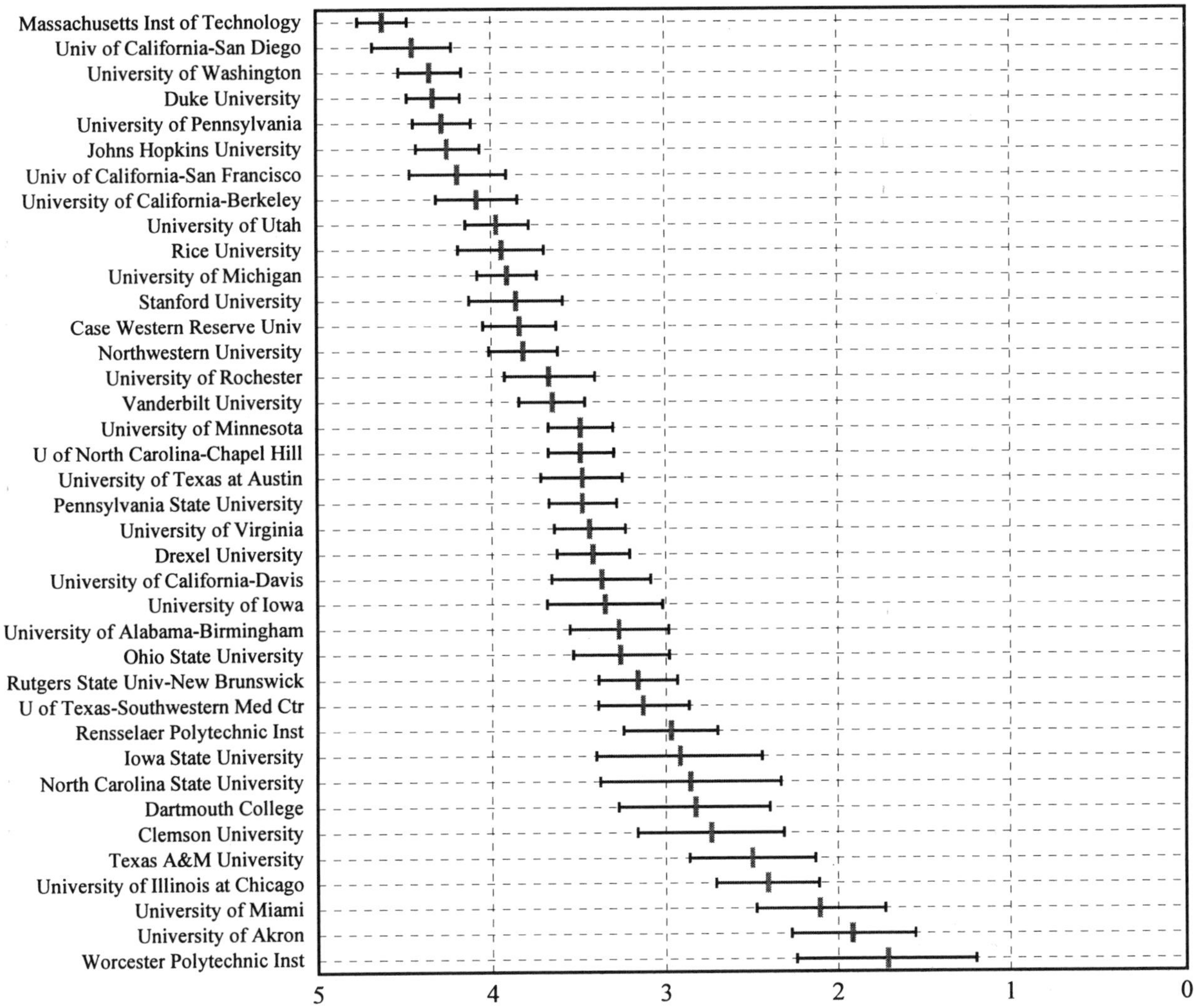

Source: National Survey of Graduate Faculty

Appendix Figure Q - 7 Means and Confidence Intervals for the Scholarly Quality of Program Faculty Ratings of the 179 Programs in Cell and Developmental Biology

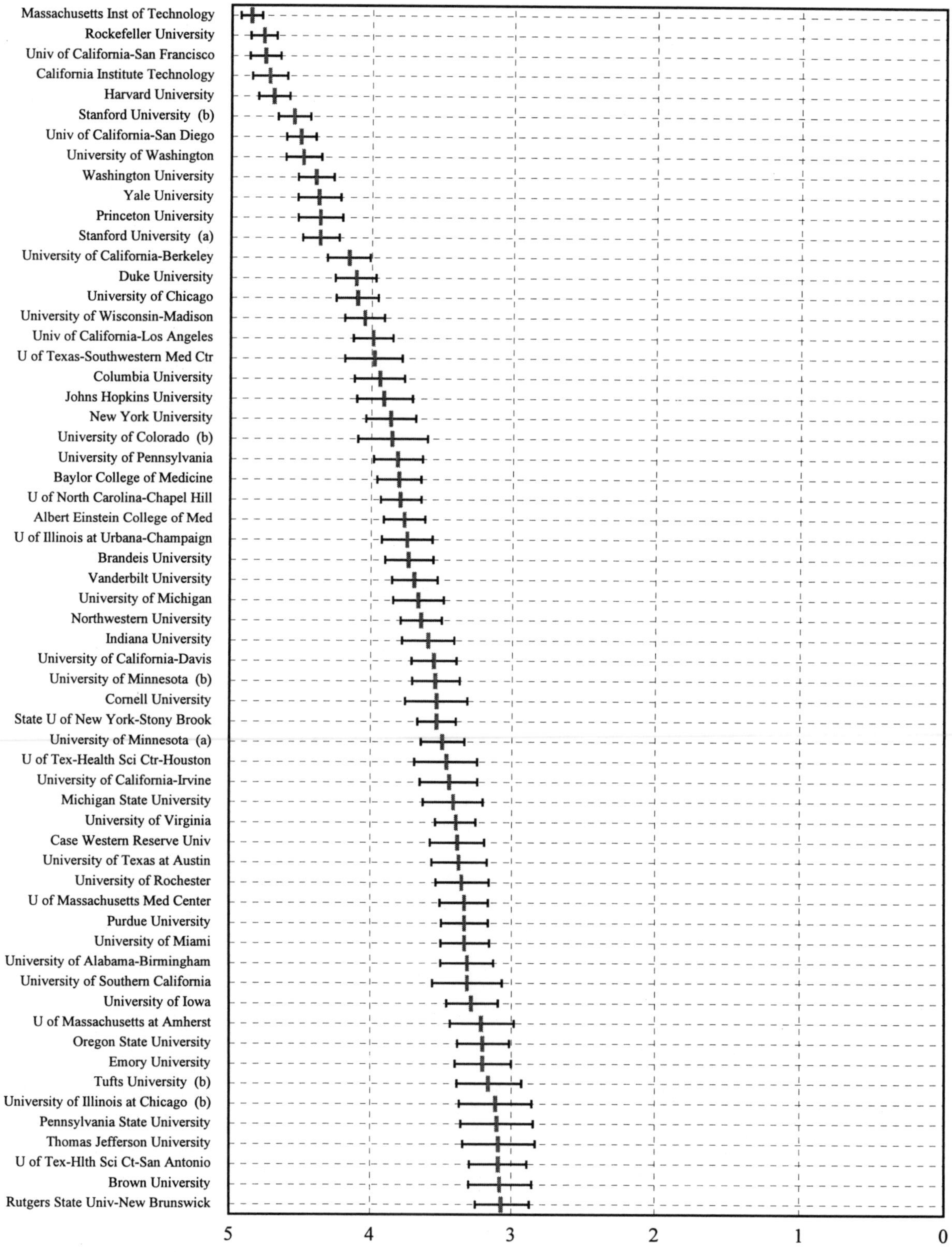

Appendix Figure Q - 7 Cell and Developmental Biology (Continued)

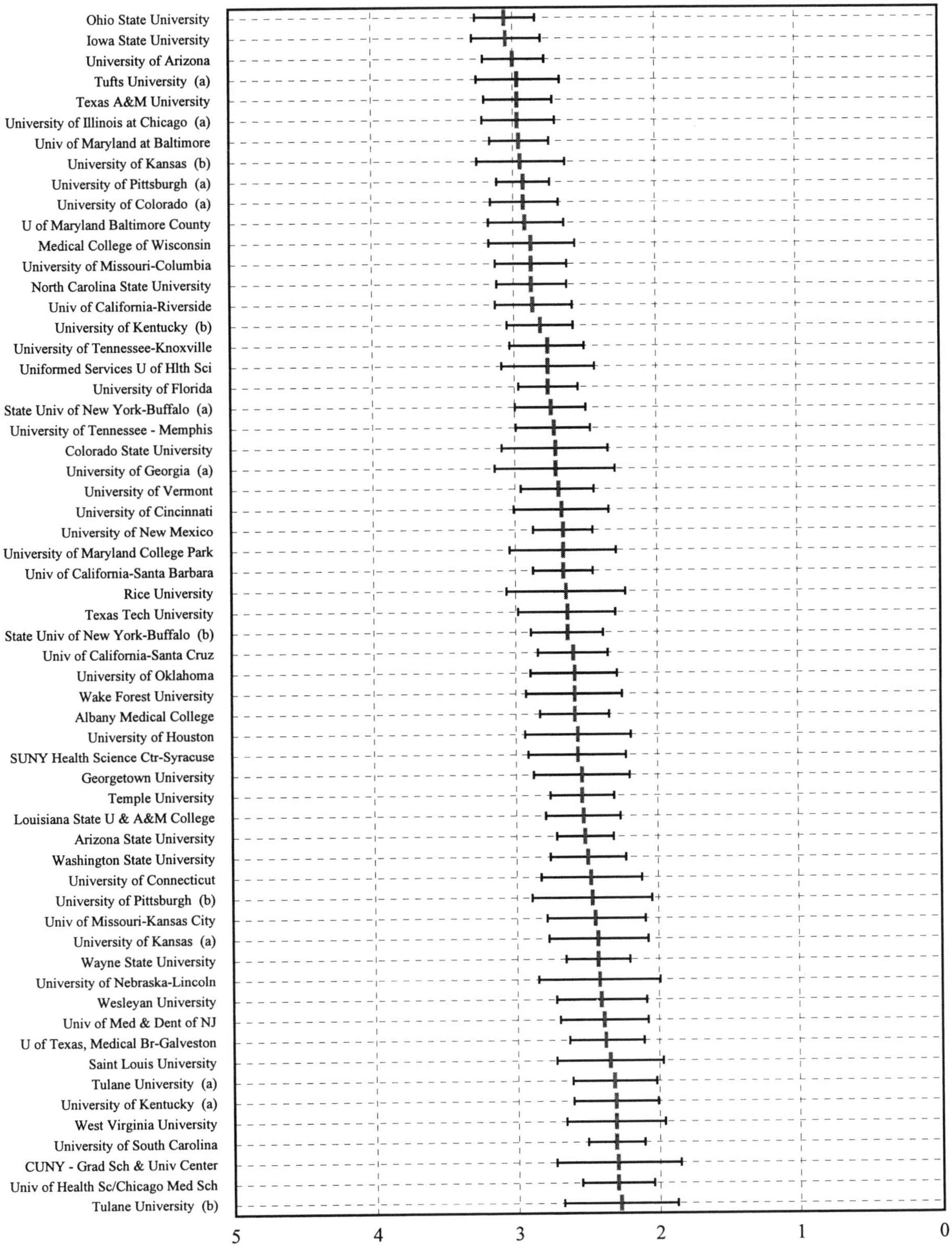

Appendix Figure Q - 7 Cell and Developmental Biology (Continued)

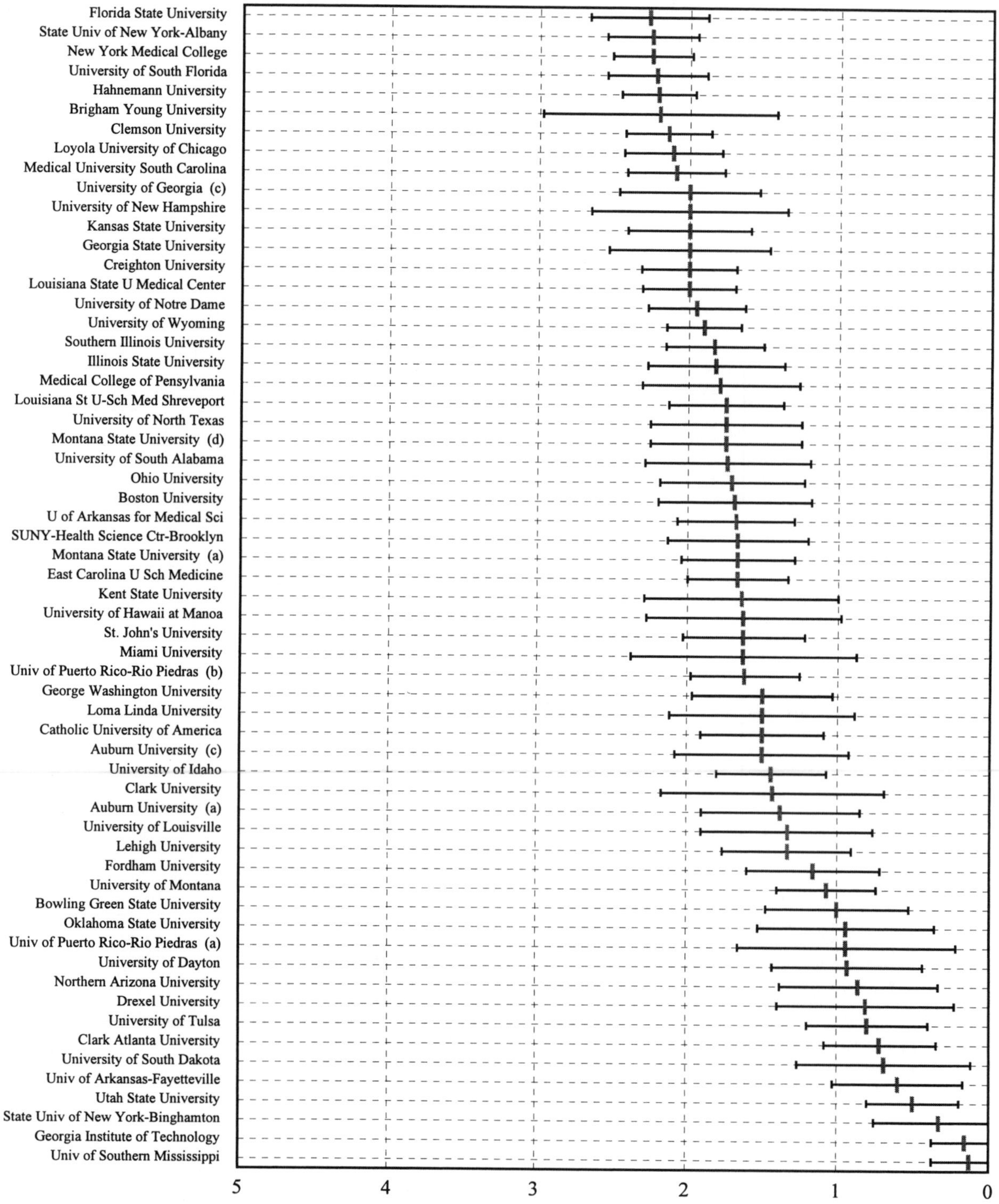

Source: National Survey of Graduate Faculty

Note:
(a) School of Arts and Sciences
(b) School of Medicine
(c) School of Veterinary Medicine
(d) School of Agriculture

Appendix Figure Q - 8 Means and Confidence Intervals for the Scholarly Quality of Program Faculty Ratings of the 93 Programs in Chemical Engineering

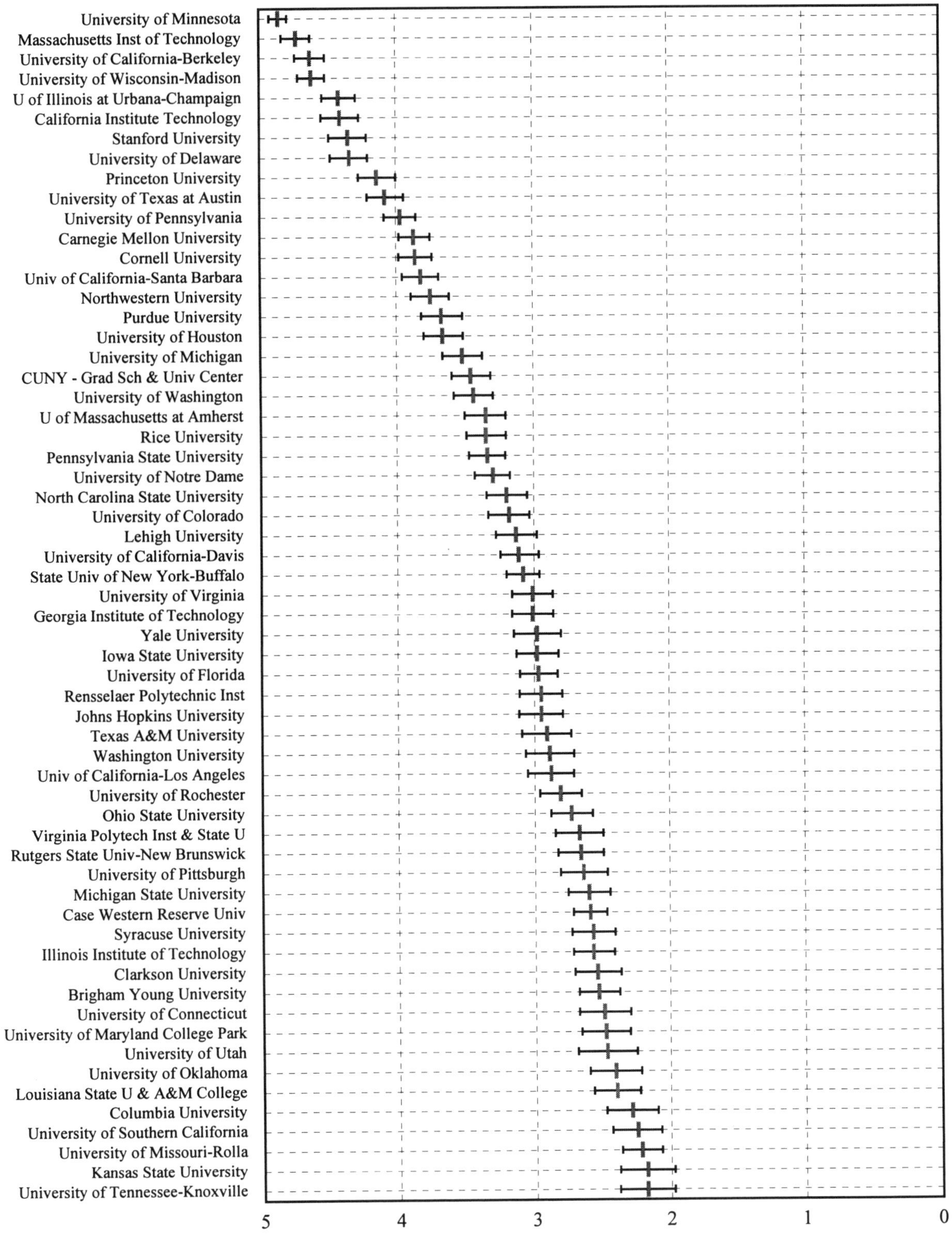

Appendix Figure Q - 8 Chemical Engineering (Continued)

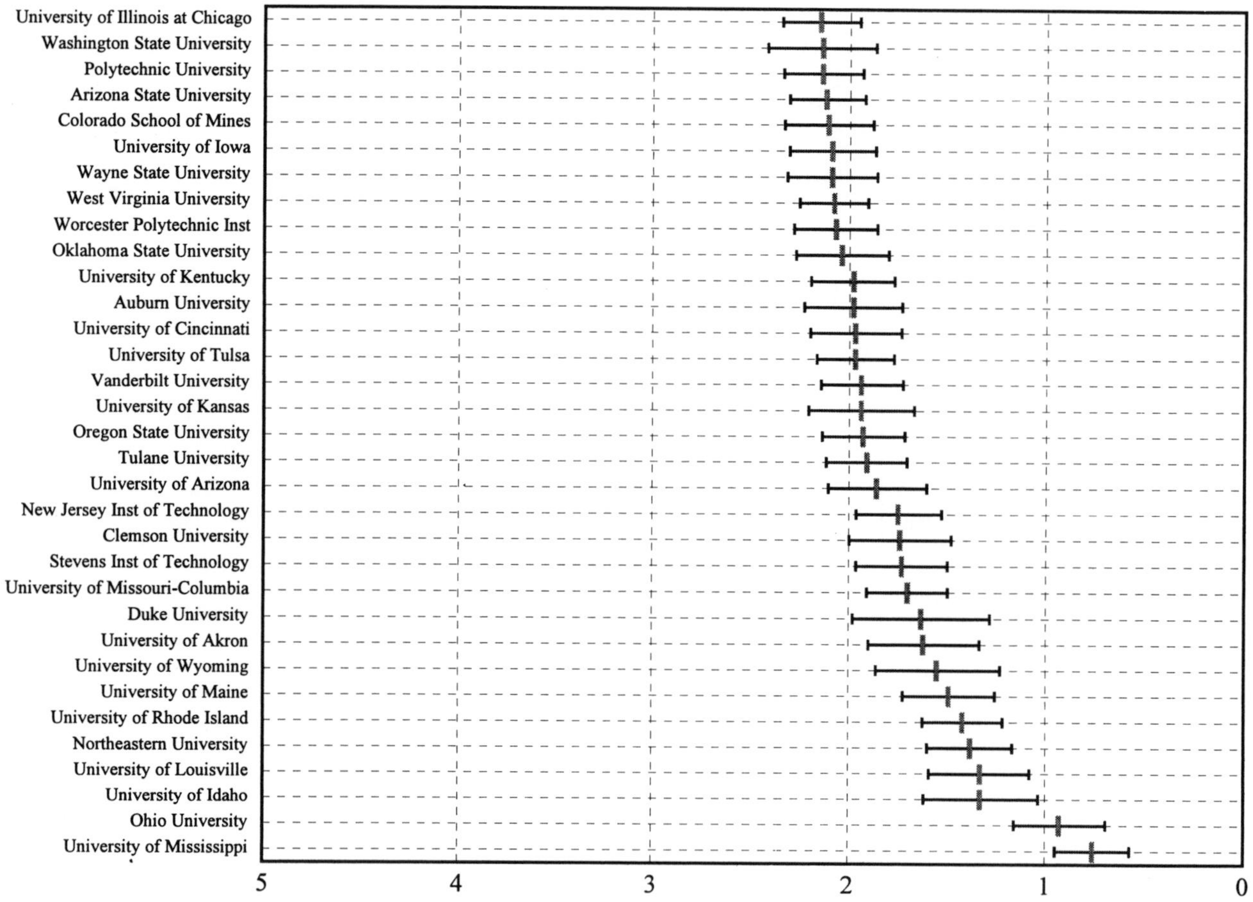

Source: National Survey of Graduate Faculty

Appendix Figure Q - 9 Means and Confidence Intervals for the Scholarly Quality of Program Faculty Ratings of the 168 Programs in Chemistry

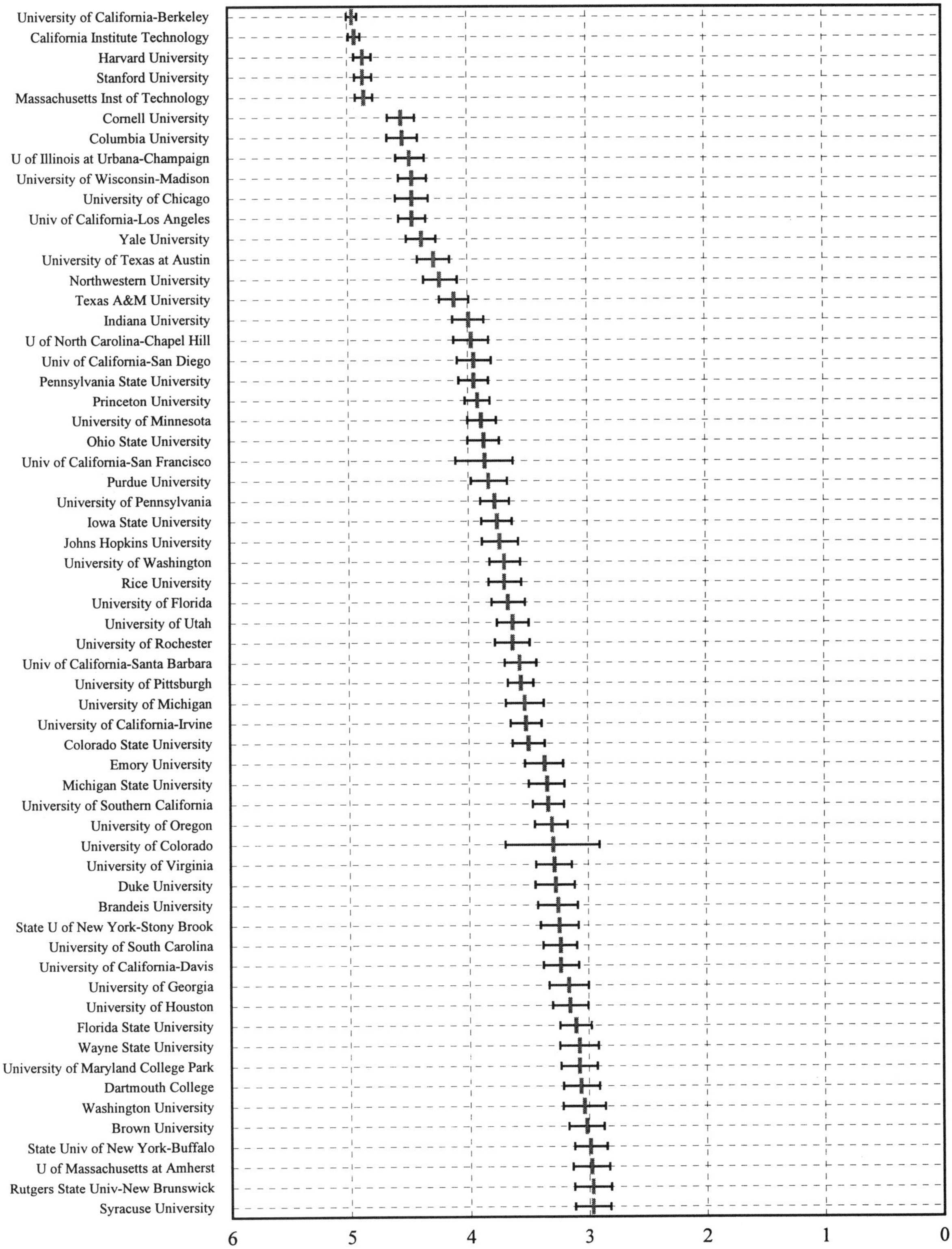

Appendix Figure Q - 9 Chemistry (Continued)

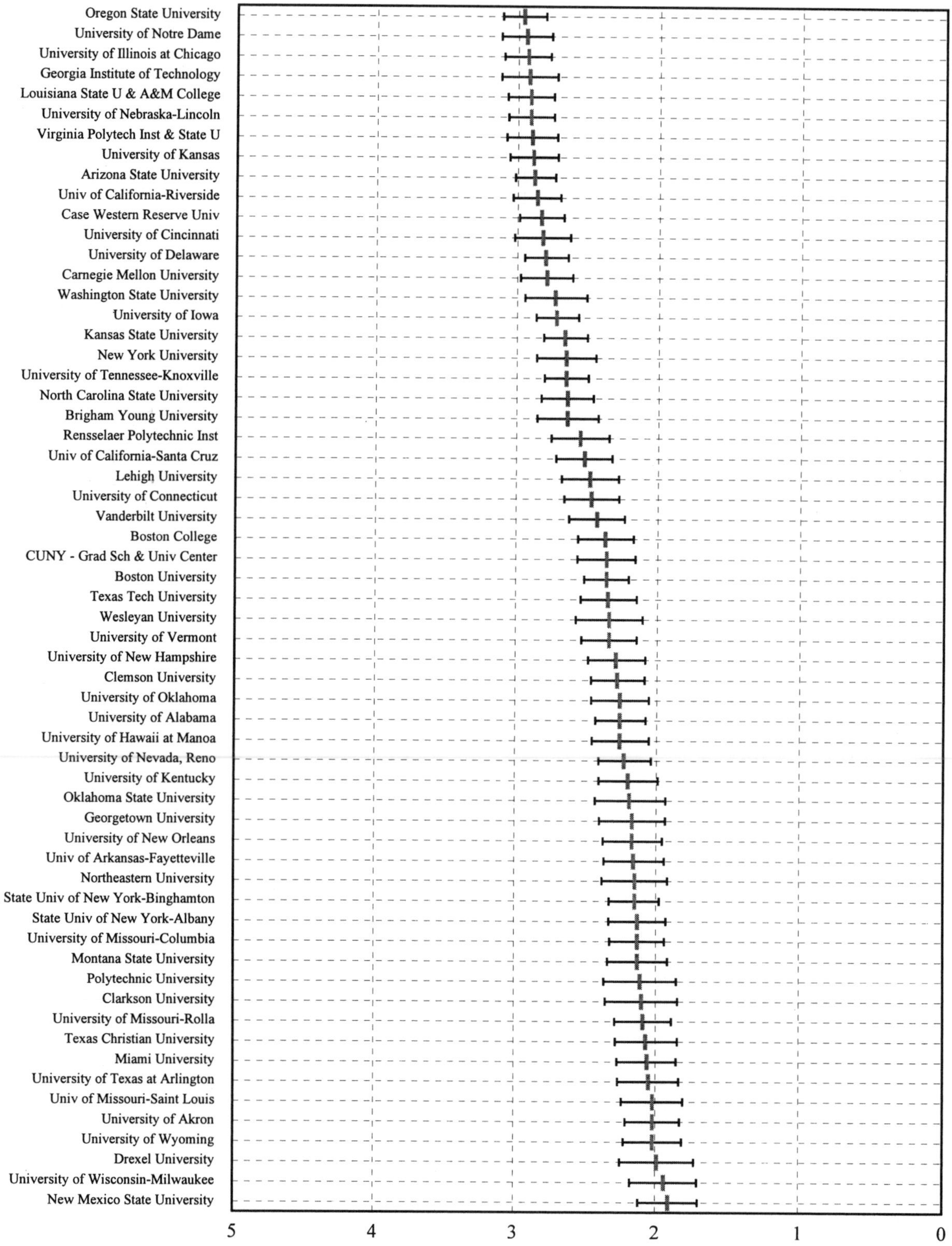

Appendix Figure Q - 9 Chemistry (Continued)

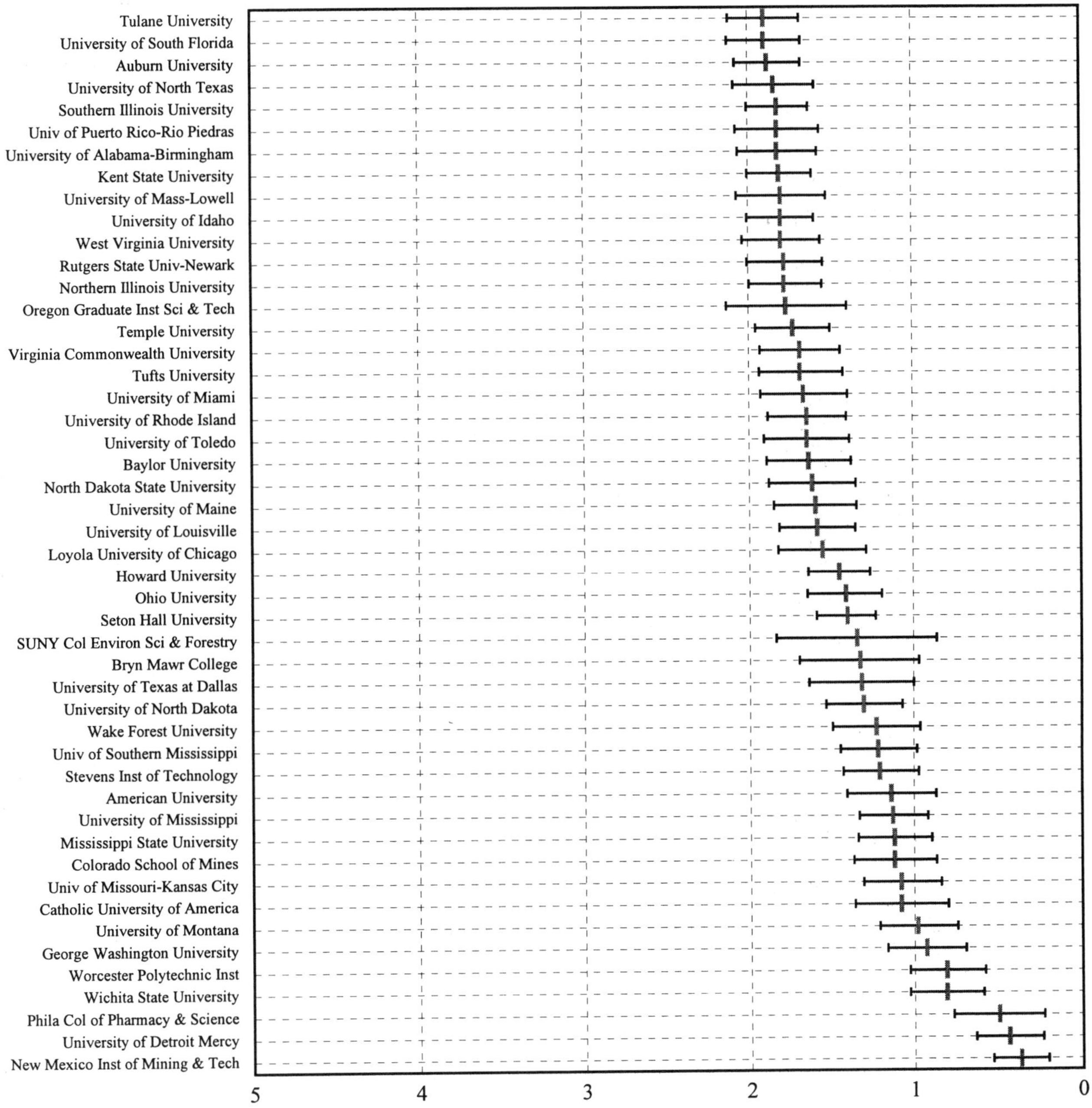

Source: National Survey of Graduate Faculty

Appendix Figure Q - 10 Means and Confidence Intervals for the Scholarly Quality of Program Faculty Ratings of the 86 Programs in Civil Engineering

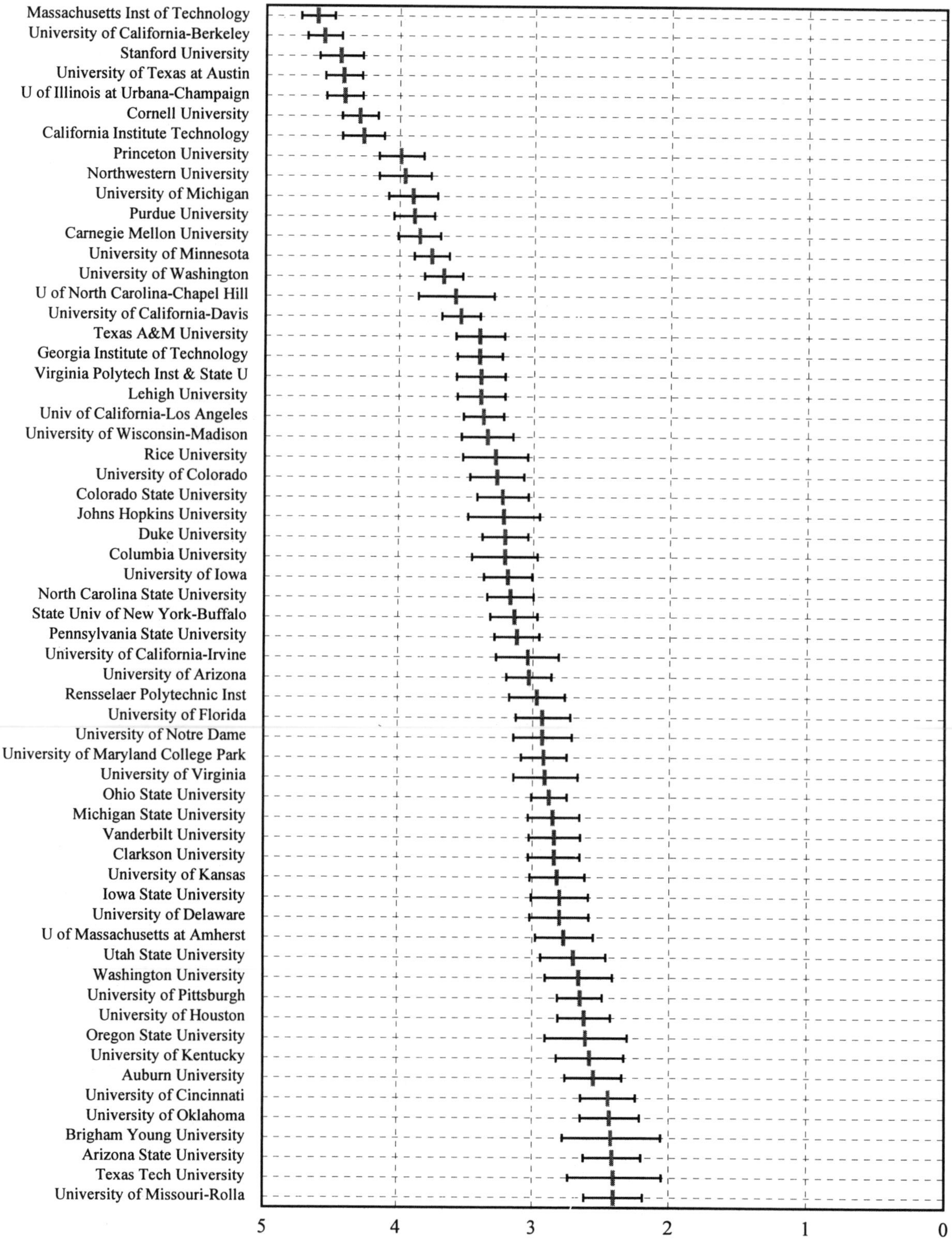

Appendix Figure Q - 10 Civil Engineering (Continued)

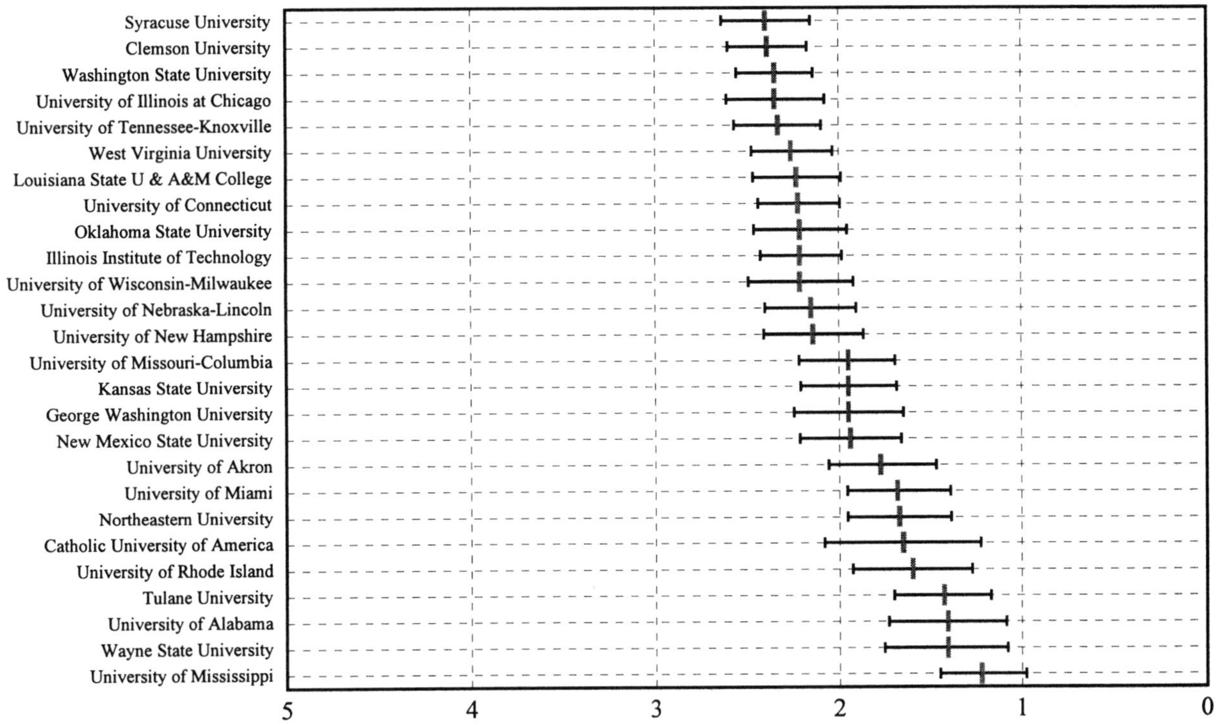

Source: National Survey of Graduate Faculty

Appendix Figure Q - 11 Means and Confidence Intervals for the Scholarly Quality of Program Faculty Ratings of the 29 Programs in Classics

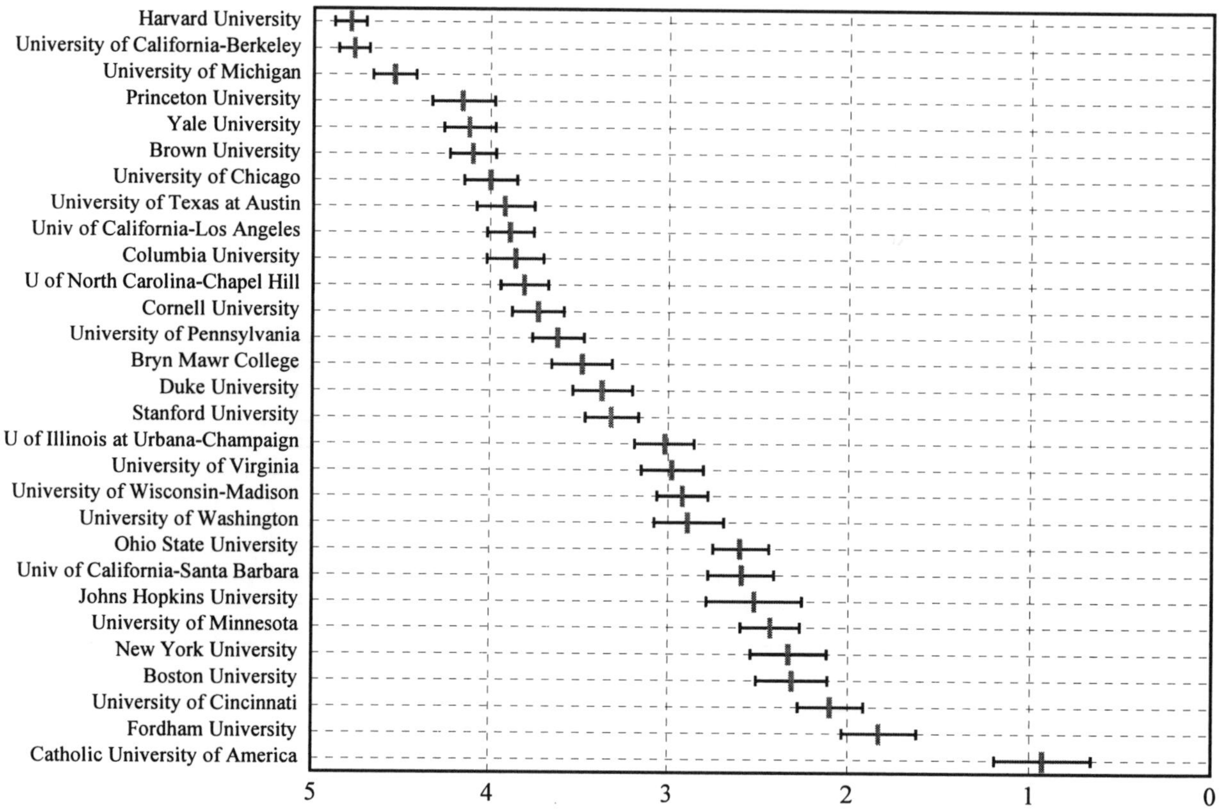

Source: National Survey of Graduate Faculty

Appendix Figure Q - 12 Means and Confidence Intervals for the Scholarly Quality of Program Faculty Ratings of the 44 Programs in Comparative Literature

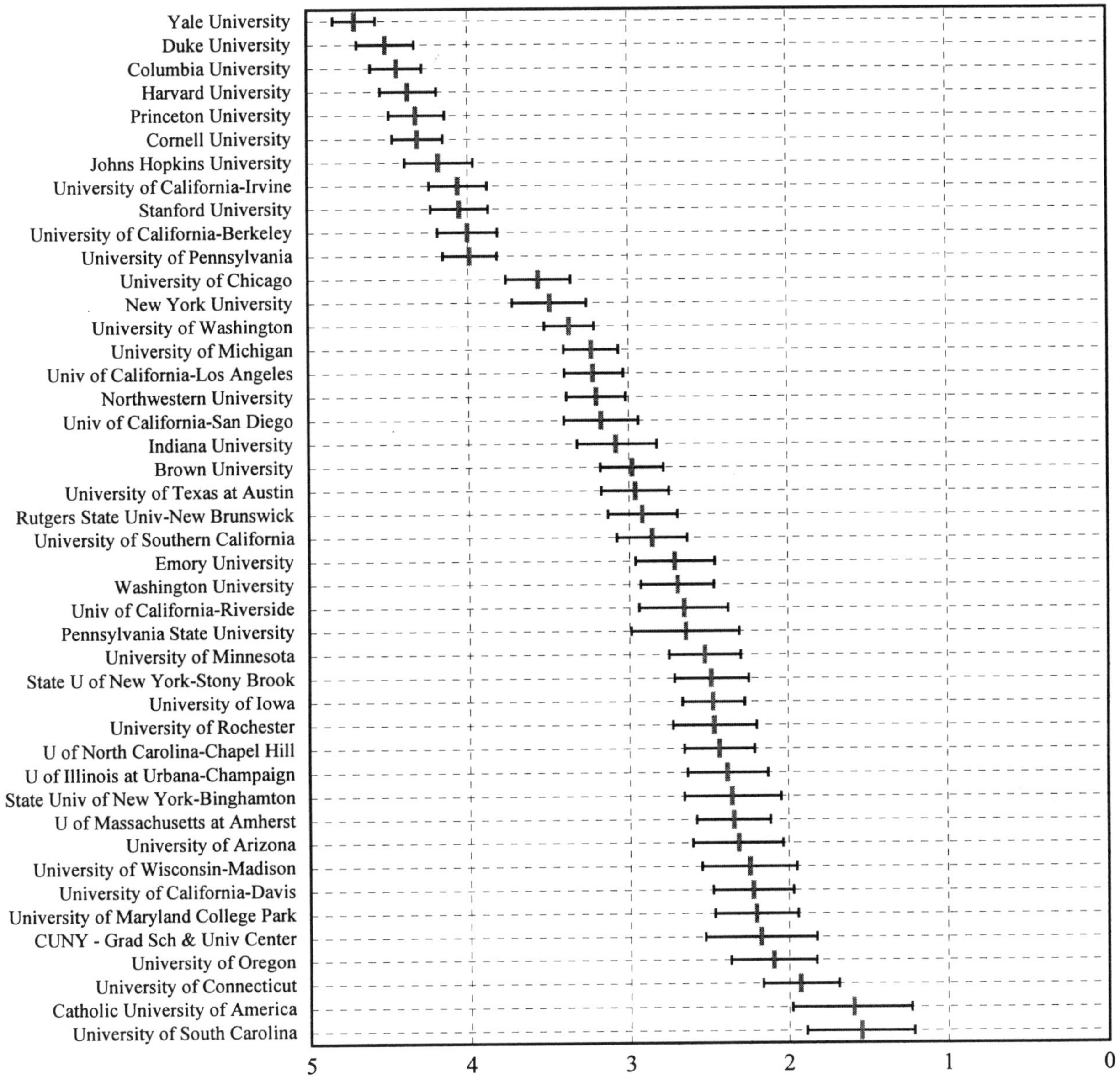

Source: National Survey of Graduate Faculty

Appendix Figure Q - 13 Means and Confidence Intervals for the Scholarly Quality of Program Faculty Ratings of the 108 Programs in Computer Sciences

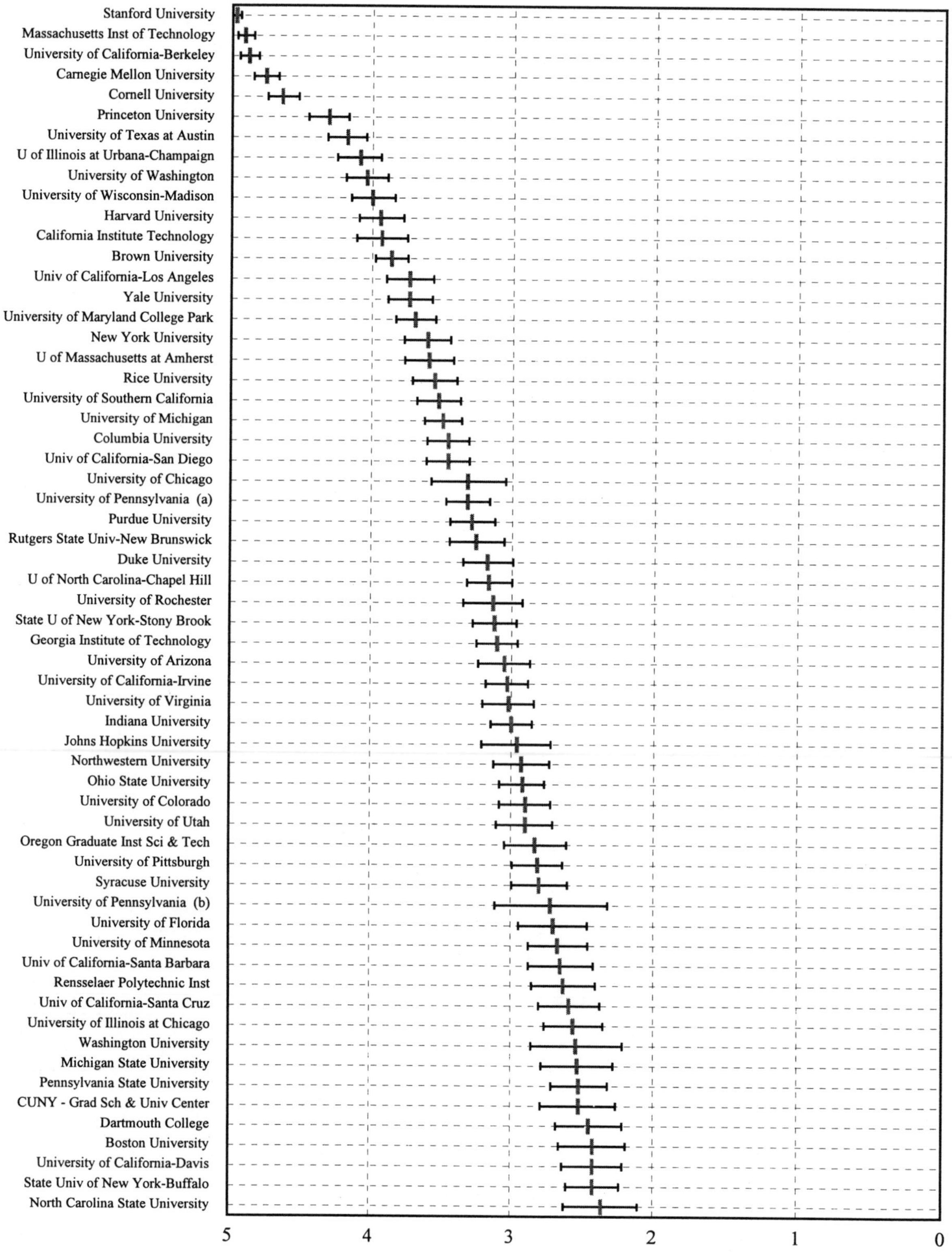

Appendix Figure Q - 13 Computer Sciences (Continued)

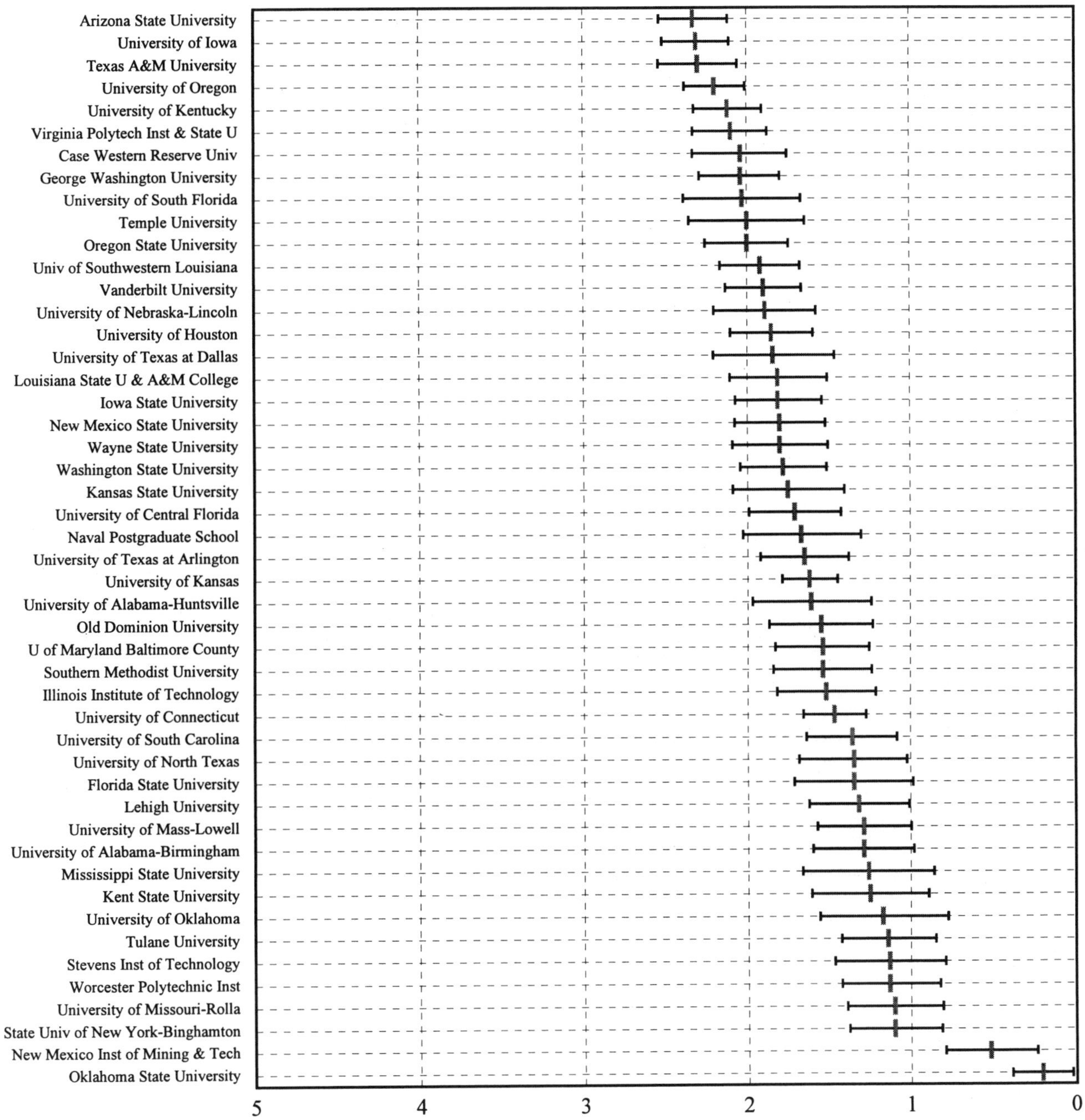

Source: National Survey of Graduate Faculty

Notes: (a) Program in Decision Sciences, Wharton sSchool
(b) Program in Computer and Information Sciences

Appendix Figure Q - 14 Means and Confidence Intervals for the Scholarly Quality of Program Faculty Ratings of the 129 Programs in Ecology, Evolution, and Behavior

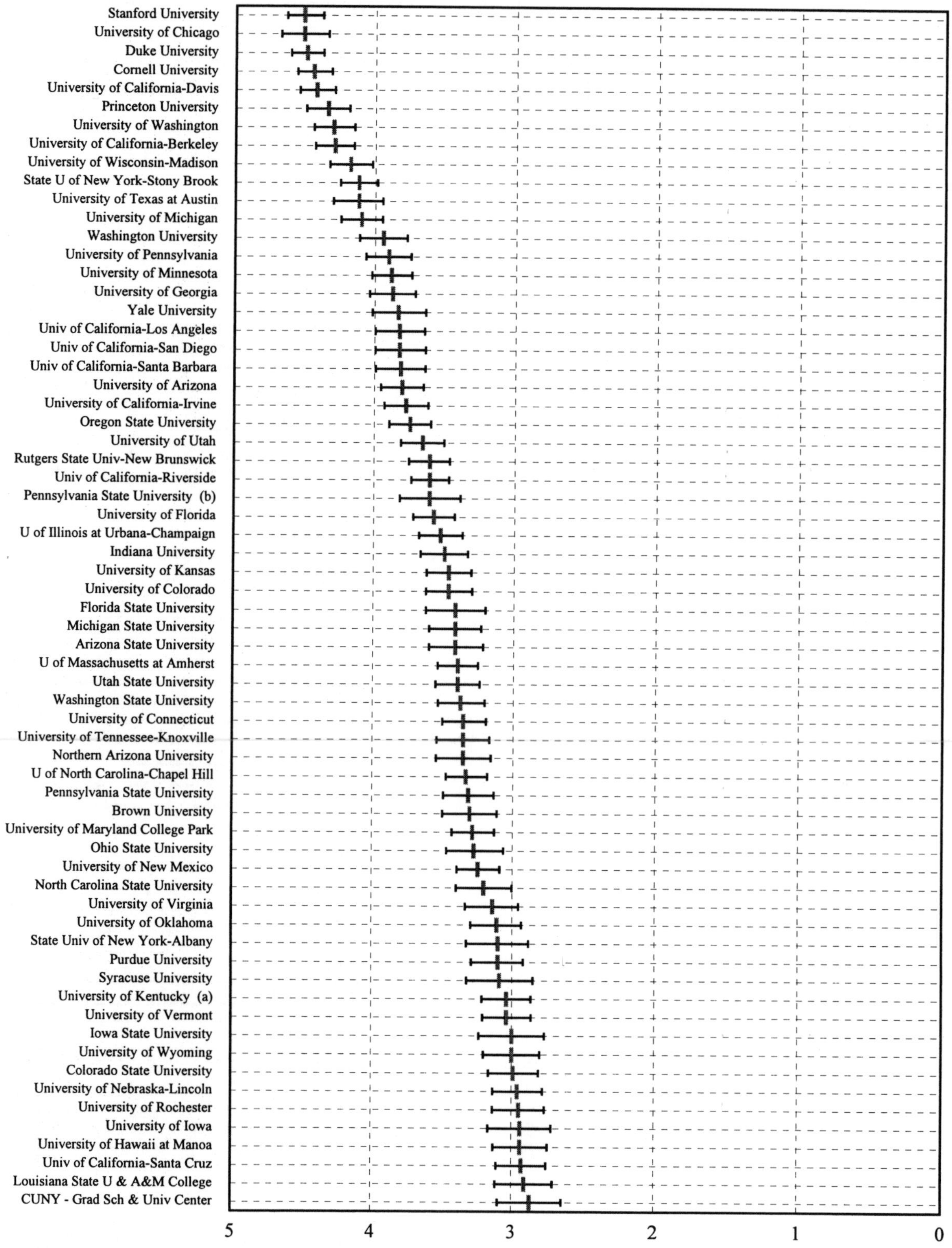

Appendix Chart Q - 14 Ecology, Evolution, and Behavior (Continued)

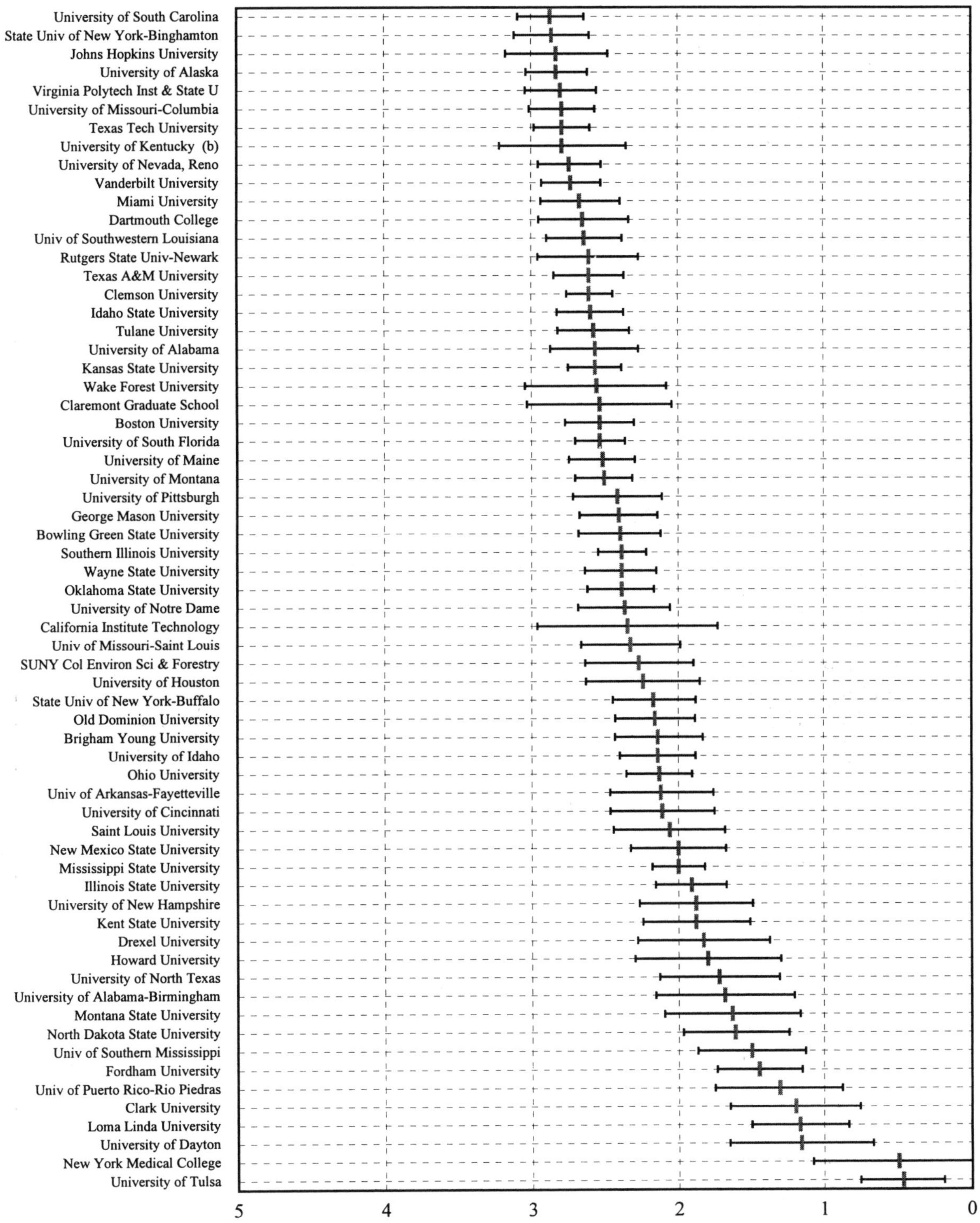

Source: National Survey of Graduate Faculty

Note: (a) School of Arts and Sciences
(b) School of Agriculture

Appendix Figure Q - 15 Means and Confidence Intervals for the Scholarly Quality of Program Faculty Ratings of the 107 Programs in Economics

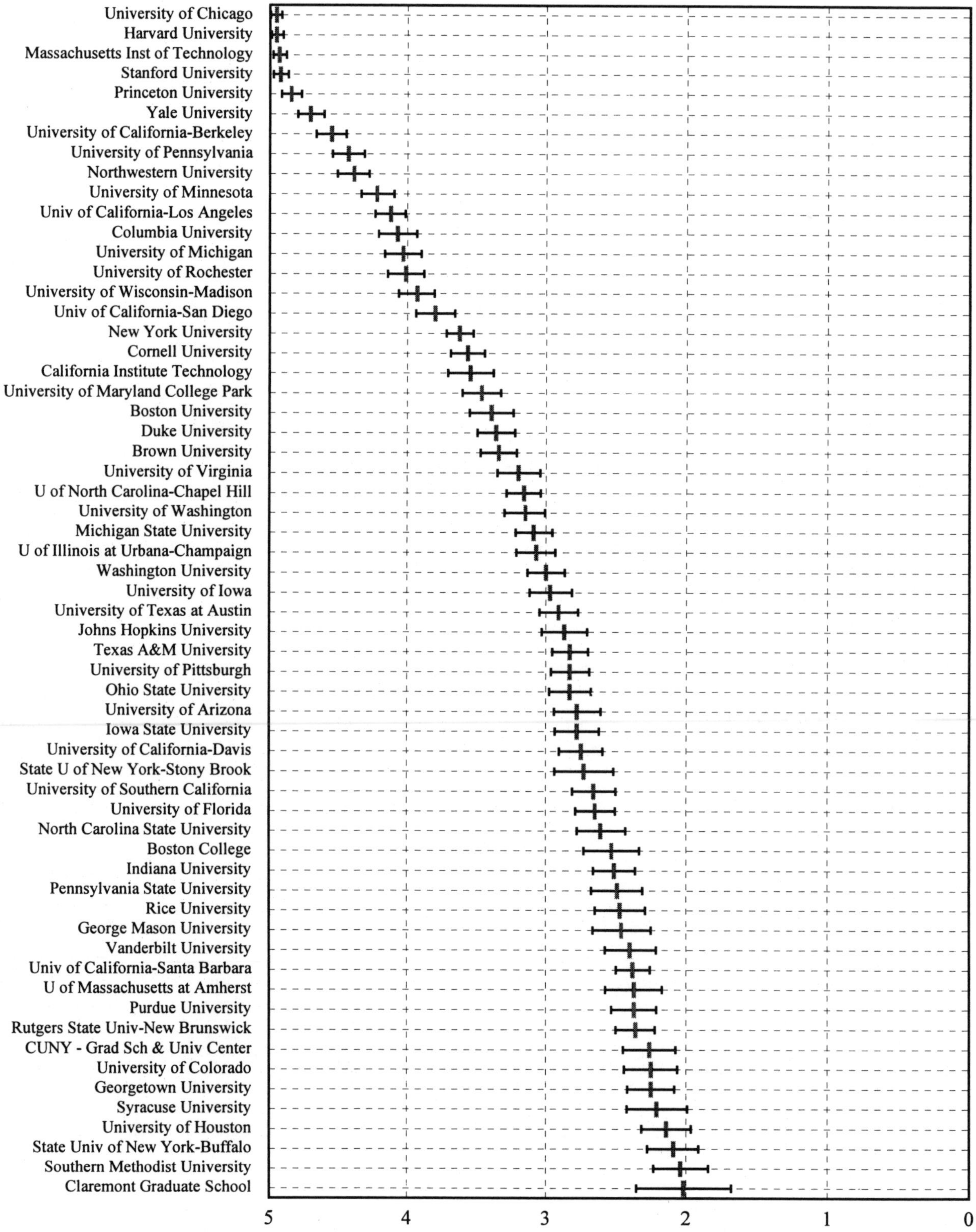

Appendix Figure Q - 15 Economics (Continued)

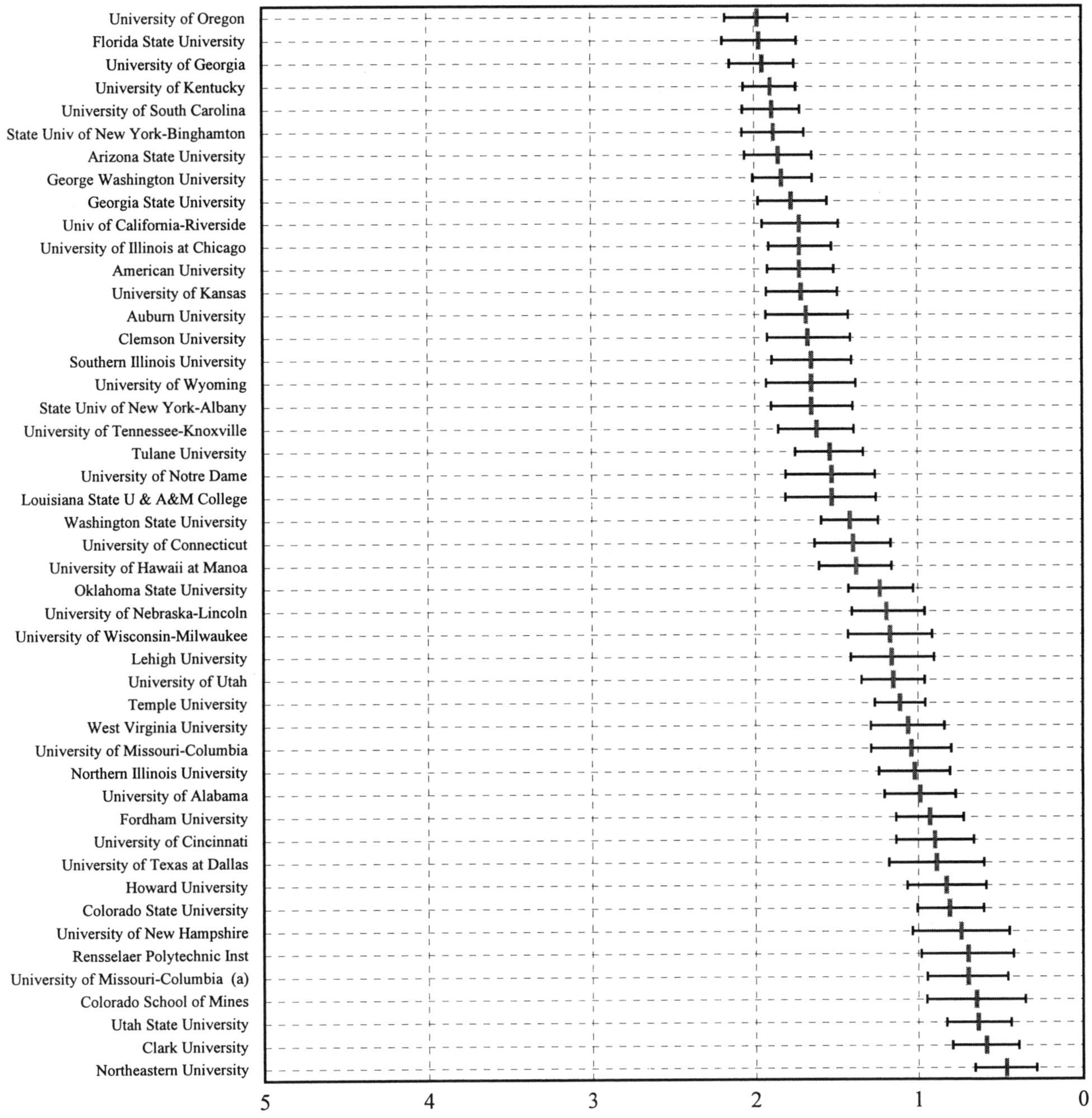

Source: National Survey of Graduate Faculty

Note: (a) Program in Agricultural Economics

Appendix Figure Q - 16 Means and Confidence Intervals for the Scholarly Quality of Program Faculty Ratings of the 126 Programs in Electrical Engineering

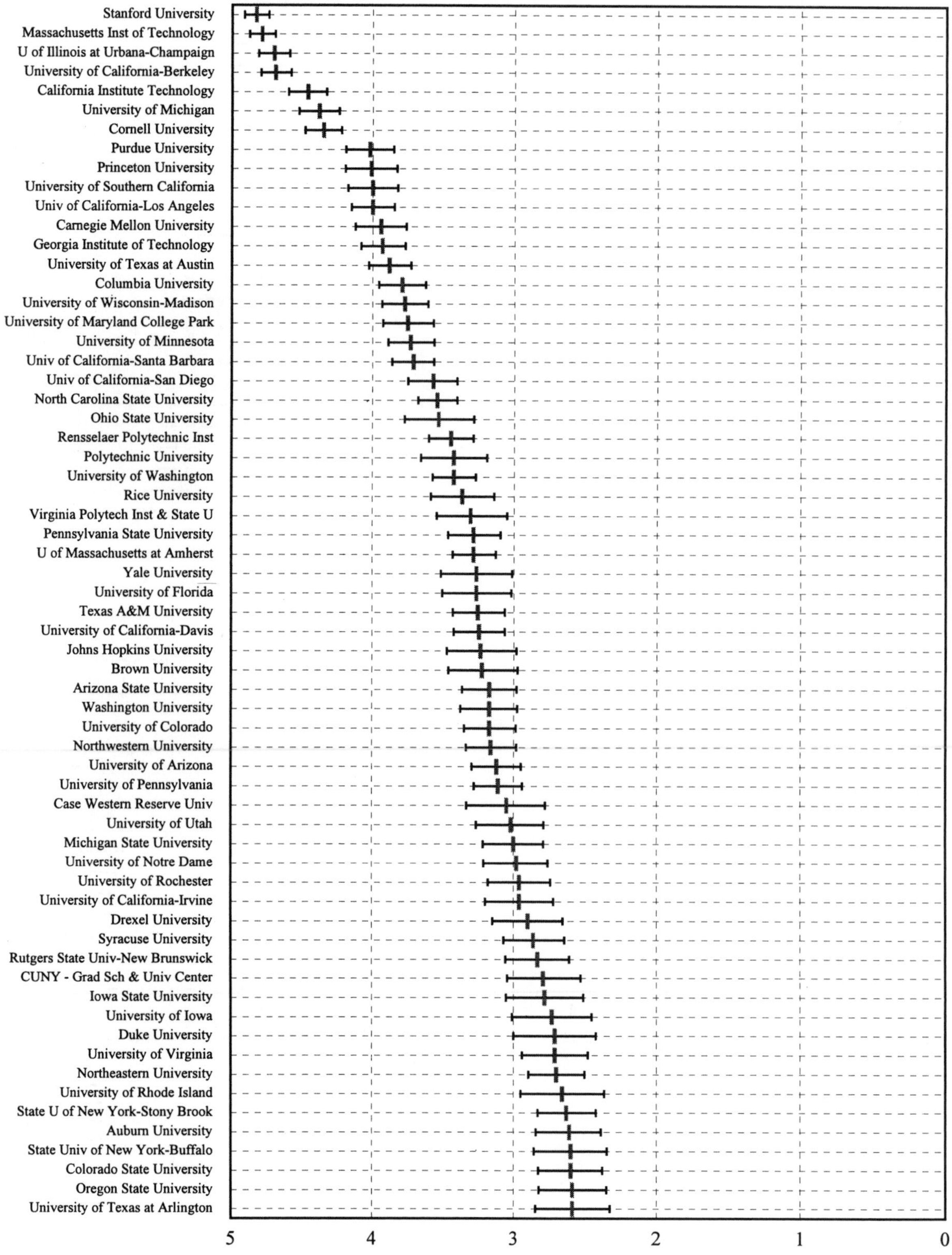

Appendix Figure Q - 16 Electrical Engineering (Continued)

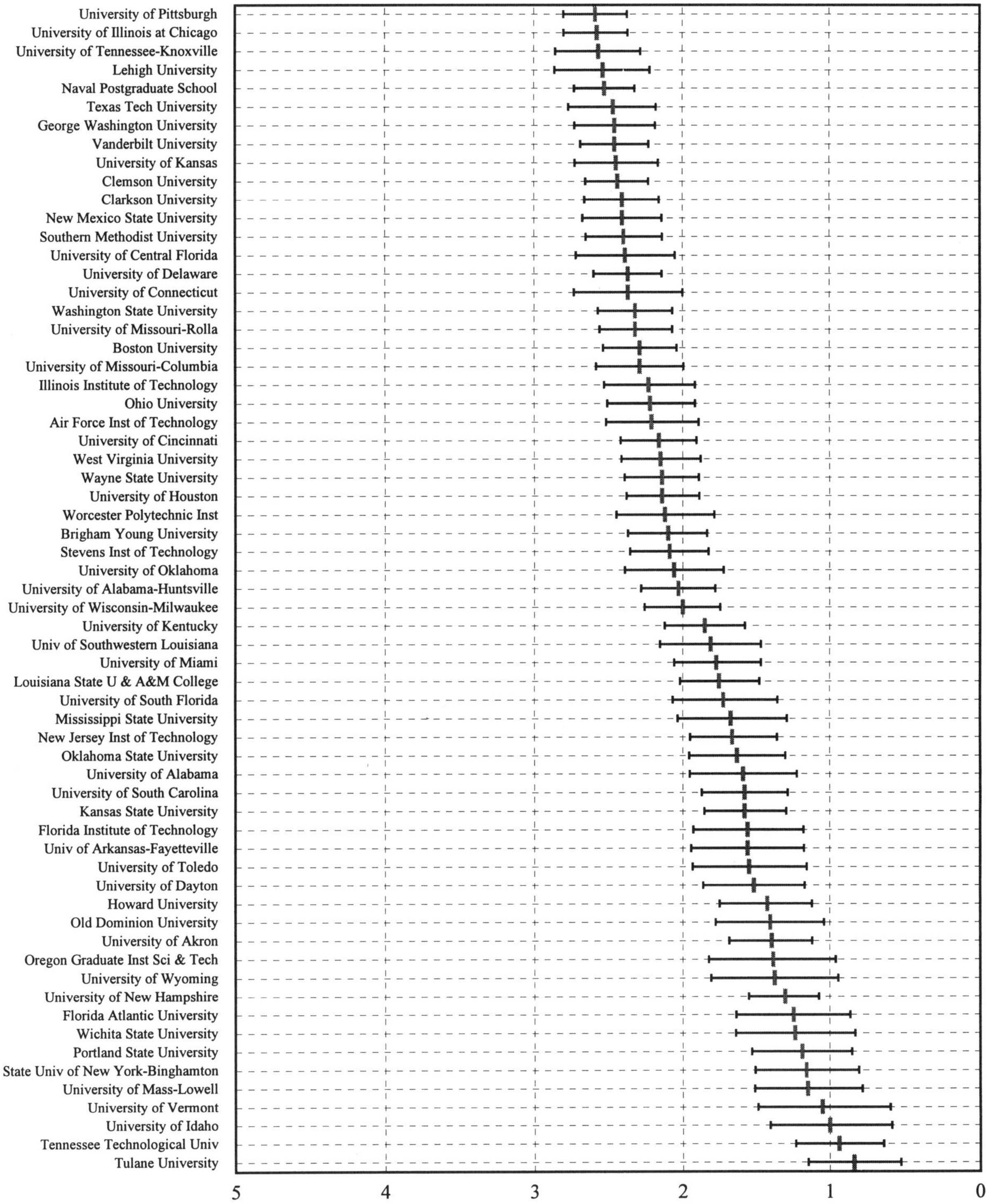

Source: National Survey of Graduate Faculty

Appendix Figure Q - 17 Means and Confidence Intervals for the Scholarly Quality of Program Faculty Ratings of the 127 Programs in English Language and Literature

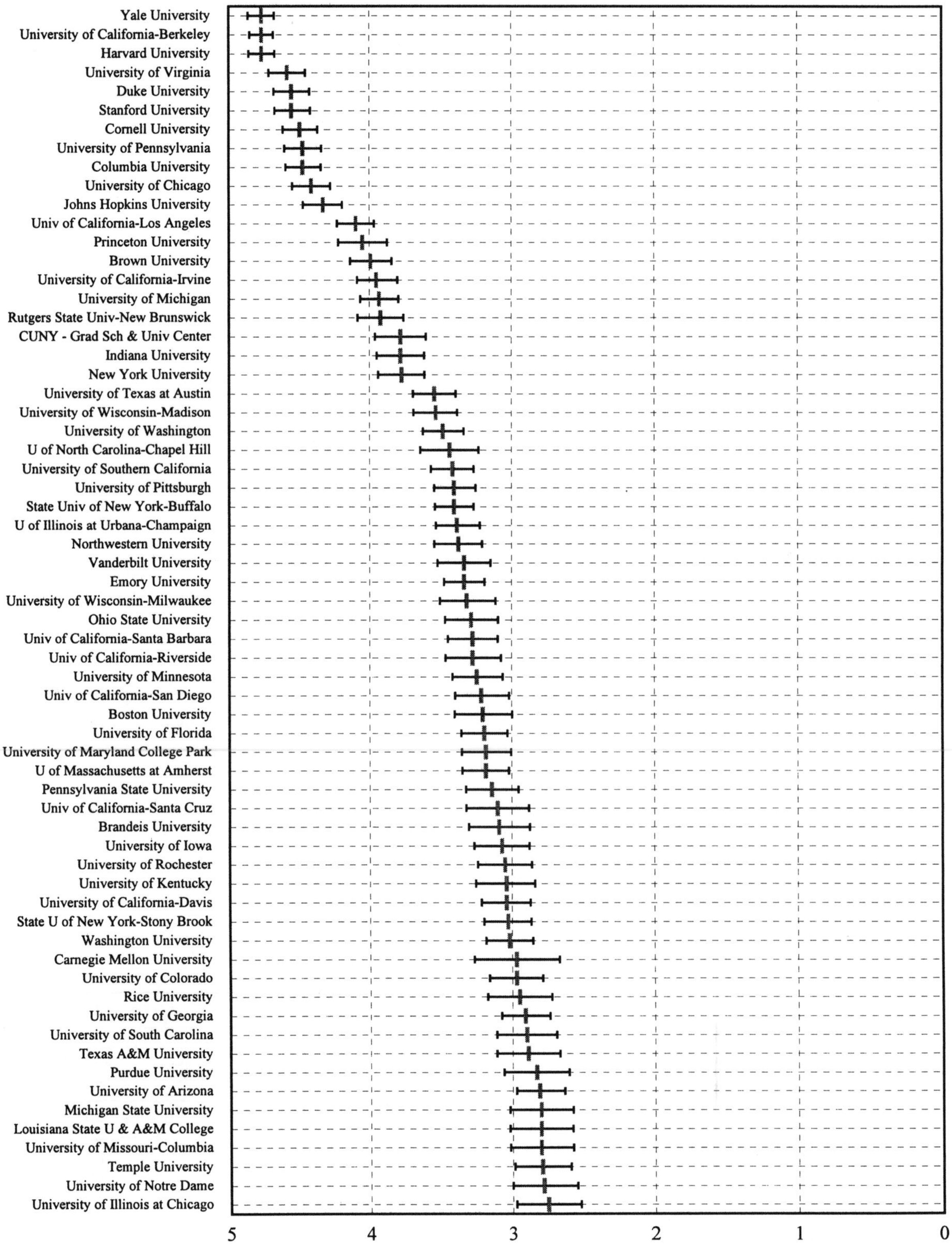

Appendix Figure Q - 17 English Language and Literature (Continued)

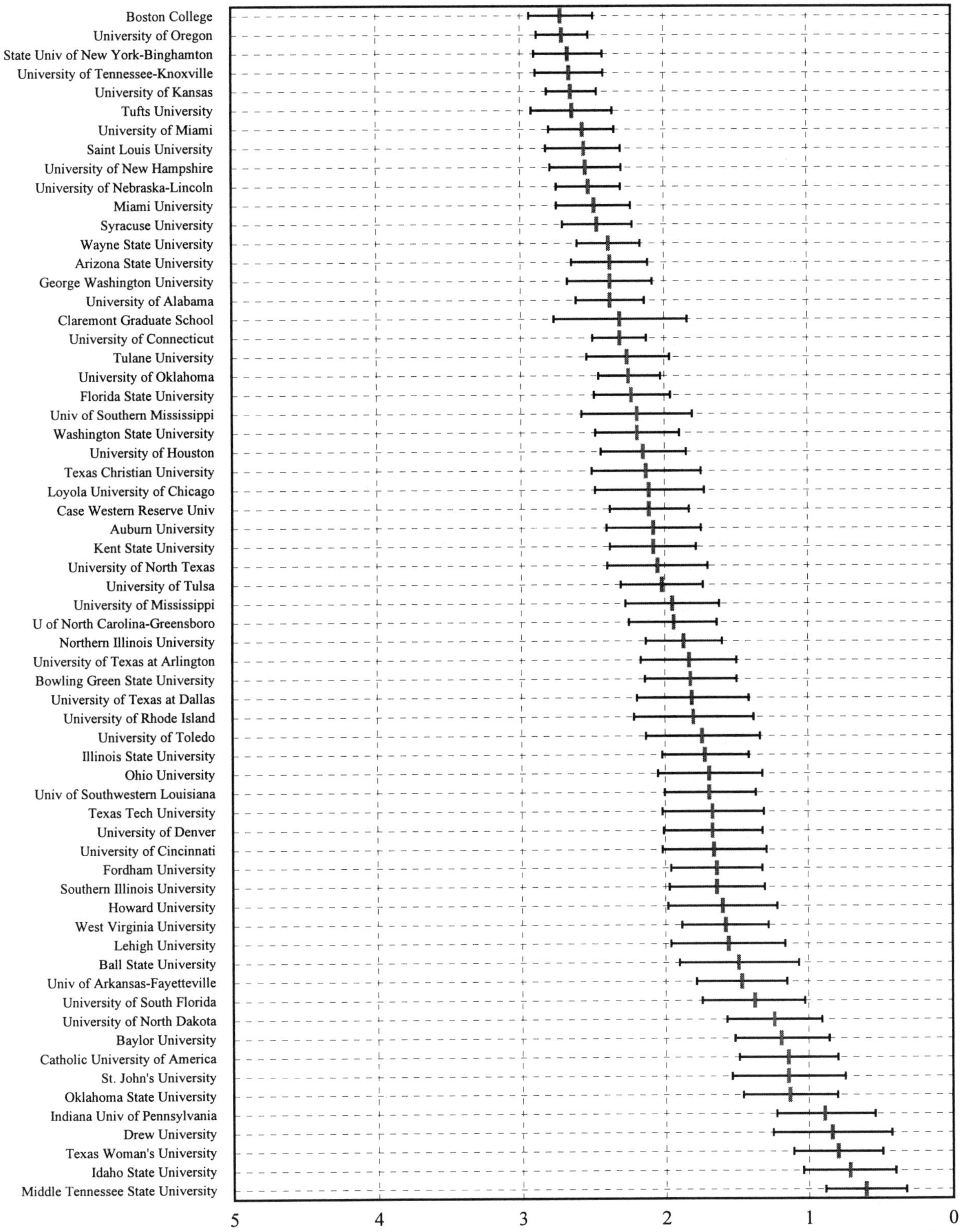

Source: National Survey of Graduate Faculty

Appendix Figure Q - 18 Means and Confidence Intervals for the Scholarly Quality of Program Faculty Ratings of the 45 Programs in French Language and Literature

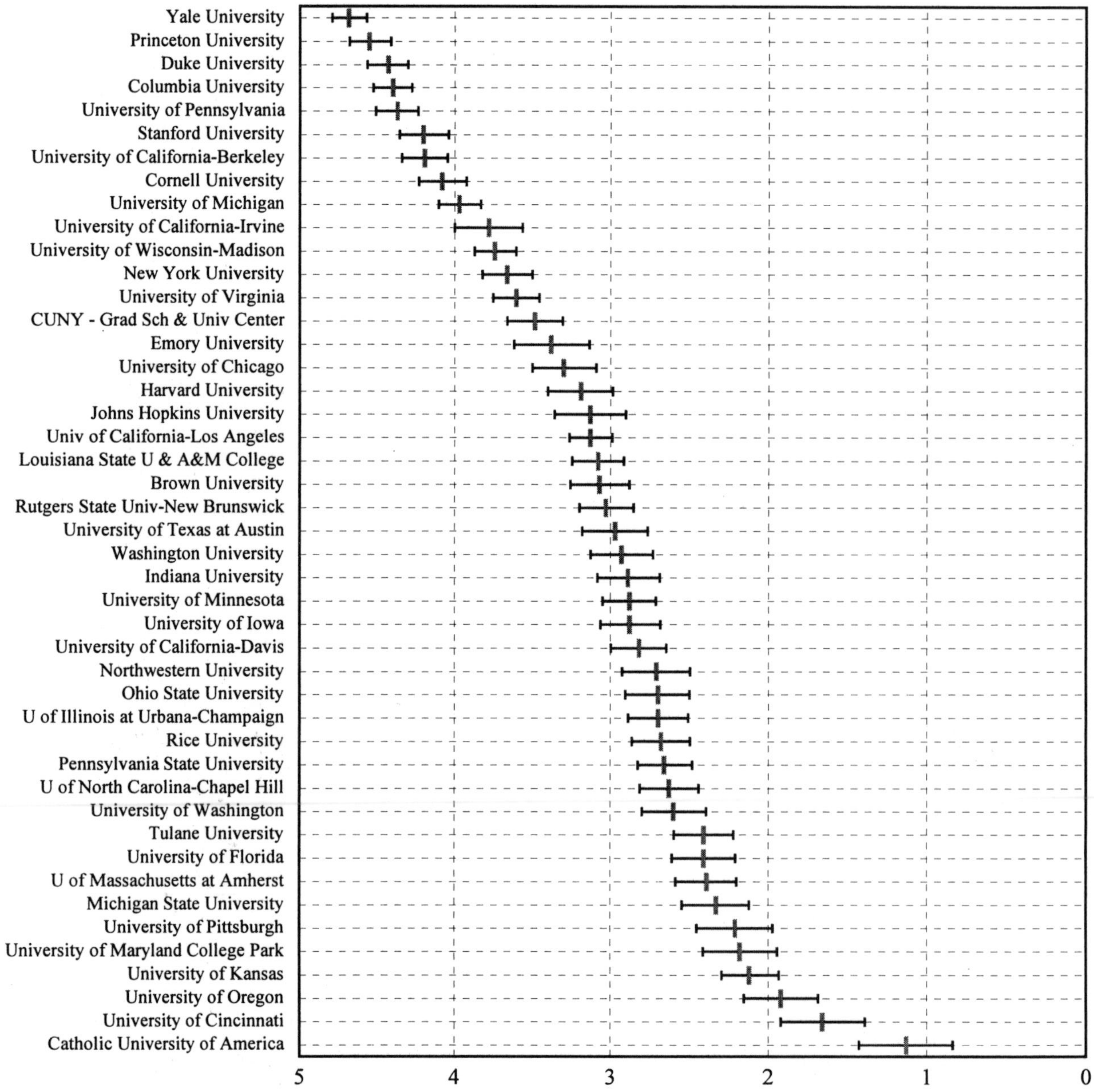

Source: National Survey of Graduate Faculty

Appendix Figure Q - 19 Means and Confidence Intervals for the Scholarly Quality of Program Faculty Ratings of the 36 Programs in Geography

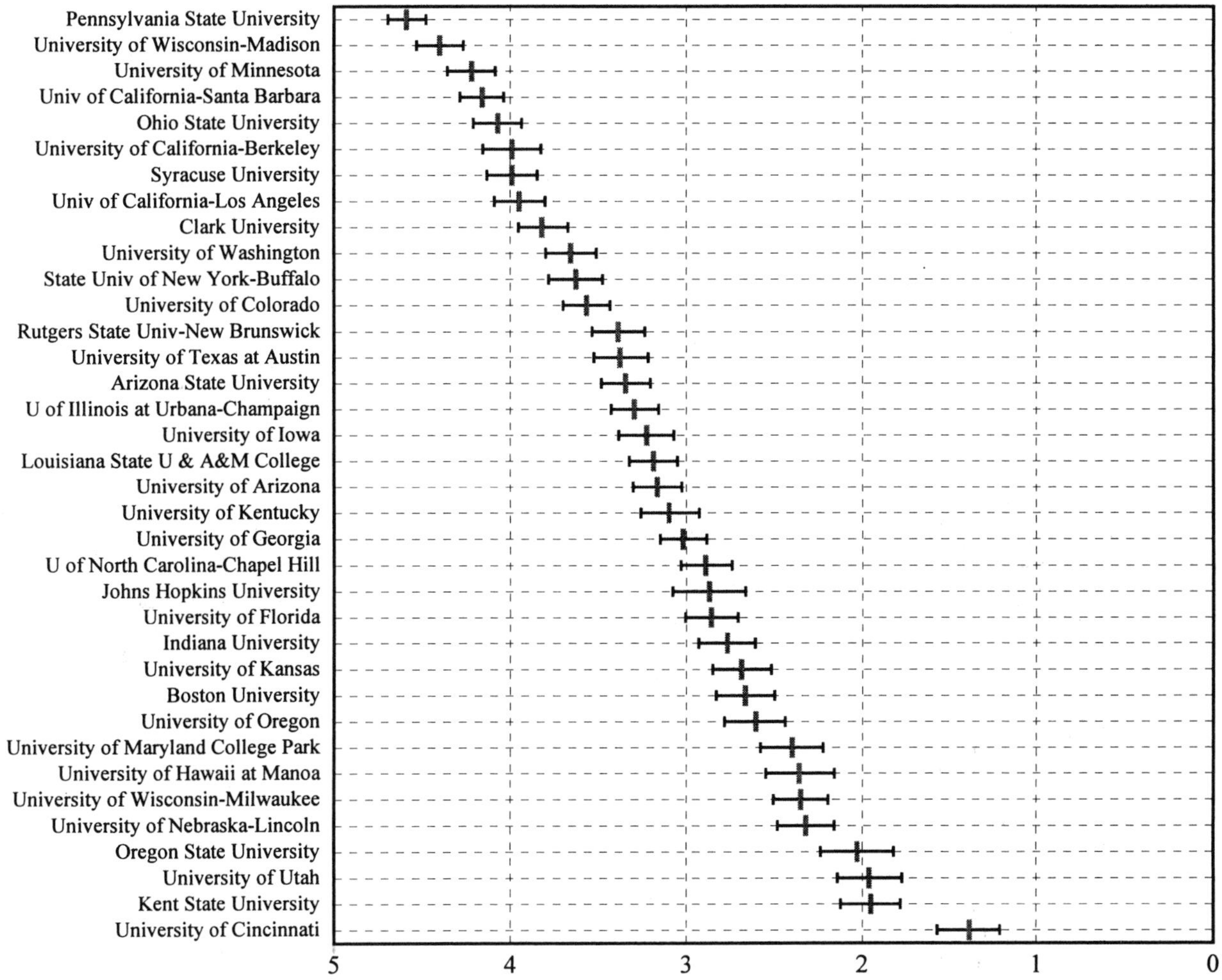

Source: National Survey of Graduate Faculty

Appendix Figure Q - 20 Means and Confidence Intervals for the Scholarly Quality of Program Faculty Ratings of the 100 Programs in Geosciences

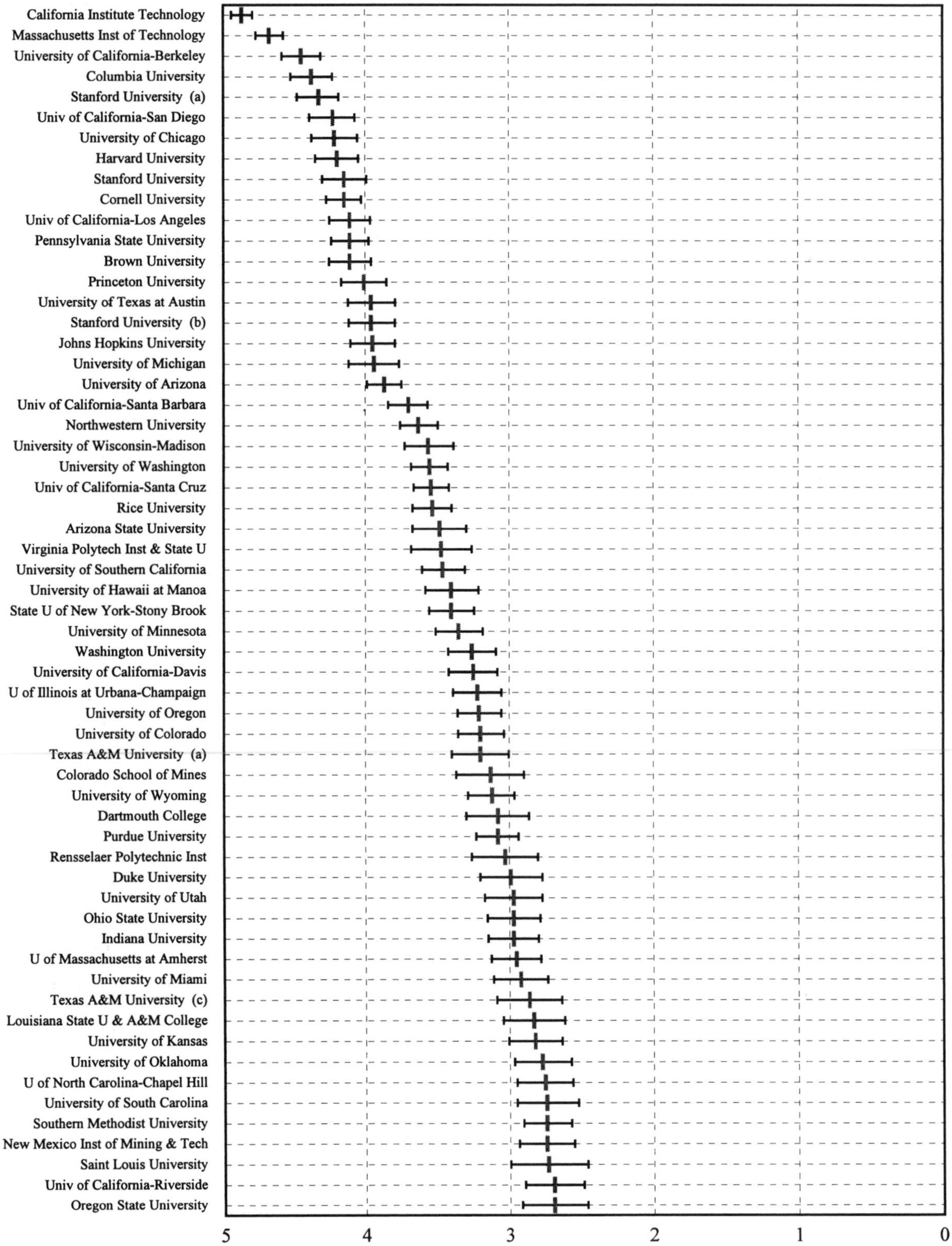

Appendix Figure Q - 20 Geosciences (Continued)

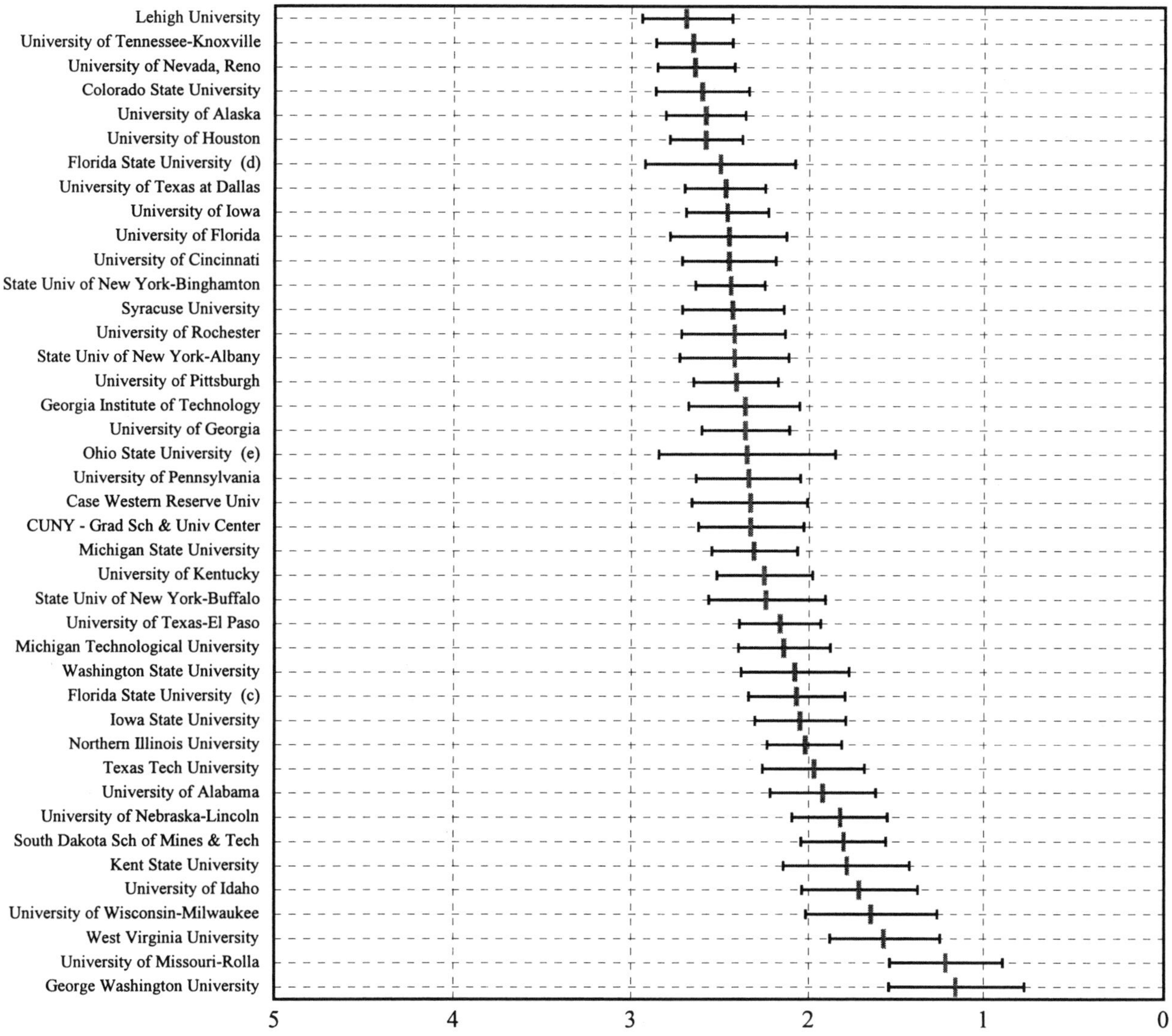

Source: National Survey of Graduate Faculty

Notes:
(a) Program in Geophysics
(b) Program in Applied Earth Sciences
(c) Program in Geology
(d) Program in Meteorology
(e) Program in Geodetic Science and Surveying

Appendix Figure Q - 21 Means and Confidence Intervals for the Scholarly Quality of Program Faculty Ratings of the 32 Programs in German Language and Literature

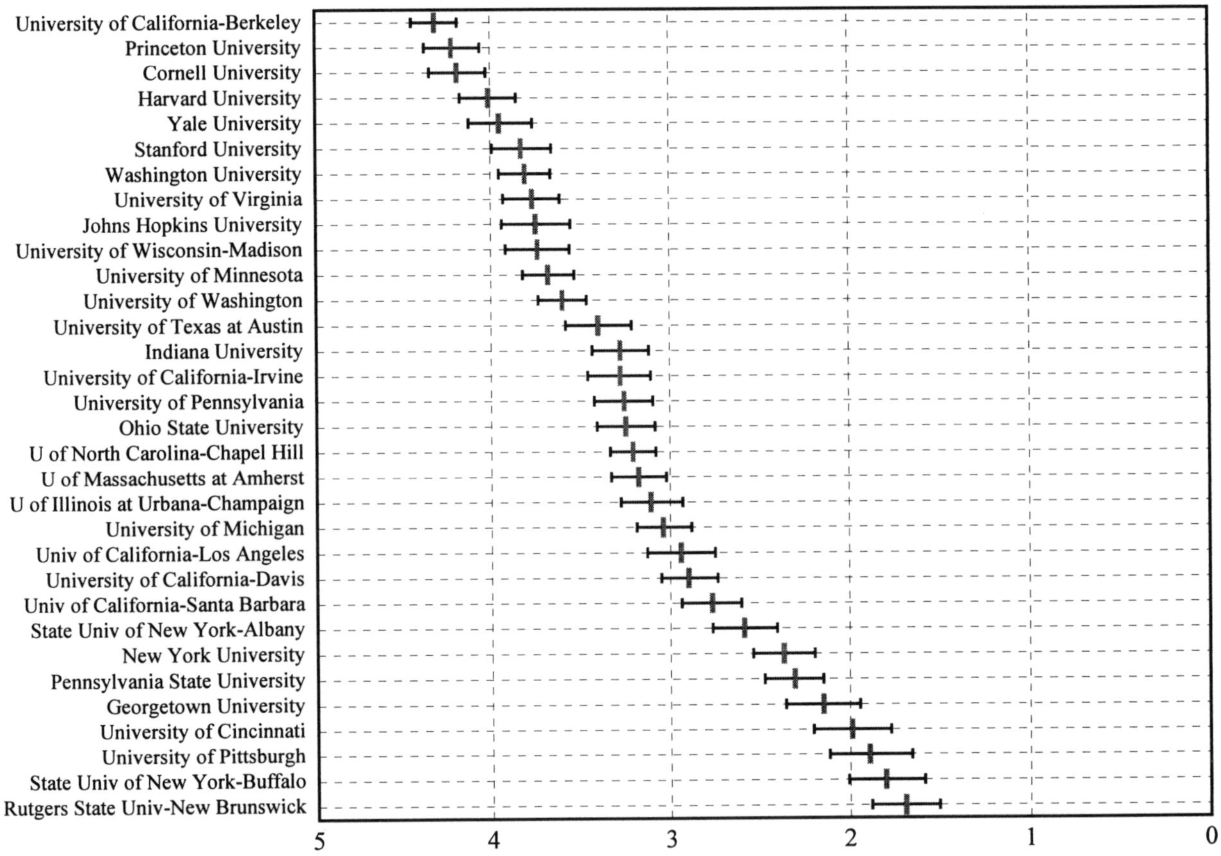

Source: National Survey of Graduate Faculty

Appendix Figure Q - 22 Means and Confidence Intervals for the Scholarly Quality of Program Faculty Ratings of the 111 Programs in History

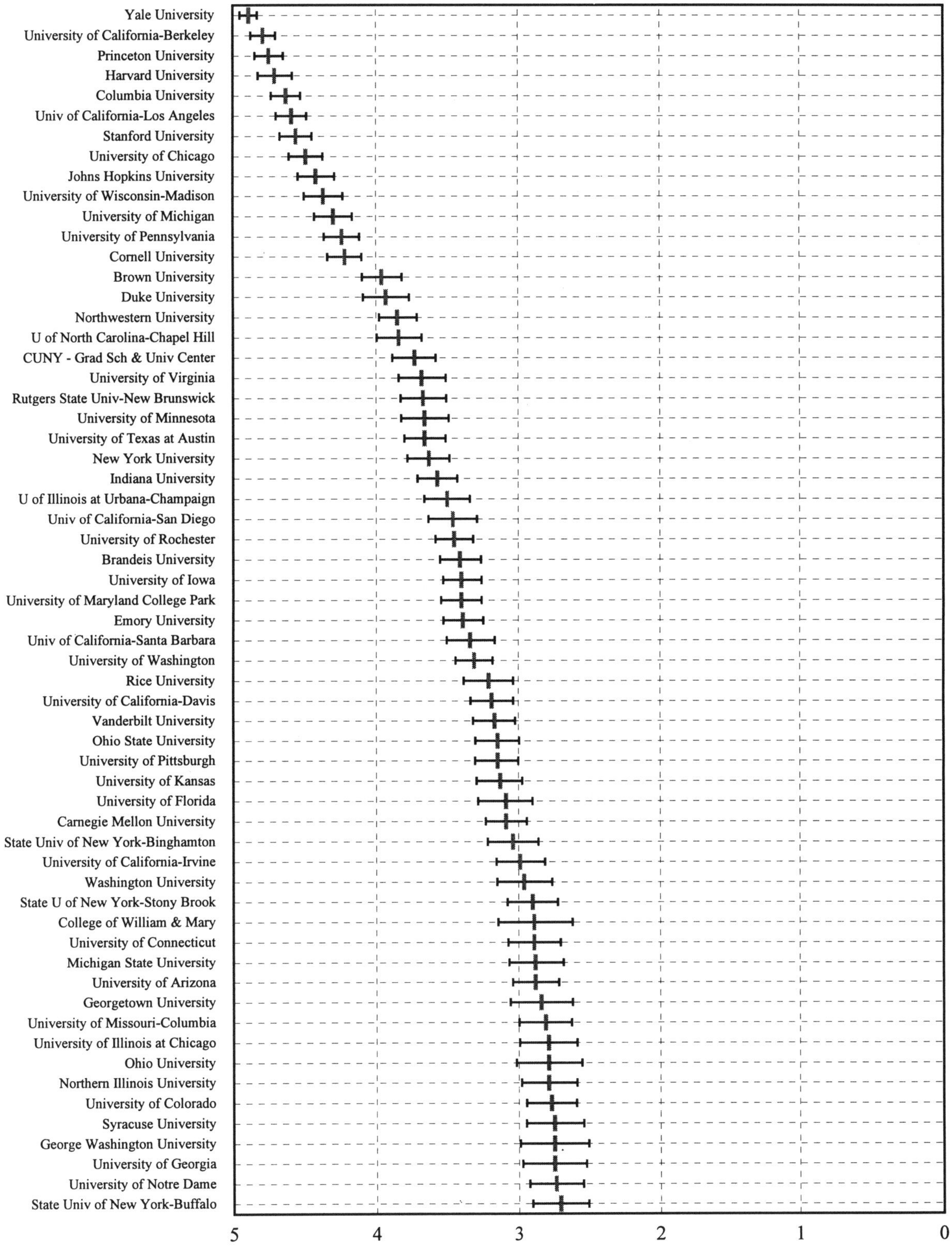

Appendix Figure Q - 22 History (Continued)

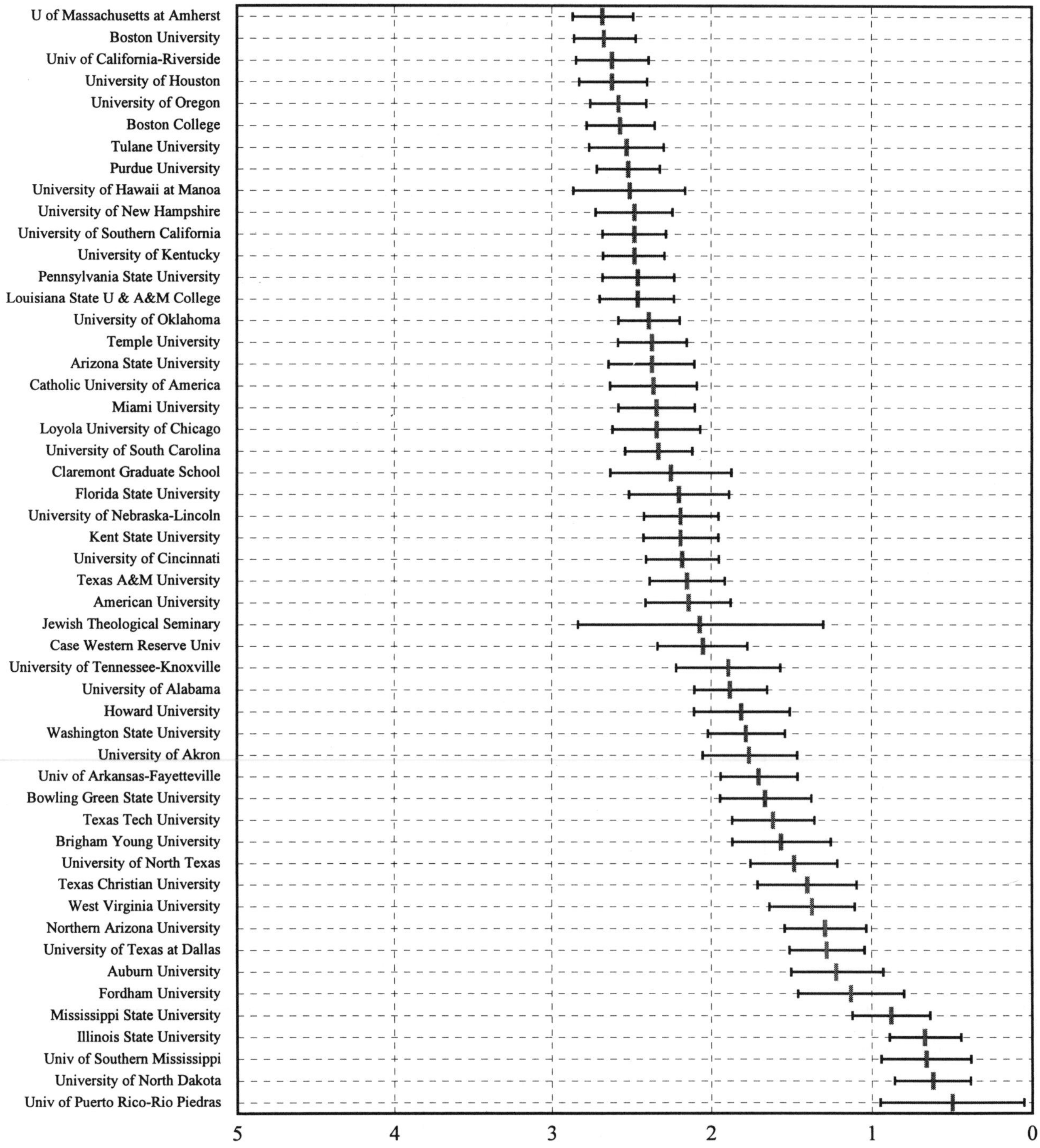

Source: National Survey of Graduate Faculty

Appendix Figure Q - 23 Means and Confidence Intervals for the Scholarly Quality of Program Faculty Ratings of the 37 Programs in Industrial Engineering

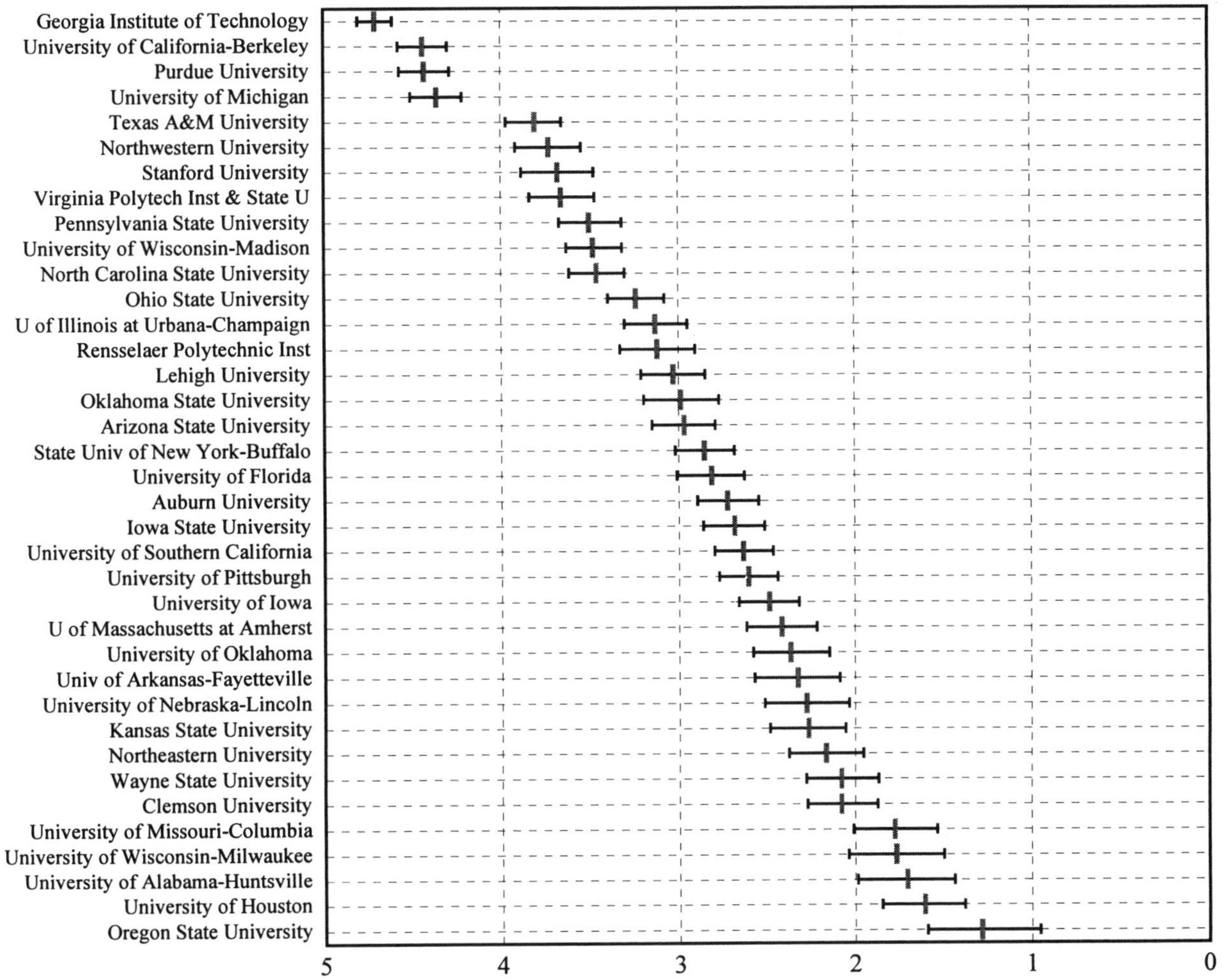

Source: National Survey of Graduate Faculty

Appendix Figure Q - 24 Means and Confidence Intervals for the Scholarly Quality of Program Faculty Ratings of the 41 Programs in Linguistics

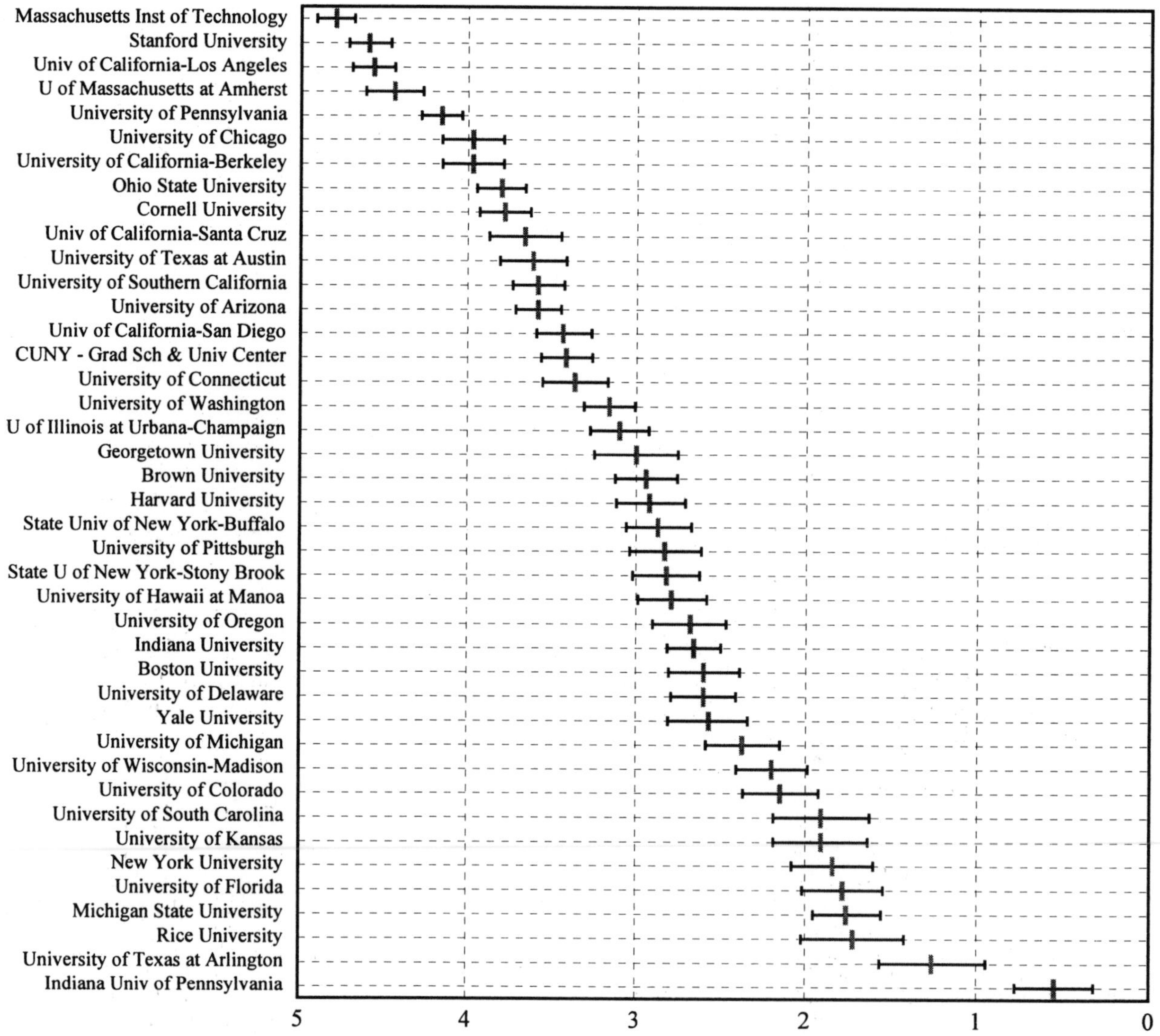

Source: National Survey of Graduate Faculty

Appendix Figure Q - 25 Means and Confidence Intervals for the Scholarly Quality of Program Faculty Ratings of the 65 Programs in Materials Science

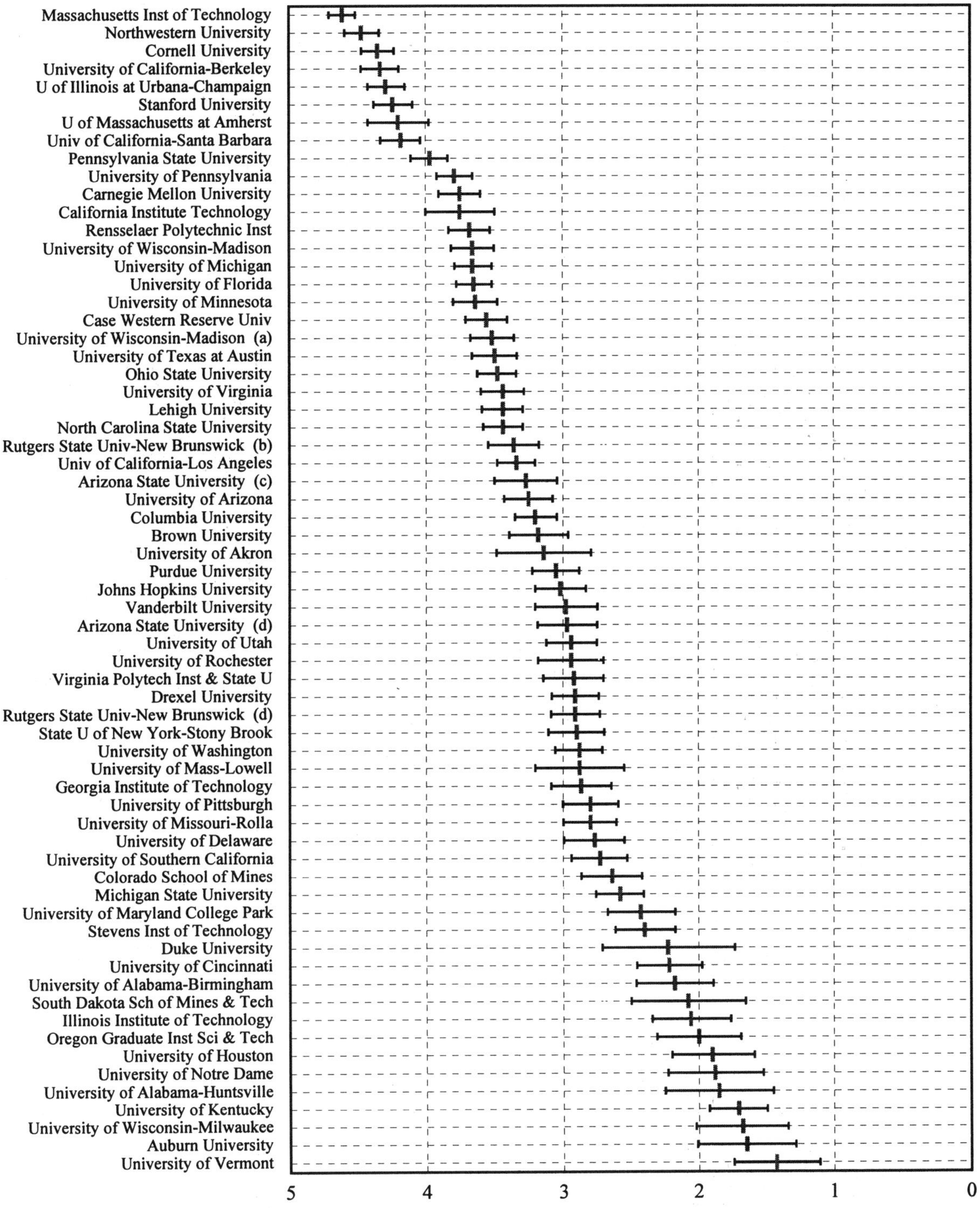

Source: National Survey of Graduate Faculty

Notes:

(a) Program in Metallurgial Engineering
(b) Program in Ceramic Science and Engineering
(c) Program in Science and Engineering of Materials
(d) Program in Material Science and Engineering

Appendix Figure Q - 26 Means and Confidence Intervals for the Scholarly Quality of Program Faculty Ratings of the 139 Programs in Mathematics

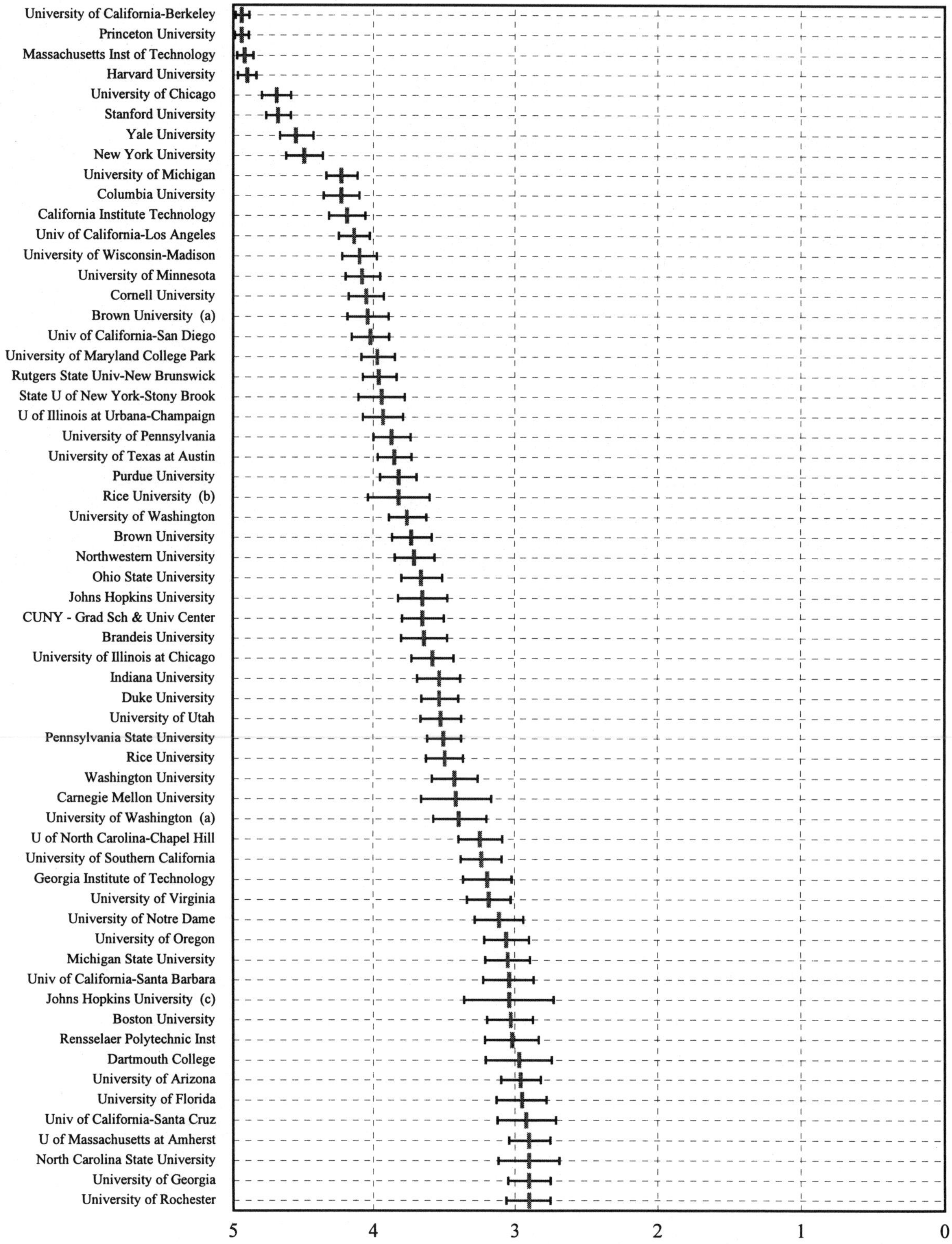

Appendix Figure Q - 26 Mathematics (Continued)

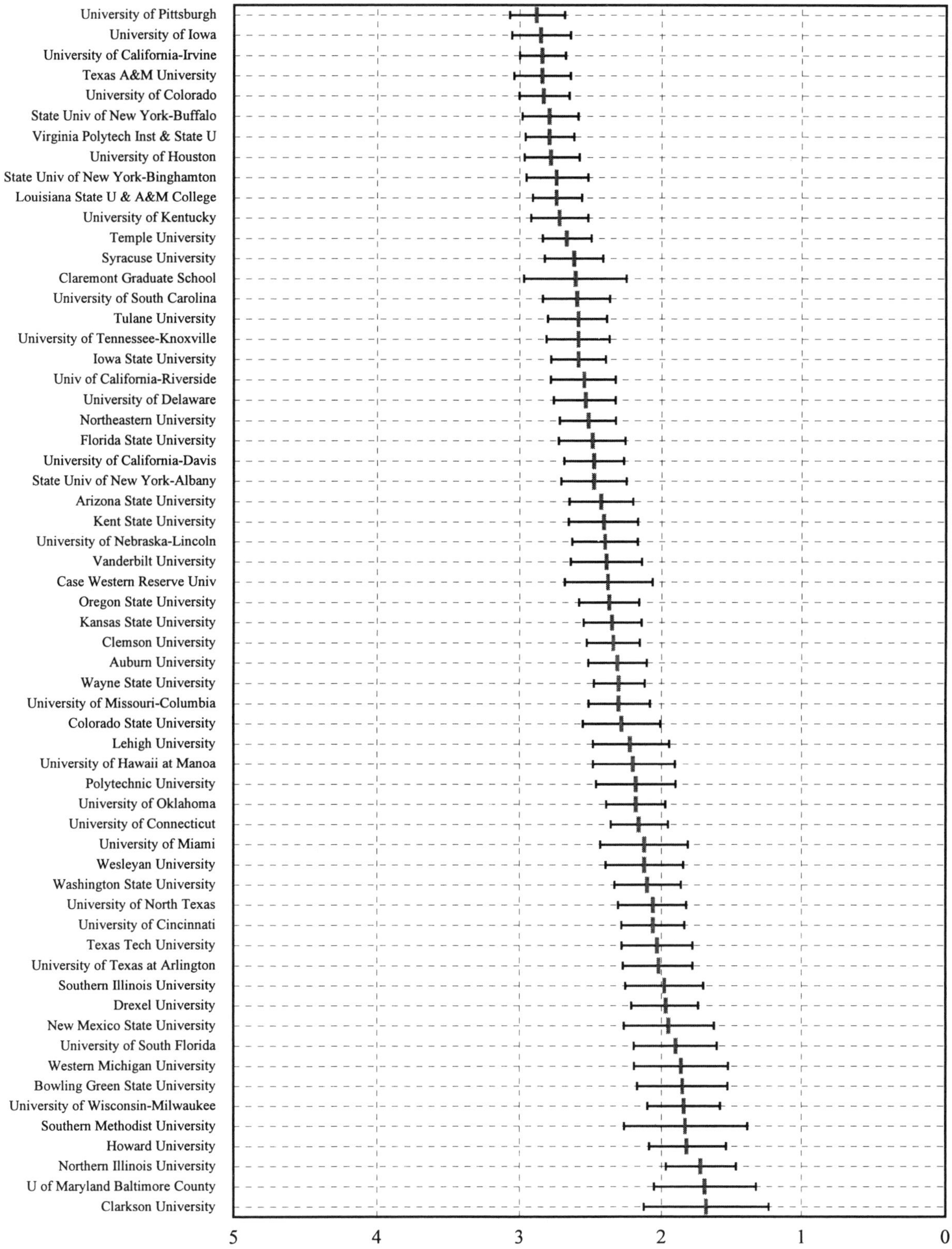

Appendix Figure Q - 26 Mathematics (Continued)

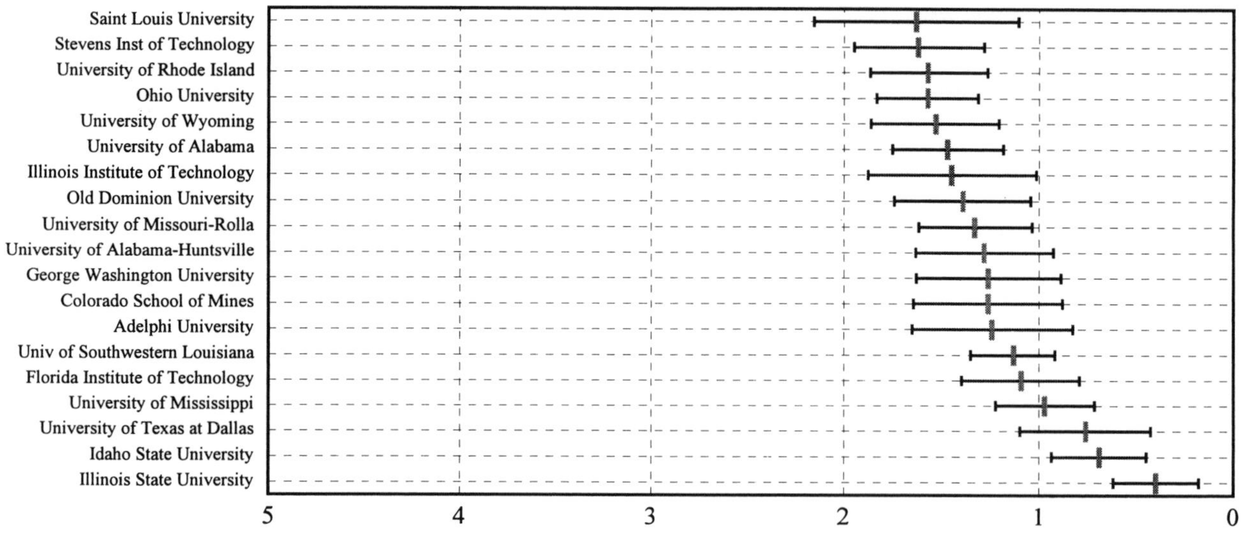

Source: National Survey of Graduate Faculty

Note:
(a) Program in Applied Mathematics
(b) Program in Computational and Applied Mathematics
(c) Program in Mathematical Sciences

Appendix Figure Q - 27 Means and Confidence Intervals for the Scholarly Quality of Program Faculty Ratings of the 110 Programs in Mechanical Engineering

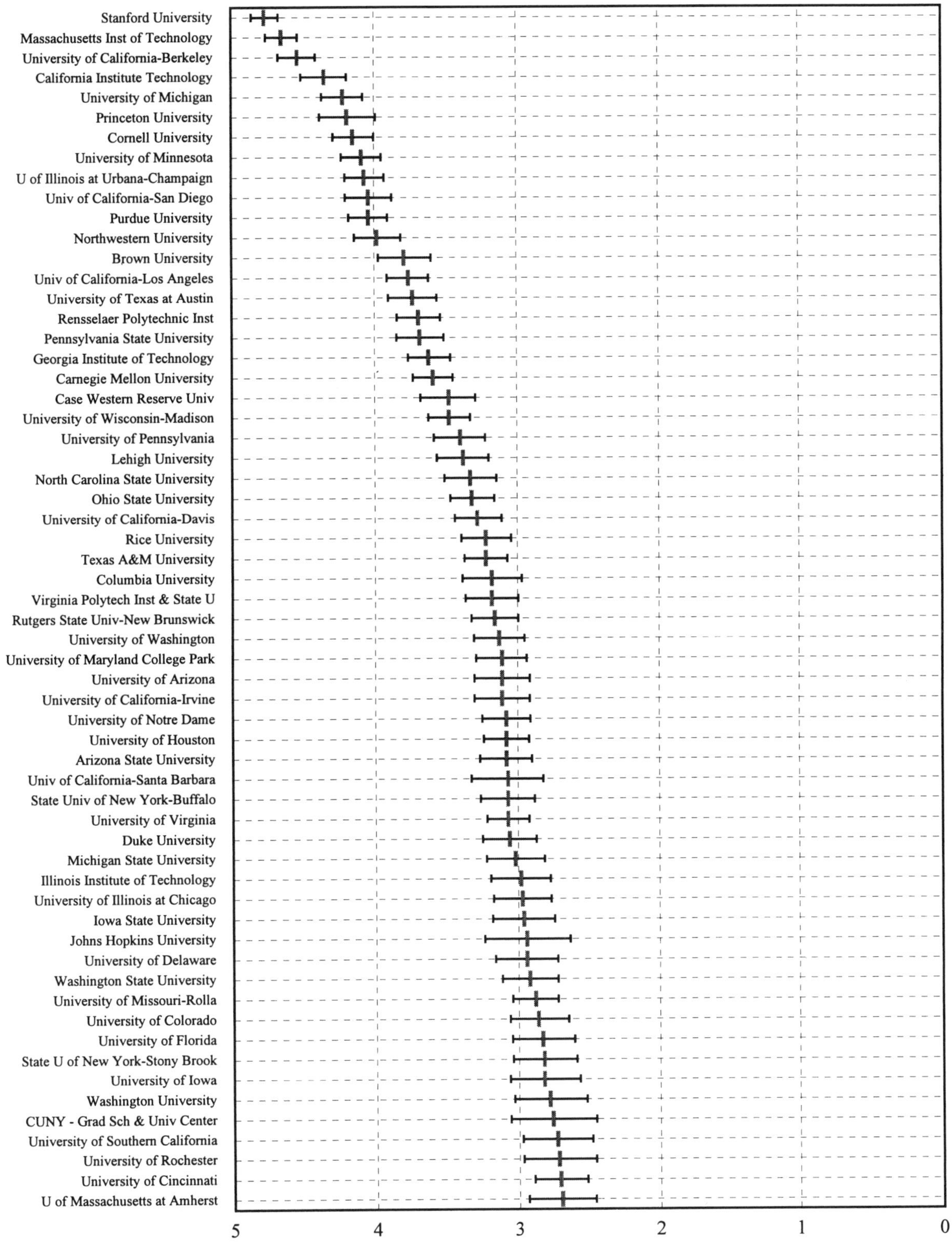

Appendix Figure Q - 27 Mechanical Engineering (Continued)

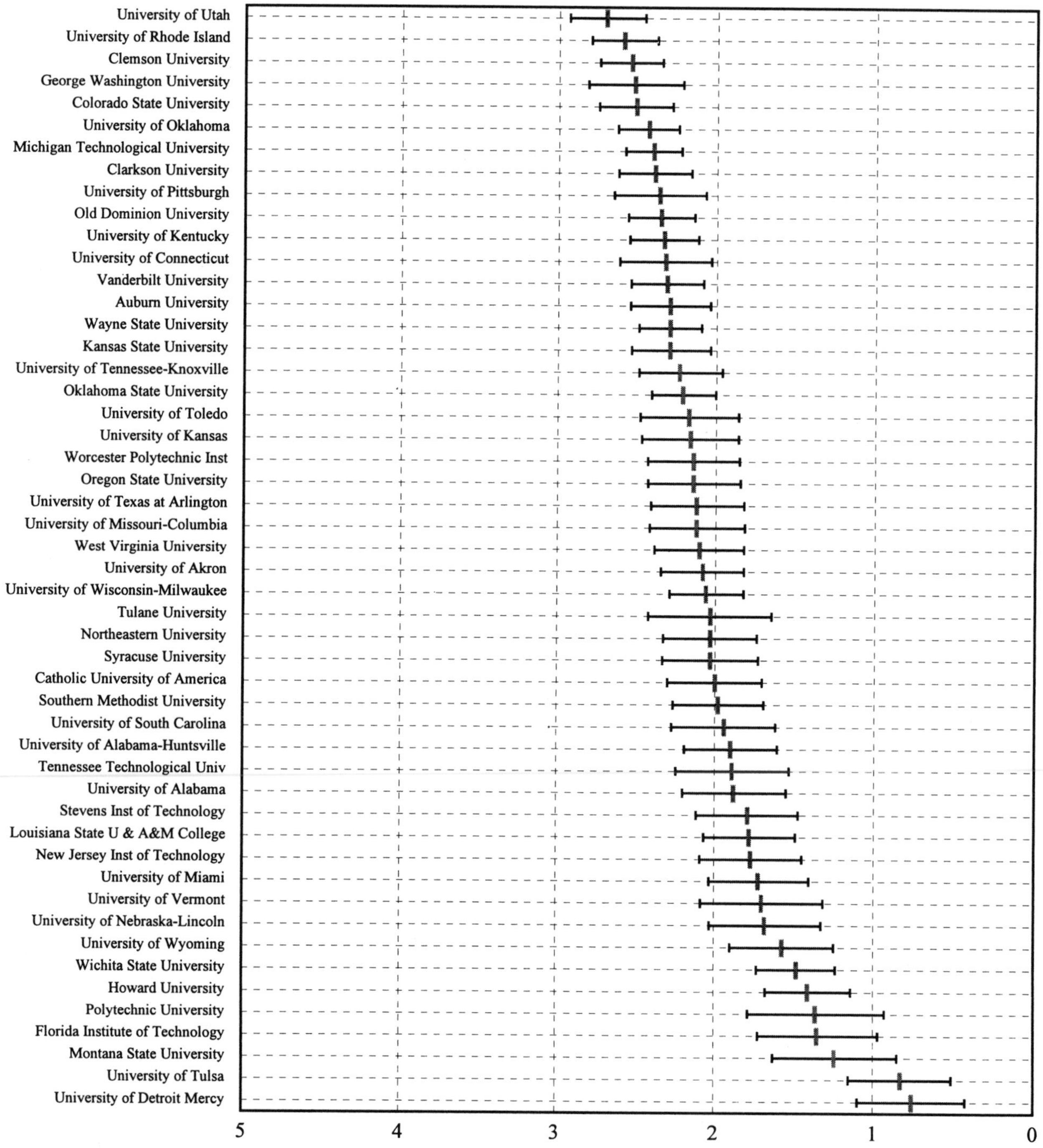

Source: National Survey of Graduate Faculty

Appendix Figure Q - 28 Means and Confidence Intervals for the Scholarly Quality of Program Faculty Ratings of the 103 Programs in Molecular and General Genetics

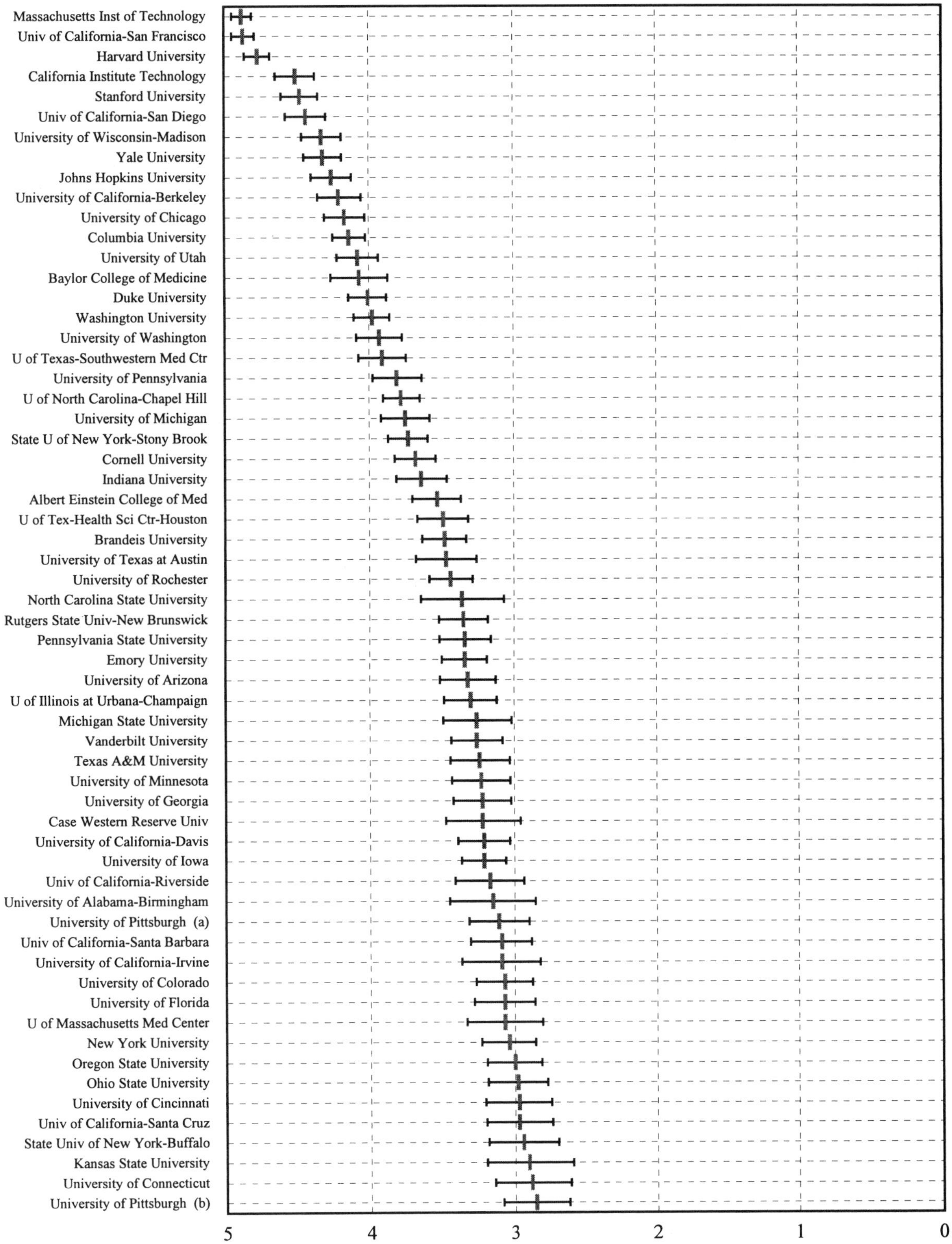

Appendix Figure Q - 28 Molecular and General Genetics (Continued)

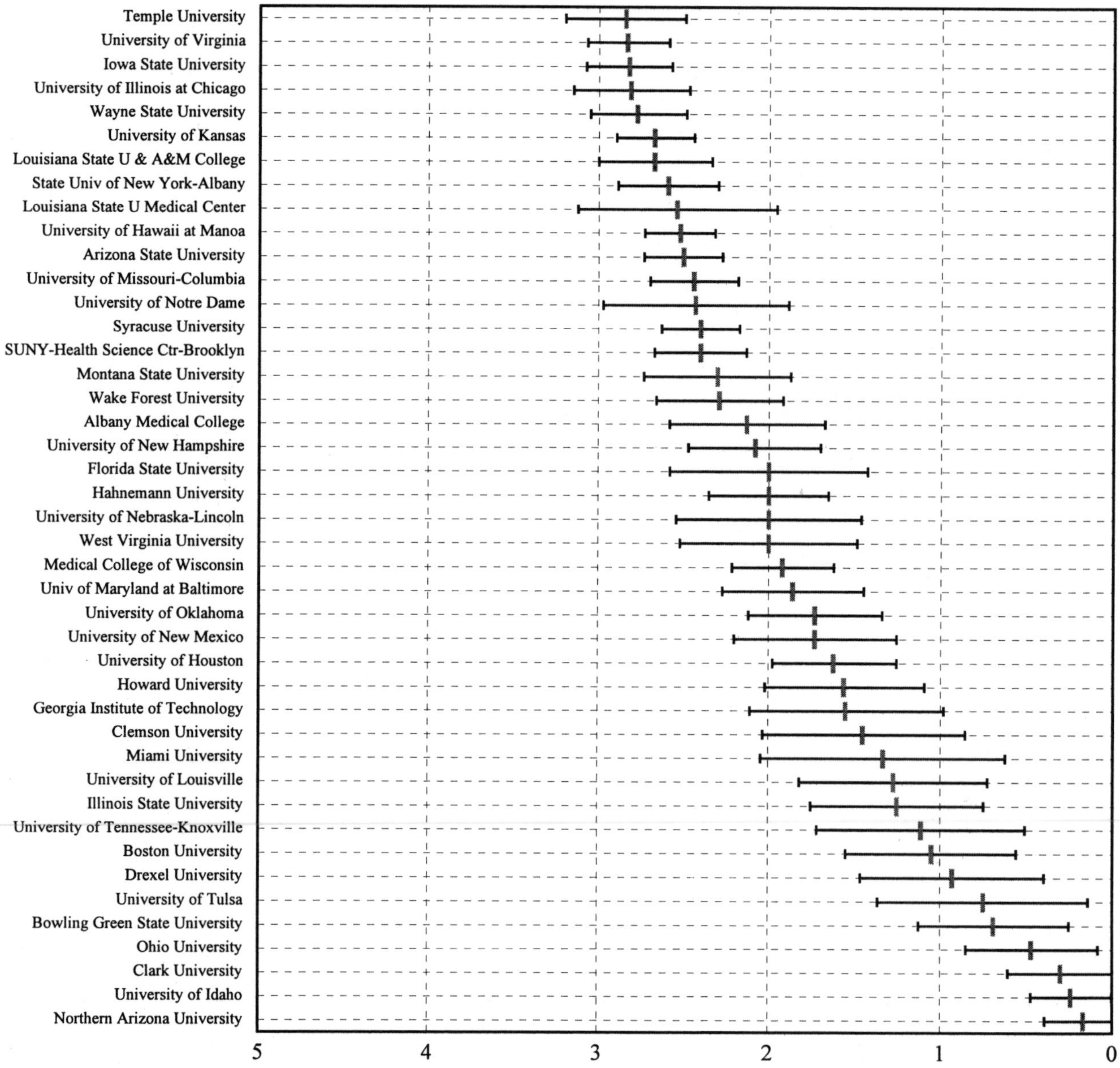

Source: National Survey of Graduate Faculty

Note: (a) School of Medicine
(b) School of Public Health

Appendix Figure Q - 29 Means and Confidence Intervals for the Scholarly Quality of Program Faculty Ratings of the 65 Programs in Music

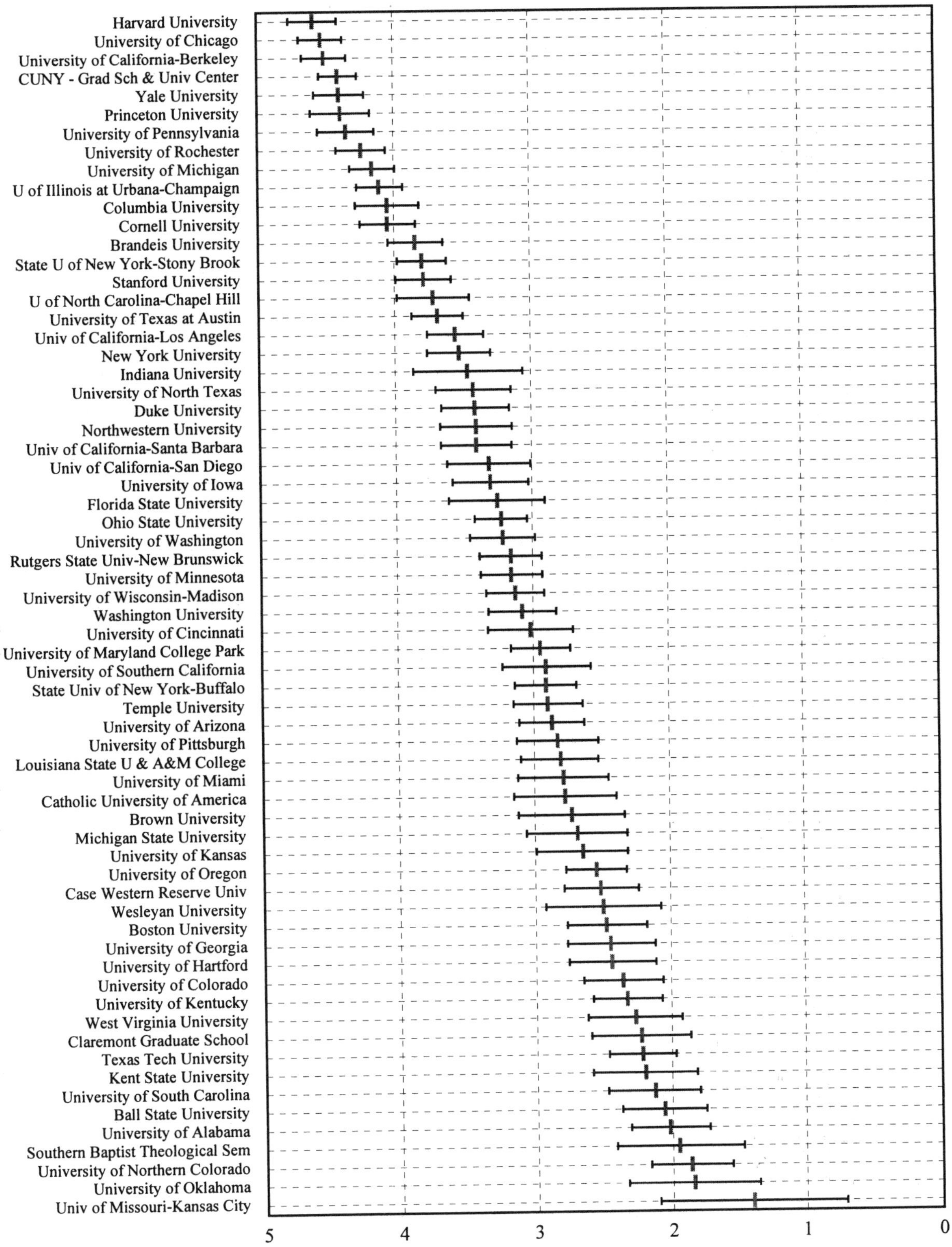

Source: National Survey of Graduate Faculty

Appendix Figure Q - 30 Means and Confidence Intervals for the Scholarly Quality of Program Faculty Ratings of the 102 Programs in Neurosciences

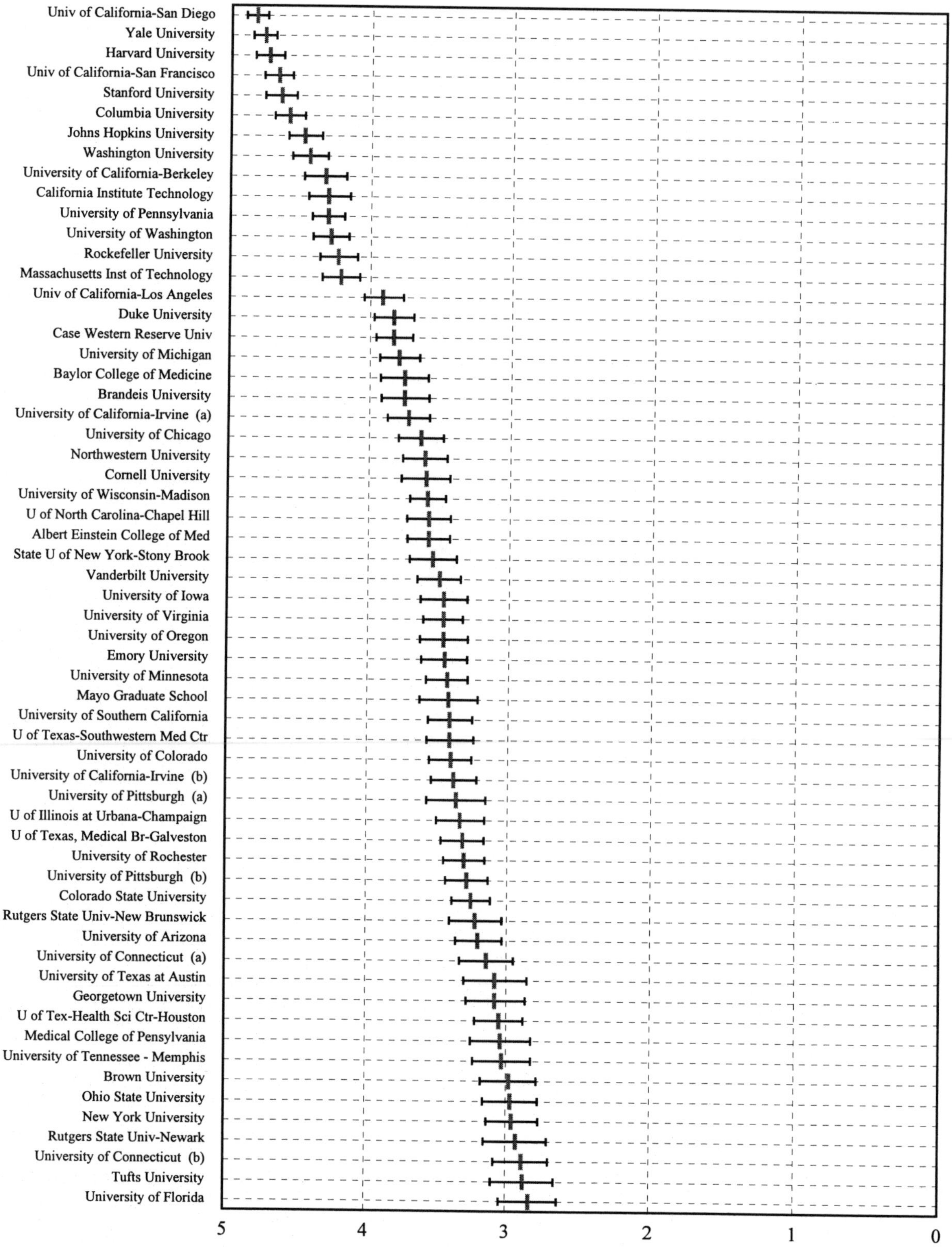

Appendix Figure Q - 30 Neurosciences (Continued)

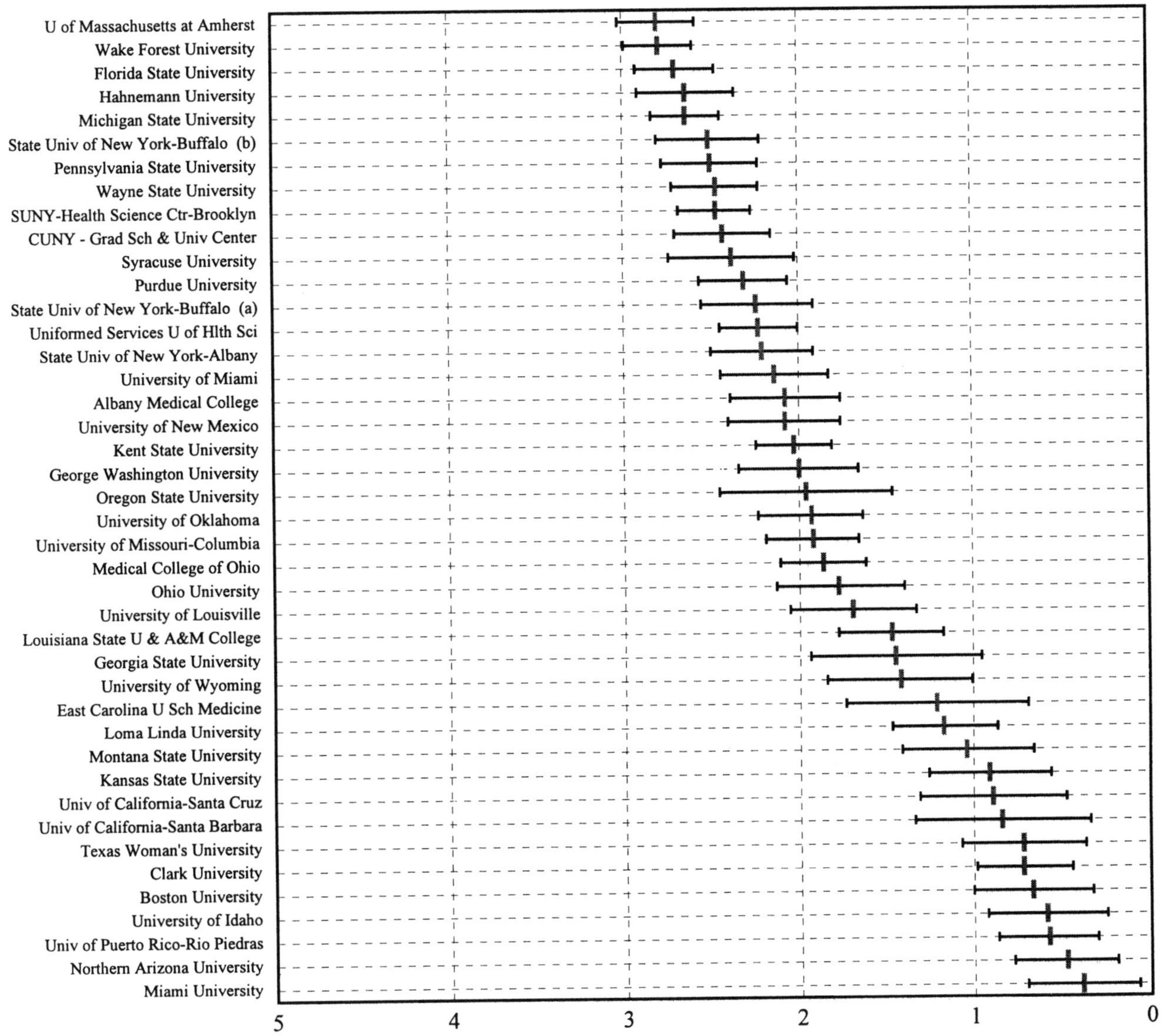

Source: National Survey of Graduate Faculty

Note: (a) School of Arts and Sciences
(b) School of Medicine

Appendix Figure Q - 31 Means and Confidence Intervals for the Scholary Quality of Program Faculty Ratings of the 26 Programs in Oceanography

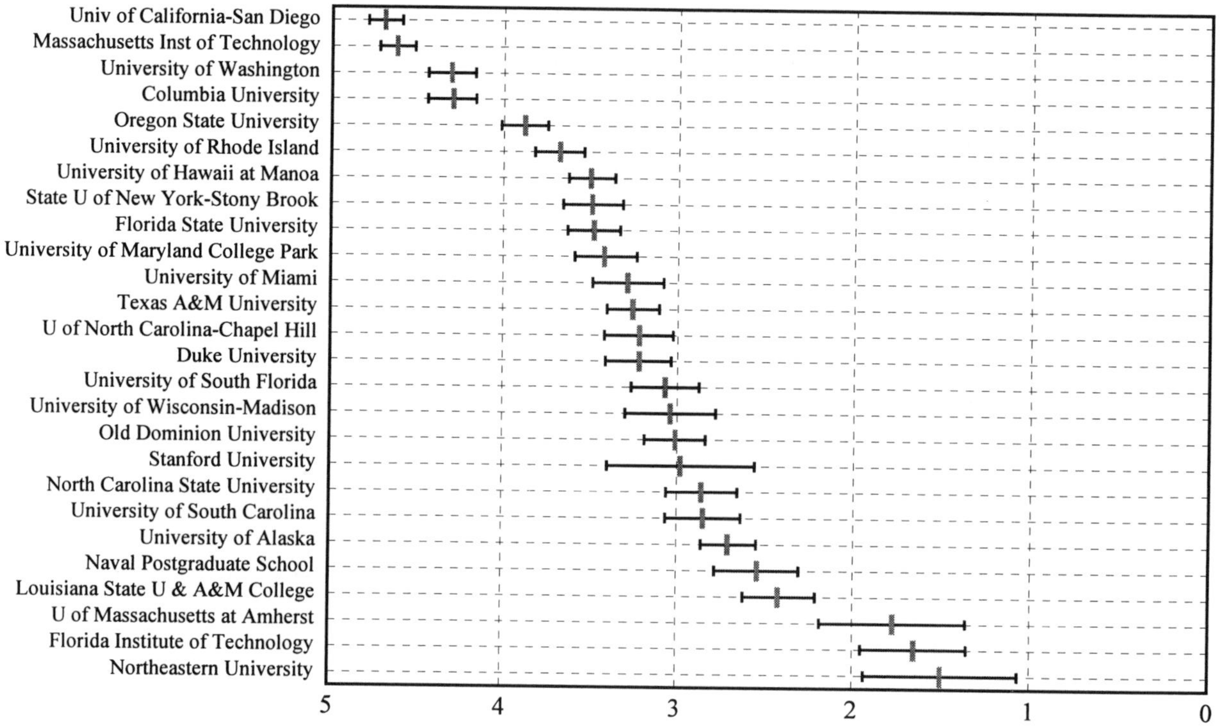

Source: National Survey of Graduate Faculty

Appendix Figure Q - 32 Means and Confidence Intervals for the Scholarly Quality of Program Faculty Ratings of the 127 Programs in Pharmacology

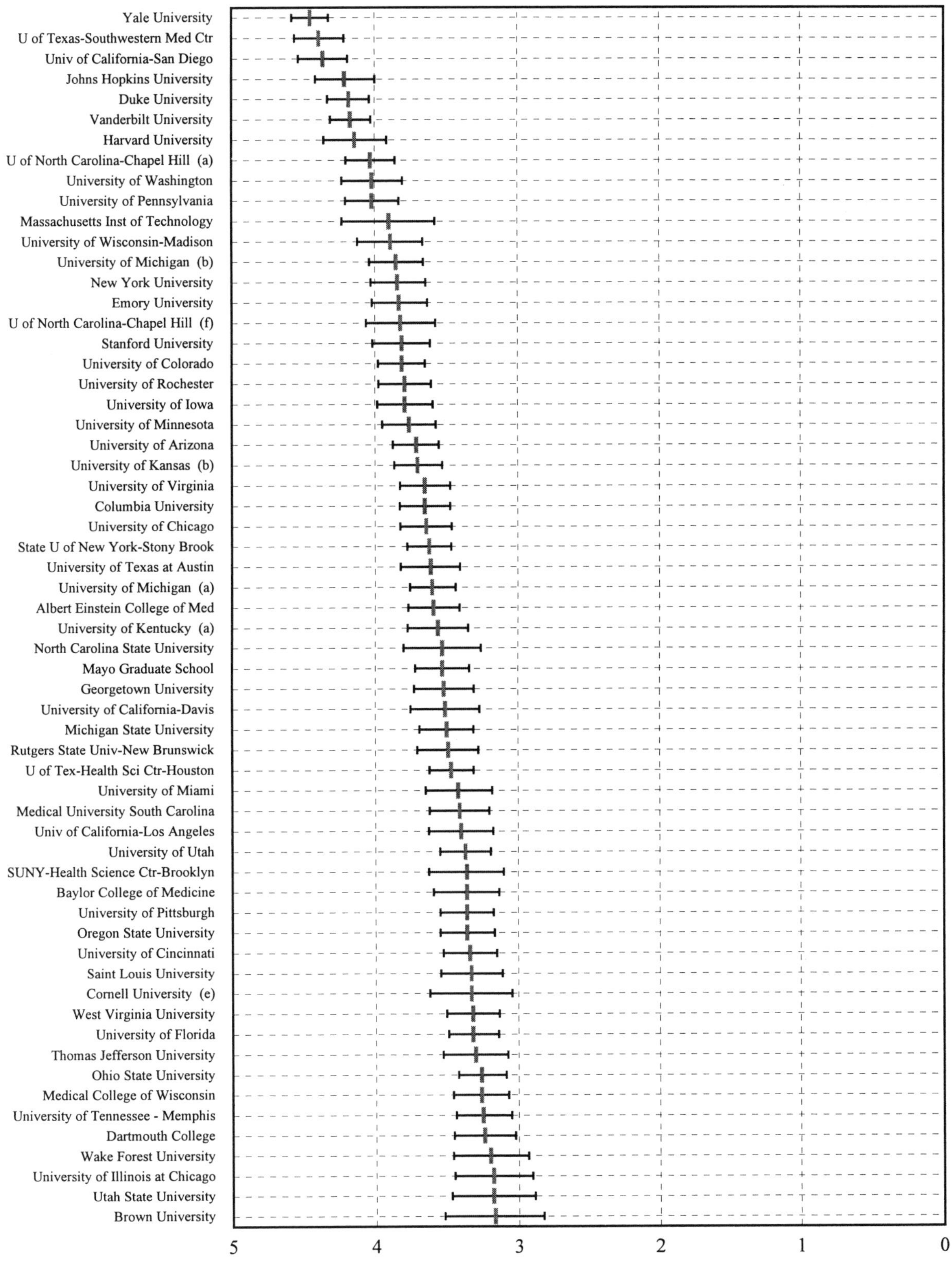

Appendix Figure Q - 32 Pharmacology (Continued)

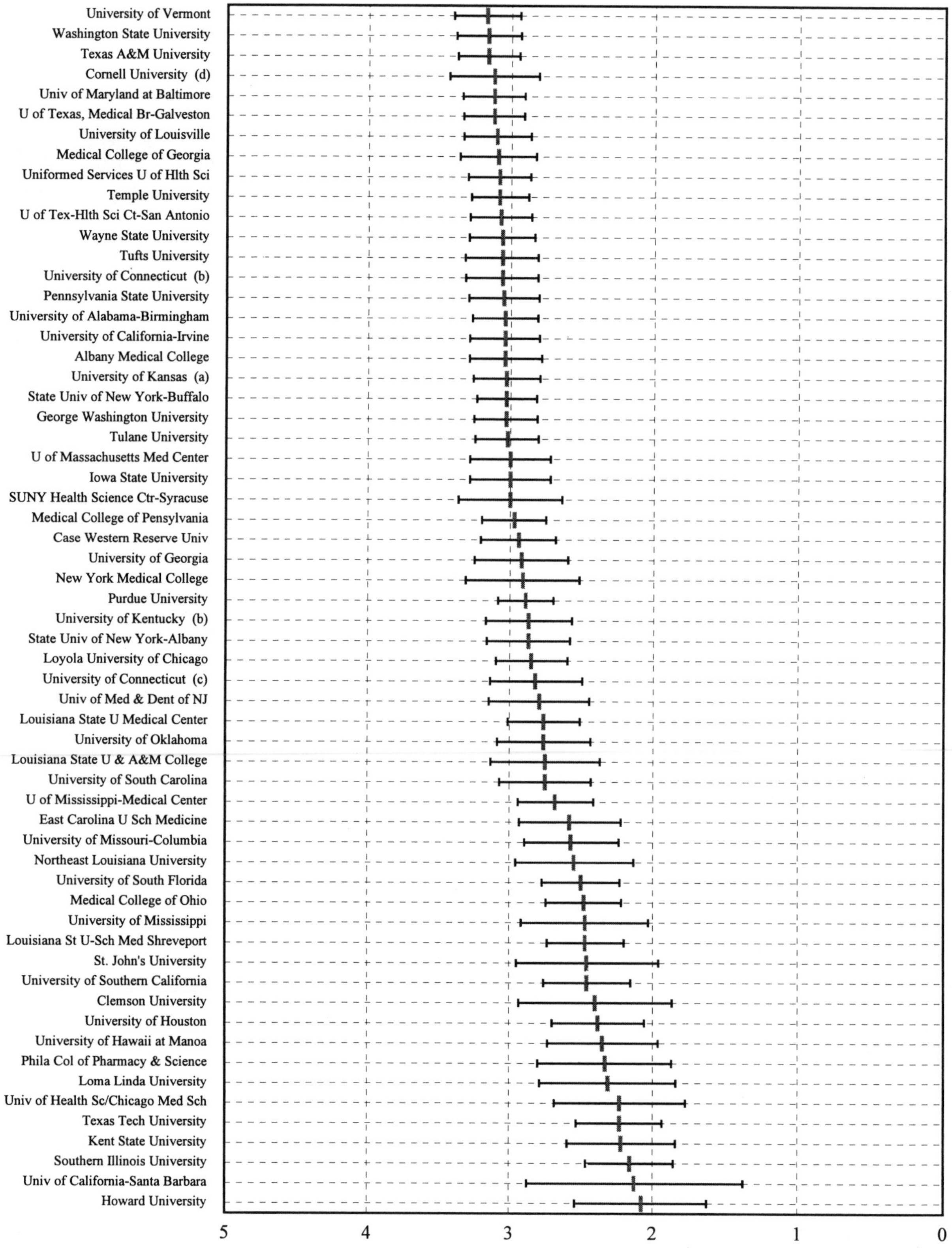

Appendix Figure Q - 32 Pharmacology (Continued)

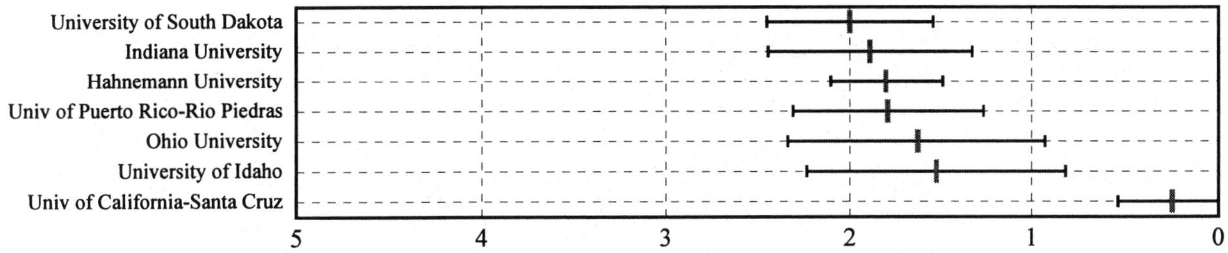

Source: National Survey of Graduate Faculty

Note:
(a) School of Arts and Sciences
(b) School of Medicine
(c) School of Pharmacology
(d) School of Veterinary Medicine
(e) School of Engineering
(f) Interdisciplinary with the Schools of Medicine, Pharmacology, and Public Health

Appendix Figure Q - 33 Means and Confidence Intervals for the Scholarly Quality of Program Faculty Ratings of the 72 Programs in Philosophy

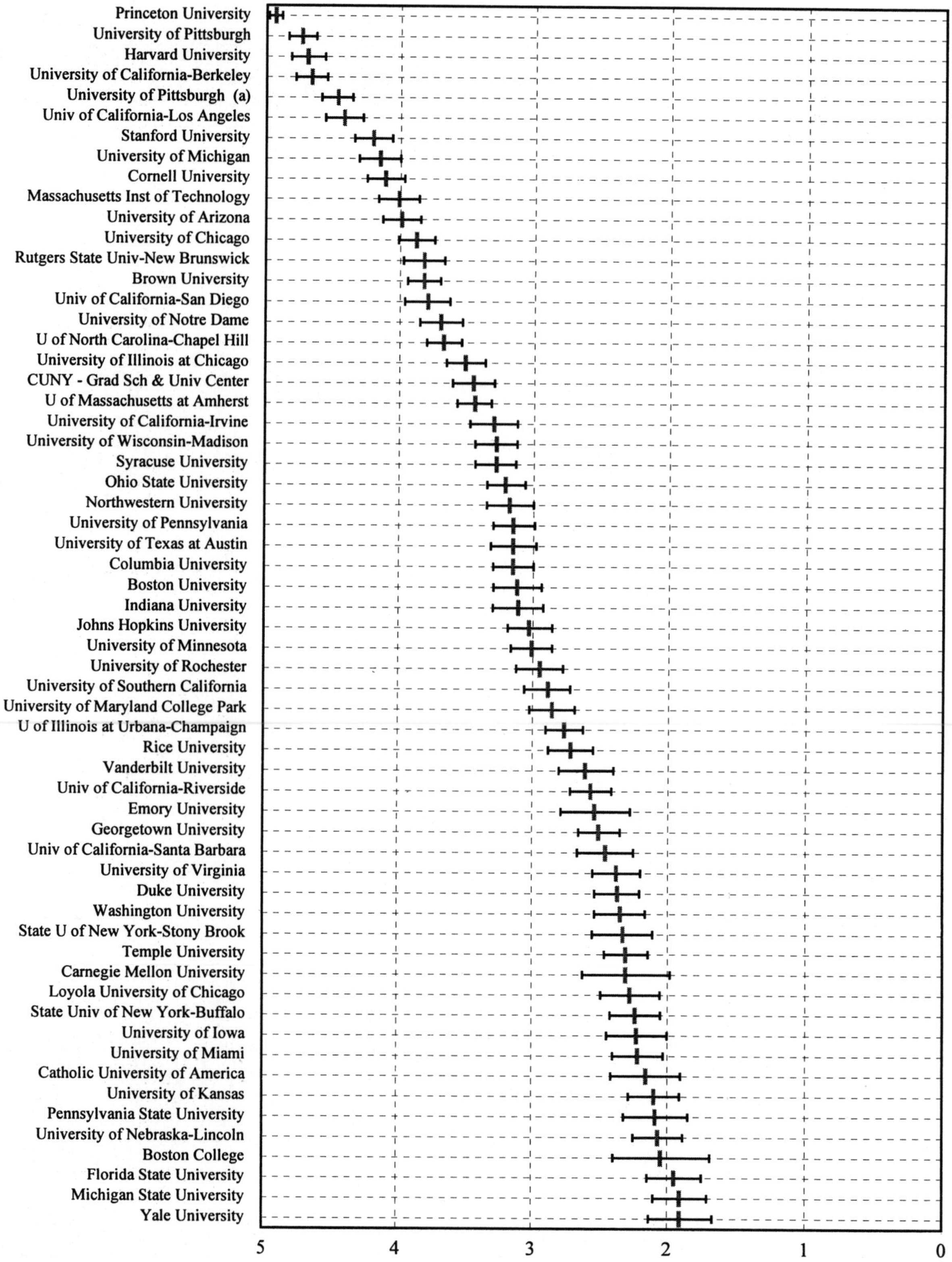

Appendix Figure Q - 33 Philosophy (Continued)

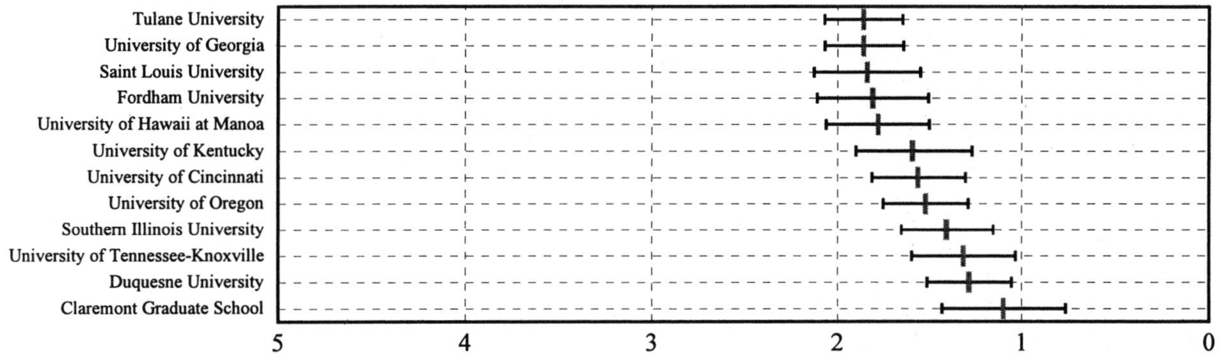

Source: National Survey of Graduate Faculty

Note: (a) Program in History and Philosophy of Science

Appendix Figure Q - 34 Means and Confidence Intervals for the Scholarly Quality of Program Faculty Ratings of the 147 Programs in Physics

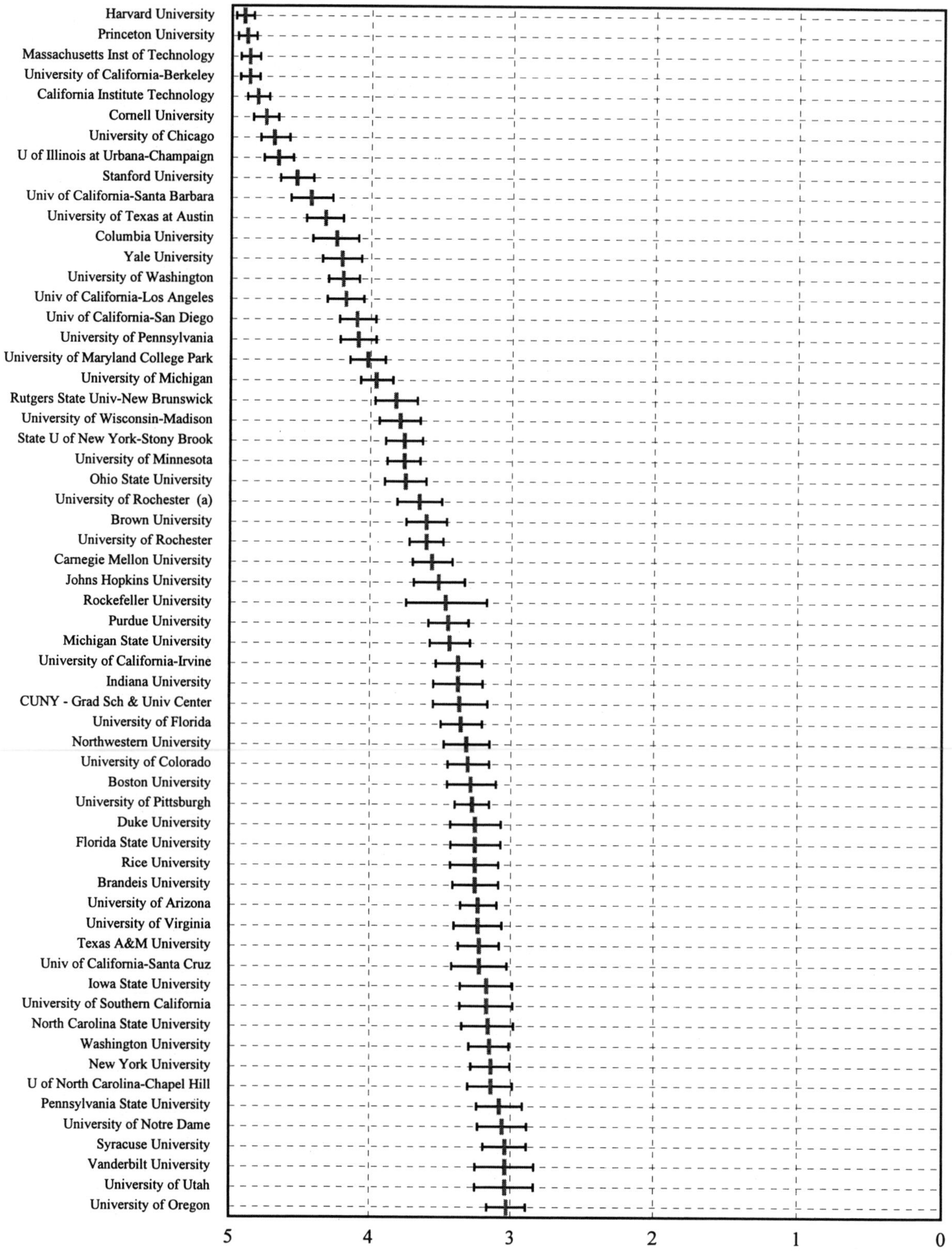

Appendix Figure Q - 34 Physics (Continued)

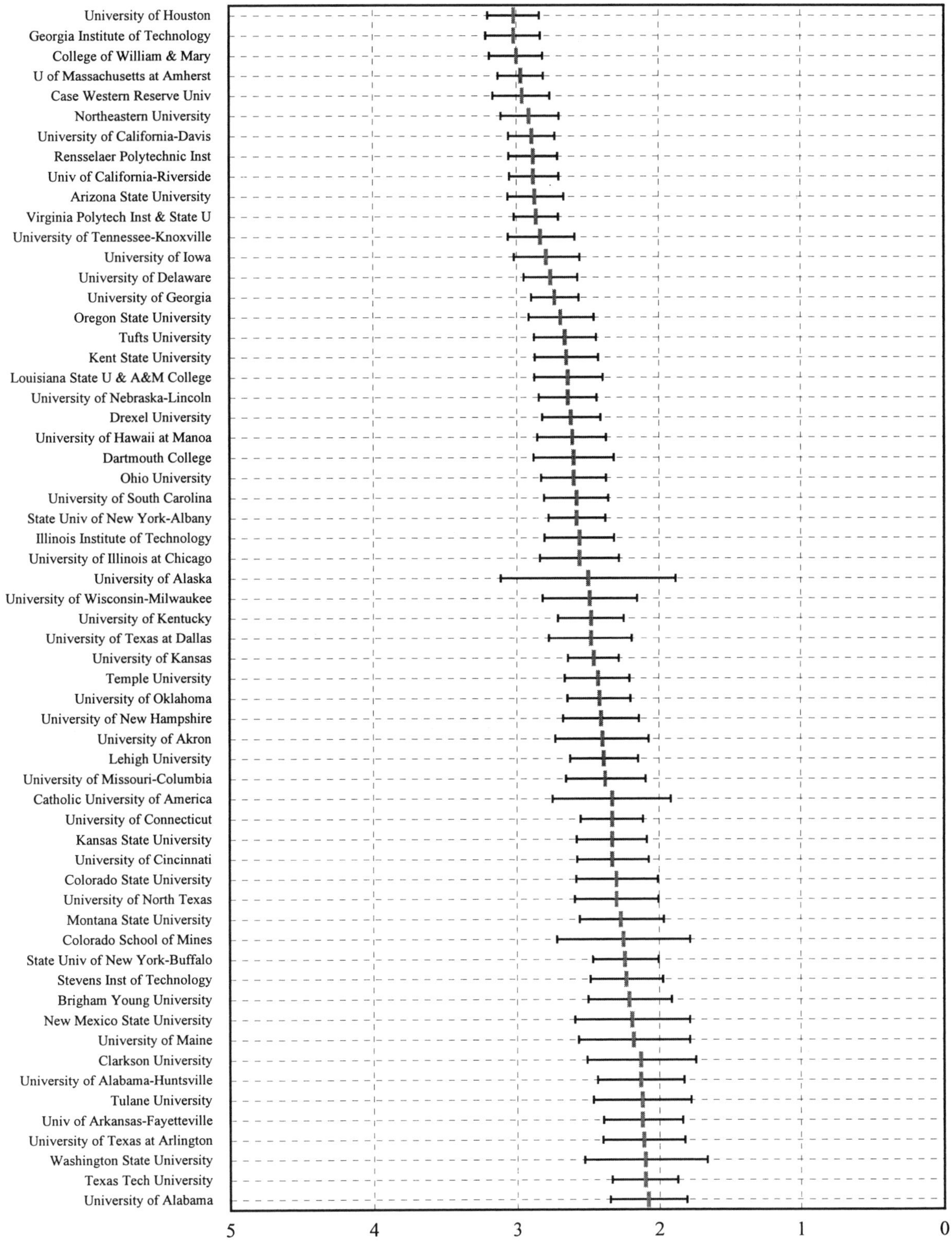

Appendix Figure Q - 34 Physics (Continued)

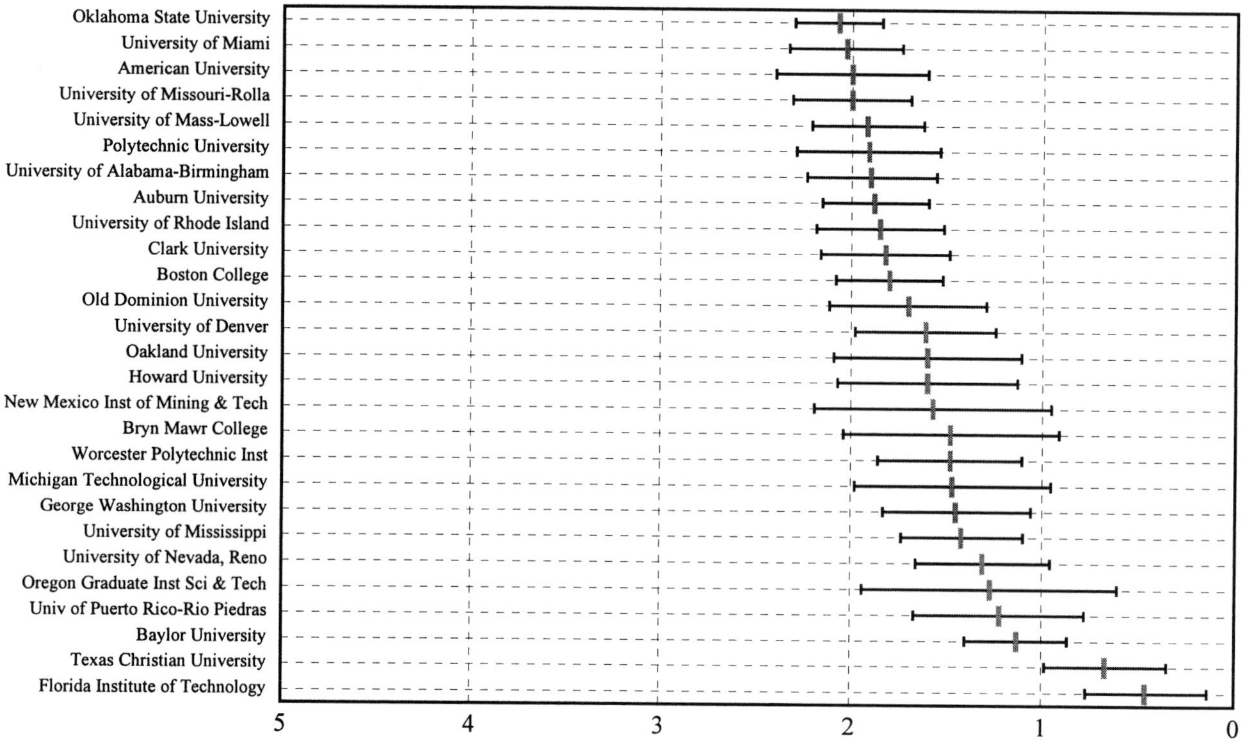

Source: National Survey of Graduate Faculty

Note: (a) Program in Optics

Appendix Figure Q - 35 Means and Confidence Intervals for the Scholarly Quality of Program Faculty Ratings of the 140 Programs in Physiology

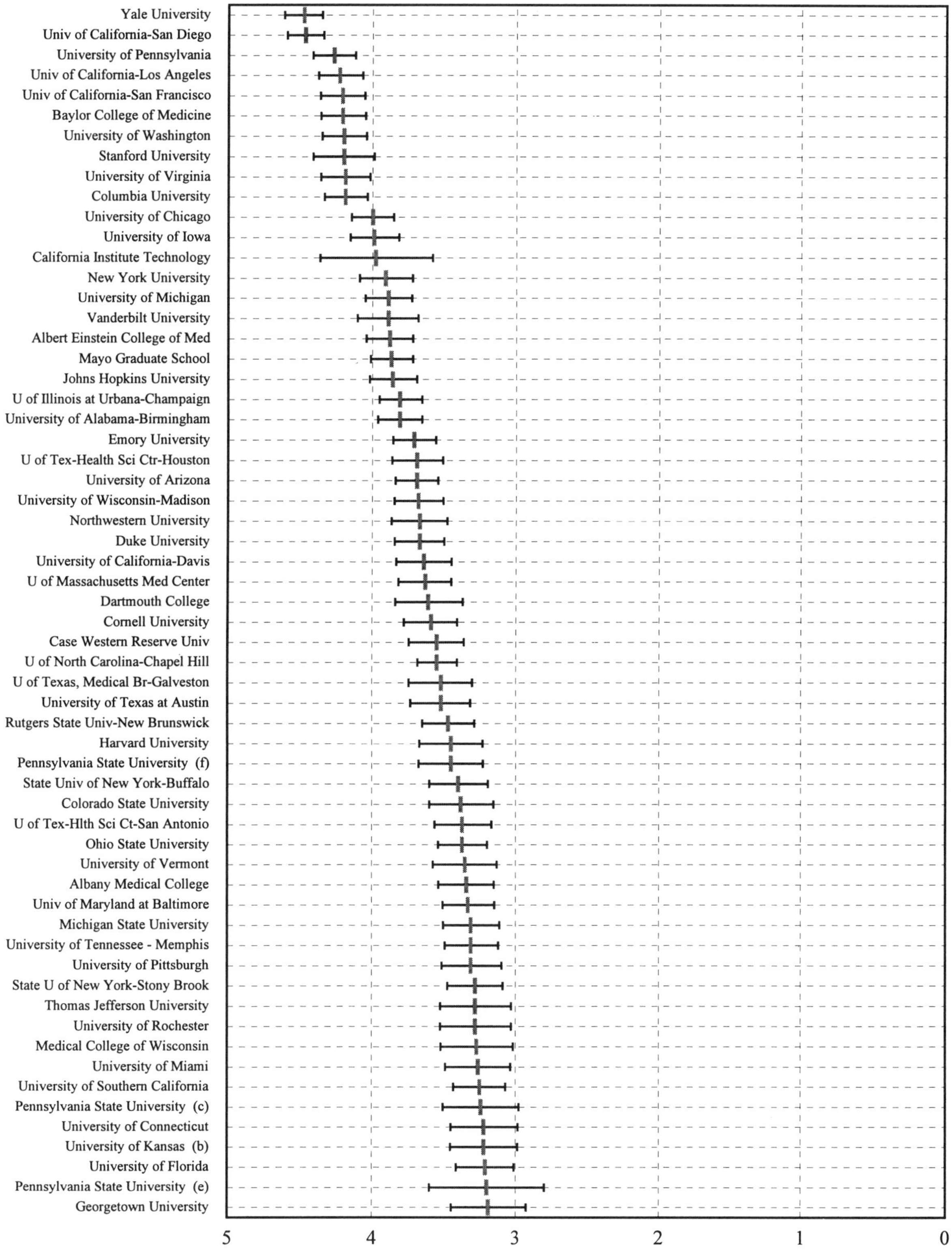

Appendix Figure Q - 35 Physiology (Continued)

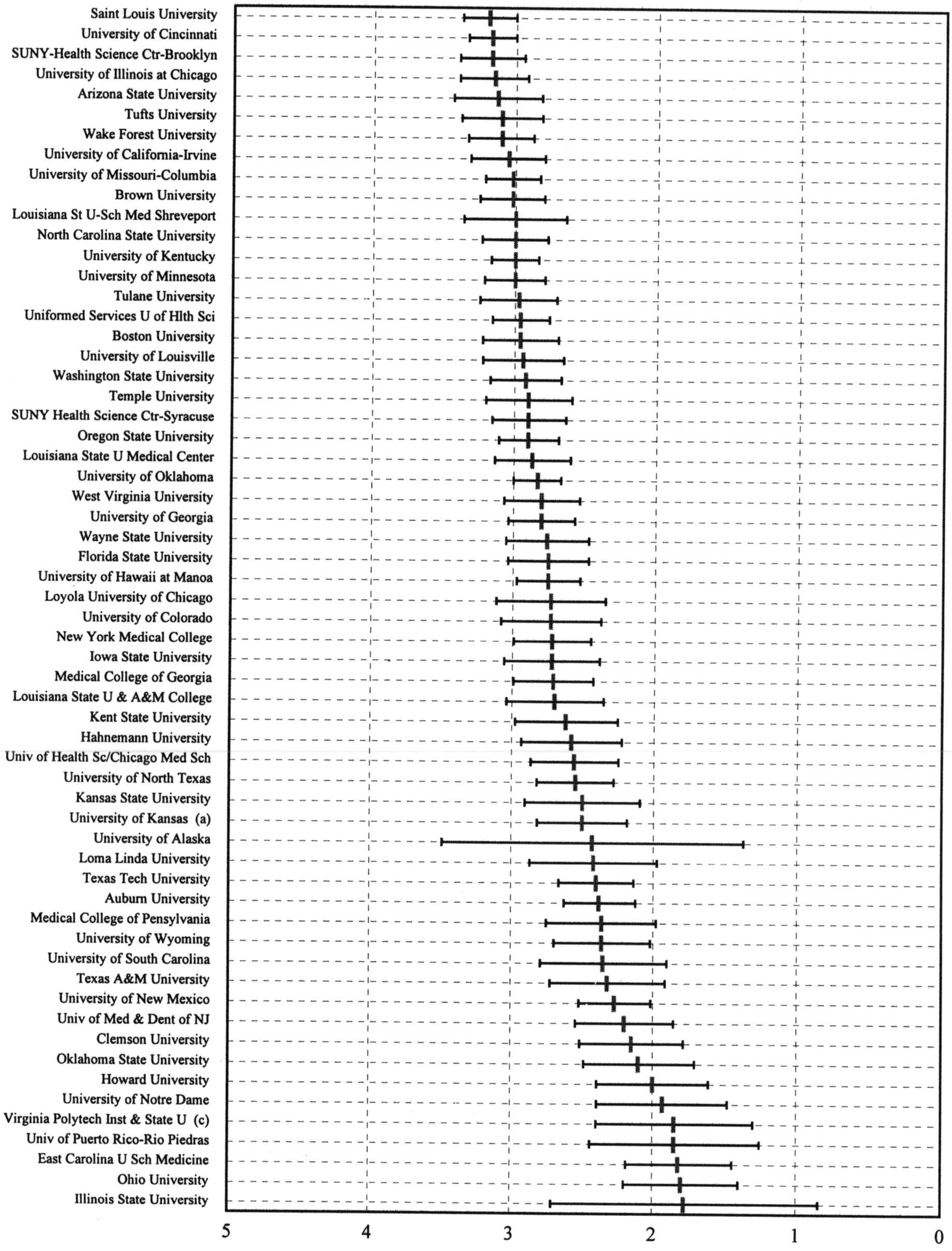

Appendix Figure Q - 35 Physiology (Continued)

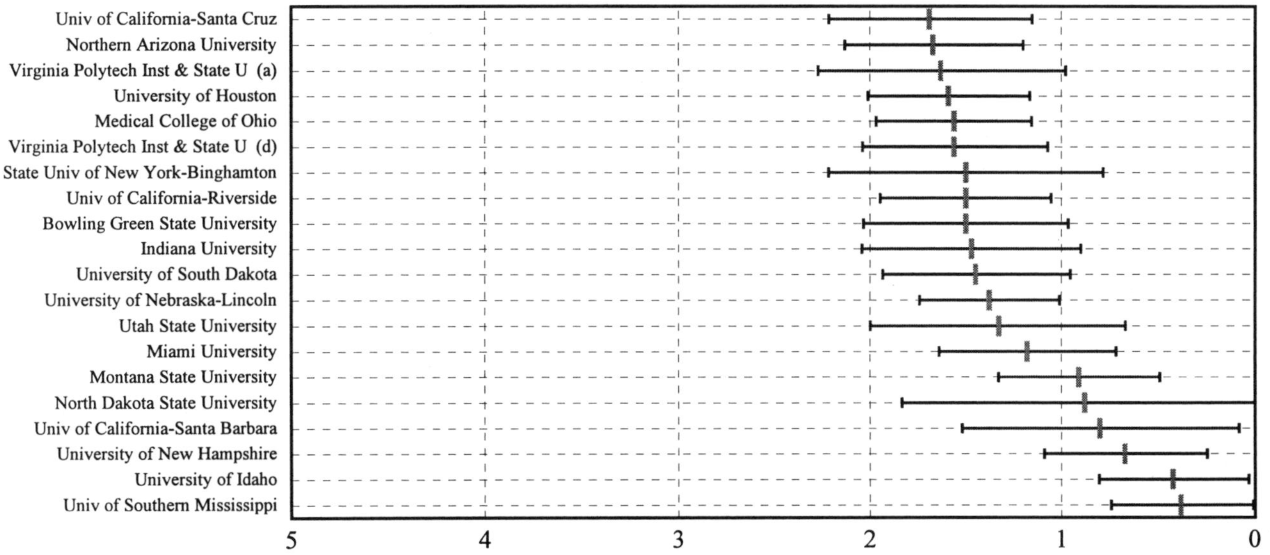

Source: National Survey of Graduate Faculty

Note:
(a) School of Arts and Sciences
(b) School of Medicine
(c) School of Agriculture
(d) School of Veterinary Medicine
(e) Interdisciplinary with the Schools of Agriculture and Arts and Sciences
(f) Interdisciplinary with the Schools of Agriculture, Arts and Sciences, and Medicine

Appendix Figure Q - 36 Means and Confidence Intervals for the Scholarly Quality of Program Faculty Ratings of the 98 Programs in Political Science

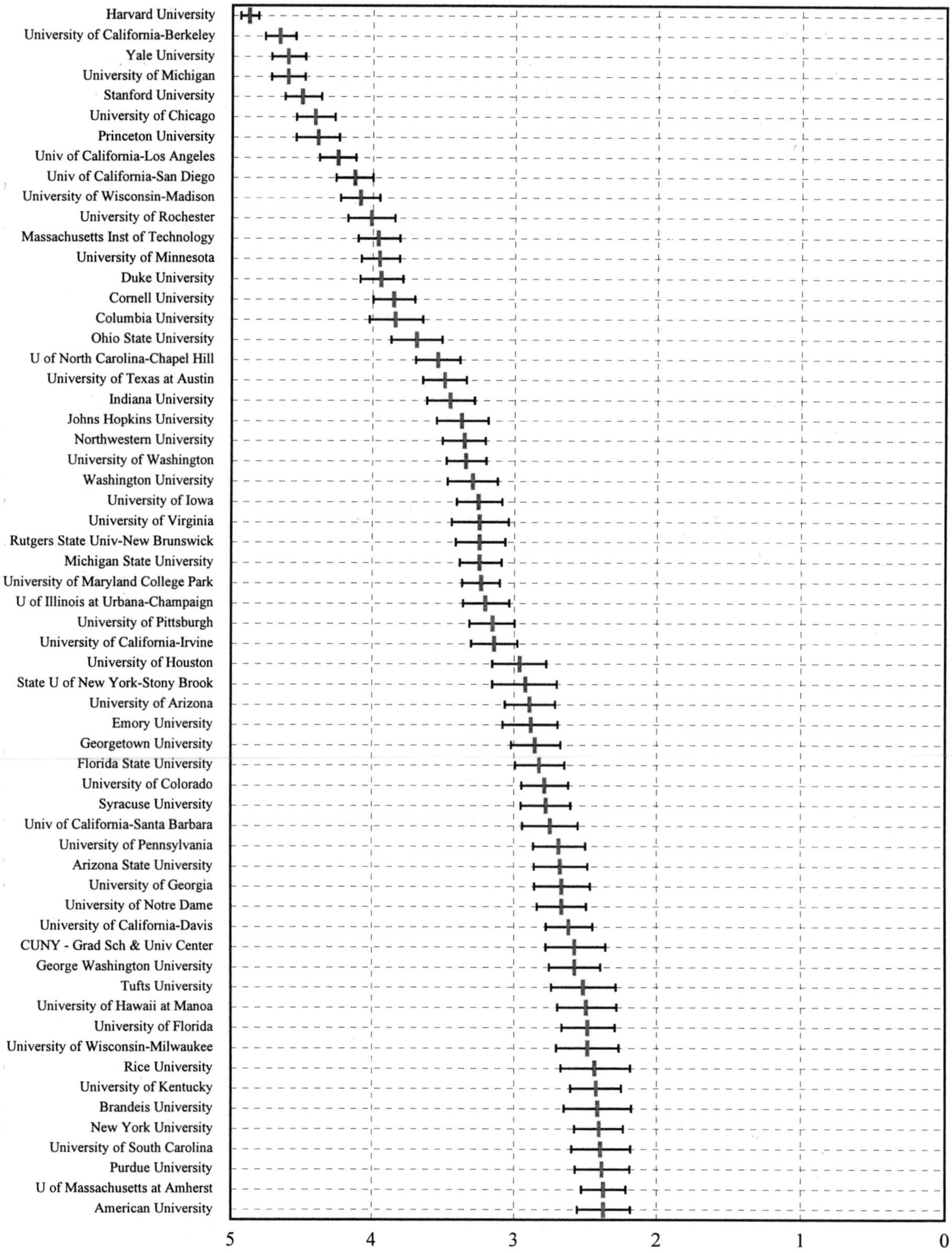

Appendix Figure Q - 36 Political Science (Continued)

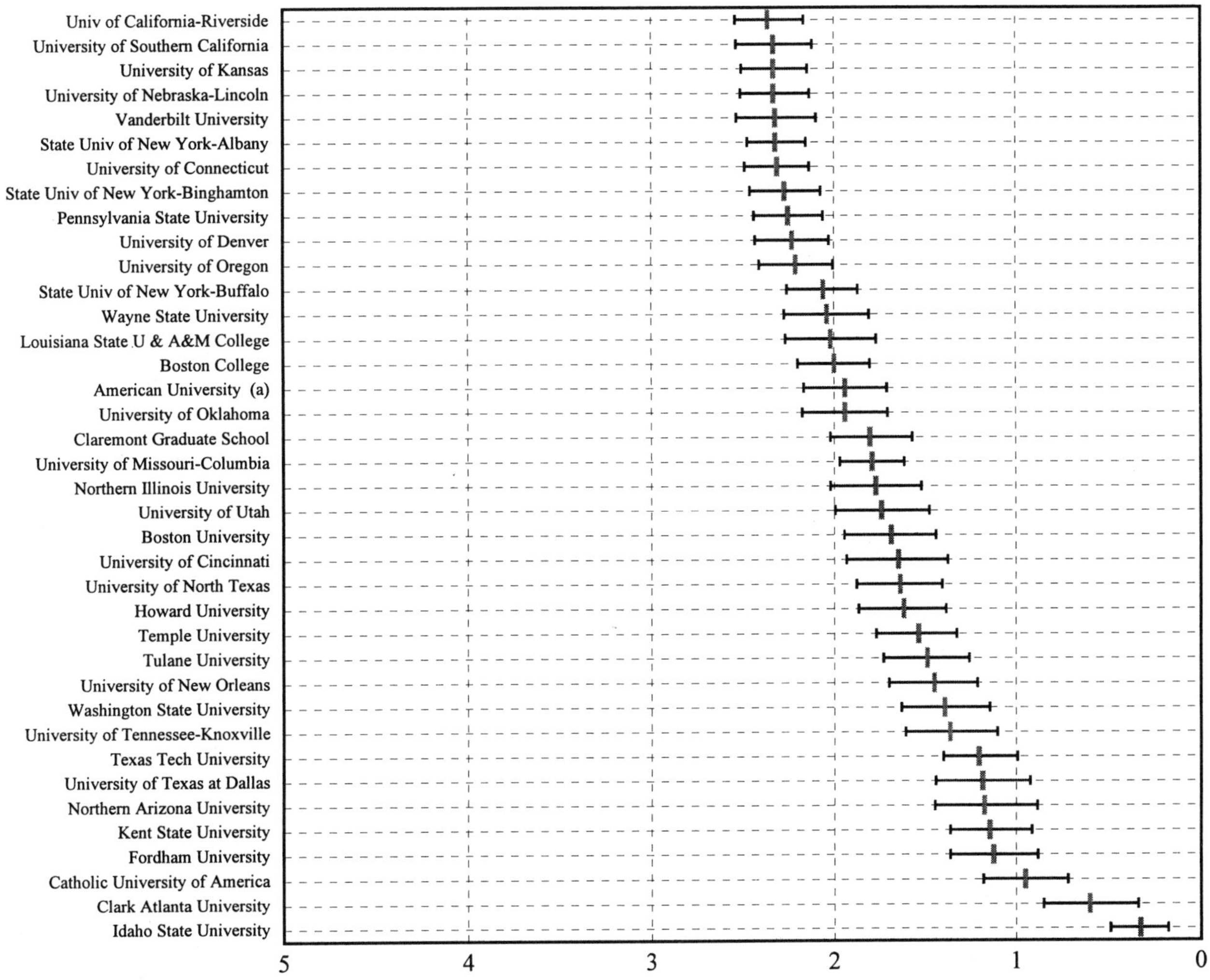

Source: National Survey of Graduate Faculty

Note: (a) Program in International Relations

Appendix Figure Q - 37 Means and Confidence Intervals for the Scholarly Quality of Program Faculty Ratings of the 185 Programs in Psychology

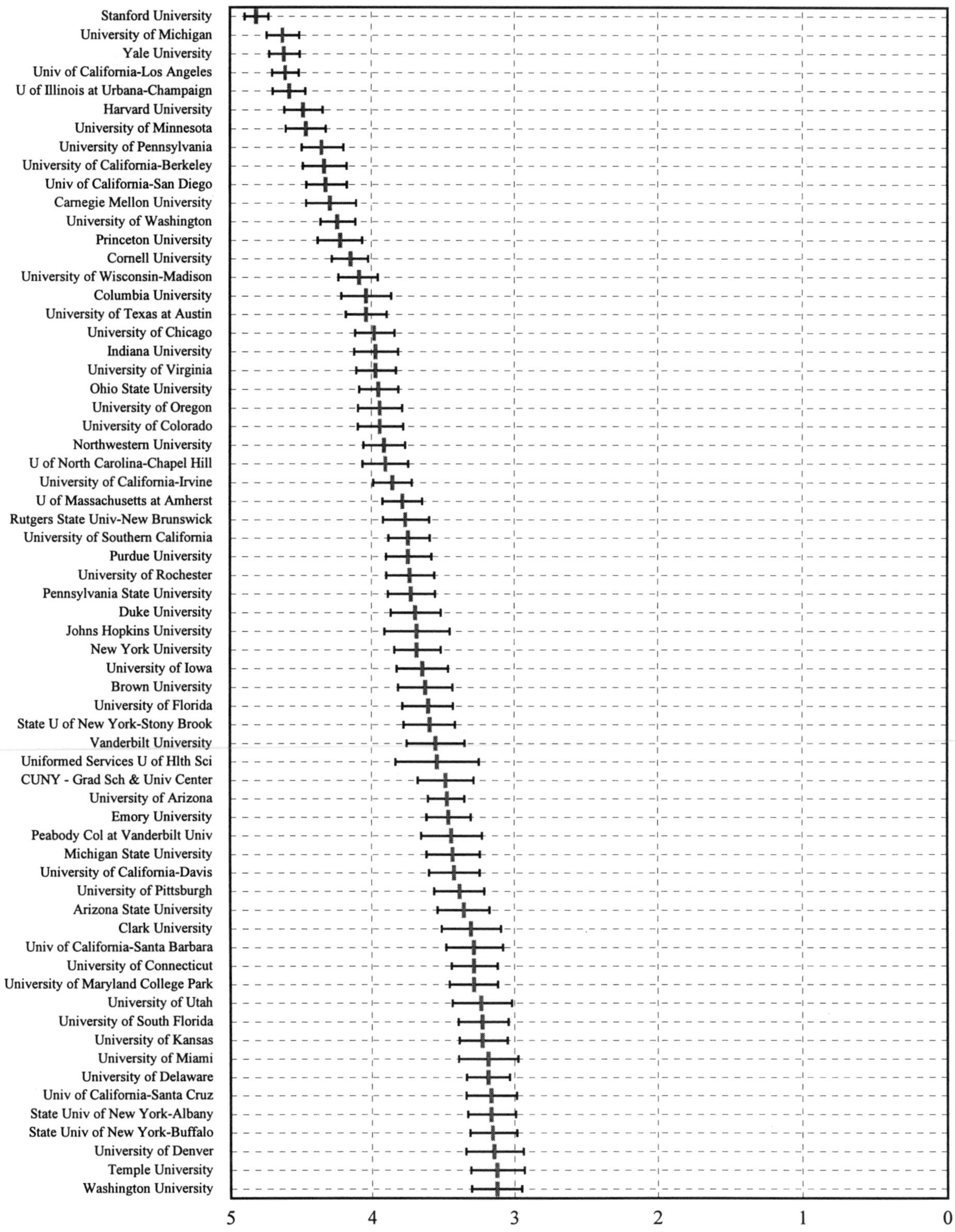

Appendix Figure Q - 37 Psychology (Continued)

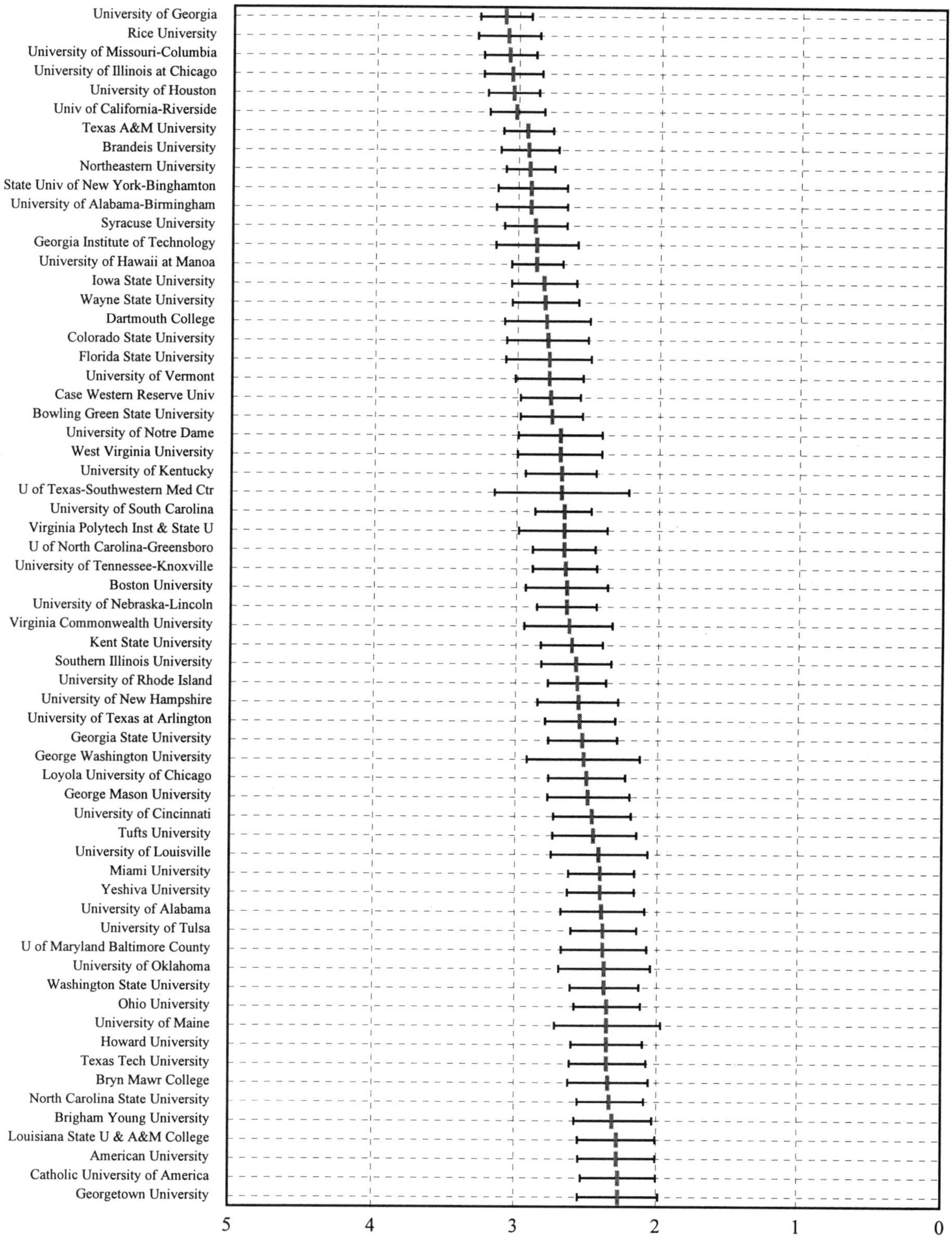

Appendix Figure Q - 37 Psychology (Continued)

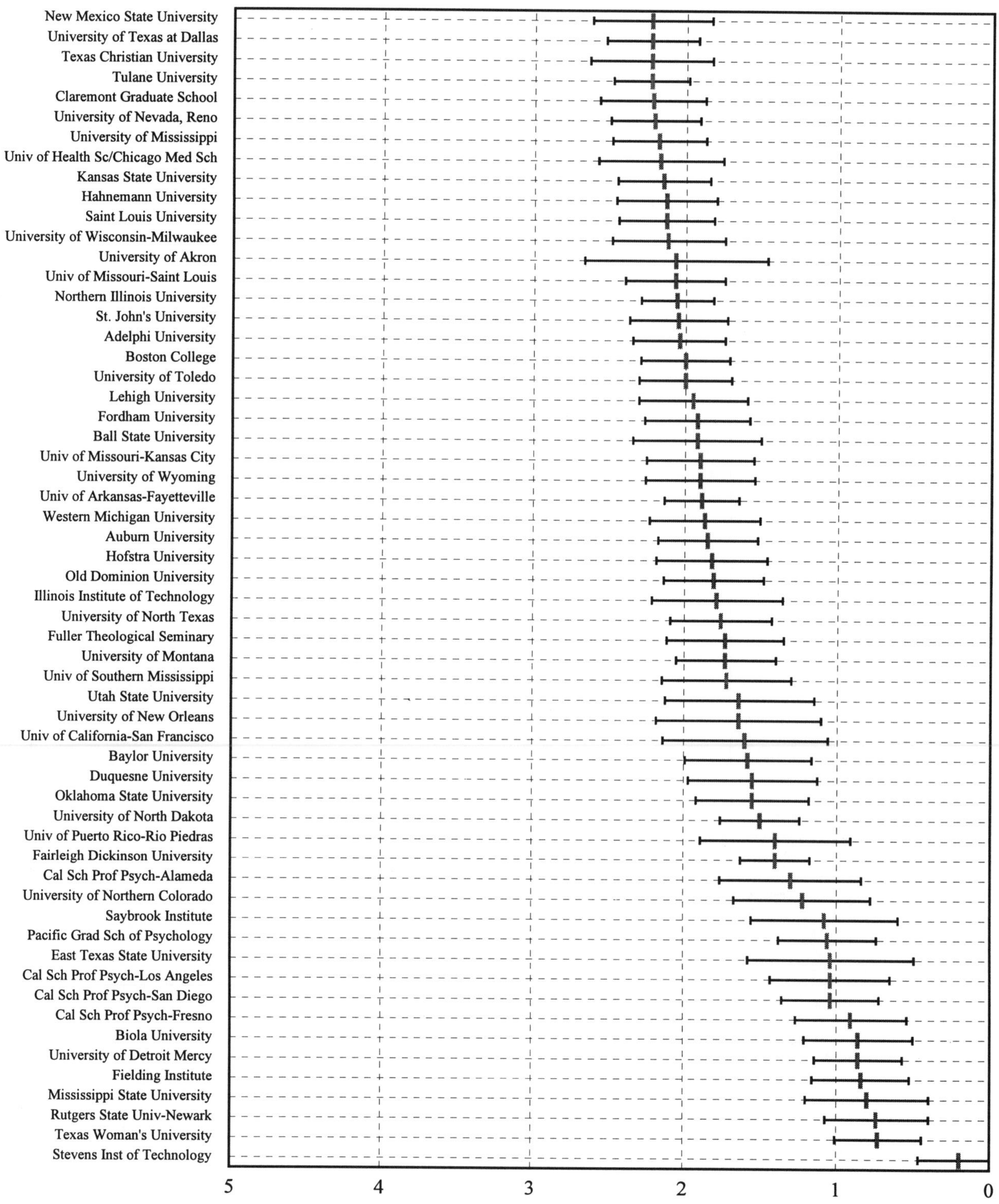

Source: National Survey of Graduate Faculty

Appendix Figuer Q - 38 Means and Confidence Intervals for the Scholarly Quality of Program Faculty Ratings of the 38 Programs in Religion

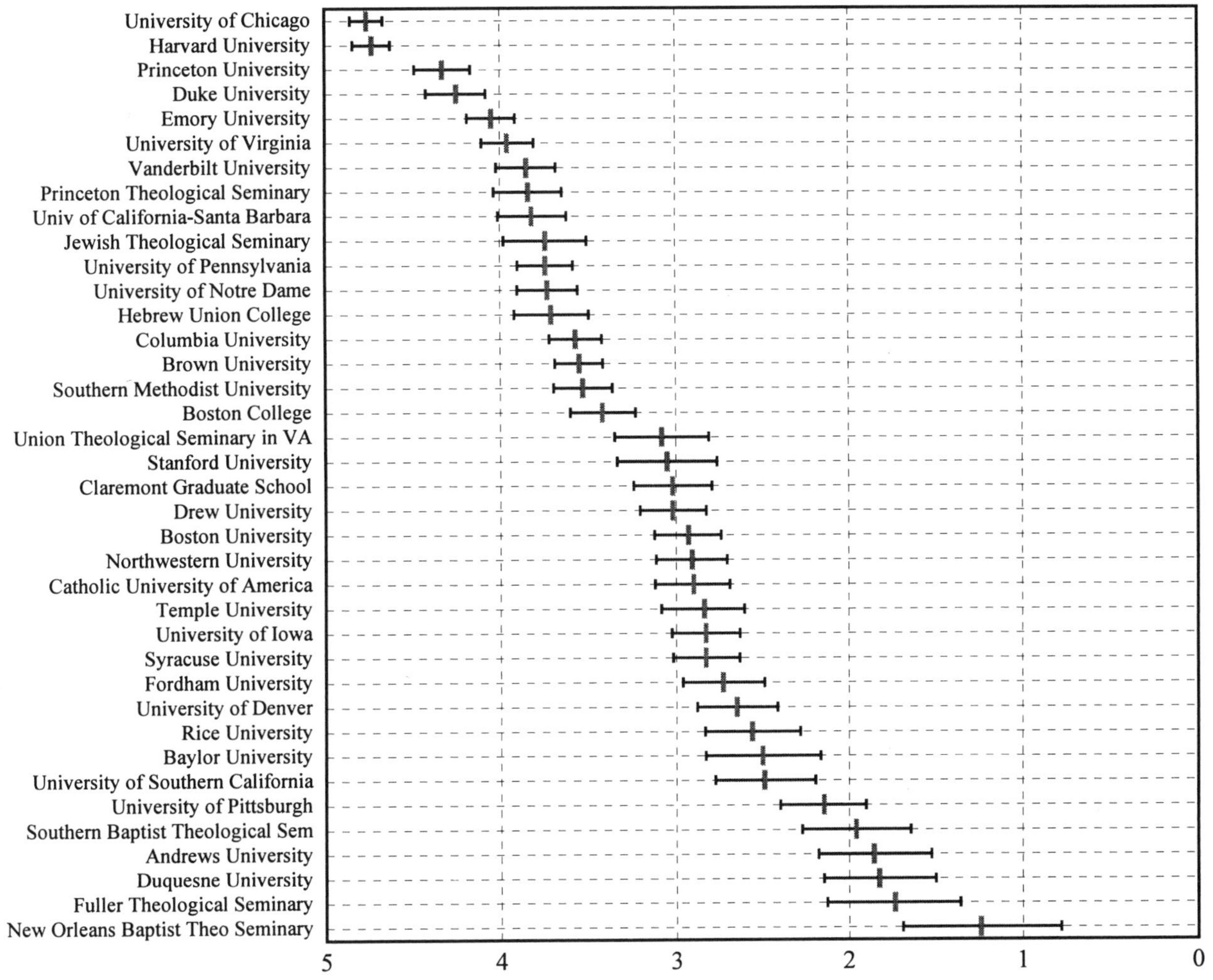

Source: National Survey of Graduate Faculty

Appendix Figure Q - 39 Means and Confidence Intervals for the Scholarly Quality of Program Faculty Ratings of the 95 Programs in Sociology

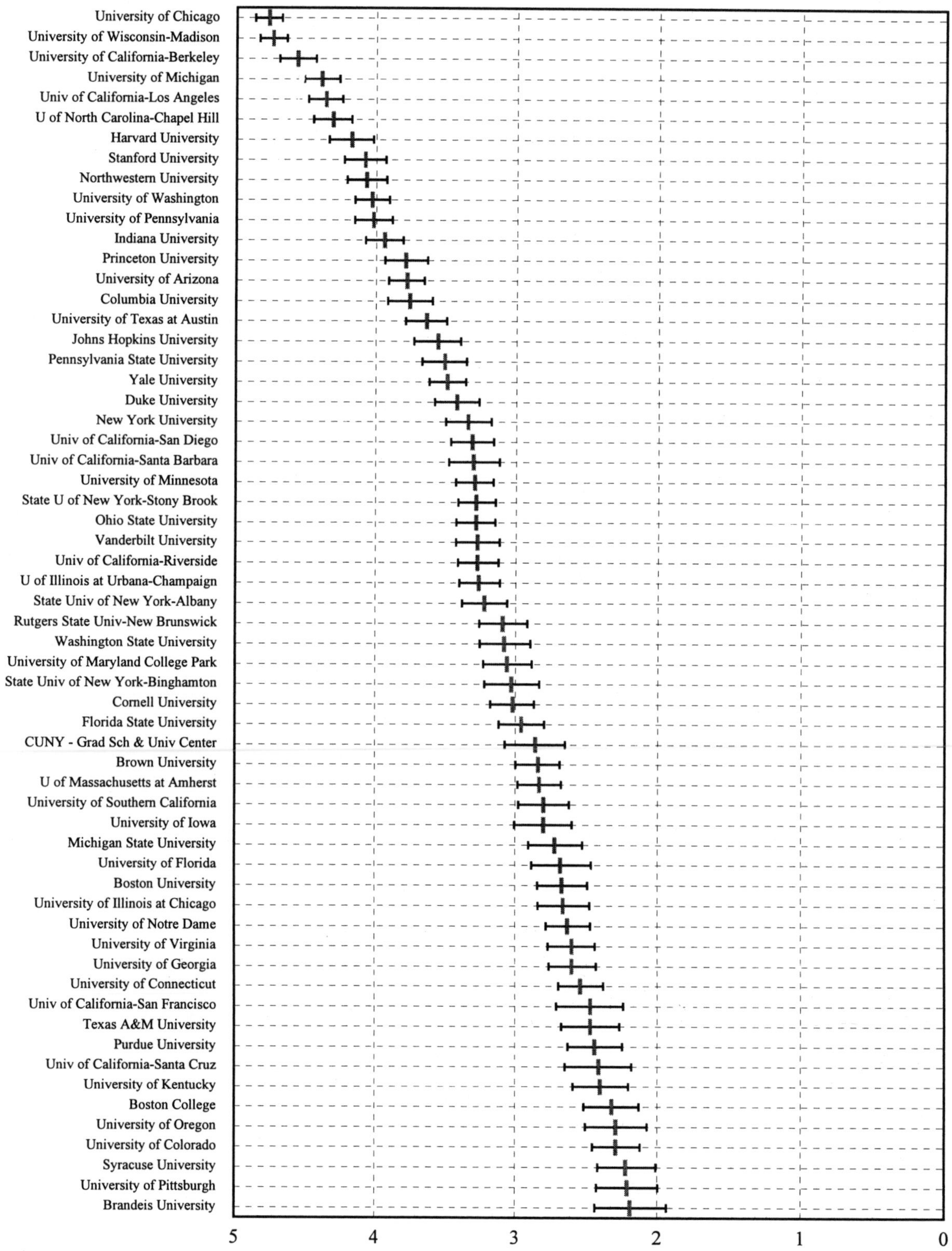

Appendix Figure Q - 39 Sociology (Continued)

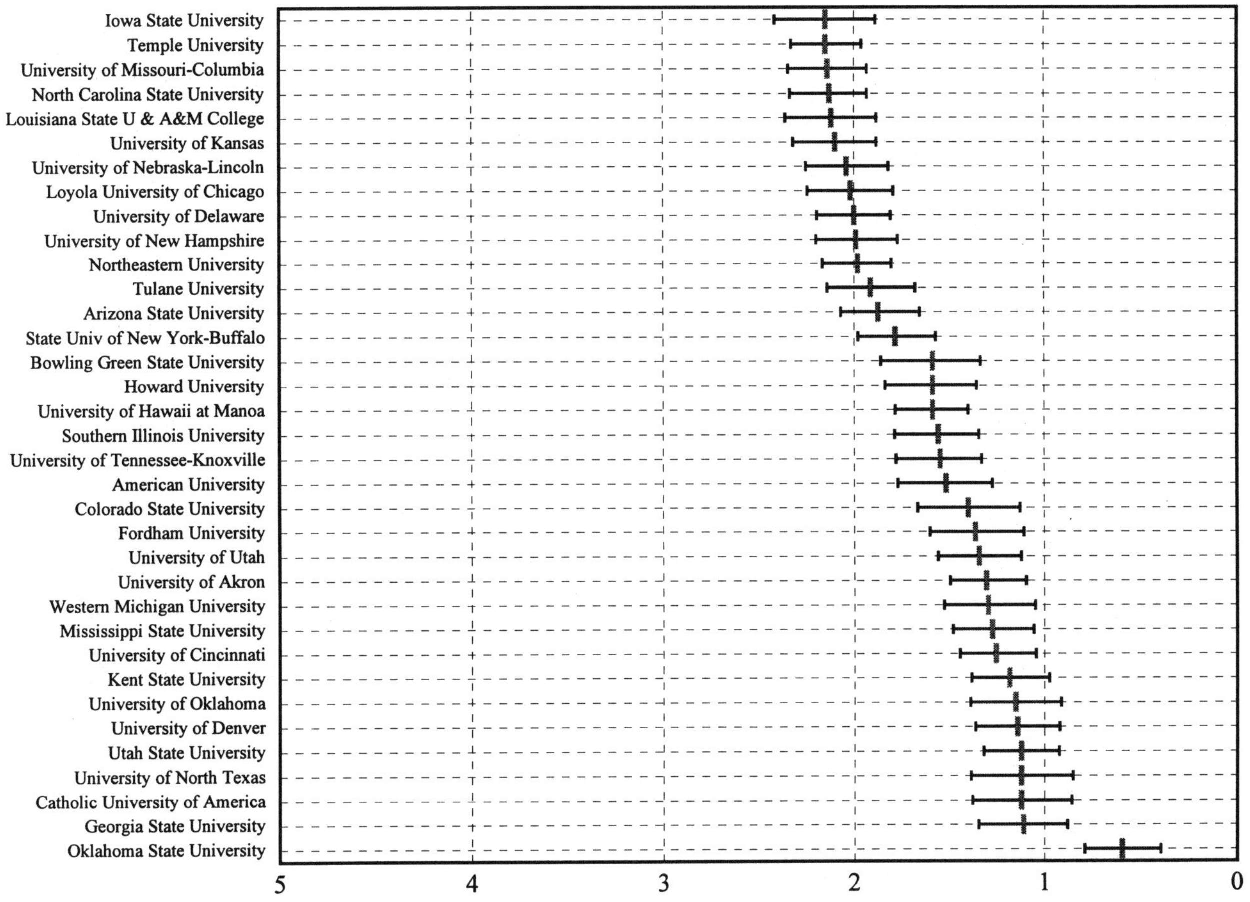

Source: National Survey of Graduate Faculty

Appendix Figure Q - 40 Means and Confidence Intervals for the Scholarly Quality of Program Faculty Ratings of the 54 Programs in Spanish and Portuguese Language and Literature

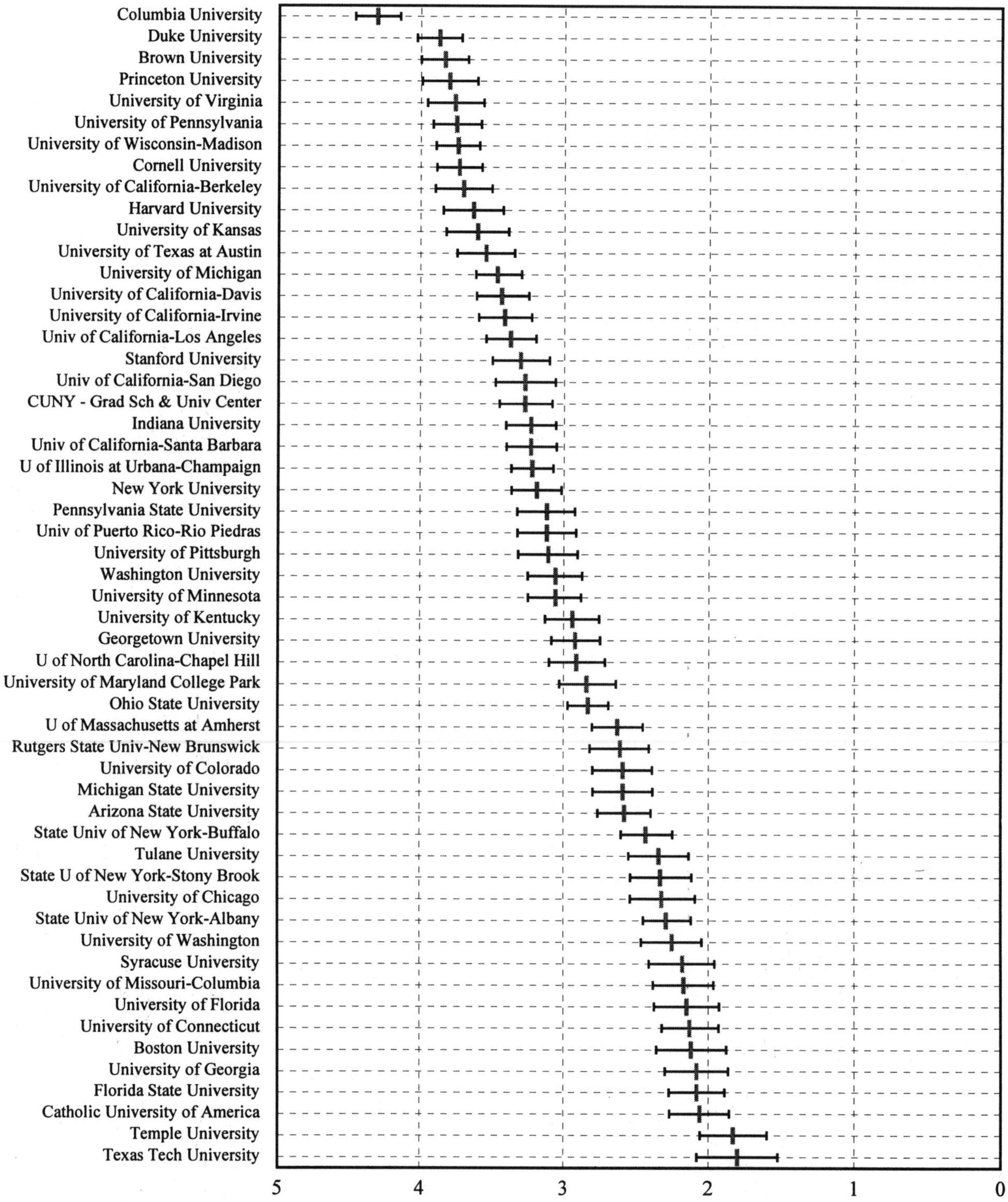

Source: National Survey of Graduate Faculty

Appendix Figure Q - 41 Means and Confidence Intervals for the Scholarly Quality of Program Faculty Ratings of the 65 Programs in Statistics and Biostatistics

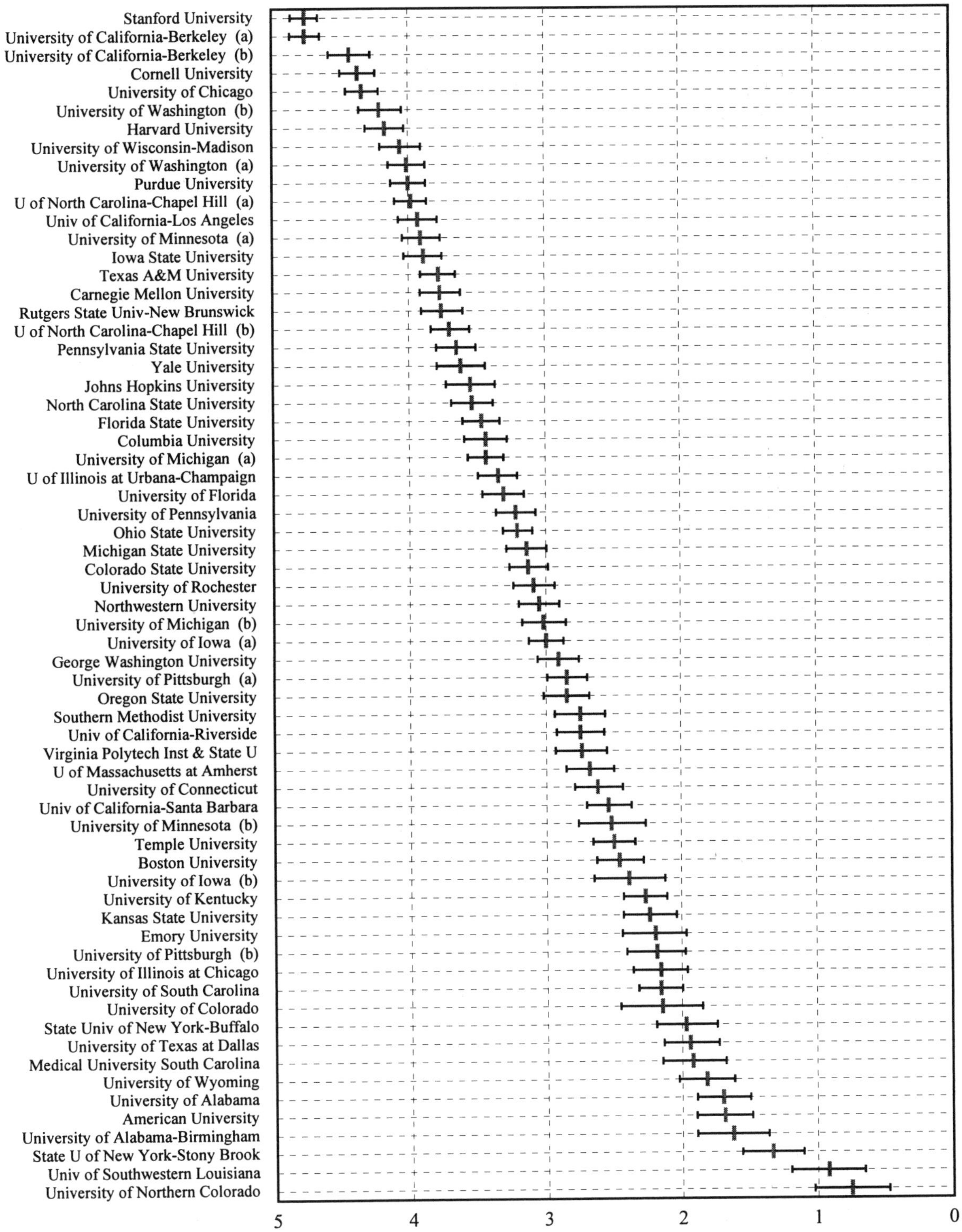

Source: National Survey of Graduate Faculty

Note: (a) Program in Statistics
(b) Program in Biostatistics

APPENDIX R

Change in Magnitude of Selected Measures

The following tables were produced for the twenty seven fields common to both the 1982 and 1993 Studies (see Appendix C). The table documents change along four dimensions: Size of Program Faculty, Number of Program Graduates, Median Years to Degree from Entering Graduate School and Quality Rating of Program Faculty. For each field, programs that were included in both studies were compared by dividing the programs into quarters based on their 1982 Quality Rating of Program Faculty and computing for each quarter of the four measures the 1982 average, the 1993 average and the average change from 1982 to 1993. In addition the averages for all programs in both studies and the average for all programs common to both studies is given. The appendix ends with a technical note prepared by Brendan Maher on the matter of analyzing change.

Appendix Table R - 1 Change in Magnitude of Selected Measures for Programs in Anthropology Appearing in Both the 1982 and 1993 Studies by 1982 Quality Grouping

Number of Program Faculty [1]

	1982 Quarters				
	Top	Second	Third	Fourth	Average
Average Number of Faculty, Fall 1980	26.63	17.50	13.94	11.25	17.33
Average Number of Faculty, Fall 1992	28.06	21.63	17.50	13.94	20.28
Change in Average Number of Faculty	**1.43**	**4.13**	**3.56**	**2.69**	**2.95**

Number of Program Graduates [1]

	1982 Quarters				
	Top	Second	Third	Fourth	Average
Average Number of PhD's, Acad Yrs 1975-80	52.00	26.81	21.81	15.25	28.97
Average Number of PhD's, Acad Yrs 1987-92	43.31	22.75	17.63	11.19	23.72
Change in Average Number of PhD's	**-8.69**	**-4.06**	**-4.18**	**-4.06**	**-5.25**

Median Years to Degree from Entering Graduate School [2]

	1982 Quarters				
	Top	Second	Third	Fourth	Average
Average Median Years to Degree, Acad Yrs 1975-79	7.88	8.23	8.34	8.81	8.26
Average Median Years to Degree, Acad Yrs 1986-92	10.83	11.62	11.42	12.40	11.57
Change in Average Median Years to Degree	**2.95**	**3.39**	**3.08**	**3.59**	**3.31**

Quality Ratings of Program Faculty [3]

	1982 Quarters				
	Top	Second	Third	Fourth	Average
Average Rating of Program Faculty Quality, 1982	3.87	2.98	2.45	1.93	2.80
Average Rating of Program Faculty Quality, 1993	3.86	3.18	2.89	2.17	3.02
Change in Average Program Faculty Quality	**-0.01**	**0.20**	**0.44**	**0.24**	**0.22**

Sources: 1 Institutional Coordinators.
2 Doctorate Records File.
3 National Survey of Graduate Faculty 1993 and Jones, Lindzey and Coggeshall, 1982.

Appendix Table R - 2 Change in Magnitude of Selected Measures for Programs in Art History Appearing in Both the 1982 and 1993 Studies by 1982 Quality Grouping

Number of Program Faculty [1]

	1982 Quarters				
	Top	Second	Third	Fourth	Average
Average Number of Faculty, Fall 1980	21.00	10.67	11.44	12.33	13.66
Average Number of Faculty, Fall 1992	21.13	11.33	14.67	11.33	14.43
Change in Average Number of Faculty	**0.13**	**0.67**	**3.23**	**1.00**	**0.77**

Number of Program Graduates [1]

	1982 Quarters				
	Top	Second	Third	Fourth	Average
Average Number of PhD's, Acad Yrs 1975-80	50.50	17.33	9.44	6.67	20.14
Average Number of PhD's, Acad Yrs 1987-92	37.38	17.00	11.22	10.44	18.49
Change in Average Number of PhD's	**-13.13**	**-0.33**	**1.78**	**6.67**	**-1.66**

Median Years to Degree from Entering Graduate School [2]

	1982 Quarters				
	Top	Second	Third	Fourth	Average
Average Median Years to Degree, Acad Yrs 1975-79	9.42	8.59	9.92*	9.00*	9.17
Average Median Years to Degree, Acad Yrs 1986-92	12.19	11.48	13.31	13.51	12.63
Change in Average Median Years to Degree	**2.77**	**2.89**	**3.39**	**4.51**	**3.46**

Quality Ratings of Program Faculty [3]

	1982 Quarters				
	Top	Second	Third	Fourth	Average
Average Rating of Program Faculty Quality, 1982	4.39	3.19	2.54	1.72	2.92
Average Rating of Program Faculty Quality, 1993	4.30	3.28	2.95	2.20	3.15
Change in Average Program Faculty Quality	**-0.09**	**0.09**	**0.41**	**0.48**	**0.23**

Sources: 1 Institutional Coordinators.
2 Doctorate Records File.
3 National Survey of Graduate Faculty 1993 and Jones, Lindzey and Coggeshall, 1982.

* The average is based on fewer than four values.

Appendix Table R - 3 Change in Magnitude of Selected Measures for Programs in Chemical Engineering Appearing in Both the 1982 and 1993 Studies by 1982 Quality Grouping

Number of Program Faculty [1]

	1982 Quarters				
	Top	Second	Third	Fourth	Average
Average Number of Faculty, Fall 1980	16.05	12.32	12.47	9.47	12.48
Average Number of Faculty, Fall 1992	18.95	15.11	13.89	10.47	14.37
Change in Average Number of Faculty	**2.89**	**2.79**	**1.42**	**1.00**	**1.89**

Number of Program Graduates [1]

	1982 Quarters				
	Top	Second	Third	Fourth	Average
Average Number of PhD's, Acad Yrs 1975-80	34.37	15.74	15.05	8.11	17.87
Average Number of PhD's, Acad Yrs 1987-92	76.05	36.63	27.79	16.47	38.45
Change in Average Number of PhD's	**41.68**	**20.89**	**12.74**	**8.36**	**20.58**

Median Years to Degree from Entering Graduate School [2]

	1982 Quarters				
	Top	Second	Third	Fourth	Average
Average Median Years to Degree, Acad Yrs 1975-79	5.53	5.96	5.97	6.95	5.94
Average Median Years to Degree, Acad Yrs 1986-92	6.18	6.76	7.06	7.26	6.82
Change in Average Median Years to Degree	**0.65**	**0.80**	**1.09**	**0.31**	**0.88**

Quality Ratings of Program Faculty [3]

	1982 Quarters				
	Top	Second	Third	Fourth	Average
Average Rating of Program Faculty Quality, 1982	4.03	2.85	2.37	1.65	2.70
Average Rating of Program Faculty Quality, 1993	4.08	2.99	2.41	1.95	2.83
Change in Average Program Faculty Quality	**0.05**	**0.14**	**0.04**	**0.30**	**0.13**

Sources: 1 Institutional Coordinators.
2 Doctorate Records File.
3 National Survey of Graduate Faculty 1993 and Jones, Lindzey and Coggeshall, 1982.

Appendix Table R - 4 Change in Magnitude of Selected Measures for Programs in Chemistry Appearing in Both the 1982 and 1993 Studies by 1982 Quality Grouping

Number of Program Faculty[1]

	1982 Quarters Top	Second	Third	Fourth	Average
Average Number of Faculty, Fall 1980	32.70	25.09	21.67	15.79	23.76
Average Number of Faculty, Fall 1992	34.58	26.74	22.85	16.32	25.07
Change in Average Number of Faculty	**1.88**	**1.65**	**1.18**	**0.53**	**1.31**

Number of Program Graduates[1]

	1982 Quarters Top	Second	Third	Fourth	Average
Average Number of PhD's, Acad Yrs 1975-80	110.76	52.97	31.94	19.35	53.49
Average Number of PhD's, Acad Yrs 1987-92	147.63	71.68	45.18	23.53	71.20
Change in Average Number of PhD's	**36.87**	**18.71**	**13.24**	**4.18**	**17.71**

Median Years to Degree from Entering Graduate School[2]

	1982 Quarters Top	Second	Third	Fourth	Average
Average Median Years to Degree, Acad Yrs 1975-79	5.41	5.65	6.26	6.27	5.90
Average Median Years to Degree, Acad Yrs 1986-92	6.28	6.56	7.04	7.52	6.85
Change in Average Median Years to Degree	**0.87**	**0.91**	**0.78**	**1.25**	**0.95**

Quality Ratings of Program Faculty[3]

	1982 Quarters Top	Second	Third	Fourth	Average
Average Rating of Program Faculty Quality, 1982	3.96	2.91	2.18	1.46	2.62
Average Rating of Program Faculty Quality, 1993	4.09	3.14	2.43	1.76	2.85
Change in Average Program Faculty Quality	**0.13**	**0.23**	**0.25**	**0.30**	**0.23**

Sources: 1 Institutional Coordinators.
2 Doctorate Records File.
3 National Survey of Graduate Faculty 1993 and Jones, Lindzey and Coggeshall, 1982.

Appendix Table R - 5 Change in Magnitude of Selected Measures for Programs in Civil Engineering Appearing in Both the 1982 and 1993 Studies by 1982 Quality Grouping

Number of Program Faculty [1]

	1982 Quarters				
	Top	Second	Third	Fourth	Average
Average Number of Faculty, Fall 1980	36.60	21.25	15.75	10.94	20.89
Average Number of Faculty, Fall 1992	37.27	26.63	18.94	13.94	23.98
Change in Average Number of Faculty	**0.67**	**5.38**	**3.19**	**3.00**	**3.10**

Number of Program Graduates [1]

	1982 Quarters				
	Top	Second	Third	Fourth	Average
Average Number of PhD's, Acad Yrs 1975-80	54.13	16.63	14.44	8.38	22.91
Average Number of PhD's, Acad Yrs 1987-92	81.47	33.50	26.50	18.88	39.43
Change in Average Number of PhD's	**27.34**	**16.88**	**12.06**	**10.50**	**16.52**

Median Years to Degree from Entering Graduate School [2]

	1982 Quarters				
	Top	Second	Third	Fourth	Average
Average Median Years to Degree, Acad Yrs 1975-79	6.44	7.14	6.84	6.88	6.81
Average Median Years to Degree, Acad Yrs 1986-92	7.89	7.92	8.58	8.27	8.27
Change in Average Median Years to Degree	**1.45**	**0.78**	**1.74**	**1.39**	**1.46**

Quality Ratings of Program Faculty [3]

	1982 Quarters				
	Top	Second	Third	Fourth	Average
Average Rating of Program Faculty Quality, 1982	4.00	2.95	2.42	1.75	2.76
Average Rating of Program Faculty Quality, 1993	4.02	3.24	2.73	2.36	3.08
Change in Average Program Faculty Quality	**0.02**	**0.29**	**0.31**	**0.61**	**0.32**

Sources: 1 Institutional Coordinators.
2 Doctorate Records File.
3 National Survey of Graduate Faculty 1993 and Jones, Lindzey and Coggeshall, 1982.

Appendix Table R - 6 Change in Magnitude of Selected Measures for Programs in Classics Appearing in Both the 1982 and 1993 Studies by 1982 Quality Grouping

Number of Program Faculty [1]

	1982 Quarters				
	Top	Second	Third	Fourth	Average
Average Number of Faculty, Fall 1980	15.14	13.14	9.29	8.00	11.39
Average Number of Faculty, Fall 1992	15.57	17.86	12.29	7.57	13.32
Change in Average Number of Faculty	**0.43**	**4.72**	**3.00**	**-0.38**	**1.93**

Number of Program Graduates [1]

	1982 Quarters				
	Top	Second	Third	Fourth	Average
Average Number of PhD's, Acad Yrs 1975-80	17.14	8.86	10.71	6.57	10.82
Average Number of PhD's, Acad Yrs 1987-92	17.14	8.43	8.14	4.86	9.64
Change in Average Number of PhD's	**0.00**	**-0.43**	**-2.57**	**-2.20**	**-1.18**

Median Years to Degree from Entering Graduate School [2]

	1982 Quarters				
	Top	Second	Third	Fourth	Average
Average Median Years to Degree, Acad Yrs 1975-79	7.04	8.67*	6.83*	11.17*	7.68
Average Median Years to Degree, Acad Yrs 1986-92	8.54	8.79	9.71	15.03	10.52
Change in Average Median Years to Degree	**1.68**	**0.11**	**2.93**	**3.02**	**2.86**

Quality Ratings of Program Faculty [3]

	1982 Quarters				
	Top	Second	Third	Fourth	Average
Average Rating of Program Faculty Quality, 1982	4.27	3.64	2.81	1.93	3.16
Average Rating of Program Faculty Quality, 1993	4.33	3.70	2.92	2.24	3.30
Change in Average Program Faculty Quality	**0.06**	**0.06**	**0.11**	**0.35**	**0.14**

Sources: 1 Institutional Coordinators.
2 Doctorate Records File.
3 National Survey of Graduate Faculty 1993 and Jones, Lindzey and Coggeshall, 1982.

* The average is based on fewer than four values.

Appendix Table R - 7 Change in Magnitude of Selected Measures for Programs in Computer Science Appearing in Both the 1982 and 1993 Studies by 1982 Quality Grouping

Number of Program Faculty [1]

	1982 Quarters				
	Top	Second	Third	Fourth	Average
Average Number of Faculty, Fall 1980	23.07	13.79	16.93	10.80	16.16
Average Number of Faculty, Fall 1992	38.57	21.86	22.86	17.73	25.12
Change in Average Number of Faculty	**15.50**	**8.07**	**5.93**	**6.93**	**8.96**

Number of Program Graduates [1]

	1982 Quarters				
	Top	Second	Third	Fourth	Average
Average Number of PhD's, Acad Yrs 1975-80	31.43	13.54	9.85	10.14	16.41
Average Number of PhD's, Acad Yrs 1987-92	77.86	38.00	32.17	21.07	42.04
Change in Average Number of PhD's	**46.43**	**24.46**	**22.32**	**10.93**	**25.63**

Median Years to Degree from Entering Graduate School [2]

	1982 Quarters				
	Top	Second	Third	Fourth	Average
Average Median Years to Degree, Acad Yrs 1975-79	6.52	6.20	6.08	7.16	6.47
Average Median Years to Degree, Acad Yrs 1986-92	7.64	7.73	8.79	9.17	8.35
Change in Average Median Years to Degree	**1.12**	**1.53**	**2.71**	**2.01**	**1.88**

Quality Ratings of Program Faculty [3]

	1982 Quarters				
	Top	Second	Third	Fourth	Average
Average Rating of Program Faculty Quality, 1982	3.83	2.68	2.23	1.37	2.53
Average Rating of Program Faculty Quality, 1993	4.24	3.34	2.72	2.00	3.06
Change in Average Program Faculty Quality	**0.41**	**0.66**	**0.49**	**0.63**	**0.53**

Sources: 1 Institutional Coordinators.
2 Doctorate Records File.
3 National Survey of Graduate Faculty 1993 and Jones, Lindzey and Coggeshall, 1982.

Appendix Table R - 8 Change in Magnitude of Selected Measures for Programs in Economics Appearing in Both the 1982 and 1993 Studies by 1982 Quality Grouping

Number of Program Faculty [1]

	1982 Quarters				
	Top	Second	Third	Fourth	Average
Average Number of Faculty, Fall 1980	31.33	26.48	20.29	17.43	23.88
Average Number of Faculty, Fall 1992	36.52	30.10	23.29	18.71	27.15
Change in Average Number of Faculty	**5.19**	**3.62**	**3.00**	**1.28**	**3.27**

Number of Program Graduates [1]

	1982 Quarters				
	Top	Second	Third	Fourth	Average
Average Number of PhD's, Acad Yrs 1975-80	81.43	38.67	32.95	22.95	44.00
Average Number of PhD's, Acad Yrs 1987-92	82.38	41.24	31.43	22.57	44.40
Change in Average Number of PhD's	**0.95**	**2.57**	**-1.52**	**-0.38**	**0.40**

Median Years to Degree from Entering Graduate School [2]

	1982 Quarters				
	Top	Second	Third	Fourth	Average
Average Median Years to Degree, Acad Yrs 1975-79	6.83	6.98	7.45	7.71	7.24
Average Median Years to Degree, Acad Yrs 1986-92	7.67	8.02	9.03	9.16	8.47
Change in Average Median Years to Degree	**0.84**	**1.05**	**1.58**	**1.45**	**1.23**

Quality Ratings of Program Faculty [3]

	1982 Quarters				
	Top	Second	Third	Fourth	Average
Average Rating of Program Faculty Quality, 1982	4.06	2.55	1.75	1.06	2.36
Average Rating of Program Faculty Quality, 1993	4.18	2.89	2.15	1.36	2.64
Change in Average Program Faculty Quality	**0.12**	**0.34**	**0.40**	**0.30**	**0.28**

Sources: 1 Institutional Coordinators.
2 Doctorate Records File.
3 National Survey of Graduate Faculty 1993 and Jones, Lindzey and Coggeshall, 1982.

Appendix Table R - 9 Change in Magnitude of Selected Measures for Programs in Electrical Engineering Appearing in Both the 1982 and 1993 Studies by 1982 Quality Grouping

Number of Program Faculty [1]

	1982 Quarters				
	Top	Second	Third	Fourth	Average
Average Number of Faculty, Fall 1980	41.52	22.86	16.71	15.26	23.88
Average Number of Faculty, Fall 1992	47.29	33.10	24.67	22.91	31.78
Change in Average Number of Faculty	**5.76**	**10.24**	**7.95**	**7.65**	**7.90**

Number of Program Graduates [1]

	1982 Quarters				
	Top	Second	Third	Fourth	Average
Average Number of PhD's, Acad Yrs 1975-80	74.33	25.52	18.19	12.48	32.16
Average Number of PhD's, Acad Yrs 1987-92	144.57	57.43	37.81	28.26	66.12
Change in Average Number of PhD's	**70.24**	**31.90**	**19.62**	**15.78**	**33.96**

Median Years to Degree from Entering Graduate School [2]

	1982 Quarters				
	Top	Second	Third	Fourth	Average
Average Median Years to Degree, Acad Yrs 1975-79	6.46	6.72	6.62	6.86	6.65
Average Median Years to Degree, Acad Yrs 1986-92	7.18	7.21	7.85	7.87	7.54
Change in Average Median Years to Degree	**0.72**	**0.49**	**1.23**	**1.01**	**0.89**

Quality Ratings of Program Faculty [3]

	1982 Quarters				
	Top	Second	Third	Fourth	Average
Average Rating of Program Faculty Quality, 1982	3.79	2.89	2.31	1.67	2.65
Average Rating of Program Faculty Quality, 1993	4.02	3.27	2.73	2.34	3.07
Change in Average Program Faculty Quality	**0.23**	**0.38**	**0.42**	**0.67**	**0.42**

Sources: 1 Institutional Coordinators.
2 Doctorate Records File.
3 National Survey of Graduate Faculty 1993 and Jones, Lindzey and Coggeshall, 1982.

Appendix Table R - 10 Change in Magnitude of Selected Measures for Programs in English Language and Literature Appearing in Both the 1982 and 1993 Studies by 1982 Quality Grouping

Number of Program Faculty [1]

	1982 Quarters				
	Top	Second	Third	Fourth	Average
Average Number of Faculty, Fall 1980	43.29	31.92	30.13	21.96	31.72
Average Number of Faculty, Fall 1992	46.21	37.72	31.42	24.44	34.87
Change in Average Number of Faculty	**2.92**	**5.80**	**1.29**	**2.48**	**3.15**

Number of Program Graduates [1]

	1982 Quarters				
	Top	Second	Third	Fourth	Average
Average Number of PhD's, Acad Yrs 1975-80	91.21	48.48	34.21	25.08	49.48
Average Number of PhD's, Acad Yrs 1987-92	61.54	43.44	26.42	21.96	38.22
Change in Average Number of PhD's	**-29.67**	**-5.04**	**-7.79**	**-3.12**	**-11.26**

Median Years to Degree from Entering Graduate School [2]

	1982 Quarters				
	Top	Second	Third	Fourth	Average
Average Median Years to Degree, Acad Yrs 1975-79	7.92	9.00	9.61	9.99	9.12
Average Median Years to Degree, Acad Yrs 1986-92	9.90	10.95	12.34	12.75	11.49
Change in Average Median Years to Degree	**1.98**	**1.95**	**2.73**	**2.76**	**2.37**

Quality Ratings of Program Faculty [3]

	1982 Quarters				
	Top	Second	Third	Fourth	Average
Average Rating of Program Faculty Quality, 1982	3.98	2.87	2.20	1.29	2.57
Average Rating of Program Faculty Quality, 1993	4.07	3.22	2.70	1.88	2.96
Change in Average Program Faculty Quality	**0.09**	**0.35**	**0.50**	**0.59**	**0.39**

Sources: 1 Institutional Coordinators.
2 Doctorate Records File.
3 National Survey of Graduate Faculty 1993 and Jones, Lindzey and Coggeshall, 1982.

Appendix Table R - 11 Change in Magnitude of Selected Measures for Programs in French Language and Literaure Appearing in Both the 1982 and 1993 Studies by 1982 Quality Grouping

Number of Program Faculty [1]

	1982 Quarters				
	Top	Second	Third	Fourth	Average
Average Number of Faculty, Fall 1980	13.90	11.91	10.50	9.55	11.43
Average Number of Faculty, Fall 1992	14.10	14.09	13.10	10.73	12.98
Change in Average Number of Faculty	**0.20**	**2.18**	**2.60**	**1.24**	**1.55**

Number of Program Graduates [1]

	1982 Quarters				
	Top	Second	Third	Fourth	Average
Average Number of PhD's, Acad Yrs 1975-80	28.30	20.82	16.10	9.18	18.43
Average Number of PhD's, Acad Yrs 1987-92	19.30	12.45	7.90	6.00	11.44
Change in Average Number of PhD's	**-9.00**	**-8.37**	**-8.20**	**-3.18**	**-6.99**

Median Years to Degree from Entering Graduate School [2]

	1982 Quarters				
	Top	Second	Third	Fourth	Average
Average Median Years to Degree, Acad Yrs 1975-79	8.96	8.56	9.31	9.43	9.01
Average Median Years to Degree, Acad Yrs 1986-92	10.03	10.15	13.10	13.47	11.69
Change in Average Median Years to Degree	**1.07**	**1.59**	**3.79**	**4.04**	**2.68**

Quality Ratings of Program Faculty [3]

	1982 Quarters				
	Top	Second	Third	Fourth	Average
Average Rating of Program Faculty Quality, 1982	3.99	3.19	2.51	2.01	2.91
Average Rating of Program Faculty Quality, 1993	4.10	3.33	2.77	2.43	3.14
Change in Average Program Faculty Quality	**0.11**	**0.14**	**0.26**	**0.42**	**0.23**

Sources: 1 Institutional Coordinators.
2 Doctorate Records File.
3 National Survey of Graduate Faculty 1993 and Jones, Lindzey and Coggeshall, 1982.

Appendix Table R -12 Change in Magnitude of Selected Measures for Programs in Geography Appearing in Both the 1982 and 1993 Studies by 1982 Quality Grouping

Number of Program Faculty [1]

	1982 Quarters				
	Top	Second	Third	Fourth	Average
Average Number of Faculty, Fall 1980	17.00	13.75	15.33	11.56	14.35
Average Number of Faculty, Fall 1992	19.50	13.75	15.44	12.33	15.18
Change in Average Number of Faculty	**2.50**	**0.00**	**0.11**	**0.77**	**0.83**

Number of Program Graduates [1]

	1982 Quarters				
	Top	Second	Third	Fourth	Average
Average Number of PhD's, Acad Yrs 1975-80	30.38	16.63	12.33	10.56	17.12
Average Number of PhD's, Acad Yrs 1987-92	22.75	14.00	14.44	9.11	14.88
Change in Average Number of PhD's	**-7.63**	**-2.63**	**2.11**	**-1.45**	**-2.24**

Median Years to Degree from Entering Graduate School [2]

	1982 Quarters				
	Top	Second	Third	Fourth	Average
Average Median Years to Degree, Acad Yrs 1975-79	7.98	8.24	9.79	8.47	8.61
Average Median Years to Degree, Acad Yrs 1986-92	10.10	9.51	9.95	12.51	10.56
Change in Average Median Years to Degree	**2.12**	**1.27**	**0.16**	**4.04**	**1.95**

Quality Ratings of Program Faculty [3]

	1982 Quarters				
	Top	Second	Third	Fourth	Average
Average Rating of Program Faculty Quality, 1982	4.05	3.34	2.78	2.05	3.02
Average Rating of Program Faculty Quality, 1993	4.13	3.20	2.86	2.38	3.11
Change in Average Program Faculty Quality	**0.08**	**-0.14**	**0.08**	**0.33**	**0.09**

Sources: 1 Institutional Coordinators.
2 Doctorate Records File.
3 National Survey of Graduate Faculty 1993 and Jones, Lindzey and Coggeshall, 1982.

Appendix Table R - 13 Change in Magnitude of Selected Measures for Programs in Geosciences Appearing in Both the 1982 and 1993 Studies by 1982 Quality Grouping

Number of Program Faculty [1]

	1982 Quarters Top	Second	Third	Fourth	Average
Average Number of Faculty, Fall 1980	20.79	15.53	17.89	11.30	16.31
Average Number of Faculty, Fall 1992	30.79	19.79	21.32	12.45	20.97
Change in Average Number of Faculty	**10.00**	**4.26**	**3.43**	**1.15**	**4.66**

Number of Program Graduates [1]

	1982 Quarters Top	Second	Third	Fourth	Average
Average Number of PhD's, Acad Yrs 1975-80	31.42	20.79	15.26	11.42	19.72
Average Number of PhD's, Acad Yrs 1987-92	50.58	29.37	22.74	12.35	28.55
Change in Average Number of PhD's	**19.16**	**8.58**	**7.48**	**0.93**	**8.83**

Median Years to Degree from Entering Graduate School [2]

	1982 Quarters Top	Second	Third	Fourth	Average
Average Median Years to Degree, Acad Yrs 1975-79	6.54	6.98	7.09	7.44	6.94
Average Median Years to Degree, Acad Yrs 1986-92	8.08	8.39	9.32	9.70	8.88
Change in Average Median Years to Degree	**1.54**	**1.41**	**2.23**	**2.26**	**1.94**

Quality Ratings of Program Faculty [3]

	1982 Quarters Top	Second	Third	Fourth	Average
Average Rating of Program Faculty Quality, 1982	4.01	3.21	2.74	2.11	3.01
Average Rating of Program Faculty Quality, 1993	4.08	3.29	2.88	2.26	3.11
Change in Average Program Faculty Quality	**0.07**	**0.08**	**0.14**	**0.15**	**0.10**

Sources: 1 Institutional Coordinators.
2 Doctorate Records File.
3 National Survey of Graduate Faculty 1993 and Jones, Lindzey and Coggeshall, 1982.

Appendix Table R - 14 Change in Magnitude of Selected Measures for Programs in German Language and Literature Appearing in Both the 1982 and 1993 Studies by 1982 Quality Grouping

Number of Program Faculty [1]

	1982 Quarters				
	Top	Second	Third	Fourth	Average
Average Number of Faculty, Fall 1980	13.57	14.13	7.75	7.75	10.71
Average Number of Faculty, Fall 1992	13.71	13.50	10.13	8.00	11.26
Change in Average Number of Faculty	**0.14**	**-0.63**	**2.38**	**0.25**	**0.55**

Number of Program Graduates [1]

	1982 Quarters				
	Top	Second	Third	Fourth	Average
Average Number of PhD's, Acad Yrs 1975-80	21.00	16.38	12.25	11.38	15.06
Average Number of PhD's, Acad Yrs 1987-92	16.71	10.13	9.63	7.25	10.74
Change in Average Number of PhD's	**-4.29**	**-6.25**	**-2.62**	**-4.13**	**-4.32**

Median Years to Degree from Entering Graduate School [2]

	1982 Quarters				
	Top	Second	Third	Fourth	Average
Average Median Years to Degree, Acad Yrs 1975-79	8.45	8.39	10.00	9.42*	8.92
Average Median Years to Degree, Acad Yrs 1986-92	9.71	9.72	11.16	12.88	10.90
Change in Average Median Years to Degree	**1.26**	**1.33**	**1.16**	**3.46**	**1.98**

Quality Ratings of Program Faculty [3]

	1982 Quarters				
	Top	Second	Third	Fourth	Average
Average Rating of Program Faculty Quality, 1982	4.34	3.67	3.20	2.38	3.36
Average Rating of Program Faculty Quality, 1993	3.82	3.48	3.23	2.34	3.20
Change in Average Program Faculty Quality	**-0.52**	**-0.19**	**0.03**	**-0.04**	**-0.16**

Sources: 1 Institutional Coordinators.
2 Doctorate Records File.
3 National Survey of Graduate Faculty 1993 and Jones, Lindzey and Coggeshall, 1982.

* The average is based on fewer than four values.

Appendix Table R - 15 Change in Magnitude of Selected Measures for Programs in History Appearing in Both the 1982 and 1993 Studies by 1982 Quality Grouping

Number of Program Faculty [1]

	1982 Quarters				
	Top	Second	Third	Fourth	Average
Average Number of Faculty, Fall 1980	40.30	31.65	24.13	17.50	28.28
Average Number of Faculty, Fall 1992	45.17	35.39	25.22	20.75	31.52
Change in Average Number of Faculty	**4.87**	**3.74**	**1.09**	**3.25**	**3.24**

Number of Program Graduates [1]

	1982 Quarters				
	Top	Second	Third	Fourth	Average
Average Number of PhD's, Acad Yrs 1975-80	93.22	42.83	26.65	20.42	45.51
Average Number of PhD's, Acad Yrs 1987-92	55.39	24.00	17.39	13.08	27.31
Change in Average Number of PhD's	**-37.83**	**-18.83**	**-9.26**	**-7.34**	**-18.20**

Median Years to Degree from Entering Graduate School [2]

	1982 Quarters				
	Top	Second	Third	Fourth	Average
Average Median Years to Degree, Acad Yrs 1975-79	8.52	9.43	9.43	9.54	9.22
Average Median Years to Degree, Acad Yrs 1986-92	10.37	12.51	13.01	12.93	12.21
Change in Average Median Years to Degree	**1.85**	**3.08**	**3.58**	**3.39**	**2.99**

Quality Ratings of Program Faculty [3]

	1982 Quarters				
	Top	Second	Third	Fourth	Average
Average Rating of Program Faculty Quality, 1982	4.13	3.01	2.29	1.44	2.70
Average Rating of Program Faculty Quality, 1993	4.18	3.20	2.60	2.01	2.98
Change in Average Program Faculty Quality	**0.05**	**0.19**	**0.31**	**0.57**	**0.28**

Sources: 1 Institutional Coordinators.
2 Doctorate Records File.
3 National Survey of Graduate Faculty 1993 and Jones, Lindzey and Coggeshall, 1982.

Appendix Table R - 16 Change in Magnitude of Selected Measures for Programs in Linguistics Appearing in Both the 1982 and 1993 Studies by 1982 Quality Grouping

Number of Program Faculty [1]

	1982 Quarters				
	Top	Second	Third	Fourth	Average
Average Number of Faculty, Fall 1980	21.63	16.43	12.00	10.88	15.30
Average Number of Faculty, Fall 1992	25.13	13.57	13.71	12.00	16.27
Change in Average Number of Faculty	**3.50**	**-2.86**	**1.71**	**1.12**	**0.97**

Number of Program Graduates [1]

	1982 Quarters				
	Top	Second	Third	Fourth	Average
Average Number of PhD's, Acad Yrs 1975-80	29.50	17.43	20.71	17.38	21.40
Average Number of PhD's, Acad Yrs 1987-92	34.00	23.71	21.71	24.50	26.20
Change in Average Number of PhD's	**4.50**	**6.29**	**1.00**	**7.12**	**4.80**

Median Years to Degree from Entering Graduate School [2]

	1982 Quarters				
	Top	Second	Third	Fourth	Average
Average Median Years to Degree, Acad Yrs 1975-79	7.48	7.96	7.94	8.41	7.86
Average Median Years to Degree, Acad Yrs 1986-92	9.62	9.30	9.88	11.12	10.00
Change in Average Median Years to Degree	**2.14**	**1.34**	**1.94**	**2.71**	**2.14**

Quality Ratings of Program Faculty [3]

	1982 Quarters				
	Top	Second	Third	Fourth	Average
Average Rating of Program Faculty Quality, 1982	4.07	3.23	2.73	1.98	3.00
Average Rating of Program Faculty Quality, 1993	4.12	3.33	3.23	2.39	3.27
Change in Average Program Faculty Quality	**0.05**	**0.10**	**0.50**	**0.41**	**0.27**

Sources: 1 Institutional Coordinators.
2 Doctorate Records File.
3 National Survey of Graduate Faculty 1993 and Jones, Lindzey and Coggeshall, 1982.

Appendix Table R - 17 Change in Magnitude of Selected Measures for Programs in Mathematics Appearing in Both the 1982 and 1993 Studies by 1982 Quality Grouping

Number of Program Faculty [1]

	1982 Quarters Top	Second	Third	Fourth	Average
Average Number of Faculty, Fall 1980	43.92	35.44	30.44	22.75	32.94
Average Number of Faculty, Fall 1992	45.69	38.11	31.41	26.43	35.23
Change in Average Number of Faculty	**1.77**	**2.67**	**0.97**	**3.68**	**2.29**

Number of Program Graduates [1]

	1982 Quarters Top	Second	Third	Fourth	Average
Average Number of PhD's, Acad Yrs 1975-80	52.58	23.52	14.19	12.29	25.27
Average Number of PhD's, Acad Yrs 1987-92	54.65	31.63	16.67	14.25	28.93
Change in Average Number of PhD's	**2.07**	**8.11**	**2.48**	**1.96**	**3.66**

Median Years to Degree from Entering Graduate School [2]

	1982 Quarters Top	Second	Third	Fourth	Average
Average Median Years to Degree, Acad Yrs 1975-79	5.76	6.36	6.97	7.38	6.54
Average Median Years to Degree, Acad Yrs 1986-92	7.10	7.60	8.42	8.72	7.97
Change in Average Median Years to Degree	**1.34**	**1.24**	**1.45**	**1.34**	**1.43**

Quality Ratings of Program Faculty [3]

	1982 Quarters Top	Second	Third	Fourth	Average
Average Rating of Program Faculty Quality, 1982	4.11	2.95	2.28	1.51	2.70
Average Rating of Program Faculty Quality, 1993	4.20	3.25	2.61	2.03	3.00
Change in Average Program Faculty Quality	**0.09**	**0.30**	**0.33**	**0.52**	**0.30**

Sources: 1 Institutional Coordinators.
2 Doctorate Records File.
3 National Survey of Graduate Faculty 1993 and Jones, Lindzey and Coggeshall, 1982.

Appendix Table R - 18 Change in Magnitude of Selected Measures for Programs in Mechanical Engineering Appearing in Both the 1982 and 1993 Studies by 1982 Quality Grouping

Number of Program Faculty [1]

	1982 Quarters Top	Second	Third	Fourth	Average
Average Number of Faculty, Fall 1980	31.32	19.79	17.68	12.85	20.31
Average Number of Faculty, Fall 1992	35.47	30.11	20.89	15.50	25.36
Change in Average Number of Faculty	**4.15**	**10.32**	**3.21**	**2.65**	**5.05**

Number of Program Graduates [1]

	1982 Quarters Top	Second	Third	Fourth	Average
Average Number of PhD's, Acad Yrs 1975-80	41.68	18.05	11.68	9.95	20.21
Average Number of PhD's, Acad Yrs 1987-92	82.63	44.53	33.11	19.40	44.58
Change in Average Number of PhD's	**40.95**	**26.48**	**21.43**	**9.45**	**24.37**

Median Years to Degree from Entering Graduate School [2]

	1982 Quarters Top	Second	Third	Fourth	Average
Average Median Years to Degree, Acad Yrs 1975-79	6.39	7.34	7.05	7.59	7.00
Average Median Years to Degree, Acad Yrs 1986-92	7.41	7.95	7.93	8.49	7.95
Change in Average Median Years to Degree	**1.02**	**0.61**	**0.88**	**0.90**	**0.95**

Quality Ratings of Program Faculty [3]

	1982 Quarters Top	Second	Third	Fourth	Average
Average Rating of Program Faculty Quality, 1982	3.86	2.92	2.49	1.87	2.77
Average Rating of Program Faculty Quality, 1993	3.95	3.18	2.78	2.16	3.01
Change in Average Program Faculty Quality	**0.09**	**0.26**	**0.29**	**0.29**	**0.24**

Sources: 1 Institutional Coordinators.
2 Doctorate Records File.
3 National Survey of Graduate Faculty 1993 and Jones, Lindzey and Coggeshall, 1982.

Appendix Table R - 19 Change in Magnitude of Selected Measures for Programs in Music Appearing in Both the 1982 and 1993 Studies by 1982 Quality Grouping

Number of Program Faculty [1]

	1982 Quarters				
	Top	Second	Third	Fourth	Average
Average Number of Faculty, Fall 1980	21.82	20.00	16.58	20.54	19.72
Average Number of Faculty, Fall 1992	23.91	26.36	22.00	17.08	22.36
Change in Average Number of Faculty	**2.09**	**6.36**	**5.42**	**-3.46**	**2.64**

Number of Program Graduates [1]

	1982 Quarters				
	Top	Second	Third	Fourth	Average
Average Number of PhD's, Acad Yrs 1975-80	29.36	50.50	26.50	22.62	32.84
Average Number of PhD's, Acad Yrs 1987-92	32.82	40.57	31.50	16.46	30.42
Change in Average Number of PhD's	**3.45**	**-9.93**	**5.00**	**-6.16**	**-2.42**

Median Years to Degree from Entering Graduate School [2]

	1982 Quarters				
	Top	Second	Third	Fourth	Average
Average Median Years to Degree, Acad Yrs 1975-79	9.02	10.35	10.40	10.11	10.01
Average Median Years to Degree, Acad Yrs 1986-92	10.61	11.27	11.63	12.11	11.43
Change in Average Median Years to Degree	**1.59**	**0.92**	**1.23**	**2.00**	**1.42**

Quality Ratings of Program Faculty [3]

	1982 Quarters				
	Top	Second	Third	Fourth	Average
Average Rating of Program Faculty Quality, 1982	4.15	3.30	2.44	1.66	2.85
Average Rating of Program Faculty Quality, 1993	4.23	3.47	2.93	2.48	3.25
Change in Average Program Faculty Quality	**0.08**	**0.18**	**0.49**	**0.82**	**0.40**

Sources: 1 Institutional Coordinators.
2 Doctorate Records File.
3 National Survey of Graduate Faculty 1993 and Jones, Lindzey and Coggeshall, 1982.

Appendix Table R - 20 Change in Magnitude of Selected Measures for Programs in Philosophy Appearing in Both the 1982 and 1993 Studies by 1982 Quality Grouping

Number of Program Faculty [1]

	1982 Quarters				
	Top	Second	Third	Fourth	Average
Average Number of Faculty, Fall 1980	15.81	15.29	13.75	12.47	14.32
Average Number of Faculty, Fall 1992	17.63	21.35	14.25	14.65	17.00
Change in Average Number of Faculty	**1.82**	**6.06**	**0.50**	**2.18**	**2.68**

Number of Program Graduates [1]

	1982 Quarters				
	Top	Second	Third	Fourth	Average
Average Number of PhD's, Acad Yrs 1975-80	26.63	24.18	17.69	13.24	20.38
Average Number of PhD's, Acad Yrs 1987-92	19.38	18.18	13.44	11.12	15.50
Change in Average Number of PhD's	**-7.25**	**-6.00**	**-4.25**	**-2.12**	**-4.88**

Median Years to Degree from Entering Graduate School [2]

	1982 Quarters				
	Top	Second	Third	Fourth	Average
Average Median Years to Degree, Acad Yrs 1975-79	7.13	7.55	8.08	8.35	7.70
Average Median Years to Degree, Acad Yrs 1986-92	8.84	9.86	10.11	10.85	9.93
Change in Average Median Years to Degree	**1.71**	**2.31**	**2.03**	**2.50**	**2.23**

Quality Ratings of Program Faculty [3]

	1982 Quarters				
	Top	Second	Third	Fourth	Average
Average Rating of Program Faculty Quality, 1982	4.07	3.01	2.30	1.59	2.73
Average Rating of Program Faculty Quality, 1993	4.14	3.11	2.45	1.97	2.91
Change in Average Program Faculty Quality	**0.07**	**0.10**	**0.15**	**0.38**	**0.18**

Sources: 1 Institutional Coordinators.
2 Doctorate Records File.
3 National Survey of Graduate Faculty 1993 and Jones, Lindzey and Coggeshall, 1982.

Appendix Table R - 21 Change in Magnitude of Selected Measures for Programs in Physics Appearing in Both the 1982 and 1993 Studies by 1982 Quality Grouping

Number of Program Faculty [1]

	1982 Quarters Top	Second	Third	Fourth	Average
Average Number of Faculty, Fall 1980	44.07	30.57	22.77	15.00	28.01
Average Number of Faculty, Fall 1992	50.07	36.36	27.07	17.39	32.62
Change in Average Number of Faculty	**6.00**	**5.79**	**4.30**	**2.39**	**4.61**

Number of Program Graduates [1]

	1982 Quarters Top	Second	Third	Fourth	Average
Average Number of PhD's, Acad Yrs 1975-80	78.54	36.79	22.10	15.82	38.25
Average Number of PhD's, Acad Yrs 1987-92	92.00	45.00	27.43	18.32	45.37
Change in Average Number of PhD's	**13.46**	**8.21**	**5.33**	**2.50**	**7.12**

Median Years to Degree from Entering Graduate School [2]

	1982 Quarters Top	Second	Third	Fourth	Average
Average Median Years to Degree, Acad Yrs 1975-79	6.54	6.79	7.40	7.59	7.07
Average Median Years to Degree, Acad Yrs 1986-92	7.07	7.40	7.75	8.28	7.63
Change in Average Median Years to Degree	**0.53**	**0.61**	**0.35**	**0.69**	**0.56**

Quality Ratings of Program Faculty [3]

	1982 Quarters Top	Second	Third	Fourth	Average
Average Rating of Program Faculty Quality, 1982	4.08	2.91	2.26	1.57	2.71
Average Rating of Program Faculty Quality, 1993	4.17	3.23	2.72	2.23	3.08
Change in Average Program Faculty Quality	**0.09**	**0.32**	**0.46**	**0.66**	**0.37**

Sources: 1 Institutional Coordinators.
2 Doctorate Records File.
3 National Survey of Graduate Faculty 1993 and Jones, Lindzey and Coggeshall, 1982.

Appendix Table R - 22 Change in Magnitude of Selected Measures for Programs in Physiology Appearing in Both the 1982 and 1993 Studies by 1982 Quality Grouping

Number of Program Faculty [1]

	1982 Quarters				
	Top	Second	Third	Fourth	Average
Average Number of Faculty, Fall 1980	34.67	24.44	15.11	11.09	20.28
Average Number of Faculty, Fall 1992	30.28	35.67	25.33	15.41	26.08
Change in Average Number of Faculty	**-4.39**	**11.23**	**10.22**	**4.32**	**5.80**

Number of Program Graduates [1]

	1982 Quarters				
	Top	Second	Third	Fourth	Average
Average Number of PhD's, Acad Yrs 1975-80	21.78	12.89	10.06	8.64	13.09
Average Number of PhD's, Acad Yrs 1987-92	20.67	12.94	12.65	9.14	13.62
Change in Average Number of PhD's	**-1.11**	**0.05**	**2.59**	**0.50**	**0.53**

Median Years to Degree from Entering Graduate School [2]

	1982 Quarters				
	Top	Second	Third	Fourth	Average
Average Median Years to Degree, Acad Yrs 1975-79	6.23	6.60	5.98	6.28	6.28
Average Median Years to Degree, Acad Yrs 1986-92	7.91	8.37	7.99	8.28	8.15
Change in Average Median Years to Degree	**1.68**	**1.77**	**2.01**	**2.00**	**1.87**

Quality Ratings of Program Faculty [3]

	1982 Quarters				
	Top	Second	Third	Fourth	Average
Average Rating of Program Faculty Quality, 1982	3.96	3.38	2.81	2.18	3.07
Average Rating of Program Faculty Quality, 1993	3.89	3.50	3.20	2.64	3.27
Change in Average Program Faculty Quality	**-0.07**	**0.12**	**0.39**	**0.46**	**0.20**

Sources: 1 Institutional Coordinators.
2 Doctorate Records File.
3 National Survey of Graduate Faculty 1993 and Jones, Lindzey and Coggeshall, 1982.

Appendix Table R - 23 Change in Magnitude of Selected Measures for Programs in Political Science Appearing in Both the 1982 and 1993 Studies by 1982 Quality Grouping

Number of Program Faculty [1]

	1982 Quarters				
	Top	Second	Third	Fourth	Average
Average Number of Faculty, Fall 1980	30.89	25.10	19.10	17.89	23.19
Average Number of Faculty, Fall 1992	35.21	27.35	20.95	19.44	25.67
Change in Average Number of Faculty	**4.32**	**2.25**	**1.85**	**1.55**	**2.48**

Number of Program Graduates [1]

	1982 Quarters				
	Top	Second	Third	Fourth	Average
Average Number of PhD's, Acad Yrs 1975-80	69.84	36.68	27.95	19.56	38.35
Average Number of PhD's, Acad Yrs 1987-92	53.84	24.00	18.30	17.94	28.26
Change in Average Number of PhD's	**-16.00**	**-12.68**	**-9.65**	**-1.62**	**-10.09**

Median Years to Degree from Entering Graduate School [2]

	1982 Quarters				
	Top	Second	Third	Fourth	Average
Average Median Years to Degree, Acad Yrs 1975-79	8.03	8.65	7.83	8.68	8.27
Average Median Years to Degree, Acad Yrs 1986-92	9.76	9.73	10.11	11.40	10.22
Change in Average Median Years to Degree	**1.73**	**1.08**	**2.28**	**2.72**	**1.95**

Quality Ratings of Program Faculty [3]

	1982 Quarters				
	Top	Second	Third	Fourth	Average
Average Rating of Program Faculty Quality, 1982	3.96	2.92	2.27	1.54	2.68
Average Rating of Program Faculty Quality, 1993	4.10	3.00	2.39	1.86	2.84
Change in Average Program Faculty Quality	**0.14**	**0.08**	**0.12**	**0.32**	**0.16**

Sources: 1 Institutional Coordinators.
2 Doctorate Records File.
3 National Survey of Graduate Faculty 1993 and Jones, Lindzey and Coggeshall, 1982.

Appendix Table R - 24 Change in Magnitude of Selected Measures for Programs in Psychology Appearing in Both the 1982 and 1993 Studies by 1982 Quality Grouping

Number of Program Faculty [1]

	1982 Quarters				
	Top	Second	Third	Fourth	Average
Average Number of Faculty, Fall 1980	45.53	31.31	23.15	17.32	29.10
Average Number of Faculty, Fall 1992	45.68	30.92	23.97	21.05	30.21
Change in Average Number of Faculty	**0.15**	**-0.39**	**0.82**	**3.73**	**1.11**

Number of Program Graduates [1]

	1982 Quarters				
	Top	Second	Third	Fourth	Average
Average Number of PhD's, Acad Yrs 1975-80	94.68	76.69	51.76	47.62	67.39
Average Number of PhD's, Acad Yrs 1987-92	75.62	61.81	53.71	72.86	66.09
Change in Average Number of PhD's	**-19.06**	**-14.89**	**1.95**	**25.24**	**-1.30**

Median Years to Degree from Entering Graduate School [2]

	1982 Quarters				
	Top	Second	Third	Fourth	Average
Average Median Years to Degree, Acad Yrs 1975-79	5.90	6.27	6.10	6.39	6.17
Average Median Years to Degree, Acad Yrs 1986-92	8.17	8.71	8.84	8.87	8.65
Change in Average Median Years to Degree	**2.27**	**2.44**	**2.74**	**2.48**	**2.48**

Quality Ratings of Program Faculty [3]

	1982 Quarters				
	Top	Second	Third	Fourth	Average
Average Rating of Program Faculty Quality, 1982	3.94	2.86	2.14	1.35	2.55
Average Rating of Program Faculty Quality, 1993	4.07	3.16	2.59	1.96	2.93
Change in Average Program Faculty Quality	**0.13**	**0.30**	**0.45**	**0.61**	**0.38**

Sources: 1 Institutional Coordinators.
2 Doctorate Records File.
3 National Survey of Graduate Faculty 1993 and Jones, Lindzey and Coggeshall, 1982.

Appendix Table R - 25 Change in Magnitude of Selected Measures for Programs in Sociology Appearing in Both the 1982 and 1993 Studies by 1982 Quality Grouping

Number of Program Faculty [1]

	1982 Quarters				
	Top	Second	Third	Fourth	Average
Average Number of Faculty, Fall 1980	27.60	23.24	20.45	15.90	21.74
Average Number of Faculty, Fall 1992	29.45	22.10	21.80	16.33	22.34
Change in Average Number of Faculty	**1.85**	**-1.14**	**1.35**	**0.43**	**0.60**

Number of Program Graduates [1]

	1982 Quarters				
	Top	Second	Third	Fourth	Average
Average Number of PhD's, Acad Yrs 1975-80	55.30	37.14	30.60	18.19	35.12
Average Number of PhD's, Acad Yrs 1987-92	36.15	26.00	19.85	15.52	24.29
Change in Average Number of PhD's	**-19.15**	**-11.14**	**-10.75**	**-2.67**	**-10.83**

Median Years to Degree from Entering Graduate School [2]

	1982 Quarters				
	Top	Second	Third	Fourth	Average
Average Median Years to Degree, Acad Yrs 1975-79	7.69	7.88	8.15	8.60	8.07
Average Median Years to Degree, Acad Yrs 1986-92	9.97	11.36	11.16	11.96	11.13
Change in Average Median Years to Degree	**2.28**	**3.48**	**3.01**	**3.36**	**3.06**

Quality Ratings of Program Faculty [3]

	1982 Quarters				
	Top	Second	Third	Fourth	Average
Average Rating of Program Faculty Quality, 1982	3.99	2.99	2.20	1.33	2.62
Average Rating of Program Faculty Quality, 1993	3.91	3.07	2.48	1.55	2.74
Change in Average Program Faculty Quality	**-0.08**	**0.08**	**0.28**	**0.22**	**0.12**

Sources: 1 Institutional Coordinators.
2 Doctorate Records File.
3 National Survey of Graduate Faculty 1993 and Jones, Lindzey and Coggeshall, 1982.

Appendix Table R - 26 Change in Magnitude of Selected Measures for Programs in Spanish and Portuguese Language and Literature Appearing in Both the 1982 and 1993 Studies by 1982 Quality Grouping

Number of Program Faculty [1]

	1982 Quarters Top	Second	Third	Fourth	Average
Average Number of Faculty, Fall 1980	13.67	9.69	11.31	8.77	10.80
Average Number of Faculty, Fall 1992	15.92	12.69	13.85	11.15	13.35
Change in Average Number of Faculty	**2.25**	**3.00**	**2.54**	**2.38**	**2.55**

Number of Program Graduates [1]

	1982 Quarters Top	Second	Third	Fourth	Average
Average Number of PhD's, Acad Yrs 1975-80	21.75	14.92	11.85	9.75	14.52
Average Number of PhD's, Acad Yrs 1987-92	19.75	14.23	14.62	10.42	14.74
Change in Average Number of PhD's	**-2.00**	**-0.69**	**2.77**	**0.67**	**0.22**

Median Years to Degree from Entering Graduate School [2]

	1982 Quarters Top	Second	Third	Fourth	Average
Average Median Years to Degree, Acad Yrs 1975-79	8.44	8.61	10.40	9.51*	9.06
Average Median Years to Degree, Acad Yrs 1986-92	10.14	10.44	11.61	11.97	11.06
Change in Average Median Years to Degree	**1.70**	**1.83**	**1.21**	**2.46**	**2.00**

Quality Ratings of Program Faculty [3]

	1982 Quarters Top	Second	Third	Fourth	Average
Average Rating of Program Faculty Quality, 1982	3.81	3.12	2.56	1.96	2.85
Average Rating of Program Faculty Quality, 1993	3.53	3.41	2.70	2.35	2.99
Change in Average Program Faculty Quality	**-0.29**	**0.29**	**0.14**	**0.39**	**0.14**

Sources: 1 Institutional Coordinators.
2 Doctorate Records File.
3 National Survey of Graduate Faculty 1993 and Jones, Lindzey and Coggeshall, 1982.

* The average is based on fewer than four values.

Appendix Table R - 27 Change in Magnitude of Selected Measures for Programs in Statistics an Biostatistics Appearing in Both the 1982 and 1993 Studies by 1982 Quality Grouping

Number of Program Faculty [1]

	1982 Quarters				
	Top	Second	Third	Fourth	Average
Average Number of Faculty, Fall 1980	19.33	14.50	13.08	9.17	14.02
Average Number of Faculty, Fall 1992	20.08	18.67	16.08	11.00	16.46
Change in Average Number of Faculty	**0.75**	**4.17**	**3.00**	**1.83**	**2.44**

Number of Program Graduates [1]

	1982 Quarters				
	Top	Second	Third	Fourth	Average
Average Number of PhD's, Acad Yrs 1975-80	26.00	12.75	14.08	7.75	15.15
Average Number of PhD's, Acad Yrs 1987-92	29.83	20.92	17.17	11.75	19.92
Change in Average Number of PhD's	**3.83**	**8.17**	**3.09**	**4.00**	**4.77**

Median Years to Degree from Entering Graduate School [2]

	1982 Quarters				
	Top	Second	Third	Fourth	Average
Average Median Years to Degree, Acad Yrs 1975-79	6.16	6.61	7.45	6.56	6.72
Average Median Years to Degree, Acad Yrs 1986-92	8.03	8.66	9.56	9.24	8.87
Change in Average Median Years to Degree	**1.87**	**2.05**	**2.11**	**2.68**	**2.15**

Quality Ratings of Program Faculty [3]

	1982 Quarters				
	Top	Second	Third	Fourth	Average
Average Rating of Program Faculty Quality, 1982	4.16	3.37	2.77	1.89	3.05
Average Rating of Program Faculty Quality, 1993	4.12	3.53	3.07	2.28	3.25
Change in Average Program Faculty Quality	**-0.04**	**0.16**	**0.30**	**0.39**	**0.20**

Sources: 1 Institutional Coordinators.

2 Doctorate Records File.

3 National Survey of Graduate Faculty 1993 and Jones, Lindzey and Coggeshall, 1982.

THE ANALYSIS OF CHANGE

A Worked Example

In this note, we examine some of the possible change analyses that may be made with the data available from the 1993 survey. For the purposes of illustration, the analysis is confined to the data on programs in English Language and Literature, and focuses mainly on the changes in assessed quality of the faculty, and their possible correlates. The base from which changes are analyzed is the 1982 database; all of the analyses draw on data published in the 1982 reports.

The strategy of the analysis consists of overall analyses of changes across all programs, followed by analyses of the same changes by bands of quality range. For this latter step, we have ranked programs according to their 1982 quality ratings, and then divided these into quarters. The Top Quarter includes the 25 percent of programs drawing the highest ranks, the other quarters composing the second, third, and fourth bands of rankings in 25 percent groupings.

Concurrent Validity of Faculty Quality Changes

Two numerical measures of change in assessed faculty quality are available. One is the computed difference between ratings given in 1993 (93Q) and the analogous ratings given in 1982 (82Q). The difference between these two ratings may then be separated into quarters, and compared in terms of their means and change.

The second measure (93C) is the rated change in quality, a judgment made by the 1993 raters. If the concept of faculty quality, and change in that quality, has a widely understood common meaning, we should expect that the two measures would produce rather similar results. Comparability of results might be looked at in two ways. One is whether or not the 1993 and 1982 ratings leave the *relative* position of individual programs more or less untouched; the second is whether or not the *absolute* magnitude of the ratings remains more or less the same. On a five-point scale, do the overall ratings and the average ratings of programs in the Top Quarter remain about the same in 1993 as they did in 1982, and so on down the remaining quarters. We turn to this first.

Computed Changes in Quality Ratings from 1982 to 1993. Figure R-1 presents the scattergram of the regression of the 1982 and 1993 ratings. The scattergram contains two lines. One, the regression line, is defined in the usual way, i.e. as the line of best least-squares fit for the data points. The other, labeled as the "No Change Line," plots the position that each program would have occupied had each received exactly the same rating in 1993 as in 1982. It is not a regression line, but a useful guide to the inspection of the greater direction of changes throughout the range of quality of the programs.

The coefficient (+0.94) indicates that the *relative* position of programs remains, overall, unchanged over the 11-year period. However, the overwhelming bulk of the programs fall above the no-change line, indicating that most programs drew higher *absolute* ratings in 1993 than they did in 1982. Visual inspection suggests that this is particularly true for programs that were lower end of the ratings in 1982, namely in the three lower quarters. This can be illustrated by the comparison of differences shown in Table R-28.

TABLE R-28 Means of Faculty Quality Ratings Over All Programs and by 1982 Quarters. English Language and Literature

Unit of Analysis	1982 Mean	1993 Mean	Difference (93-82)
Over all Programs	2.573	2.961	.388 §
Top Quarter	3.975 †	4.070 ‡	.095 *
Second Quarter	2.866 †	3.218 ‡	.352 *
Third Quarter	2.203 †	2.705 ‡	.502 *
Fourth Quarter	1.290 †	1.885 ‡	.595

Notes:
§ Difference between overall means is significant, $p < .0001$
† ‡ All vertical differences between adjacent quarters are statistically significant
* All differences between quarters in this column are significant except between the Third and Fourth Quarters.

Rated Changes in Quality: As Judged by 1993 Raters. The second measure of change in quality (93C) permits a similar analysis. The first question of importance is whether or not 93C correlates with the computed difference 93Q-82Q, employed in the previous analysis. The correlation coefficient is +0.36. While this is statistically significant in a sample of this size ($p<.0003$) the size of the coefficient itself is modest, indicating just under 13 percent of shared variance in the two measures.

For this reason it is useful to repeat the foregoing analyses, employing Rated-Change (93C) in lieu of the 93Q-82Q measure. It is helpful to be reminded that Rated Change was scaled from +1 to –1, with 0 being "no change."

The mean overall rating was +.156; the distribution of scores above and below the zero (no change) point was: 71 above, 22 below, and 5 exactly zero. If we compare this with the changes indicated in Figure R-1, we find in the latter case that 12 programs were rated lower than in 1982, the remaining 86 being rated higher than in 1982. By this comparison the standard of improvement reflected in 93C was stricter than that reflected by 93Q-82Q. Nonetheless,

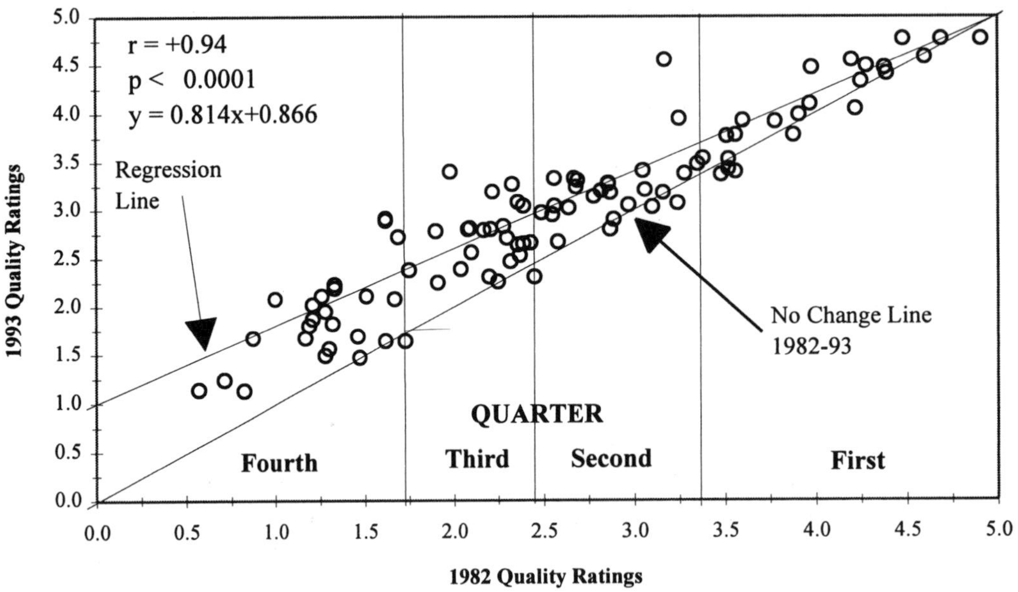

FIGURE R-1 Scattergram of the Regression of the 1982 and 1993 Ratings

the basic picture is the same, namely that the majority of programs have received substantially higher ratings for quality than they had in 1982.

Quarter analysis of 93C provides the following data. See Table R-29 below.

TABLE R-29 Mean Rated Change in Quality (93C) by 1982 Quarters

Quarter	Mean Improvement
Top	+.204
Second	+.230
Third	+.165
Fourth	+.028 *

* The only significant difference is between the Fourth Quarter and each of the other three quarters. They do not differ between themselves.

Comment. While 93C indicates the assessment that there has been a general improvement in quality over the programs as a whole, the distribution of rated improvement differs from that depicted by 93Q-82Q. The latter places the major improvement at the lowest ends of the distribution, while 93C places it mainly in the upper half of the distribution. This discrepancy, together with the low coefficient of correlation between the two measures already reported, suggests that there is limited concurrent validity to the measures, and that they are likely to reflect the operation of different factors.

Summary. The foregoing analysis suggests conclusions that differ from each other, depending upon the measure of change that is employed. The measure 93Q-82Q suggests that either (a) there has been a genuine increase in faculty quality in programs that were at the lower end of the 1982 ratings, or (b) there has been some increase in the magnitude of ratings that may be only partially or not at all related to genuine changes in faculty quality, i.e. that there has been some sort of "grade inflation." This would necessarily be most evident at the lower end of the ratings, as increases at the upper end are constrained by the ceiling of the 5-point scale that is employed.

On the other hand, 93C indicates that the major perceived improvements have been in the middle to upper ranges, with no improvement at the lower end. However, the perception that the quality of a program has changed is likely to be affected by the degree of the rater's knowledge of the program over the period in which change might have occurred. This knowledge is related to the visibility of the program, which suggests that the lower visibility of fourth quarter programs (see Table P-17) may account for the perceived lack of change. Ratings of absolute quality (93Q) on the other hand, may be influenced by other factors, such as a bias in favor of large programs.

Exploratory Analyses of Factors Associated with Quality Change

One strategy for answering the questions that are stimulated by the previous analyses consists of looking at changes in other variables known to be associated with 93Q, 82Q, and 93C to see if the changes in quality ratings are associated with changes in these factors. Total number of faculty (TF) is generally positively correlated with quality ratings, as is the total number of students (TG). Modest correlations also exist between quality ratings and Median Years to Degree (MYD)

In the 1993 data, the correlations are shown in Table R-30 as follows:

TABLE R-30 Correlations between 93Q and other selected factors, 1993 data

Variable	Coefficient
Total Faculty	+.414 Sig
Total Graduate Students	+.59 Sig
Median Year to Degree	–.539 Sig

As a particular focus of interest is the fourth quarter, we can look at the nature of the correlations that we find in that quarter.

TABLE R-31 Correlations between selected factors in 1993 and two measures of quality change. *Fourth Quarter*. English Language and Literature

Factor	93C	93Q-82Q
Total Graduates	.089 NS	+.278 NS
Total Faculty	+.453 p = .023	+.424 p = .034
Median Years to Degree, 1993	r = .061 NS	r = .004 NS

Comment: Here we see that in the Fourth Quarter, total faculty size is a reliable correlate of quality ratings, but that neither of the other two factors have significant relationships with quality. This suggests that examination of changes in these various factors will reveal possible determinants of assessed quality change.

Correlations between computed changes in Total Faculty, Total Students, and MYD and changes in quality measures. We can examine the association between computed changes in the variables presented in Table R-31 above, and changes in the two change in quality measures. These are presented in Table R-32.

TABLE R-32 Correlations between changes in quality measures and changes in other factors between 1982 and 1993

Changed Factor	93C	93Q-82Q
Total Faculty, 93-82	+0.202 Sig	+0.259 Sig.
Total Graduate Students, 93-82.	+0.209 Sig	–0.028 NS
Median Year to Degree, 93-82	–0.025 NS	+0.058 NS

Note: An additional set of analyses was computed using the ratio of Total Students to Total Faculty, a computation that was not employed in 1982. The correlations between changes in this ratio between 1982 and 1993 and quality change measures were:

93C = –.17 (NS), 93Q–82Q = +.071 (NS)

Comment: The general picture that emerges from these analyses is that changes in quality as measured by either of the two measures of change are positively associated with changes in the size of the faculty. Changes in the total of the graduate students enrolled in a program produce ambiguous relationships between the two measures of change. Rated change correlates significantly (but marginally so) while calculated change in quality is not significantly associated with increases in total students. In any event, the significant correlations are not impressive, accounting as they do for only between 4 and 7 percent of the variance in the change of quality measures.

Summary: The unambiguous conclusion from this analysis is that changes in quality, however measured, are associated with changes (increases) in faculty size. The magnitude of this association is modest, and appears insufficient to account for the observed increases in quality ratings reported in the survey.

It is important to emphasize that these concluding observations are, of course, limited to the field of English Language and Literature. The form of analysis employed here may be useful in the production of similar analyses in other fields, where the conclusions may well be quite different.

APPENDIX S

Committee for the Study of Research-Doctorate Programs in the United States

M.L. Goldberger is Dean of Natural Sciences and Professor of Physics at the University of California, San Diego, and President Emeritus of the California Institute. Dr. Goldberger served as Director of the Institute for Advanced Study, Princeton, from 1987 to 1991, and prior to that position was President of the California Institute of Technology for the period 1978 to 1987. He has held faculty positions at the University of Chicago and at Princeton University, where he was chair of the physics department and Joseph Henry Professor of Physics. Dr. Goldberger has served on several national committees, including the President's Science Advisory Committee, and has received numerous honors and awards, including membership in the National Academy of Sciences, American Academy of Arts and Sciences, and American Philosophical Society. He holds a B.S. degree from the Carnegie Institute of Technology and a Ph.D. in physics from the University of Chicago.

Brendan Maher is Edward C. Henderson Professor of the Psychology of Personality at Harvard University. He came to Harvard in 1972 as Professor of Psychology and served as department chair from 1973 to 1978 and 1987 to 1989, and Dean of the Graduate School of Arts and Sciences 1989-1992. Prior to joining the faculty at Harvard, he was a faculty member at Brandeis University, the University of Wisconsin, Louisiana State University, Northwestern University, and the University of Copenhagen. He has served on a number of committees, including chair of the Panel on Behavioral Sciences at the National Research Council, and has received numerous awards, including charter President of the Society for Research in Psychopathology. His research interests focus on language, motor, and thought disorder in schizophrenia, and on the psychopathology of delusion. Publications include eight books and over 100 articles. He received his B.A. from the University of Manchester, England, and his Ph.D. in clinical psychology from Ohio State University.

Richard Atkinson is Chancellor of the University of California at San Diego and also professor of cognitive science and psychology. He is a former director of the National Science Foundation, past president of the American Association for the Advancement of Science, and former chair of the Association of American Universities. His research has been concerned with problems of memory and cognition, and has been used to develop computer-controlled systems for instruction in the primary grades. He is a member of the National Academy of Sciences, the Institute of Medicine, the National Academy of Education, and the American Philosophical Society. He obtained a Ph.B. degree from the University of Chicago and a Ph.D. degree from Indiana University.

Norman M. Bradburn is Senior Vice President for Research at the National Opinion Research Center, and Tiffany and Margaret Blake Distinguished Service Professor, Department of Psychology, Harris Graduate School of Public Policy Studies, Graduate School of Business and the College, University of Chicago. Previously, he served as Provost of the University of Chicago. He chairs the Committee on National Statistics of the Commission on Behavioral and Social Sciences and Education at the National Research

Council. He holds B.A. degrees from the University of Chicago and Oxford University, and a Ph.D. degree in social psychology from Harvard University.

Joseph Cerny is Provost for Research and Dean of the Graduate Division at the University of California, Berkeley. He has been on the faculty of the Chemistry Department at the University of California, Berkeley since 1961, and during the period 1975 to 1979 he served as chair of the department. He has also served as Associate Director of the Lawrence Berkeley Laboratory. His honors and awards include: a Guggenheim Fellowship, and the Lawrence Award of the Atomic Energy Commission. His research interests are in low energy nuclear science. He received his B.S. degree at the University of Mississippi, and his Ph.D. in nuclear chemistry at the University of California, Berkeley.

Jonathan Cole is the Quetelet Professor of Social Sciences and Provost at Columbia University. He joined the faculty at Columbia in 1968 and served as the Director of the Center for Social Sciences from 1979 to 1987 and Vice Provost for Arts and Sciences from 1987 to 1989. His awards and honors include a Guggenheim Fellowship and Fellow of the Center of Advanced Study in the Behavioral Sciences. He has published extensively on the growth of scientific knowledge, the social organization of peer review in science, and women in the scientific community. He holds a B.S. degree and Ph.D. in sociology from Columbia University.

Jane S. de Hart joined the faculty at the University of California, Santa Barbara, as a Professor of History in January 1992. She previously was at the University of North Carolina, where she was Professor of History from 1982 to 1991 at the Chapel Hill campus and Associate Professor and Professor at the Greensboro campus from 1971 to 1982. Her honors and awards include the Victoria Schuck Award from the American Political Science Association, a Fulbright Fellowship and a National Endowment for the Humanities Fellowship. Dr. de Hart's research area is public policy and cultural/political conflict, dealing especially with arts and gender issues. She holds a B.S. degree and a Ph.D. in history from Duke University.

John H. D'Arms is Vice Provost for Academic Affairs, Dean of the Rackham School of Graduate Studies, G.F. Else Professor of Classical Studies and Professor of History at the University of Michigan. He has been Director of the American Academy in Rome, and has written on Roman social, economic and cultural history. He has served as a member of the Board of Directors of the American Council of Learned Societies, and has been appointed by President Clinton to the National Council on the Humanities. His honors and awards include a Guggenheim Fellowship and membership in the American Academy of Arts and Sciences. He holds an A.B. from Princeton University, a B.A. degree from Oxford University (England), and a Ph.D. in Classics from Harvard University.

Elsa Garmire is Director of the Center for Laser Studies and William Houge Professor of Electrical Engineering and Physics at the University of Southern California. She has held positions at the California Institute of Technology, ITT Standard Telecommunication Laboratories in England, the Electronics Research Center, NASA, and consultantships at the Aerospace Corporation and several other companies. Garmire is a member of the National Academy of Engineering as well as fellow of the IEEE, the Optical Society of America and the American Physical Society. In 1994, she won the Society of Women Engineers National Achievement Award and USC's Creativity in Research Award. In 1993, Garmire was President of the Optical Society of America. She has served on the board of directors of IEEE Lasers and the Electro-optic Society, the American Institute of Physics and American Physical Society. She was a member of the Air Force Scientific Advisory Board and the NSF Advisory Committee on Engineering. Garmire's research currently focuses on guided wave optics, nonlinear optics and III-V semiconductor device research. She holds an A.B. degree from Harvard University (Radcliffe College) and a Ph.D. in physics from the Massachusetts Institute of Technology.

Gardner Lindzey is Director Emeritus of the Center for Advanced Study in the Behavioral Sciences at Stanford. Prior to coming to the Center in 1975, he was a professor of psychology at Syracuse University, the University of Minnesota, Harvard University and the University of Texas, Austin, where he was also Chair of the Psychology Department, Vice President of Academic Affairs, and Vice President and Dean of Graduate Studies. He has served as a member of the board of directors for several foundations and professional organizations, as a member of more than 25 national committees, including the Presidential Committee for the National Medal of Science, and as president of several organizations. His contributions to social and personality psychology and behavioral genetics are presented in more than 20 books and numerous technical articles. He is a member of the National Academy of Sciences, the American Philosophical Society, the Institute of Medicine, and the American Academy of Arts and Sciences. He received his A.B. from Pennsylvania State University, and his Ph.D. in psychology from Harvard University.

Pamela Mellon is a Professor of Reproductive Medicine and Neuroscience at the University of California, San Diego. Prior to her current position she held research appointments at the University of California, Berkeley, the California Institute of Technology, Harvard University and The Salk Institute. Her honors and awards include a Mellon Assistant Professorship and the Richard E. Wietzman Memorial Award of the Endocrine Society. She is an active researcher with more than 70 published articles and contributions to books and monograms. She holds a B.A. degree from the University of California, Santa Cruz and a Ph.D. from the University of California, Berkeley.

Lincoln Moses is a Professor Emeritus of Statistics and Biostatistics at the University and School of Medicine, Stanford University. At Stanford, he has also held the positions of Executive Department Head, Associate Dean of Humanities and Science, and Dean of the Graduate School. Honors and awards include a Guggenheim Fellowship and a Fellowship at the Center for Advanced Study in Behavioral Science. He is a member of the Institute of Medicine and the American Academy of Arts and Sciences. His research areas are experimental design, biological and psychological application of statistical methods, and data analyses. He holds a B.S. degree and a Ph.D. in statistics from Stanford University.

Ernest Smerdon is Vice Provost and Dean of Engineering and Mines at the University of Arizona. He has served on the faculties of: Texas A&M University where he was a Professor; University of Florida where he was Professor of Agricultural Engineering and Department Chair; the University of Texas system where he was Vice Chancellor for Academic Affairs; and the University of Texas at Austin where he held the Janet S. Cockrell Centennial Chair in Engineering. He has on numerous occasions consulted foreign countries on problems related to his research areas: water resource development and irrigation, energy use and conservation and research administration. He received his B.S. and Ph.D. in Agricultural Engineering from the University of Missouri.

Stephen Stigler is the Ernest DeWitt Burton Distinguished Service Professor in the Department of Statistics, and member of the Committee on the Conceptual Foundations Science, of the University of Chicago. Prior to coming to Chicago, he was on the faculty at the University of Wisconsin-Madison from 1967 to 1979. His research areas are: order statistics, experimental design, and the history of statistics. He is a member of the American Academy of Arts and Sciences. He holds a B.S. degree from Carleton College and a Ph.D. in statistics from the University of California, Berkeley.

Debra W. Stewart is Dean and Professor of Political Science and Public Administration at North Carolina State University. She joined the NCSU faculty in 1974, and has written, co-authored, and edited books and scholarly articles on administrative theory and public policy. Her current research interest focuses on ethics and managerial decision making. Dr. Stewart has served as Chair of the Council of Graduate Schools and Chair of the Council on Research Policy and Graduate Education of the National Association of State Universities and Land-Grant Colleges, as well as serving on the executive committee of the Council of Southern Graduate Schools and the Board of Directors of Oak Ridge Associated Universities. Currently she is Chair-elect of the Graduate Record Examinations Board. Her educational background includes a B.A. from Marquette University, an M.A. in government from the University of Maryland, and a Ph.D. in political science from the University of North Carolina, Chapel Hill.

James Wyche is Associate Provost and Associate Professor of Biology at Brown University. He is also Faculty Assistant to the President. Prior to joining the Brown faculty in 1988, he held faculty positions at Stanford Medical School, Hunter College, and the University of Missouri-Columbia. Professional service includes membership in and chairmanship of several panels and committees for the NSF and NIH. He is an active researcher in cellular endocrinology and has published widely in this area. His educational background includes a B.S. degree from Cornell University and a Ph.D. in Genetics from the Johns Hopkins University.

INDEX

Index

This index is provided as an easy page reference to the appendix material for the individual 41 fields in the study. The abbreviated titles in the index refer to the different appendixes as follows: Change in Magnitude of Selective Measures (Appendix R), Correlations for Selected Characteristics (Appendix O), Effectiveness Ratings by Broad Field (Appendix I), Faculty Quality Ratings by Broad Field (Appendix H), Mean Scores with Confidence Intervals (Appendix Q), Relative Rankings (Appendix P), and Selected Characteristics (Appendixes J, K, L, M, and N).

A

Aerospace Engineering
- Correlations for Selected Characteristics, 428
- Effectiveness Ratings by Broad Field, 220
- Faculty Quality Ratings by Broad Field, 170
- Mean Scores with Confidence Intervals, 626
- Relative Rankings, 472
- Selected Characteristics, 282

Anthropology
- Change in Magnitude of Selective Measures, 700
- Correlations for Selected Characteristics, 429
- Effectiveness Ratings by Broad Field, 237
- Faculty Quality Ratings by Broad Field, 187
- Mean Scores with Confidence Intervals, 627
- Relative Rankings, 475
- Selected Characteristics, 352

Art History
- Change in Magnitude of Selective Measures, 701
- Correlations for Selected Characteristics, 430
- Effectiveness Ratings by Broad Field, 198
- Faculty Quality Ratings by Broad Field, 148
- Mean Scores with Confidence Intervals, 628
- Relative Rankings, 478
- Selected Characteristics, 250

Astrophysics and Astronomy
- Correlations for Selected Characteristics, 431
- Effectiveness Ratings by Broad Field, 227
- Faculty Quality Ratings by Broad Field, 177
- Mean Scores with Confidence Intervals, 629
- Relative Rankings, 480
- Selected Characteristics, 314

B

Biochemistry and Molecular Biology
- Correlations for Selected Characteristics, 432
- Effectiveness Ratings by Broad Field, 208
- Faculty Quality Ratings by Broad Field, 158
- Mean Scores with Confidence Intervals, 630
- Relative Rankings, 483
- Selected Characteristics, 386

Biomedical Engineering
- Correlations for Selected Characteristics, 433
- Effectiveness Ratings by Broad Field, 220
- Faculty Quality Ratings by Broad Field, 170
- Mean Scores with Confidence Intervals, 633
- Relative Rankings, 490
- Selected Characteristics, 284

C

Cell and Developmental Biology
- Correlations for Selected Characteristics, 434
- Effectiveness Ratings by Broad Field, 208
- Faculty Quality Ratings by Broad Field, 158
- Mean Scores with Confidence Intervals, 634
- Relative Rankings, 493
- Selected Characteristics, 394

Chemical Engineering
Change in Magnitude of Selective Measures, 702
Correlations for Selected Characteristics, 435
Effectiveness Ratings by Broad Field, 220
Faculty Quality Ratings by Broad Field, 170
Mean Scores with Confidence Intervals, 637
Relative Rankings, 500
Selected Characteristics, 286

Chemistry
Change in Magnitude of Selective Measures, 703
Correlations for Selected Characteristics, 436
Effectiveness Ratings by Broad Field, 227
Faculty Quality Ratings by Broad Field, 177
Mean Scores with Confidence Intervals, 639
Relative Rankings, 504
Selected Characteristics, 316

Civil Engineering
Change in Magnitude of Selective Measures, 704
Correlations for Selected Characteristics, 437
Effectiveness Ratings by Broad Field, 220
Faculty Quality Ratings by Broad Field, 170
Mean Scores with Confidence Intervals, 642
Relative Rankings, 510
Selected Characteristics, 290

Classics
Change in Magnitude of Selective Measures, 705
Correlations for Selected Characteristics, 438
Effectiveness Ratings by Broad Field, 198
Faculty Quality Ratings by Broad Field, 148
Mean Scores with Confidence Intervals, 644
Relative Rankings, 513
Selected Characteristics, 252

Comparative Literature
Correlations for Selected Characteristics, 439
Effectiveness Ratings by Broad Field, 198
Faculty Quality Ratings by Broad Field, 148
Mean Scores with Confidence Intervals, 645
Relative Rankings, 514
Selected Characteristics, 254

Computer Sciences
Change in Magnitude of Selective Measures, 706
Correlations for Selected Characteristics, 440
Effectiveness Ratings by Broad Field, 227
Faculty Quality Ratings by Broad Field, 177
Mean Scores with Confidence Intervals, 646
Relative Rankings, 516
Selected Characteristics, 323

E

Ecology, Evolution, and Behavior
Correlations for Selected Characteristics, 441
Effectiveness Ratings by Broad Field, 208
Faculty Quality Ratings by Broad Field, 158
Mean Scores with Confidence Intervals, 648
Relative Rankings, 521
Selected Characteristics, 401

Economics
Change in Magnitude of Selective Measures, 707
Correlations for Selected Characteristics, 442
Effectiveness Ratings by Broad Field, 237
Faculty Quality Ratings by Broad Field, 187
Mean Scores with Confidence Intervals, 650
Relative Rankings, 526
Selected Characteristics, 355

Electrical Engineering
Change in Magnitude of Selective Measures, 708
Correlations for Selected Characteristics, 443
Effectiveness Ratings by Broad Field, 220
Faculty Quality Ratings by Broad Field, 170
Mean Scores with Confidence Intervals, 652
Relative Rankings, 530
Selected Characteristics, 295

English Language and Literature
Change in Magnitude of Selective Measures, 709
Correlations for Selected Characteristics, 444
Effectiveness Ratings by Broad Field, 198
Faculty Quality Ratings by Broad Field, 148
Mean Scores with Confidence Intervals, 654
Relative Rankings, 535
Selected Characteristics, 257

F

French Language and Literature
Change in Magnitude of Selective Measures, 710
Correlations for Selected Characteristics, 445
Effectiveness Ratings by Broad Field, 198
Faculty Quality Ratings by Broad Field, 148
Mean Scores with Confidence Intervals, 656
Relative Rankings, 540
Selected Characteristics, 262

G

Geography
Change in Magnitude of Selective Measures, 711
Correlations for Selected Characteristics, 446

Effectiveness Ratings by Broad Field, 237
Faculty Quality Ratings by Broad Field, 187
Mean Scores with Confidence Intervals, 657
Relative Rankings, 542
Selected Characteristics, 359

Geosciences
Change in Magnitude of Selective Measures, 712
Correlations for Selected Characteristics, 447
Effectiveness Ratings by Broad Field, 227
Faculty Quality Ratings by Broad Field, 177
Mean Scores with Confidence Intervals, 658
Relative Rankings, 544
Selected Characteristics, 328

German Language and Literature
Change in Magnitude of Selective Measures, 713
Correlations for Selected Characteristics, 448
Effectiveness Ratings by Broad Field, 198
Faculty Quality Ratings by Broad Field, 148
Mean Scores with Confidence Intervals, 660
Relative Rankings, 548
Selected Characteristics, 264

H

History
Change in Magnitude of Selective Measures, 714
Correlations for Selected Characteristics, 449
Effectiveness Ratings by Broad Field, 237
Faculty Quality Ratings by Broad Field, 187
Mean Scores with Confidence Intervals, 661
Relative Rankings, 550
Selected Characteristics, 361

I

Industrial Engineering
Correlations for Selected Characteristics, 450
Effectiveness Ratings by Broad Field, 220
Faculty Quality Ratings by Broad Field, 170
Mean Scores with Confidence Intervals, 663
Relative Rankings, 554
Selected Characteristics, 300

L

Linguistics
Change in Magnitude of Selective Measures, 715
Correlations for Selected Characteristics, 451
Effectiveness Ratings by Broad Field, 198
Faculty Quality Ratings by Broad Field, 148
Mean Scores with Confidence Intervals, 664
Relative Rankings, 556
Selected Characteristics, 266

M

Materials Science
Correlations for Selected Characteristics, 452
Effectiveness Ratings by Broad Field, 220
Faculty Quality Ratings by Broad Field, 170
Mean Scores with Confidence Intervals, 665
Relative Rankings, 558
Selected Characteristics, 302

Mathematics
Change in Magnitude of Selective Measures, 716
Correlations for Selected Characteristics, 453
Effectiveness Ratings by Broad Field, 227
Faculty Quality Ratings by Broad Field, 177
Mean Scores with Confidence Intervals, 666
Relative Rankings, 561
Selected Characteristics, 332

Mechanical Engineering
Change in Magnitude of Selective Measures, 717
Correlations for Selected Characteristics, 454
Effectiveness Ratings by Broad Field, 220
Faculty Quality Ratings by Broad Field, 170
Mean Scores with Confidence Intervals, 669
Relative Rankings, 566
Selected Characteristics, 305

Molecular and General Genetics
Correlations for Selected Characteristics, 455
Effectiveness Ratings by Broad Field, 208
Faculty Quality Ratings by Broad Field, 158
Mean Scores with Confidence Intervals, 671
Relative Rankings, 570
Selected Characteristics, 406

Music
Change in Magnitude of Selective Measures, 718
Correlations for Selected Characteristics, 456
Effectiveness Ratings by Broad Field, 198
Faculty Quality Ratings by Broad Field, 148
Mean Scores with Confidence Intervals, 673
Relative Rankings, 575
Selected Characteristics, 268

N

Neurosciences
Correlations for Selected Characteristics, 457
Effectiveness Ratings by Broad Field, 208

Faculty Quality Ratings by Broad Field, 158
Mean Scores with Confidence Intervals, 674
Relative Rankings, 578
Selected Characteristics, 410

O

Oceanography
Correlations for Selected Characteristics, 458
Effectiveness Ratings by Broad Field, 227
Faculty Quality Ratings by Broad Field, 177
Mean Scores with Confidence Intervals, 676
Relative Rankings, 582
Selected Characteristics, 338

P

Pharmacology
Correlations for Selected Characteristics, 459
Effectiveness Ratings by Broad Field, 208
Faculty Quality Ratings by Broad Field, 158
Mean Scores with Confidence Intervals, 677
Relative Rankings, 583
Selected Characteristics, 415

Philosophy
Change in Magnitude of Selective Measures, 719
Correlations for Selected Characteristics, 460
Effectiveness Ratings by Broad Field, 198
Faculty Quality Ratings by Broad Field, 148
Mean Scores with Confidence Intervals, 680
Relative Rankings, 588
Selected Characteristics, 271

Physics
Change in Magnitude of Selective Measures, 720
Correlations for Selected Characteristics, 461
Effectiveness Ratings by Broad Field, 227
Faculty Quality Ratings by Broad Field, 177
Mean Scores with Confidence Intervals, 682
Relative Rankings, 591
Selected Characteristics, 340

Physiology
Change in Magnitude of Selective Measures, 721
Correlations for Selected Characteristics, 462
Effectiveness Ratings by Broad Field, 208
Faculty Quality Ratings by Broad Field, 158
Mean Scores with Confidence Intervals, 685
Relative Rankings, 597
Selected Characteristics, 420

Political Science
Change in Magnitude of Selective Measures, 722
Correlations for Selected Characteristics, 463
Effectiveness Ratings by Broad Field, 237
Faculty Quality Ratings by Broad Field, 187
Mean Scores with Confidence Intervals, 688
Relative Rankings, 602
Selected Characteristics, 366

Psychology
Change in Magnitude of Selective Measures, 723
Correlations for Selected Characteristics, 464
Effectiveness Ratings by Broad Field, 237
Faculty Quality Ratings by Broad Field, 187
Mean Scores with Confidence Intervals, 690
Relative Rankings, 607
Selected Characteristics, 371

R

Religion
Correlations for Selected Characteristics, 465
Effectiveness Ratings by Broad Field, 198
Faculty Quality Ratings by Broad Field, 148
Mean Scores with Confidence Intervals, 693
Relative Rankings, 614
Selected Characteristics, 274

S

Sociology
Change in Magnitude of Selective Measures, 724
Correlations for Selected Characteristics, 466
Effectiveness Ratings by Broad Field, 237
Faculty Quality Ratings by Broad Field, 187
Mean Scores with Confidence Intervals, 694
Relative Rankings, 616
Selected Characteristics, 378

Spanish and Portuguese Language and Literature
Change in Magnitude of Selective Measures, 725
Correlations for Selected Characteristics, 467
Effectiveness Ratings by Broad Field, 198
Faculty Quality Ratings by Broad Field, 148
Mean Scores with Confidence Intervals, 696
Relative Rankings, 620
Selected Characteristics, 276

Statistics and Biostatistics
Change in Magnitude of Selective Measures, 726
Correlations for Selected Characteristics, 468
Effectiveness Ratings by Broad Field, 227
Faculty Quality Ratings by Broad Field, 177
Mean Scores with Confidence Intervals, 697
Relative Rankings, 622
Selected Characteristics, 346